Cultural heritage and contemporary change
Series IIID, South Asia, Volume 12
General Editor
George F. McLean

Paths to the Divine: Ancient and Indian

Indian Philosophical Studies, XII

by
Vensus A. George

The Council for Research in Values and Philosophy

Copyright © 2008 by
The Council for Research in Values and Philosophy

Box 261
Cardinal Station
Washington, D.C. 20064

All rights reserved

Printed in the United States of America

Library of Congress Cataloging-in-Publication

George, Vensus A.
  Paths to the divine : ancient and Indian / by Vensus A. George.
  p. cm. -- (Cultural heritage and contemporary change. Series IIID, South Asia ; v. 12) (Indian philosophical studies ; 12)
  Includes bibliographical references and index.
  1. Religions (Primitive, Greek, Roman, Hindu, Buddhist, Jain, Sikh).
I. Title. II. Series.
BL41.G46 2007   2007021928
201--dc22   CIP

ISBN 978-1-56518-249-3 (pbk.)

Table of Contents

Preface   v
Introduction   1

1. Primitive Religious Traditions   5
   Introduction
   1.1. The Spiritual World of the Primitive Religions
   1.2. Primitive Religious Paths to Spiritual Beings
   Conclusion

2. Greco-Roman-Hellenistic Traditions   55
   Introduction
   2.1. Greek Religion
   2.2. Roman Religion
   2.3. Hellenistic Religion
   Conclusion

3. Hindu Tradition   131
   Introduction
   3.1. Vedic Hinduism
   3.2. Vedaantic Hinduism
   3.3. Vaishnavism
   3.4. Saivism
   Conclusion

4. Jaina Tradition   317
   Introduction
   4.1. Divinities of the Jaina Pantheon
   4.2. The Jaina Paths to the Divine
   Conclusion

5. Buddhist Tradition   411
   Introduction
   5.1. Hiinayaana Buddhism
   5.2. Mahaayaana Buddhism
   5.3. Vajraayaana Buddhism
   Conclusion

6. Sikh Tradition   561
   Introduction
   6.1. God in Sikhism
   6.2. The Sikh Path to the Divine
   Conclusion

Bibliography   623
Index   635

Preface

Within the human person there dwells a deep yearning for the Divine. Humankind, in its divergent cultural contexts and during the different stages of its history, has attempted to realize this yearning in very many ways. The actualization of the inner yearning for God in different historical, cultural and religious milieus has given rise to divergent religious paths to the Divine. Though these paths differ in the means they use to help a person to arrive at his ultimate destiny, they have the common aim of helping humans to actualize the deep inner longing for God. This book entitled Paths to the Divine: A Global Perspective endeavors to study the reality of the Divine and the paths to the Divine in the major religious traditions of humankind.

Having come to the end of the work, I recollect with gratitude every person who has helped me in accomplishing this venture. I remember with thankfulness the Very Rev. Fr. Friederich Kretz, SAC, the Rector General of the Pallottine Fathers and Brothers, for his words of encouragement and appreciation of my efforts. I specially acknowledge Dr. George F. McLean, Ph.D., professor emeritus of philosophy, The Catholic University of America, Washington D.C., for his encouragement and support from the outset of this project up to its completion. I remember with gratitude the staff of the Council for Research in Values and Philosophy, Washington D.C., for agreeing to publish this work, just as they have already published three of my books. I acknowledge gratefully the Director, staff and students of Pallotti Institute of Philosophy and Religion, Goa, India, for their constant support and for allowing me to use all the academic facilities of the Institute for working on this project. Finally, I remember gratefully the Pallottines of Assumption Province, India, for their kindness, concern and appreciation.

Vensus A. George, SAC.

Introduction

The origin of religions is shrouded in mystery. The history of religion – a science that attempts to study individual religions, their history and development - proposes a number of theories to explain the origin of religions. Most of these theories attempt to explain religion in terms of social, psychological, moral or empirical elements, instead of understanding religion from a holistic perspective. The sociological theory of religion considers religion as a product of the society and states that the sacred is simply whatever is held sacred in the society. The psychological theory of religion comprehends religion as the expression of psychic feelings towards a transcendent reality. The moralistic theory of religion views religion as something that helps a person to perform good actions and to avoid evil. The empirical theory of religion attempts to explain religion as that which helps a person to cope with the different eventualities of one's empirical existence in this world. Similarly, the animistic theory holds that religion emerges from the ancient practice of spirit worship, while the totemistic theory of religion believes that religions originate from the practice of sacrifice.

All these theories of religion give a piece-meal explanation of religion rather than one that is an integrated. As a matter of fact, the approach of each of these theories involves a certain type reductionism. For instance, the sociological theory of religion reduces the whole realm of religion to sociology, as it sees religion as a mere product of social conditions, while the psychological theory of religion reduces the total sphere of religious experience to the realm of psychological feelings. Likewise, the moralistic theory of religion reduces religion to the realm of morality, while the empirical, animistic and totemistic theories reduce religion to everyday events, belief in spirits and the sacred totem animals and plants, respectively. Hence, we fail to have a birds-eye view of religious experience, but have only a partial perception of the phenomenon of religion.

Deeper reflection reveals that every religion originates from a foundational experience of the Divine. This foundational experience is, in fact, religion in the primordial sense. The original experience is that of the founder in the case of historical religions, while it is that of the various sages and holy men in the case of cosmic religions. For instance, the foundational and original experience that forms the basis of Christian religion is Jesus's experience of union with the Father and the Holy Spirit. In a cosmic religion, like Hinduism, the original experience is that of sages and holy men, who have paved the way for the emergence of the Hindu religion. The founder of a religion, the sage or holy man, goes through the foundational and original experience of the Divine deep within. The depth experience of the Divine unseats the value system of the one who goes through this experience. He or she is overwhelmed by this experience, and total transformation is brought about in their life. They receive new insight regarding the absolute reality, human nature and destiny, and their relationship to every reality in the world.

They are impelled to preach their new convictions to others and a circle of disciples gathers around the sage, to whom the truth is communicated by way of oral teaching. In this manner, the original and foundational experience finds expression in language. As time moves on, after the death of the founder and as the disciples increase, a teaching that has stemmed from the original experience is committed to writing, thereby giving way for the emergence of the scripture of that particular religion. Over the years their scriptures are codified and commentaries are written, thereby adding new dimensions of the practice of these religions. In this manner, the original experience of the founder, as communicated in oral and written language in the context of a particular culture and society, and as accepted by a body of believers, gives way to the emergence of a particular religion. Thus, the particular religion is a concretization of the original experience of the founder in the historical and cultural context of a particular society as the original experience – the primordial religion – finds expression in a particular religion.

Now the question arises whether the nature of the experience of the primordial religion is the same for each founder or sage and thus whether the reasons for the emergence of various individual religions are the same. It is difficult to speak of the nature of primordial religion apart from the experience of each founder or sage, as the knowledge of the primordial religious experience depends on one's experience of the primordial religion. Hence the objective reality of the primordial religion, as such, is incomprehensible. But we can conclude from the similarities we find in the various religions that the experience of primordial religion of different founders and sages has a certain commonality. If the experience of primordial religion is common for all founders and sages, then it is difficult to gauge differences between various individual religions.

The differences in the beliefs and practices of each particular religion emerge from a number of factors. Firstly, the uniqueness of the personality of each founder or sage who experiences the primordial religion contributes to the distinct character of a particular religion. As the original experience captures the total personality of the founder and finds expression through it, the uniqueness of his personality places a stamp on the nature of the particular religion. Secondly, the historical, social and cultural context in which the particular religion originates and develops also plays a part in coloring the individuality of a particular religion. Thirdly, the different interpretations of the original teachings of the founder, which the later adherents of the religion develop also add to the specific character of a particular religion. In this way, even though the experience of primordial religion is the same for all founders and sages, the formulation of the content of their experience in a particular religious belief and practice is different.

A particular religion that has begun in this manner develops over a period of time into a well-organized system in order to help people arrive at the final goal of experiencing the Divine. The simplicity of the original experience gives way to the formulation of elaborate religious doctrines, mythologies, moral teachings, complicated systems of ritual practices and various techniques to achieve deep levels of spiritual existence. Theology develops as a religious science. It attempts to give theological justification for various religious doctrines and practices. Thus, the original experience of the founder or the sage, which he or she experienced and communicated, becomes a concrete way for adherents of the religion to share the original experience of the founder. That foundational and original experience of the founder is the basis of every individual religion.

The project upon which we venture, entitled *Paths to the Divine: A Global Perspective*, attempts to explore some of the major individual religious traditions of humankind, especially with a view to elaborating the nature of the Divine in these religious traditions and the paths they propose in realizing the Divine. We have chosen eleven religious traditions: Primitive, Greco-Roman-Hellenistic, Hindu, Jaina, Buddhist, Sikh, Jewish, Islamic, Christian, Chinese and Japanese and Zoroastrian. We shall study these eleven traditions in two volumes. The first volume considers the first six traditions, while the second volume considers the remaining five. Each traditions will be treated in a chapters containing: a brief introductory essay on that tradition, its perception of the Divine, the paths it proposes for arriving at the Divine, and a short conclusion.

The first volume deals with Primitive Religious Traditions. The introductory essay explores the term "primitive religion", the nature and characteristics of primitive religions and their different types. The first essay in this chapter will explore the spiritual world in the primitive religions, studying the primitive people's belief in different spiritual beings, viz., a Supreme Being, the Divinities, the Free Spirits and the Living-Dead. The second essay studies the primitive religious paths by which one comes in contact with their spiritual beings, such as, prayer and sacrifice, worship-offering of the priests, the celebration of religious festivals, respecting the sacred, living a strict moral code, offering expiatory rites, the use of a fetish and recourse to magic. The second chapter deals with the Greco-Roman-Hellenistic Tradition, which consists of three interrelated cultures, of which the most dominant is the Greek culture. The three essays attempt to explore the Greek, Roman and Hellenistic pantheons and the various means each of these religious traditions provides for their adherents to come in touch with the gods. The third chapter deals with the Hindu Tradition. Here we shall attempt to clarify the Vedic Hinduism, Vedaantic Hinduism, Vaishnavism and Saivism, in four essays. In each of them our concern is to explore the reality of God in these Hindu religious systems and the various means they provide for their adherents to experience God-realization. The fourth chapter deals with the Jaina Tradition. The introduction explores a brief history of Jainism, its scriptures, its community and its doctrines. The two ensuing essays analyze the Divinities of the Jaina Pantheon and the Jaina path to the Divine. The fifth chapter deals with the Buddhist Tradition. Its introductory essay deals with a history of the Buddhist religion, Buddhist scriptures, Buddhist community and the basic Buddhist doctrines. The three subsequent essays attempt to explore the three major branches of Buddhism, viz., *Hiinayaana*, *Mahaayaana* and the *Vajrayaana*. Our main thrust in these essays is to study the pantheon of Divinities in these three Buddhist religious traditions and the means they provide for adherents to come into contact with the Divinities. The last essay of the first volume deals with the Sikh Tradition. After the usual introductory comments, the two following essays attempt to elaborate God in Sikhism and the various Sikh paths to God.

The second volume begins with the seventh chapter and deals with the Jewish Tradition. The three essays elaborate the reality of God and the paths to God, in Jewish Orthodoxy, *Kabbalahism* – Jewish Mysticism, and *Hasidism* – Jewish Spiritualism. The eighth chapter studies the Islamic tradition. The first two essays attempt to examine the Islamic reality of God and the Islamic paths to God in Islamic Orthodoxy and Sufism – the Islamic mystical tradition. The last essay concerns the *Baha'i* faith, in both of these aspects. The ninth chapter deals with the Christian tradition. The first three essays speak of Roman Catholicism, Eastern Orthodoxy and Protestantism, while the last essay looks at the Christian mystical perception of the God and the mystical path to God. The tenth chapter deals with the Chinese and Japanese Religious Traditions, such as, Confucianism, Taoism and Shintoism. The eleventh chapter investigates the reality of God and the paths to God according to the Zoroastrian Tradition.

The conclusion will attempt a synthesis of these traditions. It will indicate possible comparative studies on various themes that emerge in these two volumes. The work includes also a select bibliography on each of the traditions taken for study.

Chapter 1

Primitive Religious Traditions

INTRODUCTION

Primitive religious traditions present themselves as an interesting topic for deeper study and analysis. It is difficult to talk about primitive religions, their origin and development, as we have very little evidence about these religions. Our attempt to understand them in terms of speculative theories, may not give us a clear picture of these religions, as the conclusions arrived at would basically be speculative and not necessarily founded on reality. Probably we would never be able to know the reality of the ultimate origins of primitive religions. This thinking makes some authors even question the use of the term "primitive" to refer to these religions. In the introductory section, we would briefly sketch the validity of the use of the term "primitive" in relation to these religions, the nature, characteristics and types of primitive religions.

I. TERM "PRIMITIVE": A VALID QUALIFICATION

The use of the term "primitive" to refer to ancient religious traditions has run into difficulties. A number of scholars raise their eyebrows at this usage. They say that the term "primitive" cannot be used to indicate these religions on two counts. Firstly, if we take the term "primitive" in the sense of 'early', 'ancient', 'original' or 'primary', it cannot refer to these religions, as primitive man and his religion in this sense disappeared from the world thousands of years ago. The people and religions that are described thus are neither original nor primary, but belong to the present era of human existence. Therefore, it is wrong to speak of the religion of living people as primitive. Secondly, the term "primitive" could mean 'old-fashioned', 'backward', 'uncouth' or 'savage'. In this sense the term "primitive" stands at the opposite end of the pole from "civilized". Thus, used in this meaning to refer to these religions, the term "primitive" can indicate that they are unsophisticated and crude in comparison with the religions of developed civilization. Such use, according to these authors, is simply on the ground of racial and ethnic prejudice, and it indicates lack of sympathy and understanding from those races, which consider themselves superior to others.[1] This thinking has led authors to look for different words to refer to these religions in their works. These religions are being referred to as "religions of non-literate peoples"[2] and "traditional religions".[3]

There is a great deal of truth in the claims of these authors. Considered strictly, we cannot speak of primitives in any part of the present world. Neither can we have direct knowledge of the earliest beginnings of religion so as to have first hand information about the true chronologically primitive religion. Besides, in the course of the development of such religions there might have occurred a number of changes, and so the present day tribal religions are not primitive in the original sense. Therefore, to make such equations would be a claim that cannot be justified.[4] Again to say that these religions are 'the religions of the savages and the uncivilized' would be totally incorrect. As a matter of fact these people are not savages, though they may not be as developed as some other cultures and their religions are not absurd, though they may not have the doctrinal clarity of some religions. The religious thought of these religions is "remarkably sensitive and often refined and intelligent. It is also highly complex, to a degree that ethnologists after more than a century of study are still struggling to clarify their complicated beliefs and ritual practices."[5]

When we use the term "primitive" to indicate contemporary tribal religions we do not equate them with the ancient religions. Neither do we say that these religions are savage and uncivilized. It is possible that a person with such a bias can read into our use of the term "primitive" a racial or ethnic prejudice. In fact, the reason for the use of the term "primitive" to the contemporary tribal societies and their religions is very different. We could mention a few. Firstly, the prehistoric people also used primitive techniques, such as, food gathering and hunting for maintaining life. The people of the tribal societies depend on such methods to maintain life. "Since their mode of life corresponds to that of the prehistoric man, it is not unnatural to try to divine what went on in prehistoric times by reading into them the experience"[6] of the contemporary tribal people. Secondly, the tribal cultures of the present "have remained from time immemorial out of general and influential contact with other peoples and as a consequence are said to possess some religious beliefs and institutions which characterized her mankind nearer the beginnings of human history than other, major religions."[7] So they are primitive in the sense that they are the closest to the ancient religions. Thirdly, in the historical religions faith is a system of belief to which one may or may not become committed. Thus here faith is a matter of personal choice. But for prehistoric man and for tribal peoples religion is essentially part of the structure of everyday existence. Everyone adheres to religion by way of custom and practice rather than of choice. Therefore, we find a greater affinity between prehistoric religions and contemporary tribal religions.[8] All these affinities between prehistoric man and contemporary tribal cultures suggest that the latter derive their lineage from the prehistoric ancestors of the human race. Since we find a number of similarities between prehistoric people and contemporary tribal people both in behavior and practice, we use the term "primitive" in an extended sense to refer to the contemporary tribal cultures and religions. Such use has no racial or ethnic bias, and it is justifiable.

Nature and Characteristics of Primitive Religion

Now we can move on to consider the nature of the primitive religion. It is not a revealed religion, nor does it have a founder. It has no Holy Scripture or prophets; the beliefs about God, prayers and forms of worship are handed down through generations by word of mouth. It is a religion of the group. Primitive peoples were so identified with their clan that they could not think apart from it. Group thoughts, custom and tradition conditioned the life of the primitive people. Often they did not have a permanent place of worship and makeshift arrangements were made for worship. The rituals were often associated with magic. Animism, spiritism, magic, totemism and sacrifice are some of the characteristic elements of primitive religion.[9]

Animism consists in attributing qualities of the soul to material objects and non-human living creatures, such as the moon, a grove of trees, mountains, rain, sky and other similar objects. When animated with the soul, they are said to affect one's personal and social life. Since power is attributed to these objects, they are often regarded as extra-ordinary and supernatural.[10] Ethnologists and anthropologists use the term *mana* to refer to the quality of the soul that is found in objects. *Mana* is a supernatural force or power that operates silently and invisibly in objects and persons. It gives tremendous power to the one possessing it. Just as electricity is capable of doing much for the benefit of man and is at the same time capable of destroying him, in the same way the *mana* is capable of effecting evil and good for man. It usually resides in the chieftain, animals, plants and certain types of rocks. Primitives believed that the *mana* can be transferred from a person to an object, as an arrow can be endowed with it.[11] Belief in animism made the primitives worship natural objects such sun, moon, stars, rivers, clouds, winds and trees, besides revering animals such as tigers, crocodiles and snakes. The reasons for the practice of animism among the primitive people are the recognition of the secret powers possessed by these soul-filled realities, the good things they gave and the fear of the hurt they might do.[12]

Spiritism is an improvement over animism. In animism the souls are linked with an object, an animal or a place. But in spiritism the souls are not bound in this manner, but rather they are free to move about as they wish. According to spiritism, a soul that is bound to a body, a mountain or a tree can desert the place it was and go about as it wishes and return to its original place whenever it wishes. Spiritism gave rise to fetishism. A fetish may be a stone or any object that is said to possess mysterious powers because of the presence of the spirit. When the spirit is present in the fetish, it is revered, and when the spirit is away the fetish is discarded. Primitive people believed that a great number of spirits haunted the mountaintops, rivers, forests, trees and other such places and directed the lives of people. They also believed that some spirits are malicious and do harm to people, while others are good and save people in times of troubles. The recognition of the powers of the super-sensible spirits led the primitive people to revere the spirits and offer them worship.[13]

Primitive religion is associated with magic. It is an attempt on the part of man to achieve his ends by occult and mysterious means. Man has many desires, and he attempts to achieve them by taking recourse in the power of the spirits. The magicians use magical incantations, spells, formulae and other rites to achieve their ends. The magical rites are performed usually to achieve needs related to economic prosperity, sex, removal of illness in a person, fertility of the fields and warding off evil. Therefore, a large number of magical practices are centered on food supply, women, economic pursuit and effecting clement weather. The power of magic resides in words. Therefore, the incantations are recited deliberately and formally. A magician invokes the spirits to help him achieve these ends. Magic is a strategy the primitive people used to influence the spirits and get their help for achieving their purpose. Magic was called 'white' if its purpose was benefit or protection from harm, while it was 'black' if the intention was to do an injury. Though we cannot say that the primitive religion is magical, yet many of the religious rites practiced by the primitive people are magical. For instance, eating the totem animal was considered a magical means of bringing good to the tribe. Thus, in primitive religions the magical dimension was closely related to the religious rites.[14]

Totemism and sacrifice are two other characteristic elements of the primitive religion. Totemism is based on the belief that a clan has a deep sense of kinship with creatures other than human beings. A tribe may feel related to a particular species of animal or plant. The tribe considers that animal or the plant as its *totem*. The deep sense of affinity is such that the *totem* animal or plant is considered as the ancestor of the clan. The life of the tribe is bound up with the *totem,* and is closely linked with the social well being of the people of the tribe. Therefore, the members of the tribe honor the *totem* with reverence and respect. In this manner totemism brings about genuine fellowship and social living within the members of the tribe. Totemism also has a sacrificial dimension. Generally the members of the tribe are not allowed to kill a *totem* animal, as it is sacred to them. But there are occasions of communal celebration, when the *totem* animal is sacrificed and shared by all the members of the tribe. The primitive people believe that when the *totem* animal is sacrificed, the gods and the people eat it in a common meal. Such a meal is considered as a sacrament, and they believe that it brings a bond of union among them, besides bringing strength and power to the people of the tribe.[15] Other than the totem sacrifice there was also the practice of offering expiatory sacrifices and sacrifices to appease gods. Human sacrifice was also prevalent. Offering of the firstborn children, guilty tribesmen and, in extreme cases offering of the tribal chief in sacrifice to appease the deity was also practiced. The surrender of worshipper and his self-denial is best expressed in these sacrifices. Primitive peoples believe that such sacrifices arouse the sympathy of the deity towards the worshipper.[16]

Types of Primitiave Religion

Ethnologists speak of two types of primitive religion. Firstly, the lower type, which is pure, untouched by other major religions and lacks speculative development. Besides, the lower type of primitive religion is more animist, spiritist and fetishist. The following are some of the lower type primitive religion: the Negritos of the Philippine Islands, various tribes of

Micronesia and Polynesia, the Papuans of New Guinea and the black Aruntas of Australia. To this group also belong the Andaman Islanders in the Bay of Bengal, the Kols and Pariahs of Central and South India, the Pygmies and Bushmen of Central Congo basin, the Caribs of the West Indies, and the Yahgans of the extreme south of South America. Secondly, a higher type of primitive religion developed later than the lower type. To this group belong the Samoans and Hawaiians, the Kalmuks of Liberia, the Veddas of Ceylon, the Todas of the Nilgri Hills in South India, the Bantu of South Central and Southern Africa and the Eskimos and Amerinds, i.e., the American Indians of North and South America.[17]

Ethnologists further divide the lower and the higher type of primitive religion as traditional, syncretist and spontaneous. This division is aimed at making a precise assessment of the nature of the types of primitive religion according to its origin and development. The traditional group has attempted to maintain the originality of the ancestral religion, preventing any influence from outside to change the original pattern of life and worship. Usually the traditional group is isolated, as they lived in places that are removed from the other cultures. They occupied mountainous areas or islands. The Syncretist group is more open to other cultures and religions. They often adapt forms of religious worship and practice from other higher religions. The spontaneous group is a traditional type of primitive people, who in response to the decline of their culture and religious practice, create new forms of belief and ritual and thereby attempt to maintain their own identity and originality.[18]

Now that we have made some introductory remarks about primitive religion in general, we could move on to consider, in the following two essays, the world of the Divine and of the divinities in the primitive religion and the primitive peoples' path to reach out to the Divine, respectively.

1.1. THE SPIRITUAL WORLD OF THE PRIMITIVE RELIGION

The spiritual world of the primitive religion is filled with various levels of spiritual beings. For instance, if we take the Ainu religion[19] we find there a rich variety of spirits. They use the term "*kamui*" to refer to the spiritual beings. The first group of *kamui* is considered as remote and traditional, which includes gods of the sky. It is believed that *Kando-koro Kamui*, one of the *kamui* belonging to this group, assigned *Moshiri-kara Kamui*, to create the land of Ainu. The *kamui* of this group, though not reached in many rituals, are considered as significant gods (*pase-kamui*) and are revered by the people. To the second group belong the trustworthy *kaumi* with whom the Ainu people have regular dealings. The leader of this group of *kamui* is *Shiramba Kamui*, who is referred to as "the upholder of the world", whose spirit-energy (*ramat*) vivifies every form of plant life useful to the people. There is also another *Kamui Fuchi*, whose *ramat* is manifest in the fire of the hearth, which must be kept alive and never allowed to go out. The third class of *kamui* is related to the second class of *kamui*. These are subsidiary to the former and function on their behalf. The fourth group is spirits that have animal form. Animals like bears and foxes are considered as *kamui* who can take human shape in a miraculous manner. Some of these are considered as good, while others harm people. To the fifth group of *kamui* belong the spirit-helpers, which reside in the skulls of certain *kamui* of the fourth class. The sixth groups of kamui is the evil spirits that haunt places, which are dangerous to man, such as, woods, marshes, ravines and rapidly moving rivers. The seventh group of *kamui* is the malicious spirits of disease and pestilence. The eighth class consists of *kamui* that create horror and unpleasantness in human beings.[20]

The example of the Ainu religion clearly shows that the world of the spirits in primitive religion ranges from the highest type to the lowest. In order to understand the religious perception of the primitive people it is important to consider not only their concept of the Supreme Being, but also the many divinities and spiritual beings that populate the spiritual world. The spirits spoken of in the primitive religion can be listed under four categories. Firstly, the Divine, which is the Supreme Being and the source of everything in the universe: Secondly, the divinities or the associates of the Divine created by Him and standing for His activities. Thirdly, the free spirits those are beneath the status of the divinities and above the status of men. Some of these spirits are directly created, while others are spirits of the people who lived on this earth but have completed their state of being bound to the body. They are not body-bound and are the 'common populace' of spiritual beings. The fourth category is the living dead. They are spirits that are still in the process of attaining complete death and freedom from the body-bound world. In this essay we would attempt to elaborate on these four categories of the spirit in the primitive religion.

1.1.1. THE SUPREME BEING

Though there are fetishistic and animistic elements in primitive religion, it is interesting to note that a great number of them believe in a Divine that is the Supreme Being. Some writers on primitive religion speak of this Supreme Being as a "High God". This name gives one the impression that He is distant and transcendent, so much so that He is not involved with people. These authors mention the common belief in different parts of Africa that God is 'gone away', in the sense that He is very remote from the everyday concerns of ordinary people, to substantiate their idea of a "High God". They cite a myth, which says that there was a time when the sky, where God dwelt, was so near that it could be touched. But one day a woman took pieces of sky and cooked them in the soup. This angered God and He withdrew into the present distance. Since He has 'gone away' from the people, He no longer concerns Himself with human affairs. Another reason they give to justify their claim is the relative absence of rituals for the High God. On the one hand they speak of a Supreme Being and, on the other hand, there are not many ritual observances for the Divine. These writers claim that the possible reason for this is the remoteness and transcendent nature of the High God. Since He is uninvolved with the everyday life of the people, the rituals people offer do not concern him much. Therefore, He is also spoken of being existing beyond the firmament too exalted to be contaminated by the affairs of the ordinary people.[21] Though there may be a certain amount of truth in the claim of these writers, the study of primitive religion gives one a clear perception of primitive peoples' belief in a Supreme Being, who is the Supreme Sprit, who rules over lesser spirits and gods. He is described as governing the natural forces, creating souls, men and all other things in the universe. This Great Spirit is considered as the First Cause and the creator of the world. Besides, myths about God's anger and His distance, though simplistic and naïve, communicate the primitive peoples' belief in the numinous nature of God as the Holy Being. God, as the Holy Being, stands over against man in an exalted level, which is symbolized by distance. It also points out God's perfection and man's incapacity for perfection.[22] Thus, the distance and transcendence of God perceived by the primitive people, in fact, does not make the Supreme Being a "High God", but only points to the exalted nature of the Supreme Being and His holiness in comparison with the human being who is limited and imperfect.

Other writers speak of syncretism as the reason for the notion of the Supreme Being in primitive religion. Syncretism consists in primitive religions coming in contact with developed religions and accepting developed notions of the divinity from these developed religions. In other words, syncretism implies borrowing developed concepts of God and religious practices from the developed religions. According to these authors the idea of the Supreme Spirit as the creator of the universe present in primitive religion does not go back to the primeval history of the primitive religion, but rather is borrowed from one or the other developed religions. These authors cite the example of the primitive religion of Rhodesia as greatly influenced by the Jewish religion. They believe that the God *Lesa* is the creator of mankind that the first parents sinned and, as the result, death came into the world. Besides they also practice some customs that are distinctively Jewish, such as not eating certain types of meat, offering the first fruits, and concern over legal defilement, which are very similar to that mentioned the Book of Leviticus. There are also archeological evidences to show the presence of the Jewish community and a temple of Yahweh in Africa at the end of the 6th century BC. Besides, the discovery of Jewish coins in Natal and Zululnad in the pre-Christian era also points to the influence of the Jewish religion in the African primitive religion. Those who hold for syncretism as the reason for the belief in a Supreme Being in primitive religions put forward all these evidences and thereby conclude that until being influenced by the developed religions, there is no belief in the Supreme Being in the primitive religions. This claim of these thinkers can only be made of African primitive religion that was influenced by the Jewish religious ideas, but it cannot be made of primitive religions in Asia and other places, where no such syncretism can be established. The presence of the notion of a Supreme Being, even in religions where no syncretism can be established, clearly indicates that the experience of a Supreme Divinity is part and parcel of the belief of the primitive religion.[23]

One may object to the belief in a Supreme Divinity in the primitive religion, because God is presented in the myths as having wife, children, servants and messengers. Besides, He is described as having other gods as his partners and agents in the act of creation; for instance, the Semang of Malacca believe that *Ta Pedn*, the all-seeing creator God, who lives in heaven with His spouse. He also has a counterpart, who is manifested in thunder. The Siberian religion speaks of the Sky-God as the Supreme Being and that seven other gods stand beside Him and assist Him. Another myth from the Congo tribal religion speaks of God once living in the middle of Africa with His three sons, of which one was white, the other was black and the last was a gorilla. Again God is described as having a body, head, eyes, ears, mouth, arms and legs. The Supreme Being cannot be supreme if these qualities are attributed to Him. In understanding myths of the primitive religion, especially regarding the Supreme Being, we must keep in mind the fact that myths express primitive peoples' belief about God in graphic form. Myths speak of God in picture language and through symbols. Therefore, it is not necessary to accept every detail found in the myths. They are often stories told to communicate truth about God's spiritual direction of the universe to very simple and illiterate people. Besides, expressing the reality of the Supreme God in human language always involves physical imagery, and speaking of Him in negative terms as invisible and indescribable. Therefore, we must understand myths of the primitive religions metaphorically, looking for the underlying truth communicated by the myths rather than the feasibility of every detail contained in the myth.[24] From what we have said it is clear that the myths of primitive religions in no way disprove the existence of the belief in the Supreme Being among the primitive people.

Having established the truth about the fact of primitive religious belief in a Supreme Being, we can move on to talk about the nature, attributes, the ways of the Supreme Being and the images used by the primitive people to speak of Him/Her.

1.1.1.1. THE NATURE OF THE SUPREME BEING

The Supreme Being exists by Himself. He is different from any type of creature, as the latter are caused while He is the uncaused cause of everything. He has a pre-eminent place in the universe, as the universe depends on Him. The pre-eminence of God makes Him greater than any creatures, whether it is spirit or man. The greatness of God makes Him mysterious and incomprehensible. No one is able to know Him or understand His nature. The essential nature of the Supreme Being is one. Myths, which speak of God as related to wife, children and associates must be taken in a metaphorical sense. In fact God is the unity beyond all diversity and duality. God is not only the creator, but also the principle of unity that holds every duality such as heaven and earth, sun and moon, day and night, man and woman, together. The essence of God is present everywhere and sustains everything. Though He is given a number of attributes, He is beyond all such attributes. He is often not represented by a figure, as no figure is capable of depicting His real nature. That is probably the reason why people of tribal religions do not use statues or image in honoring the Supreme Being. But the Supreme Being is seen as one directing every moment of peoples' lives and as having a great deal of influence. Thus, primitive people had some form of belief in the providence of God.[25]

A look into the belief of the Ewe people of Upper Guinea illustrates a number of aspects we mentioned regarding the nature of the Supreme Being. They associated the Supreme Being with the visible sky. The blue of heaven is His veil and the clouds His dress and ornaments. The thunder is the sound of His voice. These expressions about God must be taken in the metaphorical sense. They give the Supreme Being, the name *Mawu* or *Mahou*, but they do not describe His attributes. *Mawu* is considered as the one reality behind the multiplicity that is experienced in the world. They never represent *Mawu* in figure; there are hardly any images or statues in relation to which worship is offered to *Mawu*. Worship is offered to Him by looking at the western sky as the sun is setting. People confide, as it were, to the setting sun the message they wanted to give to *Mawu*. The Ewe people depend on *Mawu* for everything in their life, as He directs their life and has a great deal of influence its affairs. A person who does not pronounce the name of *Mawu* as he rises in the morning is considered as equivalent to a beast. During the day they frequently pronounced the name of *Mawu*. When they faced any danger in their life, they always call on to Him for help, speaking His name aloud. If they gain any unexpected benefit, they attribute it to the good *Mawu*. When a person is accused falsely before a tribunal or court, they use the expression '*Mawu* knows my soul'. When faced with death the Eve people do not address any lower spirits, but call on *Mawu*, their Supreme Deity, to have pity on them.[26] The primitive people of Rhodesia believe in a Supreme Being, whom they call *Lesa Mukulu*. The name literally means God, the Supreme Being. They point to the superiority of their God over everything by saying that He is not in need of their offerings of flour and meat. They indicate their faith in His providence by saying that when *Lesa* cooks food there is no smoke and He gives food when they least expect it.[27]

In this manner for the primitive people, God, the Supreme Being, was the source of everything in the world including the other spirits on whom they depended and worshipped. During the most significant moments of their life they took recourse to the Supreme Being rather than to inferior deities.

1.1.1.2. ATTRIBUTES OF THE SUPREME BEING:

The nature of God is further elaborated when we consider the attributes given to Him in primitive religion. Some of the qualities attributed to the Supreme Being in primitive religion correspond to the names given to God in the developed religions. Of these attributes many point to the transcendent nature of the Supreme Being. Most of the primitive peoples associate the Supreme Being with the vault of heaven or the sky. Their speaking of God as in the sky indicates His transcendence and superiority over everything in the universe. As the Supreme Being, He is described as the omnipotent and all-powerful being. A few other titles given to the Supreme Being spell out further the quality of omnipotence. "Creator", "allotter", "the giver of rain and sunshine", "the one who made the great forests", "maker of souls" and the "one who exists by himself" are some of such titles. Thus, for most primitive people, God is the creator and ruler of everything that exists. He is beyond all the thanks and praise we offer Him. He is the ancient of days who is from the beginning. God is the everlasting being who has no limits and who is fullness and abundance. The Zulu people attribute the Supreme Being such names as "the one who bends down majesties", "the irresistible" and "the one who roars, thereby striking the nations with terror".[28]

Many other primitive people describe the Supreme Being in His transcendent and all-powerful aspect, and consider creation as God's natural and primary function. The Dinka people of Southern Sudan call the Supreme Being *Nhialic*, which means 'that which is above in the sky'. They refer to *Nhialic* as the creator. The Ga people, who live in Accra, Ghana, believe in a most powerful Supreme Spirit, whom they call *Naa Nyonmo*. They believe that He lives in the sky. He is the creator of everything. He created the heavens first and then the earth. Along with the earth, he also created the waters and all other things on earth. In creating the waters the *Naa Nyonmo* created the sea.[29] Many of the tribal people of Eastern Africa believed in a Supreme Being, whom they called *Mulungu*, which means 'He above' or 'He in heaven'. The (A)kambe people consider *Mulungu* as the creator of everything, who lives in heaven. He is superior to the spirits of the dead and all the forces of nature. For the Kikuyu of Kenya *Mulungu* is the creator of everything. He shows His power in the sun, the moon, the stars, the gale, the rain and the rainbow. To (Ba)konko people of Kongo territory, *Nzambi* is the creator of the world and of the humankind. For the tribal people of Western Cameroons *Nyambe* has created the earth. The Semang people of Malacca believe in a creator God, whom they call *Ta Pedn*. The North American Indians believe in a Great Spirit, who is the creator, whose strength manifests and permeates everything. The Araucan people of South America believe in the Supreme God, who is called 'the Lord of mankind', 'the Lord of the land' and 'the blue King'. The last title refers to the fact that He is associated with the sky. He is seen as the creator, giver of life and fertility. He is also responsible for the well-being of humanity.[30]

Besides, the many indications regarding the all-powerful, transcendent and creative aspect of the Supreme Being, there are also a number of references to God as present everywhere; He is immanent in the world. We find God is described in primitive religion as omnipresent, 'the one who is met everywhere', 'the great ocean whose headdress is the horizon', the wise one, 'the great pool contemporary of everything', 'the one who fills everything' and 'the one who brings round the seasons'. All these attributes bring to the fore the nearness of God to His people. Most of the primitive people experienced the immanence of God in physical and natural terms.

They spoke of God's presence in big trees, in thickets, on mountains and rocky places and in rivers and streams. His immanence makes the people experience Him as many, though He is one, as He is available to everyone in the life situation of each person. God is said to be invisible in ordinary times, but people can experience Him before they die. The voice of the immanent God is heard when the bush burns or the wind blows.[31] The Maori people, who belong to the Polynesian tribes and who live on the islands in the South Pacific Ocean, believe in the Supreme Being, whom they call *Io*, which means 'the innermost part'. For them *Io* is the Supreme Power (*atua*). He lived before anything else lived. They consider *Io* as the innermost part of everything that lives in the sky and on earth. For them, *Io* is 'the source of all knowledge' (*Io Wananga*), 'the spring-water of life' (*Io Te Waiora*) and 'the face that cannot be seen" (*Io Mata-ngaro*). Thus, the Maori people consider their Supreme Being as the immanent principle of life and activity, as He is the innermost of everything in heaven and on earth.[32]

Besides considering the Supreme Being as transcendent and immanent, the primitive people also attribute to Him moral and humane qualities. In addition to being supremely great, omnipotent, omniscient and present everywhere, He is kind towards people. In His providence He deals with people in great benevolence. He is spoken of as the God of destinies, the kindly disposed, the God whose providence watches over all like the sun, the God who is full of pity, the father of babies and the great friend. He is considered not only as the creator of the world, but also as the one who established the laws of the society. Justice, truth and equity exist in society only where people live in obedience to Him. Such beliefs about the moral nature of God are reflected in the Akan people giving God the title "the one on whom men lean and do not fall".[33]

In expressing the benevolent nature of God and His universal goodness the Rhodesian tribal people compare their Supreme Being, *Lesa Mukulu*, with a blacksmith who caters to the needs of all and with a tailor who makes cloth for everyone. He is also invoked as the God who upholds truth. People often call on *Lesa Mukulu* to justify their truthfulness. For instance when their truthfulness is questioned they say "may *Lesa* strike me dead if I lie". Their Supreme Being, *Lesa*, is also referred to as one who preserves their health and as the one who punishes the evildoer.[34] The Eve tribal people also call on their Supreme Being *Mawu* to proclaim their truthfulness and innocence. When falsely accused before a tribunal they cry out "*Mawu* knows my soul". For them *Mawu* is good, always ready to help them and ready to forgive them. So, when faced with troubles of life, they call on Him saying "*Mawu* help me, I ask you". Before anyone dies he asks *Mawu's* forgiveness by saying "*Mawu* have pity on me". The tribal people of Congo and Angola call on their Supreme Being, *Nzambi's* conscience, to be their witness when faced with untrue accusations. They use His name to pledge oaths.[35] The Selknam tribe of the South American Indians of Tierra del Guego believes that the Supreme Being, *Temaukel* lives in heaven. Though He is invisible, He sees everything and is the guardian of the moral life of the people.[36]

All these examples show clearly that the primitive people not only believed in the Supreme Being, but also attributed to Him moral qualities. Thus, they experienced the Supreme Being as the benevolent Deity who, though at a distance, exercised overall control over everything in the world and had true concern for peoples' welfare.

1.1.1.3. THE WAYS OF THE SUPREME BEING

Though the Supreme Being is experienced as transcendent, immanent and the guardian of morality, sometimes the primitive people questioned the manner in which God treated them. They did not understand the ways of God, as these were incomprehensible and inscrutable. Myths of the primitive religion brought to the fore the unpredictable ways of God's dealing with them. One famous African myth narrates how God *Leza* brought a great deal of trouble for an old woman with a large family. God first smote her parents and then all her relatives. The deaths of her husband, children and grandchildren followed. Only she was left, and she hoped to die. But strangely enough she grew younger, as she ate the soul-stuff of her relatives. She decided to use her newly found powers to find where God is and to get an explanation for the way God has treated her and her family. She attempted to reach the sky where God is by making a ladder out of forest trees. Since this attempt failed, she decided to travel through every country until she found a place where heaven touches the earth, thereby providing her a road to God's dwelling place. To those who questioned her about her travels, she said that she suffered a great deal from God and she was seeking Him to get from Him an explanation for His behavior. Those who heard her speak told her that to have trouble in life is nothing strange. "No body can be free of troubles, as God's ways are incomprehensible".[37] There are also other myths that speak of God's anger and the reason for His distance from people. One such myth goes as follows. The sky, the dwelling place of God was once very near to the people. Then people could easily have contact with God. But people seem to have lost respect for God and His dwelling place, the sky, as it was so near to them. One day one woman took pieces of sky to make soup. This disrespectful behavior seemed to have made God angry and He withdrew from the earth to the present distance. There are also many myths that speak of the reason for God bringing death in the life of man. We could mention one such myth from the primitive people of Congo. Once upon a time God lived in the middle of Africa with three of His sons, one a white, the second a black and the third a gorilla. The black son and the gorilla disobeyed God. In anger God withdrew to the west with His white son and all His riches. The gorilla retired into the middle of the forest, while the black son was left in poverty, despair and ignorance. In this manner evils such as poverty and death entered the life of man.[38]

All these stories must be understood metaphorically. Though we need not take all the details of these stories as true, they all question God's role in the suffering and evil in people's lives. The primitive people wondered about God behaving with them in this manner. Their query was, 'If God is the omnipotent, omniscient and moral guardian of our lives, how can such troubles come?' If God is the creator of the universe, what is His role in the continued existence of the world and its people? The Primitive mind attempted to answer these questions by pointing to the fact that God's ways are beyond man. Therefore, they can never be known. God is the giver of destinies. His ways may appear harsh and inscrutable, but people should not be fatalistic about their lives because of the troubles. Neither should they question God's ways. They must also see that many a time God consoles them. Good things also happen in the universe. The creative work of the Supreme Being continues in His sustaining activity in the universe. Thus, the sustenance of the universe is the continuance of the creative act of God. There are many sustaining actions of God taking place in the world. He gives rain and sun. He blesses people with health and fertility. God is the deliverer and savior, as He guides everything within His providence. The troubles such as disease, poverty, drought, famine, pestilence and death must be accepted as part of the mystery of God's nature and action. Man's response to God's ways must be one of submission rather than rebellion, as God is the supreme and central moving force of the whole universe and every reality in it including man.[39] Some of the names the Maori people give to *Io*, the Supreme Being, point to their unquestioning acceptance of the ways of God. They call Him the Great, the Eternal and the Unchanging. He is looked upon as the Source of all sacred and occult knowledge; he is the Parent or the Origin of all things, while Himself being Parentless. While He is recognized as the Source of welfare and of all life, He is seen also as the Vigilant and the Withholder. As the Source of welfare and of all life, the Supreme Being sustains everything in the universe. But He is also the Vigilant One, who sees what people are and what they do. Therefore His care for people should not be taken for granted by people. As the Withholder, the Supreme Being possesses power to prevent man from gaining all his desires. The Supreme Being - as the Source that sustains everything, the Vigilant who sees the ultimate good of man and as the Withholder who has the power to give what He wishes - knows what is the best for man. Therefore, He gives and withholds at His pleasure. Thus, God is within His power to act in the way He wishes towards His people. People should not question God for His ways, but accept His will without grumbling.[40]

1.1.1.4. SUPREME BEING: ITS IMAGES

The primitive peoples use a number of images when they address the Supreme Being. Human images are used to refer to the Supreme Being. He is referred to as 'father'. The Araucans of South America spoke of their Supreme Being as 'The blue king and father' indicating that though He lived in the sky, God is their father, who cares for them. The Uitoto people of Colombia also called their Supreme Being father. They regarded Him as the creator and the one who founded religious ceremonies. There are primitive people who worship the Supreme Being in the form of female deity. The tribal people of Southern Nuba referred to their God as the 'Great Mother'. The Cagaba people of

South America believed in a female Supreme Being, considered as the mother of all men, the world, animals, fruits, rivers, thunder, the Milky Way, song, dance, sacred object and sanctuaries. Some Siberian tribal peoples believed in a female Supreme Being, whom they named as the life giving 'Mother of the Milk Lake, and 'the Progenitrix'. The Fon people consider their Supreme Being as male-female and give the name *'Mawu-Lisa'*. But generally the Supreme Being is personified as the great ruler.[41]

There are times the Supreme Being is described as a glorified ancestor or a cultural hero in order to organize creation. The functions attributed to this cultural hero are the following. Firstly, he organized the shapeless world and killed the monsters inhabiting it. Secondly, he stole fire from the sun. Thirdly, he restored the world after the great flood. Fourthly, he created humankind and ordered their lives. The cultural hero appears in many manifestations. Some North American Indian tribal people speak of three such manifestations. The first is the *Manabozho*, i.e., the Big Hare. He is the founder hero, who created the second world when the flood destroyed the first. He also killed the snake that oppressed the people. The Second manifestation is the *Coyote*, the Prairie Wolf, who was the organizer of the world. The third is the Raven, the *Demiurge*.[42]

Often God is seen as related to heavenly bodies and is at times identified with them. A great number of tribal people associate the Supreme Being with the sky, and often He is seen as identical with it. The myths that speak of God's anger and divine withdrawal clearly see Him as the one who dwells in the sky. The Eve people of Upper Guinea identify the Supreme Being with the visible sky. The aboriginal people of the Andaman Islands believe in the Supreme God, *Puluga*, who lives in the heavens in a big 'stone-built-house' and is manifested in thunder and lightening. There are other myths that identify the Supreme Being with the sun. The Ashanti people of Upper Guinea call the Supreme Being *Nyame*, which means 'the shining one'. The tribal people who live around the Gulf of Mexico consider the sun as their highest deity. The tribes of East Africa, the Gold Coast and Nigeria consider the sun as the Supreme Being. The Ge tribal people of Eastern Brazil worship the sun as the creator and the father of men. The Koryak people of Siberia worship the sun as their Supreme Deity. There are other stories where the sun is personified and seen as that which possesses the spirit of God, i.e., as the manifestation of God. The Plains Indians of North America consider the sun as that deity which can transmit the gifts of the Great Spirit of mankind. The Kaffa people of Ethiopia believe that the sun represents the fatal force of the Supreme God. Sometimes other celestial bodies are also connected with God. The Akan people of Ghana believe that the thunderbolts are God's axes, the rainbow is His bow and lightning is seen as God's weapon against the evildoers. The pygmies believe that the Supreme Being, *Khmwum*, manifests in the rainbow. The Toba-Batak people of Sumatra believe in the Supreme Being, which has three aspects. Each of these aspects represents a part of the cosmos, viz., the sky, the human world and the nether world. In the third aspect, the Supreme Being appears as the God of thunder, rain and fertility.

Their myths also speak of the cosmic tree of life that originates in the nether world and reaches up to the sky. The Supreme Being is sometimes identified with the entire cosmos represented by the cosmic tree of life.[43]

The Supreme Being is spoken of as dwelling in earthly objects and places. Certain places such as high mountains, like Mount Kenya, are said to be dwelling places, where the transcendent God is manifested to the people. Often people go up to such mountains to offer prayers and sacrifices to the Supreme Being. Groves of trees and open places are also considered sacred. The Gikuyu people pray to the Supreme Being in open places. Many unusual happenings in nature, such as earthquakes and floods, are attributed to the direct action of the Supreme Being. The regularity of nature, succession of day and night, heat and cold, and various seasons are ascribed to the Supreme Spirit. In this manner, everything in the universe comes under the concern of God, the Supreme Being.[44]

Though the Supreme Being is understood in anthropomorphic, celestial and earthly images, the primitive people give Him a prominent place in their lives. They consider Him as superior to all other spirits and the source of everything in the universe. He is seen as the guardian of moral law. He rewards the good and punishes the evildoers. John A. Hardon expresses aptly the belief of the primitive people about the Supreme Being as follows:

> The general pattern, whether in Africa or elsewhere, is that this High God [the Supreme Being] is supposed to live in the sky and is clearly soul-like. He is eternal, all knowing, and almighty without abusing his power. He acts with sovereign freedom as author of the moral law, and rewards and punishes not only in this life, with prosperity or adversity, but beyond the grace in a life after death. Unlike the gods of mythology he is asexual although mythological influences have endowed him with human emotions and traits. Such a personage inspires believers with reverence, so that they are reluctant to name him. They do not worship him in temples or through images but invoke him in spontaneous prayer in times of special need, and many offer him first-fruits in token adoration, and not as though he were the ghost of a dead person who receives food for his sustenance.[45]

After scaling through the concept of the Supreme Being in primitive religion, one wonders as to the reason for the presence of animistic belief in primitive religion even though there is a rich concept of belief in one Supreme Being. The question naturally arises, 'Which of these beliefs is more original and archaic?' Evolutionary anthropology proposed the theory that the original state of the primitive religion is animistic. From the animistic state emerged polytheism, belief in many gods. Polytheism gave way to monotheism, belief in one Supreme Being. Though this theory might sound very logical, an objective study of primitive religions reveals monotheism to be the more original. The development of animistic and polytheistic beliefs in primitive religion is the result of some form of religious decadence. In other words, the belief in one Supreme Being, which was the original creed of the primitive people, came to be overlaid by animistic, polytheistic and other elements. From this it follows that to the extent that animism, polytheism and other elements dominate the religion of the modern primitives, their religion has degenerated. The reason for our claim is the widespread presence of the belief in one Supreme Being in almost every primitive religion. This is mentioned before every other deity as the creator of the universe including other deities. Thus, there seems to be a downward movement, i.e., from the Supreme Being to many gods and to the spirits, rather than a successive upward movement of animism to polytheism and of polytheism to monotheism, as suggested by evolutionary anthropologists. But neither can we determine the extent to which monotheism was affected by animistic and polytheistic elements, nor generalize their mutual relationship, because there is such a variation of belief regarding these among the tribal religions.[46]

Our concern in this paper is not to enter into such controversies elaborately. Having considered the belief of the primitive people in one Supreme Being, before entering into the study of their belief in other spiritual beings, we raised this question in passing. Now we move on to the study of spiritual beings other than the Supreme Being in primitive religion.

1.1.2. DIVINITIES

Divinities are God's associates. They are the personifications and manifestations of the Supreme Being. They manifest the power of the Supreme Being in natural phenomena and objects. Often many names are used to refer to these groups of spirits. They are known as nature spirits, deified heroes, mythological figures, demigods, gods and ancestral spirits. The primitive people believe that God creates these divinities. Ontologically they are of the nature of spirits. They are associated with the Supreme Being and often stand for the activities of God. They display the power of God as manifestations sometimes personifications of God, at other times as spiritual beings in charge of the major phenomena of nature. Some of these manifestations take the form of the deified national hero, such as the tribal chieftain.[47] We could consider a few examples from different primitive religions.

Some African tribes believe that all events depend on two kinds of spirits, viz., the *mipaji* and the *nguru*. The *mipaji* are the spirits of the dead. The powerful ones are the spirits of the deceased chiefs. Some of are good, while others are evil. According to their nature they bring good to people or cause illness and death. Huts are built to house these spirits. They are offered food and drinks to win their favor and to ward off their anger. People attempt to reach out to these spirits through the help of magicians. By such objects as pieces of skull, jawbones and human skeleton (*kabbas*), they communicate with these spirits. Another way of communication with these spirits is for people, mostly women, to be possessed by them and to receive from them directions for action from the spirits. The *nguru* are also spirits, who attempt to control the rain, drought, famine, weather and such natural phenomena. Normally *nguru* are found in the mountains, waterfalls and riverside. They live in animals like lions, leopards, snakes and big trees. They also have the knowledge of medicine. The people communicate with these spirits, with the help of persons who possess these spirits. People also provide the *nguru* sacred huts for their use. They travel from one place to another in answer to proper incantations to make their presence felt in favor of anyone, who calls upon them for their help.[48]

The Dinka people of Sudan believe in a number of divinities associated with their Supreme Being, the *Nhialic*. Some of these associates of God are clan-divinities. The Dinkas believe that these divinities are present in the clan emblems. These emblems include many kinds of animals, birds, insects, trees, the forest, the rain, the river Nile and the planet Venus. These emblems of the clan divinities are treated with respect. Other than these clan divinities, the Dinka people also believe in a few free divinities, not connected to any particular clan. These divinities are known by personal names. Some important free divinities are the following: *Deng*, who is also known as *Dengdit,* is associated with rain, thunder and lightening. *Gerang* is a free divinity, which is associated with red-brown and brown colors in association with white. Men possessed by this divinity are believed to have the power to cure sickness. The term '*Gerang*' is the name used to refer to the first man. The free divinity *Abuk* is the symbol of kindness, thought to be a female divinity it is associated with the welfare of women. *Macardit* is considered as 'the great black one'. It is a harmful power, which brings evil and hurtful effects on men. For Dinka people this divinity is the final explanation of sufferings and misfortunes. Dinka tribal people do not think that the divinities have human forms. They associate them with emblems and think of them as operating in the great variety of natural objects. Divinities show their presence through rain, thunder, lightening and the changes of seasons. They manifest their presence in strange and unusual events. Again, the presence of the divinities is experienced when misfortunes like illness and death befall people. Divinities also manifest their presence through dreams, causing feelings of remorse or guilt and taking possession of human beings and speaking through them. [49]

The *Ashanti* people believe in a number of divinities through which the Supreme Being manifests Himself. They call them *abosom*. They are said to come from the Supreme Being and act as His servants. Their function is to be intermediaries between God and men. Major divinities take care of the tribe, while the minor divinities protect individual human beings. The Banyro people see their divinities as in charge of different aspects of the socio-political structure of the society. Thus, there are divinities of war, smallpox, harvest, health and healing, weather, lakes and cattle. Some of their minor divinities take care of different clans.[50]

The Yoruba tribal people are said to believe in 1700 divinities, which they call *orisa*. Their fields of activity are natural phenomena, objects, human activities and experiences. There are Yoruba myths, which say that these divinities offer the Supreme Being annual tribute and thereby acknowledge His Lordship. There is a hierarchy of Yoruba divinities. *Orisa-nla*, the supreme divinity, is considered as God's earthy representative. He performs creative and executive functions on behalf of God. *Orunmila* is the divinity of language. He can understand every language spoken on the face of the earth. He represents God's omniscience and knowledge. He also manifests himself through oracles of divination. He is also said to be a great doctor. *Ogun* is the divinity of iron and steel. He is called 'chief among the divinities' because he was responsible for other divinities to coming to earth. He is present everywhere and manifests himself in activities such as war and hunting where iron is used. *Sango* represents God's wrath. He is also the divinity of thunder and lightening. There are offerings to him to appease his wrath. The Walamo tribal people speak of a divinity connected with rain. He is said to dwell on a mountain. People take gifts there during drought.[51]

The tribal people of Siberia speak of the Sky-God as the Supreme Being, who is assisted by seven divinities, God's helpers. The Eskimoes believe in many spirits. Among them there are three true divinities. The first, *Sila*, the lord of the air, who is at times referred to as male, while at other time described as female. It manifests the Supreme Being's power of punishing man's sins. The second, *Sedna*, the deity of the water, is the queen of the sea mammals and the dead. She lives at her home at the bottom of the sea. According to the myth, the sins of mankind soil her and so she withholds good luck in hunting, until the *angakok*, the shaman, appeases her by combing her hair. The third is the divinity of the moon whose marriage with the sun took place at the beginning of time.[52]

Maori, the Polynesian tribal people, though they believed in a Supreme Being, *Io*, had faith in a great number of divinities, which they call *atua*. The term '*atua*' literally means 'power'. Its meaning is similar to the word '*mana*'. It can also be translated as 'strength' or 'greatness'. Thus, for them, divinities are powers that are at work in their lives. The *atua* are the invisible people. Some *atua* are the ancestors of the Maori people. They affect the lives of the people for good and for bad. Thus, they bring good things and cause evil things to happen. For instance, at times they provide plenty of food, while at other times they give very little food. *Atua* gave power to a person, a family or to a tribe. Therefore, they were respected and people always try to please them. The Maori people understood the divinities and their activities through the things that are tangible and visible. Therefore, they associated the divinities with existing things in the world, such as stars, rocks, trees, springs of water, birds and animals. Maori believed that the divinities had the power to enter these natural objects. This made them call these objects 'visible representatives of the divinities' (*aria*) and consider such objects as sacred.[53]

The Maori people divided the divinities into three categories. The first group of *atua* had greater power than the second group, and the latter had more power than the third category of *atua*. All Maori tribal people worshipped the *atua* of the first group. We could mention some important *atua* of this group. *Tane* is the father of the trees, birds and animals. He is also said to have created human beings, giving them life. The word '*tane*' means a 'man' or a 'married man'. Thus, *Tane* is the divinity that gave birth to everything in the universe. He is said to possess all the powers of all *atua*. *Tu* is the *atua* of warfare. As Maori people consider warfare a great value, they hold *Tu* in great respect. This made them dedicate the male babies to *Tu* as soon as they were born. At the time of war, prayers were offered to *Tu*, with the hope that he would help and protect them during war. *Rongo* is the *atua* of peace and agriculture. After war people offer prayers to *Rongo*. He is also prayed to during the time of planting and harvesting. The first fruits of the land after harvest were offered to *Rongo*. *Tangaroa* is the *atua* that had control over sea and all that live in it. *Tawhirimatea* is the *auta* of winds and storms. Maori people prayed to him to calm the storm and to bring good climatic conditions. *Whiro* is the *atua* of darkness and evil. He causes illness and death. He is considered as the father of all powers that attempted to harm people. Only a few tribes worshipped the second group of *atua*. To this group belong three *atua*, viz., *maru, kahukura* and *uenuku*, all of which are concerned with the welfare of the people. Some Maori tribes believed that the latter two revealed their presence in the rainbow. If a rainbow appears in front of a war party they must return home, as it indicated the absence of support from the *atua* of welfare. On the other hand, if the rainbow appears behind a war party they are encouraged to go ahead with the war plan, as it is the sign that *kahukura* and *uenuku* have shown their support for the war plan of the people. A few families worshipped the *atua* of the third category. There were a number of family *atua*. They protected the families and its members. They also performed certain tasks for the family. Maori people believed that there were some *atua*, belonging to this third group that brought harm to people also.[54]

The *Ga* people of Ghana believed in a Supreme Being, *Naa Nyonmo*. It was also their belief that *Naa Nyonmo* had many sons and daughters, who were known as *dzemawodzi*, which literally means 'gods of the world'. Thus, *dzemawodzi* are the divinities the *Ga* people believed in. Though these divinities have their abode in the sea, lagoons, mountains and other natural objects, they move about in the world. They are intelligent and powerful, as *Naa Nyonmo* handed His authority over to them. They are in active contact with the world of nature and human beings. The *Ga* people believed that each clan had its *dzemawodzi*. But all of them are not of the same rank. Some of them are more senior, while others belong to the lower order. The most senior divinity is the *nee*, the sea-god, whose wife is *afiyee*. They have many children, two of whom are *koole*, the lagoon-goddess and *ashi akle*, the sea-goddess. Some other important deities are *sakumo*, the river-god, who is also the god who leads people in war, and *la kpa*, a lagoon-god. The Ga people worshipped all these divinities. There are also other divinities, which the *Ga* people revered. They are associated with natural objects like trees and mountains, as for example the *otu* group of divinities. There are also other divinities, which the Ga people adopted from other tribes like the Fante, the Akwapim and the Ewe.[55]

All these illustrations from primitive religions clearly indicate that the primitive people believed in a great number of associate deities, besides their belief in the one Supreme Being. For some reason the primitive peoples came to believe that these divinities were closer to them here on earth and affected their lives greatly, in comparison to the Supreme Being. Therefore, they were more concerned with appeasing the divinities than focusing their attention on God. Having looked into primitive peoples' belief in the divinities, we now move on to consider the third group of spiritual beings, viz., the free spirits.

1.1.3. FREE SPIRITS

Besides their belief in the Supreme Being and the divinities, the primitive people believed in many spirits. The divinities are associates of God and belong to a relatively higher level of spiritual existence. The free spirits are common spiritual beings that come below the level of divinities and rank above the living-dead. They constitute the 'common populace' of spiritual being. There is no clear indication in the primitive religions as to how spirits came to be. There are varying beliefs among the primitive people regarding the origin of spirits. It is believed that God created some spirits as a race. They, then, like any other living creatures, continue to reproduce and add numbers to their race. But the most common belief is that human beings become spirits after their physical death. For most men, becoming spirit is their final destiny, though a few, such as national heroes, might be deified as divinities. Thus, arriving at the state of being the spirit is the final destiny of man. Some people believe that, under normal circumstances, man need not attempt to become a spirit, but automatically becomes one, just as a child becomes an adult or an adult becomes an old man. A few tribal societies hold the existence of spirits in animals and their continued living along with the human and other spirits after death. For instance the Eskimoes of North America believe that animals and natural phenomena had their spirit and called them *inua*.[56]

The spirits are called 'free spirits' because they are not body-bound. The spirits are not body-bound because they have gone beyond the horizon of the *Sasa* period, the state in which the life of physical involvement with other human beings and objects (*Sasa*) and have sunk into the *Zamani* period. Having entered the *Zamani* period, in which such physical involvement has ceased to exist, the spirits have become part of the state of collective immortality. As a result they are freed of all family ties and personal relationship with other human beings. They have lost their human names and all association with the human life once they lived. They have also grown out of the state of the living-dead. As far as men are concerned, spirits have become strangers, foreigners, outsiders, and they belong to the category of things. Therefore, often the spirits are referred to with the pronoun 'it'. Thus, becoming a spirit, as an ontological mode of existence, involves a depersonalization, a withering of human individuality, rather than a completion and maturation of the human individual. So for the primitive people death was the end of being a human being, which implies a loss of human personality, disappearance of the human name, becoming less of a person and assuming the mode of a thing, the spirit. As a result, spirits are not visible, and human beings do not see them either physically or mentally. The reality and existence of the spirits, therefore, becomes the object of the corporate belief of the primitive people.[57]

Becoming spirits involves a loss of human personality and the end of human life, which once the spirits lived. This is a social elevation in the mind of the primitive people. Spirits as a group are believed to have more power than men have. This is because the realm of the spirits is ontologically nearer to God. They fill up the ontological region of the *Zamani*, while men are still in the *Sasa* region. Thus, the spirit-mode existence bridges the ontological transcendence of God and of the divinities with that of man's existence. Therefore they can communicate with the divinities and God directly, whereas men need intermediaries to do the same. Primitive people believe that the spirits are older than men, as the spirits have already passed through the *Sasa* and reached the state of *Zamani*, while men are still in the *Sasa* state. The fact, that the spirits belong to a realm that is higher than the human realm and that they are older than men made the primitive people respect the spirits. Just as the young respected the elders, so also the primitive people respected the spirits. The social etiquette of respecting the elders was observed in the case of the relationship between the spirits and men, as men are younger than spirits.[58]

Though spirits are free, not body-bound and believed to be ubiquitous, yet the primitive people allocated different places for spirits to dwell. Some primitive people believed that spirits live in the underground, the nether-world and the subterranean region. The reason for this comes from the fact that the dead people are buried underground, and so it points to and symbolizes the new home for the departed. Therefore, the primitive people believed that the spirits lived in the subterranean region. There was also the belief among some tribal people that the spirits lived above the earth, as in the air, in the sun, in the moon or in the stars. The reason that led these people to locate the abode of the spirits in the celestial region was their belief that the spirits, having sunk into the *Zamani* state, are closer to God, who is believed to be in the sky. But the general belief of the vast majority of the primitive people regarding the dwelling of the spirits is that they live in woods, bushes, forest, rivers, and mountains and just around the villages where men lived. For instance, the Ga people of Ghana believed that spirits inhabited rivers, forests, certain trees and other natural objects. In other words, the general belief is that the spirits lived in the same geographical regions as men. The possible reason for this belief is primitive peoples' conviction that after their death they would also become spirits, and that they did not want to find themselves totally in a different environment.[59]

Folk stories speak of spirits being involved in a number of activities, such as, appearing to human beings in different forms, though they are said to be invisible to people's eyes. People believe that the spirits have a shadow form of body, with the help of which they assume forms of human beings, animals, plants and inanimate objects. Folk tales declare that the spirits are seen in ponds, caves, groves and mountains, besides outside the villages where men live. Some of the time passing activities attributed to the spirits are dancing, singing, herding cattle, working in the field and nursing their children. Spirits also appear in dreams to impart information. Specialists, such as diviners, priests, medicine men and rainmakers, consult spirits as a part of practicing their profession. There are stories that speak of the spirits playing the naughty game of calling people's names and confusing them. It is said that they derive a great deal of fun from this game. It is also believed that the spirits sleep during the day and are awake at night. Some spirits are said to be benign and good, while others are believed to be malicious.[60]

Spirit-possession is another important activity that is attributed to the spirits. In consists in the spirit taking hold of a person completely and making him act as it wishes. There are two forms of spirit possession. The first form is desirable and so is often induced through special dancing and beating of drums. When a person is possessed in this manner, the spirit communicates to the people special messages through the medium of the possessed person. The second form of spirit possession is not desirable, as it ends up in evil effects in the possessed person. In such cases the spirits cause severe torments in the possessed person, drive him out of his home and make him live in the forest. They can also lead the possessed person to jump into the fire or water, hurt himself with sharp instruments, fail to sleep for days or at times be led to do harm to others. In such possessions the spirits take hold of the personality of the possessed person and make him act as they wish. Such form of possession can damage the health of the one possessed. In some primitive societies people believe that illnesses, such as madness and epilepsy, are cause by the spirits.[61]

Due to the evils the spirits can bring on people, they look at the spirits with a certain amount of fear. People prefer not to have much contact with the spirits. As the spirits are not visible to peoples' eyes and are unpredictable in their ways of acting, people, in general, do not like to have much to do with the spirits. When the spirits attempt to harm the village or an individual person for some reason, the primitive people approached traditional doctors, diviners and magicians asking for help. These men are experts and they performed elaborate rituals to exorcise the spirit and to ward off the evil it might have brought to the people of the village or the individual person in question. Thus, though the spirits are powerful in bringing good or evil to human beings, human experts in the art of magic and medicine can manipulate and control the spirits as they wish, thereby driving away the same spirits or using them for their own advantage.[62]

1.1.4. LIVING-DEAD

Besides the free spirits the primitive people also believed in the existence of the living-dead. The living-dead is a person who has died, but who has not become a spirit. So they are different from the category of the free spirits. The living-dead shares the *Sasa* period with the human beings. Therefore, the living-dead is still in the state of personal immortality. The living-dead still lives on, as his death is not complete. Human beings have the closest link with the group of living-dead, as both live out the *Sasa* in varying decrees. The living-dead is bilingual, as the members of this group can speak the language of men and that of the spirits, divinities and God to whom they are drawing closer. They are part of their human families, and the family members and others have vivid memories of them. Thus, every member of the living-dead, as a group, is still a human being. They have not become spirits, and so primitive people do not refer to them as 'it'. But the living-dead is fast moving out of the *Sasa* and moving into the *Zamani*. The group of the living-dead includes all the departed persons up to the fifth generation. After five generations there is hardly any one who knows if the dead ancestor is still alive. When that happens, the process of death is completed as far as a particular living-dead is concerned. Then the living-dead has left *Sasa* and sunk into the horizon of *Zamani*. He is no longer remembered by name, as he is no longer a human being. Thus, the living-dead becomes a spirit, i.e., 'it', and merges into the company of spirits. To the living-dead that has sunk into the *Zamani* not much attention is paid in terms of fulfilling the obligation of the family members, as people lose contact and interest. Besides, the family members would have new generations of the living-dead to which they must pay more attention.[63]

We could briefly consider the beliefs of some primitive people regarding their living-dead. The Dinka people of Sudan believed that every human being has within him a soul or spirit, which they called *atiep*. The word '*atiep*' means 'shadow'. When a person dies, his *atiep* goes out of the body and remains near the house or the burial place. Sometimes the *atiep* appears in the dream of a family member. If any requests are made in such dreams, the family members carefully carry out the *atiep's* request. Dinka people believed that the *atiep* has the power to hurt his relatives in a number of ways. The *atiep* of the important living-dead is called *jok*. The *jok* includes ancestors of a particular clan, which could be either men or animals. *Joks* are considered almost as divinities, as they are more important than other living-dead.[64]

The *Ga* people of Ghana also believed in the spirits of the dead people. According to them everyone has a soul (*susuma*) and a spirit (*mumo*). It is the spirit that keeps one alive, whereas the soul gives him his personality. When the spirit leaves the body, a person dies. When that happens, his soul becomes a ghost (*sisa*). The ghosts live in the 'land of the ghosts', which is different from the physical world. Though different, it is a continuation of the present life. Therefore, the ghosts of the living-dead influence the lives of his family members. The Ga people believed that the living-dead could bring good as well as evil. Some of the evils the ghosts can bring are sudden death, chronic illnesses and poverty. It is believed that the living-dead is attentive to the needs of the children in a special way. If a child invokes the departed spirit for being neglected or cheated by his family members, the ghost of the living-dead promptly listens to the pleas of his child and inflicts severe punishment on the person who has cheated him. So the people feared the ghosts and took care to know their wishes, and carried them out. To ward off the evils the living-dead can bring, the Ga people also approached experts called *tsofatsemei*. This term literally means 'people of the tree roots'. These are medicine men, who, besides giving medicines, invoke all spirit powers by using sacred objects like the horns of some animals, empty clay pots and other similar objects, thereby attempting to bring about healing of mind and body. Some form of magic and witchcraft was also practiced among some of the Ga people to achieve the same purpose.[65]

The *Maori* people believed that human beings have a spirit, which they called *wairua*, besides the body. When a person dies his *wairua* continues to live and goes on a long journey. The first stage of the journey is arriving at the place at the top of New Zealand called 'the flying-off-place of spirits' (*Te Rerenga Wairua*). From there, crossing the sea, the *wairua* reaches the island of *Hawaiiki*, which is the original place of the ancestors of the Maori people. Finally the *wairua* lands at *Hine-nui-te-po*, which is the place of the god (*atua*) of death. During ceremonies for the dead, the Maori people prayed that the *wairua* of the dead person arrived at his final destiny soon. But this did not happen often. The *wairua* of the dead came back to visit the living family members. Some of these visits were for good, while others brought evil. They believed that these visits took place through a particular member of the family, a bird, an animal or other objects. The Maori people were afraid of the visits of the *wairua*. The family priest of the Maori peoples at times used the harmful *wairua* to bring harm to those whom they hated. But the tribal priests of the Maori people, who are more powerful than the family priests, attempted to send all *wairua* to their final destiny.[66]

These illustrations clearly show that living-dead, as a group, is very much involved in the life of the family members and does them a great deal of good. They have contact with their families and do communicate with the eldest member of their families. The eldest member is able to recognize the living-dead by name. They come to know and have interest at every happening in the family. The primitive people believe that those belonging to the group of the living-dead return to their families to take part in most of the major events of the family and share the food with the family members. They show keen interest in every family affair. They indicate to the members of the family some dangers that are ahead and admonish them for failure to follow the instructions they give. They are seen as guardians of the family, its customs, practices, morality and other activities. Therefore, a crime committed against a member of the family was seen as a crime committed against the living-dead of the family. In this manner the living-dead exerted a great deal of influence on the members of the family. Besides, they are of great help to the people. They are the best intermediaries between God and the human beings, as they are closer to God and belong to the same *Sasa* of man. Again they are able to speak the language of God and the language of men. As a result they can communicate the needs of men to God directly, without mediation of any others. Some primitive people also believed that all the living-dead communicate to God indirectly through the spirit of their forefathers. Therefore, the primitive people approached their living-dead with their troubles of everyday living instead of approaching God directly.[67]

Though the members of the group of the living-dead do a great deal to their family members, the relationship between them is not always very cordial, because physical death has built a certain distance between the living-dead and human beings. Besides, they believed that the living-dead not only do them good, but also harm. Therefore, peoples' reaction to the appearance of the living-dead is often twofold. On the one hand, they welcome the living-dead and show hospitality, because they need the services and benefits the living-dead can bring them. On the other hand, they would like the living-dead to move away from them and not return to them often, because the frequent presence of the living-dead makes the people feel uncomfortable and fearful. Thus the attitude of the people towards the living-dead is one of desiring to have their presence and, at the same time, their absence. The relationship that exists between the living-dead and the family members is not an inter-human relationship of cordiality, but rather one of utility. Besides, they want to appease the living-dead and keep it good humor that it does no harm to them. Prof. John S. Mbiti beautifully describes the relationship of the people to the living-dead as follows:

> When the living-dead return and appear to their relatives, this experience is not received with great enthusiasm by men; and if it becomes too frequent, people resent it. Men do not say to the living-dead: "Please sit down and wait for food to be prepared!"; nor would they bid farewell with the words: "Great so-and-so in the spirit world!" And yet these are two extremely important aspects of social friendliness and hospitality among men in African communities. The food and libation given to the living-dead are paradoxically acts of hospitality and welcome, and yet of informing the living-dead to move away. The living-dead are wanted and yet not wanted. If they have been improperly buried or were offended before they died, it is feared ... that the living-dead would take revenge. This would be in the form of misfortune, especially illness, or disturbing frequent appearances of the living-dead. If people neglect to give food and libations where this is otherwise the normal practice, or if they fail to observe the instructions that the living-dead may have given before dying, then the misfortunes and sufferings would be interpreted as resulting from the anger of the living-dead. People are, therefore, careful to follow the proper practices and customs regarding the burial or other means of disposal of dead bodies, and make libation and food offerings as the case might be.[68]

In this manner the relationship of human beings with the living-dead, though real and active, was not always cordial and friendly. Often fear, reservations and apprehensions marked such relationships. Besides, it was self-interest rather than the thought of the other that motivated these relationships.

The possible reason, for the living-dead treating the living family members harshly when they neglected to remember them, could be that the living-dead needed the assistance of the living family members, as they are living through their personal immortality in the later stages of the *Sasa* period. In other words, the living-dead, moving towards the realm of *Zamani*, needed the libations and rituals offered on their behalf by their family members. The Dahomey people on the coast of West Africa believe the following about their living-dead. When a man dies, his personal soul leaves the body and begins the journey towards the land of the dead. As he journeys, he experiences many obstacles on the way. Several rivers have to be crossed, and the boatmen have to be given offerings so that the soul can be ferried across the rivers. Unless the family members offer special rituals and oblations, the living-dead cannot cross the rivers. After reaching the land of the dead, the living-dead meets the other deceased members of the family. Even at this stage of the journey special ritual sacrifices are to be offered by the family members on behalf of the living-dead. When the living family members of the living-dead neglect their duty they thereby prevent the living-dead from moving into the next state of their existence, and they become angry and avenge the callous attitude of the family members.[69]

1.2. PRIMITIVE RELIGIOUS PATHS TO SPIRITUAL BEINGS

Our analysis of the spiritual world of the primitive people, thus far, has shown clearly the extent to which their thought and living are founded on religious feeling. Their world-view is a spiritual one. They not only attributed their origin to the Supreme Being, but also believed that from birth to death a person's life is directed and guided by the realm of the spirit. This is true not only of human beings, but also of every existing thing in this world. Their spiritual perception that life originated from God and is directed by the divinities, free spirits and the living-dead made them seek these divine realities at every moment of their lives. Therefore, primitive people made use of various means to come in contact with these divine beings and receive their blessing in every endeavor. It would be interesting to tread the path of the primitive people, in and through which they attempted to encounter the spiritual beings in the spiritual world. In this essay we attempt to explore the path, which the primitive people walked in their desire to experience the touch of the divine beings in their lives.

Though most primitive peoples believe in the Supreme Being yet regular worship is not offered to Him. For some reason He is in the background, as far as worship is concerned. There is very little ordered worship offered to God among the primitive people. There are times when He is addressed in prayer. But at other times the name of the Supreme Being is mentioned in prayers along with the divinities and other spiritual beings, but regular worship to the Supreme Being is not common. The greater part of the worship is offered to the lesser spirits. Though they seemingly receive most of the prayers and sacrifices, it is said that they carry essences of these to the Supreme Being, while keeping the externals of the offering for themselves. The spiritual beings other than God are seen as subordinated to Him and are believed to pray to God for men. That is why the name of the Supreme Being is first mentioned in some of the prayers that are addressed to divinities and other spirits. Though the Supreme Being is experienced as distant and transcendent, He is seen as the one who can be called upon in times of distress.[70] Some of the means with the help of which the primitive people attempted to encounter the divine beings are prayer and sacrifice, worship-offerings of the priests, celebration of religious festivals, respect for the sacred, living a strict moral code and offering expiatory rites. They also had recourse to the use of fetishes and magic to be in touch with the spiritual beings.

1.2.1. PRAYER AND SACRIFICE

The reasons for the offering of prayers and sacrifices are often utilitarian. Primitive people prayed for various motives. Most of these are material in nature and are aimed at safeguarding the well-being and prosperity of the tribe. For instance, the Dinka people of Sudan offered prayers and sacrifices for obtaining clement weather, such as rain and sunshine, which would help them in bringing a good harvest. They also prayed for other benefits such as protection of people and cattle, recovery from illness, relief from famine and other calamities, and for good hunting.[71] For example, the Maori people prayed invoking the spiritual beings to help court a lover, to help to kill a bird, to help one run quickly or to make the opponent run slowly and to help to mend a broken bone. They also prayed for the blessings of the divinities to remove harmful spirits from the house, to give strength and accuracy to a war spear and to help them keep things in memory. Prayers and sacrifices were also offered while dedicating a baby to the divinities, when the grace of the divinity is sought for the growth of the baby into a good adult.[72]

There are occasions when prayers are directed only to the Supreme Being. For instance, the Ewe people address prayers to *Mawu*, their God. When any danger is foreseen they instinctively call His name saying '*Mawu* help me I ask you'. When the people are blessed with any special favors they proclaimed "*Mawu* is good". When falsely accused they call on the Supreme Being to defend them saying "*Mawu* knows my soul". At the time of death the dying person directly calls on God saying "*Mawu* have pity on me".[73] The Wa-pokomo people who live on the right bank of the Tana in East Africa sometimes address prayer to the Supreme Being. In praying for a person who is ill, they say, "You are God and Master. I say to you, free this person from his sickness".[74] Another prayer for the sick person goes as follows: "This woman is ill. O God, give health to her, and to her village, and to her children, and to her husband; may she get up, hurry to work, take care of the kitchen; may happiness return, may it come from the other bank, may it come from the other bank."[75] The Dinka people of Sudan address prayers to their Supreme Being, the *Nhialic*. One of their prayers seeking the good life from the Supreme Being reads as follows: "You, *Nhilalic*, …let us walk in health, …that there should be no fever, and no other illness should seize people, that they may all be well. And if my clansman travels, then let him complete his journey without sickness, and let no evil befall him or anybody. And you, *Nhialic*, do not bring evil upon us … *Nhialic* will be pleased with us and we will pray to *Nhialic* that there may be no bad thing… "[76] But more often the Supreme Being is invoked in prayer along with other lesser divinities. In most of such prayers the Supreme Being is mentioned first. The Wa-pokomo ritual prayer seeking peace goes as follows: "O God, we ask You! O Manes, we ask You! O Ancestors, we ask You! Grant us peace. Grant us tranquillity, … He who bewitches our village, may die. He who utters evil spells against us, may he die. …We also ask for some fish, may the fish come. Thus eating, let us eat in peace."[77] Another prayer, in which, the Supreme Being and lesser divinities are invoked while cultivating the land reads: "O God, I beg of You. I am going to cultivate this field. Very well, it is in order to have things to eat that I may have life and health. Come *Manes*! I till this field that the grain may spring up abundantly and that I may harvest it when it is ripe."[78] One of the prayers the Dinka people of Sudan address to *Nhialic* and to other divinities goes as follows:

> *Nhialic*, you are called by my words, because you look after all people. You are greater than anyone and all people are your children. And if evil has befallen them you are called to come and join with them in it also. And you … come, help. O you *Flesh*, the divinity of *Pagong* if you are called then you will indeed hear me and you, *Awar grass*, you will hear. And you, *Flesh* of my father, and *Fig-tree* of my father, and *Head carrying-ring* of my father, you will hear.[79]

Often prayers are said in the context of sacrifice. The primitive people believed that life, health, strength and vitality are gifts of God and of the divinities, and so they attempted to gain them through prayer and sacrifice. Though prayers are addressed to the Supreme Being, generally sacrifices are not offered to Him. For instance the Maori tribal people do not offer sacrifices to their Supreme Being, *Io*.[80] But the Dinka tribal people offer sacrifices, such as killing a bull or an ox, to their Supreme Being, *Nhialic*.[81] Again, the ordinary Ewe people do not offer any cultic ritual to honor their Supreme Being. But some wealthy tribal Ewe people practice a form of cultic sacrificial worship, even though no killing is involved in this right, to honor *Mawu*, their Supreme Being. They believe that they are *Mawu's* favored people, as He has blessed them with wealth. In order to reanimate the devotee's fervor for the Supreme Being and to enhance zeal for recruiting new devotees for *Mawu* they take in small doses of poison at the right moment, which does not cause death but brings a certain amount of inconvenience to the devotee.[82]

Generally all the primitive people offered sacrifices accompanied by prayers mostly to the divinities and spirits of the ancestors. The offerings sacrificed ranged from food items to animals. For instance, the Dinka people offered beer, milk, sheep, oxen, bulls and chicken to appease the divinities and the ancestral spirits.[83] The Maori people usually sacrificed food items, a bird, a fish or some small animal. The first fish caught while fishing was killed and offered to the divinity of the sea, *Tangaroa*. On important occasions, such as in time of war, the Maori practiced human sacrifice. It is offered usually to the god of warfare, *Tu*. Human sacrifices are offered to gain *Tu's* favor and to thank the god of warfare for the success achieved during wartime. They chose the enemy who was captured and enslaved during war as the offering to be sacrificed. Before the priest made the sacrifice he picked up the offering with both hands and raised it above his head. Calling upon the divinity, he placed the offering on the ground by the sacred tree or the object. Then the offering was killed. Thus, in the Maori worship prayer and sacrifice went hand in hand.[84]

The Dinka people of Sudan also perform sacrifices accompanied by spoken prayers. They invoke all the clan-divinities, free-divinities, the ancestral spirits, and at times the Supreme Being, *Nhialic*, during the sacrifices. Those who say the prayers hold a fishing spear in their hands. They pronounce with great emphasis short phrases expressing the needs of the people, such as 'I call upon you because my child is ill' or 'I do not want words of sickness', while thrusting the spear at the animal to be sacrificed. The people who participate in the sacrifice repeat the words of the leader of the sacrifice. Such repetition of the short phrases creates a powerful effect upon those who are present at the sacrifice. The leader of the sacrifice expresses deep feeling, which attracts the others to get involved in sacrifice that is taking place.[85]

On certain important occasions, especially in moments of crisis and trouble, the Dinka acts of prayer and sacrifice continue for a long period of time. There are four stages in such prolonged sacrificial prayer. The first stage is the description of the problem people are facing in their lives. Here the leader speaks aloud the things that cause anxiety. We could mention a prayer of the Dinka people, in which the problem that troubles the people is addressed to *Nhialic*:

> Why is it, O *Nhialic*, that when one son is left alive alone out of all the children his mother bore, you do not help him, that he may be in health? You *Nhialic*, if you have left ...[him] behind to beget children, and he now becomes ill, we have refused (to accept) the illness in him. For ...[he] has no sister born with him, and no brother born with him, and if *Nhialic* does not help him to bear his children, then the children will become the children of the mother. And you, *Nhialic*, you are the great person, father of all people, and if a man has

called upon you, you will strengthen his arm, that no evil may befall him.[86]

In this manner one's petition is placed before the Supreme Being or the divinities. Having done the act of describing the trouble, the leader of the sacrifice leads the community to the second stage, confession of the past sin. It consists in the people who are present at the sacrifice acknowledging the past acts of evil, if they were the cause of the present trouble. A typical prayer of confession of sins reads as follows: "And you (divinity) of my father, if you are called, then you will help me and join yourself with my words. And I did not speak (in the past) that my children should become ill; that quarrel is an old matter."[87] The offering of praise to the divinities follows the confession of the past sin. Praise is offered in the hope that the prayers of praise would please the divinities and would make them listen to the needs of the people. The act of praise often takes the form of singing hymns of honor and ox-songs of young men. The final stage is the expulsion of the misfortune. This is done among the Dinka people by identifying the misfortune with the animal, for instance an ox, to be sacrificed. The sacrificing of the animal with which the misfortune of the people is identified would bring about the sending away of the misfortune from the Dinka territory. The Dinka people pray at the time of the sacrifice of the ox as follows:

> And you, ox, it is not for nothing that we have tethered you in the midday sun, but because of sickness, to exchange your life for the man, and for the man to stay on earth and for your life to go with the illness. You, *Nhialic*, hear my speech, and you, clan-divinity, hear my speech, and you, illness, I have separated you from the man. I have spoken thus: "You leave the man alone, you have been given the ox called *malith*.[88]

Other than these forms of sacrifices accompanied by prayers, there were also sacrifices offered in the community of the primitive people during which the *totem* is sacrificed as a communal act of worship. The *totem* is often a species of animal, which is seen as being bound up with the life of a tribe. The *totem* animal is very much linked with the social well-being of the tribe. Therefore, that particular tribe deifies and worships the *totem*. The *totem* animal is said to be the divine ancestor, who brings cohesion and unity among the people of the tribe. Thus, the *totem* is seen as the embodiment of the oneness of the group and the guardian of its well-being. On certain solemn and important occasions the people of the tribe sacrifice the *totem* animal. After the sacrifice, the whole community shares the flesh of the *totem* animal in a common meal. The *totem* sacrifice and the eating of the *totem* animal are believed to have sacramental significance, as they provide bond of union among the people of the tribe, besides uniting themselves with spiritual beings. The *totem* sacrifice fills the people of the tribe with strength and power.[89] In this manner, prayers and various forms of sacrifice helped the primitive people to come in contact with the Supreme Being, the divinities and other spiritual beings.

1.2.2. WORSHIP-OFFERING OF THE PRIESTS

Other than using prayers and sacrifices, some primitive people made use of the worship-offerings of the priests to establish contact with the spiritual beings of the divine world. In such primitive societies there was a well-established system of priesthood, in which the priestess, usually the wife of the priest, and other helpers assisted the priest in offering worship on behalf of the community. We will consider briefly the priesthood that existed in the primitive religion of the Ga people in Ghana and in Shamanism, which is the ancient natural religion of the Korean people. We would also describe the worship with the help of which they attempted to encounter their divinities. Usually in these primitive religions the purpose of the worship offered is to promote communion between the divinity and man, and to bring about the well-being of the community.

1.2.2.1. THE RELIGION OF THE GA PEOPLE IN GHANA

The Ga people considered the priest, whom they called *Wulomo*, as the spokesman of a particular divinity. So he is usually the *Wulomo* of a particular deity. For instance, the priest of the god *Dantu* is called *Dantu Wolomo*. The *Wulomo* does not possess the spirit of the god whom he serves. His functions are performing rites in the temple, offering worship in the shrine of the god on behalf of the people and interpreting the messages that come from the god through other people. Because the *Wolomo* performs these functions and comes in contact with the divinity directly, he must be different from the ordinary people in a number of ways. He must be a person who lives a genuine by moral life. There were a few taboos that he must follow in order that he is not contaminated by the dirt (*mudzi*). He must not see a dead body and if, by chance, he sees one, rituals must be performed to cleanse him. The *Wulomo* should not eat any food until the sun rises. While eating he should not utter a word. He is forbidden to eat salt, though he can eat food cooked in water from the sea. All these and similar taboos are aimed at keeping the priest of the Ga people pure, holy and a person consecrated for divine functions. After the *Wulomo*, the second in rank is the *Woyoo*, who is usually the wife of the priest. The term '*Woyoo*' means 'god's woman'. She helps the *Wulomo* to offer worship at the shrine. Some of the functions she performs are purifying the shrine by burning incense, preparing the food that is to be offered to the god on a holy day, acting as the medium through which the god speaks to the people. In performing the last function the spirit of the god possesses her, she becomes wild and at times she falls into a trance. On such occasions, she speaks in different languages, even those she has not learned. The message from the god may be a happy one, a warning and a command to do something or to refrain from doing something. The *Wolomo* often interprets and explains to the people the messages received through the help of *Woyoo*. The third in the order of priesthood is the *Agbaayei* and *Agbaahii*. They are servants who serve at the temple in different ways. The *Wulomo* can delegate some of his functions or those of the *Woyoo* to the *Agbaayei* and *Agbaahii*.[90]

Having clarified the priesthood in the primitive society of the Ga people, we could take a look at the regular worship that the priest offers at the shrine of the sea-god, *Nae*. The shrine of *Nae* is a clean room in the home of the *Wulomo* of *Nae*. Usually the *Wulomo*, his wife, children and other extended members of his family live in this homestead. The house is located nearly 200 yards from the sea. It is painted white. The days holy to *Nae* are those in which regular worship is offered. These holy days are Tuesdays, Fridays and Sundays. On the night before and at the dawn of the holy day the *Woyoo* purifies the house of the *Wulomo*, in which the shrine is situated by burning incense. The purification is carried out to remove any *mudzi* that might be in the house when the god visits the shrine. Usually the *mudzi* can be caused when a dead body is seen or touched and a menstruating woman comes into the house. After the incense burning at the dawn, the *Wulomo* and the *Woyoo* have a ritual bath in the holy water, which the *Wulomo* consecrates by placing two kinds of leaves in it. After the bath the couple and their assistants dress in pure white. Then the worship offering begins. The *Wulomo* pours a libation with gin. He calls upon *Nae* three times. When he is convinced of the presence of *Nae*, he addresses prayers and petitions to *Nae* on behalf of different people who belong to the Ga community. Prayers are offered on behalf the fishermen, farmers, traders, government officials and the sick. Besides, prayers are offered to obtain good things of life, such as health, grain, money and children. The *Wulomo* repeats these prayers three times. When the prayer ends, the officiating *Woyoo* prepares food for the god, viz., *kpekple* [91] mixed with red and white palm oil. She sprinkles the food at the shrine, in the courtyard of the house and in the surroundings of the homestead. The members of the *Wulomo's* house or any outsider who wishes to partake in the food eats the remaining food. The members of the clan and the people present can take the holy water, which could be used for the bath or for washing the face. The Ga people believe that the use of the holy water for the bath or for washing will cleanse them from all ailments, especially ailments of the mind and spirit.[92]

1.2.2.2. SHAMANISM

Shamanism gives an important role to the priest in worship. He is known as Shaman. The Korean word used to address the Shaman is *Moodang*. There are two types of Shamans. The first group of Shamans became Shamans either by heredity or by learning. They receive their training and education from master Shamans. They pass through some initiation rites before they begin functioning as Shamans. The Shamans of South Korea belong to this group. The second group became Shamans by choice. They are considered as gifts of gods. When the gods choose one to be a Shaman, he experiences dreams and ecstasies. As one experiences the gods in dreams and ecstasies, a Shaman 'stands outside' the normal everyday experiences in the physical world and becomes aware of the powers and truths, which cannot be grasped through the normal functioning of the senses. The people of Central and North Korea believe that their Shamans are gods' gifts.[93]

The task of the Shamans is to bring about communion between the gods and men through worship. Shamanism believes that it is the gods who rule over man and nature. Therefore, good and evil, life and death come from the gods. Hence the control of nature and that of man's destiny is possible only if man has a genuine relationship with the gods, who have power over everything. By worship offerings, the Shamans attempt to persuade the gods to act according to man's wishes. Thus, through various ceremonies of worship the Shamans invite gods, make them happy, listen to their commands and warnings, and obey them. The ceremonies of Shamanism have three aims. Firstly, ceremonies are aimed at eliminating evil fortune and bringing down the blessings of the gods. The second aim of ceremonies is to expel evil spirits and to cure diseases by the intervention of the gods. Finally the ceremonies are performed to comfort and to purify the souls of the dead. This is done to help them reach the other world, thereby preventing them from causing disasters in this world. Thus the ceremonies aim at removing every calamity and bringing blessings of the gods, thereby creating a happy world here on earth for people, by recourse to the power of the gods.[94]

To bring about these aims, the Shamans worship and serve the gods by singing and dancing in a ceremony of worship called the *Kut*. There are two forms of *Kut*. The first one is related to the cycle of a human person and his growth, while the second is related to the cycles of various seasons of the year. The first *Kut* consists in performing various ceremonies of worship that help the individual to have recourse to the blessing of the gods at different stages of his life. We could mention a few of such ceremonies. When a person marries, the Shamans perform the 'ceremony of detection'. It is aimed at getting rid of every misfortune in the life of the couple and to pray for the blessing of the gods on the couple, as they begin their new life. When a woman conceives a child, the Shamans hold a ceremony to propitiate the god of new life and to pray for the safe birth of the child and for the security of his growth. Throughout the life of the individual as he grows from childhood to old age, the Shamans conduct ceremonies of worship periodically to pray for a long and happy life without illness, and to obtain riches and honors in full measure. The Shamans also offer ceremonies of worship when a person dies in order to assure his safe journey and entrance into the other world.[95]

The Second *Kut* relates to the ceremonies of worship offered throughout the cycle of the seasons of the year, for instance, the ceremonies held in spring in order to pray for the elimination of the evil fortune and for a plentiful harvest. At the time of the First Moon the people of the village gather together to perform the ritual of 'treading on the earth God' to prevent misfortune. Again, when the crops are ready, a special ceremony is performed to please the agricultural gods and to pray for an abundant harvest. In the same way the Eighth Moon and the Tenth Moon were considered as times of thanksgiving, during which a ceremony of worship was held for the new harvest.[96] Usually the *Kut* of this second type consists of twelve parts symbolically referring to the twelve months of the year, though at times it has more or less than twelve parts.[97]

We will state briefly what is done in each of the twelve parts. The first and second parts are aimed at purifying the place of ritual and calling down various gods. The third part is a prayer of protection. The fourth part is aimed at the expulsion of evil spirits. The fifth part consists in inviting the god of wealth, *Taegam-sin*, and praying to him for the blessing of wealth. In the sixth part *Chesok-sin*, the Buddhist guardian god, is invited, and prayer is made to him for long life. The seventh part is a prayer for peace. The eighth and the ninth parts are prayers for the expulsion of the evil spirits and a prayer for protection respectively. In the tenth, eleventh and twelfth parts the Shaman worships the guardian gods and offers sacrifices to various spirits to prevent every evil consequence. Each of the parts in the full ritual of twelve parts follows the same pattern. Firstly, the Shamans invoke the god who is the object of ritual, which is done with an invitation song that calls people to worship. Secondly, the Shamans sing and dance to a special tune and rhythm to please the god who is already invited. Thirdly, when the singing and dancing reaches a violent level, the Shamans enter a state of trance and ecstasy. At this state they are in communion with the gods and convey messages from the gods. It could be an utterance of warning and command or a promise of blessing. Fourthly, the Shamans send the gods back to their places by singing songs of praise and by dancing.[98] In this manner, ceremonies of worship are means with the help of which primitive people encounter the divine spirits.

1.2.3. THE CELEBRATION OF RELIGIOUS FESTIVALS

Besides using the worship offering of the priests as a means to come in contact with the divinities, primitive people also used the celebration of religious festivals as occasions of contact with their deities. Festivals also had a social meaning for the primitive people; at festival time the whole community reunites. People of the community, who had gone to different places for work, return to their homes. People from the neighboring towns and villages also come to participate in the festivals and receive the blessings of the gods. As a result the towns are full of strangers. Besides, festival is a time of family reunion and for meeting friends. During festival time every family mourns the dead, disputes between the families are settled and there is a general jubilation. The community as a whole experiences the presence of the divine in their life at the festival time.[99] We shall mention a few festivals of the primitive people through which they experienced the divine beings.

The most popular festival the Ga people of Ghana celebrated is the annual *Homowo* festival. The word '*Homowo*' literally means 'hunger hooting'. It is a harvest festival in which, after the rich harvest, people 'cry the hunger out'. They rejoice in the abundance of food, which is the blessing of the gods. *Homowo* festival begins on the first or the second Monday in the month of May and ends in September. The festival is celebrated in different towns of the Ga people. Religious ceremonies are performed throughout the festival. The festival begins with the ceremony in which the priests of the gods who are honored till the plot of land sacred to the gods. Then with the help of their assistants they raise a garden tool and point it to the sky. As this act is done, the *Wulomo* addresses a prayer to *Naa Nyonmo*, the Supreme Being of the Ga people.[100] The prayer goes as follows:

> Lend ears, lend ears, lend ears!
> Lord God, we beseech Thee,
> Let there be rain, let there be dew,
> That the earth may be fertile,
> That grain may grow,
> That there may be plenty for all.
> Life! Life!
> We are praying life for all.
> Let one year go and another year come to meet us alive! [101]

The *Wulomo* repeats the prayer three times to the Supreme Being. The purpose of this rite, accompanied by triple repetition of the prayer, is to thank the Supreme Being and the gods, ask for their blessing for the fertility of the soil, pray for the increase of the family and plead the gods to guard against misfortune. Other than the spiritual celebration of the rituals in the shrines, in every home people prepare the traditional food called *kpekple* and serve it with palm nut soup and fish. People celebrate the arrival of the bountiful blessings of the gods with gaiety. [102]

The Swazi people of South Africa celebrate a six-day festival called *Incwala*. They believe that during this festival the king dies and gains new life and strength, which he, in turn, transmits to the people of his kingdom. During these days the king remains in an isolated place, while dances in special costumes are performed. On the fourth day the king eats food made of the new grain. Then the people are permitted to eat of the new grain. Symbolically expressing the king's gaining of new life a green gourd is thrown out for the people to catch. Fresh herbs are also used at the rites. During these six days no people from the kingdom are permitted to shed blood or to carry arms. Through this festival the Swazi people believe that their king receives new life and strength from their gods and transfers it to them, thereby bringing about a communion between the gods and the people.[103]

The Ainu people of North Japan, who revered the bear as sacred, celebrate the bear festival as their greatest festival during the year. The festival begins with the ritual of killing a bear cub accompanied by various ceremonies. The skull of the bear is placed in a special place in the house with an *inao* or *inau*, which is a stick that is made of living wood, with shavings attached and arranged into a tassel or a garland. This stick serves as a sacred offering to the gods. The *inau*, when used at the ritual, is imbued with the sacred power (*ramat*), which is a form of spiritual energy. Since the *inau* is made of living wood it is filled with the power of the terrestrial spirit, *Shriamba Kaumi*. Through the sacred power and the spiritual energy present in the *inau*, the gods can be worshipped, revered and placated. The Ainu people believe that by the celebration of the bear festival, with this special ritual of killing the bear, the gods enter the house as guests, as the bear, the Lord of the animals, returns to the gods' abode in heaven. In this manner the blessings of the gods are brought to the people by the visiting gods.[104] The Koryak tribal people of Siberia celebrate a similar annual bear festival. Besides, they also hold a wolf festival during which a wolf is sacrificed. When the wolf is killed at the sacrifice, a man dressed in wolf skin walks around the sacrificial fire while beating a drum. This is a typical hunting rite, which aims at seeking the blessings of the gods for success in hunting or to thank the gods for the success in the hunting mission.[105] The *Aztecs* of Mexico celebrated an annual festival for their sun god, *Tonatiuh*. This festival commemorated the sun's struggle with the evil powers, its death and rebirth. During the festival these aspects were enacted in dances. Besides, the festival included the sacrifice of a prisoner by tearing his heart from the living body and raising it towards the sun god. By celebrating this festival, the Aztecs believed that they would receive the bountiful blessings of the sun god, *Tonatiuh*.[106]

In this manner the celebrations of various festivals, accompanied by special rituals to the gods, besides preserving the unity of the community, served as an important means for primitive people to establish and to maintain contact with the divinities.

1.2.4. RESPECTING THE SACRED

Respecting all that are considered to be sacred is a means through which the primitive people came in contact with the spiritual beings. The sacredness, whether it belongs to a thing, a person or a practice, depends on people's beliefs that these bring them in touch with divine beings. In the primitive societies the sacredness is associated with the word '*tabu*', from which the English word 'taboo' derived. It is a Polynesian expression, which is used to describe something that is forbidden, as it is considered sacred or as it is something that defiles that which is sacred. What is believed to be the *tabu* is full of sacred power. Therefore, a profane person must keep away from it. If an unworthy person approaches the *tabu*, he would have to bear the consequence. For instance, sacred persons, such as priests must handle the sacred objects. If ordinary people attempt to do what a priest is expected to do, it is dangerous for them. In the same way a village chieftain is considered as a *tabu*, because he has an important religious, social and political position among the tribal people. A person is called to avoid these types of taboos, because these are sacred.

Besides, at times people and things are considered taboos because they are believed to be essentially evil. Anything involving blood, women during the period of menstruation, a newborn baby, a warrior on the eve of a battle, a person who is dying and a dead body are a few examples of this type of *tabu*. These are to be avoided not because they are sacred, but because they defile the sacredness and purity in a person.[107] In the sense we have spoken, *tabu* or the sacred could be attributed to people, things and places. We could elaborate these sacred realities, by giving a few illustrations from the religion of the primitive people.[108]

The sacred people are generally the priests. The Maori people of Polynesia set their priests apart as they believed them to be sacred. They treated the priests with great respect and reverence, because the priests talked to the divine spirits on behalf of the people and the divinities gave messages for the people through them. Among the priests some were respected more than others, as the former were more sacred than the latter. The more sacred priests were treated differently. People would not touch these priests. They fed them by placing food in their mouth. The touch of their shadow was believed to be sacred. The less sacred priests were often the priests of the family divinities, who manifested their weakness by practicing witchcraft and magic.[109] In most of the primitive African societies, the living-dead were considered as taboos. They are still persons, who are yet to become free spirits and therefore able to affect the life of the people positively or negatively. Various rites were performed to keep in contact with the living-dead. These rites involved the offering of food, other articles and the pouring of beer, milk, water, tea or coffee. Prayers, invocations and instructions to the living-dead often accompanied these offerings and libations.[110] In some other primitive societies on some important occasions a small bird, a sheep or an oxen is killed and the blood is allowed to soak the graves of the living-dead.[111] In this manner people were considered as sacred, and these sacred people meditated the contact with the divine and the sacred beings.

The primitive people also considered things as sacred and taboos. For the Maori people anything could become sacred. For instance a tree, a stone, a part of the sea, a piece of land, a piece of human hair, a walking stick, a spring of water could be considered as *tabu*. These taboos, besides effecting contact with the divine, also had some social function of regulating the behavior of the people that it did not offend the other. By making certain things taboos, the Maori community prevented the greedy from using up certain birds, fruits or similar things. The Maori people also considered the birth of a baby, sickness, warfare and death as taboos, because these were associated with spiritual powers (*atua*).[112]

In some primitive societies, relics of the dead are considered as objects of religious care. In some societies the people preserved a part of the skull of the dead, painted it red and preserved it in a container made of bark from a certain tree on which the picture of the dead was drawn. The Loango people of the Congo and the Melanesians of New Guinea even made real statues of the dead and placed them above the relics in niches at the back of the public house of the village. On certain occasions, they also built makeshift altars in front of the statues for presenting offerings to the dead.[113] Thus, in the primitive societies many things were considered to be taboos. With the help of these taboos they encountered the divinities and regulated the social life of the people.

The primitive people also believed certain places to be sacred and forbade any profane activities being performed in those sacred places. The tombs of the ancestors and cemeteries were considered sacred places. The veneration of these places was believed an act of religion. People built little houses where the souls of the departed could come and rest. Small altars were built near these tombs to offer sacrifices to appease the spirits of the ancestors. The Maori people had the practice of burying their dead in the caves and considering these places of burial as sacred places. In the tribal societies of East Africa small huts were erected at the crossroads for the spirits of non-human origin. These huts were considered sacred places, as they were the shrines of these divinities, and people offered sacrifices of flour, grain and other objects in these huts.[114]

Similarly, sacred enclosures were made to honor the Manes (*Ikigabiro*). These enclosures consisted of a round place of several meters over which fine grass was planted in the form of a bed and the center of which a fig tree was planted. The divinity of the community was invited to come and rest. This sacred place was used to offer sacrifice to the divinity. The sick and the dying were placed in this bed of grass that they might be cured of their illnesses.[115] Other places, such as rivers, springs, sea, earth and mountains are also considered as sacred. In these places, dedications to the gods, ritual washing of purification and similar rites are performed. Some of such sacred waters are believed to be curative.[116]

Various rituals are also done in these sacred places. For instance, while fishing the fishermen of Gabon, in equatorial Africa, when they catch the first fish of the day, cut the fish open carefully, remove the internal organs and throw them into the waters as the first fruit offering for the spirit of the waters. In the same way, it is a common practice among the primitive people, when they take any fermented drinks like beer or wine, to pour a little on the ground as a libation sacrifice to the spirits of the earth.[117]

From what we have said, it is clear that in most of the primitive societies the people had a sense of the sacred. They set apart persons, things and places as sacred. The purpose of these sacred realities was to help them come in touch the divine powers that their personal and social life in the community might be guided properly.

1.2.5. LIVING A STRICT MORAL CODE

In most tribal societies there is some form of moral code that directs the behavior of the people. These moral codes vary depending on tribal customs, the geography of the place where people lived, the contact of the people with other cultures and their religious beliefs. Religious beliefs played a great role in the moral consciousness of the people. Often it is fear of the Supreme Being that made people be moral. In some primitive societies certain moral transgressions, such as incest, were considered a sin against the

Supreme Being, which breaks man's relationship with the divine. It was also their belief that for such sins the whole community would be punished. Thus, the primitive people believed that these moral codes have a religious sanction and their violation is not merely a social offense, but also a religious offense. As a result, the infringement of the moral law of the tribe is believed to bring divine punishment on the people. Illness and similar troubles were seen as punishments for the violation of the moral code. Therefore, living a strict moral code was considered a means of establishing genuine contact with the divinities and avoiding divine punishments.[118] The following are some of the moral practices prevalent among the primitive people.

In many primitive cultures marriage was considered an area of moral prescriptions. Often there were a great number of prohibitions associated with marriage. Blood relatives were not allowed to enter into a married relationship. Adultery was considered evil, and severe punishments were given when the prescriptions regarding adultery were violated. There were moral customs that regulated the relationship between married partners. For instance, a conjugal relationship was not permitted when the wife was pregnant and while she nursed the child. Similarly, the partners were not allowed to have conjugal relationships during the time of war and hunting. There were prescribed norms for divorce. For instance, a man could divorce his wife for laziness, suspicion of magic and adultery, while the wife could divorce her husband if cruelty was done to his mother-in-law.[119]

Since marriage and sexuality were such an important area of moral sanction, in many primitive societies there were initiation rites, by which the young were admitted to the circle of adults and made full members of the community. These rites include isolating the young people for a period of time, during which practical instructions were given regarding sexual, moral and religious matters. Then they were put to test by heavy trials and painful treatment, before they were admitted into the circles of the adult members. During such initiation rites, the tribal people of the Sudan and the Equator performed circumcision of the boys and clitoridectomy of the girls. Usually the boys and the girls were initiated separately. In this manner the young were prepared for accepting adult life and married responsibility.[120]

Besides the regulations directing sexual and marital life, there were also other restrictions, which the native traditions prescribed on the primitive tribal people. For instance, using abusive language, poisoning someone, any form of murder and calumny were punishable before the family or the tribal tribunal. The native tradition of the Bavili people prescribes five types of prohibitions. The first of these concerns the Supreme Being. The second regulates the practice of the magical divination. The third deals with mothers correcting their children. The fourth concerns observing each fourth day by abstaining from certain types of occupations. The fifth deals with duties and ceremonies which a woman had to follow regarding premarital and marital morality. In many primitive traditions, breaking any of the prescriptions does not require free and voluntary consent. Any form of violation, whether voluntary or not, is punishable.[121]

In this way in most primitive societies living a strict moral code was not seen merely as a means to regulate the social life of the people. Rather it was viewed as a means to reach out to the divine, for the violation of the moral code not only disrupted the relationship between man and the divinities, but also brought their condemnation. Thus, for most primitive peoples moral living was a bridge between the gods and men.

1.2.5. EXPIATORY RITES

Man is human and limited. Therefore, he is not always able to follow the directions of the gods and of the society in living the moral codes. In spite of his good intentions, he often fails and offends the divine and brings evil on himself and the community. So, having offended the gods, one wishes to rectify one's relations with them at the earliest opportunity. Besides, every commonly accepted transgression must be atoned in order to avoid divine punishment not only on the individual who has committed the evil, but also on the community to which he belongs. Hence, every primitive society had one or the other form of expiatory rite, with the help of which the primitive people appeased the offended divine spirit. The expiatory rites express the total surrender of the offender to the gods and his attitude of self-denial. Besides, in offering expiatory rites, the person who displeased the gods recognizes his fault and wants to make amendment for the wrong he has done. In doing so he not only frees himself from the punishments of the divine spirits, but also re-establishes his broken relationship with the god he has offended.[122] We shall briefly consider some of the expiatory rites that were practiced in different primitive societies.

The *Kikuju* people practiced a purification rite called *ko-tahikio*. The literal meaning of this word is 'to vomit one's sin'. According to ethnologists, this practice was prevalent among these people until recently, when they came under Christian influence. *Ko-tahikio* is aimed at freeing the offender from the evil he has done and bringing him the peace of mind he yearns for after violating the taboo. It is conducted in the following manner. It usually takes place in the open air at some isolated place in the village. At the appointed time, those persons who have transgressed the law of the gods come either individually or together before the leader of the tribe. They sit on the ground and shout aloud the various evils they had done. If the faults are so grave and personal that they cannot be said in public, then they go far away from the village and accuse themselves of the crime they have committed before a sacred pole. When they return they carry on their heads wood equivalent to the sins they have confessed. The primitive people of Tahiti performed similar expiatory rites, which included a number of expiatory prayers and sacrifices that expressed a genuine spirit of humility.[123] At the concluding ceremony the priest addressed the supreme God with the following prayer: "Hearken, O God, to our petition with food. Here is the sacrificial pig for thee, a sacred pig, a pig without blemish. It is a pig of atonement, to set free the sinful man.

Here also is the fat, small eating, for thee and the gods here in thy presence, O God, accept it. This is our petition, hearken unto us."[124]

The *Ga* people of Ghana practiced elaborate expiatory rites to make amends for the wrong done by the people. The priest of the sea-god (*Nae Wulomo*) performs special rites to *Nae* on behalf of people, who have offended him and have come to receive his pardon. There are a number of ways a person can offend *Nae*. For instance, taking the name of the god in vain, failing to carry out a promised vow and cursing in his name amount to offending the god. Offenses, such as curses, are considered very grave, as they prevent peoples' efforts to increase the well-being of the society at large. Since such offenses go against the wishes of the god himself, they cannot be pardoned without taking some form of life. When a person confesses his sin, he is expected to bring different things for sacrifices, depending on the nature of the offense. Often he is asked to bring a goat and two birds, a male and a female. The time of expiatory rites are considered as very solemn occasions among the Ga people. Before the rite begins, the *Wulomo* and others, who take part in it, purify themselves. After purification, the *Wulomo* calls out the names of *Naa Nyonmo*, *Asase Afia*, *Nae* and other gods who are affected by the offense to come down and make themselves present. He then describes the offense to the gods. He places his request, on behalf of the offender, to accept the sacrifice, pardon the offender and to spare his life. Then the offender is brushed from head to toe with the birds that are offered. It is believed that this symbolic gesture takes away the offense.[125]

At the next stage, the *Wulomo* strangles the head of one of the birds and tears it open with his hands and toes. The dead bird is thrown up as everyone watches it in silence. If the bird falls with the breast up, it is a sign that the offense is forgiven. If this does not happen, it is believed that the sin is not pardoned. Then the *Wulomo* discerns the reason for what happened. It could be that the person has not confessed all his sins, or it may be due to the faulty performance of the ritual. It could also be because some of the gods offended by the evil are not invoked. Having identified the reason the *Wulomo* sets it right. Then he repeats the strangling, tearing open and throwing up of the bird, until it falls with its breast up, which is the sign that the divinities are satisfied and pleased with the offender.[126]

Then the goat, which symbolizes the offender, is sacrificed. The life of the offender is given back as the goat dies. Some of the blood collected from the goat is placed in the big bowl containing holy water, with which the offender is given a ritual bath. Now the offender is completely pardoned and purified. As a result the blessings of the gods rest on him. After the sacrifice the body of the goat is skinned and cut into pieces. One of the limbs is given to the sacrificer. He is not allowed to eat of the meat, but his relatives can eat. Those present at the expiatory rite, the priests and the servants of the gods eat the rest of the meat.[127]

The Dogon people in the French Sudan celebrate a six yearly expiatory ceremony called *Sigui*. This ceremony and the celebrations associated with it lasted for about 20 days. The ceremony consists in renewing the Big Snake made of wood, which the people worship. The people sacrificed a dog and a chicken in order to enable the spirit to enter the new snake. Heavy beer drinking marked the celebration. For it is believed that the drinkers are acceptable to the ancestral spirits, whose vital forces are in a state of disorder due to death. The goal of this ceremony is to expiate the sins of the young people who have brought about the death of the founding ancestors. It is believed that this ceremony, besides expiating the sins, renews the strength and vitality of the ancestral spirits and of the people of the society. If anyone, due to illness, violating the taboos or in any other way loses the vital force of life, it is restored to him as a result of this expiatory rite. The vital forces of the ancestral spirits and of the people are restored and revived by placing the blood of the sacrificial animal on the top of the altar. Thus, this ceremony brings about the expiation of sins, revival of the vital force in the ancestral spirits and communion of the people with the divine spirits and the well-being of every member of the society.[128]

Thus in the many primitive societies we find the people having recourse to expiatory rites, which included the calling upon the divinities who were offended, confession of sins, offering of prayers and putative sacrifices to the offended spirits. This, in turn, restored the purity of the offender, established the lost communion between the divinities and the people and brought about the genuine well-being of the community.

1.2.6. USE OF FETISH AND MAGIC

Primitive people believed in animism, which consists in accepting the power of the spiritual forces to control and direct their lives. For instance, the Dogan people believed that their Supreme Being, *Amma*, had given each individual a soul and a *nyama*, which is a certain force or energy. After the death of the individual, the soul joins the ancestral spirits, while the *nyama* continues to remain in the world for generations. The tribal people of Ruanda call the spiritual force given to them by God as *imana*.[129] Though these powers are immaterial and bodiless, they are believed to be residing in bodily objects. When inhabited by these spiritual powers, these objects become very potent and are capable of bringing good luck or misfortune to the people. The belief in animism made the primitive people to use of fetish and magic to control these powers and use them for their advantage. Thus, the use of fetish and magic became means of contact with the divine spirits, warding off the evil they could bring and obtaining the good fortune they can effect in the live of the people. In this section, we attempt to elaborate the use of fetish and magic as means of contact with the divine powers.

1.2.6.1. USE OF FETISHES:

The animistic belief of the primitive people led them to believe in the power of fetishes. The term 'fetish' seems to have derived from the Latin *'facticius'* and the Portuguese word *'feitico'*, which meant an amulet. The word seems to have been first used by the Portuguese adventurers when they met with these practices among the primitive people.[130] They used this term to mean "symbolic (or real) repositories of supernatural power, ... [which] serve as the psychological function of objectifying the primitives' belief [in the power of the spirits to control their lives]."[131] Describing a fetish, John A. Hardon says the following:

> A fetish is a common object of no value in itself but which the primitive keeps and venerates because he believes it is the dwelling-place of a spirit. This can be anything: a stone, root, vase, feather, log, shell, colored cloth, animal's tooth, snake's skin, box, an old rusty sword. However the term is specially applied to those more or less crude representations, generally in wood, though sometimes in metal or clay, consecrated to various *genii* [powers] that flourish in the religions of Western Africa.[132]

Of themselves, these objects are powerless, but what makes them powerful is the presence of the spiritual powers. Therefore, no object or human representation is considered an effective fetish until it is consecrated to a supernatural power through the hands of persons, whom primitives call 'medicine men', and from whom it receives its power. For instance the Ga people of Ghana call these 'medicine men' *tsofatsemei*, which literally mean 'people of tree roots'. They are herbalists, who treat physical illnesses. Since the Ga people believed that every illness has a spiritual side, they treated not only the physical ailment, but also the corresponding spiritual illness. Therefore, *tsofatsemei* were also believed to be spiritual men, who had the power to invoke the spirit-powers to heal the spiritual side of the patients. For this purpose these 'medicine men' consecrated objects to the sacred powers. Thus, what makes a fetish extra ordinarily potent is the mysterious spell sung over it at its ritualistic consecration to one or the other supernatural powers by the *tsofatsemei*. When the spiritual powers are withdrawn from these objects, then the objects become ordinary and powerless.[133]

There are different types of fetishes. The first type of fetish consists of any object symbolic of a certain spirit, who may be invoked in a given time and circumstance. It is believed to defend the people against evil. The second type is the family fetish, associated with the worship of the ancestors. It consists of remains of the dead, such as, the skull bones, hair, tooth or any such relic. The value of these fetishes depends on the association of the members of the family with the living-dead, whose fetish they are. They protect the family, tribe or the clan. There is a third type of fetish, which is used for conducting black magic and spells, to bring about illnesses and to take revenge on others. It is aimed at bewitching spirits as a means to call down malicious powers to bring about harm in the lives of the people.[134]

Besides fetishes, the primitive people used amulets and talismans. These are different from fetishes, though they belong to the same category.

A fetish is believed to be animated, conscious and efficacious because a supernatural power inhabits it. But the amulet (*grigri*) is a lifeless object, which a person carries wherever he goes. Though no spirit inhabits an amulet, it is believed to have some secret and intrinsic powers to preserve the well-being of the person carrying it. In the same way, no spirit inhabits a talisman. But it exercises magical effects on events and happenings of the people who use them. The secret power and magical effects of amulets and talisman come from special ceremonies done over them before they are given to the people for use. Their effectiveness depends on their type, and the spells and formulae used during such special ceremonies. The main difference between an amulet and a talisman is that while a person carries the former wherever he goes, the latter is placed on the door of the house, inside the home and at crossroads outside the village.[135] Thus, for the primitive people, the use of fetishes, amulets and talismans effectively brought about the contact between them and the divine beings.

1.2.6.2. THE USE OF MAGIC:

Besides the use of fetishes, the use of magic played a great role among the primitive people in their effort to come in touch with the spiritual realities. In magic one makes use of the powers of nature to bring about certain effects with the help of certain occult observances that have a religious appearance. Magic also could mean establishing contact with the invisible spirits and affecting their secret influences in different aspects of a person's life. In magic, one attempts to bring about an effect that is much greater than the effort he has put in. In other words, magic is seen as a shortcut to achieve ends that are much greater than the means. Besides, a magician in practicing the art of magic often calls upon the influence of the lesser spirits, while giving them an importance they do not deserve.[136] Thus magic "is a generic term which describes the effort to produce an effect by means that are disproportionate to the result expected, through the invocation of lesser spirits as though they were divine."[137]

The primitive people distinguish between natural and supernatural magic. Natural magic is based upon the belief that in nature there are many objects, which have hidden and curative properties that can satisfy every need of the people and ward off every evil that can plague them. Often to identify these objects was a problem for the primitive people. With knowledge not fully developed, coupled with the animistic beliefs, the primitive people, instead of rightly exploring the forces of nature, took recourse to superstitious cults that implied charms, omens, the art of divination, prohibitions and taboos. Those who practiced the form of natural magic attempted to diagnose, treat and to heal the evils in people and societies and were known as 'diviners' or 'seers'. Since natural magic's purpose was to bring benefit and to protect from harm it was often known as 'white magic'. On the other hand, supernatural magic is a religion by itself, that had its own form of worship, incantations, evocations, rites, sacrifices, priests and special meeting places. Persons who practiced the supernatural magic, viz., the sorcerers and the witches, attempted to charm, bait, bewitch, poison and prowl, thereby effecting various consequences in the individual and the societies. Since supernatural magic is often associated with harmful effects on the people, it is called 'black magic'.[138]

Though sorcery and witchcraft belong to the same category of the supernatural magic, they are not exactly the same. Sorcerers do their magical practice as individuals. In practicing sorcery, the sorcerer performs magical rites, pronounces incantations, special formulae and uses typified gestures. When these are done the magical effect takes place despite the personal qualities of the sorcerer who performs the magical ritual. Thus, sorcerers are professionals in the art of the performance of magic, whom people consult when they want to injure an enemy or to take revenge on a rival. Their practice of magic as an evil art does not necessarily make them evil. On the other hand, the primitive people believed that witches are evil by their very nature. Witches are witches by birth. Unlike the sorcerers, who effect evil others only by the performance of magic, the witches not only effect the evil by the rituals they perform, but also because of the spontaneous effect of the wickedness of their persons. The witches form secret societies and practice their trade of witchcraft as a collective organization. They practice their trade at night, when their victims are asleep. At the hoot of the owl, which is their sacred bird, the witches are said to leave their corporeal bodies, which lie asleep in their huts and join in meeting with other witches in their spirit bodies. In such meetings they converse with the evil spirits and invoke them against the victims of their witchcraft. Such acts of the witches "spiritually masticate the souls of the victims", which in turn bring them bodily harm depending on the malice of the evil intended, while the witches were at their midnight session. Therefore, the primitive people hated the witches more than the sorcerers. In general, in the primitive societies all those who performed any form of 'black magic' were looked on with contempt and at times punished for the evil they brought upon the people.[139] In this manner, magic, in it various forms, was used in the primitive societies to come in contact with the divine beings, to win their favor and to prevent them from harming the people.

In this essay we have highlighted the various means with the help of which the primitive people attempted to encounter the divine beings. They are prayer and sacrifice, worship-offering of the priests, celebration of religious festivals, respecting the sacred, living a strict moral code, offering expiatory rites, the use of fetish and the performance of magical rites. Some of these means are very sublime, while some others belong to a lower order. But all these practices are found among the primitive people, and each in its own way helped them to establish and maintain their relationship with divine beings.

CONCLUSION

Our consideration of the religion of the primitive people brings to light that their *Weltanschaung* is spiritual. They do not distinguish between the sacred and the secular, as every dimension of their life is linked with the invisible world of the spirits. Therefore, they believe that their life is not totally in their hands, but rather it depends on God and other lower divine beings. Since they are not able to determine their destinies independent of these spiritual beings, the primitive people are often moved by an attitude of fear towards these divine realities. As a result, the primitive peoples' approach to religion is utilitarian and egoistic. It is utilitarian because they wanted to be at the safer side as far as the divine beings are concerned, as displeasing the divinities may not turn out to be good for them. It is egoistic because preserving themselves from the anger of the deities becomes their main religious concern. Thus, the prayers addressed to the gods, the sacrifices offered and all other forms of worship are characterized by selfish motives. Some of such motives are obtaining food, victory over enemies, averting an evil and freedom from an illness. Besides, there is great deal of materialism inherent in the primitive religion, as the object of most of peoples' prayers and worship is winning material favors from the divinities. So they take great care to appease the divine spirits and to ward off their anger. Since fear of the divinities dominated primitive peoples' religious attitude, pleasing the gods became one of the primary tasks of religious worship.

Though we find that fear of the gods is a significant motive that directed the life of the primitive people, still we find that it is not the only motive that guided their lives with the divine beings. Most of the primitive people believed in the Supreme Being, and their attitude towards Him is not always one of fear. They considered the Supreme Being as one who really cared for them and attributed many moral qualities to Him. They called upon the Supreme Being, at the most difficult moments in lives and believed that He would never let them down. They offered Him prayers in praise, and thanked Him for His goodness. In the same way, peoples' attitude towards lesser divinities is not always one of fear. They believed in the power of the divinities to help them and offered prayers of thanks for the blessings received. Thus, we find elements of genuine religious motivation in the religious attitude of the primitive people.

Primitive religions provided various means to establish contact with the divine realities. The variety of ways provided helped people to keep in touch with the divinities and seek their blessings at different seasons of the year and different stages of life. Besides opening people to divine blessings, these religious rites also built up genuine bonds among the people of the family and the clan. In this manner, in spite of the limitations that we find in the primitive religions, there is a great deal of richness inherent in them. Though they are primitive in their nature and expressions, without any doubt they led people to God and established a living relationship between the divinities and the people.

NOTES

1 Cf. E. Bolaji Idowu, "Errors of Terminology", *The Ways of Religion: An Introduction to the Major Traditions*, ed. Roger Eastman, 2nd ed. (Oxford:

Oxford University Press, 1993), pp. 425-426.
2 Cf. Helmer Ringgren and Ake V. Stroem, *Religions of Mankind: Today and Yesterday*, (Philadelphia: Fortress Press, 1967), p. 3.
3 Cf. David A. Brown, *Guide to Religions* (London: SPCK, 1980), p. 14.
4 Cf. John A. Hardon, *Religions of the World*, Vol. I (New York: Image Books, 1968), p. 22.
5 Ibid.
6 Ninian Smart, *The Religious Experience of Mankind*, (New York: Fount Paperbacks, 1977), p. 45.
7 John A. Hardon, Vol. I, p. 22.
8 Cf. Ninian Smart, pp. 45-46.
9 Cf. Rama Shanker Srivastava, *Comparative Religion*, (New Delhi: Munshiram Manoharlal Publishers Pvt. Ltd., 1974), p. 28.
10 Cf. John A. Hardon, Vol. I, p. 30.
11 Cf. Ninian Smart, p. 48.
12 Cf. Rama Shankar Srivastava, pp. 29-30.
13 Cf. Ibid., pp. 30-32.
14 Cf. Ibid., pp. 32-34. Cf. also John A. Hardon, Vol. I, pp. 40.
15 Cf. Ninian Smart, pp. 56-57. Cf. also Rama Shankar Srivastava, pp. 34-35.
16 Cf. Rama Shankar Srivastava, pp. 35-36.
17 Cf. John A. Hardon, Vol. I, pp. 23-24.
18 Cf. Ibid., p. 24.
19 The people of the Ainu religion are a technologically backward aboriginal people, who live on Hokkaido, Sakhalin, and the Kurile Islands in the Pacific Ocean, north of Japan. Traditionally they lived by food gathering, hunting and collecting edible plants and berries. Cf. Ninian Smart, pp. 50-51.
20 Cf. Ibid., pp. 52-53.
21 Cf. Ibid., pp. 54 –55, 60.
22 Cf. Ibid., pp. 53- 54, 55, 61.
23 Cf. Ibid., pp. 26, 28-30.
24 Cf. E. Geoffrey Parrinder, "God in African Belief", *The Ways of Religion: An Introduction to the Major Traditions*, ed. Roger Eastman, pp. 429, 432. Cf. also Helmer Ringgren, pp. 22, 24. Cf. also Ninian Smart, pp. 60-61.
25 Cf. E. Geoffrey Parrinder, p. 430. Cf. also John A. Hardon, Vol. I, p. 25.
26 Cf. John A. Hardon, Vol. I, p. 25. Cf. also Helmer Ringgren, p. 8.
27 Cf. John A. Hardon, Vol. I, p. 26. Cf. also Helmer Ringgren, p. 8.
28 Cf. E. Geoffrey Parrinder, p. 430. Cf. also Helmer Ringgren, p. 8.
29 Cf. David A. Brown, pp. 16, 18, 26,27.
30 Cf. Helmer Ringgren, pp. 8-9, 22, 30.
31 Cf. E. Geoffrey Parrinder, p. 430.
32 Cf. David A. Brown, pp. 36-37, 40.
33 Cf. E. Geoffrey Parrinder, pp. 430-431.

34 Cf. John A. Hardon, Vol. I, p. 26.
35 Cf. Ibid., pp. 25, 28.
36 Cf. Helmer Ringgren, p. 33.
37 Cf. E. Geoffrey Parrinder, p. 431.
38 Cf. Ninian Smart, pp. 60-61.
39 Cf. E. Geoffrey Parrinder, p. 431.
40 Cf. Esdon Best, *The Maori*, Vol. I, (Wellington: Publication Board of Maori Ethnological Research on behalf of the Polynesian Society, 1924), pp. 87-88.
41 Cf. E. Geoffrey Parrinder, pp. 431-432. Cf. also Helmer Ringgren, pp. 24, 33.
42 Cf. E. Geoffrey Parrinder, p. 431. Cf. also Helmer Ringgren, pp. 30-31.
43 Cf. E. Geoffrey Parrinder, p. 432. Cf. also Helmer Ringgren, pp. 8, 9, 22, 24, 25, 30, 33.
44 Cf. E. Geoffrey Parrinder, p. 432-433.
45 John A. Hardon, Vol. I, p. 30.
46 Cf. Ninian Smart, pp. 71-74. Cf. also John A. Hardon, Vol. I, pp. 30-31.
47 Cf. John S. Mbiti, "Divinities, Spirits, and the Living-Dead", *The Ways of Religion: An Introduction to the Major Religions*, ed. Roger Eastman, p. 443.
48 Cf. John A. Hardon, Vol. I, p. 27.
49 Cf. David A. Brown, pp. 18-19. Cf. also John S. Mbiti, p. 444.
50 Cf. John S. Mbiti, pp. 443-444. Cf. also Helmer Ringgren, pp. 24, 29.
51 Cf. ibid.
52 Cf. ibid.
53 Cf. David A. Brown, p. 37, 38.
54 Cf. Ibid., pp. 37-38.
55 Cf. Ibid., pp. 27-28.
56 Cf. John S. Mbiti, pp. 444 -445. Cf. Helmer Ringgren, p. 29.
57 Cf. John S. Mbiti, p. 445.
58 Cf. John S. Mbiti, pp. 445-446. Cf. also David A. Brown, p. 28.
59 Cf. Ibid.
60 Cf. John S. Mbiti, pp.m446-447
61 Cf. Ibid.
62 Cf. Helmer Ringgren, p. 19. Cf. also John B. Mbiti, pp. 445, 447.
63 Cf. John B. Mbiti, pp. 448-449.
64 Cf. David. A. Brown, p. 19.
65 Cf. Ibid., p. 28.
66 Cf. Ibid., pp. 39-40.
67 Cf. John B. Mbiti, p. 448.
68 John B. Mbiti, p. 449
69 Cf. John A. Hardon, Vol. I, p. 32
70 Cf. E. Geoffrey Parrinder, pp. 433-434.

71 Cf. David A. Brown, p. 21. Cf. also Helmer Ringgren, p. 25.
72 Cf. David A. Brown, p. 42.
73 Cf. John A. Hardon, Vol. I, p. 25.
74 Cf. Ibid., p. 37.
75 Ibid.
76 David A. Brown, p. 23.
77 John A. Hardon, Vol. I, p. 37.
78 Ibid., pp. 37-38.
79 David A. Brown, pp. 21-22.
80 Cf. Ibid., p. 42.
81 Cf. Ibid., p. 23.
82 Cf. John A. Hardon, Vol. I, pp. 25-26.
83 Cf. David A. Brown, p. 21.
84 Cf. Ibid., pp. 42-43.
85 Cf. Ibid., p. 21.
86 Ibid., p. 22.
87 Ibid.
88 Ibid., pp. 22-23.
89 Cf. Rama Shanker Srivastava, pp. 34 -35.
90 Cf. David A. Brown, pp. 29-31.
91 *Kpekple* is the traditional food of the Ga people. It is made from corn-dough. Cf. ibid., p. 31.
92 Cf. Ibid., pp. 32-33.
93 Cf. Ibid., p. 47.
94 Cf. Ibid., pp. 46-47.
95 Cf. Ibid., pp. 47-48.
96 Cf. Ibid., p. 48.
97 Cf. Ibid., pp. 45-46.
98 Cf. Ibid., pp. 48-50.
99 Cf. Ibid., p. 31.
100 Cf. Ibid.
101 Ibid.
102 Cf. Ibid.
103 Cf. Helmer Ringgren, pp. 11-12.
104 Cf. Ibid., pp. 22-23. Cf. also Ninian Smart, pp. 51-52.
105 Cf. Helmer Ringgren, p. 25.
106 Cf. Ibid., 34.
107 Cf. Ninian Smart, pp. 55-56.
108 Cf. David A. Brown, p. 43.
109 Cf. David A. Brown, p. 43.
110 Cf. John S. Mbiti, p. 447.
111 Cf. John A. Hardon, Vol. I, p. 38.
112 Cf. David A. Brown, p. 43.
113 Cf. John A. Hardon, Vol. I, p. 36.
114 Cf. John A. Hardon, Vol. I, p. 38. Cf. also David A. Brown, p. 43
115 Cf. John A. Hardon, pp. 36-37. Cf. also David A. Brown, p. 43.

116 Cf. John A. Hardon, Vol. I, p, 38. Cf. also David A. Brown, p. 43.
117 Cf. Ibid.
118 Cf. David A. Brown, pp. 40-41. Cf. also Helmer Ringgren, p. 18.
119 Cf. David A. Brown, p. 41.
120 Cf. Helmer Ringgren, p. 13.
121 Cf. John A. Hardon, Vol. I, p. 41.
122 Cf. Rama Shankar Srivastva, pp. 35-36.
123 Cf. John A Hardon, Vol. I, pp. 41-42.
124 Ibid., pp. 42
125 Cf. David A. Brown, pp. 33-34.
126 Cf. Ibid.
127 Cf. Ibid.
128 Cf. Helmer Ringgren, p. 12.
129 Cf. Ibid., pp. 18-19.
130 Cf. John A. Hardon, Vol. I, p. 35.
131 Ibid.
132 Ibid., p. 33.
133 Cf. Ibid., pp. 35-36. Cf. also David A. Brown, p. 28.
134 Cf. John A. Hardon, Vol. I, pp. 33-34.
135 Cf. Ibid., p. 34.
136 Ibid., p. 40.
138 Cf. Ibid., pp. 38-39, 40.
139 Cf. Ibid., pp. 39-40. Cf. also David A. Brown, pp. 28-29.

Chapter 2

Greek-Hellenistic-Roman Traditions

INTRODUCTION

The Greek, Hellenistic and Roman cultures could be considered a single tradition, as they have so much in common in spite of their divergence. Greek culture, in its antiquity, was not homogeneous and integrated, but rather was a hybrid reality. It was the result of the coming together of a number of immigrant Greek tribes, such as, the Ionians, the Achaeans and the Dorians, since 2000 BC. The characteristic elements of the tribal people were fused to form what we call the Greek culture. In the centuries that followed, Greek culture and civilization developed through the Geometrical Period, the Archaic Period and the Classical Period to achieve its own identity and to influence the thinking and way of life of many other cultures. Though the Hellenistic and the Roman cultures have emerged outside the Greek mainland, still they have the characteristic marks of Greek culture. The Hellenistic culture originated out of the manifold contacts of the Greeks with the East, starting from the time of Emperor Alexander the Great, and his invasion of the East, about 300 BC. It continued through the Roman and Christian era up to the time of the Christian Roman emperor Constantine the Great, about 300 AD. Thus, the Hellenistic cultural and religious movement was a mixed civilization, in which the Greek, the Oriental and, to some extent, the Roman cultures influenced each other. But the dominant influence was that of Greek culture. Roman culture, though originated and developed independently of Greek culture, came under its dominance when Roman Emperor Agustus made Greece a province of the Roman Empire. Though Greece lost its political independence in being part of the Roman Empire, it gained its cultural and religious dominance over the Roman culture and religious practice. Since this contact between the Greek and Roman cultures, the civilization of the Roman Empire became Greco-Roman, in which the Greek element was dominant.[1]

In view of this inter-relatedness of the Greek, the Hellenistic and the Roman cultures and their common base as one tradition, in the ensuing essays we will make an attempt to unfold their religious beliefs and practices. We will take up for consideration the Greek and the Roman religions first and then the Hellenistic religion, as the latter has the influence of both the former religions, as well as of the oriental religions. In doing so, our main focus will to understand their gods and the various means the people of these religions used in their desire to come into contact with the Divine. In other words, our concern is to know the concrete paths these religions proposed to experience the divinities in which they believed.

2.1. GREEK RELIGION

Our knowledge of Greek religion depends, to a great extent, on the information the poets, philosophers and historians furnish, as it has no sacred writings of its own. The two classical poets from whom we gather a great deal of data about the Greek gods and religious practice are Homer and Hesiod. The two epics of Homer, viz., *Iliad* and *Odyssey*, both of which are said to be written during the 8th century BC, speak of the Olympic gods adorned in their court. But one would wonder how much of it really reflects the actual religious belief of the 8th century BC and how much of it need to be attributed to the poetic imagination and literary stylization of the poet. Hesiod, lived in the 7th century BC, and dealt with a number of religious themes in both of his poems. In his *Theogony*, he grouped the gods in genealogical tables and organized myths about their origin. His second book, *Works and Days*, contains rules regarding moral and religious taboos, purification precepts and rules for agriculture. Besides these major sources, there was a series of hymns attributed to Homer, known as the *Homeric Hymns*; the so-called *Palaecastro Hymn* from Crete also speaks of the cultic practices of the people of Greece. The works of the later poets also contain information about the religious situation of the time. Pausanias's description of Greece provides details about the sanctuaries and local cult practices. In many of his works, Plutarch provides us with material regarding Greek religion. The archeological finds, such as, temples, pictorial representations, vase paintings, sculptures, coins and inscriptions also complement the literary sources in supplying knowledge about the religious life of the people of Greece.[2]

Since Greek religion does not have a scripture that guides the faith of its adherents, it is a religion of piety and worship rather than a religion of doctrinal belief. It is common worship that united the people rather than a common profession of a doctrinally formulated faith. This does not mean that people had no faith at all, but only that their faith was implicit and non-formulated. This faith was not based on any sacred scriptures or explicitly formulated doctrinal creed. Neither was there any professional clergy who defended the faith, interpreted stories about the gods and officially taught doctrine and morality. The priests of ancient Greece had the right and duty to perform certain sacrifices and ceremonies in the temples. Often a priest was a priest of a particular temple and performed the rites at that temple. He had nothing to do with doctrinal teaching or moral instruction. Therefore, in ancient Greece, religion and piety was that of the ordinary people. There was no clericalism and the religion was genuinely lay-centered.[3] In this manner, though there was genuine religious spirit in the practice of religion, still it was free and informal. A.H. Armstrong in describing the religious life of the people of ancient Greece notes:

> In the ancient [Greek] world we are not dealing with a "religion" in any sense in which we normally understand the term nowadays. There is no scripture, no church, and no

body of authoritative interpreters of the tradition. The stories that the poets told about the gods and the way in which they expressed the common pieties certainly deeply colored people's imaginations and influenced their feelings about the gods. But they were not in any way authoritative. Poets could and frequently did disagree with each other about the gods, and anyone was free to disagree with the poets. The cults were the foundation of all piety, but there was much in them that never got into poetry. The old-fashioned way of speaking Homer as "the Bible of the Greeks" was decidedly misleading. And if there was no Bible, there was no church either. There was no organized religious community distinct from the general communities of families, villages, cities, and peoples and no clergy with the special function of safeguarding and interpreting a tradition arising from a scripture. Priests were representatives of the families or the officers of the state whose business was to perform certain ritual functions, not to teach or to guide the development of spirituality. ...So the ancient spirituality [of the Greeks] is bewilderingly free and various.[4]

In spite of the free spirit that prevailed among the people in their religion and religious practice, the Greeks were not 'secular', as every aspect of their life was permeated by religion. They visualized the world as filled with the divine presence of the spirits and gods. People were reminded of this truth by the public ceremonies in cities and the villages, and the domestic rites offered at the homes, farms and family graves.[5] The ancient Greeks believed in gods and felt deeply about them. They attempted to experience the divine power of these gods through the worship and prayer they offered to gods.[6]

In the first part of this essay we will make an attempt to understand the world of the gods among the Greeks, while in the second part we will endeavor to explore the paths the Greek people used to come in touch with these divinities.

2.1.1. GODS OF THE GREEK PANTHEON

The prominent characteristic of the Greek gods is their humanity. The gods are presented in terms of human beings. While artists represent the gods as idealized human figures, the poets depict them as powerful and valiant, though at times limited by human faults and frailties. In other words, there is a great deal of anthropomorphism in the manner in which the Greeks speak of their gods. This does not mean that there is no difference between the gods and men. The gods are greater and more powerful than men. They are beautiful, immortal, eternally youthful, raised above the suffering and sorrow that torment men and living a carefree and peaceful life in a place that is far above the dwellings of the human.[7] In exploring various gods worshipped and prayed to by the people of Greece, in this section, firstly we would try to understand the nature of the gods of the Greeks. Having done this, we would expound the relationship between the gods and human beings. Finally, we seek to comprehend the individual gods, to whom the Greeks, as a people, were devoted and whom they honored in their worship.

2.1.1.1. NATURE OF THE GREEK GODS

Though the Greek gods, described in some of the ancient Greek poems, might seem, to a modern rational mind, as falling below the standards demanded of truly divine beings, people perceived them as embodiments of power. The ancient Greeks experienced the divinity as power. Gods deserved worship because they were more powerful than human beings. It does not mean that every god was omnipotent and stood outside the world and acted on this world. Gods were often perceived as powers, in this world, that are potent enough to help or harm people, though at times limited by the powers of other gods.[8]

The power of the gods was eternal and everlasting, as they were immortal. Immortality is another fundamental difference between the gods and human beings. The immortal nature of gods does not necessarily mean that they have no origin. As a matter of fact the myths often describe the strange birth stories of the gods. In the ancient Greek poems, immortality and eternity often refer to the deathless and endless nature of the gods rather than the absence of origin. Eternity, as a state without beginning and end, was the product of later philosophical thinking. Therefore, once the gods were born, they lived without experiencing death. From the ancient times Greeks believed that their gods were immortal, eternal and everlasting. This divine immortality implied that the gods lived a life of perpetual youth, beauty and strength. They were free from any form of evil humans experience in this world. The gods were unaffected by old age and sickness. Though they many experience occasional pain or grief, these could never affect them permanently. For instance, they could be hurt in a fight; they could experience pain at the death of a human being they loved, but these hurts and pains would soon pass away, as they returned to their permanent state of peace and joy. The ancient poems gave two reasons for the immortality of the gods and their perpetual youthful existence. The first reason was that, unlike the humans in whose veins run blood, the gods had a different fluid, viz., *ichor*, running in their veins. Besides, the gods had special food and drink, viz., *ambrosia* and *nectar*. Secondly, the home of the gods, Mount Olympus, was a place of light and peace. Thus, the fluid that ran in the veins of the gods, the food they ate and their dwelling place made them immortal and kept them youthful.[9]

Some ancient poems attributed immorality to the gods. They were said to be doing everything that was considered as shameful among men, such as, stealing, committing adultery and deceiving each other. A number of philosophers, like Xenophanes, criticized too human a portrayal of the gods in the poems of Homer and Hesiod. Such poetic presentations were not to be taken literally, but rather must be taken allegorically. The simple reason for so doing is that poetry is not sacred scripture. The authors of the poems have attributed to the gods, the human behaviors of kings and nobles. On the other hand, the gods were seen as exercising their power to maintain the world order, which automatically implies moral order. Offenses involving solemn oaths, grave offenses against the family and offenses against strangers and suppliants were seen as direct insult to the gods. The gods were said to punish those who violated the world order. Besides, we see that the gods did take care of families, villages and cities. They also cared for individual humans. All these indicate that the gods were moral, and the immoral character of gods indicated in the ancient poems must be understood in an allegorical sense.[10]

2.1.1.2. RELATIONSHIP BETWEEN THE GODS AND THE HUMANS

From what we have said about the nature of the gods, it is clear that the gods are superior to human beings in a number of ways. The gods are more powerful than men. While the gods are immortal and eternally young, humans have to undergo many pains in life and finally experience death. The gods are said to be the moral guardians of the universe: they are morally superior to human beings. Nowhere in the ancient poetry do we find a sense of human jealousy expressed when man sees himself in relationship with the gods. Man does not feel resentment when he experiences the gods as superior to him. As a matter of fact, as the worshipper of the gods, humans looked at these powerful beings with a sense of wonder, as they lived in perpetual youthfulness and beauty in their world of light, far removed from the sufferings and pains of this earthly existence. His attitude towards the gods was one of pleasure, admiration and deep affection; there is no envy on the part of humans about the gods.[11]

But some of the gods, described in the ancient poems, who have "the beauty ...of the sun, the sea, the wind, the mountains, great wild animals, splendid, powerful and dangerous realities that do not come within the sphere of morality"[12] are in no way concerned about the human race. In other words, it seems that the gods do not love humans, and the human race cannot depend upon them for their kindness and favor. They seem to recent the success and happiness of human beings and attempt to bring disaster on any person who makes progress either in power or prosperity that might take one to the superhuman level. Thus, the ancient poems seem to say that the gods are envious of man and look for occasions to cause trouble. But, philosophers from the time of Plato often did not accept this claim of the ancient poems about divine envy, as it would go against the moral goodness of the gods. So they were critical of the claims of the ancient poems regarding divine envy.[13]

The piety of the ordinary people was not too rigid in its understanding of the relationships of the gods to men. Ordinary people believed that the gods could be relied upon to be kind and concerned, while at the same time they could not be relied upon. In other words, the ordinary people believed that the gods had a love-hate relationship with them. As a community or as individuals, people felt that they had a special relationship with particular gods, which involved loving care on the part of the divine and affection and gratitude on the human side. This sense of being looked after by the gods, though it often could not be justified rationally, was an essential dimension of the religious life of the Greek people. We find numerous examples to illustrate this in the ancient poems. As a community, the Athenians felt the love and protection of the goddess *Athena*. As an individual, Odysseus experienced that he was under the care and protection of the goddess *Athena*, who looked after him. In both of these cases, the Athenians and Odysseus experienced the divine care and kindness and responded to the goddess who loved and cared for them with affection and gratitude.[14]

While people experienced this sense of being looked after by the gods, they also were afraid of the gods, as they were dangerous and their actions were unpredictable. The anger of the gods might strike and destroy individuals, families and cities. Often the people were not able to find a reason for the divine anger and destruction. Because of the unpredictable nature of the gods, fear of the gods was an essential dimension of the religious life of the Greeks. Such fear made the people wonder if the gods really cared for them.[15]

The relationship of the gods to humans is paradoxical. While man experiences the care of the gods, he also experiences their condescension. On the one hand he feels that he is looked after, and on the other hand he feels that he is cheated. He sees the gods as loving him and at the same time encounters their hate and dislike for him. This twofold aspect of the love-hate relationship of the gods to human persons is beautifully expressed in Homer's *Odyssey*. After the shipwreck Odysseus was swimming to safety. The sea-god *Poseidon* is doing all within his power to thwart the safety of Odysseus. This action indicates Poseidon's hatred for Odysseus, as the former is happy at the death of the latter. A river goddess, *Leucothea*, was supportive of Odysseus's effort to escape from the trouble. The loving presence, guidance and inspiration of the goddess *Athena* were very much with Odysseus. As he comes to the mouth of the river, which is the only safe way for him to reach the shore, Odysseus prays to the river-goddess he has never known or met before. Though he is a stranger to her, the river-goddess checks her current, holds back the waves and makes the path of the swimmer smooth, thereby bringing him to safety at the mouth of the river. Thus, the relationship of the gods to men implies a certain amount of mystery. Man is never be able to understand the mystery of the ways of the gods.[16]

2.1.1.3. INDIVIDUAL GODS OF THE GREEK PANTHEON

The ancient Greeks regarded their gods as the immortal controllers of the world of nature and all it contained. Since the gods were the guardians of nature there was a type of departmentalization, each god looking after a certain aspect of nature. For instance, there was the god of weather, the god of the sea, the god of the underworld and many often gods seeing to the smooth running of world. Besides the departmentalization of gods, the Greeks categorized their gods in two groups, viz., the *Olympian* gods and the *Chthonian* gods, the former are the gods of the heavenly realm of nature, while the latter are the gods of the earthly realms of nature. This twofold categorization of the Greek gods should not be taken as a strict grouping, as there are certain gods who intermediate between the heavenly and the earthly realms of nature. If we press this division too hard we would find it difficult to place those intermediate gods in any of these groupings. Besides, we must not think that one group of gods is superior to the other. This division does not point to superiority or inferiority of the gods, but rather it indicates only that the gods who belong to these two groups care for the heavenly and the earthly aspects of the world.[17] The gods of the Greek Pantheon can be ordered under these two headings.

2.1.1.3.1. The Olympian Gods

The *Olympian* gods lived in the divine Mount of Olympus, which was in Northern Greece. They were believed to be 'heavenly', as they lived in the high places and cared for the higher realms of nature.[18] The following are some of the major gods and goddesses who made their home in the great Mount of Olympus.

2.1.1.3.1.1. Zeus

Zeus was supreme among the *Olympian* gods. He ruled the *Olympian* aristocracy. As a matter of fact he was supreme among the whole galaxy of the Greek gods. He was the sky-god, who took care of the meteorological phenomena of nature. He was the god of the vault of heaven. He makes the sky to be clear one day, cloudy and rainy another day, and the thunder to strike on the earth another day. Thus, *Zeus* exercised great power over the clouds, rain and thunderbolts.[19] He was seen as the king of the gods and humans. The Greek term *"theos"* was a synonym for *Zeus*.[20] He was considered as the one who weighs everything in the universe and keeps everything in perfect balance. "*Zeus*, whosoe'er he be – if by his name it well pleaseth him to be invoked, by this name I call to him – as I weigh all things in the balance, I can conjecture none save '*Zeus*'."[21] He was also seen as the culmination and end of all the gods, as all gods are identical with him. "*Zeus* is air, *Zeus* is earth, *Zeus* is heaven, yea, *Zeus* is all things and whatsoever transcendeth them."[22] In this manner, *Zeus* was seen in the ancient poems as the one who brings unity and balance both in the world and among the gods. Thus, we find an element of monotheism in the figure of *Zeus* within the Greek Pantheon.[23]

Homer and Hesiod considered Zeus as the god who awarded fate (*moira*) to all men. At times fate is described as a kind of universal order independent of *Zeus* and at other times personified and spoken as three *moiras* in the poems of these two authors. This way of speaking of fate is a consideration of fate from the human point of view, as it is experienced in human lives, without taking into account its origin. Thus, for both of these authors, *Zeus* was, indeed, the controller fate who meets out to each person his share in life.[24] A quotation from Hesiod's *Work and Days* illustrates this truth with clarity:

> Tell of *Zeus* your father and chant his praises. Through him mortal men are famed or unfamed, sung or unsung alike, as great *Zeus* wills. For easily he makes strong, and easily he brings the strong man low; easily he humbles the proud and raises the obscure, and easily he straightens the crooked and blasts the proud, *Zeus* who thunders aloft and has his dwelling most high.[25]

Though *Zeus* was a great and exalted god, he was too high, mighty and his reign so universal that he did not arouse much personal devotion from the people. In the ancient poems we find rare mention of *Zeus* as being friends with and caring for individual persons. Generally speaking, many Greeks, whether they were ordinary people, kings or emperors, believed that *Zeus* was not personally concerned about them. As a result not many of them chose *Zeus* as their personal god, but rather settled upon more approachable gods to be their divine patrons and guardians. This did not mean that *Zeus* was insignificant to the Greeks. He was believed to be the one who gave divine unity and order to the whole universe. It was the responsibility of *Zeus* to see that this universe remained a cosmos with order and regularity, and that it did not become chaos. It was he who saw that each kingdom on earth remained a kingdom and did not become anarchy and despotism. Therefore, *Zeus* was not far away from this world, but he was very much in the world. It is *Zeus* who balances the scales and sets the weights in them, thereby guiding history, whether human, natural or national, to its final destiny.[26]

2.1.1.3.1.2. Hera

Hera was *Zeus's* permanent wife. According to legends, *Zeus* had to court her for 300 years, before she would marry him. Her betrothal to *Zeus*, *hieros gamos*, was celebrated each year. This celebration is associated with the ancient fertility rites. She was looked upon as a model of human marriage. She was a motherly figure, who presided over a number of concerns related to women. *Hera* was believed to be the protectress of marriage, married women, children and the home. She often appears in stories of the gods as a betrayed wife, troubling girls because *Zeus* was in love with them.[27]

2.1.1.3.1.3. Athena

Athena, commonly known as *Pallas Athena* (Maiden *Athena*), is the daughter of *Zeus*. She was the patroness of the city of Athens, which derived its name from her. She was born out of her father's forehead in a full-grown state. She was believed to be the personification of the sagacity or the practical insight (*metis*) of her father, *Zeus*. In the earliest times Athena was depicted as a young girl. But as the city of Athens grew, she was also presented as an older woman. In the course of time, she was represented, as the matronly figure under whose protection the city of Athens flourished in the civilized world. *Athena* was a virgin and was uninterested in sex. She was believed to be the calmest, the most rational and self-possessed goddess, full of practical wisdom. She was the patroness of household craftsmen, as well as of statesmen and leaders. She was also a warrior goddess, a champion and leader of her people in war. Often she was represented as fully armed for battle and, indeed, was terrifying. She was armed with shield, lance and aegis (*aigis*), which is a protective weapon consisting of a metal mounted collar bearing terrifying images. As a goddess, she was capable of bringing together active strength and shrewd action. As a result, she could defend the individuals and communities for whom she cared against their enemies, at the same time protecting peaceful occupations, such as crafts and arts. It was believed among the Greeks that *Athena* invented the flute. But, in a typically womanly fashion, she spurned the use of this musical instrument, when she saw her face disfigured as she puffed up her cheeks to blow on it. She cared for the people she loved and helped them to overcome their trials and troubles. But she also punished those who disregarded her. For instance, she helped the Greeks to win Troy, but she avenged those Greek heroes who failed to pay her befitting homage. *Athena* was said to have established the rule of law and the concept of mercy in the trial that freed Orestes from the Furies after he had murdered his mother at *Apollo's* orders. It was believed that the olive tree was *Athena's* gift to mankind. She was especially remembered and venerated in Athens for this gift. The owl is *Athena's* bird. As a goddess, she was cool and unaffected by the allurements of love. She remained an eternal virgin. We find the same calmness and control in the cults offered to *Athena*, which are bereft of all exaggerations.[28]

2.1.1.3.1.4. Apollo

Apollo was the greatest of the sons of *Zeus*. He possessed solar features, as he was originally a sun god. He was said to be pure, holy and the shining one. His nature was marked by the qualities of light, truth, and exacting clarity, striving for insight, moderation and order. *Apollo* is associated with the fundamental Greek teachings, such as, "know thyself" and "nothing in excess". It was believed that he set things in order, sometimes by using means that are horrifying. When someone broke the order by grave human offenses, *Apollo* purified the offender both ritually and morally. As the god of purification, the purity he bestowed on man healed both his body and soul. Thus, *Apollo* was the god of law, justice and order. He also healed people of their diseases. He is also believed to ward off evil. But the arrows he held in his hands often said to brought illness and even death. Thus, we find him ambivalent in these twofold characteristics of warding off evil and bringing illness and death. He protected adolescents who were admitted to the state of adulthood, as they consecrated their long hair to him. *Apollo* also instilled athletic spirit in humans. He and his close associates, the *Muses,* were inspirers of *mousike*, which in Greek refers to the whole range of realities related to the cultural life of human beings, such as, poetry, music, dance, philosophy and the whole of human culture. *Apollo* had a special closeness to his father *Zeus*. This closeness is not one of personal love and relationship, but a functional closeness, in that he is the spokesman for his father and the king of the gods, *Zeus*. As a spokesman for *Zeus*, *Apollo* was the god of prophecy. He unveiled what was hidden in the past and what lay in the future through oracles at Delphi, Didyma, Claros and many other shrines. Through the oracles he revealed and declared the divine order in the world. *Apollo* was more distant in his relationship with people. He represents a spiritual orientation that is dominant in Greek religion, viz., sense of balance and moderation, which stresses the distance between the gods and men. *Apollo's* personality as a distant god represents this dimension of the spirituality of the Greek religion. *Apollo* was one of the most majestic of the Olympian gods. He was the patron of truth, archery, music, medicine and prophecy.[29]

2.1.1.3.1.5. Poseidon

Poseidon was the god of the sea and earthquakes. His name means 'the Lord or the Spouse of the Earth'. He was believed to be the consort of the earth-goddess. Certain epithets speak of him as the Lord of earth and fertility. But in historical times *Poseidon* was the ruler of the water, the ocean and the rivers. His symbol was the trident. It was believed that he gave horses to men. In certain myths he himself appeared as a horse. According to Homer, he had his palace built of 'gleaming gold' deep in the Aegean Sea. The Greeks prayed to *Poseidon* to be kind to them as they voyaged in ships through the sea.[30]

2.1.1.3.1.6. Artemis

Artemis was the virgin goddess of the moon. She was the twin sister of *Apollo*. Like her brother *Apollo*, she was the pure and the holy one. She was a fresh, pure, sweet maiden. She was the mighty huntress and the 'rainer of arrows'. As a goddess of hunt, the nymphs accompanied her. Night, the time of shining moon, belonged to her. She was the guardian of the cities, of young animals and of women of all ages. Women prayed to *Artemis* for easy childbirth, as she was the midwife at the birth of her own twin brother Apollo. She could be harsh and unsympathetic. A clear example of her stern nature was seen in her act of blocking the passage of the Greek army to Troy, because Agamemnon boasted that he was better than *Artemis*, and demanding that he sacrifice to her his daughter.[31]

2.1.1.3.1.7. Aphrodite

Aphrodite was the goddess of love and beauty. According to the poet Hesiod, she presided over 'girlish babble and tricks'. She was known for her rapture, embrace and caresses. In places she walked flowers sprang up, doves and sparrows flew over her. She bore many children to *Ares*, her lover. Significant among them were Fear and Terror. She had the power to tempt even wise gods. She was said to have tempted *Zeus*, making him forget his love for *Hera*, his bride.[32]

The goddess *Aphrodite* and her son *Eros* represented the powers of passionate sexual love. The Greeks used the name of *Eros* to refer to passionate sexual love. Sexual love is a great universal force. We find in many myths of world origin that the world emerges from coupling divine powers and sexual generation. In such myths *Eros* appears as an important power. *Aphrodite* and *Eros* were the embodiment of sexual charm and excitement. The power of these two deities and their influence on animal and human life was universal. It included regular mating, married love and disorderly sexual passion. *Aphrodite* and *Eros* were felt to be present in various manifestations of sexual love, whether they were regular or irregular, serious or superficial. The dove, the myrtle and the pomegranate were the symbols associated with the goddess *Aphrodite*. She was also revered as the goddess of the sea and the flowering nature.[33]

2.1.1.3.1.8. Ares

Ares was the God of war. He represented brute force, violence and the tumult of battle. His symbol was the vulture. His parents, *Zeus* and *Hera,* had a deep dislike for him. But *Hedes*, the god of the underworld, befriended Ares. Ares needed many people to fight wars, so he increased the population of the underworld. He was involved in a love affair with *Aphrodite*. *Hephaestus*, the husband of *Aphrodite*, caught them in the act, with the help of an invisible net. In this manner, *Ares* became an embarrassment for the gods. Though he was a lifelong warrior, he was not always successful in his battles. Once the giants captured him, while *Heracles* and *Diomedes* wounded him thrice and once, respectively. As a symbol of war and the evils associated with it, viz., the death, suffering and sorrow, the Greeks held *Ares* in great awe, but he was never the object of their adoration.[34]

2.1.1.3.1.9. Hermes

Hermes was a pastoral god. He was believed to be capable of increasing the herds of cattle. He was the patron of flocks. But from the myths we come to know that he increased the herds of cattle by stealing his brother *Apollo's* cattle. This made him the patron god of the thieves, rogues and mischief-makers. After stealing the cattle from his brother's flocks he tried to escape. As people attempted to find him, he confused his pursuers with the help of an ingeniously devised false trail. Due to his ingenuity in confusing people in the journey, he became the patron god of the wayfarers. When he was caught he protested and defended himself by saying that he was too young to perform the act of stealing. This ability to be a trickster earned *Hermes* the honor of being the patron god of commerce, the market place, orators and writers.[35]

2.1.1.3.1.10. Hephaestus

Hephaestus was the god of fire and the patron of artisans. According to a legend, his mother *Hera* expelled him from Mount Olympus because she could not bear to see his lameness. He produced many marvels. One such marvel was the creation of the first woman, Pandora, into whom the gods breathed life. It was believed that on Mount Olympus he built for himself a shining bronze palace. It was said that a number of mechanical servants managed this mansion.[36]

2.1.1.3.1.11. Hestia

Hestia was the goddess of home and hearth. She manifested in the world in fire. As a goddess of home and hearth, she received a share of all the sacrifices performed in the house.[37]

2.1.1.3.2. The Chthonian Gods

The *Chthonian* gods included all the other gods, who did not belong to the *Olympian* family of gods. The Greek term "*chthonioi*" literally means "those of the earth". The phrase "those of the earth" does not mean that the gods, who belong to this group are evil powers or enemies of gods. The *Chthonian* gods are not to be identified with earth-born enemies of the gods in Greek mythology, viz., the giants and monsters. The gods who belong to this group are gods by their right and they belong to the divine society of the gods. These gods are considered to be 'earthly', as they occupied the subterranean realms and were involved with the fertility of the earth, the realm of death and similar realms associated with the nether world.[38] Now, we shall consider some of the major gods who belong to this group.

2.1.1.3.2.1. Demeter

Demeter, though shebelonged to the *Chthonian* group of gods, established herself among the *Olympian* gods. She was a fertility goddess, who provided plentiful crops, grains and fruits. Her name means 'earth mother' or 'corn mother'. The fact she was the mother of earth and a fertility goddess is clearly indicated in the ancient poems. The following quotation from Aeschylus indicates this truth:

The holy heaven yearns to wound the earth, and yearning layeth hold on the earth to join in wedlock; the rain, fallen from the amorous heaven, impregnates the earth, and it bringeth forth to mankind the food of flocks and heards and *Demeter's* gifts; and from the moist marriage-rite the woods put on their bloom.[39]

In Eleusis, *Demeter* was worshipped as the goddess of the seed and the subterranean regions. A myth speaks of her quarrel with Hades, the god of the underworld. Hades had abducted and taken to the nether world *Persephone*, the daughter of *Demeter*, who was also known as *Kore*. This was done with the permission of the great god Zeus. The sorrowing mother waited for a long time for the return of her daughter. Finally the god *Hilios* told her that *Hades* would not return her daughter. Filled with anger *Demeter* brought all life to a standstill by not letting the earth produce its fruits and allowing famine to take control of the earth. At this juncture, *Zeus* intervened and brought about a reconciliation by proposing a compromise according to which *Persephone* would remain for one third of the year with Hades in the underworld as his spouse, while the remaining two thirds she would spend with her mother on earth. Thus, the time between the harvest season and the planting season, when the fields are empty, *Persephone* was said to be in the subterranean region. When she was with her mother *Demeter* on the earth, the fields would bear fruit. *Persephone*, therefore, was the goddess of darkness and light, the lower world and the upper world.[40]

2.1.1.3.2.2. Dionysus

Dionysus was another significant god of the Greeks, though he was not included among the *Olympian* groups of gods. He was believed to be the god of Wine, fertility, joyous life and hospitality. It was believed that he was a Thracian god by origin, and that his cult, which flourished in Asia Minor, spread from there to Greece. According to legends *Dionysus* was the son of *Zeus* by a mortal mother. *Hera*, the wife of *Zeus*, moved by jealousy, destroyed *Dionysus's* mother and drove Dionysus mad. He wandered about the earth accompanied by satyrs, sileni and maenads, as well as nymphs. He had a number of manifestations. Among his manifestations, as the highest male principle, a bull represented him. As a fertility god, he was associated with trees, fruits and particularly wine. Often he was represented along with Wine. He was believed to have gifted the Greeks with Wine. The most significant manifestation of *Dionysus* was that of god of ecstasy and rapture. Thus, in many of the mystery cults associated with *Dionysus*, there were wine drinking and orgiastic ceremonies.[41]

In the Orphic mystery cults *Dionysus* appeared in a totally different manifestation. Here he was presented as a mystic and an ascetic rather than as a god to whom orgiastic ceremonies are offered. According to Orphic myths, *Dionysus*, under the name *Zagreus*, was the son of *Persephone* and *Zeus*. His father, *Zeus*, wanted *Zagerus* to rule the whole world. But this could not happen, as the dreadful Titans, a race of ancient giants killed the infant *Zagerus* and ate his *flesh*. Zeus, in his anger, sent down thunderbolts, destroyed the Titans and reduced them to ashes. The human race was formed from these ashes. Man was both evil and good, because he was made up of the ashes of the Titans, who were evil, and the flesh of the good infant god, *Zagreus*. But, in fact, *Zagreus* was not dead, as the goddess *Athena* succeeded in rescuing his heart. *Zeus* swallowed the heart of *Zagreus*, which the goddess *Athena* rescued, and he was reborn as the son of the earth goddess, *Semele*. The rebirth of *Zagreus* brought hope of a purified new life for man. This new life was achieved though the union of man with *Zagreus*, the 'once-more-living god'.[42]

Having these two aspects of ecstasy and mysticism in his personality, Dionysus represents a major spiritual orientation of the Greek religion, viz., the ecstatic-mystical trend. This spiritual trend attempts to help the devotee to come into communion with the divine in two ways that are seemingly contradictory, viz., the way of ecstasy, rapture and orgiastic ceremonies, and the path of asceticism and mysticism. If a sense of balance were brought about between these two paths, a richer experience of the divine would be possible for the devotee.[43]

2.1.1.3.2.3. Minor Chthonian Gods

In Greek mythology, we find a number of minor *Chthonian* gods. There was the thunder-god, *Zeus Chthonos*, who sent rain and fertility to earth. Often he was represented as a serpent. We could mention *Hades*, the god of the realm of death. He was considered to be merciless and unconquerable. When he entered someone's life, there was no way that person could win over *Hades*. Hardly any worship was offered to *Hades*. Often he was identified with Pluto, the god of wealth, as treasures were hidden in the ground. Other best-known *Chthonian* beings were the *Heroes* (*heros*). They were acknowledged as strong human beings who lived on earth. It was believed that though they are dead, they have the power to assist the humans still living here on earth. *Heracles* was among the well-known Heroes of Greece, who accomplished twelve labors entrusted to him. Some cults are associated with the Heroes, as well.[44]

2.1.1.3.3. Other Spiritual Beings

Beyond the *Olympian* and *Chthonian* gods, there were other gods who were significant because of their place in Greek mythology. These gods are not included in the above categorization, but they do appear in Greek mythology and literature. *Helios* was the sun god, who moves across the vault of heaven. *Eos* was the goddess of dawn. *Aeolus* was the god of the wind. Pan was a pastoral god who protected the herds. He was represented with goat's ears, beard and a horned brow. He was said to play the syrinx, a shepherd's flute. The *Dioscuri* (*Zeus's* boys) were a pair of twins acting as helpers especially when there was a shipwreck. In Sparta this pair of twins was associated with the moon goddess *Helena*. *Eileithyia* was the goddess of childbirth. She was believed to be a manifestation of *Artemis*.[45]

Besides believing in the gods, the Greeks believed that nature was filled with various sorts of supernatural beings, such as, satyrs, sileni and nymphs. There were different types of nymphs, who were the followers of Artemis: the mountain nymphs (*Oreads*), the tree nymphs (*Dryads*) and the nymphs of springs (*Naiads*). Besides, there were the centaurs, which were half horses and half men.[46]

Other than believing in the gods, the Greeks also believed in the survival of the soul (*psuche*), after the bodily life had come to an end. The soul that survived death, after a prolonged journey through the vast sheet of water, reached the underworld (*Hades*), which was a dark and sad place, where the souls of the dead exist in vague and unsubstantial shadows. Deep below the realm of death, was the realm of Tartaores, where the wicked suffer punishment. A few selected people reached the *Elysium*, which was the place of eternal spring. The Greeks also believed in the spirits of the dead that were harmful, known as *Keres*. These spirits of the dead had to be appeased. One of such festivals that attempted to appease them was *Anthesteria*. It was believed that the *Keres* took part in this festival. The festival was closed with the phrase, "out Keres! The Anthesteria is over". The notion of better life after death developed from the Elusian mysteries, which was supplemented by the philosophical ideas about the immortality of the soul. Orphism also believed in immortality.[47]

So far we have been exploring the nature of the Greek gods, their relationship to the humans and the various gods of the Greek Pantheon. In the next section, we shall inquire into the various ways and means the Greeks used to come in touch with the divinities they honored and whose blessings they sought.

2.1.2. GREEKS PATHS TO THE DIVINE

The Greeks believed that they had a deep relationship with their gods. They maintained this relationship by communicating with the various gods in whom they believed. The various forms of worship they offered to the gods helped them to come in contact with the divinities. The mediation of the priest played an important role in establishing contact between the gods and the people. The sacred places were the dwelling places of the gods and so they formed the locus of people's meeting with the divine. Offering prayers and sacrifices, organizing festivals and taking part in various forms of mystery cults also helped the Greeks to be in touch with the gods. Sometimes the Greeks took recourse to oracles to know the divine will and acted according to the directives they received from the gods through the oracles. Genuine moral living as per the will of the gods and making atonement and expiation for their failures were some of the ways that helped the Greeks to encounter their gods.

We shall elaborate some of these paths that brought the people of Greece to come closer to the gods and to experience their blessings.

2.1.2.1. MEDIATION OF THE PRIESTS

There was no official clergy in the Greek religion, as the division between the secular and the religious spheres was not made. But professional help was available to those who wished to worship the gods, because in Greece by and large worship was well organized. The priesthood was more hereditary, even though it was not official. In ancient Greece, the king was in charge of worship. In the city of Sparta, for example, the king presided over sacrifices in the name of the state. Later on, an official of the state took care of worship matters on behalf of the king. For instance, we find that, in the city of Athens, an official called *Basileus* oversaw religious worship and performed some cultic function. Some cultic practices took place in the families, and the obligation of presiding over such cults passed on from one generation to the next in the family circle. In general, sacrifices and other rites were officiated by priests or priestesses often chosen by the gods. There was no necessary correspondence between the sex of the divinities and the priests who officiated at their temples. For instance, *Apollo*, a male god, chose Pythia as the priestess of his temple at Delphi, while he preferred a priest to serve his temple at Ptoon. The tenure of such priests or priestesses lasted, in some cases, for a whole lifetime, while in other cases only for a particular period of time. But the functions they performed were limited to the particular deity, who chose them to be priests or priestesses. Besides, they served only in the particular temple they were chosen to serve. They were regarded as officials of the state. In Greece, there was also a special type of priesthood, in which a person performed priestly ministry, while carrying on with a secular profession. In the Greek society, priests, priestesses and prophets enjoyed high social status.[48]

Priests, priestesses and prophets played very important roles in the religious life of the Greek people. Though the priests of the Greek religion were neither professional clergy, who were the authorized interpreters of the sacred scriptures, nor official teachers of doctrine and morality, they definitely were intermediaries between gods and the people. They spoke to the gods on behalf of the people and announced the will of the gods to the people, especially through oracles. They performed specific sacrifices and ceremonies, thereby opening the world of the gods to the people and made the gods more accessible. Though the priests of Greek religion were not teachers of faith, their role as priests, the position they held in the liturgical life of the Greek society and their understanding of cult and ceremonies did help in the development of local piety in the Greek society.[49]

2.1.2.2. SACRED PLACES

Sacred places, such as local sanctuaries, temples and shrines, were vital in the religious life of the Greeks. They were believed to be the places where the gods dwell. Though gods were said to be present everywhere, their presence was special in the sacred places. So the sacred places were the actual meeting places of the gods and the people. Besides, prayers and sacrifices were offered to the gods in the vicinity of the sacred places, as the gods could also participate in the cultic rites and bless the people. In the earliest days, the Greeks believed that groves, caves and mountaintops were sacred places and worshipped the gods there. But over time a number of local sanctuaries emerged all over the country. They were usually places where a sacred stone, a sacred tree or something similar was found. They were attached to houses, farms and streets. In some cases the family graves were seen as sanctuaries, where the cult of the ancestors continued for many generations. Such sanctuaries produced in the people a sense of the divine, as they believed that the gods manifested themselves there. The feeling experienced by those who visited the sanctuaries was a mixture of astonishment and fear before the sacred, which was expressed by the Greek word "*thambos*".[50]

Building temples for the gods was a later development in the history of Greek religion. Initially the gods had no temple of their own, but shared the king's palace. A precinct (*temenos*) attached to the palace was allotted to the god. It contained altar, temple or the place for the deity (*naos*) and other sacred articles. *Naos*, which meant 'dwellings' or 'temples', housed the image of the god, which was usually made of wood. No ritual was associated with the image in the *naos*, though at times it was paraded before the people. The ancient kings performed sacred rites often outside the precinct allotted to the god, in the royal residence. Later much larger temples were built for the gods. Temples always had a rectangular chamber (*naos*), where the image of the deity was placed in the innermost part facing the entrance. Besides, there was an antechamber. A fenced-in sacred compound (*tenemos*) or a sacred groove surrounded the temple. One or more altars were placed there. The larger part of the temple complex, including the inner chambers, was to be used only by the cult officials. Other people could gather only outside the temple, where the altars were placed, as cult took place only outside the temple. Most of the temples were opened only once or twice a year, for temples were considered to be the dwelling places of gods and their premises for services and worship.[51]

Other than the local sanctuaries and the temples there were the shrines, which also were considered sacred places. Shrines were little country places of worship. They were less elaborate than the temples. Often they did not have altars, but they were provided with subterranean chambers or pits for the offerings. There were some Pan-Hellenic shrines, where all the Greeks gathered to celebrate the festivals of their gods. Shrines also included the oracular shrines like the one at Delphi and the shrines built to honor the Heroes.[52]

The sanctuaries, temples and the shrines provided a sacred atmosphere for the people of Greece. They believed that the gods dwelt in these places and made them sacred. They did not believe that a sanctuary, a temple, a shrine, a sacred precinct or an enclosed area set apart became automatically sacred. In other words, one did not make the place sacred by building a temple, setting up an altar or placing an image there. On the contrary, the temple was built because the place was felt to be holy. It was the presence of the gods in the sanctuaries, temples and the shrines that made these places holy, not vice-versa.[53] Sophocles of Colonus, one of the great tragedians of the fifth century BC, in his *Oedipus at Colonus*, describes the natural beauty and religious sacredness of the local sanctuaries of his native village as follows:

> This place is holy, with its strong growth of laurel, olive and vine and crowds of nightingales, which fly and sing beautifully within it. ... All this place is holy: Poseidon's majesty possesses it, and it is the fire-bearing god, the Titan Prometheus: the place where you stand is called the brazen threshold of this land, the bulwark of Athens: and the nearby glades boast the horseman, Colonus, as their lord, and bear his name, all together called after him: this is what the place is like, a stranger, not honored in story but more by living with it.[54]

The sense of the sacredness of the sanctuary, the temple or the shrine was expressed in and maintained by the fact that no public worship took place inside these holy places, for they were the sacred dwelling places of the gods. The main sacrificial rites took place under the sky at the great altar outside the main door of the temple, which remained open during the ceremony, symbolically expressing the participation of the god at the worship.[55] Thus, the sacred places, such as, the sanctuaries, the temples and the shrines represented the presence of the gods to the people and provided the opportunity to encounter the gods in whom they believed.

2.1.2.3. PRAYER AND SACRIFICES

Homer, in his poems, speaks of people offering prayers to the gods. Prayers usually began by the devotee singing the praises of the divinity to whom he was praying. Then he indirectly mentioned his devotion and piety to the god. Finally, he placed his petitions and needs before the deity. Most of the prayers were offered to obtain a particular favor from the god or to ward off difficulties and troubles. If a person prayed to the *Olympian* gods, he stood with arms raised, palm upward towards the sky. But, if the prayer was made to the *chthonian* gods, the person stood with his arms downward, pointing to the earth.[56]

Prayer and sacrifices accompanied each other. Hesiod, in his poems, refers to daily morning and evening prayers that accompanied the sacrifices. Such prayers and sacrifices must be done with purity achieved through various forms of ablutions. He says: "Sacrifice to the deathless gods purely and cleanly, and burn rich meats also, and at other time propitiate [ask for favor] them with libations and incense both when you go to bed and when the holy light has come back."[57]

Sacrifices were made to the *Olympian* gods usually at dawn. They were offered on the large altar that stood, under the open sky, at the entrance of the temple, i.e., at the east, in the *tenomos*. The sacrificial gift to the gods, placed at the altar, was a sign of the worshipper's devotion and piety towards the gods. Different animals were considered holy to different gods and the offerings were made accordingly. For instance, *Athena* preferred heifers, *Hera* was offered cows, *Poseidon* preferred horses, while *Zeus* and *Apollo* wanted bulls. In Homeric poems it is mentioned that the ritual washing of the offering, sprinkling of the barley grains and making a token offering of the hair preceded the actual act of sacrifice. The sacrificial victim must be without blemish, in order that the gods were not offended. Generally the sacrifices made to the *Olympian* gods were convivial sacrifices (*hiera*). In such sacrifices, part of the sacrificial animal was burned and offered to the gods, while the priest and the devotees ate the other part in the sacrificial banquet.[58] Homer in his *Iliad* describes a *hiera* offering as follows:

> Then having prayed and thrown the barley-grains
> They raised the victims' head and cut their throats
> And skinned them and cut portions from the thighs,
> Wrapped them in fat, and laid new meat on them;
> All these the old man burned upon the billets,
> And poured the red wine on them while beside him
> The young men held in hand five-pointed forks.
> And when the thigh-pieces were wholly burned,
> And they had tasted of the inner meat,
> They cut the rest up small and spitted it
> And broiled it carefully, and drew off all.
> Now when they had made
> The banquet ready, then they fell to feasting,
> And lacked for nothing at the feast they shared. ...
> So all day long they soothed
> The god with song, the youths of Achaeans,
> Rising a lovely paean, and extolling
> The Archer-god [*Apollo*]; and he took pleasure in listening.[59]

There was a marked difference in the manner in which sacrificial offerings were made to the *Chthonian* gods. The altars for the sacrifices were low. At times they were also performed in a cave or a pit. In this manner, the entire setting of the rite indicated that the sacrifice was oriented towards the earth and not the sky. Unlike the sacrifices to the *Olympian* gods, the time of the sacrifice was evening rather than morning. Usually black victims were offered. For instance, goddess *Demeter* was offered a black pig. They were offered total by burned offerings (*sphagia*), in which the entire sacrificial offering was burned and offered to the gods; there was no sacrificial banquet attached to the sacrifice to the *Chthonian* gods.[60]

Every household had certain cultic obligations to be followed, for instance, libations to the goddess of hearth and offerings to *Zeus* for protection of the house, ceremonies performed at the birth of a child in the family, funeral ceremonies when a member of the family died and the annual commemoration of those who have died from the family. Many such offerings were bloodless sacrifices. They included offering libations of milk, honey, wine and similar things. Animal and bloody sacrifices preceded battles, treatises and similar happenings in the community.[61] In this manner, prayers and sacrifices played a great role in the Greek people experiencing and encountering the gods in whom they believed and whose favor they desired to obtain.

2.1.2.4. FESTIVALS

The celebration of various festivals added color to the religious, political and cultural life of the people of Greece. Festivals were not merely religious acts. They also served as occasions of official political functions, such as welcoming foreign emissaries and recognizing the achievements of the citizens. Festivals also did a great service to the cultural life of the people. For instance, drama had its origin in the festivals. They also included athletic competitions and recitals of poetry and music. Though festivals helped Greek society in a number of ways, they were also a great means for people to encounter the divinities they worshipped. That was the reason for festivals being associated with the local sanctuaries, temples and shrines. During festivals, people were involved in ritual singing and dancing, in which they were dressed as animals. Fertility cults and cults of death were also associated with festivals. It is very difficult get the full details of all the festivals celebrated in Greece. Some historians of religions say that there were as many as 70 festivals in the city of Athens. Some of these festivals have archaic elements. Therefore, they were very different from the *Olympian* religion in spirit. But there were also festivals associated with the *Olympian* gods.[62] In the city of Athens there was a calendar of festivals, which spelt out clearly the number of festivals celebrated during the different months of the year.

During the first month of the year there was the *Hecatombs*. It consisted of offering one 100 oxen to *Apollo*. The *festival of Cronus*, which consisted of the masters serving the slaves, was celebrated in the same month. The *Panathenaea* was the national festival of the Athenians to honor their goddess *Athena* and offer her sacrifice. Another purpose of the festival was to provide the ancient wooden statue of *Athena*, which was housed in the Old Temple, a new robe specially made by the women of Athens, and to carry it in process on a ship. It was celebrated during summer every fourth year. In the fourth month two festivals were celebrated. The first one is the *Pyanepsia*. It consisted of the cooking of the pulse, which is a special dish cooked of beans. During this festival the children carried fruits, cakes and tufts of wool decorated with little 'maypoles' (*eiresione*), olive or laurel branches in procession.

These were later kept above the door of the house, where they were allowed to remain till the following year. The second festival celebrated in the same month was the *Thesmophoria,* to honor goddess *Demeter.* It was celebrated at the beginning of sowing season. The celebrants of this festival were the married women. Having purified themselves for three days, they descended into the caves, where pigs had been thrown as offerings together with a snake and phallus-shaped cakes at the *Arrephoria* a few months earlier. The remains of this offering were now brought out and placed on the altar, after which they were mixed with the sowing seed. This was done to pray to the goddess *Demeter* for a good harvest.[63]

In the seventh month the *Hieros Gamos* of *Zeus* and *Athena* was celebrated. It symbolized the bringing together of heaven and earth. In the eighth month of the year, the *Anthesteria,* the festival of flowers was celebrated. It was celebrated in honor of *Dionysus.* This festival was celebrated for three days and it had the elements of fertility cult and commemoration of the dead. The first day was 'the festival of opening of casks'. It consisted of the wine from the previous year's harvest was tasted. The second day was 'the festival of jugs', which involved the consecration of the new wine in a general festival of joy. The same day was celebrated *Dionysus'* marriage to the wife of the king Archon. On the third day sacrifices were made to the spirits of the dead and *Hermes,* the god of the dead. In the tenth month a cult-dance was organized to honor *Artemis.* Girls disguised as bears performed these dances. In the same month *Thargelia* festival was celebrated in honor of *Apollo.* This was the original harvest festival of the first fruits. This festival also included rites of expiation, atonement and purification. In the eleventh month the *Urban Dionysia* festival was celebrated in the city of Athens. It was the greatest festival of god *Dionysus.* At the end of the ritual the image of *Dionysus* was carried in a procession to the theater of *Dionysus,* where it presided over the dramatic contests. In the last month of the year the *Dipolia* for *Zeus* as the protector of the city was held. The sacrifice performed at this festival also had the element of expiation and atonement.[64]

In this manner, the celebration of festivals, besides performing social, cultural and artistic functions, also provided the people of Greece with an opportunity to come in touch with the gods, offer them worship, receive their blessings and be purified of their sins through expiatory sacrifices.

2.1.2.5. MYSTERY CULTS

While the worship offered to the *Olympian* gods constituted an important dimension of the public religious life of the Greeks, the mystery cults provided a personal dimension of faith to the Greek religious life. At times these latter mystery cults exerted a greater influence in the life of the ordinary Greeks, than the official worship of the *Olympian* gods.[65] Three major mystery cults were prevalent in Greece during this time. Two of these cults were associated with *Dionysus*: one was an orgiastic cult dedicated to *Dionysus* as the god of the vine (*Bacchus*); the other was the ascetic orphic cult related to another manifestation of *Dionysus* under the name *Zargeus*. The third was the Eleusinian mystical cult associated with the two goddesses *Demeter* and *Kore*. In this section, we would briefly analyze these three mystery cults, as they provided the people with opportunities to communicate with their gods.

2.1.2.5.1. Orgiastic Dionysian Cult

This cult was an ecstatic and violent form of mystery rite. It was dedicated to *Dionysus*, under the name *Bacchus*, the lord of the vine. It usually took place in remote places, such as mountains or groves. Seemingly it was women (*Maenads*), who performed this rite. The devotees of god *Bacchus* gathered on the mountains and engaged themselves in wild dancing and singing accompanied by drinking wine. They were seized by a sacred frenzy (*enthusiasmos*), and went on dancing, singing and drinking in the glow of troches, until they found a sacrificial animal, which was usually a goat or a bull. Having found the sacrificial victim that they considered identical with *Bacchus*, they tore it and ate the raw flesh of the animal. The cult ended with the eating of the raw flesh of the sacrificial victim. With the help of drinking, dancing, singing and eating of the flesh of the animal identified with their god, the devotees experienced a state of divine intoxication, in which they felt their identity with *Bacchus*, the lord of the vine.[66] Euripides, who made this cult immortal in his work *Bacchae*, describes the *Dionysian* orgiastic cult as follows:

> To raise for Bacchos [*Dionysus*] my cry...
> Blessed is he, who favored of heaven,
> Skilled in the mysteries of the gods,
> Makes holy his life,
> Gives his soul to the chorus,
> As over the mountains he dances to Bacchos
> In cleansing service...
> Servant of Dionysos...
> Joyful on the mountain –
> When from the rushing dancing throng
> Sinks he to the ground,
> With his holy fawnskin round him,
> Pursuing blood, slaughter of goats,
> Joy of raw flesh devoured...
> Fixed to the wand, leaps madly,
> With running and dancing
> Rousing his roving followers -
> Stirring with cries -
> Casting to heaven his flowing hair.
> Mid Bacchic shouts he thunders.[67]

Those, who upheld the tradition of harmony and proportion inherent in the Greek culture, criticized the orgiastic *Dionysian* cult for its lack of temperance and the wildness involved in its practice. This cult degenerated, especially in the Hellenistic and Roman times, into a religious dining club for well-to-do ladies, losing its original religious fervor.[68]

2.1.2.5.2. The Orphic Dionysian Cult

The orphic cult was based on the myth of *Zagreus*, who was another manifestation of *Dionysus*.[69] Orphism was based on this dualistic doctrine of man as good and evil. Evil is associated with the body. It was expressed by the Greek phrase "*soma sema*", i.e., "the body is the tomb". Therefore, the main thrust of the orphic cult was to liberate one's spirit from the entanglements of the body through the practice of asceticism. Great emphasis was given to purification and living ascetically. They were vegetarians and held that eating animal's flesh was an abomination. The underlying beliefs of orphism were the essential immortality of the soul, hope of new life for those who conquer the body in this life and eternal punishment for the wicked in the nether world. The more one purified oneself, the more one would be able to liberate the divine in man from the clutches of the body. For the orphic devotee, life in this world was shadow living, the aim of which was a continuous purgation for the sins and evils inherent in the human condition. In so doing, one prepared oneself for the life to come in the real world. Thus, a true orphic seeker hoped for blessed life in Elysium after his death. This was possible for man, because the god *Zargeus* was a living god, whose victory over death made future life possible for all true seekers.[70]

Orphism could be seen as a reform movement within the *Dionysian* religion. It was a reaction from within against the orgiastic *Dionysian* cult, which indulged in drinking, shouting, dancing and eating raw meat of sacrificial victim. Orphism, by stressing discipline, asceticism and moral living, attempted to renew the *Dionysian* religious tradition in Greece.[71]

2.1.2.5.3. The Eleusinian Mystical Cult

This cult was based on the myth of the goddess *Demeter* and her daughter *Kore* and their relationship with *Hermes*, the god of the nether world.[72] This cult was practiced in Eleusis every year in the autumn in honor of *Demeter* and *Kore*. Though originally this cult was associated with fertility rites, later those who practiced this cult were concerned with a happy life after death. It was a mystical rite in which the initiates, known as *Mystes*, were admitted to the ceremonies, which were kept religiously secret. As a result of these secret ceremonies, the *Mystes* gained depth, mystical experience and achieved spiritual renewal. The rite was not open to all, but only to the group of chosen initiates. The *Mystes* gathered in Athens and spent the night fasting. Then, they purified themselves and their sacrificial victims, viz., pigs, by bathing in the sea.[73]

On the following day the great procession from Athens to Eleusis began. In the front of the procession the image of the god *Iacchos*, who was identified with *Dionysus-Bacchus*, was carried. The procession moved slowly and singing accompanied it as to moved on. A number of stops were made for various offerings in different places. When it was dark the procession continued by the light of torches and reached Eleusis, where the mystery festival was celebrated under the leadership of "He who shows holy things" (*Hierophant*). The celebrations had three parts, viz., the *legomena* (the recital), the *dromena* (the doings) and the *deiknumena* (the shown). Firstly, 'the recital' consisted of partly repeating various formulae and partly enacting dramatically different parts of the *Demeter-Kore* myth. Secondly, 'the doings' were performances of rites, which had to do with the handling of certain sexual symbols related to a 'sacred wedding' between heaven and earth. The formula used at the time of the performance of rites '*hue! Kue!*' meant 'rain! Become pregnant!' The doings end with the announcement of the birth of the child. Thirdly, 'the shown' was an ear of corn, which probably symbolized an infant in the basket. The mystery cult left the initiates with deep psychological depth, giving them hope of eternal life. Just as the new corn grows and brings new life, in the same way the mystical cult the initiates went through would lead them to new life in the next life.[74] Homer points to this belief of the *Mystes*, when he says the following:

> Happy is he among men on earth who has seen these mysteries; but he who is uninitiated and who has not part in them, never has lot of them like good things once he is dead, down in the darkness and gloom. ...Right blessed is he among men on earth whom they [*Demeter* and *Kore*] freely love: soon they do send Plutus as guest to his great house, Plutus who gives wealth to men.[75]

Though the ceremonies involved in the cult were kept secret, the main aim of this cult was not learning new mystical knowledge about the divine or to receive any new revelation; but rather it was intended to bring about a genuine spiritual transformation within the initiate. Once they went through the sacred and mystical ceremonies and experienced inner renewal and transformation, the initiates returned to Athens, garlanded and serene. This mystery cult continued both in the Hellenistic and Roman period as an expression of the personal dimension of religion. A number of Roman emperors became *Mystes*. This cultic movement came to a close, when Alaric, the Goth, destroyed the temple at Eleusis in the fourth century BC.[76]

Without any doubt these three mystery cults gave a personal touch to the religious life of the people of Greece. They, in their own way, attempted to direct and lead people towards the gods. They instilled in people the yearning for mystical union with the gods and brought about renewal and transformation in their lives by the touch of the divine.

2.1.2.6. ORACLES

Another important means that was used in Greek religion to enter into communication with the gods was the oracles. In the oracles people could come in real contact with the divinities and know their will regarding various affairs of social, political and religious life of the people of Greece. In the oracles the gods spoke through their priest/priestess, which then the priests interpreted for the people. Manifesting the will of the gods through oracles did not take place everywhere, but was limited to some important oracular shrines.[77]

There were a number of such shrines in Greece, but the most important one was the oracular shrine of the god *Apollo* at Delhip, on the southwest ridges of Mount Parnassus. In this shrine there stood a naval stone (*Omphalos*), which was regarded as the center of the earth. In the inner chamber (*Adyton*) of the shrine was the seat of the oracle. There was a deep opening in the ground from which drugging gases were said to emerge. Pythia, the oracle priestess of *Apollo*, took her seat on the tripod over the deep opening. She very soon moved into an ecstatic state that was caused by the fumes that emerged from the deep opening. While she remained in the ecstatic state, she uttered words, which the priests would make into versified answers to the questions that were asked to the god *Apollo*. Another important oracular shrine was that of the god *Zeus* at Dodona. Here, *Zeus* was said to make his will known in the rustling of the leaves on the sacred oak tree, which the priests interpreted.[78]

The oracles were addressed to the individuals and to the nation. They played an important role in the life of individuals and that of the nation, because people believed that every aspect of the life of the people and the nation at large was subjected to the approval or the disapproval of the oracles. All pronouncements on religious issues, such as recognition of the veracity of a cult, establishment of new laws guiding worship or religious practice and all such religious issues came under the sanctions of the oracles.[79] Thus, oracles were indeed a great means through which the gods communicated their will to the people, and people came in contact with their divinities.

2.1.2.7. MORAL LIVING

Living a genuine moral life formed an important aspect of the Greek religious living. The Greeks believed that the gods would never disown a person who was committed to living a moral life, but rather he would win their favor. Moral living involved that a person lived out the twofold attitudes of moderation and justice towards the gods and his fellowmen respectively. Firstly, genuine moral life called for man cultivating a right moral attitude towards the gods. Greek religion considered the gods as divine helpers of the humans on earth. But they themselves were 'the blessed ones'. They were beyond the cares of earthly life. A pious Greek considered the existence of the gods in bliss and beauty as a positive value.[80]

Thus, Greek religion stressed the distance and the difference between the gods and men. Therefore, man should always be aware of his place in relation to the gods. Man should neither ignore the gods, nor should he take the place that belonged to the gods; to do so would be a very grave sin. The Greeks referred to this attitude of man to the gods with the Greek word "*hubris*". It consisted in overcoming with pride, striving beyond what the gods have granted and being unwilling to bow to the will of the gods. The Greeks believed that if a person fell prey to "*hubris*", he would be liable to the retribution (*nemesis*) of the gods.[81] We read in *The Odes of Pindar*: "Seek not then to become a god. ...The lot of mortals befits mortal men."[82] Therefore, man should accept himself as a mortal human being with his limitations. He should accept the wise principle of moderation (*sophrosune*) as the highest virtue and practice it. In Sophocles we find an excellent description of the attitude man should have. To quote:

> Warned by these sights, Odysseus, see that thou
> Utter no boastful word against the gods,
> Nor swell with pride if happily might of arm
> Exalt thee o'er thy fellows, or vast wealth.
> A day can prostrate and a day upraise
> All that is mortal, but the gods approve
> Sobriety and forwardness abhor.[83]

The two of the precepts inscribed in the temple of *Apollo* at Delphi, viz., "Know thyself" (*Gnothi Seauton*) and "Nothing too much" (*Meden agan*), also points to the same truth. The first precept brought to man's awareness the fact that he is limited, while the second one advised him to avoid extremes and excesses.[84] Thus, genuine moral living implied that man recognize his limitations and bow his will to that of the gods.

Secondly, while living the attitude of moderation towards man's relationship with the gods, man also must cultivate the attitude of true justice towards his fellowmen. Living a just life meant that man practiced reciprocity. It consisted in doing to others what others did to him. We need to be kind to the one who was kind, helpful to the one who was helpful and give to the one who gave to us. The gifts received must be reciprocated with return gifts. Hesiod speaks, in his *Work and Days*, about the pleasure and joy of giving to those who give. At the same time, he reminds us of the demand of justice that we do not give to those who do not give. To quote him: "Be friends with the friendly, and visit him who visits you. Give to one who gives, but do not give to one who does not give."[85] Thus, in one's social dealings with one's fellowmen, one must be just and reciprocal. When a person lived these twofold moral attitudes towards the gods and his fellowmen, he would be open to the divine and become worthy of their blessings. In this way moral living becomes a genuine path to the divine.

2.1.2.8. PURIFICATION AND EXPIATION

Living a moral life implied that a person got himself purified whenever he defiled himself in one or the other way. Defilement could be external or internal. It would be external when associated with bodily impurity, while it would be internal when it meant that man had violated the laws of the gods and sinned. While the former implied the purity of the body, the latter called for purity of heart.[86] We will consider briefly the twofold defilement and the means to remove them in the following section.

External defilement was associated with impurities related to childbirth, sex life, death and similar taboos. When the laws concerning taboos were violated, a person was defiled. It could happen through physical contact with a person or thing considered as impure and capable of defiling, such as, a dead body or a woman in the period of menstruation. The external defilement could be removed and the person could achieve purification by way of ablutions, such as washing, sprinkling water considered to be holy or prayer by the priest. A person could prevent himself from such defilement by following the laws regarding the taboos. Hesiod, in his *Work and Days*, gave a number of measures that could be taken to protect a person from such external impurities.

> Do not expose yourself befouled by the fireside in your house, but avoid this. Do not beget children when you are come back from ill-omened burials, but after festivals of the gods. ... Never cross the sweet-flowing water of ever-rolling rivers afoot until you have prayed, gazing into the soft flood, and washed your hands in the clear lovely water. Whosoever crosses a river with hands unwashed of wickedness, the gods are angry with him and bring trouble upon him afterwards.[87]

The internal defilement implied absence of genuine inner purity, i.e., the absence of purity of heart. Hesiod recommended that all the sacrifices to the deathless gods must be made "purely and cleanly".[88] What he meant here was that the one who sacrificed must be free from all sinfulness and he must have the inner attitude of purity of heart. The removal of one's sins and attaining a pure heart could be made possible by the performance of expiatory rites.

In the Greek religion, there were not many elaborate forms of expiatory sacrifices. But there were a few expiatory sacrifices aimed at helping people to atone for the sins they have committed. One such expiatory rite took place at the *Thargelia* festival celebrated in honor of *Apollo*. On the first day of the festival two men (*Pharmakoi*) were decorated with figs. Then they were whipped with twigs and were taken in procession all around the city. When the parading of the *Pharmakoi* was completed, they were banished from the city. It was believed that all the sins of the whole city's people were placed on the shoulders of these two men and was disposed of with their banishment. Thus, the *Pharmakoi* became the offering for the sins of the people of the city. People believed that by the performance of this rite they were internally purified of all their sins and achieved the purity of heart, which would make them capable of standing before the gods "purely and cleanly".[89]

The *Bouphonia* (the slaying of the ox) ceremony was celebrated at the festival of *Dipolia* for *Zeus* as protector of the city. This ceremony contained some expiatory elements. During the ceremony an ox was sacrificed. The priest, after having killed the sacrificial victim, had escaped from the sacrificial scene. Then, the ax the priest used to kill the sacrificial animal was charged with murder. Thus, the sin of murdering the animal, which, in fact, belonged to the priest and those who were performing the sacrificial rite, was placed over the ax; in the process, people's sins were expiated. As a result, the people could stand before the gods without a guilty conscience.[90]

In this manner, purification rites freed all external defilement from the people and the expiatory sacrifices of offering removed the sinfulness of people and made them acceptable before the gods. Thus, purification ceremonies and expiatory rites, indeed, effected genuine communication between the gods and the people. These rites brought a touch of the gods to the lives of the people.

The Greek religion, thus, had a rich spiritual tradition. Though the religion was polytheistic, an element of monotheism was found in the personality of the god *Zeus*, who was seen as superior to the other gods. Besides, the personalized form of worship in some of the mystery cults was supplemented by external public worship. There were spiritual traditions within the Greek religion that were eccentric and out of the way, like the *Dionysian* orgiastic cult. At the same time, there were also traditions that were mystical like the later *Dionysian* cult and the Eleusinian rites. Then, there was the *Apolonian* tradition that upheld the principle of moderation and a sense of balance proclaiming the distance between gods and men. The people were offered a number of paths to encounter the divinities. The mediation of the priests, sacred places, prayers and sacrifices, festivals, mystery cults, oracles, moral living, the purification ceremonies and expiatory rites played a very significant role in helping the people to come in contact with their gods. The Greek religious tradition was rich in content and practice.

2.2. ROMAN RELIGION

The Roman religion, like the Greek religion, does not have sacred writings or purely religious texts. So, our knowledge of the religions depends, to a great extent, on evidences that are external. We come to know a great deal about the Roman religion from archeological findings, such as, temples, images of the gods, and tombs. Inscriptions from the temples (*leges templorum*), festival calendars (*fasti*) and seven bronze tablets with the collection of cult precepts (*Iguvian Tables*) are some of the other sources of evidence. The third source of evidence comes from the writings of historians, poets and the church fathers. To this group belong *De agri cultura* of M. Porcius Cato Major, *Historia naturalis* of C. Plinius Major, *Noctes atticae* of A. Gellius, *Rerum resticarum libri tres* and *Antiquates rerum divinarum* of M. Terentius Varro, *Fasti* of P. Ovidius Naso, *De natura deorum, De haruspicum responsis* and *De divinatione* of M. Tullius Cicero, *Saturnalia* of A. Th. Macrobius and some of the writings of the church fathers, such as St. Augustine.[91]

The Romans believed that everything was under the direction and guidance of the gods. While recognizing and acknowledging the subordination of every reality in the world to the gods, they did not visualize a religious situation in which they were totally dependent on the gods. Thus, Roman religion, while accepting the role the gods played in the destiny of the world, including humans, also held for the role of human beings in shaping their destiny and that of the world. Therefore, the religion of the Romans was not a religion of grace. Rather it was a religion based on mutual trust (*fides*) between the gods and the human beings. The purpose of Roman religion was to obtain the collaboration and good will of the gods. In other words, the Romans wanted their religion to help them secure 'the peace of the gods' (*pax deorum*).[92]

The peace that religion would bring them did not consist in achieving mere mental calmness, but rather it involved receiving power from the divinities to master the unknown forces that make them anxious and to help them live successfully. As a result, two important religious attitudes characterized the religion of the Romans, viz., *religio* and *pietas*. The former stood for the awe or anxiety people felt in the presence of the unknown realm of the spirits, including the gods, while the latter referred to the meticulous sense of duty with which they treated their gods and each other. Thus, the Romans believed that if they trusted their gods and did scrupulously what was due to the gods, the god, in turn, would treat them with trust and give them 'the peace of the gods', which would make them succeed in their lives. So, the exact performance of ritual and cultic acts became the important dimension in the Roman religion.[93]

Since Roman religion considered the gods as helpers, whose cooperation was very vital for success in people's lives, it did not have any mythology associated with the gods. The Romans did not constitute divine families of the gods, so their gods generally are childless. The Romans lacked the Greek pictorial imagination for seeing their gods in an anthropomorphic way and attributing myths to their origin and activities in the world. In this Greek sense, there was no mythology in Roman religion. The pseudo-mythology found in Roman religion was often nationalistic and family legends clothed in mythical dress, due to Greek influence. For instance, the narrative about the four initial kings of Rome, who represented various functions in society, had a pseudo-mythical dimension. Romulus, the young divine prince, introduced *auspicial* which stood for the ruler-function of the society. Numa Pompilius, the priest-king, introduced the *sacra* and the calendar, and was representative of the sacred function in the society. Tullus Hostilius, 'the inimical', who expanded the power of Rome, symbolized the warrior function in the society.

Ancus Marcius, who consolidated the kingdom, founded the *Larentalia*, 'the festival of the farmstead' and introduced the *Venus* cult, exemplifying the stabilizing function in the society.[94]

Romans recognized the periodic intervention of the gods in human history, but they did not attempt to mythologize such entrance of the gods into human history. Again, there were not many myths associated with the performance of cultic rites. Similarly, the Roman religion did not have creeds or articles of faith. No Roman needed to believe in particular doctrines about the gods. All that he was called to do was to perform the religious rite according to the prescribed rules. As long as he had done this, he was free to think of the gods, as he liked. The absence of creed also did away with the emotional element in the act of worship of the gods.[95]

Roman religion had a long history of development. The simple and nature centered worship of the earliest Roman religion was open to various influences from outside. The first such influence came from the Etruscans, as they controlled Roman territory at least for some time. The Etruscan religion influenced the Roman religion greatly and the importance Romans gave to the performance of the ritual without any doubt came from the Etruscan practice. The Etruscan practice of divination, which involved the inspection of sacrifice and interpreting the will of the gods by using the liver and the entrails of the sacrificial animal, became very popular in the Roman religion. Some other areas of influence included the plan, appearance and decoration of the temples; representing the gods in human images; and rites and ceremonies. The Romans also owed the origin of the Roman religious calendar to the Etruscans.[96]

The second influence was that of the Greeks. The Romans were already used to Greek religious customs during the Etruscan period. Contact with the Greek religion reinforced anthropomorphism in the Roman religion, which in turn led to a certain amount of mythologizing of the gods. A number of Greek gods were admitted into the Roman Pantheon under the Roman names. Certain Greek gods were compared with the Roman gods. Pairing of male and female deities also took place. A number of Greek ritual practices were imported into Rome. For instance, the special rite of inviting the gods of the conquered cities to abandon their homes and to migrate to Rome, called *evocatio*, was introduced. Another right called *lectisternium*, which was a sacrificial banquet in which the images of pairs of god were exhibited in reclining position before tables spread with food and drink. To avert pestilence, a rite called *supplicatio*, was introduced, in which people went around the temple and prostrated themselves, as did the Greeks. Later this practice was also done to celebrate war victories.[97]

The third influence came from the introduction of mystery cults into the Roman religious practice. The most significant of such rites was the cult of the Great Mother (*Magna Mater*) of Asia Minor, *Cybele*, who was represented by the carved black stone and the worship of *Bacchus-Dionysus*. Castrated priests performed orgiastic rites for the Great Mother, while women performed similar rites for *Bacchus*. There were also similar cults of *Isis* and *Mithras*.

The introduction of such mystery cults brought a crisis in the religious life of the people, which made the government either prevent the Romans from participating in such mystery rites or suppress such cultic celebrations.[98] Finally during the imperial epoch, when Augustus became the emperor, he revived many of the ancient cults and religious practices. Besides, he also was instrumental in introducing the imperial cult that defied the emperor of Rome. Thus, Roman religion, from its very beginnings until the imperial times, was a national religion. But it was never forcibly imposed on other nations and peoples. It always remained open towards other religions.[99] Some of the developments in the Roman religion that took place after Augustus will be dealt with under our consideration of the Hellenistic religion.

Following upon the above introductory comments on Roman religion, we shall move on to consider the gods of the Romans and the various means of the Roman people in order to encounter the divinities, communicate with them and win their help for successful living.

2.2.1. ROMAN PANTHEON

Historians of religion have made numerous attempts to categorize the Roman gods. One classification from Roman times attempted to group the gods into the *Di Indigetes* and the *Di Novensides*. The former stood for the indigenous gods, while the latter referred to the gods who have newly arrived from other towns and cities. Some scholars interpret the same division differently. According to their interpretation the *Di Indigetes* was a group of ancestral gods or a group of gods with a special kind of ritual. The term '*indigetes*' derived from the word '*indigetare*', which means 'to invoke'. The *Di Novensides* was a group of nine gods. The word '*novensides*' came from the term '*novem*', which means 'nine'. Another grouping spoke of *Di Coelestes* (the heavenly gods), *Di Terrestres* (the earthly gods) and *Di Inferni* (the fire gods). But the exponents of this classification did not assign various gods to these groupings. Another classification that was proposed during the modern period distinguished the Roman gods between celestial Indo-European gods and *Chthonian* indigenous Pre-Italic gods. But proper distribution to these groupings was also not done.[100] Here we attempt a tentative twofold classification of the Roman gods, viz., the earliest Roman gods and the later Roman gods.

2.2.1.1. THE EARLIEST ROMAN GODS

In the earliest stages the Romans deified various functions. They believed that the divinities were operative in human activities like birth and in the phenomena of nature, such as the movement of the sun. Thus, there came about the worship of functional deities and veneration of objects of nature. They believed that there were sacred powers behind these functions and objects. They used the term '*numen*' to refer to these powers that make the functions and objects sacred. Originally this term meant half-impersonal divine forces that controlled the various phenomena or were manifested in them. They resided in trees, rocks, birds, beasts, the grass of the fields and the lightning in the sky. They were neither moral nor immoral, having an affinity to man, and could help or harm men, depending on the manner in which they were treated.[101]

The job of the earliest Roman religion was to organize rituals to please each *numen* in such a way that its powers could be used for the benefit of man.[102] The word '*numen*' literally means 'nodding' (*nutus*) or 'beckoning indicating a command'. These meanings of the term '*numen*' suggest that the 'nodding' and the 'beckoning that indicated a command' must come from a volitional being, i.e., from a god (*deus*). Thus, we find expressions, such as, *numen dei* and *numen deorum*, were recorded from a very early date.[103] Therefore, we could say that behind the belief in functional deities and the veneration of objects, there was inherent the belief in the gods, whose 'nodding' and 'beckoning' made the '*numen*' operative in functions and objects. Consequently, from the earliest times the Romans believed not only in powers and forces expressed in functions and objects, but also in the gods. In this section, we could briefly consider some of the earliest gods the Romans believed in and worshipped.

2.2.1.1.1. Jupiter, Mars and Quirinus

Prominent among the earliest Roman gods was a triad, viz., *Jupiter*, *Mars* and *Quirinus*. These three gods were given their own priests, known as *flamines majores* (the highest priests) to conduct their cult. The chief among the triad of gods was *Jupiter*. He was a sky-god, who lived in the vault of heaven and on the hilltops. Like the Greek god *Zeus*, *Jupiter* was the lord of the atmosphere, lightening and rain. The sun was said to be his eyes. Since his concern was caring for the atmospheric phenomena, with the help of sun and rain, he was believed to be the giver of fertility. *Jupiter* was also believed to be the god who brought victory over enemies. He was also the god of celestial light (*Lucetius*). Besides, he was considered to be the god of fate, who sends auspices to men. He was also said to be the god of justice, who oversees oaths and contracts. As *Jupiter* performs this function, he was called *Dius Fidius*, i.e., a deity representing the juridical aspect of the sovereign's function. *Jupiter* was known all over Italy, especially for his local functional manifestations. Like the Greek god *Zeus*, he also manifested himself as a *Chthonian* god who was involved with the nether world. As the national god of the expanding Roman Empire, *Jupiter* was addressed as 'the best and the greatest' (*Optimus Maximus*) of all gods.[104]

The second of the triad was *Mars*. He was primarily a god of war. The weapon associated with him was the spear. Many of the cults dedicated to *Mars* clearly manifested his warlike nature. Besides protecting the state against the enemies, he was also said to be the god of health and strength, who preserved the fields and herds against disasters and damages. The cults associated with *Mars* were aimed at purification and warding off evils. Later

Mars was identified with the Greek god of war, *Ares*. Besides he was believed to be the father of Romulus.[105]

The third of the triad was *Quirinus*. He was commonly known as 'the peaceful *Mars*' or 'the *Mars* who presided over peace'. As the name "*Quirinus*" suggested that he was the god of the people, i.e., the civil members of the society. But, he was also presented as possessing warlike qualities and often represented as being armed with a lance. Originally he was believed to be the patron god of Quirinal village. Later he was believed to have been the god that Romulus became when he ascended into heaven.[106]

2.2.1.1.2. *Janus* and *Vesta*

The other two earliest divinities were *Janus* and *Vesta*. *Janus* was the god of entry or doors (*janua*), i.e., of all beginnings. He was often referred to as 'the creator', 'the god of gods' and 'the origin of gods'. We do not find any god equivalent to *Janus* in the Greek Pantheon. Probably the worship of *Janus* originated from a divine power that regulated the passage over running water. It could also have emerged from the sacred doorways, like those found on the art of Bronze Age Mycenae. *Janus* originally stood for the magic of the door of a private hut, and later it was adapted into the state religion. *Janus* was said to be the first king of Latium and the founder of civilization. His priest, *rex sacrorum*, perpetuated the office of the ancient monarchy. *Janus* was worshipped in a small shrine near the Forum. The shrine consisted of a vaulted arch with doors on two sides. Often the armies were consecrated there before beginning a war. The doors of this shrine would be closed only in times of peace. During war the doors of the shrine were kept open. This custom goes back to the ancient war magic that required the armies to march out for battle though a properly sanctified route. *Janus* was represented as having two faces, referring to his nature as the door, that let one in ahead and behind.[107]

Vesta was the goddess of the domestic hearth. But her place in the cult of the state was very important. In her temple in the Forum, a fire burned continuously and it was watched over by six virgin priestesses, the *Vestals*. She was the goddess of purity and so was remote from anything associated with death. She also had connection with the making of flour and bread. Near the sacred hearth the *Vesta*, there was a cupboard called *penus*, in which provisions were stored. The sacred animal associated with her was the ass. *Vesta* was endowed with the important function of being the sacred protector of Rome. She was one of the most honored divinities of the city Rome, and her feast was held during mid-June.[108]

2.2.1.1.3. *Manes, Indigetes, Lares and Penates*

The *Manes* were the collective powers that consisted of the spirits of the dead ancestors. They were referred to as 'the good people', as they were of help to the members of the families or the clans, of which they were a part. As the guardians of their clans and families, these dead men and women were called *Di Parentes*. Reverence for such ancestral spirits formed the core of Roman religious and social life. The *Indigetes* included the ancestral spirits and other deified powers that controlled the destiny of Rome. For instance, *Aeneas*, whose mythical immigration from Troy led to the foundation of the city, was referred to as *Indigetes*. The *Lares* were the guardians of boundaries, the protectors of family estates and believed to be related to the *Manes*. They were worshipped inside every home in the domestic shrine (*lararium*) and wherever people had properties and estates. When the state took over their worship, they were moved from the shrines in the homes and the boundaries of properties to shrines at the crossroads. Then they were worshipped as the guardian spirits of the whole community (*Lares Praestites*). The *Penates* were the guardians of the storage cupboard. They ensured that there was enough to eat in the home. Originally the *Penates* were associated with the *Dioscuri* (*Castor* and *Pollux*), the twin-gods. According to some legends, *Aeneas* brought them to Italy from Lavinium when the early Romans annexed the city. As the guardians of the store they were worshipped in every home. Later they, too, were moved from the homes to the state. When this happened, the *Penates* were regarded as the national protectors (*Penates Publici*).[109]

2.2.1.2. THE LATER ROMAN GODS

While the worship of the gods of the earliest times continued during the later period, there were a number of new gods that were accepted and worshipped in different part of the Roman Empire. In this section, we would consider the gods people worshipped especially during the period of the kings and the period of the Roman Republic.

2.2.1.2.1. Diana and Fors Fortuna

The two deities who became popular at the time of the kings were *Diana* and *Fors Fortuna*. The Roman monarch Servus Tullius popularized these deities. *Diana* was an Italian wood goddess. She was also considered as a moon goddess and the guardian of nature and women and the sender of fertility. Women who wanted to have children prayed to *Diana*. Originally she was worshipped in her temple, which was a sacred groove at Aricia, on the lake of Nemi, in Latium. Her priest, *rex nemorenss* (king of the groves) obtained his office by killing his predecessor with a holy branch. In the course of time, she was identified with the Greek goddess *Artemis*. The temple dedicated to *Diana* on the Aventine Hill, with her statue was built in imitation of the temple of *Artemis* in Ephesus. The other deity, *Fors Fortuna,* was originally a farming deity. Later she came to represent fortune and luck. There was a myth, which spoke of *Fors Fortuna* as the daughter of *Jupiter*, the god of fate who sent auspices to people. Her temple across the river Tiber was one of the few temples where the slaves could come and worship. There were also oracular shrines of *Fors Fortuna* at Antium and Praeneste. Hellenistic Greeks identified *Fors Fortuna* with the goddess *Tyche*, the patroness of cities and goddess of Fortune.[110]

2.2.1.2.2. Juno, Minerva, Volcanus, Saturnus, Hercules, Faunus, Neptunus and Vejovis

The goddess *Juno* was considered to be the protector of woman. Her chief function was to supervise the lives of women, especially their sexual lives. In Italy she was also believed to be the warlike goddess of the town of Lanuvium in Latium. Later on, due to the Greek influence, she was identified with *Hera*, the consort of *Zeus*. As a result *Juno* was attributed the quality of being the consort of *Jupiter*, who was identified with the Greek god *Zeus*. *Minerva* was the goddess of art and handicrafts. She protected the craftsmen and artisans. She was identified with the Greek goddess *Athena*, the daughter of *Zeus*. As a result, *Minerva* was also seen as the daughter of *Jupiter*. *Volcanus* was the god of fire, who was identified with the Greek blacksmiths' deity *Hephaestus*. *Saturnus* was a fertility and agricultural god, identified with the Geek god *Cronus*, the Father of *Zeus*. Both *Volcanus* and *Saturnus* were worshipped in open altars in Rome before they had temples. *Hercules* was the god of traders. The center of the *Hercules* cult was the Great Altar (*Ara Maxima*) in the cattle market, inside the boundaries of the primitive Palatine settlement. The name of the god *Hercules* was derived from the Greek *Heracles*, whose worship was propagated in Southern Italy by the traders. The traders venerated *Heracles's* journeys, labors and his power to prevent any form of evil. Such a god was necessary to keep peace in the market, where all sorts of people came. Though the *Hercules* cult might have begun as a private cult, it received a public dimension very soon. *Faunus* was a pastoral deity, who protected and increased the cattle herds. *Neptunus* was the god of the sea and springs. *Vejovis* was the god of the nether world. Originally this function of being the god of the nether world was attributed to *Jupiter* in his *Chthonian* aspect. Later the Romans transferred this function to *Vejovis*. In this sense *Vejovis* was associated with *Jupiter*.[111]

2.2.1.2.3. Ceres, Apollo, Venus, Tellus, Flora, Pomona and Anna Perenna

Ceres was an Italian deity, who presided over the generative powers of nature. She was the goddess of growth and grain. She also manifests in her personality, strong elements of a death divinity. *Ceres's* was identified with the Greek fertility goddess *Demeter*. *Ceres'* installation in Rome was due to the influence of the Greek colony of Cyme (Cumae), from which the Romans imported grain during the famine. In this temple *Ceres* was worshipped in association with two other deities. The first one was *Liber*, a fertility god identified with the Greek god *Dionysus*. The second one was the counterpart of *Liber*, a female deity called *Libera*, who was identified with the Greek goddess *Kore*. Another god introduced in Rome, due to the influence of the people of Cumae, was *Apollo*. The people of Cumae believed *Apollo* to be the god of prophecy. But the people of Rome saw *Apollo* as the god of healing, as the *Apollo* cult was introduced in Rome at the time of the epidemic. Later Emperor Augustus accepted *Apollo* as his patron and that of the Empire, thereby converting *Apollo* into a Hellenistic god of peace and civilization. Another goddess introduced into the Roman Pantheon was *Venus*. The term '*venus*' meant 'blooming nature'. So *Venus* was considered to be the protector of the orchards. She gained prominence because of the legend that she was the mother of *Aeneas*, the ancestor of Rome. She was identified with the Greek goddess *Aphrodite*. *Tellus* was called *Terra Mater*. She was the goddess of growth, vegetation and the queen of all living beings, especially the wild animals, as she gives life and receives the dead. *Flora* was the goddess of flowers. *Pomona* was the goddess of fruit. *Anna Perenna* was the goddess in whose honor the New Year festival was celebrated.[112]

2.2.1.2.4. The Abstract Divinities

The latest gods to be added to the Roman Pantheon were the abstract divinities, i.e., divine powers representing various qualities. These were either personifications of the qualities and functions of some of the major gods or independent attributes accepted as gods. For example, *Fides* (faith or loyalty) was seen as an attribute of the Latin-Sabine god of oaths, *Semo Sanctus Dius Fidius*. Similarly *Victoria* (victory) was attributed to *Jupiter*; *Pavor* (awe) was ascribed to Mars; and *Saturnus* was qualified as *Ops* (plenty). But in a number of cases the qualities themselves were seen as divine powers. For instance, *Concordia* (concord), *Pietas* (piety), *Justitia* (justice) and *Salus* (well-being) were some of the qualities considered to be divine powers. Many of these divine qualities had their own temples, where worship was offered to them. The Roman people believed that these divinities were actual realties, objects of worship and external divine forces that work upon their devotees, effecting in them the qualities the name described.[113]

2.2.1.2.5. Other Spiritual Beings

St. Augustine in his *City of God* speaks of a multitude of special gods, whom the Roman priests invoke on special occasions. Thus, there existed a series of gods for tilling the field. The priests invoked *Vervactor* for the first ploughing, *Redarator* for the second ploughing and *Isitor* for the sowing. Similarly different gods were invoked at different stages of a child's growth. For instance, *Cunina* was the protector of the cradle, *Rumina* taught the child how to suck and *Statulinus* taught the child to stand.[114] These deities are original to Roman religion. These gods were not objects of any cult or worship, but they were invoked at special vocations. Besides, the Roman people also believed that just as there were patron divinities for families and clans, there were also patron spirits for each individual human being. The patron spirit of a man was called *Genius*, while the patron spirit of a woman was *Juno*. There was also the worship of *Sol* (the sun), as *Sol Invictus* (the unconquerable sun) and its ally *Mithras*.[115]

Besides, belief in various gods, the Romans also believed in life after death. We have already seen that there was a form of ancestral worship among the Romans, for they believed in the continued living of the spirit of the ancestors, such as *Manes*, *Indegetes*, *Lares* and *Penates*. Thus, the people of the Roman religion believed in life after death. But they were not very clear as to what exactly was the nature this life, unless one believed in some of the mystery cults that had a clear idea as to the nature of the next life. Their attitude towards the dead was cautious hope that they would do the good to the living and fear that some of them might do the living some harm. In other words, some of the dead were believed to be good, while others were believed to be evil and harmful to the living. Such harmful dead people were known as *larvae* or *lemurs*. Such evil spirits were propitiated through special rites and offerings. The dead were believed to be dependent on the living for their livelihood. This belief made the Romans fill the graves of the dead with gifts and food. The idea of an underworld realm of death, or a happy after life in the stars or in happy isles, was a later belief that came about through the Greek or the Oriental influence.[116] The Romans had an elaborate burial rite. Though cremation was used at an earlier time, later burial of the dead body became more common. When a person died, a professional undertaker prepared the body for burial or cremation. The body was adorned with the insignia of the office held by the dead person. The body was taken in a long procession, which consisted of family members, professional mourners and actors wearing the death masks of the ancestral spirits. Music accompanied the ritual. The poor were buried in the common pits, the rich in elaborate roadside tombs. There were also joint burial places that held a number of urns in niches. Graves and tombs were inviolable. They were protected by supernatural powers and taboos.[117]

We have been examining the world of the gods in which the Romans believed. The Roman people were very religious minded and saw the role of the gods in their lives. They wanted the blessings of the gods in order that they would be successful in their lives. They attempted to communicate with the divinities, in whom they believed. In the next section, we attempt to elaborate the various paths the Romans used to get in touch with the divinities and to open themselves to the blessings of gods.

2.2.2. ROMAN PATHS TO THE DIVINE

In Roman religion, cult was very well organized. A number of cultic practices were performed at the domestic level, while others were done in the level of various kin groups (*gens*), fraternity groups (*sodalitates*) and the state level. The foundation of all Roman cultic practices was the belief that there existed a contract between the gods and men that was reciprocally binding. Every rite performed was aimed at giving the gods *debitos honores*, i.e., 'appropriate honors'. The gods must receive what was due to them, in order that they could also give what was due to men. This juridical way of thinking was responsible for the strict performance of the cults in all detail, even using the exact words and actions that were prescribed.[118] The Romans made use of a number of means to get their due from the gods and to give the gods their due. In this section, we shall attempt to elaborate the various ways they used to encounter their divinities, to give them what was due to them and to receive what was due to them from the gods.

2.2.2.1. PRIEST: THE INTERMEDIARY BETWEEN THE GODS AND MEN

The domestic cult was centered on the goddess of the hearth, the *Manes*, the *Indigetes*, the *Lares*, the *Penates* and the *Genius* of the head of the household. The responsibility of such domestic cults rested on the father of the family (*pater familias*). Thus at the domestic level, the father of the family took the role of the priest and mediated between the gods and the members of the family. There were kin group (*gens*) cults, which the leader of the kin group presided over. There were also certain fraternities (*sodalitates*), which were entrusted with a particular cult. For instance, *Luperci* and Patrician *Salii* (Salians) were associated with the cult of *Mars*. Another fraternity was *Fratres Arvales* (Arval Priest/Brothers). Which performed cultic sacrifices accompanied by dances to an agrarian divinity called *Dea Die*; they also invoked *Mars*.[119]

But in general, the king performed all types of sacred functions. Since the time of the Republic, the priestly function of the king was distributed among a number of sacerdotal officials of the state. One of them, *rex sacrorum* (king of the sacred rites), with his consort *regina sacrorum* (queen of the sacred rites), took over the remaining sacred powers, which the Republican officials did not assume. Thus *rex sacrorum* and his colleagues became powerful and exercised a great deal of control over the sacred law and in the dating of the sacred calendar. The *rex sacrorum*, besides his many functions, was also the guardian of the cult of *Janus*. In the course of time, their power weakened, as the secular officials took over the sacred powers.[120]

After the *rex sacrorum*, next in rank were the three *flamines majores*, who were priests of the special cults to *Jupiter*, *Mars* and *Quirinus*. The priest of *Jupiter* was known as *flamen Dialis*, the priest of *Mars* was called *flamen Martialis* and the priest of *Quirinus* was the *Quirinalis*. The priest of *Jupiter*, *flamen Dialis*, was expected to follow a number of purification and taboo precepts dating back to very early times, suggesting sacral kingship.[121] The following quotation clearly indicates some of the taboos of the priest of *Jupiter*.

> It is unlawful for the priest of *Jupiter* to ride upon a horse, or to look upon the army on parade outside the city boundary. ...The *flamen* might not take an oath. He might not wear a ring, unless it was perforated and without a gem. No fire must be taken from his house except for a sacred rite. If a fettered suppliant entered his house he must be freed, the

bonds being drawn up to the roof and thence lowered into the street (to prevent a second defilement of the door?). He had no knot in his headdress, or girdle or in any part of his dress, which must have been decidedly awkward. In his head he wore an olive twig... His barber must be a free man... He must not touch or even name a she-goat, raw flesh, ivy or beans, nor walk beneath a wine arbor. He must eat only unleavened bread. For him every day is a holiday. ...He might not go out without his cap... If his wife, known as *flaminica*, dies he abdicates his office, and his marriage has been dissolved only by death, (a rare condition in Rome, where divorce was so easy).[122]

In this manner, the life of a *Flamen Dialis* was very restricted. Since the taboos were considered as absolute, life was rather hard for the priests of *Jupiter* in the Roman religion.

Other than the *rex sacrorum* and *flamines majores*, whose duties were professional and technical, every other priestly function in Rome was held as a part time post. The people who held such posts were men who were politically prominent. Since these posts brought social distinction and political prestige, they were keenly contested. These priests were formed into four guilds or colleges: The college of *Pontifices*, the college of *Auguries*, the college of *Quindecimviri Sacris Faciundis* and the college of *Fetiales*. *Pontifex Maximus*, the head of the state clergy, presided over the college of *Pontifices*. He was elected, not chosen, from among the existing *Pontifices*. He resided in the ancient palace, as he was also the hair of some royal functions. The task of this college of *Pontifices* was to oversee how the calendar, the laws, ritual performance and the religious traditions were observed.[123]

The second clerical institution in Rome was the college of *Auguries*. The name '*auguries*' might have been derived from the practice of magic in fertility cults. Probably it meant 'increasers'. The *Auguries* performed the task of discerning if the gods approved or did not approve an action. They used various means to determine the will of the gods, which will be elaborated in the next section. The college of *Quindecimviri Sacris Faciundis* had the task of looking after the foreign rites, adoption of strange gods and cults, and supervising them. The college of *Fetiales* was concerned with various aspects of international relationships, such as declaration of war and making treaties of peace. The leader of this college, *Pater Patratus*, saw to it that such acts of international relationships were done according to divine right (*jus divinum*). There were also officials called *Epulones*, who supervised religious feasts. There were twelve *flamines minores*, who were in charge of the cult of different particular deities. There were also six *Vestal* virgins, chosen from the old partisan families, who looked after the shrine and the fire of goddess *Vesta*. They lived in the house of *Vestals* with a number of taboos. The *Vestals* were chosen when they were six to ten years old. They were expected to serve as *Vestals* for thirty years. During the years they serve as *Vestals*, they had to live a life of perfect chastity. If their chastity was violated, they were buried alive in an underground chamber. It was said that the vestals must spend the first ten years of their service learning their duties; the second decade was used to practice them and the final ten years were spent teaching those duties to the new recruits. Once they completed the thirty years of service, a *Vestal* was free to get married and lead a normal life. *Pontifex Maximus* was in charge of the supervision of the affairs of the *Vestal* virgins.[124]

The elaborate organization of the priesthood in Roman religion was aimed at helping people to perform various cultic rites, using the help and expertise of the priest, at the levels of the family, kin group, fraternity group and the state. Priests, at all these levels, helped people to offer cults to the gods in the proper manner as prescribed by the sacred law and tradition, that people may honor gods and give them their due. In doing so, people would communicate with their gods, live in the state of *pax Deorum* and obtain what was due to them from the gods. In this manner priests of the Roman religion were intermediaries between the gods and men and served as a path to the divinities.

2.2.2.2. SACRED PLACES

In the early Roman religion, sacred places as temples and sacred objects as divine images were absent. The word '*templum*' was derived from the Etruscan language. Originally it meant a specific area in the sky, which the priest delimited for the gathering of auspices and the interpretation of omens. Later on this area was projected to the earth, and then '*templum*' meant a piece of ground set aside as sacred and consecrated to the gods. There was no sacred building for worship in this place allotted to the gods. Often the gods were worshipped in the open, by the sacred grove (*lucus*) set apart as sacred, on an altar erected for the purpose of sacrificing to the gods. At a later stage, small shrines were built around the site where the altar was. Finally larger temples were built using solid materials. For the Roman people the temple was something sacred, as it was the dwelling place of the gods. The presence of the god in the temple was represented by the divine image.[125] The importance the Romans gave to the temples was clearly shown in the celebration of the anniversaries of the vows to build temples and the conscientious remembrance of the days of the dedication of the temples. Thus, from the early stages of Roman religion, sacred places such as sacred groves, altars, shrines and temples played a very important role in helping people to encounter the divine and receive their blessings.

2.2.2.3. PRAYER AND SACRIFICE

The Romans were very articulate in their prayer and meticulous in the offering of sacrifices. The prayers of the Romans had a structured form. They were said like repeating a formula. The prayers must be recited without any alteration according to the definite wordings prescribed. A little change would destroy the intended result. If a person made a mistake by altering a word or a sentence, he must start the prayer from the beginning. The prayer must be clear and distinct. The name of the gods to whom the prayers were addressed must be the correct name of the deity. Any mistake made in this regard was believed to offend the gods. At the same time, prayer was not magical. In prayer the favor of the god was invoked, but no attempt was made to force the deity. Prayer was not a pledge (*votum*) to place demands on the gods, but rather it was a pact between the gods and the devotee. The worshipper promised the gods an offering in return for the favor for which one asked. Prayer at times could be *devotio*, in which, for instance, an army general might dedicate himself as a sacrifice to the gods that he might obtain a victory. Prayers were made for obtaining from the gods material gifts, health, prosperity, fertility and victory in war. They could also be made for the purpose of reconciliation with the gods when they were angry and to propitiate for one's sinful behavior. The language used in prayer was often unintelligible, archaic and obscure. Thus they often provide information about the early Latin language.[126] A prayer offered to *Mars* by the *Salii* fraternity reads as follows: "O, Planter God [*Mars*], arise. Everything, indeed, have I committed unto thee (as Opener). Now art thou the Doorkeeper; thou art the Good Creator, the Good God of beginnings. Thou wilt come specially, thou the superior of these kings."[127] To quote another prayer of the *Fratres Arvales*: "Help us ye Lares! Let not blight and ruin, O Mars, haste upon the multitude. Be satiate, fierce Mars, leap the threshold, stay thy scourge! Summon ye in turn all the gods of sowing [Semones]. Help us O Mars! Huzza, Huzza, Huzza!"[128] Some of the sentiments expressed in these prayers were fear of the god, need for his help and the request for his support.[129]

The characteristic mark of the offerings of the Roman people was that the prayers were accompanied by sacrifices. The following prayer to *Mars* clearly indicates the relationship between prayers and sacrifices in the Roman religion:

> Father Mars, I pray and beseech thee that thou be gracious and merciful to me, my house, and my household; to which intent I have bidden the *suovetaurilia* (a pig, a ram, and a bull) to be led around my land, my ground, my farm; that thou keep away, ward off and remove sickness, seen and unseen, barrenness and destruction, ruin and unseasonable influence; and that thou permit my harvests, my grain, my vineyards, and my plantations to flourish and to come to good issue, preserve in health my shepherds and my flocks, and give good health and strength to me, my house, and my household. To this intent, to the intent of purifying my farm, my land, my ground, and of making expiation, as I have said, deign to accept the offering of these suckling victims; Father Mars, to the same intent, deign to accept the offering of these suck lings.[130]

In the historic era of Roman religious life, sacrifices were regulated in minute detail. Sacrifices did not have to be of animals, as there were bloodless offering of bread, fruit, milk, honey or wine. But animal sacrifice was considered to be more effective than the bloodless sacrifice. The pig was the commonest victim of sacrifice. On certain important occasions a sheep and an ox were added. Before an animal was sacrificed, it was dedicated to the gods by rubbing the victim's head with flour mixed with slat (*mola sala*). After the animal was killed the entrails were examined. Then they, along with the heart, liver and kidneys, were sacrificed to the gods as a burnt offering, while participants in the offering ate the other parts of the animal. Human sacrifice was not common in Rome. But, in expressing his *devotio*, a general in war might offer himself to the gods in order to achieve victory in the war. Sacrifices were distinguished by three categories, viz., *hostiae honorariae*, *hostiae piaculares* and *hostiae consultatoriae*. The first were the sacrificial offerings made to honor the gods and to gain their friendship. The second were offerings made in expiation of a trespass, whether it was a ritual or a moral one. The third were the divinatory offerings, through which one attempted to interpret the intentions and will of the gods by scrutinizing the entrails of the sacrificial animal.[131]

Another rite performed, in historic times, was the games (*ludi*), which involved chariot racing, dancing and military exercises. The best-known *ludi* was the *Ludi Romani*, which was celebrated on the 13th of October. It included a banquet in honor of *Jupiter* and a solemn procession from the Capitol to the *Circus Maximus*. Another important *ludi* was the *Ludi Seculares* performed at the time of the consecration of the new *saeculum*, i.e., an era of 110 years, in order to make the gods bestow their favor on it. Though these games had a secular character, they were religious rites, as the gods were invoked, prayers were offered to them and the blessings of the gods were sought during the games.[132]

In this manner, prayers, sacrifices and other rituals played an important role in the lives of the Roman people in their attempt to encounter the divinities. These were important paths the Roman religion used to contact the gods and to achieve the *pax deorum*.

2.2.2.4. FESTIVALS

Festivals played an important religious function of bringing the gods and men together, thereby renewing the contract that existed between them. Festival days were moments in which the Roman people called on their gods, made amends for their failures of breaching the covenant with the divinities and opened themselves for the blessings the gods could bring to them. The Roman religion had an elaborate calendar of festivals, which was based on the calendar of the Etruscans. It contained 58 regular festivals. These included first, the 45 *Feriae Publicae*, which were celebrated on the same day every year. They were fixed and unmovable festivals. *Lupercalia* (February 15) and *Saturnalita* (December 17) were examples of *Feriae Publicae*. Second, there were the monthly festivals, such as *Ides*, in honor of *Jupiter* and the *Kalends of March*, which was sacred to *Mars*. Third, there was, then, the *Feriae Conceptivae*, the dates of which were fixed each year by the proper authority. *Feriae Latine*, which was celebrated on the Alban Mount, by the end of April, was an example of *Feriae Conceptivae*.[133]

Having mentioned the general classification of festivals of the Roman calendar, we could mention some of the individual festivals. Three festivals were celebrated in honor of *Jupiter*, which were connected with wine and the grape harvest. The most significant of these festivals was the *Meditrinalia*, which was celebrated on October 11, explicitly for honey and wine. Another festival celebrated on 15th February was the *Lupercalia*. Originally it was a ritual aimed at keeping the wolves (*lupi*) out if the herds. It also had an element of fertility ritual. Certain young men stripped naked, except for a girdle of goat skin, and, carrying flails of goat hidden in their hands, known as the *Luperci*, ran all around the palace settlement, making it secure against the evil spirits and other aggressors. As the young athletes progressed, they gave a tap with the goat flail to any woman they encountered, thereby giving her a dose of this doubly powerful male medicine. It was believed that barren women touched during the holy chase, escaped of the curse of sterility. The 24th of February was the festival called *Regifugium*, i.e., the flight of the king, in which the *rex sacrorum*, after killing the sacrificial victim, disappeared from the scene of the sacrifice. Nothing is known about this festival except that it was celebrated as a festival. Perhaps the killing of the sacrificial victim was considered a crime.[134]

There were a number of festivals celebrated to appease *Mars*, the god of war and, to ward off evil. Three festivals involving horse chariot races were celebrated in honor of *Mars*. The first two, celebrated on February 27 and March 14, were called *Equirria*, while the third, held on October 15, was known as *Equus October*. In the last of these festivals, the horse that was on the right hand side of the winning team at the race was sacrificed to *Mars* in Campus Martinus. The neck of the horse was adorned with a wreath of bread, probably for the growth of crops. The blood was given to the *Vestals* for purification. The tail of the horse was cut off, and a runner carried it to the *Regia*, the old royal palace, where it was hung up to drip blood onto the altar. Two rival teams fought over the head of the horse. The meaning of this gruesome rite has not been clear. The *Salii*, the 'leaping' priest of *Mars*, performed another festival in honor of *Mars*. It involved dance, brandishing of spears and clashing of the holy shields (*ancilia*). The priests were dressed like the ancient Latin soldiers, while dancing invoked, besides *Mars*, *Saturnus* the god of sowing. The aim of this festival and the rite accompanied were to expel all the evil spirits that have entered the city during winter and to stimulate growth of the crops. Some other festivals of *Mars* were: the *Armilustrium*, which was celebrated on 19th March, which consisted of the cleaning and dedication of arms; *Ambravalia* in the month of May, for the protection of fields and crops; and the *Suovertaurilia*, which involved offerings of a pig, a ram and a bull. The latter was a festival of purification and expiation. Another festival celebrated on the 15th of March was *Anna Perenna's* festival, which was a popular New Year festival when the old *Mars* was driven out and people drank together to a good year.[135]

During the month of April, there were a number of agricultural festivals. On April 15, there was the festival called *Fordicidia*, in which a pregnant cow was sacrificed to the earth goddess *Tellus*, and the unborn calf was burned. This was done probably to secure fertility of the earth and better production of the crops. On April 19, there was the festival called *Cerialia*, when foxes with burning torches attached to their tails were set off, probably in order to prevent damage from the burning heat of the sun. Again there was the festival in which a pig was sacrificed to *Tellus* and *Ceres* before the harvest. On April 21 was celebrated as *Palilia*, to honor *Pales*, a god who preceded the foundation of Rome. The rite involved the lustration of cattle before they left the winter pastures for the wilder runs of the hills, similar to the lustration of the army before it left for a campaign. On April 23, there was celebration of *Vinalia*, to seek the protection of the vines. On the 25th of the same month, when the new ear was beginning to form, the evil spirit (*Robigus*) was formally propitiated.[136]

In the month of May there were no major festivals other than those indicated earlier. In mid-June there was the festival in honor of goddess *Vesta*, when the temple and the *penus* (the storage cupboards) had their annual cleaning. The water used for the cleaning was not drawn from the public wells but from the sacred springs. On this day, the asses were garlanded with flowers and given a holiday. The purification symbolizes the readiness to receive the grain of the new crop. During July a few minor festivals were celebrated. During August there were the *Consualia* and *Opiconsiva* festivals, on the 21st and 25th respectively. Both were related to storing of the new crop. In between these two festivals the *Volcanalia* was celebrated, the aim of which was to ward off the accidental fires, which occurred in the hot dry weather of the summer. Until the autumn sowing was over, the festival calendar was free, other than the few we mentioned earlier. On December 17 was celebrated the festival *Saturnalia*, which was preceded and followed by a second *Consualia* on December 15 and *Opalia* on December 19 respectively. *Saturnalia* and the other two festivals that went before and after it were related to the agricultural activities of sowing and reaping. This feast was celebrated with various processions under the leadership of a king of fools elected for the day. On this day the masters served the slaves. It was a feast of merriment and enjoyment. People exchanged gifts with each other, as they gladly celebrated the end of the work year.[137]

In this manner, the elaborate liturgical calendar and the various festivals touching different aspects of the life of the Roman people played a very important role in establishing contact between them and their gods. The festivals of the Roman religion regularized and organized the religious life of the people so much so that they could not but be in touch with their gods, at least at some time of the year. Thus, the religious festivals of the Romans were indeed genuine paths to the divine.

2.2.2.5. MYSTERY CULTS

The official Roman religion was rather formal and bound by strict regulations for conducting rites and ceremonies. Therefore, it lacked emotional content. Hence the ordinary man preferred the spirituality of the mystery cults, which satisfied the need for affective element in his reaching out to his god. There were five cults that were very popular in the Roman world at this time, most of which emerged in Rome due to influences from outside the Roman Empire, viz., the cult of *Cybele*, the cult of *Bacchus-Dionysius*, the cult of *Isis*, the cult of *Mithras* and the emperor cult.[138]

2.2.2.5.1. The Cult of Cybele

The Cult of *Cybele*, an Asian fertility goddess, was one of the significant mystery cults of the Roman period. She was identified with *Rhea*, the wife of *Cronos* and the mother of the gods. In Rome she was known as the *Magna Mater* (the Great Mother). Her cult was brought to Rome by official Roman invitation during the Second Punic War, 204 BC, hoping that it would help the Roman cause during the war. She was worshipped at Pessinus in the form of a black stone, which was believed to have fallen from heaven. This stone was sent to Rome and set up in a temple at the Palatine Hill. With her came her consort *Attis*, who castrated himself at her service. Like him her priests, the *Galli*, castrated themselves in order to serve her at the temple. The *Cybele* worship included orgiastic dancing, during which her devotees pricked and slashed themselves with swords and knives, turning the rite into a blood bath. The state interfered and regulated the worship of the Great Mother, at the same time forbidden the Roman citizens from participating in such rites. The restrictions on the Roman citizens to be associated with this cult were so strict that the procession held in honor of the goddess on April 4 was fully a foreign affair. But the Roman *Praetors* celebrated in honor of the goddess the Great Games (*Megalesia*). Later some of these restrictions were removed and the goddess *Cybele* gained a great number of followers.[139]

2.2.2.5.2. The Bacchus-Dionysius Cult

A second mystery cult that was popular in Rome was the *Bacchus-Dionysius* cult. According to Euripides a lowborn Greek, a sacrificing priest and prophet, introduced the cult in Rome. He was a man with a gainful occupation while he was the leader of this cult. He was an expert in hidden and nocturnal rites. In the initial stages of the sect, only a few, mostly women, were initiated. But later it was open to women and men. In the same way, wine and feasts were added to the original religious cult. The inclusion of wine, women and men led the cult to wrong paths. Drinking, wild dancing, cries of ecstasy, noise of drums and symbols, and the presence of men and woman gave the cult a wild and orgiastic tone. Since the whole experience was kept secret, a great deal of unwanted happenings, such as, as making false witness, false seals and wills, preparing false evidence against the other, which in turn led to violence, poisonings and slaughters within the cult. The government attacked all these dissident practices which led to the unauthorized holding of *Bacchanalia* mystery cults. The Roman Senate gave approval only to small groups to conduct *Bacchanalia*, when applications were made. Though the *Bacchus-Dionysus* cult had an original religiosity, it was lost over the course of time.[140]

2.2.2.5.3. The Isis Cult

A third cult that gained prominence in Rome was the *Isis* cult. *Isis* was a fertility goddess. She was far more gracious and gentle than *Cybele*. Originally *Isis* was an Egyptian goddess, but she was Hellenized, before being introduced into Rome. Most of her devotees were Roman women. The initiates of this cult went through elaborate and mystical rites. These rites were said to last for ten days and ended after a nightlong religious dramatization of the story of the death and resurrection of *Isis's* husband *Osiris*. His rebirth, which was miraculous, was achieved by the efforts of *Isis*, especially through her deep grief. This dimension of the cult gave the devotees an emotional appeal. It was believed that the reconstruction of the event through religious dramatization would bring about rebirth to her devotees and finally lead to the achievement of immortality. Unlike the *Cybele* and *Bacchus-Dionysus* cults, the *Isis* cult was more mystical and sober and appealed to the genuine inner feelings of the Roman people.[141] In his famous work, *Metamorphoses* (*The Golden Ass*), Apuleius speaks of the religious feeling the goddess *Isis* evoked on the devotee as follows:

> You indeed, holy one, the perpetual preserver of human kind, and always generous in fostering morals, grant the sweet affection of a mother to the misfortunes of the wretched. Neither day nor any quiet time of night, nor indeed any moment passes by that is not occupied by your good deeds. You protect men by land and sea: when you have driven off the storms of life, you stretch out your saving right hand. With it you draw back the threads of the fates, however inextricably they are twisted together. You soften the storms of Fortune, and restrain the harmful passage of the stars. ...You rule the globe, you light the sun, you rule the world, you tread down Tartarus. The stars answer to you, the seasons return, the godheads rejoice, the elements serve you. At your nod, breezes blow, clouds nourish, seeds germinate, seedlings grow. The birds, passing in heaven, tremble at your majesty. ... But I am poorly provided with talent for reporting your praises. I have no property for providing sacrifices. My voice is not rich, for saying what I feel about your majesty. A thousand months, and as many tongues, are not enough,

nor is an eternal succession of unwearied speech. Therefore, I shall make it my care to bring about the only thing that I can do, who am indeed religious, but in other respects a poor man. I shall form an image of your divine countenance and of your most holy godhead, and I shall always keep it hidden within the secret places of my breast.[142]

2.2.2.5.4. The Cult of Mithras

A fourth cult that was popular among the Romans, especially among the military class was the cult of *Mithras*. The origin of the god *Mithras* was not clearly known but Probably was of Iranian origin. When Rome came in contact with this cult, *Mithras* was associated with Persian Zoroastrianism. He was the deity of truth and light. Those who followed this cult believed that the world was divided between the good, powers of light *(Ahura-Mazda)*, and evil, powers of darkness *(Ahriman)*. *Mithras* was often associated with *Ahura-Mazda* and the Sun god. He, as the god of light, was represented as surrounded by the signs of the Zodiac in the heavens slaying a bull, which was a living embodiment of brute force. Being the god of light and truth, he fought against all forms of evil. Every follower of *Mithras* joined his god in fighting against evil. The cult of *Mithras* was a man's cult, as it demanded that members be rigorous and virile. It emphasized a sense of fraternity and fighting for the cause of good. With this twofold orientation the cult spread within the Roman army. It became so army based that by the third century AD every soldier belonged to this cult. The members of the cult were initiated in a purification rite similar to Christian Baptism and participated in a common ritual meal. Another rite associated with the cult of *Mithras* was *taurobolium*. It was a revolting rite, which consisted in drenching a neophyte with the blood of a bull slaughtered above him. This rite symbolized the regeneration of the neophyte. The cult of *Mithras* expected from its adherents the highest moral sense and discipline. This probably was the reason for its growth among the Roman army.[143]

2.2.2.5.5. The Emperor Cult

A fifth cult popular in the later religious history of Rome was the emperor cult, which propagated the worship of the emperors. The origin of this cult in Rome also has been due to the influences from the oriental cultures. It began with the deification of the dead emperors, as a form of remembering them. Later it was applied to the living emperors as well. A deified emperor became the symbol of the empire, and worship of the emperor came to signify the loyalty of the people towards the empire, and unity of all citizens under the emperor. Emperor worship also gave the Roman religion an inner meaning as well as external form.[144]

There were some misgivings about what some of these mystery cults contributed to the religious life of the Roman people. But, a number of them gave a personal touch to the Roman religious practice catering for the affective and emotional aspect of man's reaching out to the gods, which was lacking in the traditional Roman religion. In this way, the mystery cults supplemented the traditional Roman religious practice.

2.2.2.6. ORACLES AND DIVINATION

In the Roman religion the oracles were a collection of ancient cryptic writings. According to legend, they entered the Roman religious life in nine *Sibilline* Books. But, by the time Romans got them, they were reduced to three. The myths about the origin of the books say that a prophetess (*sibyl*) brought them to Rome. She tried to sell all nine to one of the early Etruscan kings. He showed no interest in buying them, and the offended *sibyl* burned three books. Again she came to sell the remaining six books. But the king again showed no interest in the books. Offended by the king's lack of interest, she burned three more books. The *sibyl* came a third time to sell the last three books. The king was curious and bought the three books for the same price as the nine books. These oracles played an important role in determining the will of the gods. They in a very special way promoted the true welfare of the state. They were consulted only on matters of great importance and during the time of national emergencies, such as, a plague, a famine, as during a critical moment in a war or similar situations. The directions given in an oracle were not solutions to the problem itself, but rather the guidance of the oracles pertain to how one could get the attention of the gods in such a moment of national importance. The consultation of the oracles was undertaken only at the Roman senate's orders. The actual consultation was accomplished through the official priests, who were appointed for this purpose. The actual content of the oracles was kept a mystery.[145]

Divination was another means of establishing the will of the gods on any matter of great importance. In Rome divination became associated with birds. The Latin term '*auspicia*', i.e., 'taking auspices', literally meant 'birdwatching'. It consisted in interpreting the will of the gods regarding various undertakings of the state by observing the movement of the birds. According to a legend, Romulus and Remus decided which of them should lay out the city by watching the flight of vultures. Remus, facing in one direction, saw six of them, while Romulus, facing in another direction, and saw twelve vultures. The latter claimed the honor on the basis of the numerical superiority of the vultures. Later divination involved the use of chicken. It was said that during the first Punic War the commander of the Roman fleet, Cladius Pulcher, took from a flock of a sacred chickens. He expected to read good or bad omens from the manner in which the bird pecked the feed. The chicken refused to eat. In a fit of anger, he threw the sacred chicken in the sea, with the cynical remark that if it did not want to eat it drink water. The loss of Cladius Pulcher at the war to the Carthaginians was attributed to his impious act towards the gods, and when he returned he was punished for his impiety. Thus, divination was given a very important place in Roman religion, so much so that taking recourse to such divination was indispensable to every state act. But the responsibility for the decision rested not with the priests, but with the presiding state official, who was said to 'possess the auspices'. The Etruscan method of divining from the liver and entrails of animals (*haruspicina*) was also very popular in Rome.[146]

2.2.2.7. MORAL LIVING

Two moral ideals, viz., *religio* and *pietas* characterized the moral life of the Roman people. The *religio* involved a sense of reverence people felt before the gods that came from the awareness that everything in the world is governed by the will of the gods. It also implied a feeling of being happily dependent on the higher powers and a desire to accept their will in all dimensions of human life. The Romans expressed this sentiment by using expressions such as, "with gods' help" (*Dis juvantibus*), "by the grace of the gods" (*Dis faventibus*) and "the gods be willing" (*Dis volentibus*). Thus, *religio* made the Roman people do nothing without knowing the will of the gods and relying on the support of the gods. *Pietas* referred to the meticulous sense of duty that characterized the life of the Roman people. It made them to give the gods their due. In having reverence for the gods and doing their duty towards them harmony with the gods (*pax Deorum*) was preserved. The Romans believed that if such a relationship with the gods were established, the gods would also maintain their part of the contract and give to men their due. Thus, The Romans stressed a sense of moderation in their relationship with the gods, especially in the cultic practices. Violation of moderation would lead to what the Romans called '*superstitio*' (superstition). When this moderation was violated in some of the mystery cults, the state intervened and stabilized such cults. These moral attitudes made the pious Roman seek the help of the gods in times of crisis and to be grateful to them for the blessings they bestowed.[147]

Besides regulating the relationship of the Roman people to their gods, the attitudes of *religio* (reverence) and *pietas* (duty) directed the moral living of the Roman people among themselves. These principles guided the moral fabric of the family and the clan groups. *Pater familias* had the legal control over each Roman family. He made major decisions regarding the everyday life of the members of the family. Later family councils took over most of the task of the *pater familias*. Similarly, reverence and duty were the center the relationships of members within the clan. The institution of marriage within Roman society, which was seen as a contract between the families and the partners, was founded on these twofold moral principles. The patron-client association, that became an institution in the Roman society in the later times, was founded on these twofold moral principles. It was a mutual assistance arrangement between the wealthy and the needy, but useful followers. Under this relationship the rich person offered his clients benefits such as protection in lawsuits and other monetary benefits. In return, the patron received political support, manifestation of gratitude and open show of respect and loyalty whenever the patron and the client met each other. The client addressed the patron not by name, but referred to him a *dominus* (master). We find this patron-client relationship spread over various sections of the Roman society. For instance, the generals were patrons of the people they conquered. Similarly, wealthy masters patronized artists and writers. But in all such cases it was related to matters of politics and economics. Even the master-slave relationship in Roman society was built upon the principles of *religio* (reverence) and *pietas (duty)*. Finally, the relationship between the citizens and the state, emperor and the people, the governors and the governed depended on these principles. With these principles guiding the family, clan, associations, class and the state life of the Roman people, a sense of moderation was achieved in every dimension of their lives. This would establish a harmony among the people, which in turn brought about the *pax populorum* (peace among the people), similar to the *pax Deorum*.[148] In this manner, the principles of *religio* and *pietas* guided the god-man and man-man relationships in Roman society. Therefore, genuine moral living not only opened man to the gods, but also opened man to his fellowmen.

2.2.2.8. PURIFICATION AND EXPIATION

Another important characteristic of Roman religion was the clear distinction it made between the sacred and the secular. This was clear from the fact that the days of the year were divided in the Roman calendar as *fasti* and *nefasti*, i.e., the days in which business can be transacted and the days in which the business might not be done, respectively.[149] The former were secular days for doing one's everyday business, while the latter were sacred days dedicated to the gods. On such holy days, one freed oneself from normal and routine life and spent the day in honor of the gods by participating in festivals, prayers and sacrifices. As a person took part in cults and sacrifices on the sacred days, he had to must purify himself. Ritual cleanliness and purity were very vital to make one's sacrifices acceptable to the gods. Tibllus points to the need for ritual purity, as one stands at the presence of the deities, in his work *Elegies*. To quote him: "Ye too I bid stand far away – let none be nigh the altar to whom Love's goddess gave her pleasures yester-night. The powers above ask purity. Clean be the raiment that ye come in, and clean the hands to take the waters from the spring."[150] The idea of purity before the divinities became very clear in the context of the taboos associated with the *Vestals* of goddess *Vesta* and the *Flamen Dialis*, the priest of *Jupiter*. The *Vestals* and *Flamen Dialis* were given elaborate directions to keep them pure, and if for some reason they violated these taboos, severe sanctions were given. For instance, if the *Vestals* violated the vow of chastity any time during the 30 years of service to the goddess *Vesta*, they were buried alive in an underground chamber. All these speak for the importance of purity in the life of a devotee and the need for purification when one has failed the gods by defiling oneself, in the Roman religion.[151]

The idea of purification after defilement takes us to the expiation one must undertake to make oneself pure before the divinity. Prayers and sacrifices are made not only to obtain material gifts, health, prosperity, fertility and victory, but also to reconcile one with the gods and to calm their anger, especially after some sort of defilement. Such sacrifices are called expiatory sacrifices. For instance, *suovetaurilia*, which consists in offering a pig, a ram and a bull to *Mars*, was done in expiation of one's defilement and sin. Besides expiating one's sinfulness through *souvetaurilia*, it is offered to purify one's farm and one's land.[152] Again the offerings made to the gods in the Roman religion were classified in three categories, viz., *hostiae honorairae, hostiae piaculares* and *hostae consulatoriae*. Of these three, the second one, *hostiae piaculares*, was specifically a category of expiatory offerings to the gods. These were offered in expiation for a transgression, whether it was ritual or moral, that had tainted a person's inner purity and tarnished his personality. It was the belief of the Roman people that such expiatory sacrifices would free the person from his defilements and make him acceptable before the gods. In other words, expiatory sacrifices were true means of recapturing the original purity a person enjoyed before he was defiled, thereby justified before the gods, whom he had offended.[153] Thus, purification and expiation were true means used in the Roman religion to encounter the divinities and to open oneself to their blessings, especially after one had offended the gods.

The Roman religion was a religion that recognized the influence of the gods in every sphere of the life of a human person and the community. It called people to cultivate a sense of reverence for the gods and give to them what was their due. In the process it helped the devotee to establish a harmonious and peaceful relationship with the gods. When a person achieved this peaceful relationship with the divinities, the deities would favor him and shower their blessings on him. These attitudes of reverence and sense of duty not only linked man to the gods, but also man to his fellowmen. Thus, helping a person to achieve genuine peace with the gods and with his fellowmen was the true goal of the Roman religion. It proposed a number of paths, such as, priest – the intermediaries between the gods and men sacred places, prayers and sacrifices, celebration of the festivals, mystery cults, use of oracles and divination, genuine moral life, purification and expiation. All these paths helped the people of the Roman religion to establish a harmonious relationship with the gods (*pax Deorum*).

2.3. HELLENISTIC RELIGION

The conquests of Alexander the Great opened the Greek world to the Orient. This opening led to the spread of Greek civilization in the whole of the Eastern Mediterranean and the Orient. There took place the intermixing between the Greek and the Egyptian, the Mesopotamian, the Persian and, to a certain extent, the Indian cultures. The interaction among these cultures brought about a cosmopolitan civilization in which, though the Greek element was dominant, there was the substantial presence of Oriental components. From the time of the Roman Emperor Augustus, Roman culture was drawn also into this interaction of cultures. The involvement of Rome continued until the emergence of Christianity as the religion of the Roman Empire under the Emperor Constantine the Great. Thus, the multinational civilization that began with the Greek Emperor Alexander the Great and ended with the Roman Emperor Constantine, the Great, was known as Hellenism. Hence, in its final form Hellenism was constituted of the Greek culture, the Oriental cultures and Roman culture.[154]

The Hellenistic period was one of the most creative periods in the history of religion. It was a time of spiritual revolution in the Greek and Roman Empires. The ancient Greek and Roman religions continued to exist but were modified in many ways. During this period a number of old cults died, while others were totally transformed, and new religious movements emerged. Many of these cultic movements had two forms of existence, one in the land of their origin and the other in the Diaspora, viz., in the cosmopolitan cities, such as, Greece and Rome, where the people were immigrants. In the homeland the religious cult was tied up with local loyalties, such as, the expectation of a messianic personality, who would deliver them from the Greco-Roman political, cultural and religious domination. There was a revival of the religious cult by way of interpretation of the sacred texts in relation to the present context, restoration of temples and rejuvenation of mythical traditions. The messianic hope and revival activity led to the emergence of wisdom literature that spoke of the hidden purposes of the deity and apocalyptic writings that announced the dramatic intervention of the gods in human and natural events. In all such revivalism that was taking place in the religion of the homeland, Greek thinking exerted a great deal of influence.[155]

In the Diaspora, there were two circles of believers, viz., the inner and the outer circles. The inner circle consisted of full-time adherents of the cult. They were usually first generation immigrants from the native land. For them the deity was indigenous and special. They continued to use the native language, even in worship. The outer circle consisted of the second and the third generation immigrants or non-ethnic converts, for whom the religion was not native. They were also alien to the language of the ethnic group and so used only Greek or Latin. There was a need to translate or paraphrase the ancient sacred texts of these religious cults into Greek or Latin. The concerns of these ethnic groups and converts living in the Diaspora were different from those of the people of the homeland. Though they were sentimentally attached to some pilgrimage centers in the homeland, their beliefs were very different. They practiced esotericism, i.e., secrets known only to the members, to achieve visions, epiphanies and manifestations of god. The members of the inner circle did this by using native language and sticking to the informal oral traditions of the native land, while the members of the outer circle achieved this by allegoric interpretation of the sacred texts, formulating dogma, creed, codes, rules for conversion and admission.[156]

Thus, there grew up new religious communities around secret and mystery cults. As a result, the main thrust of the religion of the Diaspora was not messianic hope for the nation, but rather individual salvation. Thus, religion was not something into which one was born, but rather it was a personal choice, that grew out of personal conviction. One entered and become a member of the cult by personal choice and going through the secret mystery rite, following strictly the rules for conversion and admission into the cult. Along with the individualism that was felt in religious matters, the old nationalistic and patriotic sentiments were giving way to a cosmopolitan attitude.[157]

This cosmopolitan attitude had a great influence on man's perception of religion and his ultimate destiny. The educated person gave up the practice of traditional religions and embraced Philosophy as a substitute to religion. Philosophical schools, such as, Stoicism, Epicureanism and Neo-Platonism had tremendous impact on the educated classes. The insecure and changing conditions of the time made many people believe in pessimism and fatalism, as the traditional religion did not make much sense to them. The archaic religions of the Mediterranean world conceived the cosmos as a network of relationships, in which each one had his place and was called to accomplish an appointed role. Therefore, through astrology, divination and oracles, man discerned the unchangeable patterns of the gods and attempted to bring his world into harmony with the divine cosmos.[158]

Unlike these archaic religions, the main focus of the Hellenistic religion was neither having a place in this world, nor conformity to the designs of the gods, but escape, salvation and liberation from the evil world in which one was imprisoned. The characteristic element of the religion of the Hellenistic period was dualism. Man wanted to flee from the tyranny of this world and to rise to another world of freedom, peace and joy. He believed that he was an exile in this world and his true home was the Beyond. Therefore, he sought ways and means to return to the original world to which he belonged. He realized that in order to return to his true world, he must strip off this world, its gods, his body, and awaken the spirit that had descended from the world beyond. Man must know who he had been before this earthy existence, what he had become here on earth, where he was going and from what he was to be redeemed in order to attain true bliss. In other words, when a person having realized his origin, identity and destiny, shunned this earthly existence and moved to the world-beyond-this-world, he could experience true liberation. This perception of his destiny made man not to be worried about securing his place in this world or to be concerned about establishing peace with gods of this world, but to look for ways and means through which he could transcend this world. A number of mystery cults provided occult and secret means to achieve man's liberation. Religious philosophies, such as Manichaeism and Gnosticism, which considered matter as evil and the spirit as good, helped man to achieve liberation by shunning the pleasures of the world and opening oneself to the true '*gnosis*' (knowledge).[159]

Before we move on to talk about the various ways used by people of the Hellenistic period to transcend the present world of pain and sorrow and arrive at the world beyond, we must briefly study the Hellenistic gods.

2.3.1. HELLENISTIC PANTHEON

The individualistic approach to salvation, the cosmopolitan outlook, the new spirit of the Hellenistic age and the foreign influences led to the transformation of the gods of the archaic religions and the cultic rites associated with these gods. Many of the ancient *Chthonian* fertility gods and their agricultural cults, which expressed renewal of the community related to the fertility concepts, were changed considerably. These very cultic rites and the enactment of the seasonal drama associated with the cult, instead of expressing the celebration of the promise of renewal for the land and the people, signified the destiny, fortune, and the salvation of the individual after death. The collective and community-oriented agricultural rites became a mystery, i.e., an experience of salvation set aside only for the select few. Some of these cults were interiorized to refer to the liberation of the divine soul within man. As the result, they became dualistic, sharply distinguishing between the body and the soul. It was believed that the soul alone was initiated through the rite, thereby it might be freed from the body and regain its rightful mode of spiritual existence. In Gnostic mysteries, i.e., the esoteric dualistic cults that viewed matter as evil and spirit as good, the soul, which was good but fallen, was redeemed by the divine intervention during the cultic activity. In this manner, the perception of the gods and their cults changed greatly during the Hellenistic period.[160]

In the changed scenario, there was a quest for a god who had universal acceptance. Already an element of monotheism was present in the archaic religions, especially relating to certain deities, such as *Zeus*. These ideas were taken further during the Hellenistic period. Deities, who were previously associated with national destiny, such as *Zeus* and *Isis*, were raised to a transcendent status and considered as supreme deities, whose power and ontological position were far above the other gods. They were believed to be gods of the Beyond. The truly religious man wanted to stand before this one true God of the true world beyond this world. We find the Stoics identifying *Zeus* with this universal order.[161] The Stoic writer, Cleanthes, in his famous *Hymn to Zeus* speaks of *Zeus* as the god of the universal order and the father of mankind whom everyone must call in time of need and obey. To quote:

> Most glorious of immortals, many-named
> Almighty Zeus, creation's primal Lord,
> Whose lawful government is over all.
> Hail! – for we mortals unto thee may speak.
> We are thine offspring ...
> Lo the whole world revolving round the earth
> Obeys the lead and wills to do they will...
> Thou hast so welded all things into one.
> Joined good with evil, that there runs for ever
> One law through all which bad men scorn and scape. ...
> But thou Zeus, giver of all, with they black cloud

And glittering gold, save men from folly's bane.
O, father, cleanse our souls, grant us to find
Wisdom wherewith thou governest all aright.[162]

This quote clearly states the prime place given to *Zeus* as the universal Supreme Being, who was seen as the controller of everything in the universe.

Similarly the goddess *Isis* was a deity, who had a claim of universal status as a Supreme Being. The Roman author Apuleius clearly presents this claim as follows:

> I am she that is the natural mother of all things, mistress and governess of all the elements, the initial progeny of worlds, chief of the powers divine, queen of all that are in hell, the principal of them that dwell in heaven, manifested alone and under one form of all the gods and goddesses. At my will the planets of the sky, the wholesome winds of the seas, and the lamentable silence of hell be disposed; my name, my divinity is adored throughout all the world, in divers manners, in variable customs, and by many names. For the Phrygians that are the first of all men to call me the Mother of the gods at Pessinus; the Athenians, which are sprung from their own soil, Cecropian Minerva; the Cyprians, which are girt above by the sea, Paphian Venus ... and the Egyptians, which are excellent in all kind of ancient doctrine, and by their proper ceremonies accustomed to worship me, call me by my true name, Queen Isis.[163]

Another such self-predication, in which the goddess *Isis* proclaims herself as the Supreme Being, who has total control over even fate, was found in the Ios and Andros Inscriptions.

> I am Isis, the mistress of every land... I laid down laws for mankind and ordained things that no one has power to change. I am the eldest daughter of Kronos. I am the wife and sister of Osiris, the king... I divided the earth from heaven. I made manifest the paths of the stars. I prescribed the course of the sun and the moon... I made justice mighty. I brought together man and woman... I ordained that parents should be beloved by their children... I revealed initiations to mankind. I taught mankind to honor the statues of the gods. I founded sanctuaries of the gods... I ordained that truth should be regarded as beautiful... I conquer Fate, Fate hearkens to me.[164]

In the same way, monotheistic belief was linked with the sun god. Astrology considered the sun as the supreme of the fate-governing celestial bodies. Since the sun was regarded as the sovereign, that has sway over everything in the universe, the Roman Emperors propagated a solar cult. In the course of time they began to see themselves as the representatives of the sun. Emperor Aurelianus built a magnificent temple to the invincible sun (*Sol Invictus*) in the Campus Martius in Rome. In doing so he made the sun-cult the imperial religion.[165]

The cosmopolitan mind-set of the period allowed a great deal of interchange of gods and their cults among the religions. As the result, the practice of translating the names of the native gods in Greek or Latin was in vogue. For instance, many of the Oriental sky gods were worshipped in their native lands as *Zeus* or as *Jupiter*. Similarly many of the foreign gods entered the Greek and Roman pantheon. For example, the worship of *Cybele, Magna Mater*, was introduced into Rome in the year 204 BC. New gods were created and new cults were formed in the bringing together of different elements of the Greek, the Oriental and Roman religions. To cite an example, Ptolemy I, the Greek successor of Alexander the Great and the ruler of Egypt, created a half Greek and half Egyptian god known as *Sarapis* and organized a cult in his honor. The name '*sarapis*' was derived from *Osorapis*, a god who combined the attributes of *Osiris* and the sacred bull-god *Apis*. Similarly gods from different religious traditions were identified. For example, the Phrygian fertility god *Sabazios* was identified with *Dionysus*.[166]

Some of the other gods worshipped and in whose honor cults were offered were *Mithras* and *Attis*. While *Mithras* was a solar and fertility deity, *Attis*, the consort of *Cybele*, the Great Mother, was a fertility god who dies and returns to life.[167] The emperors were also worshipped as gods. Initially this honor was given to emperors only after their death. But later, even the reigning emperor was given worship.[168] Another goddess who was revered with awe and fear was *Tyche* (Fate). She was the goddess of fortune, who had the power to allot fortune or misfortune, good or evil. *Tyche* was the patron goddess of newly built cities. Since Fate ruled over everything and had absolute sway, people were at the mercy of fate. These made the people look for ways and means to escape the domain of Fate and achieve salvation.[169]

2.3.2. HELLENISTIC PATHS TO THE DIVINE

The issue of man's quest for salvation and the desire to free him from all that blocks his genuine liberation takes us to the study of the Hellenistic paths to the divine. Man's reaching out to the world-beyond-this-world in personal piety consisted either in preparing himself to ascend through the planetary spheres to the realm of the transcendent deity or calling the deity down to earth to reveal himself in epiphany or vision. The purpose of the ascent of man to god and the descent of god to man was the effecting of salvation (*soteria* or *salus*) in man. In the Hellenistic religion a number of techniques were used to bring about this ascent of man or descent of god. These techniques were made available to the initiates of the mystery cults. People looked upon mystery cults as a means of attaining salvation. Besides, there were other means such as priesthood, sacred rites, festivals and expiatory rites, in the context of the mystery cults that helped the people to experience personal salvation. In this section, we will elaborate those paths the people of Hellenistic times used to have the touch of the divine in their lives.

2.3.2.1. MYSTERY CULTS

Mystery cults provided individuals a means to feel religious experience and the healing touch of god, which the official religions did not offer. Their origin goes back to the tribal societies, where ceremonies were performed to initiate the members of the tribe or the clan into the social and religious life of the tribe or the clan. But during the Hellenistic period, in the Greco-Roman world, mystery cults began as private religious societies (*thiasoi*). These religious societies were dedicated to the worship of a particular deity. Though they began as immigrant associations, they developed into religious organizations, which included people from all walks of life. While admission to these groups was voluntary, the members had to pay a certain amount of money to be members. The members had to submit to the collective authority of the group and live the strict moral code of the group. These groups had regular meetings, which included cultic ritual, common dances and a common sacramental meal. The members, taken into the group through a secret cult, were known as *mystes*. They were taught techniques that would help them to experience the manifestations of the gods in their personal life and to achieve salvation. Usually these techniques were kept secret among the members of the society. The one who introduced the *mystes* was called *mystagogos*. Other leaders of the group included *hierophantes* (revealer of holy things) and *dadouchos* (torchbearer). Besides giving the members a sense of belonging, the mystery cult helped the initiates experience personal salvation.[170]

A number of mystery cults that were adhered to in the Greek and Roman religions continued during the Hellenistic period. The *Demeter-Kore* mystery cult[171] that flourished at Eleusis survived the Roman period and continued though the Hellenistic times. The heart of this fertility and mystery cult, in which the death and resurrection of corn was dramatically represented, was to effect the process of renewal within the *mystes*. Similarly, the two forms of Dionysian mystery cults, viz., the orgiastic cult of *Bacchus-Dionysus*, commonly known in Rome as *Bacchanalia*,[172] and the orphic mystical cult of *Dionysus-Zagreus*[173] also were popular in the Hellenistic religious scene. While the predominant appeal of the *Bacchanalia* cult was the union experienced with the deity in ecstasy, the orphic mystic cult of *Dionysus-Zagreus* by focusing on the death and coming to new life of the god, promised the *mystes* a blessed and happy new life after death. In the same way, the mystery cult of *Cybele*, the Great Mother and her consort *Attis*,[174] which was popular in the Roman religious practice, continued to exert influence in the Hellenistic period. The mystery cult of the Great Mother and her relationship to *Attis* symbolized during the Hellenistic times the relationship of mother earth to her children, which impressed upon the *mystes* the personal certainty of being united with the goddess.

Other than the cults we mentioned so far a few other mystery cults that were in vogue during the Hellenistic religion. The significant ones were the *Attis* mysteries, the *Isis* mysteries, the *Mithras* mysteries, the imperial mysteries and the *Sol* mysteries. We shall briefly consider each of these cults in the following section.

2.3.2.1.1. The *Attis* Mysteries

The main focus of this cult during the Hellenistic period was more on *Attis* rather than on *Cybele*, the *Magna Mater*. Thus, in the Hellenistic religion, it was more a mystery cult of *Attis* than the Great Mother, even though she was remembered in a significant way in each of the rites performed. According to myths, *Attis* castrated himself in the service of the Great Mother, and died. Though his rising to new life was not indicated in the myths, it has been suggested that he was brought back to life, which links *Attis* to the growth of flowers and trees. *Attis*, thus, appears to be a fertility god who dies and returns to life. Thus, the *Attis* mysteries once again affirmed to the *mystes* the hope of new life.[175] There was a special initiation ceremony arranged for the *mystes*, in which the general public was not permitted to participate. It involved a kind of confession of sin (*symbolum*) and a sacred meal. But we do not have the details of this cult of the *mystes*, as there was a shroud of secrecy around such mysteries. Another rite enacted during the cult of *Attis* was the *taurobolium*, which was a type of baptism by blood. In this ceremony the hero, who might be a king or any other private person, was seated in a pit, which was covered with perforated planks. Then a bull was placed over the planks and killed. The blood of the sacrificed bull was allowed to drip on the hero. It was believed that this rite brought divine power in the hero. He was greeted and worshipped by those present at the ceremony. The person who went through such a ceremony was called '*renatus*', i.e., 'born anew'. Usually this ceremony was performed for personal benefit of the emperor or any private individual. There were elaborate festivities associated with the *Attis* mysteries that were open to the general public.[176] We will consider the festivals associated with the mystery cults.

2.3.2.1.2. The *Isis* Mysteries

Another mystery cult that was popular during the Hellenistic period was the cult of the goddess *Isis*.[177] The *Isis* cult had its origin in the mythology of ancient Egypt. The Greek successors of Alexander the Great and the rulers of Egypt introduced the cult of *Sarapis*. The name '*sarapis*' originated from that of *Osorapis*, a god who combined the qualities of *Osiris* and the sacred bull god *Apis*. The cult center of *Osorapis* was at Memphis in Lower Egypt. *Apis*, after his death, was transformed into *Osiris*, thus gaining immortality, which he offered to his devotees. The worship of *Sarapis* (*Osiris*) combined

Egyptian and Greek elements and became very popular in Rome. Three deities were involved in the cult, viz., *Sarapis* (*Osiris*), *Isis*, his wife and *Horus*, their son. The dominant of the three was the goddess *Isis*.[178]

We have a clear description of what the *Isis* mystery cult was about in the famous book *Metamorphoses* (*The Golden Ass*) of Apuleius. Here the author recounts the story of a certain Lucius, who, due to his scandalous adventures with a sorceress, was turned into an ass. He was turned back into a human being at the festival of *Isis*, due to the miraculous grace of the goddess. After the instruction of the *Mystagogos*, he went through a cleansing baptism. Then he fasted for ten days, after which the initiation took place.[179] Lucius expressed the transformation he went through at the initiation as follows:

> Thou shalt understand that I approached near unto hell, even to the gates of Proserpine [Latin name for Persephone], and after that I was ravished through out all the elements. I returned to my proper place: about midnight I saw the sun brightly shine, I saw likewise the gods celestial and the gods infernal, before whom I presented myself and worshipped them.[180]

The next day Lucius was dressed in a religious habit and twelve stoles. Besides, he wore the Olympian Stole, carried a torch and a wreath of flowers with palm leaves on every side, like rays placed on his head. In this apparel he appeared before the community, and those present greeted him as a god. A banquet followed.[181] This story points to the fact that one could subdue one's animal nature, clarify his spiritual perceptions and become godly through the grace of goddess *Isis*. During the ceremonies Lucius saw the brightness of the light at the midnight. Probably this refers to the Egyptian belief that the sun god voyaged through the nether-regions during the night. Twelve stoles might refer to the twelve hours of the night. His wearing a wreath and being seated closer to the throne of the goddess *Isis* pointed to his deification. In other words, it was indicative of his movement from a life of darkness and death to a life of rebirth and new life with godlike qualities. In gratitude for what the goddess had done for him, Lucius acknowledged the goddess as the savior of mankind and was devoted to her throughout his life.[182]

Thus, the splendor of the cultic act, the secrecy with which the rites were performed, the significance of personal ethics and purity involved in the *Isis* cult, made a deep impression on the initiates and made the cult more attractive and popular. For this reason the cult of *Isis* spread in the Greek empire from 300 BC, and a number of *Isis* shrines were built in Greece during this period. In the Roman world, the *Isis* cult was in vogue from 100 BC. *Isis* was a very popular goddess among the Roman emperors. As late as fourth century AD, this cult was received favorably, so much so that even in the Christian era the private cult of *Isis* could be found in Rome.[183]

2.3.2.1.3. The Mithras Mysteries

Probably, the mysteries of *Mithras*[184] originated in Iran. *Mithras* was the most significant of the Iranian gods. He was considered to be the god of the sun, as he belonged to the realm of powers of light (*Ahura Mazda*). *Mithras* was believed to be the eye of *Ahura Mazda*, who ruled over the earth by beholding everything in the universe. He was also acknowledged as the god of contract and mutual obligations. The 15th century BC treaty between the Hittites and the Mitanni invokes *Mithras* as the god of oaths, who mediates and brings people together. As the solar deity beholding everything, *Mithras* could function as the guardian of oaths and treatises. He was also the god of the justice, which a king guarantees. Whenever people observed justice they venerated *Mithras*. He was also believed to be the god of war. He was engaged in a great struggle between good and evil, in which he was victorious. Besides, *Mithras* was the guardian of the mutual obligation between the king and his warriors. According to a myth, *Mithras* was born from a rock in a cave. The central point of this myth was that as the god of war, to assure his victory over evil and to renew every form of life, *Mithras* was said to have hunted and sacrificed a great bull, which was the prototype of the living world of nature. Through this sacrifice nature was made fertile, and useful plants and animals came to be in the world. In this manner, *Mithras* was also considered as a fertility god who brings everything back to life through the death of the bull.[185]

A rite associated with the *Mithras* mysteries was the *taurobolium*, which consisted of the ritual slaughter of a bull. This rite repeated and commemorated the original act of *Mithras*. This bull-killing rite went back to the ancient New Year festival and spoke of *Mithras*'s activity as the savior, who liberates the devotee from fate (*heimarmene*) and its power. The *mystes* were baptized in the blood of the sacrificed bull. The baptism of blood allowed them to participate in the life-giving properties of the sacrificial bull, which was believed to fructify nature by bringing forth corn and vine from its side. A sacramental meal of bread and wine followed the slaying of the bull and the ritual baptism in the blood of the bull in memory of the divine banquet *Mithras* himself enjoyed after slaying the great bull. It was supposed to give the initiates power, immortality and strength against all forces of evil. The cult of *Mithras* was conducted in small underground sanctuaries that had stone seats fitted to the wall along the sides. In the front, a stone with the representation of *Mithras* as the bull slayer was fitted to the wall, serving as the altar. The atmosphere of the sanctuary was made intense and refined by some form of lighting.[186]

The initiation of the *mystes* included 'a pledge to the standard' (*sacramentum*), a test of courage and the handing over of a sword. There were a number of levels of initiation depending on the degree of growth in godliness the initiate manifested. There were seven levels of initiation, each of them taking the initiates to higher and higher levels of spiritual existence. They were *Corax* (Raven), *Nymphus* (Bridegroom), *Miles* (Soldier), *Leo* (Lion),

Perses (Persian), *Heliodromus* (Courier of the Sun) and *Pater* (Father). The lowest in the rank was the *Corax* and the highest the *Pater*. The *Corax* were the servants of the community during the sacred meal of bread and wine. These stages helped to keep the fervor of the *mystes* and enabled them to ascend to the deeper experience of *Mithras*.[187]

The cult of *Mithras* was unique in that, unlike other mystery cults, it was only open to men. Therefore, it did not present itself as a universal faith. *Mithras*, who had won victory over every form of evil, was considered to be the Unconquered and Unconquerable (*Invictus*). Hence, the cult symbolized the courage, success and confidence of the soldier. The ethics of the *Mithras* mysteries required self-control, determination and other virtues associated with a soldier. The *Mithras* cult never stood in opposition to the official religion of the state. It was more polytheistic rather than monotheistic. Though *Mithras* was supreme in the eyes of an initiate, who could lead one to the state of immortality through the cultic rite, yet other deities were recognized. For these reasons, the cult of *Mithras* gained wide acceptability in the Roman Empire, especially in the rank and file of the Roman army during the Hellenistic era. The patronage given on the part of the emperors contributed a great deal to its spread in the Roman army. The influence of this cult was so great that from the second century AD, the Roman emperors began to assume for themselves the title *Invictus* that was given to *Mithras* and which led to the emergence of an imperial cult.[188]

2.3.2.1.4. The Imperial Mysteries

The Hellenistic period saw the emergence of the imperial mysteries[189] due to the Oriental influence. In the ancient Near East, kingship was considered as sacred. So it was natural that the Syrians and the Egyptians believed in the Greco-Macedonian emperors as semi-divine beings, as they did not consider the structure of the society in an abstract manner distinguishing the state from religion, but rather saw the whole political spectrum in the person of the king. For them the king was the symbol of the security and help they could derive from the gods. This belief led to the emergence of mystery rituals called 'Royal Mysteries', especially in Egypt. Traditional Egyptian religion believed that the reigning Pharaoh was an incarnation of *Horus*, the sun god. His mother or wife was an incarnation of *Isis*, the Heavenly Queen. The diseased father of Pharaoh was an incarnation of *Osiris* (*Sarapis*), the god of fertility.[190]

The Greeks very soon submitted to this mixture of politics and religion. Emperor Alexander, even when he was alive, was greeted as a divine person, both in the Orient and in Greece. After his death he was given a regular cult in Alexandria. The successors of Alexander, though they did not claim the homage given to the divinities, were given such homage. In the course of time the emperor and certain members of his family received officially recognized cult with its priest and temples. The emperors were given divine names, like, 'Savior' (*Soter*) and 'Rescuer', as they protected the state and its people from the enemies. They were also called *Epiphanes*, as they manifested the deity. The emperors wore a radiant crown that symbolized their divine nature. The family of the emperor was called 'a sacred house' (*hiera oikia*). Initially it was a matter of the personal choice of the emperor, but later imperial mysteries became an official institution.[191]

The Oriental and Greek practice of the imperial cult continued also in Rome, though initially it might have been related to some of the sacred functions the king of Rome performed. In the early stages of emperor worship in Rome, the worship was never directly addressed to the reigning emperor but to his *genius* (spirit), and only after the death of the king was he raised to the realm of the gods (*apotheosis*). But the situation changed as the reigning emperors claimed divinity and divine homage. For instance, Julius Caesar demanded divine worship. With Augustus, imperial mysteries became a sacred institution in Rome. He was given divine names, such as, 'savior', 'god', 'venerable' and 'majestic'. A few emperors like Nero were represented as wearing the radiant crown of the Sun god. Emperor Domitian claimed for them the divine title 'lord and god' (*dominus et deus*). Worship of the emperor had become the sign of loyalty to the Roman Empire. Thus, emperor worship had its political consequences as well.[192]

In addition, the emperor mysteries led to the theologizing of kingship. The emperor was believed to be a son of the gods, such as *Jupiter* or *Apollo*. Thus, the kings became manifestation (*epiphanes*) and the presence of the gods (*praesens divus*) here on earth. Legends and myths were written describing the divine parentage of the emperors. For instance, Augustus was believed to be the deputy and image of *Jupiter*. Therefore, he was said to be the ruler of the world and the globe was part of his royal emblem. It was also believed that the sovereignty of the emperor influenced the progress of the year and the order of nature. Thus, with the ascending of the emperor to the throne, there began a new era that had its impact on nature and the fertility of nature. The reason for the influence of the king on nature at his assuming the kingly office was that he was elected as a prince to accomplish the functions of the gods here on earth. As the king was the representative of the gods here on earth, he must imitate the gods in the exercise of his power, and his commands were binding on his subjects. This idea of kinship did not change, even after the introduction of Christianity in the Roman Empire by Emperor Constantine the Great. In Christianized Rome the emperor became the deputy and representative of God and Christ. He was the defender of the Church. The empire became the dominion of the king by the grace of God.[193]

The imperial cults had played a number of political and religious functions in the Greco-Oriental-Roman world. Politically they helped the king to hold his nation and its people together. The king was the soul of his nation and its unifying force. He was the vital spirit (*spiritus vivans*) of the nation and its people. Since the king was the visible manifestation and living expression of the gods, religion became concrete and real to the people. They could reach out to the gods and get their blessings through the king. In this way the imperial mysteries had a significant impact on the religious life of the people of Hellenistic times.

2.3.2.1.5. The Sol Mysteries

Imperial mysteries had an impact in the propagation of the worship of the sun god. The sun was considered supreme among the celestial bodies that governed fate. Many emperors preferred the solar cult, as they began to see themselves as symbols and representatives of the sun here on earth. Just as the sun was supreme in the celestial sphere, in the same way the kings saw themselves supreme here on earth. So a number of emperors gave importance to the *Sol* mysteries. In Syria the sun cult gained great significance. Emperor Elagabalus, also known as Heliogabalus, of Syrian descent, introduced the sun worship in Rome. This cult consisted in the worship of the sun in the form of a meteorite. It was given the name *Sol Invictus Elagabal*. Though the emperor wanted to make this worship official in the empire, he did not succeed in this endeavor. But the emperor Aurelianus later elevated *Sol* to the highest rank among the gods in the empire. Many sanctuaries of the *Sol* were built, especially the beautiful temple in the Campus Martius in Rome, dedicated to the *Sol Invictus* (the invincible sun). The solar festival *natalis invicti* (the birth of the invincible sun) was celebrated at the winter solstice, December 26. Thus, the sun cult became the imperial religion in the Roman Empire. It was said that the Roman emperor, Constantine the Great, wavered between the *Sol* and Christ, and at the early stages his policy allowed both the *Sol* mysteries and Christianity to coexist. Later, having accepted Christianity, he was instrumental in fixing Christmas day on December 25, the day on which the festival of the sun god *natalis invicti* was celebrated. Thus, the *Sol* cult was one of the most popular cults in the Hellenistic times.[194]

Mystery cults had an important place in the religious life of the people of the Hellenistic age. Each of the mysteries we have dealt with had its specificity and uniqueness, though there might be some common elements. For instance, the *taurobolium* rite of sacrificing a bull and baptizing the initiate with its blood was found in the cult of the Great Mother, in the cult of *Attis* and in the cult of *Mithras*. Though we might find such similarities among the various mystery cults, we would never be able to establish a theology common to them. But all the mystery cults were concerned with helping the initiates to experience rebirth, transmission of divine life and offering an emotional appeal that was missing in the official religion.

Similarly, each of the mystery cults catered to the spiritual needs of the different groups of people within the Hellenistic society. There was no cult that satisfied the spiritual needs of all sections of the society. For instance, middle class city people preferred the orgiastic cult of Dionysus, which included drinking, dancing and merriment. The Goddess *Isis* cult was popular among the people of the lower middle class, especially in the seaports of Greece and Rome. Most of the followers of the cult of the Great Mother were craftsmen. Soldiers and imperial officials favored the *Mithras* mysteries. The

Sol mystery cult was dear to the emperors. Thus, the mystery cults were true paths that guided different sections of the society. One could choose the cult that suited one's temperament and character and with its help achieve the true liberation one desired to achieve in one's life.

2.3.2.2. PRIESTHOOD

Priests facilitated the people's path to ascend to the divine and to experience the manifestation of the divine. In the mystery cults the priesthood was not as organized as that of the official religion. Generally the priests of *Dionysus-Bacchus* were wealthy laymen, who had done well in business. The priest who introduced the orgiastic *Dionysian* cult in Rome was a lowborn Greek priest and prophet, who had a gainful occupation. The priests called the *Galli* guided the community that practiced the cult of the Great Mother. The chief priest of the cult was the *Archgallus*. They were eunuchs, who castrated themselves at the service of the Great Mother. They wore female garb, kept long hair, and perfumed with oil. They guided the members of the cult in celebrating the goddess's rites, which included music and dancing. When the cult members got frenzied with music and dancing they performed acts of self-scourging, self-torture and self-laceration. Other than the priest there were the priestess and other minor officials, such as bearers of the tree (*dendrophori*), the bearers of the reed (*cannophori*) the bearers of the statue of the deity (*lecticarii*). During cultic processions, they took their respective places according to their importance in the rank and file of the cult. In Egypt, where the *Isis* cult originated, the higher levels of priestly service were reserved for people who were born in the priestly caste. Therefore, to be born in the priestly caste was far more important than talents and skills. This led to the lessening in the quality of priests. But there were also groups of laymen elevated to priestly service. They were inferior in rank to the members of the priestly class. They served as porters (*pastophori*) of the holy shrines. But in the Greece and Rome of Hellenistic period the *pastophori* replaced the caste priests and served as the leaders of the communities.[195] Thus, the priesthood contributed a great deal to the spiritual well being of people in the Hellenistic religion.

2.3.2.3. INITIATION RITES

The mystery cults prescribe elaborate initiation ceremonies in preparing the *mystes* to enter into the spirit of the cult. These preparatory rites fill the initiate with the sense of mystery and awe, in the process leading to greater and deeper spiritual experience. For instance, the *Isis* mysteries prescribe fasting for ten days, which includes abstaining from eating meat, drinking wine and having any form of sexual activity. The candidates to be initiated into the cult were separated from the common people. They were given special accommodation in the sacred precincts of the community center. They were called 'the chastely living ones' (*hagneuontes*). Besides, these initiates were expected to sign an oath of secrecy, which would bind them not to talk to others about the inner happenings at the gatherings of the members of the cult. There was also a ritual baptism, which symbolically pointed to the transformation that would be effected on the person, as he was initiated into the cult. This transformation reminded the initiates of the realties of death and resurrection.[196]

Therefore, the initiation rites involved exaggerated forms of acting out these realities, in order to give the candidates an experience of dying and resurrection. For instance, the candidates were symbolically buried, shut up in a sarcophagus, drowned in water, decapitated, mummified or deprived of their entrails to let them go through the experience of death. Similarly, in the orphic mystery cult of *Dionysus-Zagreus* there was a rite in which the heart of a sacrificial victim, which was often a child, was roasted and given to the initiates to be eaten. The baptism ceremony was conducted either by water or fire. In order to achieve the fire effect sulfur torches, which burned while taken out of water, were used. Similarly, light effects, writings and scripts were made to appear on the walls of a dark room. A circle of light was made to appear over the head of the priest officiating in the ceremonies. In the *Dionysian* and *Isis* mysteries, at times, the initiation was completed with a rite of 'sacred marriage'. The priest, speaking from the statue of the deity, ordered an unsuspecting woman to come to the temple and be the concubine of the deity. The priest played the part of the deity. Music, dancing and similar frenzies accompanied the initiation rites. Some of these latter acts performed at the rite, such as, acts with light effects, music, merriment and the 'sacred wedding' brought to the mind of the initiates the reality of the new life to which they were called by their initiation into the cult.[197]

All these means were used to bring about in the initiates a sense of mystery, which in turn would make them recognize the grace of the divinity that sustained them and would make them rise to higher levels of spiritual experience. In this way, the various elements involved in the initiation rites served as paths to the manifestation of the divine in their lives.

2.3.2.4. FESTIVALS

Festivals were occasions in which the glory and grace of the deities were manifested to the members of the mystery cults. The cults of *Dionysus*, *Demeter-Kore*, *Isis* and *Cybele*, the Great Mother had organized festivals according to the seasons of the year. These festivals were derived from the ancient tribal festivals and were closely associated with the sowing and reaping of corn and the production of wine. The *Dionysian* festivals were related to the vintage and tasting of wine, while the *Demeter-Kore* festivals were linked with the sowing and harvesting of corn. Thus, the festivals of these two mystery cults were connected to each other.[198]

In Egypt, the cult of *Isis* had three seasonal festivals, caused by the cycle of the River Nile, viz., inundation, sowing and reaping. The greatest festival was on the occasion of the flooding of the River Nile, breaking the summer heat. It was considered the New Year's Day. There were also two other solemn festivals of sowing and reaping. In the Roman Empire the festivals of *Isis* were held on December 25, January 6 and March 5. The most significant of these was the one celebrated on March 5. Apuleius, in his book *The Golden Ass*, described this festival in detail. The festival was celebrated in the city of Corinth. It was a spring festival and was celebrated at the beginning of the maritime season. A ship was carried on a cart and taken through the city in procession. The priest of *Isis* carried the insignia of the goddess, while the candidates, initiates and the members of the cult followed him in procession, wearing bright clothes and masks. The procession went up to the sea, and all returned to the temple after the ship was let into the sea. In the temple, initiation ceremonies, ceremonial meals and dances were organized.[199]

In the city of Rome, the cult of the Great Mother had a grandly celebrated spring festival in which renewal of life was commemorated and enacted. Closely related to the cult of the Great Mother, in Hellenistic times, were the festivals of the *Attis* mysteries. Each year at the spring equinox, a vernal festival of *Attis* was celebrated. On March 22 was celebrated an *arbor intrat*. It consisted in cutting down of a pine tree, carrying it to the temple and decorating it with ribbons and flowers. The decorated tree symbolized the god *Attis*. March 24 was the *dies sanguinis*. On this day the priests (*galli*) of *Attis* performed ecstatic dances accompanied by the sound of cymbals. While dancing they cut themselves with knives and let the blood sprinkle at the altar of the Great Mother. On March 25 was celebrated the *hilaria*. The name '*hilaria*' means joy and jubilation. But nothing is known about the reason for this jubilation. Nether do we know anything about the rites of the day. Probably the reason for joy and jubilation was the return to life of the god *Attis*. On March 26 was the day of rest (*Requietio*). On March 27 was the day of *Lavatio*. It consisted in carrying the symbol of the Great Mother, viz., the black stone, in a carriage and taking it to the river Almo to be bathed with the carriage. The washing of the stone probably symbolized the participants of the festival were washed of all iniquities and raised to a new life with the gods once again. This festival of *Attis* and that of the Great Mother were meant not only for the initiates and members of the cult, but also for anyone who wished to participate in it.[200]

The most important festival of the *Sol* mystery cult, viz., the *natalis invicti* (the birth of the unconquerable sun), was celebrated at the winter solstice on December 25, as from that day the length of the day began to increase. This festival announced the rebirth of the sun god, which promised new life to everyone who believed in the *Sol Invictus*.[201]

Thus, the celebration of the various festivals associated with the various mystery cults provided the people occasion to come in touch with the divinities of various mystery cults. They were sacred events during which the deity of the mystery cult manifested his/her presence to the devotees and instilled in them the hope of new life. Therefore, they were moments of joy, happiness and jubilation.

2.3.2.5. EXPIATION

In the spirituality of the Hellenistic mystery cults, doing expiation for one's sin was an important element. Before initiation and baptism a confession of sins was expected of the candidate. In some mystery cults the candidate narrated the story of his faults from the time of his birth up to the time of baptism in the cult, which brought about rebirth in the life of that person. The community of devotees of the cult listened to the confession of the candidate. It was believed that the rite of baptism would bring about an internal cleansing of the sins of the candidate, would change his life for the better, would enroll him in the service of the savior god and would make him worthy of new birth. The *Isis* cult, for instance, gave a great deal of importance to expiation in the life of neophytes. They were expected to fast for ten days, abstain from meat, wine and sexual activity. They must be separated from common people and live in a separate house closer to the temple. All these were aimed at helping the initiated make amends for the sins of the past. Expiation was necessary for being a genuine devotee of the cult, that it was capable of transforming a person in the image of the deity were clearly shown in the story of Lucius, which Apuleius narrated in his book *The Golden Ass*. Though Lucius had committed a great many sins in his past life, the life of expiation he undertook as the initiate of the *Isis* cult transformed him into a god, giving him a throne next to the heavenly queen *Isis*.[202]

Similarly, we find in the orphic cult of *Dionysus-Zagreus* importance was given to expiation. The aim of an orphic devotee was to liberate his soul from bodily entanglements through ascetic practices, and thereby to attain immortality in the next life. The body was considered as the tomb in which the soul was buried. So the task of the initiate was to free his soul from the body. Therefore, for the orphic neophyte, what was more important was the next life rather than the present life. Life here on earth must be lived as a continuous purgation, expiating and making atonement for the sins and evils that are inherent and implicit in the human condition.[203] The *Lavatio* rite associated with the *Attis* mystery cult, in which the black stone, the symbol of the Great was washed in the river Almo, also had an element of expiation of one's sins and iniquities.

Thus, we find that the mystery religions of the Hellenistic times stressed the importance of expiation for one's sins as the means to the new life promised to the initiates and members of the mystery cult.

In short the Hellenistic era presented a religious situation that could be called a religious syncretism. It was a time of transition and interchange in the religious realm. No absolutes were followed in one's religious affiliation. It was a time of religious freedom and religious pluralism. From among the many religious cults one could choose what one found most helpful for one's spiritual journey. Even the state allowed a great deal of religious freedom. It interfered in the religious life of a cult only if it believed that the cult in question affected the normal life of the citizens and their peaceful existence within the state. The emergence of individualism, coupled with the cosmopolitan spirit, broke the nationalistic sentiments and narrow outlook, and facilitated the recognition and acceptance of truth, wherever it was found, especially in the sphere of religion. This, in turn, led to the lessening of interest in formal religion, which was less personalized, and the emergence of more mystery cults. Mystery cults, besides giving each individual the sense of belonging to a social group of likeminded people, took care to elevate the religious feelings of the initiate, opening him to the manifestation of the deity of the cult in his personal life. The social good feeling that came from the sense of belonging to the group and the spiritual transformation brought about through the personal experience of the deity, gave the individual a tremendous sense of meaning in his life. Besides, the mystery cults did not prevent the initiate from living a normal life in the society. As a result, the life of the person became more integrated, as he was genuinely open to himself, to the divine and to others in the society, without any force from any quarters and purely of his personal choice. Though there were a number of abuses in the mystery cults and other religious movements of the Hellenistic era, they provided an atmosphere in which an individual could choose his path to the divine, pursue it with genuine freedom and enjoy its fruits in his personal and social life.

CONCLUSION

We have surveyed through the whole spectrum of the religious life of the people of the Greco-Hellenistic-Roman tradition. It is an ancient tradition, rich in its beliefs, diverse in its religious practices and resilient as open to, and integrative of, the diverse cultures that constitute it. A deeper look at this religious tradition reveals two religious elements, viz., a formal and established structure of worship and an informal and personal approach to the divine. We find the meticulously established system of gods in the Greek and Roman Pantheon, each god taking care of and having control over one or the other aspects of nature. The worship of these gods is so carefully planned and scrupulously followed. In the formal and state-controlled religion of Greece and Rome, we find a number of examples to illustrate this fact. However, not all were satisfied with formal religion, which did not suit the religious sentiments of all the adherents. People wanted something more than a well-established formal religious structure and practice as such structures often lacked the true spirit of religion, they want something more that would satisfies their personal and inner yearnings for a deeper experience of the divine. This dissatisfaction with formal religion and the inner yearning for depth experience in the sphere of religion makes man move towards informal forms of worship. In the Greco-Hellenistic-Roman tradition, the mystery cults provided this informal and personal approach to religious experience.

If we take a fleeting look at the history of this rich tradition, we find that both of these trends to religious experience, viz., the formal and the informal, have coexisted from the beginning. In the Greek and Roman religion, the formal element is very strong, so much so that the informal element, viz., the mystery cults, had to struggle for survival. We find official condemnation of some of the mystery cults and preventing the Roman citizens from taking part in some. But, as history progresses and as we come to the later Hellenistic period, we find a situation in which there is a near-rejection of the formal religion, as people choose a cult to experience the liberation they longed for. In this stage, the state officially approved the mystery cults and supported their practice. Thus, we find the history of the Greco-Hellenistic-Roman religious tradition moving from formal to informal religion, from a religion of structure to a religion of inner experience, from a national religion to a multinational religion, and from a religion-for-all-attitude to a religion-for- me-attitude. In brief, in the early moments of the history of this tradition the formal dominated, while towards the end of its history, the informal had taken supremacy over the formal.

NOTES

1 Cf. Helmer Ringgren, pp. 210-212.
2 Cf. Ibid., pp.212-213.
3 Cf. A.H. Armstrong (ed.), *Classical Mediterranean Spirituality: Egyptian, Greek, Roman* (London: SCM Press Ltd., 1986), p. xvii.
4 A.H. Armstrong, "The Ancient and Continuing Pieties of the Greek World", *Classical Mediterranean Spirituality: Egyptian, Greek, Roman*, ed. A.H. Armstrong, p. 73.
5 Cf. A.H. Armstrong (ed.), *Classical Mediterranean Spirituality: Egyptian, Greek, Roman*, p. xvii.
6 Cf. A.H. Armstrong, "The Ancient and Continuing Pieties of the Greek World", p. 73.
7 Cf. Helmer Ringgren, p. 213.
8 Cf. C.M. Bowra and the Editors of Time-Life Books, *Classical Greece* (United States: Time-Life International (Nederland) N.V., 1966), p. 17. Cf. also A.H. Armstrong, "The Ancient and Continuing Pieties of the Greek World", p. 74. Even though power was that which separated the gods from men, this gulf was never so great that it could not be bridged. Ancient Greek poems speak of men, who were considered to be descendants of gods, who were often referred to as "Heroes" and were given worship similar to that of gods. Poets mention two such Heroes, namely, Heracles and Asclepius, who were believed to have passed beyond humanity completely after their deaths and to have become gods without any qualification. They were worshipped and loved just as any other gods. Besides, there were cases of a human being of fully human parentage, being given the status of a god after his death. To cite an example, Brasidas, the Spartan general, was worshipped as a god in the city of Amphipolis, which he delivered from the Athenians. The Hellenistic and Roman cult of the worship of kings as gods derived from this ancient practice. Cf. Ibid.
9 Cf. Ibid., pp. 75-76.
10 Cf. Ibid., pp. 79-81.
11 Cf. Ibid., p. 76.

12 Ibid.
13 Cf. Ibid., pp. 76, 78.
14 Cf. Ibid., p. 78.
15 Cf. Ibid., p. 79.
16 Cf. Ibid., pp. 78-79.
17 Cf. Helmer Ringgren, p. 213. Cf. also A.H. Armstrong, "The Ancient and Continuing Pieties of the Greek World", pp. 91-92.
18 Cf. Ibid.
19 Cf. A.S.F. Gow, ed. & trans., *Theocritus*, Vol. I (London: C.U.P., 1950), p. 137. Cf. also Ninian Smart, p. 317.
20 Cf. Helmer Ringgren, p. 214.
21 W. H. Smyth (ed. & trans), *Aischylus*, Vol. II (London: Leob Library, W.Heinemann, 1950), p. 19.
22 Ibid., p. 403.
23 Cf. Helmer Ringgren, p. 214.
24 Cf. Ibid.
25 Hugh Evelyn White (ed. & trans.), *Hesiod, the Homeric Hymns, and Homerica*, (London: Leob Library, W.Heinemann, 1914), p. 3. In later thinking, due to the influence of philosophical speculation, fate was seen as a force independent of gods, to which both the gods and the humans were subjected. Cf. Helmer Ringgren, p. 214.
26 Cf. A.H. Armstrong, "The Ancient and Continuing Pieties of the Greek World", pp. 81-82.
27 Cf. Helmer Ringgren, p. 215. Cf. also C.M. Bowra, p. 180.
28 Cf. C.M. Bowra, p. 180. Cf. also Helmer Ringgren, p. 215. Cf. also A.H. Armstrong, "The Ancient and Continuing Pieties of the Greek World", pp. 83-84.
29 Cf. C.M. Bowra, p. 180. Cf. also Helmer Ringgren, pp. 215-216, 219. Cf. also A.H. Armstrong, "The Ancient and Continuing Pieties of the Greek World", pp. 84-85.
30 Cf. also Helmer Ringgren, p. 216. Cf. also C.M. Bowra, p. 181.
31 Cf. also Helmer Ringgren, p. 216. Cf. C.M. Bowra, p. 180.
32 Cf. C.M. Bowra, p. 180
33 Cf. A.H. Armstrong, "The Ancient and Continuing Pieties of the Greek World", pp. 85-87. Cf. also Helmer Ringgren, p. 216.
34 Cf. C.M. Bowra, p. 181. Cf. also Helmer Ringgren, p. 216.
35 Cf. Ibid. Cf. also Helmer Ringgren, pp. 216-217.
36 Cf. C.M. Bowra, p. 181.
37 Cf. Helmer Ringgren, p. 216.
38 Cf. Ibid., p. 213. Cf. also A.H. Armstrong, "The Ancient and Continuing Pieties of the Greek World", pp. 91-92.
39 W.H. Smyth, ed. & trans., *Aischylus*, Vol. II, p. 395.
40 Cf. Helmer Ringgren, p. 217.
41 Cf. Ninian Smart, pp. 319-320. Cf. also Helmer Ringgren, pp. 217-218.
42 Cf. Ninian Smart, pp. 320-321.

43 Cf. Helmer Ringgren, p. 219.
44 Cf. Ibid., 214, 220.
45 Cf. Ibid., p. 219
46 Cf. Ibid.
47 Cf. Helmer Ringgren, pp. 228-229.
48 Cf. Helmer Ringgren, p. 222.
49 Cf. A.H. Armstrong (ed.), *Classical Mediterranean Spirituality: Egyptian, Greek, Roman*, p. xvii.
50 Cf. Helmer Ringgren, p. 222. Cf. also A.H. Armstorng, "The Ancient and Continuing Pieties of the Greek World", p. 69.
51 Cf. Ibid.
52 Cf. A.H. Armstrong, "The Ancient and Continuing Pieties of the Greek World", pp. 69-70.
53 Cf. Ibid.
54 Ibid., p. 70.
55 Cf. Ibid.
56 Cf. Helmer Ringgren, p. 223.
57 Hugh Evelyn White, pp. 27, 29.
58 Cf. Helmer Ringgren, pp. 222-223.
59 Sir William Moris (trans.), *The Iliad of Homer*, (London: O.U.P., 1934), pp. 17-18.
60 Cf. Helmer Ringgren, pp. 220, 223.
61 Cf. Ibid., pp. 222-223.
62 Cf. Helmer Ringgren, p. 224. Cf. also Ninian Smart, p. 318.
63 Cf. Helmer Ringgren, p. 224.
64 Cf. Helmer Ringgren, pp. 224-225.
65 Cf. Ninian Smart, p. 319.
66 Cf. Helmer Ringgren, p. 218. Cf. also Ninian Smart, pp. 319-320.
67 W.D.C. Guthrie, *The Greeks and their Gods*, (London: Methen, 1950), pp. 151-152.
68 Cf. Martin P. Nilsson, *The Dionysiac Mysteries of the Hellenistic and Roman Age* (Acta Instituti Antheniensis Regni Sueciae 8.5; Lund: Gleerup, 1957), pp. 146-147. Cf. also Ninian Smart, p. 320.
69 Cf. Section No. 2.1.1.3.2.2.
70 Cf. Helmer Ringgren, pp. 229-230. Cf. also Ninian Smart, pp. 320-321.
71 Cf. Helmer Ringgren, p. 230.
72 Cf. Section No. 2.1.1.3.2.1.
73 Cf. Helmer Ringgren, p. 226. Cf. also Ninian Smart, pp. 323-324.
74 Cf. Ibid.
75 Hugh Evelyn White, p. 323.
76 Cf. Ninian Smart, p. 324.
77 Cf. Helmer Ringgren, pp. 225-226.
78 Cf. Ibid.
79 Cf. Ibid.
80 Cf. Helmer Ringgren, p. 227.

81 Cf. Ibid.
82 F.A. Paley (trans.), *The Odes of Pindar* (Cambridge: Deighton Bell & Co., 1868), p. 243.
83 F. Storr (ed. & trans.), *Sophlcles*, Vol. II, (London: Loeb library, William Heinemann, 1919), p. 19.
84 Cf. Helmer Ringgren, p. 227.
85 Hugh Evelyn White, p. 29.
86 Cf. Helmer Ringgren, p. 228.
87 Hugh Evelyn White, p. 57.
88 Cf. Ibid., pp. 27, 29.
89 Cf. Helmer Ringgren, p. 225.
90 Cf. Ibid.
91 Cf. Helmer Ringgren, pp. 238-239.
92 Cf. Ninian Smart, p. 325.
93 Cf. Ibid. Cf. also John Pinsent, "Roman Spirituality", *Classical Mediterranean Spirituality: Egyptian, Greek, Roman*, ed. A.H. Armstrong, p. 157. The sense of duty towards the gods that characterized the Roman religion gave rise to the emergence of 'the divine law' (*jus divina*), which directed what must be done and what must be avoided in the performances of rituals. Though there was hardly any moral element in the divine law initially, as time went by, the sense of duty contained in the divine law became a means of binding the relationships in the family and the state, in the process, giving rise to the Roman law. Thus, the whole fabric of the Roman law that developed later owes its origins to the piety practiced in the early Roman society. Cf. Ninian Smart, p. 325.
94 Cf. Helmer Ringgren, pp. 239, 243-244.
95 Cf. Ibid.
96 Cf. Ibid., pp. 250-252. Cf. also John Pinsent, "The Roman Spirituality", pp. 171-172, 175 -176. Cf. also Steward Perowne, p. 53.
97 Cf. Ibid.
98 Cf. Ibid.
99 Cf. Ibid.
100 Cf. Helmer Ringgren, pp. 239-240.
101 Cf. also Moses Hadas and The Editors of Time-Life Books, *The Imperial Rome*, U.S.A.: Time-Life International (Nederland) N.V., 1968, p. 121.
102 Cf. Ibid.
103 Cf. Helmer Ringgren, p. 239.
104 Cf. Ibid., pp. 240-241. Cf. also John Pinsent, "Roman Spirituality", pp. 181-183. Cf. also Stewart Perowne, *Roman Mythology*, (London: Hamlyn, 1988), pp. 13-15, 17-18.
105 Cf. Ibid.
106 Cf. Ibid.
107 Cf. Helmer Ringgren, p. 240. Cf. also John Piscent, "Roman Spirituality", p. 189. Cf. also Steward Perowne, p. 18.
108 Cf. Helmer Ringgren, p. 242. Cf. Steward Perowne, p. 30.

109 Cf. Ibid., p. 242. Cf. also John Pinsent, "Roman Spirituality", p. 182. Cf. Steward Perowne, pp. 30, 46, 47-48.
110 Cf. Helmer Ringgren, pp. 241, 242-243.
111 Cf. Ibid., pp. 241, 242-243, 250. Cf. also Stweard Perowne, pp. 12, 15, 17, 47.
112 Cf. Ibid., pp. 241-242. Cf. also John Pinsent, "Roman Spirituality", pp. 183-185. Cf. also Steward Perowne, pp. 51-53.
113 Cf. Helmer Ringgren, p. 251. Cf. also John Pinsent, "Roman Spirituality", p. 182.
114 Cf. Saint Augustine, *The City of God*, trans. Gerald G. Walsh, et al. (New York: Image Books, 1958), IV, 8.
115 Cf. Helmer Ringgren, p. 243. Cf. also John Pinsent, "Roman Spirituality", pp. 192-193. Cf. Moses Hadas, p.122.
116 Cf. Helmer Ringgren, p. 249-250.
117 Cf. Moses Hadas, p. 88.
118 Cf. John Pinsent, "Roman Spirituality", pp. 155-156. Cf. also Helmer Ringgren, p. 244, 247-248. Cf. also Moses Hadas, p. 80.
119 Cf. Helmer Ringgren, pp. 244, 247-248. Cf. also Moses Hadas, pp. 79-80.
120 Cf. Helmer Ringgren, pp. 247. Cf. also Steward Perowne, pp. 30-34.
121 Cf. Ibid.
122 Steward Perowne, pp.32-34.
123 Cf. Ibid., p. 247. Cf. also Moses Hadas, p. 125. Cf. also Steward Perowne, p. 30.
124 Cf. Ibid.
125 Cf. Ibid., p. 248.
126 Cf. Ibid., pp. 244-245. Cf. also John Pinsent, "Roman Spirituality", p. 156.
127 R.G.Kent (ed. & trans.), *De Lingua Latina*, vol. II, (London: Leob Library, W. Heinemann, 1938), p. 295.
128 J. Wight Duff, *A Literary History of Rome*, (London: Leob Library, 1960), p. 58.
129 Cf. Helmer Ringgren, p. 248.
130 V.D. Hooper and H. Ash (eds. & trans.), *De Re Rustica*, (London: Leob Library, W. Heinemann, 1934), pp. 121, 123.
131 Cf. Helmer Ringgren, p. 245-246.
132 Cf. Ibid., p. 246. Cf. also John Pinsent, "Roman Spirituality", pp. 158-161.
133 Cf. Steward Perowne, 35-46.
134 Cf. Helmer Ringgren, pp. 246, 247. Cf. also Steward Perowne, pp. 30, 37.
135 Cf. Helmer Ringgren, p. 246. Cf. also Steward Perowne, pp. 37,39.
136 Cf. Helmer Ringgren, p. 246. Cf. also Steward Perowne, p.41.

137 Cf. Steward Perowne, pp. 41, 44-45. Cf. also Helmer Ringgren, p. 247.

138 Cf. Moses Hadas, p. 127. We make a more elaborate study of some of these mystery cults in the next essay on Hellenistic religion.

139 Cf. Ibid. Cf. also Steward Perowne, pp. 62, 70. Cf. also John Pinsent, "The Roman Spirituality", pp. 172, 174-175.

140 Cf. John Pinsent, "Roman Spirituality", pp. 176-177. Roman authorities had clamped similar restrictions on worships of Judaism and Christianity, as the Roman believed that these two religions were also similar cults. In the same way, a number of other cults, such as the *Isis* cult, were also restricted. Cf. Ibid. p. 177. Cf. also Moses Hadas, p. 126.

141 Cf. Moses Hadas, p. 127. Cf. also John Pinsent, "Roman Spirituality", pp. 177-178.

142 Apuleius, *Metamorphoses*, 11.25. Translation taken from John Pinsent, "Roman Spirituality", pp. 177-178.

143 Cf. Moses Hadas, p. 127. Cf. also Steward Perowne, pp. 105-109.

144 Cf. Moses Hadas, pp. 125-126.

145 Cf. Moses Hadas, p. 125.

146 Cf. Ibid., pp. 123-124. Cf. also Helmer Ringgren, p. 250.

147 Cf. Helmer Ringgren, pp. 248-249.

148 Cf. Moses Hadas, pp. 79-84.

149 Cf. Ibid., p. 124.

150 J.P. Postgate (trans.), *Catullus, Tibullus, and Pervigilium Veneris*, (London: Leob Library, W. Heinemann, 1919), p. 253.

151 Cf. Moses Hadas, p. 125. Cf. also Steward Perowne, pp. 30-34.

152 Cf. H. Ash, pp. 121, 123.

153 Cf. Helmer Ringgren, pp. 245-246.

154 Cf. Ibid., p. 252.

155 Cf. Ibid., p. 253.

156 Cf. Ibid.

157 Cf. Ibid.

158 Cf. Ibid., pp. 253, 255-257, 263-269.

159 Cf. Ibid.

160 Cf. Ibid., pp. 260-269.

161 Cf. Ibid., p. 254.

162 Ibid. p. 256.

163 Apuleius, *The Golden Ass*, trans. S Gaselee, (London: Leob Library, W. Heinnemann, 1922), pp. 545-547.

164 Wallis Budge (trans.), *Osiris*, Vol. II, (London: Medici Society, 1911), pp. 289-292.

165 Cf. Helmer Ringgren, p. 255.

166 Cf. Ibid., pp. 253-254. Cf. also Ninian Smart, p. 331.

167 Cf. Helmer Ringgren, pp. 261-262. Cf. also Ninian Smart, pp. 333-334.

168 Cf. Helmer Ringgren, pp. 257-259.

169 Cf. Ibid., pp. 253,255.

170 Cf. Ibid., pp. 224, 226, 260.
171 Cf. 2.1.2.5.3.
172 Cf. 2.1.2.5.1. Cf. also 2.2.2.5.2.
173 Cf. 2.1.2.3.2.
174 Cf. 2.2.2.5.1.
175 Cf. Helmer Ringgren, p. 261.
176 Cf. Ibid., p. 262.
177 Cf. 2.2.2.5.3.
178 Cf. Ninian Smart, p. 331.
179 Cf. John Pinsent, "Roman Spirituality", p. 177. Cf. also Helmer Ringgren, p. 260. Cf. also Ninian Smart, pp. 331-332.
180 Apuleius, *The Golden Ass*, trans. S. Gaselee, pp. 581-582.
181 Cf. Helmer Ringgren, p. 261.
182 Cf. Ninian Smart, p. 332. Cf. also Helmer Ringgren, p. 261.
183 Cf. Helmer Ringgren, p. 261.
184 Cf. 2.2.2.5.4.
185 Cf. Ninian Smart, p. 333. Cf. also Helmer Ringgren, p. 262.
186 Cf. Ninian Smart, pp. 333-334. Cf. also Helmer Ringgren, pp. 262-263.
187 Cf. Helmer Ringgren, p. 262. Cf. also Ninian Smart, p. 334.
188 Cf. Ninian Smart, p. 334.
189 Cf. 2.2.2.5.5.
190 Cf. Helmer Ringgren, pp. 257-258.
191 Cf. Ibid.
192 Cf. Ibid., p. 258.
193 Cf. Ibid., pp. 258-259.
194 Cf. Ibid., p. 255.
195 Cf. John Pinsent, "Roman Spirituality", p. 176-177. Cf. also Helmer Ringgren, p. 251.
196 Cf. Helmer Ringgren, pp. 220-230, 260. Cf. also Ninian Smart, pp. 320-321.
197 Cf. Ibid.
198 Cf. Helmer Ringgren, pp. 218, 226. Cf. also Ninian Smart, pp. 319-320, 322-325.
199 Cf. Helmer Ringgren, pp. 260-261.
200 Cf. Ibid., pp. 261-262.
201 Cf. Ibid., p. 255.
202 Cf. Ibid., pp. 260-261.
203 Cf. Ninian Smart, pp. 320-321.

Chapter 3

Hindu Tradition

INTRODUCTION

John A. Hardon begins his essay on Hinduism saying that it "can be better described than defined",[1] as it "is more a league of religions than a single religion with a definite creed".[2] One needs to describe Hinduism because it is not a faith to which everyone must subscribe but collection of different beliefs regarding the Reality behind the universe and the individual. A single definition of Hinduism is not possible because it has multiple of doctrines, differing sects and varying practices. Besides, it has no founder or authoritative body to regulate and define the limits of orthodoxy.[3] Thus, it is more a cosmic and natural religion that emerged over a long period of time than a historical religion founded at a particular time. Besides, Hinduism is a personal religion, which one lives by personal preference rather than as imposed by an external authority. For this reason, S. Radhakrishnan says: "There has been no such thing as a uniform, stationary, unalterable Hinduism whether in belief or practice. ... [It] is movement, not a position; a process, not a result; a growing tradition, not a fixed revelation."[4] This does not mean that Hinduism has no common authoritative sources on which it is founded and basic principles that guide the lives of its adherents. In this introductory section we explore the common sources and foundational principles of Hinduism.

1. THE SOURCES OF HINDUISM

The authoritative sources of Hinduism are the Hindu Scriptures, viz., the *Sruti* and the *Smrti*. *Sruti* means 'what is heard'. It is eternal and impersonal truth, which is revealed to the sages (*rishis*) in their moments of contemplation. The rishis have nothing to do with its composition and expression. They reproduce what is heard and echo it to others. *Smrti* means 'recollection' or 'tradition'. It includes all the other sacred texts that have their origin from human sources, but which depend on *Sruti* for their validity. Thus, the authority of the *Smrti* is derived from that of the *Sruti*. Therefore, while the former is considered as the primary authority, the latter is believed to be secondary source of Hinduism.[5] We shall elaborate a bit more on these two bodies of writing that form the basis of Hinduism.

1.1. THE SRUTI

The *Sruti*, when written down, are called the *Vedas*. Thus, *Sruti* and the *Vedas* are one and the same. The only difference consists in that the former is what is heard, while the latter is a written record of what is heard. The *Vedas*, therefore, are "collections of very ancient texts which were composed in the course of centuries and which reflect the various aspects of religious life in India up to the appearance of Buddhism."[6] Since they were collected over a long period of time the *Vedas* are also called *Samhitaas* (collections) of which there are four. The first is the *Rig Veda*, which contains a collection of praises of different gods. The second, *Saama Veda*, is a collection of hymns that are chanted during sacrifices. The third is the *Yajur Veda*, which is a collection of sacrificial formulas. The fourth, *Atharva Veda*, includes a collection of charms and magical formulas.[7]

Each of these *Vedas* contains four types of texts, viz., the *Mantras*, the *Braahmanas*, the *Aaranyakas* and the *Upanishads*. The *Mantras* are hymns and praises. The *Braahmanas* are texts that deal with ritual, sacrifices and the tasks of the priests. The *Aaranyakas* or forest texts emerged as a reaction against the ritualism and sacerdotalism exalted in the *Braahmanas*. They insist on the internal rather than the external dimension of sacrifices and are propounded by hermits in the forests. The *Upanishads* contain mystical sayings revealing deep spiritual truths. They form the core of the *Vedas* and so are called *Vedaanta*, i.e., the end of the *Vedas*. Thus, in the *Rig Veda* collection we have the *Aitareya* and the *Kaushiitaki Braahmanas*, the *Aitareya* and the *Kaushiitaki Aaranyakas*, and the *Aitareya* and the *Kaushiitaki Upanishads*. In the *Sama Veda* there are the *Pancavimsa*, the *Chaandogya* and the *Talavakaara Braahmanas*, and the *Chaandogya* and the *Kena Upanishads*. *Yajur Veda* contains the *Taittiriiya* and the *Satapatha Braahmanas*, the *Taittiriiya* and the *Brhad Aaranyakas* and the *Taittiriiya*, the *Mahaanaaraayana*, the *Kathaka*, the *Maitrayaniia*, the *Svetaasvatara*, the *Brhadaaranyaka* and the *Isha Upanishads*. In the *Atharva Veda* we find the *Gopatha Braahmana* and the *Mundaka*, the *Prasana* and the *Maandukya Upanishads*. The *Mantra* texts are found throughout the four *Vedas*. Again the subject matter of the *Vedas* is divided into three major sections, viz., the *Karmakaanda*, the *Upasanakaanda* and the *Jnanakaanda*. The first deals with rituals and sacrifices. The second is concerned with worship and devotion. The third is focused on attaining the highest knowledge of the Divine. All the other texts that are not included in the above consideration of *Sruti* would be included in the secondary sources of Hinduism, viz., the *Smrti*,[8] to which we turn our attention in the next

1.2. THE SMRTI

The *Smrti* (tradition) refers to all the other religious texts that do not belong to the canon of *Sruti* and that recognize the *Vedas* as the final authority. This can be understood in a strict sense and in a broad sense. Taken strictly, *Smrti* consists of the texts known as the *Suutras*. They are short formulas and attempt to explain systematically the various branches of Vedic wisdom. The *Suutras* are divided into six disciplines, known as the 'limbs of the *Vedas* (*Vedaangas*). They are: *Suutras* that deal with astronomy (*Jyotisha*), *Suutras* that study etymology (*Nirukta*), *Suutras* that analyze grammar (*Vyaakarana*), *Suutras* that treat prosody (*Chandas*), *Suutras* that go into phonetics (*Siksaa*) and *Suutras* that consider ceremonies (*Kalpa*). Of these six *Suutras*, the most important is the last, viz., the *Kalpa Suutras*. They include three types of texts: *Srauta Suutras* that talk about sacrificial ritual, the *Grhya Suutras* that take up the domestic ceremonies and the *Dharma Suutras* that are concerned with the social behavior of various castes and the rules for the various stages of life.[9]

In the broad sense the *Smrti* literature comprises the following texts: the Codes of Law (*Dharma Saastras*), the Epics (*Itihaasas*), the Chronicles and Legends about gods (*Puraanas*), the Theological Treatises of Worship (*Aagamas*) and the Schools of Philosophy (*Darsanas*).[10] The Codes of Law contain detailed instructions to all classes of people in the society as to their specific duties in the given conditions of their existence. The great lawgivers of the Hindu tradition are Manu, Yaajnavalkya and Paraasara. The Epics are the well known *Raamaayana* and *Mahaabhaarata*. These two books expound the traditional Hindu domestic, social and national ideals through the various characters of these Epics. The *Bhagavad Giitaa*, which is a part of the *Mahaabhaarata*, orders the performance of public duty despite personal loss and sorrow. In this manner, the Codes of Law and the Epics explicitly state the Hindu *Dharma*, contained in the *Vedas*, in the context of the life of the people[11]

The *Puraanas*, originally, referred to narratives about gods and their deeds, the genealogies of kings and the lives of sages. But later, when various sects of popular Hinduism emerged, *Puraanas* were used to propagate the beliefs of each sect. Thus, the *Puraanas*, as we have them now, are sectarian texts. It is in this body of texts that the doctrine of *Avataara* has its complete development. There are 18 major *Puraanas*, divided into three categories, each related to one of the three gods (*Trimurti*).[12] The *Puraanas* related to Vishnu are the *Vishnupuraana*, the *Naaradapuraana*, the *Bhaagavatapuraana*, the *Garuudapuraana*, the *Padmapuraana* and the *Varaahapuraana*. The *Puraanas* that speak of Brahmaa are the *Brahmaandapuraana*, the *Brahmavaivartapuraana*, the *Maarkandeyapuraana*, the *Bhavisyapuraana*, the *Vaamanapuraana* and the *Brahmaapuraana*. The *Puraanas* that are linked to Siva are the *Matsyapuraana*, the *Kuurmapuraana*, the *Lingapuraana*, the *Sivapuraana*, the *Skandapuraana* and the *Agnipuraana*. According to Hindu tradition, there are another 18 subsidiary *Puraanas*, besides the 18 major ones.[13]

The *Aagamas* are the theological treatises of the various sects. They deal with the worship of the gods of the different sects and prescribe detailed courses of discipline, which the worshipper is expected to follow in order to experience the blessings of the deity. So, like the *Puraanas*, the *Aagamas* are sectarian scriptures. Depending on the deity to whose worship the *Aagamas* directed the devotee, we could speak of three categories of *Aagamas*: Firstly, the *Paancaraatra Aagamas*, which is the scripture of Vaishnavism. They proclaim the glory of Vishnu as god. They form the basis for various forms of Vaishnava Philosophy and religious practice. Secondly, *Saiva Aagamas* forms the scripture of Saivism, as a Hindu religious sect. They declare and sing the praises of Siva as god. They also form the basis for the school of Philosophy called *Saiva Siddhaanta*. Thirdly, *Saakta Aagamas* (*Tantras*) is the scripture of Saaktism. It believes that the Supreme Being possesses eternal power (*Sakti*) out of which all things have been created. The *Tantras* contain a mixture of philosophy, occultism, mysticism, magic, ritual and ethics. They announce the Supreme Deity as the Mother of the universe and worship her under one of the many names she has as the *Devii* (goddess). In spite of the differences we find in the *Aagamas* of these sects regarding the forms and methods of worship, they are very much Vedic in spirit. Therefore, they are considered as valid scriptures. The most significant element of these sectarian scriptures is the volume of devotional poetry in the popular languages of the country. Thus, the *Aagamas* succeeded in bringing the religion to the hearts of ordinary people.[14]

The *Darsanas* are the philosophical systems. They are six in number. Just as *Puraanas* and *Aagamas* are meant for the common people and have an appeal to the heart, in the same way, the *Darsanas* are meant for the scholar, and their appeal is to logical understanding. The *Darsanas* developed in the same way as the *Vedaangas*. The founder of the particular *Darsana* would compile the doctrine of the school in the form of *Suutras*. The pupils memorized these *Suutras*. Then the master attempted to explain the meaning of the *Suutras* to the pupils. The founders of the six *Darsanas* are the following. Gautama is the founder of *Nyaaya Darsana*; Kanaada is the founder of *Vaiseshika Darsana*; Kapila is the founder of *Saamkhya Darsana*; Patanjali is the founder of *Yoga Darsana*; Jaimini is the founder of *Miimaamsaa Darsana* and Baadaraayana is the founder of *Vedaanta Darsana*. These six systems are considered orthodox, as they recognize the authority of the *Vedas*.[15]

All these secondary scriptures (*Smrti*), viz., the *Dharma Saastras*, the *Itihaasas*, the *Puraanas*, the *Aagamas* and the *Darsanas*, derive their validity from the *Vedas* (*Sruti*), which are the fountainhead of the Hindu religion and culture. They are only developments of the *Vedas* over the period of time. Vedic *Rishis* and kings are the source of the first four bodies of writings. In the same way, Vedic forms of meditation and prayer give rise to the *Bhakti* doctrines of the later sects of Hinduism. Similarly, each of the *Darsanas* has its roots in the *Vedas*. The philosophical speculations of the *Vedas* form the *Vedaanta Darsana*. Vedic sacrifices shape the *Miimaamsaa Darsana*. From the cosmology and psychology of the *Vedas* develop the *Samkhya Darsana*. Achieving the religious experience of the *Vedas* leads to the foundation of the *Yoga Darsana*. Vedic metaphysical reflections fashion the logical reasoning of *Nyaaya Darsana* and metaphysical categories of the *Vaiseshika Darsana*.[16] As all the later scriptures have their origin in the *Vedas*, they also have only one aim, viz., to help the seeker to experience the Divine. Making this point D.S. Sharma says:

> And, Just as all our scriptures have a common source, they have a common aim. Their aim is to make man a perfect spirit like God and one with Him. With that aim in view they try to create political and social institutions, which will help

the spiritual development of every man according to his capacity. They rouse his imagination and quicken his intellect and form his character and thus guide him along the steep and difficult path of ascent that leads to God.[17]

Since the scriptures of Hinduism have a common source and have a common aim of helping the seeker to ascend to his spiritual destiny, they also propose some basic principles to guide the aspirant in his journey to the Divine. Now, we turn our attention to these guiding principles of Hinduism.

2. EARTHLY PRINCIPLES FOR HINDU DAILY LIFE

We will see how the Hindu sense of inner transcendence makes paths to God of the four structures of daily life, namely, the doctrines of Karma, Samsaara, the ends of life (*Purusaarthas*), the stages of life (*Aasramas*) and caste (*Varnas*). We will treat these in inverse order.

2.1. THE DOCTRINE OF CASTE

Caste is a very complex social reality. For centuries it was a dominant factor in the social system of the Hindus. One belonged to a caste by heredity one was born into a caste. People of a particular caste generally practiced the same profession. There were marriage and food taboos for various castes. The caste had the power to impose sanctions on any of its members, who violated the taboos.[18]

In ancient Hindu society, this was more a racial division of classes, rather than the strict caste system of the later period. The Sanskrit term used to refer to the class was '*Varna*', which means 'color'. The names used to refer to the four classes, viz., the *Braahman*, the *Kshatriiya*, the *Vaisya* and the *Suudra*, meant the white color, the red color, the yellow color and the black color respectively. The racial element involved in the ancient division of society is also clear from the fact that lightness or darkness of complexion became a basis for the organization of the society.[19] As time went by, it became more rigid, and a religious sanction was attached to the classes, thereby paving the way for the emergence of strict castes. The traditional account of the origin of the caste is found in the *Rig Veda*. It reads:

> With three-fourths *Purusha* [the Supreme Being] went up: one fourth of him again was here. Thence he strode out to every side over what eats not [the inanimate beings] and what eats [the animate beings]. ... When they divided *Purusha* how many portions did they make? What do they call his mouth, his arms? What do they call his thighs and feet? The *Braahman* was his mouth, of both his arms was made *Raajanya* [*Kshatriiya*]. His thigh became the *Vaisya*; from his feet the *Suudra* was produced.[20]

This passage from the *Rig Veda* clearly points to a society in which the divinely appointed kings (*Kshatriiyas*) were rulers. They were the groups of kings, warriors and aristocrats who undertook the task of protecting treasure and life. The *Braahmans* counseled them in all matters of governing, interpreted the moral and religious behaviors of the kings and other classes. They were religious teachers and performed the religious duty of sacrificing and assisting others in their sacrifices. The agriculture and all forms of trade remained in the hands of the *Vaisyas*. So they were traders, merchants and people engaged in similar professions. The *Suudras* were expected to serve the members of the other three castes. People who belonged to the first three castes were known as the twice born (*Dvijas*) and they had the privilege of going through the initiation rites (*Upanayana*) and wearing the sacred thread. The *Suddras* did not have this right, as they were the conquered people and so considered the slaves of the other castes.[21] Though the doctrine of caste is discriminatory, it did provide the ancient Hindu society with a social organization that helped the progress of the Hindu civilization.

1.2. THE DOCTRINE OF STAGES OF LIFE

Just as Hinduism attempted to regulate the social life of the people with the help of the doctrine of caste, it aimed at ordering the whole span of life of an individual, who belonged to any of the first three castes, with the help of the stages of life (*Aasramas*). There are four *Aasramas* that direct the lifespan of the member of the twice-born caste, viz., the student stage (*Brahmacaarya*), the stage of the householder (*Gaarhasthya*), the stage of the hermit in the forest (*Vaanaprasthya*) and the stage of the ascetic (*Sannyaasa*).

The student (*Brahmacaarii*) begins his student life with the initiation ceremony (*Upanayana*). He is under the guidance of the *Guru*. He stays with the *Guru*, serves the *Guru* and studies the sacred scriptures. The student is expected to abstain from wine, meat, perfumes, garlands, sweetmeats and women. He is to wear no ointments and shoes, nor to use an umbrella. Lust, anger and greed are some of those qualities he must avoid in his life. He is not allowed to dance, sing or to play a musical instrument. He must shun slander, gossip, gambling and untruth. He must not get into an argument or strike anybody. He must sleep alone in continence. All these practices help the boy to become a sturdy and energetic youth, besides giving him the concentration required to study the scriptures.[22]

After completing the student life, the *Brahmacaarii* presents gifts to his *Guru* and returns home. He marries and becomes a householder (*Grhasta*). The life of the householder is very central, as all the other *Aasrmas* find their support in the *Grhasta*. He practices duties to the gods, the ancestors, the *Braahmins*, the family members and the lower animals. The householder practices virtues, such as hospitality, almsgiving, industry and truthfulness, besides remaining faithful to the ritual and social duties prescribed by his caste. The householder also sees to it that the fathers, brothers, husbands and brothers-in-law honor the women at home. Thus, the life of the householder consists in performing various duties.[23]

When a householder sees his skin wrinkled, his hair white and his grandchildren, he must retire from the world and go to the forest, thereby becoming a hermit in the forest (*Vaanaprastha*). He, either alone or with his wife, leaves the house. He goes to the forest to spend his days in prayer, austerity and performance of sacrifices. He is expected to follow numerous restrictions. He must not take food raised by cultivation, but be satisfied with roots, flowers and fruits. He must not eat honey, flesh and mushrooms. He must wear wornout clothes, which he collects from others. These ascetic and sacrificial practices, along with the study of the scriptures, help the *Vaanaprastha* to attain complete union with the Supreme Soul.[24]

Having spent time in the forest, the *Vaanaprastha* becomes a wanderer freeing himself from all of attachments, thereby becoming a wandering ascetic (*Sannyasii*). He lives by begging. He has no shelter for himself. His attitude towards the world and life is one of total indifference. He desires neither life nor death. He waits for the appointed time, just as a laborer waits for his wages. His eyes guide his feet, truth purifies his speech, and reason governs his conduct. He accepts insults without retaliation and makes no enemy, as he knows that his body has no value. He blesses those who curse him. He finds delight in the Supreme Being and is indifferent to pleasure and pain. Having no companion except the Divine, he wanders here on earth in search of final liberation.[25]

In this manner, starting from the student stage, a twice-born passes through the stages of the householder and forest dweller, and finally arrives at the state of the hermit, which helps him to experience unity with the Absolute. The *Aasramas* regulate only the lives of those who belong to the first three castes and ignore the *Suudras* totally. In the same way, women also are excluded from the *Aasramas*. Thus life is always linked with men: as a child she is subjected to her father; as a young woman she depends on her husband; and when her husband dies she is taken care of by her sons.[26] So women are expected to acquire qualities that would help them to be good children, wives and mothers. Thus, the *Aasramas* exclude the last group in the caste ladder, viz., the *Suudras*, and women as capable of achieving the final state of union with the Supreme Being, by going through the prescribed stages of *Brahmacaarya*, *Gaarhasthya*, *Vaanaprasthya* and *Sannyaasa*. In spite of this limitation, they provide guidance for a person on the way to God.

2.3. THE DOCTRINE OF ENDS OF LIFE

Hinduism speaks of the different ends of human life, as a human seeker cannot arrive at selfless action (*Nishkaamakarma*) without effort and struggle. A human person is a composite of qualities (*Gunaas*), such as *Tamas* (darkness), *Rajas* (energy) and *Sattva* (truth and light). Depending on which of these qualities predominate in a person and his functioning, his activities are good or evil. Man can have different goals in life, depending on the influence of these *Gunas*. If one aims at satisfying the desires of one's sensuous nature, one's end in life is pleasure (*Kaama*). On the other hand, if one attempts to achieve power and material possessions, one's goal is wealth (*Artha*). Likewise, if a person seeks sound moral life as the ultimate purpose of his existence, one's aim in life is duty (*Dharma*). When a person rises above the grip of the three *Gunas*, attempts to free himself from bondage and rebirth, thereby aiming at achieving total freedom, his end in life is liberation (*Moksha*). Of these four *Purusaarthas*, the ultimate one is the attainment of *Moksha*. In order to achieve this ultimate goal of *Moksha*, a seeker must direct his desire for pleasure and possession, viz., the first two ends of *Kaama* and *Artha*, within the limits of moral law, i.e., *Dharma*. Thus, Hinduism is not puritanistic, as it does not deny the value of the first two ends of life. But rather Hinduism expects the householder to fulfill these two ends of life according to the principle of *Dharma*, thereby gradually purifying himself to achieve the final state of liberation in *Moksha*.[27] In this manner, "by glorifying the householder and sanctioning his pursuit of wealth (*Artha*) and pleasure (*Kaama*), Hinduism does justice to the flesh as well as to the spirit of man."[28]

2.4. THE DOCTRINE OF KARMA-SAMSAARA

The doctrine of *Karma* is the characteristic feature of the Hindu religious belief. It is an impersonal cosmic mechanism, which makes the present existence flow from the deeds of the past existence, the past being determined by the actions of the previous existence. The foundational reason behind the doctrine of *Karma* is strict retribution for one's actions. A man reaps what he sows. The moral law of *Karma* is comparable to the physical law of causation. When a person places his hand on the fire, the hand is burned. In the same way, when a person constantly performs an evil action, like stealing, he becomes more and more a thief. According to the law of *Karma*, the inequalities of life are not due to God, but are due to our past deeds. The mental and moral tendencies a person acquires in a particular life determine the nature and characteristics of his next life. The consequence of the law of *Karma* is the time-process called *Samsaara*, which is the state in which a person finds himself as the result of the good or evil done in the past. In the *Samsaara* state, a person is under the grip of his past *Karma*, so much so that what he thinks, plans and does are conditioned by his past thoughts, plans and actions.[29]

Hindu scriptures speak of three types of *Karma*, viz., the *Samciita Karma*, the *Aagaami Karma* and the *Praarabdha Karma*. The *Samciita Karma* is the *Karma* accumulated from the previous lives of a man that has conditioned his present character and inner tendencies. It is possible for a person to reform his character and pull up his evil tendencies with the help of moral education and discipline. The *Aagaami Karma* is the *Karma* that is accumulated in the present life and which will bear fruit in the life of the person in the future. The task of freeing oneself from this type of *Karma* is fully in the hands of the person. If a person, knowing the consequences of his action, chooses the right manner of living, he will speed up his movement towards perfection, in the process freeing himself from *Aagaami Karma*. The *Praarabdha Karma* is that part of the past accumulated *Karma* that has begun bearing fruit in a person's present life. For instance, a person's gender, family ties, bodily condition and other circumstances of his present life. These conditions cannot be changed, however hard a person tries. Therefore, *Praarabdha Karma* must be accepted and lived through.[30]

The task of a true Hindu, firstly, is to free himself from the grip of the *Samciita Karma*, which determines his character and inner tendencies of the present *Samsaara* existence. This freedom is achieved by way of genuine moral disciple, asceticism and penance. Secondly, the seeker of God-experience must take care to regulate the *Aagaami Karma*, which determines his future existence by an authentic plan for his present moral, life as he lives out the state of present *Samsaara*. In doing so, he is able to accumulate good *Karma* in living the present *Samsaara* existence, which in turn, leads him to a perfect living in the future. Thirdly, the aspirant seeking perfection must accept the *Praarabdha Karma* and live through it in all humility and resignation. In doing so, the seeker of God is able to achieve freedom from all types of *Karma* and to free oneself from *Samsaara*, thereby experiencing the Divine, which is the highest goal of human living. Thus, the law of *Karma* does not lead one to despair, as it reminds the aspirant that, though the fruits of the past actions determine his present condition and the present *Karma* conditions his future existence, he is free to take the necessary action both to remove the effects of the past *Karma* and to regulate the effects of the present *Karma*. Like a farmer who can either till the land given to him and cultivate the desired crop or allow it to be a wasteland, in the same way the seeker of God is free to accept the land of his present *Samsaara* and make it a means to God-realization or to get lost in it. In this manner, the law of *Karma* not only speaks of determination and retribution, but also speaks of the individual person's power to change his destiny and to achieve the realization of God, with the help of human effort and the grace of God.[31]

In this introductory section to our chapter on the Hindu tradition, we have attempted to show the common sources and foundational principles of Hinduism, in spite of the fact that it is divergent and many-sided. In the ensuing essays we elaborate the divergent character of Hinduism, by examining Vedic Hinduism, Vedaantic Hinduism, Vaishnavism and Saivism.

3.1. VEDIC HINDUISM

The *Vedas* form the basis of Hindu religion. All the later developments we find in the Hindu religious beliefs and practices are present in an embryonic form in the *Vedas*. But the Hinduism of the Vedic times is different from the later Hinduism in a number of ways. The gods who were held in high honor in Vedic Hinduism seem to lose their significance in later Hinduism. For instance, *Indra*, who was a prominent god in the Vedic hymns, loses his importance in the later Hinduism. Besides, the Vedic Hinduism is simple, less speculative and more pastoral. In this essay we attempt to consider the major features of the Vedic perception of gods, examine into the gods and goddesses of the Vedic Pantheon and elaborate the paths Vedic Hinduism used to come in touch with these gods and goddesses.

3.1.1. MAJOR FEATURES OF VEDIC PERCEPTION OF GODS

The Pantheon of gods we find in the Vedic literature is highly unstructured. The interest of the *Rig Veda* is to sing the praises of the gods in the ritual context rather than to present in detail their origins and deeds. Unfortunately, even from the cultic context we are not able to figure out many details about the gods. Therefore, it is difficult to reconstruct a lucid mythology of the Vedic gods.[32] Despite this difficulty the Vedic hymns give us some understanding of the deities of the Vedic period. From them we can identify a few significant features of the Vedic perception of gods. In this section we make an attempt to outline some of these features that are characteristic of the way the Vedic seers perceived the divinities.

3.1.1.1. ANTHROPOMORPHISM

The simplicity of the people of Vedic times made them consider that the gods were like humans. Thus, for them the gods are essentially human in nature. They require food and drink, fight wars, experience happy times and sorrowful moments in their lives.[33] Thus, we find anthropomorphism in their conception of the gods. Though the gods are similar to men in nature, they are endowed with supernatural powers. They are immortal. Some reasons given for their achieving immortality are the practice of austerity, drinking of the *Soma* juice[34] and the activities of the Fire god (*Agni*).[35]

Since Vedic people considered the gods in terms of humans, they also believed that the gods, like human beings, must originate from a pair, having a male and a female element. Thus, all important gods of the Vedic period and those gods who came to prominence in the post-Vedic Hinduism are believed to have been brought to existence by the common parents, viz., the god of the sky (*Dyaus*) and the goddess of the earth (*Prthivii*). They form a divine couple, becoming the universal father and mother of all the gods[36] and the created world.[37] In the *Rig Veda* we read: "*Dyaus* is my Father, my begetter: kinship is here. This great earth [*Prthivii*] is my kin and Mother. Between the widespread world-halves is the birth-place [of the gods and the created world]: the Father laid the Daughter's germ within it."[38] These two deities are so interdependent that they are always part of the dual compound *Dyaavaaprthivii*, the Sky-Earth. They sanctify each other through their relationship.[39] Together they are said to kiss the center of the world.[40] There is an indication in the *Rig Veda* that these two were together and were separated at the decree of *Varuna*.[41] But they came together again when *Dyaus* fertilizesd *Prthivii* with abundant rain and blessed the universe.[42] There is a hymn in the *Rig Veda* that speaks of the god *Suurya* as the son of *Dyaus* and *Prthivii*. To quote:

Thus Heaven and Earth, bestow prosperity on all sustainers of the region, Holy Ones and wise. Two Bowls of noble kind: between these Goddesses the fulgent Sun, travels by fixed decree. ... Son of these Parents, he the Priest with power to cleanse, Sage, sanctifies the worlds with his surpassing power. Thereto for his bright milk he milked through the days that party-colored Cow and the Prolific Bull. Among the skillful Gods most skilled is he, who made the two world-halves which bring prosperity to all; Who with great wisdom measured both the regions out, and stabilized them with pillars that shall ne'er decay.[43]

From the fact that the people of Vedic times perceived the gods in terms of humans, even relating to their origin, clearly points to the anthropomorphism present in the Vedic conception of the gods.

3.1.1.2. NATURALISM

Besides the anthropomorphism, which we find in the Vedic understanding of the gods, we notice also the deification of natural phenomena. Celestial natural phenomena, like the sun, sky, moon, rain, air, thunder and lightening are deified and given godly qualities. Similarly, terrestrial objects like fire, earth, plants and rivers are considered to possess divine nature. In the same way, natural realities like the dawn and the night are seen as divine. The origins of many of the Vedic gods, in this manner, can be traced to the phenomena of nature. Thus, the deification and worship of nature and her various elements are significant characteristics the Vedic Hinduism.[44] The naturalism present in the Vedic perception of gods does not mean that the people of Vedic times did not have a genuine experience of the Divine. On the contrary, their experience of the Divine in manifold realities of nature only points their mystical perception of all natural realities as manifestaions of the Divine. The trends to unify gods which we find in the Rig Vedic hymns points also to the depth-level experience of the Divine by the people of Vedic times particularly in and through the natural phenomena.

3.1.1.3. MONOTHEISTIC TRENDS

Though Vedic Hinduism is seemingly polytheistic, there are monotheistic elements. In the Hindu religion of the *Vedas*, we find a strong trend towards the unification of many gods and their functions in the one. Firstly, in the hymns of the *Rig Veda*, there is a tendency towards an interrelationship of gods. This interrelationship often amounts to a comingling of gods, in which one merges into the other and emerges from the other. For instance, water is said to be divine. But from the waters of the clouds emerges the fire of lightening. Similarly fire in its descent to the earth enters into water. Thus, water contains an element of fire, and so the god *Agni* is said to be the son of the waters. In this manner, we find the unification of the divine elements of fire and water in *Agni*.[45] We find another statement in the *Rig Veda* to illustrate this point. "Thou at thy birth art *Varuna*, O *Agni*; when thou art kindled thou becomest *Mitra*. In thee, O Son of Strength, all Gods are centered. *Indra* art thou to man who brings oblation."[46] Secondly, there is an amalgamation of functions and powers of the various gods. For instance, *Agni* repells demons by fire, while *Indra* performs the same function with the help of thunderbolts. Similarly, *Varuna*, *Indra* and *Vishnu* can perform the task of moving through the earth, the air and the sky, the first as the upholder of the physical order of the universe, the second as the great active god, the third as one who strides through the world.[47]

The merger of persons and the functions of the gods break down the domains and boundaries of the different gods. The activities of these gods seem to emerge from a much deeper and foundational reality, to which every god is a manifestation. In each god the same function of the foundational reality is accomplished in a different way, depending on the type of manifestation that god is. There are a number of indications in the *Rig Veda* to point to this truth. We quote a few texts to illustrate this point. "They call him *Indra*, *Mitra*, *Varuna*, *Agni*, and he is heavenly nobly-winged *Grautmaan*. To what is One, sages give many a title: they call it *Agni*, *Yama*, *Maatarisvan*."[48] "Him with fair wings though only One in nature, wise singers shape, with songs, in many figures."[49] In these texts the terms 'Him' and 'One', to which various names are given, refer to the foundational reality, of which all the gods are manifestations. The foundational reality, which is referred to by the terms 'Him' and 'One' is the Divine Being, the One Supreme Spirit that is the source of everything in the universe. Thus, in the religion of the *Rig Veda* we find a strong tendency towards monotheism, in spite of the seeming polytheism.

Again the hymns of *Rig Veda* exhibit a tendency to exalt one god as supreme over the others, though the hymns recognize many gods. Here, the particular divinity invoked is considered supreme and absolute. He is treated as the only object of worship and the only god who can satisfy the desires of the worshippers. All the supreme qualities of the other gods are attributed to him.[50] For instance, *Indra* is described as the giver of life to Sun, Dawn and Heaven, the slayer of *Vrtra* and her mother *Daanu*, the King of all that moves and moves not, the invisible Wealth-giver and the one who raises the Sun in the morning.[51] Similarly, other gods like *Agni* and *Varuna* are praised. This attitude can be described as "one-god-at-a-time-ism". Though many gods are acknowledged, within the context of a particular hymn a given god is addressed as supreme.[52] Swami Harshananda, while recognizing such a tendency in the Vedic hymns to exalt one god over all others, says that this attitude only expresses the devotee's singular devotion to his chosen deity (*Ishanishtha*), through whom the Absolute Being is worshipped and praised.[53] Thus, the tendency of the Vedic hymns to praise a deity over the others, in fact, amounts to the worship of the Absolute Divine Spirit that is manifested in every deity, which the devotee worships through his chosen deity (*Ishtadevata*).

This monotheistic trend is clearly manifest in the hymn of *Rig Veda*, commonly known as the '*Purusha Suukta*'. *Purusha* is the embodied spirit, i.e., Man personified. It is regarded as the soul of the universe, the personal and life-giving spirit in all living beings. It is a being that is one with all created beings. It contains within itself the whole universe, what was and what is yet to come. *Purusha* is the Lord of the immortal world of the gods that grows because of the sacrificial offerings of men. The whole universe emerges in the context of the great general sacrifice the gods offered, having *Purusha* as the victim of sacrifice. From this sacrifice emerged the seasons, forests, every creature of the air, animals both wild and tame. The different *Vedas*, the caste divisions within the society and all living beings originated also from this sacrifice. Besides, the sacrifice of *Purusha* generated the celestial, the atmospheric and the earthly regions and the gods, such as, the Moon, the Sun, *Indra*, *Agni* and *Vaayu*. Thus, all that exists – from the least to the greatest – including the gods - came from the *Purusha*, who is all.[54] Since this hymn sees the whole universe and even the gods as emerging from the *Purusha*, it indicates the monotheistic trend that is found in the Vedic Hinduism.

The hymn of the *Rig Veda* dedicated to 'the Unknown God' (*Ka*), clearly points to the tendency towards monotheism in the Vedic religion. In fact, this hymn attempts to show the superiority of *Prajaapati*,[55] as the Lord of the Universe. A number of questions are raised as to who (*ka*) is the source of the origin of the universe and all it contains. *Prajaapati* is presented as the answer to these questions. He appears as the Giver of vital breath, the Ruler of all the moving world, the Lord of men and cattle, the Maker of the regions of the world and all they contain, the Generator of worship, the God of the gods, the Heaven's Creator, the one who comprehends all created things. Thus, *Prajaapati* is the creator God par excellence and the Supreme Being. In the *Rig Veda* many of the Vedic gods lose their functional importance, and there is a strong movement towards the unification of the functions of the various gods in the one. This tendency leads to monotheism.[56] Hence in *Prajaapati* of the Vedic Hinduism, we find all the semblances of the monotheistic God. It is from this monotheistic tendency that we find in the Vedic religion that the philosophical enquiry leading to the discovery of the Absolute *Brahman* in the *Upanishads* has its origin.[57]

From our consideration in this section, we conclude that, in the Vedic Hinduism there is an underlying monotheism. Swami Harshananda puts this truth as follows:

> The variety of the deities [of the Vedic Hindu Pantheon] is as fascinating as it is bewildering. However, as long as we do not forget that the divine form we worship is an embodiment of the attributes that reveal the Supreme Principle in one way or other, we are on safe ground. This knowledge should develop into an intense awareness of the Reality that is at the back of everything in the universe.[58]

3.1.2. GODS OF THE VEDIC PANTHEON

Our consideration of the perception of the *Vedas* about the gods, takes us to the topic of the classification of the gods in the Vedic Pantheon. The Vedic sages attempted to classify the gods of the Vedic Pantheon based on their conception of the universe. They perceived the world as constituted of three regions, viz., the upper region, the middle region and the lower region. The sky (*Svar*) represents the upper region, the atmosphere (*Bhuva* or *Antariksha*) stands for the middle region and the earth (*Bhur*) denotes the lower region. Accordingly, the Vedic gods are grouped into the gods of the sky, the gods of the atmosphere and the gods of the earth. Though this division seems very simple and clear, if accepted, it would lead to further confusions, as some of the gods engage in different activities each of which could pertain to different spheres. For example the activities of the god *Agni* are expresses as burning fire in the terrestrial region, as lightening in the atmospheric region and as bright light in the upper region of the universe. If we go by this triple division of the gods, *Agni* must be included in all three regions. Thus, we cannot accept this triple division to classify the Vedic Pantheon.[59]

In this essay we attempt to classify the gods of the Vedic Pantheon, following an approach that is in line with the suggestion made in the *Rig Veda*. The goddess *Vaak* says: "I travel with the *Rudras* and the *Vasus*, with the *Aadityas* and All-Gods [*Visvedevas*]. I wander. I hold aloft both *Varuna* and *Mitra*, *Indra* and *Agni*, and the Pair of *Asvins*."[60] In this verse from the *Rig Veda*, the principal gods are mentioned first collectively and then individually. Our approach in exploring the Vedic Pantheon is the same. Firstly, we endeavor to explore the various groups of gods mentioned in the *Vedas*. Secondly, we move on to study the major individual male and female gods. Thirdly, we unravel the tendency toward unification of the gods and monotheism as found in the *Vedas*.

3.1.2.1. GROUP OF DEITIES

The above quoted verse from the *Rig Veda* speaks of four groups of gods. They are *Rudras*, *Vasus*, *Aadityas* and *Visvedevas*. There are also some other smaller groups of gods mentioned in other texts of the *Vedas*. In this section, we explore these groups of gods.

3.1.2.1.1. Rudras

There are differing views as to the number of gods included in the group of deities called the *Rudras*. Some say they are 11 in number and are actually principles of life, viz., the 10 vital breaths (*Praanas*) and the mind. But others say that they are eight in number. The names of the eight are *Bhava, Sarva, Isaana, PaspathiI, Bhima, Ugra, Mahaadeva* and *Rudra*.[61]

The most significant god of this group is the *Rudra*. He is tall and has a well-built body. His body is brilliant and his color matches the golden ornaments he wears. He has long, braided hair. Thus, though he is not a predominant deity in the *Rig Veda*, he has a marked individuality and a colorful appearance. The origin of *Rudra* is not very clear. According to mythology it is said that when he was born, he wept. *Prajapati*, his father asked the reason for his weeping. The child replied that he wept because he had no name. Then *Prajapatii* named him *Rudra*. The root '*rud*' means 'to weep'. Besides, the word '*rudra*' means 'the howler', 'the roaring one', 'the terrific one', 'the red one' and 'the remover of pain'. He is also considered as the god of the thunderbolt and of storms. He is also the god of wild communities living in the mountains and forests, who give themselves to anti-social activities.[62]

Thus, *Rudra* is a god who howls and roars. He is a terrible god, who instills fear in others. He holds a number of weapons, of which the bow and arrow are prominent. With his bow and arrow he spreads disease and death. In the early popular mythology *Rudra*, the red one, not *Yama*, was believed to be the god of death. Even the gods fear him, as he is believed to be the strongest one. His anger can never be appeased. Therefore, the best one can do is to pray that his anger is directed against someone else, especially one's enemies. He is invoked in prayer that he may not destroy people, their horses, cattle and fields. He is given flattering attributes, such as, 'the destroyer' (*Hara*) and 'the Lord of the Livestock' (*Pasupati*), in order to placate him, thereby prevent him from doing harm. Therefore, most of the cults offered to *Rudra* are aimed at satiating him and averting his dangerous, destructive presence.[63]

Though *Rudra* is terrible and fearsome, he is merciful and benevolent to humanity.[64] Though furious, he is mild; though he curses, he blesses. He is a god who sends sickness on men and cattle and he is the physician who cures people's illnesses with the many of remedies at his disposal. He even heals people of illnesses sent down on them by other gods. [65] Though there is a preventive purpose in the *Rudra* cult, there are prayers offered to *Rudra* that seek his genuine blessing. To quote from *Rig Veda*:

> By worship of the Gods we, O Bounteous One, O *Rudra*, gain they grace, Ruler of Valiant men. Come to our families bringing them bliss: may we, whose heroes are uninjured, bring the sacred gifts. Hither we call for aid the wise, the wanderer, impetuous *Rudra*, perfecter of sacrifice. May he repel from us the anger of the Gods: verily we desire his favorable grace.[66]

In *Rudra* of the Vedic period the opposites meet, but are not totally reconciled. As a result, despite the gracious and merciful overtones to his character, he still remains a god, who is terrible and fearsome.[67] Sometimes he is identified with the god *Agni*. *Rudra* is spoken as the father of *Martus*, another class of Vedic deities. Some of the names attributed to *Siva*[68] in the later mythological writings, such as, *Kapardin* and *Mahaadeva* are attributed to *Rudra* in the *Rig Veda*.[69] Thus, *Rudra* is the most significant god of the first group of gods called the *Rudras*.

3.1.2.1.2. Vasus

The *Vasus* are another group of deities mentioned in the *Vedas*. The term '*vasu*' comes from the Sanskrit root '*vas*', which means 'to dwell', 'to cause to dwell' and 'to shine'. Therefore, the *Vasus* are deities, who represent all spheres of extension, space and height. They are considered to be chief attendants of the god *Indra*. So their movement and activities are associated with *Indra*. The eight *Vasus* are: *Dhara* (the earth), *Anala* (the fire), *Ap* (the waters), *Anila* (the wind), *Dhruva* (the polestar), *Soma* (the moon), *Prabhaasa* (the dawn) and *Pratyuusha* (the light). As each of the *Vasus* is associated with one or the other elements of nature, they are believed to be the personifications of the different natural phenomena.[70]

3.1.2.1.3. Aadityas

The *Aadityas* is another collection of deities. The name '*Aaditya*' is another name for the Sun god (*Suurya*). Therefore, *Aadityas* are a group of gods associated with the Sun. They are said to be imperishable eternal beings that are the gods of light. They manifest and sustain all aspects of light and luminosity in the universe. The *Aadityas* are believed to be personifications of the laws that rule the universe and human society. They direct, regulate and control relationships among human beings, besides guiding their associations with the forces of nature. There are differing opinions as to their number. The *Rig Veda* speaks of six *Aadityas*, while most of the *Braahmanas* consider them to be eight. The *Satapatha Braahmana* says that the *Aadityas* are twelve in number, and in the later Hindu mythological literature they are always twelve. Their names are: *Mitra* (the friend), *Varuna* (one who encompasses and binds), *Aaryaman* (the destroyer of foes), *Daksha* (the skillful), *Bhaga* (the gir), *Amsa* (the liberal), *Tvashtr* (the shaper), the *Savitr* (the vivifier), *Puushan* (the nourisher), *Saktra* (the mighty), *Vivasat* (the resplendent) and *Vishnu* (the pervader). The twelve *Aadityas* associated with twelve aspects of the Sun spread over the twelve months of the year and so are portrayed as the twelve spokes of the wheel of time.[71]

3.1.2.1.4. Visvedevas

The term '*visvedevas*' literally mean 'all the gods'. It is not clear what is actually intended in the use of this word. Some authors suggest that this group might have included all the gods whose names are not specifically mentioned in prayers. Whatever may be its origin gradually this group evolved into a collection of gods similar to the groups we mentioned earlier. The *Visvedevatas* are said to be the protectors of the eternal moral law (*Rita*). They destroy the enemies of their devotees. They protect every good person and provide auspicious dwelling places. They give the kings control over their enemies. Later Hindu mythology speaks of the *Visvedevatas* as 10 in number. They are: *Vasu* (the dwelling place), *Satya* (the truth), *Kratu* (the will), *Dak-*

sha (the Skill), *Kaala* (the time), *Kaama* (the desire), *Dhrti* (the forbearance), *Kuru* (the ancestor of the *Kurus*), *Puruuravas* (a dwelling place in the atmosphere) and *Madravas* (the cry of joy). The *Visvedevatas* are said to be young and handsome. The offerings of the devotees easily appease them.[72]

3.1.2.1.5. Maruts

The *Maruts* are the group of stormgods. They are sportive and move about brilliantly in their chariots, unopposed by anyone. The *Maruts* are said to move about illuminating the clouds in the spotted deer (*Prishati*), their animal. With the help of the spears and draggers they hold, they produce the thunderbolt. The glittering ornaments that adorn them cause lightening. It is said of the *Maruts* that they had surpassing strength as soon as they were born, that they thundered and swept over the whole sky, driving away clouds from all corners. Their strength makes men and mountains tremble.[73] The god *Rudra* is believed to be their father.[74] They are referred to as "the boys of *Rudra*" (*Rudrasya Maryah*),[75] "the many youths of *Rudra*"[76] and "the offspring of *Rudra*".[77] Though *Maruts* are born of *Rudra*, they are always associated with *Indra*, who is the principal stormgod. It is with the help of the *Maruts* that *Indra* fights against *Vrtra*. They used the same weapon as *Indra*. Generally the *Maruts* are invoked in the plural.[78] Prayers are addressed to the *Maruts* in praise of their mighty power and asking for their bounteous blessings. We quote a prayer addressed to this group of gods in the *Rig Veda*:

> The *Maruts*, who with the golden tires of their wheels increase the rain, stir up the clouds like wanderers on the road. They are brisk, indefatigable, they move by themselves; they throw down what is firm, the *Maruts* with their brilliant spears make (everything) reel. We invoke with prayer the offspring of *Rudra*, the brisk, the pure, the worshipful, and the active. Cling for happiness-sake to the strong company of the *Maruts*, the chasers of the sky, the powerful, and the impetuous. The mortal whom ye, *Maruts*, protected, he indeed surpasses people in strength through your protection. He carries off booty with his horses, treasures with his men; he acquires honorable wisdom, and he prospers. Give, O *Maruts*, to our Lords strength glorious, invincible in battle, brilliant, wealth-acquiring, praise-worthy, known to all men. Let us foster our kith and kin during a hundred winters. Will you then, O *Maruts*, grant unto us wealth, durable, rich in men, defying all onslaughts? – Wealth a hundred and a thousand-fold, always increasing? – May he who is rich in prayers (the host of the *Maruts*) come early and soon![79]

3.1.2.1.6. Asvins

The *Asvins* are a group of two gods. They are called the twins. They are always spoken of, and praised, together. What these two gods represent is not clear. While some say that the *Asvins* stand for the earth and the sky, others say that they correspond to night and day. A third group is of the opinion that the *Asvins* embody the moon and the sun.[80] According to an Aryan myth, the *Asvins* were not gods initially, but were kings, who lived an itinerant life as helpers of mankind. As helpers of mankind they achieved such extraordinary merit, that after a pact with the god *Indra*, they were elevated to the position of the *Devas*. They, thus, became 'the helper gods' (*Dhishnya*), who sent prosperity and happiness to all. Their chief characteristic is that they constantly strive to bring good to others. They are also called 'the healers' (*Naasatyas*), as they are expert physicians, who bring healing and rejuvenation. They also help people to come together in marriage. Childless parents pray to the *Asvins* for the boon of children. He is also supplicated for food, wealth, health and protection from enemies.[81] A hymn from the *Rig Veda* highlights these characteristics of the *Asvisn* as follows:

> When, *Asvins*, ye equip your very mighty charriot, bedew, you Twain, our power with honey and with oil. To our devotion give victorious strength in war: may we win riches in the heroes' strife for spoil. ... Bring hither nourishment for us, ye *Asvins* Twain; sprinkle us with your whip that drops with honey-dew. Prolong our days of life, wipe out our trespasses; destroy our foes, be our companions and our Friends. Ye store the germ of life in female creatures; ye lay it up within all living beings. ... Leeches are ye with medicines to heal us, and charioteers are ye with skill in driving. Ye strong, give sway to him who brings oblation and with his heart pours out his gifts before you.[82]

In their varied activities as helpers, a number of other 'prosperity gods' assist the *Asvins*. For instance, the god *Puushan*, the protector of roads and pastures, help them in many ways. That is why the *Asvins* are invoked along with the gods *Puushan* and *Aryaman* during the Vedic wedding ritual. Thus, with the *Asvins*, *Puushan* and *Aryaman* become part of this group of gods.[83]

Another goddess associated with the *Asvins* is the goddess *Suuryaa*, the daughter of the sun god *Suurya*, sometimes also known as *Savitr*. According to mythology the *Asvins* were wedded to the goddess *Suuryaa*, after they had won a race. The *Asvins* are often described as riding in a chariot with her and in winning her, they are said to have achieved all their desires.[84]

3.1.2.1.7. Dyaavaaprthivii

The *Dyaavaaprthivii*, the Sky-Earth, is another group of two deities, who are always found together. This group includes the sky god *Dyaus* and the earth goddess *Prthivii*. They form a couple and a dual compound *Dyaavaaprthivii*, who become the universal Father and Mother of the gods and the whole created order.[85] Other than the role of being the Parents of the gods and the world, the *Dyaavaaprthivii* are praised for the supportive role they play in the lives of the people. The Sky-Earth is said to uphold and support all things in the universe, as they are broad, wide and remain motionless.[86] The waters they produce are described as fat, full, fertile and nourishing everything that is in the world. Besides, they provide dwelling places for every creature.[87] The *Dyaavaaprthivii* are prayed to for protection from people from danger, to forgive them and expiate their sins[88] and to bring people a sense of security and happiness.[89] The Sky-Earth represent a realm of abundance and safety, a realm that is guided by *Rta*, the eternal moral order, which strengthens and nourishes every reality in the universe.[90]

Having mentioned some of the group of gods found in the Vedic writings, we move on to consider the individual Deities that appear in the Vedic texts.

3.1.2.2. INDIVIDUAL DEITIES

The *Vedas* speak of a number of individual deities. In the Vedic writings the gods play a more dominant role than the goddesses. Though a number of female deities are praised in the *Rig Veda*, none of them gets the importance that is given to some of the male deities such as *Agni*, *Soma* or *Indra*. Only the goddess *Ushas* is accorded the importance that is given to the second level male deities, such as *Varuna* or *Mitra*. Therefore, in Vedic Hinduism, the male deities form the center of religious practice.[91] In this section, we will attempt to explore briefly all the major gods and goddesses of the Vedic period. For the sake of clarity, we take up the study of the gods first and then proceed to analyze Vedic goddesses.

3.1.2.2.1. Vedic Gods

Some of the major male deities, whose names appear in the Vedic hymns, are *Indra*, *Agni*, *Varuna*, *Soma*, *Suurya*, *Vaayu*, *Vishnu* and *Yama*. In this section, we briefly study their main features and functions.

3.1.2.2.1.1. Indra

Indra is the chief deity of the Vedic Period. His importance is shown in that nearly one fourth of the hymns of the Rig Veda sing his praises. He is the most individualized god of the Vedas and finds a concrete existence among the gods. He is the most significant god of the atmosphere (Antariksha). Indra is believed to be the god of the storm, the one who brings rain and dew. His consort is Indraanii. She is also known as Sacii, which means a helper.[92]

Indra had many with a number of other Vedic gods. He is closely associated with Soma, who is an earthly god. He is fond of the Soma juice and from drinking the Soma juice receives all the energy needed for his various daring deeds. A hymn highlights this point: "O, Soma-drinker, thunder-armed, friend of our lovely featured dames, and of our Soma drinking friends. Thus, Soma-drinker, May it be; thus, friend, who wieldest thunder, act to aid each wish as we desire".[93] His love for the Soma juice is so much that in order to get this energizing drink from his father Dyaus, he seized his father by the foot and killed him.[94] While drinking the Soma juice he enjoys the company of Agni.[95] Besides, Indra and Agni are similar in nature. Indra is said to generate Agni, and the latter is found in the waters. There are hymns that praise both of these gods in common. They are considered to be twins, born of the same parents, viz., Dyaus and Prthivii, impetuous in strength and addressed as partners.[96] Indra is also associated with the troops of storm-gods called the Maruts. They follow him wherever he goes. He is also identified with Suurya. "Suurya is he: throughout the wide expanses shall Indra turn him, swift as car wheels hither, like a stream resting not but ever active: he has destroyed with light, the black-hued darkness".[97] Though Indra has good relationships with a number of gods, his relationship with the god Varnua is not cordial. Though there are texts from Rig Veda that speak of them as working together,[98] there was no lasting peace between these two gods. The rivalry reaches it peak, when Varuna asserts his primacy over Indra, assuming all the qualities of Indra for himself.[99] A similarity between both of these gods is their ability to bind their enemies and imprison them with their magical powers.[100]

Indra is the good of absolute strength.[101] He is a warlike god, brutal in the expression of his strength. With his power and might, he is said to have separated the earth and sky.[102] He is armed with the thunderbolt (*Vajraaydha*). His awe-inspiring valor is praised in many of the Vedic hymns. *Indra's* feats are, indeed, many. He killed, *Vrtra*, the dragon, and his mother *Daanu*, who were blocking the course of water. Having drunk *Soma* juice, he slew them with a thunderbolt and set free the water, which fertilizes the earth. In accomplishing this task, *Indra* made use of a 'bond' to bind *Vrtra* without cords, using his magical power of imprisonment.[103] We read in the *Rig Veda*:

> I will declare the manly deeds of *Indra*, the first that he achieved, the Thunder-wielder. He slew the Dragon, then disclosed the waters, and cleft the channels of the mountain torrents. ... Impetuous as a bull, he chose the *Soma*, and in three sacred beakers drank the juices. *Maghavan* grasped the thunder for his weapon, and smote to death this first-born of the dragons. ...Then he humbled the strength of *Vrtra's* mother: *Indra* hath cast his deadly bolt against her. The mother was above, the son was under, and like a cow besides her calf lay *Daanu*. Rolled in the midst of never-ceasing currents flowing without a rest forever onward. The waters bear off *Vrtra's* nameless body: the foe of *Indra* sank to during darkness.[104]

As he released the water, by defeating the cloud-demon *Vrtra* with the help of the thunderbolt, he is known as the rain god. *Indra* also clipped the wings of the mighty mountain. He also recovered the cows of the gods that the demons had abducted. As the war god, he became a symbol of royal power and hence warriors worshipped him before they went to the battlefield.[105]

Indra has been equated with the Supreme God. "*Indra* is the sovereign Lord of Earth and Heaven; *Indra* is the Lord of waters and mountains; *Indra* is the Lord of the prosperous and sages; *Indra* must be invoked in rest and effort".[106] He is also spoken as the one who gives life to many other gods. "When, *Indra*, thou has slain the dragon's firstborn, and overcame the charms of enchanters, ... giving life to Sun and Dawn and Heaven, thou foundest not one foe to stand against thee".[107] *Indra* is the royal king of everything in the universe. "*Indra* is King of all that moves and moves not, of creatures tame and horned, the Thunder-wielder. Over all living men he rules as *Sovran*, containing all as spokes within the wheel".[108] In all his manifestations the god *Indra* represents the natural phenomena of rain released from the dark clouds, supported by lightening and thunder, and nourishing all creatures both living and non-living. In some of the temples, *Indra* is depicted in a human form with four arms, riding on his animal, the celestial elephant called *Airaavata*.[109]

3.1.2.2.1.2. Agni

Agni is the god of fire. He is the second most important of the Vedic gods after *Indra*. Since Vedic Hinduism was mainly sacrificial, *Agni*, as the god of fire, held an important place. This is clear from the fact that over 200 hymns are devoted to his praise in the *Rig Veda*.[110] The fire god is the mediator and messenger between the gods and men, between the divine world and the human world. He carries the offerings of men to the gods and brings to men the blessings of the various gods.[111] So *Agni* is believed to be the first priest and minister of sacrifice. The first hymn in the *Rig Veda* highlights this priestly role of the god *Agni* as follows:

> I laud *Agni*, the chosen Priest, God, minister of sacrifice, the *hotar* [the first sacrificial priest] lavishest of wealth. ... *Agni* the perfect sacrifice, which thou encompassest about. Verily goeth to the gods. May *Agni*, sapient-minded Priest, truthful, most gloriously great, [the] God, come hither with the Gods. ... Ruler of sacrifices, guard of Law eternal, radiant one, Increasing in thine own abode. Be to us easy of approach, even as a father to his son. *Agni*, be with us for our weal.[112]

Though *Agni* is a minister and priest of sacrifice, who is with man as his kinsman, he is god to all men.[113] He is a great god, all knowing, all powerful, all merciful and surpasses everything in greatness.[114] He is praised as the Supreme God, the creator, the sustainer and the all-pervading spirit. He is born in heaven, in the atmosphere and on the earth, and is manifest on the earth as *Agni*, in the atmosphere as lightening and in the sky as the Sun. So all gods are said to be his manifestations.[115] "He [*Agni*] is the meeting place of gods and men and the bond of union between them, pervading everything in heaven and atmosphere and earth as Sun, lightening and fire, he is none the less the 'navel of the earth'."[116] There are references in the Vedic texts that all gods join together and worship *Agni*, who is supreme over all the gods. The *Rig Veda* says: "Three times a hundred gods and thrice a thousand, and three times ten and nine have worshipped *Agni*."[117] The *Atharva Veda* speaks of *Agni* as the all-pervading primordial reality that is present everywhere and sustains the entire creation. To quote: "*Agni* (fire) is in the earth, in the plants, the waters hold *Agni*, *Agni* is in the stones; *Agni* is within men, *Agnis* (fires) are within cattle, within horses. *Agni* glows from the sky, to *Agni*, the god, belongs the broad air. The mortals kindle *Agni*... The earth, clothed in *Agni*, with dark knees, shall make me brilliant and alert".[118] He is described as the "child of heaven",[119] and as "one born in the highest heaven".[120] He is identified with "the light of heaven".[121] The fire god, thus, is "ageless, immortal, insurmountable, in possession of all strength and an untiring conqueror".[122]

Even though the fire god is exalted in heaven and on earth,[123] he is also considered to be their child.[124] The *Rig Veda* speaks of *Agni* as the supreme lord above all the gods[125] and as their common "infant".[126] Hence, *Agni* is both god and minister.[127] Thus, we find that these opposing qualities of greatness and smallness, old age and childhood, might and humility are unified in the person of the fire god. Though mighty and heavenly, he descends to the earth as the mouth of the gods to devour the oblations men make, and as god he brings down on man the blessings of the gods.[128] He is the heart of every household. In domestic worship, he is described as the guest of the house, father, brother, son and at times even as mother.[129] He is also addressed as the "Lord of the house".[130] Hence, the fire god is the immortal who lives among the mortals in every house and delights in the oblations of mortal men. He is the protector who removes every evil and a helper in all moments of troubles. Without the fire god, life could not be sustained.[131]

There are a number of mythical stories about the birth of the god *Agni*. His mythical parents are *Dyaus* and *Prthvii*.[132] He is also said to be the child of all gods, whose father he is as the ever-present reality in the universe.[133] At the setting of the Sun, *Agni* is said to unite himself with the rays of the Sun.[134] In a hymn, the *Agni* is referred to as the *Suurya*.[135] According to another myth *Agni* was born when two fire sticks were struck, as he was dormant in them. Of these two fire sticks, the upper one was male, while the lower stick was female. As force is needed for his birth from these two fire sticks, he is known as the son of Strength.[136]

In the temples, *Agni* is presented as an old man with a red body. He has two heads, a large stomach, six eyes and seven arms. His arms hold objects, such as, spoon, ladle and fan. He has seven tongues, four horns and three legs. His hair is braided he wears a garment and the sacred thread (*Yajnopavita*). Two consorts, *Svaahaa* and *Svadhaa* attend the god *Agni* on either side. His banner is smoke, and he uses a ram as his vehicle. In this depiction, the god *Agni* is presented in an anthropomorphic way.[137]

3.1.2.2.1.3. Varuna

Varuna is one who encompasses the whole world. His name is derived from the Sanskrit root '*vr*' which means 'to contain' or 'to encompass'. The bright blue sky, that is behind the atmosphere, the realm of *Indra*, is the dwelling place of *Varuna*. He is the god of the night sky, who is above the conflicts in which *Indra* is engaged. *Varuna* has a natural basis and probably he is the personification of the sky.[138]

He is associated with a number of gods. The Sun is said to be his eyes.[139] *Varuna* is also described as fixing the Sun in the heavens[140] and as giving a special pathway for the Sun to travel.[141] Another god *Varuna* is closely in relationship with is *Mitra*, the fair god of the day-sky, who is benevolent, omnipresent, always meting out justice and righteousness. *Mitra* is always invoked along with *Varuna*. Sometimes in invocation and prayers, they are joined as *Mitraavaruna*. Other names given to them together are 'the dual kings' (*Raajaanau*) and 'the protectors of cosmic order' (*Rtasya Gopau*). *Varuna* is also associated with the Moon.[142]

Varuna is the creator of all beings. All happenings in the universe are 'the holy operations' of *Varuna*. Creation does not mean production of everything out of nothing; rather it means the ordering of already existing matter into an intelligible form according to the cosmic order (*Rta*). He does this creative act with help of 'the creative power', which is in his control. In this manner, *Varuna* is the creator of heaven and earth, but neither heaven nor earth can contain him, as he encompasses everything. He is the lineal descendant of *Dyaus Pitar*, the father god and there is no hair of the father god *Dyaus* other than *Varuna*. Therefore, he is 'the supreme ruler' (*Samraaj*) of the universe. He is given heavenly and royal attributes. The universe and every clan of the world are said to be his garment. He is transmundane, in total control of every happening and living in the highest world.[143]

Though he lives in the distant world, *Varuna* constantly keeps an eye on every corner of the earth. He is feared because he sees everything with a thousand eyes. He even knows what is said in confidence.[144] He sends his messenger, the Sun, to oversee every happening and report to him. *Varuna's* companion, *Mitra*, supervises and sustains everything. *Varuna's* wisdom, knowledge, providence and power clearly demarcate him from all the other gods. As the sustainer of the universe, he 'measures the universe'. His special power keeps the sea from overflowing despite the fact that all the rivers flow into the sea. By directing *Vaays*, the god of air, *Varuna* is said to sustain life by giving rain and crops. He is not only concerned with the order of the physical universe, but also governs the moral order of the universe (*Rta*). In maintaining the cosmic moral order, *Varuna* has the power of binding and loosing, punishing and forgiving. These functions of *Varuna* are part of his role as the sustainer of the universe. He is omniscient, and so he is able to observe man's truth and falsehood. He punishes those who transgress the moral order. When men sin he visits them with his wrath and binds the wicked with fetters. He forgives and loosens the fetters of the one who repents and changes his life. It is said that *Varuna* not only forgives the sin one has committed, but also the sins of one's father.[145]

Varuna, thus, is the god of the sky, who is presented in the Vedic hymns as the creator and sustainer of the universe. He maintains the stability and nobility of the cosmos. He is represented in temple art differently. In some of the temples, he is depicted as riding on a crocodile. In two of his four hands he holds the serpent and a noose (*Paasa*). He is also shown as riding in a chariot drawn by seven swans. In this representation, he holds the lotus, the noose, the conch and a vessel of gems in his four hands, and an umbrella covers his head.[146]

3.1.2.2.1.4. Soma

Soma is another god who has an important place in the Vedic period. He is a powerful divinity, because he presides and animates the *Soma* plant, the juice of which is used in sacrifices as a libation to the gods and as a beverage for the worshipper. The consuming of the *Soma* juice brought great power to the gods and gave spiritual significance and holy dynamism to the worshipper. For instance, the god *Indra* gained all his power from the drinking of the *Soma* juice.[147] The importance of the god *Soma* is indicated in that the whole of the ninth chapter of the *Rig Veda* is dedicated to singing his praises. He is also addressed as *Indu* and *Soma-Pavamaana*. At times he is also praised as the Supreme Being. *Soma* cures illnesses in men, gives them joy and leads them to immortality. He rules over human minds and activates speech in human beings. It is believed that he has the power to make ordinary men into wise sages (*Rshis*). Therefore, at times he is called 'the lord of speech' (*Vacaspati*). The god *Soma* is also praised as the creator of the worlds and as the one who rules over the mountains.[148] In the later hymns of the *Rig Veda*, *Soma* is identified with the moon. Thus, *Soma* becomes a personification of the moon, which is in turn identified with the god *Varuna*, the heavenly lord. Hence the moon is considered to be the great storehouse of the sacred *Soma* juice and the shining distillation of the heavens, which is the very essence of the god *Varuna*. Thus, *Soma* and *Varuna* are closely associated with each other.[149]

3.1.2.2.1.5. Suurya

Suurya is praised in the *Rig Veda* as 'the god who knoweth all that lives', 'the light that is most excellent' and 'the loftier light above the darkness.[150] In six hymns *Suurya* is addressed using differing tiles: *Savitar, Pushan, Bhaga, Vivasvan, Mitra* and *Vishnu*. As *Savitar*, he is the stimulator of everything. He establishes people in their respective places and gives life and energy to guide people in the right path. *Pushan* points to the Sun as the pastoral deity and describes his benevolent power. It points to the nourishing and life-supporting aspect of the Sun. He destroys the evil ones with the discus he wears. He represents the impartial nature of the Sun god, who looks upon everyone with an equal eye. He points to the extreme generous nature of the

Sun and his readiness to protect people. *Bhaga* stands for *Suurya* as presiding over the forenoon. *Vivasvan* originally stood for the rising Sun and later came to be regarded as the first sacrificer and an ancestor of the human race. *Mitra's* connection to the Sun is not that clear in the *Rig Veda*, as he is more associated with the god *Varuna*. Still the relationship between *Mitra* and *Surrya* can be inferred to as both of them are related to *Varuna*: the former oversees the activities of *Varuna*, while *Suurya* is said to be the eye of *Varuna* that spies over the whole universe. Thus, *Suurya* and *Mitra* are related to each other in their relationship to *Varuna*. *Vishnu* is another deity associated with *Suurya*. Many of these aspects of the Sun belong to the group of deities called the *Aadityas*.[151]

Suurya is extremely brilliant and rides on a beautiful chariot drawn by seven horses. He is described as the celestial bird (*Garutman*) that flies in the sky, as a jewel in the sky and as the red ball of the sky. *Suurya* is the active force in the universe, as he is the power that gives light, produces day and night, gives power and strength to living beings, makes them active, and destroys their laziness and disease. He is the god of life, and he gives and prolongs life. Hence, he is prayed to for children. *Suurya* is the child of *Dyaus* and *Prthivii*. He is the priest who sanctifies the whole universe by his power and ever-pervading presence.[152]

3.1.2.2.1.6. Vaayu

Vaayu is the god of the wind. He is the personification of air and life-breath (*Praana*). He is the lord of the atmosphere (*Antriksha*). Hence he is associated with and shares his power with the god *Indra*. He moves around the atmosphere in a chariot pulled by horses. Depending on the number of horses he allows to pull his chariot, he produces ordinary currents of wind, a storm or a cyclone. The movement of his chariot warns everyone of the arrival of the god *Vaayu* with roars of the storm. But he, himself, is invisible, and no one is able to see him. Being an active god, like *Indra*, *Vaayu* is fond of *Soma* juice. Depending on the amount he drinks, he is able produce powerful storms and cyclones. Not only does he activate the physical atmosphere with varying currents of wind, but he is also the basis of life in every creature, as he is the lord of vital breath. In bodies he is the source of five life-breaths (*Pancapraana*). It is also said of him that, like *Rudra*, he is a physician who can cure people of illness and diseases. In temple art he is portrayed as blue in color and as having four hands. In two of his hands he holds a fan and a flag, while the other two hands show *Abhaya Mudra*, indicating his protection, and *Varada Mudra*, denoting granting gifts to his devotees.[153]

3.1.2.2.1.7. Vishnu

Vishnu, the Supreme Deity of the Vaishnava tradition of later Hinduism, finds a secondary place in the Vedic hymns. The name '*Vishnu*' could have derived from three possible Sanskrit roots: Firstly, from the root '*vi*', which signifies 'a bird', secondly, from the root '*vis*', which means 'the active one', thirdly, from the roots '*vi*' and '*snu*', which means 'crossing the back of the world' or 'crossing the earthly regions'.[154] All these three uses indicate that *Vishnu* is a god who is active and pervading the earthly and heavenly regions. He is spoken as a friend of the god *Indra*. Vedic hymns also mention him as a solar deity and an aspect of *Suurya*, who covers the whole universe with his rays.[155]

In Vedic hymns *Vishnu* is addressed as 'the one who has great strides' (*Urugaaya*) and as 'the one who covers the universe in three steps' (*Trivikrama*). The *Rig Veda* says: "Like a dread beast he [*Vishnu*] wanders where he will. Haunting the mountains: in his three wide paces all worlds and beings (*Bhuvans*) dwell".[156] The threefold 'wide paces' have been interpreted differently. Firstly, it can be seen as threefold manifestations of light in the three regions of the universe: in the form of fire on the earth, lightening in the atmosphere and the brightness of the Sun in the heaven. Secondly, the three steps could also signify the Sun as it marches on three times a day, viz., dawn, day and dusk. Thirdly, it could also be taken as that with the first two steps *Vishnu* measures out the earth and the atmosphere, while with the third, he goes beyond the atmosphere, the ken of the birds, to the sublime realms of the heavens. Whichever may the explanation we accept, it would point to the fact of *Vishnu* being the greatest in the whole universe.[157] He is said to be eternally youthful and handsome. The Sun is referred to, at times, as his discus. *Vishnu* is extremely kind and generous to his devotees, and he is pleased by the offerings and sacrifices made to him.[158]

3.1.2.2.1.8. Yama

The term '*yama*' means 'to restrain', 'to curb' and 'to control'. Hence the god *Yama* is the controller, restrainer, the one who curbs. He determines one's life in this world. He was the first person to die and depart to the celestial world, so he is the god of the dead. The departed spirits live in his presence. He has two fierce dogs with four eyes and wide nostrils. They guard the path of the departed souls on their way to the kingdom of the god *Yama*. According to myths, *Yama* is not only the god of death, but also the judge of the people on earth. He is known as the *Dharmaraaja*, because he rewards and punishes justly the dead, who come to his kingdom. In his task as the judge of the dead, *Citragupta*, his recorder, assists *Yama*. In temple art' he is presented as green in color. He wears a red garment and holds a mighty mace and noose. During his travels he rides on a male buffalo.[159]

3.1.2.2.2. Vedic Goddesses

In the last section, we explored the male deities of the Vedic period. They dominated the scene. The female deities played secondary roles, either as helpers or supporters of the male deities. While the male gods were at the center, the female deities were at the periphery. Some of the significant goddesses of the Vedic period are *Ushas, Prthivii, Aditi, Sarasvatii, Vaak, Nirrti* and *Raatrii*. There are a few minor gods who are mentioned individually or collectively. In this section, we explore the nature, characteristics and functions of these goddesses.

3.1.2.2.2.1. Ushas

Ushas is the goddess of dawn. She reveals herself in the coming of the light to the world. In the *Rig Veda* she is described as a radiant young maiden riding on shining chariot. She is referred to as 'the Daughter of the Sky', 'the Lady of the Light', 'the Bounteous One', 'the Excellent One' and 'the Mighty One' invoked by the *rishis* of old. She is described as one who impels life and is the source of the breath of life in every living creature. For instance, it is *Ushas* who awakens every man and leads him to his daily pursuits. She is also addressed as 'the Mother of Cows', who, like a cow that yields its udder for the benefit of people, bears her breast to bring light into the world, thereby removing the darkness that envelopes the universe. In doing so, she rouses all life, sets everything in motion and sends people off to their daily duties and tasks.[160]

As the goddess of dawn, she brings forth light and is followed by *Suurya*, who urges her onward. She is also addressed as the spouse of *Suurya*. Traversing though the sky at the urging of the god *Suurya*, *Ushas* is associated with *Rta*, the cosmic, social and moral order of the universe. She observes what people do and uncovers the dark elements in their life, according to the principles of *Rta*, the moral and cosmic order. In this sense, she is said to be the eye of the gods, who sees everything in the universe. But she is never invoked to forgive human beings their transgressions. Instead, *Ushas* is addressed to drive away punishment. As the guardian of *Rta* she is also mentioned as the foe of chaotic forces which threaten the cosmic order and who ushers in all that is auspicious and good for man.[161]

Though *Ushas* is referred to as a young and beautiful maiden, she is also described as the mother of the gods, who provides food to make them happy. She is also said to be the mother of the *Asvins*. She is also addressed as the mother of her petitioners, who tends everything and cares for everyone as a good matron. She blesses her petitioners with every good. *Ushas* is honored as the goddess of the hearth, who keeps every family in her providence.[162] In meting out the blessings to her devotees, she follows the directives of *Rta*, the cosmic order. She wakes up all living creatures and leads them on. But she does not disturb those who sleep in death. She is mistress and maker of time, as she daily reminds people of the limited time they have in this world, with each dawning of the day. So people pray to *Ushas* for long life and many blessings here on earth.[163] To quote a prayer to *Ushas* from the *Rig Veda*:

> She [*Ushas*] hath shone brightly like a youthful woman, stirring to motion every living creature. ... Bearing the Gods' own Eye, auspicious Lady, leading her Courser white and

fair to look on, ... Draw nigh with wealth and dawn away the foeman: prepare for us wide pastures free from danger. Drive away those who hate us, bring us riches: pour bounty, opulent Lady, on the singer. Send thy most excellent beams to shine and light us, giving us lengthened days, O Dawn, O Goddess. Granting us food, thou hast all things precious, and bounty rich in chariots, ... and horses. O *Ushas*, nobly-born, Daughter of Heaven, ... Bestow on us vast and glorious riches.[164]

3.1.2.2.2.2. Prthivii

Prthivii is the goddess of earth, i.e., the terrestrial sphere, the abode of every living creature. In the *Rig Veda*, she is always associated with *Dyaus*, the sky-god. We have already elaborated this aspect of the goddess *Prthivii*. In the *Atharva Veda*, we find a hymn that is dedicated to the goddess *Prthivii* alone, and no mention is made of *Dyaus*. Interestingly, in this hymn the goddess is the main focus and a number of gods are associated with her. She is said to support *Agni*, as she is clothed in *Agni*. *Indra* is described as her mate, who protects her from every agitation and commotion that happens on the earth.[165] The *Asvins* have measured out the course of the earth, and *Vishnu* has stepped out to the earth.[166] The gods *Parjanya*, *Prajaapati* and *Vishvakarman* are described as either protecting *Prthivii*, providing for her or as her consorts.[167] The associations of the male gods with her make her unique, important and a goddess on her own right. She is presented as the fertility goddess, who nourishes every creature that lives upon the earth.[168] *Prthivii* is the mother, who supports within her the tribes of men and the manifold breathing and moving things. She provides food for all of them, the good and evil, the demons and the gods. She is compared to a mother who pours forth milk for her son.[169] The fragrance and beauty of the goddess *Prthivii* are manifested in the loveliness and charm of men and women, in the steeds and heroes, and in the luster that is in each maiden.[170] David Kinsley sums up the place of the goddess *Prthivii* in the *Atharva Veda* as follows:

> *Prthivii* is a stable, fertile, benign presence in Vedic literature. She is addressed as a mother, and it is clear that those who praise her see her as a warm, nursing goddess who provides sustenance to all those who move upon her firm, broad expanse. The *Rig Veda* nearly always links her with the male god *Dyaus*, but in the *Atharva Veda* and later Vedic literature she emerges as an independent being.[171]

3.1.2.2.2.3. Aditi

The goddess *Aditi* is mentioned in the *Rig Veda* only eight times.

Each of these references to her does not give us a clear picture of what her actual nature is. Like, *Ushas* and *Prthivii*, who represent natural phenomena, such as dawn and earth, *Aditi* represents no natural phenomenon. There are hardly any references to her physical features in the Vedic hymns.[172] The name *Aditi* is derived from the root '*daa*', which means 'to bind' or 'to fetter'. So '*A-diti*' means 'the unbound one' or 'the free one'. Not only is she free, but also she is said to free her devotees from all that hinders them, especially sin and illness. In this task of binding and loosing, the role *Aditi* plays is similar to that of the god *Varuna*.[173] As the one who frees a petitioner, *Aditi* plays the role of the guardian of *Rta*, the cosmic moral order. She enforces the principles of *Rta* to support and help his devotee, thereby keeping the universe free from chaos.[174] The most outstanding attribute given to her in the Vedic hymns is motherhood. She is described as the mother of the *Aadityas* and *Indra*. She is referred to as "the mother of kings" and as "the mother of the gods". Interestingly, though mentioned as mother, *Aditi* does not have any male consort.[175] In her role as the mother, *Aditi* is identified with the cosmic cow, because, like a cow, she provides nourishment, the sacred drink *Soma* that is invigorating and redemptive.[176] As a mother she often guards her devotee, provides him safety, gives him wealth and blesses him abundantly.[177]

3.1.2.2.2.4. Sarasvatii

The goddess *Sarasvatii* is associated with the *Sarasvatii* River of the Vedic times, which has since disappeared. *Rig Veda* mentions her as mighty and powerful, having waters that break down the mountains. Her waters surpass all waters in greatness, and she is said to be inexhaustible, as her source is the celestial ocean. *Sarasvatii* is not a mere river, but a heaven-sent stream that blesses the earth, atmosphere and the celestial regions.[178] Since she makes all three regions of the world fertile, she is called the bountiful (*Subhaga*) and the best of all mothers.[179] People petition her "for wealth, vitality, children, nourishment, and immortality. She quickens life, is the source of vigor and strength, and provides good luck and material well-being to those whom she blesses."[180] It is said that unmarried men, who long for wives and sons, pray to her for food and progeny.[181] As a protector of the petitioners, she is called an iron fort and a sheltering tree.[182] *Sarasvatii* is also closely related to the Vedic cult, as she is said to be the participant, the witness and the guardian of the cult. She is also associated with *Idaa* (*Ila*) and *Bhaaratii*, the sacrificial goddesses and *Mahii* and *Hotraa*, the goddesses of prayer. She is also said to destroy those who abuse the gods and the slayer of *Vrtra*, the demon of chaos.[183] *Sarasvatii* is known for her purifying presence. She is described as cleansing men, purifying them with holy oil and removing their defilements.[184] *Rig Veda* also speaks of *Sarasvatii* as 'the inciter of all pleasant songs', 'the inspirer of all gracious thoughts' and 'the one who brightens every pious thought".[185] In doing so, it anticipates "her later nature as a goddess of inspiration, eloquence and learning."[186] In this aspect *Sarasvatii* is similar to the goddess *Vaak*, whom we consider in the next section.

3.1.2.2.2.5. Vaak

Vaak is the goddess of speech. She reveals herself through the various attributes of speech. She inspires the sages, makes a person belong to the priestly class with the powerful ritual speech, and stirs a person to truth by sustaining the *Soma*, the drink of vision and immortality.[187] David Kinsley describes the goddess *Vaak* as follows:

> She is the mysterious presence that enables one to hear, see, grasp, and then express in words the true nature of things. She is the prompter of and the vehicle of expression for visionary perception, and as such she is intimately associated with the...[sages], and the rituals that express or capture the truths of their visions. In an important sense she is an essential part of the religio-poetic visionary experience of the ... [sages] and of the sacrificial rituals that appropriate those visions.[188]

As one who bestows visions, the goddess *Vaak* is referred to as 'the Heavenly Queen', 'the Queen of Gods', 'the Gladdener', 'She who streams with Sweetness' and 'One who bestows vital powers'.[189] Like the other Vedic goddesses, *Vaak* is benign and bounteous. She is the mother who brings everything into being through naming them. Besides, she is said to provide light, strength, nourishment and growth. She is often addressed as 'the Heavenly Cow' that gives food and vigor to the gods and men.[190] *Vaak* also facilitates relationships between people, enabling them to see and recognize each other as friends, thereby building up a genuine and loving community.[191] Thus, *Vaak* is the goddess, "who provides ... the lofty, discerning vision of the ... [sages]; ... the ritual formulas of the priest; and ... the everyday language of people which enables them to establish themselves as the community of friends."[192]

3.1.2.2.2.6. Raatrii

Raatrii is the goddess of night, the sister of *Ushas*, the goddess of dawn. In the *Rig Veda*, they both are said to be lovely maidens and at times are referred to as twin sisters. David Kinsley describes the roles of these two goddesses in keeping the order of the universe as follows:

> They are called weavers of time and mothers of eternal law. In their alternating cyclical, and endless appearance, they represent the stable, rhythmic patterns of the cosmos in which light and dark inevitably follow each other in an orderly predictable manner. Together they illustrate the coherence of the created order: the ordered alternations of vigor and rest, light and dark, and the regular flow of time.[193]

As the goddess of the night, *Raatrii* is described as the security and comfort of the people during the dark hours of the night. She is generally presented as a benign goddess. She is praised as the light-giver during the night, with the help of the stars. She is honored for giving rest to all creatures and for providing life-sustaining dew. Prayers are addressed to *Raatrii* to protect people from the common dangers of the night. For instance, she is asked to keep away thieves, wolves and other creatures that can harm people in the night. Thus, *Raatrii*, besides guarding the night, protects people from the dangers of the night.[194] Despite her benign nature, some texts in the *Rig Veda* refer to her as bringing harm to people. For instance, she is described as being chased away by *Agni* and *Ushas*. She is referred to as barren and gloomy, in comparison with her bright sister *Ushas*.[195] In spite of these passing references, the goddess *Raatrii* is basically benign and bounteous towards her petitioners.

3.1.2.2.2.7. Nirrti

Unlike the other Vedic goddesses, *Nirrti* possesses no benign qualities. Whenever she is mentioned in the *Rig Veda*, the concern of the text is not to seek her protection, but rather that she be driven away, as she represents death, ill luck, decay, need, anger, cowardice, old age and destruction. Even when other gods are prayed to for life, wealth, food and continued long life, the refrain "Let *Nirrti* depart to distant places" is also invoked. Thus, *Nirrti* is a goddess with whom no one would like to have contact, as she represents all that is evil and disastrous.[196]

3.1.2.2.2.8. Other Minor Female Deities

Other than these major female deities, we do find references to a number of minor female deities in the *Rig Veda*, all of whom are benign in nature. *Puramdhi*, *Paarendi*, *Raakaa* and *Dhishanaa* are associated with bounty, riches, wealth and abundance. *Sinivaalii* is said to be the goddess of the family and is prayed to for progeny. *Ila*, *Bhaaratii*, *Mahii* and *Hotraa* are goddesses of sacrifice and prayer and are invariably grouped with the goddess *Sarasvatii*. There is mention of the goddess *Suuryaa*, the daughter of the Sun-god (*Suurya*), who is said to be in relationship with the *Asvins* and with a few other gods. *Aranyaanii* is the goddess of the forest. *Rig Veda* also mentions about the consorts of famous Vedic gods, such as *Indraanii*, *Varunaanii* and *Agnaani*. Except for *Indraanii*, most of these goddesses have independent characters of their own. Even the former is overshadowed by the powerful presence of her male consort god *Indra*.[197]

3.1.3. VEDIC PATHS TO THE DIVINE

We have been considering the gods and goddesses of the Vedic Pantheon. In this section we discuss the various paths the people of the Vedic period used to encounter the gods they believed in, receive their blessings and ward off any evil they might bring to man. Some of the paths that helped the people to come in touch with the divinities were daily prayers and practices, domestic cults, priesthood, sacrifices, temple worship, moral living, expiation and purification, and sacramental acts. Besides, there were other special observances, such as astrology, omens, auspicious days in the week and the month, charms to appease demons, ghosts and wandering spirits – aimed at warding off the evil that can come to man's life through the actions of the divine beings. We briefly consider each of the paths in this section.

3.1.3.1. DAILY PRAYERS AND PRACTICES

The daily life of a genuine Hindu is completely directed and controlled by various rituals and practices. This is not only true of a Brahmin, who belongs to the highest caste of the Hindu society, but also true of the members of the other castes. A study of the course of a *Braahman's* daily prayers and practices would give us a clear perception of the daily ritual duties of the all the Hindus. Daily prayers and practices include the bath (*Snaana*), the morning worship (*Praatah-sandhya*), the morning oblation (*Homa*), the spiritual reading (*Svaadhyaaya*), the propitiation ceremony (*Tarpana*) and the worship of the deity (*Deva-puujana*). We briefly consider each of these stages.

The *Snaana* ceremony begins on waking up. Usually a *Braahman* rises before the sunrise. As he comes out of his bed, the right foot must touch the ground first. Once he is out of the bed, he avoids looking at any inauspicious thing like a dead body, and an inauspicious person such as a widow, a sweeper or a barren woman, so as not to pollute his day. He would rather gaze at a ring, cow or a little child, believed to be auspicious. He rinses his mouth three times and coils his holy thread round his neck and over the right ear. He then does his morning ablutions, wears the holy thread round his neck and breaks his silence. He cleans his teeth, washes his mouth and venerates the sun with a bow. After his bath, preferably in a river, he says a prayer to the gods, the ancestors and the sages.[198]

When the *Snaana* is complete, the morning worship (*Praatah-sandhyaa*) begins. The *Braahman* is expected to complete it before sunrise. While seated on a low seat, facing east, with his sacred thread hanging from his left shoulder, he sips water, utters sacred formulas (*Mantras*) over the ashes he has brought with him and marks with them his forehead, arms, ribs and the legs. Having tied his hair, closing one nostril after the other, he exhales and inhales, repeating the sacred *Gaayatrii Mantra*. He closes both the nostrils, bows his head and repeats the same invocation four times. He repeats the whole process three times. When he has completed the process, he makes his intention (*Sankalpa*) to be purified of his sins. He sprinkles water to chase away the demons and pours more water as a symbol of being freed from demons for the sun to rise, which is followed by a prayer to the sun. The *Gaayatrii Mantra*[199] is repeated 108 times on a rosary, counting the beads. The morning worship is completed with different positions of the fingers to indicate different petitions.[200]

Then begins the morning oblation to the fire god, known as the *Homa*. It consists in the offering of *ghee* (purified butter), curds and rice to the fire. This oblation to the fire god must go before the first meal. The spiritual reading (*Svaadhyaaya*), with another detailed ritual, follows the *Homa*. The *Braahman* places his right hand successively on the mouth, the eyes, the ears, the nose, the lips, the top of head, the chin, the forearms, the navel and the back. The purpose of the placing of the hand on all these parts of the body is to get the protection of the gods. After he repeats the *Gaayatri Mantra*, the sacred scripture is briefly read. The ceremony's three propitiations (*Tarpana*) come after the spiritual reading. The ceremony consists of three propitiations, viz., the propitiation of the gods (*Deva-tarpana*), the propitiation of the sages (*Rishi-tarpana*) and the propitiation of the ancestors (*Pitr-tarpana*). In propitiating the gods the *Braahman*, after sipping water, sits facing the east, his sacred thread hanging over his left shoulder, as he pours water from his straightened fingers. In propitiating the sages he faces the west, his sacred thread hanging round his neck, and pours water between his two little fingers, while he holds his hands in the form of a cup. In propitiating the ancestors, he sits facing the south, his holy thread hanging from his right shoulder, and pours water between the base of the thumb and the first finger of his right hand.[201]

The final ritual a *Braahman* is expected to do is the worship of the deity (*Deva-puujana*). It takes place in a small room, in the home, reserved for the image of the favorite god (*Ishtadevataa*) and other gods. The various articles used for worship, such as a bell, copper vessel, spoon, sandalwood paste, incense and other similar things are also kept in this room. The first ceremony in the worship of god is the blessing of the water to be used for the worship, which takes place as follows. The *Braahman* holds his right hand over the copper vessel containing the water. He bends down the forefinger and moves the hand up and down, reciting the name of the great pilgrimages and the holy rivers. Then, holding his hand in the form of a cow's udder over the water to symbolically represent the coming down of the nectar, the blessed water is sprinkled over all the articles used for the worship. The prayers said and the gestures of worship depend on the deity, who is worshipped. The *Braahman* ended the *Deva-puujana* with a prayer, in which he asks for the forgiveness of his sins.[202]

Since the practices are elaborate, an abbreviated ritual, including the essential elements, viz., bath, morning worship, morning oblation, spiritual reading and worship of god, is at times used. The Hindus, even if they do not go through all these elaborate daily practices, remain faithful to the daily recital of the *Gaayatrii* invocation. A prayer is also said in the afternoon and in the evening. In the performance of all these daily practices, the members of the family are not bound to participate. Usually the head of the family performs these rites in the name of every member of the family.[203] Thus, the everyday life of a devout Hindu is centered on the recitation of various prayers and performance of different rituals, which helped them to be in touch with gods.

3.1.3.2. DOMESTIC CULT

Besides, the daily prayers and practices, which the *Braahman* performs on behalf of and in the name of every member of his family, there are also some common domestic cults, in which each member of the family participates. Some of these rites are very elaborate. Usually the *paterfamilias* (*Grhapati*) conducted these rituals with the assistance of the other members of the family. When he is absent, the mother of the household (*Grhapatinii*) officiated at the rites. In some of these sacrifices, *ghee* and vegetables are the principal offerings.[204]

The main sacrifices ordinarily included in the domestic cult are five in number. The first is the sacrifice to the gods (*Devayajna*). It consisted of the whole family joining in offering various forms of sacrifices accompanied by prayers to the *Ishtadevataa* of the family and to other deities. The second is the sacrifice to the ancestors (*Pitryajna*). In this form of sacrifice, the ancestors of the family are remembered and appeased. The third is the word offering (*Brahmayajna*), which consists in the recital of sacred texts from the *Vedas*. The fourth is the offerings to man (*Manushyayajna*). It consists in practicing hospitality by offering food to the guests who come to the house. The fifth is the offerings to beings (*Baliyajna / Bhuutyajna*). It involves feeding various forms of living beings. In practicing offerings to beings, the householder leaves food on the ground, on the doorstep and other common places with the intention of feeding birds, worms and animals, in which the dead are likely to have been incarnated. The fivefold sacrifice which the *paterfamilias* is expected to practice are related to the fivefold duties he is called to accomplish, as a householder, with the help of his family members. In the performance of these *Yajnas* every member of the family actively participates and assists the *paterfamilias*.[205] The domestic cult, besides keeping the family together, provides a path to come in touch with the gods in whom the family believes.

3.1.3.3. PRIESTHOOD

The priestly function predominantly rests with the *Braahman* caste. But not all *Braahmans* are priests, as many of them take up other professions as means of livelihood. At the same time no one except a *Braahman* can be a priest. But the *Braahman* priests do not have the freedom to perform rites for all the castes. The Vedic Hindu religion provides a unique example of priestly civilization. Ritual worship is so dominant that even arts and sciences are subordinated to it. The priests composed most of the Vedic literature. Everyone depended on the sacrificial performance of the priests. The priests of the Hindu religion are essentially household priests. Even when priesthood was considered hereditary, the caste of the *Braahmans* never formed itself into a unified hierarchical clergy, as we find in some other religions.[206]

Though we do not find a well-organized hierarchical structure among the Hindu priests, still priesthood is considered as a profession among the Hindus, and there are distinctions of status within the profession. At the top of the order are the priests, who are the teachers of Hindu philosophy and the consultants on the sacred law. This group of priests gives expositions in mythology, recites and comment on religious texts, and holds debates and discussions in philosophy and logic for the edification of the public. They also performed and supervised significant ritual celebrations in the homes of their clients. Second in the order are the priests who performed seasonal worship for standardized fees. They are general practitioners of the profession and are experts in their work. The third in the hierarchy are the family priests (*Kula-purohit*), who give their services to orthodox and well-to-do families. They attend to all the important events in the family, such as births, initiations, weddings and last rites for the dead. In a sacred place set apart in the house, they officiate at all the worship and baths, anoint and propitiate the images of the family and other deities. At times they also perform the functions of astrologer, physician, exorcist and the adviser of the family in all matters. *Kula-purohits* are considered superior members of the domestic staff of the families they serve. The last in the order is the temple priests, who serve at the temples.[207]

The professional priest of Hinduism must have a working knowledge of the Sanskrit language, as he has to chant the Vedic texts at the sacrificial rites. Besides, they must be familiar with the sacred literature, as they must be able to find the right texts when they want to recite them. They must also have a thorough knowledge of liturgy of worship connected with different gods and goddesses, and the rites related to the everyday lives of the people. In performing the various rites and chanting the *Mantras* they can always make use of the appropriate texts or pause to consult them. But they must take care to pronounce the words correctly and to make the appropriate gestures, in order that the efficacy of the incantations are not lost. Besides, they must have some knowledge of astrology. They learn all the complicated liturgical worship from their elders in the family, rather than through formal study. The priest has no role towards his clients other than performing the ritual worship for them. He has no responsibility for the spiritual or moral welfare of those whom he serves. Neither does he perform the task of caring for the poor, the destitute or the sick. His task is professional. He performs the ritual sacrifice professionally and does nothing else for his client.[208]

In performing various ritual worships, the Hindu priest assists the people to open their lives to the gods, to appease them through the sacrifices he offers, and brings down the blessings of the gods on the people with the power of the sacrifices he performs. Thus, the priest becomes a medium through whom the encounter between the gods and man is brought about. Hence, the priesthood is a path that leads people to god.

3.1.3.4. SACRIFICES

From the time of the *Vedas*, sacrifices (*Yajnas*) played an important role in establishing contact between the people and the gods. A Hindu understands by the term "*Yajna*" various things. For instance, reading from the sacred scripture is considered a sacrifice to a *Braahman*. The propitiation offering to one's ancestors and morning oblation of *ghee*, curds and rice to the fire god (*Homa*) are said to be sacrifices. Feeding animals is believed to be a sacrifice made to the elements. Similarly hospitality is looked upon as a sacrifice made for human beings.[209] Usually, sacrifices are not offered in thanksgiving, but are oblations made to the gods. Hence, sacrifices are offered to obtain different material and spiritual blessings, such as health, prosperity, increase of cattle, offspring and good fortune, and other similar good things from the gods.[210] To bring about the efficacy of the sacrifice, the one who sacrifices must fast before the sacrifice. So about the one, who sacrifices it is said that 'the gods live with him' (*Upavasanti*), and the sacrificial day is called 'the fasting day' (*Upavastha*).[211]

In general the offerings of the sacrifices include animals, vegetables, milk and *ghee*. The most important offering during the Vedic period is *Soma*, the drink that leads to immortality. *Rig Veda* confirms the sacredness of this drink when it says that every moment of the preparation of this drink is sacred, regulated minutely, and even the stones of the press are objects of sacred invocations.[212] This drink is closely associated with the god *Indra*. Those who take part in the cult in which *Soma* is offered and drink of it at the sacrifice are said to become the incarnation of *Indra*, drinking the *Soma* and killing the demons.[213]

The elaborate ritual involved in the Vedic sacrifice is based on the belief that ritual sacrifice is vital for the sustenance of the order of nature, human society and history. It is with the help of sacrifice that every happens in nature, such as, the rising of the sun, the rainfall, the growth in plants and the procreation in animals, takes place. It is because the sacrifices have the power to strengthen the will of the gods and man's capacity for achieving public good and private ends. Sacrifices are believed to consolidate the social order, such as, the caste system, the family, city and state. In the course of time, the sacrifices gain such great prominence that it is forgotten to which god it is offered thereby it becomes a fate-controlling act. It is no longer the gods guarding the *Rta*, the cosmic moral order, but the sacrifices become 'the protector of the order' (*Rtasya Gopa*). The one who sacrifices becomes 'the mortal hero' who can even command a great god like *Agni* through the effectiveness of the sacrifice.[214]

In the Vedic period, a number of elaborate sacrifices were performed on different festivals and other occasions. Some of the sacrifices are the *Agnihotra*, the *Agnishtoma*, the *Agnicayana*, the *Sautraamanii*, the *Mahaavrata*, the *Mahaarudra*, the *Gaayatrii-purascarana*, the *Asvamedha*, the *Purushamedha* and the *Raajasuuya*. We briefly consider each of them.

The *Agnihotra* is the fire worship. It is an important sacrifice, which every *Braahman* and *Vaisya* head of the family has the duty of seeing carried out, every morning and evening. It requires only one priest. It consists in the milk of a cow that has delivered a bull-calf, is purified with a special grass called '*kusa* grass', mixed with water, carried around the fire and finally poured on the fire. It is believed that *Prajaapati* founded the *Agnihotra* sacrifice and created all things through it. It is the belief of the Hindus that if anyone regularly performs this sacrifice, he would save himself from fire and death. Through this sacrifice one can obtain control over everything.[215]

The *Agnishtoma* is the fire hymn sacrifice. It is usually performed in the spring season, when the *Soma* plant is pressed and becomes *Soma* juice. The enactment of this sacrifice required the services of 16 priests. It includes the sacrificing of a goat and the correct recitation of Vedic *Mantras* for several days. At the beginning of the *Agnishtoma* sacrifice, the one who organizes the sacrifice, the son, grandson and the parents are expected to come to the place of worship in a procession. The organizer of the sacrifice must give about 100 cows, besides giving his daughter in marriage to the priests. The *Agnishtoma* sacrifice is performed to produce plentiful *Soma* during the spring season.[216]

The *Agnicayana* sacrifice is called 'the building-up of fire-bricks'. It is a ritual that lasts for one full year. The mythology associated with this sacrifice says that gods were mortal, and they tried a number of sacrifices to gain immortality, but did not succeed in attaining immortality. Then *Prajaapati* taught them to build an altar to *Agni* in the right way, and they offered the *Agnicayana* sacrifice, which brought them immortality. Thus, the performance of this sacrifice is said to preserve one from death and help one to attain immortality. It is also believed that it can save a person from the disastrous 'second death' (*Punar-mrtyu*), which consists in the dead man dying a second death, before he is reborn. *Agnicayana* rite involves blood sacrifices and fire ceremonies. The one who sacrifices is bound by a number of taboos, such as not being out of his house when it is raining, eating the meat of fowls and other similar restrictions.[217]

The *Sautraamanii* is a special sacrifice made to *Indra*, the benevolent protector. The sacrifice involves a number of peculiar rites. It includes a libation of a special drink called *suraa*, in which a hair each of a lion, a tiger and a wolf are placed, as well as a goat, a sheep and a bull, aimed at appeasing the gods of creation, sustenance and destruction. At the end of the sacrifice, the one sacrificing sits on the skin of a tiger with a gold disc on his right leg and a silver disc on the left leg, to gain control over the sun and the moon, respectively. As he sits, thus, he is sprinkled with melted fat, while he proclaims that he possesses royal power.[218]

The *Mahaavrata* is a great sacrifice that involves a number of rituals. It takes place usually at the winter solstice. It consists of the priest officiating at the sacrifice (*Hotr*) balancing in a swing, and young women dancing, while the drums and lutes are played. There is another rite in which an *Arya* and a *Sudra* fight over a white skin. Besides, there is a ritual wedding ceremony, during which highly obscene dialogue is used. Every rite involved in the *Mahaavrata* sacrifice is aimed at pointing to, marking and assisting the change of season at the winter solstice.[219]

The *Mahaarudra* is a sacrifice, specially offered to the god *Rudra* and is believed to have the power to wash the sins of the one who offers this sacrifice, whether he is living or dead. The performance of the sacrifice requires 11 officiating priests (*Hotr*), one guide (*Aacaarya*), one protector (*Brahmaa*), one scriptural guide (*Sadasyapati*), one to supervise the correct recitation and pronunciation of the *Mantras* (*Ganapati*) and one general supervisor (*Upadrastr*). Besides, there is the need for four *Braahmans* as doorkeepers, to keep the demons away. The fire lit as the sacrifice begins must burn continually until the sacrifice comes to an end, which is usually either five or eleven days. The important rite of the sacrifice is the installation of the images of the god *Rudra* and his attendants. Though the worship goes on without stop, every evening there is a special 'waving of the lamps (*Aarati*).[220]

The *Gaayatrii-purascarana* is a sacrifice, which consists in the recital of the *Gaayatrii Mantra*. A householder is expected to repeat the *Gaayatrii* invocation over two million times during his lifetime. As a person comes to the close of life and realizes that he has not completed the required number, he may perform the *Gaayatrii-purascarana*. A number of priests sitting around the burning fire recite the *Gaayatrii Mantra*, while pouring the *ghee* on the fire. The sacrifice continues until the required number is completed.[221]

The *Asvamedha* is the Horse Sacrifice. It is said to be the greatest of all the sacrifices. It is usually celebrated either in February or in March. Its performance begins at the presence of the king, four queens and 400 helpers. There are elaborate preparations for this sacrifice. The king keeps a vigil for one night in silence. He, then, proves that he can remain chaste by lying naked between the legs of his favorite spouse (*Vaavaataa*). There are differing opinions as to how long he should practice chastity in this manner. Some sources say that it is for one day, while others say that it is for one year. Similarly, a stallion is chosen and let loose with 100 horses. Four hundred men are assigned to see that it does not lose its purity, either by bathing in unclean water or mating with other mares, for one year. When the stipulated time is passed the stallion is taken for the sacrifice. Twenty-seven days of fasting are required before the sacrifice begins. The stallion is decorated with pearls and harnessed to a golden carriage. Then it is allowed to be excited at the sight of mares and at the cries of different animals, after which it is strangled to death. The four queens stand around the dead horse while it is covered. The leader among the queens (*Mahishii*) goes under the cover and places the horse on her lap. Then follows the exchange of questions and answers between the king, the queens and the priests, during which highly obscene remarks go on between the priests and the queens. The horse is cut into four pieces. A number of other bloody sacrifices are also made, of which the final one is the killing of 21 cows. The festival comes to a close, with a right involving the criminals. The purpose of this sacrifice is to increase power, piety and fertility to the highest level. The importance given to the sexual dimension in the *Asvamedha* sacrifice is parallel to the *Soma* intoxication in some of the sacrifices offered to *Indra*. *Prajaapatii* is said to be both the sacrificial victim and the one who sacrifices in the *Asvamedha*.[222]

The *Purushamedha* is the human sacrifice. There are legends and myths that speak of this form of sacrifice. The classical example is the legend of Sunahsepa. The legend goes as follows: A king had a hundred wives. But he had no son. The god *Varuna* promised that he would give him a son, provided that he would sacrifice his son to the god. *Varuna* gave the king a son, whom he called Rohita. But later *Varuna* asked him back in sacrifice. A *Braahman* sold his own son Snuahsepa to be sacrificed in the place of Rohita. The king gave a hundred cows in payment for the boy. The sacrifice of Snuahsepa began with the assistance of his own father, who performed a number of other sacrificial functions for additional payment. Finally, the goddess *Ushas* saved the boy before he was actually sacrificed. It is said that in the *Agnicayana* ritual a man and four other animals are sacrificed. But the actual happening of *Purushamedha* is not traceable. *Purushamedha* is said to be the most distinguished and effective of all the sacrifices, as it is the one who sacrifices equates himself with *Prajaapati*, who is both the victim and the one who sacrifices.[223]

The *Raajasuuya* is the rite of 'Anointing of the King'. The ritual goes as follows: the King is seated on a wooden throne covered with a skin of a tiger. He is sprinkled with flour, butter and similar things. He plays dice with a priest and wins the game. Then he econducts a fake raid on a herd belonging to a kinsman, in order to regain his virility, which he is said to have lost. An integral part of the rite is a *Hotr* narrating the Sunahsepa to the king. The legend points to the readiness of the *Braahman* to sacrifice his son in the place of the prince, to strengthen the kingship. The *Raajasuuya* sacrifice is not only meant for the anointing of the king as he ascends to the throne, but also aims at strengthening the monarchy.[224]

The various sacrifices we have described have helped the people of the Vedic time to come in touch with the gods, and brought their blessings down upon earth, thereby bringing stability in the order of nature, to society and the history of the human beings.

3.1.3.5. TEMPLE WORSHIP

In the early Vedic times there were no temples and so temple worship was not in vogue. Offerings were laid out in the fields and in the 'the sacred tombs' with 'the sacred straw' (*Barhis*).[225] Later temple worship became common. A Hindu temple basically is not a place of public worship. But rather it is the sanctuary of a god or a goddess. The innermost chamber of the temple is the *Sanctum Sanctorum*, in which the image of the presiding deity of the temple is placed, surrounded by the shrines of lesser important gods and goddesses. The priest treats the god, as if he is a living person. He is awakened with sweet sounding music. Then he is bathed, usually the reflection of the deity in a brass plate. After the bath, the god is dressed, served a light meal and made ready to give audience to the pilgrims. Later in the day he is served a substantial meal, his dress is changed and he is put to rest. Before sunset he is given another light refreshment, change the clothes, a light waving ceremony (*Aaratii*) conducted and he is retired for the night's rest.[226]

Therefore, there is no strict liturgical service in the sense of public ceremony, in which the sacraments are administered to the people. The priest performs the ceremonies alone without people's actual participation in the ceremonies. People come to the shrine, read from the holy book, recite the beads, sing religious songs or listen to religious instructions, but do not actually take part in the ceremonies the priest offers. The private worship of the people consists in offering prayers and oblations. In response the gods give people audience (*Darshan*). People give their offerings to the priest, bow before the image of the god, go around the temple, their right side turned towards the deity, and finally carry home a part of the offering that has been presented to the god (*Prasaada*). This usually takes place between the regular intervals of the priestly ritual. Thus, the religious practice that takes place in the temple is private in character, both on the part of the priest and the people.[227]

In this way, worship in the temple truly opens the people to the gods and the gods to the people. Thus, temple worship provides a genuine path to the people to experience the divinities and to receive their blessings.

3.1.3.6. MORAL LIVING

Vedic Hinduism, by its very nature, affirms life in all its form. All the various daily practices of a Hindu, the domestic cult and the sacrifices he offers are aimed at strengthening and preserving life in nature, in the state and in the family. Besides the various ritual performances of his choice (*Ishta*), there are the moral observances (*Puurta*) that helped the individual to obtain long life on earth and a prosperous life for all posterity. The importance of moral life is clearly shown, already in the Vedic times, in the truth that after death man would reap what he has sown. Thus, *Ishta* and *Puurta* are the cardinal commands of the Vedic Hinduism.[228] This is clearly indicated in a hymn from the *Rig Veda* that addresses the dead as follows:

> Go forth; go forth upon the ancient pathways whereon our sires of old have gone before us. There shalt thou look on both the Kings enjoying their sacred food, God *Varuna* and *Yama*. Meet *Yama*, meet the Fathers, meet the merit of free or ordered acts in the highest heaven. Leave sin and evil, see anew thy dwelling, and bright with glory wear another body.[229]

This hymn from *Rig Veda* points to the fact that the dead person not only meets the ancestors, the kings and the gods, but also encounters the previous good deeds done here on earth, whether they are ritual observances or moral commands. Besides, it also points to the fact that if a person leaves sin and evil and lives a genuine moral life, he possesses a new dwelling and wears another bright glorious body. By implication, it also means that if a person lives a life of sin and evil, i.e., an immoral life, he may not possess the blessings of a new dwelling and a new body. Thus, in this hymn from the *Rig Veda*, the concept of *karma* is already implied, though it is not clearly stated. Hence, in the Vedic concepts of *Ishta* and *Puurta*, viz., sacrifice and moral living respectively, especially in the latter, the law of *Karma* is present in seed form, which developed in the later Vedic literature.[230] From what we have said it is clear that Vedic Hinduism did perceive genuine moral living as a path to encounter the gods and enjoy their blessings, not only here on earth, but also in the life after this life.

3.1.3.7. EXPIATION AND PURIFICATION

Failure in performing the sacrifices according to the rules and not living a genuine moral life make a person commit sin. Thus, there is the need for expiation for one's sin, thereby effecting the purification within the person. Thus, expiation and purification have to do with the removal of sin. In the *Rig Vedas* we find a number of terms used to refer to evil and sin. The terms '*Paapa*' and '*Paapam*' are general terms, and they indicate an evil. '*Paasa*' means a fetter or a snare, while '*Amhas*' stands for distress and anxiety. '*Enas*' means a moral wrongdoing or a ritual inaccuracy the consequence of both is sin. '*Aagas*', '*Heda*' and '*Hedana*' mean an offence. '*Viloma*', '*Kilvisa*' and '*anrta*' indicate a ritual mistake, injury, guilt and offence. All these terms point to various kinds of evils, such as, disease, death, misfortune, calumny, enmity and sin. Therefore, in the *Rig Veda* there is a vague conception of sin and no clear distinction between sin and other forms of evil is made.[231]

But there are texts in *Rig Veda* that speak of sin materialistically as a stain, in which a person is enmeshed and which can be washed away by water, fire and the holy law of *Varuna*. To quote: "Whatever sin is found in me, whatever evil I have wrought, if I have lied or falsely sworn, Waters, remove it far from me."[232] Similarly sin is described as being removed by fire. "I, by address, by blame, by imprecation, have committed sin, awake or sleeping, [all] hateful acts of mine, all evil doings may *Agni* bear away to distant places."[233] Likewise the holy laws of *Varuna* are said to remove sin. "Loosen the bonds, O *Varuna*, that hold me, loosen the bonds above, between and under. So in thy holy law, may we be made sinless."[234] Thus, though the *Rig Veda* has a concept of sin, it is more in a general and unspecified sense that the term 'sin' is used. But, in the other *Vedas* the concept of sin is more specified. For instance, in the *Atharva Veda* speaks of illness as a punishment for sin, while the *Yajur Veda* speaks of ritual sin that is more important than the violations of the moral law.[235]

The idea of expiation for and purification of one's sin is clearly expressed in the hymns of *Rig Veda* that present *Varuna* as the moral god, who governs the world according to *Rta*. Wrongdoings, such as, disobedience, false speech, negligence in worship, gambling and cheating in games are considered as sins against *Varuna*, the Lord of *Rta*, and need to be expiated in order to receive the Lord's forgiveness and thus, be purified. The following beautiful expiatory prayer addressed to the god *Varuna* clearly expresses the sentiments of the devotee, who has realized his sinfulness:

> If we have sinned against the man who loves us, have ever
> wronged a brother, friend, or comrade, [the] neighbor ever

with us, or a stranger, O *Varuna* remove from us the trespass. If we, as gamesters cheat at play, have cheated, done wrong unwittingly or sinned of purpose, [cast] all these sins away like loosened fetters, and, *Varuna* let us be thine own beloved.[236]

Another hymn that expresses the devotee's deep sentiments of sorrow, repentance and the desire for mercy from the Lord and King *Varuna* reads as follows:

Let me not yet, King *Varuna*, enter into the house of clay: Have mercy, spare me, Mighty Lord. When, Thunderer! I move along tremulous like a wind-blown skin, [have] mercy, spare me mighty Lord. O Bright and powerful God, through want of strength I erred and went astray: Have mercy, spare me, Mighty Lord. Thirst found thy worshipper though he stood in the midst of water-floods: Have mercy, spare me, Mighty Lord. O *Varuna*, whatever the offence may be which we as men commit against the heavenly host, [when] though our want of thought we violate thy laws, punish us not O God, for that iniquity.[237]

Having experienced the forgiveness of the Lord and having been purified by his healing touch, the seeker expresses his trustful love for the Lord, the desire to be united with Him and to serve Him like a slave. The following hymn communicates these sentiments:

With mine own heart I commune on the question how *Varuna* and I may be united. What gift of mine will he accept unangered? When may I calmly look and find his gracious? ... What, *Varuna*, hath been my chief transgression, that thou wouldst slay the friend who sings thy praises? Tell me Unconquerable Lord and quickly sinless will I approach thee with mine homage. ... Slavelike may I do service to the Bounteous, serve, free from sin, the Lord inclined to anger. This gentle Lord gives wisdom to the simple: the wiser God leads on the wise to riches. O Lord, O *Varuna*, may this laudation come close to thee and lie within thy spirit. ... Preserve us evermore ... with blessings.[238]

These texts from the *Rig Veda* clearly point to the fact that recognition of one's sin and evil, and the desire and prayer for expiation, opens one to the forgiveness of the Lord, thereby effecting purification within one. Having been purified by the forgiving touch of the Lord, the seeker desire to be united with the Lord in love and friendship. Thus, expiation for one's sin and the resultant purification truly indicates that the people of the Vedic time used to come in contact with the divine.

3.1.3.8. SACRAMENTAL ACTS

Genuine purification in the life of the Hindu is usually brought about with the help of the sacramental acts (*Samskaaras*), which are domestic rites. The term "*Samskaara*" is derived from the Sanskrit root "*Samskrgan*", which indicates 'purification'. Impurities are of two types, namely, bodily impurities and spiritual impurities. A *Samskaara* is a rite that has the power to remove both of these types of impurities. The purifying effect of the *Samskaaras* can even help a dead person in his next life.[239] The following description points to the nature of the *Samskaaras*:

> The word "*Samskaara*" has its own peculiar associations gathered round it through its long history. It means religious purificatory rites and ceremonies for sanctifying the body, mind and intellect of an individual, so that he may become a full-fledged member of the community. ... [They] also combine a number of preliminary considerations and rites and other accompanying regulations and observances, all aiming at not only the formal purification of the body but at sanctifying, impressing, refining and perfecting the entire individuality of the recipient. The *Samskaaras* with their paraphernalia were regarded as producing a peculiar indefinable kind of merit for the man who underwent them.[240]

The question of the origin and the purpose of the *Samskaaras* are also not very clear. Their origin may be attributed to popular superstitions or to people's recognition that the *Samskaaras* are moments in and through which the life of an individual can be opened to the blessings of the gods. Spelling out some of the purposes of the *Samskaaras* could throw some light on this point. Some of the popular purposes are the removal of the hostile influences, the attracting of favorable influences, and the gaining of material goods - like cattle, progeny, long life, wealth and prosperity. Besides, the *Samskaaras* serve as moments of self-expression, in which the householder makes known his happy feelings, for instance, during the marriage ceremonies or his painful feelings at the funeral ceremonies. The performance of the *Samskaaras* also contributes to the cultural, moral and spiritual life of an individual, the formation of his personality and his relationship to the community and the family to which he belongs, as the *Samskaaras* cover every stage of a person's life here on earth, from his birth to his death. All these various purposes might have led to the development of different *Samskaaras* of Hinduism.[241]

There are a number of elements that go to make the complex *Samskaaras* of Hinduism. The most prominent element is fire, as it is lit before every *Samskaara* begins. Prayers, appeals and blessings make the second element of *Samskaaras*. These are part of every stage of the performance of the *Samskaaras*. Prayers and appeals are usually made for one's own good, while the blessings are made for the good of others. The third constituent is sacrifices, which are offered in the beginning and throughout the course of the *Samskaraas*. Fourthly, they included lustrations, which consist of bath, sipping water and sprinkling of water over persons and things. The fifth constituent of *Samskaaras* is orientation, which implies taking certain positions and directions while they are being performed. Symbolism is the sixth element. Every act done during the *Samskaara* has an inner meaning, which is expressed through external symbols. Seventh, while performing the *Samskaaras*, before and after, one is expected to follow certain taboos. Observing the taboos strictly is essential for obtaining the merit of the *Samskaaras*. Magic is the eighth element. It is believed that the performance of certain actions and repetitions of certain formulas automatically brings about the results intended. Ninth, divinatory methods, especially astrology, as a means to know the will of the supernatural beings, formed are an important part in the *Samskaaras*. Tenth, a number of cultural elements are included in the *Samskaaras*. All these elements and their combinations provide an atmosphere of spiritual significance to the *Samskaaras*, which, in turn, elevates and sanctifies the recipient.[242]

Though the term "*Samskaara*" does not appear in Vedic literature, the reality it stands for is of Vedic origin. Even though the whole range of *Samskaaras* has developed later, the *Rig Veda* speaks of *Samskaaras* related to conception of the child, wedding and funeral.[243] There is a difference of opinion regarding the number of the *Samskaaras*. For instance, the *Dharmasaastras* considers the number as 40. But the generally accepted number is 16, listed under five major headings, covering the entire range of the life of an individual from birth to death. The first are the pre-natal sacramental acts (*Gaarbha Samskaaras*), which include the conception (*Garbhaadhaana*), the quickening of male child (*Pumsavana*) and the hair-parting (*Siimantonnayana*). The second category, the childhood sacramental acts, (*Saisava Samskaaras*) consists of the birth ceremonies (*Jaatakarma*), the name-giving (*Naamakarna*), the first outing (*Nishkramana*), the first feeding (*Anna-Praasana*), the tonsure (*Chuudaa Karana*) and the boring of ears (*Karnavedha*). The third group, the educational sacramental acts, comprise the following: the learning of the alphabets (*Vidyaarambha*), the initiation (*Upanayana*), the beginning of Vedic study (*Vedaarambha*), the shaving of beard (*Kesaanta*) and the end of studentship (*Samaavartana*). The fourth is the sacramental act of Marriage (*Vivaaha*), while the fifth is the funeral sacramental act (*Antyesti Samskaara*).[244] We briefly consider each of them.

3.1.3.8.1. Pre-Natal Sacramental Acts

The pre-natal *Samskaaras* guide the life of the child from its conception up to the time of its birth, by opening it to the influences of the gods. The first pre-natal sacramental act is the conception (*Garbhaadhaana*). It is a rite though which a man places his seed in a woman. It consists in the woman receiving the semen of her husband in her womb. It also involves the husband and the wife making an offering to the sun, accompanied by the prayer "O faithful wife, give birth to a son who will live long and will perpetuate our line". Conception as a *Samskaara* is based on the idea that beneficial gods helped in begetting children. It presupposed a well-established home, a regular marriage and desire for children. The rite points to the fact that conception is not merely an accidental reality in the life of a couple, but rather that it is a calculated procedure, done in all religious sincerity, to produce the best possible progeny. The second pre-natal *Samskaara* is the rite aimed at quickening the male child (*Pumsavana*). It is usually done three months after conception, once the couple has ascertained the conception. It consists in the consecration of the child in the womb, accompanied by Vedic hymns, so that the gods would bless the couple with the male child. Usually this rite is performed when the moon is in the male constellation, a time that is favorable for a male issue. Besides, a few drops of the juice of the banyan tree are placed in the right nostril of the pregnant woman for the birth of a son. A dish of water is placed on her lap to symbolize the life and spirit of the would-be male child. The hair-parting (*Siimantonnayana*) is the third pre-natal *Samskaara*. This rite is said to protect the mother and the child from evil demons, bring prosperity to the mother, keep her in good cheer and bring long life to the unborn child. This rite is performed when the pregnancy is in the fourth, sixth and eighth months. The wife is seated on the western side of the fire, the husband parts her hair upwards, with a number of objects like *Darbha*-grass, porcupine's quill with three white spots, a stick of the *Viiratara* wood and a spinning needle, while chanting *Mantras*. A number of other ceremonies followed. These three *Samskaaras* belonged to the pre-natal period.[245]

3.1.3.8.2. Childhood Sacramental Acts

The pre-natal *Samskaaras* are followed by *Samskaaras* of childhood, which aim at helping the child at its birth and its growth throughout the childhood years. In this section we consider briefly some of the childhood *Samskaaras*.

3.1.3.8.2.1. Birth Ceremonies

The first of the childhood *Samskaaras* is birth ceremonies (*Jaatakarma*). All care is taken to find a suitable place for the delivery. Once the child is born, before the severing of the navel cord, the birth ceremonies are performed. It involves a three-fold rite. The first is *Medhaajanana*, aimed at the production of intelligence. It consists in the father giving the child *ghee* and honey with his fourth finger and with an instrument of gold, while saying the *Mantras*. The second rite is the *Aayushya*, which aims at giving long life to the newborn baby. They involve saying various prayers to prolong the child's life and to strengthen his breath. Lastly the father performs another rite for the fruitful marital and pure life of the child. Blessing the mother for bearing a strong son follows. Then the father cuts the navel cord, washes the child and gives it to the mother for breast-feeding. A few other ceremonies follow. When all the ceremonies are over, *Braahmans* are given gifts and the distribution of alms take place.[246]

3.1.3.8.2.2. Naming of the Child

The second childhood sacramental act is the naming of the child (*Naamakarana*). As a general practice this ceremony is performed on the tenth or the twelfth day after the birth of the child. Secretly naming the child on the day of birth would be an exception to this rule. In the later period, this rite is performed any day between the tenth day after the birth and the first day of the second year. As a preparation for this rite, the house is washed and purified, to remove the impurities caused by birth. The mother and the child are also bathed. The mother, having covered the child with pure cloth and wetted its head with water, standing on the right side of her husband, places the baby in the hands of the father. Offerings are made to *Prajaapati* and the deities of the constellation, viz., *Agni* and *Soma*. Invocations are made depending on the day and the birth sign of the child. The father, then, writes two different names on two stones and lights a small oil lamp before each. The name must be chosen before the lamp flame grows. The directions given in choosing the name, based on the caste and gender of the child, must be followed. The father pronounces two *Mantras*, while touching the mouth, the nose, the eyes and the ears of the baby. Then he whispers the name of the baby in the mother's left ear and the child's right ear, after which he places the child back in the mother's lap. The rite ends with feasting the *Braahmans*, respectfully dismissing the gods and the ancestors to their respective places.[247]

3.1.3.8.2.3. The First Outing

The third childhood sacramental act is the first outing (*Nishkramana*). It is a rite by which the child is introduced to the outside world. During this rite the help of the gods is sought for the protection of the child from natural and supernatural dangers, as it is introduced to the world outside the security of its home. It is generally performed when the child is about four months old. The father and mother of the child perform this rite for the child. On the day of performing this *Samskaara* a square portion of the courtyard, open to the sun, is plastered with clay and cow-dung. The sign of good fortune (*Svastika*) is made on the plastered portion and grains of rice are scattered over it. The child is decorated and brought to the family deity in the house, and the deity is worshipped by singing with instrumental music. The guardians of the eight directions, viz., the sun, the moon, the *Vaasudeva* and the sky are also propitiated. The mother of the child hands it over to the father, and it is carried out into the open air with sounds of conch-shell and the recital of the Vedic hymns. At the time of the actual exposition of the child to the open air the father of the child says the following prayer: 'Whether the child is conscious or unconscious, whether it is day or night, let all the gods led by *Indra* protect the child'. Then the child is taken to the temple for worship, where the child is made to bow to the gods, and the *Braahmans* bless the child. The maternal uncle brings the child home, and it is given gifts.[248]

3.1.3.8.2.4. The First Feeding

The first feeding (*Annapraasana*) is the fourth childhood sacramental act. It is the act of giving solid food to the child and weaning it away from its dependence on the mother's milk. Food is a life-giving substance, and there is something mysterious about it as life emanated from it. As the child is going to take food, the help of the gods is sought to infuse in the child the source of energy. It is usually done between the sixth and eighth months for a boy and between the fifth and seventh months for a girl. On the day of feeding, the sacrificial food is cleansed and cooked, with appropriate verses from the *Vedas*. An oblation is offered to the goddess *Vaak*, praying for speech for the child. Another oblation is made for the vigor and strength of the child. The father of the child makes four more oblations that the child may be gratified through all the senses within the bounds of morality. Finally the father feeds the child silently. The ceremony ends with the feasting of the *Braahmans*.[249]

3.1.3.8.2.5. Tonsure

The fifth childhood sacramental act is the tonsure (*Chuudaakarana*). It consists in shaving off the hair of the child. It is done usually between the first and the third years. On an auspicious day, the mother takes the child, bath and clothed with a new garment that is not yet washed. She places the child on her lap, as she sits down to the west of the sacrificial fire. Then the father performs oblations and partakes of the sacrificial food, moistens the head of the child with water, uttering prayers. The next stage of the rite is shaving the head of the child with razor, with prayers for non-injury to the child. Thirdly, the father hides the hair away along with cow-dung, that the enemies of the family may not use it as an object of magic. The final stage of the rite is the keeping of the top-hair. It is believed that keeping the top-hair prolongs the life of the child. The *Samskaara* ended with giving presents to the teacher and the barber.[250]

3.1.3.8.2.6. Piercing the Ears

The last of the childhood sacramental acts is piercing the ears (*Karnavedha*). It is a rite in which the child's ears are pierced. Though initially it was done for wearing ornaments, later it took religious meaning. This *Samskaara* was done for protection from diseases and for decorative purposes. It is usually done between the third and the fifth years, though it can be done before. Usually a professional needle-maker or the goldsmith performed this

Samskaara. It was performed on an auspicious day. The child seated facing east. At the time of the ceremony it was given some sweetmeats. At first the right ear was pierced, followed by the left and accompanied by prayers. The *Samskaara* ended by feeding the *Braahmans*.[251]

3.1.3.8.3. Educational Sacramental Acts

These childhood sacramental acts took care of the different stages of a person's childhood. As a child grows into a boy and moves towards his adulthood, another set of *Samskaaras* come to a person's aid, viz., the educational sacramental acts. Here we elaborate the different educational *Samskaaras*.

3.1.3.8.3.1. Learning of the Alphabets

The first of the educational *Samskaaras* is the learning of the alphabets (*Vidyaarambha*). The performance of this sacramental act marked the beginning of the child's formal education. Usually it is performed when the child is five years old, but for serious reasons it can be postponed up to the seventh year of the child. But it must be performed before the initiation ceremony. An auspicious day is fixed, when the sun is in the northern hemisphere, to perform the *Samskaara*. On the stipulated day, the child is bathed and well-dressed. Propitiation to many gods is made, after which a *Homa* is offered. Then the child sits facing west, while the teacher sits facing east to begin the *Vidyaarambha Samskaara*. It consists of learning to write and to read. Saffron or other substances, like rice, are scattered on a silver plank and the child writes the first alphabet with a golden pen or with a pen specially made for the occasion, while salutations and prayers are offered to the gods. The child venerates the teacher, and the teacher makes the child read thrice what it has written. The child presents clothes and ornaments to the teacher and makes three circumambulations round the gods. The *Braahmans* are given the sacrificial fee, and they bless the child. At the end the teacher is presented with a turban. The *Samskaara* ends with the dismissal of the gods to their respective places.[252]

3.1.3.8.3.2. Initiation

The second educational sacramental act is the initiation (*Upanayana*). It is a rite by which a young boy begins his preparations for taking up the responsibilities of a householder in the future. It includes being a student, studying the *Vedas* and other sciences, serving his teacher, learning social obligations and responsibilities, and living a strict life of celibacy. The *Atharva Veda* calls the teacher '*Aacaarya*' and the student '*Brahmachaari*'. *Upanayana Samskaara* is meant only for the boys of the twice-born castes. A *Braahman* boy is initiated when he is eight years old, the *Kshatriiya* boy at his eleventh year, and the *Vaisya* boy when he completes his twelfth year.

The father of the boy chooses the teacher. The night before the initiation, the candidate is smeared with a yellow substance. Then a silver ring is tucked in the hair on the top of his head. He spends the whole night in absolute silence. This is a mystic act to remind him of his second birth. The next morning he has his last meal with his mother.[253]

On the day of initiation, which is usually an auspicious day, the boy's head is shaved, except for the lock of hair on the top of his head (*Silkhaa*), has a bath and wears an undergarment (*Kaupiina*) to cover his private part, which reminds him of the life of celibacy he is going to take up. He is also given a silk dress of one piece, which he wears for the ceremony. The teacher, then, ties a girdle around the waist of the candidate, which is aimed at protecting his purity and chastity. Next comes the most important rite of investing the student with the Sacred Thread (*Yajnopaviita*). Placing the Sacred Thread over the boy, the teacher recites appropriate *Mantras* praying for the strength, long life and illumination of the boy, while this boy looks towards the sun. After the Sacred Thread is given, the boy is presented with a deer skin (*Ajina*) and a staff, the former for the purpose of sitting while studying and meditating, the latter for protection as he ventures into the forests, especially when it is dark.[254]

Having equipped the student with the necessities of a student life, a series of symbolic acts are performed. Firstly, the teacher, with his joined hands fills the joined hands of the student with water. Then they both pour out the water from their hands while *Mantras* are recited. It is a symbol of the purification of the student. Secondly, the student is asked to look at the sun and learn from it unswerving duty and discipline. Thirdly, the teacher touches the right shoulder, the navel, the heart and the left shoulder of the student, symbolically reminding him of the need for complete harmony and a whole-hearted communion between the teacher and the initiate. Fourthly, the student is asked to mount a stone, accompanied by prayers. This rite symbolically admonishes the student to cultivate the firmness of determination and strength of character, which are essential for a student life. When these symbolical rites are completed, the teacher takes charge of the student. Reciting the relevant *Mantras*, the teacher holds the hand of the candidate and asks for his name. When the student says his name, he further asks, whose pupil he is. The student replies that it was he. The teacher corrects him saying, "*Indra's* pupil thou art; *Agni* is thy teacher, I am thy teacher". With these words the teacher accepts the boy as his student. Then he gives the student some commandments, which are practical advice for his life. The teacher teaches the *Saavitri Mantra* to the student. Then comes the rite of the first kindling of the fire and feeding the sacred fire with *ghee*, while the teacher teaches the student the *Gaayatrii Mantra*. After this rite the boy goes a to his mother and asks for arms, by addressing her 'lady'. With this the initiation ceremony ends, and the student makes the teacher's house his home and lives by his directions and guidance.[255]

3.1.3.8.3.3. Vedic Study

The beginning of the Vedic Study (*Vedaarambha*) is the third educational *Samskaara*. It is performed after the *Upanayana* and immediately before the student begins his study of the *Vedas*. An auspicious day is fixed for the performance of this *Samskaara*. Before the actual rite begins, a number of preliminary ceremonies are performed. The teacher makes the Sacred Fire and invites the student to be seated on the western side of the fire. General offerings are made. Depending on which *Veda* is going to be studied, two measures (*Aahutis*) of *ghee* are offered to different gods. For instance, if the *Rig Veda* is going to be taught, the offering of *ghee* is made to earth and *Agni*; if the *Yajur Veda*, to the sky and *Vaayu*; if the *Saama Veda*, to *Dyau* and the sun; and if *Atharva Veda*, to the quarter and the moon. If all *Vedas* are going to be studied, all the gods are propitiated with the *ghee* offering. Besides, *Homa* is offered to *Brahman*, *Chhandas* and *Prajaapati*. Finally, the teacher pays the fee (*Dakshinaa*) to the officiating *Braahman* and begins teaching the *Veda*.[256]

3.1.3.8.3.4. Shaving of the Beard

The fourth educational sacramental act is the shaving of the beard (*Kesaanta*). It is a *Samskaara*, which consecrates the first shaving of the student's beard. It is performed when the student arrives at age sixteen and marks the beginning of youth and the end of the boyhood days. The consciousness of manhood dawns upon the youth with the appearing of the beard and moustaches on the face. He needs, now, to be watchful over his youthful impulses. *Kesaanta Samskaara* reminds the student once again of his vow of *Brahmacaarya*. The actual procedure is similar to that of the *Chuudaakarana Samskaara*. The only difference is that in the *Kesaanta Samskaara* it is the beard and the moustaches, while in the former the head is shaved. *Mantras* are recited as the barber does the shaving. After the performance of the *Samskaara*, the student is expected to renew his vow of *Brahmacaarya* and to live a strict life of continence for one year. On this occasion, the student offers a cow to the teacher.[257]

3.1.3.8.3.5. The End of Studentship

The last of the educational *Samskaaras* is the end of studentship (*Samaavartana*). The term '*samaavartana*' means 'returning home from the house of the teacher'. It is performed to terminate the student life. Having finished his studies, the student is in an important stage of his life. This *Samskaara* opens the student's life to the grace of the gods at this important juncture in his life. It is normally performed when the student is about 24 years old. On the day of the *Samskaara* the student shuts himself up in a room throughout the morning. By afternoon, he comes out of the room, embraces the feet of his teacher and pays his last tribute to the Vedic fire by putting fuel on it. Then he bathes in the eight vessels of perfumed water. The number eight suggested the arrival of blessings from the eight quarters of the earth. After the bath, he gives up the clothes he wore as a student, wears new, unwashed clothes and other ornaments, as he is going to begin a more active life in the world. To the one who wishes to spend his life as a scholar is given a bamboo-staff as a security. He is also dressed in new attire and taken in a chariot or on an elephant, and introduced by the teacher as a scholar, who would get many students to teach. [258]

3.1.3.8.4. Sacramental Act of Marriage

Marriage (*Vivaaha*) is the most significant Hindu *Samskaara*, as it unites two people in love and relationship, thereby establishing a family. The marriage rite is very elaborate.[259] We consider here only the essentials of this *Samskaara*. Before the actual marriage takes place, there are a number of preliminaries. The choice of the bride and the bridegroom is the duty of the parents. They have the help of the middleman (*Ghataka*) in this task. Once the initial contacts are made between the families of the bride and the bridegroom, they make a verbal promise (*Vaagdaana*) that is binding on the parties, unless there is any cheating involved. Then, the members of both the families visit each other and exchange gifts. During these visits they discuss the matter of dowry. But there is no meeting between the bride and the bridegroom. An astrologer is consulted to fix the date and time of the marriage.[260]

The actual wedding ceremony has two parts, viz., the giving away of the bride (*Sampradaana*) and the wedding rite proper (*Paanigrahana*). The *Sampradaana* begins with the bridegroom being taken to the room, where the *Vivaaha Samskaara* is to take place, accompanied with shouts of joy. He is made to sit on a low seat opposite the bride's father (*Sampradaataa*). Two *Braahmans* representing the two families assist at the *Samskaara*. The genealogies of the bride and the bridegroom are read out. The bride's father officially announces his decision to choose this young man as his son-in-law. Then he is given gifts, which symbolize his new status in the bride's family and the prosperity, which the bride's family wishes him. Now the bride, who is seated on a flat seat, is carried on the shoulders of four relatives and brought to the place of the ceremony with loud cries of joy. This may be the first time that the bride and the bridegroom see each other face-to-face (*Subhdarsana*). A married woman, a mother of living sons, then, ties together the right hands of the bride and the bridegroom with *Kusha* grass. The bride's father, having held the left hand of her daughter, sprinkles her with scented water. Sprinkling holy water on the tied right hands of the bride and the bridegroom, the bride's father says: "I give away this my daughter decked with clothes and ornaments and devoted to *Prajaapati*". The bridegroom accepts the bride with the word '*Svasti*'.[261]

Once the bride's father gives his daughter to the bridegroom, the wedding ceremony (*Paanigrahana*) begins. It takes place before a Sacred Fire. After a few introductory rites and oblations, the bride places her hand on the bridegroom's right shoulder, while the bridegroom pours *ghee* on the fire, invoking the gods for the prosperity of the new home he is going to begin with his bride. The bride is made to mount a stone, and the bridegroom takes her round the fire and says: "Tread on this stone; like a stone be firm". After this, the bride offers grain to the fire. At this moment, the guests are invited to bless the bride. The *Paanigrahana*, which literally means 'seizing the hand', which forms the core of the wedding ceremony, consists in the following. The bridegroom, while supporting the folded hand of the bride with his left hand, seizes the bride's right thumb with his right hand and recites prescribed *Mantras*. These *Mantras* are prayers for children, harmony in the family and happiness in the married life. With this act they become husband and wife. While seated in front of the fire, the husband and wife promise to live together. The husband, then, leads his wife outside the door and points out to her the pole star, which is accompanied by repetition of prayers on the part of the husband and wife. Following this, the husband touches the heart of the bride, and reaching over her right shoulder, says: "I bind your heart and mine with the knot of truth. May your heart be mine, may my heart be yours. May *Prajaapati* join you to me". The husband and wife then take seven steps together. Through this act symbolically they give their marriage consent. After it is performed, the marriage is regarded as legally complete. When the wedding ceremony is over, the family of the bride throws a grand meal for the members of the family of the bridegroom and the guests. As is customary, after a day or two the bride leaves her house and joins the family of the husband, where she now belongs.[262]

3.1.3.8.5. Funeral Sacramental Act

The funeral rite (*Antyesti Samskaara*) is the last sacramental act in the life of a Hindu. It not merely concludes the life of a devout Hindu, but also opens his life in the next world. So it has a great significance in the Hindu religious life. It is the belief of the Hindus that death does not bring about the annihilation of a person, as his soul lives on. Hence, the attitude of the survivors towards the dead is a mixture of dread and love. Though they loved the dead, yet they were afraid that the dead would do them some harm. This is the reason for offering propitiations for the dead. The bodies of the dead are usually cremated, though there are references to burial. There was also the custom of first cremating the body and then burying the ashes.[263]

There are a number of references in the *Rig Veda* and the *Atharva Veda* as to the manner in which the funeral rite had to be done. When a person dies we are told that we must try to revive his breathing-in and out-breathing by praying to *Brihaspati* and to the *Asvins*, the physician gods. *Agni* is prayed to snatch the dying man from the lap of *Nirrti*, the goddess of destruction. Then we are told to commit the dying man to the seven sages, who can bring him back to life. When all attempts to revive the life of the dead man are done, we must prepare for the funeral rite.[264] It begins with washing the dead body of the person. After he is washed, the big toes of the feet must be tied together with a bunch of twigs. It is done to prevent the dead walking back to the house after the corpse is sent out.[265] Then the corpse is removed from the house and carried on a cart drawn by two bulls, while the relatives and professional mourners accompany the funeral bier.[266] When the funeral bier has reached the burning ground, the dead body is taken out of the cart and dressed before the cremation. The face of the dead person is covered with the skin of a cow and the staff, which the dead person has been using, is taken from his hands.[267] Then the corpse is placed on the funeral pyre. The widow, whose husband has died, symbolically lies down on the funeral pyre by the side of her husband's dead body and bids him goodbye.[268] A goat is sacrificed, as the funeral pyre is lit up, while the women express their grief.[269] The various parts of the dead man's body are directed to go to appropriate places, depending on the merit of the person. For instance, the eye is directed to go to the sun, the spirit to the wind and other parts to the waters to find their home in plants.[270] After the burning of the body, the bones are collected and buried. In some cases, a funeral monument is erected over the buried bones.[271] The actual funeral rite ends with a farewell address, in which a close relative or friend of the dead person condoles his death narrating the many good things the dead person has done while he was alive.[272]

When the funeral is over, the survivors bathe themselves to purify the pollution caused by the funeral fire. As they arrive home from the funeral ground, a pure sacrificial fire is lighted in the house to remove the impure fire. The power of the pure fire drives the corpse-eating fire (*Kravyaada*) that is invoked for cremation out of the house. Similarly, the *Graahi* fire, that holds fast to the house when a woman's husband dies, is also send out of the house.[273] The survivors, having purified themselves and the house, offered various propitiatory oblations and sacrifices to the dead, to aid the dead to attain the life of the spirits. These include asking forgiveness for the human frailty of the dead, that they may deserve and become worthy of a share of the *Soma*, that they may dwell in glowing light with *Agni*, that *Agni* may take them to their proper place, that *Agni* may give these offerings to the dead person, and they may be granted the world of the spirits and their body.[274] When the dead person is propitiated and prayed for, the survivors return to their normal living, which includes feasting, dancing and laughter.[275]

In the *Rig Veda* and the *Atharva Veda*, we find a clear statement of the four main parts of the *Antyesti Samskaara*, viz., the washing of the corpse and piling of the funeral pyre (*Smasaana-chiti*), the burning of the corpse (*Abhishinchana*), the water oblations (*Udaka-karma*) and the propitiatory rites (*Saantikarma*). A number of additions have come about in the course of time, but in essence *Antyesti Samskaara* has remained as we find it in the *Vedas*.[276]

The *Samskaaras* open the totality of a person's life from birth to death, especially the key moments of transition and change, to the grace of the gods. In doing so, they serve as a great means through which a Hindu could come closer to the gods and the gods he believed in could come closer to him. In this manner, the *Samskaaras* are true paths to the divine.

9.9.9.9. SPECIAL OBSERVANCES

Other than the *Samskaaras*, there are a number of practices that have a great deal of influence on the lives of the people. They helped people to open themselves to the good the gods provide and to avoid evil influences, which the planetary movements, the demons and spirits cause. In this section, we briefly consider some of such special practices.

In their daily practical living the Hindus gave immense importance to astrology and omens. No significant event in the life of a Hindu passes without consulting an astrologer. Whether it is birth, choosing a partner in marriage or choosing a profession, a Hindu approaches an astrologer to compose the horoscope, which becomes a sacrosanct document, for any move he makes in his life. For instance, a person may choose a profession, even though he may have no aptitude for it, if his horoscope says that his prosperity consists in that particular profession. Similarly, two people can get married only if their horoscopes are in agreement. Hindus also give an important place to following the omens in their life.[277]

Secondly, these are regulations regarding auspicious and inauspicious hours of the day, days of the week and weeks of the month that direct the daily life of the Hindus. For instance, Monday is inauspicious for the purchase of cloth and shoes and starting a journey eastward, while it is auspicious for birth and wedding. Tuesday is not good for sowing any seed, entering a new house or opening a new shop. Traveling northward on this day would be inauspicious. Wednesday would be a lucky day for the birth of a son, but an unlucky day for the birth of a daughter. It is good day to start a court case or to buy clothes. Thursday is auspicious to send the child to a new school. To travel southward would be inauspicious. Friday is a good day to buy land and trees. One must avoid traveling westward. Saturday is a bad day for most things one undertakes, but it is good to begin a friendship, to engage a servant and to move to a new house. Sunday is a good day to study the *Mantras* and to travel. Similarly, certain days of the month are considered auspicious, while others are inauspicious. In a lunar calendar the month is divided into two fortnights, viz., the bright fortnight (*Suklapaksha*) and the dark fortnight (*Krshnapaksha*). The eleventh day (*Ekaadasii*) of each fortnight is the holiest day, and it brings luck to any task undertaken on that day. Usually the first, fourth, ninth and fourteenth days of each fortnight are inauspicious. The full moon day (*Puurnimaa*) is auspicious, whereas the moonless day (*Amaavaasyaa*), which is dedicated to the ancestors, is not auspicious. Neither sowing nor marriages take place on that day. In this manner, each day of the week and month is regulated and people are scrupulous in following these directions regarding what is auspicious and inauspicious.[278]

Thirdly, most Hindus believe in demons, ghosts and wandering spirits. The *Atharva Veda* is full of charms, spells and incantations that would ward off the evils these spirits can bring to men. The wearing of amulets and talismans help one to avoid the evils of these wicked spirits. Talismans and amulets contain an image of god or a small bit of paper or a bark of a tree on which the spell is written. They are very helpful to drive away the evil spirits. The *Atharva Veda* praises the power of amulets and talismans.[279] People use other methods, such as, placing the skull of a cow smeared with vermillion, the burnt skull of a dog, an old shoe or a thorny twig placed on a wall to scare off the devils. Again, placing a sickle under the bed, beating the drums, blowing a conch-shell and keeping a scare-devil in the field are believed to frighten away the evil spirits. The spirits that cannot be warded off must be propitiated. People do it by providing them a home and worship. A stone surrounded by a few small stones, smeared with vermillion represents these spirits. The regular worship offered to them consists in washing the stones, smearing *ghee* and new vermillion and offerings of fruits and sweetmeats. It is believed that these spirits protect those who worship them in time of troubles, especially during pestilence. There are some most dangerous spirits, which need to be propitiated through bloody sacrifice. The worship of these spirits consists in a devil-dance, accompanied by loud music, during which the spirits take possession of a person and use him as a 'medium' to communicate oracles. The use of exorcism to ward off the spirit that possesses people was also common. The methods used included physical violence and the recital of *Mantras*. Magic was also used as a means to free oneself from these wicked spirits or to win their favor.[280]

These are a few of the practices that serve the people as means to come in contact with divine beings, being open to their blessings and to protect themselves from the troubles that the evil spirits can bring in their lives. Thus, though some of these means are not as good and honorable as they should be, yet they are paths that opened the people to the divine.

Vedic Hinduism is simple and deeply religious. The daily prayers and practice help a Hindu to build up his personal relationship to the gods. The domestic cult strengthens the religious fabric of the family. Priesthood, sacrifices, temple worship and moral living guide the social and national framework opening it to the influences of the divine. Acts of expiation, purification and the *Samskaaras* while purifying the individual, open every important stage of his life, from birth to death, to the powerful guidance of the gods. Other special observances free a person from fear and give him a sense of confidence in every move he makes in his life. Thus, Vedic Hinduism, in spite of its limitations, is, indeed, a religion of rich beliefs and life-sustaining religious practices.

2.2 VEDAANTIC HINDUISM

Our study of the Vedic Hinduism clearly shows that in the Vedic religious belief about the divinity, there is a move from polytheism to monotheism. A number of hymns of the *Rig Veda* points to this transition. To quote: "They call him *Indra, Mitra, Varuna, Agni*... To what is One, sages give many a title: they call it *Agni, Yama, Maatraisvan*."[281] Again the famous *Purusha Suukta* hymn of the *Rig Veda* presents the *Purusha* as the primordial Man, who contains in himself the whole cosmos, which he brings into being as the one who sacrifices and the sacrificial victim.[282] The hymn addressed to the unknown God (*Ka*) questions the origin of the universe and speaks of an anonymous god, who became the golden egg (*Hyrayanagarbha*) in the beginning and brings about everything in the universe. The hymn ends by identifying the unknown God with *Prajaapati*.[283] The creation hymn of *Rig Veda* goes much further than the unification of the gods the previous three hymns aim. It reads as follows:

> Then was not non-existent nor existent: there was no realm of air, no sky beyond it. What covered in, and where? And what gave shelter? Was water there, unfathomable depth of water? Death was not then, nor was there aught immortal: no sign was there, the day's and night's divider. That One Thing, breathless, breathed by its own nature: apart from it was nothing whatsoever. ...All that existed then was void and formless: by the great power of Warmth was born that Unit. Thereafter rose Desire in the beginning, Desire the primal seed and germ of Spirit. Sages who searched with their hearts' thought discovered that existent's kinship in the non-existent. ...Who verily knows and who can here declare it, whence it was born and whence comes this creation? The Gods are later than this world's production. Who knows then whence it first came into being? He, the first origin of this creation, whether he formed it all or did not form it, Whose eye controls this world in the highest heaven, he verily knows it, or perhaps he knows not. [284]

In describing creation, this hymn says that creation comes about by the activity of One Supreme Being. Before the Supreme Being brings creation into being, there was nothing that existed. Even the gods are said to be later than the process of the world's becoming. To the question as to the manner in which the creation takes place, the hymn gives a two-fold answer. Firstly, creation comes about by the power of Warmth. Secondly, Desire is the basis of the creative process. The hymn ends with an ironic statement that the Supreme Being may or may not know about the creative process. Through the ironic conclusion of the hymn, the poet suggests that there could be a reality higher than the Supreme Being, who is the principal source of the creative process.[285]

Thus, the transition towards the unification of many gods into one continues throughout the *Rig Vedic* hymns, and towards the end of the Vedic period, especially in the *Upanishads*, there arrives on the religious scene the monism of the Vedaantic Hinduism, which takes the place of monotheism. This essay attempts to elaborate the nature of the divinity, its relationship to man's destiny and the paths that are proposed to help man to come in union with the divinity during the period of the end (*Anta*) of the *Vedas*.

3.2.1. THE DIVINITY AND MAN'S DESTINY IN VEDAANTIC HINDUISM

The way the divinity is perceived in Vedaantic Hinduism has a great influence on the manner in which the destiny of man is conceived, as the destiny of man is linked to his relationship to the divinity. Therefore, before we can consider the paths, which lead man to achieve his destiny in the divinity, we need to unravel the nature of the divinity and its relationship to man's destiny. Hence, in this section, we elaborate the nature of the divinity in Vedaantic Hinduism and man's destiny as interpreted in the thoughts of the three scholastic thinkers, Shankara, Raamaanuja and Madhva.

3.2.1.1. NATURE OF THE DIVINITY IN VEDAANTIC HINDUISM

The term, Vedaantic Hinduism of the *Upanishads* used to refer to the divinity, is '*Brahman*'. It appears for the first time in the *Rig-Veda*. Here, it means a sacred word, hymn or utterance. Initially it stands for a 'spell' or a 'prayer'. Gradually the word '*brahman*' acquires the meaning of the mysterious power of prayer, which can bring about what one wishes to achieve. *Brahmanaaspati* is considered as the Lord of prayer. In the *Braahmanas*, '*brahman*' denotes a ritual food offering, the chant of the *Soma* singer, magical formula, duly completed ceremony, chant and the sacrificial gift together, and the recitation of the *Hotr* priest. Therefore, it is considered omnipotent. In the later thought, '*brahman*' means wisdom or sacred knowledge (*Veda*) and its expression a hymn and incantation. In this sense, it is used to refer to the hymns of the *Rig Veda* and the *Atharva Veda*. Since divine origin is attributed to '*Veda*' or '*Brahman*', it comes to be known as the first created thing (*Brahmaprathamajam*) and is treated as the creative principle and the cause of existence.[286]

Having clarified the meaning of the term '*brahman*', we move on to see how the reality called *Brahman* is understood in the *Upanishads*. The sages of the *Upanishads* understand the reality of *Brahman* from two levels of experience, viz., the transcendental and the phenomenal. In the transcendental perspective, *Brahman* is viewed as the unitive principle, in which all the differences of the subject and the object merge into a non-dual consciousness. In the phenomenal level, *Brahman* is associated with the universe that is diverse. A person's experience in both of these planes is real, if seen from the points of view of the respective stage. But what is experienced in one stage as true may be invalidated, when it is seen from the perspective of the other.[287] We could briefly analyze the nature *Brahman* in both of these aspects, as described in the *Upanishads*.

3.2.1.1.1. Transcendental Brahman

The *Upanishads* speak of the transcendental *Brahman* as devoid of any qualities (*Nirviseshaa / Nirgunaa*). As qualifying characteristics are totally absent, the *Upanishads* designate the absolute *Brahman* by the neuter 'it'.[288] As *Brahman* is without qualities, it is completely incomprehensible. Since it is not comprehensible, it is known through the negative method of 'not this, not this' (*neti, neti*). Therefore, we could not give any positive description of the transcendental *Brahman*, but rather we can say only what it is not. The knowledge of a thing arises through the senses, the mind and the intellect. Since *Brahman* cannot be reached through these media, it is impossible to explain what it is to a disciple. "There [in the realm of the *Brahman*] the eye goes not, nor the mind; we know not, we understand not, how one can teach this."[289] The indescribability of *Brahman* results in the Upanishadic sages giving it conflicting descriptions. *Brahman* is never stirring, yet it is swifter than the mind. Thought it is subtler than the atoms, it is greater than the great. It is said to be sitting down, but it travels far. Similarly, though it is lying down, it goes everywhere. These conflicting qualities ascribed to *Brahman* cancel each other and leave us with the idea of a pure consciousness free from all attributes. The realization of this pure consciousness is the supreme purpose in the life of every human person.[290]

The indescribable and pure-conscious *Brahman* is above the known and the unknown, but it is not unknowable. In other words, though we cannot categorize *Brahman* either as known or as unknown, to say that we cannot know it would be wrong. The implied reason behind this claim of the *Upanishad* is that though the knowledge of *Brahman* cannot be attained by logic, it is known in the teaching of the ancients that comes to us through the tradition and through mystical experience.[291] This truth is clearly stated in the following passage from the *Kena Upanishad*:

> That which is not expressed through speech but that by which speech is expressed; that, verily, know thou, is *Brahman* ... That which is not thought by the mind but by which they say, the mind ... (thinks); that, verily, know thou, is *Brahman* ... That which is not seen by the eye but by which the eyes ... (see); that, verily, know thou, is *Brahman* ... That which is not heard by the ear but by which the ears...(hear); that, verily, know thou, is *Brahman* ... That which is not breathed by life, but by which life breathes; that, verily, know thou, is *Brahma.*[292]

Besides, the transcendental *Brahman* is all-pervasive, as it is in everything and everything is in it. The *Upanishads* speak of *Brahman* as identical with speech, eye, breath, ear, mind and the heart. It is also described as food, water, ether and all other elements. All these indicate that nothing is outside *Brahman*.[293] Again it is identified with space. *Brahman* is said to be the space outside a person and a space within in a person.[294] Yet it is free from the limiting adjuncts of space and time. It is supra-cosmic, eternal, spaceless and timeless spirit that supports all the worldly manifestations of space and time. *Brahman* is the source of activity behind the various cosmic forms and movements. *Brahman* is compared to salt melted in the water. Though salt is invisible, it is present and felt in every drop of water. In the same way, *Brahman*, though invisible, is the directing force of everything in the universe.[295] Swami Nihilananda describes the transcendental *Brahman* as follows:

> [Transcendental] *Brahman* is the negation of all attributes and relations. It is beyond time, space, and causality. Though it is spaceless, without it space could not be conceived; though it is timeless, without it time could not be conceived; though it is causeless, without it the universe, bound by the law of cause and effect, could not be conceived to exist. Only if one admits the reality of pure being as the unchanging ground of creation can one understand proximity in space, succession of time, and interdependence in the chain of cause and effect.
> ... *Brahman* is not a philosophical abstraction, but it is more intimately known than any sense-object. It is *Brahman* that, as the inner consciousness, makes perception of sense-object possible. *Brahman* is the intangible reality that unifies all the discrete objects in the phenomenal universe, making it appear a cosmos and not chaos.[296]

Thus, the *Upanishads* declare *Brahman* as the unitary and supreme reality that is hidden from the senses, but which remains identical and persists through change, and the knowledge of which frees a human person from his finitude. This perception of *Brahman* suggests the deep relationship between the human spirit and the foundational spirit that guides this universe, which the former aspires to attain.

3.2.1.1.2. Phenomenal Brahman

The phenomenal *Brahman* is endowed with qualities (*Saviseshaa / Sagunaa*). The *Upanishads* attribute the pronoun 'He' to refer to the phenomenal *Brahman*. Another term used to speak of *Brahman* in the phenomenal aspect is *Iishvara*, which means 'the Lord'. *Iishvara* is the all-powerful Lord of all and the ruler of the universe. He bestows all blessings and is adored as the personal god. The whole universe is under his mighty rule. He is the inner ruler of creatures, who guides their activities, but he is totally different from the creatures he governs. *Iishvara* in association with *maayaa* and its constituents, the three *Gunaas,* brings about everything in the universe including the various aspects of his Godhead. Thus, *Maayaa* gives rise to the conception of *Iishvara*, as the creator (*Brahmaa*), the preserver (*Vishnu*) and the destroyer (*Siva*). These three gods are nothing other than *Iishvara* with reference to the three *Gunaas*. When *Maayaa*, in its *Sattvic* aspect, limits *Iishvara*, i.e., *Sattva* as the predominating limiting conditions (*Upaadhi*), it is called *Vishnu*. He sustains and preserves the cosmic order. When *Iishvara* has *Maayaa* with

Rajas as the dominant *Upaadhi*, it is called *Brahmaa*. He is the creator of the cosmic order. When *Maayaa* dominates *Iishvara* with *Tamas*, it is called the *Siva*. He is the destroyer of the universe. Thus, *Iishvara* with the help of the *Sattva* preserves, with the help of *Rajas*, creates and, using *Tamas*, destroys. *Iishvara* is the Lord of creation, preservation and destruction. In him the universe lives, breathes and disappears. The phenomenal *Brahman* is said to be the womb from which the universe comes into existence, where it is sustained and to which it returns at its destruction. Thus, during periods of creation, preservation and destruction, the universe is said to be not distinct from *Brahman*. He is the God, who pervades all the regions of the universe. Creation and destruction are said to be the breathing of *Iishvara*. When he exhales, the world of names and forms appears, and when he inhales, it ceases to exist. Thus, the phenomenal *Brahman* is the innermost essence of everything and it is he who sustains everything in its being.[297]

Iishvara is not only the controller of the physical nature and the moral life of the humans. His providence is extended to every aspect of the moral life of a person. Thus, good and evil acts produce their respective fruits under his supervision. We should not conclude from the above statement that God is responsible for the good and evil men do. When man is separated from God, he sees good and evil, just as one perceives darkness and light only when he is separated from the sun, which is light. God is not affected by good or evil. We need light to see things. In the same way, God is the light with guidance of which good and evil actions are performed. But God is not doing the good or evil but only helps the action as light helps one to see. If a person uses the light of God for evil, one does evil. On the other hand, if one uses God's light for good, one performs a good action. A man is judged according to the fruits of his actions. The Law of *Karma* preserves the moral order, and God is the administrator of this law, just as civil authority administers the civil law.[298] Thus, *Iishvara* is the all-knower, as he is the witness of all animate and inanimate objects in the universe. He has universal Lordship, as he gives rewards and punishments to finite beings according to the merits of their actions (*Karma*). *Iishvara* has total control over all, because he directs all the physical and mental propensities of finite beings.

The Vedaantic Hinduism of the *Upanishads* presents this dual perspective of the divinity as a matter of fact manner. It sees no real conflict between the transcendental and the phenomenal *Brahman*, as *Brahman* can be viewed from the phenomenal and transcendental points of view. When the world of sense perception is looked upon as real, *Brahman* would be described as the all-powerful and all knowing creator, preserver and the destroyer. But seen from the transcendental perspective, for instance, as in a state of deep meditation, one experiences *Brahman* as Pure Consciousness and loses oneself in it. In the *Upanishads*, we find texts to support both of these experiences of *Brahman*. The lack of precision and clarity in the Upanishadic perception of the divinity, viz., *Brahman*, later led thinkers to a great amount of confusion, both regarding their understanding of the nature of *Brahman* and man's relationship to *Brahman*, in the process bringing about conflicting views on man's destiny. In this section, we will briefly consider three major scholastic interpreters of Vedaanata, viz., Shankara, Raamaanuja and Madhva, whose perception of the nature of *Brahman* and its relationship to man made them propose different theories regarding man's ultimate destiny.

3.2.1.2. MAN'S DESTINY IN VEDAANTIC HINDUISM

Shankara proposes a Non-dualistic (*Advaitic*) interpretation of Vedaanta, which makes him consider *Brahman* as *Nirgunaa* and the whole world, including *Iishvara* and the empirical existence of man, as unreal from the perspective of *Brahman*. Thus, for him man's destiny consists in the recognition of his identity with *Brahman*. Raamaanuja proposes a Qualified Non-dualism (*Visishtaadvaita*), which holds for a Non-dual *Brahman*, but qualified by the world and individual spirits that form his body (*Sariira*). Raamaanuja, while not denying the reality of the world and the individual soul, denies the *Advaitic* distinction between absolute *Brahman* and *Iishvara*. Thus, he holds for the reality of God, the *Sagunaa Brahman*, the soul and the material world. In doing so, he upholds the unity of God and the dependence of man and world. The destiny of man, for Raamaanuja, consists in the soul acquiring qualities similar to God. Madhva proposed a Dualism (*Dvaita*), which holds that there is a fundamental distinction between God and man. The soul of each man is distinct from that of another man and God. The destiny of man consists in the liberation of the soul the sorrows of the present life and it knowing its true nature. We could expose the views of these three interpreters of Vedaanta in detail.

3.2.1.2.1. Shankara

Shankara, being a Non-dualist, understands *Brahman* as the absolute and transcendental being, which is Pure Consciousness. He derives the word '*brahman*' from the root '*brihati*', which means 'to exceed' (*Atisayana*) and has the meaning of eternity and purity. So the term '*brahman*' etymologically means that which is absolutely the greatest, the eternal and the pure.[299] '*Brahman*', therefore, denotes "that first ... reality from which the entire universe of our experience has sprung up."[300] Thus, *Brahman* signifies the absolute and unlimited reality, which forms the substratum and the foundation of the world as we know, and on which everything depends for its existence. *Brahman* is self-sufficient and does not depend on anything else for its existence. Hence it must be a spiritual entity, since matter is not self-sufficient, but is limited and subject to change. George Thibaut, in his introduction to the *Vedaanta-Suutras*, says that whatever exists is in reality one, and this one universal being is called *Brahman*. This being is absolutely homogeneous in nature. It is pure Being, Intelligence and Thought. Intelligence or thought is not predicated of *Brahman* as its attribute, but constitutes its substance. *Brahman* is not a being that thinks, but thought itself. It is absolutely destitute of qualities, and whatever qualities are conceivable can only be denied of it.[301]

So we cannot grasp *Brahman* with our empirical experience. *Brahman* is *a priori* and cannot be grasped by *a posteriori* experience.

Though the ultimate *Brahman* is indescribable in empirical language, the sages attempt to give some descriptions of *Brahman* that would help the seeker to continue the process of assertion about *Brahman*. The process of assertion provides the seeker with the material needed for contemplation and meditation, which would lead to the realization of *Brahman*. Some of the definitions of *Brahman* are the following. *Brahman* is:

- Eternal (*Nitya*). This means that *Brahman* is not bound by time.
- Imperishable, deathless and changeless.
- Immaculate (*Suddha*), i.e., *Brahman* is not affected by any limiting adjuncts. Just as electricity works through different equipments and yet remains unaffected, so is also *Brahman*, who though functions through everything visible, is unaffected by it.
- Liberated (*Vimukta*), i.e., it is not affected by any bondage and enjoys supreme and everlasting freedom.
- One (*Ekam*). Though due to superimposition, the phenomenal world is projected on *Brahman*, it remains untouched by them. Just as a dream is an expression of mind, so also the plurality of the phenomenal world does not make *Brahman* many, but it remains one. When knowledge dawns, the plurality vanishes and only *Brahman* exists.
- Unbroken bliss (*Akhandaanantam*). Unlike the passing joys derived from material things, the bliss of self-realization is absolute and eternal. Therefore, the supreme bliss is unbroken and everlasting.
- Non-dual (*Avayam*). Though we refer to *Brahman* as one, we cannot consider it as a unit. The concept of unit would bring in the idea of composition of parts and so a limitation on *Brahman*. So *Brahman* is described as non-dual.
- All pervading (*Saravagata*). It alone exists and it exists everywhere. If it were not so there would be a place where *Brahman* has no access, and it would limit *Brahman*. So it is limitless and all pervading.
- Formless (*Niraakaara*). Since it is all pervading and existing everywhere, it is beyond form. Having a form limits a being. So limitless *Brahman* is formless.
- *Satyam – Jnaanam – Aanantam* (truth, knowledge and infinity). *Brahman* is *Satyam*, because it is that which remains the same at all times – in the past, the present and the future. *Brahman* as truth is ever the same and unchanging. *Brahman* as *Jnaanam* is absolute knowledge. We cannot have knowledge of *Brahman*, as we have knowledge of sound, smell, taste, joys and sorrows. But *Brahman* is unconditional knowledge. Knowing *Brahman*, in the sense of experiencing (*Anubhava*) is self-realization. *Brahman* is endless and infinite. Waves have temporary existence, but the sea is permanent. In the same way, the world of phenomenal experience is passing and *Brahman*, the infinite and the endless is the substratum upon which the world appears.[302]

Shankara repeatedly speaks of and strongly defends the absolute, unchangeable and attributeless nature of *Brahman*, alluding to many texts in the scripture, which point to the *Nirgunaa Brahman*.[303] Commenting on the Upanishadic text, "as a lump of salt is without interior or exterior, entire and purely saline taste, even so is the self (*Brahman*) without interior or exterior, entire and pure intelligence alone",[304] Shankara points to the oneness of *Brahman*. In the lump of salt there is nothing other than salt, so, too, *Brahman* is nothing other than itself. It is the absolute being without a second.[305] Shankara uses the example of the sun reflecting in water and appearing as many, in order to bring home the same truth. He says that just as the reflection of the sun in water increases with the increase of water and decreases with its reduction, it moves when the water moves, and it differs as the water differs, so is the self. The sun seems to conform to the characteristics of water, but in reality the sun never has these increasing or decreasing qualities. So also, from the highest point of view, *Brahman* always retains its sameness, and seems to conform to such characteristics as increase and decrease of the limiting adjunct, owing to its entry into such an adjunct as a body.[306]

We can give a few more illustrations to indicate the unitary, unchanged and unaffected nature of *Brahman*. Many candles can be lit from the one flame of a candle. The flame of the first candle is not less because it has given light to many candles. In the same way, though infinite names and forms are drawn from *Brahman*, it remains ever the same. Again cotton is made into thread and cloth. Thread is drawn from cotton and thread is woven into cloth. But the reality of cotton is in both of these forms, viz., both in the thread and the cloth. Similarly, the projections of names and forms of this material world on *Brahman* do not alter the nature of *Brahman*. It remains as it is without any change. We can also illustrate the uniqueness of *Brahman* by analyzing the phenomenon of dreams. Dream objects and dreamer are an internal projection upon the mind of a person. Varieties of things emerge from a person's mind and form the dream. The emergence of the dreams does not make any difference to the mind. The mind remains unchanged and unaffected by the dream, even though both the dream objects and the dreams are aspects of the mind. The dreamer would not realize that dream objects and the dreams are simply aspects of the mind unless he wakes up from the dream. Once the dreamer wakes up, he realizes that the unchanging reality behind the external manifestations is the mind. In the same way, varieties of beings are nothing but different aspects of *Brahman*. As long as a person is caught up in the phenomenal existence, he does not see the unity behind the multiplicity. When one wakes up to the noumenal level, one experiences the one non-dual *Brahman*.[307]

For Shankara, *Brahman* is a principle of utter simplicity. There is no duality in *Brahman*, for no qualities are found in the concept of *Brahman*. It is also simple in the sense that it is not the subject of inner contradictions, which would make it changeable and transitory. Though he uses logic and arguments to understand the nature of *Brahman* and to speak of it, still, for him, *Brahman*, in its reality, is not a metaphysical postulate that can be proved logically, but it must be experienced in silence.[308] Thus, *Brahman* is one: It is not a 'He', a personal being; nor is it an 'It', an impersonal concept. It is that state which comes about when all subject-object distinctions are obliterated. Ultimately, *Brahman* is a name for the experience of the timeless plentitude of Being.[309]

Shankara's understanding of *Brahman* makes him consider the human person from this absolute perspective. For him, the true spirit of man is not the empirical ego, but the *Aatman*. The term '*Aatman*' comes from the Sanskrit root '*an*', which etymologically means to breathe. So '*Aatman*' is the breath of life. In the course of the usage, it was referred to mean life, soul, self or the essential being of an individual. Shankara derived '*Aatman*' from the Sanskrit root, which meant 'to obtain', 'to eat or enjoy' or 'to pervade all'. So for Shankara, '*Aatman*' is the principle of an individual's life, the soul that pervades his being, his breath (*Praana*) and his intellect (*Prajnaa*), and which transcends all these. Negatively put, *Aatman* is that which persists and remains, when the non-self is removed. In the Rig-Veda there is a reference to the unborn (*Ajo Bhaagah*) and the immortal element in man. This element in man is *Aatman*. The body, the mind, the life and the intellect are forms and external expression of the *Aatman*.[310]

Therefore, for Shankara, *Aatman* is the deathless, birthless, eternal and real substance in every individual soul. It is the unchanging reality behind the changing body, sense organs, mind and ego. It is the spirit, which is pure consciousness and is affected by time, space and causality. It is limitless and without a second.[311] In order to understand the true nature of *Aatman*, one must discriminate the innermost self from the outer physical and mental coverings, just as one separates the rice from the husk or exposes the pure white kernel from the coconut by removing the outer husk.[312] *Aatman* is distinct from the body, sense organs, the mind, intellect and desires (*Vasanaas*), and at the same time is the substratum of all activities that emanate from these physical and mental faculties. Though *Aatman* is the activity principle, it ever remains detached and independent of these activities. It is a witness to all these activities. In the same way, the all-pervading *Aatman* directs all the three states of consciousness, namely, the waking state (*Vishva*), the dream-state (*Taijasa*), and the state of deep-sleep (*Praajna*). The basic underlying principle, which witnesses all these three states of one's existence and the activities of the physical and mental faculties, is the pure consciousness (*Chaitanyam*), the self. It is because of the presence of this ultimate substratum that the body, the senses, the mind and the intellect function properly. At the same time, the self is not identified with any of these and not affected by the changes that take place in the body, senses, mind and intellect. Thus, the self belongs to a level higher than these three states, i.e., the Fourth State. In the Fourth State, the self is pure consciousness like a homogenous piece of gold. The Fourth State is nothing else but to be witness of the three states, being unaffected by the changes that take place in these states.[313] Therefore, *Aatman* is the "unrelated witness of the experiences of the three states, which include a man's diverse activities."[314]

Shankara gives the following illustration to clarify the nature of the self, especially in its role of being the witness to all activities of body, senses, mind and the intellect, viz., the analogy of a king's court. In the court, the king sits on his high throne as the observer of the activities of his ministers, councilors and all the others present. But because of his majesty as the king, he is unique and different from all. So, too, the self that is pure consciousness dwells in the body as a witness to the functions of the body, mind and other faculties, while at the same time it is different from them by its natural light. Thus, the witness is the absolute consciousness, the unchanging intelligence that underlies the finer and the grosser bodies. It is neither *Iisvara* nor the *jiiva*, but it is *Aatman*, which is untouched by the distinction of *Iishvara* and *jiiva*.[315]

Shankara also gives a number of other illustrations to show the absolute nature of *Aatman*. An ignorant person may identify the clay with the pot and gold with an earring, forgetting that the pot and the earring are not clay and gold respectively, but rather they are only forms of manifestation of clay and gold. Similarly one may identify the empirical ego with *Aatman* without knowing the real nature of *Aatman*.[316] Again out of a person's ignorance, he may attribute blueness, concavity and similar qualities to the sky, even though the sky does not have any such qualities. In the same way a person walking in a desert may perceive water in a mirage by wrong perception. Likewise in semi-darkness one can perceive a human figure in a post. All such perceptions are illusory. Illusion also is the perception of *Aatman* as identical with the elements of this world.[317] Just as perceptions of a castle in the air and a second moon in the sky are illusory, so also is the perception of *Aatman* as identical with the world is unreal.[318] All these illustrations point to the basic and absolute nature of *Aatman*. The following Upanishadic statement bears witness to this fact. "That imperishable is the unseen seer, the unheard hearer, the unthought thinker, the ununderstood understander. Other than It, there is naught that hears; other than It, there is naught that thinks; other than It, there is naught that understands."[319] Thus, *Aatman* is the Absolute Consciousness.

From the Advaitic perspective of Shankara, the terms '*Brahman*' and '*Aatman*' basically denote one and the same underlying principle: the former stands for the underlying and unchanging principle of the universe; while the latter refers to the unchanging reality in the individuals. Both of these terms are used in the *Upanishads* and understood by the interpreters as synonyms. They are even interchanged in the same sentence to mean each other. Commenting on the Upanishadic statement "Who is *Aatman*? What is *Brahma*?"[320] Shankara remarks: "By *Brahman*, the limitations implied in the *Aatman* are removed, and by the *Aatman* the conception of *Brahman* as the divinity to be worshipped is condemned."[321] Thus, for Shankara, both *Brahman* and *Aatman* are one and the same. He comments on this point in his *Brahma-Suutra Bhaashya* as follows:

> As to that *Brahman* does exist as a well-known entity – eternal, pure, intelligent, free by nature and all knowing and all-

powerful. For from the very derivation of the word '*Brahman*', the ideas of eternity, purity, etc., becomes obvious ... Besides, the existence of *Brahman* is well known from the fact of Its being the self [*Aatman*] of all; for everyone feels that his self exists, and he never feels, 'I do not exist'. Had there been no general recognition of the existence of the self everyone would have felt, 'I do not exist'. And that self is *Brahman*.[322]

Again, Shankara reiterates this fact in his book *Viveekachuudaamani* as follows:

What can break the bondage and misery in the world? [It is the] knowledge that *Aatman* is *Brahman*. ... Realize *Brahman*, and there will be no more returning to this world. ... You must realize absolutely that *Aatman* is *Brahman*. Then you will win *Brahman* forever. He is the truth. He is existence and knowledge. He is absolute. He is pure and self-existent. He is eternal, unending joy. He is none other than the *Aatman*.[323]

Both of these declarations of Shankara clearly indicate the fact that he perceived *Brahman* and *Aatman* as one and the same. Following the comment of Shankara very closely, S. Radhakrishnan records the following regarding the relationship between *Brahman* and *Aatman*:

Just as, in relation to the universe, the real is *Brahman*, while name and form are only manifestations, so also the individual egos are the varied expression of the one universal self. As *Brahman* is the eternal quiet underneath the drive and activity of the universe, so *Aatman* is the foundational reality underlying the conscious powers of the individual, the inward ground of human soul. There is an ultimate depth to our life below the plane of thinking and striving.[324]

This Advaitic teaching is not a mere fabrication of the ingenious mind of Shankara, but it has a foundation in the *Upanishads*. According to the *Upanishads*, *Aatman* is the principle of individual consciousness, while *Brahman* is the super-personal foundation of the cosmic universe. The separation between the two soon vanishes in the Upanisahadic teaching and both of these principles are identified, as *Brahman*, the first principle of the universe is known through *Aatman*, the inner self of man.[325] *Chaandogya Upanishad* states this truth: "Verily this whole world is *Brahman*. ... This soul of mine within the heart, this is *Brahman*."[326] Again the Upanishadic sayings - - "That person who is seen in the eye, He is *Aatman*, that is *Brahman*",[327] "This is your self that is within all",[328] "This is the internal ruler, your own immortal self"[329] and "That is truth, that is the self and That thou art"[330] - - all indicate the identity of the *Aatman* with *Brahman*. From what we have said it is clear that *Brahman-Aatman* doctrine is deeply founded in the teaching of the *Upanishads* from the earlier times and which reached its culmination in the teachings of Shankara.[331] Thus for Shankara, the relationship between *Brahman – Aatman* and the created world, including the *Jiivas*, would be expressed in the phrase the substratum and the superimposed appearance (*Adhishthaana-aaropyabhaava*). Therefore, the destiny of man consists in removing the superimposed appearance and realizing the identity between *Brahman* and *Aatman*.

3.2.1.2.2. Raamaanuja

According to Raamaanuja, the term '*Brahman*' denotes the Supreme Person (*Purushottama*), who is by his very nature free from all imperfections (*Doshas*) and possesses many auspicious qualities (*Kalyaanagunas*). Thus, the word '*Brahman*' stands for the Being, whose greatness is matchless both in essence and other qualities. Such a being is the Lord of all (*Sarvesvara*), and the word '*Brahman*' is primarily used to refer to this being.[332] The above statement points to the fact that unlike Shankara, Raamaanuja holds for *Brahman* possessing qualities. Speaking about the essence of *Brahman*, Raamaanuja distinguishes between two types of essences, viz., the *Svaruupa* and the *Svabhaava*. The *Svaruupa* refers to the unchanging aspect of the Divine nature, while *Svabhaava* points to the aspect of Divine nature that can change. From the former emerges the positive perfection of *Brahman*, while the latter refers to *Brahman* being free from every kind of imperfections. With this distinction of Divine nature, Raamaanuja indirectly indicates its primary and secondary qualities.[333]

Raamaanuja mentions five qualities that belong to the *Svaruupa* nature of *Brahman*, called 'defining attributes' (*Svaruupa-Niruupana-Dharma*). They are True Being (*Satya*), Knowledge (*Jnaana*), Infinity (*Anantatva*), Bliss (*Aananda*) and Purity (*Amalatva*). *Satya* describes *Brahman* as possessing unconditioned (*Nirupaadhika*) existence, thereby distinguishing him from non-intelligent matter and from intelligent beings associated with matter, which are subject to change. *Jnaana* describes what *Brahman* is, i.e., Pure Consciousness (*Jnaanaikasvaruupa*). It refers to the state of permanently uncontracted knowledge. Thus, *Jnaana* distinguishes the Supreme Being from the released souls, whose knowledge was at one time contracted. *Aananda* elaborates further the nature of consciousness that the Pure Being is. *Brahman* is not merely the consciousness that is bliss, but also a consciousness that enjoys bliss. Thus, *Brahman* is said to be Consciousness and Bliss (*Jnaanaa nandaikasvaruupa*). *Anantatva* describes the essential nature of *Brahman* as free from the limitations of time and space. This quality excludes the eternally free souls (*Nityas*) from the definition of *Brahman*, as they are finite. *Amalatva* points to the fact that *Brahman* is free from evil (*Apahata-paapmatvam*) and free from *Karma* (*Apahata-karmatvam*). According to Raamaanuja, the five defining attributes in fact define the one essence of *Brahman*. The secondary qualities bring to light the other changeable qualities of *Brahman*. They are Omniscience (*Jnaana*), Strength (*Bala*), Sovereignty (*Aisvarya*), Power (*Sakti*), Courage (*Viirya*) and Light (*Tejas*). Raamaanuja also speaks of some other qualities, such as, Dignity (*Gaambhiirya*), Generosity (*Audaarya*) and Mercy (*Kaarunya*). All these primary and secondary qualities, which Raamaanuja attributes to *Brahman* clearly indicate the emphasis he gives to the perfections of God.[334] Besides attributing primary and secondary qualities to *Brahman*, Raamaanuja also gives a number of Divine Names. He calls *Brahman* the Supreme Person (*Purushottama*), the Supreme Lord worthy of worship (*Bhagavaan*), *Naaraayana* and *Vishnu*. His purpose in giving names to *Brahman* is to indicate the personal dimension of God, thereby giving an emotional touch to worship. With a personal name the devotees would be able to address the Lord in a one-to-one relationship and reach out to him in loving relationship, even though he is the most Perfect Being.[335]

Brahman, though perfect in himself, has a relationship to finite beings. He reveals himself in creation. The souls and the created world are expressions of *Brahman*. Thus, he is the material and efficient cause of the universe. *Brahman* is the material cause, since he is the primordial being, eternally differentiated into Self and body out of which the manifest-universe has come forth. He is the efficient cause, as he is the intelligent being who orders and governs each new creation. The universal causality is the fundamental mark of Divine supremacy over the world. Thus, *Brahman* is the causal substance and everything comes out of him. Even though the souls and the material world are real and distinct, they always depend on God. As to the reason for the creation of the world, Raamaanuja accepts the traditional view that it is the sport (*Liilaa*) of God. Thus, the creation is God's spontaneous self-expression.[336]

Though the Supreme Being is related to the souls and the world so intimately by way of causality, he is not affected by the limitations and imperfections of the created beings. Neither are the limitations of the created world due to the act of the creator. Evil exists in the world because the souls are free to choose good or evil, and their choices accumulate the fruits of the actions (*Karma*). *Brahman* is the Lord of *Karma*. He measures out to all according to this law. So reward and punishment, in accordance with the law of *Karma* are part and parcel of a person's life here on earth. But God is also a merciful protector and a savior. He is ready to shower his abundant graces on anyone who comes to him in devotion and love. It is this merciful and saving function, which makes God descend on earth in various manifestations (*Avataaras*).[337]

Raamaanuja accepted that what the *Upanishads* say about the Supreme Self (*Paramaatman*) is also applicable to individual finite selves (*Jiivaatmaa*), as they are the modes of the Supreme Self. But he accepted this Upanishadic truth with a few qualifications. Firstly, in case of the finite self, the divine nature can be obscured by ignorance, which results in the bondage of *Karma*. While the finite selves can be in a state of impurity, the Supreme Self always has the defining attribute of *Amalatva*. Secondly, *Anantatva* as a defining attribute belongs only to the Supreme Self. The finite selves, after liberation from bondage (*Samsaara*), attain only the infinity of knowledge and not the infinity of God. In spite of these qualifications, Raamaanuja holds that the finite selves have the same essential nature as the Supreme Self. In explaining *Brahman's* relationship to the souls as the material and efficient cause Raamaanuja uses a number of analogies. One of the analogies used is that of the body and soul. A body that is animated by the soul is coordinated and subservient to soul that animates it. Besides, it is only though the body that the soul could express its activities. Though the soul and the body are inseparable and form a type of unity, yet they are distinct. In the same way, God and the soul, which is his body, are related. Thus, *Brahman* is the Supreme Self that ensouls the human souls, which is his body. Similarly Raamaanuja compares the relationship of *Brahman* with the souls with the substractum (*Aadhaara*) and the supported (*Aadheya*); the ruler (*Niyantaa*) and the ruled (*Niyaamya*); the inner controller (*Antaryaamii*) and the controlled (*Niyaamyam*); and the owner (*Sesha*) and the owned (*Seshii*).[338] The greater the awareness a self has about its relationship with *Brahman*, and the more it uses the disciplines of devotion and meditation, the more it acquires qualities similar to the Supreme Self.[339] Thus, for Raamaanuja the destiny of man consists in becoming similar to *Brahman*, the Supreme Being, by acquiring the manifold qualities of *Brahman*.

3.2.1.2.3. Madhva

Unlike Shankara, who speaks of the unity of every other reality in the *Brahman*, and Raamaanuja, while acknowledging the element of difference between *Brahman*, souls and the world, reduces it to a mere intrinsic modality of the substantial identity, Madhva stresses the element of radical difference and denies the substantial identity of *Brahman*, the souls and the world. The foundational presupposition of Madhva is that "the very fact a being is, it is different from other beings". The inner unity within a being automatically implies that it is different from other beings. For instance, by knowing who Devadatta is, I also know that he is different from a jar, a tree or another man. Thus, Madva holds for a philosophy of difference. He speaks of five-fold differences, viz., difference between: *Brahman* and souls, *Brahman* and world, souls and souls, souls and world, and each object of the world and all other objects. These five-fold differences allow diverse external relationships, but do not allow the reality of an intrinsic community. Thus, for Madva, the dualist, there is no unity, but only duality and plurality in the universe. As a result, Madva holds for the separate existence of *Brahman*, the souls and the world.[340]

According to Madhva, the most fundamental aspect of *Brahman* is his independence (*Svatantra*). *Brahman* is the Lord, who is completely independent in his Being. He is absolutely independent and unutterable in majesty. In order to be independent and majestic in his Being, *Brahman* must be absolutely perfect. The nature of *Brahman* includes two aspects, viz., the perfection of Being (*Sarvagunapuurnatvam*) and the freedom from all limitations (*Sarvadoshagandhavidhuratvam*). Firstly, *Brahman's* nature as the perfection of Being must be understood in terms of an unlimited pervasion in time, in space, and fullness of attributes. For Madhva, *Brahman* alone possesses this three-fold perfection. As the one who possesses the fullness of attributes, *Brahman*, though Pure Consciousness (*Tat Saarabhuutam Cinmaatram*) possesses an infinite number of most excellent differences (*Viseshas*), which are found in him in perfect identity. Similarly, he possesses a purely spiritual body (*Vigraha*), which he can manifest at will in the incarnations *(Avataara)*, while remaining one and undivided. Thus, *Brahman* is immutable. He is above all change, limitation and loss of his powers. He is so absolutely self-contained, uniform and self-sufficient that no external factors affect his nature. He has no peer, nor superior, for he transcends all such divisions. His Form consists of absolute consciousness and unlimited bliss. This means that *Brahman* has a spiritual form with its own instruments of knowledge and bliss. Thus, for Madhva, the Divine nature is not only all knowing, but also self-luminous. In other words, not only does God know everything, but he also knows that his knowledge is all embracing. Secondly, *Brahman*, besides being the fullness of perfection, is also free from all limitations. He is free from ignorance, dependence, being liable to misery, material defilement and equality with, or inferiority to, others. Besides, he is undimmed by time, space and various states of his existence. He is the Supreme Lord, Super Consciousness, who is absolutely free from all evils. While describing all these qualities of *Brahman*, Madhva takes special pains to point out that these attributes of *Brahman* are transcendental and trans-empirical, even though they are empirical designations. The implication of what Madhva says here is that though we use these empirical terms to refer to God's qualities, the terms must be used analogously of God, the souls and other entities of this world.[341]

The world is a creation of *Brahman*. It is as real as *Brahman*. He is omnipotent, as he has the means to develop any world he wishes, not out of necessity, but as a way of play or self-expression. Creation comes from holy will. For Madhva, God is not a mere artificer (*Brahmaandakulaala*) of the creation, but rather he is the very source (*Apaadaana*) of its being and becoming, as it arises out of what entirely belongs to *Brahman*, viz., the *Prakrti*. Though *Prakrti* exists eternally, it is characterized by a passive dependence and gives itself to *Brahman* as an instrument in his hand, with the help of which he gives existence (*Sattaa*) to all particular beings. Thus, objects, deeds, time, natural dispositions and souls never exist without relation to him. Hence, the utter majesty of *Brahman* is revealed in the created order by the eight-fold cosmic determinations, namely, evolution, permanence, involution, direction, knowledge, rebirth, bondage and release. As the complete efficient cause of creation, he penetrates and resides in nature as its inner controller. Consequently, creation is entirely *Brahman's*, as it rests on him, acts by him and is totally governed by him. While God is the efficient cause of creation, he is not the material (*Upaadaana*) cause, as it is through *Prakrti* that he brings about the creation. Thus, *Prakrti* is the material cause of creation. According to Madhva, the only sense in which creation can be said to be a creation of God is if creation is seen as an eternal act of God. In other words, for reasons known to him, God has chosen to evolve a world from souls and matter, co-existent with him. Thus, creation is nothing else but an eternal dependence of one beginningless on another, which is a more powerful one. In order to uphold the supremacy of God over creation, Madhva would say that if God wishes, he could reverse the process and effect creation out of nothing.[342]

For Madhva, the soul is a finite creature of conscious experience which has as its own unique essence spiritual consciousness. It is without parts, yet it has an indivisible identity that comes from its spiritual nature, which is unalloyed bliss and pure intelligence, though, when embodied, these qualities may be clouded. Thus, the soul is essentially of the nature of *Brahman*, but dependent on him and finite. Though one could say that the activity of the soul is its own, yet in its very activity it is dependent (*Asvatantra*) on the Lord. He penetrates into souls and resides as their inner witness and guardian. *Brahman* is the immanent energizer of all that a soul does, and the soul individualizes the all-embracing activity of the Lord in its own life. Thus, a soul depends on *Brahman* for its existence, consciousness and activity.[343] There are infinite numbers of souls. Madhva classifies them into three groups: the salvable souls (*Muktiyogya*), the ever-transmigrating souls (*Nitya-samsaarin*) and the damnable souls (*Tamoyogya*). The grace of God helps the first two groups of souls to move towards liberation, while the souls of the last group, by their choice, allow themselves to be condemned.[344]

Speaking of the relationship between the soul and *Brahman*, Madhva uses a number of analogies. According to him, a soul is said to be an image (*Abhaasa*), a reflection (*Pratibimba*) and a broken off particle (*Bhinna Amsa*) of *Brahman*. The concept of the soul as image, reflection and a particle of God should not be taken in the Advaitic sense of a false appearance, but rather it must be taken in the gross physical sense. So, it is an actual image, reflection and a particle that is referred to here. For Madhva, the relationship between *Brahman* and the soul is sacred and inviolable. It is a relationship that is true for all time, forms the core of the soul and, therefore, never could be done away with. Being an image, a reflection or a particle of *Brahman* is a natural and essential characteristic (*Svalakshana*) of the soul and this relationship is an intrinsic relationship (*Nirupaadhikasambandha*). Without this relationship the soul would cease to exist. Madhva uses the analogy of the sun, raindrops and the rainbow to illustrate this relationship. Just as the raindrops manifest the beauty that is concealed in the white rays of the sun in the rainbow, in the same way every soul as an image, a reflection and a particle of *Brahman* that has the potency to manifest the Divine light and transmit it.[345] Our reflection on the relationship between *Brahman* and the soul clearly indicates the destiny of man. It consists in a person becoming consciously aware that he, as the soul, is truly an image of *Brahman* and must attempt to realize his own nature, as the soul that is the image of God. When this realization dawns in a person, he is able to transcend the troubles of the present life and become the true reflector of the true nature of *Brahman*, whose image is he.

3.2.2. VEDAANTIC PATHS TO THE DIVINE

In the last section we elaborated the nature of the divinity in the Vedaantic Hinduism of the *Upanishads* and its interpretations in the scholastic thinkers Shankara, Raamaanuja and Madhva. Shankara visualized a unitary approach in his understanding of the divinity, according to which he proposed a Non-dual *Brahman* as the only Reality and the world as unreal. Raamaanuja put forward a qualified Non-dual *Brahman*, to whose identity the soul belongs though distinct from *Brahman*. Madhva proposed a Dualism in which *Brahman* and the soul are distinct entities. The former is the efficient cause and the latter is the effect of the causality of God. Though distinct, the soul is a real image of *Brahman*. In the Shankarite perception of divinity, man's destiny consists in moving towards an identity with the Divine Reality. In Raamaanuja's view of God, the destiny of man consists in a person attempting to become similar to God to whose identity he belongs. In Madhva's vision of God, the destiny of man consists in his becoming aware of his true nature as the soul, that is the image of God. These perceptions of the divinity and the destiny of man in Vedaantic Hinduism have given rise to new paths to experience the divine reality. Though many of the Vedic paths to the gods are still in vogue in the popular practice of Hinduism, specific forms of paths have emerged as the result of the varied visions of the divinity and the destiny of man. For instance, Shankara's approach to *Brahman* has led to the emergence of the Path of Knowledge (*Jnaanayoga*), while Raamaanuja recommends the Path of Devotion (*Bhaktiyoga*). Madhva offers to his disciples the Path of Unselfish Action (*Karmayoga*), besides the *Bhaktiyoga*. All of them propose the Path of Disciplining the Mind (*Raajayoga*) as an aid to meditation and God-realization. Each of these paths is suited to people who are of different temperaments and character. In this section, we elaborate these Vedaantic Paths to the Divine.

3.2.2.1. PATH OF KNOWLEDGE

The *Jnaana* path to self-realization is meant for a person who is rational and whose head dominates his heart. As a result, such a person is more intellectual and discriminative, while less emotional and impulsive. He is not moved by his feelings, as his intellect is able to view events impartially. A man of intellect is not satisfied in postulating a God and worshipping Him. He looks for arguments to justify such postulation. The significant characteristic of a person with an intellectual mind is his ability to discriminate between the phenomenal and the transcendental. He has the propensity for deeper meditation and experience of the transcendental self.[346] Thus, *Jnaanayoga* is designed for a person of intelligence, who can ask fundamental questions about this universe and draw answers out of his reflection. The knowledge he acquires is not merely intellectual, but experiential and existential. The *Jnaana* path is described as '*Nitya Anitya Viveeka Vichaara*', i.e., 'the discrimination between the eternal and the temporal by way of reflection'. Thus, *Jnaanayoga* constantly attempts to distinguish the permanent from the impermanent, the noumena and the phenomena, the transcendental and the terrestrial, the real and the unreal, so that the seeker of knowledge can realize the ultimate knowledge of *Brahman* as identical with *Aatman*.[347] For Advaitins the *Jnaana* path is the only way for direct experience of *Brahman*, as only true knowledge can remove ignorance. Hence, the *Jnaana* path involves a deep understanding of the illusory nature of the phenomenal world and the fundamental oneness of everything in *Brahman*. Besides, it implies a discriminative consciousness that would enable the aspirant to break through the appearance superimposed by ignorance and to realize the underlying absolute reality behind the manifold world of everyday experience.[348] In order to study the scriptures and thereby remove the ignorance, Shankara proposes certain physical, moral and intellectual preparations. The physical preparation aims at helping the seeker to attain full control over his body. This is done by what Vedaantins call *Hathayoga*. The moral preparation has for its goal the purification of the mind by removing all inclinations to evil. The intellectual preparation intends to grasp the full import of the scriptures with the intellectual study of the scriptural texts. We now elaborate these three in detail.

3.2.2.1.1. Hathayoga: Physical Preparation

The term '*Hathayoga*' comes from two Sanskrit terms '*Hatha*' and '*Yoga*'. The term '*Hatha*' means violence, force and oppression. The word '*Yoga*' means a technique prescribed for the removal of the tendencies (*Vaasanas*) of the body and the mind. Thus, *Hathayoga* means physical disciplines which an individual undertakes, and which involve a certain amount of violence, force or oppression to the body. Therefore, the practice of *Hathayoga* involves a certain amount of compulsion, either administered by others or by the person himself. The aim of *Hathayoga* is to purify the tendencies of the body and mind so that the intellect can begin to reason, thereby enabling the aspirant to study the scripture. Many practices, such as different forms of self-torture, standing on one leg, holding up arms, inhaling smoke with head inverted, piercing different parts of the body with sharp instruments and similar practices are included in the *Hathayoga*.[349] It increases vitality in the body, gives good health and preserves a great amount of energy within the aspirant, as *Hathayoga* opens the aspirant for the life-process of the cosmic *Praana*.[350]

Though there are many practices included in *Hathayoga*, its two main limbs are posture (*Aasana*) and breath-control (*Praanaayaama*). Posture consists in placing the body in various positions that would lead to the discipline of the bodily system. *Aasana* helps the body to get rid of the restlessness that blocks deep reflection and concentration. Posture brings the entire physical organism of the aspirant under the control of his will. It is different from other types of physical exercises, as its aim is to make the body fit for the highest type of experience. The *Hathayogin* keeps his body free from all impurities, his nervous system intact and gains control over the different muscles of the body by the practice of the *Aasanas*.[351] Besides, the practice of the *Aasanas* brings about equipoise of all the limbs of the body (*Dehasaamya*), which is conducive to the experience of total absorption in the *Brahman*.[352]

Genuine practice of posture helps the aspirant to the practice of the second limb, breath-control (*Praanaayaama*). With this method the aspirant controls the vital power of breathing, which is the basis of organic life. It keeps under check one's inhalation and exhalation. For Patanjali, the founder of the Yoga System, *Praanaayaama* involves controlling the motion of inhalation and exhalation. There are three steps in breath-control. The first one is *Puraka*, which consists in taking in breath; the second is *Kumbahaka*, which means to hold the breath taken in for some time in the lungs; and the last step is *Rechaka*, which is to throw out the breath retained in the lungs during the second stage. It was Patanjali's opinion that the mind would be naturally controlled if one practices the restraining of breath and thereby prevents the mind's communication with the external world. But, Shankara does not subscribe to Patanjali's view. He holds that the breath is entirely dependent on the mind and not the mind on breathing. Therefore, by restricting the breathing one cannot restrain the mind. On the contrary, the control of the mind would effectively bring about restraining the breath. So the aspirant, instead of wasting his energy in his attempt to restrain the breath, must always try to control the mind. When the mind is controlled, it automatically lead to restraining the breath.[353] Shankara defines *Praanaayaama* as the "restraint of all modifications of the mind by regarding all mental states like *Citta* as *Brahman* alone…"[354] Thus, for an Advaitin, *Praanaayaama*, if practiced as advocated by Shankara, can lead to complete control over the modifications of the mind (*citta-vritti*). It helps the aspirant to control instincts, passions and impulses that disturb the peace of mind, thereby opening the seeker to mental and spiritual discipline.[355]

3.2.2.1.2. Moral Preparation

If the intellect is able to understand the import of the scriptural statements, it must be pure. The knowledge of *Brahman* revealed in the scripture, though expressed in terms of duality, still is the highest knowledge that can be known by the human intellect in the empirical realm. This knowledge cannot be grasped if the intellect is not open to understanding eternal truth. Just as a stained mirror does not reflect things clearly, so an impure mind cannot grasp *Brahman* intellectually from the study of the scriptures. Shankara uses an analogy to illustrate this truth. Fire, by its nature, is able to burn wood. But if the wood is wet, fire is not able to burn it. In the same way, intellect, though it is able to know and understand the import of the scriptural statements, because it is clouded by passions and attachments to things, does not grasp *Brahman* from the study of the Vedic aphorisms (*Mahaavaakyas*).[356] So it is important that under the guidance of the Guru an aspirant go through a course of moral preparation before he makes a serious attempt to study the scripture.

The moral preparation consists of the practice of four disciplines called the instruments of spiritual knowledge (*Sadhanachatushtaya*). They aim at preparing the inner personality of the aspirant so that he be able to get the best out of the study of the scripture. The first discipline is the destruction of sins through the practice of austerities (*Tapobhih Ksinapaapaanaam*). It envisages two types of disciplines at the physical level, viz., a negative discipline, which aims at preventing sensual dissipation by exercising self-control and a positive one that utilizes the conserved energy to move towards the highest ideal of self-realization.[357] Thus, the first spiritual discipline, the discipline on the physical level, with its positive and negative practices, destroys sins and inclination to sin in the aspirant and generates in him purity of body and mind. The second spiritual discipline aims at restraining the aspirant on the level of the mind. It is aimed at bringing in the seeker a calmness of mind (*Saantaanaam*). It fundamentally consists in not allowing the mind to get lost in objects, whether past, present or future by removing its attention from the senses which are mind's gateways to the world of objects, thereby attaining mental peace and tranquility.[358] The third spiritual discipline is one that focuses on the intellectual level, and aims at freeing the aspirant from all desires (*Viitaraaginaam*). It consists in disciplining the intellect so as to withdraw one's attention from the material layers of one's personality and to concentrate on *Brahman*, which would effect the cessation of all imperfections in a person, and so bring about the end of all desires that disturb and agitate the mind.[359] The fourth is the discipline at the spiritual level. It is the consequence of the first three disciplines, viz., disciplines of the body, the mind and the intellect. It aims at creating in the aspirant a yearning for liberation (*Mumukshuunaam*). In this discipline the mental energy generated by the disciplines of the body, the mind and the intellect is conserved and directed for gaining liberation (*Moksha*). It involves the rejection of all worldly desires and substituting the desire for gaining spiritual liberation.[360]

These four spiritual disciplines – the disciplines at the physical, mental, intellectual and spiritual levels – help the aspirant move from the world to *Brahman* and to substitute worldly desires with desires for liberation. In going through these four disciplines, there is a genuine moral preparation of the aspirant. As the result of these practices the aspirant becomes a qualified person (*Adhikari*) to begin the study of the scriptural texts. In the process the *Adhikari* acquires four qualities. They are the following: the discrimination between the real and the unreal (*Viveeka*); detachment from the unreal, i.e., renunciation (*Vairaagya*); the practice of six-fold virtues (*Shadsampatti*) – calmness (*Shama*), self-control (*Dama*), self-settledness (*Uparati*), forbearance (*Titiksha*), faith (*Shraddha*) and complete concentration (*Samaadhaana*); and hunger for self-realization (*Mumukshvata*).[361] Each of these qualities morally prepares the student for the study of the scriptures and, therefore, they can be considered, as moral conditions required of the student, before ever he can undertake the deliberate and serious study of the scriptures.

3.2.2.1.3. Intellectual Preparation

The moral disciplines purify the intellect of the aspirant, freeing him from all passions and attachment, so that he can give himself uninterruptedly to the study of the scriptures. In the stage of intellectual preparation the role of the *Guru* is especially significant. Fully qualified students cannot venture into the vast ocean of scriptural learning, unless a competent *Guru* leads them into it. Even a person, who is well versed in the scriptures, should not undertake the journey towards *Brahman* without the guidance of a *Guru*. Therefore, for Shankara, the instructions of the *Guru* are absolutely necessary for knowledge of *Brahman*, whether the aspirant is a person with scriptural knowledge or a qualified beginner (*Adhikari*). Every seeker of knowledge of *Brahman* must sit at the feet of the proper and competent *Guru*, who is a spiritual guide, an authority on the Vedas, desireless and sinless. Thus, the *Guru* is a true teacher of knowledge of *Brahman* to anyone who wishes to make the journey towards *Brahman*.[362] The seeker of knowledge of *Brahman* should approach such a *Guru* in the spirit of humility and service, and with suitable gifts in his hands.[363] When a student approaches the *Guru* in this manner, he instructs the pupil on *Brahman* and prepares him for the knowledge of *Brahman*. Mundaka Upanishad states: "Unto him [the pupil] who has approached in due form, whose mind is tranquil and who has attained peace, let the knowing (teacher) teach in its very truth that knowledge about *Brahman* by which one knows the imperishable person, the true."[364] Thus begins the intellectual preparation, for the qualified student, at the feet of the *Guru*. To study the scripture and understand its import and meaning calls for three stages, viz., hearing (*Sravana*), reflection (*Manaana*) and meditation (*Nidhdhyaasana*). They constitute the objective intellectual conditions for the removal of ignorance.

Hearing implies the idea of being taught. At the first stage of understanding the meaning of the Vedaantic statements, the competent teacher introduces the aspirant to the teachings of Advaita. Thus, *Sravana* is the initiation of the aspirant to the traditional Vedaantic doctrine transmitted and passed on by the teachers. *Sravana*, at the same time, is the mental activity, which helps the understanding of the Upanishadic texts, leading to their only import, i.e., *Brahman*. *Sravana* is not a mere hearing the truth about *Brahman* from the teacher or from the scriptures in a blind manner. It involves on the part of the aspirant ascertainig what is heard. Thus, in *Sravana* the student ascertains and establishes the true import of the scriptures, viz., "*Brahman* is one without a second".[365] Without a genuine ascertaining, *Sravana* would be fruitless. This ascertaining is achieved by an examination of the texts through six tests or characteristic signs, namely, commencement and ending, repetition, uniqueness, result, eulogy and reason.[366] We shall briefly clarify each of these texts. The first is commencement and ending. Commencement involves the presentation of the subject matter to be taught to the student, in *Sravana*, at the beginning of a section, that the aspirant clearly comes to know the topic of his study. In the ending the same truth is restated, not as a hypothesis but as a verified fact that the student knows with certainty. The second test, the repetition, consists in frequent presentation of the subject matter in different parts of the section. It is aimed at helping the student to become more and more aware of the import of the subject matter by ascertaining each time it is repeated. The third is uniqueness of the subject matter. It consists in the subject matter of a section not being available through any other source of knowledge, but can be understood only in relation to the study of the scriptures. The fourth is the result. It is the utility of the subject matter of the section for the qualified student to move into the higher stages of *Brahman*-realization. In other words, the result consists in the utility of the subject matter, for its attainment. The fifth test, eulogy, consists in praising the subject matter in different parts of the section. It is aimed at instilling in the student a desire to listen attentively and to inculcate in him its significance. The last test is reason, which consists in demonstrating the subject matter with rational arguments. It helps the qualified student to understand the thinking behind the subject matter and to understand its import, which in the last analysis would lead to the right ascertaining of the meaning of the subject matter.[367] By the use of these six tests, the student makes a deep effort to understand the import of the subject matter that he heard from the teacher or read from the *Vedas*.

Sravana is followed by reflection (*Manaana*). The *Kena Upanishad Bhaashya* speaks about the second intellectual condition required for the removal of ignorance, viz., *Manaana*, as follows:

> After being addressed by the teacher, the disciple (*Shyshya*) sat at the solitary place [*Vijana-desha*] and attended to nothing else (*Ekaanta*), concentrated his thoughts (*Saamhita*) and pondered over the meaning of *Aagma* [the traditional teaching pointed out by his *Guru*], arrived at a conclusion through reasoning, made it [the teacher's instructions] his own experience, went back to his teacher and explained: 'I think, I now know *Brahman*'.[368]

This passage clearly shows the nature and function of *Manaana*. It is a mental activity, which consists in the employment of favorable arguments for the removal of the apparent contradictions that might arise during the study of the scripture against other means of valid knowledge. The truth pointed out by the teacher is difficult to grasp and seems to contradict the ordinary perception and knowledge obtained from the *Pramaanas* other than the scripture. Thus, it is very important that the aspirant strengthen his conviction at this stage, by looking for rational basis for the teaching received from the teacher in *Sravana*. Professor Ramamurthi clearly points out the role of *Manaana* as follows: "The purpose of it [*Manaana*] is to fortify one's conviction of the truth from the scripture and to rid oneself of all doubts ... Another important function of reflection is to make one comprehend the real meaning of the scriptural statements by consistently interpreting them so that the apparent inconsistencies are resolved."[369] The continuous reflections involved in *Manaana*, though performed with the aid of reasoning, must be subservient to the teaching of the *Upanishads*, on the secondless reality of *Brahman* that is known through *Sravana*.[370] At the stage of *Manaana*, the aspirant makes use of the negative method of Advaita Vedaanta, viz., *Apavaada*, which consists in the elimination of what is not, in order that one may attain the truth about that particular thing. By negating the attributes of the non-self, one attains the true nature of *Aatman* and by negating the world of names and forms one attains the knowledge of *Brahman*, the absolute reality.[371]

Thus, the negative method completely does away with all false attribution of *Brahman*, and thereby paves the way for true knowledge.

The final stage leading to the complete removal of ignorance and thus, to the direct realization of the self is meditation (*Nididhyaasana*). If an aspirant, having heard the teacher, is successful in his reflection and is intellectually convinced of his identity with *Brahman*, then he is ready to strive for the direct realization. *Nididhyaasana* is a mental activity consisting in withdrawing the mind from all other things and concentrating it on *Brahman*.[372] Meditation is not a concentration of oneself on *Brahman*, as an external of separate entity. It is an activity of the mind "in which the mind is turned completely inward, and is firmly fixed on the inner self and its identity with *Brahman* till one's finitude and individuality is dissolved."[373] Hence, meditation involves a continuous and unbroken thought on *Brahman*, that flows like a line of flowing oil,[374] and the exclusion of all thoughts. For Shankara, therefore, meditation consists in "remaining independent of everything as a result of the unassailable thought 'I am verily *Brahman*' ... and [which] is productive of supreme bliss."[375]

Nididhyaasana has two forms, viz., *Samprajnaat-samaapatti* and *Asamprajnaat-samaapatti*. *Samprajnaat-samaapatti* is a form of meditation in which the aspirant experiences modifications of consciousness while meditating on the *Mahaavaakyas*. In this type of meditation there are two stages. The initial stage is characterized by the knowledge of the modification of mental consciousness that originates while meditating on the Vedaantic statements. The aspirant, therefore, is conscious of himself, the meditator and the witness of the modification that has taken place in the consciousness and of the modification created by the meditation on the scriptural axiom at that particular moment. The later stage of *Samprajnaat-samaapatti* is free from all thoughts regarding the origin of the modification that is produced in the consciousness, as the result of meditation on the *Mahaavaakya*. Since meditation is intense at this stage, the temporal and spatial marks of modifications are not available to the consciousness of the meditator. The aspirant is only aware of himself, as the witness, and the modifications produced by his meditation on the Vedaantic aphorisms.[376] *Asamprajnaat-samaapatti* is a state of meditation, in which the consciousness of the aspirant practicing meditation is not characterized by any modifications. In it, there is no sense of duality, as all modifications produced by the meditation on the scriptural axiom have ceased to exist. As there is no subject-object distinction in this meditation, the *Aatman* becomes the subject and object of the meditation, as the identity without any modifications is arrived at as the result of *asamprajnaat-samaapatti*.[377]

The practice of meditation is facilitated by the aspirant's focus on the four *Mahaavaakyas* while meditating. Meditation must begin with the statement of definition (*Lakshana Vaakya*), viz., 'Consciousness is *Brahman*'

('*Prajnaanam Brahmaa*'). This aphorism fixes the mind of the meditator on the thought that consciousness in the individual (*Aatman*) and the consciousness underlying the entire universe (*Brahman*) are one and the same. In other words, meditating on this aphorism the aspirant recognizes existentially that the same consciousness is the substratum of the microcosm and the macrocosm. Thus, the meditation on the statement "Consciousness is *Brahman*" envelops the depth of the aspirant with the experience that the consciousness ever remains the one homogeneous reality, whether it be in the cosmos or in the individual. With the deep awareness of the oneness of the ultimate reality, the aspirant moves on to the meditation of the statement of advice (*Upadeesha Vaakya*), viz., 'That art Thou' ('*Tat Tvam Asi*'). It asserts that the one ultimate reality (That) is the pure self (Thou) that is the core of one's personality that lies beyond the five sheaths (*Koshas*) of matter. In this manner the meditation on the second *Mahaavaakya* makes the aspirant experience the oneness of the infinite *Brahman* and *Aatman* within him. Being convinced that the supreme reality is nothing but his own self, the aspirant moves on to the meditation of the statement of practice (*Abyhaasa Vaakya*), viz., 'This Self is *Brahman*' ('*Ayamaatama Brahmaa*'). The meditation on this practical formula makes the aspirant realize *Aatman*, which activates him as the same *Brahman* who vitalizes the entire universe. Thus, the aspirant discovers the identity between the self and the all-pervading *Brahman*. The conviction arrived at by the meditation on the third *Mahaavaakya* makes the aspirant experience the truth of the statement of experience (*Anubhava Vaakya*), viz., 'I am *Brahman*' ('*Aham Brahmaasmi*'). This statement is a pronouncement of realization. He knows now experientially that he is the all-pervading *Brahman* and that the duality is totally removed. The 'I' referred to in the fourth *Mahaavaakya* is different from the 'I' experienced in the waking state, dream state and the state of deep sleep. The 'I' of the *Anubhava Vaakya* is the supreme self, identical with *Brahman*. In this manner, the practice of meditation, facilitated by the *Mahaavaakyas*, leads to self-realization.[378]

In the states of *Sravana* and *Manaana*, the aspirant studies the scriptures, analyses the meaning of the Vedaantic aphorisms and discriminates the perishable body, mind, intellect and plurality of the world from the imperishable self. Having done this, the aspirant negates the perishable world and asserts the imperishable self as real, repeatedly bringing to his awareness that "I am supreme *Brahman*".[379] The latter task of assertion is done by the practice of meditation, which takes the aspirant to the experience of the fundamental identity of *Aatman* and *Brahman*. Thus, by repeated exercise of meditation, one moves to greater depth of absolute consciousness. This consciousness of identity with the absolute *Brahman* removes all the effects of ignorance. By focusing more on the inner self, by way of meditation the aspirant makes the inward journey, until he experiences his absolute identity with *Brahman*, in the state of release (*Samaadhi*), thereby becoming a *Jnaanayogi*.

The *Bhagavad Giitaa* says that the *Jnaanayogi* possesses the qualities of humility (absence of pride), integrity (absence of deceit), non-violence, patience, uprightness, service of the teacher, purity (of body and mind), steadfastness and self-control. He is indifferent to the objects of sense, is self-effacing and perceives the evil of birth, death, old age, sickness and pain. He is not attached to son, wife, home and the like. He is equal-minded to both the desirable and the non-desirable. The *Jnaanayogi* is devoted to the Supreme Being, is wholehearted in his discipline, prefers a solitary place and dislikes crowds of people. Besides, he is constant in his knowledge of the spirit, perceives the end of true knowledge and knows that all that is different from it is non-knowledge.[380]

3.2.2.2. PATH OF DEVOTION

Bhaktiyoga is meant for a person who is more emotional in nature, whose heart dominates his head. Such a person is more emotional, devotional and impulsive, while he is less rational, intellectual and discriminative. One who follows *Bhaktiyoga* chooses a personal God (*Ishtadeevata*) and pours out his personal love and devotion to the Lord by making use of *Mantras*, *Bhajans* and chants, which make him single-minded in his attachment to the Lord. This, in turn, frees him from worldly attachments and leads him to God-realization.[381]

The term '*Bhakti*' is derived from the Sanskrit roots '*Bhaaj*' and '*Bhooj*'. The former means 'to serve', while the latter conveys the meaning 'to share' or 'to participate. The two words that derive from these roots are '*Bhajan*' and '*Bhojan*', which mean 'a hymn sung in praise of the Lord's name' and 'a meal taken together' respectively. These words indicate that '*Bhakti*' implies genuine service of the Lord, which involves singing his praises and a loving attachment to the Lord, with an intimacy and union of hearts. Generally the term '*Bhakti*' is translated as 'devotion', which connotes faith, love, loving surrender, devotional attachment and piety. A term related to '*Bhakti*' is '*Puujaa*', which signifies adoration, reverence and worship. Both of these words point to a personal relationship and an existential attitude of dependence and piety. God is the supreme object of *Bhakti* and *Puujaa*. We offer *Pranaama*, which involves lesser degrees of reverence and devotion to our motherland, parents, spiritual teachers and holy men.[382]

Having clarified the term '*Bhakti*' etymologically and seen its relation to a few related terms, we move on to explain the meaning of *Bhakti* as a path to God-realization. *Bhakti* is a loving attachment to God, an intense love of God. It is a longing for God for its own sake. It is surrender in trusting appropriation of the grace of the Lord. It is a love, which, without seeking results, is dedicated to the Lord. *Bhakti* is a profound experience that negates all desires and fills the heart of the devotee with genuine love of God. In it, one is supremely attached to the Lord. The *Bhakti* path emphasizes humility, readiness to serve, compassion, tenderness and gentle love. The devotee experiences a sense of utter humility and longs to surrender himself, to renounce his self-will and to give himself to the Lord in utter prostration of the self. This attitude of self-surrender emerges the devotee's perception of God's goodness. Thus, in the *Bhakti* path, the devoted soul draws near to God by contemplating His power, wisdom and goodness, and by constant remembrance of the Lord with a devout heart. The contemplation and remembrance of the Lord makes the *Bhakta* talk about the qualities of God with others, sing His praises with his fellowmen and perform all his actions in the service of the Lord. Therefore, *Bhakti* is not a mere over-emotional or sentimental enthusiasm that the devotee feels within himself, but rather it calls for true service of the Lord by serving others in need.[383] Radhakrishnan comments on this point as follows: "*Bhakti* is not merely the 'flight of the alone [the devotee] to the Alone [God]', the soul's detachment from the world and attachment to God, but is active love for the Divine who enters into the world for redeeming it."[384] Therefore, a true *Bhakta* expresses his devotion to the Lord by incarnation into the world for the service of others.

A person who has achieved the state of *Bhakti* is perfect (*Siddha*), immortal (*Amrta*) and fully satisfied (*Trpta*). He is totally free from sorrow, hatred and passion. He is at peace and his mind is centered on the Lord. A *Bhakta*, free from all affections, transcends his selfishness and does his every activity, both sacred and profane, with dedication to the Lord. He is single-hearted in his actions; renounces the obstacles to devotion; practices only those duties and observances that are in agreement with his dedication to the Lord; and is intensely attached to the worship of the Lord.[385] The *Bagavad Giitaa* describes the true devotee as follows:

> He [the *Bhakta*] ... has no ill will to any being, ... is friendly and compassionate, free from egoism, and self-sense, even-minded in pain and pleasure and patient. ...[He] is ever content, self-controlled, unshakable in determination ... He from whom the world does not shrink and who does not shrink from the world and who is free from joy and anger, fear and agitation ... He... has no expectation, is pure, skilful in action, unconcerned, and untroubled ... has given up all initiative (in action) ... He... neither rejoices nor hates, neither grieves nor desires, and ... has renounced good and evil, he ... is thus devoted. ... He...(behaves) alike to foe and friend, also to good and evil repute and ... is alike in cold and heat, pleasure and pain and ... is free from attachment. He ... holds equal blame and praise, ... is silent (restrained in speech), content with anything (that comes), ... has no fixed abode and is firm in mind, that man ... is devoted.[386]

Thus, the path of devotion leads the devotee to a state of steadied consciousness, in which nothing disturbs or annoys him. In such a *Bhakta*, there is no ulterior motive except God alone (*Ahaitukii*). He relies purely on the grace and love (*Tat-krpaa*) of the Lord. A devotee is dedicated and consecrated (*Nivedita*) to the Lord. He offers himself and surrenders (*Arpita*) to the Lord: he belongs (*Tadiiya*) to the Lord. The *Bhakta* is said to be full of the Lord, whose very self he becomes (*Tanmaya*). The true follower of the path of devotion is able to arrive at such a deep level of spiritual existence, because he fixes his mind on the Lord with supreme faith (*Sraddhaa*). Thus, faith is the basis of *Bhakti*. Faith is an attentive inner vision, through which the Lord illumines the human mind with his divine light. Constant practice of the fixation of mind with faith, which involves a concentration on the Lord and a personal attachment to Him, makes the devotee experience deep spiritual union with the Lord. As the *Bhakta* surrenders his mind to the Lord in faith, he rests secure in the profound peace (*Samaadhaana*), which is a state of steadied consciousness, where he experiences the totality of his existence in the Lord.[387]

The spiritual authors distinguish between two types of *Bhakti*, viz., the imperfect devotion (*Aparaa Bhakti*) and the perfect devotion (*Paraa Bhakti*). Imperfect devotion is a preparatory form of devotion, which is qualified and mixed with personal interest of the seeker. It is not guided by true motivation, as worldly interests and personal ambitions mar the quality of this type of devotion. The practice of *Aparaa Bhakti* comes out of a sense of duty, consciousness and formalism. Imperfect devotion can be further divided into types, depending on the preponderance of the three *Gunaas*, viz., the *Sattva*, the *Rajas* and the *Tamas*, and based on the motives that animate the devotee in his devotion. Depending on the *Gunaas*, we can speak of three types of imperfect devotion, viz., the *Taamasika* devotion, the *Raajasika* devotion and the *Saattvika* devotion. The *Taamasika* devotion consists in people approaching the Lord in devotion to succeed in their sinful undertakings. The *Raajasika* devotion involves praying to the Lord for naturally desirable things, such as, children, fortune, reputation and power. The *Saattvika* devotion is that which makes a person pray unselfishly for the welfare of others and to achieve perfection in his spiritual life.[388]

Based on the motives that animate the devotee, imperfect devotion can be classified into three, viz., the *Aarta* devotion, the *Jijnaasu* devotion and the *Arthaarthi* devotion. The *Aarta* devotion consists of seeking the Lord's favor in times of danger, sickness and trouble. Thus, an *Aarta* devotee remembers the Lord in his affliction and implores the Lord in his sinfulness for mercy. He begs the Lord to free him from his trouble. Though this form of devotion is clouded by selfishness, it brings one nearer to God. The *Jijnaasu* devotion implies praying for knowledge of God from the study of the scriptures out of intellectual curiosity. Though selfishly motivated, this devotion turns one to God. The *Arthaarthi* devotion makes the devotee seek from the Lord the favor of His grace. Though these different forms of the *Aparaa Bhakti* lack right motivation, they lead people to God, as they gradually bring about the purification of the devotee's mind.[389]

There is a nine-fold step in the attainment of this imperfect devotion. The steps are: listening to the praise of the Lord (*Sravana*), singing His praise (*Kiirtana*), pious remembrance of the Lord (*Smarana*), serving the Lord's feet (*Paada-sevana*), adoration (*Arcanaa*), salutation and praise (*Vandanaa*), worship of the Lord as one's master and Lord (*Daasya*), worship of the Lord as a friend and companion (*Sakhya*) and self-dedication of the devotee (*Aatma-nivedana*).[390]

The perfect devotion (*Paraa Bhakti*) is the superior and purer type of devotion. It is described as motiveless, pure, absolute, primary, transcendent and perfect, as it consists of pure affection for the Lord. It is based on completely selfless love (*Prema*) of the devotee for the Lord. Such a pure love makes the devotee open to the Lord with single-hearted attachment and brings to the devotee perfect peace and spiritual joy. There are 11 forms *Paraa Bhakti* can take. A *Bhakta*, in reaching the perfection of devotion, can achieve it in any one of these forms according to his temperament and vocation. At the same time, each of these forms involves an ascent in the attitude of mind (*Bhaava*) of the *Bhakta*.

- First, the devotee is attached to the contemplation of God's attributes and greatness (*Guna-maahaatmya-aasakti*) in His outward manifestations.
- Second, the devotee's contemplation of the beauty of God (*Ruupa-aasakti*) as He is in Himself.
- Third, the love of adoration (*Puuja-aasakti*) and fixing the mind on God.
- Fourth, the devotee's love of contemplation (*Samarana-aasakti*) and loving remembrance of the Lord.
- Fifth, a more personal relationship between the *Bhagavaan* and the *Bhakta*, and the latter approaches the former with the love of the servant for the Lord (*Daasya*).
- Sixth, the mutuality of relationship between the Lord and the devotee, based on the love of friendship (*Sakhya*).
- Seventh, parental affection (*Vaatsalya*).
- Eighth, spiritual espousal (*Kaantaa-aasakti*), in which God is considered as the divine spouse, and the devotee assumes the attitude of a loving wife.
- Ninth, the devotee's self-consecration (*Aatma-nivedana*), which implies the entire surrender of self to the Lord, who is his Beloved.
- Tenth, the love of absorption (*Tanmaya-aasakti*), which consists in the devotee completely becoming the object of his contemplation. In this mode of devotion the devotee experiences the whole world as being filled with the Lord, whom he loves.
- Eleventh, love in separation (*Parama-viraha-aasakti*), in which the devotee, for whom nothing but the Lord exists, feels the agonizing pain of being separated from the Lord. This sublime form of *Bhakti* is not a means to attain salvation (*Mukti*), but is salvation itself. The heart of such a devotee is permanently established in the Lord. The pain of separation (*Vihara*) is the highest form of union that the liberated soul, tied to his material body, (*Jiivan-mukta*) experiences with the Lord, which at the same time is a yearning for total union with his Beloved Lord in heaven (*Videha-mukti*).[391]

Some spiritual authors call these two stages of devotion *Bheda-upaasana* and *Abheda-upaasana*. This division focuses on the nature of the union that exists between the devotee and the Lord in the two stages of *Bhakti*. In *Bheda-upaasana* a difference between the devotee and the Lord is kept in view. The *Bhakta*, in this state, while enjoying the delights of the union in love, experiences his separation from the Lord. But *Abheda-upaasana* is a state in which the identity of the devotee with the Supreme Lord is kept in view. Here, the *Bhakta* gradually loses himself in the object of his love and worship. Thus, in the latter state, there is the possibility of identity-consciousness, as life in the world does not seem anything more than the mental life of the devotee. Such an identity-consciousness can take place in two different processes, viz., the process of sinking and the process of expansion. In the sinking process, the devotee feels that his soul is placed in the all-pervasive consciousness. Feeling the immanence of the bliss, the *Bhakta* surrenders his self completely. The complete surrender brings about psychological and spiritual transformations in the devotee. He experiences every mental modification in a new vision and meaning, as everything is viewed in relation to the Infinite Lord. There is complete delight and deep satisfaction in the soul. The intensity of devotion in love and the inner delight and satisfaction makes the finite self-consciousness forget itself and be absorbed in the immanent Infinite Consciousness. The process of expansion consists in the gradual realization, in the devotee, that he is the immanent principle of the *cosmos*. When this realization takes over, the devotee no longer feels that he is placed in the vastness of the *cosmos*, but rather finds the entire universe to be a reflection of his own being. In other words, he feels within himself the totality of existence. In the process, his sense of finite personality dissolves into the Infinite Consciousness.[392]

In the attainment of *Bhakti*, especially in its higher form, the grace of the Lord plays a very important role. It is not merely the efforts of the *Bhakta* that effect in him *Paraa Bhakti*, but also the grace of the Lord. The divine grace (*Anugraha*) facilitates the devotee to free his self from the bondage of sin, awakens devotion in the heart of the devotee, brings about the gracious indwelling of the Lord in his heart and leads him to the final beatific communion with the Lord. *Bhakti* is a gift from the Lord to those who have responded to His love. While the grace of the Lord elevates and transforms the devotee, his cooperation and response to the Lord's inviting love is necessary for the full flowering of true *Bhakti* in him.[393]

There have been controversies regarding the question of the mutual relationship between the role of the grace of God and the cooperation of the devotee in obtaining *Bhakti* and through it salvation. Some emphasize reliance on the grace of God (*Prapatti*), so much so that they propose passive surrender to God's action on the soul, while others warn against presuming the grace of God and advocate that man must cooperate with the grace of God by living a life of virtue in order to obtain true devotion. Two groups of the disciples of Raamaanuja, known as the 'Cat group' and the 'Monkey group', propose two analogies in explaining this point. The 'Cat group' stresses the role of God alone in the attainment of salvation through *Bhakti*. According to this group, just as a cat carries the kitten by holding it up by the scruff of the neck, the grace of God brings the *Bhakta* to true devotion and through it to salvation. Therefore, the effort of the devotee does not matter at all for salvation through the path of devotion. The 'Monkey group', on the other hand, emphasizes the role of the devotee along with the grace of God. For this group, just as the little monkey holds on to the mother monkey as she transports the baby from one place to the other, the devotee must cooperate with the grace of god to arrive at true devotion.[394]

Thus, salvation through the path of devotion calls for the grace of God and the cooperation of the devotee. The grace of God comes to the *Bhakta* through his openness to the mediation of the *Guru* and holy men. The devotee's invocation of the Lord's Name (*Naama-japa*) is another powerful means to obtain the grace of God. Besides, the devotee's good deeds, such as, the practice of virtues like detachment and humility, avoidance of the company of evil people, unselfish performance of his personal and social duties, fidelity to prayer and the faithful fulfillment of similar obligations, make the devotee worthy of the grace of God. In this manner, the devotee's cooperation with the grace of God leads him to the path of true devotion.[395]

Raamaanuja, one of the great teachers of *Bhaktiyoga*, proposes the following seven disciplines as necessary for the true development of *Bhakti* in the devotee.

- First, the lover of God must be careful about his food habits. When food is pure, the mind becomes pure. Food influences one's mind. Certain kinds of foods dull the mind, while others excite the mind. For instance, heavy meals induce laziness of the mind. Similarly, drinking alcohol excites the mind of a drunkard, and he loses control over his mind. Food should be free from dirt and dust. It should not have any contact with the saliva of another person. An impure person should neither cook nor serve the meal.
- Second, the devotee should be free from extreme attachment to material objects, as they lead him to entanglement with the world. He must consider material things as means rather than ends.
- Third, the devotee must practice *Bhakti* tirelessly. Whether he is in a low or high situation, he must be constant in his devotion. It must move towards God uninterruptedly, just as oil flows uninterruptedly when poured out from the jar. When the devotee feels dryness in his heart, he must take recourse to devotional hymns (*Bhajans*).
- Fourth, the devotee must learn to be unselfish towards others, for selfishness can never lead one to cultivate divine love. One can learn to be unselfish by performing good actions to the benefit of others.
- Fifth, the devotee must practice purity, which includes truthfulness, straightforwardness, compassion, non-injury and charity. By being truthful, one becomes like God, for God is Truth. Straightforwardness means being simple and guileless as an innocent child. The practice of compassion helps the devotee to control greed and selfishness. The devotee practices non-injury

when he does not hurt others in thought, word and deed. Charity consists in going to the extent of hurting oneself in helping others. The practice of purity in all these aspects makes the devotee gain divine grace.

- Sixthly, the devotee must avoid despondency and gloominess. True devotion is not one of dejection and melancholy. Cheerfulness is the heart of true devotion and it comes from the devotee's faith in God.

- Seventh, the devotee must avoid excessive merriment, because it makes his mind inconsistent and indecisive, which, in turn, may lead to sorrow. According to Raamaanuja, the practice of these seven preparatory disciplines on the part of the devotee helps him to walk on the path of genuine *Bhakti*.[396]

3.2.2.3. PATH OF UNSELFISH ACTION

The path of unselfish action (*Karmayoga*) is proposed for persons of mixed temperaments, viz., persons who are both emotional and rational. These are energetic personalities who have an inherent orientation towards activity, work and service. The path of *Karma* calls for the simultaneous use of one's head and heart. A *Karmayogi* dedicates his activities in love and devotion to the Lord. The willing surrender of his life in generous service calls him to live a life of sacrifice and action. For such a life of action, it is necessary to work towards eliminating selfish motives and intentions that stem from animal instincts in man. Besides, the aspirant must learn to do everything he does without any self-interest. In the process, he sheds his personality off worldly thoughts and pleasures, purifies his mind and turns his attention to the contemplation of the Supreme Self, which is the source of his love and service.[397]

In order to attain this path of perfect action, the seeker of the *Karma* path must not reject action itself, but must let go of his personal likes (*Ragga*) and dislikes (*Dwesha*) in performing his action. One should not do an action because one likes it; nor should one give up certain actions because one dislikes it. One must learn to overcome one's whims and fancies in performing actions. Thus, the greatest enemies of man are his likes and dislikes, for they make even the highest type of activity meaningless. The activities that emerge from likes and dislikes are called negative actions. Negative actions produce desires (*Vasanas*). When desires are denied they turn into anger. Thus, desire and anger are one and the same. They are enemies of the genuine path of unselfish action, and they cause spiritual degradation and devolution. It is important that we avoid negative actions. Avoidance of negative actions does not consist in rejecting what one likes or forcing oneself to do something one does not like. Rather it consists in performing actions without any personal preferences, i.e., not allowing oneself to be carried away by one's likes and dislikes.[398] The *Bhagavad Giitaa* says: "Therefore, without attachment, perform always the work that has to be done, for man attains to the highest by doing work without attachment."[399] Radhakrishnan comments on this point as follows:

> It is not possible for us to abstain from action. Nature is ever at work and we are deluded if we fancy that its process can be held up. Nor is cessation from action desirable. Inertia is not freedom. Again, the binding quality of an action does not lie in its mere performance but in the motive or desire that prompts it. Renunciation refers not to the act itself but to the frame of mind behind the act. Renunciation means absence of desire. ... [Thus] ... *Giitaa* advocates detachment from desire and not cessation of work.[400]

Thus, the *Karma* path involves that its seeker must guide his actions with the help of intellectual discrimination. Instead of rejecting work, he must deny negative actions that increase desire in the seeker. This calls for a discriminative reflection on the part of the aspirant of the *Karma* path before he performs his actions. He must pause, think and analyze his attractions and repulsions regarding the actions he is going to perform in a given situation. He must obtain a sense of objectivity and must use his discriminating intellect to judge and decide on a proper course of action, irrespective of his likes and dislikes. In so doing, the seeker of *Karmayoga* would not only prevent the perpetuation of negative actions in his life, but also would be able to remove them from his life, thereby achieving a sense of objectivity in choosing and performing his actions.[401]

Once a person brings about a sense of objectivity and steadiness by removing acts of likes and dislikes, he must cultivate positive activity. In the words of the *Giitaa*, positive activity consists in acting dynamically, surrendering all one's actions to the Lord, allowing one's thoughts to rest on the Supreme Self. Such action must be free from egoism, hope and feverish excitement.[402] This verse from *Giitaa* speaks of twofold characteristics of positive activity, viz., acting dynamically so as to use one's body, mind and intellect purposefully, resting on the Supreme Lord; and not allowing the energies produced by dynamic action to be dissipated in an unproductive manner. The first characteristic involves engaging in constant action, using the body, because action builds up energy in the body, while inaction weakens a person's body. In performing the action one's thoughts must rest on the Lord, always becoming aware that the Inner Self is the foundation of one's actions. In this manner, one builds up mental stamina and intellectual ability for work. Thus, positive activity consists in building up one's body, mind and intellect, so that the person is ready for genuine action. Secondly, once the energy of a person is built up by dynamic action that is resting on the Lord, the person must see that the energies, thus built up, should not be lost. There are three outlets that dissipate energy, viz., egoism, hope and excitement. Egoism and self-interest can vitiate a person's sense of purpose. So one must see that self-interest does not lead a person astray from the path of disinterested action (*Nishkaamakarma*). Again, hope of enjoying the fruits of one's actions can de-rout a person from good intentions. A person, who seeks the path of *Karma*, must detest craving for enjoyment. Besides, excitement brings unrest in a person's sphere of activity. An excited person cannot be fully responsible for his duties and responsibilities. Thus, egoism vitiates the past, by focusing on a person's past activities; the hope of enjoyment dissipates a person acting purposefully in the future; and excitement disturbs the present activity. When a seeker of the *Karma* path performs a dynamic action, resting his thoughts on the Lord, and prevents egoism, hope and excitement to vitiate the energy in the threefold temporal dimensions of his life, he becomes a *Karmayogi*.[403]

There are two motivations that move the *Karmayogi* to give himself in unselfish action in the spirit of detachment from results, by rejecting the worries of the past, anxieties of the future and the excitements of the present. They are his dedication to God and his love for humanity. The *Giitaa* calls the *Karmayogi* to dedicate himself to God, especially in performing *Nishkaamakarma*, by using phrases, such as, "Doing continuously all actions whatsoever, taking refuge in me…", "Surrendering in thought all actions to me…" and "Resigning all thy works to me…".[404] Again we read: "Abandoning all duties, come to Me alone for shelter. Be not grieved, for I shall release thee from all evil."[405] These texts from the *Giitaa* point to the first motive of dedication to God that moves the *Karmayogi* to selfless action. He, listening to the invitation of the Lord to surrender to Him, willingly and completely takes shelter in His love. Commenting on the last text Radhakrishnan says:

> If we destroy confidence in our own little self and replace it by perfect confidence in God He will save us. God asks of us total self-giving and gives us in return the power of the spirit, which changes every situation. … If we are to realize our destinies, we must stand naked and guileless before the Supreme. … When we turn to Him and let Him fill our whole being, our responsibility ceases. He deals with us and leads us beyond all sorrow. It is an unreserved surrender to the Supreme who takes us up and raises us to our utmost possible perfection. … When we wait on God without words and desire only His taking hold of us, the help comes.[406]

Thus, total dedication to God and the desire to do His will, moves the *Karmayogi* to surrender himself to the Lord. This loving surrender, in turn, gives him the courage to do every action he does without desiring its fruit.

The second motive is *Karmayogi's* love for and dedication to humanity (*Lokasamgraha*). The term '*Lokasamgrah*' means world-maintenance. It stands for the unity of the world. It also means the interconnectedness of communities and societies. The *Karmayogi*, called to work to remove the physical misery and moral degradation found in individuals and societies, thereby attempts to establish the genuine brotherhood of mankind. The *Karmayogi* is not a man merely lost in varied activities of the everyday changing world (*Kshara*); he is an ideal man, who works to reconcile all possibilities of the world without getting involved in it. Though he lives in the world, he lives as if he is not of the world. He lives in this world as a stranger. He exists in the world, but he is the citizen of the heavenly world. He is the doer of actions, yet not a doer, as he is fully detached from the fruits of his action. The *Karmayogi* does not deny the fruits of the action, but he rather welcomes them. But he directs the fruits of the action not towards himself, but rather towards the good of his fellowmen. The purpose of his action is to make every man happy, to make this world a better world and to make human society more humane and just. With this purpose, the *Karmayogi* becomes a social activist, who works earnestly for the welfare of others. He endures troubles and hardships to maintain peace and order in the human society.[407]

Thus, the *Karmayogi* reaches the highest degree of perfection by his performance of actions with perfect detachment. That is the reason that *Giitaa* calls a *Karmayogi*, who is moved by these two-fold motives to perfect action, a perpetual monk (*Nitya Samnyaasin*).[408] The *Karmayogi* remains unaffected by personal advantages or disadvantages in his action. He enjoys spiritual freedom without resorting to inactivity. His freedom is such that neither desire nor anger has any effect on him. He constantly fights the battle in defense of truth and justice. But he, in no way, is affected by his struggle for truth. Like a lotus leaf, which is in the water, the *Karmayogi* is fully in the world. But just as the lotus leaf is always above the water, he is also above the passions of this world. His spirit of detachment is of a high degree so that he remains totally unstained regarding the purity of his intentions and the sincerity of his commitments. In this manner, *Karmayoga* becomes a true path to the salvation of man.

3.2.2.4. PATH OF DISCIPLINING THE MIND

Raajayoga is the king of all other *Yogas*. It attempts to discipline the mind, which is the most important aspect of God-realization. Every other *Yoga*, concerned about God-realization, makes use of the principles of *Raajayoga* to help its adherent to discipline his mind. In that sense, we can truly call it the king (*Raja*) of all other *Yogas*. The mind is the cause of the phenomenal existence and man's varying conditions of life. The goal of *Rajayoga* is the restraint of mental fluctuations (*Citta-vritti-nirodha*). *Citta* includes all aspects of the mental faculty. The *Vrittis* are right knowledge, wrong knowledge, verbal delusion, sleep and memory. *Nirodha* is the restraint of these mental fluctuations. By *Nirodha* of *Citta-vritti* the concentration of the mind is achieved, which, in turn, leads to a state of release (*Samaadhi*) where the seeker experiences his oneness with the Divine. *Raajayoga* is different from *Hathayoga*. The latter is the physical *Yoga*, while the former is the mental *Yoga*. While the former attempts to discipline the mind, the latter aims to discipline the body. Where *Hathayoga* ends, the *Raajayoga* begins. Therefore, they cannot be separated, and they are interdependent.[409]

Thus, *Raajayoga* deals in detail with the process of restraining thought waves and helps one attain the Super-conscious state. It enables the one who practices it to have a vigorous and healthy mind, strong will power, power of concentration, self-control and various psychic powers. The philosophical background of *Raajayoga* is dualistic, as it recognizes reality as constituted of material nature (*Prakrti*) and the Spirit (*Purusha*). But the practice of various steps of *Raajayoga* eventually bridges this duality and leads to the realization of God-experience, as, by its practice, multiplicity and fragmentation of consciousness are abolished, and integration, unity and wholeness of personality are achieved. It helps the aspirant to silence the senses and mind, and to make the inward journey until he comes to the divine center within, where he can encounter the indwelling spirit and become one with it.[410]

The *Raajayoga* proposed by Patanjali has eight limbs (*Ashtaangayoga*). The eight limbs are: self-purifications (*Yama*), virtuous practices (*Niyama*), posture (*Aasana*), breath-control (*Praanaayaama*), withdrawal of senses (*Pratyaahaara*), concentration (*Dhaaranaa*), meditation (*Dhyaana*) and absorption (*Samaadhi*). The aspirant ascends in the *Yogic* ladder as he practices these eight steps and becomes a *Raajayogi*. Of these, the first five steps are external aids. The first of these two limbs aims at cultivating in the aspirant of *Raajayoga* moral qualities, while the third, fourth and the fifth help him to control his body and senses. The last three are internal aids, as they attempt to discipline the mind, develop concentration and lead to final state of liberation.[411] We elaborate each of the *Ashtaangas* of the *Raajayoga* in the following section.

3.2.2.4.1. Self-purifications (Yama)

The first limb of *Raajayoga* is *Yama*, which consists of five general disciplines of self-purification. They are the very foundation of *Raajayoga*. Without genuine self-purification, we cannot build a superstructure of mental discipline. These restraints are universal practices, and so are not limited to class, circumstance, place and time. A true aspirant of *Raajayoga* must practice them always and everywhere, in thought, word and deed. The first is non-injury (*Ahimsa*), which involves not harming others by thoughts, words and deeds. Second, non-lying (*Satya*), which consists in maintaining identity between thoughts, words and deeds. Third, non-stealing (*Asteya*), i.e., giving up the desire for other's things. Fourth, continence (*Brahmacarya*), i.e., abstaining from sexual intercourse and lustful thoughts. Fifth, non-covetousness (*Apaarigraha*), i.e., freeing oneself from all forms of greed. It also involves the aspirant not accepting any gifts that would make his mind impure, thereby likely to stand in the way of meditation.[412] The practice of the discipline of self-purifications leads the aspirant to the practice of the following virtues.

3.2.2.4.2. Virtuous Practices (Niyama)

The second limp of *Raajayoga*, *Niyama* consists in the practice of five virtues. The first is cleanliness (*Sacca*), which consists of external and internal purity. External purity is cleanliness of the body, house, food and similar things that belong to the physical environment in which a person lives. External purity is maintained by washing away the external dirt, by following the taboos and by avoiding things that would defile a person physically. Internal purity consists in purity of thought, mind and heart. It also involves freeing one's actions from the cravings of the ego. The second is contentment (*Samtosa*), which is the joyful acceptance of what comes in life. It is the spirit of non-possessiveness. Though the aspirant does not possess many things in life, he is not sad, but rather is joyful. Joy results from inner satisfaction and the unruffled peace one possesses. Contentment is vital for concentration, for the mind of man who is not contented always wanders. The third is austerity (*Tapas*); practice of mortification. It is an inward reality and a positive orientation towards higher values. It is expressed in self-control and the renunciation of all that stands as obstacles to the spiritual journey. Austerity is practiced in relation to body, speech and mind. The practice of these threefold austerities helps the aspirant to acquire various *yogic* powers. The fourth is the study of the scriptures (*Svadhaaya*). It consists in the aspirant of *Raajayoga* undertaking the study of the scriptures and studying them meditatively. It entails the contemplative reflection on the *Mahaavaakyas* and the eternal syllable '*Aum*'. The fifth is the remembrance of the Lord (*Iishvara-pranidhana*). This requires a meditative attention to the Lord both in prayer and in all the household duties which aspirant is expected to do every day. It calls for true knowledge of, and loving devotion to, God.[413]

3.2.2.4.3. Posture (Aasana)

The aspirant of *Raajayoga*, having prepared himself morally with the help of *Yama* and *Niyama*, takes the first step towards bringing harmony between the body and the mind by way of disciplining the body with the help of posture. *Aasana* means steady (*Stira*) and pleasant (*Sukha*) posture. For Patanjali, 'steady' means that one is able to keep the chest, neck and the neck erect and equal to the other parts of the body. It also means that one is capable of remaining in a particular posture motionless for a long period of time. 'Pleasant' stands for the posture being comfortable. It means that our body is free from tension and is relaxed, that our mind can concentrate without being distracted by the movements of the body. One can arrive at the goal of steady and pleasant posture only by constant practice. Regular performance of the *Aasana* removes restlessness of the body, cures a number of illnesses and keeps the body healthy and strong, and checks the wandering nature of the mind.[414]

3.2.2.4.4. Breath-control (Praanaayaama)

Once the steadiness of posture is established one must move on to the regulation of breath. *Praanaayaama* comes from two Sanskrit words '*Praana*' (vital breath) and '*Yama*' (control). Thus, *Praanaayaama* means regulation of vital breath, i.e., the life force. Breath is the external manifestation of the internal, subtle and all-pervading vital breath, which is in man. By the practice of *Praanaayaama*, through the regulation of external breathing, one enters into the deep rhythm within man and regulates this underlying vital force.[415]

According to Patanjali, it consists in the regulation of inhalation and exhalation. It is a conscious control over one's rhythm of breathing. In the light of what Patanjali has said, a number of common breathing exercises are proposed. They are: inhalation (*Puraka*), retention of breath taken in (*Kumbaka*), exhalation (*Recaka*), suspension of breathing after having breathed out the air taken in (*Sunyaka*), and complete stoppage of in-breathing and out-breathing for some time (*Aksepin*). One could begin with inhalation and exhalation; then move on to the practice of retention of breath, after which begin practicing suspension of breathing after having breathed out the air taken in; and finally one could attempt to practice the stoppage of breathing in and breathing out. When a person practices the stoppage of breathing in and breathing out for a long time, he arrives at the state of absolute retention (*Kevela Kumbaka*), which is a perfect form of *Praanaayaama*.[416]

There are also two forms of *Praanaayaama*. They are *Agarbha Praanaayaama* and *Sagarbha Praanaayaama*. This division is based on non-attachment or attachment of meaning to the rhythm of breathing. If the aspirant attaches no meaning to his breathing, it is *Agarbha Praayaanama*. This is a simple awareness of breathing. In it the aspirant moves into concentration by conscious awareness of his breathing. But in the *Sagarbha Praanaayaama* the practice of breathing is done attaching meaning to the act of breathing. The aspirant gives meaning to his breathing. There are various ways in which can do this. For instance, as the aspirant breathes in, he could imagine that he is breathing in the divine qualities, such as mercy, love, joy and forgiveness entering his body-mind-spirit system. In the same way, as he breathes out, one could picture expelling evil qualities, such as lust, anger, greed and jealousy out of his body-mind-spirit system along with the out-going breath. Similarly, one could mentally repeat '*Aum*' or any other word that evokes spiritual significance, as one breathes in and out. In this way, one makes simple breathing an *Agarbha Praanaayaama*. The practice of various forms of *Praanaayaama* keeps the mind steady so that it can be fixed on any point. The practice also purifies the nerves and the mind and destroys *Karma*. The constant practice of *Praanaayaama* helps the aspirant observe perfect *Brahmacaarya*.[417]

3.2.2.4.5. Withdrawal of Senses (Pratyaahaara)

Pratyaahaara consists in silencing the senses. The senses are silenced when the senses are withdrawn from their respective objects. By their nature, the senses have continuous connection with objects and thus open the mind to the outside world. However, when the mind is turned outward through the senses, it gets lost in the mental fluctuations because in knowing an object the mind assumes the form of that multiple and changing object. Hence when the senses are withdrawn from their respective objects, the mind is unable to assume the form of any object and in the process the mind becomes focused. Thus, *Pratyaahaara* consists in removing the focus of the mind's attention from the senses. In other words, in *Pratyaahaara*, the aspirant is helped to withdraw the sense organs from the respective objects, which happens only when the mind does not allow it to be modified into objects by shutting down the senses. When this happens, the sense would follow the mind just as the bees follow the queen bee. For, when the mind is restrained by the silencing of the senses, the senses follow the direction of the mind.[418]

Thus, the practice of *Pratyaahaara* helps the aspirant to achieve supreme mastery over the senses. As a result, one is able to experience sense objects without likes and dislikes. It frees the mind from distractions and makes it focused, thereby helping the aspirant in concentration and meditation. By preventing distractions and helping the aspirant in concentration, *Pratyaahaara* gives him the facility to reach the state of silence even amidst noise. Just as a tortoise can withdraw all its limbs at once, in the same way, the aspirant can withdraw his sense from all objects by the practice of *Pratyaahaara*, leading him to the state of concentration.[419]

3.2.2.4.6. Concentration (Dhaaranaa)

Even after the senses are silenced in *Pratyaahaara*, the mind need not be fully silenced and concentration is achieved, because the images the mind received from the senses are stored in memory and imaginations. Therefore, the mind can wander from one image or thought to another, in the process assuming the form of that image or thought. Thus, to silence the mind totally one must silence the internal organs, such as, memory and imagination. This can be done when the mind does not work on these stored images and thoughts. *Dhaaranaa*, in the first place, attempts to stop these modifications of the mind in the level of thoughts and images. The cessation of the modification of the mind based on memory and imagination leads to attention (*Ekaagraha*). It is a positive attempt to fix the mind on one object. Those who begin the state of attention begin by choosing an object of their liking upon which to fix their attention. One could use any sense object, the sorrowless condition of the mind, the sacred syllable '*Aum*', the pure mind of a god-man, the wonderful experience of the dream state or any chosen favorite object - to fix the attention of the mind, while one is engaged in *Dhaaranaa*.[420] Constant practice of fixation of the mind on a specific object in *Dhaaranaa* leads the aspirant to the state of meditation.

3.2.2.4.7. Meditation (Dhyaana)

When *Dhaaranaa* is unbroken and continues for a long time, it becomes *Dhyaana*. According to Patanjalai, *Dhyaana* is the steadied evenness of the mind in concentration. The oil flows from the jar continuously and without any interruption. In the same way, the mind in *Dhyaana* is engaged, in an uninterrupted manner, in the object of one's meditation. Thus, in meditation, the awareness of God has become a living foundation from within. As a result, one has a unitary vision of reality and an undivided awareness of the presence of the divine. Thus, *Dhyaana* is experiencing the divine at the center always and everywhere. There is a habitual flow of God's presence in his life. Though the one who meditates is involved in various activities, the divine presence envelops him. The union of divine and human consciousness in meditation is not only due to human effort, but also is the result of the activity of God.[421]

There are two types of meditation, viz., gross meditation (*Sthula-dyaana*) and subtle meditation (*Sukshma-dyaana*). In gross meditation, one materially contemplates the image of the deity. Again in *Sthula* meditation, the aspirant feels absorbed in a word or a sentence with his favorite deity (*Ishtadevata*). The word illumines the mind of the meditator, remaining in the back of his mind as a seed, and helps him to experience the *Ishtadevata* not only at the intellectual level, but also at the emotional level. In this form of meditation, the role of the aspirant is greater, as his meditation either on the image or the word of the *Ishtadevata* leads him to the experience of the Deity. Besides, the Deity is experienced at the sensory level. But in subtle meditation there is no image of the Deity and it being experienced in the sensory level. In *Sukshma* meditation no specific word of the *Ishtadevata* is remembered, but the mind is pulled into the experience of the Unmanifest and the Infinite. Though the aspirant fails to experience what he seeks, yet in a mysterious way the presence of the nameless and formless absolute is powerfully felt. Thus, in this form of meditation, the divine spirit is that which leads the human spirit, and therefore the role of the former is greater than the latter. In both of these forms of meditations, the aspirant experiences the steady and unbroken presence of the Lord. In the *Sthula* meditation there is the positive experience of the Lord at the sense level. In the *Sukshma* meditation the presence of the Lord is not in any form, image or word, but is at a much deeper level as the Unmanifest and Absolute Reality.[422]

3.2.2.4.8. Absorption (Samaadhi)

The *Dyaana* becomes *Samaadhi* when the thinker and the object of thought, the meditator and the object of meditation become identical. In the state of absorption the distinction between one who contemplate and that which is contemplated fade away. The aspirant, at this stage is not conscious of any form of object. It is a state in which the seeker has discovered the purpose of the journey. *Samaadhi* is, thus, the state of the total absorption of the seeker in the divine. Arriving at this stage is the goal of a *Raajayogi*. He has a number of qualities. He enjoys genuine freedom. He is free from desire, anger and fear. He accepts friend and foe, fame and blame, pain and gain with an equal mind. The *Raajayogi* is one who has crossed over to the other side and so, though he lives inside the river physically, nothing of this world affects him. His presence is pleasing and peace- emanating. He achieves infinite knowledge, which is like the sun. He sees without eyes, tastes without the tongue, hears without ears, smells without nose and touches without hands. His thoughts are miracles, as he wills everything to come into being. He is entirely free from the effects of the three *Gunas*. Thus, there is total transformation of the seeker in the state of *Samaadhi*.[423]

There are a number of stages of *Samaadhi*. The first is discursive absorption (*Savitarka-samaadhi*) in which one is perfectly absorbed in the meaning of a saying of the Lord and develops argumentative thinking in support. When an aspirant is absorbed in the flow of such thinking, he is said to have discursive *Samaadhi*. The second is the absorption of thought (*Savicara-samaadhi*). When the aspirant advances in meditation, he may not need argumentative thinking to be convinced of the meaning of scripture. The moment he reads or remembers a word, his attention is totally on that word alone, and the meaning of that word overwhelms him without any help from argumentative thinking. So in the *Samaadhi* of thought the seeker gets lost in the word of the *Ishtadevata* without any discursive argumentative thinking. The third is thoughtless absorption (*Avicara-Samaadhi*). Here, the aspirant is not even dependent on a word or thought formed by the word of the *Ishtadevata*. In this state, the thoughtless awareness of God takes him to stillness and absorption. The fourth is seedling absorption (*Sabiija Samaadhi*) in which the seeker even gives up the particular form of thought. Yet the seed of such thought may still linger in the memory of the seeker. The fifth is awareness absorption (*Samprajnata Samaadhi*). In this stage there is no image of God, a thought or the seedling of thought that guides the seeker, but pure awareness of the presence of God, which takes hold of him. But even here as sense of self is present, it is also called determinate absorption (*Savikalpaka Samaadhi*). The last is mindless absorption (*Asamprajnata Samaadhi*) where there is no support for the mind. The mind is fully at rest in a total state of steady consciousness. All impressions and I-consciousness are entirely destroyed. There is no distinction between the seer, the seen and the sight. It destroys all impressions of the mind and other mental functions. It is said even to wipe away the *Karma* that determines the state of one's present life (*Praraabdha-karma*). Since the subject-object duality is wiped away, the mind becomes non-existent, which is also called indeterminate absorption (*Nirvikalpa Samaadhi*). This is the highest end of *Raajayoga*, which gives absolute freedom to the seeker. When this form of absorption is achieved, the process of *Ashtaangayoga* is complete.[424]

In this essay we have looked into the Divinity of Vedaantic Hinduism and the path proposed to establish relationship with the Divinity. Unlike Vedic Hinduism, in Vedaantic Hinduism the Divinity is considered as one, either an Absolute Impersonal *Brahman* or a theistic God, who is usually addressed as *Iishvara*. The difference in the perception of the Divinity means that make the scholars of Vedaantic Hinduism view man's destiny differently, for this is achieved according to his varying relationship with the Divinity, viz., identity, similarity and duality. The outlook on man's destiny proposes differing paths that help man to achieve his final destiny, depending on his nature, temperament and character. The four paths proposed, viz., the *Jnanayoga*, the *Bhaktiyoga*, the *Karmayoga* and the *Raajayoga*, though different are not opposed to each other, but rather are mutually complementary. Thus, in Vedaantic Hinduism we find a systematized and personalized approach to

God-experience. Though Shankarite non-dualistic interpretation of the *Upanishadic* teaching on *Brahman* and man's destiny as an identity of *Brahman* and *Aatman* formed the mainstream thinking, the monotheistic teachings of Raamaanuja and Madhva became more popular. The monotheism of Vedaantic Hinduism found popular expression in the later religions of Vaishnavism and Saivism. In the following two essays, we will explore the beliefs and practices of these two religions.

3.3. VAISHNAVISM

Vaishnavism is one of the most significant religious sects of Hinduism. In the course of its history, it has developed into a full-fledged philosophical system and religion within the Hindu tradition. As a philosophical system it enunciates the sound philosophical theories stated in the *Upanishads*. At the same time, Vishnavism expounds distinctive theological doctrines, based on philosophical theories. The sources of Vaishnavism in its philosophical aspect are the *Upanishads*, *Vedaanta Suutras*, (especially as interpreted by Raamaanuja) and the *Bhagavad Giitaa*. The theological and religious aspects of Vaishnavism are developed in the *Itihaasas*, *Puraanas*, *Vaishnava Aagamas*, *Paancaraatra* treatises, the Hymns of the Tamil *Aalvars*, and in a number of other similar works.[425]

Vasihnavism is one of the oldest religions of India. It is a monotheistic system that upholds *Vishnu* as the ultimate reality (*Paratattva*). It teaches that devotion to the Lord *Vishnu* leads one to the realization of one's ultimate goal (*Parampurushaartha*). Vaishnavism is an ethical and religious discipline that leads man to his final destiny.[426] As a religion it is very popular. Many kings and sages have patronized it. It has a multitude of adherents. Some of the main features of Vaishnavism, as a religion and practice, are the following: firstly, it is strictly monotheistic. People who are attached to this religion worship *Vishnu* as the Supreme God. Secondly, Vaishnavism believes in the incarnation (*Avataaras*) of the Lord *Vishnu*. Thus, it believes that *Vishnu* is not a mere spectator of the world process, but upholds the what is good in the human society and removes all that is evil He descends among men. The third characteristic of Vaishnavism is that it proposes *Bhakti* as the way to attain salvation. The *Bhakti* way envisages the establishment of a deep relationship of communion between the *Bhakta* and the *Bhagavaan*. The *Bhakta* is deeply devoted to the Lord, while the Lord is deeply concerned about the devotee and showers on him His graces (*Anuraaga*). Fourthly, Vaishnavism advocates the practice of non-injury (*Ahimsa*) towards every living creature, as it is the supreme way to realize the God, who is truth. This belief is clearly shown in the fact that all types of animal sacrifices are discarded. Fifthly, Vaishnavism makes a clear distinction between God, man and the world. God is the author of the latter two and they depend on Him. Sixthly, enjoyment of the presence of God is the ultimate goal of Vaishnavism. The grace of God, which is natural (*Svaabhaavika*) and unconditional (*Nirhetuka*), is vital for the attainment of this goal. God only waits for His devotees to come to Him that He can bless them with His grace. Finally, Vishnavism gives great emphasis to the development of the moral and mystical dimensions of man, by way of *Bhakti*. With the help of *Bhakti* spirituality, Vaishnavism helps man to move beyond caste barriers. In doing so, it offers even to the untouchables (*Suudras*) the privilege of knowing God and achieving liberation.[427] Having clarified the basic features of Vaishnavism, by way of introduction, we could move on to analyze the Vaishnavite understanding of *Vishnu* as the Supreme Being, and the paths proposed by Vaishnavism for coming in contact with the Lord *Vishnu*.

3.3.1. *VISHNU*: THE SUPREME GOD OF VISHNAVISM

Vishnu is not a very important god in Vedic times. But he is not merely a general deity (*Devataa-Saamaanya*) but belongs to a group of solar gods known as the *Aadityas*. The twelve *Aadityas* associated with twelve aspects of the Sun god spread over the twelve months of the year and so are portrayed as the twelve spokes of the wheel of time. Thus, without any doubt, *Vishnu* is a Vedic Deity, who is associated with light and life and to whom Vedic hymns are addressed. He is often referred to as the God who is willing and able to bring abundant blessings on the worshippers. To *Vishnu* are attributed qualities such as, 'one who confers welfare' (*Svastida*), 'the cause of welfare' (*Svastikrt*) and 'one who gives happiness' (*Sukhada*).[428]

The *Rig Veda* speaks of *Vishnu* as taking three steps (*Trivikarma*) over the universe, thereby maintaining fixed ordinances for the preservation of the universe. Similarly, *Vishnu* is said to take three strides that covers all the worlds where beings (*Bhuvans*) live. Probably the 'three strides' is a reference to the rising, the transition and the setting of the Sun. It can also mean the three-fold manifestations of light in the form of fire on earth, lightening in the atmosphere and the sunlight in the heavens. Thus, it is justifiable to think that *Vishnu* worship is a continuation of the worship of the Sun god, who holds an important place in the Vedic pantheon.[429] In the *Braahmanas* and *Upanishads*, *Vishnu* attains a prominent place. Speaking of the three strides of *Vishnu*, the *Satapatha-Braahamana* explains it in terms of a myth. The gods, losing their superiority over the *Asuras*, agree with them regarding the division of the world, that they would have as much as *Vishnu*, the dwarf, could cover in three steps. The *Asuras* agree to the proposal, seeing the dwarf nature of *Vishnu*. But, *Vishnu*, in three steps, occupied the whole universe, thus defeating the *Asuras*, the enemies of the gods. He does so with the help of chanting sacred hymns and the performance of sacrifices.[430] Thus, in the *Braahmanas*, *Vishnu* is referred to as 'the personification of sacrifice' and as 'the son of *Dharma*', which gives Him the supreme place, both in the sacrificial and moral life of the people. Similarly, the *Katha Upanishad* speaks of the supreme abode of the all-pervading *Vishnu* as the goal of human existence.[431] In this manner, though *Vishnu* is not a very important deity in the early Vedic period, he gains considerable prominence in the later Vedic period, especially in the *Braahmanas* and the *Upanishads*. The emergence of the *Bhakti* Movement and the theism propagated by some of the interpreters of Upanishadic teaching bring

Vishnu to an eminent position, and from then on He is acknowledged as the Supreme God. In the following section, we elaborate the nature and attributes of *Vishnu* as believed in Vaishnavism, *Vishnu* in his incarnations (*Avataaras*) and the symbolic representation of Lord *Vishnu* in stone-pieces called *Saalagraama*.

3.3.1.1. NATURE AND ATTRIBUTES OF VISHNU

Etymologically, the name '*Vishnu*' derives from the root '*vish*', which means 'to pervade'. The term '*Vishnu*' has a number of meanings in its derivation. Firstly, it means 'He who pervades the universe'. This meaning speaks of *Vishnu* as the all-pervading Soul (*Paramaatman*). There is no limit to the presence of the Lord in the universe. Just as liquidness pervades in the water, warmth pervades in the fire, saltiness pervades in the salt and sweetness pervades in the suger, *Vishnu* pervades everything in the universe. Secondly, *Vishnu* is 'He who supplies water to the world'. *Vishnu* is the one who truly sustains every living being in the universe. Thirdly, *Vishnu* stands for 'He who unites the devotee to Him'. This refers to the compassionate, tender feeling the Lord has towards his devotees. He is benevolent to all His law-abiding devotees. Fourthly, *Vishnu* is 'He who enters the body of every living being'. *Vishnu* is the inner Soul (*Jiivaatman*) that enlivens and animates every living being. It is He who is the core of human personality, the source of the growth of a seed into a plant and the life force in everything. Fifthly, *Vishnu* is 'He in whom everything has its entry'. *Vishnu* attracts every living being into His limitless body. Just as fishes live in the water, so also every reality finds its existence in *Vishnu*. Sixthly, *Vishnu* is 'He whose body is the largest of all'. Vishnu's body is limitless. Seventhly, *Visnu* is 'He who exhibits His might against *Asuras* and sin'. Hence, He is the transcendent and the immanent reality in the universe. *Vishnu* is the inner cause and the power by which everything exists. He is the *Aatman*, who manifests itself through body, mind and intellect as the individual, while the same *Vishnu* pervades the entire universe as *Brahman*. Thus, *Vishnu* is the supreme and all-pervading Reality that is responsible for the sustenance, protection and maintenance of the world.[432]

Vishnu is addressed as *Naaraayana*. The term '*Naaraayana*' is a compound of two words: '*Naara*' and '*Ayana*'. The term '*Naara*' is again derived from '*Nara*', which means 'a collection of men'. The term '*Ayana*' means 'a resting place'. Taken in this sense, '*Naaraayana*' means the abode or the resting place of men, i.e., the ultimate goal of every human person. Again '*Nara*' is derived from '*Na*' and '*Ra*', which, when taken together, mean 'never perished'. Viewed in this sense, '*Naaryaana*' refers to the Imperishable Spirit behind the universe. Some other scholars say that the term '*Naaraayana*' has a Dravidian origin. It derives from three Dravidian words: '*Naar*', '*Ay*' and '*An*'. The first word '*Naar*' is equated with the Dravidian '*Niir*' which means 'water'. '*Ay*' means 'to lie in a place'. '*An*' is the Dravidian, male, personal termination. If we combine the meaning of these three words '*Naaraayana*' applies to a male deity who is supposed to reside on the waters.[433] From the analysis we have done so far, we derive the following meanings of *Naaryaana*. Firstly, He is one who makes the causal waters His abode. Secondly, He is the one who is the abode of all human beings. Thirdly, He is the one who makes the hearts of human beings His abode. Finally, He is the one who is the final goal of all human beings. Thus, *Naaryaana* is the only Supreme Lord of the universe. Nothing exists without Him, as He is the cause (*Kaarana*) as well as the effect (*Kaarya*) of creation. Just as the ornament of gold is not different from gold itself, similarly there is no distinction between God as the cause and the effect.[434]

Vaasudeva is another name given to *Vishnu*. It comes from the Sanskrit '*Vas*' which means 'to reside'. So *Vaasudeva* is one who abides everywhere and who is the source of everything. When the suffix '*Deva*' is added to '*Vaasu*', it implies 'to shine forth'. So, *Vaaudeva* is one who shines forth (*Diivyati*), untouched by defects, though He abides everywhere. Thus, *Vaasudeva* is the everywhere-abiding, perfect Reality, who enjoys involvement with the created universe and whose praises the celestial beings sing. Therefore, the name '*Vaasudeva*' brings out the essential characteristics of the ultimate Reality. The other two names given to *Vishnu* are *Brahman* and *Bhagavaan*. Etymologically, the term '*Brahman*' means 'that which grows' or 'that which causes to grow'. Thus *Brahman* implies that which is infinite. The term '*Bhagavaan*' means Supreme Being, who is endowed with the essential attributes of the absolute Reality. Hence, Vaishnavism considers that the names '*Vishnu*', '*Naaraayana*', '*Vaasudeva*', '*Bhagavaan*' and '*Brahman*' bear the same meaning and denote the Supreme Reality referred to in the *Upanishads*, and He is the God of Vaishnava religion.[435]

As the transcendent, supreme and all-pervading Reality, *Vishnu-Naaraayana-Vaasudeva-Bhagavaan-Brahman* is said to possess a number of attributes. According to Raamaanuja the attributes of the Supreme Being are countless (*Asamkhyeya*). *Vaamana Puraana* reiterates the same truth by saying that the attributes of God are immeasurable. But *Paancaraatra Samhitaas* and *Vishnupuraana* speak of six essential attributes (*Shadgunas*), which portray the Supremacy of *Vishnu*. They are knowledge (*Jnaana*), power (*Sakti*), strength (*Bala*), lordship (*Aisvarya*), energy (*Viirya*) and splendor (*Tejas*). Of these six the first two, viz., *Jnaana* and *Sakti* are regarded as the most important ones, as the Supreme God must be omniscient and omnipotent. The other four attributes are only different aspects of the former two. Besides these essential qualities, there are a number of secondary qualities (*Niruupita-svaruupa-viseshana*) of the Lord *Vishnu*, which are nothing else but different aspects of the essential qualities. Raamaanuja speaks of 19 of them. They are intimate communion with the devotee (*Sausiilya*), tender affection (*Vaatsalya*), soft-heartedness *(Maardava)*, straightforwardness (*Aarjava*), friendly disposition (*Sauhaarda*), equal treatment (*Saamya*), compassion (*Kaarunya*), enchanting beatitude (*Maadhurya*), incomprehensible character (*Gaambhiirya*), generosity (*Audaarya*), skillfulness (*Caaturya*), steadfastness (*Sthairya*), courage (*Dhairya*), fortitude (*Saurya*), valor (*Paraakrama*), ever desired (*Satyakaama*), firm resolve (*Satyasankalpa*), feeling of having fulfilled the obligation (*Krtitva*) and feeling of satisfaction even with the smallest good deed (*Krtanjnataa*). All these essential and secondary qualities point to the auspicious and glorious nature of the Supreme Being, which Vaisnavism proclaims as the personal God.[436]

We find a beautiful description of *Vishnu-Naaraayana*, the Supreme God, in His heavenly abode, narrated in *The Institutes of Vishnu*.[437] The context of the narration is the Goddess of the Earth looking for help to sustain Herself, as *Ganaardana* (*Vishnu*), the chief of the gods, who has sustained the earth so far, has become invisible. Assuming the form of a beautiful woman, She seeks the advice of Kasyapa, the great sage. He advises her to go to the abode of *Vishnu*, the ocean of milk (*Kshiirasamudra*). The Goddess of Earth saluting the sage reverently, proceeds to the abode of *Vishnu*, arrives there and encounters the glory of *Vishnu-Naaraayana*.[438]

After the destruction of the universe of the previous cycle[439] and before creation of the next cycle, the *Vishnu-Naaraayana* enters into a yogic sleep (*Yoga-nidra*). The body of the great serpent (*Sesha* or *Ananta*) is coiled to form *Vishnu's* bed. The serpent has a thousand heads, and its hood is turned inward looking at its coiled body. The serpent bed holding *Vishnu-Naaraayana* is floating over the ocean of milk. As He sleeps, one of His legs is resting on the lap of His consort *Lakshmi*, who is gently pressing it. As *Naaraayana* is dreaming of His next cycle of creation in His yogic sleep, a lotus springs forth from His navel along with the god *Brahmaa* sitting on it. When *Vishnu* awakes from His yogic sleep, he instructs *Brahmaa* to proceed with the act of creation of the new cycle.[440]

The glorious sight of *Vishnu-Naaraayana* overwhelms the Goddess of the Earth. She kneels down and thanks *Vishnu* for His benevolence towards all living beings. She, then, praises *Vishnu*, using many names, such as, 'Lord of gods', 'O brilliant Chief of gods', 'One who annihilates the enemies of the gods', 'the Sovereign of the world', 'the Supreme Spirit', 'the One who knows the *Mantras*', 'the Invincible', 'the Great Soul of the universe', 'the Omnipresent', 'the Great Lord of all creatures', 'the Preceptor of the *Suras* and the *Asuras*', 'the Destroyer of *Madhu* and *Kaitasa*', 'the Teacher of religious rites' and many other similar names. Then She expresses her desire to learn form *Vishnu* those secret ordinances with which He guides the created universe. According to the direction of *Vishnu*, the Goddess of Earth sits at ease and listens to the sacred precepts that come out of the mouth of *Vishnu*.[441] In His lengthy exhortation to the Goddess of Earth, *Vishnu-Naaraayana* speaks of the various laws with which He directs the personal life of the individual, the social life of the community, the spiritual life of the ascetic and the hermit, duties related to the different castes and stages of life, the practice of the *Samskaaras*, penances to be done in expiation for the sins and many similar directives with which He maintains the everyday order of the universe. Toward the end of His address, *Vishnu* says that meditation on Him leads a person to be united with His Spirit.[442] When *Vishnu* finishes His exhortation, the Goddess of the Earth kneels and bows Her head before Him and says:

O *Bhagavat*! Four (out of the five) grosser elements are receiving their support from thee, and are constantly about thee: the ether, in the form of shell; the air, in the form of the discus; the fire, in the form of the mace; and the water, in the form of the lotus. Now I also desire to attend upon thee, in my own shape, as the ground which *Bhagavat's* feet tread upon.[443]

When *Vishnu* accepts the wish of the Goddess of the Earth, she expresses her happiness by offering the God of the gods, *Vishnu-Naaraayana*, a litany of praises.[444] This narration clearly points to the supremacy of *Vishnu* as the God of the universe.

In the common icon form, *Vishnu* is represented in blue color (*Niilameghasyaama*), and clothed in yellow garb. He wears a crown and stands upon a lotus. He has four arms holding the conch (*Sankha*), the discus (*Cakra*), the mace (*Gada*) and lotus (*Padma*). He wears a necklace with the famous gem *Kaustubha* dangling on a lock of hair (*Sriivatsa*) on the left chest. He also wears a garland of gems or fragrant flowers (*Vaijayantii*). Each of these has a symbolic meaning. The blue color of *Vishnu* indicates His infinite stature. The color blue is associated with the infinite and the immeasurable entities, such as, the sky and the ocean. Since *Vishnu* is the all-pervading cosmic power, He is depicted in blue. He wears a yellow garb. The color yellow is usually attributed to the earth, as anything that is buried in the earth for a long period of time becomes yellow in color. *Vishnu*, blue in color and clothed in yellow, stands for the descent of the infinite, immeasurable and the transcendent Reality to the earthly realm. The crown on *Vishnu's* head represents His supreme sovereignty and Lordship over the entire universe. He has power over everything. He maintains and protects all things. *Vishnu* stands upon a lotus. The lotus points to eternal Truth. Standing on the lotus means that any god-man who wishes to realize union with *Vishnu* must base himself on the substratum of the Supreme Truth, *Vishnu*.[445]

The four hands represent the four quarters of the universe and so refer to the absolute power of *Vishnu* over the whole universe. The conch stands for the five elements that make up the universe. The discus indicates the cosmic mind. The mace is symbolic of the cosmic intellect and the lotus points to the evolving world. Thus, the world is constituted of the five elements, the mind and the intellect. *Vishnu* is the absolute master of the world. The curl of hair represents all objects of enjoyments. The gem *Kaustubha* stands for the enjoyer. The garland symbolizes the subtle elements (*Bhuuta-tanmaatras*). On the personal level, one must move from the gross level of the duality of the enjoyer and the enjoyed to the level of subtle elements. The conch can be seen as *Vishnu's* call to everyone to live a noble and pure life, which the lotus represents. The mace is meant to warn those persons who do not heed the call of the Lord to change their ways. The discus points to the inevitable end that would befall those who choose to live an unholy life. Those who listen to *Vishnu's* call live a life of contentment here on earth and reach the abode of *Vishnu* in the life to come.[446]

Our consideration of the nature and attributes of *Vishnu* is not complete if we do not say anything about His consort, Goddess *Lakshmi*. As *Vishnu's* consort, she manifests the characteristics of steadfastness, submissiveness and loyalty. She manifests the characteristics of a model Hindu wife. She is often represented as kneeling before *Vishnu* to massage His feet. When she is depicted along with *Vishnu*, she is shown as smaller than *Vishnu* and as having two arms instead of the four arms she usually has when she is shown alone. Thus, *Lakshmi* represents righteous behavior, orderly conduct and correct social observance. She is a model of social decorum as *Vishnu's* wife. Besides, the goddess *Lakshmi* is inseparable form the Lord *Vishnu*. She is ever at His side in every form *Vishnu* takes. In all His incarnations, *Lakshmi* accompanies *Vishnu*. For instance, it is *Lakshmi* who appears in the form of Sita and Radha in the incarnations of *Srii Raama* and *Srii Krshna* respectively. Thus, there is permanence about the relationship between *Vishnu* and *Lakshmi*.[447] Besides, she symbolizes the power, wealth and glory of this world. The Goddess of the Earth, after her conversation with *Vishnu*, addresses Goddess *Lakshmi* as follows:

> O charming lady! Thy hands are as beautiful as the expanded red lotus. Thou art holding the feet of him [*Vishnu*] ... Thou art constantly residing in ... [*Vishnu's*] abode... Thou art repose (final liberation), the highest among the (four) objects of human pursuit; thou art *Lakshmi*; thou art a support (in danger); thou art *Srii*; thou art indifference (the freedom from all worldly pursuits and appetites, which is the consequence of final emancipation); thou art victory; thou art beauty; thou art splendor (of the sun and moon personified); thou art renown; thou art prosperity [as goddesses of wealth, power and glory]; thou art wisdom; thou art the power of expression; thou art the purifier. ... As the first of the gods (*Vishnu*) pervades the whole aggregate of three worlds ... even so doest thou, O black-eyed bestower of gifts. Yet I enquire for the dwelling, in which thy superhuman power is residing.[448]

In responding to the praise of the Goddess of the Earth, Goddess *Lakshmi* says that though she resides in many places and does many great things, her glory consists in being a seeker of her consort *Vishnu*. She says thats he constantly holds Him in her mind and does everything according to His instruction. To quote:

> I am constantly at the side of the brilliant destroyer of *Madhu*, O goddess, who shinest like gold. But learn from me, where I reside (besides). O supports of the world, from the

instruction of him [*Vishnu*], whom I constantly reflect upon in my mind, and who the virtuous call the husband of *Srii*, and from my own recollection. ... I always reside in the destroyer of *Madhu* [*Vishnu*]. ... I do not remain separated from *Purushottama* [*Vishnu*] for a single moment.[449]

This statement from Goddess *Lakshmi* clearly shows her divine personality and the nature of her relationship with her consort *Vishnu-Naaraayana*, who is the source of all her powers.

3.3.1.2. VISHNU IN HIS INCARNATIONS

Vishnu-Naaraayana, the Supreme God, as the maintainer and preserver of the universe, takes recourse to various incarnations (*Avataaras*) in accomplishing His task of maintenance of the world. The term '*Avataara*' is composed of two Sanskrit words: '*ava*', which means 'down' and '*tr*', which has the meaning 'to pass'. Again '*Avataara*' is said to derive from the Sanskrit root '*avatr*', which suggests the meaning 'to descend'. Thus, *Avataara* literally means 'to pass down', 'to come down' and 'to descend'. *Bagavad Giitaa* uses words such as 'birth' (*Janman*), 'coming into being' (*Sambhava*), 'creation' (*Srjana*) and 'appearance' (*Praadurbhaava*) to express the idea of incarnation. In the incarnation, the God is said to 'assume an animal or a human form' or 'enter into an animal or a human body'.[450]

In Vaishnavism, *Avataara* means the descending of the Supreme God, *Vishnu-Naaraayana*, from His heavenly abode and coming down to earth, taking upon Himself either an animal or a human form. It consists not merely in God assuming various forms, but incarnating Himself with the specific purpose of destroying the wicked and protecting the righteous. When righteousness (*Dharma*) declines and unrighteousness (*Adharma*) increases, the Supreme Lord creates Himself. The Supreme Being, though unborn and eternal, He embodies Himself in this world to overthrow the forces of ignorance and selfishness. Whenever there is serious trouble in society, materialism is invading people's hearts and the sense of wisdom lost, the Lord descends on earth to establish equilibrium, wisdom and righteousness. Thus, the purpose of the descending of God in *Avataara* is to raise man to the divine level and to inaugurate a new society, by destroying the evil in it. The goal of *Avataara*, therefore, is the victory of love and mercy over hatred and wickedness, *Dharma* over *Adharma*, truth over falsehood, the good over evil. It is to actualize such a goal that God descends on earth.[451] In the next section, we consider briefly the major *Avataaras* of *Vishnu-Naarayana* and the way the *Vishnu-avataaras* are arranged.

3.3.1.2.1. Major Incarnations of Vishnu

Vaishnavism believes in five forms of incarnations of *Vishnu-Naarayana*, viz., *Paara-avataara*, *Vyuuha-avataara*, *Vibhava-avataara*, *Ar-*

caa-avataara and *Antaryaami-avataara*. *Paara-avataara* is the descend of the transcendental Supreme Being, who is present everywhere (*Vibhu*) as personal God for the purpose of helping individual souls in their meditation and offering of divine services. *Paancraatra Samhitas* describes *Vishnu* in this form of incarnation as possessing the six essential attributes, a spiritual body (*apraakrta-sariira*), decorated with divine weapons and ornaments, and surrounded by His consorts, divine attendants, eternally released souls (*Nityasuuris*) and souls released from bondage (*Muktas*). *Vyuuha-avataara* is the manifestation of the Supreme Being in four different forms, viz., *Vaasudeva*, *Samkarshana*, *Pradyumna* and *Anirudha*. Each *Vyuuha* is attributed specific functions, such as, creation of the universe, sustenance of the universe, dissolution of the universe and promulgation of spiritual knowledge. This form of incarnation is described in detail in the *Paancaraatra* treatises. *Vibhava-avataara* is the manifestation of the Supreme Lord, assuming bodies similar to those of human beings and other living beings. *Arcaa-avataara* means the descending of God for the purpose of worship in man-made idols in response to the ardent prayers of human beings. *Saattvata Samhitaa* of the *Paancaraatra* treatises speaks of this form of *Avataara*. *Antaryaami-avataara* as the manifestation of God is the indwelling in a subtle divine bodily form (*Vigraha-visishta*) in the inner recess of human hearts for the purpose of meditation.[452]

The third form of incarnation, viz., the *Vibhava-avataara*, stands for the descending of *Vishnu-Naaraayana*, assuming human or animal bodies. The *Mahaabhaarata* contains two lists of *Vibhava-avataara* of *Naaraayana*: the first enumerates six incarnations, while the second speaks of only four incarnations. In the later works the number is gradually extended. The *Bhaagavatapuraana* speaks of as many as 24 incarnations of *Vishnu*, while *Pancaraatra Samhitaas* speaks of 29 *Avataaras*. *Ahirbhudhnya Samhitaa* enumerates 39 incarnations of the Lord *Vishnu*.[453] But the major incarnations of *Vishnu* are accepted as 11,[454] of which 10 have already taken place and the last one is yet to come. The 11 incarnations of *Vishnu* are the following: the Fish-incarnation (*Matsyaavataara*), the Tortoise-incarnation (*Kuurmaavatara*), the Boar-incarnation (*Varaahaavataara*), the Man-lion-incarnation (*Narasimhaavataara*), the Dwarf-incarnation (*Vaamanaavataara*), the *Raama* with an axe in hand- incarnation (*Parasuraamaavataara*), the *Srii Raama*-incarnation (*Sriiraamaavataara*), the *Balaraama*-incarnation (*Balraamaavataara*) the *Srii Krshna*-incarnation (*Sriikrshnaavataara*), the *Buddha*-incarnation (*Buddhaavataara*) and the last and the yet-to-come incarnation is the *Bhagavaan-Kalki*-incarnation (*Kalkiavataara*).

3.3.1.2.1.1. Fish-incarnation (Matsyaavataara)

At the end of the last cycle (*Kalpa*), as *Brahmaa* takes repose, there occurs the *Brahmaa* Dissolution of the world. It is submerged under water. The *Vedas* are out of the mouth of the sleeping *Brahmaa*. A strong demon called *Danavaraaja Hayagriva* steals the *Vedas* and torments the followers of the *Vedas*. The Lord *Vishnu*, being aware of the happening, appears as a fish to rescue and deliver the *Vedas* and the followers of the *Vedas* from the clutches of the evil demon. *Vishnu* appears as a small fish to the renowned King Satyabrata, who is a follower of the *Vedas*, as he takes his bath in the sea. The fish asks him to rescue it from larger fishes that can swallow it. So the King brings the fish to his palace. Surprisingly the fish grows so fast that it has to be put back in the sea from where it was brought. Before the mysterious fish departs to the sea, it imposes an obligation on the King. It predicts that there is going to be a deluge, and only the King and his family will survive it. So the King must board a boat, carrying with him seeds of grains and living creatures. The King does the command of the Divine Fish. As the boat is tossed in the storm, the King and the seven sages (*Saptarsiis*) who are mind-born sons of *Brahmaa* and their families take recourse to saying devotional prayers. The Lord *Vishnu* appears to them in the form of the Fish to pronounce the *Attama Tattva*, which the King and the sages hear with great attention. They are saved from the deluge. In the mean time, the Lord *Vishnu* slays the demon *Danavaraaja Hayagriva* and restores *Vedas* to *Brahmaa*, who comes out of repose after the purposive dissolution of the universe.[455]

3.3.1.2.1.2. Tortoise-incarnation (Kuurmaavatara)

The prominent gods and the demons wish to have nectar (*Amrta*) from the Ocean of. Milk. They undertake an expedition, searching for *Amrta*. As the gods and the demons begin the task of searching for the nectar, the Ocean of Milk starts churning (*Samudramathana*). This, in turn, leads to the sinking of the mount *Mandaracal*, which has been supporting the ocean. The Lord *Vishnu* takes the form of the Tortoise, supports the mountain from underneath, prevents the mountain from sinking, thereby establishing equilibrium in the universe. The *Kuurmaavataara*, by protecting the world from its downfall, points to the fact that *Vishnu*, the Supreme God, is the preserver, sustainer and cultivator of all that we have among ourselves.[456]

3.3.1.2.1.3. Boar-incarnation (Varaahaavataara)

Most of the scriptures of Hinduism acknowledge the earth being submerged under deep waters and being rescued and re-established to its original shape by the intervention of the Supreme God. But there can be differences of opinion among the scriptures regarding the manner of rescue and the nature of the intervention of God. Vaishnavism believes that when the earth is in the sunken state, it is the Lord *Vishnu* who incarnates as the young robust Boar (*Varaaha*), delves deep into the waters and brings the earth on its tusks. Besides, the incarnated Boar drains the fluid surface and re-establishes the earth on the dry surface. It is said that the Boar is black in color and has a hundred arms. The Boar is so large that the earth is only as large as the size of its span. As the Divine Boar lifts the earth out of the waters, it slays *Hiranyaaksha*, the demon, as the latter prevents the rescuing process. The Boar incarnation of the Lord *Vishnu* symbolically exhibits the supremacy of the all-powerful *Vishnu-Naaraayana* to free every *Jiiva* that is marooned in the deluge of sin and to help to shape its future with faith and hope.[457]

3.3.1.2.1.4. Man-lion-incarnation (Narasimhaavataara)

Prahlaada is a great devotee of the Lord *Vishnu*. His father, Hiranyakasipu, a non-believer in the existence of the omnipotent and omnipresent God, severely tortures Prahalaada for his piety. In spite of his repeated appeals, the threats and troubles of his father continue. Even when Prahlaada is submitted to terrible tortures, he remains steadfast in his devotion to *Naaraayana*. Hiranyakasipu ties up his son Prahlaada on a pole to be tortured and killed. He laughs at his son asking him to invoke the God he believes in to come and save him, as he is going to die. Prahlaada, pointing to a pole, says that the Lord *Naaraayana* pervades the whole universe and that He can come out of that pole and protect him from death. Hiranyakasipu takes his sword and by one stroke breaks down the pillar. At this juncture the Lord *Vishnu-Naaraayana* assumes the form of a Man-lion (*Narasimha*), emerges out of the broken pole, slays Hiranyakasipu and protects the life of Prahlaada, His devotee, Lord *Vishnu*, places Prahlaata on the throne of his father and vanishes from the spot. *Narasimha* is the combination of man, the best of the higher creatures and lion, the best of the lower creatures. The upper part of his body is that of the lion and the rest is that of a man. *Narasimha* is the embodiment of the divine attribute of valor. His *Mantra* is said to be powerful to destroy enemies and remove evil. Warriors and kings are devoted to the *Narasimhaavataara* of Lord *Vishnu*. This incarnation of *Vishnu* points to His omnipresence and all-seeing nature. Besides, it declares that God does not spare the self-conceited and insolent persons who trouble His devotees, who are pure, innocent and devoted.[458]

3.3.1.2.1.5. Dwarf-incarnation (Vaamanaavataara)

King Bali, the grandson of Prahlaada is a virtuous man. He propitiates the goddess of fortune by hard austerities. By the boon of the goddess of fortune, Bali conquers the three worlds, driving the gods out of heaven. As a result, the god *Indra* is dispossessed of his heavenly kingdom. Bali expresses boastfulness, pride and conceit in all his actions, as he is the most powerful king in the world. He does not listen to the advice his grandfather, Prahlaada, renders him. The goddess *Aditi*, the mother of *Indra*, requests *Vishnu-Naaraayana* to help with the situation. With the desire to help the gods and to protect righteousness on earth, Lord *Vishnu* incarnates, through *Aditi* as the Dwarf (*Vaamana*), a young *Braahman* boy. He approaches Bali, who at that time decides to be generous to all who come to him for the success of the sacrifice he is performing, and asks for a gift of land that he can cover with three steps. Bali agrees to give the land *Vaamana* requests. The Lord *Vishnu*, incarnated as *Vaamana*, with the first and second steps covers the heaven and earth, and with the third step he pushes Bali to the underworld. Hence *Vishnu-Naaraayana* is designated as the one who encompasses the world in three big steps (*Trivikarama*). This incarnation of *Vishnu* points to the truth that just as God has to assume the form a dwarf and do the act of begging to win over the evil, Similarly, a true devotee must be able to humble himself to achieve great things. Again, it symbolically teaches that a true devotee of the Lord *Vishnu* can conquer every problem in life with the power of the spirit of the Lord.[459]

3.3.1.2.1.6. Raama with a Battle Axe-incarnation (Parasuraamaavataara)

King Arjuna of the Haihai clan, by his worship of *Sri Dattatreya*, a partial incarnation of Lord *Vishnu*, gains two boons: his body possesses thousand arms and he cannot be defeated. These gifts fill Arjuna with excessive physical powers, invincible mental powers, abounding wealth, bravery and the power of having everything at his command. Such an achievement makes him self-conceited, proud and self-assertive. As a result, he uses his abilities to do much evil, especially to the *Braahmans*, who were wealthy, educated and totally in control. This leads to a war between the *Braahmans* and the *Kshatriyas*, in which the *Braahmans* are routed. In hearing about the happenings, *Parasuraama*, one of the sons of the sage, Jamadagni, taking the battleaxe, which he always holds in his right hand, kills king Arjuna and trounces the *Kshatriyas* and establishes the rule of the *Braahmans*. *Parasuraama* is held as the incarnation of *Vishnu-Naaraayana* mainly for the reason that he has undertaken inconceivable sacrifices to fight against evil and to establish the rule of law for his people. His success in an unequal war with King Arjuna also points to the presence of the power of the Supreme Lord in him.[460]

3.3.1.2.1.7. Srii Raama-incarnation (Sriiraamaavataara)

Srii Rama is the son of king Dasaratha of the Iksvaku clan. His three younger brothers are Lakshmana, Satrughana and Bharata. To fulfill a promise his father made to Kaikeyii, the mother of Bharata, he renounces being the ruler of his kingdom and spends 14 years in the forest in exile, along with his wife, Sita, and brother, Lakshmana. During their forest dwelling, Raavana, an *Asura* king kidnaps Sita. *Srii Raama* destroys the kingdom of Raavana, kills him and liberates his wife from his custody. Later he comes back to his kingdom and takes over as the ruler of the kingdom. When Sita becomes pregnant, people of the kingdom question her sexual integrity, as she was in the harem of Raavana for about ten months. Though *Srii Raama* knows about her integrity, bowing to public opinion he banishes her but secretly makes arrangements for her to stay at the *Ashram* of the sage, Vaalmiiki. From then on *Srii Raama* lives the life of a bachelor, thinking about his banished wife. Sita gives birth to twins, Kusa and Lava. Later Sita and the son are brought to the kingdom to assist in the performance of *Asvamedha* sacrifice. As the ceremony is in progress, people question the propriety of performing the sacrifice with the help of a wife whose moral life is questionable. Succumbing to their pressure, *Srii Raama* requests his wife to prove her innocence publicly. On hearing this, Sita falls unconscious and dies. The mother earth gives way to her. She enters the ground and never comes out again. *Srii Raama* made a golden statue of his wife Sita and continues the performance of the sacrifice. It is said that over 100 *Asvamedhas* have been offered in his lifetime. *Srii Raama* establishes a constitution for the better governance of the country and the people that lasts more than 11,000 years after his death.[461]

Srii Raama is considered as an *Avataara* of *Vishnu-Naaraayana* for a number of reasons. Firstly, he voluntarily sacrifices military and kingly power to uphold morality. Secondly, unlike the kings of his time, he takes only one wife, remains faithful to her and, after her death lives on with her fond memory. Thirdly, he holds morality in so high esteem that he is ready to sacrifice his queen Sita, whom he loves and whose loss is a great pain throughout his life. Fourthly, *Srii Raama* establishes peace and stability in his kingdom, provides a well-organized rule of law and destroys everything that is evil. Fifthly, He patronizes Vedic religion and the performance of sacrifices. Sixthly, he is the patron of the *Varnaastrma Dharma*, as he follows it very strictly in his life. Though he loves the outcastes, he keeps himself away from them to preserve the purity of the *Aashramas*. Besides, he strengthens the *Aashramas Dharma* by allotting instruction to uphold the traditional law of piety. All these point to the fact that *Srii Raama* is, in fact, an incarnation of *Vishnu-Naaraayana*. The name of *Srii Raama* is called *Taaraka-mantra*, as it takes one across the ocean of transmigration.[462]

3.3.1.2.1.8. Balaraama-incarnation (Balaraamaavataara)

Balaraama is the son of Vasudeva and Devakii, the elder brother of *Krshna*. His name literally means *Raama*, the Strong (*Bala*). He assists his brother *Krshna* in stopping the misdeeds of his uncle Hamsa. He accomplishes a number of military victories, especially over the kings who are hostile to the Vedic religion. His great deeds include the slaying of the ape *Dvivida*, the demon *Dhenuka*, capturing the ramparts of Hastinaavati, the capital city of the Paandavas, and changing the course of the river Yamunaa. There is a myth that describes the serpent *Sesha* coming out of *Balaraama's* mouth at the time of his death, providing the reason to believe that he is the incarnation of the serpent *Sesha*, that forms the dwelling place of *Vishnu-Naaryaana* in the Milk-Ocean. The weapon associated with *Balaraama* is the plough (*Hala*). Therefore, some authors suggest that he is an agricultural hero raised to the status of an *Avataara* of *Vishnu* in the course of time. *Balaraama* can truly be called an incarnation of *Vishnu*, because fighting the enemy for the right cause in a most appropriate manner is his significant characteristic. All through his life he showed enthusiasm and courage to enforce laws of morality and religiosity.[463]

3.3.1.2.1.9. Srii Krshna-incarnation (Krshnaavataara)

Bhaagavatapuraana beautifully sets the background for the appearance of *Krshna* as an incarnation of *Vishnu-Naaraayana*. The kings of the time are non-believing despots. Since they do not accept the religion of the *Vedas*, they begin to harass the innocent people under every pretext. One example of such evil kings is king Hamsa, the brother-in-law of Vasudeva. Seeing the situation, the Mother Earth pleads for *Brahmaa's* help. Realizing the pitiable condition of the earth, *Brahmaa*, along with *Siva*, the three-eyed god, the Mother Earth and other gods reach the shore of the Milk-Ocean to meet *Vishnu-Naaraayana*. They propitiate *Vishnu* by pronouncing Vedic hymns and ask Him to help in changing the condition of the earth. *Vishnu-Naaraayana* is pleased with the request and promises that He will be born in the house of Vasudeva for protecting the pious and punishing sinners.[464]

Srii Krshna is born in this miraculous way, but has to grow away from his parents in the cowherd village at the bank of river Yamuna, in order that he escape the evil hands of Hamsa. As a cowherd boy, *Krshna* takes life with the utmost delight, enjoying the company of his friends and the local shepherd women (*Gopis*). He has such an extraordinarily charming nature, that he is able to cast a spell on all. He is often referred to as the 'stealer of the hearts of girls'. He is a man who takes his life in the spirit of sportfulness, involving himself totally in everything he undertakes, and is thus, able to instill enthusiasm in the most disinterested persons. Lord *Krshna*, therefore, is the greatest enemy of all that can block true development in a person. *Srii Krshna*, with the help of his elder brother, *Balaraama*, kills his wicked uncle, Hamsa and places the father of Hamsa on the throne, destroys all other wicked kings and establishes the Vedic religion to its glory. Later he plays an important role in the war of Kurushetra and establishes true justice. He dies an unnatural death, at the ripe age 125 when a poisonous arrow hits his leg.[465]

Srii Krshna is considered as the full incarnation (*Puurnavataara*). We read in the *Bhaagavatapuraana* as follows: "But Lord *Krshna* is the Supreme Being himself and all these, parts and smaller parts of the Supreme Being who give happiness to the world (when it is) troubled by the enemies of *Indra* (i.e. demons) in every epoch."[466] He is believed to be the full incarnation of *Vishnu-Naaraayana* for the following reasons. Firstly, he is an ardent champion of the Vedic religion. Secondly, he regards *Braahmans* as living deities and does not hesitate to offer them reverence and worship. For instance, while at the peak of his power, he washes the feet of a poor *Braahman* called Sudaaman, touches them with his head and anoints them with sandal paste. Thirdly, *Srii Krshna* destroys evil wherever he finds it and establishes good instead. Fourthly, all his actions are aimed at raising the life of the people materially, morally and spiritually.[467]

3.3.1.2.1.10. Buddha-incarnation (Buddhaavataara)

Gautama Buddha, the son of Suddhodana, belongs to the royal family of Kapilavastu. Though he is brought up in the luxury of the royal palace, his heart is not at ease. He is keen to find solutions to the suffering of mankind. Leaving the palace, he comes to the hermitage at Kapila and studies the *Samkhya* system of philosophy. Later he leaves the hermitage, travels through various countries, and arrives at the Uruvilva village in the district of Gaya. He sits there under a pippal tree. After six years of meditation, he attains perfect knowledge (*Bodha*), thus solving his intellectual questions and mental agonies. In his teachings, he denies the authority of the *Vedas*, existence of God and the caste system. But he calls people to discriminate between right and wrong by using the reason that is given to man alone. Initially the teaching of the *Buddha* is not acceptable to the elite Hindus, but later they accept his teachings, especially in seeing its similarity with the *Samkhya* philosophy. In the course of time, he is considered as one of the major *Avataara* of *Vishnu-Naaraayana*.[468]

The reasons for the acceptance of *Buddha* as an incarnation of *Vishnu* are the following. Firstly, *Buddha* attempts to remove the evils in the world and bring happiness to the lives of the people. Secondly, he does it by way of cessation of desire, the cause of suffering, and by way of an eight-fold path of right living. Thirdly, the followers of Buddhism believe in the incarnation theory and say that there have been 24 *Buddhas* before *Gautama Buddha*, and he is the 25th *Buddha*. Fourthly, the basic tenets of *Buddha* are very much in agreement with the *Samkhya* philosophy. All these indicate that the teachings of the *Buddha* are not contrary to the genuine spirit of the *Vedas*. Fifthly, the political situation of foreign invasions called for the unification of the diversities of the whole nation, motivating the Hindus to accept *Buddha* as one of the incarnations. Sixthly, in order to prevent the spread of Buddhism in the country by making it part of Hinduism, the Hindus may have included *Buddha* into the pantheon of the *Avataaras* of *Vishnu*. In the Hindu iconography *Buddha* seems to have disappeared after the 15th century. Whatever the reason, it is a fact that *Buddha* is believed to be an incarnation of *Vishnu*.[469]

3.3.1.2.1.11. Bhagavaan-Kalki-incarnation (Kalkiavataara)

Bhagavaan-Kalki is the last of the *Avataaras* of *Vishnu* that is yet to come. He comes at the end of the present age (*Kaliyuga*). At the end of the *Kaliyuga* even good men will have to face opposition to perform worship. They will suffer in the hands of despotic rulers. The basic elements of Vedic religion will be under attack. People of the first three *Varnas* will become hypocritical, pretentious, showy, jealous and self-centered. *Sudras* will be powerful. There will be no genuine worship left in the world. The whole population will be totally deviated from the right path. *Dharma* will be destroyed and *Adharma* will reign supreme in the world. On the repeated supplications of the oppressed people, the Lord *Kalki* will come riding on a white horse, with a drawn sword, to bring the world under the reign of *Dharma* and to re-establish it in all its glory. *Bagavaan Kalki* will be born at the house of a *Braahman* named Vishnuyasas, living at a village called Sambhala. He may appear in different forms by the power of his *Maayaa*. The form he takes and time he comes are secrets known only to the Lord. But, when he comes, he will crush the evils and establish the rule of law and piety. He will organize people in his able guidance, train them militarily and destroy all the despotic kings, crushing them in battle. When all evil from the world is rooted out, he will establish peace and stability all over the earth. He will set up a world empire. He will be head of the administration. He will give everyone the freedom to practice the religion he likes. The spirit of the Vedic religion will be the guiding force. The worship of Lord *Vishnu-Naaraayana* and his incarnations will be popular in every part of the world. All will live in peace and joy.[470]

We have seen all the major incarnations of the Lord *Vishnu-Naaraayana*. *Avataaras* of God take place in regular cycles and often at fixed intervals, according to God's plan and the needs of the world. When God incarnates into the world, he conquers all enemies of good people with the power of his compelling personality and boundless wisdom. In doing so he establishes religion in its original purity. Before he leaves the world he prepares his disciples, who become illumined teachers of his mankind. Again, when the need arises for such an intervention God does not shrink back from the responsibility. The intervention of God in the world we call incarnation, and it goes throughout his man history.[471]

3.3.1.2.2. Arrangement of the Vishnu Incarnations

The various incarnations of the Lord *Vishnu* are positioned corresponding to the progressive development of creation. In the beginning of the world, it is filled with water. Therefore, the first incarnation of *Vishnu* is in the form of the Fish. Then the dry land appears. Hence the second incarnation is that of the Tortoise, which can move both in water and on dry land. The development of the world progresses into successive stages of animal life in the forests, life of wild humans who lived the principle 'might is right', the life of cave men, the occurrence of early civilization and the fully developed civilization - characterized by family and domestic organization, social and political organization. The intervention of *Vishnu-Naaraayana* in the world also moves in an ascending order, as the life of the people grows more complex. The ascending involvement of God with man in the world is represented by the other incarnations of *Vishnu*, viz., the Bore incarnation, the Man-lion incarnation, the Dwarf incarnation, the *Raama* with a battle Axe incarnation, the *Srii Raama* incarnation, the *Balaraama* incarnation, the *Srii Krshna* incarnation, the *Buddha* incarnation and the yet-to-come *Kalki* incarnation. It is striking to note that the progressive incarnations of *Vishnu* takes place in historical persons rather than in animal forms that do not have a historical background.[472]

3.3.1.3. THE SAALAGRAAMA: THE EMBLEM OF LORD VISHNU

The *Saalagraamas* are colored, rounded and polished stones with a hole containing the fossil of tiny molluscs, marked with specific signs. They are considered emblems of *Vishnu*, on which He can be lawfully worshipped. The *Puraanas* and other sacred books narrate a number of myths regarding the origin of *Saalagraama*. We mention just one of them here. Once a demon king named Sankhacuuda drives out the gods and occupies their place in heaven. At the request of the gods, *Vishnu-Naaraayana* agrees to kill the demon, but is prevented from doing so on account of the queen of Sankhacuuda, Tulasii, who is a devoted to the Lord. As the oppression of Sankhacuuda increases, the Lord *Vishnu* kills him with His discus. The widowed queen, in her anger, curses the Lord *Vishnu* and turns him into a stone. When the Lord pacifies her, Tulasii modifies her curse and wishes that He becomes a particular type of stone-pieces. A particular type insect on the Saalagraama Mountain forms these stone-pieces, which are found in and around the river Gandakii. Tulasii declares that if anybody lawfully worships the Lord *Vishnu* in such a stone piece, he would obtain his goals. Showing respect to the chaste widow, Lord *Vishnu* agrees to be transformed into stones and to stay around the river Gandakii.[473]

The myth has to be understood allegorically. The king Sankhacuuda stands for the *Asura* rulers, who are anti-Vedic in their beliefs. They oppress the righteous people, who follow the Vadic religion. Under such oppressive rulers, the devotees of the Lord *Vishnu* are not able to offer public worship to the Lord for a long period of time, as any form of public expression of faith in the Lord can be dangerous to their lives. With a desire to renew the people's devotion to the Lord and to keep their faith alive, especially during such difficult times, the believers of the Lord *Vishnu* invent the new form of worship of the Lord in the *Saalagraama* stones. Since these stone-pieces are small and hard, they can be easily shifted from place to place, concealed at any place, if need be, even in water. As a result, while secretly carrying on the worship of the Lord *Vishnu*, the devotees could protect themselves from the soldiers of the *Asura* kings. It is probable that, at this time, the worshipers of the Lord *Vishnu*, at least some leading members, might have settled near the Saalagraama Mountain. Therefore, they are familiar with *Saalagraama* stone-pieces. Since the stone has special markings and openings, people believe that the creator of these stone-pieces is God and that they are given these stones to perpetuate His worship. Initially they do so earnestly, and over the period of time stories and traditions are formed regarding the origin and organization of the *Saalagraama* stones.[474]

As the worshipping community increases, there is the need for more *Saalagraama* stones. Probably a number of interest groups emerge in the believing community. The worshippers of different *Avataaras* of the Lord *Vishnu* begin to worship *Saalagraama* stones attributed to the different incarnations of *Vishnu*, such as, *Srii Krshna*, *Balaraama*, *Srii Raama* and others. So the *Saalagraama* stones available at the Gundakii riverbed are not sufficient for the devotees. Thus, the need arises for finding other places, from where the *Saalagraama* stones can be collected. The Vaishnava community comes up with the idea of recognizing the stones-pieces available at the Dvaarakaa region as a new type of *Saalagraama*, which is given the name *Dvaarakaasilaa*. In order to make the latter type of stone acceptable to the people, a certain amount of denouncing the value of the original *Saalagraama* stones has taken place. But over the period of time these two types of *Saalagraama* stones are accepted as emblems of *Vishnu* worship. The original *Saalagraama* is called from then on *Gandakiisilaa*, while the later one is called *Dvaarakaasilaa*. Both of these types are further divided into different categories, depending on from where they are collected, to which of the incarnations of *Vishnu* they are attributed, their color and other qualities. There also comes about specifications as to the worship of different *Saalagraama* stones bringing the worshipper different results, such as, enjoyment and salvation (*Bhukti-mukti*), kingship of heaven, wealth, destruction of enemies, fulfillment of one's desire and other similar results. In this manner, there arrives on the scene a complicated system of classifying the *Saalagraama* stones and the regulation of their worship in various Vaishnava sects.[475]

The *Saalagraama* is believed to be so holy that the people of only certain *Varna* could worship *Vishnu* through their use. For instance, the *Braahmans* have the right to touch a purified *Saalagraama* stone and to worship on it. But he is forbidden to do this form of worship until he is purified with the sacred rite of investiture with the sacred thread (*Upanayana*). The *Kshtriyas*, *Vaisyas* and upper class *Suudras* have no right to touch the *Saalagraama* stone while they worship. But they can worship the sacred stone, without touching it. The lower class *Suudras*, the women of all castes and the outcasts have neither the right to touch a *Saalagraama* stone nor to offer it worship. The concession that is made to the last group is that they can worship the sacred stone through a *Braahman* priest. All such regulations are aimed at upholding the sanctity of the *Saalagraama* and the worship of *Vishnu* through it.[476]

Our study of the nature and attributes of *Vishnu*, *Vishnu* in his incarnations and the *Saalagraama* as the symbol of the Lord *Vishnu* clearly manifest the personality of *Vishnu-Naraayaana*, the Supreme God of Vaishnavism. The Lord *Vishnu* has a dignified and definite personality. He has an image of His own and all His *Avataaras* are depicted in icons. His consort goddess *Lakshmi*, other female gods and goddesses associated with the Lord *Vishnu*, and the god *Garutmaan* (*Garuda*), the bird-vehicle of Lord *Vishnu* do not infringe on His prerogatives, but remain subordinate to Him. Goddess *Lakshmi* and Sita, the wife of *Srii Raama*, are gentle, heroic and morally admirable. Thus, *Vishnu-Naaraayana*, the Supreme God of Vishnavism, is truly a Supreme Person of remarkable character.[477]

3.3.2. VAISHNAVA PATH TO THE DIVINE

Vishnavism proposes a number of paths to help the devotees of the Lord *Vishnu* to express their devotion and love to Him, thereby paving the way for genuine encounter between the Lord and the devotee. Some of the paths are the following: the practice of total self-surrender to God (*Prapatti*), the practice of loving devotion to God (*Bhakti*), the practice of non-injury

(*Ahimsaa*), the ritual acts of worship (*Upacaaras*), the practice of initiation, the temple worship, the practice of private devotions, the celebration of festivals and the practice of moral virtues. In the section, we elaborate these paths in detail.

3.3.2.1. THE PRACTICE OF TOTAL SELF-SURRENDER TO GOD (PRAPATTI)

The term '*Prapatti*' is derived from two Sanskrit words '*Pra*', which means 'to move' and '*Pad*', which means 'in the best manner'. Thus, literally '*Prapatti*' means to move on the path of God-realization in the best manner. As a means to *Moksha*, it implies total self-surrender to God. It consists in placing the burden of caring for our spiritual life in the care of God (*Aatma-nikshepa*). Besides, it implies seeking God as one's only place of safety (*Saranaagati*). In *Prapatti* the devotee recognizes his inability to move towards the path of God-realization and seeks the help of Divine Power with fervent prayer. The devotee is fully conscious that none other than the Supreme Being is able to protect him from the quagmire of earthly existence and counts on the grace of God for achieving his spiritual goals. *Bhakti* is different form *Prapatti*. *Bhakti* is a loving devotion to God, which involves fixing one's mind on God. Thus, to practice *Bhakti* one needs to have true knowledge of God and serving the Lord by way of works. Thus, *Bhakti* is a rigorous discipline. But, *Prapatti* is a total self-surrender of the devotee to the Lord. *Prapatti* is the easiest method of attaining salvation, as it only involves unburdening all one's concerns and worries on God.[478]

Besides cultivating a yearning for liberation (*Arthitva*), the devotee must fulfill two conditions in order that he can be eligible for the practice of *Prapatti*. Firstly, the devotee must experience within himself an absolute inability to move towards salvation (*Aakincanya*). Secondly, he may not aspire for any other goal than *Moksha* (*Ananya-gatitva*). When these two conditions are found in a seeker, he is able to undertake the six-fold disciplines (*Shadvidhaa-saranaagatih*). They are the following. Firstly, there must be a determined will on the part of the devotee to perform only such acts that please God (*Aanukuulya-sankalpa*). Secondly, he must refrain from all acts that displease God. (*Praatikuulya-varjana*). Thirdly, the devotee experiences a deep sense of humility, as he knows that no means can lead him to *Moksha* other than the grace of God (*Kaarpanya*). Fourthly, The devotee has absolute and unshakable faith in God as the only protector (*Mahaa-visvaasa*). Fifthly, The devotee must make a request to God and seek His protection formally (*Gpotrtva-varana*). Sixthly, The devotee must entrust the task of protecting the devotee to the care of God. (*Aatma-nikshepa*).[479]

When a devotee makes total self-surrender, through the six-fold discipline, he is able to renounce the three-fold egoism that characterizes his life. Firstly, he renounces that he is the agent of action of self-surrender (*Kartratva-tyaaga*). Secondly, he rejects that the action of self-surrender belongs to him (*Mamataa-tyaaga*). Thirdly, he denounces that the fruit of the action of self-surrender is for him (*Phala-tyaaga*). He declares that he is not the person who does the act of self-surrender, as it is God, who gives the capacity for action. The idea that self-surrender does not belong to him comes from the awareness that it is only the grace of God that let him do it. The idea that he is not the enjoyer of the fruit of self-surrender comes from the awareness that it is only a condition, in relation to which the grace of God brings about *Moksha*. When these three-fold renunciations help the devotee to empty himself of sense of self, he is able to make the act of total self-surrender, which, in turn, directly leads him to the experience of liberation.[480]

We can speak of different types of *Prapatti* based on the mode of its observance. The first type of *Prapatti* is called *Ukinishta-prapatti*. Here, the *Guru* prescribes a prayer and the devotee, by reciting the prescribed prayer, moves towards true *Prapatti*. The second form is called *Aacaary-nishtha-prapatti*. In this form the *Guru*, on behalf of the individual, performs the prescribed rite, which helps him to move towards *Prapatti*. There are other prescribed ritualistic procedure modes of observance that lead a seeker to genuine *Prapatti*. Despite the varying forms and prescribed procedure, the attainment of *Moksha* is guaranteed only when the *Prapatti* of the devotee opens himself to the grace of God. Once the total surrender is made, the devotee can live in peace for the rest of his life, without any fear of rebirth. Thus, unlike *Bhakti*, which is a lifelong process, *Prapatti*, as a means to *Moksha*, is performed only once. The *Guru's* role is vital on the path of *Prapatti*.[481]

3.3.2.2. PRACTICE OF LOVING DEVOTION TO GOD (BHAKTI)

Bhakti is the intense love of God (*Paramapremaruupa*). It is trusting in the grace of the Lord. It involves loving the Lord without seeking results, such as, enjoyments and fruits of one's actions. But it is not an extinction of one's desires and actions, but rather the concentration of one's actions and desires in God. *Bhakti* is a religious path that leads us to God and provides us with a way of life. It does not mean mere enjoyment of ecstatic trances by being close to the Lord *Vishnu*, but it also calls for performing one's duties in life. It implies the study of the scriptures, as, in order to be devoted to the Lord, one must know the Lord.[482]

Therefore, Raamaanuja speaks of a seven-fold moral and spiritual discipline (*Saadhana- saptaka*) as necessary for those who wish to follow the path of devotion. They are *Viveka, Vimukta, Abhyaasa, Kriyaa, Kalyaana, Anavasada* and *Anuddharsha*. *Viveka* is the purification of the body (*Kriyaasuddhi*) by means of pure food, which, in turn, leads to spiritual concentration (*Dhruvasmrti*). *Vimukta* is the cultivation of mental detachment that is essential for meditation on the Lord. *Abhyaasa* consists in attaining bodily purity and mental calmness as a means to cultivate the presence of the indwelling Lord that the mind may become more centered on the Lord. *Kriyaa* is the performance of the five-fold moral duties that they may develop in to meditation on God. *Kalyaana* consists the practice of virtues, such as, truthfulness, integrity, compassion, benevolence and non-violence. *Anavasada* is fortitude, which frees one from despair due to disappointment and remembrance of sorrows. *Anuddharsha* consists between the mean between excessive joy (*Atisamtosha*) and the total absence of joy (*Asamtosha*). When a person practices these *Saadhana-saptaka* there happens in him a harmonious development of his thought, feeling and will. This, in turn, leads the devotee to fix his mind on the Lord in meditation and facilitates the cultivation of the true *Bakhti*.[483]

In the cultivation of devotion to the Lord *Vishnu*, the devotee gradually makes progress, assuming different sentiments (*Rasa*) towards the Lord. There are five types of *Rasa* that the devotee can take on. They are *Saanta Rasa, Daasya Rasa, Sakhya Rasa, Vaatsalya Rasa* and *Madhura Rasa*. *Saanta Rasa* is a state in which the devotee abandons all his worldly ties and concentrates the totality of his feelings and faculties on the Lord *Vishnu*. This sentiment makes the devotee so detached that he is not concerned about the attainment of salvation, enjoyment of heaven and relationship with the Lord. There is no trace of 'mineness' in the devotee, as he does not consider the Lord as the master, friend, son, or as the husband. He experiences the Lord *Vishnu* in essence, as the embodiment of consciousness, infinite power and bliss. In the *Daasya Rasa* there is the feeling of personal attachment, as the devotee considers himself as the servant and the Lord as the Master. Therefore, there exists between the Lord and the devotee a respectful distance. The devotee approaches the Lord like a humble servant. *Sakhya Rasa* involves the sentiment of friendship with God on the part of the devotee. The sentiments of detachment and distance that are characteristic of the *Saanta Rasa* and *Daasya Rasa* respectively are absent in the sentiment of friendship. God becomes a lover and an associate to the devotee. In *VaatsalyaRasa* the sentiment is deeper than the former three. The devotee looks upon the Lord *Vishnu* as his own son. The devotee approaches the Lord with the love of a mother towards the Lord, consoling, nursing, scolding and even beating. The Lord is considered as a small boy. In *Madhura Rasa* the devotee has single-minded devotion to God, like that of a wife to the husband. It is the highest expression of love between the devotee and the Lord. It implies all the properties of the previous four *Rasas*. Here one experiences the deep sense of unity and intimacy with God.[484]

Though many of the teachers of Vaishnavism stress different *Rasas* when speaking of the devotee's relationship to the Lord *Vishnu*, the dominant *Rasa* is that of the servant (*Daasya*). Great Vaishnava schools, such as the Qualified Non-dualism of Raamaanuja, the Assam Vaishanvism of Shamkaradeva, the mysticism of Maadhavadeva and the Tamil Vaisnavism of the Alwars, advocate the *Daasya Rasa Bhakti*, which stresses the servanthood of the devotee and the mastership of God. Thus, the devotee is advised to surrender himself completely to the Lord, who is the compassionate master (*Dayaasiila*), with an attitude of a selfless and faithful servant. The love involved is love of a master and that of a slave. It is not the love of a lover to the loved. Another image used to refer to the *Bhakta* is 'the hired laborers of the *Bhaagavat*'. The image of the wage-earning servant indicates the wish to earn merit by serving the Lord. The characteristic elements of *Daasya Rasa*

Bhakti are spirit of humility and self-surrender to the Lord in service. According to Raamaanuja, the service of the servant of the Lord is not servility, but is the free self-gift of the devotee that flows from genuine love of the Lord. It is this *Rasa* that is present in the *Bhakti* of Bharata, Lakshmana and *Hanumaan* towards *Srii Raama*. When a devotee possesses this attitude of service, he is not only open to the Lord, but also toward every other human person. *Daasya Rasa Bhakti* always maintains the conditional duality between the master and the servant, the Lord and the devotee. Since the servant always knows that he is a servant, service becomes easier. His only concern is to serve the Lord. Such a service frees the devotee from all worry and anxiety. He is equally free from anger, desire and fear, as he is balanced in the Lord and enjoys peace and tranquility. Thus, the final goal of the *Daasya Rasa Bhakta* is not to experience complete union of self-annihilation with the Lord, but to be overwhelmed by a complete state of security and bliss under the protection of his master.[485]

Bhakti is attained by the practice of nine stages of devotion. Firstly, the devotee listens (*Sravana*) with rapt attention to discourse about the Lord. Secondly, he chants (*Kiirtana*) the praises of the Lord. Thirdly, the devotee remembers (*Smarana*) the form (*Ruupa*), the sport (*Liilaa*) and the name (*Naama*) of the Lord with love and devotion. Fourthly, the devotee serves at the feet (*Paadasevana*) of the Lord. Fifthly, he worships (*Archana*) the Lord with total self-surrender. Sixthly, the *Bhakta* offers genuine acts of homage (*Vandana*) to God. Seventhly, he approaches the Lord with the attitude of a servant (*Daasya*), which helps him to serve the Lord and his fellowman. Being the *Daasya* for the Lord makes the devotee not only do acts of service to the Lord (*Bhagavat-kainkarya*), but also is willing to do service to Godly men (*Bhaagavata-kainkarya*). The service of the latter with genuine detachment amounts to the service of the Lord Himself. Eighthly, the devotee establishes genuine love of friendship (*Sakhya*) with the Lord. Ninthly, the devotee surrenders himself (*Aatmanivedana*) completely to the Lord. The devotee can with the mercy of God practice all of these stages of *Bhakti* at once, or in suitable combinations. For instance, Assam Vaishnavism of Samkaradeva proposes the combination of *Sravana* and *Kiirtana* as the most suitable combination for the attainment of devotion to the Lord, as persons irrespective of caste, creed, age or state of life can use them easily. The role of a spiritual guide (*Guru*) is necessary to lead the devotee to the goal of *Bhakti*, by way of instruction and guidance.[486] The practice of *Bhakti* thereby establishes genuine contact between the Lord *Vishn* and His devotee.

3.3.2.3. PRACTICE OF NON-INJURY (AHIMSAA)

Devotional Vaishnavism gives importance to the practice of *Ahimsaa*. *Puraanas* state that a devotee of *Vishnu* never commits any forms of violence, specially those acts that involve killing. It is said that God does not dwell in the heart of the one who indulges in any form of killing. Similarly, it is said that the Lord is pleased with those persons who neither inflict any pain nor commit slaughter of animals. It is believed that King Vasu Uparicara, a devout worshipper of the Lord *Vishnu*, is said to have performed *Asvamedha* sacrifice without any animals being slaughtered.[487] Samkaradeva of Assam Vaishnavism opposes all forms of bloody sacrifices involving large-scale killing of animals. He says that one who cuts animals in sacrifice is destined to hell. Condemning the killing of animals in *Durga* sacrifices, he says that the one who worships *Durga* with animal sacrifice, the one who organizes the worship, the one who cooks the sacrificial flesh, the one who eats the cooked meat, the one who decapitates the animal and the one who buys animal for sacrifice are responsible for the letting of the blood of the animal. A true Vaishnavite, who loves his Lord, does not harm any creature, including insects and worms.[488]

In Vaishnavism, *Ahimsaa* means not only the non-killing of animals for sacrifice, but also it means not injuring anyone by thought, word and deed. It is the basis of genuine moral life. *Bhagavad Giitaa* says that a perfect *Yogi* is one who sees equality of others with oneself (*Aatma-aupamya*). Just as he desires good to himself, he desires good to all. He embraces all things in God. He wishes no harm to others, just as he does not wish any harm to himself. As a result, he is able to consider all as equal to himself. Such a person rejoices in doing what is good for others, as he is filled with love and compassion. Therefore, the true meaning of *Ahimsaa* is not merely avoiding something that is negative, i.e., non-killing. Rather it is something that is positive, as it consists in recognizing the image of the Divine in every creature, seeing them with equal mindedness and being compassionate to them. According to Vaishnava sages, the path of *Ahimsaa* is said to bring about more merits from God than performance of sacrifice or asceticism.[489] Thus, the practice of *Ahimsaa* opens the devotee to live his life with thoughts for others and the Lord. In this manner the genuine practice of *Ahimsaa* establishes genuine contact between the Lord and the devotee.

3.3.2.4. PRAYER (JAPA)

Vaishnavism lays great stress on *Japa*, as it is one of the best ways to express the *Bhakti* of the devotee. It consists in the devotional recitation of sacred syllables, formulas and names of the deity. *Vishnusmmrti* calls prayer *Japa-yajna*, just as ritual sacrifice is called *Vidhi-yajna*. The implication of raising prayer to the status of a sacrifice (*Yajna*) is to indicate that *Japa* is as good as ritual sacrifice to enter into a deep relationship with the Lord *Vishnu*. Prayer can take two forms, viz., the oral recitation of the sacred syllables or their mental recitation (*Maanasa-japa*). Since *Japa* is considered as an effective means of God-realization, it accompanies the external ritual worship of icons of gods (*Vaahyayaaga*). Similarly, *Maanasa-japa* is also part of the internal ritual worship (*Maanasayaaga*), which involves the visualization of a mental image of the deity and worshipping it, with the help of symbolic hand gestures (*Mudraa*) and the placing of the sacred letters in different parts of the body (*Nyaasa*). Recitation of prayer is believed to be a very powerful means to experience the power of the Lord in the life of the devotee. *Vishnusmrti* says that *Japa* is ten times more meritorious than ritual sacrifice. The immense power of *Japa* is manifested in that the Lord *Vishnu*, when all methods fail, takes recourse to His *Mantric* form (*Mantramaya-ruupa*) for killing the demons, *Madhu* and *Kaitabha*. The efficacy of *Japa*, in the sense of recitation of *Mantras*, is emphasized in the Vedic and the Tantric traditions. The shift in emphasis from costly ritual sacrifices to simple *Japa* contributes a great deal to the popularization of *Vishnu* worship, especially among the masses. Since *Japa*, in its different forms, is the best way to express the sentiment of *Bhakti*, ordinary people use *Japa* to express their devotion to Lord *Vishnu*. Thus, we find that the unbroken recitation of the names (*Naamasankiirtana*) of *Srii Raama* and *Srii Krshna* is a popular religious practice, believed to be an effective means of devotion to these two *Avataaras* of Lord *Vishnu*.[490]

Samkaradeva, an exponent of Assam Saivism, proposes *Japa* in the form of *Naamadharma*, as a practical method of the practice of *Bhakti*. He says that *Naamadharma* is the supreme religion of the present age (*Kali-yuga*). It consists in chanting the name of God with undeviated devotion. When the name of the Lord is chanted with the accompaniment of musical instruments, it produces inner vibrations in the soul of the devotee, which, in turn, evoke intense feelings of devotion to the Lord. *Naamadharma* is so easy a method that everybody can practice it, irrespective of his caste, age, state of life, time or place. According to Samkaradeva, though one begins the recitation of the name of the Lord mechanically, in the course of the practice one effectively cultivates the sentiments of *Bhakti*, as the name of the Lord is identical with the Lord, and through the very recitation, the Lord would take hold of the devotee and fill him with true devotion. Since supreme devotion (*Parama Bhaakti*) comes from the grace of God, a devotee must utter the name of the Lord without worrying about the result of his practice of *Naamadharma*. When the devotee makes himself ripe for the supreme devotion by the constant practice of *Naamadharma*, the Lord grants it to him. According to Samkaradeva, the practice of *Japa*, in the form of *Naamadharma*, frees the devotee from all his sins and leads to true salvation.[491] Hence, the genuine practice of prayer helps the devotee to experience the Lord and His power in his life. Thus, *Japa* is a great means Vaisnavism uses as an aid to God-realization.

3.3.2.5. RITUAL ACTS OF WORSHIP (UPACAARAS)

Puraanas speak of three modes of worship, viz., Vedic, Tantric and *Misrita*, which is a combination of the former two. Vedic worship involves the worship of images. It requires the recitation of various *Mantras* during the performance of the act of worship. But the recitation of the *Mantras* is superficial, and it has nothing to do with the rite itself. In all probability, the use of *Mantras* is a later addition to the original ritual. The second form of worship is Tantric. The Pancaraatra Vaishnava cult contains a number of Tantric elements. It emphasizes the use of magical and mystical formulas and the offering of meat, wine, honey, fish and distilled liquor to attain mundane desires and supernatural powers. The popularization of *Ahimsaa* in Vaishnavism brings about a change in the offerings people use at the ritual worship. Some of the offerings the devotee use at worship are rice cooked in milk (*Paayasa*), parched cereal food of various kinds, curds (*Akshata*), rice mixed with either sesamum or peas and flowers. The third form of worship mentioned in the *Puraanas* is the mixture of the Vedic and Tantric worship[492]

Another term often used to refer to worship is '*Puujaa*'. Some authors opine that the term '*Puuja*' is derived from the Tamil term '*Puusu*' which means 'to smear' or 'to daub'. According to this interpretation of the term, the main feature of *Puujaa* is washing and sprinkling the image of the deity with water, honey or curds. It also means daubing the image with red paint in remembrance of the bloody sacrifices of the earlier days. Some other scholars are of the opinion that the term '*Puujaa*' is derived from two Dravidian words "*Puu*' and '*Cey*'. The former means 'flower', and the latter means 'to act'. Thus, '*Puujaa*' refers to the act of offering flowers to the deity. Taken in this sense, *Puujaa* means the flower-ritual. The earliest description of *Puujaa* that we find in the *Vishnusmrti* combines both of these meanings. It describes the actual act of *Puujaa* as follows. It begins with the invocation and welcoming of the deity. Then water is offered for the washing of the hands and feet, for sipping and for bathing (*Arghya*). The offering of incense, ornaments, garments and flowers to the deity follows the washing ceremony. The deity is, then, worshiped with lamps. While *Vishnusmrti* prescribes the use of Vedic *Mantras* at the *Puujaa*, while *Grhya Suutra* of the Vaikhaanasas recommends the muttering of eight and twelve syllabled sectarian *Mantras* when *Puujaa* is done. The *Vishnudharmottara* lays down the use of the betel leaf (*Taambula*) in *Puujaa*. With the identification of *Vishnu* with popular deities like *Naaraayana* and *Vaasudeva*, the use of Vedic *Mantras* at the *Puujaa* became a regular practice. The injunctions regarding the participation of people of different *Varnas* in *Puujaa* also are prescribed. For instance, men of the three upper *Varnas* were allowed to participate in the *Puujaa*, while the women and the *Suudras* did not have access to the ritual worship.[493] Thus, the practice of various forms of ritual worship assisted the worshipper to encounter the Lord.

3.3.2.6. PRACTICE OF INITIATION

Unlike the Vedic worship, in which, there are injunctions regarding the restriction of certain group of people in worship, in the Tantric form of worship everyone is free to participate, irrespective of caste, sex and age. All persons who approach to be initiated are to be initiated, whether they are children, women or the *Suudras*. The Pancaraatra Vaishnava sect has its own initiation rite, known as *Diikshaa*, which is very different from the *Upanayana*. In order to qualify oneself as a fit person to worship *Vishnu*, one must go through the *Diikshaa*, which a qualified preceptor conducts. The *Diikshaa* is a 'rite of knowledge' that provides for worship of the great Tantric circle (*Mahaamandala*) in the initiation ceremony of a rich person. The poor are simply initiated by the word of mouth through the kindness of their spiritual preceptor and by making offerings of sesamum. There are two types of *Diikshaas*: the ordinary (*Saamaanya*) and special (*Visesha*). The special initiates are five types, viz., the *Samayajnas*, the *Putrakas* the *Saadhakas*, the *Aacaaryas* and the *Desikaas*. The *Samayajnas* are initiates who remember the *Mantras* and observe all the traditional rules. They are proficient in traditional Tantric practices. Devoted men and unmarried girls can become the *Samayajnas*. The *Putrakas* are the second in the hierarchy of the initiates. The *Saadhakas* are initiates who abandon all family ties and other relationships and attempt to accomplish the *Mantra*. They live in forests, lonely places or in temples of *Naaraayana*. Even if they live in their homes, they are freed from forms of worldly attachments and endeavor to attain the desired *Mantra*. The *Aacaaryas* are those who have attained the desired *Mantra*. Their initiation brings their identification with the highest principle (*Brahma*). The *Desikaas* are women initiates. They hold the highest place among the special initiates. They are considered as the women followers (*Bhaagavati*) of the *Bhaagavat*. The date best suited for conducting the Pancaraatra initiation ceremony is the twelfth day of a lunar fortnight (*Dvaadasii*) of the month of *Kaarttika*. The practice of keeping the initiation ceremony secret from the unbelievers is strictly followed. Only the faithful are invited for the initiation ceremony. When the ceremony is concluded, gifts are distributed among the Pancaraatra Vaishnavas.[494]

An initiated Pancaraatrin is expected to dedicate himself to the worship and service of *Vishnu* from early morning to late night. His day is divided into five parts (*Pancakaalas*). He is duty-bound to perform the five-fold daily religious practices (*Pancakala-prakriyaa*) each day. They are: *Abhigamana*, *Upaadaana*, *Ijyaa*, *Svaadhyaaya* and *Yoga*. The *Abhigamana* is the first act to be performed in the morning. The term '*Abhigamana*' literally means approaching the temple of God with one's mind, speech and body concentrated on the deity. It implies that the initiate finishes his bath and the morning prayer (*Sandhyaa*). Then he enters the place of worship, either in the temple or in the home, with the totality of his being centered on God, who is present in the holy place. When he is in the holy place, he prostrates himself before God, while reciting a prayer and then offers a formal worship to God. The main purpose of this simple act of adoration before God in the morning is to seek the grace of God to carry out the rest of the divine service of the day successfully. The second religious duty of the day is *Upaadaana*, which is the obtaining of material for worship, such as, flowers, fruits and the needed material for the worship of God. This is usually done immediately after the *Abhigamana*. The third act is *Ijyaa*, the actual worship (*Aaraadhanaa*) of *Vishnu*. It is usually done in the forenoon. For a Vaishnava initiate, the act of *Ijyaa* is mandatory. It is considered as the most meritorious act of the day. It is said that to take a meal without performing this act of worship of God is sinful. There are six stages in the act of worship. The first stage is *Mantraasana*, which involves the worshipper offering himself to God and seeking his blessings as he begins the worship. He offers water in a small spoon to the deity three times, to wash the hands and feet and for sipping. This completes the external and internal purification. The second stage is the *Snaanaasana*, which is the act of bathing the idol, while reciting the *Purusha-suukta*. The third stage is the *Alamkaaraasana*, which consists in decorating the idol with clothes, flowers, ornaments and sandal paste. During this stage the idol is venerated with incense and a lighted lamp. Basil (*Tulsi*) leaves and flowers are offered with the recitation of Vedic *Mantras*, Vaishnava *Mantras* or the names of *Vishnu* (*Naamaavalii*). The fourth stage is *Bhojyaasan*, which involves offerings of cooked food to the idol. The fifth stage is *Mantraasana* where the idol is presented with fruits, betel leaves and camphor light. It concludes the adoration of the Lord with the recitation of hymns. The sixth stage is *Paryankaasana*, which is putting the idol back to rest. When all the worship is done, the initiate prostrates himself before God and with utter humility seeks God's forgiveness for the sins committed. The fourth act is *Svaadhyaaya*. It is the hearing, meditating, discoursing and studying of the sacred scriptures. The time between the forenoon and the sunset is used for the study of the scriptures. The fifth act of the day is *Yoga*. The initiate, after he completes his night prayers and dinner, sits down to contemplate on God until he goes to sleep, so that he can feel that he rests in the Lord. The *Pancakaala-prakriyaa* is prescribed as a strict and rigorous discipline, for the purpose of making the Lord *Vishnu* the major preoccupation of the initiate's life.[495]

  The initiated person is expected to practice five sacraments (*Panca-Samskaara*). They are: *Tapa*, *Uurdhva-pundra*, *Naama*, *Mantra* and *Ijyaa*. The first *Samskaara* is *Tapa*, which consists in wearing the mark of the conch (*Sankha*) and discus (*Cakra*), the two weapons of the Lord *Vishnu*, on the left and right shoulder blades of the initiate. In order to make the marks on both the shoulders of the initiate, one uses heated pieces of silver or copper engraved with the conch and discus. These two symbols are chosen to be marked on the shoulders of the initiate as the former indicates auspiciousness, whereas the latter signifies the spiritual energy that wards off evil. The preceptor performs preliminary rituals (*Homas*) in the consecrated fire before the actul rite of *Tapas* is carried out. It is the most important of the five sacraments, as it makes the initiate a formal worshipper of *Vishnu* and makes him qualified to recite the esoteric *Mantras*. The second is *Uurdhva-pundra*. It consists in the initiate marking his forehead and different parts of his body with the sectarian *Uurdhva-pundra* mark, which is in the shape of *Vishnu's* feet. This implies placing a vertical middle line on the forehead and quadrangular mark around the vertical line on the forehead. Similar quadrangular marks are placed on the heart, belly, arms and neck with ashes after the sacrifice or worship. Usually an orthodox Vaishnava initiate makes twelve *Pundra* marks over his body. The meaning of the *Uurdhva-pundra* mark is the following: The middle line of the mark symbolizes the *Aatman*. The quadrangular mark around the middle line signifies the union one's self with the supreme soul. Thus the placing of the *Uudhva-pundra* mark on the forehead constantly reminds the devotee of his call to God-realization, and placing them on different parts of the body has for its goal the acquiring of bodily purity. The third is *Naama*, which involves giving the initiated person a name that is connected with *Vishnu*, which conveys the sense of 'lordship' or 'ownership' of the Lord *Vishnu* over the initiated and that the initiate become the Lord's servant (*Vishnu-daasa*). After the naming ceremony, the initiate is known by his new name. The fourth is *Mantra*, in which the initiate is imparted esoteric Vaishnava *Mantras*. They contain a few sacred syllables that are spiritual in character. The *Guru* orally transmits them and the initiate keeps them secret. The fifth is *Ijyaa*, which is the formal instruction of the mode of worship of God (*Yaaga*). Here, the *Guru* formally instructs the initiate as to the form of worship, such as the use of *Saalagraama* stones or any other form he should use in his worship of *Vishnu*.[496] Organizing initiation rites, continuing the faith of the initiates with the help of the community of initiated persons and the practice of the various duties and other rites definitely provided a genuine path for coming in touch with the Lord *Vishnu* and entering into a deep relationship with Him.

3.3.2.7. TEMPLE WORSHIP

In spite of the popularity of *Bhakti*, *Japa* and other similar practices among the Vaishnavites, worship at the temple is widely practiced. People offer worship at the temple for obtaining good health, long life, prosperity, merits in religious living and for passage to heaven. The performer of temple worship pays the *Braahmans* fee (*Dakshinaa*) for the performance of the worship. Temple worship is offered before the image of Lord *Vishnu* or before the icons of any one of His *Avataraas*. But worship can also be given to the *Saalagraama* stones in the temple. There are special instructions as to the manner of installation of images in the temple. Initially the images are made of wood, clay and stone. But later images, made out of metals, became popular. Ritual offerings before the images of the deities, singing, dances and the use of musical instruments form an important element of temple worship. According to *Vishnudharmottara*, dedication to the Lord, by way of singing, dancing and playing musical instruments is much more meritorious than offerings of flowers and food (*Naivedya*). Such acts of worship at the temple fulfill all desires, and one gains merits equal to that of performance of sacrifices. Thus, the building of temples, having maids (*Daasiis*) and priests (*Karmakaras*) attached to them, are essential to keeping the devotion of the people for the Lord alive. The method of worship at the temples is different from the way worship is done at home, as the former is much more elaborate than the latter. The temple priests are trained to perform ritual worship in the temples.[497]

3.3.2.8. PRACTICE OF PRIVATE DEVOTIONS

There are a number of private devotional practices, which a true Vaishnavite may perform either individually or within the context of his family. We mention just four of such practices, viz., worship at home, observing vows, the practicing of placing *Pundra* marks on the forehead and offering devotion to the Lord *Vishnu* by the veneration of *Saalagraama* stones. Each of these devotional practices serves as a genuine path to establish a loving relationship between the devotee and the Lord *Vishnu*. We briefly consider each of these.

A devotee of the Lord *Vishnu* not only worships at the temple, but also offers his homage to the Lord at home. Originally worship was given to the image of the Lord in the temple. The installation and worship of the image of the Lord at home is a later development and is popular. The images meant for household worship are made of metals, such as, gold, silver or brass. Images made of clay, wood or stone are not to be used in home-worship. Already in the Epic period, household shrines were becoming more common. Wealthy people worship in shrines situated within the compound of their houses. But these shrines are not situated within the living rooms. In these shrines, the family-worship takes place. But, for individual worship, it is permitted to build a niche at the head of the bed, where the person can install the image of his favorite deity (*Ishtadevata*).[498]

Another popular private devotional practice a true Vaishnavite takes up is the observing of vows (*Vratas*). It consists in total or limited abstinence from food and the execution of certain acts of worship. Practice of vows involves selection of a date, lying on the ground as a penance, appointing of the priest for the performance of the act of worship, fasting and listening to pious stories. The *Puraanas* mention a large number of vows, such as, fasting, making pilgrimages to holy places, the practice of certain penances and other similar acts. There are a number of references to people taking up the vow of fasting. For instance, queen Balasrii engages in fasts with great devotion. Similarly, we hear from Kaalidaasa that the mother of Sushyanta observes a fast for four days. In the Sangam age, in order to gain the favor of the deity, people fast in the precincts of the *Vishnu* temple.[499]

Another popular devotional practice many adherents of Vaishnavism follow is the placing of the *Pundra* (*Urdhva-pundra*) mark on the forehead and different parts of the body. Originally it is one of the *Panca-samskaaras* the initiates are expected to practice. But later, it becomes a common practice among all Vishnavites. There are differences in the manner in which the adherents of different sects place the *Pundra*. The Vadakalais Vaishnava sect wears the *Pundra* in the shape of a single foot of *Vishnu* in the 'U' with a curve formed at the bottom of the forehead right above the nose. The Tenkalais Vaishnava sect put on the mark in the 'Y' shape, symbolizing the two feet of *Vishnu* with a separate mark on the nose symbolizing the footstool for His feet to rest. They both use white soft clay to make the mark. Generally speaking the *Pundra* should be in the shape of a flame (*Varti-dipaakrti*), the leaf of a bamboo (*Venu-patraakrti*), a flower bud or the shape of *Vishnu's* feet (*Hari-paadaakrti*). Usually it is placed every morning after the bath. It is believed that for the fruitfulness of the religious ceremony it has to done with the *Pundra* mark on the forehead. Thus, the use of *Pundra* mark is a sign of true devotion to the Lord *Vishnu*.[500]

The worship of the Lord in the symbol of *Saalagraama* stones is another devotional practice common among the devotees of the Lord *Vishnu*.

The worship of *Saalagraama* stones is said to bring many merits in the life of the worshipper. For instance, when a person duly worships a single stone in a place, it is able to purify an area up to three *Yojanas*, i.e., twenty- four miles, on each side. Any believer of the Lord *Vishnu* who breathes his last within that area is absolved of all his *Karma* and attains salvation. The Vaishnavites also keep the *Saalagraama* stone where they perform the *Samskaaras*, in order that the fruits of the *Samskaaras* truly benefit the performer. If a person donates a *Saalagraama* stone, the one who donates is freed from all his sins of one year. The washing of the *Saalagraama* stone, according to the ritual laws with devotion, liberates a person from troubles, such as, diseases, poison, fire and thieves. If a person sips a drop of water or milk in which the *Saalargaama* is washed at his death, it gains for him a place in the abode of the Lord *Vishnu*. If a person tells a lie by touching the *Saalagraama* stone, he experiences great sufferings while still alive and punishment in hell after he dies. It is said that the daily worship of the *Saalagramma* stone, with due devotion, helps a devotee acquire merits equal to what one obtains by the performance of one thousand *Raajasuuya* sacrifices. Since the *Saalagraama* stone is sacred and powerful, its right worship can be of great help to the life of the devotee of *Vishnu*. As a result, the worship of the Lord *Vishnu* in the *Saalagraama* is so popular among the Vaishnavites.[501]

3.3.2.9. CELEBRATION OF FESTIVALS

The devotees of the Lord *Vishnu* celebrate a number of festivals. The times of festivals are occasions in which the Vaishnava devotees as a community and as individuals experience deeply the touch of the Lord in their lives. They celebrate the festivals by worshipping in the temple and at home, both with spiritual fervor and genuine joy. The most significant of them are the ancient festival of *Caaturmaasya*, the *Janmaashtamii*, the birthday of *Srii Krshna*, and the *Raamanavamii*, the birthday of *Srii Raama*. We briefly consider each of the festivals.

3.3.2.9.1. Caaturmaasya Festival

The ancient festival of *Caaturmaasya* is celebrated by the Vaishnavites with gaiety. It commemorates the Lord *Vishnu's* going to sleep on the eleventh of the bright fortnight of the month of *Aashaadha* for four months and waking up again on the eleventh of the bright fortnight of the month of *Kaarttika*. During the sleep of Lord *Vishnu* the rain god, *Indra*, does his work of watering the whole earth. The important aspects of this festival are the day on which *Vishnu's* slumber commences (*Sayanii*), the day of *Vishnu's* awakening (*Prabodhanii*), the eleventh of the fortnight (*Ekaadasiis*) and its culmination in the *Mahaakaarttika-Puurnimaa* day. Originally all these elements are linked with the fertility cult. The time of the festival is connected to the periods of sowing and reaping rice and sugarcane crops. On the fifteenth of the bright fortnight of the month of *Kaarttika*, the women worship the implement they use for preparing grain (*Sakata*) and the wooden mortar used for cleansing rice (*Uluukhala*) with sugarcane. On the day of *Vishnu's* awakening (*Prabodhanii Ekaadasii*), the women fix five sugarcane shoots on the kitchen door and perform worship with edibles prepared with sugarcane products. This ancient festival is given a thorough Vaishnavite color and is popularized.[502]

3.3.2.9.2. Janmaashtamii Festival

Janmaashtamii, the birthday of *Srii Krshna* is another important Vaishnava festival, as he is believed to be the most significant *Avataara* of Lord *Vishnu*. *Srii Krshna* was born in the *Duparyug*, just before the *Kaliyug*, the age in which we find ourselves. His birthday falls on the eighth day of the dark fortnight in the month of *Bhadon*, i.e., sometime in July or August, during the monsoon season. *Janmaashtami* is celebrated on two days: on the actual day of his birth in the prison at Madhura and on the next day when he is discovered in the house of Nand and Yashoda at Gokul, having escaped from the evil hands of Hamsa, his maternal uncle.[503]

The celebrations begin on the first day with depicting scenes from the life of Lord *Krshna* through cribs and decoration, both in the homes and in the temples. If a person is not able to make the crib or other decoration he can keep idols of *Krshna* and other gods from the *Puujaa* room of the house and keep them out in the living room on a specially made altar. Since *Krshna* is the main deity of the festival, his idol or picture is placed at the center and is garlanded. Most devotees fast on this day in waiting for the Lord's birth. They have only one meal, known as *Phalar*, around two to three in the evening. They can take tea or coffee any time of the day. In the afternoon the food of blessing (*Prasad*) is prepared. It consists of the same edibles, which the new mother is given after childbirth, which is called *Paggi-hui-meva*. Fruits like bananas, guava and apples can be added to the *Prasad*. By midnight the whole family sits around the specially prepared crib or alter where the idol or picture of *Srii Krshna* is placed. A lamp is lit in front of the altar. At the stroke of the midnight, the exact time of *Srii Krshna's* birth, the whole family welcomes the Lord. The Lord is welcomed at his birth by applying sandal paste (*Teeka*) on the idol. Then *Puujaa* begins. It consists in sprinkling the idol with water, which follows the showering of the idol with flowers, a kind of red powder (*Roli*), rice and a few other things. When the sprinkling and showering ceremonies end, the idol is incensed (*Aarati*), while the bell is rung. Thus, the birth of the Lord is commemorated.[504]

The festivities continue on the following day. In the evening of the second day the family members gather around the altar of Lord *Krshna* and sing hymns (*Bajans*), with the accompaniment of musical instruments to praise his name. The children are encouraged to bring their talents to the fore at this gathering. At the stroke of midnight on the second day, all stand to sing a special hymn to the Lord, while incensing is done accompanied by the ringing of the bell. Then flowers are showered on the main idol of Lord *Krshna*. *Prasad* is distributed to all present. The worship of the Lord is followed by a good vegetarian meal. In this manner, the festival of *Janmaashtamii* is celebrated at home. During these two days people also visit temples to worship the Lord.[505]

3.3.2.9.3. Raamanavamii Festival

Raamanavamii is the birthday of *Srii Raama*, through whom the Lord *Vishnu* incarnates into this world to re-establish *Dharma*, that Raavana, the *Asura* king has destroyed. This *Avataara* takes place on the ninth day after the new moon in the waxing moon (*Sukul Paksh*), i.e., sometime in the month of April. As a devotional practice people undertake a fast the day before the actual celebration. On the day of fast, they take only one meal, the *Phalar*. *Srii Raama* is born in the afternoon, and so the *Puujaa* is performed in the afternoon. It is arranged in a large room, with the idols of *Srii Raama* kept in the middle. The idols of Sita, Lakshman, and Hanuman are kept on either side of the idol of *Srii Rama*. From the morning, *Bhajans* are sung in praise of the Lord. Before the *Puujaa*, the male member is welcomed by applying *Teeka*, while the female members are welcomed with a *Bindi*. Everyone sprinkles the idols of gods with water, which is followed by showering of *Roli*, rice and other things. The birth of *Srii Raama* is heralded with singing *Bhajans* in praise of the Lord, that accompanies the incensing and ringing the bell. All stand for the incensing ceremony. Then water from the river Ganga is mixed with plain water and is sprinkled over all present, while all recite a response: 'A drop of water on me and all the illness and sickness of the body are driven away'. They continue singing more *Bajans*. Then *Prasad* is distributed to all present for the *Puujaa*. Thus, the birthday of *Srii Raama* is celebrated with great devotion and piety.[506]

3.3.2.10. PRACTICE OF MORAL VIRTUES

The practice of moral virtues is an important means to experience God-realization in the life of a devotee. Vaishnavism fundamentally accepts the qualities of the godlike person enumerated in the *Bhagavad Giitaa*. Some of the virtues mentioned in the *Giitaa* are the following: fearlessness, purity of mind, wise apportionment of knowledge and concentration, charity, self-control, uprightness, non-violence, truth, freedom from anger, renunciation, tranquility, aversion to fault finding, compassion to living beings, freedom from covetousness, gentleness, modesty, steadiness, vigor, forgiveness, fortitude, purity, freedom from malice and freedom from excessive pride.[507] In the light of these directives of *Giitaa*, Vaishnava sages like Raamaanuja and Samkaradeva, propagated the value of moral life for the cultivation of genuine devotion to the Lord. Some of the cardinal virtues (*Saadhaarana Dharmas*) they propose are self-control, detachment, endurance, humility, compassion, social service and giving gifts. We briefly consider these virtues that lead a devotee to a deeper attachment to the Lord *Vishnu*.

Self-control helps the momentum of spiritual progress in the devotee. It is a *sine qua non* for spiritual life. It helps the devotee to discipline his senses, body and the mind. Self-control is not self-torture, it only implies self-mastery and moderation in everything one does. Self-control leads to genuine concentration of the mind on the Lord. The immediate consequence of self-control is detachment. It consists in doing everything without any desire and craving for the results of the work. When detached we do everything as servants of the Lord. True detachment leads to endurance. Endurance becomes easy for a person who is totally detached from pain and gain, joy and sorrow, success and failure. Endurance calls for being patient and tolerant in the most difficult situations. A devotee is able to effect real good through endurance. A person, who has acquired the first three virtues, viz., self-control, detachment and endurance, cannot but be a humble person. Humility consists in the devotee considering himself as the lowliest of the lowly. A humble man is able to control the psychic ego that blocks genuine religious attitudes. The practice of true humility makes the devotee transcend his self-centeredness and move towards others in compassion. The virtue of compassion or loving kindness is the foundation of all moral virtues. It consists in being thoughtful of others in their suffering and pain. A compassionate person goes out of his way to see the other in need and to give a helping hand to the needy. Therefore, true compassion leads a person to social service. To serve man by way of social service is equivalent to serving God. The practice of social service calls the devotee to practice the giving of gifts (*Daanadharma*), which is nothing else but an active benevolence. Thus, the practice of all these cardinal virtues attunes a devotee with a mind-set that takes him out of his self-centered living to others and to God. [508]

In this essay we have seen Vaishnavism as a monotheistic religion. It has a rich concept of God. The *Vishnu-Naaraayana*, the Supreme God of Vaishnavism, is a God who is concerned about and involved in the world. Though He is transcendent, He makes Himself immanent in the world through His incarnations. This is clear from the fact that He is ready to enter into a deep personal devotion with His devotees. *Vishnu*, as the preserver and sustainer of the universe, upholds the moral and spiritual well-being of every human person. It is His desire to maintain the moral equilibrium between *Dharma* and *Adharma*, that makes Him incarnate in the world. Besides, developing a rich concept of God, Vaishnavism also provides a number of paths for the devotee to move towards the Lord *Vishnu*. The various paths, such as the practice of total self-surrender, the practice of loving devotion to God, the practice of non-injury, the ritual acts of worship, the practice of initiation, the temple worship, the practice of private devotions, the celebration of festivals and the practice of moral virtues, are sure ways to the realization of *Vishnu*. Many of these paths are so universal and easy that any ordinary person can practice them without extraordinary efforts. The simplicity of their practice has made Vaishnavism appealing to even average persons, which, in turn, makes it a religion that is popular among the masses. The *Bhakti* spirituality inherent in the Vaishnava religion and practice makes it a religion acceptable to all. In the next essay we make an attempt to elaborate the other popular monotheistic religion, viz., Saivism.

3.4. SAIVISM

Like Vaishnavism, Saivism is a Hindu religious sect that is centered on the belief that the Lord *Siva* is the Supreme Spirit, who not only pervades the entire universe in absolute form (*Paramaatman*), but also dwells within every living being in his existential form (*Jiivaatman*). Saivism exalts the Lord *Siva* as the Supreme Being and personal God to whom worship is offered and who bestows wisdom and salvation to anyone who approaches Him. According to believers of Saivism, the Lord *Siva* is supreme over all gods, and the latter, including *Brahmaa* and *Vishnu*, the other members of the trinity of gods, are subordinate to the Lord *Siva*. The adherents of Saivism are distinguished from that of other Hindu sects by a horizontal *Tilaka* mark they place on the forehead and their wearing of rosaries of *Rudraaksha* berries.[509]

The origin of Saivism is not easily traceable and is shrouded in mystery. It is generally accepted that it is an upshot of a pre-Aryan, i.e., Dravidian primitive religion that belongs to the Mohenjo-Daro and Harappa civilazation. But in its historical growth Saivism emerged as the result of the coming together of both the Dravidian and the Aryan religious elements. Though very little is known about its origins and initial development, since the seventh century A.D., it contributed greatly to the ethos of the Hindu religious practice and worship. The rise of Saivism to prominence is related to the decline of the importance of Buddhism and Jainism in the sixth century A.D. One of the reasons for the weakening of Buddhism and Jainism is the attack these two religious movements received at the hand of the Hindu revivalists, especially the zealous Saivas. The burning of the Bodhi-tree at Gayaa, which the Hiuan-Tsang narrates in his diaries, is a clear instance that illustrates the religious animosities between the Hindu and other religious movements of the time. Similarly, the Tamil Saiva saints, the *Naayanaars*, attack Buddhist and Jaina teachings as lies in their Saivite hymns.[510]

Though Saivism itself is a sect within Hinduism, over the course of its development we find the emergence of a number of Saiva sects. The followers of the *Viirasaiva* sect, also known as the *Lingaayatas*, distinguish themselves from other Saiva sects by wearing the symbol of *Linga* drawn of ashes on their bodies and by worshipping the *Sivalinga* daily. This is known as *Lingaacaara*. Besides, they practice four other religious practices, viz., practice of good conduct (*Sadaacaara*), the service of the Lord (*Bhrtyaacaara*), daily worship of the Lord *Siva* (*Sivaacaara*) and the religious practices in a body at sacred places (*Ganaacaara*). The founder of this sect is Vrshabha. *Viirasaivism* rejects the caste system and the practice of Braahmanical rites. The members of the *Viirasaiva* sect are instructed to marry within the sect. Widow remarriage is not appreciated in the sect, but rather the widows are expected to live a strict ascetical life engaging in the sacred duty of worshipping the Lord *Siva*. The *Viirasaivas* also practiced some form of initiation ceremony.

They are divided into four classes, viz., the priests (*Jangamas*), the pious (*Siilavants*), the traders (*Banjigs*) and the ascetics (*Pancamasaalins*). The *Viirasivas* avoid meat and drink, as they are strict vegetarians. Besides they have the practice of burying their dead instead of cremating.[511]

The *Mahaavratins* is another Saiva sect. The name suggests that the members of this sect are observers of the great vow. They practice extraordinary vows, such as eating food that is placed in the human skull and placing on their body ashes of the cremated human corpses. They worship the female principle, which at times degenerates into licentious orgies. There are those who follow the *Hatha Yoga* very rigorously as a way of life. The skull-bearers (*Kaapaalikas*), the black faces (*Kaalaamukhas*) and the *Yogins* with split-ears (*Gorakhanaathiis*) are some who belong to this sect of *Mahaavratins*.[512]

Another Saiva sect is the *Paasupatas*, who adore the Lord *Siva* as *Pasupati*. According to a myth that is found in the *Linga* and *Vaayu Puraanas*, the Lord *Pasupati* assumes the form of a mendicant, called Nakuliisa, and spends his time serving the people. In the course of time, he chooses four disciples, viz., Kusika, Gaargya, Mitraka and Rushta, who are well-versed in Vedic lore and of high moral standard, and passes on to them the responsibility of preaching the doctrines of the *Paasupatas*. They, in turn, give this responsibility to their disciples.[513] The *Paasupata* sect of Saivism is associated with a *Yogi* from the region of Baroda, called Lakuin. According to him, the *Paasupatas* are those who attain the state of ecstacy by means of strict asceticism and violent practices. They realize their last end by the knowledge of five categories. Firstly, the effect (*Kaarya*). It consists in knowledge (*Vidyaa*), organs of knowledge (*Kalaa*), and the individual soul (*Pasu*). The individual soul is called *Pasu*, which litterally means cattle, because, like the cattle, the individual soul is fettered by matter (*Paasa*), from which it needs to be liberated. Secondly, the cause (*Kaarana*), which is identified with the Lord *Siva*, who is called *Pati*. He is made of energy and controls everything in the world. Thirdly, the union of the *Pasu* and the *Pati* (*Yoga*), which is obtained through the practice of ritual and meditation, and through pure abstract consciousness. Fourthly, the injunctions to arrive at the *Yoga* (*Vidhi*), which consists of two elements, viz., the vows (*Vratas*) and the means (*Dvaaras*). The *Vratas* are placing ashes on the body, sleeping on the bed of ashes and the worshipping *Siva* – with the help of a lagugh, a song, a dance, prostration and prayer. The *Dvaaras* are snoring, trembling, limping, mimicking a lover, acting and speaking without much sense. Fifthly, the end of the misery (*Duhkhaanta*). It consists in acquiring *Yogic* powers that are beyond the capability of ordinary men and the total distruction of any form of misery. Since the *Paasupata* Saivism stresses the importance of asceticism in attaining the ultimate goal of life, it hardly sees the need for the grace of the Lord.[514]

More sober and devotional worship of the Lord *Siva* is found in the Savism of the *Aagamas* and that of the 63 Tamil saints called the *Naayanaars*. The Savism of the *Aagamas* dates from seventh centruy A.D. and is based on the canon of 28 texts (*Aagamas*) and the 198 auxiliary treatises (*Upaaagamas*), which originated either in the north or south India, known as the

Tradition. According to this form of Savism, the Lord *Siva* is beginningless and all-knowing reality. His power (*Sakti*) is the source of everything in the universe. The souls are eternal and possess the spiritual energy (*Citsakti*) that makes them capable of knowledge and action. But they are actually prevented from exercising these powers, as they are fettered by threefold impurities (*Malas*), viz., ignorance (*Aanava*), actions and their effects (*Karma*) and the cosmic illusion (*Maayaa*). Only the grace of the Lord (*Anugraha*) can liberate and free the souls from these fetters and help them achieve the realization of their true nature, i.e., their identification with the Lord *Siva*. The Savism of the Tamil saints, the *Naayanaars*, is found in their poetic writings. The most imporant *Naayanaars* are Appar, Sambandar Sundarar and Manikavaasakar. They present Savism as a universal religion of loving devotion (*Bhakti*) to the Lord *Siva*. According to them, faith and loving devotion to the almighty Lord *Siva* opens the devotee to His grace (*Arul*) and removes all forms of darkness (*Irul*) and leads to endless fellowship and communion with the Supreme Lord. This spiritual goal is not limited to people of any caste or creed, but to everyone who love the the Lord *Siva* with undivided heart. Thus, for these Tamil *Naayaanars* Savism is a religion for all.[515]

The *Saiva Siddhaanta* is the monotheistic philosophy of religion that grew outside the Brahmanic tradition, both in Tamil and Sanskrit in the first half of the 13th century A.D. Its expression in Tamil is based on 14 texts, which include the *Siva-Jnaana-Bodham* of Meykandar, *Siva-Jnaana-Sittiyar* of Arulnandi and the eight complementary texts attributed to Umaapati. As a philosophy of religion, *Saiva Siddhaanta* attempts to understand the relationship of God to souls and the world. It speaks of three eternal and real substances, viz., God (*Irai*), souls (*Uyir*) and the world that fetters the souls (*Kattu*). The Sankrit equivalent to these Tamil terms are *Pati*, *Paasu* and *Paasa*. The *Irai* is the Lord *Siva*, the source of everything. The *Uyir* is the soul that is endowed with knowledge, volition and action. The *Kattu* is the world that binds the soul with threefold impurities of ingorance, effects of action and the illusion of the empirical reality. The *Saiva Siddhaanta* proposes threefold paths to get out of this binding, viz., service (*Caarya*), worship (*Kriyaa*) and meditation (*Yoga*). When each of these three paths is animated by loving devotion (*Bhakti*) to the Lord *Siva*, the soul is disposed to receive the gratuitous gift of divine knowledge (*Siva Patijnaana*), which in turn makes union with the Lord *Siva* possible. Such a realized soul is filled with the Lord *Siva* (*Sivamaya*), though it does not become the Lord *Siva* Himself.[516]

Another important Saiva sect, the Kashmir Saivism, appears in the early ninth century A.D. It is based on three group of texts called the Triple Instruction (*Trika Saasana*) of Kashmir Saivism, viz, the *Agamasaastras* of Vasugupta, *Spandasaastra* of Kallata and the *Pratyabhijnaanasaastra* of Somaananda. Kashmir Saivism is a monistic philosophy, which considers the Lord *Siva* as the only reality. He is pure Intelligence, Infinity and Transcendence, and is the underlying substratum of the universe which He emmanates by his power (*Sakti*) through the process of self-denial and self-forgetting. The emanation of the world is not merely an illusory self-modification (*Vi-*

varta) of the Lord *Siva*, but an illumination (*Aabhaasa*) in which the finite reality is brought forth, while the Lord *Siva* remains unaffected. The products of the emanation have the reality which they seem to possess. They constitute 36 categories (*Tattvas*) and fall under three groups, viz., pure (*Suddha*), pure-impure (*Suddhaasuddha*) and impure (*asuddha*). The first is the *Paramasiva* who is pure light (*Prakaasa*). The second is the finite souls (*Purushas*) The last is the material nature (*Prakrti*). The finite soul, though identified with the Lord *Siva*, due to the three-fold bonds (*Paasa*) of *Prakrti* considers itself as imperfect. The soul can get out of this state of *Paasa* only by the process of self-recognition (*Pratyabhijnaa*), which is an instantaneous intuition of pure consciousness (*Pratibhaa*). Thus, the soul is awakened, realizes its true nature and becomes one with the Lord *Siva*.[517]

In the previous pages, we have considered Saivism in a general way, as a religion that has emerged in the Hindu tradition and its significant sects. Having done this by way of introduction, we move on to the main intent of this essay, viz., the God of Saivism and Saiva paths to the Divine.

3.4.1. *SIVA*: THE GOD OF SAIVISM

The historical development of Saivism points to Dravidian and Aryan elements. These elements are nothing other than the blending together of the characteristics of a Dravidian deity and an Aryan deity, who forms the God of later Savism. The Dravidian deity is *Siva*, while the Aryan deity is *Rudra*. The Dravidian element is clearly evidenced from the portrayal of a deity that appears on a roughly carved seal excavated from Mohanjo-Daro and Harappa. The seal dipicts a three-faced male figure with a horned headdress seated on a low platform in the meditation posture amidst six animals, viz., an elephant, a tiger, a rhinoceros, a buffalo and two longhorned antelopes. One can see in this personage the possible prototype of the Dravidian deity *Siva*. Many of the characteristics that Saivas attribute to the later God of Savism are found in the deity. For instance, the three faces correspond to the later representation of *Siva* with three, four or five faces, and having three eyes denoting insight into the past, present and the future. His *Yogic* posture is similar to the perception of the later *Siva* as an ascetic and the prince of *Yogis* (*Mahaayogin*). His presence among the aminals reminds us of the quality of the later *Siva* being seen as the Lord of the cattle (*Pasupati*). His horned headdress is comparable to the trident (*Trisul*), which forms the royal insgnia of the later *Siva*. According to some other scholars, *Siva* is a figure of Dravidian origin, who assimilates the old Dravidian deity *Seyyan*, the red god of war and the son of the victorious goddess *Koravai*. Probably his cult had its beginning in the mountains of northwest India, and spread quickly to the south and the rest of India.[518] If we accept the latter suggestion, it would mean that besides the characteristics of being a contemplative and protector of cattle, the Dravidian *Siva* also had the characteristic of destruction and terror, as he is also seen as the god of war and bloodshed. Thus, we do find a certain amount of contradictory elements,viz., calmer and terrifying aspects, in the personality of the Dravidian deity *Siva*.

The Aryan element of the later God of Saivism is represented in the Vedic god *Rudra*. *Siva* is not strictly a proper name in the *Rig Veda*, but rather it is an adjective meaning the quality of being auspicious that is applied to various gods. It is also applied to *Rudra* once. *Rudra* is a minor deity, the red one and the howler. In the *Rig Veda* he is associated with the Fire-god (*Agni*) and is related to the destructive energies and is said to the father of *Maruts*, the gods of the violent winds. He is a man-slayer, who is full of malevolence. He is often prayed to avert his dangerous presence and spare the worshipper from lightning, storm, fever, cough and poison, as he is like a wild beast.[519] *Rig Veda* also speaks of a milder aspect of *Rudra*. He is said to shower blessings on men and cattle, to grant remedies for disease and to heal the sick. In this sense, *Rudra* is *Siva*, the auspicious.[520] Similarly *Atharvaveda* speaks of the twofold contradictory characteristics of *Rudra*. He is said to be the benign (*Bhava*) and the malignant (*Sarva*). He is said to be the punisher of sinners and the killer of the demon, *Vrtra*. At the same time it is said of him that he carries thunderbolts, his weapon, and brings terror everywhere.[521] In spite of the auspicious nature attributed to him in the *Rig Veda* and the *Atharvaveda*, *Rudra* is more a fear-inspiring deity, who is appeased rather than prayed to by means of rituals that are full of prohibitions and taboos.[522]

The Vedic *Rudra* over the history completely merges with the richer and complex personality of Dravidian *Siva*, probably due to the similarity of both of these deities, as they possess both mild and a terrifying aspects. Though *Siva* is given the function of dissolution in the Trinity of gods, he is considered as the Creator, as destruction leads to reproduction and new life. This may be the reason that the Lord *Siva* is often represented by the *Linga*, a symbol of new life rather than destruction. Similarly, the representation of *Siva* as half male and half female also points to the generative dimension of the Lord *Siva*.[523] From what we have said, it is clear that the *Siva*, the God of Savism, is in fact *Rudra-Siva*, a blending together of the characteristics and elements of the Aryan god *Rudra* and the Dravidian god *Siva*.[524] These two names, *Rudra* and *Siva*, are used as equivalents. Yet theoretically *Rudra* represents the fearful and terrifying element, while *Siva* embodies the peaceful and auspicious aspect. In this section, we elaborate the nature and characteristics of the Lord *Siva*, the God of Saivism.

3.4.1.1. NATURE OF SIVA

The Lord *Siva* can be considered as the Absolute Being and in relation to his functions, viz., His activities in the world. The former leads us to study the Lord *Siva* in Himself, while the latter lets us view Him in his powers (*Saktis*). In this section, we elaborate the nature of the Lord *Siva*, in these twofold aspects.

3.4.1.1.1. Siva in Himself

Siva is not to be considered as a third person. But He is the pure Cosmic Consciousness, that is the substratum of every reality in the universe. As it is in the Lord *Siva* that every reality is based, He must be seen as the true First Person. If I am the lower self, He is my higher Self. Just as the waves are individualized water and the vast expanse of ocean that underlies the waves is their foundation, so also the Lord *Siva*, is the First Person on whom my individual first person stands. In this sense, *Siva*-realization is fundamentally Self-realization, i.e, the realization of the higher Self on which my self is founded.[525]

Siva, as the foundational reality, is the absolute (*Nirapeksha*). As the absolute, He is independent (*Anapeksha*). He exists by Himself, without any dependence (*Apekshaa*) on anything else. He is unborn (*Aja*) and beginningless (*Anaadi*). As the world is relative (*Saapeksha*), it depends on *Siva* for its existence and sustenance. He is the material cause (*Upaadaana*) and the efficient cause (*Nimitta*) of the world. Everything in the world is a self-manifestation (*Prasaara*) of *Siva*. The created world is not a superimposition (*Adhyaasa*) on *Siva* from outside, but it is a free self-projection (*Aabhaasa*) of *Siva*. He is the pure unity and non-duality that pervades the whole universe. Though *Siva* is non-dual in Himself, all variety in the world comes from Him. Just as the liquid present in the egg of the peacock (*Mayuuraandarasavat*), though colorless, effects a variety of colors in the newly hatched bird, in the same way, though in *Siva* there is no variety, He causes all variety in the world. But, unlike the egg of the peacock, the world is not potentially present in seed form in *Siva*. Creation is a spontaneous free act (*Spanda*) of the Lord *Siva*, without any factor from within or without determining it.[526]

Though the absolute *Siva* causes determinations in the world by His spontaneous creation of every reality in the world, He Himself is indeterminate (*Nirvisesha*) and transcendent (*Anuttara*). When we say that the Lord *Siva* is indeterminate, we mean that He cannot be determined, grasped and judged by our intellect. Besides, our intellect can judge only that which has determinations, predications and qualifications that can be grasped by our understanding. *Siva* is indeterminte in the sense that He does not possess qualities that our understanding can grasp. This is because, as the highest reality, the Lord *Siva* transcends the categories of reality (*Tattvas*) and is beyond the categories of understanding (*Vikalpa*). Thus, the Lord *Siva* is indeterminate, as He is beyond the categories of understanding (*Nirvikalpa*) and without qualifications (*Nirguna*). What we have said does not mean that the indeterminate Lord *Siva* cannot be known at all. We have only said our reason and categories of understanding cannot grasp the indeterminate *Siva*. But, He can be known with the help of intuitive and immediate (*Aparoksha*) knowledge, called *Praatibha-jnaana* that is supra-intellectual and supra-rational.[527]

There is a seeming contradiction in the personality of the Lord *Siva* in that on the one hand He causes determinations in things of the world and appears through them as finite, while on the other hand, He is indeterminate and transcendent. This is possible because *Siva*, as the absolute, enjoys complete freedom (*Svaatantrya*). His freedom is a total freedom. He is free to appear the way He wishes, to appear in a different way and not to appear at all. If the Lord *Siva* is only transcendent, beyond appearances and not free to appear the way he wishes, then His freedom would be restricted. The freedom of *Siva* involves *a freedom from* and *a freedom to*. The former means that *Siva* is untouched by the world of appearances, while the latter implies the ability of the Lord *Siva* to act in whatever way He wishes. The light has no color of its own, and so it can assume different colors by passing through different colored glasses. The water has no shape of its own. Hence it can adopt to the different shape of the containers in which it is placed. In the same way, the formless and pure Lord *Siva* can take on as many forms as He likes. In the examples of light and water, it is the external conditions that make them different forms, but in the case of the Lord *Siva* the various forms He assumes are self-created, self-projected and free manifestations. Thus, there is no contradiction in the indeterminate *Siva* assuming determinate forms.[528]

The absolute freedom of the Lord *Siva* presupposes that He is absolute Self-consciousness, as freedom is the very nature of the light of consciousness. Self-consciousness is essentially the awareness of one's own existence. When one attempts to know one's existence, one does not have to differentiate oneself from others, for to know oneself one does not have to be aware of others. Hence, the Lord *Siva*, though non-dual and pure unity, is Self-consciousness. It is natural for absolute Consciousness, i.e., the Lord *Siva*, to become aware of Himself, as Self-consciousness is the foundational activity (*Aham-vimarsa*) of Consciousness. Just as the very nature of light is self-illumination, so also the nature of absolute consciousness is Self-consciousness. If Self-consciousness is lacking in the absolute Consciousness, then He would be no better than unconscious matter, as He would remain indifferent to the fear and love of the worshippers. Hence when considered from the spiritual point of view, absolute Consciousness, devoid of Self-consciousness, would be unthinkable. Therefore, the absolute Lord *Siva*, who is the Supreme Self (*Puurna Aham*) must be pure Self-consciousness. He is perfection (*Puunatva*), freedom (*Svatantrya*), infinity (*Bhuumaa*) and bliss (*Aananda*).[529]

The absolute non-dual *Siva*, the pure Self-consciousness, is the absolute Person. Being a person does not mean that one has a specific physical form, for one can be a person even without a body. A divine person can be without form (*Niraakaara*) or with a given specific form (*Saakaara*). But having a form is not necessarily a qualification of being a person. The essence of a person is that he is a self-conscious being. The Lord *Siva* is a person because He is absolute Self-consciousness. Even when *Siva* is in the state of pure non-duality, absolute Self-consciousness and absolute Personhood are possible because of the natural inner dynamism (*Vimarsa*) of *Siva*. Thus, *Parama Siva* is both impersonal and personal. These are two aspects of the absolute *Siva*. The Lord *Siva* is impersonal because of *Prakaasa*, while He is personal because of *Vimarsa*. *Prakaasa* stands for the pure, changeless and witness aspect of the universal Consciousness, while *Vimarsa* indicates the power which gives rise to self-consciousness, will, knowledge and action. It also gives the subject the facility to know himself in perfect freedom from all forms of affections. The former can be compared to a pure mirror which serves as a background for the reflection of objects, while the latter represents the power of the mirror to give rise to reflections. *Prakaasa* and *Vimarasa* go hand in hand and together they represent the Self-luminous (impersonal) and Self-conscious (personal) aspects of reality. Thus, in so far as He is indeterminate and transcends all manifestations, He is impersonal. In so far as the absolute *Siva* assumes the form of conscious being, presides over its own powers and rules over the works of its own nature, He is the absolute person and a personal God. Thus, *Parama Siva* is both impersonal and personal, being and becoming, transcendence and immanence, the unqualified and the qualified, because it is the integral unity of *Purusha*, the transcendental aspect of the absolute Lord (*Siva*) and *Prakrti*, the self-manifesting power of the Lord (*Sakti*).[530] Our consideration of the the Lord *Siva* in Himself takes us to the topic of His *Sakti*. In the next section, we delve into the analysis of the Lord *Siva* in his *Sakti*.

3.4.1.1.2. Siva in His Sakti

We begin our study of the Lord *Siva* in His *Sakti*, by giving an etymological clarification of the term *Sakti* and its synonyms, viz., *Kriyaa, Vimarsa, Svaatantrya* and *Spanda*. *Sakti* literally means power, force or energy. It is something that facilitates a thing for its activity. *Sakti* does not imply performance of actual activity as such, but it only means a capacity for and potentiality to perform an activity. When the potentiality for activity contained in *Sakti* is actualized into an activity, we call it *Kriyaa*. *Kriyaa* involves the accomplishment of a function, a movement, a flow or a dynamism. Thus, *Kriyaa* is an actual activity. *Kriyaa*, by its very nature belongs to the consciousness (*Citi*), as it is the consciousness which actualizes a potentiality. *Vimarsa* is the activity of the consciousness, viz., thinking. It suggests the activity of the Lord *Siva*, which is not physical even at the level of the creation of the world, as *Siva's* creative activity is nothing but a mental projection of His absolute Consciousness, as dream is a projection of the finite consciousness. Thus, *Vimarsa*, as a mental *Kriyaa*, is also knowledge (*Jnaana*). Such a *Kriyaa* of the Lord *Siva*, that flows out of *Vimarsa* is *Svaatantrya*, i.e., an act that emerges out of complete freedom, unconditoned and unbound. Condtions and compulsions for performing an activity can come either from external circumstances or from inner urges and desires of the performer. Since the Lord *Siva* is perfectly free (*Svatantra*) from external and internal comuplsions, He can choose to act, not to act or to act in the way He likes. The Lord *Siva's* state of complete *freedom-to-act* we call *Svaatantrya*. Again the *Kriyaa* of the Lord *Siva* that comes out of total *Svaantantrya* is not an effortful action, but a natural and spontaneous activity. Such an activity is called *Spanda*. The term *Spanda* carries with it the meanings of freedom, spontaneity, free flowing and effortlessness. Thus, the *Kriyaa* that emerges from *Spanda* is is an effortless, spontaneous, and free-flowing action. The *Spanda-kriyaa* is the most perfect term to refer to the *Sakti* of the Lord *Siva*.[531]

Having clarified the word *Sakti* and its synonyms, we move on the analysis of the nature of *Siva-Sakti*. *Siva-Sakti* is different from moral action (*Karma*) which involves voluntariness and effortfulness. When a person makes a moral choice, he has to exert his will and make an effort to accomplish that action. The *Kriyaa* that comes out of the *Sakti* of *Siva* is an effortless activity, as it is spontaneous and natural. There is freedom and no binding factor involved while the activity is performed. The activity flows from within the Lord *Siva*. Since *Kriyaa* is free-flowing and effortless (*Spanda*), it is different from an ethical action. Since *Kriyaa* emerges from *Spanda*, it is different from *Karma*, which is an effortful voluntary activity. While *Kriyaa* is spontaneous, effortless and free-flowing action, *Karma* is effortful and volitional ethical action. Similarly *Siva-Sakti*, though automatic and spontaneous, is not the same as mechanical activity. External factors determine and condition an activity that is mechanical. For instance, the movement of a fan, which is a mechanical activity, depends on switching it on, the availability of electricity and similar conditions. In the same way, conditions, such as inner obsessions and compulsions, move an activity that is psycho-neurotic. So, *Siva-Sakti* is different from all these forms of activities. The play of a child is an illustration from our experiences that has certain amount of similarity with a *Kriyaa* emerging from *Siva-Sakti*. A child plays not due to any motives, as it is natural for a child to play. Its act of play is not effortfully willed, mechanically conditioned and due to internal compusions. Play is a spontaneous and free-flowing act on the part of the child, for it plays for the joy of playing. The *Sakti* of *Siva* is operative in creation in a similar fashion. The creative act springs automatically, freely and without any compulsions out of *Siva-Sakti*, like the free-play of the child.[532]

We have clarified the nature of *Siva-Sakti*. The next point we must raise is the relationship between *Siva* and His *Sakti*. *Siva* and *Sakti* are not two realities and not even two parts of the same reality, but rather they are identical. Neither is *Sakti* an attribute of *Siva*, but the former is of the very nature (*Svaruupa*) of the latter. When *Siva* is conceived as dynamic, it is *Sakti*. The water and the current of water are one and the same. The term *water* connotes the *being of water*, while the term *current* connotes the *flow of water*. But in reality the terms *water* and *current* are one and the same. Similarly *Siva* and His *Sakti* are one. They both denote the absolute Consciousness, the source of everything in the universe, but *Siva* connotes the being of the absolute Consciousness, while *Sakti* connotes the *Kriyaa* of the very same absolute Consciousness. Thus, the difference between *Siva* and *Sakti* is only connotative and not denotative. But *Sakti* does not exist independent of *Siva*, as He is the place of its rest. *Sakti* produces its effects only because it rests in *Siva*, for it belongs to Him. Therefore, *Sakti* is nothing but the nature of *Siva*. This relationship between *Siva* and *Sakti* is beautifully depicted in the symbol of *Ardhanaariisvara*. In this symbol the male (*Siva*) and the female (*Sakti*) are represented not as two persons, but as one, i.e., half of the image is that of *Siva* and the other is of *Sakti*. Though a limited representation, it symbolizes the real nature of *Siva* and *Sakti*, viz., the unity of *Siva* and *Sakti* (*Siva-Sakti-Saamarasya*).[533]

Sakti, as the power of the supreme *Siva*, is one. But we can speak of it as many with reference to the different ends it produces. The burning power of fire and the cooking power of fire, as power, are one and the same, even though from the point of view of the results produced they can be spoken as two separate powers. Similarly it is with the *Siva-Sakti*. Since the Lord *Siva* has the freedom to manifest Himself in various activities, we can speak of different forms of *Sakti*. But in reality *Sakti* is one and identical with *Siva*. Saiva Tantric tradition describes five kinds of *Sakti*, viz., *Cit-sakti, Aananda-sakti, Icchaa-sakti, Jnaana-sakti* and *Kriyaa-sakti*. Of these five types of *Sakti*, the first two *Cit-sakti* (power of awareness, illumination or knowledge)and *Aananda-sakti* (power to enjoy the state of bliss) are called *Svaruupa-sakti*, as they belong to the transcendental (*Paraa*) level of Ultimate Consciousness (*Puurna Aham*), where there is no world and no creation. They correspond to the transcendental categories (*Tattvas*) of *Siva* and *Sakti*, which are one and non-dual. Hence, the first two forms of *Sakti* belong to the stage of pure unity, where there is no object consciousness and all is *Siva* (*Siva-pramaataa*). The other three types of *Sakti* describe the process of creation in the hierarchical order. The *Icchaa-sakti* stands for the the desire of the Lord *Siva* to create the world as His manifestation, spontaneously and effortlessly. The *Jnaana-sakti* represents the next step of ideation, i.e., the full mental picture of what is to be created by the mind of the Lord *Siva*. The *Kriyaa-sakti* consists in the actual creation of the world as the mental projection (*Aabhaasa*) of *Siva*, by externalizing the mental picture of the world He has in His mind. Thus, as the result of these three forms of *Sakti*, there emerges in this world various levels differentiation between subject and object, and objects among themselves.[534]

The Saiva Tantric texts and tradition express the *Siva-Sakti* with the help of various symbols, myths and allegories. Since the term *Sakti* is grammatically feminine, the symbols of *Sakti* are in the female gender. Besides, of the two parents of a child the father is associated with reason that guides and disciplines, while the mother is associated with the heart, the seat of emotions and feelings. Though reason controls activity, the power of acutal activity comes from the emotional side of personality, represented in the person of the mother. Hence, the mother, the person of the heart, is made the symbol of *Sakti*, while *Siva* is represented as male. Therefore, *Sakti* is personified consort of *Siva*, i.e., the female half of His essence. In every one of *Siva's* charcteristics, *Sakti* is not only His partner, but also adds greater intensification to the attributes of *Siva*. A few of such characteristics of *Sakti are*: as distructress she is *Kaalii*; she typifies beauty in the personality of *Umaa*; as the reproducer, she is represented by the *Yoni*; as the mother of the universe, she is *Jaganmaatri*; as the female ascetic, she is the *Yogini*; as the malignant being delighting in blood, she is *Bhairavii* and *Durga*; and as the mountaineer, *Paarvati*. Thus, the Saiva Tantric tradition has developed a wide range of deities through whom the *Sakti* worship is perpetuated.[535]

3.4.1.2. CHARACTERISTICS OF SIVA

In the last section, we have looked into the nature of the Lord *Siva* in

Himself and in His *Sakti*. Though the Lord *Siva* transcendent, pure, changeless and attributeless in Himself, through His *Sakti* He unfolds Himself in this world. In this section we move on to analyse the characteristics of the Lord *Siva*, which, indeed, are as the result of the manifestation of His *Sakti*.

3.4.1.2.1. Siva: The Lord of Yoga

The practice of *Yoga* leads to harmony between the body and mind, besides taking the one who practices it to the mystic state of spiritual union with the absolute. The Lord *Siva* is the perfect example of contemplation. He is the ideal ascetic, who has attained the highest perfection and innumerable powers through the practice of austerity and yogic. The yogic practices of the Lord *Siva* are uninterrupted, and He is the great master of *Yoga*, whom the *Yogins* of all times meditate upon. Hence, He is called the *Mahaatapaah* and the *Mahaayogi*. In His character as the *Mahaayogi*, He is depicted as an austere half-naked (*Dig-ambara*) ascetic, whose body is smeared with ashes and whose hair is matted. He is immovably fixed to one spot and is seated in the perfect yogic posture under a banyan tree. As the *Yogi*, the Lord *Siva*, while meditating, takes the *Samabhavee-mudra*, which consists in keeping his eyes neither fully closed nor fully open. It points to the fact that while He is deeply rooted in the inner Self, He has not forgotten His duties towards the world. This is what an ideal *Yogi* is expected to be. Thus, the Lord *Siva*, as the *Mahaayogi*, represents the supreme state of perfection in man, which is truly both God-consciousness and man-consciousness.[536]

3.4.1.2.2. Siva: The Fire That Destroys and Liberates

As the supreme *Yogi*, the Lord *Siva* has attained innumerable powers. Among those powers, is the power to destroy and liberate. In the *Braahmanas* and *Puraanas* the aspect of the fire power that destroys and liberates is personified in *Rudra-Siva*. For the *Satapatha Braahmana* speaks of *Rudra* as the all-pervading subtle fire.[537] In this aspect the Lord *Siva* is believed to have the power of devastation that destroy things. He is identified with sickness, death and all forms of power that destroys the earth. As a destroyer, He is called *Hara*, which literally means the one who carries away. The *Hara* in his most terrible form appears as the *Bhairava*, who is said to take 64 different manifestations. The Lord *Siva* is not only the fire that destroys, but also a fire that liberates. Often *Rudra-Siva* is said to perfom healing and curative functions. He is said to be the remover of all forms of pain – physical, mental and spiritual – that are found in the world. Thus, He is also a fire that inspires and animates all living things in the world. A myth speaks of *Brahmaa*, the creator of the universe, who desires to destroy the whole world, as living beings have multiplied and suffocated the earth. The Lord *Siva* mediated to avoid the total destruction by inducing *Brahmaa* to substitute total destruction of the world with individual death. Because of this benign attitude towards the people of the world, the Lord *Siva* is known not only as the power that destroys, but also the one who liberates, creates and preserves.[538]

3.4.1.2.3. Siva: The Auspicious Lord

Since the Lord *Siva* is the light that not only destroys but also liberates, there is an auspiciousness about Him. He restores and re-creates, even after the destruction. He is described as not terrifyng, but a kindly protector of the mountains and one who does not wish to injure a man or things. All these qualities point to the peaceful and humane face of the Lord *Siva*. Eight qualities – independence, purity, self-knowledge, omniscience, freedom from evil, boundless benevolence, omnipotence and bliss – are attributed to the Lord *Siva*. His greatness is unlimited. Though as Pure Consciousness He is incomprehensible to human mind, yet He is available to human beings in their need with His benevolent presence.[539]

3.4.1.2.4. Siva: The Source of Knowledge

The Lord *Siva* is believed to be the source of all knowledge, becuse in Him all the three aspects of energy, viz., understanding (*Jnaana*), will (*Iccha*) and action (*Kriyaa*) are totally integrated. *Siva* is called the never-diminishing-personality (*Akshara-purusha*), because the totality of knowledge is integrated within His personality. Language is said to have begun in Him. All forms of understanding and communication among people depend on Him. There are four ways that lead a person to understand reality. Firstly, the *Yoga*, which leads a person to inner awareness and harmony among the different aspects of his personality. Secondly, the theoretical cognition of reality, which forms the foundation for all types of practical action. Thirdly, the study of language, by which one is able to synthesize verbal symbols with reality and the ideas that represent them. Fourthly, music, which helps one to recognize the relation of numbers to ideas and forms. All these ways of understanding and many varieties of knowledge that emerge from them are released in the cosmic dance of the Lord *Siva*. His knowledge is comprehensive and immediate, as neither biological, mental or external conditions limit His knowledge. Hence, every enlightenment comes from the Lord *Siva*. Therefore, He is the model of all forms of intellectual achievement.[540]

3.4.1.2.5. Siva: The Font of Joy

Aananda-sakti is one of the *Saktis* of the Lord *Siva*. *Aananda*, the state of bliss and joy, is the ontological state of being of *Siva*. It is the changeless state, which is far removed from the physical level. It is the infinite state in which the Lord *Siva* is in the infinite joy of inwardness. It is an attributeless state, as the Lord *Siva*, the absolute Consciousness, is fully with Himself. But, it is a conscious state of joy, as the absolute *Siva* abides in His changeless state of joy. It is the state of identity, a state of affairs and the present continous existence of the Lord *Siva*, as the *Aananda*. It can neither be described as a state that belongs to *Siva*, nor can *Siva* be said as being in this state, but rather the state of joy is the Lord *Siva* Himself. As a result, it cannot be symbolized or expressed in our human communications. But it can be shared and experienced, when seekers of the Lord *Siva* move towards their Lord by the practice of *Saadhana*. The Puraanic thinkers call this state of the Lord *Siva* as *Sambhuu*.[541]

3.4.1.2.6. Siva: The Hermaphrodite

The Lord *Siva* is the underlying *neutral* and changeless reality, the undifferentiated absolute Consciousness, who is the foundation of every change and becoming. The hermaphrodite reality is one which is independent of all distinctions of male and female, the phenomenal and the non-phenomenal, and yet forms the basis of all such distinctions. The *Puraanas* speak of the Lord *Siva* as the hermaphordite reality, though distinctionless within Himself, letting the distinctions of the manifold world spring up from Him. The Puranic thinkers interpreted and represented this hermaphrodite aspect of the Lord *Siva* in various ways. One such symbolic expression is the figure of *Arthanaariisvara*, the half-male and half-female representation of *Siva* and His *Sakti*. Another such symbol is the *Phalus* (the male reproductive part) and the *Yoni* (the female reproductive part). A third, a more anthropomorphic metaphor, is that of the union between *Siva* and His many consorts, such as, *Parvati*, *Umaa* and others. All these symbolisms express the truth that the variety of this universe stems from the the Lord *Siva* through His *Sakti*. To explain this point very picturesquely, the *Puraanas* apply the mythological story of creation by way of the sexual union between *Prajaapati* and his daughter to *Siva* who, by His eternal union with His *Sakti* creates the world. The *Puraanas* also use another more sacrificial symbolism to expound the hermaphrodite characteristic of *Siva*, according to which the male principle is represented as Fire, the devourer of the offering, and the female principle is the *Soma*, the devoured offering. In this symbolism, the hermaphrodite is the embodiment of the cosmic sacrifice, through which the universe emerges out of the Lord *Siva*.[542]

3.4.1.2.7. Siva: The Third of the Puraanic Triad

The *Puraanas* depict the Lord *Siva* as the third of the triad of deities, the other two being *Brahmaa* and *Vishnu*. The function attriubted to *Siva* is that of the destroyer of the universe, while the other two are said to perform the creative and preserving functions respectively. Making *Siva* part of the triad of gods does not diminish His importance and status. The *Puraanas* do take care that the importance of the Lord *Siva* is not lost, though He is placed as the last in the triad of deities. A myth to this effect is narrated in the *Linga Puraana*. The Lord *Vishnu* addresses *Brahmaa* as His son. To this *Brahmaa* replies that He is the grandfather of all. In reply *Vishnu* asserts that *Brahmaa* came out of the naval of *Vishnu* in the vast waters, and so He is the father of *Brahmaa* and the grandfather of all others. While the dispute was going on, there arose between them a pillar of fire, the symbol of the Lord *Siva*, which they both could not identify. In order to identify the nature of this pillar of fire, *Brahmaa* takes the form of a swan and flies to find the top of the piller, while *Vishnu* takes the form of a bear and dives down into the bottom to find its termination. Both of them are disappointed, as they could find neither the top nor the end of the pillar of fire. This story clearly points to the primacy and significance the Puraanic thinkers gave to the Lord *Siva*, who is not to be reduced to an aspect (*Amsa*) of either *Brahmaa* or *Vishnu*.[543]

3.4.1.2.8. Siva: The Leader of the Flock

The followers of the Lord *Siva*, in their spiritual journey experience Him as the leader of the flock (*Pasupati*). For them, He is the ideal and the realized personality, who has become so with the help of His great asceticism and Yogic practices. He is free from all fetters (*Paasa*), such as, the principle of arrogance (*Aanava*), the accumulated effects of actions (*Karma*) and the illusion of the phenomenal world (*Maayaa*). The human soul (*Pasu*), on its journey here on earth, is like the cattle bound by all these forms of fetters. The Lord *Siva* (*Pati*) shows the fettered human soul the way these fetters can be unbound, with the help of His *Sakti*, which is released through the practice of *Yoga* and asceticism. Thus, as the human soul struggles through life to recognize its own inwardness and to free itself from the anguish, pain and desire that come as a result of the three-fold fetters, the Lord *Siva*, shines forth as the leader, who has already walked the way. When the human soul recognizes him as its *Pati* and attempts to live the example of the leader, it also can attain the ideal which the leader of the flock has already attained in His personality. Thus, experiencing the Lord *Siva* as the leader of the flock (*Pasupati*) is not an experience that can be empirically verfied or analyzed, but rather it is an experience that each soul on its way to *Siva*-realization spiritually recognizes.[544]

3.4.1.2.9. Siva: The Time

The Sanskrit term *Kaala* means black. It also means due season or time. The ordinary signification of the term is time. Everything in this world exists in time, as it is the first condition of existence of the universe. Time brings about and destroys things. Similarly, time effects the good and the evil. No one on earth can conquer time, as it seems invincible. As the Lord of disintegration, dissolution and devastation, the Lord *Siva* is identified with all eternal time. In this form His consort is the terrible goddess *Kaalii*. As the eternal time, all time and all that happens in time depends on the Lord *Siva*. But He Himself is not bound by time, as eternal as He is, He has no beginning and no end.[545]

3.4.1.2.10. Siva: The Great Dancer

The most popular depiction of the the Lord *Siva* is that of the King of Dance (*Nataraaja*). He performs the cosmic dance which preserves the equilibrium and balance of the creative and destructive dimensions. He dances standing with the right leg over the body of the dwarf demon (*Apasmara Purusha*), who symbolizes the ignorance that characterizes unenlighened souls and which the Lord *Siva* subdues. The lifted left leg points to the Lord leading all creatures to deliverance. The upper right hand hold a small drum (*Damaru*), which regulates the rhythm of the cosmic process and which involves the five activities of the Lord *Siva* (*Pancakrtya*), viz., creation of the universe (*Srishti*), preservation of the universe (*Sthiti*), destruction of the universe (*Samhara*), concealing His essence behind the garb of manifestations (*Tirodhana*) and bestowing grace to the devotee (*Anugraha*). The first four stages of the world process are done for the sake of the last. In other words, helping the devotee and blessing him with the graces of the Lord is the ultimate purpose of the cosmic process. In all these the Lord remains unchanged and unaffected. The upper left hand makes the half-moon posture (*Ardha-chandra-mudra*) holding a tongue of flame, an instrument of destruction, that indicates the end of mundane existence. Both the lower hands are held in protective posture (*Abhaya-mudra*) and grace-bestowing posture (*Varada-mudra*), bestowing protection and salvation to the devotee. The seven streams of water coming out of each side of the head remind us that the Lord *Siva* is the one who releases the river Ganges in seven streams from His hair (*Gangaadhara*). The ring of flames that surrounds the dancing Lord (*Prabha-mandala*) points to the life process of the universe that is taking place within *Siva*, the Prime Mover, in an uninterrupted manner, while He Himself remains as the Unmoved Mover. Thus, the Lord *Siva*, as the *Nataraaja*, manifests Himself as the Supreme Lord of the universe.[546]

3.4.1.3. EMANATIONS OF SIVA

Having looked into the characteristic of the Lord *Siva* in the last section, we now move on to consider His emanations. Unlike the Vaishnavas, the Sivas do not claim incarnations (*Avataara*) of the Lord *Siva*, but they do speak of His various emanations. Over 1008 emanations of *Siva* are spoken of in different *Puraanas*. Often the Lord *Siva* appears to devotees in the form in which he worships the Lord. Similarly the Lord *Siva* takes the form that is required to save a soul. These emanations are expressions of the grace of the Lord. But both the *Linga* and the *Siva Puraanas* speak of five special emanations (*Pancaanana*), viz., *Iisaana, Tatpurusha, Aghora, Vaamadeva* and *Sadojaata*, each of which are related to the five cosmic functions of the Lord *Siva*. The *Iisaana* is the highest aspect. It is also called *Sadaasiva* and is turned towards the zenith. On the physical plane, it represents the deity that rules over the sky, while in the spiritual sphere, it is the power of *Siva* that grants liberation. *Tatpurusha* faces the east. It stands for the power that dominates the air.

It represents forces of darkness and obscurity in the spiritual realm. *Aghora* faces the south, rules over the fire and stands for the power that absorbs and renovates the universe. *Vaamadeva*, faces the north, rules over the the element of water and takes care of preservation. *Sadyojaata*, faces west and represents the creative power of *Siva*.[547]

3.4.1.4. ICONOGRAPHIC DEPICTION OF SIVA

Corporeally the Lord *Siva* is depicted as having five faces or as having one face with three eyes. The presence of three eyes denotes his insight into the past, the present and the future. He wears the crescent moon on His head. Hence, He is known as *Chandra-sekara*. It points to measuring time by months. There is a serpent wound round His neck, which indicates the endless cycle of recurring years. A necklace of skulls (*Kapaalin*) with many serpents adorns His person, which connotes the eternal changing of ages and the successive dissolution and regeneration of the universe. He carries the Ganges above His forehead and allows it to flow in a calm way, so that the earth may not be crushed by the weight of the falling stream. This gained for the Lord *Siva* the name *Gangaadhara*. His throat is blue, due to the fact that He drinks the deadly poison *Halaahala* out of pity for mankind, which otherwise could have destroyed the universe on its production at the churning of the ocean. Hence He is called *Niilakantha*. The Lord *Siva* rides on a white bull called *Nandi*, which symbolizes creative sexual energy. In order to fight against the powerful demons, such as, Pura, Tripura and Andhaka, the Lord *Siva* is armed with a trident (*Trisuula*), a bow (*Ajagara*), a thunderbolt (*Vajra*) and an axe (*Parasu*). He also holds in His hands a noose (*Paasa*) to bind His enemies and a drum (*Damaru*) to keep time while dancing. He wears an elephant's skin as His garment and a tiger skin around His waist. He besmears His body with ash (*Vibhuuti*) as a sign of purification, penance and the sublimation of biological sex. He also wears a garland of *Rudraaksha* berries, which represents His concern, sorrow and anger. Thus, the iconographic representation of the Lord *Siva*, gives the devotee a solemn and an awe-instilling presence.[548]

3.4.1.5. SIVALINGA: THE EMBLEM OF SIVA

The Lord *Siva* is the ithyphallic God, whose emblem is the *Sivalinga*. Even some of the worshippers of the Lord *Siva* see this emblem only as an archetype of the male generative organ, which is seen along with the *Yoni*, the female generative organ. But for others, *Sivalinga* is an image of the generative process of the universe, viz., the rhythmic creation and destruction of the universe in different cycles. The Sanskrit word *Linga* literally means a mark, a sign or a symbol. Thus, it is the symbol of *Siva*, the supreme Reality, in Himself and in the manifestations of His *Sakti*. Probably the worship of *Sivalinga* has its origin from the Dravidians, for whom it is a symbol of the supreme reality, the Lord *Siva*. The river Narbmada contains marble-like elongated, stones shaped as an ellipsoid, having two sides formed due to the running waters. The Dravidians saw in the cylindrical ellipsoid with its two foci the representation of the Lord *Siva* and His *Sakti*, the former the immanent, the latter manifest. The *Sivalinga* is fixed in such a way that the lower half is embedded into the ground, which represents the invisible substratum, the supporter of the upper half, i.e., the supreme Reality, the Lord *Siva*, while the upper half appears above the earth which stands for the manifest, the *Sakti*. Thus, for the Dravidian mind, the *Sivalinga* clearly represents both the unmanifest and the manifest aspects of the absolute Reality.[549]

Though *Sivalinga* is an emblem of the Lord *Siva*, as it denotes the various aspects of the absolute Reality, it points to the triad of gods (*Trimurti*), viz., the *Brahmaa*, the *Vishnu* and the *Siva*, and their respective functions of creation, maintenance and destruction respectivly. Thus, the *Trimurti* are represented in the *Sivalinga*. Therefore, the *Sivalinga* has three parts. The lowest part is square and is hidden in the pedestal. It is called the *Brahmaa* part (*Brahmaa-pitha*). The octagonal part that the *Yoni* grasps is the *Vishnu* part (*Vishnu-pitha*). The cylindrical part that stands out above the *Yoni* is the *Siva* part (*Siva-pitha*). Thus, at the root of the *Sivalinga* is the *Brahmaa*, in the middle is the *Vishnu* and above both of them is the Lord *Siva*. Thus, the *Linga* represents the true Divinity (*Maheshwara*). Because it represents the totality of Godhead, mysterious and indescribable power is attributed the the *Sivalinga*.[550]

The *Puraanas* and the *Tantra* literature speak of different types of *Sivalinga*. They are original (*Akrtrima*) and man-made (*Krtrima*). The former are river banks and mountainous areas, while the devotees make the latter. They are made of metals, earth, stone and other similar materials. As the use of *Sivalingas* became popular, they were further divided into movable (*Cala*) and immovable (*Acala*). The former are made in such a way that they can be moved from place to place for devotional worship, while the latter are firmly established in particular places for public worship, such as, the *Sivalingas* that are worshipped at palaces or temples, those worshipped in ordinary houses and those worshipped in open places. With the further increase in the popularity of the worship of *Sivalinga* among the people, there is the increase in the types of *Sivalingas* used for worship. Besides, it is believed that the worship of many *Sivalingas* together brings to the worshipper greater blessings from the Lord. For instance, the one who desires wealth may worship 50,000 earthern *Lingas*. Similarly, a person who desires to have a son may worship 1,500, while the one who wishes to have a daughter worships 300 *Sivalingas*. Thus, there emerges a detailed regulation regarding the intended goal of the worshipper and the number of intended *Sivalingas* to be worshiped. In this way the worship of the *Sivalingas* became very popular among the devotees of the Lord *Siva*.[551]

3.4.2. SAIVA PATH TO THE DIVINE

So far in this essay we have been exploring various aspects of the Lord *Siva*, the supreme God of Savism, as He is in Himself and as manifested in His *Sakti*. Now our concern is to look into the ways in which the believers in the Lord *Siva* attempt to experience Him. Saivism is so divergent, as there are various sects and differing traditions. We find a number of means to experience the Lord *Siva*. In this section we move on to elaborate these Saiva paths to the Divine.

3.4.2.1. WASHING THE ICON OF SIVA

The believers of Lord *Vishnu*, while worshipping Him, take recourse to adorn the icon of the Lord *Vishnu* with fine dress, beautiful ornaments and similar decorative articles, because He is fond of being decorated (*Alankara*). Similarly, the Lord *Siva* is fond of being washed (*Abhisheka*). As washing is essential to the worship of *Siva*, we find in the *Siva* temples a pot made of copper or brass with a hole in the center which is kept hanging over the image of *Siva* or the *Sivalinga*, and water or other materials used for the *Abhisheka* falling on the image or the *Sivalinga* uninterruptedly. The washing of the image of the Lord *Siva* and the *Sivalinga* pouring over it water or other materials used for washing is called *Abhisheka*. Some of the materials used for *Abhisheka* are the following: water, milk, melted butter (*Ghee*), curd, honey, coconut water, rose water, sandal paste, scented oil, sugarcane juice, lime juice, water extracted from *Kusa* grass, waters from the sacred rivers and sea water. Different materials are used for *Abhisheka* in order to obtain different blessings from the Lord *Siva*. For instance, one does the *Abhisheka* with pure water to get rain. The milk-*Abhisheka* is done to free oneself from illnesses, to attain cows, to obtain a son and for barren women to beget children. The *Kusa*grass water-*Abhisheka* frees one from all forms of diseases. A person who desires to attain *Moksha* does the *Abhisheka* with the water taken from the sacred rivers. After one uses any of these materials for *Abhisheka*, pure water is poured on the image of the Lord *Siva*. While doing the *Abhisheka*, various types of short prayers (*Mantras*), from texts such as, *Rudri, Purushasukta, Chamaka, Mahaamrityunjaya Japa* and other texts, are chanted in a particular rhythm and order. In order to do the *Abhisheka* rightly and without interruption, one needs to memorize the words from *Rudri* (*Rudripatha*) and other texts. Just as different materials for *Abhisheka* are prescribed for obtaining different blessings from the Lord, similarly there are the detailed prescriptions as to the number of *Rudripathas* to be said in order to obtain the said blessing. The use of the right material for the *Abhisheka* and the recitation of the right number of *Rudripathas* make the *Abhisheka* most effective, as such a combined offering greatly propitiates the Lord *Siva*.[552]

When the *Abhisheka* is done with a deep inner attitude (*Bhaava*) and devotion (*Bhakti*), the devotee's mind is concentrated and his heart is filled with the image of the Lord *Siva*. His egoism vanishes, he is ready for self-sacrifice and self-surrender, and he experiences the immense joy of being devoted to the Lord. The regular practice of *Abhisheka* leads a devotee to the greatest and the highest *Abhisheka* of pouring waters of pure love on the *Aatmlinga* that dwells in his heart. Besides, *Abhisheka,* done along with the recitation of the *Rudripatha* in the name of a person, brings him good health and well being. *Abhisheka* cures incurable diseases, bestows health, brings wealth and prosperity, blesses one with progeny and helps one obtain many blessings from the Lord. Mondays and the thirteenth day of the fortnight (*Pradosha*) are special days of the Lord *Siva*. They are the most auspicious days for performing *Abhisheka* and other forms of offerings to the Lord *Siva*. Similarly, doing *Abhisheka* on the *Sivaraatri* day is very effective.[553]

3.4.2.2. RECITAL OF THE GREAT SIVA-MANTRA

A *Mantra* is that which removes all obstacles and miseries of the one who meditates on it, besides bestowing on him eternal bliss and immortality. The great *Siva-mantra* (*Mahaamantra*) is composed of five letters (*Pancakshara*), viz., the *Namassivaaya*. The devotees of the Lord *Siva* believe that the *Pancakshara* is the best among the seven chores of *Mantras* and central to the one thousand *Mantras* of *Rudra-siva*. The meaning of *Namassivaaya* is the following: *Namah* means the prostration or the profound adoration the *Jiivaatman* offers. *Siva* stands for the Lord *Siva*, who is the *Paramaatman*. The term *Aya* denotes the identity (*Aikyam*) of *Jiivaatman* and the *Paramaatman*. Hence *Namassivaaya* means the same as the great Vedaantic aphorism "That art Thou" (*Tat Tvam Asi*), which signifies the identity between the individual soul and the supreme soul. Again the five letters of the *Pancakshara-mantra* indicate the actions (*Pancakrityaas*) of the Lord *Siva*, viz., creation (*Srishti*), preservation (*Sthiti*), destruction (*Samhara*), veiling (*Tirodhana*) and blessing (*Anugraha*). Similarly the five letters point to the five elements that constitute this material universe, viz., ether, earth, air, fire and water. Thus, the *Pancakshara-mantra* stands for the Lord *Siva* as the unmanifest Reality in Himself and in His manifest aspect of *Sakti*. In this manner, it takes us to the true being of the Lord *Siva*. There are five forms of the *Pancakshara-mantra*. They are: the *Sthula* form – *Namassivaaya*, the *Sukshma* form – *Sivaaya Namah*, the *Kaarana* form – *Sivaaya Siva*, the *Mahaakaarana* form – *Sivaaya* and the *Mahaamanu* form – *Si*.[554]

Before one begins practicing the *Pancakshara-mantra,* one takes a bath or at least washes one's face and feet. Wearing *Bhasma* and *Rudrakshamala*, the devotee sits in a preferred Yogic posture, facing either east or north. He repeats silently the *Pancakshara-mantra* and meditates on the Lord *Siva*. While meditating, he keeps the image of the Lord in his heart or in the space between the eyebrows. Another way of doing the *Pancakshara-mantra* is *Pancakshara-mantra*-writing. Here the aspirant writes down in a notebook the *Mantra* for about half an hour daily. He writes the *Mantra* in ink clearly, observing strict silence (*Mouna*). Any language could be used for writing the *Mantra*. The seeker must repeat the *Mantra* mentally as he writes it. Writing leads to greater concentration. In this manner, if one practices meditation on the *Pancakshara-mantra*, either by way of reflection or writing, on a regular basis, at least for sometime during the day, it effects a great transformation in the person. The heart of the meditator is purified. His sins and past *Karmas* are removed. In the course of time he becomes what he meditates, *Naamas-sivaaya*, i.e., one with the Lord *Siva* (*Siva-yoga-Nishtha*), and enjoys the eternal bliss of *Sivaanandam*.[555]

3.4.2.3. MEDITATION ON THE LORD SIVA

Meditation on the Lord *Siva* is another means to arrive at oneness with the Lord. There are two forms of meditation proposed for the devotee. The first one is called *Sagunaa* meditation, which is preparatory in nature. Just as one who practices shooting initially aims at a large target and then slowly moves on the smaller targets, similarly the *Sagunaa* meditation prepares the way for the deeper level meditation called *Nirgunaa* meditation. The *Sagunaa* meditation consists in concentrating on an object of the devotee's desire. For the first three to six months he attempts to gaze (*Trataka*) on either a picture or an icon of the Lord *Siva*. Having practiced the physical gazing on the Lord, the seeker of *Siva* moves on to meditate on the mental picture of the Lord, keeping the picture between the eyebrows (*Trikuti*) or in the heart. The meditator moves slowly over the different parts of the picture: the elephant skin round the waist, then to the necklace, the *Rudraaksha* beads, beautiful blue neck, calm and meditative countenance, half-closed meditative eyes, the mysterious third eye, the matted locks that carry the river Ganges, the cool crescent moon, the trident and the drum. Then he fixes his mind either on the face or the feet of the Lord, and repeats the process as many times as possible. The meditator can also see and feel the Lord as present in every object in the universe, repeat one or the other *Siva-mantras* and think of the Lord as omnipresence, omnipotent and omniscience. If this practice of meditation is done a half-hour to two hours daily for about two years, the seeker is established in meditation and has communion with the Lord.[556]

When the meditator is established in the form of *Sagunaa* meditation, he can move to the practice of *Nirgunaa* meditation. It is a meditation on the Lord *Siva* as the all-pervasive, unmanifest aspect. Here the seeker meditates on the Lord, without any form, attributeless, eternal, infinite *Saccidananda*, the Pure Consciousness. While concentrating on this absolute *Siva*, the meditator attempts to identify himself with the transcendental *Svaruupa* of *Siva*. In this identification process, the meditator feels with his heart, thinks with the head and experiences with his soul the true identity with the Lord *Siva*. At the same time, he negates the body idea by repeating the *Sivoham*, which means 'infinitely I am', 'all light I am', 'all joy I am', 'all glory I am', 'all power I am', 'all knowledge I am' and 'all bliss I am', many times. When the meditator does this form of meditation with constant effort and zeal, he realizes the total identity with the Lord *Siva*, the absolute Consciousness.[557]

3.4.2.4. WORSHIP OF THE LORD SIVA

Usually the Lord *Siva* is worshipped in the form of *Sivalinga*. *Siva-bhaktas* at times offer worship to five deities including the Lord *Siva* (*Pan*-

cayatana Puja). The other deities remembered at the *Puuja,* along with the Lord *Siva,* are *Ganesa, Parvati, Suuryanarayana* and the *Saligraama* of these deities. Before one begins the *Puuja* of the Lord *Siva,* one arranges all the necessary things: *Bael* leaves, incense, light, camphor, sandal sticks, fresh water, plenty of flowers, food offerings to the Lord, a chosen form of liquid for the *Abhisheka,* a seat to sit upon, a bell, a conch and other things required for the *Puuja.* On the day of the *Puuja,* one who offers the *Puuja* arises before sunrise, washes his face, takes a bath and wears the special cloth, which is usually worn for *Puuja.* Once again, he washes his feet before entering the beautifully decorated *Puuja* room. As he enters the *Puuja* room, he chants the name of the Lord, glorifies the Lord by singing hymns in His praise and prostrates himself before Him. He sits on the special seat and commences the worship. Firstly one performs the purificatory rite in the prescribed method, which includes purification of the water vessel (*Kalasa*), the conch (*Sankha*), the Lord's seat (*Pitha*) and oneself (*Aatma*). The *Abhisheka* of the Lord's image or the *Sivalinga* follow along with the recitation of words from various sacred texts. After the *Abhisheka* the image of the Lord is decorated with sandal paste and flowers. Then comes the adoration (*Arcana*) of the Lord, which is done by repeating various *Siva-mantras*. One is expected to do daily 108 to 1008 *Arcanas.* The waving of the lighted Lamp (*Deepaarati*) follows. Usually various forms of *Deepaarati,* such as, waving one, three and five lighted lamps, besides the burning camphor light are done. While these *Deepaaratis* are done, the bell is rung and the conch is sounded. Then food offerings are given to the Lord. When all these forms of worship are completed, hymns in praise of the Lord *Siva* (*Siva-stotras*) are sung, during which one needs to begin the real internal worship (*Maanasa Puuja*) of the Lord. It consists in offering everything to the Lord and feeling that one is a mere instrument in the hands of the Lord. It also involves cultivating *Nimitta Bhaava,* i.e., the attitude of doing everything with the one intention of obtaining the divine grace of the Lord *Siva.* The *Maanasa Puuja* calls for deeper mental concentration on the Lord and a heart to heart communication of love between the *Bhakta* and the Lord. When this attitude is achieved at the worship of the Lord *Siva,* the seeker has the deep experience of the presence (*Darsana*) of the Lord in the innermost recess of his heart. In this manner, the worship of the Lord *Siva* truly takes the devotee to the Lord's presence. Usually after the *Puuja,* the food offered to the Lord is distributed among the *Bhaktas* as the sacred food (*Prasaad*). The sacred ash (*Vibhuti*) is also taken as *Prasaad* and applied on the forehead with devotion.[558]

3.4.2.5. PRACTICE OF VARIOUS DEVOTIONS

There are a number of devotional practices, which the *Bhaktas* do that purify them from all evils (*Maalas*) and lead them to the Lord *Siva.* Some devotionals are the use of the *Prasaad,* making pilgrimages, devout perambulations (*Parikramas*) and the practice of the fourfold *Saadhanaa,* viz., *Chari-*

yai, *Kiriyai*, *Yoga*, and *Jnaana*. Now we briefly consider each of these devotions that serve as genuine paths to the experience of the Lord *Siva*.

The *Prasaad* consists of those food and other items offered to the Lord during *Puuja*. They are believed to contain the power of the Lord in whose honor they are placed at the altar of the Lord. For instance, the sacred ash (*Vibhuuti*) is the *Prasaad* of the Lord *Siva*. It is applied on the forehead with great devotion, and small portions of it can also be taken in. Similarly, the red powder used at the worship (*Kumkum*) is considered as the *Prasaad* of *Sri Devii*, the *Sakti* of the Lord *Siva*. It is not usually taken in, but is applied at the space between the eyebrows. Likewise, *Tulsi* leaf, flowers and other food items offered at the worship are believed to be powerful *Prasaad*. Usually leaves and flowers are not taken in, but the food items are taken in. Usually people carry *Prasaad* to their dear ones at home after they offer *Puuja* at the temple. *Prasaad* is believed to purify sins bestow the Lord's grace, as it is the embodiment of the power (*Sakti*) of the Lord. Those who sincerely take the *Prasaad* experience the effects of the power of the Lord in their lives. It is said to cure incurable diseases. It brings peace, prosperity and joy. It energizes, strengthens and brings life into the devotion of the seeker of the Lord, if it is taken with deep faith and trust in the Lord. The Saiva religious practice provides a very important place to *Prasaad* in the life of a devotee of the Lord *Siva*, as no significant religious function ends without the distribution of the *Prasaad*.[559]

Another important religious practice, which a devout Saiva undertakes is the pilgrimage. Often pilgrimages are made on foot, and so it is very beneficaial physically. Besides helping physical health, pilgrimages also bring many spiritual blessings to the seeker. They lead to the destruction of sin in the life of the devotee and the acquisition of virtue, as, during such long and arduous pilgrimages, the mind of the devotee is fixed on the Lord, whom he is going to meet when he reaches the place of pilgrimage. Such fixation of the mind on the Lord for a long period of time helps the seeker to understand the relative nature of this *Samsaara* existence. This, in turn, brings a love for renunciation (*Vairaagya*) and a desire for liberation. The seeker, therefore, during his pilgrimage days looks in a special way for means of *Siva*-realization. Such seeking of means makes him perform his daily obligatory religious rites (*Nitya-naimittika-karmas*) well and also to practice other true religious means for God-realization, such as, reading the scriptures, reflecting on them and mediating on the truths reflected upon. Thus, a pilgrimage to *Kailas*, the seat of the Lord *Siva* can turn out to be a permanent acquiring of the means (*Parampara Saadhanaa*) of God-realization, as it causes purification of the mind (*Citta-suddhi*) and effects in one the desire for meditation (*Nididhyaasana*). For a householder, who is caught up with the world, such a pilgrimage can turn out to be a great means to experience the Lord of their lives deeply in the innermost recess of the heart. Besides, he may clarify his doubts and come out of his anxieties by opening them to the *Saadhuus* and *Sannyaasins* he meets during his journey. In this manner, the devotional practice of pilgrimage can be physically and spiritually fulfilling. True *Bhaktas* undertake it with great devotion and preparation.[560]

The *Parikrama* is a holy walk taken around a holy place, viz., a moundain peak, a sacred pond (*Tirtha*), a place of pilgrimage or a large area considered as sacred by tradition. When *Parikrama* is done to cover a large circuit, it is called *Pradakshina*. It is usually done by a large number of devotees at the time of certain festivals, even though such walks can also be taken at any time. Even shorter circuits, like a walk taken around a temple, around a sanctuary of the icon of a deity in a temple, around a *Tulsi* plant or a Pipal tree, taken with a holy purpose, are considered as *Parikrama*. Sometimes people also practice more difficult forms of *Parikrama*, which involves greater physical exertion and strain. Some of such forms are: lying on the floor and rolling along the entire route, proceeding slowly, prostrating after taking a few steps, and covering the whole route by placing one foot in close proximity to the other. These forms of *Parikrama* are undertaken as a penance, as fulfilling a vow taken earlier or as a spontaneous expression of zeal and fervor for the Lord *Siva*. What matters most in the *Parikrama* is not the physical aspect of the place, but the spiritual power the place symbolizes and the presence of the Lord that the devotee experiences in making the walk. The maximum spiritual benefit is derived depending on the mental attitude and motive of the devotee. The devotee takes a bath, wears clean clothes, places a *Tilak* of *Kumkum* or smears sacred ash on the forehead, wears a *Rudraaksha Maala* around his neck and begins the *Parikrama*. On the way he participates in the meetings (*Satsanga*), the *Saadhuus* and the *Sannyaasins*, thereby gaining valuable knowledge. He also takes holy dips in the sacred ponds and rivers on the way, thus washing away many of his sins. He also has the opportunity to open himself to the Lord's *Darsana* in many shrines on the way. The hardships and discomforts involved in making the *Parikrama* make him develop patience and endurance. Besides, the spiritual vibrations one receives from these holy acts purify the evil tendencies within the devotee. In doing all these things, his mind is elevated to the Lord. Thus, *Parikrama* serves as the *Saadhanaa* that elevates the body, mind and spirit of the one who makes it, thereby making him truly experience the Lord *Siva* in his inmost being.[561]

Another four-fold *Saadhanaa* of devotion and love towards the Lord that aims at the destruction of egoism in the devotee is the practice of *Chariyai*, *Kiryai*, *Yoga* and *Jnaana*. The external worship of the all-pervading, eternal and supreme God is called *Chariyai*. It consists of erecting temples, cleaning them, making garlands of flowers, singing the praises of the Lord, burning lamps in the temples, making flower gardens and doing similar things in devotion and love to the Lord. The required initiation for this practice is called *Samaya Diikshaa*. The worship of the cosmic form of the eternal Ruler of the universe, both externally and internally, is called *Kiriyai*. It involves performing the *Puuja* and the *Arcanas* to the Lord both in the temples and at home. The one who performs this devotional act must perform both the external act of ritual worship and the internal act of *Maanasa Puuja*. *Yoga* is the worship of the Lord *Siva* as formless and pure Consciousness. It calls for the restraint of senses and internal contemplation. Both *Kiriyai* and *Yoga* are initiated with an initiation called *Visesha Diikshaa*. The direct realization of the Lord *Siva* with the help of the *Guru* is called *Jnaana*. It helps the seeker to understand the true significance of *Pati, Pasu* and *Paasa* and to become one with the *Siva* through constant meditation on Him. The initiation that brings about *Jnaana* is called *Nirvaana Diikshaa*. By the practice of the four-fold *Saadhanaa* of devotion the aspirant frees himself from the three-fold *Paasa* that binds him, viz., egoism (*Aanava*), fruits of action (*Karma*) and illusion of the world (*Maayaa*). Having freed himself from various fetters, being guided by the *Guru* and the grace of the Lord, the devotee grows in faith, child like trust and devotion in his attitude towards the Lord *Siva*. Beginning from the attitude of a servant towards his master (*Daasya Bhaava*), he moves to that of a son towards his father (*Vaatsalya Bhaava*), to that of a friend (*Sakhya Bhaava*) and finally to that of wife to that of a husband (*Madhurya Bhaava*) in his attitude towards the Lord *Siva*. This movement makes him become one with the Lord *Siva*.[562] Thus, all these devotional practices, in the final analysis, lead to genuine union between the Lord and the devotee.

3.4.2.6. INITIATION CEREMONY

We have a made reference in the last section to the initiation of the devotees into the practice of the four-fold *Saadhanaa* of devotion and love, viz., *Chariyai, Kiryai, Yoga* and *Jnaana* by different forms of initiation ceremonies (*Diikshaas*), viz., *Samaya Diikshaa, Visesha Diikshaa* and *Nirvaana Diikshaa*. We find a similar three-fold rite of *Diikshaa* rite in the Viirasaiva sect of Saivism. According to them, the *Diikshaa* rite opens a devotee of the Lord *Siva* to attain the state of union with Him, by freeing him from three different worldly bondages. Such an initiated man can never be considered as a layman (*Pasu*). The initiation rite is called *Diikshaa*, because it facilitates a person is to enlightenment in the Saiva philosophy and frees him from the bondages this world imposes on him. The Viirasaivas speak of three forms of the *Diikshaa* rite. They are the *Vedhaa-diikshaa*, the *Mantra-diikshaa* and the *Kriyaa-diikshaa*. In the *Vedhaa-diikshaa* a person is initiated simply by the touch of his *Guru's* palm on his head. By this simple touch of the *Guru*, the initiate is transformed into a new person, in the process acquiring the knowledge of the Saiva system of philosophy automatically. The second, the *Mantra-diikshaa*, involves a mere verbal instruction given to the initiate by the teacher. What the teacher gives the initiate verbally is an incantation (*Mantra*). The *Kriyaa-diikshaa* is performed with a prescribed ritual.[563]

It is the spiritual teacher who initiates the disciple into *Kriyaa-diikshaa*. The teacher of the Viirasaiva sect must be a *Braahman* who belongs to one of the five famous families (*Gotras*). He is bound to do five sacred duties daily, viz., the muttering of the sacred incantations (*Japa*), austerities (*Tapas*), worship (*Arcana*), meditation (*Dhyaana*) and the reading of sacred philosophical teaching (*Jnaana*). The teacher fixes a holy time in a solar or lunar day in a holy month to initiate his disciples in the *Kriyaa-diikshaa*. At the appointed time, before the assembly of the invited devotees of the Lord *Siva*, the disciple to be initiated is brought according to the prescribed rules. Before he arrives at the place, he takes a holy dip in water, cleanses his face and teeth, and dresses in white. As he arrives, the teacher escorts him to the specially marked place (*Mandala*). He sits facing east. The teacher sits by his side facing north. Five pitchers filled with water, representing the five ancient *Aacaryas* of the Viirasaiva sect, are placed in front of the disciple to be initiated. A piece of cloth colored with sacred ashes is also placed before the disciple. The teacher makes the disciple pronounce the name of the Lord *Siva* and to meditate upon the Lord. Then he, along with a few priests, sprinkles the body of the disciple three times with the water taken from the five pitchers, pronouncing sacred incantations. The teacher then performs a number of rites and formalities. He then mutters in a low voice a *Mantra* consisting of five letters in the right ear of the disciple being initiated. Since this *Mantra* is only for the initiate, it is said in such a way that nobody else hears it. The most important act at the initiation ceremony is the placing of the sacred thread on the shoulders of the disciple. As the result of holding this sacred thread, the initiated disciple becomes free from all his sins and other forms of misfortunes. In this manner, the *Kriyaa-diikshaa* gives the initiated a special status in the Viirasaiva society, as he is facilitated by his initiation to move towards the Lord *Siva* and to attain the highest state of *Siva*-Consciousness. Thus, the initiation ceremony, in deed, is a special path that leads the initiated towards union with the Lord *Siva*.[564]

3.4.2.7. TANTRIC MEANS TO SIVA-REALIZATION

In the Tantric Saiva tradition, there are two branches, viz., the Right-hand Doctrine (*Upaaya-saadhanaa*) and the Left-hand Doctrine (*Kaula-saadhanaa*). Both of them have *Siva*-realization as the goal of their respective *Saadhanaas*. But the former attempts to arrive at this goal by some form of negation of the world, along with the positive means (*Upaaya*) of spiritual practice, while the latter endeavors to arrive at the same goal by accepting the world positively and using the world as a means to achieve it. This is because the Right-handed Doctrine considers the world as a mere projection (*Aabhaasa*) of *Siva*-Consciousness, while the Left-handed Doctrine sees everything in the world as filled with *Siva* (*Siva-mayaa*). As a result, the former transcends the world, by way of negation of the world, to reach *Siva*, while the latter embraces the world as a reality and looks through the world to arrive at *Siva*. Concretely it means that *Upaaya-saadhanaa* views base nature and its tendencies as evil, and shuns them to reach the goal of *Siva*-realization, while *Kaula-saadhanaa* accepts them as good and sublimates them to reach the goal of *Siva*-realization. In the following section, we make an attempt to explore the paths of these two Tantic Saiva traditions.

3.4.2.7.1. Right-hand Doctrine

According to the Right-hand approach, *Siva*-realization is basically a state of Self-realization, as the innermost Reality behind every individual is *Siva*. One's Sivahood is veiled temporarily due to the ignorance (*Anjaana*) and impurity (*Mala*) of the world. When the veils of ignorance and impurity are removed, one realizes his true Self, i.e., *Siva*. The path of attaining Self-realization, thereby *Siva*-realization, by removing ignorance and impurity, is called *Upaaya*. The *Upaaya*, the path or the means to liberation is the self-effort the seeker of *Siva* offers on his part for the process of Self-realization. But, according to Saiva tradition, the grace of the Lord *Siva* (*Anugraha*) must supplement the human effort of *Upaaya*. Thus, whatever human effort achieves, it achieves with the grace of God. The nature of the grace of God is such that it is free flowing from the bounty of God, and it is completely motiveless. In other words, the Lord showers his graces on the devotee not for His benefit, but rather for the benefit of the souls. Yet the grace of God is not given arbitrarily, but is given only to the one who deserves it. Thus, *Siva*-realization is the combined effect of the grace of God and human effort (*Upaaya*). *Upaaya* is a means because it does contribute to the realization of our true nature, even though the grace of God is involved in the process. The tantric Saiva tradition speaks of three categories of *Upaayas*, viz., the inferior means (*Aanavopaaya*), the medium means (*Saaktopaaya*) and the supreme means (*Saambhavopaaya*).[565] We attempt to clarify each of these *Upaayas* in detail, starting from the lowest to the highest.

3.4.2.7.1.1. Inferior Means

The *Aanavopaaya* is the external physical means. It is the lowest of all the three *Upaayas*. It operates in the external world of difference and duality. Hence, it is called *Bhedopaaya*. All forms of external worship, including ritual worship, fall within the category of *Aanavopaaya*. It is a means that is concerned with the individual person with a body (*Nara*). It is also called *Naropaaya*, as it is related to man who performs all his activities with the help of the body. We call it *Kriyopaaya*, as it involves external activity (*Kriyaa*) and emerges from the *Kriyaa-sakti*. It is comparable to the practice of physical *Yoga*, such as *Haathayoga*, posture (*Aasana*), breathing (*Praanaayaama*) and other similar Yogic stages.[566]

One form of the actual practice of *Aanavopaaya* involves the process of concentration on different physical functions of the person, such as breathing (*Uccaara*), organs of sensation (*Karana*), contemplation (*Dhyaana*) and concentrating on some particular place (*Sthaana Prakalpanaa*). Firstly, concentration on breathing consists in the aspirant continuing breathe deeply and finding out the center between two breaths, viz., the incoming breath and the outgoing breath. This central point is the ending point of the incoming breath, the beginning point of the outgoing breath, and the center point of the whole span of the breath. The practice of *Uccaara* helps the seeker to cultivate a deep quality of concentration. Secondly, concentrating on the organs of sensation (*Karana*), which consists in practicing one-pointedness with the help of a sense. For example, concentrating one-pointedness with the sense of sight implies that the devotee looks at an icon of the Lord *Siva* for a long time, without even blinking the eyes. Such a concentration leads to an unbroken awareness of the Lord. If one practices *Karana* with the sense of hearing, then one listens to the sound of a *Mantra*, for instance, repeating the sound again and again. Similarly *Karana* can be practiced with the help of other senses. Continuous practice of one-pointedness *Karana* leads to deeper levels of concentration in the seeker of the Lord. Thirdly, *Dhyaana* is another form of *Aanavopaaya*. It consists in contemplating on some point. There are lower and higher forms of *Dhyaana*. For instance, contemplating the Lord *Siva* in the form of *Sivalinga* is a lower form of *Dhyaana*. On the other hand, when the seeker contemplates the lotus in his heart, or on the meaning of a *Mantra*, such as, *So'ham* or *Siva*, he does a higher form of *Dhyaana*. The *Sthaana Prakalpanaa* is another form of *Aanavopaaya*, in which the seeker concentrates on a particular place, either in the outside world or in one's body. In the body one concentrates on three places, viz., between the eyebrows (*Bhruumadhya*), on the pit of the throat (*Kanthakupa*) on the heart (*Hridaya*). Thus the devotee places the image of the Lord in any of the three places in his body and concentrates on it. All these forms of *Aanavopaaya* remain in the individual person and exist in him.[567]

Since *Aanavopaaya* deals with the external activity of worship and concentration, what makes it more effective is the spiritual feeling a person attaches to these activities. Mere external performance of activities does not bring any good to the person. If these external activities involved in *Aanavopaaya* are coupled with the inner spiritual fervor, they produce much fruit for the seeker of the Lord *Siva*, especially by dissolving the ego in all the actions and leading to the higher Self.[568]

3.4.2.7.1.2. Medium Means

The medium means is *Saaktopaaya*. This is called so because it involves thinking (*Vimarsa*). But the thinking involved is deliberate (*Vkalpaatmaka*) thinking, which implies exerting one's will (*Sankalpa*) and making effort (*Adhyavasaaya*). This form of *Upaaya* involves deliberate mental activity. As it belongs to the level of *Jnaana-sakti* and originates from it, *Saaktopaaya* is also called *Jnaanopaaya*. So one has to contemplate, assimilate and think over and over again in the mind. Therefore, in the state of *Saaktopaaya*, one does not recite *Mantras* nor is one aware of using breathing, concentrating on a particular spot, or any similar means; rather what is thought of in the mind as an idea is held in the unity of mind, i.e., in the state of unity-in-difference. Thus it is also called *Behdaabhedopaaya*. In *Saaktopaaya* the seeker is expected to practice centering between thoughts or actions. This calls for cultivation of firmness of awareness that is continuous. Only by maintaining the unbroken chain of awareness can the aspirant effect a balance between one thought and another, between a waking state and the dream state, between one step and the next and between one breath and the next. If his awareness is loose and faulty, and not continuous, he falls back into the lowest *Upaaya*, viz., *Aanavopaaya*. All forms of mental recitation of an idea, such as, meditation, contemplation and concentration fall into the category of *Saaktopaaya*. Since there is deliberate and voluntary thinking in the state of *Saaktopaaya*, there is the sense of 'I-ness', ego and doing something (*Abhimaana*) in this state.[569]

3.4.2.7.1.3. Supreme Means

The supreme means is *Saambhavopaaya*, which is the spiritual *Yoga* that involves direct dissolution of one's ego and feeling one's unity with all in universal love. Unlike *Saaktopaaya*, which is a state of continuous thoughtfulness, *Saambhavopaaya* is a continuous state of thoughtlessness, wherein the seeker realizes that he is the real 'I', the *Parama Siva*, and finds the whole universe reflected from within his own consciousness. The seeker's experience of the seeing the whole world as his own projection is not a deliberate thinking done as in *Saaktopaaya*, but rather it comes to him automatically and spontaneously (*Nirvikalpa*). Since, in the *Saambhavopaaya* state, the thinking is neither created nor deliberately willed, but comes automatically, this highest state of existence can be arrived at only after the seeker passes through the first two states of *Aanavopaaya* and *Saaktopaaya*. Such a state emerges from the *Iccaa-sakti*. So *Saambhavopaaya* is also called *Iccaaopaaya*. When a seeker reaches the *Saambhavopaaya* state, he can enter the state of Sivahood at will, as he is completely attuned to *Siva* (*Siva-samaavesa*). As the seeker merges in the consciousness of the Lord, the total unity between the seeker and the Lord is achieved. Hence, *Saambhavopaaya* is also called *Abhedopaaya*. Since *Upaaya* aims at arriving at the highest state of unity, only those seekers who have attained a highly developed stage of awareness are permitted to follow this path.[570]

Speaking of the relationship between these three categories of *Upaayas* Swami Lakshman Lee says the following:

> In *Aanavopaaya* the strength of your awareness is such that you have to take the support of everything as an aid to maintaining and strengthening your awareness. Though you concentrate on the center you need to take the support of two things for concentrating on that center. In *Saaktopaaya* your awareness is strengthened to the extent that only one point is needed as a support for your concentration and that point is the center. In *Saaktopaaya* you begin with the center and then become established in that center. In *Saambhavopaaya* the strength of your awareness is such that no support is needed. There is nowhere to go, just reside at your own point. The rest is automatic.[571]

This statement clearly shows that these threefold *Upaayas* are three types of *Upaayas*, meant for three classes of people of different mental abilities and spiritual evolution. At the same time, they are not three independent types of *Upaayas* having no relationship to each other. As a matter of fact, they are hierarchically ordered and each of the lower can be seen as a preparatory step towards the one immediately higher. Thus, we can say that *Aanavopaaya* is a means to arrive at *Saaktopaaya* and *Saaktopaaya*, is a means to reach the highest state of *Saambhavopaaya*.[572]

These threefold *Upaayas* lead a seeker on his way to *Siva*-realization. In doing so, they call the seeker to negate the world. Firstly, the world is dispossessed of its independent and real existence, as it is reduced to a mere manifestation of the Lord *Siva*. Secondly, by making it a projection of the Consciousness of *Siva*, its materiality is denied. Thirdly, the multiplicity of the world is given up in order to be consistent with the unity of the Lord *Siva*. Fourthly, in the stage of *Saambhavopaay*, the world is reduced to a reflection and projection of the seeker's own higher self. Fifthly, *Saaktopaaya* and *Aanavopaaya* ask the seeker to see the world as an expression of *Siva* (*Sivabhaavanaa*). Sixthly, the ignorance and impurity an individual experiences in his life is attributed to the illusory nature of the world (*Maayaa*).[573]

In this manner, the *Upaaya-saadhanaa*, the Right-hand Doctrine of Tantric Saivism, while giving three-fold positive means, viz., *Aanavopaaya*, *Saaktopaaya* and *Saambhavopaaya*, to reach towards *Siva*-realization, also calls for negation of the world and its influences on the spiritual journey in order to arrive at the final states of *Anupaaya* and *Pratyabhijnopaaya*. *Anupaaya* literally means 'no means'. It refers to the state of Transcendence (*Anuttara*). At this stage all distinctions such as the worship, the worshipper and the worshipped are obliterated. Similarly, at this state there is no going anywhere, no doing anything, no applying any technique, no practicing anything and no making effort, as one takes nothing, leaves nothing, but takes everything as it is. There is nothing other than the unity consciousness, in which everything happens spontaneously (*Spanda*) and naturally. It is the state of complete relaxation and bliss, in which the Self is totally relaxed (*Aatma-visraanti*). The state of *Anupaaya* is attributed to and emerges from the *Aananda-sakti* of the Lord *Siva*, and so it is referred to as *Aanandopaaya*. The *Pratyabhijnopaaya* is the end of the Saiva Tantric process of Self-realization. It is referred to in the Saivite Tantra literature in different ways: Self-recognition (*Aatma-pratybhijnaa*), knowledge of the Self (*Aatma-jnaana*), experience of the Sivahood (*Siva-nubhuuti*) and liberation (*Moksha* or *Mukti*). It is related to the *Cit-sakti* of the Lord *Siva*, which helps the seeker to recognize that he is eternally the Lord *Siva*. *Anupaaya* and *Pratyabhijnopaaya* are, strictly speaking, not two states, but belong to the state of Pure Unity of absolute *Siva*-Consciousness, which is the ultimate goal of the Saiva Tantric path to the Divine.[574]

3.4.2.7.2. Left-hand Doctrine

The left-hand Doctrine of the Saiva Tantric tradition, commonly known as the *Kaula-saadhanaa*, is the little known but the most criticized *Saadhanaa* of Tantrism. It is the most misunderstood and the least appreciated, because it is a secret technique (*Rahasya-vidhi*), the practice of which has been always kept secret. It has been handed down from the *Guru* to the disciple and is never made known to the general public. The reason for the secrecy attached to the practice of *Kaula-saadhanaa* is that it may not fall into the hands of unqualified persons, who might abuse it. In spite of the trouble taken to prevent its abuse, in real practice *Kaula-saadhanaa* has been abused and used as a means to enjoy physical pleasure of illicit sex, and so it is branded as a form of perversion. For this reason, *Kaula-saadhana* is known, in the Indian tradition, as the Left-hand way (*Vaama-maarga*). But the Kaulas accept this name for some other reason. The term *Vaama* means 'the left half'. By this term they mean the left half or the female side of the Lord *Siva*, viz., his *Sakti*, which is expressed in the half-male and half-female representation of *Siva* and *Sakti* (*Ardhanaariisvara*). In this representation the left half depicts the *Sakti* of Lord *Siva* in half-female form. Thus the term *Vaama* comes to mean one of the many names given to *Sakti*. Hence, *Vaama-marga* stands for the worship of the left half of *Siva*, viz., His *Sakti*.[575]

Kaulism as a school of Saiva Tantric thought reacts to the Puritanism of Vedic religion, which considers many things in the world as impure and identifies impurity with unholiness. There is a difference between something being unclean and it being unholy, i.e., religiously impure. Cleanliness or uncleanliness is a secular value, while holiness or unholiness is a religious value. It is wrong to equate these totally different spheres of existence. In the Vedic religion, for instance, an untouchable (*Suudra*), even if he has washed his body and wears clean clothes, is considered impure, in the sense of unholy. Similarly, taking wine, fish, meat and the whole realm of sexuality are considered impure, meaning unholy. This makes an orthodox Vedic believer not only abstain from these things, but also think that coming close to these things would make him unholy. Kaulism, in principle, is condemning this puritanistic trend of looking at certain things of this world as unholy in the orthodox Vedic religion. The Kaulas attempt to show the religious purity or holiness of even things that are unclean, as they believe that unclan things are not necessarily unholy.[576]

Reacting to the religious Puritanism inherent in the orthodox Vedic religious practice, the Kaulas profess to find divinity even in the most profane objects and activities, and to use them as powerful tools to discover the Divine that is present in everything. Therefore, for them, the entire world is an extension of the Lord *Siva* and is directly connected with Him. The world is *Siva* and *Siva* is the world. Since the Lord *Siva* is directly reflected in everything through His *Sakti*, everything in the world becomes a medium for coming into contact with *Siva*. Thus, the external world (*Bahih*), the woman (*Sakti*), the male-female couple (*Yaamala*), the body (*Deha*), the process of breathing (*Praana-patha*) and the workings of the mind (*Mati*) become the media to realize the Lord *Siva*. Therefore, there is nothing mundane and unholy. Every reality is holy and can reveal the Lord *Siva*. The profane realities of the orthodox Vedic religion, such as, wine, meat, fish, parched grain and sexual intercourse are considered profound means for the *Siva*-realization. The goal of *Kaula-saadhanaa* is the sublimation of all desires, i.e., raising all the lower desires to the highest level, and using them as a means to experience the Lord *Siva*. Sublimation involves not taking an antagonistic attitude towards our desires, but accepting them as good and holy, raising them to higher levels and giving them creative expressions of love, creativity and aesthetic activity.[577]

Among the various media that reveal the Lord *Siva*, the most significant, according to *Kaula-saadhanaa*, is sexual energy (*Kaama-sakti*). It is not limited to genital sex expression alone, but rather it is the general energy of pleasure (*Aananda-sakti*), which is the basis of every form of joyful activity. Sexual energy is the very same energy of the universe that is responsible for all forms of creative expression in different areas of life. It expresses itself in the gross form as the genital sex act and in the sublimated form as love and aesthetic enjoyment. In the Saiva Tantric tradition, sexual energy is symbolized as a coiled serpent (*Kundalinii*) that is seated face downward at the base of the sex-organ in the body (*Muulaadhaara-cakra*). Its downward awakening leads to the lowest expression of the sex energy, i.e., the physical enjoyment of sex. *Kaula-saadhanaa* aims to awaken the *Kundalinii*, cause it to raise its face upward, ascend through the chain of *Cakras* in the body and finally be united with the Lord *Siva* in the *Cakra* at the top of the head (*Sahasraara-cakra*). The ascending of the *Kundalinii* is the figure the *Kaula-saadhanaa* uses to refer to the process of sublimation of the sex energy from the gross level of physical enjoyment to the highest level of the divinity. *Kaula-saadhanaa* believes that the great power of sex energy is wasted as long as it remains at the gross level, but if it is sublimated and transmuted to the higher level, it can find manifold, powerful expressions.[578]

As against the contemptuous attitude of the puritanistic ascetic traditions towards sex energy, the Kaula ritual asks its adherents to cultivate an attitude of sacredness towards sex. Only with such an open attitude can one sublimate the sexual energy. *Kaula-saadhanaa* instructs its followers to begin by developing a feeling of reverence towards the sex act and by acquiring a feeling of love towards the sex partner. Cultivating an attitude of respect for sex that is based on one's belief in its sanctity, helps a Kaula initiate to take a distanced attitude towards the sex act. This, in turn, calms one's inordinate desire to indulge in sex compulsively. The sexual act or feelings associated with it are not considered as evil. The Kaula initiate is neither in an attitude of confrontation with the whole realm of sexuality nor suppressing it. Kaulism admonishes its initiate neither to hate sexuality as sinful and base, nor to use it for self-gratification. The aim of *Kaula-saadhanaa* is to teach its adherents the mean between these two extremes, thereby moving towards its sublimation. In the initial stages of the practice of *Kaula-saadhanaa*, one may depend on physical sex, but as one progresses one is expected to cultivate an attitude of healthy detachment towards physical sex. Besides, the motive of the ritual sexual act (*Maithuna*) is not self-gratification or enjoyment of pleasure (*Bhoga*), but it is done as an offering to the deity, i.e., as a religious act. The man and woman involved in the ritual sexual act are worshipped as *Siva* and *Sakti* respectively. For the Kaulas the sacredness of and respect for sexuality is beautifully expressed in the phallic worship of the male sex organ (*Linga*) and the female sex organ (*Yoni*). Similarly, the worship of *Kaama-deva*, as the god of sex, on the festival day of *Vasantapancamii* and the worship of the serpent, a symbol of sexual energy, on the festival of *Naagapancamii* also expresses the truth that sexuality is holy and that it needs to be raised above the physical level. Hindu mythology affirms this truth, when it speaks of the Lord *Vishnu* as resting on the divine serpent, *Sesha*; the snake as an ornament adorning the Lord *Siva* and the earth as resting upon the hood of the divine serpent, *Sesha*. Thus, for the Kaulas, the cultivation of the attitude of sex as something holy and not profane and approaching it respectfully is the first step. It brings in the Kaula initiate a respectful distance and detachment towards the sexual act, thereby helping to sublimate the sexual energy.[579]

Secondly, *Kaula-saadhanaa* prescribes to develop deep love for one's sex partner. The man is instructed to visualize his sex partner as his own *Sakti*, while the woman is taught to see her man as her own *Siva*. This perception leads them to nurture a sense of identity with each other. Such an experience of oneness makes them wish what is best for each other and to feel that the other is one's own self. When this happens between the partners, there develops in them an intense love for each other, which makes them see the spiritual beauty in each other, bringing in the process deep joy and satisfaction that belongs to a level much higher than the physical level. Thus, true love between the partners automatically makes them sublimate their sexual energy into higher energy. Sex becomes only a symbol of this deep love that exists between them. As a result, the sensuality associated with lower forms of sex vanishes and genuine integration of their personality takes place, as they are able to move easily from the pleasant (*preya*) to the good (*Sreya*). They are no more caught up in what is merely pleasant in each other, but are able to see the true goodness and spiritual beauty of each other. Thus, the cultivation of the attitudes of the sanctity of sex and genuine love for the sex partner automatically lead to the sublimation of sex energy, in the process opening in the partners deeper levels of experience such as love, aesthetic enjoyment, creativity in everything they do and even *Siva*-realization.[580]

All the Saiva traditions, including *Kaula-saadhanaa*, consider *Siva*-realization as the state of liberation (*Moksha*). The sublimation of sexual energy frees man from the level of the pleasant and takes him to the level of the good, in the process cultivating in him a desire for moving towards the true good. Besides, it releases in man the free flow (*Spanda*) of the highest form of love, i.e., unselfish and other-centered love. When the seeker (*Saadhaka*), having sublimated his sex energy by the use of *Kaula-saadhanaa*, moves toward the true good, with unselfish and altruistic love in all spontaneity, he cannot but reach the ultimate center of his existence, viz., his true Self (*Siva*). Thus the Kaula path leads the seeker to *Siva*-realization, through the sublimation of sexual energy.[581]

In moving to the goal of *Siva*-realization, the *Kaula-saadhana* proposes three stages, viz., the stage of the animal (*Pasu*), the stage of the hero (*Viira*) and the stage of the divine (*Divya*). Each of these stages is meant for different groups of people (*Adhikaariis*). The stage of the animal, which is the lowest among the three, is meant for people who are still in the state of selfishness regarding their attitude towards sex, and their sexual orientation remains in the crude physical level. *Kaula-saadhanaa* suggests initiating only married couples (*Yaamala-diiksha*) to this stage. The stage of the hero calls for a high level of sex sublimation. He is called a hero, because he is above every selfishness and capable of loving anyone as his own self. Only when a person has achieved such a mental attitude is he initiated into the hero stage, where extra-marital relationship is allowed. The stage of the divine is the highest stage. Here all ego of the *Saadhaka* has totally vanished. He has attained a state in which he has moved from the pleasant to the good. Besides, he has attained the state of free flowing altruistic love. Such a person has no need for physical sex, as he can feel deeply the intensity of love without physical union. The *Divya*, thus, has achieved the highest level of sex sublimation. One who attains this state is a Self-realized person (*Jiivanmukta*). In making this threefold division of people, *Kaula-saadhana* clearly points to the varying spiritual levels of different persons and admonishes that the initiate should have the necessary spiritual acumen to cope with the demands of a particular stage of the *Saadhanaa*. It is the *Guru*, who needs to judge the spiritual status of a person, before he is initiated into a particular stage. For this reason, the *Kaula-saadhana* was kept secret and not taught to the general public. If this strict discipline in judging the different levels of competence of the people (*Adhikaarii-bheda*) is not maintained in the practice of this *Saadhanaa*, many things may go wrong. Kaulism says that following the Kaulic path is more difficult than moving on the edge of a sword, riding on a tiger and wearing a serpent. The Kaulic literature criticizes sternly those who violate this admonition and use *Kaula-saadhanaa* for sensual enjoyment.[582]

In this manner, *Kaula-saadhanaa* proclaims the ideal of the sanctity of the world and sexuality. It claims that accepting them as holy and transforming them would help one to transcend them without denying them their true value, thereby facilitating the seeker to arrive at his life's destiny, i.e., the realization of the Lord *Siva*.

3.4.2.8. CELEBRATION OF FESTIVALS

In the religious life of a devout Saivite, festivals are significant moments to open the self to the grace of the Lord *Siva* and to experience His benevolence and love. Festivals with their special forms of worship charge the total atmosphere with religious fervor. Some of these festivals are related to places of pilgrimages, which make the people visit these holy places during the festival days. In this section, we consider some of the Saivite festivals.

One of the festivals celebrated with great religious devotion is the lighting festival at Arunaacalam, which is another name for Thiruvannamalai. It is believed that on the top of the Hill at Arunaacalam, the goddess *Parvatii*, the consort of Lord *Siva*, performed penances and visualized Him as *Arunaacalesvara*, the Lord of Arunaacalam. For this reason this place is considered a very important holy place of the Saivities. This place, situated in Tamilnadu, is famous for its festival of light. It consists in lighting the *Kartigai Diipam* every year at the month of *Kartigai* (November). It is lighted on the day when the full moon falls in a star named *Kartigai* (*Kartigai Nakshatram*), at about 5:30 in the evening. On the top of the hill there is a big hollow rock. It is filled with melted butter (*Ghee*), oil and camphor. A big wick is put in the oil and lighted. It burns continuously for three months. During the day, a veil is put around the light. At about 5:30 in the evening, when the *Kartigai Nakshatram* dawns, a firework (*Bhaana*) is sent towards the light in the hill through the sky. The man in charge of lighting the *Diipam* removes the veil as he sees the firework. People see the light and worship, *Siva*, the Lord of the light at Arunaacalam, chanting the *Mantra* '*Harahara, Harohara*'. It is said that the light may be seen from as far as 16 miles away from Arunaacalam. The light burning at the top of the hill at Arunaacalam represents the Lord *Siva*, who is the Supreme Soul (*Parmaatman*). The firework (*Bhaana*) dispatched towards the light though the sky is symbolic of the individual soul (*Jiivaatman*), which is engaged in meditation and contemplation. The veil that is removed by the one in charge of the light, is the ignorance (*Avidya*). Just as the *Bhaana* removes the veil that covers the light and makes everyone see the light, similarly the removal of ignorance from the individual soul, by meditation and contemplation leads it to merger with the Supreme Soul, *Siva*, the Light of lights. Thus, the festival of lighting at Arunaacalam brings to every Saivite the message that the Lord *Siva* is the self-effulgent (*Jyotis-Svarupa*) Light of lights, Sun of suns. One who sees this Light of lights that is burning eternally in the cave of one's heart through constant meditation attains immortality. It is believed that this light has great spiritual powers. Anyone who beholds this light is said not to have any future births. The *Yogi*, who perceives this light during his meditation, is believed to merge with the Lord *Siva* in *Nirvikalpa Samaadhi*. During the three months, when the light is kept burning, thousands of people visit Arunaacalam to have a *Darsana* of the Lord *Arunaacalesvara*, the Light of lights.[583]

Another important Saiva festival is the *Mahaasivaraatri* that commemorates the wedding day of Lord *Siva* and *Parvatii*. It falls on the 13th day (*Thrathshi*) of the waning moon in the month of *Phagun* (Feruary-March). This festival is celebrated with great gaiety and religious fervor by the Saivites of Kashmir. They celebrate it for 16 days, but the actual wedding of *Siva* and *Parvati* is celebrated for four days, viz., from the 12th to the 15th day. Already from the 11th day, actual preparations for the *Puuja* begins by way of decorating the *Puuja* room, getting earthen pots (*Gaggars*) ready with *Puuja* offerings and similar activities. On the 12th day, special *Puuja* is done to Lord *Ganesh*. The 13th day is the actual wedding day of *Siva* and *Parvatii*, i.e., the day of *Mahaasivaraatri*. Special *Puuja* and elaborate ceremonies involving the sounding of conch shell, waving of lamps (*Aarti*) and singing of hymns in praise of *Siva* and *Parvatii* are done on this day. On the 14th day, the father, mother, brother and sisters invite the daughters and sons-in-law for a special meal. The meal is sumptuous, consisting of meat, fish, chicken and vegetables. The sons-in-law are given money for a drink (*Pyala*). Children in the family are given money to buy gifts. On this day people greet each other and send sweets and *Prasaad*. The 15th day is the end of the wedding festivities. The earthen pots and other things used for *Puuja* are collected and immersed in the nearest river or lake. In other parts of Northern India, the celebration of this festival is confined to the temples and is celebrated only on the 14th and 15th day of the waxing moon. The priests perform *Puuja* with the accompaniment of chanting of the *Mantras*. People visit temples to honor the Lord *Siva* and his consort *Parvatii*, especially by performing *Abhisheka* and *Parikrama* to the *Sivalinga*. They also undertake a fast in preparation for the festival. This festival of Lord *Siva* is celebrated with great religious fervor.[584]

There are a number of festivals that honor the Lord *Siva*, especially in the aspect of His *Sakti*. These festivals aim at worshipping the Mother aspect of the Godhead, which is a source of power, prosperity and learning. One such festival is *Vijaya Dasami*. It falls on the tenth day of the bright half of the lunar month of *Asvina*. It is a soul-stirring festival that proclaims the victory good over evil that God the Mother brings about in the lives of Her children. It is on this day that boys are put in school and taught their first lessons. Similarly, the aspirants are initiated on this day. Besides, it is on this day that every artisan does *Puuja* to his instrument of work (*Aayudha Puuja*). In performing this *Puuja* to the instrument of his work, the artisan recognizes the *Sakti* behind the instrument and worships the Mother (*Devii*) for his success, prosperity and peace. Similarly, there are a other festivals honoring the Mother aspect of God, celebrated in different names in different parts of the country. They are *Dassera*, *Durga Puuja*, *Navaraatri* and *Gauri Puuja*.[585]

The celebration of various festivals in honor of the Lord *Siva* and His *Sakti* is, indeed, a great means to come in touch with the power of the Lord in its manifestations. Therefore, these festivals do serve as true paths to encounter and experience the Lord *Siva*, the supreme God of Saivism.

In this essay on Saivism, we have explored the origin of Saivism and the development of its various sects, by way of introduction, and have proceeded to explore *Siva*, the Lord of Saivism and the various paths different Saiva traditions propose for *Siva*-realization. Saivism as a religion is founded on the conception of *Siva* as the supreme God, who is related to the world through His power. Though He is transcendent Pure Consciousness in Himself, He gives Himself to the devotee as his unique personal God, omnipotent, omniscient, the only Lord and cause of the universe, in whom the devotee can find solace in times of his trouble and pain. Though eternally existent in His uniqueness in Himself, the Lord *Siva* is immanent in every reality, especially in the hearts of human persons, and directs them to their final destiny of being one with Him through the power that is operative in the world. Thus, Saivism presents its God, *Siva*, as both transcendent and immanent, impersonal and personal, eternal unqualified existence and temporal qualified presence. Thus, *Siva* is the God whom sages can approach through contemplation, while the ordinary people can arrive at Him through simple ways of worship. Similarly, the various types of paths Savism uses to encounter its God move from simple forms of devotions to more complex practices that call for great disciplining of human body, mind and spirit. For instance, practices, such as *Abhisheka*, the recital and writing of the great Saivite *Mantra*, the offering of *Puuja* to the Lord *Siva*, devotional practices – such as, taking of the *Prasaad*, making of pigrimages, taking of *Parikramas* – and the celebration of the festivals are so simple and easy that any ordinary individual can practice them, encounter the Lord *Siva* and enter into union with Him. On the other hand, the practice of *Nirgunaa* meditation and the Saiva Tantric practice, both in the right-hand and left-hand approach, call for much greater physical, mental and spiritual discipline. Saivism is a religion that believes in a God who is open to all, both to the great and to the small. Similarly, it proposes a path of religious practice that can take to God people of differing physical, mental and spiritual competence (*Adhikaarii-bheda*). Without any doubt, Saivism is a religion for all.

CONCLUSION

We have elaborately explored the Hindu tradition in the above four sections, viz., Vedic Hinduism, Vedaantic Hinduism, Vaishnavism and Saivism. These clearly manifest the divergent nature of the Hindu religious tradition. Firstly, we find this divergence relating to the development of the concept of the Divine in the four phase of the Hindu religious tradition. Vedic Hinduism proposes a multitude of gods, yet we find that there is a tendency in the early Vedic literature to move towards the unification of gods into one God. In the hymns of *Rig Veda*, we have a number of references to this unification. For instance, a hymn speaks of an 'Unknown God'. *Prajaapati* is mentioned as the God of all, and the *Purusha Suukta* also speaks of one God. In the mystical tradition of Vedaantic Hinduism this tendency of unification of the gods into one God moves further and a non-dualism emerges, which sees ultimate Reality as the One, with its transcendental and phenomenal aspects. But towards the end of the Vedaantic period, with the development of the *Bhakti* cult in the writings of Raamaanuja, Madhva and others, there is again a definitive movement towards clear monotheism. Vaishnavism and Saivism represent this monotheistic tradition. Even these monotheistic religious traditions of Vaishnavism and Saivism in their view God both are transcendental and immanent aspects. The concept of the *Avataara* of Lord *Vishnu* in Vaishnavism and the concept of *Sakti* of the Lord *Siva* in Saivism point to the immanent aspect of the supreme God as active in the world respectively.

Similarly, the paths proposed to reach the Divine are also different, even though there are similarities. In Vedic Hinduism, daily prayers and practices, domestic cult, priesthood, sacrifices, temple worship, moral living, expiation and purification, sacramental acts and other special observances - like astrology, omens, auspicious days in the week and the month, charms to appease demons, ghosts and wandering spirits – play an important role in helping people to ward off the evil that comes in their lives and to lead them to God. In the mystical Vedaantic Hinduism, though many of the Vedic paths to the gods are still practiced in popular Hinduism, specified paths to reach the Divine emerge due to the way the Divine is perceived. Four major paths to the Divine viz., the Path of Knowledge (*Jnaanayoga*), the Path of Devotion (*Bhaktiyoga*), the Path of Unselfish Action (*Karmayoga*) and the Path of Disciplining the Mind (*Raajayoga*) emerge as an aids to meditation and God-realization. Each of these paths is suited to people who are of different temperament and character. Similarly, if we turn our attention to the Vaishnava and Saiva religious traditions, we find, though many of the paths of both Vedic and Vedaantic Hinduism are found in them, still the attitude of *Bhakti* towards the Lord *Vishnu* is dominant in Vaishnavism, while devotion to the *Sakti* of the Lord *Siva* is the central religious attitude of Saivism. Thus, we find many differences in the paths people use in the different phases of the religious life of Hindu tradition.

Despite these diversities of Hindu religious beliefs and practices, the foundational unity in the Hindu tradition pervades. This foundationl unity consists in the deep spiritual perspective with which the whole universe is viewed and understood. In fact, it is this spiritual perspective that makes it possible for seemingly contradictory elements of beliefs and practices to co-exist and to be integrated into a system. The long history of Hindu religious tradition has many times made such integration. For instance, as a reaction against the ritualism of Hinduism, Jainism and Buddhism emerge, threatening its existence as a religion. But Hindu religious tradition has integrated the Jain and Buddhist elements so well that both of these religions lose their significance within the country of their birth. Thus, the underlying spiritual perspective of reality helps Hinduism to adopt such diversities and adapt them suitably so as to make an integrated whole, in the process, giving each adaptation sufficient autonomy.

Besides, the religious practice of Hindu tradition is not without aberrations that have social and cultural implications. The religious practice of the Hindus, over history, has cultivated an exaggerated sense of purity that considered some people and things as permanently impure and unholy. This has led to the social evil of the caste system and untouchability. Likewise, many superstitious practices that are prevalent in the Hindu society have their origin in the Hindu religious practice. We find Hindu religious practice degenerating into eroticism, authorizing religious cults that involve seduction and sex abuse in the name of religion. This form of anomaly is clearly seen in the Vaishnava *Krshna-bakti* cult and the Saiva *Sakti* cult, which in some form is present even today in the practice of keeping temple maids (*Deevadaasiis*). Over the centuries these evils and many other practices such as bride burning (*Sati*) and child marriage are perpetuated in the name of religion, giving them a religious sanction.

Without any doubt these defects mar the sanctity and richness of the Hindu religious tradition. But such eccentricities are not uncommon in any religion. It has to do more with the men and woman who practice the religion rather than the religion itself. These abnormal practices creep up, develop and mature in the life of a religion because of the selfishness of people, who interpret the directives of the religion to their own personal advantage. Over its history, Hindu religious tradition has recognized many such evil practices and changed them, due to the efforts of the great saints who revived it. Hinduism believes God as working in history and upholding the values that sustain the universe. We can hope that such interventions of God in history will remove the existing evils in the Hindu religious tradition and make it serve as a means that leads people to God.

NOTES

1 John A. Hardon, Vol. I, p. 47.
2 D.S. Sharma, *What is Hinduism?* (Madras: G.S. Press, 1939), p. 10.
3 Cf. Jesuit Scholars, *Religious Hinduism: A Presentation and Appraisal*, (Allahabad: St. Paul Publications, 1964), p. 23.
4 S. Radhakrishnan, *The Hindu View of Life* (New York: Macmillan, 1927), p. 91.
5 Cf. D. S. Sharma, *Essence of Hinduism* (Bombay: Bharatiya Vidya Bhavan, 1971), pp. 11-12. Cf. also Jesuit Scholars, p. 31. There are differences between the various sects of Hinduism as to the books included in *Sruti* and *Smrti*. Just to give an illustration of this controversy, we could mention the *Gita*, which some sects consider as *Sruti*, while others consider it as *Smrti*.
6 Jesuit Scholars, p. 31.
7 Cf. Ibid.
8 Cf. Ibid., pp. 31-33. Cf. also S.D. Sharma, *Essence of Hinduism*, p. 11.
9 Cf. Jesuit Scholars, p. 34.
10 Cf. D.S. Sharma, *Essence of Hinduism*, p. 12.
11 Cf. Ibid., pp. 12-14. Cf. also Jesuit Scholars, pp. 34-35.
12 This division should not be understood strictly, as many legendary stories and mythological narratives about a god are found also in *Puraanas* that do not refer to him directly. This categorization of the *Puraanas* is more open and general. Cf. Jesuit Scholars, pp. 35-36.
13 Cf. Jesuit Scholars, p. 35. Cf. also D.S. Sharma, *Essence of Hinduism*, pp. 14-15.
14 Cf. D.S. Sharma, *Essence of Hinduism*, pp. 15-16. Cf. also Jesuit Scholars, p. 36.
15 Cf. D.S. Sharma, *Essence of Hinduism*, pp. 16-18.
16 Cf. D.S. Sharma, *Essence of Hinduism*, pp. 18-19.
17 Ibid., p. 19.
18 Cf. Jesuit Scholars, p. 114.
19 Cf. Ibid., p. 115. Cf. also Ninian Smart, p. 89.
20 Ralph T.H. Griffith (trans.), *The Hymns of the Rig Veda* (Delhi: Motilal Banasidass Publishers Private Limited, 1986), X, 90, 4: 11-12 (Hereafter: RV).

21 Cf. K.M. Sen, *Hinduism*, (Middlesex: Penguin Books, 1975), pp. 27-31. Cf. also Jesuit Scholars, pp. 114-116.
22 Cf. G. Buehler, *The Laws of Manu, The Sacred Book of the East*, F. Max Mueller (ed.), Vol. 25, (Delhi: Motilal Banarsidass, 1979), II, 177-80 (Hereafter: LM).
23 Cf. LM, III, 55-103.
24 Cf. Ibid., VI, 1-32.
25 Cf. Ibid., VI, 45-49.
26 Cf. Ibid., V, 148.
27 Cf. Jesuit Scholars, p. 111. Cf. also S.D. Sharma, *Essence of Hinduism*, pp. 39-40.
28 D.S. Sharma, *Essence of Hinduism*, p. 40.
29 Cf. Jesuit Scholars, pp. 108-109. Cf. also D.S. Sharma, *Essence of Hinduism*, pp. 53-54.
30 Cf. S.D. Sharma, *Essence of Hinduism*, pp. 55-56.
31 Cf. Ibid., pp. 54-55, 56-59.
32 Cf. David Kinsley, *Hindu Goddesses: Visions of the Divine Feminine in the Hindu Religious Tradition*, (Delhi: Motilal Banarsidass, 1986), p. 6.
33 Cf. RV. I, 175: 2; IV, 16: 5.
34 *Soma* juice is the drink that brings immortality. It is extracted from the roots of the *Soma* plant, which is yellow in color. The sacred juice is obtained by pressing the roots through a woolen filter into a container having milk and water. It is an exhilarating drink that gives supernatural power and immortality to the gods. Some authors are of the opinion that though it is an exhilarating drink, it is not intoxicating liquor. The reason they give is that the Vedic texts consider drunkenness as one of the seven heinous sins that one should avoid. Besides the preparation of the *Soma* juice differs from the way liquor is made. Vedic hymns also speak of *Soma* as a deity of the terrestrial region. We will elaborate on *Soma* as a deity later. Cf. R.C. Zaehner, *Hinduism*, (London: Oxford University Press, 1966), p. 21. Cf. also N.B. Pavgee, "*Soma* Juice is not Liquor", *Proceedings and Transactions of the Third Oriental Conference* (Madras: University of Madras, 1924), pp. 70, 71. Cf. also RV, IX, 97: 14; 96: 22-24; 100: 2.
35 Cf. RV, IX, 100: 5-6; III, 9: 1.
36 Cf. Ibid., I, 85: 1-11.
37 Cf. Ibid., I, 159: 1-5.
38 Ibid., I, 164: 33.
39 Cf. Ibid., IV, 56: 6.
40 Cf. Ibid., I, 185: 5.
41 Cf. Ibid., VI, 70: 1-6.
42 Cf. Ibid., 56: 1-7.
43 Ibid., I, 160: 1, 3-4.
44 Cf. Kurien Mathothu, *The Development of the Concept of Trimuurti in Hinduism*, (Palai: St. Paul's Press Training School, 1974), p. 11.
45 Cf. A.B. Keith, p. 88.
46 RV, V, 3: 1.

47 Cf. Kurien Mathothu, p. 9. Cf. also RV, I, 22: 17.
48 RV, I, 164: 46.
49 Ibid., X, 114: 5.
50 Cf. Ninian Smart, p. 90.
51 Cf. RV, I, 32: 4, 5, 9, 15; 33: 2, 8.
52 Cf. Ninian Smart, p. 90.
53 Cf. Swami Harshananda, p. 167.
54 Cf. RV, X, 90: 1-16. Cf. also Kurien Mathothu, pp. 51-52.

55 The name *'Prajaapati'* is formed from two Sanskrit words *'praja'* and *'pati'*. The former means 'offspring', 'children', 'progeny' and 'procreation' while the latter means 'lord', 'master', 'husband' and 'king'. So *Prajaapati* is the Lord of creatures, the one who presides over procreation and the protector of life. He is the Supreme Being, who is above all the Vedic gods. Cf. Kurien Mathothu , p. 45, Fn. 58.

56 Cf. RV. X, 121: 1-10. Cf. also Kurien Mathothu, pp. 45-46.
57 Cf. A.B. Keith, p. 58.
58 Cf. Swami Harshananda, pp. 164-165.

59 Cf. A.B. Keith, *Religion and Philosophy of the Veda*, (London: Oxford University, 1925), p. 87. Cf. also Kurien Mathothu, pp. 6-8.

60 RV, X, 125: 1.

61 Cf. Swami Harshananda, *Hindu Gods and Goddesses*, (Madras: Sri Ramakrishna Math, 1982), p. 13. In the later Hindu literature these eight *Rudras* represent the eight aspects of the *Rudraa-Siva*. Cf. Ibid.

62 Cf. Ibid., p. 12. Cf. also Kurien Mathothu, p. 27.

63 Cf. Helmer Ringgren, p. 308. Kurien Mathothu, p. 27. Cf. also RV, IV, 3: 6.

64 Cf. RV, II, 33: 5. Many authors say that this quality of *Rudra* being merciful and benevolent is a post-Vedic quality. The Svetaasvatara Upanishad considers him as 'the god with the white mule' and is devoted to praising *Rudra* as the one God. Cf. Helmer Ringgren, p. 308. Other thinkers consider the attribution of gracious qualities to *Rudra* as an attempt on the part of the Vedic poets to give him a place in the group of major gods of the Vedic period. Cf. Kurien Mathothu, p. 28. But we could say that the milder and auspicious qualities are not altogether missing in *Rudra*, though he is a terrible god, who 'spites like a wild beast'.

65 Cf. RV, II, 33: 2, 7.
66 Ibid., I, 114: 3-4.
67 Cf. Kurien Mathothu, p. 28.

68 The name *'Siva'* is not found in the *Rig Veda* as the name of a god. In fact, *Siva* is a pre-Aryan deity. It is due to the contact with the Aryan civilization, that the pre-Aryan *Siva* became *Rudra* in the *Vedas*. Cf. Ibid.

69 Cf. Swami Harshananda, pp. 12-13.
70 Cf. Ibid., p. 17.
71 Cf. Ibid., p. 7.
72 Cf. Ibid., p. 19.
73 Cf. RV, I, 37: 1-15.

74 Cf. Ibid., X, 81: 1.
75 Cf. Ibid., VII, 56: 1.
76 Cf. Ibid., I, 64: 2.
77 Cf. Ibid., I, 64:12.
78 Cf. Kurien Mathothu, p. 21, fn. 21.
79 Cf. RV, I, 64, 11-15.
80 Cf. Swami Harshananda, p. 10.
81 Cf. Ibid. Cf. also Helmer Ringgren, p. 309.
82 RV, I, 157: 2, 4 -6.
83 Cf. Ibid., X, 85: 1- 47
84 Cf. Ibid., VIII, 29: 8; 8:10.
85 Cf. David Kinsley, p. 8.
86 Cf. RV, I, 185: 1-2.
87 Cf. Ibid., I, 22:13-16.
88 Cf. Ibid., I, 185: 8.
89 Cf. Ibid., X, 63: 10.
90 Cf. Ibid., I, 159: 1-5.
91 David Kinsley, pp. 6-7
92 Cf. Swami Harshananda, p. 10. Cf. also Helmer Ringgren, p. 306. Cf. also Kurien Mathothu, p. 19.
93 Cf. RV, I, 30: 11-12.
94 Cf. Ibid., IV, 18: 12; III, 48: 4.
95 Cf. Ibid., I, 21: 1, 3.
96 Cf. Ibid., V, 86: 3-5.
97 Cf. Ibid., X, 89: 2.
98 Cf. Ibid., VII, 82 – 85.
99 Cf. Ibid., IV, 42: 1-10.
100 Cf. Kurien Mathothu, p. 21.
101 Cf. RV, I, 29: 2.
102 Cf. Ibid., X, 89: 1.
103 Cf. Ibid., II, 13: 9; 30: 2.
104 Ibid., I, 32: 1, 3, 9-10.
105 Cf. Swami Harshananda, pp. 10-11.
106 RV, X, 89: 10.
107 Ibid., I, 32: 4.
108 Ibid., I, 32: 15.
109 Cf. Swami Harshananda, p. 12.
110 Cf. Ibid., p. 8. Cf. also Kurien Mathothu, p. 23.
111 Cf. RV, IV, 1: 1; IX, 91: 18.
112 Ibid., I, 1: 1, 4-5, 8-9.
113 Cf. Ibid., V, 24: 4.
114 Cf. Ibid., VIII, 91: 9.
115 Cf. Ibid., V, 3: 1-3.
116 Cf. Ibid., I, 59: 2. Cf. also Swami Harshananda, p. 8.
117 Ibid., III, 9: 9.
118 Maurice Bloomfield, *Hymns of the Athava-Veda, Sacred Books of*

the East, ed. F. Max Mueller [Hereafter: SBE], Vol. 42 (Delhi: Motilal Banarsidass, 1979), XXII, 1: 19-21 (Hereafter: AV).

119 Cf. RV, VI, 8: 2; I, 143: 2.
120 Cf. Ibid., VI, 49: 27
121 Cf. Ibid., X, 88: 6; VIII, 44: 29.
122 Cf. Kurien Mathothu, p. 23.
123 Cf. RV, VII, 7: 5.
124 Cf. Ibid., X, 1: 2.
125 Cf. Ibid., VIII, 91:17.
126 Cf. Ibid., VI, 7: 4.
127 Cf. Ibid., V, 22: 2.
128 Cf. Cf. Kurien Mathothu, pp. 23-24.
129 Cf. RV, V, 18: 1. Cf. also Kurien Mathothu, p. 25.
130 Cf. Ibid., VII, 15: 7.
131 Cf. Swami Harshananda, p. 8.
132 Cf. RV, X, 2: 7.
133 Cf. Ibid., VI, 7: 4.
134 Cf. Ibid., V, 37: 1; VII, 2: 1.
135 Cf. Ibid., IV, 2: 5.
136 Cf. Ibid., I, 127: 4: VII, 1: 1. Cf. also Kurien Mathothu, p. 24.
137 Cf. Swami Harshananda, p. 8.

138 Cf. Ibid., p.15. Cf. also Helmer Ringgren, p. 305. Cf. also Kurien Mathothu, p. 16, Fn. 37. Cf. also Ninian Smart, p. 91.

139 Cf. RV, X, 37: 1; VII, 61: 1; 63: 1, 5.
140 Cf. Ibid., VI, 87: 1.
141 Cf. Ibid., I, 24: 8.

142 Cf. Helmer Ringgren, pp. 305-306. Cf. also Swami Harshananda, p. 15.

143 Cf. Kurien Mathothu, p. 17. Cf. also Helmer Ringgren, p. 305. Cf. also RV, VIII, 41: 7.

144 Since *Varuna* spies on everyone and everything in the universe, sometimes he is depicted as the unpredictable and a malevolent god from whom men pray to be saved. Sometimes he is also identified with *Rudra*, the destroyer, from whom no one can flee. To quote from *Atharva Veda*: "He that should flee beyond the heaven far away would not be free from king *Varuna*. His spies come hither (to the earth) from heaven, with a thousand eyes do they watch over the earth." AV, IV, 16: 4. Cf. also Helmer Ringgren, p. 305.

145 Cf. Kurien Mathothu, pp. 17-18. Cf. also Ninian Smart, p. 91. Cf. also Helmer Ringgren, p. 305. Cf. also Swami Harshananda, pp. 15-16. Cf. RV, I, 24: 14-15; VII, 89: 3.

146 Cf. Ninian Smart, p. 92. Cf. also Swami Harshananda, p. 17.
147 Cf. Ninian Smart, p. 93.
148 Cf. Swami Harshananda, p. 13.
149 Cf. RV, IX, 100: 2. Cf. also Ninian Smart, p. 94.
150 Cf. RV, I, 50: 1, 10.

151 Cf. Ibid., I, 22: 5; 23: 13; 24: 5; 46: 13; III, 59:1; VI, 53-59. Cf. also Kurien Mathothu, p. 13. Cf. also Swami Harshananda, pp. 14-15.
152 Cf. Kurien Mathothu, pp. 13-14. Cf. also Swami Harshananda, p.15. Cf. also RV, I, 160: 3.
153 Cf. Swami Harshananda, pp. 17-18.
154 Cf. A.B. Keith, p. 109. Cf. also Kurien Mathothu, pp. 28-29.
155 Cf. Swami Harshananda, p. 18.
156 RV, I, 154: 2. Cf. also Swami Harshananda, p. 18.
157 Cf. Kurien Mathothu, p. 29. Cf. also R.C. Zaehner, p. 34.
158 Cf. Swami Harshananda, p. 18.
159 Cf. Ibid., p. 19-20.
160 Cf. RV, I, 48: 1-16; 92: 1, 4-5.
161 Cf. Ibid., III, 61: 1-7; VII, 75: 1-8; I, 113: 12.
162 Cf. Ibid., I, 113: 12; III, 39: 3; VII, 81: 1-6; VI, 64: 6.
163 Cf. David Kinsley, pp. 7-8. Cf. also RV, VII, 77: 5.
164 RV, VII, 1, 3-6.
165 Cf. AV, XII, 1: 6, 11, 18, 19.
166 Cf. Ibid., XII, I: 10.
167 Cf. Ibid., XII, I: 42, 60, 61.
168 Cf. Ibid., XII, 1: 27, 29.
169 Cf. Ibid., XII, 1: 4, 10.
170 Cf. Ibid., XII, I: 25.
171 David Kinsley, p. 9.
172 Cf. Ibid.
173 Cf. RV, II, 27: 14; VIII, 67: 14.
174 Cf. Ibid., I, 136: 3.
175 Cf. Ibid., II, 27: 1-17; I, 113: 19.
176 Cf. Ibid., I, 153: 3.
177 Cf. Ibid., I, 106: 7; 94: 15. In the *Braahmanas* the goddesses *Aditi* and *Prthivii* become practically identified. Cf. Julius Eggeling, *The Satapatha-Braahmana* [Hereafter: SB], SBE, Vol. 12, (Delhi: Motilal Banarsidass, 1978), II, 2, 1, 19.
178 Cf. RV, VI, 61: 2, 8, 11-12; VII, 95: 1-2; V, 43: 11.
179 Cf. Ibid., II, 41: 16.
180 David Kinsley, p. 11.
181 Cf. RV, VII, 96: 4-6; I, 164: 49.
182 Cf. Ibid., VII, 95: 1, 5.
183 Cf. David Kinsley, pp. 11, 15.
184 Cf. RV, I, 3:10; VI, 61: 3; X, 17: 10.
185 Cf. Ibid., I, 10-12.
186 David Kinsley, p. 11.
187 Cf. RV, X, 125: 1-8.
188 David Kinsley, pp. 11-12.
189 Cf. RV, VIII, 89: 10; III, 53: 15-16.
190 Cf. Ibid., VIII, 89: 11; IV, 1: 16.
191 Cf. Ibid., X, 71: 1-11.

192 David Kinsley, p. 12.
193 Ibid., p. 14.
194 Cf. RV, I, 34: 1; V, 5: 6; X, 127: 6. Cf. also AV, XIX, 47: 2; 48: 3, 6; 49: 4.
195 Cf. RV., X, 3: 1; 172: 4; I, 92: 11; 122: 2
196 Cf. Ibid., X, 59: 1-4. Cf. also David Kinsley, p. 13.
197 Cf. David Kinsley, pp. 14 -17.
198 Cf. Jesuit Scholars, p. 150. Cf. also John A. Hardon, Vol. 1, p. 73.

199 The *Gaayatrii* invocation reads as follows: "*Asotama sat gamaya; Tamasyoma joythir gmaya; Mirthyoma amirtham gamaya; Om Shanti, Shanti, Shanti.*" It is rendered in English as " Lead me from untruth to truth; Lead me from darkness to light; Lead me from mortality to immortality; Oh Peaace, Peace, Peace".

200 Cf. Jesuit Scholars, pp. 150-151. Cf. also John A. Hardon, Vol. 1, p. 73.
201 Cf. Jesuit Scholars, p. 151. Cf. also John A. Hardon, Vol. 1, pp. 73-74.
202 Cf. Jesuit Scholars, pp. 151-152. Cf. John A. Hardon, Vol. 1, p. 74.
203 Cf. Jesuit Scholars, p. 152. Cf. also. John A. Hardon, Vol. 1, p. 74.
204 Cf. Helmer Ringgren, p. 319.
205 Cf. Ibid.
206 Cf. Jesuit Scholars, p. 142. Cf. also Nirad C. Chauduri, *Hinduism: A Religion to Live By*, 5th Impression, (Oxford: Oxford University Press, 1999), p. 164.
207 Cf. Nirad C. Chauduri, pp.164 -165. Cf. also Jesuit Scholars, p. 143.
208 Cf. Nirad C. Chaudhuri, pp. 166-167.
209 Cf. John A. Hardon, p. 74.
210 Cf. Helmer Ringgren, p. 315.
211 Cf. Ibid. Cf. also SB, I, 1, 1, 7.
212 RV, X, 175: 1-4.
213 Cf. Helmer Ringgren, p. 315.
214 Cf. Ibid., pp. 315-316. Cf. also RV, IV, 15: 5; 51: 8.
215 Cf. Helmer Ringgren, p. 316.
216 Cf. Ibid., pp. 316-317.
217 Cf. Ibid., pp. 317, 324.
218 Cf. Ibid., p. 317.
219 Cf. Ibid.
220 Cf. Jesuit Scholars, p. 152.
221 Cf. Ibid.
222 Cf. Helmer Ringgren, pp. 317-318.
223 Cf. Ibid., p. 318.
224 Cf. Ibid.
225 Cf. Ibid., p. 315.
226 Cf. Jesuit Scholars, pp. 153-154. Cf. also John A. Hardon, Vol. 1, p. 75.

227 Cf. Jesuit Scholars, pp. 153, 154. Cf. also John A. Hardon, Vol. 1, pp. 74-75.
228 Cf. Helmer Ringgren, pp. 320-321.
229 RV. X, 14: 7.
230 Cf. Ibid., p. 321-322.
231 Cf. Jesuit Scholars, p. 122. Cf. also Helmer Ringgren, p. 322.
232 RV, I, 23: 22.
233 Ibid., X, 164: 3.
234 Ibid., I, 24: 15.
235 Cf. Helmer Ringgren, p. 323. Cf. also Jesuit Scholars, p. 123. A clear classification of sin is found in the Sacred Law of the Hindus (*Dharma Sastras*). It classifies sins as the sins beyond classification (*Ati-pataka*), the great sins (*Maha-Pataka*), the mortal sins (*Anu-pataka*) and the venial sins (*Upa-pataka*). Besides giving this classification, it also lists sins included in each of these groupings and prescribes detailed expiatory measures. Cf. Nirad C. Chaudhuri, pp. 198-200.
236 RV, V, 85: 7-8.
237 Ibid., VII, 89: 1-5.
238 Ibid., VII, 86: 2, 4, 7-8.
239 Cf. Rajbali Pandey, *Hindu Samskaaras: Socio-Religious Study of the Hindu Sacraments*, (Delhi: Motilal Banarsidass, 1987), pp. 15-16. Cf. also Jesuit Scholars, p. 159.
240 Rajbli Pandey, pp. 16-17.
241 Cf. Ibid., pp. 25-35.
242 Cf. Ibid., pp. 36-47.
243 Cf. Ibid., pp. 1, 15, 17.
244 Cf. Ibid., pp. xvii - xxvi, 17-24.
245 Cf. Ibid., pp. 48-69. Cf. also Jesuit Scholars, p. 159.
246 Cf. Rajbali Pandey, pp. 70-77. Cf. also Jesuit Scholars, pp. 159-160.
247 Cf. Rajbali Pandey, pp. 78-85. Cf. also Jesuit Scholars, p. 160.
248 Cf. Rajbali Pandey, pp. 86-89.
249 Cf. Ibid., pp. 90-93.
250 Cf. Ibid., pp. 94-101.
251 Cf. Ibid., pp. 102-105.
252 Cf. Ibid., pp. 106-110.
253 Cf. Ibid., pp. 111-140. Cf. also Jesuit Scholars, p160-161.
254 Cf. Ibid.
255 Cf. Ibid.
256 Cf. Rajbali Pandey, pp. 141-142.
257 Cf. Ibid., pp.143-145.
258 Cf. Ibid., pp.146-152.
259 For an elaborate study of *Vivaaha Samskaara* Cf. Ibid. pp. 153-233.
260 Cf. Jesuit Scholars, p. 162.
261 Cf. Ibid., pp. 162-163.

262 Cf. Ibid., pp. 163-164.
263 Cf. Rajbali Pandey, pp. 234-243.
264 Cf. AV, VII, 53: 1-7.
265 Cf. Ibid., V, 19: 4, 12.
266 Cf. Ibid., VIII, 1: 19; IX, 2: 11.
267 Cf. Ibid., XVII, 2: 57-60.
268 Cf. RV, X, 18: 7. Cf. also AV, VIII, 3: 1-2.
269 Cf. AV, VIII, 2: 4, 8. Cf. also RV, X, 16: 4.
270 Cf. RV, X: 16: 3.
271 Cf. Ibid., X, 18: 11, 13.
272 Cf. Ibid., X: 14: 7-8.
273 Cf. AV, XII, 2: 39-44.
274 Cf. RV, X, 15: 1-14.
275 Cf. Ibid., X, 18: 3.
276 Cf. Rajbali Pandey, pp. 245-274.
277 Cf. Jesuit Scholars, p. 155.
278 Cf. Ibid., pp. 155-156.
279 Cf. AV, VIII, 5: 1-22; X, 3: 1-25, 6: 1-35.
280 Cf. Jesuit Scholars, pp. 156-157.
281 Cf. RV, I, 164: 46.
282 Cf. Ibid., X, 90: 1-16.
283 Cf. Ibid., X, 121: 1-10.
284 Ibid., X, 129: 1-7.
285 Cf. Ninian Smart, pp. 95-96. Cf. also Kurien Mamothu, pp. 50-51.

286 Cf. Radhakrishnan, S., *The Principal Upanishads*, 3rd impression, (London: George Allen & Unwin Ltd., 1969), pp. 52-53. Cf. also Kurien Mathothu, pp. 33-34.

287 Cf. Swami Nihilananda, *Hinduism: Its Meaning for the Liberation of the Spirit*, (Madras: Sri Ramakrishna Math, 1982), p. 29.

288 Cf. Kurien Mathothu, pp. 31-32. Cf. also Swami Nihilananda, p. 30.

289 Cf. "*Kena Upanishad*", *The Principal Upanishads*, ed. Rathakrishnan S., I, 3 (Hereafter: Ke.U.).

290 Cf. Swami Nihilananda, *Hinduism: Its Meaning for the Liberation of the Spirit*, p. 31.

291 Cf. Ke.U., I, 4.

292 Ibid., I, 5-9.

293 Cf. "*Brhad-aaranyaka Upanishad*", *The principle Upanishads*, ed. Radhakrishnan S., IV, 1: 2-7(Hereafter: BU). Cf. also "*Taittiriiya Upanishad*", *The Principal Upanishads*, ed. Radhakrishnan S., III, 1: 1 (Hereafter: TU).

294 Cf. "*Chaandogya Upanishad*", *The Principal Upanishads*, ed. Radhakrishnan S., III, 12: 78 (Hereafter: CU).

295 Cf. BU, II, 4: 12.

296 Swami Nihilananda, *Hinduism: Its Meaning for the Liberation of the Spirit*, pp. 34-35.

297 Cf. Ibid., pp. 36-38. Cf. also Kurien Mathothu, pp. 32, 40-41. Cf.

also. Mahendranath Sircar, The *System of Vedic Thought and Culture*, (New Delhi: Anmol Publications, 1987), p. 128.

298 Cf. Swami Nihilananda, *Hinduism: Its Meaning for the Liberation of the Spirit*, p. 37.

299 Cf. Swami Gambhrananda, trans., *Brahma-Suutra Bhaashya*, 3rd ed., (Calcutta: Advaita Ashrama, 1977), I, 1: 1, pp. 11-12 (Hereafter: BSB). Cf. Also Radhakrishnan, S., *The Principal Upanishads*, p. 52.

300 Ramkant A. Sinari, *The Structure of Indian Thought*, (Illinois: Charles E. Thomas Publisher, 1970), p. 67.

301 Cf. George Thibaut, trans., *Brahma-Slutras*, (Mayavata: Advaita Ashrama, 1948), pp. xxiv-xxv (Hereafter: BSB, Thaibaut).

302 Cf. Shankara, *Aatmabhoodha [Knowledge of the Self]*, trans. A. Parthasarathy, 3rd ed., (Bombay: Vedaanta Life Institute, 1960), no. 36, pp. 74-76 [Hereafter: AB, Parthasarathy]. Cf. Also A. Parthasarathy, *Vedaanta Treatise*, 3rd ed., (Bombay: Vedaanta Life Institute, 1989), pp. 304-307.

303 In interpreting the Upanishadic texts, Shankara is of the opinion that one must accept only those texts, which speak of *Brahman* without qualities and forms. "But other texts speaking of *Brahman* with form", he says, "have the injunctions about meditations as their main objectives. So long as they do not lead to some contradictions, their apparent meaning should be accepted. But, when they involve contradictions, the principle to be followed for deciding one or the other is that those that have the formless *Brahman* as their main purport are more authoritative than the other, which have not that as their main purpose. It is according to this that one is driven to the conclusion that *Brahman* is formless and not its opposite." Cf. BSB, III, 2: 14, p. 612.

304 BU, IV, 4: 13.

305 Cf. BSB, III, 2: 16, pp. 613-614.

306 Cf. Ibid., III, 2: 18-20, pp. 615-617.

307 Cf. A. Parthasarathy, *Vedaanta Treatise*, pp. 303-304. Cf. Also Shankara, *Aprokshaanubhuuti(Self-realization) of Sri Shankaraachaariya*, trans. Swami Vimuktananda, (Calcutta: Advaita Ashrama, 1977), no. 64, p. 36 [Hereafter: AI].

308 Baskali asked Bhava three times about the nature of *Brahman*. The latter remained silence all three times. Finally he replied: "I have already spoken, but you cannot comprehend that self is silence". BSB, III, 2: 17, p. 614

309 Cf. Eliot Deutsch, *Advaita Vedaanta – A Philosophical Reconstruction*, 2nd ed., (Honolulu: The University Press of Hawaii, 1962), p. 9.

310 Cf. Radhakrishnan S., *The Principal Upanishads*, p. 73.

311 Cf. Shankara, *Self-knowledge (Aatmabhooda)*, trans. Swami Nihilananda, (New York: Ramakrishana Vivekananta Center, 1980), p. 118 (Hereafter: AB, Swami Nihilananda).

312 Cf. AB, A. Parthasarathi, no. 16, pp. 34-37.

313 Cf. Ibid., no.18, pp. 39-40.

314 Cf. AB, Swami Nihilananda, p. 133.

315 Cf. Ibid., p. 136. Cf. also Mahendranath Sircar, pp. 156-157.

316 Cf. AI, no. 60, p. 43.

317 Cf. Ibid., no. 61, pp. 34-35.
318 Cf. Ibid., no. 62, p. 35.
319 BU, III, 8: 1.
320 "*Chaanduukhya Upanishad*", *The Thirteen Principal Upanishads*, ed. Hume R.E., (New York: Princeton University Press, 1973), V, 9: 1, p. 234 (Hereafter: Ch.U.).
321 Paul Deusen, *The Philosophy of the Upanishads*, (New York: Dover Publications Inc., 1966), Pp.86-87.
322 BSB, I, 1: 1, pp. 11-12. Cf. also BU, II, 5: 19.
323 Shankara, *Crest-Jewel of Discrimination (Viveka-Chudaamani)*, trans. Swami Prabhavananda and Christopher Isherwood, 3rd ed., (California: Vedanta Press, 1978), p. 66 (Hereafter: VC).
324 Radhakrishnan S., *The Principal Upanishads*, pp. 73-74.
325 Cf. Ibid., p. 77.
326 CU, III, 14: 1.
327 BU, I, 4: 10
328 Ibid., III, 4: 1.
329 Ibid., III, 7: 3
330 CU, VI, 8: 7
331 S. Radhakrishnan, basing himself on the authority of A.B. Keith, claims that no one can deny that *Brhaman-Aatman* doctrine has a long history, originating from the Rig Veda, developing in the Brahmanas and culminating in the Upanishads. Cf. Radhakrishnan S., *The Principal Upanishads*, p. 77, fn. 3.
332 John Braisted Carman, *The Theology of Raamaanuja*, Indian Reprint, (Bombay: Ananthacharya Indological Research Institute, 1981), p. 67.
333 Cf. Ibid., pp. 88-91.
334 Cf. Ibid., pp. 98-113.
335 Cf. Ibid., pp. 158-166.
336 Cf. Ibid., pp. 114-123.
337 Cf. Ibid., pp. 176-186.
338 Cf. Ibid., pp. 124-175.
339 Cf. Ibid., pp. 93-94.
340 Cf. Jesuit Scholars, pp. 69-70.
341 Cf. B.N.K. Sharma, *Philosophy of Srii Madhvaacaarya*, (Delhi: Motilal Barsidass, 1986), pp. 323; 329 -33o, 343-348. Cf. also Jesuit Scholars, 70.
342 Cf. B.N.K. Sharma, pp. 324-325; 349-350. Cf. also Jesuit Scholars, pp. 70-71.
343 Cf. B.N.K. Sharma, pp. 253-263. Cf. also Jesuit Scholars, p. 71.
344 Cf. B.N.K. Sharma, pp. 290-305. Cf. also Jesuit Scholars, p. 71-72.
345 Cf. B.N.K. Sharma, pp. 306-319. Cf. also Jesuit Scholars, p. 71.
346 Cf. A. Parthasarathy, *Vedaanta Treatise*, p. 178.
347 Cf. Ibid., p. 186.
348 Cf. Mahendranath Sircar, pp. 219-220.

349 Cf. A. Parthasarathy, *Vedaantic Treatise*, p. 179.
350 Cf. Mahendranath Sircar, pp. 229-230.
351 Cf. Ibid., p. 230.
352 Cf. AI, no. 115, p. 61.
353 Cf. Ibid., nos. 119-120, pp. 63-64.
354 Ibid., no. 118, p. 62.
355 Cf. Mahendranath Sircar, pp. 230-231.
356 Cf. Shankara, "Statasloki", *The Works of Shankara*, Vol. XV (Srirangam: Srivanivilas, 1910), no. 40.
357 Cf. AB, Parthasarathy, p. 2.
358 Cf. Ibid., p. 3.
359 Cf. Ibid.
360 Cf. Ibid.
361 Cf. Ibid., p. 4.
362 Cf. CU, VI, 14: 2. Cf. also "*Mundaka Upanishad*", *The Principal Upanishads*, ed. Radhakrishnan S., I, 2: 11 (Hereafter: MU).
363 Cf. MU, I, 2:12.
364 Ibid., I, 2: 13.
365 Cf. Swami Nihilananda, trans, *Vedaantasaara of Sadaananda Yorindra*, (Calcutta: Advaita Ashrama, 1968), no. 182, p. 111 (Hereafter: VSS).
366 Cf. Ibid., nos. 183-184, p. 112. Cf. Also BSB, I, 1: 4, pp. 25, 30, fn. 62, 69.
367 Cf. VSS, nos. 185-190, pp. 112-115.
368 Shankara, "*Kena Upanishad Bhaasya*", *Upanishad Bhaasyas (Aitareeya, Iisha, Kaatha, Kena, Mundaka, Prasana and Taittiiriya Upanishads)*, trans. Swami Gambhirananda, Vol.2, (Calcutta: Advaita Ashrama, 1957), II, 1: 4, p. 25, fn. 62 (Hereafter: Ke.U.B.).
369 Ramamurthi A.: *Advaitic Mysticism of Shankara*. West Bengal: The Center of Advanced Study in Philosophy, Vishva Bharati, Shanti Niketan, 1974, p. 72.
370 Cf. VSS, no. 191, pp. 115-116.
371 Cf. AB, Swami Nihilananda, p. 42. Cf. Also VSS, no. 137, p. 86.
372 Cf. BSB, I, 1: 4, p. 25, fn. 62
373 Ramamurthi A., p. 72.
374 Cf. Radhakrishnan S., *The Bhagavadgiitaa*, 15th Impression, (New Delhi: HarperColins Publishers India Pvt. Ltd., 2000), XIII, 24 (Hereafter: BG).
375 AI, no. 123, p. 165.
376 Cf. Mahendranath Sircar, pp. 246-247.
377 Cf. Ibid., p. 247.
378 f. AB, Parthasarathy, pp. 60-62.
379 Cf. Ibid., pp. 63-64.
380 Cf. BG, XIII, 7-11, pp. 304-305.
381 Cf. A. Parthasarathy, *Vedaanta Treatise*, p. 178.
382 Cf. BG, p. 60. Cf. also Jesuit Scholars, p. 243.
383 Cf. BG, pp. 60-62. Cf. also Jesuit Scholars, pp. 243-244.

384 BG, p. 62.
385 Cf. Jesuit Scholars, p. 243.
386 Cf. BG, XII, 13-19, pp. 296-298.
387 Cf. Ibid., XII, 2, 20, pp. 291, 299. Cf. also Jesuit Scholars, pp. 243-244.
388 Cf. Jesuit scholars, pp. 244-245.
389 Cf. Ibid.
390 Cf. Ibid.
391 Cf. Ibid., pp. 244, 246.
392 Cf. Mahendranath Sircar, pp. 222-225.
393 Cf. Jesuit Scholars, pp. 247-248. Cf. also Ninian Smart, pp. 172-173.
394 Cf. Ibid.
395 Cf. Ibid.
396 Cf. Swami Nihilananda, *Hinduism: Its Meaning for the Liberation of the Spirit*, pp. 110-111.
397 Cf. A.Parthasarathy, *Vedaanta Treatise*, pp. 178-179. Cf. also Mahendranath Sircar, pp. 221-222.
398 Cf. A. Parthasarathy, *Vedaanta Treatise*, pp. 189-190. Cf. also BG, III, 36-43, pp. 147-150.
399 BG, III, 19, p. 138.
400 Ibid., pp. 67-68.
401 Cf. A.Parthasarathy, *Vedaanta Treatise*, p. p. 190.
402 Cf. BG, III, 30, p. 145.
403 Cf. A. Parthasarathy, *Vedaanta Treatise*, pp. 190-191.
404 BG, III, 30, p. 145; XVIII, 56-57, p. 372.
405 Ibid., XVIII, 66, p. 378.
406 Ibid.
407 Cf. Ibid., pp. 69-73, III, 20, p. 139.
408 Cf. Ibid., V, 3, p. 175.
409 Cf. H. Kumar Kaul, *Aspects of Yoga*, (Delhi: B.R. Publishing Corporation, 1994), p. 76. Cf. also Sri Swami Sivandanda, *Science of Yoga*, Vol. 5, (Tehri-Garhwal: The Divine Life Society, 1981), p. 19.
410 Cf. Sri Swami Sivananda, *Science of Yoga*, pp. 1-5.
411 Cf. Ibid., pp. 5-6. Cf. also H. Kumar Haul, pp.. 76, 78.
412 Cf. Sri Swami Sivananda, *Science of Yoga*, pp. 7-12. Cf also VSS, no. 201, p. 120.
413 Cf. Sri Sivananda Swami, *Science of Yoga*, pp. 13-18. Cf. also VSS, no. 202, p. 120.
414 Cf. Sri Sivananda Swami, *Science of Yoga*, pp. 19-22.
415 Cf. Ibid., pp. 23-27.
416 Cf. Ibid., pp. 27-31.
417 Cf. Ibid., pp. 30-31.
418 Cf. Ibid., pp. 33-34. Cf. also VSS, no. 205, p.121.
419 Cf. Sri Swami Sivananda, *Science of Yoga*, pp. 34-35.
420 Cf. Ibid., pp. 36-45.

421 Cf. Ibid., pp. 46-50.
422 Cf. H. Kumar Kaul, p. 78.
423 Cf. Sri Swami Sivananda, *Science of Yoga*, pp. 51-54.
424 Cf. Ibid., pp. 55-62.
425 Cf. S.M. Srinivasa Chari, *Vaishnavism: Its Philosophy, Theology and Religious Discipline*, (Delhi: Motilal Banarsidass Publishers Private Limited, 2000), pp. xxvi-xxviii, 35-39.
426 Cf. Ibid., p. 1.
427 Cf. H.V. Sreenivasa Murthy, *Vaishnavism of Samkaradeva and Raamaanuja*, (Delhi: Motilal Banarsidas, 1973), pp. 9-14.
428 Cf. H.V. Sreenivasa Murthy, p. 9.
429 Cf. RV, I, 22: 17-18; I, 154: 2. Cf. also H.V. Sreenivasa Murthy, pp. 9-10. Cf. also Kurien Mathothu, p. 29.
430 Cf. SB, I, 2, 5, 1-7.
431 Cf. H.V. Sreenivasa Murthy, p. 10. Cf. also "*Katha Upanishad*", *The Principal Upanishads*, ed. Radhakrishnan, I, 3: 9 (Hereafter: KU).
432 Cf. Rabindra Kumar Siddhantashastree, *Vaishnavism through the Ages*, (New Delhi: Munshiram Manoharlal Publishers Pvt. Ltd., 1985), pp. 5-7. Cf. also Swami Harshananda, p. 26. Cf. also A. Parthasarathy, *The symbolism of Hindu Gods and Rituals*, (Bombay: Vedanta Life Institute: 1989), p. 35.
433 Cf. H.V. Sreenivasa Murthy, pp. 10, 104. Cf. also Suvira Jaiswal, *The Origin and Development of Vaishnavism*, (New Delhi: Munshiram Manoharlal Publishers Pvt. Ltd., 1981), p. 33.
434 Cf. H.V. Sreenivasa Murthy, p. 105. Cf. also Swami Harshananda, pp. 27-28.
435 Cf. SM. Srinivasa Chari, pp. 132-134.
436 Cf. Ibid., pp. 185-199. Cf. also Sreenivasa Murthy, p. 13.
437 Julius Jolly, trans., *The Institutes of Vishnu*, SBE, Vol. 7, (Delhi: Motilal Banarsidass, 1977), (Hereafter: TIV).
438 Cf. Ibid., I, 19-38.
439 Cf. Ibid., I, 1-18.
440 Cf. Ibid., I, 39-43, 50. Many authors give different allegorical interpretations to this particular scene of the *Yoga-nidra* of *Vishnu-Naaraayana*. For two such interpretations refers to the following references. Cf. Swami Harshananda, pp. 28-29. Cf. also A. Parthasarathy, *The Symbolism of Gods and Rituals*, pp. 35-38.
441 Cf. TIV, I, 45-65.
442 Cf. Ibid., II –XCVII
443 Ibid., XCVIII, 2.
444 Cf. Ibid., XCVIII, 3-102.
445 Swami Harshananda, pp. 29-30. Cf. also A. Parthasarathy, *The Symbolism of Hindu Gods and Rituals*, pp. 38- 40.
446 Cf. Ibid.
447 Cf. David Kinsely, pp. 26, 28-29. Cf. also S.M. Srinivasa Chari, pp. 160-166. Though a number of Vaishnava sects would recognize the submis-

siveness of *Sri Lakshmi* to *Vishnu* and her permanent relationship with Him, a few other Vaishnava sects do not subscribe to this view. For instance, the Paancaraatra and Srii Vaishnava sects of Vaishnavism consider *Lakshmi* as a goddess on a par with *Vishnu*. They consider *Lakshmi* as infinite (*Vibhu*) by her essential nature. She is said to play a central role in creation. Besides, to her are attributed all the functions of the *Trimurthis*. She is identified with the *Sakti* of *Vishnu*, thereby presented as a dynamic power associated with the origin, growth and sustenance of every reality in the universe. *Lakshmi* is also believed to be a powerful and compassionate intermediary between the devotee and the Lord *Vishnu*. Cf. David Kinsley, pp. 29-32. Cf. also S.M. Srinivasa Chari, pp. 166-175.

448 Cf. TIV, XCIX, 3-4, 6.

449 Ibid., XCIX, 7-8, 22-23.

450 Cf. BG, IV, 5; V, 6-8. Cf. Kurien Mathothu, p. 66. Cf. also Suvira Jaiswal, p. 130.

451 Cf. BG, IV, 5-8; X, 12, 40. Cf. also Kurien Mathothu, pp. 66-67. Cf. also Suvira Jaiswal, pp. 130-131. Cf. also R.K. Pandey, *The Concept of Avatars* (Delhi: B.R. Publishing Corporation, 1979), pp. 7-10.

452 Cf. S.M. Srinivasa Chari, pp. 212-228.

453 Cf. Suvira Jaiswal, pp. 130-131. Cf. Rabindra Kumar Siddhantashastree, *Vaishnavism through the Ages*, pp. 85-106. Cf. also S.M. Srinivasa Chari, pp. 218-222.

454 In listing the major *Avataaras* of Lord *Vishnu*, there are a number of discrepancies. Authorities list differ. Some authorities consider, *Krshna* as *Vishnu* Himself and do not include *Krshna* in the list of major incarnations, and *Buddha* takes the place of *Krshna*. On the other hand, the *Vishnu, Bhaagavata* and *Brahmavaivartta Puraanas* count *Krshna* as the full-fledged incarnation and include him in the list of major incarnations, keeping *Balaraama*, the elder brother of *Krshna* out of the list. But in the daily worship of the *Braahmanas*, *Balaraama* is counted as the eighth incarnation of *Vishnu*. Besides, we find varieties of *Saalagraamas* representing *Balaraama*, while others represent *Krshna*. Taking into account these facts, we can arrive at the conclusion that originally *Balaraama*, as the elder brother of *Krshna*, is included in the list as the eighth incarnation, but with the passing of time the supporters of *Krshna* replace the latter with the former as the eighth incarnation. In some other lists, *Buddha* replaces *Balaraama*. In our presentation of *Avataaras* of *Vishnu*, we include the incarnations of *Balaraama, Krshna* and *Buddha*. Thus, we have a list of 11 *Avataaras*, of which 10 have already taken place, while the eleventh is yet to take place. Cf. Swami Harshananda, pp. 42, 44. Cf. also Rabindra Kumar Siddhantashastree, *Vaishnavism through the Ages*, pp. 75-76. Cf. also R.K. Pandey, pp. 10-12.

455 Cf. R.K. Pandey, pp. 23-24. Cf. also Swami Harshananda, p. 31.

456 Cf. R.K. Pandey, p. 22. Cf. also Swami Harshananda, p. 31.

457 Cf. R.K. Pandey, pp. 19-20. Cf. also Swami Harshananda, pp. 33, 35.

458 Cf. R.K. Pandey, p. 24. Cf. also Swami Harshananda, p. 35. Cf.

also Rabindra Kumar Siddhantashastree, *Vaishnavism through the Ages*, pp. 54-56.

459 Cf. R.K. Pandey, p. 25. Cf. also Swami Harshananda, p. 35. Cf. also Rabindra Kumar Siddhantashastree, *Vaishnavism through the Ages*, pp. 58-62.

460 Cf. Swami Harshananda, p. 38. Cf. also R.K. Pandey, pp. 26-28. Rabindra Kumar Siddhantashastree, *Vaishnavism through the Ages*, pp. 62-67.

461 Cf. R.K. Pandey, pp. 28-29. Rabindra Kumar Siddhantashastree, *Vaishnavism through the Ages*, pp. 67-74.

462 Cf. Rabindra Kumar Siddhantashastree, *Vaishnavism through the Ages*, pp. 74-75. Cf. also Swami Harshananda, p. 38.

463 Cf. Swami Harshananda, pp. 39, 42.

464 Ganesh Vasudeo Tagare, trans., *The Bhaagavata Puraana, Ancient Indian Tradition & Mythology*, ed. J.L. Shastri, vol. 10, Part 4, (Delhi: Motilal Banarsidass, 1988), X, 1: 1-69 (Hereafter: BP). Cf. also Rabindra Kumar Siddhantashastree, p. 77.

465 Cf. R.K. Pandey, pp. 42-43. Cf. also Rabindra Kumar Siddhantashastree, *Vaishnavism through the Ages*, pp. 76, 78-80. We find a difference in the personality of *Srii Krshna* as he is presented in various *Puraanas* and in the *Bhagavat Giitaa*. The *Puraanas* depict erotic and amorous sport of *Krshna*. For instance the *Bhaagavatapuraana* speaks of *Krshna's* amorous adventures with the *Gopi* women of the Cowherd village. The other works like *Harivamsa* and *Vishnupuraana* confirm this truth. The *Brahmavaivartapuraana* narrates *Krshna's* love affair with Radha, his mistress and 900,000 *Gopis*. This trend of seeing *Krshna* in his sexual orgies continues in the famous book of Jayadeva, the *Giita-Govinda*. But the *Krshna* of *Bhagavat Giitaa* is very different. He is a person caught up with the sense of duty and teaches the obligation of performing the duty to Arjuna. He declares himself as the Supreme Being and the only God, who is there to assist the true devotee. The *Krshna* of *Giitaa* speaks of himself as God, as *Allah* does in the *Quran* and *Jesus* does in the *Bible*. Thus, we find a striking difference in the two-fold portrayal of the personality of *Srii Krshna*. In the *Kishna* of *Bhagavat Giitaa*, the love between the devotee and *Krshna* is characterized by '*agapae*', while in the *Puraanas*, the love between the Lord and the devotee is marked by '*eros*'. Cf. Nirad C. Chaudhuri, pp. 261-282.

466 BP, Part 1, SBE, Vol. 7 (Delhi: Motilal Banarsidas, 1986), I, 3: 28.

467 Cf. Rabindra Kumar Siddhantashastree, *Vaishnavism through the Ages*, pp. 78-79.

468 Cf. R.K. Pandey, 29-30. Cf. also Rabindra Kumar Siddhantashastree, *Vaishnavism through the Ages*, pp. 80-83. Cf. also Swami Harshananda, pp. 42-46.

469 Cf. Ibid.

470 Cf. Rabindra Kumar Siddhantashastree, *Vaishnavism through the Ages*, pp. 83-84. Cf. also R.K. Pandey, p. 30. Cf. also Swami Harshananda, p. 42.

471 Cf. Kurien Mathothu, pp. 68-69.
472 Cf. Ibid., pp. 69-70.
473 Cf. Rabindra Kumar, Siddhantashastree, *Vaishnavism through the Ages*, pp. 16-17.
474 Cf. Ibid., pp. 20-22.
475 Cf. Ibid., pp. 22, 27-49.
476 Cf. Ibid., pp. 24-26.
477 Cf. John Clark Archer, "Hinduism", *The Great Religions of the Modern World*, ed. Edward. J. Jurji, (Princeton: Princeton University Press, 1967), p. 84. Cf. also Swami Harshananda, pp. 57-59.
478 Cf. S.M. Srinivasa Chari, pp. 260-268.
479 Cf. Ibid., pp. 268-272.
480 Cf. S.M. Srinivasa Chari, pp. 268-274.
481 Cf. Ibid., pp 274-275.
482 Cf. H.V. Sreenivasa Murthy, pp. 131. Cf. also Suvira Jaiswal, p. 122.
483 Cf. H.V. Sreenivasa Murthy, pp. 141.
484 Cf. Ibid., pp. 156-158. The sentiment of love, which is the essence of the *Bhakti* involved between the Lord and the devotee, in some *Krshna*-cults takes erotic forms. There are attempts made in some of the *Puraanas* to sanctify the adulterous sexual love of *Krshna* for the *Gopis* and his sexual orgies with his consort Radha. Thus, in some *Krshna*-cults there is an irreconcilable dichotomy between *Bhakti* and eroticism. Often in such cults, the *Madhura Rasa*, though it means 'sweet sentiment', is taken to mean 'erotic sentiment'. The sexual intercourse, accompanied by kissing, biting, scratching, squeezing of the breasts, waving of the hips and orgasm, *Krshna* has with either the *Gopis* or with Radha, is interpreted as the symbolic expression of the mystical union of the devotee with God. Perhaps in the name of devotion to God, a great deal of immorality is sanctified in such cults. In fact, such attempts lack the true spirit of *Vaishnavism* as a religion. Cf. Nirad C. Chaudhuri, pp. 269-282.
485 Cf. H.V. Sreenivasa Murthy, pp. 15-19, 159-163. Cf. also Sluvira Jaiswal, pp. 122-123. Cf. also S.M. Srinivasa Chari, pp. 249-254.
486 Cf. H.V. Sreenivasa Murthy, pp. 164-174. Cf. also S.M. Srinivasa Chari, pp. 316-322.
487 Cf. Suvira Jaiswal, pp. 123-124.
488 Cf. H.V. Sreenivasa Murthy, pp. 181-182.
489 Cf. BG, VI, 32; V, 25. Cf. also H.V. Sreenivasa Murthy, pp. 181-182.
490 Cf. Suvira Jaiswal, 161-162.
491 Cf. H.V. Sreenivasa Murthy, pp. 144-149.
492 Cf. Suvira Jaiswal, pp. 152-155.
493 Cf. Ibid., pp. 155-156.
494 Cf. Ibid., pp. 156-158, 159. Cf. also S.M. Srinivasa Chari, pp. 306-307.

495 Cf. S.M. Srinivasa Chari, pp. 3011-316. Cf. also Suvira Jaiswal, p. 158.
496 Cf. Ibid., pp. 158-161. Cf. also S.M. Srinivasa Chari, pp. 306-311.
497 Cf. Suvira Jaiswal, pp. 162-163. Cf. S.M. Srinivasa Chari, p.315.
498 Cf. Suvira Jaiswal, pp. 163.
499 Cf. Ibid., pp. 165-166.
500 Cf. S.M. Srinivasa Chari, pp. 309-310.
501 Cf. Rabindra Kumar Siddhantashastree, *Vaishnavism through the Ages*, pp. 22-24.
502 Cf. Suvira Jaiswal, pp. 163-165.
503 Cf. Om Lata Bahadur, *The Book of Hindu Festivals and Ceremonies*, (New Delhi: UBSPD, 1997), pp. 117-119.
504 Cf. Ibid., pp. 119-121.
505 Cf. Ibid., p. 121.
506 Cf. Ibid., pp. 75-81.
507 Cf. BG, XVI, 1-3.
508 Cf. H.V. Sreenivasa Murthy, pp. 193-191. Cf. S.M. Srinivasa Chari, pp. 322-329.
509 Cf. Rabindra Kumar Siddhantashastree, *Saivism through the Ages*, (New Delhi: Munshiram Manhorlal Publishers Pvt. Ltd., 1975), p. vii. Cf. also Jesuit Scholars, p. 251.
510 Cf. Jesuit Scholars, p. 251.
511 Cf. Rabindra Kumar Siddhantashastree, *Saivism through the Ages*, pp. 151-162. Cf. also Jesuit Scholars, p. 254. Cf. also Jadunath Sinha, *Schools of Savism*, (Calcutta: Jadunath Sinha Foundation, 1975), pp. 176- 200.
512 Cf. Jesuit Scholars, pp. 254-255.
513 Cf. Rabindra Kumar Siddhantashastree, *Saivism through the Ages*, p. 165.
514 Cf. Jesuit Scholars, p. 255. Cf. also Rabindra Kumar Siddhantashastree, *Saivism through the Ages*, pp. 165-169. Cf. also Jadunath Sinha, pp. 104- 129.
515 Cf. Jesuit Scholars, pp. 255-258.
516 Cf. Ibid., pp. 258-260. Cf. also Jadunath Sinha, pp. 126-153.
517 Cf. Jesuit Scholars, pp. 260-261. Cf. also Rabindra Kumar Siddhantashastree, *Savism through the Ages*, pp. 128-150. Cf. also Jadunath Sinha, pp. 25-103.
518 Cf. Jesuit Scholars, pp. 251-252, 254. Cf. also Kurian Mathothu, p. 26, Fn. 73.
519 Cf. Jesuit Scholars, p. 252. Cf. also RV, I, 164:46; II, 33:1, 11; IV, 3:6;VII, 35:6.
520 Cf. Jesuit Scholars, p. 252. Cf. also RV, II, 33: 2, 5, 7,12.
521 Cf. Rabindra Kumar Siddhantashastree, *Saivism through the Ages*, pp. 3-4. Cf. also AV, IV, 28:3; X, 1:23; XI, 2:12.
522 Cf. Jesuit Scholars, p. 252.
523 Cf. ibid.
524 Cf. Kurien Mathothu, p. 82.

525 Cf. Kamalakar Mishra, *Kashmir Savism: The Central Philosophy of Tantrism*, (Delhi: Sri Satguru Publications, 1999), pp. 95-97.
526 Cf. Ibid., pp. 97-104.
527 Cf. Ibid., pp. 105-109. Cf. also Ibid., pp. 78-84.
528 Cf. Ibid., pp. 111-113. Cf. also L.N. Sharma, *Kashmir Saivism*, (Delhi: Bhatatiya Vidya Prakashan, 1996), pp. 178-179.
529 Cf. Kamalakar Mishra, pp. 118-121, 124-126. Cf. also L.N. Sharma, pp. 179, 181, 193-201.
530 Cf. Kamalakar Mishra, pp. 122-123. Cf. also N.L. Sharma, pp. 183, 201-202.
531 Cf. Kamalakar Sharma, pp. 143-145.
532 Cf. Ibid., pp.128-129.
533 Cf. Ibid., pp. 127-128, 135-138. Cf. also L.N. Sharma, pp. 281-282, 283-290.
534 Cf. Kamalakar Mishra, pp. 137-143. Cf. also L.N. Sharma, pp. 290-295.

535 Cf. Kamalakar Mishra, pp. 145-147. Cf. also Jesuit Scholars, p 253. For a detailed consideration of *Sakti* as the goddess: Cf. also Swami Harshananda, pp. 80-129. Over the years the Saiva Tantric *Sakti* worship has developed into a right-hand and a left-hand. The right-hand *Sakti* worship views *Sakti* as the clean and unselfish mother of mercy, from whom devotees derive deep personal satisfaction and move towards the realization of perfect union with the divinity. But the left-hand *Sakti* worship, known as the *Vaamaacara*, displays all forms of evil practices in the name of worship of the goddess *Sakti*. They offer bloody sacrifices, including human sacrifices. In the name of ritual worship of the goddess, they practice robbery and deceit. Their worship includes indecent orgiastic rites, which are magical in meaning. In such rites goddess *Sakti* is worshipped through sexual union, in imitation of goddess *Bhairavii* (*Sakti*), who is in eternal sexual union with the god *Bhairava* (*Siva*). They use names such as *Tripuraa*, *Tripuraa-bhairavii*, *Thirpurasundarii*, *Sundarii* (the beautiful), *Vaamaa* (the better half) and *Sodasii* (the damsel of 16 years) to refer to the *Sakti*-goddess *Bhairavii*. Divine *Sakti* is also worshipped as a beautiful goddess, whom they call *Sarvesvarii* (the queen of all). The worship of the *Sakti* goddess included the use of animal flesh, fish, grain, wine and woman. The left-hand *Sakti* cult, thus, perpetuates all forms of evil in the name of worship of *Sakti*. Cf. John Clark Archer, "Hinduism", *Great Religions of the Modern World*, ed. Edward J. Jurji, pp. 83-84. Cf. also Kamalakar Mishra, p. 146. Cf. also Swami Nihilananda, *Hinduism: Its Meaning for the Liberation of the Spirit*, pp.156-157.

536 Cf. Frederick L. Kumar, *Philosophy of Saivism: An Existential Analysis of its Underlying Experiences*, (New Delhi: Oxford & IBH Publishing Co. Pvt. Ltd. , 1988), p. 57. Cf. also Kurien Mathothu, pp. 89-90. Cf. also A. Parthasarathy, *The Sumbolism of Hindu Gods and Rituals*, pp. 22-23.

537 Cf. SB, IX, 1, 1,1.

538 Cf. Frederick L. Kumar, pp. 58-59. Cf. also Kurien Mathothu, p. 83.

539 Cf. Frederick L. Kumar, pp. 59-60. Cf. also Kurien Mathothu, pp. 83-84. Cf. also MU, II, 1-4.
540 Cf. Frederick L. Kumar, pp. 60-61. Cf. also Alain Danielou, *Hindu Polytheism*, (London: Routledge & Kegan Paul, Ltd., 1964), p. 200.
541 Cf. Frederick L. Kumar, pp. 61-62. Cf. also Alain Danielou, p. 202.
542 Cf. Frederick L. Kumar, p. 62. Cf. also Kurien Mathothu, pp. 86-87. Cf. also Alain Danielou, p. 203.
543 Cf. Frederick L. Kumar, pp. 63-64.
544 Cf. Frederick L. Kumar, pp. 64-65. Cf. also Jesuit Scholars, pp. 258-260. Cf. also Kurien Mathothu, pp. 93-94.
545 Cf. Kurien Mathothu, pp. 82-83.
546 Cf. Kurien Mathothu, pp. 84-86. Cf. also A. Parthasarthy, *The Symbolism of Hindu Gods and Rituals*, 29-34.
547 Cf. Kurien Mathothu, pp. 91-92. Cf. also Swami Harshananda, p. 70.
548 Cf. Jesuit Scholars, pp. 252-253. Cf. also Frederick L. Kumar, 67-71. Cf. also Sri Swami Sivananda, *The Lord Siva and His Worship*, (Tehri-Garhwal: The Divine Life Society, 1984), pp. 120-129.
549 Cf. Kurien Mathothu, pp. 87-88. Cf. also A Parthasarathy, *The Symbolism of Hindu Gods and Rituals*, pp. 107-108. The worship of *Sivalinga* can be traced back to the worship of primitive stone symbols, existing as early as the Neolithic age. Many such symbols were discovered during the excavations in Mohenjo-Daro. From this we can conclude that the Dravidian religion is familiar with the worship of at least some forms of *Sivalinga*. Cf. Kurien Mathothu, pp. 87-88.
550 Cf. Kurien Mathothu, p. 88. Cf. also Sir Swami Sivananda, *The Lord Siva and His Worship*, pp. 143-144.
551 Cf. Rabindra Kumar Siddhanrtashastree, Saivism through the Ages, pp. 70-84.
552 Cf. Sri Swami Sivananda, *The Lord Siva and His Worship*, pp. 58-63.
553 Cf. Ibid., pp. 59-61.
554 Cf. Ibid., pp. 131-132.
555 Cf. Ibid., pp. 132-133, 139.
556 Cf. Ibid., pp. 133-134.
557 Cf. Ibid., pp. 134-135.
558 Cf. Ibid., pp. 135-138.
559 Cf. Ibid., pp. 150-151.
560 Cf. Ibid., pp. 150-153.
561 Cf. Ibid., pp. 153-156.
562 Cf. Ibid., pp. 48-51.
563 Cf. Rabindra Kumar Siddhantashastree, *Saivism through the Ages*, p. 157.
564 Cf. Ibid., pp. 157-159.
565 Cf. Kamalakar Mishra, pp. 329-339. Cf. also Swami Lakshman

Jee, *Kashmir Savism: The Secret Supreme*, (Delhi: Sri Satguru Publications, 1991), p. 33.

566 Cf. Kamalakar Mishra, pp. 344-345.
567 Cf. Swami Lakshman Jee, pp. 36-39.
568 Cf. Kamalakar Mishra, pp. 345-347.
569 Cf. Ibid., 342- 344. Cf. also Swami Lakshman Jee, pp. 35-36.
570 Cf. Swami Lakshman Lee, pp. 31-33. Cf. also Kamalakar Mishra, pp. 341-342.
571 Swami Lakshman Jee, p. 39.
572 Cf. Kamalakar Mishra, pp. 347-349.
573 Cf. Ibid., pp. 351-352
574 Cf. Kamalakar Mishra, pp. 80, 338-340, 354-362. Cf. also Swami Lakshman Lee, p. 40.
575 Cf. Kamalakar Mishra, pp. 363-364, 365-366.
576 Cf. Ibid., pp. 366-367.
577 Cf. Ibid., pp. 364-365, 367-368.
578 Cf. Ibid., pp. 365, 368-369.
579 Cf. Ibid., 369-372.
580 Cf. Ibid., pp. 372-376.
581 Cf. Ibid., pp. 376-377.
582 Cf. Ibid., pp. 377-278.
583 Cf. Sri Swami Sivananda, *Lord Siva and His Worship*, pp. 236-239.
584 Cf. Om Lata Bahadur, pp. 42-51.
585 Cf. Sri Swami Sivananda, *The Lord Siva and His Worship*, pp. 339-347. Cf. also Om Lata Bahadur, pp. 158-190.

Chapter 4

Jaina Tradition

INTRODUCTION

The Jaina tradition has provided the world with a humanistic religion (*Dharma*) and a scientific philosophy (*Darsana*), commonly known as Jainism (*Jaina-dharma*). Jainism, as a religion, attempts to effect the highest development of the human soul, always maintaining the purity of the means and the end, as it cleanses one's head and heart, thought and conduct equally. As a philosophy, Jainism explains the various categories of fundamental truths that constitute this universe. One who holds for the tenets of the Jaina tradition as a religion and philosophy is called a Jaina. Strictly speaking a Jaina is a follower of a *Jina*, i.e., a spiritual conqueror. He is a human teacher, who totally conquers the effects of *Karma* and crosses the ocean of suffering through asceticism, moral and spiritual discipline and achieves omniscience (*Kevalajnaana*). Having achieved this state, he preaches the doctrine of salvation (*Moksha*) to help others to tread the path he has walked. Such a spiritual conqueror is called *Tiirthankara*, which means a guide or a ford-maker. A *Jina* is not the founder of a religion, but he is only a teacher of a path that has been taught by other teachers before him. The function of each *Tiirthankara* is to re-animate the tradition that has existed from time immemorial, so that it makes more sense to the present and the future generations. The teaching of *Tiirthankara* is received neither through a revelation from God, nor with the help of any magic, but rather it is the result of the reflection of the *Tiirthankara* on the earlier teaching of the said tradition. It is believed that the Jaina tradition is the consequence of the teachings of a number of *Tiirthankaras*.[1] Jainism, therefore, is the religion that helps one to conquer the *Karma-samsaara* cycle under the guiding influence of the lives and teachings of the *Tiirthankaras*. In this introductory section, we endeavor to give a brief history of Jainism, its scriptures, it believers and its philosophy.

1. A BRIEF HISTORY OF JAINISM

The Jaina tradition is a very ancient one and thus has a quite long history. We cannot endeavor to gauge it fully in a few pages. Yet in our consideration of the history of Jainism, we make an attempt to understand its origin and development, the emergence of schisms and various sects, and its decline.

1.1. ORIGIN AND DEVELOPMENT OF JAINISM

The Jainas claim that Jainism is the oldest religion in the world. As some people see it, it is neither a branch of Vedic religion nor that of Buddhism, but belongs to a pre-Aryan tradition, viz., the *Sramana* or the *Aarahata* tradition, that is much older than these two. The *Aarahata* tradition does not accept the authority of the *Vedas*, denies performance of animal sacrifices (*Yajnas*) and upholds the practice of non-violence (*Ahimsaa*). During period of the *Vedas* and the *Aaranyakas*, the *Aarahata* tradition is known as the *Vraatya Parampraa*, as the sages of this tradition follow the practice of observing vows (*Vraatya*). For instance, *Atharva Veda* calls a *Vraatya* one who practices continence (*Brahmacaarii*), a performer of special good deeds (*Visishta Punyasiila*), a scholar (*Vidvaan*) and one who is respectful in the world (*Visvasammaanya*). There are archaeological evidences to show that the sages, whom the *Rig Veda* refers to as *Vaatarasanaamunis*, belong to the *Aarahata* tradition. Since the *Aarahata* tradition is nothing other than the Jaina tradition, these sages are none other than the *Tiirthankaras*, in whose teaching the Jaina tradition originates. It is also clear from the fact that up to the time of the Lord Mahaaviira, Jaina literature refers to the *Tiirthankara* with the term *Aarahat*. All these indicate that the Jaina tradition is very ancient and independent, and that it cannot be considered as an appendix to any other tradition.[2]

It is the belief of the Jainas that their ancient religion, its ideas and practices developed in the teachings of 24 *Tiirthankaras*. They are Rshabhadeva or Aadinaatha, Ajitanaatha, Sambhavanaatha, Abhinandana, Sumatinaatha, Padmaprabhu, Suparsvanaatha, Chandraprabhu, Suvidhinaatha, Siitalanaatha, Sreyaamsanaatha, Vasupuujya, Vimalanaatha, Anantanaatha, Dharmanaatha, Saantinaatha, Kunthunaatha, Aranaatha, Mallinaatha, Munisuvrata, Naminaatha, Neminaatha or Arishta Neminaatha, Paarsavanatha and Mahaaviira. It is said that each of these *Tiirthankaras* were taught after long intervals of time between each other. They are also described as possessing extra-ordinary size and seemingly lived for many years. The first *Tiirthankara*, Rshabhadeva, is said to have taught 72 arts to men and 64 to women, besides initiating them to the Jaina way of life. His successors followed his example and continued the task he had begun. Though there is mythology associated with each of the *Tiirthankaras*, the fact that they are historical and that there existed a succession of teachers, in whose teaching the Jaina tradition emerged, need not be doubted. This is because a critical study of the growth of the religio-philosophical ideas of India leads us to definite conclusions about the presence of the pre-Vedic culture and religion in Eastern India. It is possible to think that the *Tiirthankaras* and the predecessors of Buddha might have belonged to this tradition and made all efforts to preserve the continuance of this tradition against the attacks of the Vedic tradition.[3]

Though one may raise the issue of the historicity of the early *Tiirthankaras*, the fact that the last two *Tiirthankaras*, namely Paarsavanatha and Mahaaviira, are historical figures is an undeniable fact, as historical Jainism begins with them. Paarsavanatha belonged to a kindly family in Banaaras, lived a carefree life until he is 30 years old and then renounced the world. Practicing asceticism for 83 days, he received enlightenment on the 84th day under a Dhaataki tree near Banaras. His mother and wife became his first disciples. He preached his teachings for 70 years and died at the age of 100 on

Mount Sameta Sikhara, near the Bengal-Bihar border. His essential teachings are: not to take a life, not to tell a lie, not to steal and not to own property. The 24th *Tiirthankara*, Mahaaviira, is the most significant of all. His original name is Varthamaana. He belonged to a kingly family at Kundagraama, a suburb of Vaisaali. For 30 years, he liveed the life of a householder. For 12 long years he continued to be a monk and attained omniscience under a Saala tree on the bank of the river Rjupaalikaa near Jrmbhikagraama. For the next 30 years he preached as the *Tiirthankara*. The main elements of his teaching are: many-sided viewpoint, non-violence and non-possession; equality of all without caste or creedal differences; giving high status to women and the removal of animal sacrifices. He also added a fifth negative prescription to the four of Paarsavanatha, viz., not to indulge in sensual pleasures. Many illustrious emperors were his disciples, converted at his hands. He attained *Nirvaana* at the age 72 in a place called Majjhima Paavaain. Before his end, he delivered 55 lectures and recited 36 unasked questions (*Uttaraadhyayana-suutra*).[4]

Since the death of Mahaaviira, the *Ganadharas*, the chief disciples of Mahaaviira guide the Jaina community. They all belong to the *Braahman* caste and are converts to Jainism. Instead of moving from lay state to the state of mendicant monks, which is the normal practice in Jainism, they all take monastic vows on the very day of their conversion. Similarly, they adopt the practice of nudity as per the direction of Mahaaviira. There are 11 *Ganadharas* the chief of them is Indrabhuuti Gautama. The others are Agnibhuuti, Vaay-ubhuuti, Akampita, Aarya Vyakta, Sudharman, Manditaputra, Mauryaputra, Acalabhraataa, Metraaya and Prabhaasa. Of these 11 *Ganadharas*, a few of them died before the death of Mahaaviira, while a few others died at the same year of Mahaaviira's death. Some of them attained the state of omniscience early, after which they did not perform the function of the *Ganadharas*. With the exception of Indrabhuuti, Gautama and Sudharman, none of the others really guided the Jaina community as leaders. After the death of Indrabhu-uti Gautama, Sudharman took over as the leader of the community. He died in his 100th year and with him the first generation of disciples of Mahaaviira came to an end. It is said that Sudharman was the last to achieve the state of omniscience. For the next century and a half, the successors of Sudharman carried on the oral tradition. Some of the important persons of this period were Prabhava, Sayyambhava, Yasobhadra and Bhadrabaahu, in whose time the Jaina community moved from Magadha to Mysore due to famine, which over the next few years led to the loss of the Jaina canon of books, the emergence of a major schism and the division of the Jaina community into two major groups.[5]

1.2. THE EMERGENCE OF SCHISM AND VARIOUS SECTS OF JAINISM

Since the time of Mahaaviira, there have come about eight major schisms (*Nihnava*) within the Jaina community, some of which were resolved, while the others keep the Jaina community divided into major sects and subsects. The reasons for the schisms are either difference in a doctrinal matter or a controversy pertaining to the practical life of the Jaina monks. The first schismatic died unrepented, while the initiators of the second to the fifth schisms repented, correct their views and returned to the Jain community. But the sixth and the seventh schisms were never retracted, and their initiators living outside the Jain community maintain their views. The eighth schism brought about a major division of the Jaina community into two groups. Thus, the Jainas do not represent a united religious community.[6]

The first two of these schisms took place during Mahaaviira's lifetime itself. The first one originated from Mahaaviira's son-in-law, Jamaali. He differed in saying that an influence is considered as over when it is completed. He died without accept his error and thus he was not redeemed. A monk named Tishyagupta is the source of the second schism, which refuted Mahaaviira's doctrine that the soul includes all the atoms of the body. He was corrected and he returened to the fold. The third schism came from the disciples of a monk called Aashaadha, who propose the doctrine of indistinguishability, namely, that the ascetics and gods must be treated without distinction. They were excommunicated, but later King Balabhadra corrected their views and received them back into the Jain church. Asvamitra's theory that all beings disappear one day was the fourth schism. Later when he offered an apology for his errors the excommunication placed on him was removed. The fifth schism came from Ganga's teaching that two contradictory sensations such as hot and cold can be experienced simultaneously. He was expelled from the Jain church, but confessed his mistake and atoned for it. The initiator of the sixth schism was a monk named Rohagupta who proposes a third class of reality, non-life (*Nojiiva*), besides the usually recognized Jaina categories of living beings (*Jiiva*) and lifeless beings (*Ajiiva*). According to the Jainas, the *Vaiseshika-darsana* stems from such a theory. No retraction was made regarding this sixth schism. The seventh schism came from Goshtaamaahila, who claimed that the soul does not completely merge with *Karma*-matter, which only touches the soul. If there is such a merging of Karmic matter and the soul, salvation cannot be attained, as the former cannot be removed from the latter. He also proposed that the vow of renunciation should not be taken for a short period of time, but for an unlimited period. The Jaina church assembly rejected this position and excommunicated the schismatic, as he did not retract from his stand.[7]

The eighth schism is the major one that divides the Jaina community into two groups, viz., those clothed in the air (*Digambaras*) and those clothed in white (*Svetaambaras*). This schism has lasted ever since. The former group follow the strict discipline, while the latter group is more lax in their practice of Jaina discipline. Both the groups accuse each other as the cause of the division. The reasons for the division are both historical and dogmatic. The historical reason may be related to half of the monks moving out of the monastery in Magadha in Bihaar to Mysore in Karnataka, during the famine, under the leadership of Bhadrabaahu, while the rest remained in Magadha under the leadership of Sthuulabhadra, a pupil of Bhadrabaahu. This separation and the existing difficult conditions in Magadha did not provide ideal conditions for the strict practice of Jaina teachings. To cope with the situation, the council of Paataliiputra made a number of alterations both in the canon of scriptures, dogmas and practices. When the migrated monks returned home, they found the changes unacceptable, as the initial practice had changed greatly. The already existing tensions between the more liberal disciples of Parsavanatha and stricter followers of Mahaaviira added fuel to the fire that came as the result of the historical situation related to the famine and the migration of the monks. All these historical factors brought about irreconcilable differences between the group of *Digambharas* and the *Svetaambaras*.[8]

The differences that came between these two groups within the Jaina community due to the said historical reason widened for dogmatic reasons and their consequences in the practical life of the Jaina monks and the nuns. Some differences in the area of dogma and practice are the following: the canon of scriptures, the nature of the omniscient *Jina*, the role of nudity in holy life, the position of women and differences in the practice of begging and eating habits. Firstly, there is a difference of opinion between these two groups regarding the canon of scriptures. The *Digambaras* believe that the canon of scriptures, over the period of time, was completely lost and so does not exist now. But the *Svetaambaras* acknowledge that the main parts of the canon of scriptures have come down and are available to them up to the present day. The final editing of such a canon seems to have taken place in the year 980 A.D., about 993 years after the death of Mahaaviira, under the chairmanship of Devarddhi Gani in the city of Valabhii in Gujarat. Secondly, there is a difference between both the groups regarding the nature of the omniscient *Jina*. *Digambaras* hold that *Jina* has no worldly activities and bodily functions, such as, eating, drinking and similar activities. He preaches by means of a magical, divine sound. The *Svetaambaras* consider the *Jina* as involved in normal human activities and functions, while at the same time possessing omniscient cognition. Thirdly, they also differ regarding the role of nudity in the life of a monk. *Digambaras* consider nudity as an absolute necessity in the life of the mendicant monk, as it frees him from shame and sexuality, thereby helping the monk to attain a state of total nakedness of body, mind and spirit, which, in turn, leads him to *Moksha*. The *Svetaambaras*, while denying attachment to clothing, point to the optional nature of the practice of wearing clothes.[9]

Fourthly, both the groups differ on the point of the position of women in the Jain community. *Digambaras* deny that women possess the body that is necessary for attaining salvation. Therefore, they must be born as men before they can attain salvation. *Svetaambaras* consider that women, as they are now, can attain salvation, as do men. The differing views of both groups on women attaining *Moksha* are related to the nudity question. The idea of women going about nude, especially during their menstrual cycle, is socially unacceptable in Indian society. In fact, none of the Jaina groups allow their women followers to go about unclad. While the *Digambaras* see it as a reason for their automatic disqualification from *Moksha*, the *Svetaambaras* do not see any difficulty, as wearing some necessary cloths does not deter one from attaining *Moksha*. Finally, there are differences between the monks of these two groups regarding begging and eating habits. The *Svetaambara* monks carry small pots and beg from house to house and take what they have collected to the monastery and eat there, as they are not expected to enter a house to eat. Besides, they beg for two to three meals a day. The *Digambara* monks carry no bowl, but collect the food in their upturned palms (*Paani-paatra*). They can enter a house and eat, without prior invitation, as part of their begging trip. But they do not use any plates to eat. They eat only one meal a day. These dogmatic differences and their practical consequences have aggravated the historical situations in such a way that no reconciliation is possible between these two Jaina groups, which brought about the final breakup between these groups by the end of the first century A.D., i.e., in the early 80's.[10]

Over the years the *Svetaambaras* and the *Digambaras* have further divided into various schools (*Ganas*), sub-classification of schools (*Kulas*) and branches (*Saakhaas*). The *Svetaambaras* use the term *Gaccha* to refer to their sub-groups, while the *Digambaras* use the terms *Sangha* and *Panthiis* to refer to their sub-groups. The *Svetaambaras* are further divided into two main groups, viz., the idol-worshippers and the idol-rejectors. Though there are minor variations in the beliefs and practices of these two groups of *Svetaambaras*, the common element is that the idol-worshipers used idols for worship, while the idol-rejectors are hostile to idol worship. The idol-worshippers are the following: *Upakesa-Gaccha, Kharatara-Gaccha, Tapaa-Gaccha, Paarsvacandra-Gaccha, Paurnamiiyaka-Gaccha, Ancala-Gaccha* and *Aagamika-Gaccha*. The idol-rejectors are the following: *Lonkaa-Gaccha, Veshadharas, Vandhyas, Sthaanakavaasiis* and *Teraapanthis*. The *Digambara* sects can be divided into two, the original community (*Muula-Sangha*) and the present day schools. The original community has its orthodox and heterodox *Sanghas*. The orthodox *Sanghas* are four in number. They are the following: *Nandi-Sangha, Sena-Sangha, Simha-Sangha* and *Deva-Sangha*. Each of these *Sanghas* is further divided into a number of sub-schools. The ascetics of these *Sanghas* carry a fan of peacock feathers and are greeted with the word *Dharmavrddi*. The heterodox *Sanghas* of the original community are also four in number: *Draavida-Sangha, Yaapaniiya-Sangha, Kaashthaa-Sangha* and *Mathuraa-sangha*. Of the four heterodox *Sanghas*, it seems that only *Kaashthaa-Sangha* exists today. The present day *Digambara* sects are *Visvapanthiis (Bispanthiis), Teraapanthiis, Ternapanthiis, Gumaanpanthiis* and *Totaapanthiis*. Thus, we find manifold groups of Jaina sects.[11]

1.3. DECLINE OF JAINISM

In the course of time, Jainism as a religion begins to lose its influence among the people for many reasons. The diverse sects within Jainism and their antagonism towards each other definitely weaken its significance. The spread of Buddhism in India and the attack of the Buddhism on Jainism is another reason for its decline. Jainism suffered a great deal under the Islamic rulers. The revival of Hinduism by many great sages like Kumarila,

Paths to the Divine 323

Shankara, Ramaanuja and Madhva is another cause of its losing its significance. Similarly, the emergence of Vaishnava *Bhakti*-cult, the Saiva *Sakti*-cult and the *Bhakti*-movement, initiated by thinkers such as Kabiir and others, also exerted effect on the decline of Jaina religious culture. Although these attacks against Jainism have brought about a decline in Jainism in terms of the number of believers, still Jainism has its place as a religion in the land of its birth unlike Buddhism. Jainas could continue their religious practices under the British rule of India and after the independence of India from British rule. Many efforts are being made presently to revive the Jaina religion and culture. In spite of all these efforts, the number of believers in Jainism continues to decline.[12]

2. JAINA SCRIPTURES

The Jainas have maintained a rich literary tradition. Many of the Jaina-writers belong to the class of the monks. Though they are wandering monks, the literary spirit is high among them. They used the monsoon months, when the rains restricted their movement, to carry on their literary activities. Here we attempt to provide a general view of the canonical literature (*Aagama*) and the post-canonical expositions (*Anuyogas*) of Jainism in general, without getting into the controversies of the canon of the different sects of Jainism. The ancient books are written in a language called Ardhamaagadhii. The *Svetaabaras* texts are found in a language called Mahaaraashtrii Prakrit, while the *Digambaras* use another dialect called Sauraseni Prakrit.[13]

2.1. CANONICAL LITERATURE

The canonical literature (*Aagama*) of the Jainas is known differently: sermons of the *Nigrantha* (*Nigantha-paavayaana*), basket of *Ganadharas* (*Gani-pidaga*), scriptural knowledge (*Suya-naana*) or doctrine (*Siddhaanta*). They consist of three groups of texts, known as the *Puuva*, the *Anga* and the *Angabaahya*. We briefly consider these three groups of texts.

2.1.1. The Puurvs

The *Puurvas* literally means the old texts. They consist of 14 ancient works, which are said to have their origin from the time of Parsavanatha. All these texts are lost to the Jaina tradition. But we find brief descriptions about them in the later works, especially in the twelfth *Anga*, called *Drshtivaada*. The fourteen texts of the *Puurva* are the following: *Utpaada, Agraayanii, Viirya, Astinaastipravaada, Jnaanapravaada, Satyapravaada, Aatmapravaada, Karmapravaada, Pratyaakhyaanapravaada, Vidyaanuvaada, Kalyaanavaada, Praanavaada, Kriyaavisaala* and *Lokabindusaara*. Some of the contents of the *Puurva* texts are the following: speculations on the nature of the cosmos, doctrines about the bondage of the soul in matter, discussion about contemporary philosophical schools, Jaina astrology and astronomy, and esoteric methods of attaining Yogic and occult powers. It is believed that most of the materials contained in the *Puurva* texts are transmitted until the time of Mahaaviira, through oral tradition, and he teaches these doctrines which the *Ganadharas* systematize and put to writing. Perhaps because of the esoteric nature of the *Puurva* texts or as they are incorporated into the *Anga* texts, not many Jainas have taken the trouble to memorize them. It is said that the last person who learned the whole of the *Puurva* texts by heart was Bhadrabaahu, the leader of the Jaina community at Magadha, who later headed the migrant community of monks in Mysore. After him, the complete knowledge of the *Puurva* is lost to the Jain community, though they have its knowledge as it is found in parts of the *Angas*.[14]

2.1.2. The Angas

The term "*Angas*" means limbs. These texts are called *Angas* because they are seen as parts of the body of the Jaina scripture. It is believed that the *Anga* texts originate in the teachings of Mahaaviira and they are free from later sectarian conflict. They include twelve books, of which the first eleven books survive, while the twelfth book that contains the summary of the *Puurva* texts is no longer extant. The twelve *Angas* are the following: *Aacaaraanga-suutra, Suutrakrtaanga, Sthaanaanga, Samavaayaanga, Bhqagavatii Vyaakhyaaprajnapti, Jnaatrdharmakathaa, Upaasakadasaah, Antakrddasaah, Anuttaraupapaatikadasaah, Prasnavyaakrana, Vipaakasruta* and *Drshtivaada*. The 11 *Angas* deal with four areas of Jaina life, viz., the ecclesiastical law, the examination of false views, the basic Jaina doctrine and the narratives for the edification of the laity. The 12th *Anga*, which is lost, contains the summary of the teachings of the *Puurva* texts.[15]

2.1.3. The Angabaahya

The term "*Angabaahya*" literally means 'outside the limbs'. Therefore, they are subsidiary books of the canon. They do not originate either in the teaching of Mahaaviira or the *Ganadharas*, but from certain elders (*Sthaviras*), who are mendicant authors of a later date. Before the division of Jainism into *Digambaras* and *Svetaambaras* this collection was known as the Miscellaneous (*Prakiirnaka*), containing 18 texts that were mostly used for the confessional rites. They reached the present form probably after the *Svetaambara* council of Valabhi. This collection contains 34 books, which are divided into five groups, viz., *Upaanga, Chedasuutra, Muulasuutra, Prakiirnakasuutra* and *Cuulikaasuutra*.[16]

The *Upaangas* are subsidiary to *Angas*. They consist of 12 texts, viz., *Aupapaatika, Raajaprasniya, Jiivaajiivaabhigama, Prajnaapanaa, Suuryaprajnapti, Jambuudviipaprajnapti, Candraprajnapti, Nirayaavalii, Kalpaavatamsikah, Pushpikaah, Pushpacuulikaah* and *Vrsnidasaah*. The *Upaangas* contain mostly narratives addressed to the laity. Some of these narratives include the description of the grand reception Kind Kuunika gives to Mahaaviira, the dialogue between a Jain mendicant named Kesi and King Paaesi about the existance of the soul, a discussion of two modes of being, a discussion about the holy assembly of the *Tiirthankara*, many stories about lay people involved in good and evil actions and reaping their respective fruits, and other legends and stories that edify a lay person on his path to salvation.[17]

The *Chedasuutras* are a group of texts that is known as the Jaina Book of Discipline (*Vinaya Pitaka*). This collection consists of six texts. They are the following: *Acaaradasaah, Brhatkalpa, Vyavahaara, Nisiitha, Mahaanisi-itha* and *Jiitakalpa*. Some of these works are attributed to Bhadrabaahu. These texts basically deal with the ecclesiastical law regulating the life of a Jain as a layman, laywoman and a monk. They describe various offences and corresponding expiations, qualifications required as a leader, different types of disrespect shown to elders, various austerities that can lead one to *Moksha*, the stages the layman should go through as he progresses in spiritual life, rules for monastic life, codification of monastic law and similar disciplinary matters.[18]

The *Muulasuutras* are four in number. They are *Dasavaikaalika, Uttaraadhyayana, Aavasyaka* and *Pindaniryukti*. They contain various essays that deal with the basic elements of monastic life, such as, non-violence, austerity, begging habits of the mendicant monk, various conducts that are not permitted in the mendicant community, the duty of the mendicant not to hurt six forms of living beings and the need to practice compassion. They also contain dialogues, parables and catechisms. Similarly they maintain that a mendicant monk's sacrifices are not external, but internal, and calls for not being angry, not to dishearten, but to pardon and to show mercy. The next group of works included in the *Angabaahyas* are *Prakiirnakasuutras*. They are a collection of ten short texts called the *Miscellaneous*, viz., *Catuhsarana, Aturapratyaakhyaana, Bhaktaparijnaa, Samstaaraka, Tandulavaicaarika, Candravedhyaka, Devendrastava, Ganividyaa, Mahaapratyaakhyaana* and *Viirastava*. They contain detailed descriptions of the rituals associated with the preparation for a holy death. The rituals are the following: taking the four refuges, renunciation by the sick, renunciation of food, preparing the death-bed, contemplation on rice – the condition for living, retaining consciousness at the last moment of life, praise of *Jinas* by the king of gods, knowledge of propitious times for monastic activities, renunciation at the time of death and praising the Lord Mahaaviira. The final group of *Angabaahyas* are the *Cuulikaasuutras*, which consist of two texts, viz., *Nandii-suutra* and *Anuyogadvaara-suutra*. They include a summary of most of the canonical books. In short, the last collection of *Angabaahyas* is an appendix to the *Aagamas*.[19]

2.2. POST-CANONICAL EXPOSITIONS

The post-canonical expositions (*Anuyogas*) are different from both the canonical texts and the commentaries on them. They are the compositions of various *Aacaaryas*, who are learned monk-scholars. They belong to both the *Digambara* and the *Svetaamabara* traditions. The writings of these

Aacaaryas of both traditions, when put together, form the largest collection of non-Vedic Indian literature, called the *Anuyogas*. In the *Digambara* tradition, the *Anuyogas* have always enjoyed canonical status. The collection is divided into four categories, which sometimes are referred to as the four *Vedas* of the Jainas. They are *Prathamaanuyoga, Karnaanuyoga, Caranaanuyoga* and *Dravyaanuyoga*.[20]

The *Prathamaanuyoga* is the primary exposition. It contains biographies of *Jinas* and other famous mythological personalities, which form the basis of popular Jaina religious life. These texts have contributed greatly to the popularisation of Jainism among the masses. The *Karanaanuyoga* contains expositions on technical matters and deals with the sciences of antiquity, such as, cosmogony, cosmology and astronomy. The *Caranaanuyoga* is an exposition on discipline. It confines itself to the exploration of rules that pertain to the life of a layperson and that of a mendicant. The *Dravyaanuyoga* deals with the study of substances, i.e., the existent realities. It touches upon every aspect of Jaina philosophy, viz., ontology, epistemology, psychology and other sciences. The fourth *Anuyoga* also includes *Stotras*, poetical hymns in praise of various *Jinas*, either individually or collectively. In these *Stotras*, the *Jinas* are praised for preaching the doctrine. Hence in glorifying the *Jinas*, these philosophical poems glorify their doctrines, while criticizing the doctrines of the opponents. Thus, these *Stotras* have a completely philosophical orientation. While emphasizing to the intellectual aspects of the Jaina religious life, these *Stotras* sustain the cultic life of Jainism.[21]

The main purpose of these post-canonical expositions of the *Aacaaryas* is to develop a sense of missionary zeal among the monks to propagate the religion they believed in, giving them a sound intellectual background in the doctrines the *Jinas* taught. At the same time, they wanted to animate the faith of the laity, caring for their spiritual needs through popular stories and biographies of the *Jinas* and other mythological figures, comparable to the ones mentioned in the Hindu *Epics* and the *Puraanas*. Thus at the heart of these *Anuyogas* lies the intention of protecting the religion of the Jainas from the attacks of Hinduism and to make Jainism as popular as Hinduism so that it can appeal to the masses, at the same time strengthening the faith of the Jain monks and nuns, so that they can become true missionaries of the faith.[22]

3. JAINA COMMUNITY

The Jaina community is well organized. It consists of four orders (*Tiirthas*), viz., the order of monks (*Saadhus*), the order of nuns (*Saadhviis*), the order of laymen (*Sraavakas*) and the order of laywomen (*Sraavikaas*). Already in his lifetime, Mahaaviira had formed these four *Tiirthas*. It is said that in Mahaaviira's lifetime about 14,000 monks, 36,000 nuns, 159,000 laymen and 358,000 laywomen were members of these four orders. According to the plan of Lord Mahaaviira, the spiritual leadership and organization of the four *Tiirtha* remain in the hands of the monks, to whom the other three orders are subordinate. But the monks and the nuns have their livelihood from the pious donations from the laymen and laywomen. This is the genius of Mahaaviira that formed the last two orders and organized them to assist the first two orders. Possibly this is the reason that Jainism really took root in the land of its birth, unlike Buddhism. There is a great bond between the members first two and the last two orders. Though the orders of laymen and laywomen are under the spiritual care of the monks and the nuns, yet the laypeople have a great deal of influence over the monks and the nuns, as the latter depend on the former for the material things in life. From this point of view, the laypeople are called the parents of the ascetic. The monks and the nuns are advised not to burden the lay people in this matter. They are expected to be like the bees. Just as a bee is not bound to any flower, so also the monks and the nuns should not be attached to any type of food and should be ready to eat whatever the laypeople are able to provide. In addition, the laypeople are able to check the power-crazy, money-loving monks and nuns, thereby helping them to remain faithful to the chosen path of religious life. If the monks and nuns deviate from living the life of the vows they profess, the laypeople interfere and ask them to give up their life of consecration and the signs of their consecration are taken away from them. Thus, the spiritual dependence of the laypeople on the ascetic and the material dependence of the ascetic on the laypeople regulate extreme forms of behavior in both the groups. This cordial of relationship between the four orders is the foundation of the true religious life of the Jaina community. In this manner, the cooperation and mutual dependence of the laity and the consecrated people in Jainism provide a healthy atmosphere for the growth of *Jaina-sangha*.[23]

The first two orders, i.e., the orders of the monks and the nuns, are meant for men and woman who wish to renounce the world. They must lead a life of penance and religious meditation. They are also expected to practice various forms of ascetical practices and to take special vows. A number of conditions are prescribed before they can enter the orders of monks and nuns. For instance, people with physical deformity, those given to sensual pleasure, those who are convicted under the law, murderers and people of similar category cannot become monks and nuns. Many such conditions are prescribed so that unworthy persons may not enter these two orders. Thus, the members of these two orders live a life of discipline, and every detail about their daily living is strictly prescribed.[24]

The last two orders, i.e., those of laymen and laywomen, consist of householders who cannot renounce the world as monks due to their lives in the world, and devout women whose household duties do not allow them to become nuns. But they attain their salvation by living modified rules. The members of these two orders take upon themselves small vows, which influence their conduct greatly. They are not allowed to take any form of food that would make them sinful. The members of the last two orders are forbidden certain foods, alcoholic drinks, unfiltered water and similar food that would involve the killing of small living organisms. Similarly, they are not allowed military service, hunting, fishing, the making and selling of weapons, ivory works, trading animals and similar works that go against the principle of non-violence. So the Jainas usually take to trade up trade in cloth, pearls, corns, banking and other similar professions. They have the duty of hearing the preaching of Jaina monks and nuns, and living those edicts in the lives. They are expected to practice the virtue of generosity in an extraordinary manner, as they have the duty to look after the material needs of the monks and nuns, besides maintaining religious institutions like monasteries, temples, other centers for care for animals (*Paanjraapols*) and the like. The laywomen do a great deal of service to holy men and women, thereby expressing their generosity, while laymen contribute generously to the cause of religion. They believe that a life in the simple form of asceticism and a life of generosity lead them to the attainment of *Moksha*. All sorts of people who can voluntarily do the above-mentioned duties are allowed to enter the orders of the laymen and laywomen. It is said that in Mahaaviira's time, even kings and nobles were delighted to be part of these two orders of hearers.[25] In this manner, the Jaina community is a well-knit, self-sustaining and coherent organization.

4. JAINA PHILOSOPHY

The Jainas explain the fundamentals of their philosophy with the help of nine categories, viz., *Jiiva* (living reality), *Ajiiva* (non-living reality), *Punya* (merit), *Paapa* (sin), *Aasrava* (channels of *Karma*), *Bandha* (bondage), *Samvara* (impeding *Karma*), *Nirjaraa* (wiping out *Karma*) and *Moksha* (salvation). The *Digambaras* recognize all nine categories, while the *Svetaambaras* speak of only seven categories, as they leave out the categories of *Punya* and *Paapa*, saying that they are included in the latter ones.[26]

Now let us make an attempt to explain briefly the basic truths of Jaina philosophy, with the help of these nine concepts. They see this universe as made up of twofold substances (*Dravyas*), the *Jiiva* and *Ajiiva*. The former is the souls that are uncreated, imperishable, knowing and active substances, while the latter is inanimate realities, such as space, time, motion, rest and matter, which are also eternal and uncreated. The mixture of these two types of realities makes up the world, as we know it. For the soul to recover its natural infinitude, it has to separate itself from *Ajiiva*. The performance of good actions leads to *Punya*, while the performance of evil actions, viz., all forms of killing lead to *Paapa*. There are 18 different sins and 82 fruits of sin. These sinful actions and their fruits (*Karma*) enter the *Jiiva* through the medium of the *Aasravas* and accumulate there. Jainas speak of 42 *Aasravas*, such as the senses, emotions and the like. There are also eight types of *Karma* that affect the condition of the soul differently and entangle it with *Ajiiva*. We can speak of many types of *Jiivas*, depending on its involvement with *Ajiiva*. Thus, *Karma* is the link between the *Jiiva* and the *Ajiiva*. As a result the soul is bound (*Bandha*) to *Ajiiva* and enters into the *Samsaara* state of living, which involves transmigration of the soul and the cycle of rebirth after death. There are two ways to free the soul from its bondage to *Ajiiva*, viz., to check the inflow of new *Karma* (*Samvara*) and to destroy the accumulated *Karma* (*Nirjaraa*). To bring about these two ways to remove *Karma*, the Jaina tradition proposes moral and cultic paths, which we will elaborate below. When the *Jiiva* ascends from the grip of *Ajiiva*, by the removal of *Karma*, it achieves *Moksha*, which is a state of perfection, enlightenment, deliverance and the end of all misery.[27]

Another important aspect of Jaina philosophy is the systematic exposition of their logic (*Pramaana-saastra*). It rests on two principles, viz., the doctrine of non-absolutism (*Anekaantavaada*) and the doctrine of partial truths (*Nayavaada*). These theories declare that a particular statement is true from one point of view, while it is invalid from another. For instance, a person may consider the forest as a collection of trees, while the other may consider it as one reality, i.e. as forest in general. Similarly, the total life of a tree, from its springing out of the seed to its bearing fruit, can be seen as a continuous flow, while it can also be grasped as different moments of successive emerging elements. Both of these views are neither totally true, nor totally false, as both are true from different points of view. Thus the Jainas speak of seven perspectives from which a thing can be viewed, and each of the views made are true from their respective standpoints. These seven modes (*Paryaas*) of assertion are: affirming the existence of something from one point of view (*Syaad asti*); denying it from another standpoint (*Syaan naasti*); affirming both existence and non-existence with reference to at different times (*Syaad asti naasti*); affirming both existence and non-existence at the same time would mean that one cannot speak of a thing (*Syaad avaktavyah*); the impossibility of affirmation of existence under some circumstances (*Syaad asti avaktavyah*); similarly, the impossibility of the affirmation of non-existence under different circumstances (*Syaan nasti avaktavyah*) and the impossibility of affirming both existence and non-existence from a third point of view (*Syaad asti naasti avaktvyah*). What the Jainas attempt to drive home by speaking of these seven modes of affirmations is that one should not consider a thing absolutely as existing everywhere, at all times, in all ways and in the form of everything, as the truth of a thing is partial, and so it is to be viewed from different perspectives. This logic of perspectives helps them to bridge the gulf between the two extreme forms of doctrines and to bring about a reconciliation and synthesis.[28]

We have been looking into a general overview of Jaina tradition, its history, its scriptures, its community and its philosophy by way of introduction. Now we move on to our main intent, viz., to consider the reality of Divinity in Jainism and the paths proposed by the Jainas to arrive at the state of the Divine. The ensuing two sections explore these two topics.

4.1. DIVINITIES OF THE JAINA PANTHEON

Jainism does not believe in a theistic God, who is the creator, ruler and destroyer of the universe. The Jainas strongly attack the various theories the theists propose for the explanation of the world's origin, viz., the absolutely perfect God creating this world out of nothing, the eternal God as the organizer of this world with the help of eternally existing souls and matter, the whole universe as the illusion (*adhyaasa*) superimposed on the supreme Being due to the power of *Maayaa* and the world as the manifestation (*Aabhaasa*) of the *Sakti* of the supreme Lord. They give prolonged arguments to show the meaninglessness of all the claims of the various Indian theistic systems of thought.[29] The Jainas, thus, do not see the need for a God to be the author of this universe. They say that since the world is eternal and self-produced, there is absolutely no reason for one to fall back to any eternal Beings to explain the origin of the world. They consider the world as eternal because the basic nature of the world is unchangeable and there occur only partial alterations in the world of reality. These passing changes in the world can be effected from within the inner dynamism of the world itself. The unalterable law of *Karma*, to which even the gods must be in agreement when they act explains the differences among the living beings and their respective destinies. Thus, the Jainas do not visualize a God of theism on whom the world depends for its origin and continuance.[30]

While vehemently denying the reality of the world-creating and world-ruling God, unlike the theists, the Jainas have no aversion to speak of eternally existing blissful super-mundane beings in their system of thought. Strictly speaking we cannot speak of them as atheists, even though the theists may attribute to them the name 'atheists', as they deny the reality of the God of theists. Thus, the Jainas recognize a multitude of divinities, some belonging to the Hindu pantheon and include them in their religious worship. Besides, their cosmography speaks of the divinities of the various world regions, while hagiography refers to different types of spiritual beings that appear during different eras of world history. Though the popular Jainism includes worship being offered to these various divinities, the strict Jaina religious practice considers all these forms of worship as less important and offers the greatest worship to the *Tiirthankara*, who in fact is the true divinity, who overcomes the hold of *Karma* and achieves the state of *Moksha*.[31] Now, let us consider the various types of divinities that form the Jaina pantheon.

4.1.1. DIVINITIES ENUMERATED IN THE HANDBOOK OF RITUAL

The popular Jaina handbook of ritual catalogues a great number of deities to whom worship is offered. This list includes the sons, fathers and mothers of *Tiirthankaras*, the *Ganadharas* – the first disciples of the *Tiirthankaras*, prominent *Svetaambara* nuns who attained salvation and a number of later saints who are worshipped due to their piety. Jainas also worship a number of super-mundane beings whose level of perfection is lesser than the above-mentioned, but who manifest great concern for the people of this world. In this context, mention is to be made of the two heavenly companions of the *Tiirthankaras*, viz., the spirit (*Yaksha*) and the goddess of doctrine (*Saasanadevataa*). It is the belief of both the *Digambaras* and the *Svetaambaras* that a *Yaksha* and a *Saasanadevataa* stand at the side of all the 24 *Tiirthankaras*, though there are differences in the names given to each of them. Worship is offered to these 24 *Yakshas* and 24 *Saasanadevataas*. In Jaina iconography the *Yakshas* and the *Saasanadevataas* are depicted as standing along with the *Tiirthankara* they serve. In some of such depictions, they are represented like the Hindu deities, *Brahmaa, Kumaara, Kubera, Varuna, Kaalii* and *Gaurii*. They are also given the names of these Hindu gods and goddesses, whose representations they share. There is also the mention of 16 goddesses of learning (*Vidyaadevataas*), who are described as special deities of the Jainas. The great sage Hemachandra of *Svetaambara* tradition gives them the following names: *Rohinii, Prajnpatii, Vajrasrnkhalaa, Kulisankusaa, Cakresvarii, Naradattaa, Kaalii, Mahaakaalii, Gaurii, Gaandhaari, Savaastramahaajvaalaa, Maanavii, Vairotyaa, Acchuptaa, Maanasii* and *Mahaamaanasikaa*.[32]

Besides these, the handbook of ritual mentions a number of deities, who belong to the Hindu pantheon. Various books refer to different names of the Hindu deities. For instance, Vardhamaana Suuri's *Aacaaradinakara* gives the following names: *Indra, Agni, Yama, Nirrti, Varuna, Vaayu, Kubera, Iisaana* and the *Naagas*. The same text also mentions different gods connected with different houses of the moon, viz., *Brahaspati, Pitras, Yoni, Aryamaa, Visvakarmaa, Mitra, Jala, Visvadevas, Vishnu, Vasus, Ajapaada, Ahirbudhnya* and *Puushaa*. Similarly, Sukhalaajii's *Pancapratikramana* speaks of another eight gods as the guardians of the world (*Lokapaalas*), viz., *Soma, Yama, Varuna, Kubera, Indra, Aaditya, Skanda* and *Vinaayaka*. The nine gods associated with the nine planets, viz., Sun (*Suurya*), Moon (*Candra*), Mars (*Mangala*), Mercury (*Budha*), Jupiter (*Guru*), Venus (*Sukra*), Saturn (*Sani*) and Nodes (*Raahu* and *Ketu*) are also stated. There is a reference to the *Genii* of the animal-circle and the houses of the Moon (*Nakshatras*). Patron gods of the temples (*Kshetrapaala*), countries (*Desapaalas*), cities (*Nagarapaalas*) and villages (*Graamadevataa*) also find a place in the Jaina pantheon.[33]

The Jainas also worship a number of female deities. Six goddesses are specifically referred to, viz., *Srii, Hrii, Bhddhi, Dhrti, kiirti* and *Lakshmii*. According to the *Digambara* tradition, these goddesses live on the islands of six big mountains of Jambuudviipa. The goddess *Sarasvatii*, the goddess of learning, enjoys an exalted place in the Jaina pantheon. She is also known as *Srutadevataa*. The 14 *Puurvas* and the 12 *Angas* of the Jaina scriptures are said to be her limbs and ornaments respectively. Thus, *Sarasvatii* is considered as one who presides over the Jaina scriptures. She is known as *Jinavani*. She is invoked to dispel the darkness of ignorance due to the karmic matter concealing right knowledge (*Jnaanavaraniya-karma*). Her symbols are the swan – which is her mount-manuscript, rosary, water vessel, vina and *Varada-mudra*. In iconographic depictions she is represented with two and four hands. The four-armed *Sarasvatii* seems to have enjoyed the greatest veneration among the *Digambara* and *Svetaambara* sects. Her name appears twice in the group of 24 *Yakshis*, viz., as the *Yakshi* of *Jina* Abbhinadana and *Jina* Suparsvanatha. She is also considered the goddess of music and dance. Worship is also offered to various Mother-goddesses. The ritual texts mention the worship of the patron goddesses of caste (*Jnaatidevii*) and clan (*Kuladevii*). Similarly veneration is given to holy animals, serpent-gods, holy trees – like those that are holy to the *Tiirthankaras*, holy places – like temples and holy symbols – like images and books.[34] Thus, we find in the Jaina worship a great number of gods and goddesses of their own, besides the ones borrowed from the Hindu pantheon.

4.1.2. DIVINITIES OF THE COSMOGRAPHIC WORLD REGIONS

In order to speak about the divinities that inhabit the cosmographic world regions, we must first consider the Jaina perception of the organization of the cosmos. Hence, in the first section we consider the Jaina cosmography and the inhabitants of the various regions. In the second section, we delve into the study of the various divinities that belong to these regions.

4.1.2.1. JAINA COSMOGRAPHY

Cosmography is the study of the general plan of the cosmos. It becomes the object of Jaina philosophical speculation mainly for practical and religious reasons. The basic motivation behind Jaina cosmography is not the scientific analysis of the structure of the world, but rather it is more soteriological and salvational, as it provides the conceptual background for the Jaina vision of the bondage of *Jiiva* and its path to liberation. The Jainas believe that other than what is known about the visible world, every detail that is contained in their cosmography is not known through rational speculation, but rather it is arrived at by way of contemplation.[35]

The Jainas conceive the universe as situated in space, which is divided into two parts, viz., the cosmos (*Lokaakaasa*) and the void (*Alokaakaasa*). The former constitutes the cosmos of enormous extent, filled with all forms of life, starting from the highly vulnerable to inadvertent and deliberate violence, plants, animals, humans, hell-beings and gods, while the latter consists of absolute empty space, which neither the material nor the spiritual reality can penetrate. The Jainas visualize the cosmos (*Lokaakaasa*) as a firmly fixed, multi-storied structure of unchangeable shape and limited size, though it is much larger than human beings can imagine. Its dimensions can be measured with the help of a measure called a rope (*Rajjuu*), which is equal to uncountable numbers of *Yojanas*, a standard Jain measure, which is equal to eight miles. The height of the entire structure of the cosmos is 14 *Rajjuus*. The breadth from north to south is seven *Rajjuus*. The breadth from west to east, at the lowest position, is also seven *Rajjuus*, but it decreases, till it measures one *Rajjuu* in the height of seven *Rajjuus*, which is the center of the entire structure. The breadth increases from this point and reaches on expansion of five *Rajjuus* in the middle of the remaining part and then decreases again till it is one *Rajjuu* at the highest position. This total structure covers a space of 343 cubic-*Rajjuus*. Three atmospheres surround the entire structure of the world, viz., an atmosphere of dense water, an atmosphere of dense wind and an atmosphere of thin wind. This massive structure of the universe is divided into four parts. The netherworld (*Naaraka-loka*) occupies the lowest part of the universe – in which there are the hells; the middle-world (*Madhya-loka*) is placed at the center – where the human beings live; the heavenly world (*Devaloka*) is found above the middle world – where the gods live and at the top of them all is the world of the redeemed (*Siddha-silaa*) – which is the abode of liberated souls. Running from top to bottom is the shaftlike zone called *Trasanaadii*, in which only the multi-sensed beings (*Tras*) can exist. A number of metaphors are used to describe this gigantic structure of the cosmos. We mention the one Vinayavijaya gives in his book *Lokaprakaasa*. According to him, the universe can be compared to a human being standing with legs stretched out, feet apart and arms akimbo, i.e., hands are placed on the hips, while the elbows are bent outwards. In this figure, the netherworld is imagined as lying in the region of the lower parts of the body below the hip, the middleworld is placed in the region of the hip, the upper part of the human body forms the heavenly world and the head forms the abode of the liberated souls. This vast, self-contained universe that is uncreated and has no end, provides the setting for the infinite number of beings (*Jiivas*) living in it to move from bondage to liberation through the cycle of birth to death and death to birth.[36]

The netherworld consists of seven levels of hell, having a total of 49 stories and 8,400,000 hells. The seven levels are the following: the shine of jewels (*Ratna-prabhaa*), the shine of pebbles (*Sarkaraa-prabhaa*), the shine of sand (*Vaalukaa-prabhaa*), the shine of mud (*Panka-prabhaa*), the shine of smoke (*Dhuuma-prabhaa*), the shine of darkness (*Tamah-prabhaa*) and the shine of great darkness (*Mahaatamah-prabhaa*). Except for the first two stories of the first level of the netherworld, viz., the *Ratna-prabhaa*, all the other levels are meant for punishing the souls that have sinned in their previous lives. It is said that the hells of the first four levels are hot, while the fifth is partially cold and the last two levels are the coldest. The hell-dwellers (*Naaraki*) are born by way of manifestations, i.e., suddenly coming out of the holes in the wall and falling into the hell. Their complete evolution takes place in one *Muhuurta*, which is equivalent to 48 minutes. They have a karmic and metamorphic body, with a grey appearance and are unsymmetrical in structure, and are hermaphrodites. They land in different levels of hells depending on their sins in past lives. Being in the lower levels of hell means they have to suffer greater suffering. They undergo various forms of sufferings, such as, that come from the atmosphere in the hell, the *Naarakis* cause to each other, special punishments inflicted on them for their past sins and various ill-treatments that come from the evil *Asuras*. Interestingly all the hurts and the wounds the hell-dwellers receive never kill them. They heal very fast so that their bodies are ready to for new suffering. The hell-dwellers die when they have gone through and completed the various punishments their past *Karma* prescribes. Their souls leave the decayed bodies and assume a new existence as an animal or a human being. Thus, for the Jainas hell is a place of purification rather than eternal condemnation.[37]

Above the netherworld lies the middle world, which is the world of humans and animals. It is one *Rajjuu* broad and long. The mount Meru is the center of the middle world. At the base of Mount Meru, there is the circular continent called Jambuudviip, which is divided into seven regions, six mountains separating them from the south to the north. The first of the seven regions is Bharat, the South Asian world, the only region that is physically accessible to us. Fourteen rivers originate from the six mountains and make the Jambuudviip a fertile place. A ring-formed ocean of salt surrounds the Jambuudviip. Similarly, there is a series of innumerable (*Asankhyaat*) circular continents surrounded by different types of oceans. Of these, the first two continents, Dhaatatkii Khanda and Pushkaravaradviipa, have inhabitable areas. A portion of habitable land in the Jambuudviip and the other two continents is known as 'the land of enjoyment' (*Bhogbhuumi*). Humans who are found in the *Bogbhuumi* are born as twins and are similar to those that existed in the world during the paradisiacal stage. Their lives are spent in a state of continuous sensuous enjoyment. They live without any struggle, as the trees there magically fulfil every wish of those who live there. There is no premature death here. As a result, asceticism cannot be practiced here, *Tiirthankaras* do not appear, and liberation is not possible to those who live here. Another portion of the inhabitable land is known as 'the land of endeavor' (*Karmabhuumi*), in which our region is included. The humans who live here have to earn their living through hard work, and premature death is possible. Besides, this area has the propensity for asceticism and reflection. *Tiirthankaras* are born here and liberation is possible. The most interesting aspect of the Jaina cosmography of the middle world is not its complicated physical geography, but its moral geography, which helps man to overcome the influences of *Karma* and attain salvation. Thus, we find that the motivation behind the cosmography of the Jainas is more salvational than scientific.[38]

The beings of the middle world (*Jiivas*) are of two types, viz., those that can be liberated (*Mukta*) and those that cannot be liberated (*Samsaarii*). The former are those that have shed every form of Karmic matter, while the latter are those still in the bondage of *Karma*. The *Samsaarii* class is further grouped into beings that cannot move at their own volition (*Sthaavar*) and beings that can move about at their own will (*Tras*). The first class of *Samsaarii* beings, viz., *Sthaavar* group of beings usually have only one sense, viz., the sense of touch. They are: the earth bodies (*Prithviikaay*), the water bodies (*Apkaay*), the fire bodies (*Teukaay*), the air bodies (*Vaayukaay*) and plants (*Vanaspatikaay*). The last of these categories of the *Sthaavar* group, viz., the plants, can be divided into two classes: those in which there is only one soul (*Pratyek*) and those that contain infinite souls in a given body (*Saadhaaran*). The latter are further divided into gross (*Baadar*) and subtle (*Suksham*). The Jains are not allowed to have diets of gross plant products, such as, potatoes, carrots, onions, garlic and yams, as they are believed to have many souls besides containing tiny beings called *Nigods*. The second class of *Samsaarii* beings is the *Tras* beings that can move at will. They are classified into different groups depending on the senses they have: the *Vaklendriy* class have two to four senses, while the *Pancendriy* class has five senses. Animals with less than five senses belong to the former class, while five-sensed animals and the humans belong to the latter class. The humans can be womb-born (*Garbhaj*) or born by spontaneous generation (*Sammuurchim*). The latter originate from various impurities, which the womb-born humans produce, such as, excrement, urine, phlegm or semen. They are without intelligence and cannot be detected with our senses. They die in a *Muhuurta*, i.e., in about 48 minutes, without being able to develop the full characteristics of a human body. Just as the Jaina belief in plants with multiple-souls leads them to specific forms of vegetarianism, similarly the belief in the spontaneous emergence of humans also makes them prescribe ascetic practices. In comparison to the hell-dwellers, plants, animals and humans experience less misery. But birth as an animal or a plant is not something desirable, because the human form of existence and having a human body is vital for the attainment of liberation. Though not all human may arrive at the final state, it is only possible for humans. Therefore, being born as a human has significant consequence.[39]

Above the middle world lies the world of gods, which is the destination of those who live a virtuous life. The area, which the deities inhabit, is contained within the shaft-like *Tras-naadii*. Between the lowest heaven and the terrestrial world is the gap, where the planetary and stellar bodies move around the summit of Mount Meru. The heavenly region that begins directly over the crown of Mount Meru is called the *Vaimaanas*. It consists of 12 paradises (*Kalpas*), viz., *Saudharma, Aisaana, Maahendra, Brahmaloka, Latanka, Mahaasukra, Sahasraara, Aanata, Pranata, Aarana* and *Acyuta*. Then there are the nine heavens forming the head of the human shaped universe called *Graiveyakas* and the five last levels of heavens known as *Anuttaras*, viz., *Vijaya, Vaijayanta, Jayanta, Aparaajita* and *Sarvaarthasiddha*. Thus, there are 26 separate paradises placed one above the other. Above the highest of these paradises, the *Sarvaarthasiddha*, is situated the *Ishtapragbhaara*, the final resort of the liberated souls.[40]

Now that we have elaborated the basic structure of the of the universe, including the layout of the world of the gods, we can move on to speak of the divinities who live in this world in the next section.

4.1.2.2. DIVINITIES OF THE WORLD OF GODS

The gods and goddesses resemble the hell-dwellers, in the manner of their coming to be and the type of body they have. They come to be by way of manifestation (*Upapaata*). They suddenly appear at a place where they are supposed to be born as the result of their previous *Karma*. It is said that when they are born, they appear on divine beds in the form of 16-years-old youths. As long as they live they remain young, and their lives are very long in comparison with the humans. They have fine metamorphic bodies. Their bodies do not have blood, meat or bone. Their bodies are beautiful, luminous and free from all forms of illnesses. Since they have metamorphic bodies, they do not eat as human beings do. When they desire food, it automatically enters their bodies in the form of pure atoms (*Pudgals*). When they are born and when they die, they are not subject to any forms of pollutions (*Suutak*) associated with birth or death The gods are said to know of their death six months before it takes place, and when it happens the atoms of their bodies melt away like camphor, leaving no smell or dirt. The fundamental difference between the gods and the hell-dwellers is that while the former are rewarded for the merits (*Punya*) of their virtuous acts in the previous life, the latter are punished for the evil acts of their earlier existence. As a result, the gods and goddesses cannot suffer from any forms of evil. Their lives are full of pleasure, fun and frolic. They enjoy the magnificent palaces of the heavens. Their conduct could be good or bad. Self-discipline is impossible for them, because as soon as they wish something, their desire is totally fulfilled. In comparison with human beings, the gods and the goddesses have special powers. Some Jainas believe that the deities can assist humans, although some gods, belonging to lower categories, can also harm them. Once their *Karma* is completed, their souls leave their bodies, and they are born elsewhere in the earthly regions depending on the *Karma* of their godly existence.[41]

The gods of the *Devaloka* are divided into four categories, viz., the *Bhavanavaasiis*, the *Vyantaras*, the *Jyotishkas* and the *Vaimanikas*. Usually the bodily feature of the first three groups is black, dark, grey or fiery, while that of the last group is fiery, yellow or white. These four categories of gods are further divided into a number of subclasses of various ranks and grades, though this hierarchical structure varies from one category to the other. We mention the general hierarchical structure that is followed in different categories, starting from the highest to the lowest, and their variations. The order is as follows: the kings (*Indras*), the princes (*Saamaanikas*), the dignitaries of the state (*Traayastrimsas*), the treasures (*Paarishadyas*), the bodyguards (*Aatmarakshas*), the policemen (*Lokpaala*), the warriors (*Aniikas*), the citizens (*Prakiirnakas*), the servants, the riding animals, such as, horses, lions or birds (*Aabhiyogyas*) and the common people (*Kibishikas*). The ranks of the dignitaries of the state and the policemen are not found among the *Vyantaras* and the *Joytishkas*. These differences in rank are absent in the highest subclasses of the *Vaimaanikas*. The members of different ranks look very different in their physical features, size of the body, the clothes they wear and other matters. Of these ten ranks, the kings (*Indras*) are the most significant gods. It is said that there are 64 kings in the world of gods. Of these 20 rule the *Bhavanvaasiis*, 32 the *Vyantaras* and its sub-category, two for the *Jyotishkas* and the ten for the 12 paradisiacal regions. The *Indras* and their consorts, *Indraaniis*, play important roles in the ritual worship of the Jainas.[42] We briefly consider the various categories of the gods in the following sections.

4.1.2.2.1. Bhavanavaasiis

The *Bhavanavaasiis* are the lowest of the four categories of gods. Their name literally means 'those who dwell in palatial buildings' (*Bhavana*). They live in the uppermost stories of the *Ratna-prabhaa* of the netherworld, and are untouched by the pains of hell. Their look is like that of beautiful young people. For this reason they are referred to as '*Kumaara*', i.e., princes. There are ten classes of *Bhavanavaasiis*. They are: the demon-princes (*Asura-kumaara*), the serpent-princes (*Naaga-kumaara*), the eagle-princes (*Supar-*

na-kumaara), the wind-princes (*Vaayu-kumaara*), the island-princes (*Dviipa-kumaara*), the ocean-princes (*Udadhi-kumaara*), the princes of directions (*Dik-kumaara*), the lightning-princes (*Vidyut-kumaara*), the thunder-princes (*Stanita-kumaara*) and the fire-princes (*Agni-kumaara*). Two *Indras* rule over each class, one from the north and the other from the south. Every *Indra* has several main wives and many subordinate wives. He has under his control seven armies consisting of seven divisions. He commands each division with the help of a commander. The armies include infantry, horses, elephants, bulls, chariots, musicians and actors. The features of this group of gods are black, dark, grey and fiery.[43]

4.1.2.2.2. Vyantaras

The *Vyantaras* are subterranean demons and demi-gods that live in the intermediate level between the uppermost level of hell and the middle world. Some of them also live in certain regions of the *Ratna-prabhaa* of the netherworld. They also inhabit jungles and caves. It is believed among the Jainas that this group of deities can help human beings, but some of them can also be malicious and do harm to men. The following are some of their classes: the spirits (*Kinnaras*), the goblins (*Kimpurushas*), the large serpents (*Mahoragas*), the *Genii* playing music (*Gandharvas*), the spirits of treasures (*Yakshas*), the monsters (*Raakshasas*), the ghosts (*Bhuutas*) and the demons (*Pisaacas*). Two *Indras* rule over each of these classes and their subclasses. They have a large royal household and seven armies. Their features are black, dark, grey and fiery.[44]

4.1.2.2.3. Jyotishkas

The *Jyotishkas* are planetary deities. They dwell on the earth and in the heavens above. According to Jaina cosmography, these deities encircle the Meru Mount clockwise at a height of 790 to 900 *Yojanas* over the plains of Jambuudvippa, Dhaatakiikhanda and half of Pushkaradviipa. They are said to travel in chariots drawn by lions, elephants, bulls and horses. The *Jyotishkas* are of two types viz., the moving and the stationary. The moving *Jyotishkas* are of four types, viz., suns, moons, planets and moving stars (*Nakshatras*). The stationary *Jyotishkas* are the fixed stars. According to the Jainas, there is an equation of a great number of fixed stars, 28 *Nakshatras*, 88 planets and one moon for every sun.[45]

4.1.2.2.4. Vaimaanikas

The *Vaimaanikas* are the most important among the four groups of gods, who inhabit the world of gods. They are called so because they live in the mobile palaces (*Vimaanas*) of the upper world. These mobile palaces have the size of a large township and are adorned with precious stones. Between these *Vimaanas*, there are the feeder-*Vimaanas* through which they move about in space. The *Vaimaanikas* are divided into two types, viz., the *Kalpopapans* and the *Kalpaatiitas*. The *Kalpopapans* are the lowest among the *Vaimaanikas*, and they are born and live in paradises (*Kalpas*) in the lower heavens. They occupy the first and second levels of the heavens, though they may visit the other parts of the heavens. They perform the celebrations of the *Tiirthankaras*. Besides, they live in organized societies with various ranks starting from *Indra*. The *Kalpaatiitas* are the deities without paradises, who live in the higher levels of the heavens. They are two types, viz., the *Graiveyaks*, who live in the nine stories of the upper heavens above the *Kalpopapans* and the *Anuttars*, who live in the five still upper stories the heavenly world. These second groups of *Vaimaanikas* are superior to the former. They neither participate in any form of ritual nor live in an organized society. These gods are similar to one another and all have the title *Ahamindra*, i.e., 'I am *Indra*'.[46]

The *Vaimaanikas* are radiant in their appearance and youthful. It is said that they have no shadow, do not shut their eyes, and their nails and hair do not grow. Their minds are always fresh, and they are always joyful. The higher the regions of the heavens, where the gods live, the greater is their lifespan, their knowledge and power. But the bodies of gods who live in the higher regions are smaller than the ones who live in the lower heavens. The feature of the gods who live in the first region is fiery, yellow in the second and the third regions, and from then on white. Similarly there are differences among the various levels of the *Vaimaanikas*, regarding their sexual orientation and expression. The lower classes of the *Vaimaanikas* satisfy their sexual desire by bodily mating. For the gods of the second level it is enough to embrace, kiss or to touch their consorts to feel sexual satisfaction. In the next stage, mere looking at the beauty of each other fulfils them sexually. The gods of the higher levels feel sexual satisfaction when they hear the sweet voices of their consorts. In the next level the gods feel the joy of sex when they fondly think of each other. In the highest level, especially among the deities without *Kalpas*, i.e., the *Kalpaatiitas*, love life assumes a finer form, and they have hardly any erotic desires. Thus, in the higher regions of the heavens there are no goddesses.[47]

Jainas believe that both believers and unbelievers can be born into the *Kalpa* heavens if they have good *Karma* to their account. Similarly, the good life associated with ascetical practices can lead a person to be born into the *Graiveyaka* regions of the heavens. When the gods have completed their lifespan in heaven, according to the demands of the past *Karma*, death takes hold of them. The gods who live right faith in their life in heaven can be born as human beings and move towards attainment of salvation at their next birth after life in heaven. The gods who live in the five *Anuttara* regions of the higher heavens are believed to have the right faith and the fourth stage of virtue. Others are born at lower stages, as earth beings, plants or animals.[48]

In this section, we have looked into the Jaina cosmographic world regions and the gods who belong to the world of gods. Now, we turn our attention to the Jaina hagiography, which speaks of the holy men who have appeared in the unfolding of the world history.

4.1.3. DIVINITIES OF JAINA HAGIOGRAPHY

The study of the holy men and saints of Jaina history implies the study of the Jaina perception of world history, as it is in the history of the world that holy men emerge. Therefore, before we can consider the Jaina hagiography, we must analyze the Jaina concept of world history. Hence, in the first section we look into the Jaina perception of world history, while in the second we study the various holy men who have manifested in history.

4.1.3.1. JAINA CONCEPTION OF WORLD HISTORY

Just as the Jaina cosmography visualizes this universe as an immensely vast structural whole occupying a large amount of space, similarly the Jaina conception of world history envisions the cosmos and everything in it as moving through inconceivably large periods of time. Though in most parts of the cosmos the general temporal conditions remain forever the same, in the *Karmabhuumi* regions of the universe time moves through repetitive and gradual sequences of ascending and descending world periods. These changes, in turn, effect cycles of physical and moral rise and decline. In other words, as a result of the emergence of the ascending and descending world periods, there come about changes in the climate, vegetation of the land, size of the body, lifespan and virtuous life of the inhabitants, which, make life better or worse.[49]

The Jainas postulate two world periods, which come one after the other and continue to take their turn eternally, viz. the descending period (*Avasarpinii*) and the ascending period (*Utasrpinii*). The former begins with the best possible conditions of life and becomes gradually worse, until it reaches a state of total destruction, while the latter commences with the worst condition of the cosmos, moves up progressively and finally reaches the best possible state of existence. Each of these world periods is divided into six eras, the duration of which is fixed and unchangeable. The basis of the division is how 'happy' (*Sukhamaa*) or 'unhappy' (*Dukhamaa*) is the condition of existence in a given era. The six eras of the descending world period are the following: the happiest era (*Sukhamaa-sukhamaa*), the happy era (*Sukhamaa*), the happy-unhappy era (*Sukhamaa-dukhamaa*), the unhappy-happy era (*Dukhamaa-sukhamaa*), the unhappy era (*Dukhamaa*) and the unhappy-unhappy era (*Dukhamaa-dukhamaa*). The six eras of the ascending world period are the following: the unhappy-unhappy era (*Dukhamaa-dukhamaa*), the unhappy era (*Dukhamaa*), the unhappy-happy era (*Dukhamaa-sukhamaa*), the happy-unhappy era (*Sukhamaa-dukhamaa*), the happy era (*Sukhamaa*) and the happy-happy era (*Sukhamaa-sukhamaa*). These descending and ascending world periods are considered as one cycle, each of which forms a half-cycle. These two world periods, taken together, are referred to as 'one turning of the wheel of time' (*Kaala-cakra*). The six eras of every period or the half-cycle are called the spokes (*Ara*) of the wheel of time. The one turning of the wheel of time, i.e., the passing of one descending and one ascending period, takes approximately 20 *Koraakorii Saagaropamas*. One *Koraakorii* is equal to ten million multiplied by ten million. The term *Saagaropan* or *Saagar* stands for a unit of time. The obscure and difficult calculation of time the Jainas allot to each cycle only points to the inconceivable period of time involved for the completion of a cycle. According to the Jaina thinkers the wheel of time keeps turning in an unalterable regularity, having no beginning and no end. As a result, the descending period and the ascending period follow one another uninterruptedly and eternally.[50]

The descending period begins with the happy-happy era, which is the best of all eras. During this era, the earth is filled with beautiful trees and plants, the air sends out fragrance and human beings are white as snow. There are no caste and class distinctions, as all are equal and live contentedly. There are no illnesses or dissatisfaction among the people, as all their needs are met without any effort, with the help of ten wish-trees (*Kalpadruma*). The size of the body is large and their lifespan is long. The children are born only just before the parents die. As soon as the children are born the father dies by yawning, while the mother dies by sneezing. They are born as twins, as a boy and a girl. They are united for a lasting companionship of life. They take just 49 days to grow up and so need no parental care. People live on fruits and they eat a very small quantity of food once in three days. When people die, they are born as gods in the world of gods. This era lasts for four *Koraakorii Saagaropamas*. In the happy era the conditions of life are similar to the former, but there is a sizable drop in happiness and virtue. The size of the body is smaller and the lifespan decrease. Hence they eat once in two days and a greater quantity of food is taken. The children take 64 days to grow. Here, too, those who die are reborn in the world of gods. The second era lasts for three *Koraakorii Saagaropamas*.[51]

The happy-unhappy era brings still further deterioration of living conditions. The size of the body becomes smaller. The wish-trees begin to disappear. People have to eat every day the fruits of the tress to sustain life. The children take 79 days to grow up. As there are not enough fruits for everyone, a division of people into classes and land divisions comes about. Greed and passion in people increase and moral life declines. Unlike the previous two eras, those who die are reborn in any of the three worlds. This period lasts for two *Koraakorii Saagaropamas*. The unhappy-happy era brings situations that are worse. The wish-trees cease to exist. People have to work hard daily to find food for their sustenance. Body size becomes still smaller and lifespan decreases. Illnesses and misfortune become widespread. Moral life deteriorates further. This period lasts for 42,000 years less than a *Koraakorii Saagaropama*. The Jainas say that this period ends three years and eight and a half months after Mahaaviira's death. The unhappy era is the present era in which we live. It is said that it is going to last for 21,000 years. This period is believed to bring extreme climatic conditions, which result in floods, draughts and famine. Life span and body size decrease further. Greed and bloodshed are on the increase, as rulers torment their subjects, and evil men persecute the holy men. People totally forget the scriptures and religious values.[52]

The sixth era of the descending cycle is the unhappy-unhappy era. It brings the most horrible conditions. The world is total chaos in this period. The days are very hot and the nights are very cold due to the activity of the sun and moon respectively. Body size and life span reduce drastically. People live on fish and tortoise meat. These difficult conditions continue for 21,000 years, at the end of which is total devastation due to acid rain for 49 days. Thus, comes to the end the first half-cycle of the one wheel of time, i.e., the descending period. Then begins the next half-cycle, the ascending period with the unhappy-unhappy era, moves through the unhappy era, unhappy-happy era, happy-unhappy era, happy era and reaches the happy-happy era, reversing the conditions brought about in the descending period. Thus ends the one turning the wheel of time, which initiates the next wheel of time with its own descending and ascending periods. In this manner, the progress of world history goes on eternally.[53]

4.1.3.2. JAINA HAGIOGRAPHY

Jainas believe that in this cyclic movement of time – descending and ascending periods of world history – a number of great and holy men appear to direct the destinies of people, especially during those eras when life is difficult and hard-going for people. According to Jaina hagiography these holy men appear during the happy-unhappy era and the unhappy-happy era of the descending period. Similarly they are manifest in the world during the unhappy-happy era and the happy-unhappy era of the ascending period. The happy-happy era and the happy era of the descending and ascending periods do not require holy men, as the conditions of life are so good. The unhappy-unhappy era of the descending and ascending periods provides the worst environment of existence, which is not conducive for the emergence of holy men. The Jaina hagiography enumerates the coming of 63 great men (*Salaakaa-purushas*) in each of the descending and ascending periods. These are 24 *Tiirthankaras*, 12 *Cakravartiis* and 27 heroes, who include nine *Baladevas*, nine *Vaasudevas* and nine *Prativaasudevas*. To this list we could also add the *Kulakaras*, the immediate predecessors of the *Tiirthankaras* and a few others who are insignificant in comparison to the 63 holy men. Though the *Kulakaras* are predecessors to all the others, many of the 63 holy men who have lived in the present descending period are contemporaries, living either a few years ahead of or later than the others.[54]

In our consideration of the holy men whose names are stated in the Jaina hagiography in the present section we look into the *Kulakaras*, the *Cakravartiis*, the three groups of heroes in detail and mention in passing the insignificant ones, and in the next section, which is exclusively given to the reflection on the *Tiirthankaras*, study about the *Tiirthankaras*.

4.1.3.2.1. Kulakaras

The *Kulakaras* are the immediate predecessors of the *Tiirthankaras*.

They are known as the patriarchs. They appear in the initial stages of the happy-unhappy era of the descending period. The *Svetaambaras* speak of only seven *Kulakaras*, while the *Digambaras* mention that they are 14, and refer them with the name *Manus*. They are the following: Pratisruti, Sanmati, Kshemankara, Kshemandhara, Siimankara, Siimandhara, Vimala-vaahana, Cakshushmaan, Yasasvaan, Abhicandra, Candraprabha, Marudeva, Prasenajit and Naabhi. The last of these *Kulakaras*, Naabhi, is the father of Rshbhadeva, the first *Tiirthankara*. During the time of the *Kulakaras* there take place a number of changes in the lives of the people, their living conditions, availability of food, and such. These patriarchs help the people to cope with the changing situations. General moral degradation takes place during this period and the patriarchs establish moral laws to guide the lives of the people. Animals become more savage, and the people are taught the use of sticks and stones to protect themselves from the ferocious animals. Due to the non-availability of food, in-fights emerge among the people. To cope with this, the patriarchs introduce the division of land among the people. With the coming of changes in the geographical conditions of the land and with the emergence of hills and rivers, the patriarchs instruct the people to build roads and to use boats to cross the hills and rivers respectively. With the disappearance of wish-trees and the appearance of ordinary earth plants, the patriarchs educate the people to use the products from plants as food, by using fire to cook the food. In this manner, the patriarchs play a great role in helping the people to adjust to and cope with the changing situations. In doing so, they lay the foundation for a more organized social structure and coherent social living among the people of their time.[55]

4.1.3.2.2. Cakravartiis

A *Cakravartiis* is an imperial ruler who has control over a part of the world. He maintains a high position in the world. He achieves the honor of being the *Cakravartii* because of the good actions of his past existence. He is also revered due to a passionately cherished wish (*Nidaana*) from the previous life. He is born in a kingly family, grows with all good things in life, excels in arts and sciences and acquires 36 qualities of body and mind. He destroys all his enemies, becomes victorious in battle and then is crowned as *Cakravartii*. Gods and *Genii* serve and praise him as the *Cakravartii*. As a ruler, 14 gems and nine treasures support him, to acquire and to maintain that controlling position. Of the 14 gems, seven are with one sense, while the others are with five senses. The gems with one sense are: a discus – a war weapon that is hurled against the enemy and that returns to the hand of the sender after accomplishing the task (*Cakra*), a staff that can bore hole on earth (*Danda*), a sharp sword (*Khadga*), a glittering sun-umbrella (a symbol of dignity) (*Chatra*), a hide that cannot be pierced (*Carma*), a dazzling gem – that illumines dark night, brings victory and cures wounds (*Mani*) and a shining dice (*Kaakinii*). The seven gems with five senses are: the commander (*Senaapati*), the chamberlain (*Grahapati*), the architect (*Vaarddhaka*), the house priest (*Purohita*), the elephant of great power (*Gaja*), the beautiful horse (*Asva*) and the most beautiful woman (*Strii*). The nine treasures (*Nidhis*) could refer to the nine branches of sciences. It could also refer to the nine different treasures. They are: houses (*Naisarpa*), rice and corn (*Paanduka*), ornaments (*Pingalaka*), 14 gems (*Sarvaratnaka*), clothing (*Mahaapadma*), determination of time for astrological predictions (*Kaala*), mines of metals and precious stones (*Mahaakaala*), weapons (*Maanavaka*) and poetry, drama and music (*Sankha*). With the help of these gems and treasures the *Cakravartii* rules over his part of the world for a long period of time, enjoying all the pleasures of life, power and glory. At the end of his life, some renounce their life and are liberated, while others either arrive at the world of gods for their good *Karma* or go to hell for their evil deeds. The names of the 12 *Cakravartiis* are the following: Bharata, Sagara, Maghava, Sanatkumaara, Santi, Kunthu, Ara, Subhuuma, Mahaapadma, Harisena, Javasena and Brahmadatta.[56]

4.1.3.2.3. Heroes

Baladeva, Vaasudeva and *Prativaasudeva* are three heroes, who are valiant men. They appear usually simultaneously. In one world period they appeared nine times. Thus, they were 27. *Baladeva* and *Vaasudeva* are half-brothers, i.e., sons of a king from two different wives. *Prativaasudeva* is their rival.[57] Let us consider each of them briefly.

Baladeva is also sometimes called *Balabhadra*. He is bright and white in body color. He wears a blue and black robe. There are differences of opinion among the *Digambaras* and the *Svetaambaras* regarding his insignias. The *Digambaras* hold that a chain of precious stones, two clubs and a ploughshare are his emblems, while the *Svetaambaras* say that his insignias are a bow, two different clubs (*Gadaa* and *Musala*) and a ploughshare. Usually his mother announces his appearance in the world through her four dreams. *Baladeva* assists his brother, *Vaasudeva* against the attacks of *Prativaasudeva* and helps his brother to become the half-emperor (*Ardha-Cakravartii*). After the death of his brother *Vaasudeva*, *Baladeva* renounces the world, as he finds no more happiness in the world, and attains *Moksha*. The nine *Baladevas* of our age are: Acala, Vijaya, Bhadra, Suprabha, Sudarsana, Aananda, Nandana, Padma (Raama) and Balraama.[58]

Vaasudeva is the younger brother of *Baladeva*. Though younger, he is presented in the legends as possessing a much stronger personality than that of his elder brother, *Baladeva*. While *Baladeva* is of a gentler character, *Vaasudeva* is a more powerful fighter and possesses a commanding instinct. His advantaged position comes from the fact that his mother has seen seven dreams about his birth. His bodily complexion is dark blue. He usually wears a robe of yellow silk. He also wears a *Sriivatsa* mark on his chest and carries a white sun-umbrella, a fly whisk and a *Garuda*-banner. There is difference of opinion between the *Digambaras* and the *Svetaambras* regarding his insignias. The *Digambaras* carries a bow, a conch, a discus, a sword, a sceptre, Sakti, and a club as his insignias, while the *Svetaambaras* speak of the seven emblems of *Vaasudeva*, viz., a conch which he only can blow (*Pancajaanya*), a discus (*Sudarsana*), a club (*Kaumodakii*), a bow (*Sarnga*), a sword (*Nandaka*), a wreath of seasonal flowers of the season (*Vanamaalaa*) and the precious stone (*Kasturba*). *Vaasudeva*, with the help of his brother *Baladeva*, gains victory over his opponent, *Prativaasudeva*, and kills him in war. Then, he crowns himself as the half-emperor (*Ardha-Cakravartii*) and enjoys the pleasures of the world with his numerous wives. When he dies he goes to hell on account of the evil *Karma* he has acquired due to his life of violence, war and pleasures of life. The nine *Vaasudevas* of our age are: Triprshta, Dviprshta, Svayambhuu, Purushotama, Purushapundariika, Datta, Lakshmana and Krshna.[59]

Prativaasudeva is an evil ruler, but very powerful and mighty in strength. His mother announces his birth through one dream she sees. His life is very closely associated with the half-brothers, *Baladeva* and the *Vaasudeva*. As the name suggests *Prativaasudeva* is the opponent of *Vaasudeva*. *Prativaasudeva* battles against *Vaasudeva* and captures a large part of the Bharata-land and demands obedience of the *Vaasudeva*. *Vaasudeva* accepts the challenge of *Prativaasudeva* and goes for battle with the assistance of his elder brother *Baladeva*. The brothers defeat *Prativaasudeva* in battle and kill him. After his death *Prativaasudeva* goes to hell to atone for his evil deeds. The nine *Prativaasudeva* of our age are: Asvagriiva, Taaraka, Meraka, Madhu, Nisumhba, Bali, Prahlaada, Raavana and Jaraasandha.[60]

In the foregoing sections we have taken a detailed look at the ritual books, the cosmography, the world history and the hagiography of the Jaina tradition to consider the divinities mentioned there. Having done that we move on to consider the true Divinity of Jainism, viz., the *Tiirthankara*, in the next section.

4.1.4. TIIRTHANKARA: THE TRUE DIVINITY OF JAINISM

The deities of the heavenly world, according to the Jaina tradition, are in a state of continuous enjoyment. They represent every type of worldly happiness in a perfected state. They have special powers, which ordinary human beings do not enjoy. The Jaina tradition affirms such a state of the heavenly beings, as such a state is achieved as a result of the good *Karma* of the past. Some of these deities are given a place in the Jaina worship in the guise of doorkeepers (*Dvara-paalas*) or as guardian deities (*Saasana-devataas*), meeting the emotional needs of the weaker sections of the Jaina laity. Their lifespan in the world of the gods is very long in human terms. But their happiness there is transient, and they must fall from heaven once they accomplish their *Karma*. Besides, as gods they cannot attain the supreme goal of liberation. To achieve this goal they must again be born as human beings. Thus, the gods of the Jaina pantheon are limited and not supreme. Similarly all the holy men we have spoken about in the Jaina hagiography, except the *Tiirthankaras*, are men, who have to live out the effects of their *Karma*, in the next life, in heaven, in hell or work out their salvation through renunciation of the world and the practice of asceticism. The only person who is beyond the hold of *Karma* is the *Tiirthankara*, who is the true Divinity of Jainism.[61] In the following sections we explore the nature and characteristics of a *Tiirthankara*, the ranks of the liberated and the abode of the liberated.

4.1.4.1. NATURE OF TIIRTHANKARA

The term '*Tiirthankara*' comes from the term '*Tiirtha*'. This term has two meanings. The primary meaning of the term '*Tiirtha*' is 'a ford' or 'a crossing place'. Taken in this sense *Tiirthankara* refers to 'an establisher of a ford', 'a maker of a crossing-place' or 'a pioneer who initiates a way'. So *Tiirthankara* is one who makes a crossing-place through the ocean existence (*Samsaara*). He himself walks through it and attains the state of liberation (*Nirvaana*), a state free from all sorrows. In doing so, he establishes and initiates the way for others that they can also go this way without any danger, cross over the state of *Samsaara* and achieve the ultimate goal of existence, viz., liberation. So *Tiirthankara* is not just the one who is given a way to attain salvation, but also one who leads others, by his own example, to walk the path he proposes. The secondary meaning of the term '*Tiirtha*' is 'a community the *Tiirthankara* establishes. In this sense, *Tiirthankara* is the one who establishes the Jaina community with its four orders, viz., the monks (*Saadhus*), the nuns (*Saadhviis*), the laymen (*Sraavak*) and the laywomen (*Sraavikaas*). When the *Tiirthankara* is no more in the world, this community he establishes becomes, as it were, the ford or the crossing place through which one can be sure of attaining liberation. In this community, the monks and the nuns represent the teachings of the *Tiirthankara* in the manner of their lives, while the laymen and the laywomen are the listeners, who hear and live the teachings of the *Tiirthankaras* in their lives. If we put together the implications of the primary and secondary meanings of the term '*Tiirtha*', *Tiirthankara* is a human being who by his own effort conquers *Karma* and all its effects in his life, establishes a way to salvation, walks through it, teaches others to walk through it and founds a community of four orders to assist others to walk through this path to salvation in the future.[62] Lawrence A. Babb makes this point with of clarity. To quote him:

> A *Tiirthankar[a]* is a human being. He is, however, an extraordinary human being who has conquered the attachments and aversions that stand in the way of liberation from worldly bondage. By means of his own efforts, and entirely without the benefit of being taught by others, he has achieved the state of omniscience in which all things are known to him – past, present, and future. But, before final attainment of his own liberation, ...[he] imparts his self-gained liberating knowledge to others so that they might become victors, too. Thus, he establishes a crossing place for other beings.[63]

Though a *Tiirthankara*, as a ford-maker, propounds the doctrine from his own insights and crosses over the *Karma* by his own effort, he is not the creator of a new teaching. The doctrines of Jainism exist from time immemorial and never cease to exist. A *Tiirthankara* only understands and interprets those already existing teachings to his contemporaries in the light of his insight and experience. The validity of the teachings of the *Tiirthankara* does not depend on logical arguments, but on his omniscience. A *Tiirthankara* propounds his teachings only for the purpose of attainment of liberation from worldly bondage. Thus, a *Tiirthankara* is a holy prophet, who proclaims the ancient holy doctrine to his contemporaries in a new way, thereby leading them to salvation, inspiring them both by his preaching and example.[64] For this reason, when a new *Tiirthankara* emerges, the disciples of the former *Tiirthankara* accept the new *Tiirthankara* and his teaching. Mahaaviira's teachings are, for instance, based on the doctrines of his predecessor, Paarsavanatha. But the former gives a new stricter interpretation of the latter's teachings and reforms the four orders the former has established. A clear illustration of this is seen in the disciple of Paarsavanatha's accepting the teaching of Mahaaviira and becoming his disciple.[65]

When a human person, following the path of asceticism and renunciation, having bound all other forms of *Karma* finally binds the *Tiirthankara-naama-karma*, which helps him to attain the status of an *Arahata*, he becomes a *Tiirthankara*. The pre-conditions required to bind the *Tiirthankara-naama-karma* are the following. Firstly, the person must attain the perfection of faith. Secondly, he must acquire the quality of reverence for all. Thirdly, he must be persistent in following the vows he has taken and the precepts according to his state of life. Fourthly, he makes every effort to acquire true knowledge. Fifthly, he must cultivate an attitude of sadness over the evils that exist in the world. Sixthly, he must practice charity and asceticism according to his capability. Seventhly, he must be ready to help the community. Eighthly, he learns to cultivate love for *Arhatas*, masters, wise men and their teachings. Ninthly, he must observe the six necessary duties of daily life (*Aavasyakas*) faithfully. Tenthly, in his thought he must have high regard for attaining salvation and its path. Finally, he must have deep affection for the followers of true religion. When these attitudes take hold of a seeker of *Moksha*, he has within himself all the requisites necessary to bind the *Tiirthankara-naama-karma*. When this type of *Karma* is bound, the person becomes a *Tiirthankara*.[66]

Tiirthankaras are also known as *Jinas*, as they are the conquerors of all *Karmas*, freeing them from love and hatred. The battle they wage is not an external one, but an internal one. They renounce the world and conquer all that the world can offer in order to become true spiritual victors. The name *Jina* is not only given to the *Tiirthankaras*, but also to all saints who have attained omniscience, such as the *Ganadharas*, the first disciples of *Tiirthankaras*. Therefore, to distinguish *Tiirthankara Jinas* from other *Jinas*, the *Tiirthankaras* are addressed as *Jinesvaras*, i.e., 'Masters among the *Jinas*'. A *Tiirthankara* is also known as *Arihanta*, which means 'destroyer of enemies', i.e., the one who destroys all eight *Karmas*. Another name attributed to *Tiirthankra* is *Aruhanta*, which means one who has killed the roots of all *Karmas*. He is also called the *Arahata*, i.e., the venerable or being capable of veneration, because the *Indras*, the kings of the gods of the heavenly world, come down to the earth and worship the *Tiirthankara* at the time of the five great events of his life, viz., his conception, birth, renunciation of the world, attainment of omniscience and going into *Nirvaana*, while the other gods pay their homage from heaven. Jaina legends extensively speak of the *Indra* of the *Sudharma* region of the *Vaimaanika* gods, known as *Sakra*, who alerts the gods of heaven by ringing a bell on all these five occasions in the life of a *Tiirthankara* and invites them to pay homage to the true Divinity.[67]

4.1.4.2. CHARACTERISTICS OF TIIRTHANKARA

Having looked into the nature of a *Tiirthankara*, in the last section, now we move on to some of the characteristics that are related to the state of a *Tiirthankara*. Firstly, a *Tiirthankara* is a true human being like any other in the world. Therefore, before he achieves the exalted state of enlightenment, his life is very much the same as that of any other human being. He goes through numerous births and rebirths depending on his past *Karma*. It is said that Mahaaviira, the 24th *Tiirthankara*, goes through not less than 26 different births before he becomes the *Tiirthankara*. We mention a few of his previous births. He is born as a god in the heavenly world a number of times. He takes birth as the grandson of the first *Tiirthankara* – Rshbhadeva. Later he comes into the world as the *Vaasudeva* Triprshta, after which he is said to be in the seventh hell for the sins he committed as the *Vaasudeva*. In the next birth, he is born as a horrible lion in hell. There he becomes human being, and finally, on his 27th birth, he is born as Mahaaviira, who is to become the *Tiirthankara*.[68] In this way, though destined to be a *Tiirthankara* he has to make his way towards his destiny, as does anyone else.

Secondly, the birth in which a person is going to be born as the *Tiirthankara* is proclaimed with the help of 16 dreams.[69] It is the mother of the to-be-born *Tiirthankara* who sees the dreams and proclaims his birth. The first dream presents the image of a white elephant that has a sound like that of thunder. In the second dream, she sees a white bull. The image of the third dream is that of a white lion. In the fourth dream two wreaths of beautiful and fragrant flowers are shown. In the sixth dream, the moon shining as white is shown. The sun shining red is the object of the seventh dream. In the eighth dream, the mother of the *Tiirthankara* sees a banner of two fishes fixed to a golden staff decorated with the feathers of a peacock. The content of the ninth dream is two golden containers of pure water. In the tenth dream, she sees a lotus pond in which ducks, fish and other water animals move about. In the 11th dream is shown an ocean of milk with its waves crowned by foam. A throne decked with gems is seen in the 12th dream. The 13th dream portrays one of the mobile, heavenly palaces of the gods (*Vimaana*), where the gods make heavenly music. A palace of the *Asuras* is shown in the 14th dream. The content of the 15th dream is a large heap of jewels that is as big as Mount

Meru. The 16th dream shows the image of fire shining white. The mother of the *Tiirthankara*, who sees these dreams, proclaims them to all around, and everyone comes to know that a *Tiirthankara* is going to be born.[70]

Thirdly, as a general rule a *Tiirthankara* is born to a royal family and grows up in every way like a member of the regal household. Of the 24 *Tiirthankaras* of the present world two are born in the Hari family, while all the others are born in the Ikshvaaku. After the birth, the boy grows up in the pomp and glory that befit a prince. Five nurses attend to him as a baby. As he grows up, he masters all the sciences and the arts, enjoys all earthly pleasures in a virtuous manner, marries a princess and becomes a father. He also takes up stately responsibilities. In short, his life goes on in every way as that of a member of a royal family.[71]

Fourthly, every *Tiirthankara* renounces the pomp and glory of the royal life at one stage, accepts asceticism as the way of life and attains purity of nature. The joys and comforts of kingly life do not lead the prince destined to be a *Tiirthankara* astray. He realizes that the pleasures of this world are worthless and futile. Often there occurs in the life of the young prince some external event that turns this wish to renounce the world into a decision. He gives away his treasures in arms, puts away his regal clothes and ornaments, tears his hair in five strands and leaves for the forest. There he neglects his body, spends his time in meditations, fasts, practices asceticism, makes pilgrimages and moves from place to place. This helps him to acquire purity of nature.[72] The purity of nature is explained with the help of 21 metaphors as follows:

> As no water adheres to a copper pot, no collyrium to the mother of pearls, so no sin adheres to a saint; his course is unchecked like that of life; like the sky, he does not need support; he does not know any obstruction like the wind; his heart is pure like water in autumn; like a lotusleaf nothing can make him dirty; he has withdrawn his senses from the world like a turtle its limbs; he wanders alone like a rhinoceros; he is free like a bird; he is always like a griffin (*Bhaarunda*); he is brave like an elephant, strong like a bull, unconquerable like a lion, unshakeable like the Mandara-mountain, profound like the ocean, pure like the moon, of shining power like the sun, as pure as gold, he endures everything like the earth and shines like fire.[73]

Fifthly, his attaining purity of nature frees him from 18 different deficiencies. They include obstruction in giving and receiving, in vigor, in enjoyment and profiteering. Similarly the *Tiirthankara* is freed from laughing, preference, dislike, fear, nausea, greed, heterodoxy, ignorance, sleep, conceit, love and hatred. The removal of these deficiencies makes him acquire 34 virtues, which are related to the body. Having been freed of deficiencies and acquiring various virtues, the *Tiirthankaras* acquires four infinities and 19 insignias. The four infinities are: infinite perception, infinite knowledge, infinite power and infinite bliss. The 19 insignias are the following: There is a holy wheel (*Dharma-cakra*) hovering in the air in front of him. He is adorned with two flywhisks, one lion throne with a stool for his feet, three sun umbrellas and a banner fitted with precious stones. Three precious walls surround him. He appears to look at everyone in all four directions. There is an Asoka tree near him. The trees are leaning towards him. While the heavenly drums resound, cooling airs move around him. The birds fly on his right, which is a favorabe omen. The sky rains down fragrant water and colourful flowers. His hair, beard and nails do not grow. The four classes of gods who belong to the heavenly world listen to him. The various seasons delight him by giving different flowers. Everything he perceives with his senses is pleasant. Besides, a male spirit (*Yaksha*) and a female spirit (*Yakshinii*) attend to every *Tiirthankara*. Similarly a male main pupil (*Ganadhara*) and a female mainpupil (*Aaryaa*) serve him.[74]

Sixthly, overcoming all forms of *Karma* and acquiring transcendental knowledge (*Kevala-jnaana*), the *Tiirthankara* becomes the omniscient (*Kevalii*). At this the gods revere him, and he preaches first to the gods in the precious festive hall (*Samavasarana*). Beings of all worlds simultaneously hear his preaching. Then the *Tiirthankara* roams about everywhere to propagate the true religious doctrine. He preaches in a language, which is without syllables (*Anaksharii*) and convinces his listeners in an extraordinary way. One of the *Ganadharas* translates his preaching to people in their local language. The speech of the *Tiirthankara* is said to have 35 qualities. Some of these qualities are the following: purity, loftiness, affability, thunderous sound, echo, honesty, harmony, momentousness, consistency, erudition, unequivocalness, irrefutability, power of conviction, logical connection, ability to act according to circumstances, fidelity to truth, absence of confusion and verbosity, self-praise and captiousness, propriety, extraordinary mildness and charm, excellence, leniency, sublimity, persistence with what is right and useful, grammatical correctness, freedom from intrigue, causing amazement, exquisiteness, absence of excessive slowness, variety of figures of speech, use of attributes, energy, clear pronunciation of sounds, words and sentences, uninterrupted flow and ease. The preaching of the *Tiirthankara* wins over thousands of disciples. Many of them join the orders of monks, nuns, laymen and laywoman.[75]

Finally, the *Tiirthankara* completes the task of bringing many people to his true doctrine and leading them to a holy way of living. He wishes to shake off his *Karma* completely and decides to achieve *Nirvaana*. He stops taking food and drink completely. He gives up his mortal life and in the process sheds all his *Karmas*. Then he goes to the world of the liberated to be eternally there and to enjoy bliss for ages to come. *Indra*, the king of the gods bathes the body of the *Tiirthankara* in the water of the milk ocean and adorns it. The gods place him on a pyre of sandal and aloe. The heavenly *Genii* set it on fire. The gods are said to erect a *Stuupa* of precious stones over the mortal remains of the *Tiirthankara*. Thus ends the mortal life of the *Tiirthankara*.

But he lives eternally in the bliss of the world of the liberated. His teachings and example continue to support many to walk the way he walked and to achieve the ideal of the true Divinity.[76] All we have said about the nature and characteristics of the *Tiirthankara* is best summed up in the following prayer addressed to the *Tiirthankara*:

> You I salute at various times, the Lord *Arihanta*. What kind of a Lord is He? He knows what is passing in the mind of every man. He knows what is going on at various times. He sees all the fourteen worlds as though they are in his hands. He is endowed with these six qualities: boundless knowledge, insight, righteousness, austerity, patience, strength. He is endowed with thirty-four kinds of uncommon qualities. He is endowed with speech. He has one thousand and eight auspicious marks. He is free from eighteen sins and endowed with the twelve good qualities. He has destroyed four of the hardest *Karma*, and the four remaining *Karma* are powerless. He is longing to get *Moksha*. He dispels the doubts of souls with *Yoga*. He is endowed with body, with omniscience, with perfect insight, and has the before-mentioned righteousness. He has the highest kind of *Sankita*, which is permanent; he has *Suklalesyaa, Sukladhyaana, Suklayoga*; he is worshipped, adored and saluted by the sixty-four *Indra*. He is the most learned *Pandit*. He is endowed with these and other endless qualities.[77]

4.1.4.3. RANKS OF THE LIBERATED

In the last two sections we have explored the nature and characteristics of a *Tiirthankara*. In this section, we investigate the different stages a seeker of liberation walks through in order to achieve the final state of liberation. We can also speak of them as the different ranks a human being, as an ascetic, may hold before he finally arrives at the end of his life's journey. The ascetics who complete these five ranks are called in the Jaina tradition the five supreme deities (*Panca-Paramesvara* or *Panca-Parameshthins*). A special worship, known as *Namaskaara-mantra*, is exclusively offered to them, as these beings are in fact the only beings really worthy of veneration.[78] We must not think that every ordinary monk should gain these ranks before he attains *Moksha*, as even without holding these ranks a monk can reach the liberated state. But it is generally easier for those who hold these ranks to attain deliverance than for the others, because these offices help them to acquire the qualities conducive to the liberated state. Starting from the lowest, the five ranks are the following: the ascetic (*Saadhu*), the instructor (*Upaadhyaaya*), the master (*Aacaarya*), the omniscient (*Arahata*) and the perfect one (*Siddha*).[79] We now briefly consider each of these ranks.

The first is the *Saadhu*, who is an ordinary ascetic. If he belongs to the *Digambra* tradition, he wears no clothes and lives in the forest. He spends his life in meditation and is totally lost to the world. He eats once a day and removes the hair on the head as it grows. If he belongs to the *Svetambara* tradition, he moves from place to place. He is dressed in white. A *Saadhu* lives a life of strict asceticism and inner discipline.[80]

The second stage to which an ascetic can rise is *Upaadhyaaya*, an instructor or a teacher. He is an unusually intelligent monk, who is chosen from among the monks to instruct the other monks on the Jaina doctrine and scriptures. He must be well versed in the scriptures, which the laypeople and the monks are expected to know. For the Jainas all studying and teaching involve austerity. If the instructor does his studying and teaching with no thought of acquiring merit, it helps him to remove (*Nirjaraa*) certain *Karma*.[81]

The third rank, which is higher than the former, is that of an *Aacaarya*, who is a master or a superior. In some Jaina sects the older members are chosen for this rank, while in other sects abilities are considered in selecting the *Aacaarya*. He is a person of high dignity and so always travels with the accompaniment of a minimum of two *Saadhus*. Depending on the fame of the *Aacaarya*, the number of *Saadhus* who accompany him also increases. He is the master of the Jaina community (*Sangha*) and holds the power to excommunicate the members for religious offences. In everything, he is like the other monks. For instance, he wears the same dress, eats the same food and follows the same rules as his fellow monks. But at times he may have a seat that is a bit higher than the others. The occasion of the choice of an *Aacaarya* is a day of great joy for all. Laypersons come to the *Apaasaro* to take or renew the 12 vows.[82] He is expected to possess 36 qualities: "He controls five senses; he is chaste in nine ways; he keeps the three *Gupti*; he is free from the four *Kshaaya*; he keeps five great vows; he observes the five rules of conduct; and he maintains the five *Samiti*..."[83]

The fourth stage is that of the *Arahata*, i.e., the omniscient. The *Arahata* is the *Tiirthankara*. He, by contemplation and asceticism, attains omniscience and reaches the irreversible state of freedom from the bonds of *Samsaara*. He attains perfection of knowledge, perfection of speech, perfection of worship and absolute security, as no illness comes where he is. As he is still in the body, he is able to teach what he has perceived through his omniscience and guide others to cross over the *Samsaara* existence, as he himself has crossed over. Though the state of *Tiirthankara*, is strictly lower than the next stage, i.e., the *Siddha*, yet it is considered more important, as the *Tiirthankara* is still in the world of physical existence, and so he still serves as a ford-maker. He is the *Jina*, the spiritual victor, the true Divinity of Jainism, to whom the highest worship is offered.[84]

The final stage is that of the *Siddha*. When the *Tiirthankara* sheds all *Karma* associated with his body and attains *Nirvaana*, he becomes the *Siddha*. He is a being "without caste, unaffected by smell, without the sense of taste, without feeling, without form, without hunger, without pain, without sorrow, without joy, without birth, without old age, without death, without body, without *Karma*, enjoying an endless and unbroken calm."[85] *Siddha* has the following characteristics: He has absolute knowledge, faith, insight, righteousness and competence. He can become minute or gigantic, if he decides to do so. He can move about, as he likes. He has 108 attributes, which the Jainas recited using rosary beads. Since the *Siddha* has no body he is not prayed to or worshipped. Even praying his hundred and eight attributes is aimed at stirring up one's spiritual desire of arriving at the state of *Nirvaana* and achieving the *Siddha* hood, rather than asking any favor from the *Siddha*.[86]

The Jainas speak of 15 different types of *Siddha*. The one, who has been a *Tiirthankara* before he becomes a *Siddha*, is called a *Jina-siddha*. A non-*Tiirthankara*, who becomes *Siddha*, is called an *Ajina-siddha*. One who becomes a *Siddha* after he has made four *Tiirthas* is known as a *Tiirtha-siddha*, while one who becomes a *Siddha* without preaching and founding the *Tiirthas* is known as an *Atiirtha-siddha*. One who becomes a *Siddha* without first being an ascetic is labelled as a *Grihalinga-siddha*. If a non-Jaina becomes a *Siddha*, he is called an *Anyalinga-siddha*. One who follows the path of asceticism and attains *Siddha* hood is termed a *Savilinga-siddha*. A man who has become a *Siddha* is described as a *Puullinga-siddha*. A woman who becomes a *Siddha* is called a *Striilinga-siddha*. A person who is neuter and has become a *Siddha* is identified as a *Napumsakalinga-siddha*. If one becomes a *Siddha* due to the influence of the *Guru*, he is known as a *Buddhabohii-siddha*. If a particular thing influences a person to become a *Siddha*, he is called a *Pratyekabuddha-siddha*. If a person influences himself in becoming a Siddha, he is called as *Svayambhddha-siddha*. If a person attains *Siddha*-hood alone, he is called as an *Eka-siddha*. If many achieve *Siddha* hood at the same time, then they are called *Aneka-siddha*.[87] Now that we have considered the *Panca-Paramesvara* of Jainism, we move on to make a brief description of the abode of the liberated *Siddha*.

4.1.4.4. ISHTAPRAGBHAARA: THE ABODE OF THE LIBERATED

The abode of the liberated is the glorious region of the *Istapraagbhaara*. It is situated 12 *Yojanas* above the *Sarvaarthasiddha* heaven. It resembles an open sun-umbrella. It is eight *Yojanas* high in its highest place. It is whiter than milk, more glittering than gold and purer than the crystal. There is a circular crystal rock called *Siitaa* or *Siilaa*. It is at a distance of one *Yojana* from the border of the world and the non-world. The redeemed *Siddhas* live in the uppermost part for eternity and enjoy the supernatural happiness of liberation from the bonds of *Samsaara*.[88]

In this essay we have looked into the Divinities of the Jaina pantheon. Though Jainism does not believe in an almighty Creator-God, who is involved in the world through his incarnations and the power of his grace, unlike many theistic religions, it has a rich concept of the sacred. While Jainism believes in the reality of the soul that moves towards its salvation through asceticism and holiness of life, it does not recognize the need for a supreme Deity on whose divine ordinances and manifestations the holiness of the soul has to depend. Jainism proclaims the centrality of man in working out his salvation and the holiness of his life. It holds that man, coming to grips with his *Karma*, overcomes its effects on his life by way of asceticism and the practice of virtue, thereby becoming a *Jina*, a spiritual conqueror. He achieves this goal not in one birth, but with the help of a series of births and rebirths, in the process enjoying his life as a god in the heavenly world or purifying himself in hell, depending on his *Karma* of the past existences. Thus, the various gods that appear in the Jaina pantheon or the holy men whose names are mentioned in the Jaina hagiography are bound by *Karma*. Therefore, they play very insignificant roles in Jaina religious belief and practice. The real Divinity of Jainism, therefore, is not these gods and holy men, but the *Jina*, the *Arahata* or the *Tiirthankara*, i.e., the spiritual victor, who has crossed over the ocean of *Samsaara* and attained the state of omniscience (*Kevala-jnaana*), by overcoming every effect of *Karma* and teaching others to do as he has done. He is the worthy and the venerable one to whom worship is offered. The Jainas do not consider the *Jina* or the *Tiirthankara* as a theistic God, or worship him as such. Nor do they expect the grace of the *Jina* to carry them to the highest heavens. The relationship between a Jaina and a *Jina* is strictly impersonal, as the latter, having achieved the state of *Siddha*, is indifferent to whether his teaching is accepted or rejected. Nor does a *Siddha* influence the character or the career of a Jaina. Every Jaina works out his salvation through the power of his insights and asceticism. In this effort, the teaching, example and inspiration of the previous teacher, *Arahatas*, called the *Tiirthankaras* or *Jinas*, help him. Therefore, walking the moral path of a *Jina* and offering him cult only reminds of the Jaina the path the *Jina* has walked and which he needs to walk. These concluding remarks to the first section take us to the Jaina path to the Divine.

4.2. THE JAINA PATHS TO THE DIVINE

The last section reiterated the Jaina truth that the true Divinity of Jainism is the *Tiirthankara*, who is neither an incarnation of God, nor a strange being in the divine creation. He is an ordinary human being who by his insight and effort raises himself to the level of the Divine. Jainism does not believe in the descending of God, i.e., the incarnation of God (*Avataarvaada*), but rather it proclaims the ascending of man to Godhood (*Uttaraavaada*). In moving from a human existence that is limited and subjected to deterioration and arriving at the godly life of the Omniscient that knows no deterioration, a human soul walks a strict path of moral discipline and religious worship. The purpose of this path is not to arrive at an almighty God and be united with him or to get his favors and graces, as theistic traditions hold, but to develop a human being's internal spiritual qualities and excellences to such a degree that he becomes the Godhead. When this full flowering and complete development of a human soul's spiritual powers takes place any human soul can become an Omniscient, *Tiirthankara* or a *Jina*. Similarly, living the moral path given by a *Tiirthankara* or offering him cultic worship is not done with the intention of being united with him, or obtaining his mercy, assistance and graces. Rather such moral acts, done in imitation of the *Tiirthankara* or the cult offered in his name, become occasions for the one who lives a moral life or worships to be reminded of the ultimate goal in life, i.e., to achieve the ideal of the *Tiirthankara*, whose life he is imitating and whose name he is honouring through his worship. These practices have no objective goal, but only have the subjective goal of becoming a liberated soul. Thus, the sole aim of the Jaina path to the Divine is to help the human person to remove every form of *Karma* and to become himself Divine.[89] The Jaina path to the Divine has two aspects, viz. moral and cultic. In the next two sections, we explore the moral and the cultic dimensions of the Jaina path to the Divine.

4.2.1. MORAL PATH

The fundamental moral teachings and practices of Jainism are summed up in what they call the Three Jewels (*Ratna Traya*), viz., Right Knowledge (*Samyak Jnaana*), Right Faith (*Samyak Darsana*) and Right Conduct (*Samyak Caaritrya*). Right Knowledge consists in the right perception of the Jaina religious truths, as they exist. For instance, when one knows what virtue is or what vows one ought to practice, one has the Right Knowledge. It must temporally precede the other two, unless one has the knowledge of something one cannot believe in it or live by it. The second Jewel is the Right Faith. It consists in holding the truth as truth and the untruth as untruth. It is of central importance, for unless one believes in what one knows, one cannot follow it in one's life. Faith is the foundation of living, as the latter flows from the former. Right Conduct is the third Jewel of the Jaina creed. It consists in living one's life in the light of Right Knowledge and Right Faith. For instance, keeping the five vows absolutely (*Sarvacaaritrya*) is the Right Conduct for a monk, while keeping the same vows partially (*Desacaaritrya*) is the Right Conduct for a layperson. If Right Conduct does not accompany the former two, they lose their value and worth.[90]

Practicing Right Conduct in the light of Right Knowledge and Right Faith can be vitiated due to three evils, which the Jainas call poisonous arrows (*Salya*). They are the following: fraud (*Maayaa Salya*), false belief (*Mithyaatva Salya*) and covetousness (*Nidaana Salya*). The first evil arrow, fraud, consists in a person living his life, whether in its social and religious aspect, as directed by intrigue or deceit. It takes away the merit of even holy actions, such as fasting and asceticism. The second poisonous arrow, false belief, implies a person holding a false god as true, a false *Guru* to a true one and taking false religion to be true religion. This, indeed, is a poisonous arrow that kills every form of good actions, as acceptance of a false *Tiirthankara* as a true one, a false *Guru* as a true *Guru* and false religion as true can lead a person totally astray from the possibility of doing any good. For this reason, a Jaina repeats in his everyday devotions the definition of a true *Tiirthankara*, a true *Guru* and a true religion. Covetousness is the third poisonous arrow that destroys Right Conduct. It consists in not having right motivation when a person performs a good action. For instance, if a person entertains a selfish, vindictive or revengeful thought as he performs a good action, he loses the merit of the good action by virtue of his wrong motivation. In this manner, the three poisonous arrows of fraud, false belief and covetousness can shoot down, as it were, every good action.[91]

The task of the moral path is to help a Jaina to live the Three Jewels in the fullest way in his life. The moral path aims at freeing a person from ignorance and from all these poisonous arrows so that he can practice the implications of Right Knowledge, Right Faith and Right Conduct in every dimension of his earthly existence, whether it be social, relational, religious or cultural. Again, the moral path helps a Jaina to live the demands of the Three Jewels according to his state of life. For instance, if a person is called to live the life of a householder, he is expected to live the Three Jewels in a partial way (*Desacaaritrya*), while if one is to live the Three Jewels as a monk, one is called to practice it completely (*Sarvacaaritrya*). The former is known, in Jaina parlance, as 'the path of the householder or the listener' (*Sraavakadharma*), while the latter is known as 'the path of the ascetic (*Sramanadharma*). The moral path, thus, directs the life of a Jaina, giving him detailed guidance as to how the demands of the Three Jewels are to be lived in the life of a householder and an ascetic, and the level to which these groups are expected to live them.[92] In this section on the moral path, we attempt to unfold the moral path of the householder, the ascetic and the 14 levels of spiritual progress (*Gunasthaana*) in the context of which a Jaina is called to live his journey of life until he achieves the final goal of liberation.

4.2.1.1. PATH OF THE HOUSEHOLDER

A householder is a person who belongs to the last two orders of the Jaina community, viz., the orders of the layman or the laywoman. A layperson living in the world amidst his various activities can live the teachings of the *Jinas* only partially. Therefore, their moral life is expected to be different from that of a monk. In this section, we elaborate the moral path that directs the life of 'the listener' or 'the householder'.

4.2.1.1.1. Removal of Bad Habits

The first precept that is demanded of a good householder is that he makes an effort to give up some of the bad habits that usually mark his life. The bad habits he is called to relinquish are the following: gambling, meat-eating, consuming intoxicating drinks, visiting prostitutes, committing adultery, hunting and stealing. Coming out of these bad habits is the *sine qua non* condition for becoming a listener (*Sraavaka*) in the Jaina community. Getting rid of these bad habits strengthens the will of the householder. His evil inclinations are curbed. A better sense of direction is achieved in his life, and he is oriented towards doing good actions.[93]

4.2.1.1.2. Path of Religious Development

The positive element of practicing various good qualities must follow the negative element of removal of the bad habits from the life of the householder, in order that he achieves religious development. Therefore, the Jaina moral path proposes the practice of 35 good qualities, called *Maargaanusaarii*, so that the layperson builds within him the inner capacity to follow the Jaina-*Dharma*. The practice of these 35 qualities initiates him in the path of religious development. They are the following: The householder must earn his living by honest means. He admires and imitates the conduct of cultured persons (*Sishta Purushas*). He marries off his sons and daughters to persons of good moral conduct of his class, but belonging to a different sub-caste. He is afraid of committing sin. He must follow the customs of his country. He never speaks evil of any one, especially of the rulers. He lives in neither secluded nor too open a residence. It must be situated in a good locality. The house must not have too many entrances. He must always keep the company of the good. He must respect his parents. He must avoid any place of evil reputation that destroys his peace of mind. He should not do anything that invites people's condemnation. He must adjust his expenses according to his income. He wears clothes befitting his economic condition. Developing eight good qualities of the intellect, he listens to religious discourse (*Dharma-sravana*) daily. When he suffers from indigestion, he does not eat. He eats only at fixed times with contentment. He should pursue the human ideals (*Purusaarthas*) - viz., economic well-being (*Artha*), fulfilment of desires (*Kaama*), fulfilment of duties (*Dharma*) and freedom (*Moksha*) in such a way that one does not come in the way of the other. He should respect guests (*Atithis*), saints (*Saadhus*) and the poor (*Diina*). He should not indulge in a wrong course of action (*Duraagraha*). He should have a partiality for good qualities, and he must imbibe them wherever he finds. He should not act against the prevalent customs of the times and place. He should enter a deal only after fully weighing his capabilities and weaknesses, knowing well that he should not indulge in any action that is beyond his power. He is humble and respects men who are of good conduct and more knowledgeable than he. He must discharge the duty of providing for and bringing up those under his charge. He should be farsighted, insightful and act only after sufficient reflection. He must have a discriminative knowledge and be able to distinguish between what is good and what is not good for him. He must make himself dear to people through good conduct and service. He must be thankful for what is done to him. He must be ashamed to do an action that is not proper. He must be mindful and merciful. He must be of serene disposition. He must be ever ready to serve others. He must always gain victory over six internal enemies, viz., sensuality (*Kaama*), anger (*Krodha*), greed (*Lobha*), infatuation (*Moha*), pride (*Mada*) and jealousy (*Maatsarya*). Finally, he must keep his five senses under control. These 35 qualities, indeed, lead a householder in the true path of religious development.[94] The removal of bad habits and the practice of the path of religious development strengthen the householder internally so that he is able move further in his spiritual journey and take the practice of the 12 vows. We turn our attention to the householder's practice of vows in the next section.

4.2.1.1.3. Practice of Twelve Vows

A householder takes upon himself three sets of vows, viz., the smaller vows (*Anuvratas*), the attributive vows (*Gunavratas*) and the educative vows (*Sikshaavratas*).

4.2.1.1.3.1. Smaller Vows

This group of vows includes a set of five vows. They are: *Ahimsa, Satya, Asteya, Brahmacarya* and *Parigraha-tyaaga*. The first is *Ahimsa* or *Praanaatipaata-viramana-vrata*, which consists in desisting from killing or injuring a living being intentionally, whether it is a human being, an animal or any other living creature. Though the practice of this vow does not prevent a king from leading his army to defend his kingdom, it prevents one fighting with a lunatic or a blind man, who has hurt one unintentionally. The vow forbids the killing of weak creatures, like mosquitoes or any troublesome insects. The vow also forbids five provocative actions in one's treatment of animals, viz., tying them too tightly, beating them without mercy, cutting their limbs, overworking them and failing to feed them properly. The second is *Satya* or *Mirshaavaada-viramana-vrata*, which consists in desisting from telling gross lies, i.e., one must speak the truth. By taking this vow, the Jaina layperson is required to give up falsehood and exaggeration, especially in matters pertaining to a woman. It also calls for telling the truth and acting honestly in all forms of commercial activities, such as buying, selling and exchanging. This vow also prevents a person from giving false witness against anyone. In order to practice this vow well, the Jaina layperson is advised to guard against five activities, viz., rash speech, revealing secrets, running down one's wife, giving false advice (forgery) and falsifying accounts or forging documents. The third is *Asteya* or *Adattaadaana-viramana-vrata*. It consists in desisting from gross stealing. This vow prevents a Jaina householder from falling into the temptation of any form of stealing. He must avoid the following five activities: buying stolen property, encouraging another to steal, working in any way against the Government, using false weights and measures, adulterating goods or selling them falsly as samples. The fourth is *Brahmacarya* or *Maithuna-viramana-vrata*, which consists in desisting from adultery or sex relations with any woman other than one's wife. It calls for a man to be absolutely faithful to his wife and to be content with her. This vow is broken in five ways: consummating marriage with a young child or forming a temporary connection with a woman whom it is impossible to marry, unfaithfulness before marriage, matchmaking or marriage brokerage, excessive sexual indulgence and evil talk. The last vow is *Parigraha-tyaaga* or *Parigrah-viramana-vrata*, which consists in desisting from one's desire to possess. In other words, one must be satisfied with what one has. In taking this vow, a Jaina householder sets certain limits to what he can possess and sticks to the limit he has set for himself. In taking this vow he does not transgress the limit fixed in houses and fields, silver and gold, coins and grain, two-footed and four-footed creatures, furniture and plenishing.[95]

4.2.1.1.3.2. Attributive Vows

The attributive vows are aimed at helping the householder to live the five smaller vows in a deeper and fuller way. They are three in number, viz., *Dig-vrata*, *Upabhoga-paribhoga-vrata* and *Anarthadanda-vrata*. The *Dig-vrata* consists in a layman taking upon himself to extend his journeys in each direction up to a certain point. They believe that by setting bounds to one's travels, one is restricting the area in which one can sin. This vow is broken in five ways: descending too low, climbing too high, going obliquely, increasing the fixed limits, and forgetting these limits. The *Upabhoga-paribhoga-vrata* consists in assisting people to keep their vows against lying, covetousness and stealing by limiting the number of things a person can use. In practising this vow, a layperson normally agrees to use only 26 things. In trying to keep this vow, he must guard against eating certain forms of food and doing certain types of commercial activities, both of which are associated with the killing of different forms of life. The principle behind this vow is that nothing should be enjoyed if it is obtained by harming living beings. The *Anarthadanda-vrata* is taken to guard against unnecessary evils. Firstly, this vow involves promising never to hope that evil may come upon someone or think evil of any one (*Apadhyaana*). Secondly, one does not take life by careless use of things and weapons (*Pramaada Caryaa*). Thirdly, one promises not to keep actual weapons, but also those things that can be used as weapons, thereby causing damage to any form of life (*Himsaadaana*). Fourthly, one promises never to use one's influence for evil or persuade anyone else to do the same (*Paapopadesa*). This vow is broken if a person does the following things: writes an immoral book, sells evil medicines or indulges in evil conversation, takes part in buffoonery, indulges in vile abuse, leaves one's weapons lying about when loaded or in any way is careless about them, and thinks too much about eating and drinking.[96]

4.2.1.1.3.3. Educative Vows

The educative vows are aimed at encouraging the layperson to perform his religious duties, by helping him to be faithful to various religious performances. Unlike the small vows and attributive vows which must be undertaken once and for all, the educative vows are to be repeatedly done, as they are meant for a limited period of time. They are four in number: *Saamayika-vrata*, *Desaavakaasika-vrata*, *Poshadha-vrata* and *Atithi-samvibhaaga-vrata*. The *Saamayika-vrata* consists in the layperson taking upon himself the duty of meditating totally undisturbed for one or several *Muhuurtas*, i.e., 48, 96 or one 144 minutes as he fixes it previously. This vow also involves a commitment on the part of the one meditating that he does not sin, lead others to sin or sin in the space of the whole world by mind, speech or body. Usually the meditation is done in the morning, noon and evening. Morning meditation is given more importance. Usually meditation is done in the temple or *Apaasaro*. If the idol of the *Tiirthankara* or a *Guru* is there, the meditator kneels thrice before to ask permission and to perform the *Aavartana*, which consists in making a circle before his face from right ear round to the left ear, covering his mouth with a piece of cloth and repeating the *Tikkhutto*, which is a short prayer of adoration of the *Tiirthakara* or the *Guru*. If no idol or *Guru* is there, the meditator kneels towards the northeast, the direction of the *Mahaavideha*, where the *Tiirthankaras* live, asking permission and repeating the *Tikkhutto*. The meditation ends after the fixed time by repeating a special prayer (*Paatha*), in which the one meditates, referring to the five special faults he may have committed during meditation, viz., failing to control one's thoughts, failing to control one's mind, failing to control one's actions, failing to observe the fixed time, and not repeating the *Paatha* correctly.[97]

The *Desaavakaasika-vrata* is taken for a particular day. On this day the person fixes a limit for moving about, both in mind and body. It also involves not using his five senses to commit sin. The person also promises that, within the fixed limit he does not enjoy anything he has vowed not to enjoy. Neither does he transgress this vow, nor does he lead others to transgress it, by mind, speech or body. To keep this vow, a person must avoid five actions, viz., not to increase the number of things used, not borrowing from others, not sending servants to fetch something, not getting the needed thing by making signs to others and not attracting the attention of others to get the thing needed. In *Poshadha-vrata* the householder promises to fast through 24 hours on certain days of the month, without touching either food or water. He also commits no sin and observes celibacy. In this way, a layperson shares in the life of the monk and the nun, who belong to the first two orders of the Jaina community. This is usually done four times a month. Five actions that one avoids to keep this vow are: neglecting to search the cloths for any forms of life, failing to remove it carefully when it is found, carelessly injuring any insect life, not fasting as one has vowed and sleeping during the day without meditating. The *Atithi-samvibhaaga-vrata* consists in promising to give the monks and nuns any of the 14 things they can accept without blame, viz., food, drink, fruits, chopped betel-nuts (*Sopaarii*), clothes, pots, blankets and towels. Besides, He promises to give things they can borrow and return, such as, seats, benches, beds, quilts and medicine. This vow includes the householder giving these things and seeing the need without being asked. In fulfilling this vow, the layperson must avoid actions, such as giving the monk water that is not boiled, bread hot from the fire, bread on which a green vegetable has rested or that has gone bad, and giving it through a servant instead of themselves giving it.[98]

Some laypersons take a 13th vow, the vow to accept death by starvation (*Santhaaro*), besides the already mentioned 12 vows. Usually older persons, whose bodies are frail, take this vow. But at times completely healthy and young persons take this vow to attain super-mundane salvation by the greatest act of renouncing their life. While suffering great pain and thirst before his death, his friends and relatives encourage him carry out his decision with resolve. After his death, one who has done *Aanthaaro* is called *Samaadhistha* and is held in the highest honor.[99]

4.2.1.1.4. Special Observances

By practicing the 12 vows, the householder achieves a high state of spiritual life. His life becomes simple and self-controlled. Thus, he moves towards the practice of 11 special observances (*Pratimaas*), which are stages of perfection. Living these 11 *Pratimaas* makes the life of the householder almost like that of a monk. We now briefly consider each of these special observances. The first is the *Darsana-prtimaa*, which consists in the layperson undertaking to worship the true Divinity, the *Tiirthankara*, to reverence the true *Guru* and to accept the true doctrine, i.e., the Jaina-*Dharma*. The second is the *Vrata-pratimaa*, in which he promises to observe the 12 vows accurately. In the right time he also accepts the 13th vow, viz., *Santhaaro*. The third is the *Saamaayika-pratimaa*, which enables the householder to practice three meditations daily. The fourth is the *Poshadhopavaasa-pratimaa*, which helps the householder to fast six times a month, viz., on the eighth and fourteenth of each fortnight, besides the full-moon night and the one dark night. The fifth is the *Sacitta-tyaaga-pratimaa*. It consists in abstinence from all uncooked vegetables. Thus, he avoids the killing of any forms of life. The sixth is the *Raatri-bukhta-tyaaga-pratimaa*, which consists in avoiding eating and drinking between sunset and sunrise. This helps him to avoid unknowingly swallowing an insect during the night hours. The seventh is the *Brahmacarya-pratimaa*, which consists in avoidance of sexual intercourse, even with his wife. This also includes avoiding anything, like using scent on his body, so as to avoid arousing his wife sexually. The eighth is the *Aarambha-tyaaga-pratimaa*. It involves giving up all worldly activities, such as, building a house or taking up a trade, that entails injury to living beings. The ninth is the *Parigraha-tyaaga-pratimaa*, which implies giving up all forms of attachment to worldly goods. He must distribute his possessions to his children and to charity. He must prepare himself for the hard life ahead by not allowing his servants to wait on him, thereby attempting to live a life without ambitions. The tenth is the *Anumati-tyaaga-pratimaa*. It is the renunciation all forms of special cooking for oneself, giving away the proper food prepared for him and eating only what others give or what has been left over. Here the layperson almost lives like a monk who lives by begging. He does not get involved household matters, keeping his mind totally free for spiritual considerations. The 11th is the *Udishta-tyaaga-pratimaa*, which consists in the layperson accepting monks dress and looking for a temple or a place of solitude to meditate undisturbed. If such a householder takes shelter in a temple, he is called *Kshullaka Sraavaka*, and if he goes to a place of solitude like the forest he is called *Ailaka Sraavaka*. In this state he follows the rules laid down in the scriptures for *Saadhus* and is held in high respect.[100]

When a Jaina householder arrives at the state of living the *Pratimaas*, he is said to acquire 21 qualities, which make him a perfect Jaina gentleman. These qualities are the following:

> He [the perfect Jaina gentleman] will always be serious in demeanour; clean as regards both his clothes and his person; good-tempered; striving after popularity; merciful; afraid of sinning, straightforward, wise; modest; kind; moderate; gentle; careful in speech; sociable; cautious; studious; reverent both to old age and old customs; humble; benevolent; and, finally, attentive to business.[101]

Thus, an ideal Jaina householder (*Grahasta*) or a layman (*Sraavaka*) is a storehouse of virtues. His life is a mature and ideal life. Such a person can pass to the ascetic stage (*Sramana-dharma*), by way of initiation and practicing of the five great vows. We turn our attention to the path of an ascetic in the next section.

4.2.1.2. PATH OF THE ASCETIC

The Jaina ascetic begins his path to liberation with his initiation (*Diikshaa*) into the order of the monks. The path of the ascetic to salvation involves that he aims at two things, viz., to prevent and stop the accumulation of Karmic matter in his soul and to bring about the complete purification of the soul from Karmic matter. When the accumulation of Karmic matter is prevented and it is purified from the soul, it cannot but move towards salvation. In order to achieve these two goals, the ascetic undertakes a number of moral practices. We explore these moral practices in this section.

4.2.1.2.1. Path of Prevention and Stoppage of Karma

According to the Jainas, there is a constant influx (*Aasrava*) of new Karmic matter into the soul. This influx takes place in 42 ways, through our senses, passions and various types of activities. The *Tiirthankaras* by their teaching and example show how a soul can prevent the influx of Karmic matter and effectively bring about its stoppage (*Samvara*). It calls for strict observance of a number of moral practices on the part of the ascetic.[102] In this section, we study some of those observances with the help of which the influx of Karmic matter can to stopped.

4.2.1.2.1.1. Practice of Five Great Vows

An ascetic is expected to keep the same vows as a layperson, but their scope is much greater when the ascetic practices them. Therefore the vows of the householder are called 'small vows (*Anuvratas*), while the vows of the ascetic are known as the great vows (*Mahaavratas*). The vows are the following: *Ahimsa, Asatya-tyaaga, Asteya-vrata, Brahmacarya-vrata* and *Aparigraha-vrata*. *Ahimsa* demands from the ascetic not to destroy any living being, whether it is a single-sensed, two-sensed, three-sensed, four-sensed or five-sensed being. Even a careless killing of any of these forms of living beings is considered a violation of the vow. Therefore, an ascetic must take care while he walks, as he can trample creatures while walking. Similarly, when he receives alms he must see that the food does not contain any living creatures. Thus, the vow of *Ahimsa* calls the monk to exercise self-control, examine things taken and inspect things before he eats and drinks. *Asatya-tyaaga* – the vow of truthfulness – consists in the ascetic taking great care to speak what is pleasant, wholesome and true. It implies that the monks do not speak without deliberation, do not speak when angry, do not speak when avarice is the motive, do not speak when they are afraid and do not speak falsehood even for fun. *Asteya-vrata* is the vow of non-stealing. It consists in not taking what is not given. In living this vow, the monk should ask permission for the use of anything each time he uses it. When one does not ask permission to use a thing, one presumes that the thing belongs to him. Such behavior goes against the practice of this vow. *Brahmacarya-vrata* is the vow of chastity. It calls for avoiding every type of behavior that leads to sexual stimulation and temptation in the area of sexuality. The monks should take the following precautions: they should not talk to women; they should not look at the form of a woman, they should not even recall a former sexual amusement or pleasure; they should not eat or drink in excess or eat highly spiced dishes; they should not live in the same building where there is a woman, a female animal or a eunuch. *Aparigraha-vrata* consists in renouncing all love for anything or any person. The practice of this vow calls for cultivating the attitude of indifference to everything our senses give us. This vow foreshadows the attitude of *Siddha*, who is affected by nothing. This vow is maintained by the following: renouncing all liking for pleasant touch, taste, smell, beauty, literature and oratory, and for all objects of the five senses; and renouncing hatred for unpleasant objects. Some sects, like the *Svetaambras* take a sixth vow called *Ratribhojana-tyaaga*, which consists in not taking any food at night, lest unknowing they take the life of insects and small creatures.[103] Thus, the practice of the *Mahaavratas* controls the influx of *Karma*, as it focuses the monk on the higher values related to liberation of the soul.

4.2.1.2.1.2. Practice of Five Cautions

The practice of cautions (*Samitis*) helps the monks to live the great vows in a fuller way. The *Samitis* are positive and outward activities based on discriminative knowledge. There are five cautions. They are: *Iiryaa-samiti, Bhaasha-samiti, Eshanaa-samiti, Aadaananikshepanaa-samiti* and *Parithaa-panikaa-samiti*. The first is *Iiryaa-samiti*, which consists in taking a cautious approach to everything the monk does, in order that he does not kill any form of life. It involves that the monks avoiding field paths and keeping to highways where an insect can be easily seen and avoided. This often requires the monks to take longer routes rather than shortcuts. They are called to examine the road before they take each step. Similar care should be taken while sitting and sleeping. The second is *Bhaasha-samiti*. It consists in doing outward actions that control and regulate one's words. The monks must speak kindly and never inflict pain by their speech. A monk should not reveal what the laypeople have confessed to him. If he breaks the seal of confession, it is a great sin. Threatening one by speech, making fun of others and teaching a false doctrine are sinful actions that go against the right use of words. The third is *Eshanaa-samiti*. It is is the caution connected with eating. A monk is allowed to use only 14 kinds of things, which include what he wears, eats and drinks. All regulations regarding begging come under this category of cautions. For instance, during the rainy season the monks do not go out to beg. Nor can they make the layperson suffer because of their begging. A monk must avoid all intoxicants, butter and honey. The fourth is *Aadaananikshepanaa-samiti*. It is concerned with keeping everything clean, lest insects or other small creatures are killed. Careful dusting of books before one opens them, the stool before one sits on it, keeping the room clean where one keeps water, and sweeping the hearth and the wood before burning it. All these cautions are necessary to prevent life being lost. The last is *Parithaapanikaa-samiti*. It deals with the careful disposal of waste material so as to avoid the killing of life. This type of caution calls the monk to beg only the amount of food he needs for the day, never to keep food and water overnight, not to waste food, and to dispose of waste in such a way as not kill any form of life.[104] By performing positive action with the help of *Samitis*, thereby living the *Mahaavratas* fully, the flow of Karmic matter is restricted.

4.2.1.2.1.3. Practice of Three Disciplines

The practice of disciplines or restraints (*Guptis*), that control bad tendencies in the human person, must accompany the positive external actions that are involved in the practice of *Samitis*. These disciplines are the rules for controlling the mind, speech and body. The *Guptis* are three types: those that discipline the mind (*Manogupti*), those that discipline speech (*Vacanagupti*) and those that discipline the movements of the body (*Kaayagupti*). The *Manogupti* controls the mind in three ways: not indulging in uncontrolled grief, anger, joy or anxiety (*Asatkalpanaaviyogi*); not showing partiality, thinking of the rich and the poor alike, fixing one's mind on doing kindness and obeying the tenets of religion (*Samataabhaavinii*); and one must think regularly about one's own soul and of the saints who have attained omniscience (*Aatmaaraamataa*). The *Vacanagupti* controls the speech of a person in two ways: by strictly following the vow of silence for certain days (*Maunaavalambi*) or by speaking as little as possible, i.e., only when it is absolutely necessary (*Vaakniyami*). When speaking, one must cover the mouth with a piece of cloth to prevent injuring the *Jiiva* of the air. The *Kaayagupti* controls the movements of the body, thereby restraining the influx of Karmic matter. This is done as per the directions of the scriptures (*Yathaasuutraceshtaaniyami*). When a person advances and becomes the omniscient, he is able to maintain the state of absolute immobility of the body (*Ceshtanivritti*). The keeping of these *Guptis* protects the ascetic from every temptation, as all movements and activities that distract him are restrained and disciplined. As a result he enjoys genuine peace of mind. Thus, the practice of various forms of disciplines helps an ascetic to restrict the flow of Karmic matter in the soul.[105]

4.2.1.2.1.4. Practice of Ten Duties

The practice of ten duties of the monk must accompany the practice of five cautions and three restrictions. There are ten duties the monk must assiduously live out in his life, in order that he can effect the stoppage of Karmic matter from flowing into his soul. The duties are the following: Firstly, *Kshama*, which consists in controlling of anger and acquiring the quality of forgiveness towards those who have given him offense. It also involves learning to be considerate towards the mistakes and shortcomings of others. The second duty is *Maardava*. It is the practice of humility and the suppression of pride and arrogance in one's dealings with others. A monk who practices this duty is sweet and gentle in the manner in which he treats others and never takes pride in his status, caste or clan. Thirdly, *Aarjava* is simplicity of life and frankness in speech and action. It is opposed to intrigue, deceit, deception and cunningness in speech and action. The monk practising this duty does not indulge in telling direct or indirect lies and does not use words that carry two meanings. The fourth is *Nirlobhataa*, i.e., freedom from greed and avarice. It also involves cultivating the attitude of desirelessness and contentment with what one has. The fifth duty is *Tapas*, which consists in the practice of fasting and other forms of austerities. Sixthly *Samyama*, which consists in controlling and subduing the mind, speech and body. It also guards the monk against taking his life casually, carelessly or in any way he likes. The seventh duty is *Satya*, i.e., speaking the truth with openness and meekness. Sometimes speaking the truth may hurt the other, but the monk must learn to tell the truth lovingly and without hurting the feelings of others. The eighth is *Sauca*. It requires the monk to be pure and clean. It includes the purity of body, mind and the inner spirit of the monk. It frees the monk from all that is dark, impure and unholy in him. The ninth duty is *Akimcintatva*. It is the practice of complete detachment from relatives, friends and property. The monk looks at nothing as his possession and no one as related to him. The tenth duty is *Brahmacarya*, which is the practice of celibacy and continence. It consists in acquiring full control over one's sensuality. Serious practice of these duties effectively brings about the stoppage of *Karma*.[106]

4.2.1.2.1.5. Practice of 12 Great Reflections

The practice of 12 great reflections also assists the ascetic to effectively bring about the averting of the inflow of *Karma*. *Anitya-bhaavanaa* is the reflection that everything in the world is impermanent, momentary, transient and ephemeral. All happiness vanishes like a dream. Therefore, one should not feel unhappy about renouncing everything that belongs to the world. *Asarana-bhaavanaa* consists in the thought that every being, starting from the lowest to the highest gods, ends up in death. In this world there is only misery, which continues from one birth to the other, and no one can truly give us protection. Only the practice of the *Dharma* the *Tiirthankaras* teach can help us to rise above the cycle of birth and death and lead us towards liberation. *Samsaara-bhaavanaa* is a meditation on the nature of the *Samsaara* state. It involves thinking about the *Samsaara* state as a rented house in which beings come and go or to see it as a stage in which everyone plays different roles each time. In *Ekatva-bhaavanaa* one thinks that we come unaccompanied into the world, unaccompanied we go from the world and unaccompanied we bear the consequences of our *Karma*. Here one thinks that he is alone in this world, and he has to be responsible for all that he does. *Anyatva-bhaavana* is a reflection in which one remembers that the soul is the true reality, and it is separated from the body, even though, due to ignorance, all identify the soul with the body. *Asauca-bhaavanaa* makes a monk realize that his body is composed of unclean materials, such as, faces, urine, blood, flesh, fats, bones, marrow, semen and similar things. Besides, it is the residence of many bad habits. When the soul touches the bodies, they are soiled by it. Thus the object of this reflection is to make us despise our bodies. *Aasrava-bhaavanaa* reminds the monk that in man's earthly existence *Karma* constantly flows into our soul through the channels of activities, passions and senses, as a result of what we have done in earlier births. *Samvara-bhavana* keeps the monk informed that the inflow of *Karma* can be checked and hindered by thesoul's own efforts. *Nirjaraa-bhaavanaa* tells the monk that mortifications, performing austerities and good actions can check the inflow of *Karma*, expiate the effects of *Karma* in the soul and make it pure as gold that is purified in the fire. *Loka-bhaavana* is the reflection on the nature of the universe. It reminds the monk that the world is eternal and indestructible: under his feet is hell, he belongs to the middle world, above his head is the heavenly world of gods. All who belong to these three worlds undergo death and rebirth, and at the top of it all is the world of the *Siddha*, the world of those who never pass through rebirth. *Bodhidurlabha-bhaavanaa* tells the monk that achieving liberation is the most precious and the most rare possession. It can only be achieved in the world, when one is born as a human being. Since the monk is born as a human being in his present life, he must make use of this opportunity to the fullest and take the first step in the pathway of religion, moving upward to the course of liberation. Lastly, *Dharma-bhaavanaa* is a reflection in which the monk is reminded that the teachings of the sublime *Jinas* is to keep the Three Jewels and to follow thankfully the law of the Jainas. This teaching is the only friend, the friend of those who do have no friend and the only protection from hell and a bad rebirth. One who meditates on these 12 reflections is compared, in Jaina scriptures, to a ship in water that is reaching the shore beyond misery.

Thus, these reflections are capable of causing the stoppage of influx of *Karma* in the life of a monk.[107]

4.2.1.2.1.6. Endurance of 22 Difficulties

Another path to stop the influx of Karmic matter is to suffer hardships (*Pariishahas*) patiently. Lord Mahaaviira himself advised his monks to endure 22 difficulties as means to stop *Karma*. We briefly mention them here and what they imply for a monk. A monk must be ready to endure hunger (*Kshudhaa-pariishaha*), if he is not able to get his daily food blamelessly without violating any one of the 42 faults. He should be ready to suffer thirst (*Trishaa-pariishaha*), if he cannot get boiled water, as he may destroy some form of life. A monk must suffer cold (*Siita-pariishaha*) without wishing the sun to rise, that a fire were lighted or that he had more clothes to cover himself. Neither should he warm himself at the fire or light a fire. Similarly, he must endure heat (*Ushna-paariishaha*) without fanning himself, getting into the river to cool himself or longing to pour cold water on his body. When the monk is meditating, if an insect stings him (*Damsa-pariishaha*), he must endure it without any irritation and doing no harm to the stinging insect. He also must suffer want of clothing (*Vastra-pariishaha*), be ready to go with or without clothing, totally unaffected by it. A monk must be indifferent to where he stays (*Arat-pariishaha*), as he wanders about in his journeys. An ascetic must endure the temptations that come from women (*Strii-pariishaha*), renouncing all liking for a woman's company. He must be ready to change his residence (*Caryaa-pariishaha*) and not to stay in a place more than 29 days, except during the rainy season. In choosing the place for meditation, he must select a place that is most inconvenient (*Naishidhikii-pariishaha*) and meditate keeping his eyes and limbs totally immobile. He must be ready to sleep anywhere, even under a tree using a plank of hard wood as his bed (*Sayyaa-pariishaha*). A monk also checks his *Karma* by patiently listening to the abusive language people use against him or the doctrine he believes in (*Aakrosa-pariishaha*) as he wanders about in hostile places. Similarly, accepts ill treatment and any beating he might receive (*Vadha-pariishaha*) from people who are against the Jaina-*Dharma*. Patient endurance of the shamefulness of begging, especially those who are wealthy before they have chosen the path of the ascetic (*Yaancaa-pariishaha*) truly arrests the inflow of *Karma*. He must endure the failure of getting food while begging (*Alaabha-pariishaha*), hoping that he may get something on the next day. He patiently accepts all forms of illness that might come in his life (*Roga-pariishaha*) as punishments for the sins of the past life. Enduring the scratches one receives from grass and thorns as one moves about in the forest and the cheerful acceptance of the pain associated with it (*Trinasparsa-pariishaha*) is a great remedy for arresting the Karmic matter. Enduring the discomfort of not washing his body and clothes in running water, not allowing his mind to rest on the joy and refreshment of a good bath, but patiently accepting the horror of feeling dirty in his body (*Mela-pariishaha*). Practising total indifference to the praise a monk receives (*Satkaara-pari-*

ishaha). Similarly, repressing the feeling of being puffed up when a person realizes his achievement in one or other area of his life (*Prajnaa-praiishaha*). Resisting the temptation of being downcast at the thought of one's ignorance or failure and sternly repressing such feelings (*Anjaana-pariishaha*). Finally, a monk must be ready to sacrifice his life for the sake of religion. He must willingly endure martyrdom, giving up his belief in Jaina-*Dharma* (*Samyaktva-pariishaha*). The patient endurance of all these 22 difficulties speedily brings about the cessation of *Karma* in the life of a monk.[108]

4.2.1.2.1.7. Practice of Six Essentials

The practice of six essentials (*Shadaavashyaka*) also helps the monk to focus his attention on liberation, which, in turn, effectively check the inflow of Karmic matter. These are essential religious practices, which a Jaina, including the monks, is expected to do without fail daily. These six essentials are the following. Firstly, *Saamaayika*, which demands of the monk to sit at fixed times for meditation, reminding himself of the unity of all beings (*Samataabhaava*), in the process, overcoming the mere verbal distinctions (*Saavadavyaapaara*) that may be there. The second is *Caturvimsatistava*, which is sung in the praises of the 24 *Tiirthankaras* with great dedication and devotion. In the third, *Vandanaa*, the monk remembers prayerfully the great ascetics (*Sramanas*) who have lived the *Mahaavratas* to a heroic degree. Fourthly, *Pratikramana*, which involves reviewing the manner in which one practices self-control and remove all defects in character with the help of retrospective introspection. The fifth is *Kaayotsarga*. It is renouncing the sense of possession regarding one's body. It also involves abandonning one's love for one's body, thereby allowing the soul to rise above the body. Finally, *Pratyaakhyaana* consists in giving up, for a fixed period of time, certain food or other things the monks use daily. The daily practice of these essentials helps the ascetic to move towards his liberation, by bringing about the stoppage of the inflow of *Karma*.[109]

4.2.1.2.1.8. Practice of Five Degrees of Good Conduct

The monks are also expected to follow five degrees of good conduct, to arrest the inflow of *Karma*. The first degree is *Saamaayika-caaritra*. It involves two things, viz., to give up evil conduct and to turn to do good actions, especially to the practice of meditation during different times of the day. To do this, the monks have to keep their minds in the state of calmness and indifference. The second is *Chedopasthaapanaa*, i.e., repentance. It consists in recognizing all one's limitations, confessing them to the *Guru* and doing the penances prescribed. The re-taking of the vows, which is a kind of re-ordination or re-initiation (*Navii-diiksha*) of the monk, follows the act of repentance. The third is *Parihaaravisuddha-caaritra*. It consists in attaining purity of mind, by the painful process of caring for all living beings, by service given in a dedicated manner to the saints and by the practice of special penances.

Each of the Jaina sects performs this duty with some variations. The fourth is the *Suukshmasamparaaya-caaritra*. It involves the general detachment of the monk from everything that is worldly, as all the passions have died away. The passions are expressed only in subtle forms. The fifth degree of good conduct is *Yathaakhyaata-caaritra*, in which all passions are weaned away from, and the highest degree of moral determination is achieved. As a result, a person who has arrived at the fifth degree of good conduct is ready to achieve complete freedom from passion, which automatically leads to the stoppage of the influx of new Karmic matter into the soul.[110]

4.2.1.2.2. Asceticism: Path of Overcoming All Karmas

When the monk, with the help of the above-mentioned religious practices, stops the influx of new *Karma* into the soul, his next task is the intentional destruction of all *Karmas* (*Sakaama-nirjaraa*) that have accumulated in his soul from past existences, have taken root there and have attained the condition of maturity (*Vipaaka*). According to the Jainas, the overcoming of all *Karmas* is a very slow and tedious task. They compare it with the slow draining out of water through a porous jar. But the annihilation of *Karma* can be quickened in an artificial way, just as the ripening of raw mangoes or bananas can be brought about by the application of heat artificially. Jainas believe that one of the great means, with the help of which the destruction of all *Karmas* can be accelerated, is asceticism (*Tapas*). But, in order that the practice of asceticism truly leads to salvation, it must be practised in the right manner. The practice of 'foolish asceticism' (*Baala-tapas*)[111], which the heretics and ill-informed persons practice, though it may have some good effects on the person like meditation done in a wrong manner, may not help one to attain salvation. The right practice of asceticism burns up, as it were, the seeds of all *Karma* with its glow, in the process qualifying the soul to attain salvation. Asceticism is of two types, viz., external or bodily (*Baahya-tapas*) and internal or spiritual (*Aabhyantara-tapas*).[112] In the next two sections, we clarify each of these types in detail.

4.2.1.2.2.1. External Asceticism

The external asceticism is related to the body. In this form of asceticism, the monk deprives and mortifies the body of something. There are basically six forms of bodily asceticism. The first is fasting (*Anasana*). It can be done for a fixed period (*Itvara*), for a day or for 30 days. In this case one is deprived of only food, but one drinks water. Fasting can also be done for the rest of one's life (*Yaavatkathika*). If a monk decides to fast for the rest of his life, he neither takes food nor water. Usually the latter form of fasting is done near the end of a monk's life, and finally leads him to death by starvation. The second external asceticism is reduction of food (*Unodarii*), in which a part of the food is given up daily. For instance, a monk may give up daily a mouthful of food, gradually decreasing the quantity of food he eats. The third is restriction of food (*Vritti-sankshepa*). It can be done in four different ways: by restricting the number of food items a person eats (*Dravya*); by limiting the number of places from which he obtains food (*Kshetra*); by reducing the number of times he eats (*Kaala*) and limiting the food taken under certain circumstances, such as, food given by a particular person or given in a particular posture (*Bhaava*). The fourth bodily asceticism is the giving up of tasty food (*Rasa-pratiyaaga*), such as, melted butter, milk, sugar, molasses and other similar foods one enjoys. The fifth form of asceticism is the avoidance of everything that leads the senses into temptation (*Samailiinataa*). It can be done in four ways: by controlling the senses (*Indriya-samaliinataa*); by subduing anger, deceit, pride and greed (*Kashaaya-aamaliinataa*); by subjugating the exercise of intellect, speech and body – such as, keeping silence, sitting in a cramped position; and by being careful not to live in a place where a woman lives (*Viviktacaryaa*). The last external asceticism is mortification of the flesh (*Kaaya-klesa*). It consists in enduring all forms of irritations and pains on the body, such as, sitting for meditation in great heat and cold, renouncing the care of the body, avoiding scratching oneself when one gets an itching sensation either from insect bites or from the sharp blade of the grass one may sit on, not spitting out when one feels like spitting, removing the hair by pulling it out and doing many similar things to mortify the body. Thus, external asceticism consists in voluntarily and joyfully enduring all sorts of hardships related to the body.[113]

4.2.1.2.2.2. Internal Asceticism

The practice of internal asceticism accompanies the practice of external asceticism. There are six forms of internal asceticism. The first is confession and penance (*Praayascitta*). Every morning and evening the monk must confess his sins (*Padiikamanum*) in a general way using the formula 'May my sins be forgiven'. He must confess his sin to the chief *Guru* and do the penance prescribed in the scriptures. Usually such confessions are made fortnightly (*Pakhii-padikamanum*), quarterly (*Comaasi-padikamanum*) and annually (*Samvatsarii-padikamanum*). If a monk commits a serious sin, he must confess it immediately, as the longer he waits the greater the inflow of *Karma* is. On the other hand, repentance and confession of sin lead to the destruction of all seeds of *Karma*. The second internal asceticism is showing reverence (*Vinaya*) to all who deserve. It is shown towards: those who are superior in Knowledge (*Jnaana-vinaya*); those who have greater Faith (*Darsana-vinaya*); and those who are of Right Conduct (*Caaritra-vinaya*). Similarly, reverence must be shown at: the level of the mind, and expressed in the attitude of humility towards the superiors (*Mana-vinaya*); in the level of speech, manifested in politeness (*Vacana-vinaya*); in the level of bodily service (*Kaaya-vinaya*); and in the level of customs and practices as prescribed in the religious books (*Kalap-vinaya*). To this last belongs the reverence the wife shows to her husband in the Jaina household. The third internal asceticism is social service rendered with great zeal to masters, teachers, monks, community, laypeople, the sick and the needy (*Vaiyaa-vrttya*). The fourth internal asceticism is study (*Svaadhyaaya*). The study of the scriptures, by way of reading, catechising, reciting, meditating and preaching calls for a great deal of internal discipline, concentration and self-denial. Such an exercise of the discipline of study raises the soul towards salvation by drying up the seeds of *Karma*. The fifth internal austerity is the practice of indifference with regard to the body, its passions and the temptations that come to it from outside (*Utsarga*). It also involves the denial of all bodily needs and the total neglect of the body, which finally leads to voluntary death by starvation.[114]

The last of the internal asceticisms is meditation (*Dhyaana*). It is the fixation of thought for a period of 48 minutes (*Muhuurta*). The practice of meditation requires discipline both of the body and the mind. Right posture of the body and perfect concentration of the mind for a *Muhuurta* each, a few times a day, is a great help to dry up the seeds of *Karma*. The Jainas speak of four types of meditation. They are the following: the melancholy meditation (*Aarta-dhyaana*), the bad meditation (*Raudra-dhyaana*), the meditation on religious teaching (*Dharma-dhyaana*) and the pure meditation (*Sukla-dhyaana*). Of these four types, the first two types of meditations do not promote salvation, as they accumulate rather than destroy *Karma*. But the last two types of meditations do promote salvation by the destruction of *Karma*. We briefly consider each of these meditations. The *Aarta-dhyaana* consists in constantly thinking about some unpleasant event that has taken place in a person's life, like grieving for the one who has died. It can be done in four ways: thinking of the pleasant thing one has lost (*Ishta-viyoga*); thinking of some unpleasance one has experienced (*Anishta-samyoga*); thinking of an illness (*Roga-cintaa*); and thinking of a wish, which one wants realized in the future (*Nidaanaartha*). This type of meditation is found in the people who belong to the first to the sixth levels of the moral path (*Gunasthaanas*). The *Raudra-dhyaana* is a form of meditation, which is directed towards the four different types of worldly goods, viz., murder, lying, theft and preserving material goods. Thus, in this meditation, one is thinking of how one can better one's worldly position by way of achievement, position and power. It is found in beings that have reached the fifth *Gunasthaanas*. The *Dharma-dhyaana* is a meditation in which one thinks of the religious teaching that is found in the sacred scriptures. It is usually directed towards: the holy doctrine (*Ajnaavicaya*); the fact that something that does not belong to the realm of the soul, *Karma*, prevents the fuller development of its nature (*Apaaya-vicaya*); the consequences of the *Karma* on the soul (*Vipaaka-cicaya*); and the structure and the nature of the universe (*Samsthaana-vicaya*). The third form of meditation is found in people who are between the seventh and twelfth *Gunasthaanas*. Last is the *Sukla-dhyaana*, the pure meditation, which truly destroys all *Karmas*. It has four stages. They are directed towards: the conduct and contradictions in the process of the world, such as, growth and decay, soul and matter. (*Prthaktva-vitarka*); the soul sustains all changes (*Ekatava-vitarka*); the suppressing activity which still exists in minimal degree (*Suukshma-kiryaa-pratipaati*); and the complete liberation of all *Karmas*. The first stage of pure meditation is found in people who belong to the eighth to eleventh *Gunasthaanas*; the second state found in the people of the twelfth level; the third in the 13th and the last state comes in the 14th *Gunasthaana*, immediately ahead of liberation.[115]

When a Jaina ascetic follows the path that is proposed for him, he maintains a dwelling place of perfection, and a rich variety of good qualities adorn his life. Jainas believe that such a perfect monk possesses 27 qualities. A Jaina *Maagadhii Sloka* describes an ideal monk as follows:

> The true ascetic should possess 27 qualities, for he must keep the five vows, never eat at night, protect all living things, control his five senses, renounce greed, practice forgiveness, possess high ideals, and inspect everything he uses to make sure that no insect life is injured. He must also be self-denying and carefully keep the three *Gupti*, he must endure hardships in the 22 ways and bear suffering till death.[116]

4.2.1.3. FOURTEEN LEVELS OF MORAL PATH

So far we have looked into the various elements of the moral path, which is to be followed both by the laypeople and the monks to be freed from all *Karmas* and to attain salvation. Jainas speak about 14 levels, known as *Gunasthaanas*, through which the soul passes before it arrives at the state of liberation. These *Gunasthaanas* represent varying levels of moral existence, starting from complete dependence on *Karma* to total detachment from *Karma*. The 14 *Gunasthanas* also point to the decreasing of sinfulness and the increasing of purity that takes place in the life of the person as he moves nearer his final goal. Though the soul ascends through these levels, it can slip and fall into a lower level after moving into a higher one, but soon it gets back to the higher levels. A soul may experience number of births and rebirths to complete these 14 levels and to achieve liberation, depending on the quickness with which the inflow of *Karma* is stopped and all the *Karmas* are destroyed.[117] In this section, we attempt to consider each of these *Gunasthaanas*.

4.2.1.3.1. Level of Falsity

The first level is *Mythyaatva-gunasthaana*. Here the soul is totally under the control of *Karma* and is fully detached from the truth. The soul's view of reality is totally false. Just as a blind man is not able to distinguish between the ugly and the beautiful, so also one who is in this stage is not able to differentiate between the real and the unreal. In the initial stages of this level, a person makes mistakes in such a way that others notice him making the mistake (*Vyakta-mithyaatva*). But as a person moves into this level, he continues to do the wrong action so spontaneously that it is not obvious to others (*Avyakta-mithyaatva*). Thus, the religious worldview of the one in this stage is one of complete heterodoxy. Just as an intoxicating drug mars the true vision of a person, so also a person is so caught up in *Karma* that he is blind to his mistakes.[118]

4.2.1.3.2. Level of Simple Awareness of Truth

The second is *Saasvaadana-samyagdrshti-gunasthaana*. In this level the soul begins to be aware of the difference between the true and the false (*Granthibheda*). But as soon as it becomes aware of the differentiation it forgets it, due to the cares and compulsions of the *Karma* (*Upasamasankita*). As a result, it is not able to put into practice the knowledge it has gained. When one has simple awareness of the distinction, the soul moves into the second level, but only to slip back into the first level. Thus, at this level the soul has a taste of the right faith, but is not able to remain in this except for a short time. This state is compared in the Jaina scriptures to fire hidden under ashes. Just as the fire hidden under the ashes may blaze all of a sudden, in the same way the passions erupt and mar the brief vision of faith achieved, making the soul slip back into the first *Gunasthaana*. Thus, the primary condition of the soul in this level is one of falsehood rather than truth, though the awareness of the truth is present for a short while.[119]

4.2.1.3.3. Level of Half-truth and Half-falsehood

The third is *Samayg-mithyaadrshti-gunasthaana*. It is a stage of mixed faith. Here the soul oscillates between truth and falsehood. It is an uncertain condition, as at one moment the soul sees the truth as truth, but in the next moment it doubts the truthfulness of what it knows. This state is compared to the state of a man on a swing which sometimes moves towards the state of balance, but at other times tends towards the faulty situation. It is also compared to the mixture formed when curd and sugar are brought together (*Sriikhanda*), which is half sour and half sweet. So also this third level of the moral path presents the soul in a half-true and half-false situation. But a person does not remain too long in this mixed state of faith. Depending on the condition of the weight of truth or falsity respectively, the soul either moves into the fourth *Gunasthaana* or slips back into the second level.[120]

4.2.1.3.4. Level of True Faith

The fourth is *Avirata-samyagdrshti-gunasthaana*. It is a state of true faith. A person arrives at this level either through the influence of his past *Karma* or through the teaching and guidance of his *Guru*. The soul at the fourth level develops a liking for the principles the *Tiirthankaras* have preached, which is called truth faith. A person, who reaches this state, is able to control anger, pride and greed. Besides, he achieves five good things as he arrives at this level, viz., the power of curbing anger (*Sama*); the realization that the world, where one reaps the result of *Karma*, is evil and that one should have no affection for it (*Samavega*); the realization that his wife and children do not belong to him (*Nirveda*); the realization that he must help others in their trouble (*Anukampaa*); and complete faith in *Jina* and his teachings (*Aasthaa*). Though a person may achieve a lot of good in the fourth *Gunasthaana*, he is not ready to take any of the 12 vows, as the influences of anger, pride and greed have not totally left him.[121]

4.2.1.3.5. Level of Merit

The fifth is *Desavirata-samyagdrshti-gunasthaana*. It is the level of merit, for until the fourth *Gunasthaana*, that which occupied the thoughts of the person is Right Faith, but from now on his involvement is with Right Conduct. Thus, in this state a person is ready to practice the 12 vows, which deal with his actions. The fifth level has three parts. Firstly, the seeker of *Moksha* promises not to take intoxicants, eat meat and constantly repeats the salutation in praise of the Five Great Ones (*Panca Paramesvara*). Secondly, he takes the 12 vows, lives honestly, and performs the six essential rules of daily life, viz., worships the *Tiirthankara*, serves the *Guru*, studies scriptures, controls the senses, performs austerities and gives alms. Thirdly, he advances further and performs the following actions: eats once a day, keeps perfect chastity, gives up social life and even his own wife, eats nothing that possesses life and finally desires to become a *Saadhu*. This is the highest level a layman can and is expected to reach in his life. If he moves further than this state, he becomes a *Saadhu* and continues to climb the rest of the steps of the ladder of the moral path.[122]

4.2.1.3.6. Level of the Initiation to the Professed Ascetic

The sixth is *Pramatta-samyata-gunasthaana*. It is the initial level of the ascetic. Only an ascetic can ascend to this level. At this level even the slightest passions are destroyed. Only a few negligences (*Pramaatta*), such as, pride, enjoyment of the senses, sleep, gossip, torrents of the soul in the world and the like remain. If a person living in this level does not indulge in any of the negligences more than 48 minutes at a time, his soul moves towards the seventh level. But if a person over-indulges in these *Pramaatta*, he slips back into the lower levels.[123]

4.2.1.3.7. Level of Complete Self-discipline

The seventh is *Aparamatta-samyata-gunasthaana*. In this level, complete self-discipline without negligence is arrived at in the seeker of salvation. In such a person, anger is totally destroyed and a person achieves a state of quiescence. A slight degree of pride, deceit and greed remain. The soul is able to concentrate more, as its power to meditate increases as the result of the presence of total self-discipline and the absence of bad qualities that distracts a person or leads him to sleep are absent. Besides, every form of negligence is totally absent in this stage. Thus, a great deal of spiritual progress takes place in this seventh level.[124]

4.2.1.3.8. Level of Unique Purity of the Soul

The eighth is *Apuurva-karana-gunasthaana*. It is the level in which the seeker of salvation achieves total purity of the soul (*Aatma-suddhi*). The man who arrives at this eighth level experiences a deep inner joy, which he has never experienced before. Just as anger totally disappears in the seventh level, now pride gives way. His power to meditate by the use of *Yoga* increases immensely. It is a highly elevated state that only a very few arrive at it. The one who reaches this level is called 'Unique'.[125]

4.2.1.3.9. Level of Total Absence of Impure Tendencies

The ninth is *Anivrtti-baadara-samparaaya-gunasthaana*. In this level, the total destruction of deceit takes place. Besides, the person achieves total control over his sexual instincts. For all practical purposes he become sexless, as he is totally untouched by impure tendencies. But one great difficulty still remains and continues to affect the monk at this level that is the memories of his actions and dealing before he has accepted the life of an ascetic. Thus, though there are still difficulties to overcome, the ninth level represents a high level of perfection.[126]

4.2.1.3.10. Level of Subtle Struggle

The tenth is *Suukshma-samparaaya-gunasthaana*. At this stage, the ascetic loses his sense of humor, beauty, sound and form. His perception of pain, fear, grief, disgust and smells also change. He becomes totally indifferent to all that this world can give him. In this level, anger, pride and deceit do not appear at all and there is no struggle in coping with sexual instinct. Only greed appears to a limited degree. Except for this deep-rooted passion of greed, other passions become practically extinct in the tenth stage. So the seeker has to struggle with this subtle passion.[127]

4.2.1.3.11. Level of Restraining of Greed

The 11th is *Upasaanta-kashaaya-viitaraaga-chadmastha-gunasthaana*. It is a critical stage, as the progressive movement on the path or the retrogressive movement downward on the ladder of the moral path depends on the way the seeker of *Moksha* deals with the sin of greed. If he restrains it, by way of severe ascetical practices, he is ready to go into the 12th level. At his death he is born as a god in the *Anuttara* region of the heavenly world (*Anuttaravaasii Deva*), and he knows that he becomes the *Siddha* after he takes one more birth as a man. On the other hand, if he is not able to make greed extinct at this stage, he goes down in the ladder to the sixth or the seventh level, sometime to even lower levels depending on the level of greed he still has.[128]

4.2.1.3.12. Level of Cessation of Greed

The twelfth is *Kshiina-Kashaya-viitaraaga-chadmastha-gunasthaana*. When a soul totally destroys the passion of greed, it moves into the 12th *Gunasthaana*. Though there may be other forms of *Karma* in the soul, they have little power to bind the soul at this level. If a person dies at this level, the soul at once passes through the next two stages and enters a liberated state immediately. According to the *Digambara* tradition, the soul achieves the first two levels of pure meditation (*Sukla-dyaana*) at this level.[129]

4.2.1.3.13. Level of Tiirthankara

The 13th is *Sayogi-kevalii-gunasthaana*. At this level the seeker becomes a *Kevalii*, a *Tiirthankara* or the omniscient one. As *Sayogi-kevalii*, he knows and sees everything, and is capable of everything, though he is bound to a body. He is the true *Jina* to whom both the gods and men offer worship. He is the restorer of the Jaina religion. He goes about preaching the wisdom he has obtained through this omniscience, establishing four orders and adding many members into them. When the *Karmas* determining the length of his life (*Aayus*) are exhausted, the *Tiirthankara* enters into deep meditation, during which all activities of the mind, speech and body cease. He then moves into the 14th *Gunasthaana*, the level of *Siddha*.[130]

4.2.1.3.14. Level of Siddha

The 14th is *Ayogi-kevalii-gunasthaana*. When a seeker enters this level, the remaining *Karma* is wiped away, and he attains the state of *Moksha*, becoming the *Siddha*. He lives eternally in the land of *Siddhasiilaa*. The characteristics of *Siddha* are omniscience, boundless vision, illimitable righteousness, infinite strength, perfect bliss, indestructibility, existence without form and having a body that is neither light nor heavy. The *Siddha* state is the highest level of existence. But since *Siddhas* are free from all that is material and have lost interest in the world, they have nothing to do with the world. That is why worship is offered to the *Tiirthankara*, who still has the bodily condition and who has the interest of the people in the world.[131]

So far in this essay we have considered the Jaina moral path, which includes the path of the householder and that of the ascetic. The path is aimed at effectively bringing about the stoppage of the influx of new *Karmas* and the destruction of all *Karmas* that have taken root in the soul from past existences. This task is done in 14 *Gunasthaanas*, and might take many birth and rebirths. Besides committing themselves to a strict moral life to achieve the goal of *Moksha*, the Jainas also practice a rich cultic life to achieve the same goal. These two go hand in hand in the Jaina path to achieve the state of the true

Divinity. In the next section we enter into the exploration of the rich cultic life of Jainism.

4.2.2. CULTIC PATH

Jainism, as a religion, has a well-developed cult, with rich and meaningful rituals. It has a network of magnificent temples, shrines and other holy places, where the Jainas usually perform these ritual acts. Unlike the theistic religions, the aim of the Jaina worship-structure is not praising God to attain his graces. The goal of all Jaina religious actions is to free the soul from all Karmic matter and establish in it right conditions so that it can truly move toward attaining the state of true Divinity, i.e., the *Jina*. Thus, every religious ritual a Jaina performs in praise of the *Jina*, reminds him of his vocation to become a *Jina* himself, inspires him to emulate the example and the teaching of the *Jina* he is worshipping in the ritual, walk the path he has walked and reach the goal he has reached. There is no other motive, such as, pleasing the *Jina* or getting his graces, for which a Jaina offers worship. The worship offered to other gods and goddesses is secondary in Jaina religious practice, as they are perishable beings and are on their way to final liberation like the human beings. In such worships, they are not the true objects of worship, but they are honored as the archetypal worshippers of the *Tiirthankara*, who worship him at his conception, birth, renunciation, attainment of omniscience and *Nirvaana*. Thus their place in worship is always related to worship of the *Tiirthankara*, whom they accompany or serve. Therefore, the motive of including the gods and goddesses in worship is not to win their favor, but to emulate their example of worship in our act of worship. The center of Jaina worship is always the *Tiirthankara*, the true *Jina*, who is an example and inspiration on his path towards liberation.[132] Now that we have clarified the ultimate motive of cultic worship in Jainism, we can proceed to look into the cult-structure of the Jainas in this section.

4.2.2.1. PRAYER

The most ancient Jaina prayer is the *Namokaara Mahaa Mantra*, which the Jainas have been reciting ever since the origin of the Jaina tradition. It is not strictly a prayer, in the sense that it is addressed to obtain blessings form *Jina*, but it is a *Mantra*, which reminds the one who prays it of the ultimate goal of salvation and the various steps necessary to achieve this goal. It reads as follows: "*Namo Arihantaanam. Namo Siddhaaam. Namo Aayariyaanam. Namo Uvajjhayaanam. Namo Loe Savva Sahunaam. Eso Panca Namokaro. Savva Pavappnaasno. Mangalanamcha Savvesim. Padhamam Havai Mangalam*".[133] It is rendered in English as follows:

> I offer with humility to all perfect human beings, the *ARIHANTS*... my profound reverence for such achievement. ...
> I offer with humility to all supreme beings the *SIDDHAS*

... my profound reverence for such achievement. ... I offer with humility to all the sages who are *AACAARYAS* ... my profound reverence ... I offer with humility to all the sages who are *UPAADHYAAS* ... my profound reverence. ... I offer with humility to all the sages who are *SAADHUS* ... my profound reverence. ... These five-fold offerings and reverence of the 'enlightened souls' at various stages ... result in my resolve to take the virtuous and right path. This then will result in the removal of my KARMIC attachment and will bring me close to self-realization ... Recognition of such enlightened achievement and path to perfect knowledge fills my heart with uplifting joy and bliss ... auspicious as to spread such profound joy and bliss all around.[134]

It is the *Mantra* of self-awakening. The first five statements in the *Mantra* speak of the five stages of the development leading to *Moksha*. The first step is to renounce the world and to become a *Saadhu*, who aims at self-mastery. When self-mastery is achieved, the *Saadhu* becomes the *Upadhyaaya*, who has the right understanding of the teachings of the *Tiirthankaras*. The next stage is that of an *Aacaarya*, who represents perfect control, which involves self-discipline and guiding others to have discipline in their lives. The fourth stage is that of the *Tiirthankara*, a state of complete perfection, we can achieve in this world. Finally, the state of *Siddha* is that of the perfect bodiless one. The last four statements clearly tell what the recitation of this *Mantra* does to the one who recites it with right understanding. The recital of this *Mantra* reminds the seeker of the five states of consciousness and helps him gradually: to an awakening of the true self; to free the self from *Karma* and its effects, such as, passion, possessiveness, greed and jealousy; to the right understanding of the self; and to arrive at the highest state of consciousness. Thus, *Namokaara Maha Mantra* provides the seeker with a statement of what the ultimate liberation is, continuously reminds us of this goal and finally helps with the steps necessary to achieve the goal of *Moksha*. It is also called *Parameshthii-mantra*, as it is dedicated to the honor of the five great ones (*Panca Paramesvara*) of Jaina faith.[135]

Other than this ancient *Mantra*, there are a number hymns addressed in praise of the *Tiirthankaras*, to important teachers of the Jaina faith and other deities. Besides, Jainas use a number of other *Mantras* of one or more syllables, to which the initiated attributes meaning. Some of such *Mantras* are the following: *Hraam, Hriim, Hruum, Hrah, Yah, Kshah, Phut, Ram, Riim, Raum, Rah* and *Svaahaa*. Often such short *Mantras* are used in rituals. Not only are they recited, but they are also written.[136]

4.2.2.2. POSTURE, JAINA YOGA AND MEDITATION

According to the Jainas, the Karmic matter infests the soul, due to the activities of the body, speech and mind. The control, regulation and stoppage of activities related to these internal and external faculties are essential for putting and end to the influence of *Karma* in one's life. Therefore, the Jaina tradition gives importance to disciplining the body by way of the practice of right postures (*Kaayotsarga*), such as, sitting down with crossed legs, placing loosely hanging hands on the lap, abstaining form voluntary movements of the body, the right gesticulations of the hand (*Mudra*) during ritual, bowing, bending of knees, kneeling and other similar bodily gestures. The Jaina system prescribes fixed rules as to how these bodily movements must be done. Disciplining the body also includes the practice of the regulation of breath (*Praanaayaama*).[137]

Similarly it attempts to discipline the mind by way of the practice of *Yoga* and meditation. Parallel to the *Ashtaangayoga* of Pataanjali, the Jaina tradition gives an eight-fold path of self-discipline, which is known as Jaina *Yoga*. These eight stages of self-discipline, if practised earnestly, lead to the complete cessation of all activities and the *Karma* that these activities bring into the soul. At each stage the soul arrives at a different level of "seeing" or "enlightenment" (*Drshti*). These stages are: *Mitraa, Taaraa, Bala, Diipraa, Sthiraa, Kaantaa, Prabhaa* and *Paraa*. Of these the first four are unsteady, but the last four are more stable. The first stage brings a very faint spiritual light into the soul. In the second, the enlightenment is a little clearer, and at this stage the person is able to practice self-restraint. In the third stage, the enlightenment is more distinct and the possessor gains greater control over the various postures of the body. In the fourth stage of enlightenment, the person gets control over his breath. The fifth stage of enlightenment makes the seeker capable of deep reflection and good conduct, helping him withdraw his senses from external objects. In the sixth stage of enlightenment, one attains deep concentration of mind. The enlightenment achieved in the seventh stage helps the person to cultivate the habit of meditation, in the process giving way to the fuller development of right discrimination. The last stage of enlightenment leads the seeker to the experience of ecstasy. In this upward movement the inflow of new *Karmas* stops, the existing *Karmas* are destroyed, and the person achieves omniscience, ultimately leading him to total liberation.[138]

The practice of meditation strengthens the seeker internally in what he achieves with the help of postures and the *Yoga*. While discussing the moral path mention is made to a few forms of meditation as part of internal asceticism. Here we refer to a few practical forms of meditation that are found in the Jaina tradition. The first form is *Pindastha-dhyaana*. In this form of meditation the meditator attempts to fix his thoughts, (*Dhaaranaa*) with the help of certain images related to the elements of nature. There are five such fixations, viz. *Paarthivii-dhaaranaa, Aagneyii-dhaaranaa, Maarutii-dharanaa, Vaarunii-dhaaranaa* and *Ruupavatii-dhaaranaa*. They are the following. The *Paarthivii-dhaarana* is one in which the meditator imagines the earth as a quiet and waveless ocean of milk, in the center of which there is a thousand-leafed lotus on which is a silver throne and imagines himself as being seated on this throne of silver quietly, detached, free from love and hatred. In the *Aagneyii-dhaaranaa*, the one who meditates imagines a shining sixteen-leafed lotus growing out of his navel and the fire coming out of it burns his body and the lotus completely, leaving only the ash. In the *Maarutii-dharanaa*, he imagines that the ash that is left over as the result of the fire developes into a big storm. The *Vaarunii-dhaaranaa* is one in which the meditator imagines that there is a sudden flood that fills the whole cosmic space, and the dust of his body is totally washed away. Finally in the *Ruupavatii-dhaaranaa*, he imagines that he has become pure spirit, blessed with all divine perfections, totally detached from the elements of his body, sitting on the lion throne seeing the gods and demons bowing before his majesty. The second form of meditation is *Padastha-dhyaana*, which consists in meditating on certain *Mantras*. The third *Ruupastha-dhyaana* consists in meditating on a *Tiirthankara* as an object. Here the meditator bring to his mind the image of the *Tiirthankara*, in all his perfection sitting on the throne, preaching to gods and men, while the serving spirits fan him with the *Yak*-fan. The last form of meditation is *Ruupaatiita-dhyaana*. Here the meditator observes the real nature of his soul, as that is purely spiritual and is similar in everything with that of one of the *Siddhas*.[139] The use of these practical meditation techniques helps the physical and mental discipline one aims at through the practice of posture and *Yoga*, and, in the process, facilitates one's movement towards liberation.

4.2.2.3. WORSHIP

Worship (*Puujaa*) is mainly offered to the *Tiirthankaras*. All other forms of worship in Jainism – the veneration of other great personalities, gods of the heavenly world and deities of the Hindu pantheon – are always secondary and subsidiary to the worship of the *Tiirthankaras*. The Jainas consider a *Tiirthankara* from four points of view, viz., name (*Naama*), presentation (*Sthaapanaa*), substance (*Dravya*) and accidence (*Bhaava*). Thus, *Naama-Tiirthankara* is what is called *Tiirthankara*. *Sthaapanaa-Tiirthankara* refers to what is represented figuratively as *Tiirthankara*. *Dravya-Tiirthankara* is *Tiirthankara* as such, irrespective of the condition in which one is. *Bhaava-Tiirthankara* is a *Tiirthankara* with respect to the actual *Tiirthankara* condition. Thus, we can speak of four different forms of worship of a *Tiirthakara*: worship which involves speaking of, or listening to, the name of the *Tiirthankara*; worship that is given to the figure of the *Tiirthankara* as he appears in the spiritual eyes of the believer; the worship of the image of the *Tiirthankara* as an idol or as a mental image; and finally the worship of the *Tiirthankara* as he actually lived his life in the world. The most common form of worship is that of the *Bhaava-puujaa*, i.e., with regard to the actual condition of *Tiirthankara's* existence in the world.[140] In this section, we explore the various aspects of the Jaina worship.

4.2.2.3.1. Places of Worship

Jainas have different places of worship and the various forms of cultic practices are performed in different places. Some of these places of cult are: the *Apaasaros*, the *Stuupas*, the *Chatriis*, the temples and the shrines. The *Apaasaros* are places of shelter. They form the center of Jaina community life. The Jaina laypeople maintain and manage these places of shelter where the wandering monks and nuns stay on their journeys. It is usually built of bricks and teakwood and made of a tiled roof. They are usually 30 feet long, 15 feet broad, and are two-storied. The first floor is usually a hall used for preaching, prayers, confessions and community gatherings. The ground floor contains living rooms for monks and nuns. The real cult does not take place in the *Apaasaros*, which are shelters for living and religious instructions. The *Stuupas* are memorial monuments and usually contain the relic of some great sage or a religious teacher. So it is a place, which preserves an important aspect of the religious history of the Jainas. Usually cults are performed in the *Stuupas* in whose memory they are built. The *Chatris* are the tombs of *Sriipuujyas* or other important monks. In fact, they different from the *Stuupas* only in that the former belong to the later history of Jaina architecture, while the latter represents an early phase of the Jaina architecture. The *Chatris* cult is offered to the one whose relic it contains.[141]

The temples are the places where major Jaina cultic worship occurs. There are usually two types of temples, viz., the cave temples and the open temples. The cave temples are the most ancient ones, as the practice of carving rocks to turn them into places of cult and houses for monks has been in vague among the Jainas since fifth century A.D. Usually such cave temples are known for their sculptures of *Tiirthankaras* and decorated pillars. The most significant among the cave temples are those that are found in Ellora. The open temples are erected usually to honor the *Tiirthankaras*. They are much larger than the cave temples and usually have an open hall (*Mandapa*), a closed assembly hall (*Sabhaa-mandapa*) and the holy of holies (*Garbhagrha*), where the idol of the *Tiirthankara* who is the patron of the temple (*Muulanaayaka*) is placed. Besides, there are also arch-halls and cells, where the icons of other *Tiirthankaras*, the *Genii* serving them and other deities are also kept. All the things required for cultic worship and the wooden box for arms are also kept in the temple.[142]

The last of the places of Jaina worship are shrines (*Tiirtha*). The shrines are situated in places that are made holy by the presence of the *Tiirthankaras*. They are places where a *Tiirthankara* has spent a long period of time: the place of his birth, the place of his initiation into monkhood, the place he attains there, the state of omniscience or the place of his *Nirvaana*. Similarly, shrines are also holy places related to saints other than the *Tiirthankaras* or a place where there are important cult objects. Usually in shrines, *Puujaa* is offered on special occasions, such as on festival days or on a day that is important to the *Tiirthankara*, associated with the place. On such occasions people come from different places in pilgrimages to the shrines. Thus, shrines are more pilgrim centers than places of regular worship, though regular worship may take place there. Various Jaina sects have prescribed the number of shrines and their importance. The importance of the shrines depends on the fame of the icons of the *Tiirthankaras* or other saints, as possessing miraculous powers.[143]

4.2.2.3.2. Objects of Worship

Let us, now, explore the objects to which worship is offered and the objects used in worship. The most important objects of worship are the cult icons or statues of the *Tiirthankaras*. In Jainism, among the various sects, there are differences of opinion as to the rightness or wrongness of image worship, as some sects worship the idols, whereas the other sects do not. Without getting into this controversy, we just speak of idols as the object of worship in the Jaina temples. The statues of the *Tiirthankaras*, the main object of worship, are usually made of stone, marble or metal. Sometimes they are made of five metals (*Panca-loha*), in which silver is main component. Among the *Svetaambaras*, the icons of the *Tiirthankaras* are presented seated in the 'lotus-posture', i.e., sitting erect with crossed legs, the toes of both the feet are in resting position, the soles are turned upwards, very close to the knee of the other leg. The hands are placed on the lap, the right over the left. The statues of the Jinnas as the *Svataambaras* depict them have the eyes open and are made prominent by inserting a piece of glass or jewels. They are adorned with ornaments. But the *Digambara* icons of the *Tiirthankaras* are usually presented in a standing meditative posture, the eyes turned downward and the body completely naked. The scriptures give detailed descriptions as to the manner in which the statues are to be made. Usually the statue of the patron of the temple (*Muulanayaka*) is very large in size, while the dimensions of the statues of the *Genii* serving them, or their mothers, are much smaller. Thus, besides the statues of the *Tiirthankaras*, the icons of persons who appear in the legends of the *Tiirthankaras* are also found in the temples. Similarly, idols of *Yakshas*, *Kshetrapaalas*, *Indras*, the deities of directions, the sky, *Ganesa*, *Hanumaan*, many mother goddesses, the planets and heavenly powers are also displayed in the Jaina temples. But the primary objects of worship are the idols of the *Jinas*.[144]

The Jainas use a number of symbols to express their faith, especially during worship. Firstly, to show their identity as Jainas and to proclaim that their religion is a religion of the heart, they place the form of a heart drawn out of sandal paste between the two eyebrows. Secondly, for the Jainas, the holy thread (*Yajnopaviita*), which is made of three stands of thread, stands for the Three Jewels of Jaina faith – Right Knowledge, Right Faith and Right Conduct – and the three successions of the *Tiirthankaras* in the past, present and the future world periods. Thirdly, the 108 beads of the rosary which they pray at least five times daily stands for the 108 qualities of the five great deities (*Panca Paramesvara*): 12 of the *Arahats*, 8 of the *Siddhas*, 36 of *Aacaaryas*, 25 of *Upaadhyaayas* and 27 of *Saadhus*. Fourthly, the Jainas often use in their worship symbols such as the *Svastika*, three points and a crescent moon with a point over it. The *Svastika*, which resembles a cross, symbolizes the four stages of existence in which the soul can be born, viz., as gods in the world of heaven, as hell-beings in the world below, as animals in the world or as man. The three points symbolize the Three Jewels, viz., Right Knowledge, Right Faith and Right Conduct. The crescent moon with a point over it signifies the state of *Moksha*, the ultimate goal of every soul. Fifthly, the Jainas use eight symbols of good luck (*Mangalas*), which they usually display in temples, besides marking them on flags and banners during processions. The eight *Mangalas* are: *Svastika, Nandyaavarta, Sriivastsa-svastika,* all of which are related to the *Svastika* symbol, a powder box (*Vardhamaana*), a throne (*Bhardraasana*), a water jug (*Kalasa*), two fish (*Matsya-yugma*) and a mirror (*Darpana*). Sixthly, the wheel of the saints (*Siddha-cakra*) is a symbol that is found in every Jaina temple. It is the size of the lotus and has eight leaves, besides the center. It signifies the *Panca Paramesvara* and the four virtues. The center represents the *Arahat*, the upper leaf stands for the *Siddha*, the middle right leaf symbolizes the *Aacaarya*, the lower most leaf represents the *Upaadhyaaya* and the middle left leaf stands for the *Saadhu*. The other four leaves symbolize Right Knowledge, Right Faith, Right Conduct and Asceticism. In the temples it is usually illustrated either in silver or copper plates. It is so important that twice a year a festival is celebrated in its honor. Similarly, the Jainas use a number of other symbols, such as, sound symbols like '*Om*' and '*Hriim*', the footprints of the *Tiirthankaras*, mystic diagrams and others.[145]

4.2.2.3.3. Act of Temple Worship

The actual worship of the *Tiirthankara* and cult in his honor is usually offered in the temples. Normally there are three acts of worship in a day the first one begins about half past six in the morning, the second about ten in the morning and the third between five and six in the evening. Though there are variations in the worship forms of different sects, certain fundamental features characterize the worship of the *Tiirthankara*. We can speak of five parts in a usual Jaina temple worship. They are the following: the preparations for the worship, the washing of the idol of the *Tiirthankara* (*Snaapana*), the offering of eight-fold *Puujaa* (*Arcana*), the recitation of the names of 24 *Tiirthankaras* (*Jayamaala*) and the waving of lamps (*Aarati*).[146]

The one who offers worship in the temple (*Puujaari*) after morning ablutions and bath enters the temple wearing only three pieces of cloth. He takes along with him a plate filled with flowers, fruit, camphor, uncooked rice and incense. When he reaches the main altar of the temple, he bows down and recites the *Namokaara* litany and walks around the image of the *Tiirthankara* (*Pradakshinaa*) three times, keeping it always to his right. He then sits before the image and makes the *Svastika* on a plate or wooden plank, using rice grains, which represents the four *Samsaaric* existences. Above that, he places three points, which represents the Three Jewels. Above that he makes a small crescent with the dot over it, representing the ultimate goal of *Mokasha*. Forming these symbols before actual worship of the *Tiirthankara* shows that the aim of his *Puujaa* is to achieve ultimate liberation.[147]

After these preparations are completed, he performs the *Snaapana* ceremony, which is the *Abhisheka*, in which the image of the *Tiirthankara* is washed with sterilized water. It is a re-enactment of the ritual bath of the baby *Jina* on mount *Meru*. First it is washed with water, after which sandalwood paste and milk is poured over the image. The *Abhisheka* is completed by once again washing the image with water. Then the worshipper wipes the idol of the *Tiirthankara* and gets ready for the next phase of the ritual, viz., *Arcana*, which consists in paying homage to the *Tiirthankara* by offering eight-fold substances invoking his name. The first, the *Jala-puujaa*, sprinkling of the idol of *Tiirthankara* with water, aims at the attainment of cleanliness. The second is *Candana-puujaa*, the applying of sandal paste on the idol, for the attainment of purity. Thirdly, the worshipper offers *Akshata-puujaa*, which is the offering of the plate or the wooden plank on which the symbols – *Svastika*, three points and the creasing with a point over it that are made of uncooked rice – to the idol, for obtaining immortality. The fourth is the *Pushpa-puujaa*, the offering of flowers, which aims at achieving freedom from all passions. The fifth is the *Naivedya-puujaa*, the offering of sweets, the goal of which is attainment of contentment. Sixthly, the idol of the *Tiirthankara* is offered *Diipa-puujaa*, the waving of lamp or camphor light, for the attainment of omniscience. The seventh is *Dhuupa-puujaa*, the burning of incense, the aim of which is the attaining of great fame. The last *Puujaa* is *Phala-puujaa*, the fruit offering, for the attainment of the fruit of liberation. This part of the worship ends with offering small amounts of all eight substances in one plate (*Arghya*). The third part of the worship is the recitation of the garland of victory (*Jayamaala*), which consists in invoking the names of the 24 *Tiirthankaras*. After a few minutes of silence the worshipper chants the *Namokaara* litany, with which the entire worship is begun. The last part of the Jaina worship of the *Tiirthankaras* is the waving of the lamp (*Aarati*) with the accompaniment of the temple music. After this worship in the temple the Jaina returns home and takes his first food of the day. In the temple a similar worship is offered in the forenoon, and the evening worship is much simpler.[148]

Usually the paid ministrants (*Puujaariis*) do temple worship. Usually the community makes the payment to them. Besides, they do have a share in the offerings that come to the temple. They are normally from the *Braahmam* caste. But people belong to other castes, like the merchants (*Baniyaas*), the gardeners (*Maaliis*), farmers (*Kunabis*), the bards (*Barotas*) and other similar castes are also hired for the temple service. In the *Digambara* temple the *Puujaariis* employed are usually Jainas and believers in the *Tiirthankaras*. But the *Svetaambaras* employ in the temples non-Jainas, who are not even believers in the *Tiirthankaras*, provided they are vegetarians and non-drinkers of alcohol. At certain occasions, pious Jaina laymen take up the responsibility of performing a particular rite and do the task as something religiously meritorious. But in general practice paid *Puujaariis* perform the religious worship in the Jaina temples.[149]

The Jainas permit only those persons who are pure in every respect to participate in the worship. The worshipers, therefore, are expected to have a bath and put on special clothes, which include a loincloth (*Dhotii*), a sholderpiece (*Uttaraasana*), the cloth for covering the mouth, a cloth for sitting and a brush. Those who are permitted to wear the holy thread wear it at the time of the worship. No other objects are taken into the temple, as one is not expected to use what is used in the temple for mundane purposes. The one participating in the worship performs holy actions, places certain signs on the ear and the forehead with sandalwood paste, and draws certain lines on the arms, chest and the neck. Thus, the participants at the worship must be truly ready for it.[150]

4.2.2.3.4. Special Occasions of Temple Worship

In the last section we considered worship as it takes place on an everyday basis. But on certain occasions special rites are conducted in the temples. We mention here just three special rites, viz., the installation and dedication of a new cult idol, the renewal of the dedication of the cult image and the chariot processions.

The installation (*Pratishthaa*) of the *Jina*-idol requires elaborate preparations. After the place for the installation is neatly cleansed, an astrologically favorable time is fixed. Certain rites are performed to neutralize the influences of the evil stars. All the ascetics and holy men living in the vicinity are informed about the event and duly invited. The idol is brought to the place of installation and cleansed. Herbs are prepared for the anointing ceremony. An altar is erected where the idol is to be installed. A benediction service is performed in the house of the donor of the idol. Before the installation and the dedication service begin the patrons of directions (*Dikpaalas*) are worshipped and their cult images are installed. Four jugs of precious metals are placed on the four sides of the idol to be dedicated. It is the *Aacaarya* who performs the ceremonies as the main celebrant (*Pratishthaa-Guru*). Four assistants (*Snaatrakaaras*), belonging to different levels of the Jaina community, viz., a *Paathaka*, a *Saadhu*, a Jaina-*Braahmana* and a *Kshullaka*, assist the main celebrant at the dedication ceremony. It begins with a cake called *Bhuutabali*, prepared from a Bakula plant, which is kept in all directions, and formulas are recited requesting all forms of spirits, such as, *Bhuutas, Pretas, Pisacas, Gandharvas, Yakshas, Raakshasas, Kinnaras* and *Vetaalas* to accept this offering. Immediately after, the *Saasanadevatas* and other deities are worshipped. Then the idol to be dedicated is washed with water mixed with many ingredients, anointed with sandal paste, decorated with garlands and consecrated with herbs touching each part. The festival continues for the next eight days, during which special *Puujaas* are offered and *Mantras* are recited. Food and sweets are distributed to those present.[151]

Another important occasion is the renewal of the dedication of the cultidols of the *Jinas* or other saints. Usually such rededication takes place after a fixed number of years. The right of renewal dedication involves performing the *Abhisheka* ceremony by using water, milk, curs, honey and other similar materials. It also includes showering the idol with flowers, fruits and other things used for *Puujaa,* with the accompaniment of chanting of *Mantars* and the tunes of the temple music. Such rededication ceremonies last for a number of days, and many devout Jainas visit the place to worship the *Jina.* Another special worship of the *Tiirthankaras* consists in arranging chariot-processions (*Rathayaatraa*). Usually such processions are organized once a year. Elaborate preparations are made for the processions. The chariots are very big in size, made of wood having large wheels. They are beautifully decorated. The idols of *Tiirthankaras* are washed, dried and anointed with sandal paste. They are also decorated with ornaments. Then they are placed in the chariots and are driven by elephants and horses with all solemnity, to the accompaniment of the temple music. There is great jubilation and rejoicing among the devout Jainas on such *Rathayatraa* days. To mark the solemn nature of the celebration, on days such as the installation and dedication of the *Jina*-cult-idol and renewal of such dedications and on *Ratayaatraa* days, flags with different emblems are hoisted to honor the *Tiirthankara.* Similarly, dances with music accompaniment in the temple prescient are also organized.[152]

4.2.2.3.5. Pilgrimages to Shrines

The worship of the *Tiirthankaras* and performing *Puujaa* before their idols, especially in places that are associated with their lives, has special significance for the Jainas. For this purpose most of the Jainas undertake pilgrimages (*Tiirthayaatraas*) to various shrines dedicated to the *Tiirthankaras* to worship them there. One who plans to undertake a pilgrimage prepares very earnestly by fasting, meditation and performing works of service. During the journey he must do the following: eat only once a day, sleep on the ground, keep strict chastity and walk on foot. When he arrives at the place of pilgrimage, he is expected to worship the *Tiirthankaras* in the individual temples, perform pious exercises and offer donations for religious works. Each of the shrines where people make pilgrimages prescribes different forms of worships and performances of pious actions in order to attain maximum rewards from the pilgrimage. Often making these pilgrimages and performing the required rites are so expensive, that many people are not able to make such pilgrimages. Such people can gain the reward of the pilgrimage, without actually making it, by helping others to go on a pilgrimage. One can help a pilgrim by collecting money for the trip, accommodating a pilgrim in the home as he is journeying towards the place of pilgrimage and in ever so many ways. When a person makes the pilgrimage himself and bears the cost of another to make the pilgrimage, he is believed to attain the greatest merit. Thus pilgrimages play an important role in the life of a pious Jaina.[153]

4.2.2.3.6. Private Worship

Though temple worship is the most common form of worship of the *Tiirthankaras* among the Jainas, certain non-idolatrous sects, such as the *Sthaanakavaasiis*, often take recourse to private worship. A devout *Sthaana-*

kavaasii rises two hours before sunrise, taking his 108-bead rosary and prays the *Namokaara Mantra* saluting the *Panca Paramesvara*. Then he goes to the *Apaasaro*, wearing two pieces of clothes, sits on his prayer carpet and asks the *Guru* pardon for any life he has injured on his way to the *Apaasaro*. Then he performs the *Saamaayika*, the most significant portion of which is *karemi-bhante*, in which he vows not to sin for the next *Muhuurta* either by thought, word or deed. Then he begins the *Cauviisanttho*, i.e., the praise of 24 *Tiirthankaras*. The *Vandana*, a salutation to and prayer of forgiveness from the *Guru*, follows. If the *Guru* is not present, the worshipper turns towards the northeast – where it is believed that the *Mahaavideha*, the abode of the *Tiirthankara*, is situated – and performs the *Vandana*. Then begins the *Padiikamanum*, i.e., the confession of sin, which includes a lengthy confession of his failures: breaches of the 12 vows; sins against Right Knowledge in any of the 14 ways; sins against Right Faith in any of the five ways; violations against 25 kinds of falsehoods and 18 classes of sins; and sins committed against the *Panca Paramesvara*. Having confessed his sins, the worshipper sits crosslegged and repeats the *Namokaara Mantra* and the *Karemi-bhente*. Then he performs the *Kaausagga*, which consists in arresting all bodily functions and voluntary movements of the body, in order to purify one's soul and to remove all sins from it. Finally he takes the vow of *Pacakhaana*, which consists in vowing to abstain from four kinds of food, viz., food, drink, fruits and spices, for a fixed period of time. He then listens to the preaching in the *Apaasaro* returns to the house after giving arms to the *Saadhu* and the poor. Then he takes his breakfast and goes to work. During the day he finds some time to read the scripture, according to the directions of his sect. In the evening, if possible, he goes to the *Apaasaro*, confesses his sins of the day (*Devasiya Padimamanum*), sings praises (*Sajhaaya-stavana*), and vows not to eat until sunrise. Before he sleeps, he prays the *Namokaara Mantra* five times and prepares for a good death by repeating the *Santhaaro-paatha*, which reminds him that he may not wake again. Thus, the private worship covers the whole day and keeps the person's life centered on the path of the *Tiirthankara*.[154]

4.2.2.4. INITIATION RITES

Initiation rites play an important role in Jaina religious practice. The life story of the ascetic begins with the initiation rite (*Diikshaa*). Similarly, the monks initiate the layperson in taking the 12 vows as means to further spiritual progress. In this section, we briefly consider the initiation rite of an ascetic and the way a layperson is initiated into taking his vows in the Jaina religious life.

When a layperson desires to become a monk and to embrace asceticism as a way of life, he first gets permission from his parents, his wife or his son. Then he approaches the monastery asking permission to join the order of monks and presents himself as the candidate. He goes through a few stages of training before he can be raised to the order of monks. Firstly he is initiated as a *Brahmacaari*. The initiation rite for becoming a *Brahmacaari* consists in reciting *Mantras* and taking the vow of fulfilling the duties of self-discipline. He remains in this stage for period of three years. During this period he still has the tuft on his shaven head, and he wears the holy thread, if he has one. After patiently going through this stage, he can move into the next stage. If he desires or his superiors in the monastery do not want him to move forward in the life of asceticism, he returns to the status of householder. If he completes the stage of a *Brahmacaari*, he is initiated into the next stage called *Kshullaka*. The special initiation by which a *Brahmacaari* becomes a *Kshullaka* includes the recitation of special formulas and the duty of keeping the five great vows. An initiated person remains a *Kshullaka* for three years. The conduct of the person in this stage is one of complete self-discipline (*Saamaayika-caritra*). It is the period of the novitiate. The study of scripture is very important. Many examinations are also conducted for the *Kshullaka* during this period. If he does not pass these examinations, he returns to the lay status.[155]

After the completion of the three years the *Kshullaka* he is ready for initiation as a monk. The *Kshullaka's* initiation begins with the *Pravrajyaa* ceremony. It consists of a number of rites of different types. For the initiation an astrologically favorable day is fixed. The candidate is brought from the home of his parents in a procession accompanied by beating of drums and singing of songs. The participants of the procession are dressed for the festive occasion. Usually the candidate for the monkhood is carried in a palanquin or mounted on horseback and brought to the place of consecration. The site of the initiation is usually away from the town, under a holy tree or in the open place in front of the house of the *Guru*. An altar and a festive hall (*Samavasarana*) are erected for conducting the function. Usually the *Aacaarya* conducts the initiation ceremony. But at his absence *Upaadhyaaya* can also do this ceremony. The main celebrant of the function receives the candidate at the *Samavasarana*. *Puujaa* is offered to the *Tiirthankara* at the altar in the presence of ascetics and laypeople of both sexes. Hymns are sung and holy sayings are chanted. The candidate takes off his clothes, his ornaments and the holy thread, if he is wearing one and puts on the garment of a monk. He pulls off the hair. Others assist him in this painful process of pulling of the hair. After the recital of formulas and chants, the candidate vows to fulfil the duty of total self-discipline. He either gets a new name, adds a new name along with the old one or retains the old name, depending on the practice of the different sects. Then, the *Vaasa* ointment is rubbed on the head. While this anointing takes place, a *Saadhu* whispers a sacred *Mantra* into the ear of the initiated. This is the crucial point of the initiation ceremony. The one, thus anointed, becomes a monk. The newly consecrated monk goes around the *Samavasarana* bows to the *Guru* and the monks. The nuns, laymen and laywomen who are at the function bow to the new *Saadhu*. The festivities marking the occasion resemble those of a marriage. The one who has become the monk or his family usually meet the cost of the celebration. But if they do not have the means, the Jaina community takes care of the expenses.[156]

Similar initiation rites are performed when a person is raised to the order of the *Upaadhyaaya* and the *Aacaarya*. The rites performed on such occasions are circumambulations of the *Samavasarana*, recitations of hymns and sayings and the applying of *Vaasa* ointment. The initiation of the *Aacaarya* is done very solemnly. The dress he wears on at the occasion of his initiation is consecrated on the night before the actual initiation day. On the initiation day two seats are placed. On one the *Guru* sits, while on the other a bundle of *Aksha* is kept. After the performance of a number of rites, chanting of sayings and *Mantras,* the *Guru* whispers into the ear of the one to be ordained as the *Aacaarya*, the '*Suuri-mantra*' thrice and gives the *Aksha*-bundle. Then he is given a new name, which is usually an inversion of the old name. The new *Aacaarya* now sits on the other seat. The *Guru* and all those present worship him. He is praised highly as the upholder of Jaina doctrine. Sermons and religious worship follow. The laypeople celebrate the initiation of the *Aacaarya* in festivities for about ten days.[157]

Besides the usual initiation (*Upanayana*) ceremony,[158] by which a teacher accepts the Jaina boy as his pupil, the *Saadhus* initiate Jaina laypersons into the practice of the 12 vows. When a layperson makes spiritual progress and desires to take the vows, he goes to the *Apaasaro* and tells the *Guru* of his desire. The *Guru* instructs him about the vows and the implication of violating the vows. Then the one who makes the vow writes down the limits he is setting for himself in fulfilling each vow. Then he takes the vow for a fixed period or for life. Every day he examines himself in the practice of the vows and confesses his transgressions against the vows privately. During the annual confession, he confesses the violations against the vows before a *Guru* and accepts the penance given. He repeats his vows in the morning and evening, and reminds himself of the vows.[159]

Another vow a layperson takes is the *Santharo*, a vow to die by voluntary starvation. A person seats himself cross-legged on a stool made of *Darbha* grass facing north-east. Folding his hands he encircles his face with them and performs the *Aavartana*, and says a prayer in praise of the *Tiirthankara*. He, then, repeats the 12 vows, promising never to do evil. Having done this he repeats the *Santhaaro-paatha* as follows: "I take a vow to abstain from food and drink and fruits and *Sopaarii* as long as I live". He does not eat or drink anything until he dies. Others help him to die a holy death.[160] In this manner, both in the life of the layperson and the monks, the initiation rite plays an important role in realizing the ideals of layperson and monk.

4.2.2.5. SACRAMENTAL ACTS

Sacramental acts (*Samskaaras*) accompany the life of a Jaina from the moment of his conception. Perhaps the Jainas have borrowed some of these from the Hindu religious practice. Individual ceremonies vary in different Jaina sects. Here we attempt to consider some of the common elements. We categorize them as related to the pre-natal and childhood stages, pre-adulthood stage, adulthood stage and finally the sacramental acts for the dying and the dead. We briefly consider each of them in this section.

4.2.2.5.1. Pre-natal and Childhood Sacramental Acts

The first rite performed is *Garbhaadhaana*. It is performed when the mother is five months pregnant. The woman, whose garment is bound to that of her husband, is seated at his left, is sprinkled with consecrated water and is blessed, saying the *Saantidevii-stotra* and other holy *Mantras*, calling upon the heavenly powers to protect the mother and the child from demons, wild animals and all sorts of sufferings. The aim of this ceremony is to bring happiness and prosperity. At the eighth month of pregnancy the *Pumsavana*-ceremony is celebrated, with the aim of getting a male child. This rite is performed on a day that is favorable for getting a male child, on the fourth watch of the night under a starry sky. It consists in the *Guru* sprinkling perfumed water and blessing the pregnant mother, while chanting the *Mantras*, with the wish that the soul that is in the womb may have an easy birth and that it may bring happiness to the parents and honor to the family. The same rite is repeated in the morning.[161]

When the child is born, its umbilical cord is cut, after which both the mother and the child are bathed. An astrologer is called to write the horoscope of the child. The *Guru* performs the first rite after the birth of the child, in which he burns sandalwood and *Bulva*-wood, mixes the ash with mustard and salt, and places it in a bundle, while chanting seven times the *Mantra* to goddess *Ambikaa* and calling upon the goddess to protect the child. Then he puts a piece of iron, red sandal and a few sacramental things into the bundle and requests the oldest female member of the family to tie the bundled on the child's hand with a black thread. The aim of this rite is to protect the child from all evils and to bring auspicious life. On the third day after the birth of the child, two rites takes place, viz., *Suuryendu-darsasa* and *Kshiiraasana*-ceremony. The *Suuryendu-darsasa* rite involves the worship of the sun and the moon. In the morning the *Guru* leads the mother carrying the child to the rays of the sun and implores all happiness for the child. In the evening, in the same way, the moon is worshipped and blessings are implored. The *Kshiiraasana*-ceremony consists in the *Guru* chanting a mantra and wishing the child good health and long life, as it drinks milk from its mother's breast.[162]

On the sixth day of the birth, the *Guru* performs the rite called *Shashthii-samskaara* in the house of the child's birth, in which eight mother goddesses, viz., *Brahmaanii, Maahesvarii, Kumaarii, Vaishnavii, Vaaraahii, Indraani, Caamundaa* and *Tripuraa*, are worshipped. They are called upon to come to the house and to protect the child. Women, whose husbands are alive, stay awake with the mother and the child that night. On the next morning the *Guru* lets the mother goddesses chant the *Mantras*. Then he blesses the child by sprinkling consecrated water. On the tenth day, the rite called *Sucikarma-samskaara* is done. It consists in washing away the impurity of the childbirth from the mother and the child by a ritual bath, after which the *Guru* declares that they are pure.[163]

The name-giving ceremony takes place on the 12th day after the birth of the child. At the gathering of all the members of the family, the astrologer explains the horoscope of the child. This is followed by the worship of 12 heavenly houses and nine planets, by offering 12 and 9 each gold, silver and copper coins, and similar number of *Betelnuts,* fruits and coconuts respectively. Then the *Guru* whispers into the ear of the one of the elderly aunts the already agreed upon name of the child. Then all go to the temple where the mother and the child worship the *Tiirthankaras*, after which the aunt announces the name of the child to all in front of the statue of the *Jina.* The latter part of the ceremony also can be done at home in front of the statue of a *Tiirthankara.* The first male child's name-giving ceremony is celebrated with great pomp. The next important *Samskaara* is the cutting of the child's hair (*Cuudaakarana*). No specific time is fixed for this ceremony, as it can be done in the third, fifth, seventh or the ninth month of the first year. After the *Guru* worships the Mother goddesses, a barber shaves all the hair from the head of the child. A luck mark (*Svastika*) is placed on the forehead at the end of the ceremony. Feeding the child (*Annapraasana*) is the next significant ceremony, which is usually done after six months for boys and five months for girls. After the *Guru* performs some rites, the mother of the child feeds some of the food that is offered to the family goddesses. The last of the childhood sacramental acts is *Karnavedha*, i.e., piercing of the ear lobes. It is done when the child is three, five or seven years old. This holy action involves the worship of the Mother goddesses. A number of *Mantras* are chanted when the ear is pierced. The purpose of this sacramental act, as indicated in the *Mantras* chanted at the rite, is to prepare one's ear to hear the teachings of the Jaina religion.[164]

4.2.2.5.2. Pre-adulthood Sacramental Acts

There are two *Samskaaras* that direct the pre-adult life of a Jaina, viz., the initiation ceremony (*Upanayana*) and the beginning of study (*Adhyayana*). In the *Upanayana* ceremony the teacher formally accepts a boy, belonging to any of the first three castes, as a pupil, to teach him the duties to the gods, the sages (*Rshis*), the ancestors and to the ascetics. The boy of *Suudra* caste is excluded from this rite.[165] An auspicious day is fixed for the initiation ceremony. A few days ahead of the stipulated day, the boy takes a bath and applies on his body *Sesame* oil. On the day of initiation his hair is cut. An altar is erected in front of the house and a *Jina* idol is placed over it. After the recitation of the *Mantras* and circumambulations, the boy prostrates himself at the feet of the *Guru.* He requests the *Guru* to accept him as a pupil and teach him all duties. Then the *Mantras* are chanted, during which the *Guru* provides him with a girdle of *Munja* grass and the holy thread. Then the *Namokaara Mantra* is whispered into the ear of the initiated thrice. He is given a garment and a stick of *Palaasa* wood. The teacher teaches him his duties. Then he goes begging, and he receives gifts from the Jaina houses he visits. The duration of the pupilage differs from caste to caste. It is usually between 8 to 16 years. The ending of the studentship is done by another ceremony called *Vratavisarga*, i.e., delivery from the vow. During this rite the student gives up the stick, the clothes of the penitent and the girdle. He receives instruction from the teacher and is blessed. A cow is given to the *Guru* as a gift from the house of the initiated. On this occasion food, clothes and other articles are distributed to the monks.[166]

The *Adhyayana-samskaara* is the beginning of the study. The pupil sits on the seat of *Kusa* grass on the left side of the *Guru* in the temple or under a *Kadamba* tree. Then the *Saarasvata-mantra* is whispered thrice into his right ear. The pupil is led in a solemn procession to the *Upaadhyaaya*, who begins lessons for him. Different lessons are taught to the boys of different castes. For instance, the *Braahmans* are taught medicine (*Aayrveda*), six *Angas*, the law books and the *Puraanas*; the *Kshatryas* are taught medicine, archery, politics and the knowledge necessary for one's sustenance (*Aajiivikaa*); the *Vaisyas* are taught the law books and prudence; and to the boys of the other caste knowledge that is proper to them.[167]

4.2.2.5.3. Adulthood Sacramental Acts

In the life of a Jaina, there are two adulthood sacramental acts, viz., marriage (*Vivaaha*) and the taking of the vows (*Vratas*). Marriage is one of the most significant sacramental acts in the life of a Jaina. It begins with the betrothal. Already many years before marriage the families look for suitable partners for their children. They look for alliance with the same caste, but from a different sub-class (*Gotra*). When they find a satisfactory alliance, formal visits between the elders of both families take place, the horoscopes of both are compared, token gifts are exchanged, and agreement is made. A number of rites are associated with the betrothal. When the bride and the bridegroom come of age, an astrologer is called to fix an auspicious day for the marriage. Special rites are performed in the houses of the bride and the bridegroom to worship the eight Mother goddesses, *Ganapati, Kandrapa* and the *Kulakaras*. A day before the marriage, the bride and the bridegroom have a bath, apply special oil and perform many propitious rites. On the wedding day the bridegroom is brought in procession to the bride's house. While the procession moves on, the *Braahmans* recite the *Grahasaanti-mantra* to propitiate the bad planetary influences. After the bridegroom arrives at the bride's house a number of rites are performed. They sit next to each other, while their hands are tied together with a saffron-colored thread. The *Hastabandhana-mantra* is recited, expressing the hope that they are united forever. After several other ceremonies, the bridegroom takes the hand of the bride and leads her around the altar of fire, accompanied by the recitation of the *Mantras*. A number of rites are performed both inside the house of the bride and in the pavilion. After this everyone wishes them well and gifts are given. They are, then led to the bedroom, enjoy milk and rice together, worship the god of love and give themselves to the pleasures of love. On the following day a number of rites are again performed. The festivities continue for several days.[168]

The Jainas consider the taking of 12 vows as the most significant *Samskaara*. This particular sacramental act is different from all others in two respects. Firstly, a house priest (*Grhya-guru*), a Jaina-*Braahman* or a *Kshullaka* administers all the other sacramental acts, while an ascetic (*Nirgranthaguru Yati*) initiates one into the *Samskaara* of *Vratas*. Secondly, while the formulas of other sacramental acts are composed in the Sanskrit language, the language used the sacramental act of vows is in Praakrta, as the latter is meant for all castes. We discussed the rite with the help of which one is initiated into the sacramental act of vows in our discussion of the initiation rites. The *Samskaara* of *Vrata* is significant, as it sets the layperson on the path of asceticism and holiness, in the process leading him to the ultimate goal of *Moksha*.[169]

4.2.2.5.4. Sacramental Acts for the Dying and the Dead

There are two *Samskaaras* related to the dead person, viz., the sacramental act of dying (*Antyasamskaara*) and the funeral ceremonies. The *Antyasamskaara* is the sacramental act for the dying. The Jains consider that the dying person must be helped to die well. Therefore, when death knocks at the door of a person's life, his dear one makes all the efforts to give him spiritual consolation. They recite *Mantras* for him and encourage him to repeat the *Mantras*. When a person is nearing his death, he is advised to take the vow of *Santhaaro*, which consists in giving up all attachments to the world and its good things. Besides, it also involves not taking any food and drink until one dies. Thus, the dying person is encouraged to give away his wealth to charity and forego every form of food. The monks are called to instruct the dying person about the ephemeral nature of the world and its existence. With these forms of renunciation, the dying person is enabled to concentrate his whole attention on the *Panca Paramesvara* and to die a good death.[170]

The second *Samskaara* related to the dead person is the funeral rite. When a person dies, his body is removed from the bed, washed, anointed with perfumes and dressed in new clothes. It is placed on the floor that has been covered with a special preparation of cowdung. The dead body is arranged in such a way that the face of the dead is turned towards the north, and a lamp filled with melted butter (*Ghee*) is kept burning near the dead body. When the bier is ready, the dead body is placed over the bier, and four people carry it on their shoulders to the place of cremation, where the pyre is prepared. The funeral bier is kept on a stone to prevent killing insects and other living things. The pyre is lit, using the fire that is brought from the house of the deseased person. The mourners cry for the dead, as the pyre is being burned. When the body is reduced to ashes, all go home. The ashes of the dead person are thrown into a river by the relatives of the dead person on the third day. The mortal remains are buried near a consecrated place. Later a pyramid-shaped tomb is erected over it, and a stone pot full of water (*Kalasa*) is kept over the tomb. The dear ones of the dead person go to the temple to worship the *Tiirthankaras* and to the *Apaasaro* where the monks preach on the passing nature of the earthly life.[171]

Thus, different sacramental acts constantly assist the life of the Jaina to live his life in the world in a pious way and to move towards the path of liberation despite his personal limitation. In many of the *Samskaaras*, a number of deities are prayed to and propitiated. But, the *Tiirthankara* worship remains central in every sacramental act, reminding everyone that the path one walks is the true way to liberation.

4.2.2.6. PURIFICATION AND EXPIATION

Jainism is a religion of various *Vratas*. Both the laypersons and the monks are expected to make a number of vows. Therefore, it emphasizes the need to acknowledge one's sinfulness and to make amendment for the violation of Right Conduct, especially regarding violations of the vows. As a result, repenting for sins committed voluntarily or involuntarily is an essential aspect of Jaina religion. One expresses his repentance through confession (*Pradiikamanum*). There are different forms of confessions in vogue among the Jainas. Firstly, there is the general confession, in which, using certain formulas, a Jaina expresses his repentance. For instance, during daily meditation a pious Jaina repeats his various sins, especially those committed against the various vows, and particularly against the vow of *Ahimsa*. He usually asks pardon not only for his sins of commission, but also his sins of omission. The *Svataambaras* confess in this general way the 18 sources of sin as these sources violate the living out of the vows.[172]

Secondly, other than this general confession, the Jainas also practise the auricular confession (*Aalocana*). Here the sins are not spoken of in a general way, but special sins, particular violations and their circumstances are enumerated. Usually such confessions are made in a one-to-one encounter with another person. For instance, the layperson makes the auricular confession to his *Guru* or to a monk. The monk makes his confession to his superior. Jainism advocates the frequency of such confession, as the longer a person remains in the state of sin, the deeper the seeds of his *Karma* are rooted in his soul. Therefore, immediate repentance and confession is the best way to uproot the effects of *Karma*. For this reason, frequent confession is a must in the life of a true Jaina. The monks and the nuns confess oftener than the laypersons. Pious persons make their confessions daily, while others confess every fortnight. There is also the practice of confessing every fourth month or once a year. The minimum requirement for a Jaina is the annual confession at the last day of the year. In such auricular confessions the *Guru* gives some expiations (*Praayascitta*) to the one who confesses his sins. Expiatory penances given after auricular confessions are a way of atoning for the sin one has committed. The expiations include the performance of certain cult acts, offering prayers and doing certain acts of penance. Stricter penances are given for serious offences. For instance, for the violation of certain religious laws the spiritual seniority of a monk may be reduced. In this manner, confession of sin and the performance of expiatory penances are great ways to curtail the influences of the *Karma* in a Jaina's life.[173]

4.2.2.7. FESTIVALS

The celebrations of festivals are occasions in which a pious Jaina is reminded of his final goal in life. On such festival days, besides the external celebrations, he worships the *Tiirthankaras*, takes up special fasts, does works of charity, makes his confession and does expiation for his sins, thereby moving towards *Moksha*. In this section, we briefly consider some of the significant Jaina festivals.

One of the most significant festivals of the Jainas, that stresses the communitarian dimension of the Jaina community, is *Mahaaviira-jayanti*, i.e., the birth of the Lord Mahaaviira. It takes place on the 13th day of the waxing moon of the month of *Caitra*, which usually falls in the month of April. On this day all Jainas, regardless of the sect to which they belongs, come together to celebrate the festival publicly. Usually the festival is celebrated at the local temple of the *Tiirthankara*. The rite of the day involves the dramatic re-enactment of the five auspicious events (*Kalyaans*) in the life of Lord Mahaaviira, viz., the conception, birth, renunciation, enlightenment and *Nirvaana*. The first two events are enacted by the wealthy people of the Jaina community, taking the role of the parents of Mahaaviira and that of *Indra* and *Indraani*, the king and queen of the heavenly world. The monks present at the celebration narrate the other three events, either reading from the biography of the *Tiirthankara* or preaching. All the members join in the ritual by chanting the holy litany. While the litany is chanted, people shower flowers over the idol of the Lord Mahaaviira, and the waving of the lamp (*Aarati*) is done in front of it. The ceremony at the temple is concluded by singing Jaina hymns in praise of the Lord Mahaaviira. Banners depicting the various life events of Lord Mahaaviira are displayed in the temple precinct. After the celebration, the people return to their homes and enjoy a feast in honor of the Lord Mahaaviira.[174]

Another holiday of the Jainas is the festival of the Immortal Third (*Akshaya-trtiiya*). It falls on the day of the waxing moon of the month of *Vaisaak*, i.e., in the months of April-May. *Akshaya-trtiiya* commemorates the event of king Sreyaama giving Rshbhadeva, the first *Tiirthankara*, sugarcane juice to break his six month fast. The gods are said to have blessed the king for his holy act by showering jewels on the king's household, and, since then, he is known as 'the Immortal Third'. The Jainas celebrate this festival by undertaking fasts for six months or one year. They complete the fast usually on the day of *Akshaya-trtiiya*. The elders of the Jaina community, under the supervision of a monk or a nun, honor those devout persons who undertake such fasts on this day by feeding them spoonfuls of sugarcane juice, thus helping them to break their fasts. Such fasts are seen as genuine means for the removal of *Karma,* leading one to the rise in the ladder leading to salvation.[175]

The Scripture Fifth (*Sruta-pancamii*) is another significant Jaina festival. It is celebrated on the fifth day of the waxing moon of the month of *Jeyshtha*. It falls in the months of May or June. This festival reminds the

Jainas of the day on which the Jaina scriptures were first written down. The teachings of Mahaaviira are handed down orally. But as the monks who have committed these teachings to memory are gradually becoming less in number, there is a need to commit them to writing. *Sruta-pancamii* is the actual day on which the writing down of the scriptures is completed. The *Digambaras* and the *Svetaambaras* celebrate this festival on different days, as, according to them, the days are different. But the celebration of the festival is almost the same. On this day the Jains decorate the copies of their scriptures and display them in the temples. The people sit before such displayed scriptures, singing the praises of the *Jinas* who have preached these teachings and the monks who preserved them faithfully over the centuries. It is customary that on this festival day, biographies of the *Jinas* are printed and distributed to the people. The celebration usually concludes with a homily given by a monk or a nun, in which he or she describes the importance of the study of scriptures in the life of a pious Jaina, after which the public venerates the scriptures and the teachers. Since this festival honors the teachers of the Jaina religion and the true knowledge of the Jaina faith it is also known as *Guru-pancamii* (Teacher-Fifth) and *Jnaana-pancamii* (Knowledge-Fifth) respectively.[176]

The holiest and the most spiritually invigoratinging festival is the *Paryushana-parva*. Unlike the festivals we mentioned above, which are commemorations of some historical events and last for a day, this festival lasts for a longer period of time. The term '*Paryushana*' literally means 'passing the rainy season'. This festival is associated with the rainy season (*Caatumaasa*), and officially begins on the 14th day of the waxing moon of the month of *Aashaadha*, i.e., the months of June and July. It is only during the rainy season the Jaina monks and nuns remain in their monasteries for a longer period. This festival provides the laypersons the facility to make use of the services of the monks and the nuns to grow in their spiritual lives. It involves certain religious practices for a longer duration. This festival covers the one month and twenty days of the rainy season, when the monks, nuns and the laypersons have the time to give themselves for special religious practices. Therefore, according to the *Svetaambaras* the actual celebration of the festival lasts for a period of eight days, beginning usually on 12th day of the second half of the month of *Sraavana*, i.e., July and August, and ends with the fourth day of the first half of the month of *Bhaadrpada* (August), though the holy season continues till the 14th day of the first half of the month of *Kaarttika*. But the *Digambaras* celebrate the festival for ten days, a week longer than the *Svetaambaras*. The actual celebration of the festival, for eight or ten days, involves the members of the Jaina community observing restraints regarding food. Some people fast for the whole week, while other do so for a few days. During this week, the laypersons spend most of their time in the temples, monasteries and *Apaasaros*. The laypersons try, during these days, to emulate the lives of monks and nuns. They listen to the homilies and readings from the life of the Lord Mahaaviira. On this occasion the *Svataambaras* celebrate the birthday of Lord Mahaaviira and arrange a candle procession to mark the occasion. Giving themselves to meditation and the practice of austerities, the laypeople rededicate to the ideas preached and lived by Mahaaviira. The climax of the celebration is the ceremony of annual confession (*Samvastsarii-pradikramanum*). This day is considered as the holiest day for every Jaina. They usually fast the whole day. In the evening they assemble in the temples and make their annual auricular confession to the monks. Then they reach out to each other and ask pardon for all their offences. This is done specially to the ones they have offended. The whole ceremony ends with a prayer in which they ask pardon from every creature on this earth and offer their love and friendship. The *Digambaras* call this festival *Dasa-lakshana-parva* (the festival of Ten Virtues) as for them the ten days of the celebration of the festival involve the practice of ten virtues, viz., forgiveness, humility, honesty, purity, thoughtfulness, self-restraint, asceticism, study, detachment and celibacy. The celebration of this festival brings a great deal of joy and peace to the members of the Jaina community.[177]

Another important festival of the Jainas is *Viira-nirvaana*, i.e., the death anniversary of the Lord Mahaaviira. This day commemorates the event of Mahaaviira's giving up of his body and attaining the state of the *Siddha*. Jaina laypeople observe a 24-hour fast on this feast day and spend their time in meditation. They go on a pilgrimage to Mahaaviira's place of *Nirvaana* and keep vigil throughout the holy night. Those who cannot make this pilgrimage do the same memorial service at the local temple by lighting lamps in front of the idol of Lord Mahaaviira. The actual celebration begins early the next morning, i.e., on the first day of the waxing moon of the month of *Kaarttika* (November), just before breaking the daylong fast. The festival concludes with the solemn public recitation of the hymn addressed to the liberated beings (*Siddhas*).[178]

The *Kaarttika-puurnimaa* festival takes place at the end of the rainy season, within the fortnight of the Hindu festival of *Divaalii*. It occurs on the full moon day of the month of *Kaarttika* (December). The day after this festival the monks and nuns, who have remained in the monasteries for the rainy season, must begin their wandering life again. On this festival day the laypeople thank the monks and nuns for the spiritual assistance given during the holy season of *Paryshana*. The laypeople are also released from the various vows they have undertaken during the holy season that has just ended. This festival is celebrated by organizing a chariot procession (*Ratha-yaatraa*). The *Jina*-idol is placed in a beautifully decorated large chariot and is pulled through the streets of the city, while the large number of people, led by the monks and the nuns, follow the chariot carrying the idol of *Jina* in procession. As the procession reaches the city limits, a prominent monk preaches a homily and leads people to give generous contribution to support the religious and social service projects. When the procession returns to the temple, people return home.[179]

A significant festival, which takes place every 12th year during the month of February, is the *Baahubali-mastaka-abhisheka*. It is the head-anointing ceremony (*Mastaka-abhisheka*) of the 57-foot tall, granite statue of a Jaina saint and hero, Baahubali at Sravanabelgola, in Karnataka. Jainas believe that he is the first man to attain *Nirvaana* in our present cycle, after the *Tiirthankara* Mahaaviiraa. He is said to have meditated in a standing posture for one year before he achieved the state of liberation. This head-anointing ceremony is done every 12th year to honor this great saint. Temporary scaffolding is erected behind the statue of Baahubali with a platform on the top. From this platform the act of anointing is done. It consists in pouring bucketfuls of ointments of yellow and red power, sandalwood paste, milk, curds, melted butter and clear water over the head of the statue. The colors used represent the stages of Baahubali's progressive movement into the state of liberation. A large number of people visit this place and honor this great saint during the festival days.[180]

Another major festival celebrated that is special to the Jainas is Siddha-cakra-puujaa, i.e., the worship of the holy wheel. It is impressed on a silver or brass plate and kept in every temple. It reminds the Jaina of the stages he has to walk through on his way to salvation. It represents the Panca-Parmesvara – Saadhu, Upaadhyaaya, Aacaarya, Arihanta and Siddha, and the four virtues – Right Knowledge, Right Faith, Right Conduct and Asceticism, the goal and the means of liberation respectively. The Siddha-cakara is so important for the Jainas that the festival to honor it is celebrated twice a year, viz., in the month of Caitra (March and April) and in the month of Aasvina (September and October). In each of these celebrations the festival lasts for nine days, starting from the seventh day and ending on the full moon day. One of the solemn rites performed during the festival is the Jalayaatra. It consists in taking the Siddha-cakara in procession to a lake nearby and ceremonially washing it during the festival days. On all nine days, the Siddha-cakara is worshipped with the eightfold Puujaa. The people observe special fasts on the days of the festival.[181]

The Jainas also celebrate a number of Hindu festivals in all solemnity. The most important of such festivals that is celebrated with all gaiety is *Divaalii*. The Hindus celebrate this festival to honor *Lakshmi*, the goddess of fortune, by lighting lamps. The Jainas celebrate it in commemoration of the lighting of lamps the kings, who are the followers of Mahaaviira, had done on the day of their *Nirvaana*. But in real practice this festival has turned out to be very much Hindu in its content. On the first day of this festival (*Dhanaterasa*), Jaina women polish their gold ornaments to honor the goddesses *Lakshmi*. On the second day (*Kaaliicaudasa*) they propitiate the evil spirits by placing sweets on the crossroads. On the third day (*Amaasa*), all Jainas worship their account books (*Saaradaa-puujaa*). This consists in calling a *Braahman* to write the name '*Srii*', another name for *Lakshmi*, on the account books, in the form of a pyramid. The performance of the *Lakshmi-puujaa* follows the writing ceremony. The *Puujaa* is done in the following manner. The account book is kept on the table. The oldest available rupee coin or note and a leaf of a particular creeper are placed on the account book. A little heap of rice, Paan, betelnut and turmeric is placed in front of the account book. The account book is marked with red powder. A burning camphor lamp is waved. The account book is kept open for many hours. It is closed with the words "*Laksha-laabha, Laksha-laabha*", which means '100,000 in profits'. Thus, we see the Hindu influence in the manner, the Jainas celebrate the festival of *Divaalii*.[182]

Similarly the Jainas celebrate two more Hindu festivals, giving them a different meaning and interpretation. They celebrate the *Ganesa-caturthii*, the birthday of the elephant-headed god of prosperity on the fourth day of the first half of the month of *Bhaadrapada* (August-September). But they dedicate this festival to Gautama, the master of the *Ganadharas*, who is the main pupil of Mahaaviira. Similarly, the nine days of celebration before the *Dasaharaa*, a great *Kshatriya* festival, are dedicated to Bharata, a *Cakravartii*, who is the contemporary of Rshbhadeva, the first *Tiirthankara*. Besides, the Jainas celebrate a number of Hindu festivals along with the Hindus: the festival of *Siitalaasaatama* to honor the goddess of small pox; the festival of *Virapasali*, when brothers give presents to their sisters and the sisters bless them; the festival of *Bhaaiibiija* when sisters ask their brothers to come to their houses; the festival of *Holi* in spring during which people throw color on each other; and the festival of *Makarasankraanti* on which people give food to animals and clothe the poor. Thus, in real practice Hinduism has a considerable influence on the Jaina celebration of festivals.[183]

4.2.2.8. ASTROLOGY, SUPERSTITION, BELIEF IN SPIRITS AND DIVINATION

Though the strict Jaina religious practice is centred on the worship of the *Tiirthankaras* and other deities in relation to them, the popular Jaina religious practice, while giving the prime place in their belief system to the *Tiirthankaras*, does believe in astrology, superstitious practices, the existence and influence of various spirits on the life of a human person and in divination. In this section, we briefly explore these aspects of popular Jainism.

A popular Jaina believes in the power of the stars over his life. Astrology exerts extensive control over every aspect of a Jaina's life. Of all the heavenly powers, particularly the nine planets, the 12 signs of the zodiac and the 28 houses of the moon (*Nakshatras*) hold sway over the earth and all its creatures. The position of the planetary constellation has a significant effect on the life of the newborn. That is the reason every Jaina's horoscope is written as soon as he is born, and it is consulted before every important step he takes in his life. Again, for the same reason, the Jainas look for astrologically favorable moments for events, such as, initiation, marriage, consecration as an ascetic and the like. Belief in the power of the stars does not go against their belief in the law of *Karma*, as both are in perfect harmony with each other. Therefore, they believe that astrology can help one know the effects of *Karma* on one's future life. The Jaina theologians associate individual planets with each of the 24 *Tiirthankaras*. This belief makes the Jainas to worship the stellar constellations by the recitation of the *Mantras* and offer them appropriate appeasement and propitiations to counteract the unfavourable effects that come from them.[184]

Among the superstitious beliefs of the Jainas, the most dominant one is that of the evil eye. It is the belief that some people by their look that stems from jealousy can bring evil effect on the one in whose life something good or auspicious has happened. Usually people who are beautiful, wise and particularly lucky are exposed to the evil eye. It is believed that anything dark or bitter can avert the effects of the evil eye. For instance, if a new ornament is worn, a black thread is tied to it; if a new house is being constructed, a black mud pot is kept outside; and a child is marked with a black dot on the cheek. Similarly, on the wedding day a lemon is tied with the *Turben* of the bridegroom and to the *Saree* of the bride to ward off the effect of an evil eye on the newlywed. If a child becomes sick, it is usually attributed to the evil eye. To free the child from the effect of the evil eye and its consequent fever or illness, *Najara-bandhii* is practiced. It consists in taking smokeless burning ash or coal and placing on it mustard, salt and grain till fine smoke is made. Then it is covered and kept under the bed where the child sleeps. After a few days, when the fever leaves, the content of the pot is thrown at the junction of three roads. If an adult becomes ill due to the evil eye, the method used to get rid of the effect of the evil eye is to take some food and wave it around the head of the person who is ill and to give it to a black dog. It is believed that if the dog eats the food, the effects of the evil eye pass on to the dog. In this way, there are a number of superstitious practices to ward off the effects of the evil eye.[185]

The belief in the existence of the evil spirits (*Bhuutas*) and their capability to bring harm to people is widespread among the uneducated Jainas and particularly among women. They believe that evil spirits are active during the time of the *Divaalii* festival. To prevent them from coming to their houses, women carry water to the crossroads, make a circle with water on the ground and place a small grain cake in the circle. Similarly, they place vermilion, grain and something black into the bottom of a broken pot to guard against the coming of evil sprits. It is believed that the *Bhuutas* live in pippal trees during the last days of the month of *Sraavana*, and women water these trees to make the spirits live there happily and to prevent their coming to their homes. The Jainas believe that if the evil spirits come out of their dwelling places and visit homes of the people, they can cause different types of sufferings and illnesses. So they call priests, magicians and sorcerers to satisfy the evil spirits. A number of methods are used to ward off the evil the ghosts can bring: use of magic-*Mantras*, burning of incense, applying ash to the sick, the using of amulets and talismans, use of sorcery and black-magic, and performing other rites. Similarly, the spirits of the ancestors, especially the ones who have died suddenly due to murder, suicide or war, are believed to have the power to cause evil on family members, as the spirits of the dead ancestors may come to accomplish the purposes, which their sudden death has interrupted. The Jainas use a number of practices to propitiate and calm the desires of such ancestral spirits: a metal image of the ancestor is placed along with the house idols and is worshipped; drawing a picture of a serpent in the wall of the room where water is kept, waving it thrice with water as done in *Aarati* and offering a little cake; once a year either on the eighth or the 29th of the month of *Aasvina* offering of sweets (*Naivedya*); and keeping a lamp in a corner facing the former dwelling places of the ancestors, offering of sweetmeats to the lamp. Later the one who offers eats the sweets. In this way, belief in the evil spirits, both *Bhuutas* and ancestors, affect every aspect of the life of the Jainas.[186]

The divination of omens and that of objects and beings a person meets on his journey are widespread in the lives of the Jainas. They believe that these omens, objects and beings are favourable or unfavourable signs in a person's life. Divination attempts to interpret these omens and portents. The significant example of omens and their divinations among the Jainas are dreams and their interpretations. They distinguish nine types based on their origin: dreams that originate from worry, dreams related to illness, dreams stemming from an experience, dreams coming from the nature of the one who dreams, dreams related to what one hears, dreams starting from what one sees, dreams beginning from a religious work, dreams emerging from one's sinful condition and dreams resulting from the directions of gods or higher beings. Of these the first six types are not so relevant. But the last three bear good or bad consequences on the one who dreams. Of these dreams, there are some that are auspicious, known as the great dreams, like the ones that predict the birth of the *Tiirthankaras*, the *Cakravartiis* and other heroes. But there are also inauspicious dreams that predict some or the other evil that is going to happen. An example of this type of dream is the 16 dreams the emperor Candragupta is said to have had that predicted the famine at Magadha that lasted for 12 years. Thus, divination of such portents and signs does have a place in the life of the Jainas.[187]

This essay has explored the path Jainism proposes to achieve the state of liberation. The Jaina path to liberation has two dimensions, viz., the moral and the cultic. The former attempts to achieve the goal through reformation of one's life, while the latter attempts to achieve the same by way of worship of the *Tiirthankaras*. The motivation of both of these dimensions of the Jaina path is not to achieve liberation by way of the grace of the *Tiirthankaras*, but rather to live a moral life. The cultic practices become means and occasions through which one ascends to one's ultimate destiny. The moral path is lived on 14 levels over a number of births and rebirths, and has two major stages, viz., paths of the layperson and the ascetics. While the layperson's life takes him only to a few levels, the life of the ascetic takes him to fuller realization of the ideal of liberation. The ascetic, by his various practices, attempts to stop the influx of new *Karma* and later completely destroys all Karmic matter from his soul, thereby attempting to become a liberated soul. The main thrust of the cult is the worship of the *Tiirthankaras*. While this is the mainstream of worship among the Jainas, the worship of gods of the heavenly world, some that belong to the Hindu pantheon, planetary constellations, the spirits of the nether world, the ancestral spirits and the practice of a number of superstitions are widespread in popular Jainism. Though the motivation of the main stream of worship is the attainment of liberation, the motivation behind the latter forms of popular worship is not seemingly very genuine. When we analyze the popular religious practices, we find that achieving mundane things, winning favors from the gods, opening themselves to the graces and blessings the gods can shower upon them in everyday life situations, appeasing their anger, fear of being affected by their influence and similar motivations move the people to worship them. Thus, we find a discrepancy regarding the motivations of the mainstream worship and the popular worship. Though every Jaina gives the prime importance to the worship of the *Tiirthankara*, he cannot ignore these lower deities, as he needs them, because they provide a security for everyday living, which he does not derive from the *Jina* worship, as the *Jina* is not really concerned about the ordinary Jaina's everyday life. It seems that this inconsistency in the motivations of the orthodox *Jina* worship and popular worship of deities stems from the fact that, though Jainism does not believe in a personal God who satisfies man's everyday concerns, the ordinary Jaina has the need to depend on some super-human reality to whom he can pray, who listens to his plea and who helps him to tie over the difficulties of everyday life.

CONCLUSION

Exploring the Jaina tradition historically, we have briefly mentioned its origin, development, the major schisms and its decline. An attempt is made to unravel the gods of Jainism and the path it proposed to arrive at the Divinity of Jainism. Our unfolding of the Jaina religious tradition clearly shows the rich spiritual values – Right Knowledge, Right Faith, Right Conduct and Asceticism – inherent in Jaina religious practice. Jainism as a religion attacks the modernist tendency of making idols of pleasure, enjoyment and luxury. It proclaims that the means to true happiness is not pursuing the pleasures of life, but rather it is curbing them that lead one to the final state of *Nirvaana*. Jainism also affirms that it is the effort one makes to remove the Karmic matter from one's soul, in the last analysis, that brings one the liberation. Thus, for the Jainas the path to salvation is that which one walks alone, though others walk with him and others, like the *Tiirthankaras*, who have already walked the path, can help him by their example and inspiration. Jainism as a religion upholds the spiritual individuality of every existing reality, whether in the *Karma-samsaara* state or in the liberated state. The uniqueness of the individual soul is never lost or merged with something else, though it may take birth as different realities in successive rebirths. The respect for life and the practice of *Ahimsa* that Jainism upholds clearly portrays belief in the uniqueness of the individual reality.

Though, it is duty more than love that guides Jaina morality and spiritual living, the Jaina has a deep community feeling. The four orders – the monk, the nuns, the laymen and laywomen – and their mutual interdependence bear witness to this fact. The material dependence of the monks and the nuns on the laypeople and the latter's spiritual dependence on the former presents a relationship that is mutual, whole and complete. The generous monetary contributions the laypeople make for the cause of religious and charitable works under scores their sense of community. Probably it is because of this strong community feeling among the Jainas that Jainism, unlike Buddhism is not totally wiped away from the soil of its origin, in spite of many such attempts against it during its history.

Jainism is basically a human-centered and effort-centered religion. It believes that a person can attain his or her highest state of existence by their own effort, by the total cessation of the effects of *Karma* in their life. This belief makes it deny the existence of a Supreme God and His grace as a necessity in the life of a human person. In holding to this truth very strictly, Jainism denies the reality of religious experience as a relationship with the Supreme Being. Though mainstream Jainism upholds this truth, we see popular Jainism moving towards a religious devotionalism, especially in the worship of lower deities. In spite of this drawback, Jainism is a rich religious tradition that has contributed much to the religious life of every human being.

NOTES

1 Cf. Saahitya Vaacaspati Srii Devendra Muni Saastrii, *Jaina Religion and Philosophy: An Introduction*, (Udaipur: Srii Taarak Guru Jain Granthaalya, 1985), p. 3. Cf. also Padmanabh S. Jaini, *The Jaina Path of Purification*, (Delhi: Motilal Banarsidass Publishers Private Limited, 1998), pp. 1-3.

2 Cf. Saahitya Vaachaspati Srii Devender Muni Saastrii, pp. 3-6.

3 Cf. Ibid., pp. 11-18. Sinclair Stevenson, *The Heart of Jainism*, (Delhi: Munshiram Manoharlal Publishers Pvt. Ltd., 1984), pp. 50-58. Cf. also Narendra Nath Bhattacharyya, *Jain Philosophy: Historical Outline*, (Delhi: Munshiram manoharlal Publishers Pvt. Ltd., 1976), pp. 51-54.

4 Cf. Helmuth von Glasenapp, *Jainism: An Indian Religion of Salvation*, trans. Shridhar B. Shrotri, *Lala Sundarlal Research Series*, ed. Satya Ranjan Banerjee, Vol. XVI, (Delhi: Motilal Banarsidass Publishers Private Limited, 1999), pp. 24-37. Cf. also Naendra Nath Bhattacharyya, pp. 44-47. Cf. also Sinclair Stevenson, pp. 21-47. Cf. also Saahitya Vaachaspati Srii Devender Muni Saastrii, pp. 18-21. Cf. also Padmanbh S. Jaini, *The Jaina Path of Purification*, pp. 6-38.

5 Cf. Padmanabh S. Jaini, *The Jaina path of Purification*, pp. 42-47. Cf. also Helmuth von Glasenapp, pp. 39-40.

6 Cf. Helmuth von Glasenapp, pp. 383-384.

7 Cf. Ibid.

8 Cf. Ibid., pp. 45-46, 384-386.

9 Cf. Ibid., pp. 46-48. Cf. also Padmanabh S. Jaini, *The Jaina Path of Purification*, pp. 38-41.

10 Cf. Ibid.

11 Cf. Helmuth von Glassenapp, pp. 386-395.

12 Cf. Ibid., pp. 69-90.

13 Cf. Padmanabh S. Jaini, *The Jaina Path of Purification*, p. 47.

14 Cf. Ibid., pp. 47-48, 49-52.

15 Cf. Ibid., pp. 48, 52-55.

16 Cf. Ibid., pp. 55-56.

17 Cf. Ibid., pp. 48, 56-62.

18 Cf. Ibid., pp.48, 62-64.

19 Cf. Ibid., pp. 48-49, 64-77. The books we have mentioned constitute the basic Jaina canonical books. Many commentaries have been written on

them. The earliest of such commentaries are called *Niryktis* and *Bhaashyas*, which are written in Prakrit verse; the next collection of commentaries are called *Cuurnis* which are written in Prakrit prose, and the last the *Tiikas*, written in Sanskrit prose. The commentators lived from the 5th century A.D. to the 13th century A.D. Some of the major commentators are: Bhadrabaahu, Jinabhadra, Jinadaasa, Haribhadra, Siilaanka, Abhayadeva, Mladhaari Hemachandra and Malayagiri. Cf. Ibid., p. 77.

20 Cf. Ibid., p. 78.
21 Cf. Ibid., pp. 78-87.
22 Cf. Ibid., p. 78.
23 Cf. Helmuth von Glassenapp, pp. 368-369. Cf. also Sinclair Stevenson, pp. 66-68. Cf. Arun Pratap Singh, "The Role of Lay-Votary in Jainsm", *Perspectives in Jaina Philosophy and Culture*, ed. Shri Satish Kumr Jain, (New Delhi: Ahimsa International, 1985), pp. 109-111.
24 Cf. Helmuth von Glassenapp, pp. 372-382.
25 Cf. Ibid., pp. 370-372. Cf. also Sinclair Stevenson, pp. 66-68.
26 Cf. Helmuth von Glasenapp, p. 177.
27 Cf. Cf. Ibid., pp. 178- 240. Cf. also Sinclair Stevenson, pp. 89-192. Cf. also Jesuit Scholars, pp. 191-192.
28 Cf. Narendra Nath Bhattacharyya, pp. 162-165. Cf. Sinclair Stevenson, pp. 91-93.
29 Cf. Helmuth von Glasenapp, pp. 241-248.
30 Cf. Ibid., p. 248.
31 Cf. Ibid., pp. 248-249, 408.
32 Cf. Helmuth von Glasenapp, pp. 404-406.
33 Cf. Ibid., pp. 406-407.
34 Cf. Ibid., p. 407. Cf. also Maruti Nandan Prasad Tiwari, "Sarasvatii in Jaina Art", *Perspectives in Jaina Philosophy and Culture*, ed. Shri Satish Kumar Jain, pp. 66-71.
35 Cf. Narendra Nath Bhattacharyya, p. 140. Cf. also Lawrence A. Babb, *Ascetics and Kings in a Jain Ritual Culture, Lala Sundarlal Jain Research Series*, ed. Satya Ranjan Banerjee, Vol. XI, (Delhi: Motilal Banarsidss Publishers Private Limited, 1998), p. 44.
36 Cf. Lawrence A. Babb, pp. 38-39. Cf. also Helmuth von Glasenapp, pp. 249-252. Cf. also Narendra Nath Bhattacharyya, pp. 140-142. The *Svetaambara* and *Digambara* sects differ in their description of the measurement of the universe, but they are more or less similar in their views. Cf. Narendra Nath Bhattacharyya, pp. 141-142.
37 Cf. Helmuth von Glasenapp, pp. 258-262. Cf. Lawrence A. Babb, p. 46.
38 Cf. Helmuth von Glasenapp, pp. 252-258. Cf. also Lawrence A. Babb, pp. 39-40, 46.
39 Cf. Lawrence A. Babb, pp. 44-45, 46-47.
40 Cf. Ibid., p. 40. Cf. also Narendra Nath Bhattacharyya, p. 142. Cf. also Helmuth von Glasenapp, pp. 266-267. There are a number of minor differences in the manner the *Svetaambaras* and the *Digambaras* arrange the dif-

ferent levels of the heavenly world. They are more or less the same except that the *Digambaras* speak of a region *Anudisa*, having nine heavens, between the regions of *Graiveyakas* and *Anuttaras*. Cf. Helmuth von Gasenapp, pp. 266-267.

41 Cf. Lawrence A. Babb, pp. 47, 77-78. Cf. also Helmuth von Glasenapp, p. 262.

42 Cf. Helmuth von Glasenapp, pp. 262-263. Cf. also Lawrence A. Babb, pp. 47-48.

43 Cf. Helmuth von Glasenapp, pp. 263-264. Cf. also Lawrence A. Babb, p. 47.

44 Cf. Helmuth von Glasenapp, p. 264. Cf. Lawrence A. Babb, p. 47.

45 Cf. Helmuth von Glasenapp, pp. 264-266. Cf. Lawrence A. Babb, p. 47.

46 Cf. Lawrence A. Babb, p. 47. Cf. also Helmuth von Glasenapp, pp. 266-268. The *Digambaras* speak of a region of the upper heaven called the *Anudisa* having nine parts between the *Graiveyakas* and the *Anuttaras*. The say that in this region live a group of deities called *Lokaantika* gods, who are outside the hierarchy of gods. According to the *Digambara* tradition, these gods are divided into 24 classes. *Saarasvata, Aadtya, Vahni, Aruna, Gardatoya, Tushita, Avyaabaadha* and *Arishta* are some of the classes included in the 24. These *Lokaantika* gods are without desire. Therefore, they are called the god-saints (*Devarshis*). They serve the *Tiirthankara* when he appears on earth and are finally born as human beings and get salvation. Cf. Helmuth von Glasenapp, p. 267.

47 Cf. Helmuth von Glasenapp, pp. 267-268. Cf. also Lawrence A. Babb. P. 47.

48 Cf. Helmuth von Glasenapp, pp. 269-270.

49 Cf. Ibid., p. 271. Cf. also Lawrence A. Babb, p. 41.

50 Cf. Helmuth von Glasenapp, pp. 271-273. Cf. Lawrence A. Babb, pp. 41-42.

51 Cf. Helmuth von Glassenapp, pp. 286-337. Cf. also Lawrence A. Babb, pp. 42-44.

52 Cf. Ibid.

53 Cf. Ibid.

54 Cf. Helmuth von Glassenapp, pp. 288-289, 292-293. There are differences among the *Digambaras* and the *Svetaambaras* regarding the names of these holy men, the order of their appearance and number of such matters. But the differences are minor, as on all basic matters there is agreement. Cf. Ibid., p. 289.

55 Cf. Ibid., pp. 292-293.

56 Cf. Ibid., pp. 282-285, 288.

57 Cf. Ibid., p. 285.

58 Cf. Ibid., pp. 285-286, 288.

59 Cf. Ibid.

60 Cf. Ibid., p. 286, 288. Other than the *Kulakaras* and the 63 *Salaakapurushas*, the Jaina hagiography also speaks of a few other holy men, viz.,

nine *Naaradas*, 11 *Rudras*, 24 *Kaamadevas* and 24 fathers and mothers of the *Tiirthankaras*. These are insignificant in comparison with the ones we mentioned. Therefore, we do not go into much detail about them. Cf. Ibid., pp. 273-274.

    61 Cf. Lawrence A. Babb, pp. 77-79. Cf. also Padmanabh S. Jaini, "Jaina Concept of the Sacred", *Perspectives in Jaina Philosophy and Culture*, ed. Shri Satish Kumar Jain, pp.102-105.

    62 Cf. Helmuth von Glasenapp, p. 274. Cf. also Lawrence A. Babb, pp. 5-6.

    63 Lawrence A. Babb, pp. 5-6.

    64 Cf. Ibid., p. 7. Cf. also Helmuth von Glasenapp, p. 274.

    65 Cf. Helmuth von Glasenapp, pp. 34-35.

    66 Cf. Ibid., p. 275.

    67 Cf. Ibid., pp. 268-269, 274. Cf. also Lawrence A. Babb, p. 5. Cf. also Sinclair Stevenson, p. 39.

    68 Cf. Helmuth von Glasenapp, pp. 275, 323-324.

    69 The *Digambaras* and the *Svetaambaras* disagree as to the number of dreams. While the former speaks of sixteen dreams the latter speak of only fourteen dreams. Here we mention the *Digambara* version of sixteen dreams. Cf. Ibid., pp. 275-276.

    70 Cf. Ibid.

    71 Cf. Ibid., pp. 275, 276-277.

    72 Cf. Ibid., pp. 277-278.

    73 Ibid., p. 278.

    74 Cf. Ibid., pp. 280-281.

    75 Cf. Ibid., 278-279, 280, 281.

    76 Cf. Ibid., p. 282.

    77 Cf. Sinclair Stevenson, p. 242.

    78 We elaborate the use of *Namokaara-mantra* in worship in the next essay, which deals with Jaina path to the Divine.

    79 Cf. Lawrence A. Babb, pp. 22-23. Cf. also Padmanabh S. Jaini, "Jaina Concept of the Sacred", *Perspectives in Jaina Philosophy and Culture*, ed. Shri Satish Kumar Jain, p. 103.

    80 Cf. Sinclair Stevenson, p. 239.

    81 Cf. Ibid., pp. 39-40.

    82 Cf. Ibid., pp. 240-241.

    83 Ibid., p. 241.

    84 Cf. Ibid., pp. 171, 241-242. Cf. also Padmanabh S. Jaini, "Jaina Concept of the Sacred", *Perspectives in Jaina Philosophy and Culture*, ed. Shri Satish Kumar Jain, p. 103.

    85 Sinclair Stevenson, p. 169.

    86 Cf. Ibid., 242-243.

    87 Cf. Ibid., pp. 170-171. Cf. also Helmuth von Glasenapp, pp. 238-239.

    88 Cf. Helmuth von Glasenapp, p. 270.

89 Cf. Saahitya Vaachaspati Srii Devender Muni Saastrii, pp. 8-11. Cf. also Helmuth von Glasenapp, pp. 401-404.
90 Cf. Sinclair Stevenson, pp. 245-246.
91 Cf. Ibid., pp. 246-247.
92 Cf. Saahitya Vaachaspati Srii Devender Muni Saastrii, pp. 29-30.
93 Cf. Ibid., p. 30.
94 Cf. Ibid., pp. 30-33. Cf. also Sinclair Stevenson, pp. 243-245.
95 Cf. Sinclair Stevenson, pp. 205-210. Cf. also Helmuth von Glasenapp, p. 228. Cf. also Saahitya Vaachaspati Srii Devendra Muni Saastrii, p. 33.
96 Cf. Sinclair Stevenson, pp. 210-215. Cf. also Helmuth von Glasenapp, pp. 228-229.
97 Cf. Sinclair Stevenson, pp. 215-219. Cf. also Hemuth von Glasenapp, p. 229.
98 Cf. Ibid.
99 Cf. Sinclair Stevenson, pp. 220-221.
100 Cf. Helmuth von Glasenapp, pp. 229-230. Cf. also Sinclair Stevenson, pp. 221-224.
101 Sinclair Stevenson, p. 224.
102 Cf. Helmuth von Glasenapp, pp. 225-226, 231.
103 Cf. Helmuth von Glasenapp, p, 231. Cf. also Sinclair Stevenson, pp. 234-238.
104 Cf. Helmuth von Glasnapp, pp. 213-232. Cf. also Sinclair Stevenson, pp. 144-147.
105 Cf. Sinclair Stevenson, pp. 147-148. Cf. also Jesuit Scholars, p. 193.
106 Cf. Jesuit Scholars, p. 194. Cf. also Sinclair Stevenson, pp.151-154. Cf. also Saahitya Vaachaspati Srii Devender Muni Saastrii, p. 45.
107 Cf. Sinclari Stevenson, pp. 156-161. Cf. also Saahitya Vaachaspti Srii Devender Muni Saastrii, pp. 43-44. Cf. also Helmuth von Glasenapp, pp. 232-233.
108 Cf. Sinclair Stevenson, pp. 148-151. Cf. also Saahitya Vaachaspti Srii Devender Muni Saastrii, pp. 39-42. Cf. also Helmuth von Glasenapp, p. 233.
109 Cf. Saahitya Vaachaspti Srii Devender Muni Saastrii, pp. 42-43.
110 Cf. Sinclair Stevenson, pp.154-156.
111 Committing suicide for religious reasons by jumping down from a hill or by drowning oneself are examples of *Baala-tapas*. Such acts may have some beneficial effects for the one who has done the act, such as, rebirth in the world of the gods. But it may not lead a person to the attainment of salvation. Cf. Helmuth von Glasenapp, p. 235.
112 Cf. Cf. Ibid., pp. 234-235. Cf. also Sinclair Stevenson, p. 163.
113 Cf. Sinclair Stevenson, pp. 163-165. Cf. also Helmuth von Glasenapp, pp. 235-236.
114 Cf. Sinclair Stevenson, pp. 165-168. Cf. also Helmuth von Glasenapp, p. 236.

115 Cf. Helmuth von Glasenapp, pp. 236-238. Cf. also Sinclair Stevenson, p. 168.
116 Sinclair Stevenson, p. 238.
117 Cf. Helmuth von Glasenapp, p.221.
118 C. Ibid., pp. 221-222. Cf. also Sinclair Stevenson, pp. 185-186.
119 Cf. Sinclair Stevenson, p. 186. Cf. also Helmuth von Glasenapp, p. 222.
120 Cf. Ibid.
121 Cf. Sinclair Stevenson, pp. 186-187. Cf. also Helmuth von Glasenapp, p. 222
122 Cf. Sinclair Stevenson, pp. 187-188. Cf. also Helmuth von Glasenapp, pp. 222-223.
123 Cf. Sinclair Stevenson, p. 188. Cf. also Helmuth Von Glasnapp, p. 223.
124 Cf. Ibid.
125 Cf. Sinclair Stevenson, pp. 188-189. Cf. also Helmuth von Glasnapp, pp. 223-224.
126 Cf. Sinclair Stevenson, p. 189. Cf. also Helmuth von Glasenapp, p. 224
127 Cf. Sinclair Stevenson, pp. 189-190. Cf. also Helmuth von Glasenapp, p. 224.
128 Cf. Sinclair Stevenson, p. 190. Cf. also Helmuth von Glasenapp, p. 224.
129 Cf. Ibid.
130 Cf. Sinclair Stevenson, pp. 190-191. Cf. also Helmuth von Glassenapp, pp. 224-225.
131 Cf. Sinclair Stevenson, pp. 191-192. Cf. also Helmuth von Glasenapp, pp. 224-225.
132 Cf. Lawrence A. Babb, pp. 76-82. The imitation of the spirit and example of the *Tiirthankara* as the motive of Jaina worship is generally adhered to in the Jaina religious practice, though in the popular Jaina practice, this motive is not followed strictly. Cf. Helmuth von Glasenapp, pp. 408, 410.
133 Pravinchandra J. Shah, "Namokara Maha Mantra", *Perspectives in Jaina Philosophy and Culture*, ed. Shri Satis Kumar Jain, pp 96-97.
134 Ibid.
135 Cf. Ibid., pp. 94-95. Cf. also Helmuth von Glasenapp, pp. 410-411.
136 Cf. Helmuth von Glasenapp, pp. 411- 413.
137 Cf. Ibid., pp. 415-417.
138 Cf. Mohan Lal Mehta, "Jaina Yoga", *Perspectives in Jaina Philosophy and Culture*, ed. Shri Satish Kumar Jain, pp. 19-22. Cf. also Helmuth von Glasenapp, pp. 420-422.
139 Cf. Helmuth von Glasenapp, pp. 414-415.
140 Cf. Ibid., pp. 408-409. Cf. also Padmanabh S. Jain, *The Jaina Path of Purification*, p. 207.
141 Cf. Helmuth von Glasenapp, pp. 439-441.

142 Cf. Ibid., pp. 441-444.
143 Cf. Ibid., pp. 478-481.
144 Cf. Ibid., pp. 429-438.
145 Cf. Ibid., pp. 425-429.
146 Cf. Ibid., pp. 470-473. Cf. also Padmanabh S. Jaini, *The Jaina Path of Purification*, pp. 199-202.
147 Cf. Padmanabh S. Jaini, *The Jaina Path of Purifications*, pp. 199-200.
148 Cf. Ibid., pp. 200-202. Cf. also Helmuth von Glasenapp, pp. 238-239.
149 Cf. Helmuth von Glasenapp, p. 444.
150 Cf. Ibid., p. 445. Though the Jainas are very strict with the actual participants of the worship, they are very considerate in allowing outsiders who show interest in witnessing their ritual in the temples. They ask such spectators only to remove their shoes. Cf. Sinclair Stevenson, p. 250.
151 Cf. Helmuth von Glasenapp, pp. 473-474. The consecration of statues of other deities, the plates with mystic symbols, the holy banners and the temple itself are done more or less in this fashion. Cf. Ibid., pp. 474-475.
152 Cf. Ibid., pp. 439, 475.
153 Cf. Ibid., pp. 482-483.
154 Cf. Sinclair Stevenson, pp. 254-259.
155 Cf. Helmuth von Glasenapp, pp. 464-465.
156 Cf. Ibid., pp. 465-466. Cf. also Sinclair Stevenson, pp. 225-226. Similar initiation rites are performed to initiate. Jain nun in the second order of the Jaina community, i.e., the order of the nuns. Cf. Helmuth von Glasenapp, pp. 466-467.
157 Cf. Helmuth von Glasenapp, pp. 467-468.
158 We deal with the *Upanayana* ceremony a Jaina boy goes through in the next section, where we treat the different sacramental acts (*Samskaaras*).
159 Cf. Sinclai Stevenson, pp. 219-220. Cf. also Helmuth von Glasenapp, pp. 459-460.
160 Cf. Sinclair Stevenson, pp. 220-221.
161 Cf. Helmuth von Glasenapp, pp. 452-453.
162 Cf. Ibid., pp. 453-454.
163 Cf. Ibid., p. 454.
164 Cf. Ibid., pp. 454-455.
165 The *Suudras* have a different ceremony called the handing over of the upper garment (*Uttariiyaka-nyaasa*), which takes the place of *Upanayana*. This ceremony also involves *Mantra* chanting, giving of instructions and presentation of gifts. Cf. Ibid., p. 457.
166 Cf. Ibid., pp. 455-457.
167 Cf. Ibid., p. 457.
168 Cf. Ibid., pp. 457-459. Cf. also Sinclair Stevenson, pp. 195-200.
169 Cf. Helmuth von Glasenapp, pp. 459-460.
170 Cf. Ibid., p. 460. Cf. also Sinclair Stevenson, p. 202

171 Cf. Helmuth von Glasenapp, p. 460. Cf. also Sinclair Stevenson, pp. 203-204.
172 Cf. Helmuth von Glasenapp, pp. 417-418.
173 Cf. Ibid., pp. 418-419.
174 Cf. Padmanabh S. Jaini, ed., *Collected Papers on Jaina Studies*, (Delhi: Motilal Banarsidass Publishers Private Limited, 2000), pp. 245-247.
175 Cf. Ibid., p. 247.
176 Cf. Ibid., pp. 247-248.
177 Cf. Ibid., pp. 248-250. Cf. also Helmuth A. Glasenapp, pp. 475-476. Cf. also Sinclair Stevenson, pp. 259-260.
178 Cf. Padmanabh S. Jaini, ed., *Collected Papers on Jaina Studies*, pp. 250-251.
179 Cf. Ibid., pp. 151-152.
180 Cf. Ibid., p. 252.
181 Cf. Helmuth von Glasenapp, pp. 476-477. Cf. also Sinclair Stevenson, pp. 262. Besides, the above-mentioned common Jaina festivals, some sects have their own special festivals and fasts. For instance, the *Svetaambara* and a few *Sthanakavaasii* once a year keep a solemn fast called *Maunagyaarasa* on the 11th day of bright half of the month of *Maargasiirsha* (November-December). Similarly there is a one day fast the Jaina women observe for a happy married life. There is the practice of fasting on every full moon day. In the same way, some devout Jainas observe 12 days of every month as days of abstinence. Cf. Sinclair Stevenson, pp.261, 262-263.
182 Cf. Sinclair Stevenson, pp. 260-261. Cf. also Helmuth von Glasenapp, pp. 477-478.
183 Cf. Sinclair Stevenson, pp. 263-264. Cf. also Helmuth von Glasenapp, p. 478.
184 Cf. Helmuth von Glasenapp, pp. 447-448.
185 Cf. Ibid., pp. 448-449. Cf. also Sinclair Stevenson, pp. 264-265.
186 Cf. Helmuth von Glasenapp, pp. 448. Cf. also Sinclair Stevenson, pp. 265-266.
187 Cf. Helmuth von Glasenapp, pp. 449-450.

Chapter 5

Buddhist Tradition

INTRODUCTION

Humphreys, in the introduction to his Book entitled *Buddhism*, raises the issue of the nature of Buddhism. While acknowledging the difficulty involved in speaking of Buddhism, he gives the following description: "In one sense it [Buddhism] is man's understanding of the Teaching of Gautama, the Buddha; in another it is the religion-philosophy which has grown about that Teaching ... Buddhism is in fact a family of religions and philosophies."[1] Indeed, the term "Buddhism" stands for an extensive and multifaceted religious and philosophical tradition, the lifespan of which extends over 2500 hundred years and has adherents in different nations, both East and West.[2]

However, there are scholars, who consider Buddhism as a philosophy, a way of life and a code of ethics, but deny to it the characteristic of a religion, as Buddhism does not strictly believe in a theistic-creator God, as found in the Semitic religions, though it believes in supernatural beings and spirits. At the same time, we cannot portray Buddhism as an atheistic system, as it has nothing in common with the schools of thought that profess atheism. Strictly speaking, Buddhism is neither theistic nor atheistic, but non-theistic, for it neither affirms nor denies the reality of God, but rather ignores it. If we take a closer look at Buddhism, we find that it has the seven significant characteristics that mark any religion, viz., the practical and ritual dimension, the experiential and emotional dimension, the narrative and mythical dimension, the doctrinal and philosophical dimension, the ethical and legal dimension, the social and institutional dimension and the material dimension. Buddhism gives its adherents a system of ritual worship, spiritual experiences through meditation, legends and mythical stories, systematic formulations of doctrines and beliefs, ethical laws like the law of *Ahimsa*, social and religious institutions like the *Sangha* and places of worship like the temples and sacred sites. All these characteristics of Buddhism point to the fact that it is a religion, which appeals to the needs of peoples' hearts and heads and, in turn, leads people to their ultimate destiny.[3] In this short introduction, we attempt to explore the origin and developmental unfolding of Buddhism over its 2500-year history. Besides we also take a look at the Buddhist scriptures, Buddhist community and the fundamental beliefs of Buddhism.

1. A BRIEF HISTORY OF BUDDHISM

Buddhism, like Jainism, belongs to the renouncer (*Sramana*) tradition, which considers a life of discipline and asceticism as the ideal of life and the *Arahat* as the person, who has attained this goal in its entirety. It is a heterodox thinking that does not believe in the authority of the *Vedas*, rejects sacrifices involving the killing of animals, upholds the primacy of *Ahimsa*, values genuine and righteous moral living, denounces the superiority of human beings on the basis of birth, opens the door of organized religious life for all classes of people including women, preaches compassion for all living beings and sends out zealous missionaries to propagate its beliefs.[4] In this brief history of Buddhism, we consider its origin, its doctrinal development and the emergence of the schools, its territorial expansion, and its present status as a living religion of the world.

1.1. ORIGIN OF BUDDHISM

The immediate historical context in which Buddhism originates is the Hinduism of the fifth century B.C., which is more cultic than moralistic. Sacrifices and prayers associated with the cult have tremendous influence on the lives of the people. The cult is pictured as a ship that has the power to ferry people across the ocean of *Samsaara* to the other shore of existence. The undue importance given to the cultic and ritual worship as a means to attain liberation degenerates the religious life of the people so much so that there are reactions to this type of thinking from both Vedic and non-Vedic quarters. Some Vedic texts, especially the *Aaranyakas* and the *Upanishads*, show dissatisfaction with the cult as the only means to liberation, in the process paving the way for the emergence of the last two stages of life (*Ashramas*), viz., the *Vanaprastha* and the *Sannyasa*. The non-Vedic *Sramana* traditions staunchly reject cultic and ritualistic Hinduism. Buddhism is one of the *Sramana* sects that put up a good fight against the ritualistic Hinduism of the time. Thus, Buddhism emerges as a reaction against Hindu ritualistic religious culture and emphasized to the moral and philosophical elements of the *Vedas*.[5]

The origin of Buddhism is centered on the historical personality, who bears the name Siddhartha which means "every wish fulfilled". He belongs to the Gautama royal family of the Saakya kingdom, which is located in the foothills of the Himalayas.[6] His father is king Suddhodhana and his mother is queen Maayaa. Wonderful things are said to have taken place at the conception and birth of the child. The legends speak of Siddhartha's mother dreaming of a magnificent white elephant with six white tusks coming to her room, kneeling before her and caressing her right side with a perfect golden lotus flower. Similarly, at his birth, in the Lumbini grove, the heavens drop white and golden lotus petals, and the earth sends out fragrant scents of jasmine and sandalwood, while the gods appear, bathe the child and set him on foot. Thus, Siddhartha is an unusual child, whose birth is a great joy to the whole kingdom.[7] Although Sidhartha's mother dies seven days after his birth, the king sees that his son grows up in the palace without any lack. His life, in every way, is like that of a prince, mastering every art and enjoying every pleasure of the world. At the age of 16 he marries his cousin Yasodhara, who bears him a son whom he names Rahula. In spite of having all the pleasures of this world, Siddhartha's mind is not totally lost in them, but he lives a life of self-control.[8] During one of his pleasure excursions, Siddhartha sees an old man, a person afficted by a dreaded disease and a dead body, which disturbs him. He thinks about the evils of this world and yearns to liberate himself and others from this veil of tears. Siddhartha's father allures the son with the help of women in order to change his mind. But he rejects them, bids goodbye to his wife and son, while they are asleep and flees from the palace. Coming out of the city, he dismisses his charioteer, removes his royal robes, shaves his head and takes upon himself the life of penance, ignoring the lamentations of everyone in the palace and their repeated plea to return to the palace.[9]

Having left the palace, Siddhartha goes to the hermitage of Aaraada Kaamaala, who welcomes him and teaches him meditation techniques, including the state of trance. Denying the offer of Aaraada to become the joint leader of the group along with him, Siddhartha goesto study under Uddaka Raamaputta who teaches him deeper levels of meditation, enabling him to experience the disappearance of his consciousness. Uddaka, impressed by Siddhartha's growth in this technique, expresses his desire to learn from him this form of meditation. Siddhartha does not accept the offer, as he desires to attain enlightenment. Then he moves on to practice extreme forms of asceticism by fasting and practicing breath-control, both of which destroy his health. While the former makes him emaciated, the latter leads to severe headaches. So Siddhartha, not finding enlightenment through these extreme forms of asceticism, gives them up and chooses "the Middle Way", a life of moderation, in which the appetites are neither totally denied nor excessively indulged. He lives out this middle path by accepting a bowl of curds from a maid named Sujata and eating it, in the process scandalizing the five monks who are his companions. They leave Siddhartha in disgust. After his bath in the river, he sits at the foot of the *Bodhi* Tree in meditation, determined not to leave the place until he attains enlightenment. *Maara*, the god of evil, makes all attempts to distract Siddhartha. But he defeats *Maara* and his insinuations and attains enlightenment. Thus, Siddhartha Gautama becomes the Buddha. The gods rejoice at his attainment of *Mahaa Bodhi* and worship him. The enlightened Buddha ponders for seven weeks at the *Bodh Gaya* to decide if he has to spend his life either in seclusion and privacy or in active ministry, communicating the truth of his enlightenment. Buddha is moved by compassion for the suffering humanity and decides to become the preacher of the *Dharma* to mankind. On the night of the full moon of the month of July, he preaches his first sermon, setting in motion "the wheel of *Dharma*", thereby beginning his missionary life, which lasts for the next 45 years, until he dies at the age of 80 in the little town of Kusinaaraa.[10] Thus, the origin of Buddhism as a religion comes about.

1.2. DOCTRINAL DEVELOPMENT AND EMERGENCE OF SCHOOLS IN BUDDHISM

Buddhism, which emerges in the context of Hindu ritualism, originates and has its initial development in the person and teachings of the Buddha. Until his death, he is the point of reference on every matter regarding the faith and practice of the religion. But after his death, disagreements occur on matters regarding doctrines, monastic practice and the organization of the Buddhist community (*Sangha*). The problems become more acute as Buddha has not named a successor. The absence of a central authority, as a regulatory body, leads to the appearance of many new Buddhist traditions that differ both in doctrine and in practice.[11]

In order to avoid such an eventuality and to maintain the purity of the teaching of Buddha (*Dharma*), the early followers of Buddha convene a gathering of the monks called the Councils (*Sangiiti*)[12]. Only a week after the death of Buddha, a senior monk named Mahaakassapa, who has received a garment of the Buddha as a token of authority, takes the initiative to convene the first Council at Raajagriha. He invites 499 monks (*Bhikkhus*) to constitute the Council. Ananda, who has become an *Arahat* by then, is called to the Council, due to his closeness to the Buddha and his knowledge of the teachings of Buddha. The purpose of the Council is to establish the purity of the holy truth preached by Buddha, to determine the content of the Buddhist scriptures, to organize the order of the monks and to consolidate the tradition. In spite of the first Council, disputes and schisms continue to plague the *Sangha*. The religious practices of the monks have become questionable. The Vajjian monks of Vaisaalii have allowed ten religious practices (*Dasa Vatthuni*) – involving forbidden meal regulations, possession of a rug and receiving gifts in gold and silver – which are lax, unorthodox and against the teaching of the monastic order. The second Council at Vaisaalii is convened about 100 years after the death of Buddha, to settle the issue of the ten lax practices. The council condemns the practices, and they are rejected. After the conversion of the emperor Asoka, he convenes the third Council at Paataliputra for the purpose of examining and correcting the heretical doctrines. The Council also decides to send out missionaries to foreign countries. According to the decision of the Council, emperor Asoka sends his son and daughter as missionaries to Ceylon. Emperor Kanishka, an ardent believer in Buddhism, convenes the fourth Council in Kashmir[13] to put right the disputes and dissensions among the various sects of Buddhism that have emerged by now. Similarly, a number of councils are assembled in various countries, like Ceylon, Thailand and Burma for the same purpose of settling doctrinal differences among the different schools of Buddhism.[14]

Despite the efforts of the Councils to settle disputes among the various streams of thought within Buddhism, the doctrinal differences have only increased among the groups. Some of the controversial doctrines are the following: the nature of Buddha, the means of attaining Buddhahood, and the relationship between an *Arahat* and the Buddha. The five dogmas of Mahadeva regarding the life and nature of an *Arahat* also set in motion a great many disputes. The immediate reason behind such doctrinal controversies seems to be the attempt by a group of monks to relax the Monastic Rules and the resistance from the more orthodox monks. These differences in doctrine and practice give rise to two worldviews: the Old Wisdom Worldview and the New Wisdom Worldview. The former is more orthodox, while the latter proposes more open and freer views on all these doctrinal and practical matters. This twofold thinking gives rise to four schools of thought: the *Theravaadins* (the *Sthaviravaadins*), the *Saravaastivaadas*, the *Sammatiiyas* and the *Mahaasaanghikas*. Of these four schools, the first three belong to the Old Wisdom Worldview, while the last school belongs to the New Wisdom Worldview. Each of these schools has its sub-schools. The *Theravaadins* include three sub-schools: the *Mahaavihaaravaasins*, the *Jetavaniiyas* and the *Abhayagrivaasins*. The *Saravaastivaadas* have the following seven sub-schools: the *Muula-Sarvaastivaadas*, the *Kaasyapiiyas*, the *Mahiisaasakas*, the *Dharmaguptas*, the *Bahusrutiiyas*, the *Taamarasaatiiyas* and the *Vibhajyavaadins*. The *Sammatiiya* School has three sub-schools: the *Kaurukullakas*, the *Aavantakas* and the *Vaatsiiputriiyas*. The liberal *Mahaasaanghikas* develop into five different sub-schools: the *Puurvasailas*, the *Aparasailas*, the *Haimavatas*, the *Lokottaravaadins* and the *Prjnaptivaadins*. Thus, during the first three centuries of the existence of Buddhism, the original body of Buddhist belief was split into 18 sub-schools.[15]

The more liberal *Mahaasaanghikas* represent the New Wisdom Worldview. The term "*Mahaasasnghika*" means 'the large community' or 'the universal assembly'. As a school, it opposes the monopoly of the orthodox monks. They give importance to the laity in religious matters. They believe that the Buddha is supra mundane, raised above space and divine. Therefore he possesses no human qualities. The Buddha is free from lust, malevolence and injury. Thus, the *Mahaasaanghikas* deify the Buddhas and the Bodhisattvas. The *Mahaasaanghikas*, who follow the doctrines of Mahaadeva, hold that an *Arahat* is different from the Buddha, as the former has frailties, can be taught, has a degree of ignorance and doubt, and acquires knowledge only with the help of others. Thus, the *Arahathood* is not the final state of sanctification. In matters religious and moral discipline, the *Mahaasaanghikas* are freer than any of the other ancient schools. All these characteristics make the *Mahaasaanghikas* the forerunners of the *Mahaayaana* School. Thus, we can conclude that the *Mahaayaana* School emerges from the New Wisdom Worldview of the *Mahaasasnghikas*.[16]

Modern scholars propose a number of theories for the emergence of the *Mahaayaana* School. The most common theory is that it is an outgrowth of the New Wisdom Worldview of the *Mahaasasnghikas*. Another theory is that *Mahaayaana* emerges from the esoteric teaching, which is of interest to a small group of monks from different ancient schools of Buddhism. Another group of scholars consider the *Mahaayaana* School as a movement that has grown out of the popular *Bhakti* spirituality of the laypeople, viz., the *Stuupa* and relic worship the Buddha. More recent scholarship places the origin of *Mahaayaana* as the work of forest-dwelling monks exploring the ideals of original Buddhism. Lastly, some writers believe that *Mahaayaana* School is a cult that originates from the various *Mahaayaana Suutras*.[17]

Whatever may be its origins, the *Mahaayaana* represents a liberal religious thinking and practice that is different from the earlier Buddhist traditions. The term *"Mahaayaana"* means 'the great vehicle'. It is called so because it has for its purpose the salvation of everyone. It calls its adherents to live out the compassion (*Karuna*) of the Buddha wholeheartedly. After *Mahaayaana* emerges as a religious practice, its adherents call the earlier schools of Buddhism, especially those schools that represent the Old Wisdom Worldview *Hiinayaana*, i.e., 'the lesser vehicle'. *Hiinayaana* is called Southern Buddhism, as it has adherents in South Asia, while *Mahaayaana* is known by the name Northern Buddhism, as it has its followers in North Asia like Tibet and Japan. *Hiinayaana* is considered as being the closest to the original Buddhism, whereas *Mahaayaana* is seen as a later development based on some of the beliefs suggested in the former. The 'no-soul theory' (*Anicca-Anaatta*) of *Hiinayaana* develops into 'the theory of absolute void' (*Suunyata*) in the *Mahaayaana*. The *Hiinayaana* considers the *Mahaayaana* as the corruption of the original Buddhism, while the *Mahaayaana* views the *Hiinayaana* as an incomplete religious practice and a superficial doctrine, which is taught by the Saakyamuni to those who are incapable of comprehending the deeper truths of *Mahaayaana*.[18]

The *Mahaayaana* School was divided into a number of philosophical and religious schools after the lapse of 400 years, each of the schools stressing one or the other means of *Nirvaana*. The first of the *Mahaayaana* Schools is the *Maadhyamikas*. Naagaarjuna founded it in the year 150 A.D. It chose to go by the middle path (*Madhyamaapratipad*) between denial and affirmation. Salvation, according to this school, is achieved through wisdom understood as the contemplation of emptiness. The second school is the *Yogaacaara*, founded by Vasubandhu and Asanga about 400 A.D. It relies on introspective meditation to achieve salvation. The third *Mahaayaana* School is Tantric Buddhism, known as *Vajrayaana*, i.e., 'the Diamond Vehicle', which attempts to help the aspirant to achieve salvation with the help of powerful formulas (*Mantras*) and magical rites (*Tantras*). It has its left-handed version in the *Nyin-ma-pa* sect of Tibet. *Tantrism* emerges as result of the fusion of the *Mahaayana* and the indigenous *Shamanism*. Similarly, the *Ch'an* School, *Amidism* and other similar schools of China and Japan involve the mixture of the *Mahaayaana* and indigenous religious thinking and practice. They make use of different meditation techniques to attain liberation.[19]

The doctrinal development of Buddhism and the emergence of its various schools come about as the Buddhist missionaries cross the borders of their own countries and take the teachings of the Buddha to different lands. In this section, we briefly explore the territorial growth of Buddhism

1.3. TERRITORIAL EXPANSION OF BUDDHISM

Buddhism, from its earliest beginnings, was a missionary religion. The words of the Buddha, 'Go ye forth O *Bhikkhus* for the gain of many, for the welfare of the many, in compassion for the world', addressed to his monks within a few days of his first sermon, clearly indicate the missionary nature of Buddhism. Buddhist missionaries preach the message of Buddhism without placing any pressure on the hearers, leaving them to accept or reject it. The method of teaching is preaching and deliberating on the content of the sermon. The message is given not on the basis of the authority of the preacher, but as something that he has heard. The Buddhist *Bhikkhus* also make use of educational centers such as the *Vihaaras* and the *Mahaavihaaras* to propagate their faith. The missionary methods and zeal of the Buddhist monks opens the whole world to hear the Buddhist *Dharma*. Thus, Buddhism crosses over the borders of the land of its origin and spreads through the whole of Asia and, in recent times, makes inroads into the West.[20]

The earliest Buddhist mission, already in the time of Asoka, came to Sri Lanka. It is believed that emperor Asoka's son, Mahinda, and daughter, Sanghamitta, were the first missionaries to this Island. Buddhism, in its *Theravaada* form takes its roots in Sri Lanka with the conversion of King Tissa about 250 B.C. Both the *Bhikkhus* and the laity are known for their piety. The relic worship, i.e., the tooth of the Buddha, is popular among the Buddhists of Sri Lanka. Similarly, it is believed that the missionaries of emperor Asoka brought the Buddhist faith to the Golden Land (*Suvarnabhumi*) of Burma. The original Buddhism of Burma is more *Mahaayaanist*. But most of the masses followed a Buddhist practice that is a mixture of *Mahaayaana, Hiinayaana* and indigenous nature-spirit (*Nat*) worship. The *Theravaada* Buddhism begins to have a hold in the Burmese soil with the conversion of King Anawrahta of Pagan, who lived between 1044-1077 A.D. In the same way, in Siam, though the original Buddhism is more *Mahaayaanist*, with the conversion of the King to *Theravaada* Buddhism in the 14th century, *Hiinayaana* Buddhism becomes more popular. Likewise, until the 14th century, a religion that is a mixture of Hinduism and *Mahaayaana* was dominant in Cambodia. But later due to the Siamese influence, *Theravaada* rose to prominence.[21]

Buddhism had its foothold in Vietnam, formerly known as Campa, before the 3rd century A.D. In the early phase of Buddhism in this country, a number of *Hiinayaana* sects, such as the *Aryasammatiiyas*, the *Saravaastivaadas* and the *Sravakayaana* sect were accepted. But from the 8th century onwards, *Mahaayaana* Buddhism gains importance and continues to do so until the 15th century, when the Chinese form of Buddhism dominates. Buddhism came to the Indonesian islands of Java and Sumatra by the 5th century A.D, in the former due to the missionary zeal of an Indian monk named Gunavarman, the later due to the efforts of the King of Sri-vijaya. The initial Buddhism of these two and another ten island countries of the Southern sea is the *Hiinayaana*, though the *Mahaayaana* also is practiced. But from the 7th century, due to the guidance of the Kings of the Sailendra dynasty, *Mahaayaana* Buddhism gains ascendance in the Indonesian island nations.[22]

The Buddhism of China, Korea and Japan forms a unity because it has a common scriptural basis, i.e., the Chinese *Tripitaka*. The Korean and Japanese schools of Buddhism directly derive from the Chinese schools, though conditioned by local traditions. Buddhism entered China due to the patronage of the Kings of Han dynasty in the 1st century B.C. From China Buddhism entered Korea in the 4th century A.D. and from there to Japan in the 6th century A.D. The various schools of Buddhism that have emerged in these countries are basically *Mahaayaanist* in nature, though a number of differences can be noted among them.[23]

Though Buddhism comes to Tibet, Mongolia and Nepal in the *Mahaayaanist* form, it develops into something very new due to the influence of the local religions. For instance, in Tibet the local religion *Boen* – that advocates the worship of 'the universally good god' (*Kuntu bzan-po*), who is the creator, and a divine pair 'the lord of the white light' (*gSen-lha 'odkar*) and 'the great mother' (*Ynm-chen-mo*), with blood sacrifice, ritual cannibalism, mysteries and dancing – exerts a significant influence on the development of Buddhism. According to Buddhist tradition, Buddhism was introduced into Tibet with the help of the Chinese and Nepalese wives of Srong btans sGampo, the King of Tibet, between 630-650 A.D., in the *Mahaayaana* form. But for the next hundred years it had no impact on the lives of the people. Later, in the eighth century, the King Khri Srong-lde-brtsan invites Santarakshita, an Indian monk from the Nalanda University, to preach the message of Buddhism. The influential leaders of the *Boen* religion resisted such developments. Santarakshita left the country, due to lack of success in his efforts and expecting internal trouble in the country. At his advice, the King invites Padmasambhava, a great *Tantrist*, to re-establish the teachings of Buddhism, using the help of *Tantra*. Thus, the Tantric form of Buddhism developed, 'the Diamond Vehicle' (*Vajrayaana*), which is also called *Lamaism*. The fusion of *Boen* religion and *Mahaayaana* Buddhism gives way to *Vajrayaana* Buddhist religion and practice.[24]

Buddhism has made headway and spread into the Asian continent. But it did not make any significant inroads into the West until the middle of the 19th century. The earliest contact of the West with Buddhism is the visit of Megasthenese, the ambassador of Seleucus Nikator, the heir to the eastern part of Alexander's empire, to the court of Chandra Gupta Maurya, at his capital Paataliputra in the third century B.C. Another 13th century traveler, Marco Polo, also encountered Buddhism during his travels through central Asia to China. But their knowledge of Buddhism is limited. When the Portuguese discover the sea route to India in 1498, better contact comes about between India and the West, but the initial Western visitors show more interest in acquiring wealth and converting people to Christianity, rather than studying the pagan religion. Thus, the real western interest in Buddhism and Buddhist studies begins only by the middle of the 19th century. The knowledge of Buddhism comes to the Western world mainly through three media: firstly, the academic efforts of authors – like T.W. Rhys Davis (1843-1922), F. Max Meuller (1823-1990), Hermann Oldenberg (1854-1920), Theodor Stcherbatsky (1866-1942), D.T. Suzuki (1870-1966), Christmas Humphreys (1901-1983) and others – who introduced the true nature of Buddhism to the people of the West: secondly, the work of philosophers, poets, writers and artists – such as, the philosopher Arthur Schopenhauer of Germany (1788-1860), the poet Sir Edwin Arnold of England (1832-1904), the founders of the Theosophical Society, Colonel Henry Olcott (1832-1907) and Madame Blavatsky (1831-1891), the German novelist Herman Hesse and others – through their philosophical, poetical and cultural works, make Buddhism appealing to the Wes: thirdly, the preservation of the cultural and religious identities of the Buddhist immigrants from China, Japan, Tibet and other countries to the West, especially to the United States, by establishing their own local temples and worship system, besides forming associations like the American Buddhist Congress, has contributed a great deal in popularizing Buddhism in the West. Through these three channels, Buddhism has become a popular and accepted religion in the West today, not merely due to academic interest, but also as a practical way to experience the Divine. Thus, we find that a number of Buddhist schools, such as, *Zen*, *Joodo Shinshuu* (True Pure Land School), Tibetan Tantric Buddhist School and others, have practicing adherents in the West. Besides, gaining acceptance as a religion in the West, Buddhism is beginning to have its own autonomy as a Western religion. This is clear from the new thinking in the West that speaks of a Western Buddhism – a New Vehicle (*Navayaana*) – that would integrate with the teachings of Buddha what is best in the Western culture, science, psychology and social science. The exponents of such a view do not consider it as something deliberately formed but as a natural growth from the same root of Buddhism, viz. the Buddha *Dharma*, as *Dharma* is eternal, immortal and expresses itself differently to serve the everchanging human need. In this way, Buddhism in the West is gaining its own identity and uniqueness as a religion.[25] Having looked into the history of Buddhist thought over the 2500 years, we, now, turn our attention to the study of the Buddhist scriptures of the various Buddhist traditions.

2. BUDDHIST SCRIPTURES

The Buddha himself did not write books. Neither did his immediate followers write down the teachings of their master. The contents of the Buddha's preaching for 45 years were passed on to the next generation by word of mouth. Committing the teachings of the master to memory and passing it on by way of oral tradition continued through the efforts of the School of Reciters, for over three centuries after Buddha's death. By the third century B.C. Buddhist teachings are written on rocks and monolithic pillars. Emperor Asoka uses this method to propagate Buddhist teachings. Since Buddha places no language restrictions and allows the use any language including local dialects to communicate his teachings, Buddha's *Dharma* spread among a variety of linguistic groups. As a result, from the beginning, Buddha *Dharma* was taught in languages, such as, Paali, Prakrit, Sanskrit, Mixed Sanskrit and Apabhramsa, while the Braahmii, Kharostii, Proto-Nagari and Nagari scripts were used in rendering it to writing. Free from any linguistic barriers, Buddhism crosses the borders of the land of its origin, in the process producing authentic literature in languages, such as Chinese, Tibetan, Mongolian, Korean, Japanese, Vietnamese, Cambodian, Laotian, Siamese, Burmese, Sinhalese and many other languages and scripts. Thus, in a few centuries after Buddha's death, there emerges a variety of Buddhist literature that is extraordinarily extensive and remarkably creative.[26]

There are a number of ways the teachings of the Buddha can be classified. The ancient Indian Buddhists of the *Theravaada* tradition classify the Buddha's word (*Vacana*) into nine limbs (*Angas*): prose sermon (*Suuta*), sermons in a mixture of prose and verse (*Geyya*), explanations (*Veyyaakarana*), stanzas (*Gaathaa*), pithy sayings (*Udaana*), short utterances beginning with the words "Thus spoke the Buddha" (*Itivuttaka*), stories of former births of Buddha (*Jaataka*), reports of hyperphysical events and miracles (*Abbhutadhamma*), and questions and answers of great extent (*Vepuulla*). To these nine, the Buddhist Sanskrit texts add the following three *Angas*: accounts of heroic lives and deeds (*Avadaana*), beginnings and causes (*Nidaana*) and advices and instructions (*Upadesa*). There is another twofold, traditional classification of Buddhist literature, viz., that of *Suutra* and *Saastra*. A *Suutra* is a text that contains the original Teaching (*Saasana*) of the Teacher (*Saastaa*). In other words, a Buddhist *Suutra* is the actual words the Buddha spoke. A *Saastra*, on the other hand, is an explanatory treatise written by later masters. For instance, the writings of Nagarjuna, Vasubandhu and others are considered to be *Saastras*. Some philologists of Buddhism attempt to classify Buddhist scriptures on the basis of the languages in which they are written. A fourth way of classifying Buddhist scriptures is on the basis of the accepted canons of different branch of Buddhism.[27] In this section, we attempt to elaborate on the Buddhist scriptures that form the foundation of Buddhist doctrine and practice, basing ourselves on the accepted canons of the three living traditions of Buddhism, viz., the *Hiinayaana*, the *Mahaayaana* and the *Vajryaana*.

2.1. HIINAYAANA SCRIPTURES

The *Hiinayaana* scriptures include both canonical and non-canonical texts. In this section, we make an attempt look into the canonical texts in detail and to consider briefly the non-canonical books that form the basis of the *Hiinayaana* sects of Buddhism.

2.1.1. CANONICAL TEXTS

The earliest Buddhist canon is known as 'the three baskets' (*Tripitaka*). It is the three major collections of sacred Buddhist texts. These texts are preserved in the Paali language. The Paali *Tripitaka* is the oldest of the Buddhist scriptures. The *Tripitaka* are the following: the *Vinaya-Pitaka*, *Suutra-Pitaka* and the *Abhidharma-Pitaka*. Now we consider the Paali canonical scriptures in detail.

2.1.1.1. Vinaya-Pitaka

Vinaya-Pitaka is the Book of Discipline. It is a collection of rules of moral and ascetic discipline for monks (*Bhikkhus*) and nuns (*Bhikkhuniis*), who belong to the Buddhist monastic community. It deals with violations of discipline and the punishments and admonitions given according to the gravity of the failure. These rules of the *Vinaya-Pitaka* are believed to be authoritative injunctions of the Buddha on the modes of conduct, both physical and verbal. Usually a commentary on the rules forms part of the *Vinaya-Pitaka*. It consists of five books that are divided into two main sections, viz., *Suutra-vibhanga* and *Khandhaka*, and a minor work called *Parivaara*. The *Suutra-Vibhanga* includes two books: *Mahaa-Vibhanga* and *Bhikkunii-Vibhanga*. These two books speak about rules to be followed for the confession of sins (*Praatimoksha*). They also contain a verbal commentary explaining each word of the rule, the context in which the rule is promulgated and special cases that call for exemptions. The second major section, the *Khandhaka*, comprises a large series (*Mahaavagga*) and a small series (*Cullavagga*). The former deals with admission into the order, the recital of *Praatimoksha*, the modes of executing official acts of the Order, residence during retreat in the rainy season, the ceremony concluding the retreat, material for robes, rules for robes, leather for shoes, food and medicine, proceedings in case of dissensions and other similar matters. The latter transacts matters relating to reinstatements of monks, managing schisms, handling offences that come before the order, ordination and instruction for the nuns, rules regarding traveling monks, exclusion from *Praatimoksha*, the duties of teachers and novices, rules for bathing, rules regarding lodgings, rules dealing with questions that arise and other related matters. It also deals with the history of the first and the second Councils at Raajagriha and Vaisaalii respectively. The third part of the *Vinya-Pitaka* is the *Parivaara*, which is a supplementary work. It contains summaries and classification of rules that are already said in the other two sections of the *Vinaya-Pitaka*. It is compiled in the form of a catechism, having a categorization according to the subject dealt with. This is done with the aim of helping the monks and nuns to make an analytical study of the *Vinaya-Pitaka*. The *Parivaara* deals with rules of the order to regulate the conduct of the *Bhikkus* and the administrative affairs of the order. It also describes procedures for settling monastic disputes, matters of law and the constitution of monastic courts (*Sangha Vinicchaya* Committee).[28]

2.1.1.2. Suutra-Pitaka

Suutra-Pitaka is the Book of Discourses and Doctrines (*Dharma*). It is a collection of all the teachings of Buddha in its entirety. The collections are made in such a way to suit different occasions and persons of different temperaments. Though the *Suutra* collections are made with the intention of helping the *Bhikkhus* in their journey towards the divine state, they are also of help to the moral progress of the lay people. The clear statement of doctrine of the Buddha that one finds in the *Suutra-Pitaka* clarifies the true meaning of the Buddha's teaching and guards it against any distortion and misunderstanding. It consists of five collections. They are: the *Diigha-Nikaaya*, the *Majjhima-*

Nikaaya, the *Samyutta-Nikaaya*, the *Anguttara-Nikaaya* and the *Khuddaka-Nikaaya*. This classification is more a formal one with the aim of helping people to commit to memory. The basis for the division is more the size and the arrangement of the *Suutras* into long, medium and short, grouped on the basis of numerical principle.[29]

The *Diigha-Nikaaya* is a collection of long discourses of 34 *Suutras* arranged in three series (*Vaggas*), viz., the *Siilakkhandha-Vagga*, *Mahaa-Vagga* and the *Paatika-Vagga*. The *Siilakkhandha-Vagga* deals with a list of moral rules, known as the *Siilas*, and the way they help a monk to progress in three stages and finally attain the state of the *Arahat*. The *Mahaa-Vagga* contains significant legends from the life of Buddha, such as, the last days of his life, his death, the distribution of his relics, the accounts of the last seven Buddhas, especially that of the *Vipaasii* Buddha and other similar stories. The *Paatika-Vagga* is a miscellaneous collection that deals with doctrines regarding the nature of a Buddha, explaining the origin and development of the universe and the differentiation of castes. Besides, in this collection we find also the legend about the universal king (*Cakkavattin*), the 33 bodily marks of the universal king and the prophecy about the next Buddha (*Maitreya*). It also includes the spells the Four Great Kings give to Buddha to ward off evil spirits.[30]

The second collection is the *Majjhima-Nikaaya*. It is a collection of medium size discourses of Buddha. It consists of 152 *Suutras* arranged into three books (*Pannaasa*), viz., the *Muulapannaasa*, the *Majjhimapannaasa* and the *Uparipannaasa*. Each of these books is further divided into five *Vaggas*, and thus we have 15 *Vaggas* in three books. The first book, the *Muulapannaasa*, contains five *Vaggas*. They are: the *Muulapariyaya-Vagga*, the *Siihanaada-Vagga*, the *Opamma-Vagga*, the *Mahaayamaka-Vagga* and the *Cuulayamaka-Vagga*. The second book, the *Majjhimapannaasa*, consists of the following five *Vaggas*: the *Gahapati-Vagga*, the *Bhikkhu-Vagga*, the *Paribbaajaka-Vagga*, the *Raaja-Vagga* and the *Braahmana-Vagga*. The third book, the *Uparipannaasa* is divided into the *Devadha-Vagga*, the *Anupada-Vaagga*, the *Sunnata-Vagga*, the *Vibhanga-Vagga* and the *Salaayatana-Vagga*. These 152 *Suutras* of *Majjhima-Nikaaya* throw light on the different stages in the life of the monk, viz., morality, concentration and enlightenment. They also speak of Buddha's enlightenment and first preaching and other legends about his life, such as his descent from heaven, his birth, the debates he conducts with Jains, his foster mother becoming a nun, the schism of Devadatta and a number of discussions on caste. The *Majjhima-Nikaaya* also throws light on the social, political and economic life and institutions of the times.[31]

Thirdly, the *Samyutta-Nikaaya* is a collection of 7762 *Suutras* of differing length, generally short and arranged in a special grouping (*Samyutta*) according to subject matter. These groupings are collected in five major *Vaggas*. They are: the *Sagaatha-Vagga*, the *Nidaana-Vagga*, the *Khandha-Vagga*, the *Salaayatana-Vagga* and the *Mahaa-Vagga*. Each of these *Vaggas* is divided into 56 *Samyuttas* containing related subjects. The *Samyuttas* are named after the subjects they deal with. Each *Samyutta* is divided into sections, which are constituted of individual *Suutras*. The *Sagaatha-Vagga* contains 11 *Samyuttas*, with topics grouped according to the personalities appearing in them, such as, the king of *Devas*, the *Devas*, the *Brahmaa*, *Maara*, the king of *Kosala*, *Bhikkhus* and *Bhikkhunis*. These *Samyuttas* are mostly written in verse. The *Nidaana-Vagga* contains ten *Samyuttas*. They deal with the fundamental aspects of the doctrine. They treat the principle of the conditionality and interdependence of reality, its dependent origination and the 12 factors of the chain of causation. These *Samyuttas* also analyze the concrete implications of this doctrine in the practice of holy life. The *Khandha-Vaaga* is constituted of 13 *Samyuttas*. They deal with the five aggregates (*Khandhas*) that make up the nature of an existing being. The components of the *Khandhas* – matter, sensation, perception, mental concomitants and consciousness – constitute the suffering (*Dukkha*) of a being. Topics, such as, clinging to the five *Khandhas* (*Atta*), freedom from the *Khandhas* (*Anaata*), eternity and annihilation are also treated. The *Salaayatana-Vagga* is composed of ten *Samyuttas*. It deals with the six sense organs, i.e., their internal sense bases – eye, ear, nose, tongue, body and mind –, the six corresponding sense objects, known as the external sense bases – visible form, sound, odor, taste, tangible things and mind-objects – and the consciousness that arises in relation to each pair of these internal and external sense bases. As the three types of sensations arising out of these internal and external sense bases, viz., the pleasant, the unpleasant and the indifferent, are impermanent, so one needs to relinquish them to attain *Nivaana*. Practical guidance to attain this goal, viz., *Vipassanaa* meditation is also discussed in *Salaayatana-Vaaga*. The *Mahaa-Vaaga* (the Great Series) is made up of 12 *Samyuttas*. It contains the basic teachings of the Buddha both in its theoretical and practical aspects. The goal of holy life, *Arahat*, *Nirvaana*, end of all suffering, the Four Noble Truths and the Eight fold Path are some of the other topics that are found in this last *Vagga* of the *Samyutta-Nikaaya*.[32]

The fourth is the *Anguttara-Nikaaya*. It is a collection of discourses consisting of 9557 *Suutras*. It is divided into 11 shorter collections called *Nipaata*, each of which is further divided into still smaller collections called *Vaggas*, each containing ten *Suutras*. The term "*Anguttara*" means 'increasing by one item'. As the name suggests the discourses are arranged in a progressive numerical order, each *Nipaata* containing *Suutras* with its items of *Dharma*, beginning with one item and moving up by units of one till there are 11 items of *Dharma* in each *Sutra* of the last *Nipaata*. The 11 *Nipaata* are the following: the *Ekaka-Nipaata*, the *Duka-Nipaata*, the *Tika-Nipaata*, the *Catukka-Nipaata*, the *Pancaka-Nipaata*, the *Chakka-Nipaata*, the *Sattaka-Nipaata*, the *Atthka Nipaata*, the *Navaka Nipaata*, the *Dasaka Nipaata* and the *Ekaadasaka-Nipaata*. The *Anguttara-Nikaaya* is the most significant source book on Buddhist psychology and ethics. It enumerates the essential elements of the Buddhist *Dharma*, both in its theory and its practice. It also contains the names of famous disciples of Buddha, who among the *Bhikkhus*, the *Bhikkhuniis*, the *Upaasakas* and the *Upaasikaas*, has achieved pre-eminence in a particular sphere of religious attainment or meritorious activity. For instance, the Venerable Saariputta and the *Bhikkhunni* Khemaa excell in intuitive wisdom and knowledge (*Pannaa*); the Venerable Mahaa Moggallaana and *Bhikkhunni* Uppalavanna in supernatural powers (*Iddhi*); the *Upaasaka* Anaathapindika and the *Upaasikaa* in almsgiving (*Daana*).[33]

The fifth is the *Khuddaka-Nikaaya*. The term "*Khuddaka*" literally means 'small' or 'minor'. So it is a collection of minor works. But, in fact, some of these works are neither small in size nor minor in their contents. There is a difference of opinion among the scholars as to the number of works included in the *Khuddaka-Nikaaya*. The generally accepted number is 15. The first is *Khuddaka-Paatha*, i.e., 'the reading of small passages'. It is a collection of nine short formulae and *Suutras* found in different parts of the scriptures. The second is the *Dhammapada*, i.e., 'Words of the Doctrine', a collection of 423 stanzas arranged in 26 *Vaggas*. The third is *Udaana*, i.e., a solemn utterance spoken under the influence of emotion. This collection includes about 80 utterances of Buddha, along with legends of the circumstances in which they are uttered. It is mostly written in verse. The fourth is *Itivuttaka*. It is a collection of 112 short *Suutras* in four *Nipaatas*, written in verse, and beginning with the phrase "thus it is said" ("*Iti Vuccati*). The fifth is *Suttanipata*. It is a collection of *Suutras* in five *Vaggas*, written in verse with occasional prose introductions. It contains legendary material. The sixth is *Vimaana-Vatthu*, a collection of stories about celestial mansions. It includes 85 poems in seven *Vaggas*, in which the beings reborn in heaven speak of the meritorious acts that are the cause of their reward. The seventh is *Peta-Vatthu*, which contains stories about ghosts and their unhappy existence. There are 51 poems in this collection. The eighth is *Thera-Gaathaa*, i.e., 'Verses of the Elders'. This collection consists of stanzas that are attributed to 264 elders. The ninth is *Therii-Gaathaa*, a collection that is ascribed to a hundred nuns. The tenth is *Jaataka*. It contains 547 tales about Buddha's previous births. The 11th is *Niddesa*, i.e., Exposition. It is divided into *Mahaa-Niddesa* and *Culla-Niddesa*. The former is a verbal commentary on the fourth *Vagga* of *Suutanipaata*, while the latter is a similar commentary on the fifth *Vagga* of the same book and a commentary on the first *Vagga* of the *Khaggavisaana-Suutra*. The 12th is *Patisambhidaa-Magga*, i.e., 'The Way of Analysis'. It is an analysis of various concepts, such as, knowledge, heresy, the practice of breathing during meditation and similar concepts. Both in method and material in resembles an *Abhidharma* work. The 13th is *Apadaana*, which contains lives and previous lives of monks and nuns, written in verse. The 14th is *Bhddhavamsa*, i.e., 'History of the Buddhas'. In this collection Buddha speaks to Saariputta of his first forming, in the presence of Diipankara Buddha, the resolve to become a Buddha, the life of Diipankara and the succeeding 24 Buddhas, including an account of his life. It is written in verse. The 15th is *Cariyaa-Pitaka*, i.e., 'The Basket of Conduct'. It speaks of the conduct of future Buddhas that enables them to attain ten perfections (*Paaramii*), seven of which are illustrated. It also contains 35 tales from the *Jaataka* in verse.[34]

2.1.1.3. Abhidharma-Pitaka

The term "*Abhidharma*" means 'the additional doctrine', 'the further doctrine', 'the higher doctrine' or 'the special doctrine'. It consists of further elaboration on the *Dharma* by way of a later interpretation of the original *Dharma*. The word "*Abhidharma*" is found in the *Suutras*. They speak of the monks holding *Abhidharma* discussions. We can conclude from such references that the *Abhidharma* is an analysis and expansion of the doctrinal principles that are stated in the *Suutras*. From the codification of such doctrinal principles arises 'the list of heads' (*Maatrikaa*), which, in turn, forms the basis of the *Abhidharma* Books. The *Abhidharma* texts deal with the same topics that are found in the *Suutras*. These texts are more scholastic in nature. They contain definitions, classifications and analytical details of the doctrines. *Abhidharma* texts discuss and refute many controversial opinions, which various Buddhist schools hold. The style of *Abhidharma-Pitaka* is dry and monotonous when compared with *Suutra-Pitaka*. According to tradition, Buddha thinks out the books of the *Abhidharma-Pitaka* in the fourth week after his enlightenment.[35]

The *Abhidharma-Pitaka* comprises seven works. The first is the *Dhamma-Sanganii*, the 'Enumeration of Doctrines'. It consists of stating the *Dharmas* in all categories of names (*Naama*), viz., consciousness and mental elements, and form (*Ruupa*), i.e., its corporeal aspect. Once the doctrines are enumerated, they are arranged under different heads (*Maartikaa*) to bring out their exact nature, function and mutual relationship both internally and with the outside world. *Dharma-Sanganii* begins with a complete list of heads, thereby giving us a birdseyeview of the doctrines. The second is the *Vibhanga*, the 'Book of Analysis'. It gives a closer view of the list of heads by analyzing them in minute detail. Thus, the *Vibhanga* provides complete information about the doctrines by stating the exact nature of each doctrine, its constituents and its relationship with other doctrines. It is divided into 18 chapters, each dealing with a particular aspect of the doctrine. The *Vibhanga* is considered complementary to the *Dharama-Sanganii*. The third is the *Dhaatukathaa*, the 'Discussion of Elements'. Though it is a small book, it plays an important role, along with the former two, to give one a thorough understanding of the doctrines, as it deals with the relationship of mental elements to other categories. The fourth is the *Puggalapannatti*, the 'Description of the Individuals'. It gives more weight and space to the treatise concerning the individuals. Different types of individuals are classified in ten chapters of this book, similar to the manner it is done in *Anguttara-Nikkaaya*. The fifth is the *Kathaavatthu*, the 'Subjects of Discussion'. It aims at discussing and refuting the heterodox doctrines of the various schools of Buddhism, rather than directly dealing with the abstruse nature of *Dharma*. The sixth is the *Yamaka*, the 'Book of Pairs'. It sets out to define and analyze the interrelationship between the doctrine and the individuals, as they exist in the world of reality (*Sankhaaraloka*), in the world of apparent reality (*Sattaloka*) and in the real-apparent world (*Okaasaloka*). The method it uses to accomplish this task is by raising pairs of questions. The logical process of conversion (*Anuloma*) and complete inversion (*Patiloma*) are applied to determine the full import and limit of a term in its relationship with others. An equivocal use of a term (*Samsaya*) is avoided by showing the manner in which the other meaning of the term in question does not fit for a particular consideration. The seventh is the *Patthaana*, the 'Book of Relations'. It is an analysis of the manifold causal relations of things in 24 groups.[36]

2.1.2. NON-CANONICAL TEXTS

Besides the canonical literature, there are the non-canonical texts in the Paali language. Some of the works are: the *Milina-Penha*, the *Nettipakarana*, Buddhadatta's Manuals on *Vinaya* and *Abhidharma*, commentaries on the Paali *Tripitaka* texts and the *Jaatakas*, the authorship of which is attributed to Dhammapala or Buddhagosha. Similarly, the chronicles of Ceylon, like the *Deepavamsa*, the *Mahaavamsa* and the *Culavamsa* are included in the list of non-canonical literature. We can also speak of the grammatical works of Kaccayaana, Moggallaana, Rupasiddhi and Saddaniti as part of the non-canonical texts. Buddhagosa's famous work *Visuddi-Magga*, an encyclopedia on early Buddhism is part of the non-canonical texts.[37]

2.2. MAHAAYAANA SCRIPTURES

The origin of *Mahaayaana-Suutras* is more obscure than the scriptures of the Paali canon. The *Mahaayaanists* claim that their scriptures have their foundation in the teachings Buddha propounded at various places during his earthly life. But the *Mahaayaana* texts themselves do not contain any details about their real origin. The *Mahaayaana* literature, in its totality, exists only in Chinese and Tibetan translations. We cannot say much about their origins from the present arrangement of the texts. Thus, whatever can be said regarding their date, authorship and authenticity is mere assumption. But the teachings found in the *Mahaayaana-Suutras* resemble the teachings of the later schools of the *Mahaasanghikas*. From this we can conclude that the teachings of the *Mahaasanghikas* have exerted a great deal of influence on the composers of *Mahaayaana-Suutras*. In all probability the most famous work of the *Lokattaravaada* Schools of the *Mahaasanghikas*, viz., the *Mahaavastu* – the Great Subject – and its contents must have given birth to the *Mahaayaana* scriptures, for, it contains the doctrine of ten stages (*Dasabhuumis*) of Buddha, the Buddha as the spiritual principle and the *Bodhisattva* ideal, which have become the main doctrines of *Mahaayaana-Suutras*. Thus the emergence of *Mahaayaana-Suutras* must have links to the texts and teachings of the later schools of the *Mahaasanghikas*.[38]

The *Mahaayaana* Schools recognize the canonicity of the *Tripitaka* only in name, as it is not given any importance in the doctrinal and practical aspects of living the Buddhist ideal. The significant sacred texts of the *Mahaayaana* canon are the following: The first book is the *Mahaavastu* of the *Lokottaravaada* School, which provides the doctrinal background for the *Mahaayaana* religious practice. Second is the *Dasabhuumika-Suutra*, which elaborates the ten stages of Buddha in the making, as stated in the book *Mahaavastu*. The *Bodhisattva-Pitaka* is another work that elaborates the same theme. The third is the *Prajnaapaaramitaa-Suutras*, 'The Book of Perfection of Wisdom'. It is a group of texts that have larger and shorter versions, as it is found in 100,000 lines, 25,000 lines, 10,000 lines and 8,000 lines. It deals with the central *Mahaayaana* theme of recognizing the emptiness (*Suunyataa*) of reality when one realizes the essential nature of Buddhahood. To this group of Wisdom Literature belongs *the Vajracchedikaa-Suutra*, 'the Diamond Cutter', which develops the doctrine of negativity in everything with the use of stringent logic. The *Prajnaaparamita-Hridaya-Suutra* and the *Maadhyamika-Saastra* that speak of the famous 'Eight Negations' also belong to the group of Wisdom *Suutras*. The fourth is the *Saddharmapundariika-Suutra*, 'the Lotus of the Good Law'. Many schools of Buddhism in China and Japan, like the *Tendai*, the *Nichiren* and the *Zen*, consider this *Suutra* as sacred and thus the object of veneration. It stresses the compassionate aspect of the Buddhas, the Buddhahood as the essential nature of every sentient creature, the varying capacities of the people to achieve this ideal due to the effect of *Karma*, the transcendent nature of Buddha and his three bodies. Besides, it manifests a theistic tendency and contains a number of spells (*Dhaaranii*). The fifth is the *Avatamsaka-Suutra*, 'the Garland *Suutra*'. It is also known as the *Buddhaavatamsaka-Suutra*. The Japanese Buddhists, especially the *Avatamsaka* and the *Kegon* sects hold it sacred. It speaks of the journey of Buddha's enlightenment and its various stages. The sixth is *Mahaaparinirvaana-Suutra*, which Buddha delivers before his death. The *Mahaayaanists* believe that it contains esoteric teachings, which Buddha did not disclose before. It also speaks of threefold spiritual practices, viz., morality (*Siila*), meditation (*Samaadhi*) and insight (*Prajnaa*). The seventh is 'the Pure Land *Suutras*, which includes the *Sukhaavatiivyuuha-Suutra* and the *Amitaayurdhyaana-Suutra*. The former has a larger and a shorter version, and they both describe paradise and proclaim that faith in Buddha's merit leads one to paradise. The latter speaks of the *Mahaayaana* faith in and worship of the supernatural reality in the person of Buddha *Amitaabha*, who leads the devotee to the state of immortality. The eighth is the *Tathaagatagarbha* texts, which include the *Tathaagatagarbha-Suutra*, the *Anuttaraasraya-Suutra*, the *Srimaalaadevi Simhanaada-Suutra*, the *Mahaayaanasuutraalamkaara*, the *Mahaayaanasamparigraha-Suutra*, the *Lankaavatataara-Suutra*, the *Gandavyuuha-Suutra* and the *Mahaayaanasraddhaa-utpaadasaastra*. This group of texts speaks of Buddha preaching a form of subjective idealism. The *Tathaagatagarbha* is the ultimate reality, which is the basis of everything in the manifest world. The ninth is the *Lalita-Vistara*. It is a Buddha biography that contains a prolonged account of the great acts of future Buddhas. The tenth is the *Vijnapti-maatra-Suutra*, 'the-idea-only *Suutras*', that speak of the mind and ideas as the only reality. The *Samdhinirmocana-Suutra* also belongs to this group. The 11th is the Meditation *Suutras*. They include the

Pratyutpanna-buddha-sammukhaavasthita-samaadhi-Suutra, the *Samaadhiraaja-Suutra* and the *Suurangama-samaadhi-Suutra*. These *Suutras* speak of various types of meditation practices.[39]

2.3. VAJRAYAANA SCRIPTURES

The Tibetan *Vajrayaana* scriptures are divided into two large groups, viz., the *Kanjur* (*b Kah' 'gyur*), 'the translated words of Buddha' and the *Tanjur* (*bs Tan'gyur*), 'the translated treatises'. While the former is the canon proper, the latter is the collection of hymns and commentaries.[40] In the next sections we elaborate these two bodies of Tibetan *Vajrayaana* sacred scriptures.

2.3.1. THE KANJUR COLLECTION

The body of sacred writings known as the *Kanjur* came about as the result of the large-scale translations of Buddhist texts into Tibetan that have been made between the seventh and 13th century. In the beginning of the fourteenth century they were collected and arranged into a collection seven to eight hundred texts in about 108 volumes. There are a number of editions of *Kanjur*, and there exists, minor variations both in the arrangement and in the number of texts that are found in each volume. The collection does not follow the Indian *Tripitaka* pattern, but rather it is divided into seven categories.[41]

Firstly, the texts deal with Monastic Discipline, which are the same as the *Vinaya* (*'Dul-ba*). Secondly, the texts speak of Perfection of Wisdom (*Sherphyin*). These include five large collections having varying lines: 100,000 lines, 25,000 lines, 18,000 lines, 10,000 lines and 8,000 lines. The shorter ones are abridged versions of the larger ones. They are written in prose. This collection also includes 18 smaller works, the most important among them being the *Vajracchedikaa-Suutra*, 'the Diamond Cutter'. The third is the *Buddhaavatamsaka*, 'the Adornment of the Buddha', (*Phal-chen*). It is a collection of *Suutras*, which speak of Buddha appearing above Mount Meru and in different heavens. This text contains a glorification of the Buddha and the career of the *Bodhisattvas*. It also elaborates the *Yogaacaara* doctrine. The fourth is the *Ratnakuuta*, 'the Jewel Peak' (*dKon-brtsegs*). It is a collection of 44 *Suutras* the qualities of a *Bodhisattva*. It also contains 700 verses of *Prajnaapaaramita-Suutra* and a striking prophecy of the decay of Buddhism both in doctrine and in morals. The fifth is the *Suutra* (*mDo*). It is a collection of about 300 unclassified *Suutras* that speak of the following topics: the list of the five Buddhas who have appeared and who will appear in the present 'good cycle', including *Maitreya*; spells to obtain rain, spells for removing eclipses and other similar topics. The sixth is the *Mahaayaana Mahaa-Parinirvaana* (*Myang 'das*). This collection includes two *Suutras* that deal with the death of Buddha. The discourse of Buddha given at his death is expanded in these *Suutras*. The seventh collection is the *Tantra* (*rGyud*). It is a large collection of *Suutras*, almost one third of the whole of *Kanjur*. The *Vajrayaana* tradition believes that the Buddha, the *Bhagavat*, or his substitute the *Vajra*-holder, the

Vajradhara, is the true revealer of the *Tantra* texts of *Kanjur*. It is divided into two sections, Firstly, the section that deals with *Tantra* proper, which is about 464 items. The texts that treat *Tantra* proper are classified into four groups: the texts regarding action (*Kriyaa Tantra*), texts dealing with performance of action (*Caryaa Tantra*), texts that explain the practice of *Yoga* (*Yoga Tantra*) and texts that speak of the practice of higher forms of *Yoga* (*Anuttara Yoga Tantra*). The *Kriyaa Tantras* are revealed on behalf of the candidates who delight in external ritual more than in inner *Samaadhi*. The *Caryaa Tantras* are given for those who take equal interest in external action and internal *Samaadhi*. The *Yoga Tantras* are meant for those who prefer the inner *Samaadhi* more, while the *Anuttara Yoga Tantras* are for those who delight only in inner *Samaadhi*. Thus, the disciples of *Vajrayaana* Tantric practices fall basically into these four groups. Similarly, these four Tantric texts classify the deities and their actions: the *Kriyaa Tantra* sees deities as laughing; the *Caryaa Tantra* represents male and female deities as gazing at each other; the *Yoga Tantra* portrays male and female deities holding their hands; and the *Anuttara Yoga Tantra* speaks of male and female gods in sexual union. These four representations correspond to the relationship of the devotee with the deities in various levels of mystical union, viz., the mystical experience of hearing the Lord based on sound, the mystical experience of seeing the Lord based on sight, and the mystical experience of being touched by the Lord based on touch. Secondly, the collection of *Tantra* texts that deals with spells (*Dhaaraniis*), which includes 262 items. The *Tantra* collection is also concerned with ritual magic, with instructions for making magic circles and for performing the spells for curing diseases, bringing rain, controlling the enemy, taming animals, increasing understanding and winning long life. *Tantra* texts also introduce female divinities and demons that provide the Buddhas and the *Bodhisattvas* with energy by their union with them. They also speak of five spells known as 'the five protections' (*Pancarakshaa*), which are very popular among the people.[42]

2.3.2. THE TANJUR COLLECTION

This is a collection of the translation of commentaries on the *Kanjur*. Therefore, it is non-canonical Tibetan texts. The *Tanjur* contains over 3500 texts in 225 volumes. It is basically divided into three parts. The first part consists of one volume, containing 64 hymns (*Stotras*). The second part includes 87 volumes of commentaries on the *Tantras*. The third part contains 136 volumes of commentaries on the *Suutras*. The last part includes commentaries on *Prajnaapaaramitaa-Suutra*, the *Saastras* of *Maadhyamikas* and the *Yogaacaarins* and scientific works belonging to the *Hiinayaana* schools. It also contains works on subjects like Logic, Grammar, Medicine, various arts and crafts, and social economics. It also includes original Tibetan works on technical subjects.[43]

Over the years the Buddhist history and the development of the scriptures have come about in the context of the Buddhist community, i.e., the body of people who believe in the Buddha and his teachings. Now, we turn our attention to the community.

3. BUDDHIST COMMUNITY

Buddhism grew out of the ancient Indian 'renouncer tradition'. Buddha himself renounced the life of a householder and chose the life of a mendicant wanderer, in order to achieve final enlightenment. Thus, the life of a renouncer, as the Buddha proposes, automatically involves the categorization of people into two groups: firstly, those who renounce the life of a householder for the sake of attaining true religiosity; and secondly, those who live in the world, who, in turn, provide generously for the material needs of food, clothing and shelter to the renouncer. Thus, the followers of the Buddha, i.e., the Buddhist community, fall into two socially distinct classes, viz., the homeless wanderers and the lay-supporters. Hence the Buddhist texts speak of four 'assemblies' (*Parishat*) of the followers of Buddha: the assembly of the monks, the assembly of the nuns, the assembly of the male lay-followers and the assembly of the female lay-followers. The former two belong to the class of the homeless wanderers, while the latter two belong to the class of lay-supporters.[44] In this section, we briefly analyze these dimensions of the Buddhist community.

3.1. ASSEMBLY OF MONKS

The assembly of the monks is often referred to as the *Sangha*. It has been the belief of the Buddhists that the *Sangha* is one of the Three Jewels (*Triratna*) of Buddhism, the other two being the Buddha and the Teachings of Buddha (*Dharma*). The *Sangha* emerged as a missionary enterprise within a few weeks after Buddha's enlightenment. As long as Buddha lives, he remains the head of the order. But after his death, there is no one leader of the Buddhist *Sangha*. Each school and each monastery within the school chooses its own leader, who is never more than the first among the equals. The life of the monastery is guided by the rules Buddha has given to the monks to live by. The monks are excommunicated for serious offences, and minor offences are confessed to the community or to the other *Bhikkhus*, for which a penalty is imposed according to the rules of the *Sangha* (*Paatimokha*). The purpose of the Buddhist *Sangha* is two-fold: firstly to provide the maximum conditions for the full development of the individual and, secondly, to teach the *Buddha-Dharma* to everyone. The second dynamic element, i.e., the perception of the *Sangha* as a missionary enterprise that becomes the means of serving every living being is something radically new to Buddhism. Buddha wants the *Sangha* to become a unique medium for the manifestation of his compassion to everyone in need. Thus, over the years the Buddhist *Sangha* has been rendering great social service to humanity, by way of philanthropic works, the education of children, care for the poor and caring for the moral and spiritual well-being of human persons. Besides, it gives the *Buddha-Dharma* a continuity and permanence, as it is through the *Bhikkhus*, who belong to the *Sangha* that the *Buddha-Dharma* is passed on by way of oral tradition. Thus, it is because of the *Sangha* that Buddhism has survived and spread as a world religion today.[45]

Another important purpose of one entering the *Sangha* is to work towards the total development of the individual person. This involves destroying every fetter that stems from desire and blocks a person from attaining enlightenment. To achieve this goal, one enters the order as a novice, goes through years of training in moral life and spiritual disciplines, becomes a *Bhikkhu* and lives his life as a homeless wanderer, begging for his food. In addition the monk spends the time available in study, meditation and teaching. When he is in the monastery, especially during the rainy season, he does his monastic chores and follows strictly the rules of community life. He owns only a few things – three robes, a waist cloth, a begging bowl, a razor, a water strainer, a needle, an umbrella, a pair of sandals, a few books, and, if he is a writer a desk equipment – and is happy with the ascetical life he has chosen. The performance of all these activities brings in the monk genuine personal development and spiritual good, which, in turn, leads to the final enlightenment when he becomes an *Arhat*.[46]

When the *Mahaayaana* form of Buddhism emerges in countries like Japan and China, there are some differences in the manner the *Bhikkhus* live in the *Sangha*. For instance, changes come about in the way the monks dress, their food habits and the way they preach. The monks begin to live a more settled life in the monasteries for most of the year rather than being wandering monks. In spite of such changes, the fundamental nature and purpose of the Order of the Monks have not changed. The monks remain individually poor, even though their monasteries have considerable wealth. They work in the field and live by the fruit of their labor. They beg to get their food. And also do the duties in the monastery, such as cleaning, mending, cooking and other similar chores. Starting from the youngest novice to the most senior *Bhikkhu*, they do the same tasks without any regard for seniority. The physical, mental and spiritual discipline they go through on a regular basis makes the monks achieve higher levels of piety and learning. Such personalities bring self-enlightenment and enlightenment to their fellow humans.[47]

3.2. ASSEMBLY OF NUNS

According to Buddhist tradition, the Buddha founded the assembly of the nuns at the request of his cousin Aananda. The first one to enter the order was Buddha's nurse. Tradition also says that Buddha showed a certain amount of reluctance to form the order. The reason for this is not the inability of women to achieve *Arahatship*, but it is his belief that admission of women to the ordination as *Bhikkhuniis* may hasten the decline of the *Bhddha-Dharma*. Tradition also points to the fact that Buddha has laid down eight special rules (*Garu-Dharma*) by which he subordinates the order of nuns to the order of the monks. Some scholars consider these eight rules as a later addition rather than the original rules given by the Buddha.[48]

But the Buddhist canon of scripture attributes the collection of verses called *Theriigaathaa* to female *Arahats*. Similarly we find in the scriptures references to great female religious teachers. While recognizing that women can become *Arahats*, some canonical traditions deny that women can ever become the Buddha. The ordination of woman to be nuns has been a controversial issue in Budhism, just as in Jainism. As early as the 11th century A.D., the assembly of the nuns totally ceased to exist in Sri Lanka. The practice of full-fledged ordination of nuns was never established in Tibetan Buddhism. But even in these two traditions a number of women keep the ten precepts of the novices, and live as novice nuns. In the Buddhist traditions, of countries like Japan, China and Korea, the assembly of nuns is well preserved. Some women resent the effort to revive the ordination practice of women in Buddhism, as it would imply the practice of eight special rules that subordinate the order of the nuns to that of the monks.[49]

3.3. ASSEMBLIES OF THE MALE AND FEMALE LAY-FOLLOWERS

Buddha perceives the need for laymen and women, and their services for the growth and development of the *Sangha*. The laycommunity consists of the male lay-disciples (*Upaasaka*) and the female lay-followers (*Upaasikaa*). A lay-follower is one who takes refuge in the Buddha, the *Dharma* and the *Sangha*. If a layperson takes refuge in the *Triratna* of Buddhism, on a regular basis, he is called a disciple of Buddha. A layperson becomes a true follower of Buddha and an adherent of Buddhism when he imitates in his everyday life the compassion of the Buddha and the *Bodhisattvas*. The compassion of the Lord can be lived, if a person practices generosity (*Daana*). The practice of generosity points to the two motivating forces of the mind, viz., non-attachment and friendliness. When the layperson practices generosity he, in fact, detaches himself from his selfishness and opens himself to others. The practice of generosity concretely means that he helps the growth of the *Dharma* by donating money, time and effort for the building of monasteries and temples, for the general support of the Buddhist monastic community and for the publication of Buddhist writings. The quality of *Daana* can also be expressed by way of giving food to a monk or to the monastery. When moral life and spiritual worship accompany the practice of generosity in this manner, a layperson truly lives the life of the disciple of Buddha.[50]

4. FUNDAMENTAL BELIEFS OF BUDDHISM

It is from the words of the Buddha and in the context of the long tradition of the *Sanghas* of the different Buddhist sects that the fundamental beliefs of Buddhism, as we have them now, developed. Since Buddhism is very divergent, having many schools and sects, the need is felt to summarize Buddhism inorder to capture the common ground of all the Buddhist schools.

The Buddhist Society, London, has punished such a summary of Buddhism in 12 propositions entitled *Twelve Principles of Buddhism*. This small document has been placed for approval before the *Sanghas* of different Buddhist traditions in all the countries, such as, Japan, Siam, China, Burma, Sri Lanka and Tibet where Buddhism is a living religion. After due consideration, the respective *Sanghas* have approved these proposals as representative of the basic beliefs of the World Buddhism. Since the *Twelve Principles of Buddhism* contains, in simple terms, what World Buddhism believes, both in doctrine and practice, we state them here as the fundamental beliefs of Buddhism.[51]

1.1. Self-salvation is for any man the immediate task. If a man lay wounded by a poisoned arrow he would not delay extraction by demanding details of the man who shot it, or the length and the make of the arrow. There will be time for ever-increasing understanding of the Teaching during the treading of the Way. Meanwhile, begin now by facing life, as it is, learning always by direct and personal experience.

1.2. The first fact of existence is the law of change or impermanence. All that exists, from the mole to a mountain, from a thought to an empire, passes through the same cycle of existence – i.e., birth, growth, decay and death. Life alone is continuous, ever seeking self-expression in new forms. 'Life is a bridge; therefore build no house on it.' Life is a process of flow, and he who clings to any form, however splendid, will suffer by resisting the flow.

1.3. The law of change applies equally to the 'soul'. There is no principle in the individual, which is immortal and unchanging. Only the 'Namelessness', the ultimate Reality, is beyond change, and all forms of life, including man, are manifestations of this reality. No one owns the life which flows in him, any more than the electric light bulb owns the current that gives it light.

1.4. The universe is the expression of law. All effects have causes, and man's soul or character is the sum total of his previous thoughts and acts. *Karma*, meaning action-reaction, governs all existence, and man is the sole creator of his circumstances and his reaction to them, his future condition, and his final destiny. By right thought and action he can gradually purify his inner nature, and so by self-realization attain, in time, liberation from rebirth. The process covers great periods of time, involving life after life on earth, but ultimately every form of life will reach Enlightenment.

1.5. Life is one and indivisible, though its ever-changing forms are innumerable and perishable. There is, in truth, no death, though every form must die. From an understanding of life's unity arises compassion, a sense of identity with life in other forms. Compassion is described as 'the Law of laws – eternal harmony', and he who breaks this harmony of life will suffer accordingly and delay his own Enlightenment.

1.6. Life being One, the interests of the part should be those of the whole. In his ignorance man thinks he can successfully strive for his own interests, and this wrongly-directed energy of selfishness produces suffering.

He learns from his suffering to reduce and finally eliminate its cause. The Buddha taught four Noble Truths: (*a*) The omnipresence of suffering; (*b*) its cause, wrongly directed desire; (*c*) its cure, the removal of the cause; and (*d*) the Noble Eightfold Path of self-development which leads to the end of suffering.

1.7. The Eightfold Path consists in Right (or perfect) Views or preliminary understanding, Right Aims or Motive, Right Speech, Right Acts, Right Livelihood, Right Effort, Right Concentration (mind-development), and, finally Right *Samaadhi*, leading to full Enlightenment. As Buddhism is a way of living, not merely a theory of life, the treading of this Path is essential to self-deliverance. 'Cease to do evil, learn to do good, cleanse your heart: this is the Teaching of the Buddhas.'

1.8. Reality is indescribable, and a God with attributes is not the final Reality. But the Buddha, a human being, became the All-Enlightened One, and the purpose of life is the attainment of Enlightenment. This state of consciousness, *Nirvaana*, the extinction of the limitations of self hood, is attainable on earth. All men and all other forms of life contain the potentiality of Enlightenment, and the process therefore consists in becoming what you are. 'Look within: thou art Buddha.

1.9. From the potential to actual Enlightenment there lies the Middle Way, the Eightfold Path 'from desire to peace', a process of self-development between the 'opposites', avoiding all extremes. The Buddha trod this Way to the end, and the only faith required in Buddhism is the reasonable belief that where a Guide has trodden it is worth our while to tread. The Way must be trodden by the whole man, not merely the best of him, and heart and mind must be developed equally. The Buddha was the All-Compassionate as well as the All-Enlightened One.

1.10. Buddhism lays great stress on the need of inward concentration and meditation, which leads in time to the development of the inner spiritual faculties. The subjective life is as important as the daily round, and periods of quietude for inner activity are essential for a balanced life. The Buddhist should at all times be 'mindful and self-possessed', refraining from mental and emotional attachment to 'the passing show.' This increasingly watchful attitude to circumstances, which he knows to be his own creation, helps him to keep his reaction to it always under control.

1.11. The Buddha said: 'Work out your own salvation with diligence'. Buddhism knows no authority for truth save the intuition of the individual, and that is authority for himself alone. Each man suffers the consequences of his own acts, and learns thereby, while helping his fellow man to the same deliverance; nor will prayer to the Buddha or to any God prevent an effect from following its cause. Buddhist monks are teachers and exemplars, and in no sense intermediates between Reality and the individual. The utmost tolerance is practiced towards all other religions and philosophies, for no man has the right to interfere in his neighbor's journey to the Goal.

1.12. Buddhism is neither pessimistic nor 'escapist', nor does it deny the existence of God or soul, though it places its own meaning on these terms. It is, on the contrary, a system of thought, a religion, a spiritual science and a way of life, which is reasonable, practical and all-embracing. For over 2,000 years it has satisfied the spiritual needs of nearly one-third of mankind. It appeals to the West because it has no dogmas, satisfies reason and heart alike, insists on self-reliance coupled with tolerance for other points of view, embraces science, religion, philosophy, psychology, ethics and art, and points to man alone as the creator of his present life and sole designer of his destiny.

Now that we have taken a look at the history of Buddhism, its scriptures, its community and its fundamental beliefs by way of introduction, in the ensuing three essays we can elaborate the three major traditions within the Buddhist tradition, viz., the *Hiinayaana*, the *Mahaayaana* and the *Vajrayaana*. In these essays our intent is to explore the reality of the Divine in these streams of Buddhism and the paths they propose to arrive at the Divine. Now, we move on to elaborate the first and the oldest Buddhist tradition, viz., the *Hinnayaana* Buddhism.

5.1. HIINAYAANA BUDDHISM

The *Hiinayaana* tradition is the oldest among the various Buddhist ways of life. The earliest of the *Hiinayaana* Schools is the *Theravaada* School, which, at the present, is considered as the *Hiinayaana* tradition, as it is the most known among the *Hiinayaana* sects. Besides, it is the most popular form of Buddhist practice in countries like Sri Lanka, Burma, Siam and others. As it is the most ancient Buddhist heritage that has come down to us over the long history of Buddhism, its teachings and tenets are closer to the *Buddha-Dharma*, which the Gautama, the Buddha, has expounded. Thus, the study of *Theravaada* Buddhist practice takes us the earliest origins of Buddhism. In this essay, in exploring the nature of the Divine and the paths to the Divine in the *Hiinayaana* Buddhism, we basically unfold the main teachings and practices of *Hiinayaana* Buddhism in its *Theravaada* expression.

5.1.1. DIVINITIES OF THE *HIINAYAANA* PANTHEON

Buddhism originates as a reaction against ritualistic and theistic Hinduism. Therefore, it does not strictly believe in a theisticcreator God. Since the main concern of Buddha is to help people to attain release from suffering, he shows no interest in the theoretical issue of the author of the universe. Thus, the *Hiinayaana* Buddhism, in its *Theravaada* form, adopts an attitude of agnosticism to the question of a personal, theistic creator God. Though *Hiinayaana* Buddhism ignores the question of a monotheistic God, it believes in many supernatural beings and spirits. In the practice of popular Buddhism, many deities are invoked for protection and help. Such practices have come about due to the interaction of Buddhist religious practice with the existing local and indigenous religions. The Buddhists do not think that prayers and invocations they offer to these deities and spirits in any way contradict their practice of Buddhist religion, as these gods and goddesses are part and parcel of the wheel of existence, subject to the universal law of *Karma*. They are higher beings, that exist in the heavenly realms due to the good actions of their past *Karma*. When they complete the effects of their *Karma*, they, too, die and are reborn in another cosmological region, depending on the fruits of their present *Karma*. As heavenly beings, they are superior to men, and humans can invoke their assistance and protection in coping with the troubles of everyday living. But the journey towards liberation is the task of every human being and none of these deities are capable of leading man to his final destiny, as they too are bound by the results of *Karma*.[52]

While denying a monotheistic God and accommodating beliefs in various deities, the *Theravaada* Buddhism also speaks of the state of *Nirvaana*, which is permanent, stable, imperishable, immovable, ageless, deathless, unborn power, bliss and happiness. *Nirvaana* is the secure refuge, the shelter and the place of unassailable safety. It is the One supreme Reality, the real Truth and the highest Good, which is the consummation of life – eternal, hidden and incomprehensible peace. The one who achieves this state is the *Arahat*. According to the *Theravaadins,* the Enlightened Buddha himself is the *Arhat par excellence*, who is the personal embodiment of the state of *Nirvaana*. In fact, according to the ancient Buddhist tradition, the *Arahat*, the attainer of *Nirvaana*, is the only one in whom the true divinity dwells, and who is worthy of veneration, as the name *"Arahat"* itself suggests, for he is the enlightened one, who has crossed the ocean of *Samsaara*, overcome the fruits of *Karma* and is an able teacher of the way he has walked.[53] In the following sections, we explore the various divinities of the *Hiinayaana* pantheon and present the *Arahat*, the one who has attained *Nirvaana*, as the true Divinity of *Hiinayaana* Buddhism.

5.1.1.1. BUDDHIST COSMOS AND ITS DIVINITIES

Though *Hinnayaana* Buddhism does not recognize the reality of an absolute Supreme Being as the originator and maintainer of the universe, and acknowledges the *Arahat* as the true locus of divinity, it does accept the existence of gods, who occupy the cosmos and various cosmological regions of this universe. Here, we shall attempt to study Buddhist cosmology and the various deities that inhabit the various cosmological regions, the totality of which comes within the purview of the wheel of life and the law of *Karma*.

5.1.1.1.1. Buddhist Cosmology

The Buddhist cosmology develops in the context of the *Karma-Samsaara* doctrine, which says that our life in this universe is an endless wandering, a continuous movement like a flow of a river. The beginning and the end of this cyclic process of birth, death and rebirth cannot be known with certainty. All living creatures are part of this cyclic movement and will continue to be born until they attain the final end, *Nirvaana*. It is difficult to determine how long a living creature's wandering continues. Often the term '*Aeon*' is used to refer to this journey in time. An *Aeon* is approximately a lifetime, i.e., the duration of time, which elapses between the origin and the destruction of a world system, which is comparable to a galaxy. The length of an *Aeon* cannot be fully grasped in terms of our understanding of time. After his enlightenment, Buddha is said to have remembered about 91 *Aeons* of his previous existences. Therefore, it is practically impossible to arrive at the duration of a living creature's *Samsaara* existence. The reason for this *Samsaara* existence is *Karma*. The past *Karma* is the cause of the present existence, while the present *Karma* determines one's future existence. Now, the question arises as to the nature of the region in which this *Samsaara* existence of all forms of living creatures takes place. This question leads Buddhist thinkers to take up the cosmological issue of the nature of the world system, which forms the locus of *Samsaara* existence.[54] In the following sections, we attempt to unfold the Buddhist universe, the six world realms and their occupants, and the three world spheres, in the process explaining the cosmological make up of the universe, which is the locus of the *Samsaara* existence from the Buddhist perspective.

5.1.1.1.1.1. Buddhist Universe

The Buddhist cosmology breaks up the universe into two categories, viz., the worlds systems and the various life forms (*Sattva*). The former are perceived as a container (*Bhaajana*), in which, the latter, the living beings, can stay, grow and develop. The worlds systems emerge as the result of the coming together of the five elements, viz., earth, air, water, fire and space (*Aakaasa*). A world system is a collection of many suns, moons, stars and other planetary celestial bodies. In the universe there are innumerable world systems, and they are found throughout the six directions of the universe, viz., north, south, east, west, above and below. The earth in which we live forms the part of the 'Galactic world system', which the Buddhists call 'the *Saaha* world'. Every world system undergoes cycles of evolution, decline and reemergence. It takes billions of years to complete a cycle. Buddhists call the duration of the cyclic process of a world system 'a great *Aeon*'. Thus, the Buddhists conceive of time as something cyclic rather than linear. In the same way, they also perceive history as something that has no overall direction and purpose, as during every 'great *Aeon*' similar conditions of life, existence and events repeat themselves. It is the belief of the Buddhists that the main reason for the changes that take place during the cyclic process is the moral status of the inhabitants. It is said that the world system that is inhabited by evil, selfish and ignorant people will decline faster than a world system whose people are good, wise and virtuous. Thus, the populaces of a world system are its caretakers as the quality of life and activity of the world depends on the quality of the moral life of its people.[55]

Though the Buddhists do not take up the origin of the universe with its various world systems as a serious philosophical issue, there are myths in the Buddhist *Suutras* that speak of the emergence, growth and development of life and activity in a world system. According to a myth the people of a world system that is destroyed are reborn in a new world system that is evolving. At the initial stage the bodies are semi-transparent and spirit-like, having no distinction of sexes. As the make up of the new world system becomes thicker these spirit-like bodies become less ethereal and over a period of time become fully physical bodies. As they acquire eating habits, there is scarcity of food. This leads to struggles for food, competition, quarrels and disputes. To preserve themselves in such an unruly situation, they elect a king to maintain peace and to equitably distribute the food. Thus, emerges socio-political life in the new world system. The life that has, thus, begun continues until the dissolution of the world system, depending on the Karmic effects of its inhabitants.[56]

5.1.1.1.1.2. Six World-Realms and Their Occupants

At the center of the world-system is the mighty mythical Mount Meru, also known as Mount Sumeru, which serves as the gigantic foundation of the world system. Seven concentric rings of mountains and seas surround Mount Meru. Beyond these mountains lie the four continents in four main directions. The southern continent is the Jambudviipa, which ordinary human beings inhabit. In the southern part of this continent is the land of the Buddha. There is infinite space below, upon and above Mount Meru. In this infinite space are built up 31 dwelling places for various living beings (*Sattva-lokas*). These 31 dwelling places are divided into six world realms of life and rebirth, in each of which a particular class of beings lives and is reborn (*Sattva*).[57] We can speak of the six world realms in relation to the living beings that occupy that particular realm. They, in the ascending order, are the following: the world realm of hell-beings (hells), the world realm of animals, the world realm of ghosts, the world realm of *Asuras*, the world realm of the humans and the world realm of the gods. We can picture the layout of the world system, with its six worldrealms and 31 dwelling places, if we compare it with a large building with 31 floors. The lowest floor is the hells, which is followed by the realm of animals, the realm of ghosts, the realm of *Asuras*, the realm of humans and 26 floors of the realm of gods. Thus, these 31 levels of existence in six world realms form the possible destination a destination in which a living being can be reborn, depending on the *Karma* of his past existence.[58]

Now that we have delineated the six world realms, we can briefly consider the inhabitants of each of these realms. The first and the lowest world realm are the hells (*Narakas*). There are about 136 hells to receive 136 types of offenders. The various levels of hells are arranged in tiers, one above the other. The occupants of the hells are the evil-doers in their past lives. Being reborn in the hells is the worst of the six ways of existence. The inhabitants of the hells are subjected to numerous torments, such as, being boiled in oil, being cut into pieces limb by limb and being frozen in very cold regions. There are usually two types of hells, viz., the hot hells and the cold hells. In the former punishment is inflicted by applying heat, while in the latter the suffering comes from the bodies being frozen. The punishment in hells is not eternal, but temporal, as the hell beings are reborn in some other world realm when they have completed the *Karma*.[59]

The second is the animal world realm. It is above the hells. It is not desirable to be reborn in this realm, as it is a life of subjugation and control. Men use animals for food and to get their work done. Besides, animals move by beastly instincts, and they lack intellectual capacity. They are not capable of bettering their situation in their existence as animals. When the *Karma* lapses, animals die and are reborn in another world realm. The third world realm is that of the ghosts, which is above the animal realm. The ghosts are the spirits of the departed human beings. They are unhappy spirits, who have developed deep attachments, which keep them bound to the earth. The ghosts are tormented by hunger and thirst, but they are not able to satisfy them. In art they are represented as creatures with large bellies and small mouths, symbolizing their insatiable hunger. They move around the outer edges of the earth and make themselves visible in shadowy forms. Once their *Karma* is completed, they are reborn in another world realm. At the fourth level is the world realm of the *Asuras*. They are also sometimes referred to as *Titans*. They are a type of demon that are moved by the desire for power. The *Asuras* are violent, impulsive and warlike creatures. They are said to be constantly at war with the gods to attain the power of the gods. But in spite of their conquests and wars, they do not find any fulfillment in their lives. Like all the other groups, at the completion of their *Karma* they are reborn in another world realm.[60]

The fifth world realm belongs to the human beings. Being reborn as a human being is considered to be very significant among the Buddhists, as it is 'the middle way' between the other world realms. In the first four world realms – the hells, the animal world, the world of ghosts and the world of *Asuras* – there is only suffering. In the world realm of gods, there is no pain, but only pleasure. But in the world realm of the humans there is an appropriate balance between pleasure and suffering. Therefore, it is not easy to be born as a humans. However, being reborn as human being is preferable to being reborn in the heavenly world of the gods, because the gods, living in ideal paradises, are hardly challenged and become complacent, and in the process, can loose sight of the need to strive for *Nirvaana*.On the other hand, living in the human world, a human has constant reminders of suffering – such as, death, old age and sickness – which, in turn, lead him to think of *Nirvaana* and move towards it. Besides, the reason and free will in humans can make them understand and live the *Buddha-Dharma*. Thus, when a person is reborn in the world realm of the humans, there is a better chance to attain *Nirvaana* than in any other world realms. If a person completes all the effects of his past *Karma* and builds up merit (*Punnya*) in the present life, he attains *Nirvaana* and completes his life as he. But if his past and present Karmic effects are not fully destroyed, is reborn in another world realm, depending on his *Karma*.[61]

The last world realm is that of the gods. The gods are above the human world realm. Gods are superior to the humans in sense that their material constitution is more refined, their emotions are much finer than that of the humans and their lifespan is much longer than that of the humans. They are subjected to less suffering, and there are hardly any reminders of suffering in their lives. They are ever happy, enjoying the fruits of their good deeds of the past existence in their present abode in heaven. But they are not immortal and eternal in their existence. When the *Karma* that takes them to their heavenly existence is completed, they also die and are reborn in another world realm, according to their present *Karma*. There are 26 levels of heavens and various grades of heavenly existence. The gods of the lower levels have limitations in comparison with the gods of the higher levels.[62]

5.1.1.1.1.3. Three World-Spheres

The 31 dwelling places of living beings (*Sattva-lokas*) in the six world realms exist in three spheres (*Cakra-vaalas*). They are vast circular planes into which are distributed the dwelling places of six classes of living beings. The first and the lowest sphere is the 'Sphere of Sense Desires' (*Kaamaavacara Cakra-vaala*). It is a sphere conditioned by sensuous desires. It includes the first five world realms – the world realm of hell beings, the world realm of animals, the world realm of ghosts, the world realm of *Asuras* and the world realm of the humans – and the first six levels of the heavenly world, i.e., the sixth to eleventh levels of dwelling places, which is the region of the lower gods. The second sphere is the 'Sphere of Pure Form' (*Ruupaavacara Cakra-vaala*). It is a state that is free from sensuous desires, but conditioned by pure form. It is a profound spiritual state in which gods perceive and communicate by way of telepathy. It forms the next 16 heavens, i.e., the 12th to 27th levels of dwelling places that form the region of the higher gods. The third and the highest sphere is the Sphere of Formlessness' (*Aruupaacacara Cakra-vaala*). It is an indescribably sublime state, beyond all shape and form. It is free from sensuous desire and not conditioned by any form. It is the abode of beings that exist as pure mental energy. It is the highest sphere in which a person can be reborn. It consists of the last four levels of the heavens, i.e., the 28th to the 31st levels of the dwelling places. Thus, the whole universe is organized into three spheres of ascending purity.[63]

5.1.1.1.2. Gods of the Heavenly World

Now that we have analyzed the Buddhist universe – in terms of world systems, world realms and world spheres – and have spoken briefly about the inhabitants of the five world-realms, viz., the hell beings, the animals, the ghosts, the *Asuras* and the humans, our concern now is to study the gods that occupy the heavenly world in detail. For the sake of clarity, we elaborate on the gods, in relation to the spheres in which they find themselves.

5.1.1.1.2.1. Gods of the First World Spheres

The realm of gods within the first sphere is called *Kaamaavacara Devaloka*, i.e., the heavenly realm in which there are sensuous desires. The gods of the heavens within this sphere are liable to sensuous desires. There are six heavens within this sphere. The first is the heaven of the Four Great Kings (*Mahaa-raajas*). The Four Great Kings are great champions, who guard the earth and the heavens against the demons (*Asuras*), who come out of the world below and attack the inhabitants of heaven and earth. They are represented as fully armed with armor and drawn swords. They guard each quarter of the heavens: *Dhrita-raashtra*, the King of *Gandharvas*, guards the Eastern quarter; *Viruudhaka*, the King of *Kumbhaandas*, is assigned to the Southern quarter; *Viruupaaksha*, the King of the *Nagas*, rules the Western quarter; and *Kuvera*, also known as *Vaisrvana*, the King of *Yakshas*, is the king over the Northern quarter. The inhabitants of this heaven, the Four Great Kings, are known as the *Mahaaraajika-devas* or the *Catur-mahaaraaja-kaayikas*.[64]

Above this lowest heaven, on the highest summit of Mount Meru is the second heaven of the first sphere, the realm of the god *Sakra*, the Rig Vedic god *Indra*, the god of the atmosphere. Though he is lower than the *Mahaa-brahmaa* and the *Maara*, he is the most popular god of the Buddhists and appears often in their legends. It is believed that the Buddha himself was born as *Indra* in some of his earlier births. Thus, *Indra*, under the name *Sakra*, is one of the most popular gods of early Buddhism. He rules over the Thirty-Three Gods (*Trayastrinsas*), who inhabit the second heaven. These include the eleven *Rudras*, eight *Vasus*, the twelve *Aadityas* and the personifications of Heaven and Earth. The third of the first sphere is the heaven of the *Yaama* gods. They preside over the periods of the day. They are called strifeless gods, as they do not take part in the war that is going on between the gods and the *Asuras* in the two lower heavens. The fourth is the heaven of 'the perfectly contented gods' (*Tushitas*). Here reside beings destined to become the Buddha. It is the belief of the Buddhists that Gautama himself is born into this heaven, in order to prepare for his birth as the Buddha. The fifth heaven is that of 'gods who constantly enjoy pleasures, which they themselves provide' (*Nirmaana-rati-devas*). The sixth heaven of the first sphere is the heaven of 'gods who constantly enjoy pleasures, which others provide' (*Para-nirmita-vasa-vartins*). These beings are called *Maaras*, the lords of sensuous desire. There power consists in exciting sensual and carnal desires in men. They tempt men to indulge in passions through the bodily senses. Another name of *Maara* is *Kaama*, i.e., desire. He is superior to all the gods of the first sphere, including *Sakra*. It is believed that there are millions of *Maaras*, who are ruled by a chief *Maara*.[65]

5.1.1.1.2.2. Gods of the Second World Sphere

The heavens of the first sphere belong to the world of sense (*Kaamaloka*) and are similar to the earth and the lower regions. The gods of this sphere have sexual feelings and they live an active life. But the heavens of the second sphere belong to a higher level. The gods who inhabit these heavens live a higher condition of existence, in which all sensuality ceases and no distinction of sex exists. These heavens belong to the plane of pure forms. So they are called world of forms (*Ruupa-lokas*).[66] Now, we turn our attention to these types of heavens.

The heavens of the second sphere, i.e., the sphere of Pure Form, are 16 in number and are divided into four groups. The first three groups have three heavens each, while the last group has seven heavens. The gods belonging to the first group are called 'gods having a *Brahmaa* form' (*Brahma-kaayika-deva*). The first and the lowest group is that of the *Brahmaa* gods. It consists of three heavens, viz., the heaven of *Brahmaa's* Retinue (*Brahma-parisajjaa-deva*), the heaven of *Brhahmaa's* Ministers (*Brahma-purohitaa-deva*) and the heaven of Great *Brahmaa* (*Mahaa-Brahmaa-deva*). The first class of gods with *Brahmaa* form is the *Brahmaa's* Retinue. They inhabit the lowest heaven of the *Brahmaa* abodes and perform the lower level functions in the world of *Mahaa-Brahmaa*. The second class of *Brahmaa* gods is the *Brahmmaa's* Ministers. They live in the second heaven of the *Mahaa-Brahmaa* worlds and perform the function of ministers of *Mahaa-Brahmaa*. The third class of gods with *Brahmaa* form is the Great *Brahmaas*. They occupy the third heaven of the *Brahmaa* abodes. They are chief among the gods with the *Brahmaa* form. Buddhists believe that Gautama himself was born as *Mahaa-Brahmaa* in four of his previous births.[67]

The second group of heavens belonging to the world of Pure Form is three in number. These three heavens are regions of light. The light that is found in these heavens does not come from the sun or the moon, but rather from the mental enlightenment of the gods who inhabit them. The gods abiding in these heavens have risen to higher levels of knowledge and intelligence. The first heaven belonging to the second group is the heaven of gods that have limited enlightenment (*Pariittaabhaa-deva*) and consists of gods whose level of radiance and enlightenment is circumscriptive. The second heaven of this group belongs to gods whose nature is of boundless and infinite light (*Apramaanaabhaa-deva*). The third heaven of the second group consists of gods, who are 'beings of the clearest light' (*Abhaasvaraa-deva*). These are gods of streaming radiance and enlightenment.[68]

There are three heavens in the third group of the world of Pure Forms. The characteristic of this group of heavens is the purity of the gods who live in them. Each of the three heavens manifests greater grades of purity. To the first heaven of the third group belong the gods of limited purity (*Pariitta-subhaa-deva*). In the second heaven of the third group live the gods of unlimited purity (*Appamaana-subhaa-deva*). The third heaven of the third group is the abode of the gods whose being is constituted of unlimited purity (*Subha-kritsnaa-deva*).[69]

The fourth group of the world of Pure Form consists of seven heavens. The inhabitants of these heavens have risen to the highest levels of pure thought. The first heaven of the fourth group belongs to the 'gods who enjoy great reward' (*Vrihat-phalaa deva*). The second heaven of the fourth group includes gods who are lost in total unconsiousness' (*Asanjni-sattva*). In the third heaven of the fourth group we find gods who make no efforts (*Avrihaa-deva*). In the fourth heaven of the fourth group live the gods who never endure any pain (*Atapaa-deva*). The occupants of the fifth heaven of the fourth group are the gods who see clearly (*Suddarsaa-deva*). To the sixth heaven of the fourth group belong the gods who are beautiful in appearance (*Sudarsino-deva*). The seventh heaven of the fourth group is the abode of the gods who are the highest of all beings (*Akanishthaa-deva*).[70]

5.1.1.1.2.3. Gods of the Third World Sphere

The heavens of the third world sphere are the highest of the heavens. They are free from sensuous desire and not conditioned by any forms. Therefore, they are called the planes of no forms (*Aruupa-lokas*). There are four heavens in the third sphere. The gods of these four heavens of the sphere of formlessness comprehend reality in increasingly finer ways. In the first heaven of the formless sphere abide 'the gods who are capable of grasping the idea of infinite space' (*Akaasaanantyaayatanaa-deva*). The second heaven of the third sphere contain 'the gods who are capable of apprehending infinite consciousness (*Vijnaanaanantyaayatanaa-deva*). In the third heaven of the formless sphere we find 'the gods who can comprehend the ideal of absolute non-existence' (*Akincanyaayatanaa-deva*). To the fourth heaven of the third sphere belong 'the gods who abide neither in consciousness nor unconsciousness' (*Naiva-sanjnaanaasanjnaayatanaa-devah*). This last stage is the highest level to which a person can be reborn. The sphere of formlessness and its increasingly sublime heavens belong to the mystical level, and one arrives at this level through higher levels of meditation.[71]

5.1.1.2. ARAHAT: THE TRUE DIVINITY OF HIINAYAANA BUDDHISM

In the previous sections, we have attempted to analyze the various levels of existence within the Buddhist cosmological system. Our consideration clearly points to the fact that the law of Karma binds all these levels of existence including the higher levels of heavenly existence. Therefore, even the highest gods of the heavenly world have, in no way, achieved the final goal of *Nirvaana*. Thus, however sublime these gods may be or how many *Aeons* their lives may extend, they are limited, bound and in need of final liberation. Hence, the only being that has achieved the highest state of *Nirvaana* is the *Arahat*, in whom the true divinity dwells and who is worthy of veneration and devotion. In the following section, we attempt to explore the reality of *Arahat*, the true divinity of the *Hinnayaana* Buddhism. Our exposition includes the nature and characteristics of *Arahat* and the relationship between *Arahat* and *Nirvaana*.

5.1.1.2.1. Nature of Arahat

The *Hiinayaana* Buddhism considers *Arahat* as the ideal man whom it wishes to produce by its *Dharma* and the one in whom its ideal of perfection totally resides. Therefore, *Arahatship* is the highest stage of development, for a Buddhist. The following quotation very clearly indicates the idea of *Arahat* in the early schools of Buddhism:

> It might be said that the connotation, which accrued to the term *Arahan* [*Arahat*] under [*Hiinayaana*] Buddhism, is a case of spontaneous generation, so different did it become in scope and depth from the meanings attached to it in any previous or contemporary system. For, to the disciples of Gotama, the *Arahan* came to mean not only the Founder of the creed, or the revealer of the religion, as it did in Jainism, nor only the person worthy of reverence and gifts, but the man or woman who, with mind always alert, having attained freedom of heart and mind, to insight and knowledge is adept (*Asekha*), is perfect, is a finished product; one who has crossed over the flood and gone beyond (*Paaragata*); who has rooted out craving and cut off desire; who has destroyed the *Aasavas*; who is versed in the threefold lore (*Tevijja*); who has won excellence in the 37 things associated with enlightenment; who has attained *Nibbaana* [*Nirvaana*]; the man or woman who has completed many other attainments, all of them implying finality. The *Arahan* has, in a word, achieved some static condition, where he is beyond the workings of what is now called the Law of Causation. He has no need of further development, of further progress.[72]

The Buddhist tradition derives the term "*Arahat*" from two words "*Ari*" and "*han*" which mean 'enemy' and 'to kill' respectively. Taken in this sense the word "*Arahat*" is 'one who slays the enemy', thereby attains freedom from the enemy. The enemy the *Arahat* kills is the totality of his 'outflows', i.e., passions. The 'outflows' here refers to sense desires, fluctuations of the mind, inner inclinations, attachments of various types, wrong views and other similar passions that flow from the five aggregates (*Skandhas*) of the mind-body system. Thus, in *Arahat* all forms of 'outflows' dry up. They dry up because, basing himself on the realization that the changing birth-death-rebirth cycle must be overcome, he exerts himself and struggles to master them. He fights against the five hindrances, viz., longing for the world, malice, sloth, distraction and doubt. He grapples with the ten fetters – belief in a permanent individuality, doubt, belief in rituals, sensual passion, malice, desire for existence in the world of form, desire for existence in the formless world, pride, distraction and ignorance – that attach him to this-worldly existence. Besides, he wrestles with three *Aasavas*: sensual desire, desire for existence and ignorance. In the same way, he wages war against various forms of deprivations (*Kilesas*), such as, greed, hatred, stupidity, pride, false views, doubt, sloth, distraction, shamelessness and recklessness. Of these the most significant are greed (*Lobha*), hatred (*Dosa*) and stupidity (*Moha*). Greed is a positive form of craving. Hatred is related to greed and consists in being hostile to what is pleasant. Stupidity is the dullness of mind, which, in turn, leads to unmeritorious actions. He rejects and becomes a foe of all conditions earthly existence, as they lead to decay, change and destruction. The *Arahat* abandons all these defilements and in this very abandonment attains *Arahatship*. On becoming the *Arahat*, his attachment to the three-fold world – the world of sense (*Kaama-loka*), the world of forms (*Ruupa-loka*) and the formless world (*Anruupa-loka*) – is destroyed and thereby moves beyond every form of existence. Thus, *Arahatship* is beyond every condition of existence we can think of. It is perfect existence, which is untouched by any form of defilements. The *Arahat* attains full knowledge (*Panna*), which while giving him the complete freedom from all false views opens him for knowing everything in its true reality. Thus, the *Arahat* becomes the Enlightened.[73]

The *Arahat*, the Enlightened, thus, becomes 'the Worthy One', i.e., 'the One deserving worship and gifts'. For this reason modern scholars prefer to derive the term "*Arahat*" from the word "*Arhati*", which means 'to be worthy of' or 'the most deserving'. Thus, the name "*Arahat*" indicates 'the One who is of highest merit' and 'the most perfect One', as he is free from every pain, every passion and from every form of attachment. He is the emancipated living man, who has transcendent faculties of knowledge – the inner eye, the inner ear, cognition of others' thoughts, recollection of previous existences, knowledge that his 'outflows' have dried up – and extraordinary powers over matter. In short, the *Arahat* is one who has nothing to learn. He has become the Worthy One, because he has lived greatly; he has done what he has had to do; he has shed his burden; and he has achieved the aim of his life. The *Arahat* is no longer bound, as he is set free from every attachment to himself. He is a person by himself and secluded, but zealous and earnest about alleviating the pains of others. He has absolute inner freedom, and so he is in full control, master of himself, self-restrained and dispassionate. He is constantly in a state of same-mindedness and is unaffected by any pain or gain, cross or crown, praise or blame. The *Arahat* is truly a liberated man, untouched by the effects of *Karma-Samsaara* existence, and worthy of worship and veneration.[74] The following quote highlights the true nature of the *Arahat*:

> Gold and a clod of earth were the same to him. The sky and the palm of his hand were to his mind the same. He remained cool (in danger) like the fragrant sandalwood to the axe, which cuts it down. By his *Gnosis*, he had torn the 'eggshell of ignorance. He has obtained *Gnosis*, the 'Super-knowledges' and the 'Powers of analytical Insight'. He became averse to worldly gain and honor, and he became worthy of being honored, saluted and revered by *Devas* (gods), including *Indra*, *Vishnu* and *Krishna*.[75]

Thus, *Arahat* is one who kills the enemy of his passions, attains emancipation and becomes worthy of veneration and worship. He is the true dwelling place of divinity, the Enlightened One, the true teacher of *Dharma* and the seat of true nobility. Now that we have elaborated the nature of the *Arahat*, as the *Hiinayaana* tradition understands, we can move on to speak of some of the qualities and powers of an *Arahat*.

5.1.1.2.2. Characteristics of Arahat

We find a number of characteristics in the *Arahat*. He, as the emancipated and perfect being, possesses a number of specific qualities that distinguish him from ordinary people. In this section, we consider the six mystical characteristics (*Abhinnaa*), the ten special characteristics (*Balaani*), the four godly characteristics (*Brahma-Vihaaras*) and a few other general characteristics of the *Arahat*.

5.1.1.2.2.1. Six Mystical Characteristics of the Arahat

There are six mystical and psychical powers and qualities associated with the enlightened person. All these characteristics involve the ability of the *Arahat* to overcome the natural obstacles and to transcend the laws of nature. We briefly consider each of these. Firstly, he possesses a number of occult powers. Though he is one individual, he is able to become many and then, once again, return to his original individuality. He is able to become visible and invisible at will. The *Arahat* can go without any obstruction through a wall or solid ground, as if he is going through the air. Similarly, he is able to penetrate through solid ground as if he swimming through the water. He is also able to walk on the water without sinking, as if he is walking on a solid rock. He has the power to travel cross-legged in the air, like a flying bird. He is capable of touching the sun and the moon with his hands and can reach with his body up to the *Brahmaa* heaven. Secondly, the *Arahat*, by bringing about the destruction of all defilements, develops a purified divine ear, with the help of which he can hear both divine and human sounds from far and near. Thirdly, he is capable of reading the mind of other persons, and knows the condition of a mind as impassioned, liberated or un-liberated. Fourthly, the *Arahatship* opens the *Arahat* to remember the full details of his previous lives. Fifthly, the *Arahat* develops a purified divine eye, with which he is able to perceive other people according to their *Karma*. Finally, having destroyed all forms of impurities and attained higher knowledge, the *Arahat* lives his liberated life through wisdom and concentration of mind, purified from all defilements.[76] In this manner, the *Arahat* acquires a number of powers after his enlightenment. The spiritual powers of the *Arahat* are described as follows:

> He [the *Arahat*] knows his previous lives; he sees the heavens and hells; he has actualized the destruction of (re-)birth; a sage, accomplished in the higher knowledges. ... He knows his mind

is completely purified; freed from all passions, beyond birth and death; complete in the religious life; (he knows) all impassioned *Dharmas*.[77]

5.1.1.2.2.2. Ten Special Characteristics of the Arahat

Other than the psychic and mystical qualities, the *Arahat* possesses ten special characteristics (*Balaani*). Firstly, an *Arahat* fully knows that the nature of conditioned existence is impermanence. This knowledge guides him in everything he does, either for himself or for others. The awareness of the impermanence of every reality makes the *Arahat* realize the ephemeral nature of conditioned reality. Secondly, the awareness of the impermanent nature of conditioned existence makes the *Arahat* look at the factors of existence as similar to charcoal, having little value. Thirdly, based on the first two qualities, the *Arahat* cultivates detachment and actualizes detachment, in the process effecting the destruction of the impermanent factors of existence. In doing so, he eliminates all the causal agents of impurities (*Aasava*). Fourthly, an *Arahat* cultivates Four Fields of Mindfulness (*Satipatthaana*). The practice of mindfulness keeps the mind's door that the mind does not slip into immoral states. Fifthly, the *Arahat* cultivates Four Right Efforts, viz., to avoid and overcome the evil, and to develop and maintain the good. Sixthly, the *Arahat* attempts to take four steps in actualizing four psychic powers, viz., desire, energy, thought and investigation. In achieving the psychic powers, along with concentration, struggle is also necessary. Seventhly, the *Arahat* cultivates the five faculties (*Indriyas*), faith, energy, mindfulness, concentration and insight. Eighthly, the *Arahat* develops the five powers of faith, energy, mindfulness, concentration and insight. Ninthly, the *Arahat* understands the seven factors of enlightenment, viz., mindfulness, investigation of Buddha's teachings, energy, joy, serenity, concentration and equanimity. Finally, the *Arahat* cultivates the Eightfold Path. These characteristics make the *Arahat* what he is and make him do what he does.[78]

5.1.1.2.2.3. Four Godly Characteristics of the Arahat

Besides the ten special characteristics, the *Arahat* possesses four godly qualities (*Brahma-Vihaaras*). They are loving-kindness (*Metta*), compassion (*Karnuna*), sympathetic joy (*Mudita*) and even-mindedness (*Upekkha*). Firstly, the *Arahat* possesses the quality of loving-kindness. It consists in the *Arahat* letting his mind pervade every quarter of the world with thoughts of love. As a result, the whole world – above, below, around and everywhere – is filled with his heart of love, in the process he realizes complete oneness with all other forms of life. This experience of unity with every reality expands his consciousness proportionately, so that he understands and loves every being so fully and totally that his heartbeat becomes the heartbeat of every reality in the universe, and his consciousness becomes that of all other forms of life. Thus, loving-kindness consists in being one with every being in the universe on the part of the *Arahat*, that he loves everything with his whole heart and the totality of his being. But it is not a passionate love of desire, but an altruistic love that emerges from the heart of the *Arahat* that is at peace.[79]

The second godly quality is compassion. In loving-kindness the *Arahat* identifies himself with others in altruistic love and in compassion; his feeling of loving-kindness within his heart finds concrete expression. In order to express his loving-kindness through compassionate action, the *Arahat* is ready to lower himself to any extent for the sake of every creature, especially his fellow human beings. Thus, compassion consists in feeling with and for the other, i.e., cultivating a feeling of sympathetic sorrow for the other's pains, and working out through concrete action ways of alleviating the pains and sufferings of others. Thus, compassion becomes the basis of every moral act of kindness that an *Arahat* performs.[80]

The third godly quality is sympathetic joy. Unlike compassion, which consists in feeling a sense of sorrow for the sufferings of others, sympathetic joy consists in being glad and joyful at the good of others. It involves the *Arahat* feeling gladness within his heart and rejoicing at the good things that happen to others. Moved by compassion, i.e., sympathetic sorrow, the *Arahat* performs actions to help others in their need. In sympathetic joy, he rejoices wholeheartedly at the good that has happened to the other as the result of his compassionate action. Thus, sympathetic joy is opposed to jealousy and envy. In envy one feels unhappy and sorry at the good of the other. But, in sympathetic joy one feels happy at the blessings that come to others and feels a sense of gladness within oneself on account of others' blessings.[81]

The fourth godly quality of the *Arahat* is even-mindedness, i.e., equanimity. It consists in the *Arahat* keeping a level head while practicing the other three *Brahma-Vihaaras*. In feeling a sense of unity with every being in the universe, moving out to them in compassionate action and rejoicing at the good that comes to them as a result, does not make him get lost in the other. He needs to acquire a sense of balance. Even-mindedness helps the *Arahat* to return from all exciting situations to a calm detachment, which involves the restoration of his mind's impersonal serenity. It also implies evolving within himself a central position towards others. Equanimity helps the *Arahat* to view others and the situations of others impartially, by effecting a balance between aversion and adulation in dealing with people, as he knows that the proximate cause of each person's action is his own *Karma*. But equanimity is not to be understood as a selfish indifference to the other's welfare. It is, rather, a balanced and impartial way of looking at every person and situation.[82]

5.1.1.2.2.4. Other General Characteristics of the Arahat

Over and above the above-mentioned qualities there are a few general characteristics of *Arahat*, to which we now turn. Firstly, an *Arahat* is endowed with great courage, boldness and inner strength. The fearlessness and courage come from the fact that the power of *Dharma* – the power of truth and goodness – resides in them. Secondly, the life of an *Arahat* is one of inner joy and peace. This is clear from the fact words – such as, sorrowlessness (*Asokam*), security (*Khemam*), purity (*Suddhi*), sublimity (*Paniitam*), peace (*Saanti*), release (*Vimutti*) – which are used to describe the state of the *Arahat*. Thirdly, the *Arahat* lives without hate, free from disease and in good health, without anxiety, free from all sorrows and with deep contentment in life.[83] So far we have looked into the nature and the various characteristics of the *Arahat*. In the next section, we look at the state of *Nirvaana* and its relationship to *Arahatship*.

5.1.1.2.3. Nirvaana and Arahatship

The final goal of *Hiinayaana* Buddhism is the attainment of the condition of the *Arahat*. The *Arahat* is one who has arrived at the state of *Nirvaana*. When the *Arahat* walks through the path of *Dharma* and crosses over the state of *Samsaara* and achieves *Nirvaana*, he is said to possess the *Arahatship* (*Arahatam*). Thus, *Arahatship* is the fruit of realizing the *Dharma*, by passing through the path, in the process breaking the bonds, putting an end to all intoxications, getting rid of hindrances and mastering the craving for metaphysical speculations. In other words, *Arahatship* is obtained in the state of *Nirvaana*, and an *Arahat* is one who has attained *Nirvaana*.[84]

The term "*Nirvaana*" literally means 'dying out', 'blowing out', 'quenching' or 'extinction'. Hence *Nirvaana* is related to the completed extinction of the three chief fires –greed, hatred and stupidity – and the total ending of all evils, viz., birth, old age, death, pain, lamentation, sorrow, grief and despair. When these forms of cessation take place, there comes about a state of release, a profound state of rest, wherein there is no pain and ignorance. It is a condition in which one is neither conscious of earth, water, fire, air, infinite space, the sphere of infinite consciousness, the sphere of void, the sphere of perception or non-perception, coming or going or standing still, falling away or rising. This state is neither fixed nor mobile. But its attainment brings an end to all the woes of earthly existence. However, the state of *Nirvaana* is not a state of total extinction of all existence, nor is the total destruction of one's individual existence; rather, it is a state in which all evils of existence that condition and limit a person vanish. In other words, *Nirvaana* is the end of maturation of the human person. When *Nirvaana* is achieved, all seeking of a person ceases, and he becomes the Enlightened. It is a state in which a person is transformed, and his life is characterized by peace, deep spiritual joy, compassion and a refined subtle awareness. Negative mental states, such as, doubt, worry, anxiety and fear are totally absent. A person who attains the state of *Nirvaana* continues to live in the world, as the Buddha did for 45 years after his enlightenment. But the *Pari-Nirvaana* results in the entire cessation of rebirth and the total extinction of all the elements of bodily existence, as it represents the state of the final death of the person. Buddhist scriptures often refer to this state of *Pari-Nirvaana* by using negative expressions, such as, 'the extinction of thirst', 'the absence of desire', 'blowing out', 'cessation', 'unborn', 'unoriginated', 'uncreated' and 'unformed'. At times, a few positive descriptions are used to refer to the final state of the *Arahat*, such as, 'the auspicious', 'good', 'purity', 'peace', 'truth' and 'the further shore'. But it is difficult to determine the exact meaning of these phrases and expressions.[85]

The immediate issue that arises is the nature of 'what is left over' after the state of *Pari-Nirvaana*. Strictly speaking, the dissolution of the body at the *Pari-Nirvaana* leaves no surviving personality, as Buddhists do not believe in the subsistent self (*Anatta*). Since the *Pari-Nirvaana* is the absolute termination of a series of conscious bodily organizations after which nothing remains, it should result in either an absorption into a void (*Suunya*) or in total annihilation. When this issue is posed to Buddha, he avoids dogmatic definitions about the state after the *Pari-Nirvaana*. For him asking about the afterlife of the Enlightened One is similar to asking 'where a flame goes when it is blown out'. In other words, the Buddha does not subscribe to absorption into void or to total annihilation. Besides, the Buddha never attempts to explain the goal of *Nirvaana*, which he himself has attained. Thus, in the last analysis, the nature of *Pari-Nirvaana* remains a mystery, except to those who have experienced it. In all probability, Buddha wants to have it that way. Buddha might have felt that his mission in life is not to squander away his time in metaphysical speculation so as to unravel the mysteries of the state of blessed existence after *Pari-Nirvaana*, rather, he must use his time to win people for its realization. For this reason, the Buddha maintains a studied silence and avoids any speculation regarding the final state of the *Arahat*, focusing on the moral dimension with the help of which one can become an *Arahat*.[86] The following quote throws further light on this point:

> The silence of the Buddha regarding an afterlife may have been meant to fulfill a purpose that is very ethical and typically Buddhist in character. Buddhism considers self-assertion in any form to be detrimental to its cause of liberation. Truly liberated persons will be so non-self assertive as to be totally disinterested in their very existence. They will be so indifferent and so detached as not to worry whether their present life is short or long, or whether they will live after death or not. Viewed in that light, the Buddha's silence on an afterlife is a way of underlining the degree of detachment required for a life of true inner peace and serenity.[87]

Since the primary goal of the seeker is *Arahatship*, by moving towards the state of *Nirvaana* and finally by attaining the state of *Pari-Nirvaana*, any form of undue speculative concern about the issue of an afterlife can easily distract him from keeping his goal and walking the path. Therefore, the Buddha, while on earth, points to the goal of *Arahatship*, which one attains in the state of *Nirvaana*, and with clarity outlines the path to achieve this goal. The *Buddha-Dharma*, with its 37 elements, places great emphasis on the path rather than the goal, as the goal is not to be intellectually grasped, but to be experienced existentially by the seeker. The *Hiinayaana* Buddhist path to the realization of *Arahatship* is our concern in the next section.

5.1.2. *HIINAYAANA* PATHS TO THE DIVINE

The ultimate goal of a Buddhist seeker, in the *Hiinayaana* tradition, is to become an *Arahat*, in whom the true divinity dwells. To achieve this goal of *Arahatship*, Buddha proposes the Four Noble Truths. They are the following: the disease of suffering that dominates every realm of existence in the universe; the desire which is its cause; the cessation of suffering, presented as the cure; and the Eightfold Path, the remedy to rise above the *Karma-Samsaara* existence. To quote:

> What, O Monks, is the Noble Truth of the Suffering? Birth is suffering, sickness is suffering, old age is suffering, death is suffering. Pain, grief, sorrow, lamentation, and despair are suffering. Association with what is unpleasant is suffering; dissociation from what is pleasant is suffering. Not to get what one wants is suffering. In short, the five factors of individuality are suffering.
> This, O Monks, is the Truth of Arising of Suffering. It is this thirst or craving (*Tanhaa*) which gives rise to rebirth, which is bound up with passionate delight and which seeks fresh pleasure now here and now there in the form of (1) thirst for sensual pleasure, (2) thirst for existence, and (3) thirst for non-existence.
> This, O Monks, is the Truth of the Cessation of Suffering. It is the utter cessation of that craving (*Tanhaa*), the withdrawal from it, the renouncing of it, the rejection of it, liberation from it, non-attachment to it.
> This, O Monks, is the Truth of the Path, which leads to the cessation of suffering. It is this Noble Eightfold Path, which consists of (1) Right View, (2) Right Resolve, (3) Right Speech, (4) Right Action, (5) Right Livelihood, (6) Right Effort, (7) Right Mindfulness, (8) Right Meditation.[88]

The first three truths of the Four Noble Truths point to the existential situation, that which causes it and its possible cure, while the last of the Four Noble Truths, viz., the Eightfold Path, in fact, proposes the actual remedy. It is the 'Middle Way' between a life of indulgence and harsh austerity, as it emphasizes 'the right', which indeed is the mean between the extremes. It is a path to self-transformation, which ultimately leads one to the final emancipation. The Eightfold Path clearly states that the way one looks at a situation, directs one's intention, speech, action and livelihood. The last three, namely effort, mindfulness and concentration are more technical and point to the emotional state required for the practice of Buddhist meditation. Thus, there are three elements with the help of which a person can bring about self-transformation in himself: wisdom (*Prajnaa*), morality (*Siila*) and meditation (*Samaadhi*). The pursuit of wisdom and the practice of morality remove ignorance and selfish desires respectively. The practice of meditation enables the seeker soar high to the state of *Nirvaana*. In short, the last of the Four Noble Truths, the Eightfold Path, proposes a threefold path, viz., the path of wisdom, the path of morality and the path of meditation, as the means to attain the final goal of *Arahatship*.[89] In the following sections, we analyze the Eightfold Path, in terms of the paths of wisdom, morality and meditation. We also consider the four stages of the path to *Arahatship*.

5.1.2.1. PATH OF WISDOM

For Buddhists 'wisdom' consists in the contemplation of the *Dharmas*, as expressed in the Four Noble Truths and other teachings of the Buddha. Wisdom observes the true meaning of the *Dharmas* and can enlighten one as to their true import. It destroys the darkness of delusion, which prevents the seeker from grasping the 'true being' of the *Dharmas*. Wisdom does not delude a seeker. It is attained by way of concentration, as the latter is the proximate cause of wisdom.[90] The full comprehension of the *Dharma*, with the help of wisdom, is vital, as its non-comprehension or wrong comprehension prevents the seeker from living a moral life and pursuing right meditation, thereby achieving the goal of *Arahatship*. Therefore, the aspirant of *Nirvaana* must follow the path of wisdom, before he attempts the other two paths, viz., morality and meditation. The path of wisdom includes Right Understanding and Right Resolve, the first two precepts of the Eightfold Path. In the next two sections, we describe these two precepts.

5.1.2.1.1. Right Understanding

The precept of Right Understanding (*Sammaa Ditthi*) refers to the proper intellectual grasp of the teachings of the Buddha. When a seeker's view of *Buddha-Dharma* corresponds to what is truly intended by the Buddha, then he is said to have Right Understanding of the *Dharma*. The Right Understanding concretely implies that the seeker of *Nirvaana* comprehends the teachings of the Buddha – the three marks of existence, the doctrine of dependent origination, the doctrine of *Karma* and the Four Noble Truths – in their original meaning, i.e., as the Buddha experiences them at his enlightenment.

5.1.2.1.1.1. Three Marks of Existence

At his enlightenment, the Buddha becomes fully 'awakened' to the truth of existence. In this 'awakening' he becomes aware of the three marks of existence. They are suffering (*Dukkha*), impermanence (*Anicca*) and the self as a fiction (*Anattaa*). The most obvious of these three is the presence of suffering in every form of existence. One condition common to all the inhabitants of the six world-realms is one or the other form of suffering. The gods experience the condition of suffering, in a remote way, as they are compelled to give up their exalted state of existence, when their *Karma* calls them to do. Besides, since they live lengthy lives of ease, comfort and happiness they forget the impermanence of life and lose sight of their ultimate goal of *Nirvaana*, which, in itself, is a form of suffering. Though the life of humans is a mixture of pain and pleasure, there is more pain than pleasure. Human suffering includes all forms of pain: physical pains – like, birth, disease, decay, death –,mental pains – such as, sorrow, lamentation, pain, grief, despair, disharmony, discomfort, irritation, friction – and all that opposes well-being, perfection, wholeness and bliss. It also implies sufferings in the philosophical sense, such as, incompleteness, insufficiency, limitation, dependence, contingency and the like. Besides, the humans can fall into a rebirth in the lower world realms. In short, human existence is full of suffering. The *Asuras* suffer from impulses and lust for power. The ghosts are tormented by endless hunger and thirst. Animals lack clarity of mind. Besides, they are helpless, as they can do nothing to change their situations. The hell- beings suffer torment and all forms of pain. *Dukhha* is the most universal element that pervades every realm of existence.[91]

The second mark of existence is impermanence (*Anicca*). This characteristic of existence expresses itself in the rising, passing, changing, becoming and disappearing of things and events. Buddhists consider the universe as moving on in a cyclic process and subject to unending changes. This mutable nature of the universe is manifested in every level of existence: at the cosmic level, in the creation and destruction of the world-systems; psychologically, in the endless desire for craving and immediate gratification; in the personal level, in the sequence of birth, death and rebirth; and in the level of the human body, a continual flux flowing in and out. We here mention a few. New skin replaces the old. New cells are formed in place of the dead ones. There is a continual change in the structure of the human body, so that when a child turns into an adult, the body of the adult is totally new in comparison with that of the child. Since the change is continuous, slow and steady, we often do not notice the impermanency of the organism. We can perceive it only when there is a total disruption of change that has been taking place in an organism. Thus, impermanency is an all-pervading reality that constitutes the very essence of existence.[92]

The third mark of existence is the fictional quality of the self (*Anattaa*). Unlike the other systems of Indian philosophical and religious traditions, Buddhism does not accept the reality of the constant, unchanging and permanent individual self, behind the psychophysical experiences. According to the Buddhists, when we reflect on an individual's complex of experiences, what we always find, in the last analysis, is a particular sense experience, a particular feeling, a particular idea, a particular wish and the consciousness, of something particular. Each of these is constantly changing. In fact, we do not experience 'the self', that is having a sum of these experiences, as what we experience is nothing other than individual changing experiences. If we abstract all the particular details of consciousness there is nothing left to experience. Without accepting a permanent self behind the complex of experiences, the Buddhists explain the psychophysical experiences in terms of the five aggregates (*Skandhas*) of physical and mental events, viz., form (*Ruupa*), feelings (*Vedanaa*), perceptions (*Samjnaa*), impulses (*Samskaara*) and consciousness (*Vijnaana*). Firstly, the form stands for the material element, i.e., our physical body, our material possessions and the physical world. Secondly, feelings refer to the mental activity that takes place in direct response to the physical stimuli that comes from the material form. We experience them as pleasant, unpleasant or as indifferent. Thirdly, the perception is the recognition and labeling of something, as the result of classifying or sorting out the form as conditioned by feelings. Fourthly, the impulses are volitional forces, such as, the desires, wishes and tendencies that come into play dependent on the perception of something. Finally, the consciousness is the awareness of oneself as having a series of perceptions and thoughts. Whatever a person thinks of anything as appropriate to him, 'the self' must fall within one of these aggregates, as nothing exists over and above these aggregates. We clarify the five *Skandhas* with the help of an illustration. A person says: "I have a toothache". Here 'tooth' is the form; feeling is the 'pain'; the perception consists in recognizing and labeling the pain of the tooth; the impulses are volitional reactions, such as, reaction to pain, fear of losing the tooth and concern over physical well-being; and the act of consciousness is the awareness of all these. The 'self' we usually presume as the subject of the toothache, does not form part of the analysis. The 'I' of the toothache is more imagined than real. The imagined self, in actual fact, may belong to the *Skandha* of consciousness or to the *Skandha* of impulses or volitional reactions, which would amount to a wrong belief in the self. Therefore, only the aggregates are real, the self is fictional.[93]

5.1.2.1.1.2. Doctrine of Dependent Origination

By holding for the *Anattaa* doctrine, the Buddhists deny the existence of a permanent and unchanging self. The issue of personal continuity is raised, both in the present existence and in the existence at rebirth. If personal continuity is not established, moral life, personal responsibility and the doctrine of rebirth cannot be philosophically justified. In attempting to establish personal continuity, the Buddhists propose the doctrine of Dependent Origination (*Pratiitya-samutpaada*). It is middle way between Eternalism (*Sassvata-vaada*) and Annihilationism (*Uccheda-vaada*). Eternalism holds for an unchanging permanent self and finds in it the foundation of every change that takes place in a person. In other words, Eternalism attempts to establish connectedness in terms of an unchanging self. But, Annihilationism says that there is no real connection between a person at one point of time and at another point of time. Thus Annihilationism denies any connection between a person's actions at different occasions.[94]

Taking the middle path, the doctrine of Dependent Origination says that only causal connectedness exists between mental and physical events that take place in the context of a person's life. The causal connectedness between physical and mental events is such that they occur in specific patterns. These patterns have the tendency to repeat themselves, thereby giving a certain amount of stability. As a result, a man remains a man for a long period of time. Thus, when a child becomes an adult, it is not the same substance that has continued over the years, but rather it is the specific clusters of physical and mental events that are linked causally over the years. Therefore, change is not to be understood in terms of a constantly existing primary substantial essence, but in terms of a causal connectedness of secondary qualities. According to the Buddhist tradition, dependent origination takes place when causality operates in terms of 12 links (*Nidaana*) of the chain of dependent series. Ignorance conditions formations; formations condition consciousness; consciousness conditions mind and body; mind and body condition the six senses; the six senses condition sense contact; sense contact conditions feeling; feelings condition craving; craving conditions grasping; grasping conditions becoming; becoming conditions birth; birth conditions old age and death – grief, lamentation, pain, sorrow and despair come into being. Thus, starting from ignorance, through 12 causal links, the whole mass of suffering originates.[95]

5.1.2.1.1.3. Law of Karma

The doctrine of dependent origination seems to have solved the issue of personal continuity in the present life, by establishing causal connectedness between the mental and physical events within the temporal sphere of the same life. But the question of personal continuity still remains in relation to rebirth. There must be something from the previous life that remains constant and is reborn in the new life. These issues require looking into the basis of personal continuity in rebirth and the role of the Law of *Karma* in transferring personal responsibility of a person from one birth to the other.

Buddhists explain the issue of personal continuity, not in terms of a permanent substantial self, but with reference to the causal connectedness of the physical and mental events of a person's life. According to them this causal connectedness of events does not stop at one's death, but emerges into a new group of causally connected events. Thus, death is the breaking up of one set of causal connectednesses, while rebirth is the building up of a new configuration of causal connectedness of events, dependent on the one that has broken up. In the emergence of the new arrangement of causal connectedness at rebirth, the mental events play a greater role than do physical events, as intention – a mental factor – of the person in the previous life determines what he is going to be in his rebirth. The new collection of causal connectedness, though related to the previous, may be of a different kind. Thus, we can speak of a man being reborn as an animal and a god being reborn as a man. Causal connectedness is not only the basis of personal continuity within a particular life, but it is also the basis of personal continuity between different lives. There is no permanently enduring substantial self, neither within a person's lifetime nor in his moving from death to rebirth.[96]

The foundation of personal continuity – by way of causal connectedness – within a particular life and from one life to the other is the Law of *Karma*. It is a natural law similar to the law of gravity. Just as, by the law of gravity, things fall to the earth, so also by the Law of *Karma* everyone's past moral actions determine the present life, and the present moral action determines the future life. According to this law, every person is the sole master of his destiny. By freely and repeatedly choosing certain types of behavior, a person cultivates a habit; habitually acting in that pattern he builds up his character; and through his character his destiny within the present and in the next life is determined. The Buddhists explain this in terms of what they call *Sankaaras*, which are character traits or mental dispositions. When a person makes moral choices (*Cetanaa*) and acts on them, the *Sankaaras* are formed. Over a period of time, they reach a state of maturation (*Vipaaka*) and bear fruit (*Phala*) in the life of the person. This fruit bearing may not be completed in a person's present life. The remaining fruits of *Karma* are accumulated and carried forward to the next life or into a continuous cycle of births and rebirths. It is these Karmic fruits accumulated from the past life that determine a person's family background, social status, physical appearance, character and personality at rebirth. Thus, a person moulds his own future, just as a potter moulds a pot, depending on his intention to do good or evil actions. Actions motivated by greed, hatred and delusion are evil, while actions that emerge from genuine intentions, such as, non-attachment, benevolence and understanding bear good fruit. At the ending of a set of causal connectednesses of events at a person's death and the emergence of a new collection of causal connectednesses of events at his rebirth, the *Sankaaras* that are formed as the result of the actions coming from good or evil intentions of the person, play an important role. It is the *Sankaaras* that implement the directive of the Law of *Karma* at the moment of transition from death to rebirth and guarantee the personal continuity of the person. In other words, the *Sankaaras* serve as the causal link between the set of causal connectednesses of events that break up at the death of the person and the new configuration of the causal connectednesses of events that emerge at rebirth, thereby assuring the personal continuity of the person over different rebirths. In the last analysis, it is then the Law of *Karma* that guarantees the stability and personal continuity of a person.[97]

5.1.2.1.1.4. The Four Noble Truths

All the Buddhist doctrines we have stated – the three marks of existence (*Dukkha*, *Anicca* and *Anatta*), the doctrine of dependent origination and the Law of *Karma* – clearly point to the concrete situation of human existence. The Four Noble Truths is another method the Buddha uses to sum up the malaise of human life. Here he starts with the actual fact of suffering in the First Noble Truth. In the second, he speaks of the motive, the reason and the cause of suffering that prevent the latter from disappearing. It is desire, one of the 12 links of the chain of independent arising, that motivates the continued presence of suffering in human life. The third speaks of the solution to the problem, i.e., the cessation of desire. When a person puts an end to desire, he restores the healthy condition in the here and now. The main concern of the Buddha is to remove all forms of suffering from the lives of the people as they live in the world, rather than making them happy in some future life. In the Fourth Noble Truth, the Buddha declares that there is the way – of wisdom, morality and meditation – with the help of which the cure of suffering can be brought about. In short, the Four Noble Truths sum up the totality of the *Buddha-Dharma*.[98]

The first of the Eightfold Paths, the Right Understanding, calls the seeker of *Nirvaana* to acquire a proper intellectual grasp of all these doctrines and the truth they contain. Having understood the truths, one also needs to reflect upon their concrete applicability in one's everyday life. The Right Understanding gives the seeker a general vision of the *Buddha-Dharma*, and orients him to live it. Thus, the Right Understanding becomes the understanding that guides the seeker in his practical and moral living.

5.1.2.1.2. Right Resolve

Right Resolve (*Sammaa Sankappo*) flows from Right Understanding. It refers to the intention of the seeker. It consists in having the right motive in living out the vision of *Dharma* one gains through Right Understanding. It includes the seeker's inner yearnings, aspirations and wishes in living out the *Dharma*. Acquiring Right Resolve calls for cultivating positive qualities and rejecting negative attitudes. Firstly, the seeker must cultivate a life of renunciation, a life of good will towards others and a life of compassion. Secondly, he must give up sense-desire, ill will towards others and violence that brings harm to others. The living of a life, in which one develops the positive qualities of detachment, good will and compassion and rejects their opposites, implies that one possesses the attitude of strictness towards oneself and the attitude of benevolence towards others. Thus, Right Resolve consists in the seeker having the motive of preferring others to himself, as he embarks on the path of morality.[99]

5.1.2.2. PATH OF MORALITY

The path of wisdom places before the seeker the ideals of the *Dharma*, thereby attempting to remove his ignorance. The path of morality invites the seeker to move towards the ideal by genuine moral living, thereby putting an end to all forms of selfishness. The moral path includes the third, fourth and the fifth limbs of the Eightfold Path, viz., Right Speech, Right Action and Right Livelihood.

5.1.2.2.1. Right Speech

Right Speech (*Sammaa Vaacaa*) consists in being honest in one's conversation with others. It also implies that one speak in a courteous, thoughtful and sensitive way. Right Speech, thus, admonishes one to practice control over one's words, so that no words of disrepute come out of one's mouth. By advocating Right Speech, the Buddha wants his followers to practice four forms of refraining with regard to their conversation with and about others. They are: refraining from false speech, refraining from divisive speech, refraining from hurtful speech and refraining from idle chatter. Firstly, one is asked to refrain from false speech. This requires that a person remain honest in his speech, not tell lies and avoids living a life of falsehood. Secondly, one is expected to refrain from divisive speech, which consists in avoid those words that break genuine fellowship with other persons. It also demands of one not to slander, detract and be calumnious. Thus, the directive to refrain from divisive speech exhorts the seeker of *Nirvaana* to be respectful of others and to use words that would enhance the reputation and good name of others. Thirdly, we are admonished to refrain from hurtful speech. Here the emphasis is not to be harsh in our words, but instead to be gentle in our speech: one should not cause any pain to others through one's words. Finally, we are asked to refrain from idle chatter. This directive expects the seeker not to waste his time in loose, meaningless and frivolous talk. He must say nothing which is not beneficial to the one to whom it is said. The Buddha, thus, wants his followers to live by the norm of Right Speech, because it has the power to transform individuals and society. A kind, gentle and courteous word does a world of good to the hearer, as it builds him up. But a harsh, hurtful and slanderous word destroys a person, as it causes suffering. For this reason, the Buddha declares the Right Speech as the norm of life.[100]

5.1.2.2.2. Right Action

Right Action (*Sammaa Kammanto*), the fourth limb of the Eightfold Path, constitutes the core of Buddhist religion and practice, as moral action is one of the central elements of Buddhism. Right Action informs a seeker about those moral practices he is supposed to do. At the same time, it directs him to refrain from doing what is not proper. The scope of Right Action includes practically the whole range of a devout Buddhist's moral life, whether he is a layperson or an ascetic. In our analysis, we briefly consider what Right Action means to a layperson, and what it means for a monk, who has renounced the world. We attempt to expose the moral path of a layman living as a householder in the world and the moral path of the monk living as an ascetic.

5.1.2.2.2.1. Moral Path of a Householder

A Buddhist householder's life is very different from that of the monk. Unlike the monk, the householder has not renounced the world. He lives and works in the world. So Buddhism proposes a moral path that is different from that of the monk. The layperson is expected to live a life based on the *Panca Siila*, the five rules of morality. The *Panca Siila* is a name given to recitation, which the *Theravaadins* use for many purposes. It is recited individually, when a person is in a Buddhist temple. It is collectively recited before a public Buddhist gathering or meeting. It begins with thrice repeated praise of the Buddha. Then comes the refuge formula, which also is repeated thrice. Finally, we have the statement of the five rules of moral life, which a householder is expected to follow. When this formula is recited either alone or as a group, it does not amount to taking an oath to God or to some other supernatural being, but rather it is only a solemn undertaking one takes upon oneself. The aim of this recitation is to train oneself in diminishing one's attachment to the error specified.[101] The recitation is as follows:

> ... Praise to the Blessed One, the Perfect One, the fully Self-Enlightened One!
> ... I go to Buddha for Refuge
> ... I go to Doctrine for Refuge
> ... I go to Order for Refuge
> ... Again I go to Buddha for Refuge
> ... Again I go to Doctrine for Refuge
> ... Again I go to Order for Refuge
> ... A third time I go to Buddha for Refuge
> ... A third time I go to Doctrine for Refuge
> ... A third time I go to Order for Refuge
> ... I undertake the rule of training to refrain from injury to living things.
> ... I undertake the rule of training to refrain from taking that, which is not given.
> ... I undertake the rule of training to refrain from sexual immorality.
> ... I undertake the rule of training to refrain from falsehood.
> ... I undertake the rule of training to refrain from liquors, which engender slothfulness.[102]

The *Panca Siila* recitation clearly outlines the spirituality a layperson is expected to follow in the Buddhist scheme of life. Firstly, a devout lay Buddhist is expected to honor the Lord Buddha. Secondly, it is his duty to take refuge in the Buddha, *Buddha-Dharma* and the *Sangha*. Thirdly, he must follow wholeheartedly the five duties of moral life: refraining from destroying life (*Praanaatipaata*), refraining from taking anything not given (*Adinnaadaana*), refraining from unchaste behavior (*Abrahmacariyaa*), refraining from falsehood (*Mrishaa-vaada*) and refraining from drinking strong drinks (*Suraa*). The first moral principle expects a layperson to identify with all forms of existence and to do nothing that hurts them. Thus, *Ahimsa* not only means the negative element of 'not injuring', but also the positive aspect of showing compassion towards all forms of existence, especially human beings. The second precept, i.e., not taking what is not given, directs a householder to give up all forms of theft. It also encourages a Buddhist layperson to use the wealth he has for the good of his fellow beings. The third calls for practicing self-discipline, so as to control the sexual instinct. It also advises a layperson to regulate his attitude towards women in such a way that she is not considered as an object of pleasure and self-gratification. The fourth precept instructs one to give up falsehood, thereby to live an honest life. Even minor forms of lying, such as deliberate inaccuracy and exaggeration must be avoided. The fifth precept asks one to avoid taking alcoholic drinks and drugs, so as to master laziness and slothfulness. When a householder performs Right Action in living out these five commandments, he acquires merit. Such merit frees him from the fruits of the past *Karma*.[103]

5.1.2.2.2.2. Moral Path of a Monk

The life of the monk is very different from that of the layperson, for unlike the householder, the monk renounces the world. Besides following the rules of life of the layperson, the monk is expected to do much more. His life as a monk begins with the initiation. The whole process of initiating a layperson to the life of a full-fledged monk involves a few stages and takes a number of years. At the first stage of initiation, a rite called *Pravrajyaa*, which means 'going forth from home'. It is a rite by which a layperson of 15 years is accepted into the first degree of monkhood, after obtaining due permission from his parents. He, then, is called a 'novice' (*Sraamanera*). Other names used to refer to him, at this stage, are 'new monk' and 'junior monk'. Any senior monk can admit a candidate as a novice. There is no need for the candidate to appear before the conclave of the monks, nor does the *Sangha*, as a body, take part in the ceremony. The rite of admission is very simple. The novice shaves off his hair, puts on the yellow robe (*tri-ciivara*) and adjusts the upper robe in such a way that the right shoulder remains uncovered. Having done this, he kneels before a senior monk and repeats thrice the three-refuge formula. In the case of *Brahaaman* who enters as the novice, he gives up the *brahmacaarii's* sacred cord (*Upaviita*) after repeating the three-refuge formula. Thus he becomes a novice. Immediately he is placed under a religious teacher (*Upaadhyaaya*), who is usually senior monk. He instructs the novice on the Ten Precepts (*Dasa-siila*), which are ten prohibitions requiring the practice of ten abstinences. They are the following: refraining from destroying life (*Praanaatipaata*); refraining from taking anything not given (*Adinnaadaana*); refraining from unchastity (*Abrahmacariyaa*); refraining from speaking falsely (*Mrishaa-vaada*); refraining from drinking strong drinks (*Suraa*); refraining from eating at forbidden times (*Vikaala-bhojana*); refraining from dancing, singing, music and worldly spectacles (*Visuuka*); refraining from the use of garlands, scents, ointments and ornaments; and refraining from the use of a high or broad beds; and refraining from receiving gold or silver. He continues as a novice for five years.[104]

After five years of life and learning as a novice, one is qualified for admission to full monkhood (*Upasampadaa*). It is a formal religious ceremony. A conclave of ten monks is required to conduct this ceremony. Before the actual ceremony begins, the novice is instructed about the rite and is given a begging bowl and the yellow monk clothes. The teacher of the novice presents him before the conclave of monks and informs them that the novice is ready to be admitted to full monkhood. Now, the novice comes forward, adjusts his upper garment so as to cover the left shoulder, bows before the feet of the assembled monks and sits on the ground before the monks. He then rises joins his hands and asks three times that he be admitted to the order of full monkhood, saying, 'I entreat the *Sangha* for full monkhood. Have compassion on me and uproot me from the world'. After the novice has made his request, the monks question him as to his fitness to become a monk. If the answers are satisfactory, the novice is admitted to become a monk. No prayer is said after the rite of admission. But he is told that he must depend on four Resources (*Nissaya*) for his life: he must live only on broken morsels; he must wear clothes taken from dust heaps; the foot of the trees will be his abode; and he must use only decomposed urine as medicine. Besides, the new monk is expected to live four chief Prohibitions: unchastity and sexual acts of any kind; taking anything not given, even a blade of grass; killing any living thing, even an ant, a worm or a plant; and falsely claiming the extraordinary powers of a perfect saint (*Uttarimanussadhamma*). Acceptance of the monkhood follows a five-year period of instruction in the entire doctrine and discipline under a well-qualified teacher, who has been a monk for a minimum period of ten years. Once these instructions end, he begins his life as a full-fledged monk.[105]

The daily life of a young Buddhist monk begins in the early morning with meditation and recitation of portions of the law. It is followed by lessons and discussions on doctrine and confessions of failures. Then he must beg for food and have the one noonday meal. He, then, takes time to rest, meditate and recite the law, while the senior monks preach to the laypeople. Sometime during the day is spent on duties in the monastery, offering flowers at sacred shrines and other such activities.[106]

The most important activity in the life of the monk in the monastery is the recitation of the law, especially those portions of the Law that deal with general confession of failures within the *Sangha*. This collection of the law is known as *Paatimokkha*. Usually the monks confess their failures in the community on the fast days (*Uposatha*). There are two fast days every month, viz., the full moon day and the new moon day. Before the actual confession of failures, the presiding monk begins the recitation of the general confessional laws, which the *Paatimokkha* collection contains, for all the monks to hear. The monks then make individual confessions to each other. Sometimes there is also the practice of public confession to the community. Whether the confession is made in public or privately to the monks, due penances are given as prescribed in the *Paatimokkha* section of the law. One is released from the effects of the sins due to the efficacy of the penances rather than due to any supernatural powers.[107]

The monk is expected to follow a great number of rules in order that his behavior corresponds to the Right Action of the Eightfold Path. The *Paatimokkha* section of the law, which is the most significant of the Buddhist monastic law, is categorized into eight sections. Firstly, there are the Four *Paaraajika* Rules, the violation of which involves permanent expulsion from the *Sangha*. Secondly, there are the Thirteen *Sanghaadisesa* Rules. These offences involve suspension from the *Sangha* and performance of a period of penances after which the monk is reinstated as the full-fledged member of the *Sangha*. Thirdly, there are the Two *Aniyata* Rules, which gives the provision for charging a monk with a violation under one or the other existing rules of the *Sangha*. Fourthly, there are 30 *Nissaggiya Paacittiya* Rules. These are offences involving expiation on the part of the monk. Besides, they involve the forfeiture of things. Fifthly, there are 92 *Paacittiya* Rules. This set of rules contains regulations that aim at the harmonious relationship among the monks and for the avoidance of luxury in clothing, eating and other practices that distracts the monk from striving towards *Nirvaana*. Sixthly, there are the Four *Paatidesaniya* Rules. These are rules, the violation of which calls for confession of failures. Seventhly, there are the 75 *Sekhiya* Rules, which are rules of training for the monks. Eighthly, there are the Seven *Adhikarana-Samatha* Rules. These rules deal with processing the cases that have come about in following the seven sets of previously said rules. Other than these eight sets of rules, there are also some other rules and practices the monk has to follow. Some of these are intended for the normal daily life of the monk and the organization of the *Sangha*. Some of these rules are added to the original collection due to the changing circumstances. There is also a set of 13 ascetical practices, known as the *Dhutangas*. They are: wearing clothes taken from the dust heap; wearing only three robes; getting food only by begging; begging from house to house; eating food only at one place; eating from one vessel only; refusing food offered after the proper time; living in the forest; living at the foot of a tree; living in the open air; living in a cemetery; taking any seat that is offered; sleeping in a sitting posture.[108]

When a layperson lives by the directives of the *Panca Siila*, his moral actions correspond to the Right Action. Similarly, when a monk's moral actions are strictly guided by the rules and regulations pertaining to his state of life as the monk, he performs the Right Action. Both the monk and the householder live the Right Action as their respective state of life demands, they Act Rightly.

5.1.2.2.3. Right Livelihood

Right Livelihood (*Sammaa Aajiivo*), the fifth limb of the Eightfold Path, is already implied in Right Action. It consists in following a trade or occupation that does not go against the principle of Right Action. Right Livelihood, thus, means that one does not earn one's living by engaging in works that can bring harm to the lives of others. Buddhism prohibits the performance of works such as production and sale of arms and lethal weapons, the slaughter of animals and human beings, the production of intoxicating drinks and their sale, and the production and sale of poisons, as their performance entails a disservice to living beings, especially to humans. Therefore, we cannot consider such livelihood as Right Livelihood. Buddha's teaching on Right Livelihood hinges on the principle that 'one should not earn without deserving'. Even though one works hard and earns one's living, the money one earns is really deserved only if the work is beneficial to others in society. Thus, any form of earning one's livelihood that is not beneficial to others and does not bring good to the society does not deserve. Thus, Buddha's teaching on Right Livelihood invites everyone to examine the means of livelihood in the light of the principle: 'No earning without deserving'.[109]

5.1.2.3. PATH OF MEDITATION

The path of wisdom enlightens the mind of the seeker about the *Buddha-Dharma*. The path of morality helps the aspirant to purify the inclinations of the senses, body and the mind, thereby bringing about a sense of self-discipline. Once the aspirant becomes ingrained in the Buddhist wisdom by way of Right Understanding and Right Resolve, and acquires true self-discipline by way of Right Speech, Right Action and Right Livelihood his heart, mind and body are free and ready to pursue the higher path of meditation, which, in the final analysis, helps the seeker to cross over the sea of *Samsaara* and arrive at the shore of *Nrivaana*. In the following section, we elaborate the path of meditation, by clarifying the last three limbs of the Eightfold Path, viz., Right Effort, Right Mindfulness and Right Concentration.

5.1.2.3.1. Right Effort

Right Effort (*Sammaa Vaayaamo*) is an important step between the levels of spiritual growth the seeker has achieved so far, by using the path of wisdom and the path of morality, and the heights he has yet to climb. It consists in gaining control of one's thoughts and building positive states of mind. Thus, Right Effort involves the right use of one's energies, so that one is able to secure the maximum results from of the efforts put in. Hence, Right Effort opens the seeker to the inner psychic realm and invites him to eliminate all psychic complexes and mental inhibitions. In so doing, it elevates the mind of the seeker to higher realms of spiritual experience. Right Effort helps the individual to do this in four ways. Firstly, it helps the individual to prevent evil thoughts from entering the mind, through the control of the senses. Three ways are suggested to control evil thoughts from entering the mind. If a particular object causes evil desires, the seeker must bring before his mind another object that might remove the evil thought and bring a good one. If the evil thought persists, visualizing the painful consequences that stem from that evil thought can prevent it from entering the mind. If that effort also does not help preventing the evil thought from entering the mind, the seeker is advised to change his or her environment. Secondly, if all efforts to prevent evil thoughts fail, Right Effort guides the seeker to remove the evil thoughts that have entered the mind. Thirdly, besides helping to prevent and remove evil thoughts, it directs the seeker to develop good and wholesome thoughts.

Finally, having helped develop good thoughts, the Right Effort leads the seeker to retain it as permanently as possible.[110]

The practice of Right Effort helps the seeker to come in touch with 'the bases of wonder-working psychic powers' (*Iddhipaada*) viz., desire, energy, thought and investigation. In actualizing these powers, struggle accompanies concentration. Besides, Right Effort assists the seeker to cultivate the five faculties (*Panca Indriyaani*), faith (*Sasshindriyam*), energy (*Viriyindriya*), mindfulness (*Satindriya*), concentration (*Samaadhi Indriya*) and insight (*Panna Indriya*), and the five forces (*Panca Balaani*) associated with them. Right Effort helps the seeker to understand the seven factors of enlightenment, viz., mindfulness (*Sati*), investigation of Buddha's teachings (*Dhammavicaya*), energy (*Viriya*), joy (*Piiti*), serenity (*Passddhi*), concentration (*Samaadhi*) and equanimity (*Upekkha*). Finally, the Right Effort supports the seeker in living the Eightfold Path in all sincerity. In this manner, Right Effort plays a very important role as the foundation for the various stages of spiritual progress sought in the path of meditation.[111]

5.1.2.3.2. Right Mindfulness

Right Mindfulness (*Sammaa Sati*), the seventh step of the Eightfold Path, consists in cultivating constant awareness. Buddha considers Right Mindfulness as the way to purify oneself, to overcome sorrow and grief, to remove suffering and misery, and to win *Nirvaana*. This is because Right Mindfulness is like a doorkeeper for the mind. Just as a doorkeeper stands at the door and does not allow any undesirable person to enter the house, in the same way, the presence of Right Mindfulness at the mind's door prevents the appearance of any immoral states of the mind. There are Four Fields of Mindfulness: Mindfulness of the Body (*Kaaya-satipatthaana*), Mindfulness of Feelings (*Vedanaa-satipatthaana*), Mindfulness of Consciousness (*Cittasatipatthaana*) and the Mindfulness of Phenomena (*Dhammaa-satipattaana*). The first or Mindfulness of the Body involves analyzing, observing and contemplating the body, focusing on breathing, physical movements, the impurities of the body and the personality of man, which is composed of *Naama* and *Ruupa*, i.e., the mind and the body. The second is the Mindfulness of Feeling, which consists in contemplating three types of feelings, viz., the pleasant feeling (*Sukha-Vedanaa*) in the physical and mental level, the unpleasant feeling (*Dukhaa-Vedanaa*) in the physical and the mental level; and the indifferent feeling (*Upekkhaa-Vedanaa*) which is a neutral mental feeling. The third is the Mindfulness of the Consciousness. This consists in contemplating on the fickle, restless and unsteady nature of the mind, and the qualities like greed (*Lobha*), hatred (*Dosa*) and delusion (*Moha*) that are found in the mind, with the view of destroying them. It could also involve meditating on the qualities opposed to the above-mentioned evils, like sacrifice (*Alobha*), friendliness (*Adosa*) and right understanding (*Amoha*), for the purpose of cultivating them. The fourth is the Mindfulness of Phenomena. In it the seeker contemplates various teachings of the Buddha, such as, the five hindrances

(*Pancanivaranaani*), the five aggregates (*Pancakkhandhaa*), the seven enlightenment factors (*Satta-bojjhangaa*), the 12 bases (*Dvaadasaayataani*) and the four noble truths (*Cattaraariyasaccaani*).[112] Thus, the practice of the various types of Right Mindfulness prepares the seeker to enter into the final step of the Eightfold Path, viz., Right Meditation.

5.1.2.3.3. Right Meditation

Right Meditation (*Sammaa Samaadhi*), the last step of the Eightfold path, consists in developing deeper levels of mental calm with the help of various techniques, thereby acquiring concentration of mind, integration of the seeker's personality and movement towards the Buddhist goal of human existence, i.e., the *Arahataship*. Right meditation, therefore, takes the seeker to the threshold of *Nirvaana*. Buddhist texts use two terms to refer to the reality of meditation, viz., "*Bhaavanaa*" and "*Yoga*". "*Bhaavanaa*", the older term, literally means 'bringing into being', 'making become' or 'cultivation'. Meditation, thus, is a basic Buddhist strategy for making oneself what one wishes to be. It stands for the mental disciplines that aim at developing and maintaining mental states that are helpful to the realization of the Buddhist ideal. The second term "*Yoga*", which means 'work' or 'effort', refers specifically to spiritual works and techniques. The Buddhist *Bhaavanaa* or *Yoga* involves contemplative techniques, which a person performs when he sits in a cross-legged posture.[113]

Buddhists hold the view that the human mind, by its very nature, is clear and pure, but it has become stained due to the activity of various defilements (*Klesas*). Some of these defilements are the five hindrances (*Niivarana*), viz., sensual desire, ill-will, fatigue and sleepiness, excitement and depression, and doubt. These hindrances mar the true beauty of the human mind. They also prevent the mind from understanding the nature of the mind and the manner in which these defilements affected the whole thought-process of the seeker. The purpose of Buddhist meditation, therefore, is twofold: firstly, to help the seeker to clear the mind off these defilements and to achieve its pristine clarity and beauty; secondly to help the seeker to have a right grasp of the nature of the mind and the manner in which they have been defiled due to the hindrances. To achieve these twofold purposes, the Buddhist tradition speaks of two types of meditation, viz., the calm meditation (*Samatha Bhaavanaa*) and the insight meditation (*Vipassanaa Bhaavanaa*). While the former helps the seeker to cultivate deep states of concentration, the latter attempts to furnish the seeker with deep insights into the wisdom of Buddhist religious beliefs. There are differences of opinion about the earliest Buddhist tradition as regards the particular form of meditation to be used to attain the state of *Nirvaana*. But the general understanding among Buddhist scholars today is that the calm meditation and the insight meditation are two aspects of the meditative path that leads to *Nirvaana*. One helps the seeker to achieve inner calmness of the mind, while the other reflects on the *Buddha-*

Dharma and provides right insights into the wisdom contained in it.[114] In the next two sections we decribed these two forms of Buddhist meditations.

5.1.2.3.3.1. Calm Meditation

Calm meditation (*Samatha Bhaavana*) aims at developing tranquility of the mind. Since body and mind are interrelated, the seeker needs to acquire calmness of the body before he can achieve an unperturbed state of mind. The stilling of the body is brought about by the use of certain postures (*Aasanas*) conducive to meditation. The traditional posture for meditation is sitting cross-legged, with the back straight, head slightly inclined and the hands resting in the lap. This posture facilitates deep and relaxed breathing, thereby bringing about genuine relaxation of the body.[115]

Once the body is silenced by the use of a comfortable posture, the next stage of calm meditation, viz., the quieting the mind, begins. The first thing to do to calm down the mind is to choose a suitable object of meditation. Later authors propose 40 subjects that can be used as the objects of meditation. They are: the ten devices (*Kasinas*), namely, earth, water, fire, air, blue, yellow, red, white, light and limited space; the ten uglinesses (*Asubha*), viz., the bloated, the livid, the festering, the cut-up, the gnawed, the scattered, the hacked and scattered, the bleeding, the worm-infested and the skeleton; the two subjects related to ugliness, i.e., repulsiveness of food and determining the four elements; the ten recollections (*Anusmrti*), namely, of the Buddha, of the *Dharma*, of the *Sangha*, of good conduct, of generosity, of the gods, mindfulness of death, mindfulness of the body, mindfulness of breathing and of peace; the four *Brahma-Vihaaras*, that is, loving kindness, compassion, sympathetic joy and equanimity; and four formless meditations (*Anruupa-Dhyaana*), viz., boundless space, boundless consciousness, nothingness and neither perception nor non-perception. Any of the topics can serve as the object of meditation. It must be chosen depending on the concrete situation, state of mind and the level of meditation one has arrived at. Having chosen the object of meditation, one needs to develop in the mind the capacity to rest undisturbed on the object of meditation. It is a very difficult task, as the mind constantly comes up with various forms of distractions. But by constant practice of concentration on the mental image of the object chosen, one can arrive at the tranquil state, where the awareness of the subject and the object ceases to exist, leading to a state of quiet, stillness and tranquility. The higher levels of concentration and constant presence of inner silence characterize this state. Anxieties, uncertainties, distractions and fears lose their grip on the mind of the seeker. He is able to be totally recollected and yet active in his everyday living.[116]

As the seeker grows in calm meditation, he rises through eight ascending stages of trance, each of which brings a different degree of stillness in his mind. Buddhists refer to it as *Jhaanas* in the Paali language, an equivalent to the Sanskrit term "*Dhyaana*". These eight stages of *Jhaanas* fall into two categories, viz., *Jhaanas* pertaining to the Sphere of Pure Form (*Ruupaava-*

cara Cakra-vaala) and *Jhaanas* relating to the Sphere of Formlessness (*Aruupapvacara Cakra-vaala*). The first four *Jhaanas* correspond to the four levels of the 16 heavens of the Sphere of Pure Form, viz., the heavens of gods having the *Brahmaa* form, the heavens of gods whose nature is light, the heavens of gods whose nature is purity and the heavens of gods who have risen to the level of the highest thought. The last four *Jhaanas* go with the four heavens of the Sphere of Formlessness, i.e., the heaven of gods capable of grasping Infinite Space, the heaven of gods capable of understanding Infinite Consciousness, the heaven of the gods who can comprehend Absolute Non-existence and the heaven of gods who are able to perceive the state of neither Perception nor Non-perception. Thus, we find that each of the cosmological regions of the heavenly world corresponds to one state of *Jhaana*. It means that the mental condition of the seeker in each of these stages of *Jhaanas* is similar to that of the gods of the parallel heavenly region.[117] We briefly describe here each of the *Jhaana* stages.

The first *Jhanna* is the lowest. It consists in fixing the mind on some object and exercising the thinking faculties of the seeker. At this stage, the mind of the seeker remains in the level of discursive thought. Rational thinking plays an important role in understanding reality, intuitive grasping of reality is lacking. But one experiences detachment, rapture, serenity and joy. In the second *Jhaana*, concentration replaces discursive thinking. The mind of the seeker is so concentrated on itself that the faculties of thinking stop functioning, resulting in experiences of rapture and joy. The third *Jhaana* consists in the continuance of the state of concentration and the lying-low of the faculties of thinking. Equanimity replaces rapture and joy. As the result, the seeker is calm and balanced. The fourth *Jhnaana* consists in the deepening of concentration. The exercise of thought has come to a complete standstill. Similarly, the consciousness of joy and rapture ceases to exist. The state of equal-mindedness continues to be present in the seeker. He also experiences a state that is beyond pain and pleasure. The seeker is freed from fetters. His mental state becomes increasingly subtle and sublime, giving way to a state called 'one-pointedness' (*Ekaggataa*). In it, the mind of the seeker is totally engrossed in the object of meditation, paving the way for absorption. When the aspirant reaches the fourth state of *Jhaana*, he experiences a number of miraculous powers. They includes: clairvoyance, which is the ability to see events occurring in far off places; clairaudience, that is the capacity to hear distant sounds; retro-cognition, i.e., to recall events and happenings of previous lives; telepathy, which is the ability to know the thoughts of others; and bi-location, i.e., the ability to be present in two places at the same time by duplicating bodies. One also may experience powers, such as the ability to fly through the air and to walk on the water.[118]

When an aspirant passes through the fourth *Jhaana*, he moves from the Sphere of Pure Form to the Sphere of Formlessness. To this sphere belong the last four stages of *Jhaana*. In the fifth, sixth, seventh and the eighth stages of *Jhaana*, the seeker becomes capable of comprehending Infinite Space, Infinite Consciousness, Nothingness, and 'neither Perception nor Non-perception, respectively. During these higher stages of *Jhaana*, many of the bodily functions become flaccid, including the suspension of breathing for a long period of time. The body and the mind are totally relaxed. A number of unusual sensations – such as, perceptions of light, feeling of floating and lightness of limbs – are experienced. The natural purity of mind is manifested. At these higher states of *Jhaana*, the mind is compared to purified gold that is flexible and moldable. The seeker having access to these levels of *Jhaana* can mold personality in the way he wishes. When he passes over the eighth stage, he attains the state of total cessation in which he touches *Nirvaana* with the body and becomes the Enlightened.[119]

5.1.2.3.3.2. Insight Meditation

Insight meditation (*Vipassanaaa Bhaavanaa*) is different from calm meditation. Unlike calm meditation – which aims at a state of peace, tranquility and stillness of the mind – the goal of insight meditation is to generate penetrating and critical insight (*Pannaa*), so that the seeker is able to understand the true import of the teachings of the Buddha. Insight meditation intends to understand the three aspects of the nature of things, viz., the impermanence and instability of reality (*Anicca*), the imperfect and painful nature of existence (*Dukkha*) and the non-reality of the self (*Anattaa*). When a seeker is critical and gains full insight into the import of these truths, he experiences freedom from these states, which is *Nirvaana*. Thus, insight meditation attempts to arrive at *Nirvaana* by way of critical reflection on the teachings of the Buddha. The method of insight meditation consists in bringing the critical faculties of the mind into full play, thereby entering into a detailed analysis of the seeker's own experience of his existence. At the initial stage, insight meditation uses the facilities of calm meditation to arrive at the concentration of the mind. When the concentration of the mind is achieved, instead of continuing in the calm state, the critical faculties of the mind are pressed into service for the attainment of true Buddhist wisdom. Thus, a seeker cannot enter into the insight meditation without arriving at the early stages of calm meditation.[120]

In the insight meditation, the seeker critically analyzes his experience of his own existence by dividing them into four categories: the physical sensations of the body, the feelings, the moods and the thoughts. Analysis of the physical sensations of the body may, for instance, begin with the awareness of breathing and the manner in which it affects the rest of the body. The aspirant becomes aware of every change that takes place in the body, such as, pain, pangs, itches, the impulse to move and to scratch. But, while becoming aware of the sensations, he must not react to any of them. He merely becomes aware of them and lets them pass. In other words, he learns to observe them without becoming involved with them. In doing so the seeker becomes aware of the passing nature of these sensations. Besides, after a period of practice, he acquires a freedom to respond to them in the way he wishes, as the pattern of stimulus-response, which underlies his usual behavior, breaks down.

Similarly, the hold of habitual behavioral patterns on the seeker weakens, and he acquires a sense of freedom to act. In the same manner, every part of the body and the sensations associated with them are opened up and analyzed. The seeker realizes that the body is nothing else but a collection of various elements and nothing more. Becoming aware of every sensation of the body and letting them pass without getting involved gives the seeker a freedom and control over the sensation. Thus, the insight meditation liberates the seeker both intellectually and experientially from the clutches of the body.[121]

When the seeker has gone over the whole of his body and its sensations, he moves to focus his attention on his feelings, whether they are pleasant, unpleasant or indifferent. In the same way, attention is paid to current moods and then to thoughts. While analyzing passing feelings, moods and thoughts, the seeker must see that he does not get lost in the fantasies and imaginations that may arise in the realm of the mind and appear in the body as sensations and feelings. He needs to observe them in a detached manner and allow them to move on. Such insightful analysis of the sensations of the body, feelings, moods and thoughts makes the seeker aware of the passing nature of every reality in the world, including his self. He realizes that there is no hidden self as he is nothing other than bodily sensations, feelings, moods and acts of consciousness. This insight regarding his true nature weakens his desires and finally destroys them completely, thereby setting off the process of Enlightenment. Genuine freedom of the body, feelings, moods and thoughts emerge within the seeker. His selfish and ego-centered emotional horizon vanishes; cravings and self-gratifications cease, other persons begin to move into the realm of his existence, and his selfishness gives way to altruism. Thus, there emerges in the seeker, a genuine sense of contentment, peace and lasting freedom. In this manner, right insight into the nature of existence leads the seeker to *Nirvaana*.[122]

5.1.2.3.3.3. Relationship between Calm and Insight Meditation

We have seen briefly the nature and the practice of calm and insight meditations. Here we attempt to analyze the nature of the relationship between these two forms of Buddhist meditations. In the practice of calm meditation, the seeker gives up the gross dimension of reality and moves towards the subtle, with the help of the eight stages of *Jhaana*. In other words, calm meditation takes the seeker from the gross bodily level to the highest level of the mind: in the process it attempts to control his attachment to the lower levels that are crossed over. Thus, the main thrust of calm meditation is acquiring higher stages of existence by the control of the lower levels. Since the focus is on attaining a state of calm, not on having right insight into the truth, there is a danger in calm meditation that one may get lost in the extra-ordinary powers that one may acquire as the result of calm meditation. Buddha, though possessing many of these Yogic powers, does not give much importance them, as too much stress on achieving them can attach the seeker to them, forgetting the goal of *Nirvaana*. Insight meditation, on the other hand, helps the seeker to see his experience of reality as inherently limited due to its characteristics of impermanence, suffering and the fictional nature of the self, by bringing into play the critical faculty of the mind through reflexive analysis. In doing so it helps the seeker have the right insight into his experience of reality, thereby leading him across and to the limitations and attainient of *Nirvaana*.[123]

There are differences of opinion among the scholars as to which of these forms of meditation are superior. Without entering into this controversy, we can say that the Buddha makes use of both calm and insight meditations and teaches his disciples to do so. Hence, it is clear that they can serve as aids to the attainment of *Nirvaana*. Though theoretically we may make the distinction between the calm and insight meditations, it seems that they are two aspects of the one meditative process, which leads one to the threshold of *Arahatship*, as the two are interdependent: Calm meditation forms the basis of insight meditation. If the mind is not calm and recollected, no reflection of the truth of existence is possible. Therefore, arriving at the initial stages of calm meditation paves the way for starting insight meditation. The higher the stage of calm meditation one has achieved, the greater the depth of insight one acquires thorough insight meditation. Similarly, insight meditation also makes calm meditation more fruitful for it points the one who has attained a higher level of *Jhaana* to the impermanence of that state, however great it may be. This helps him not to get lost in his achievements, but to strive for *Arahatship*. In the actual practice of meditation, these two techniques of calming and insight are often used one after the other within the same session of meditation. For instance, the technique of calming may be used first to effect concentration of the mind, and then the technique of insight may be applied to probe and analyze the truths of existence. A seeker may use both of these techniques a few times, one after the other, in a prolonged meditation session. These two forms of meditations are interrelated and interdependent. One, who uses these two forms complementarily, will attain the state of *Nirvaana* quickly and easily.[124]

5.1.2.4. STAGES OF THE PATH TO ARAHATSHIP

We have been looking into the *Hiinayaana* path to the Divine, by analyzing the Four Noble Truths, especially the Eightfold Path, in terms of the paths of wisdom, morality and meditation. The long journey towards *Nirvaana*, walked with the help of wisdom, morality and meditation, takes place in four stages, in which the ten fetters –delusion of the self (*Sakkaayaditthi*), doubt about the truth of the teachings of the Buddha (*Vicikiccaa*), belief in the efficacy of rites and ceremonies (*Siilabbata Paaramaasa*), sensuality or physical desire (*Kaama*), hatred or resentment (*Patigha*), desire for life in the world of matter (*Ruuparaaga*), desire for life in the spiritual worlds (*Aruuparaaga*), pride (*Maano*), self-righteousness (*Uddhacca*), and ignorance (*Avijjaa*) – are broken. The four stages of the path are the following: the stage of entering the stream (*Sotaapanna*), the stage of once returning

(*Sakadaagaamii*), the stage of no returning (*Anaagaamii*) and the stage of the Arahat (*Arahattam*).[125] We, now, consider each of these in this section.

5.1.2.4.1. Stage of Entering the Stream

The first stage of the path is that of entering the stream. Here the seeker is converted by an inner awakening. He is the beginner who has just entered the stream that flows towards *Nirvaana*. This stage involves hearing the teachings of the Buddha, enlightened reflection on the truth of the teachings and the practice of virtue. As the seeker walks through this stage, three fetters are removed from his life. They are: the delusion of the self, doubt regarding the truth of the teachings of the Buddha, and belief in the efficacy of rites and ceremonies. The first that is freed is the delusion of the self. It consists in the false belief that the individual self is real and self-existent. This false belief leads to egoism, which is the beginning of every sin. The second fetter that is removed is the seeker's doubt regarding the truths of the teaching of the Buddha. The doubt that is removed regards the end toward which the teaching of the Buddha is leading, i.e., *Nirvaana*. The third fetter that is wiped out at this stage is belief in the efficacy of rites and ceremonies. It consists in believing that the rites and the ceremonies have inner efficacy and validity, and that they help the devotee. The person who has entered this stage of the path is reborn either as a god or as a man, in his next birth, but not in a stage of existence below the world of humans. The significant characteristic of the seeker at this stage is perseverance.[126]

5.1.2.4.2. Stage of Once Returning

When the stage of those who have entered the stream is lived through, the seeker moves to the second stage, viz., the state of once returning. Those who enter this stage are reborn on this earth only once, after which they attain *Nirvaana*. At this stage the aspirant begins his fight against two fetters, viz., sensuality and hatred towards all forms of life. As he struggles through these two fetters he moves towards the third stage.[127]

5.1.2.4.3. Stage of No Returning

Those who have lived through the stage of once returning are reborn in the stage of no returning. In this stage, the two fetters, the struggle against which has begun in the previous stage, viz., sensuality and hatred towards all forms of life, are overcome. As a result, in the third stage, the seeker is free from all forms of animosities, viz., all feelings of anger, resentment, envy, jealousy, hatred and the like. It, in turn, removes the sense of isolation from all living beings, and brings in the seeker a desire to be united with all forms of life, especially humans. He is able to approach his neighbor with understanding, concern and respect. When lust and hatred are changed into higher forms of energy – such as, love, concern, respect, thoughtfulness of others and sympathy – and every mark of ill-will towards others is removed, the seeker moves into the final stage of the path.[128]

5.1.2.4.4. Stage of the Arahat

As the seeker moves into the final stage of the path, viz., that of *Arahatship*, he overcomes the remaining five fetters. The first fetter is to be overcome is the desire for separate life in the world of forms (*Ruupa-loka*), i.e., in the world of our everyday existence and in the world of the gods. When this longing is conquered, the seeker moves to remove the next fetter, the desire for separate existence in the formless world (*Aruupa-loka*). In the formless world, though the seeker is free from material forms, he is still bound to the limitations of existence. The desire for life, even in this finer form, must be wiped out before a person can attain *Arahatship*. The next fetter to be removed is spiritual pride, which consists in feeling great about his high and exalted spiritual existence. A seeker must realize the vanity of such thoughts and move away from them. When pride is rooted out, the next fetter, self-righteousness – which consists in seeing oneself and the source of all the spiritual progress that has taken place – is also removed. The removal of self-righteousness leads to the cessation of the final fetter, ignorance – which is the 'father' of all forms of suffering in existence. When ignorance ceases to exist in the seeker, perfect knowledge is born and the delusion of the self, with its egocentricity, is totally cleared off. With the realization that the self is a delusion, the seeker becomes an *Arhat*. Having lost his sense of self, the *Arahat's* consciousness becomes all embracing. He realizes his oneness with every creature, in the process, experiencing all in him and him in all. The godly qualities of loving kindness, compassion, sympathy and equal-mindedness take hold of him. All dichotomies, disparities, lacunae and opposing interest of the world of ignorance cease to exist, and get lost in the unity that he experiences deep within. The *Arahat*, thus, becomes the embodiment of all that is divine, holy and sacred.[129]

In this essay, we have unfolded the reality of the Divine and the path to the Divine, according to the *Hiinayaana* Buddhist tradition. Though the Buddhist tradition recognizes a great pantheon of gods of the cosmological world regions, the true Divine is the *Arahat*, who has crossed over the ocean of *Samsaara* and is worthy of veneration. The *Hiinayaana* tradition, in its *Theravaada* form, does not consider the *Arahat* as the one who bestows grace on the seeker. But, he is seen as the one who has walked the path and, therefore, is an authoritative guide to lead the seeker by his teaching and example. Since the *Arahat* has walked the path, the seeker can draw inspiration from him. The path towards *Nirvaana* is the personal path of the seeker, the effort to achieve it is his own, and he cannot count on the grace of any *Arahat* for that matter. But the *Arahat* has shown the way, namely that of the Four Noble Truths, especially that of the Eightfold Path, with its path of wisdom, path of morality and the path of meditation. When a seeker dares to walk this well-tested path, he can achieve *Nirvaana* and become an *Arahat*. This is the way human destiny is viewed in the *Hiinayaana* tradition, which is the oldest and the closest to the Buddhism the Buddha taught. By placing the importance on the Order of the Monks, Hiinayaana Buddhism sidelines the laity, so that one gets the impression that only a monk can become an *Arahat*. But over the centuries of development within Buddhism, the manner of viewing human destiny has changed. The *Arahatship* is no longer considered as the final stage of development of the human person; certain theistic characteristics are attributed to the Buddha; and layperson is also viewed as capable of treading the path of *Nirvaana*. Such developments take place in the New Wisdom World view of the Buddhist ideal, out of which grows the *Mahaayaana* tradition. In the next essay, we make an attempt to unravel the reality of the Divine and the paths to theDivine, in the *Mahaayaana* Buddhism.

5.2. *MAHAAYAANA* BUDDHISM

The advent of *Mahaayaana* Buddhist thought and religious practice is a revolutionary event within the Buddhist tradition. Some authors speak of the new turn that has come about as 'the second turning of the Wheel of *Dharma*', the first happening at the Enlightenment of the Buddha at Saarnaath. One must not conclude from this statement that *Mahaayaana* is a real break with the *Hiinayaana* tradition, as it basically accepts all the teachings of the Old Wisdom World view, such as, the three marks of being, the Four Noble Truths, the doctrine of dependent origination, man's responsibility for his actions, the importance of morality and the choice of the Middle Path as leading to enlightenment, the role of the Law of *Karma* in the wheel of life and the belief in the fictional character of the self. But *Mahaayaana* definitely represents a new thinking. There are a number of new elements in the *Mahaayaana* practice. The *Arahat* ideal of *Hiinayaana* is given up and the *Bodhisattva* ideal takes its place. The concept of the Buddha as an *Arahat* par excellence has given way to the doctrine of the three bodies (*Trikaaya*) of the Buddha. The distinction between the monks and the laity within the Buddhist *Sangha* breaks down especially with regard to the attainment of Buddhahood. An element of Buddhaness is said to be present in everyone, and *Nirvaana* is the realization of the Buddha-ness within oneself. Thus, the spirit of openness pervades *Mahaayaana*, in comparison with the *Hiinayaana* tradition. This spirit manifests itself in the ability of the *Mahaayaana* tradition to give and take from many other religious traditions of the time. Thus, the *Mahaayaana* tradition, while representing the continuity, also points to the change in thinking and praxis, in its relation to the older *Hiinayaana* tradition.[130] Our concern in this essay is to elaborate the spiritual beings that form part of the belief system of the *Mahayaana* Buddhism and the path it proposes to arrive at them.

5.2.1. DIVINITIES OF THE *MAHAAYAANA* PANTHEON

In the belief system of *Mahaayaana* Buddhism, there are a great number of divinities. Some of them are borrowed from the Hindu tradition. Besides, the *Mahaayaana* Buddhists also accept the gods that belong to the Buddhist cosmological world systems. They consider two classes of divine beings, *Arahats* and the *Pratyekabuddhas*, who belong to a lower rank than the *Boddhisattvas* and the Supreme Buddhas. The *Mahaayaanists* accept the last two categories of spiritual beings as belonging to the highest order. We consider all these categories of spiritual beings in this section.

5.2.1.1. DIVINITIES ADAPTED FROM HINDU TRADITION

While teaching the moral way of life to his followers, the Buddha does not prohibit them continuing their old forms of worship or urge ceasing to honor the gods of their fathers and forefathers. Buddha never in his life assumes a policy of hostility towards popular creeds and practices. He even teaches his followers never to consider their religion as superior to that of others. This policy of tolerance and universality towards other religions allows Buddha to appropriate elements of other religions existing around him and to subordinate them to his purposes. His aim is to purify and renew the existing religions, thereby establishing the *Dharma* that has been lost because of undue emphasis on the external and the accidental. Thus, we find that the Buddha regards the Hindu gods occupying places in his own conception of the universe.[131] With this open and free attitude, *Mahaayaana* Buddhism accepts the spirit manifested in the attitude of the Buddha, and over the centuries of its development has adopted a number of deities from the Hindu pantheon, of course with suitable modifications.

The Hindu god *Brahmaa* gets into the Buddhist pantheon as the *Mahaa-Brahmaa*. *Vishnu* is venerated as the *Padma-Paani* (*Avalokitesvara*), as 'the lord who looks down with pity on all men'. He performs the duty of watching over and protecting the entire Buddhist world. He also answers the prayers of the people quickly and grants them their requests. At times he is also addressed as the *Mahaa-Vishnu*. The god *Siva* is accepted into the Buddhist pantheon as the *Mahaa-Yogi*. The god *Indra*, usually appears in the name of *Sakra*, and is a popular god in early Buddhism. He is very friendly to his devotees and controls the influences of the evil deities, such as the *Maara*. The god of Fire, the *Agni*, finds a place in the Buddhist pantheon. *Antaka* is the ruler in Hell. He is sometimes identified with *Maara*, and *Yama*. *Yamaantaka*, a form of *Yama*, is also recognized. *Kanda-Kumaara*, a form of *Skanda*, the son of *Siva*, is venerated in Sri Lanka. Worship in shrines is offered to the devilish goddess *Pattini*, who is believed to protect people from the attack of smallpox. In Burma there is the worship of some good and evil *Genii*, called *Naathas*. In Sri Lanka, the worship of devils and the cult of devil dances to appease them are popular among the Buddhists. Every disease and calamity has its presiding demon, and they are believed to be servants of the Buddha.[132]

Some other supernatural beings that figure in the Hindu mythology appear in the Buddhist pantheon with some minor modifications. The first among them is the *Pretas*. They are beings similar to ghosts and goblins.

Paths to the Divine 475

They have inhabited the earth recently and are gigantic in size and fearful in appearance, having dried up limbs, hairy bodies and large stomachs. They suffer from hunger and thirst, but are not able to eat and drink due to their contracted throats. Some of them swallow sparks of fire, while others eat dead bodies and their own flesh. The *Pretas* inhabit a region of hell, above the surface of the earth or in desert places on the earth. This form of rebirth is introduced into the Buddhist pantheon, to cultivate generosity in the laity for caring for the monks. Secondly, there is a group called the *Asuras*, the evil demons, who are constantly at war with the gods. They are said to dwell under the foundations of Mount Meru, under the surface of the earth. *Indra*, their great enemy lives above them. The third group, closely related to the *Asuras*, is that of the *Raakshasas*. They are types of demon and nymph, who are enemies of the gods. They look like monsters and are very frightful, as they are said to have a man-eating capacity. They are believed to haunt cremation grounds and intercept human beings in solitary places to devour them.[133]

The fourth group is a class of malignant demons called *Piscas*, who are capable of causing all forms of evil. The fifth group is that of the *Yakshas* and the *Yakshiniis*. They are a class of good *Genii*. The *Kuvera*, the god of wealth, commonly known in Buddhist writings as *Vaisravana*, rules these *Genii*. They are represented in human form. They are generally believed to be harmless, though some myths speak of them as cruel. Legends say that they are converted to Buddhism. The sixth group is the *Naagas*, the serpent demons. They have human faces and serpent-like lower bodies. They live in regions below the earth under the waters (*Paattaala*). They are believed to be worshipers of the Buddha and friends of all Buddhists. They are usually represented as ordinary men. The *Naaga Mucalinda*, who shelters Buddha during a storm, is a real serpent. The seventh group is that of the *Mahoragas*, the great dragons, who also belong to the class of the *Naggas*.[134]

The eighth group is that of *Huuriis* of the *Indra* heaven, who are assigned to heroes killed in battle. They are called the *Gandharvas*, the celestial musicians, and are wives of the *Indras*. In sculptures they are represented as beautiful females. The ninth group is the *Kinnaras* and the *Kinnariis*. They, like the *Gandharvas*, are heavenly musicians. They are represented with human bodies on equine heads. According to the legend, Buddha, in one of his previous births, is born as a *Kinnarii*. The tenth group consists of minor deities dwelling in forests, groves and trees. Besides, there are also the *Kumbhaandas*, a class of demons, who attend the *Viruudhaka*, their king; the *Garudas*, a bird like group that is ruled by the mythical *Garuda*, the king of birds and the enemy of *Naagas*; and the *Apsarases*, the nymphs that are produced at the churning of the ocean.[135] Thus, we find a number of deities, who belong to the Hindu pantheon with their own mythologies and have made their way into the Buddhist pantheon, forming new myths and legends.

5.2.1.2. GODS OF THE COSMOLOGICAL WORLD REGIONS

Besides accepting the gods that are borrowed from the Hindu religious tradition, *Mahaayaana* Buddhism, like the *Hinnayaana* tradition, accepts 26 levels of the heavenly world and the gods who dwell in the *Kaama-loka*, *Ruupa-loka* and the *Aruupa-loka*. The gods of these three worlds are within the domain of the law of *Karma*. They are in the present state because of their past *Karma*. When they complete the fruits of their *Karma*, like any other beings of the lower realms, they die and are reborn. The *Mahaayaanists* give importance to the *Tushita* heaven, as it is the land of the *Bodhisattvas*, before they are born as Buddhas.[136]

5.2.1.3. ARAHATS

The next group of spiritual beings the *Mahaayaana* tradition accepts is the *Arahat*. *Arahatship* is the highest ideal of *Hiinayaana* Buddhism. An *Arahat* is the one who has crossed over the ocean of *Samsaara*. He enjoys six super-knowledges and ten powers. The *Arahat* is one who follows the *Buddha-Dharma*, i.e., the path of wisdom, morality and meditation, and attains *Nirvaana*. Thus, he becomes the perfect one, the enlightened. Since he is the enlightened, he is, as his name suggests, worthy of veneration. *Mahaayaana* Buddhism does not consider the *Arahat* as the highest ethical ideal. According to them, he is inferior, as he is selfish and caught up with his own salvation. Besides, they see an *Arahat* as one who is spiritually proud and arrogant about his achievements. Hence attachment to the 'I' and 'mine' are not fully shaken off. He is not able to break the distinction between himself and others. This implies that an *Arahat* has a notion of himself as distinct from others, and so he has fully achieved the realization of the fictional character of the self. Since his whole approach to salvation is more self-centered than other-centered, he is not perfect. Since he is not perfect, there is the possibility of his spiritual downfall. Thus, an *Arahat*, according to the *Mahaayaana* teaching, has still a long path ahead on the way to perfection. He is still on the way and remains a pilgrim. He needs to learn compassion and other-centeredness. If these virtues are practiced, he may move into the stage of the *Bodhisattva* and finally to the Buddhahood.[137] Hence, the *Mahaayaana* tradition sees the path of an *Arahat* as far inferior to the tradition of the *Bodhisattva,* and as something similar to that of the path of the *Pratyeka-Buddha*, which we elaborate next.

5.2.1.4. PRATYEKA-BUDDHAS

The *Mahaayaana* tradition, like the *Hiinayaana* Buddhism, accepts the spiritual quality of the *Pratyeka-Buddha*. He is a solitary saint. He has attained the state of *Niravaana* by himself and for himself. He has never been a member of a monastic order. Neither has he had an opportunity to listen to the *Buddha-Dharma*. He is a secluded hermit. The whole purpose of his effort is to effect sanctity within himself. His goal is concentration on isolated and selfish sanctity. He has no thought of others in any of his spiritual endeavors. He is absorbed in the bliss of his own salvation. Though in sanctity he is similar to the Buddhas, unlike the Buddhas, the *Pratyeka-Buddha* does not establish a teaching or an Order to let his teachings be taught to others. He just practices what he discovers by way of his meditation. He does not appear on earth at the same time as a Supreme Buddha. In spite of the sanctity of his life, he could never be given the names that are epithets of the Supreme Buddha, such as, the *Tathaagta, Bhagavat* and others, as he is a lonely figure and very different form the Supreme Buddha. As a spiritual seeker, the *Pratyeka-Buddha* finds his own way, follows and achieves the goal of *Nirvaana*. The recognition of the way of the solitary saint (*Pratyekabuddhayaana*) points to the Buddhist belief that men of good will, discipline, holiness and asceticism, can attain *Nirvaana* even though they are not in touch with the teaching of the Buddha. Though *Mahaayaana* acknowledges the path of the *Pratyeka-Buddha*, it is seen as a way similar to that of an *Arahat*, as it is self-centered. It is not the highest ideal of the seeker, as the compassion and the other-centeredness of the *Bodisattva* is missing in the *Pratyeka-Buddha*.[138]

5.2.1.5. BODHISATTVAS

Though the *Mahaayaana* acknowledges many gods of the Hindu tradition, the gods of the cosmological world realms, the *Arahats* and the *Pratyeka-Buddhas*, it holds the *Bodhisattva*, the Buddha-to-be, in the highest esteem. They are totally other-centered existences, moved by compassion for all. They are presented, in the *Mahaayaana* texts, as the ideals to be followed by the seeker on his way to *Nirvaana*. In this section, we consider the nature and characteristics of *Bodhisattva*, besides looking into a few popular *Bodhisattvas* who are venerated in the *Mahaayaana* tradition.

5.2.1.5.1. Nature of Bodhisattvas

The term "*Bodhisattva*" derives from two words, "*Bodhi*" and "*Sattva*", which mean 'enlightenment' and 'being', respectively. Thus, literally, the term "*Bodhisattva*" means 'enlightenment-being' or 'a being that seeks enlightenment'. Again the Paali word "*Satta*" is equivalent to the Sanskrit word "*Sakta*", which means 'to be attached to'. Taken in this sense, "*Bodhisattva*" means 'one who desires one's own enlightenment'. We can also consider the term "*Bodhisattva*" in relation to the term "*Sattva*", which also has the meaning of 'intention' (*Abhipraaya*), 'mind' (*Citta*) or 'heroic mind'. If this meaning of the term "*Bodhisattva*" is accepted, it means 'a being whose mental orientation is completely and totally directed towards perfect enlightenment'. These derivations of the term "*Bodhisattva*" point to one important aspect of the *Bodhisattva*, viz., the *Bodhisattva* is a being-on-the-way, a being-at-a-stage and a pilgrim being, who aims at the highest goal of becoming the Enlightened One, the Buddha. Thus, the *Bodhisattva* is a 'Buddha-to-be'. This movement that leads the *Bodhisattva* to become the Buddha, is an ascending movement from matter to spirit.[139]

In many *Mahaayaana* texts another term that is used in close association with the term "*Bodhisattva*" is the term "*Mahaasattva*", which means 'a great being whose intentions are of heroic nature'. In some texts both of these words are used as a compound *"Bodhisattva-Mahaasattva"*. As a compound these terms stand for "that being who has taken a vow to be reborn, no matter how many times this may be necessary, in order to attain the highest possible goal, that of Complete and Perfect Buddhahood, for the benefit of all sentient beings".[140] The term *"Mahaasattva"* brings to light the second aspect of the *Bodhisattva*, viz., he is a being descending from his high and exalted state to lower realms in order to raise up the lot of the sentient beings to the level of *Nirvaana*. It is the state of the spirit descending to matter. Thus, the *Bodhisattvas* are concerned with their own perfection, with the view of helping all the sentient beings with the perfection they acquire. Hence, the *Bodhisattva* is one who ascends to goal of Buddhahood and, at the same time, one who descends to the lowest level to raise up the lowly. According to the *Mahaayaana* tradition, the paths of the *Arahat* and that of the *Pratyeka-Buddha* do not have this descending, i.e., the other-centered, aspect. Thus, in the personality of the *Bodhisattva* is contained the dual movement of manifestation – the matter ascending to the spirit and the spirit descending to matter.[141]

The ascending and descending dimensions of the personality of the *Bodhisattva* relate to two important virtues that mark his nature, viz., wisdom (*Prajnaa*) and compassion (*Karuna*). It is desire for true wisdom that moves the *Bodhisattva* to make the ascending journey towards Buddhahood. It is compassion for all sentient beings that moves the *Bodhisattva* to make the descending journey towards others. In real life situations it is difficult to combine these two conflicting virtues. The seeking of wisdom often takes one away from the world, people and everything that distracts one's journey towards it. Similarly compassion and feeling for others makes one get caught up with others and their problems, in the process making concentration and the seeking of wisdom nearly impossible. The *Bodhisattva*, through skillful means, combines both wisdom and compassion, making them complementary and supportive of the other. Wisdom and compassion, supporting each other, assist the *Bodhisattva* to work for the salvation of every sentient being in the world of *Samsaara*.[142]

Wisdom lends a helping hand to compassion in guiding the *Bodhisattva*. Wisdom enables the *Bodhisattva* to realize the true nature of reality as non-dual and thereby to attain the Buddhahood. On becoming the Buddha the *Bodhisattva* gains omniscience. With this power of complete knowledge, he is able to know beforehand the way he can make his compassion for sentient beings real. Again, with the help of wisdom the *Bodhisattva* understands the essential Buddha-nature of every reality. This realization of the essential oneness of every reality makes the *Bodhisattva* identify himself with every other being, in the process destroying the distinction between self and others. It, in turn, builds up on the *Bodhisattva* a sense of solidarity with others, thereby making him ready even to risk his life for the sake of others. Finally, the realization of the unity of all makes the *Bodhisattva* recognize the unreal nature of the *Samsaara* existence, which, in turn, frees him from all forms of clinging, ego-centered activity and thought of himself. This outlook helps him to move towards others in compassion feeling their pain and trouble as his own. Thus, wisdom assisting compassion moves the *Bodhisattva* for genuine acts of kindness towards all forms of living beings. Similarly, compassion assists wisdom in its guidance of the *Bodhisattva*. As the *Bodhisattva* moves into higher levels of wisdom, he can fall prey to spiritual pride and his motives can become self-centered. He can become selfish and get caught up with himself. When this happens, it is compassion for others, which calms the flame of pride and selfishness, in the process negating the sense of the ego-self. The negation of the sense of the ego-self brings to the *Bodhisattva* a spirit of self-sacrifice. Thus, the guidance of wisdom by compassion that effects in the *Bodhisattva* self-sacrifice makes him take up any form of suffering for the benefit and well-being of others.[143] The following quotation indicates the coordinated interrelationship between wisdom and compassion:

> Great compassion ... takes hold of him. He surveys countless beings with his heavenly eye, and what he sees fills him with great agitation. ... And he attends to them with the thought that: 'I shall become a savior to all those beings, I shall release them from all their sufferings!' But he does not make either this, or anything else into a sign to which he becomes partial. This also is the great light of a *Bodhisattva's* wisdom, which allows him to know the full enlightenment.[144]

Receiving coordinated support from wisdom and compassion, the *Bodhisattva* is able to reach out to others in loving-kindness and self-sacrifice, without sacrificing his search for the genuine wisdom of Buddhahood. He descends to lower levels to manifest his compassion, yet his ascent to the heights of wisdom remains totally unaffected. Not only does he take himself to higher realms of spiritual experiences, but the also is able to take others, for whom he feels compassionate, to higher spiritual levels. In other words, he is able to pass on the seeds of his enlightenment to all he reaches in compassion and love. The following quotation clarifies the true nature of the *Bodhisattva*:

> Doers of what is hard are the *Bodhisattvas*, the great beings [*Mahaasattvas*] who have set out to win supreme enlightenment. They do not wish to attain their own private *Nirvaana*. On the contrary, they have surveyed the highly painful world of being, and yet, desirous to win supreme enlightenment, they do not tremble at birth-and-death. They have set out for the benefit of the world, for the ease of the world, out of pity for the world. They have resolved: 'We will become a shelter for the world, a refuge for the world, the world's place of rest, the final relief of the world, islands

of the world, lights of the world, leaders of the world, the world's means of salvation.[145]

5.2.1.5.2. Characteristics of Bodhisattvas

Having analyzed the nature of *Bodhisattva*, we shall speak briefly of a few of the characteristics, which further describe his nature. Firstly, with the help of many spiritual and other practices the *Bodhisattva* has cultivated, he develops a number of psychic and worldly powers. He makes use of these powers to help all the sentient beings on their way to *Nirvaana*. For instance, using his psychic ability, the *Bodhisattva* is capable of manifesting the Buddhas as a psychic creation for the spiritual benefit of the believer. Secondly, the *Bodhisattva* has the quality of becoming the vicarious savior. He, being selfless and always thinking of the salvation of others, transfers the stock of merit he has accumulated due to many of his virtuous deeds to all living creatures. He can also magnify the available merits that every living being receives as a share of the grace of the *Bodhisattva*. Thus, a person attains his salvation through the bounteous merits that come from the boundless love of the Great One (*Mahaasattva*). This belief is prevalent in the Pure Land Schools of *Mahaayaana* Buddhism. Thirdly, the *Bodhisattva* is capable of developing skill-in-means (*Upaaya*). They consist in the *Bodhisattva's* ability to adapt himself and his teachings so skillfully, that they are applicable to every level of his hearers. For instance, it is said that the *Bodhisattva* is able to visit to the hell regions in order to preach the *Buddha-Dharma* to the inhabitants of the hell regions. Fourthly, the *Bodhisattva* is capable of combining the conflicting virtues of wisdom and compassion. In doing so, the extremes of pride, ego-centeredness and arrogance that can arise in him due to rising into heights of wisdom, are avoided as is being lost in the lower realms due to his involvement with various types of sentient beings. In this manner, the *Bodhisattva* becomes a model and an ideal for the *Mahaayaana* seeker of *Nirvaana* to imitate and to learn from, on his way to the attainment of Buddhahood. Fifthly, the *Bodhisattva*, by his very nature, is self-sacrificing. His self-sacrificing quality is such that he is ready to postpone his own attainment of Buddhahood, in order to bring about the salvation of others. Because of his compassion for the suffering world and its inhabitants, he refuses to enter into the final state of *Nirvaana*, but allows himself to be reborn many times in this *Sahaa* world system in order to preach the *Dharma* and to perform works of mercy and compassion for all sentient beings.[146]

5.2.1.5.3. Some Bodhisattvas

We have briefly analyzed the nature and characteristics of the *Bodhisattvas* in the last two sections. In this section, we consider a few of the most popular *Bodhisattvas* of the *Mahaayaana* Buddhist tradition, viz., *Maitreya*, *Avalokitesvara*, *Manjusrii*, *Kshitigarbha* and *Vajra-panni*.

5.2.1.5.3.1. Maitreya

Maitreya, the Kindly One, is the most popular *Bodhisattva* and is given a celestial status both in the *Hiinayaana* and the *Mahaayaana* Buddhist traditions. He is believed to be dwelling in the *Tushita* heaven, waiting for the right time to descend into the world as the next Buddha. It is said that he appears only after 5,000 years, when the teachings of Gautama Buddha loses it power. From the *Tushita* heaven, *Maitreya* visits the world in various forms to save and to teach others. The cult of *Maitreya* takes different forms in different schools of Buddhism. For instance, in China the *Maitreya* cult is associated with those who hold for the mind-only (*Cittamaatra*) doctrine. In Kashmir, *Maitreya* worship is connected to the Kashmir schools of meditation, which emphasize visions that accompany meditation. This group emphasizes *Maitreya's* role as a visionary and inspirer who guides them in their meditation. Thus, in Kashmir, *Maitreya* becomes a 'tutelary deity' for the meditators and the patron saint of the exegetes. The meditators and the exegetes sit in prayer before the image of *Maitreya* to remove doubts and uncertainties and to receive clarity of doctrine. Similarly, they practice visualizations and recollections centered on *Maitreya*. In central Asian countries, *Maitreya* is associated with the missionary movement within Buddhism, and is believed to be patron of the missionaries.[147]

For Buddhists in general, *Maitreya* is a symbol of compassion. His future birth as the Buddha inaugurates the new beginning, i.e., the Buddhist millennium. When that happens the gods, men and every living creature become worshippers of *Maitreya*. Every form of evil will be wiped away. All will give up their evil ways. Everyone will lead a holy life under the guidance of *Maitreya* and experience abundance of joy and happiness. Thus, the birth of *Maitreya* is seen as the messianic time, and he himself is seen as the messiah who inaugurates happier times. The *Maitreya* cult paves the way for various messianic movements in China. Even in countries where *Theravaada* Buddhism is practiced, people wish to be reborn on earth after the birth of *Maitreya*, become a monk and attain enlightenment under his guidance.[148] The Sanskrit work, *The Prophecy of Maitreya* (*Maitreyavyaakarana*), describes the new era *Maitreya* inaugurates as follows:

> Gods, men, and other beings will worship *Maitreya* and will lose their doubts, and the torrents of their cravings will be cut off: free from all misery they will manage to cross the ocean of becoming; and, as a result of *Maitreya's* teachings, they will lead a holy life. No longer will they regard anything as their own, they will have no possessions, no gold or silver, no home, no relatives! But they will lead the holy life of chastity under *Maitreya's* guidance. They will have torn the net of the passion, they will manage to enter into the trances, and theirs will be an abundance of joy and happiness; for they will lead a holy life under *Maitreya's* guidance.[149]

5.2.1.5.3.2. Avalokitesvara

Avalokitesvara is one of the most significant *Bodhisattvas* of the *Mahaayaana* Buddhism. His name "*Avalokitesvara*" derives from two words "*Avalokita*", which means 'looking down' and "*Iishvara*", which means 'the lord'. Thus, *Avalokitesvara* is the *Bodhisattva*, who looks down upon every creature with compassion. His compassion for sentient beings makes him take a vow not to enter the state of *Nirvaana* unless he frees every being in the world from bondage. He watches over and protects the Buddhist world. He is known for the quickness with which he listens to the pleas of the people and answers their prayers. He is said to save people from all forms of evil, such as, fire, rivers, storms on the ocean, murderers, demons and ghosts, prison and robbers. *Avalokitesvara* is also said to remove lust, anger and stupidity. He incarnates in different forms – such as, a Buddha, a god, a monk, a householder, a boy, a girl and even as a non-human sentient being – to help, convert and save all forms of living beings. Thus, *Avalokitesvara* is the compassionate savior of the universe. He is not only concerned with enlightenment of the people, but also interested in every suffering and does his best to alleviate them. Therefore, people pray to him for help and consolation. He is the protector of the one who travels. Hence he is prayed to in moments of shipwreck. For these reasons, *Avalokitesvara* is known as 'god of mercy', 'ocean of pity (*Karunaarnava*)', 'deliverer from fear' (*Abhayam-da*), 'lord of the world' (*Lokshvara*), 'world protector' (*Loka-paala*), 'protector of the *Aaryas*' (*Aarya-paala*) and. 'lotus-handed' (*Padma-paani*).[150]

Avalokitesvara is also known for his miraculous powers. He is described as descending into hot hells and miraculously cooling of the hell regions in order to save the hell beings from their sufferings. He is said to have created the world with all the gods of the Hindu pantheon. He assigns to respective gods their place in the universe. To quote:

> From his [*Avalokitesvara's*] eyes arose the moon and sun, from his forehead *Mahesvara (Siva)*, from his shoulders *Brahmaa*, from his heart *Naaraayana*, from his teeth *Sarasvatii*, from his mouth the winds, from his feet the earth, and from his belly *Varuna*. When these gods were born from the body of *Avalokitesvara*, then he said to the god *Maheshvara*, "Thou shalt be *Mahesvara* in the Kali age, when the world of evil creatures arises. Thou shalt be called *Aadideva* (the primal god), the creator ... [and] the maker ...[151]

Yet *Avalokitesvara* does not attribute to himself the status of a god, but he speaks of himself as a man, who out of compassion for the poor of the world has become a teacher of enlightenment. In iconography, *Avalokitesvara* is represented in a number of ways. He is depicted as having 1,000 arms and 11 heads. He is again represented in a manner similar to that of the lord *Siva*, i.e., as a beautiful man wearing a diadem on his matted hair, manifesting friendliness and resembling a disc of gold. He is also represented as 'white robed'. He is also seen as wearing a crown and large earrings and a rosary, and having a halo from which other *Bodhisattvas* emerge.[152]

5.2.1.5.3.3. Manjusrii

Manjusrii is an important *Bodhisattva* of the celestial realm. The name "*Manjusrii*" means 'the one of glorious beauty'. While *Avalokitesvara* represents Buddha's compassion, *Manjusrii* manifests Buddha's wisdom. He is wisdom personified. As the lord of wisdom, *Manjusrii* is the spokesman on questions concerning ultimate truth. Though ancient in his wisdom, he is described as ever youthful, 16 years of age. He is also called *Manju-ghosha*, i.e., 'the one having a beautiful voice' and *Vaagiisvara*, 'the lord of speech'. *Manjusrii* is said to have produced the 'awakened mind' (*Bodhicitta*) Aeons ago in the presence of the previous Buddha. In producing the *Bodhicitta*, he vows to do everything he does for the benefit of the sentient beings, without any greed, miserliness or resentfulness. *Manjusrii* prefers to let go of his desire to seek enlightenment until the end of the future, for the benefit of sentient beings. With the power of the *Bodhicitta*, *Manjusrii* enters into *Pari-Nirvaana* in different regions and leaves holy relics behind for the benefit of the beings of this world. Due to the power of his meditation, he emanates as many Buddhas as are needed for the worship of the humans. He also appears as a poor person, so that human beings can gain merit through their acts of compassion and donation. As the personification of wisdom, *Manjusrii* is a source of inspiration for numerous teachers and scholars of *Buddha-Dharma*. Saakyamuni Buddha himself reveals that, in his previous life, he has studied under the tutelage of *Manjusrii*, and that the status he enjoys today as the Buddha is due to *Manjusrii*. For this reason, *Manjusrii* is known as the father and mother of innumerable Buddhas. He is also said to be the master of gods and the gods of god who live in the minds of all beings. In iconography, *Manjusrii* is represented as a young prince, who is seated on the lotus, with a sword in his right hand, held above his head, and a book in his left hand. The sword represents *Gnosis*, true knowledge that cuts off ignorance. The book represents the *Mahaayaana* wisdom scriptures, which are the source of true *Gnosis*.[153]

5.2.1.5.3.4. Kshitigarbha

Bodhisattva Kshitigarbha is often referred to as 'the earth-matrix', as he is given the particular task of caring for the earthly beings during the time between Saakyamuni Gautama Buddha and the coming of *Maitreya*, the next Buddha. *Kshitigarbha*, being closely involved with the everyday life of the people in the world, is presented as the guardian of travelers, helper of those in any form of trouble, the dead, women and children. In China, *Kshitigarbha* is associated with special rites offered on behalf of the dead ancestors. It is believed that he descends to the hell regions and brings salvation to the inhabitants of hell. Similarly he is said to assist in solving domestic problems, especially those of women. According to mythology, *Kshitigarbha*, in his previous life, is born as a woman and vows to save all sentient beings in return for the salvation of her mother from her great suffering. In Japan, he is known as *Jizoo*, who is fond of children and is concerned with the suffering of dead children. Thus, *Kshitigarbha* is a great helper of all sentient beings living in the universe. He is usually represented as a shaven-headed, dignified, but kindly monk, dressed in robes, his legs placed on the lotus, with a staff, a small medicine box and a halo. In Japan, his statues are usually displayed either on the side of the country roads or on the mountain paths.[154]

5.2.1.5.3.5. Vajra-paani

The name "*Vajra-paani*" means 'the thunderbolt-handed'. He corresponds to *Indra* and *Siva* of the Hindu pantheon. He is also called *Vajra-dhara*. He is the fieriest and most frightening *Bodhisattva*. He is the controller of demons and destroyer of all evil spirits. It is said that when the Buddha after his enlightenment visits his father Suddhodana, eight *Vajra-paanis* accompany him. In the Northern Buddhism, the *Vajra-paani* cult is very popular, but not as popular as the other *Bodhisattvas*.[155]

5.2.1.6. SUPREME BUDDHAS

When the *Bodhisattvas* achieve their final destiny they become Supreme Buddhas. According to Buddhist mythology, 24 Buddhas appeared before Gautama. These mythical Buddhas are the following: *Diipamkara, Kaundinya, Mangala, Sumanas, Raivata, Sobhita, Anavama-darsin, Padma, Naarada, Padmottara, Sumedhas, Sujaata, Priya-darsin, Artha-darsin, Dharma-darsin, Sidhaartha, Tishya, Pushya, Vipasyin, Sikhin, Visva-bhuu, Krakucanda, Kanaka-muni* and *Kaasyapa*. The last six, along with Gautama, constitute the seven principle Buddhas. Gautama is the 25th and the last of the Buddhas that have arisen up to the present *Kalpa*. There are many *Bodhisattvas* who can complete their journey and attain the state of Buddhahood.[156] The following sections study the nature and characteristics of the Supreme Buddha and look into some of the popular Buddhas of recent times.

5.2.1.6.1. Nature of Buddha

The Supreme Buddha is the one who attains perfect knowledge (*Sambodhi*). He attains the state of perfect knowledge by his own self-enlightening insight into the nature of reality. The Supreme Buddha is a perfect knower and a perfect teacher of the truth. His teaching is believed to be impenetrable and profound. He is a founder of monastic orders. The Buddha leads others by the example of his life, rather than by mere preaching. He is full of compassion. His compassion is of supernatural character as it is oriented towards the suffering of humanity. His compassion goes beyond the layers of hate and resentment, and also breaks every fetter of delusion. He possesses various powers, by which he conquers the demonic powers like that of the *Maara*. Thus, the Buddha is the true King of *Dharma* (*Dharmaraaja*). According to the *Mahaahyaana* tradition the Supreme Buddha is far superior to the *Arahats*, *Pretyeka-Buddhas* and the *Bodhisattvas*. Latter do not have the special attributes and qualities of the Buddha. As a matter of fact, the spiritual powers of the *Arahats*, *Pretyeka-Buddhas* and the *Bodhisattvas* are dependent on the enlightenment of the Buddha. In the last analysis, the Buddha-word (*Buddha-Dharma*) is that which saves the life of a person from the ill effects of the *Samsaara* existence.[157] Buddha's own description of his personality confirms his absolute nature as the Supreme Being:

> I [the Buddha] am all-subduer (*Sabbaabhibhuu*); the all-wise; I have no stains; through myself I possess knowledge; I have no rival (*Patipuggalo*); I am the chief *Arahat* – the highest teacher; I alone am the absolutely wise (*Sambuddha*); I am the Conqueror (*Jina*); all the fires of desire are quenched (*Siitibhuuto*) in me; I have *Nirvaana* (*Nibbuto*).[158]

Because of his supreme nature and the absolute power that flows from it, the *Mahaayaana* Buddhist scriptures give the Buddha titles and epithets that point to his honor, dignity, power and worth. Some of the titles attributed to the Buddha are the following: the thus-gone (*Tathagata*), the worthy (*Arahat*), the fully and completely awakened (*Samyaksambuddha*), the accomplished in knowledge and virtuous conduct (*Vidyaacaranasampanna*), the well-gone (*Sugata*), the knower of worlds (*Lokavid*), the unsurpassed guide for those who need restraint (*Anuttarah Purushadamyasaarathih*), the teacher of gods and humans (*Saastaa Devamanushyaanaam*) the awakened (*Buddha*) and the blessed (*Bhagavat*). All these titles point to the complete and perfect nature of the Supreme Buddha, and to him as being worthy of reverential homage, praise, devotion and worship.[159]

These titles that are attributed to the Buddha indicate someone who is over and above limited history. Though the Buddha is a historical figure – who has lived on the earth before 2,500 years – he is no more seen as merely historical, but also as trans-historical, as the Absolute Reality and the Supreme Being who cannot be conditioned by space-time compound. Hence, the *Mahaayaana* Buddhist tradition gives less importance to the historicity of the Saakyamuni, while giving significance to the deeper spiritual reality (*Dharma*) of the Buddha. Thus, *Dharma* becomes more identified with the Buddha. It, in turn, leads to the perception that the physical body of the Buddha, born of his parents, is something not worthy of a devotee taking refuge, as it is composed of impure constituents. Thus, the historical Buddha recedes into the background while the cosmic Buddha of the *Dharma*-realm comes to the foreground. The physical body of the Buddha is seen as the external manifestation of the absolute *Dharma-nature* (*Dharmataa*) of the Buddha – which resides in the *Dharma*-realm (*Dharma-dhaatu*) – in the world of becoming. In this manner, the natural Buddha is super-naturalized. The super-naturalization of the Buddha i.e., the doctrine which states that the Buddha in his ultimate Buddha-ness resides in the *Dharma*-realm, and that his presence in the world of becoming is only a manifestation -- leads the *Mahaayaanists* to propose a new Buddhology and to formulate the doctrine of three modes of manifestation of the absolute *Dharma*-nature or Buddha-ness. Thus, there emerges the doctrine of the 'three bodies' (*Trikaaya*) of the Buddha, namely, the essence body (*Dharma-kaaya*), the enjoyment body (*Sambhoga-kaaya*) and the transformation body (*Nirmaana-kaaya*).[160]

The *Dharma-kaaya* refers to the essence of Buddha's Buddhahood. It is the essence of the Buddha, the ultimate and purified 'Thus-ness' or 'Such-ness' of the Buddha, the true nature of the Buddha taken as a body, or the fundamental nature of the Buddha (*Svabhaavika-kaaya*). It is Buddha as identical with ultimate truth. *Dharma-kaaya* is a kind of ethereal essence of the highly sublimated nature, which is eternal and co-extensive with space. After the *Pari-Nivaana* of the Buddha, the Law (*Dharma*) he taught represents this body. Therefore, it is called 'the body of the Law'. It is the non-dual purified flow of consciousness and the essence of being a Buddha. *Dharma-kaaya* can be viewed as the collection of good mental qualities that characterize the being of the Buddha. It is what the Buddha exemplifies, the essence of the Buddha, his true nature, which is identical with the essence of all things. In other words, the essential body of the Buddha (*Dharma-kaaya*) and the fundamental aspect of the cosmos (*Dharmadhaatu*) are one and the same. In the realm of the *Dharma-kaaya* there is no physical body, as it is a spiritual essence. Hence, at the level of the body, various Buddhas cannot be differentiated. When this spiritual essence is manifested in the other two types of bodies, we can strictly speak of different Buddhas. Thus, *Dharma-kaaya* is the basis of the other two bodies of the Buddha. The latter are only the manifestations of the former in the subtle and gross levels respectively. The essence body of the Buddha belongs to the transcendental realm that is over and above the heavenly and earthly realms.[161]

The *Sambhoga-kaaya* is the second body of the Buddha. It is 'the body of complete enjoyment' or 'the body of conscious bliss'. It is less ethereal and more material than the *Dharma-kaaya*. It is not the gross body, but a subtle body. It is the glorified body of the Buddha that is decked with 32 and 80 qualities. It is in his *Sambhoga-kaaya* that the Buddha appears on the lotus throne in the Pure Land, preaching the *Mahaayaana* teaching to the great assembly of *Arahats* and *Bodhisattvas*. It is the actual Buddha in his supra-mundane form. It is to the Buddha in the *Sambhoga-kaaya* that the Buddhists offer their devotion. In the enjoyment body, the Buddha is a heavenly being animated through pure compassion and performing various activities to sentient beings. Besides, it is the *Sambhoga-kaaya* that attains Buddhahood.

Some *Mahaayaana* texts speak of two types of *Sambhoga-kaaya*: the private enjoyment body and the public enjoyment body. The former is the enjoyment body as experienced and enjoyed by the Buddhas themselves. The latter is the enjoyment body the Buddhas use for the benefit and enjoyment of others. The public *Sambhoga-kaaya* manifests itself in different ways and at different places according to the needs of sentient beings. It is the Buddha's heavenly body, located in the splendid paradise in the heavenly realm.[162]

The *Nirmaana-kaaya* is 'the body of visible shapes and transformations'. It is called 'the transformation body'. It is Buddha's earthly body, which is physical, mortal and having bodylike nature, similar to the body of any human being. In other words, *Nirmaana-kaaya* stands for the earthly body of the Buddha, through which the eternal and invisible essence of Buddha, i.e., the Buddha-ness of the *Dharma-kaaya*, is manifested at the gross level. The transformation body of the Buddha goes through the stages of birth, renunciation, enlightenment and death associated with a particular Buddha. Through the transformation body the Buddha reaches out to those beings that are unable to reach the Pure Land to listen to his preaching through his enjoyment body. Thus, through the *Nirmaana-kaaya*, the Buddhas, out of compassion, reach out to those beings that are caught up in the gross level of existence, whether it is human or animal existence. It is through the transformation body that the Buddhas manifest compassion suitable for particular people, places, times and situations. The *Nirmaana-kaaya* is a guarantee for the permanent continuance of history, as through it the Buddhas safeguard the good in the world and destroy the evil forces, thereby directing the movement of history in a balanced manner. Thus, the *Dharma-kaaya* as the absolute 'Such-ness', expresses its power of healing and reconciliation in the cosmos, when it manifests itself in and through the activities of the transformation body of the Buddhas. The *Nirmaana-kaaya* belongs to the earthly level, and its sphere of activity is the gross material world.[163]

5.2.1.6.2. Characteristics of Buddha

Having considered the nature of the Buddha, we move on to state some of the characteristics of the Buddha. The *Mahaayaana* scriptures speak of a number of characteristic marks of the Buddha. These characteristics relate to Buddha's appearance, actions, cognition, attitude and control. In all these aspects the personality of the Buddha marks the highest level of perfection.[164] We speak of the characteristics of the Buddha in 18 points.

Firstly, the Buddha possesses the four immeasurable states (*Brahma-vihaaras*). They are friendliness (*Maitrii*), compassion (*Karunaa*), sympathetic joy (*Muditaa*) and equanimity (*Upekshaa*). These four qualities make the Buddha possess an open and loving attitude towards every living being. Secondly, we find in the Buddha the altered states of consciousness, which he cultivates by various meditation techniques. They are the eight forms of liberation (*Vimoksha*), the eight spheres of mastery (*Abhibhavaayatana*) and the ten spheres of totality (*Krtsnaayatana*). Thirdly, the Buddha is non-contentious (*Aranaa*). Hence, he does not do anything that evokes controversies and contentions among the people he meets and lives with. Fourthly, the Buddha has the awareness (*Jnanaa*) that he has taken vows (*Pranidhi*) in the previous lives. Fifthly, the Buddha enjoys four types of understanding: understanding of doctrine (*Dharma*), understanding of meaning (*Artha*), understanding of grammar (*Nirukti*) and understanding of eloquence (*Pratibhaana*). Sixthly, the Buddha owns six kinds of supernatural knowledge (*Abhijnaa*): the ability to see and hear what is happening in a distant place, the ability to know what is in another's mind, the ability to remember one's and other's previous lives and the ability to know one's destroyed passion. Seventhly, the Buddha has 32 major qualities (*Lakshana*) and 80 minor marks (*Anuvyanjana*) related to the body and its appearance. Eighthly, the Buddha possesses four kinds of purifications (*Parisuddhi*). They are the purifications of the body (*Aasraya*), the mental object (*Aalambana*), of the mind (*Citta*) and of discernment (*Prajnaa*). The purification of the body consists in the ability to appear in any bodily form; the purification of the mental object means the ability to control the images that flood the mind; the purification of the mind involves mastering all meditation techniques; and the purification of discernment consists in possessing omniscience. Ninthly, the Buddha enjoys ten powers (*Dasabala*), such as, walking on the water, traveling cross-legged in the sky, going through the solid ground as one goes through the water, and other similar powers.[165]

Tenthly, the Buddha has four kinds of confidence (*Vaisaaradya*), which remove all forms of fearlessness from him. Eleventhly, the Buddha possesses the inner freedom that his physical, verbal and mental activities need not be consciously restrained. In these three areas his actions never go wrong. Twelfthly, the Buddha enjoys three-fold mindfullness, which prevents him from being over-joyous, sad or indifferent about the various events that happen in his life. Thirteenthly, the Buddha's tendencies towards improper thought, speech and action are totally erased. Fourteenthly, The Buddha is not confused as to what needs to be done for living beings, for he knows how to do the right thing at the right time in the right way. Fifteenthly, we find in the Buddha a great compassion (*Mahaa-karuna*) for all living beings, and it directs all he does for the benefit of the sentient beings. The compassion of the Buddha is omnipresent. Sixteenthly, the Buddha possesses 18 qualities that are specifically applicable to him. They include perfections of action, attitude and control, among others. Seventeenthly, the Buddha is omniscient. Eighteenthly, the Buddha possesses the following transcendental qualities, moral conduct (*Siila*), patience (*Kshaanti*), fortitude (*Viirya*), suppression of desires and ascending to profound contemplation (*Naishkaamya*), wisdom (*Prajnaa*), truth (*Satya*), steadfast resolution (*Adhishthaana*) and the absolute imperturbability which results in ecstatic quietude (*Upekshaa*).[166]

5.2.1.6.3. Some Buddhas

We have looked into the nature and characteristics of the Buddha. Now, we make an attempt to probe the most popular Buddhas. The three Buddhas we want to talk about are *Akshobhya*, *Bhaishajya-guru* and *Amitaabha*.

5.2.1.6.3.1. Akshobhya

Akshobhya is the Buddha of the Buddha Field named Abhirati, which is far away in the East. In that land, very long ago, a monk vows to follow the path of full Buddhahood. He makes a series of vows and strictly keeps them. Finally, he obtains Buddhahood. Numerous miracles accompany *Akshobhya's* attainment of enlightenment. His Buddha Field and its beauty tempts devotees to rise up to that level. In Abhirati, there is no illness, no lying, no ugliness, no smelly things. In this land there are no jails and no non-Buddhists. There is no farm and no farming. Similarly, there is no trader and no trading. Trees flower and bear fruit. They produce fragrant and beautiful garments. Food and drink appear as one wishes. There is no jealousy in this Pure Land. The women are beautiful, and they are freed from the curse of menstruation. There is happiness at all times, as the inhabitants of this land play and sing. Sentient beings are without any sexual desire in this land, as they derive their joy from the *Dharma*. *Akshobhya's* purity of life has a great impact on the purity of his Buddha Field. The realm of *Akshobhya*, Abhirati, has become a fully qualified Pure Land.[167]

Akshobhya has a great following in the Tibet. According to the Tibetan version of Abhirati, the Pure Land is without any form of sexuality. As soon a person approaches a woman with a carnal desire, it vanishes and he enters into deep meditative absorption on detachment from impurity. The women become pregnant with a mere thought. It is a wonderful land of happiness, free of all forms of danger, unpolluted, and without toil or trouble. All these blessings come from *Akshobhya's* great vows and compassion. There is no sun or moon in this Pure Land, as *Akshobhya's* great light eclipses the whole land. A mere desire for it does not take a person to this land. A life of passion and attachment does not take one there. Only those who have cultivated good conduct have access to this land. The main purpose of rebirth in this land is true spiritual growth, as it has optimum facilities for one's inner growth. Some of the facilities provided are the following: strenuous moral and spiritual cultivation; attainment of merit, which is dedicated to the future rebirth there; learning of meditation and frequenting holy people; visualization of the Buddhas in their Buddha Lands and preaching people; and vowing to be like them. All these facilities guarantee one to be reborn in the land of Abhirati.[168]

The significant element of the Pure Land of Abhirati is that its Buddha, *Akshobhya,* enters *pari-Nirvaana* by a final act of self-cremation done through internal combustion. Before that takes place, he appoints a successor, like Gautama Buddha appointing *Maitreya*. The doctrine of *Akshobhya* continues for long time after he is gone, but eventually it declines. The cult of *Akshobhya* becomes popular especially in the Tantric Buddhism of Tibet. *Akshobhya's* representation as the Buddha appears with a crown on his head; he is seated in the lotus posture, with left hand on his lap and right hand outstretched to touch the earth. In Tibet *Akshobhya* is the principal Buddha of the *Mandala*, the cosmogram, which is so important in Tantric ritual and meditation. His cult is very popular in Tibet.[169]

5.2.1.6.3.2. Bhaishajya-guru

Bhaishajya-guru has his own Buddha Field in the far off East. It is a wonderful land. Its roads are marked with gold. There are no women in this land, as all women are reborn into the superior state of men. Since all beings are male, there is a better and superior facility for spiritual advancement. *Bhaishajya-guru*, as *Bodhisattva*, takes the 12 great vows as to what he would like to achieve when he arrives at Buddhahood. These are the following: he will have 112 marks of the superior being, and he will cause all sentient beings to resemble him; his body will be flawless, and it will have the radiance of the sun; he will enable beings to achieve whatever is needed; he will enable non-Buddhists to enter the path of enlightenment and, lead the *Hiinayaanists* to the *Mahaayaana*; he will help his devotees to live perfect morality, and through his saving power, purify those who fail and prevent them from falling into lower realms; he will cure all forms of illness; he will heal everyone who suffers any form of infirmity as he ascends to the Buddhahood; he will help women who are tired of being women to become men through the power of his name; He will make everyone escape from the net of *Maara*; he will enable those who are suffering from fear of punishment to be freed off their punishment and the fears that accompany it; those who hunger and thirst will be given food to satisfy their needs; and the poor will have clothing and all their needs. Thus, *Bhaishajya-guru* brings a many material benefits to his devotees.[170]

Bhaishajya-guru is the master of healing. He is a medicine Buddha. He is the incarnation of healing in all aspects. He heals all forms of illnesses. Starting from minor illnesses – such as, cold, fever and all forms of minor aches – he heals major illnesses of the body and mind, besides helping one attain enlightenment, which is nothing else but the healing of the human condition filled with suffering and pain. In healing people of their human condition and helping them attain enlightenment, *Bhaishajya-guru* gives his devotees true insight into their condition, especially the type of *Karma* that affects them and the means to get away from the effects of the *Karma*. Using the insight and the help he offers, the devotees can attain true enlightenment easily. In this way, he helps people to attain favorable rebirth both in his own Pure Land and that of the other Buddhas. Similarly, meditative generations of *Bhaishajya-guru*, together with the recitation of the *Mantras*, are used to strengthen the effects of the medicine. Those who remember him in moments of death will truly be healed of their sinful state. *Bhaishajya-guru* is said to save those who go straight away into the lower realms. He attempts to save even the wickedest persons. Even those who have reached the hell regions can get the aid of *Bhaishajya-guru*. Thus the cult of *Bhaishajya-guru* brings a great number of material and spiritual blessings on the devotee. [171]

5.2.1.6.3.3 Amitaabha

Amitaabha is the most popular Buddha in China, Japan and the East Asian countries. He is also known as *Amitaays* and *Amida*. The *Amitaabha* cult gives rise to the Pure Land traditions. The meaning of the name "*Amitaabha*" is 'infinite light'. This name is given to him because his light is immeasurable and he illuminates numerous Buddha Fields in every direction. He is also called 'infinite life', because his life lasts for immeasurable *Aeons*. He lives this infinite life only for the benefit of sentient beings. The story of *Amitaabha's* journey towards enlightenment begins when, after listening to the sermon from the previous Buddha, he decides in his presence to attain Buddhahood. Though he is a king, he gives up the royal status and becomes a mendicant. As a *Bodhisattva*, he is known as *Dharmaakara*. He is said to have taken 46 or 48 vows and lives them through and attains Buddhahood. Some of these vows are the following: if his vows are not fulfilled he may not attain enlightenment; all who are born in his Pure Land may not return to lower levels of existence; those belonging to his Pure Land will remember past lives and will acquire miraculous powers; and the merits they acquire will be used for their rebirth in *Amitaabha's* Pure Land. These and may other wishes of *Amitaabha* comes true as he attains enlightenment and becomes the Buddha.[172]

The Pure Land of *Amitaabha* is called Sukhaavatii. It is a very beautiful land. While there is every material good in this Pure Land, it is not a sensual or earthly paradise, a place of unrestricted pleasure, but it is conducive to spiritual growth. The land of Sukhaavatii contains the realm of the heavens and the gods inhabit the heavens. The birds of Sukhaavatii, due to the power of *Amitaabha*, proclaim the *Dharma*. The trees do the same, as they are gently stirred in the soft breeze. A person is reborn into this Pure Land, by attaining 'the enlightened mind' (*Bodhicitta*). It is achieved by hearing the name of *Amitaabha*, holding him in the mind, meditating on him, thinking of him, and praying in the heart to be reborn in Sukhaavatii. Thirteen forms of meditative visualizations are used to encounter the Buddha of Sukhaavatii, *Amitaabha*. When a person does this regularly, without any form of distraction, *Amitaabha* appears at the deathbed of the seeker and leads him to the land of *Amitaabha*. Since *Amitaabha* personally helps the seeker to be reborn in Sukhaavatii, it is easy to get into this Pure Land. In the Pure Land of *Amitaabha*, a being is reborn non-sexually, as there are no women in this land. The blessed ones of the land appear seated on lotus blossoms in the presence of *Amitaabha*. The people who doubt the teachings of *Amitaabha* are reborn in closed lotuses, and they live in this manner for about 500 years, which is a form of purgatory to purify them. When the allotted time is lived out in the closed lotuses, their doubts are cleared, and they are open to the celestial vision of the Pure Land of Sukhaavatii.[173]

The cult of *Amitaabha* and the attainment of his Pure Land Sukhaavatii has become a significant religious movement in China, Japan and other countries. In the initial stages of the development of the Pure Land Schools of Buddhism, enlightenment is attained with the help of the balanced disciplines of faith and works. In the later period it develops into an extremist doctrine of salvation by faith alone. This happens, among other reasons, due to the efforts of Hoonen Shoonin (1113-1212) and Shinran Shoonin (1117-1262). These two stressed faith alone. The seeker is expected to repeat the name of *Amitaabha* with all his heart, without every stopping the recitation, whether he is walking or standing, sitting or lying down. The formula that should be repeated is *"Namu Amida Butsu"*, which means 'adoration to the Buddha *Amida*'. This practice assures the entry of the seeker in *Amitaabha's* Pure Land of Sukhaavatii. Thus, faith becomes the only reqisite for salvation. There is hardly any need for moral life and action. The whole moral philosophy of Gautama Buddha is swept away as unnecessary. If the sinner has faith in the inexhaustible store of merits the Lord *Amitaabha* possesses, he can gain salvation. The works of the seeker become superfluous and unnecessary. Thus, salvation becomes totally vicarious, due to the merits of *Amitaabha*. The *Amitaabha* cult turns out to be a *Bhakti* cult within the Buddhist tradition.[174]

5.2.2. *MAHAAYAANA* PATH TO THE DIVINE

Our study of the *Mahaayaana* tradition has taken us to the analysis of the *Mahayaana* pantheon, with its gods of differing levels. The *Mahaayaana* spiritual ideal is to tread the path of the *Bodhisattva*, which leads to the final enlightenment of attaining Buddhahood. To achieve the goal of becoming the enlightened, the *Mahaayaana* tradition proposes a number of paths, viz., the moral path, the path of meditation and the path of religious practice. In the following sections, it is our concern to analyze each of these ways and the manner in which each helps the seeker of enlightenment to achieve the goal. The walking of the paths of morality, meditation and religious practice takes the seeker through the ten stages of the *Mahaayaana* path to the Divine.

5.2.2.1. MORAL PATH

The practice of moral living is essential for spiritual progress. But an adept should not get attached to the practice of morality, as any form of attachment comes from ignorance, from which stems every form of defilement. Therefore, the practice of moral precepts must be done in relation to *Dharma*-knowledge, i.e., from the experience of detachment and dispassion. In doing so, the seeker experiences an inner calm and freedom, which, in fact, is the freedom of transcendence. In this manner, the practice of morality, as the *Mahaayaana* path to the Divine, instead of being burdensome, becomes a means to manifest and to express one's essential Buddha nature. When one practices morality with this mind-set, one not only uses moral precepts as a mere means to overcome spiritual impediments, but also as an expression of the seeker's love for all sentient beings. If morality is practiced in this manner, it becomes truly liberating, i.e., opens the person for enlightenment. *Mahaayaana* Buddhism does not adapt universal morality for all, but rather morality is aimed at helping the seeker to fulfill his social and spiritual demands in the context of his everyday living, as he moves towards the goal of Buddhahood.[175] Thus, *Mahaayaana* moral path includes the practice of six perfections, the practice of five moral precepts, the practice of Right Livelihood and the practice of the *Brahma-vihaaras*. We briefly consider each of these moral practices.

5.2.2.1.1. Practice of Six Perfections

The adept, as he begins his path towards the goal of Buddhahood, is advised to practice the six perfections (*Paaramitaas*). They are generosity (*Daana-Paaramitaa*), moral observations (*Siila-Paaramitaa*), patience (*Kshaantii-Paaramitaa*), courage (*Viirya-Paaramitaa*), meditation (*Samaadhi-Paaramitaa*) and wisdom (*Prajnaa-Paaramitaa*). The first is generosity. It consists in donating what one is and has to others. Generosity is charity. It does not mean that a person gives away what he has in surplus, but it consists in giving what one really needs to others, as the other is in greater need. When a person practices generosity on a regular basis, he is able to give up his attitudes of clinging to things. In so doing, he accumulates merit. Rooting out all forms of attachments opens in the individual a desire to give away even the merits he has acquired for the benefit of others. Thus, the practice of generosity brings to the seeker many spiritual blessings. The second is morality. Genuine practice of generosity leads the aspirant to live a good moral life. As the practice of generosity removes forms of self-centeredness and purifies a person's thoughts and emotions, his actions become moral and good. The third is patience. The path to enlightenment is a long and arduous journey. A person needs to go through a number of births and rebirths before he arrives at the end of the journey. So one of the significant perfections a seeker of Buddhahood must have is patience. He must make this journey patiently, taking one step after the other until he arrives at the goal of enlightenment. The fourth is courage. Courage is another important perfection that seekers of Buddhahood must possess. As the seeker moves on in the journey, he must face a number of trials, tribulations, temptations and struggles. He must master his own tendencies and inclinations. He needs to take a number of risks. Courage is a must to go on following the rugged path to enlightenment. The possession of courage is a great help to the adept to make this difficult journey. The fifth is meditation. The practice of meditation is another perfection the aspirant of enlightenment must acquire. Learning the art of meditative visualizations of the Pure Lands of the Buddhas, of the Buddha Fields and of the Buddhas themselves leads the adept to the attainment of 'the enlightenment of mind' (*Bodhicitta*), which finally leads one to Buddhahood. Thus, the greater the quality of the seeker's meditation, the quicker is his realization of the *Bodhicitta* and the Buddhahood. The last of the perfections is wisdom. Wisdom is the perfection that guides the other five perfections and gives them a sense of direction. Each of the five perfections has the quality of perfection, because wisdom accompanies them. The perfection of wisdom consists in the wisdom of emptiness, which constitutes the omniscience of the Buddha. The Buddhas become enlightened due to the guidance and protection of the perfection of wisdom. Therefore, the perfection of wisdom is called 'the mother of all Buddhas'. Acquiring these six perfections to the highest degree is the first step the aspirant of Buddhahood takes to journey towards its attainment.[176]

5.2.2.1.2. Practice of Five Moral Precepts

Besides the practice of the six perfections, the seeker of enlightenment must practice the five moral precepts (*Panca-Siilaani*). Each of these five principles of moral life is stated in negative terms. Therefore, they are commandments of prohibition rather than positive commandments that prescribe one to do something. Thus, the adept is asked to abstain from five types of behavior: abstaining from injuring sentient beings, abstaining from taking that which does not belong to oneself, abstaining from have sexual intercourse with a woman who is not one's wife, abstaining from false speech and abstaining from drugs and other intoxicants that make one lose his sense of balance. The third principle is only applicable to the laity, as the monks are expected to renounce marriage and to live a life of strict celibacy. Though these five precepts are stated negatively, each moral precept of abstention has a positive aspect. Thus, though stated in negative terms, they indirectly prescribe a positive way of living. The positive prescriptions indirectly stated in the abstentions are the following: kindness and compassion, generosity and renunciation, contentment and having few wishes, loving that which is true by knowing that which is false, mindfulness and awareness. These precepts must be seen as guides to train a seeker in the *Buddha-Dharma*. These commandments are not mere ethical rules one can choose to follow or not to follow. They have the binding of vows and must be adhered to strictly. To remind themselves of the duty of performing these moral precepts, it is the practice among the Buddhists to chant these moral precepts daily. The very chanting is a reminder to live them in their daily lives.[177]

In addition to the five moral precepts, the Buddhist layman is expected to practice a set of eight precepts, on special days of observance, like the fasting days. These are the following: abstaining from injuring sentient beings, abstaining from taking that which does not belong to oneself, abstaining from indulging in unchaste conduct, abstaining from false speech, abstaining from drugs and intoxicants, abstaining from taking meals at inappropriate times, abstaining from dancing, music and perfumes, and abstaining from making use of beds which either are high or comfortable. On special days of fasting and penance, a seeker is expected to live a stricter life than that on usual day. Such strict disciplinary practices keep the mind of the seeker away from entanglements in the world and remind him of the goal of his journey towards the attainment of the Buddhahood.[178]

5.2.2.1.3. Practice of Right Livelihood

The practice of Right Livelihood is closely related to the practice of the five moral precepts. It is also one of the limps of the Eightfold Path, which Gautama, the Buddha, has proposed for the way of life of the Buddhists. The commandment of Right Livelihood has two elements. Firstly, it means that one must acquire one's means of living by honest means. In other words, it means that one does not cheat or defraud anybody in earning his livelihood, but rather he makes his living by the sweat of his own body. Secondly, it means that one earns his livelihood without bringing any injury or harm to living beings. In other words, Right Livelihood means that one earns one's living in such a way that one inflicts no pain on any living being. The foundational thinking behind the precept of Right Livelihood, understood in the second sense, is the law of compassion. The law of compassion is not realizable until the motive of injury is removed from every action of a Buddhist. The universal law of compassion, which the precept of Right Livelihood upholds, is based on the doctrine, which says that the essence of every being is identical with the Buddha-nature. Since all beings are essentially identical with the divine Buddha, any action that hurts any being goes against the law of compassion. Hence anyone who violates this precept and causes injury to other living beings while earning his livelihood suffers from attaining his own enlightenment. Thus, the practice of Right Livelihood is one of the most difficult Buddhist precepts to follow in one's everyday life, as before one plans to undertake any means for earning his living, one must see that this particular work one is going to live by in no way harms any living beings. Therefore, one should have the purest motive in what he does.[179]

In order to help the average Buddhist to live this precept of Right Livelihood, the masters of Buddhism teach two meditation techniques of mindfulness, viz., *Hiri* and *Ottapa*, which are often referred to as 'the bright states'. The practice of the former makes the seeker focus on the sense of shame arising due to the performance of a harmful action that is done for the wrong reason. The practice of the latter focuses on the result of the action that is performed due to evil intention. The practice of these two techniques of mindfulness serves as the conscience-keeper for a Buddhist and prevents him from violating the precept of Right Livelihood.[180]

5.2.2.1.4. Practice of the Brahma-Vihaaras

The *Brahma-Vihaaras* are four virtues, which are often rendered in English as 'the immeasurables' or 'the divine abidings'. Taken together, these virtues are called 'right directed thought', as their cultivation brings about in the aspirant the quality of detachment, so that he loses the concept of 'I-am-ness' and develops attitudes of generosity. As a result, selfishness and egocenteredness cease to abide in a person, and godliness begins to abide in him. These virtues take the seeker to a high state of spiritual existence similar to the spiritual existence that is found in the *Brahmaa*-abode. For this reason they are called 'the immeasurables' and 'the divine abidings'. These virtues are loving kindness (*Maitrii*), compassion (*Karunaa*), sympathetic joy (*Muditaa*) and equanimity (*Upekha*).[181]

The first *Brahma-Vihaara* is loving-kindness. It is an attitude of the mind, which makes a person desire the happiness of all. Therefore, it is opposed to ill will. Loving-kindness directs one to prevail over those dimensions of one's nature that have the tendency to cause injury and pain to others. The disposition of loving-kindness is manifested in a beautiful way in the love, care and concern the mother has for her child. The second *Brahma-Vihaara* is compassion. It is the positive consequence of the practice of the virtue of loving-kindness. Compassion desires to free every living being from all forms of suffering. Hence, it is antithetical to all that is cruel and harsh. Compassion, thus, leads to the destruction of negative attitudes, such as, greed, ill will and sloth. It is a mental state in which the seeker feels deeply the sufferings and pains of others and wholeheartedly wishes them to be removed. Compassion moves the seeker to remove such sufferings with the help of good actions. The third *Brahma-Vihaara* is sympathetic joy. It stands for the joy and happiness the aspirant of enlightenment feels within himself, as he sees good and happy things are happening to others. Therefore, it is an antidote to attitudes of jealousy and envy. The last *Brahma-Vihaara* is equanimity. It consists in the seeker being even-minded towards all. It makes a person reach out to all in an attitude of serene repose and with a balanced mind. Hence, equanimity is opposed to being partial, being biased, acting on prejudice, or being one-sided. The practice of these four virtues together, indeed, creates an atmosphere of godliness in the seeker and helps him to create a true 'divine abiding' in the place of his living and to be godlike in his dealing with others.[182] The following quotation from the *Karaniiyamettaasutta* clearly brings to light the spirit of the *Brahma-Vihaaras*:

> He who is skilled in good, and who wishes to attain that state of peace... [*Nirvaana*] should act thus: he should be able, upright, perfectly upright, of pleasant speech, gentle and humble, contended, easy to support, unbusy, with senses controlled, discreet, modest, not greedily attached to families (for alms). He should not commit any slight wrong on account of which other wise men might censure him. (Then he should think): 'May all beings be happy and secure, may they be happy-minded! Whatever living beings there are – feeble or strong, long, stout or medium, short, small or large, seen or unseen, those dwelling far or near, those who are born or those who wait for rebirth – may all beings, without exception, be happy-minded! Let none deceive another nor despise any person whatever in any place; in anger or ill will

let them not wish any suffering to each other. Just as a mother would protect her only child at the risk of her own life, even so, let him cultivate a boundless heart towards all beings. Let his thoughts of boundless loving-kindness pervade the whole world; above, below and across, without obstruction, without any hatred, without any enmity. Whether he stands, walks, sits or lies down, as long as he is awake, he should develop this mindfulness. This, they say, is divine abiding here. Not falling into wrong views, virtuous and endowed with insight, he gives up attachment of sense-desires. He will not come again to any womb (i.e., rebirth).'[183]

5.2.2.2. PATH OF MEDITATION: MEANS TO THE MIND OF ENLIGHTENMENT

The practice of the moral path – the six moral perfections, the five moral precepts, the precept of Right Living and the *Brahma-Vihaaras* – strengthens the mind of the seeker by removing attachment to the body and the senses. As the mind is strengthened, it is ready for the practice of meditation. The life of meditation calls for a commitment to a life of discipline. Any meditational practice aims at training the mind. In order to train the mind through meditation, the adept should cultivate the practice of mindfulness. The practice of mindfulness helps the aspirant to observe and analyze the totality of his behavior. Thus, there comes about an interaction between good conduct and balanced concentration. When this happens, the mind is able to ensue actions that are pure, because the mind by the practice of morality is able to achieve a higher degree of purity. Various forms of meditational practices assisted by the practice of moral life, lead the seeker to experience 'the mind of enlightenment' (*Bodhicitta*), which, in turn, leads him to the final state of enlightenment.[184] In this section, we analyze a few meditational practices the *Mahaayaana* tradition uses to achieve the *Bodhicitta*, and thereby to attain the final state of Buddhahood.

5.2.2.2.1. Practice of Calm and Insight Meditation

The interactive practice of calm meditation (*Samatha-bhaavanaa*) and insight meditation (*Vipassanaa-bhaavanaa*) brings about the *Bodhicitta* in the seeker. Calm meditation consists in binding the thought of the seeker with the help of a simple object. The state of calming the mind is achieved by concentrating on the mental image of the object chosen for meditation. The only thrust of calm meditation is fixing the mind on the mental image of the chosen object. Calm meditation does not entertain conceptualized reflection or getting lost in restless mental states, but rather it focuses on balanced concentration. As a result, the mind is sharply focused and stabilized. When the mind has achieved a state of calm, the seeker begins practicing insight meditation. By the practice of insight meditation the seeker is enabled to experience the foundational teachings of Buddhism. Insight meditation – by the process of critical reflection, analysis and inspection of the doctrinal principles – reveals the true insight to the seeker, viz., the conditioned-ness and essenceless-ness of the phenomenon of life and reality. At this level, the seeker builds up conviction regarding the doctrinal truths of Buddhism and achieves true insight (*Vipassanaa*). In *Mahaayaana* Buddhism, the insight has three main sources, viz., the scriptures, philosophical reasoning and analysis, and the synthesis of interpretation and application. Thus, we have threefold insight: wisdom by listening to the scripture (*Srutamayii-prajnaa*); the wisdom by reflection, which arises by philosophical reasoning; and wisdom by meditation, which arises from insight meditation. Of these three forms of wisdom, the highest is the wisdom attained by the consistent practice of insight meditation, and in it the first two forms of wisdom are affirmed. The wisdom that is achieved through insight meditation is, indeed, the *Bodhicitta*, which leads a seeker to the Buddha-realization.[185]

5.2.2.2.2. Practice of Recollection on the Buddha

The recollection on the Buddha (*Buddhaanusmrti*) is a simple awareness meditation practice in which one attempts to experience the presence of the Buddha and to offer him worship constantly from the depth of one's heart. Firstly, it consists in bringing to the mind of the one who meditates the special qualities of the Buddha: his clear vision, his virtuous conduct, his sublimity, his omniscience, his knowledge of the world, his incomparable leadership, his ability to teach gods and men, the enlightened and the blessed nature of the Buddha. Secondly, it involves meditating on the physical features of the Buddha: his conquering of fear and dread, his web-like hands and feet, his teeth, his tongue that is long and single, his intensely blue eyes and many other qualities. The meditation on the spiritual qualities of the Buddha makes the seeker become more like him internally and spiritually, besides experiencing his spiritual presence. The recollection of the Buddha's physical features makes the aspirant aware of the physical presence of the Buddha. These twofold recollections of the Buddha make the seeker experience the personality of the Buddha in his material and spiritual dimensions. This experience is so real, that if the seeker is tempted to do something evil, he feels ashamed, as he is present to the Buddha in a one-to-one relationship. The *Buddhaanusmrti* highlights three points. Firstly, there is a connection between the recollection of the Buddha and the attainment of a higher plane of existence, a happy destiny or the plane of the Buddhas. Secondly, through the practice of *Buddhaanusmrti*, one becomes free from all fears. Thirdly, due to the practice of *Buddhaanusmrti*, the aspirant comes to feel that he is living in the presence of the Buddha himself. The *Buddhaanusmrti* has to be carried out as follows. When the seeker carries on the *Buddhaanusmrti*, he should live in seclusion. He must give up all discursive thoughts. The total concentration of the mind should be focused on the Buddha, while reciting Buddha's name singlemindedly. The body must be held erect when the recollection is carried out. While meditating, the seeker must face the direction of the Buddha. If the practice of *Buddhaanusmrti* becomes a continuous experience, it is said that one can encounter the Buddhas of the past, present and the future. The practice of the recollection of the Buddha is the easiest and quickest way to experience enlightenment.[186]

5.2.2.2.3. Meditation on the Buddha-Field

Buddhist cosmology considers space, like time, as infinite. In this infinite space, there are infinite numbers of universes, with their own world systems, extending over the ten directions, viz., the four cardinal directions, the four intermediary directions, below and above. Within this infinite space, there are regions called 'Buddha-fields' or 'Buddha-lands' (*Buddhakshetra*). They are, in the strict sense, not the places in which the Buddhas are born. They are the fields of activity of the Buddhas that have come about as the result of the compassionate activities of the Buddhas as the *Bodisattvas*. Buddhas, as *Bodhisattvas*, have created the Buddha-fields. The Buddha-fields emerge as the result of *Bodhisattva's* altruism. It is an area where the Buddha can teach sentient beings, do works of compassion for them, provide a place for their rebirth and help them to advance in their spiritual goals. Buddha-fields, therefore, are mystical universes in which the Buddhas and the people they rule and mature live. Hence, the Buddha-fields have the best conditions necessary for the spiritual progress of sentient beings, as there are the Buddhas and the *Bodhisattvas* to guide the spiritual progress. The *Bodhisattvas*, who belong to the Buddha-field, purify it and help the Buddhas exercise their activity of teaching and ruling. There are three types of Buddha-field, viz., the pure, the impure and the mixed Buddha-fields. The pure Buddha-fields are those in which the conditions of living are ideal and are conducive to the spiritual progress of the beings living there. They are happy lands, where joy radiates the life of everyone living there. For instance, the Buddha-field of *Amitabha* Buddha, known as Sukkaavatii, is a pure Buddha-field. The impure Buddha-field is one in which there is suffering, pain, absence of *Buddha-Dharma*, and lack of happiness is found, for instance the Buddha-fields that include the lower regions of the world systems – such as the hells, the domain of ghosts, the region of the *Asuras* and the like. Here there is want, pain and immorality. The mixed Buddha-fields include both good and evil. For instance, the present *Saaha* world, whose Buddha is Gautama Sidhaartha, is a mixed Buddha-field, as in this universe there is both suffering and happiness, good *Dharma* and lower forms of *Dharma*, differences of class, caste and group.[187]

Having described the nature of the Buddha-fields, we can elaborate on the practice of meditation on the Buddha-field. It is a meditative awareness of the sphere of activity of the Buddha, into whose realm a seeker wishes to be reborn. It consists in cultivating various contemplative visualizations about the Buddha and the Buddha-field that belongs to him. An example of meditation on the Buddha-field can be found in the series of 13 visualization meditations on Buddha *Amitaabha*, which Gautama Buddha teaches to Queen Vaidehii, whom her wicked son has imprisoned. The 13 visualizations are the following. The visualization meditation begins by reflecting on the setting sun in the west. Then, the seeker meditates on the Pure Land of the *Amitaabha* Buddha, its clear water, the ice and the crystal. The meditation proceeds further to focus on the ground of the Pure Land, its trees, its lakes and palaces. Now the seeker meditates on the lotus throne of the Buddha *Amitaabha*. Next the meditative visualization is centered on the *Amitaabah* Buddha who is seated on the lotus throne, flanked by *Bodhisattva Avalokitesvara* on the left and *Bodhisattva Mahaasthaamapraapta* on the right. The focus of the next visualization is centered on the form of *Amitaabah* Buddha, which follows the visualization of the forms of *Avalokitesvara* and *Mahaasthaamapraapta* respectively. Keeping these visualizations in mind, the seeker prays for rebirth in the Pure Land Sukhaavatii of *Amitaabha* Buddha. Then the seeker visualizes completely all details of this Pure Land with a fixed mind, and sees him as born on a lotus in the Pure Land of Sukhaavatii. Finally, the seeker visualizes him as present before the *Amitaabha* and the two *Bodhisattvas* in front. It is believed among the *Mahaayaana* Buddhists that constant meditative visualization of the Buddha-field of a particular Buddha brings alive in the seeker that particular Buddha and his Buddha-field, so that he in actual fact lives in that Buddha-field in spirit, and, when he dies, he is automatically reborn into the Buddha-field he has been contemplating while on earth.[188]

5.2.2.2.4. Two Meditations That Generate the Mind of Enlightenment

Bringing about a deep compassion for others in the seeker and thereby attaining 'the mind of enlightenment' (*Bodhicitta*), completely transforms a person, because from then on he behaves as a son of the Buddha. In order to motivate the initiates to generate *Bodhicitta*, the Tibetan traditions of 'the gradual path' make use of a series of meditations with the help of which the initiates are made aware of the values of renunciation, compassion and emptiness. These meditations make the initiates realize that renouncing themselves and preferring others in compassionate love, finally leads a person to experience knowledge of the emptiness of reality. The meditations begin with the fact of *Samsaara* existence. Then one moves on to reflect on the impermanence and death that mark existence, which, in turn, creates in the aspirant a desire to practice the *Dharma*. Next one meditates on *Karma* and rebirth, which gives rise to a moral basis for spiritual practice. Then, the aspirant contemplates various forms of rebirth and the sufferings of the beings that live in the six cosmological regions. It brings to the mind of the adept the ultimate unsatisfactoriness of existence. In this manner, these series of meditations make the initiates realize the emptiness of existence, renounce the self and *Samsaara* existence, and move towards others in compassion. The attainment of this realization is, indeed, the *Bodhicitta*.[189] There are two forms of meditations that are aimed at producing the *Bodhicitta* in the initiates.

The first one is called "six causes and one effect" while the second is called "exchange of self and others". We briefly consider them now.

5.2.2.2.4.1. Meditation on Six Causes and One Effect

As a preparation for doing this meditation the adept should cultivate an unbiased attitude towards all sentient beings. To bring about this attitude, he is asked to visualize a friend, an enemy and a person towards whom he has indifferent feelings. In fact all these three persons are alike, as in the endless series of birth, death and rebirth, each of them might have evoked in the adept differing feelings, just as enemies and friends change roles even in this life. In this way the initiate develops a feeling of equality towards all sentient beings. With the attitude of equal-mindedness, the initiate moves on to the meditation on 'six causes and one effect'. Firstly, he imagines the persons who have been his mothers in the infinite number of past lives he has lived. Secondly, he visualizes the goodness of the mothers that make them take upon themselves great troubles for his sake. Thirdly, he brings to his mind the thought that his mothers of various lives are, in fact, presently sentient beings in the world in different levels of existence, and they undergo a great deal of suffering. He also reminds himself that it is his duty to repay his mothers, who are sentient beings now, for all the suffering they have undertaken for him in the previous lives. Fourthly, in the light of the three reflections, he generates great love for all sentient beings and wishes them all happiness. Fifthly, he also plans to contribute to the enhancement of their happiness and the removal of their sufferings. Sixthly, he decides to take upon himself the responsibility of helping all sentient beings. Suddenly he realizes that it is nearly impossible for him to help anyone, as he is limited. Meditation on his limited condition and the desire to help all sentient beings evokes in him the desire to become fully enlightened and become a Buddha, that with all the abilities and powers of the Buddha, he can fulfill his desire to help every sentient being. This desire to become the Buddha due to compassion for others is the *bodhicitta*. Thus, six meditative steps cause one effect, viz., 'the mind of enlightenment'.[190]

5.2.2.2.4.2. Meditation on Exchanging Self for Others

The second meditation for generating *Bodhicitta* is the "exchanging self and others". As the first step of meditation, the one who meditates imagines that all are equal, in that all, like him, desire happiness and the absence of suffering. Secondly, he becomes aware that the individuality of each person in the world is as important as that of the one who meditates. He also becomes conscious of the fact that taken together all sentient beings are more important than he because they are greater in number than he. From this he concludes that if he has to choose between helping himself or helping others, he must choose to help others rather than helping himself, because he is just one and others are many. At this juncture, the adept repeats a meditation that aims at creating in him the quality of equal-mindedness. As a next step, he meditates on the faults and problems associated with taking care of himself rather than others, and the goodness that comes to him and to the world if he chooses to care for others. The result of the meditative steps taken so far is that the seeker is able to 'exchange self with others', as he realizes that the purpose of his existence is to serve others. Now the adept moves on to practice the next step, called "giving and taking". Here the seeker visualizes all the sufferings of beings in different realms. Keeping them before his mind, he imagines that he is taking on their suffering with the inhaling breath and breathing out the happiness he feels within him. In this manner, he removes the sufferings of all sentient beings and brings happiness to all because of his compassion for them. It is the belief of the Buddhists that if the last step of the meditation is practiced perfectly, the seeker can truly transfer the suffering of others and bring happiness to them. This is what the *Bodhisattvas* have achieved in their lives. The knowledge that moves them to perform this healing work in the world is the *Bodhicitta*. Thus, by the practice of the meditation on "exchange self for others" one attains the *Bodhicitta*.[191]

5.2.2.3. PATH OF RELIGIOUS PRACTICE

The *Hiinayaana* tradition stresses the self-reliance of the seeker in attaining the state of *Nirvaana*. It is the accepted belief of the *Hiinayaanists* that one's own personal effort can save him and no one can be the agent of the salvation of the other. But the *Mahaayaana* tradition, while not denying the role of the seeker in attaining his salvation, denies the attitude of exclusive self-reliance. It believes in the doctrine of merit and its use for the whole community. According to the *Mahaayaanists*, merit is a quality in a person, which ensures future benefits to him whether they be material or spiritual. Seeking merit for oneself alone amounts to a form of self-seeking, which goes against the goal of *Nirvaana*. So it is right and proper that a person who has acquired merits distributes them to other members of the community who deserve it. Thus, they accept the doctrine of the transference of merit. This means that the merit a person has acquired over a period of time can compensate the demands of the Law of *Karma* on behalf of another person, when it is transferred to him freely. Thus, the *Mahaayaana* tradition recognizes the role of saviors, like the *Bodhisattvas* and the Buddhas, whose merits are a source of salvation for their devotees.[192] The following quote illustrates this point clearly:

> Through the merit derived from all my good deeds I wish to appease the suffering of all creatures, to be the medicine, the physician, and the nurse for the sick as long as there is sickness. Through rains of food and drink I wish to extinguish the fire of hunger and thirst. I wish to be an inexhaustible treasure to the poor, a servant who furnishes them all they lack. My life, and all my re-births, all my possessions, all the merit that I have acquired or will acquire, all that I abandon

without hope of any gain for myself in order that the salvation of all beings might be promoted.[193]

In analyzing the *Mahaayaana* path to the Divine, we have looked into the path of morality and that of meditation. Morality frees a seeker from all forms of attachments, while meditational practices take him to the attainment of true insight into Buddhist wisdom. Thus, in the moral and meditational paths the role of the seeker is predominant. But, unlike *Hiinayaana*, the *Mahaayaana* tradition, besides recognizing the role of the seeker in his salvation, also accepts the role of *Bodhisattvas* and Buddhas whose merit is a means to attain salvation. Therefore, it proposes a religious path, besides the moral and the meditational paths, to help the seeker to attain his ultimate goal of Buddha-realization, by opening him to the merit of the heavenly saviors. In this section, we explore some the religious practices the *Mahaayaana* tradition recommends as a means to the attainment of the Buddhahood.

5.2.2.3.1. Practice of Bhakti

The *Mahaayaana* Buddhism presents the *Bodhisattvas* and the Buddhas as saviors of the people, who with the help of their merit bring bountiful blessings to them. These holy ones promote virtue in the believers and destroy their evil habits, such as, greed, hate and delusion, thereby guiding them to the final realization of Buddhahood. The *Bodhisattvas* and the Buddhas also bestow on the devotees material benefits: they protect earthly fortunes, ward off disasters, protect from robbers, help women to bear children, save sailors from shipwreck and do many similar acts that are beneficial to the people. The expectation and experience of these blessings make the people reach out to these holy ones with the attitude of *Bhakti*, i.e., with sentiments of faith, love and devotion. *Bhakti* involves a personal relationship between the devotees and their saviors. The attitude of *Bhakti* leads the people to dwell in the sight of the *Bodhisattvas* and the Buddhas. The help they offer to the people in realizing the final enlightenment is a sign of these holy ones' desire to be with the people and to take them to the Pure Lands of the Buddhas. Thus, *Bhakti* becomes a means to journey towards the 'Land of the Blessed'.[194]

People express the sentiments of *Bhakti* in a number of ways. Firstly, they commit themselves to live a pure life, as they wished to become like the Buddha and be part of his Pure Land in their next birth. Secondly, worship of the Buddha accumulates merit. The worship consists of praising the greatness of the Buddha, paying homage to him, feeling within a deep union with the Buddha at the very thought of him and praying to the Buddha to be reborn in his Buddha-field. Thirdly, the practice of *Bhakti* is expressed by repeating the name of the *Bodhisattva* and the Buddha with great devotion. A great number of formulas for invocation of the name of the Buddha are formulated. Some important ones are: 'homage to the Buddha *Amitaabha*', '*Om Namo Amitabhaaya*', '*Namo Amida Butsu*' and many others. Fourthly, *Bhakti* of the people is expressed through their belief in the vow of the *Bodhisattva* to save every sentient being and take it to paradise. Like the *Bodhisattva*, out of love for him, the seeker also must transfer his merits to paradise and make a vow to be reborn there. Finally, *Bhakti* is also expressed by the practice of meditation visualization on the Buddha, the practice of which truly takes the seeker to the Pure Land of the Buddha.[195]

5.2.2.3.2. Special Devotions to Bodhisattvas and the Buddhas

The attitude of *Bhakti* towards the *Bodhisattvas* and the Buddhas makes the people take up various devotional practices. The aim of the devotions is to honor these saviors and to receive their blessings. We briefly consider here some of the devotional practices people offer to some popular *Bodhisattvas* and the Buddhas.

5.2.2.3.2.1. Devotions to Avalokitesvara

One of the *Bodhisattvas* who receives the greatest honor from the people is *Avalokitesvara*. He is believed to be the most compassionate one, who immediately responds to those who call upon him with their whole mind. The most important form of devotion people offer to him is protective chanting. It consists in invoking the protection of the *Avalokitesvara* by chanting 'safety-runes' (*Parittas*). There are various types of *Parittas*: those that produce loving-kindness towards all beings; those that bring right hearing of the *Dharma* and lead people to *Nirvaana*; those that are used against particular dangers; and those that are used to ward off evil forces. The chanting of the *Parittas* or listening to them helps the people in a number of ways: firstly, it leads the people to self-confidence and a calm mind, cures psychosomatic illnesses, and makes a person alert in facing the dangers of life; secondly, it calms down a hostile person, animal or ghost and makes them well-disposed towards the chanter; thirdly, it brings immediate good results from the good actions done in the past; it opens the chanter to the protection and assistance of the various gods; and finally it brings the spiritual power of the Buddha, the compassionate protector, thereby leading a person to the realization of the Buddha.[196]   Other than *Paritta* chanting, people invoke *Avalokitesvara* by praying the '*Mani Mantra*', which reads as follows: "*Om Mani Padme Huum*". It is one of the most popular devotional acts practiced in Tibet. This *Mantra* literally means 'O jeweled-lotus lady'. "*Om*" and "*Huum*" are ancient Indian sacred sounds. '*Mani*' stands for the jewel the *Bodhisattva* holds in his hands and '*Padme*' refers to the lotus, which is his symbol. The jewel symbolizes the *Bodhisattva's* willingness to grant the righteous wishes of the devotee and the pure clarity in the depth of the minds of beings. The lotus symbolizes *Avalokitesvara's* compassion and the worldly minds of beings, which he guides to flower into enlightenment. The *Mani Mantra* is repeated in a number of ways. Firstly, it is repeated by using the rosary. Secondly, it is recited by using the '*Mani* religion wheel' or the prayer wheel, inside and outside of which the *Mantra* is written many times. Each turning of the wheel is equivalent to the repetition of all the *Mantras* on and in it. There are different types of '*Mani* religion wheels'. There are the hand-held ones, whose cylinders are about seven centimeters long. Wheels about 25 centimeters high are fixed in rows on the side of the *Stuupas* and monasteries, that people can turn them as they circumambulate these holy places. The largest wheels, four meters high and two meters in diameter, are found at the entrances of temples, on which are engraved thousands of *Mani Mantras*. Similarly there are wheels that are driven by streams or chimney smoke. In the same way, *Mani Mantras* are carved on stones that are placed on the top of the hills; they are also written on rock faces by the side of the roads; they are engraved on long walls that are built near the towns; and they are also printed on flags. It is believed that use of the wheel to recite the *Mani Mantras*, to read them and to glance at them thinking of *Bodhisattva Avalokitesvara* and his compassion, are said to generate and increase one's goodness-power, which helps the seeker to move fast into the path of Buddhahood. The use of the *Mani Mantras* is another great devotion people offer to *Bodhisattva Avalokitesvara*.[197]

5.2.2.3.2.2. Devotion to Amitaabah

Devotion to *Amitaabah* is found in every school of the *Mahaayaana* tradition, but it becomes more central in the Pure Land schools. Devotion consists in the invocation of various *Mantras* honoring *Amitaabah*: "*Nan-mo A-mit-t'o Fo*", "*Nama Amida Butsu*", "*Namo Amitaabhaaya Buddhaaya*" are Chinese, Japanese and Sanskrit versions of the most famous invocation to honor *Amitaabah* respectively. It is rendered in English as "Hail to *Amitaabha* Buddha". Sometimes it is chanted using music, while other times it is meditatively repeated. It is used as a great means of unwavering concentration on *Amitaabah*, which leads to the enlightenment attainable at *Amitaabah's* Pure Land, Sukhaavatii. Besides, its devotional recitation leads to the temporal dissolution of the ego. It is also recited using rosary beads. Some other devotional practices that are offered to *Amitaabah* are the following: chanting of the Pure Land *Suutras*; 13 meditative visualizations of *Amitaabah* and his Pure Land Sukhaavatii; worship of various Buddhas; singing hymns of praise to *Amitaabah*; vowing to be reborn in Sukhaavatii; and developing generosity and compassion by helping the needy and practicing vegetarianism. The followers of the *Jodo-Shin* school of Japan show their devotion to *Amitaabah* by the use of the *Mantra* "*Nembutsu*". It is used to facilitate the awakening of faith in *Amitaabah*. After the rise of faith in the heart of the devotee, the same *Mantra* is used as an expression of gratitude, often recited with the help of rosary beads. Its recitation also reminds people that they are only a bundle of passion in comparison to *Amitaabah*. The recitation of the *Mantra* also expresses the devotee's filial love and devotion for *Amitaabah*, who is referred to as 'the Parent' (*Oyasama*).[198]

5.2.2.3.2.3. Devotion to Bhaishajya-guru

People offer devotion to the Buddha *Bhaishajya-guru*, the master of healing. Popular devotions to him are common because of his healing powers. In China he is popularly worshipped as follows. The image of *Bhaishajya-guru* is set up on a throne. Flowers are scattered around the throne; incense is burnt, and the area is adorned with banners and pennants. Having done the preparations, the worshiper must make eight vows and keep them for seven days and seven nights. During these days he eats pure food, bathes in pure and fragrant water and wears new and clean clothing. He creates in himself an unstained and single-minded state, without any desire to harm anybody. He must have the thoughts of blessings, benefits, peace, loving-kindness, sympathetic joy and equanimity. He must sing praises to *Bhaishajya-guru*, using musical instruments while circumambulating the image of the Buddha. He must recall the merits of *Bhaishajya-guru* by studying the *Suutra* of *Bhaishajya-guru* and recite the *Suutra* 79 times. He makes seven images of *Bhaishajya-guru* and contemplates the image, so that it brings in him spiritual force and healing energy, in the process mentally merging with *Bhaishajya-guru*. This practice brings a number of material and spiritual blessings to the devotee – such as, long life, wealth, an official position, sons and daughters, freedom from nightmares and many similar blessings. Similarly, the recitation of the *Suutra* of *Bhaishajya-guru* in the ear of the dying man can lessen his suffering and take him to a favorable rebirth. Concentrating on the name of *Bhaishajya-guru* can help women in childbirth. In Japan, the *Suutra* of *Bhaishajya-guru* is recited to ward off droughts, pestilence and disasters that affect the nation; to bring protection and prosperity to the state; and longevity and health to the rulers and the people.[199]

5.2.2.3.3. Image Worship

The worship of the images (*Pratimaa-puujaa*) of the Buddha is a development in Buddhism that occured several centuries after the *Pari-Nirvaana* of the Buddha. The original Paali *Tri-pitaka* does not mention anything about the worship of images. But with the emergence of the *Mahaayaana* tradition and the worship of the images of the Buddhas, the *Bodhisattvas* and other deities became prevalent and popular. Elaborate rules are introduced to regulate the making of the images, while sophisticated rites are associated with the consecration and installation of the images in temples and other places. Due to the control of monks over the making and installation of Buddha images, some specific physical features common to all Buddha images emerge. Firstly, Gautama Buddha is always represented as clothed and not as naked, unlike the images of Mahaaviira and other Jaina saints. Secondly, the images of the Buddha have impressive tranquil features that point to complete conquest over passions and perfect repose. Thirdly, the images have long and pendulous ears, which sometimes reach to the shoulders. Fourthly, the images of the Buddha have a circle, small globe, or auspicious mark of some kind on the palms of the suspended hands, as well as on the soles of the feet. According to some authors, these symbols represent the wheel of the emperor (*Cakravartii*), the wheel of Law (*Dharma-cakra*), the cycle of causes or the continuous revolution of births, deaths and rebirths. Finally, the images of the Buddha have short knobby hair, carved so as to resemble a close-fitting, curly wig.[200] Some other features of the Buddha images are: the presentation of the Buddha as having a Nimbus encircling his head; other images represent him as rays of light or a halo surrounding his entire body; and there are images that represent the Buddha as a mendicant holding a begging bowl.[201] Thus we find a dignity and decorum that goes along with the images of the Buddha, in comparison with the images of the Hindu or Jaina religious traditions.

The images of Gautama Buddha express certain attitudes. They are classified into three groups depending on the position of the images, viz., squatting position, standing position and reclining position. The first four attitudes belong to the squatting position: the meditative attitude, the witness attitude, the serpent-canopied attitude and the argumentative attitude. The meditative attitude represents the Buddha as seated cross-legged in meditation on a raised seat under a tree with two hands placed one over the other. The witness attitude represents Gautama Buddha at the moment of achieving Buddhahood. In this attitude, he is seated cross-legged on the lion throne (*Sinhaasana*), while his right hand hangs over his right leg and points to the earth, and the left hand is placed on his left foot. There is a halo round his head and a mark on his forehead. Over the sacred tree is an umbrella. This is the most important attitude of the Buddha, as it represents the attainment of *Nirvaana*. The serpent-canopied attitude represents the Buddha seated cross-legged in meditation on the coiled body of the *Naaga Mucalinda*, the serpent demon, while he is sheltered from the violent storm by the expanded hood of the *Naaga Mucalinda*. The argumentative attitude represents Gautama Buddha seated, cross-legged, while the thumb and finger of his right hand touch the fingers of the left, as it is going through the heads of his doctrine and enforcing it by reiterations. It is also known as the teaching attitude. The next three attitudes belong to the standing positions, viz., the preaching attitude, the benedictive attitude and the mendicant attitude. The preaching attitude represents the Buddha standing erect, with his finger raised in a didactic manner. The monks of the present day maintain this attitude while they preach or read the Law. The benedictive attitude represents the Buddha in the standing position, while the hand is raised to impart a blessing. Sometimes this attitude is expressed while seated in the meditative posture. The mendicant attitude represents the Buddha standing erect while holding a round alms-bowl in his one hand and sometimes screening it with the other. The last attitude belongs to the reclining posture. It represents the Buddha lying down on his right side, with his head turned towards the north, and his right cheek resting on his right hand, about to pass into the stage of *Pari-Nirvaana*. This is another important attitude of the Buddha, as it represents his final consummation.[202]

Other than the above-mentioned images of the Buddha, there are images of him – representing him coming out of his mother's right side at his birth, the god *Brahmaa* receiving the newborn child, *Indra* standing on the right along with Buddha's mother's sister – that are found as carvings in the temples. Similarly there are a number of images of Buddha *Amitaabha*, images of Buddhas who came ahead of Gautama Buddha, the images of the *Dhyaani*-Buddhas, the *Bodhisattvas* – such as, *Maitreya, Avlokitesvara, Manjusuri, Vajra-paai* – are found and used in usual worship of the *Mahaayaana* Buddhists. There are also images of the *Dharma* and the *Sangha*, besides the Buddha. *Dharma* is usually represented as a female holding a half-blown lotus in the left hand, while the *Sangha* is represented as male. There are also the images of gods and goddesses that are borrowed from the Hindu pantheon. All forms of images and icons play important roles in the life of a *Mahaayaana* Buddhist as he journeys towards the ultimate goal of Buddha-realization. The usual forms of image worship are chanting hymns in praise of the Buddha, the offering of flowers and incense sticks, circumambulation of the images and bowing before the images in veneration. [203]

5.2.2.3.4. Worship of Sacred Objects

Besides the worship of the images, Buddhists also venerate and honor a number of objects, because they are considered as sacred. Buddhists generally classify the sacred objects in three categories: the objects that are parts of the body of the Buddha (*Saariirika*), objects the Buddha has possessed and used while on earth (*Paaribhogika*), and objects that are commemorative of the Buddha (*Uddesika*).[204] Though the authors have made this classification, it is difficult to place all the sacred objects into these categories. So we study the Buddhist sacred objects in a different grouping: the relics and the relic receptacles, the sacred footprints, the sacred trees and the sacred books.

5.2.2.3.4.1. Relics and Relic Receptacles

The Worship of relics of holy men is not customary among the Hindus. But the Buddhists consider the veneration of relics as an important way of honoring the holy men. The most important relics that the Buddhists honor are those of Gautama Buddha. It is believed that even before his death portions of his hair and nails were preserved. It is stated that at the death of the Gautama Buddha, the eight kings who are his followers come to take portions of his relics, which are equally divided among them. After he is cremated, the relics that remain are four teeth, two cheekbones and fragments of the skull. Reverence for the relics of the Buddha seems to be an ancient practice among the Buddhists. It seems that the earliest relic of the Buddha to which honor was given were his teeth. Then other parts of the body – such as, hair, nails, skull bones and cheekbones – were venerated. It is the belief of the Buddhists that the relics of the Buddha on some special occasions give out celestial light, and they have the power to work miracles. The circumambulation of the shrine that contains the relics is sufficient to stimulate their miraculous powers. The relics of the Buddha, such as parts of the body, his alms-bowl, his robe and other objects, are exhibited for public worship and veneration. There comes a need to preserve these relics from the people, who out of devotion may take away the relics. Thus, the need emerges to make proper relic-receptacles,[205] to which we turn our attention next.

It is customary at the time of the Buddha to raise heaps over the ashes of the kings, great men and sages. These heaps are called *Caityas*. A later name for *Caityas* is the *Stuupas*. In the Buddhist usage, *Caitya* stands for a relic-structure in an assembly hall, while the *Stuupa* denotes a relic-structure in the open air. Inside the *Caitya* or the *Stuupa* is the casket, which is usually made of silver, gold, stone or earthenware. It is called the *Dhaatu-garbha*. It contains the actual relic of the Buddha or the holy men. Later the structure, in which the relic casket is kept, as well as the relic casket, comes to be known as the *Daagaba*, from which the word "*Pagoda*" derives. Over a period of time large and enormous relic-repositories, i.e., the *Stuupas* are constructed. Originally the *Stuupas* were structures that contained relics, but over a period of time the votive *Stuupas* came about, containing no relics, but honoring the memory of the Buddha or another great saint. We find *Stuupas*, not only in honor of the Buddha, but also in honor of Buddha's immediate disciples, such as, Saariputta, Maudgalyaayana, Kaasyapa, Aananda and Upaali.[206]

5.2.2.3.4.2. Sacred Footprints

The footprint of the Buddha is another sacred object the Buddhists revere. In every country where Buddhism is practiced, there are the footprints of the Buddha, and they are venerated with great piety. According to a legend, the worship of the Buddha's footprints has emerged from the example of Mahaa-Kaasyappa, an immediate disciple of the Buddha, and 500 monks pay homage to the feet of the Buddha as his body is laid on the funeral pile. As they venerate the feet of the Buddha, the fire in the funeral pile ignites spontaneously. Though it is not clear when and where the practice of the footprints of the Buddha began, it is one of the most popular devotional acts amongst the Buddhists. There are a number of footprints in different countries, like India, Burma, Tibet, Mongolia and China. Generally the footprints are two to five feet long. The footprint of the Buddha found on Adam's Peak, one of the highest mountains in Sri Lanka, is supposed to have been left when he ascended to heaven from there. The footprint of Buddha found in Siam, which is given the name "*Phra Bat*", is another famous one. The soles of each foot are represented as flat, and the toes are of equal length. Each soul possesses 108 auspicious marks (*Mangala-lakshana*), and of these the principal is the wheel (*Cakra*). Some of the auspicious marks are: a spear, a trident, a book, an elephant goad, an elephant, a dragon, an ocean, a golden ship, water with lotuses, a conchshell, a four-faced *Brahmaa*, umbrella, King of *Naagas*, King of horses, King of tigers, King of birds, sun, moon, ten mountains, peacock, flag of victory, dear, fish and water jar. Around the footprint are representations of animals, inhabitants of different worlds and symbols of different kinds, pointing to the supremacy of the Buddha over every kind of reality in the universe. The worship of the footprints of the Buddha is a means to the realization of the goal of existence, Buddhahood. Prostration and kissing the place of footprints, and offering of flowers and incense sticks are the usual forms of worshipping the footprints.[207]

5.2.2.3.4.3. Sacred Trees

Another object the Buddhists consider as sacred is the tree. It is the faith of the Buddhists that each of the Buddhas attains enlightenment as he meditates sitting under a particular tree: Gautama Buddha - the Fig Tree (*Asvattha*); Kaasyappa Buddha – the banion tree (*Vat*); Kanaka-muni Buddha – *Udumbara* tree; Karku – *Siriisha* tree; Vishv-bhu – the Sal tree (*Saala*); Sikhin – *Pundariika* tree; and Vipasyin – *Paatali* tree. These seven are the principal Buddhas. The other trees, which the Indian Buddhists worship, are the mango tree (*Aamra*), the *Jambu* tree and the Asoka tree. The other two trees under which Buddha meditated after his enlightenment are the *Mucalinda* tree and the Raajaayatana-tree. The importance the Gautama Buddha gives to the worship of the trees is indicated in this legend. Gautama is said to have directed Aananda to cut off a branch from the original fig tree and to plant it in his monastery at Srasvasti. He also seems to have said that any person who worships the tree receives the same reward as if he worships the Buddha. Since the Buddhas of the past have given so much importance to the trees, Buddhists also respect and revere them. Common forms of worship of trees include bowing to the trees, circumambulation of the trees and offering gifts by binding them on the trees.[208]

5.2.2.3.4.4. Sacred Books

The Buddhists consider their scriptures, which contain the *Buddha-Dharma*, as something sacred. They are not merely venerated and revered, but they are practically deified. They are seen as intelligent and omniscient beings. While used for reading and recitation, the sacred books are give due reverence. They are wrapped in costly silk cloths. When the name of the sacred books is uttered, titles of honor are added to them. People generally bow to the sacred books as they pass by the place where they are placed. In some places the sacred books are placed in makeshift altars at the roadside and near the footpaths both for veneration and for offerings of money and other gifts.[209]

5.2.2.3.5. Sacramental Acts

Buddhism, like Hinduism, has a number of sacramental acts (*Samskaaras*), opening the life of the person, from his birth to death, to the grace of the Divine. In this section, we consider the initial domestic ceremonies related to the birth of the child, marriage ceremonies and the sacramental acts related to the dying and the dead.

The initial domestic ceremonies begin soon after the child's birth. Two weeks after the birth of the child, the astrologer fixes an auspicious day and hour for naming the child. Family members, relatives, friends and well-wishers are called for the feast. The child's head is washed for the first time on this day. A name is suggested for the child. A number of formalities are gone through in choosing the name. The parents, then, carefully take note of the exact year, month, date and hour of the child's birth to write the horoscope for the child. But the actual writing of the horoscope is done only when the child is about five or six years old. Once it is written, the horoscope becomes the prized document for doing anything in the life of the child. The parents take care of it until the child is of age to manage his own affairs. Buddhists believe that the life of a human being is fully under the guidance of the planets from his birth to death. At the age of eight, the boy attends the monastery school for his studies. His hair is cut and he learns the strict discipline and the wisdom the monks of the monastery impart. At the age of 15, either he joins the monastery as a novice or leaves the *Vihaara* to begin his life in the world as a householder.[210]

A person begins his life as a householder by going through the marriage ceremony. In Buddhist countries, the marriage ceremony is a purely civil ceremony. Only the parents of both the parties witness the ceremony. The ceremony is simple and hardly has any religious character. The most important ceremony is the festive meal given to the invited guests after the wedding. Though the ceremony has no religious coloring, still astrology plays a vital role in the arrangement of the marriage. Prior to the wedding, the compatibility of the partners is established through astrology.[211]

When a person is dangerously ill, the monk-priest is called from the monastery by offerings of flowers, oil and food. At the arrival of the monk-priest a temporary preaching place is prepared. The friends, relatives and family members of the sick man gather for prayer. The monk-priest reads the *Suutra* for protection (*Paritta*), the law for about six hours. As the *Paritta* is recited the monk holds one end of a thread, while the sick man holds the other end. It is a way of strengthening the sick man with the power of the protective changing. Then, the priest pronounces the benediction over the sick man. In case the sick man is likely to die, the priest repeats the Three-refuge formula, five commandments and the *Sati-patthaana Suutra*, which speaks of reflection on the impurities of the world, reflection on the impermanence of sensations, reflection on the thoughts and reflection on the condition of existence. In doing so, he prepares the sick man to accept his death courageously.[212]

If a person dies peacefully, he will be reborn into the next birth, without causing any trouble for the survivors. If that is the case, the monk-priest must recite a protective chanting of the *Suutras*. Alms must be given to the monk. In case the person does not die peacefully, the priest makes a crack on the skull, helping the dying man's spirit to escape from the body. Then the person's body is disposed according to his condition, state, rank and wealth. Generally the bodies of the monks are burnt. The cremation rite is done in decorated arches, which, after the ceremony, are left to fall on their own. The cremation for monks who are known for their sanctity is not immediately done, but is kept for the veneration of the people. First, the body is embalmed tightly wrapped in while cloth and then covered with gold leaf. The body is placed in an unclosed inner coffin. The outer part of the coffin is painted with scenes from the life of the Buddha. Then it is placed in a special *Stuupa* erected for this purpose, and it lies in state for several months. People come to venerate the holy man and pay money and other offerings. When enough money is collected for the cremation, an elaborate cremation rite is organized. The disposal of the dead body of the layman is very simple. He is usually buried after his death. His body, except the head, is covered with white cloths. A piece of silver or gold is placed between his teeth. If the family is poor, a copper coin or a betel nut is sufficient. It is meant for the ferry-money to cross the terrible river of death, which every dead person has to cross. When everything is arranged, a priest-monk leads the procession to the grave. As the procession moves on the musicians play mournful tunes, a troop of dancers accompany the procession dancing on the way. After the burial the monk-priest is given alms. A meal is arranged for the benefit of those who have come to offer condolences. The monk-priest again chants *Parittas* to ward off evil spirits.[213]

5.2.2.3.6. Initiation Ceremonies

Normally initiation ceremonies are conducted when the initiate is about 15 years of age, though at present in some places the candidate is admitted when he is 11 or 12 years old. Before he applies to be a novice in the monastery, he must learn the basic forms of worship, what is expected of him in the monastery and how to conduct himself in the monastery. Besides, he must give up his secular name and take up a new name in order to show that he can escape the sufferings of the present life. Having made these preparations, on the appointed day of the initiation ceremony, the initiate is dressed in his best clothes, mounted on a horse and is taken in procession thorough the streets of the town. A band of musicians, his close relatives and friends accompany him, singing and dancing. The procession takes him to the houses of all his relatives and friends, and he bids them goodbye. This is done in imitation of 'the great going forth from home' (*Mahaabhinishkramana*) of the Gautama Buddha. After the trip, the neophyte returns to his home. There the head of the monastery and other monks are gathered to receive the boy as a novice. Now the initiate removes his fine clothes and binds a piece of white cloth round his loins. Then his hair is cut off, his head is shaven and bathed. He comes before the assembly, prostrates himself before the monks, raises his hand in reverence and asks the chief monk to admit him into the brotherhood. The chief monk, then, presents him with the yellow monastic garments, which he puts on per the regulations. A mendicant's bowl is hung around his neck. The ceremony concludes with the formal declaration that the neophyte is a member of the monastery. After becoming a novice in the monastery, he performs all the rules, regulations and practices of the monastic order strictly. After years of training he is accepted as the full-fledged monk.[214]

5.2.2.3.7. Festivals

Buddhism does recognize the value of festivals as a way to experience the Divine. Usually the festivals are moments of grace, when both the individual and the community reach out to the Buddhas, the *Bodhisattvas* and other holy persons in special worship and devotion. The festivals are occasions when the community rejoices together, giving to each other the best they have. In this section, we consider some of the common festivals the Buddhists celebrate.

The most common festival the whole Buddhist world celebrates is the New Year festival. It is celebrated at different times between January and mid-April. It is usually celebrated for four days. The celebration of the New Year festival begins by cleaning the houses, as a sign of removal of all that is old. Scented water is poured on the images of the Buddha as a mark of veneration and worship. Similarly, the hands of the monks and the elderly people are washed as a sign of respect for them. In Burma, for instance New Year festival is celebrated as the water festival. On this day people throw water on each other and perform the rite of washing the icons of the Buddhas, the *Bodhisattvas* and other holy men. In countries like Thailand and Cambodia people build sand *Stuupas* in temple compounds or in the riverbeds. On the New Year day these *Stuupas* are dispersed. The dispersal of the *Stuupas* is seen as a sign of cleansing a person's past misdeeds. People on this day dedicate themselves to live the Buddhist ideals. During the New Year festival, acts of kindness are done to animals, like releasing the caged birds and rescuing fish from drying out ponds. The celebrations accompany a number of entertainments, such as boat races, kite flying, music, traditional dances and dramas.[215]

In the month of *Vesaakha*, i.e., in the month of May, the festival of *Vesaakha Puujaa* is celebrated. It commemorates Gautama Buddha's birth, enlightenment and *Pari-Nirvana* at his death. Every Buddhist sect celebrates this festival with great gaiety. On this festival occasion, the houses are decorated with garlands and paper lanterns. The roadsides and the temple campuses are illuminated. Posters and paintings depicting Buddha's birth, life, enlightenment and death are displayed on the pavements and pavilions. Free food is distributed to the poor from the roadside alms stalls. In Burma, the *Bodhi* tree is watered with scented water. The monks lead the laity to worship the Buddha image, the *Stuupa* and the temple by threefold circumambulation. The monks preach sermons on the Buddha's life that last through the night. In Korea and in China, the festival of the Birth of the Buddha is celebrated with great gaiety. On this day, the Koreans pour tea and scented water on the image of the Buddha. The Chinese celebrate by giving new life to creatures, releasing fish and birds in the water and air respectively. In Japan this festival is called *Hana Matsuri*, i.e., the flower festival. Since the birth of the Buddha takes place in a flower-laden grove, they celebrate this festival as a flower festival. On this day, they place the infant Buddha in floral shrines.[216]

Another important festival is the *Aasaalha Puujaa*. It is the festival that celebrates the renunciation and the first sermon of the Buddha. Usually this festival marks the start of the three-month period of the *Vassa* retreat, during the rainy season. The monks are present in their monasteries during this period, and they spend their time in concentration, study and meditation. Ordinations to the monkhood are conducted during this period. The laypeople deepen their commitment to the practice of the Buddhist ideals of renunciation. They avoid secular festivities, such as, marriage and the like. In their place, they observe fasting days (*Uposathas*) at the local monasteries. This period, starting with the festival of the renunciation of the Buddha, is a period of spiritual renewal in which every person attempts to increase his goodness-power potential.[217]

Another celebration the monks hold is the ceremony of blessing the water (*Pavaaramaa*). It takes place at the full moon that marks the end of the *Vassa*. After meditation and chanting, the monks place wax from a burning candle into a bowl of water and infuse into it the goodness-power they have acquired during the *Vassa* retreat, thereby making the water sacred. The water thus blessed, is sprinkled on the laity as a blessing. In Burma, on the day after the *Pavaaramaa* ceremony, the *Taavatimsa* festival is celebrated. This festival reminds the faithful of the Buddha's ascent to the *Taavatimsa* heaven, after the *Vassa* retreat, to teach his mother, and his descent from there to the earth. It is celebrated as the festival of light, as Buddha, the light of the world, has once again descended on the earth. On this festival, the houses, monasteries and the *Stuppas* are illuminated. Similarly illuminated leaf-boats are floated on the rivers. The monks go in procession, as a layman carries the image of the Buddha and an alms-bowl, symbolizing the return of the Buddha into the world. Food offerings are made to the monks. Another festival is known as the *Kathina* celebrations, at which new robes, useful goods and money are given to the monasteries. Patched clothes are also donated to the monks on this day, remembering the vow of the monks to wear rags taken from the dust heaps.[218]

Another important festival celebrated in China is the *Ullambana*. It is celebrated in the months of August and September. Non-Buddhists also takes part in the festival. It is the festival of the hungry ghosts. It is the belief of the Chinese Buddhists that the ancestors, reborn as ghosts, wander in the human world and can be a source of potential danger. When it is full moon, the monks using the goodness-power they have accumulated during their summer retreat, place food for these ghosts and chant *Suutras* for them that they may be reborn into a better life. They also burn large paper boats, which will help the hungry ghosts to ferry across the river of death and arrive at a better world. Usually the laypeople sponsor such rites. In Japan, this festival is known as 'the festival of the dead' (*O-bon*) and is celebrated in mid-July. On this day, the graves are washed and cleaned. A makeshift altar is made near the home of the dead for offerings of fresh herbs and flowers. Fires and candles are lit to welcome ancestral spirits to partake of the offering. The Buddhist priest is present at the rite to chant Suutras.[219]

5.2.2.3.8. Sacred Places

In the primary sense, Buddhist sacred places refer to the regions, which are associated with the life of Gautama Buddha. These places are sacred because the Buddha has been to these places. In other words, these places have felt the touch of his sacred presence. Taken in the secondary sense, Buddhist sacred places can also refer to the monasteries, temples, *Stuupas* and other holy sites where a Buddhist can find the presence of the Divine as he walks towards his final destiny. In this section, we consider the Buddhist sacred places in both of these senses.

The Buddhist sacred places, taken in the sense of regions associated with the life of Gautama Buddha, are the following: Kapila-vastu, Buddha-Gayaa, Saarnaath near Banares, Raaja-Griha, Sraavasti, Vaisaalii, Kausaambi, Naalanda, Sankaasya, Saaketa, Kanyaa-kubja, Paatali-putra, Kesariiya, Kusinagara. The first is Kapila-vastu, which is the birthplace of the Buddha and where he spent his childhood and youthful days. The second is Buddha-Gaya, where the Buddha gained enlightenment after prolonged meditation. Of all the sacred places, it is the most sacred as it is from here that Buddhism truly emerged. The third is Saarnaath, which is situated near Banares. It is the place where the Buddha preached his first sermon, thereby initiating the movement of the wheel of *Dharma*. The fourth is Raaja-Griha. It is the mother city of Buddhism. It is in this city that Gautama studied under his two *Braahman* teachers, viz., Aalaara and Uddaka. Gautma received the foundational religious and philosophical thinking for his future work from this place. During his lifetime he visited this place often during the three months of *Vassa*. He often meditated and preached here. It is in this place that the Buddha is said to have given instructions on the Forty-two points. Many of the plots of Devedatta against the Buddha took place in this town and Buddha's life is involved in this place in ever so many ways. The fifth place is Sraavasti, where Gautama Buddha has lived in the monastery for a long time. It is believed that he spent half of the *Vassa* retreats of his 45year life at the monastery at Sraavasti. It is a great seat of Buddhist learning. It is believed that it was in the monastery at Sraavasti that the first sandalwood image of the Buddha was installed. The sixth sacred place is Vaisaalii. It is a place where Gautama often preached and taught. He is said to have made a stop at this place on his way to Kusinaaraa, the place of his death. The seventh place is Kausaambi. It is believed that the Buddha resided here at the sixth and the ninth year of his Buddhahood, besides visiting this place many times. It is said that the sandalwood image that is found here was carved during the lifetime of the Buddha by a sculptor at the request of the King Udayana. The eighth sacred place is Naalanda, the greatest seat of Buddhist learning in ancient India. It is believed that the Buddha preached the Law here for three months. The ninth place is Sankaasya. This place is associated with the legend of Gautama's ascent to the *Trayastrinsa* heaven to preach to his mother and to his descent back to the earth. The tenth sacred place is Saaketa. It is said that the Buddha taught and preached here at the monastery for six years. The legend about the miraculous growth of the twig the Buddha used for cleaning his teeth is said to have taken place here. The 11th place is Kanyaa-kubja. It is believed that in this town the Buddha preached the sermon on 'the bitterness and vanity of life', which he compared to a bubble or foam on water'. The 12th sacred site is Paatali-putra. This place is important for two reasons: firstly, we find a footprint of the Buddha here; secondly, King Asoka built the first *Stuupa* over the ashes of the Buddha here. The 13th place is Kesariiya. Gautama Buddha is said to have preached a sermon here, in which he described one of his previous births as a *Cakravartii* king. The 14th holy site of the Buddhists is Kusi-nagara. It is the place where the Buddha attained his *Pari-Nirvaana*.[220]

Other than these major sacred places, there are also a number of *Caityas*, *Stuupas*, temples and monasteries (*Vihaaras*), which the people visited for the purpose of worship and experience of the Buddha. The *Caitas* and the *Stuupas* are basically relic-repositories and places of worship. People flock to these places to worship and seek the blessings of the Buddhas, the *Bodhisattvas* and other holy men, whose relics are preserved there. Temples are usually meant for public worship. There are two types of temples, viz., the cave temples and the larger temples in the towns. The cave temples are temples that are carved in large rocks, while the larger temples are built after much architectural planning. The temples contain beautiful and richly ornamented altars, upon which the images of the Buddhas, *Bodhisattvas* and other deities are placed. All vessels and other articles required for worship are placed in the temple. Usually in the temples there is regular worship, and the people participate at their convenience. The monasteries are the dwelling places of the monks. Buddhist scriptures speak of five kinds of dwelling place of the monks: monasteries (*Vihaaras*), houses of a peculiar shape (*Addhayogas*), storied dwellings (*Praasaada*), mansions (*Harmya*) and caves (*Guhaa*). Though these are meant for the dwelling of the monks, often they are places of worship even for the laity. People visit these dwelling places of the monks, listen to their sermons, take part in worship, make confessions for their failures and renew their commitment to the Buddha. Thus, indeed, these places can also be called sacred places.[221] Both forms of the sacred places play a very important role in building up the faith of the Buddhists as they journey towards their final destiny.

5.2.2.3.9. Pilgrimages

Pilgrimages are a common feature in the Buddhist tradition. They consist in visiting any sacred place with specific purpose in mind. Pilgrimages may be made for a number of reasons. It could be for the spiritual reason of bringing alive the events from the life of the Buddha or the *Bodhisattva*, deepening and strengthening one's spiritual aspirations. It may be for the purpose of generating the power of the good that lies hidden in the depth of one's heart, in the process becoming able to increase one's goodness-power. One may undertake a pilgrimage to be strengthened by the power of the relics of the Buddha, from the power of the *Bodhi* tree and receive protection of the deities from a particular holy place. Similarly, one may also plan to go on a pilgrimage to fulfill a vow that he takes for the good done to him by the power of the *Bodhisattva* or the Buddha. The most ancient sites to which the followers of the Buddha go on pilgrimage are the place of Buddha's birth, place of his enlightenment, the place of his first sermon and the place of his death.[222] The *Mahaa-parinibbaana-Sutta* declares, as follows, regarding the places of pilgrimage:

> There are four places, which the believing man [the believer in Buddhism] should visit as a pilgrim with reverence and awe. The place at which he can say, "Here the *Tathaagata* ... was born." The place at which he can say, "Here the *Tathaagata* attained perfect insight and enlightenment." The place at which he can say, "Here the Law was first preached by the *Tathaagata*." The place at which he can say, "Here the *Tathaagata* passed finally away in that utter passing away which leaves nothing whatever behind". ... 'And they who die, while with believing heart they journey on such pilgrimages, shall be reborn, in the happy realms of heaven.[223]

This statement clearly shows the importance of making pilgrimages to these important places of Buddhist faith. These four and other sacred places mentioned above are places of pilgrimage. If a seeker honestly prepares and undertakes this journey wholeheartedly and joyfully, he definitely receives the blessings the Buddha promises to give. This, in turn, brings many blessings that help him to march ahead on his way to the Buddhahood.

5.2.2.4. STAGES OF THE PATH TO BUDDHAHOOD

The practice of the moral path, the path of meditation and the path of religious practice bring in the seeker an inner pulsation for enlightenment. The seeker feels the deep desire for enlightenment – that has come about as the result of these threefold practices and is called 'the stage of aspiration for enlightenment' (*Adhimukti-caryaabhuumi*). Even at the stage of the aspiration for enlightenment the seeker cannot be considered as a *Bodhisattva*, as he has not achieved the state of 'the mind of enlightenment' (*Bodhicitta-caryaabhuumi*). Only when a person acquires 'the mind of enlightenment' (*Bodhicitta*), is he capable of setting his foot on the path of the *Bodhisattva*. The *Bodhicitta* is an invisible thought tendency, which creates in the seeker a firm resolution and gives him a determination to remain steadfast on his journey towards the path of enlightenment and makes him never turn back, no matter what happens in his life. Thus, in the seeker who has attained the *Bodhicitta*, there is a steadiness of mind, as there is no swinging of the mind between resolution and doubt.[224]

Hence, the *Mahaayaana* tradition distinguishes between the pre-*Bodhisattva* stage (*Prakrti-caryaabhuumi*) and the *Bodhisattva* stage (*Bodhisat-*

tva-caryaabhumi). The former stage represents the state of the seeker before the arrival of the *Bodhicitta*, while the latter stage stands for the state of the seeker after the arrival of the *Bodhicitta*. Therefore, when the *Bodhicitta* appears in the seeker, he abandons the pre-*Bodhisattva* stage and enters the *Bodhisattva* stage. The emergence of the aspiration for enlightenment (*Adhimukti*) and the attainment of the mind of enlightenment (*Bodicitta*) depend on the amount of merit the seeker has accumulated through the good deeds of his past life. The amount of time required to accumulate the necessary merits that enables the seeker to attain *Bodhicitta* and to enter the path of the *Bodhisattva* is difficult to tell. From the legendary lives of the *Bodhisattvas*, we may conclude that it may take a few *Aeons*. Besides, a great number of rebirths may also be necessary to enter the path of the *Bodhisattva*. But, when a seeker acquires the *Bodhicitta*, he moves into the first stage of the *Bodhisattva*.[225]

The path of the *Bodhisattva* takes the seeker into ten ascending stages. They are the following: the stage of the Joyful (*Parmuditaa*), the stage of the Immaculate (*Vimalaa*), the stage of the Illuminative (*Prabhaakaarii*), the stage of the Effulgent (*Arcishmatii*), the stage of the Difficult to Attain (*Sudurjayaa*), the stage of the Right in Front (*Abhimukhii*), the Far Reaching (*Duurangamaa*), the stage of the Immovable (*Acalaa*), the stage of Wholesome Thought (*Saadumatii*) and the stage of the Cloud of the Norm (*Dharmameghaa*). [226]

5.2.2.4.1. Stage of the Joyful

It is from this stage that the real career of the *Bodhisattva* begins. He becomes a member of the *Tathaagata*-family, having freed himself from various forms of defilements. Now he clearly knows his destiny of becoming the Buddha. The recognition of his destiny makes him the Joyful (*Pramuditaa*). As the Joyful, he experiences faith (*Prasaada*), pleasure (*Priiti*) fragrance (*Usi*), playfulness (*Utsaaha*) and many other positive qualities. The emergence of these qualities frees him from negative tendencies, such as, egocenteredness, hatred and anger. He possesses a temperament that is in perfect repose and stillness. With the rise of positive attitudes and the destruction of 'I-centered' qualities, the *Bodhisattva* acquires the quality of generosity (*Daana*), which makes him give away everything for the good of all beings, while clinging to nothing. In practicing generosity to a high degree, the Joyful *Bodhisattva* realizes the emptiness of the self. The realization of the absence of the self and the observance of the teachings of the Buddha (*Desanaa*) causes in the *Bodhisattva* the faculty of discrimination, which helps him to develop skillful means for doing good things for others. Besides, he also acquires a number of dispositional qualities: loving-kindness (*Maitrii*), compassion (*Karuna*), the spirit of sacrifice (*Tyaaga*), patience in the midst of troubles (*Kheda-sahishnutaa*), holy knowledge of the scriptures (*Sastra-jnaataa*) and faith (*Sraddhaa*). At this stage, the compassion he feels for others leads the *Bodhisattva* to make ten vows, with the aim of attaining complete perfection for the sake of others. The quality of generosity and other dispositional characteristics assists the Joyful *Bodhisattva* to move into the next stage of the path.[227]

5.2.2.4.2. Stage of the Immaculate

In the stage of Immaculate (*Vimalaa*) the Joyful *Bodhisattva* begins the practice of higher morality (*Adhisiila*) in three aspects: firstly, he imposes restraint on his body, speech and mind, by which he avoids all wrongdoings; secondly, he cultivates actions that are noble and virtuous; and finally, he performs actions that benefit others. The threefold practice of higher morality of the *Bodhisattva* requires: three physical abstentions – abstention from killing, stealing and sexual misconduct; four vocal abstentions – abstention from lying, slandering, insulting and frivolous speech; and three mental abstentions – abstention form greedy desire, malice and false views. Having practiced all these forms of restraint, he practices virtues that are noble and honorable, especially compassion for every living creature. Besides, he also becomes a teacher of the morality he lives, as he guides and protects the moral lives of others. Thus, he attains the purity of conduct as his behavior becomes in every sense immaculate and extra-ordinary.[228]

5.2.2.4.3. Stage of the Illuminative

When the *Bodhisattva* attains the purity of conduct by the practice of higher morality, he moves into third stage of spiritual development called the stage of the Illuminative (*Prabhaakarii*). The use of all forms of restraints and the practice of the noble virtues, especially that of compassion, in the second stage, helps the *Bodhisattva* to develop deeper levels of concentration, which give rise in him to the virtue of patience (*Kshaanti*). Patience, in the *Mahaayaana* tradition, is not a passive virtue, but is a virtue that manifests compassion and wisdom. Patience, on the one hand, helps him to understand others in spite of their limitation and to be compassionate towards them; while, on the other hand, it gives the *Bodhisattva* the wisdom to resolve conflicts of life creatively, as only a patient mind gains the true wisdom to understand the troublesome and difficult situations. Patience takes three forms. The first two forms are social in nature and point to the spirit of forgiveness towards others and the spirit of accommodation that makes one accept generously even adverse situations in life. The third form is intellectual in nature, which gives the *Bodhisattva* the capacity to study patiently and reflect critically on the doctrinal matters of the *Buddha-Dharma*, thereby providing the conditions for 'the true awakening' of the *Bodhisattva*. As a result, the *Bodhisattva* realizes that besides mere performance of good works, the right understanding of the truth of the *Dharma* is also necessary for his enlightenment. This realization makes him meditate on the four *Brahma-vihaaras*, viz., loving-kindness, compassion, sympathetic joy and equanimity, and to live them in his life. He also acquires a number of supernatural powers, such as, omniscience, clairaudience, mind reading and other similar powers. Thus, in the third stage the *Bodhisattva* acquires illumination regarding the reality of existence.[229]

5.2.2.4.4. Stage of Effulgent

The illumination of the mind the *Bodhisattva* develops in the third stage instills in him the perfection of vigor (*Viirya*) in the fourth stage of the Effulgent (*Arcishmatii*), which makes him move with fire in facing the challenges of life. This stage is sometimes called 'the radiant stage' or 'the ignited stage', indicating the energy the *Bodhisattva* experiences in his life. The virtue of vigor points to the *Bodhisattva's* self-confidence. At this stage, he has the capacity to face, encounter and resist the happenings in his life courageously. Vigor is the determination to pursue that, which is good courageously, without minding the troubles and hardships one may have to go through to attain it. The man of vigor is full of self-confidence, which consists in attaining freedom from doubts. The absence of doubt basically comes from the assurance the *Bodhisattva* receives from the right understanding of the *Buddha-Dharma*. Gaining this right self-confidence, the *Bodhisattva* is able to take initiative of his own, regarding his own spiritual enhancement and that of others. When a *Bodhisattva* achieves higher levels of vigor, he accepts all that happens in life enthusiastically, and his life has no trace of depression, laziness, slothfulness, attachment or self-contempt. As the *Bodhisattva* attains higher levels of the perfection of vigor, he moves into the fifth stage of *Bodhisattva* path.[230]

5.2.2.4.5. The Stage of the Difficult to Attain

The self-confidence and the vigor the *Bodhisattva* attains on the fourth stage leads him to the fifth stage, which is described as the stage that is difficult to attain (*Sudurajayaa*). In this stage, the *Bodhisattva* masters the perfection of meditation (*Dhyaana*), thereby attaining true Buddhist wisdom, which is also referred to as 'insight'. Buddhism speaks of three types of wisdom that come from three sources: firstly, the wisdom by listening that comes from the study of the scriptures (*Srutamayii-prajnaa*); secondly, the wisdom by reflection, that comes from philosophical reasoning and analysis (*Cintaamayii-prajnaa*); thirdly, the wisdom by meditation, that comes from the practice of meditation (*Bhaavanaamayii-prajnaa*). The last of these three is the highest form of wisdom, and the former two are confirmed in the third form of meditation. Buddhism makes use of two types of meditation to achieve the highest wisdom, viz. calm meditation and insight meditaion. The former helps the seeker to calm his mind by way of concentration, while the latter uses the calm mind to arrive at the highest insight, on the *Buddha-Dharma*. In this manner, the *Bodhisattva* moves towards attaining what is most difficult to attain, the true Buddhist insight.[231]

5.2.2.4.6. Stage of the Right-in-Front

By the practice of calm and insight meditation in the fifth stage, the *Bodhisattva* attempts to come in touch with true Buddhist wisdom. The sixth stage, known as the Right-in -Front (*Abhimukhii*), is the stage of the perfection of wisdom. In attaining perfect wisdom one understands the principle of sameness as causeless, single, unborn, discrete, pure primordiality, inexpressible, neither affirmed nor negated, similar to dreams and of the sameness of existence and non-existence. It also means that he grasps the doctrine of dependent origination, self as fictional and the meaning of emptiness. Perfect Buddhist wisdom, thus, consists in the realization of the ego-self as non-existent, realizing the emptiness (*Suunyata*) of reality. Realizing the impermanence and emptiness of everything, the *Bodhisattva* goes beyond the state of thought construction (*Vikalpa*), meditation (*Dhyaana*), the object of meditation (*Dheya*), releases (*Vimoksha*), powers (*Bala*), super-knowledges (*Abhijnaa*), defilements (*Klesa*) and suffering (*Dukha*). Having attained mastery over wisdom, the *Bodhisattva* can abandon the world if he wishes and enter into the peaceful state an *Arahat* experiences. But, since he has lost his attachment to everything in the world and has developed great compassion for the sentient beings of the universe, the *Bodhisattva* refrains from entering the selfish *Nirvaana* of an *Arahat*. Instead he remains in the sixth *Bodhisattva* stage and attempts to develop skillful means, entirely for the purpose of working for the welfare of all sentient beings. Thus, in the remaining stages of the *Bodhisattva* existence, concern for others moves him to perfect himself, so that, by perfecting himself and acquiring more powers, he can work for the betterment of others. With this motive the *Bodhisattva* moves to the seventh stage.[232]

5.2.2.4.7. Stage of the Far Reaching

The seventh stage is called the stage of Far Reaching (*Duurangamaa*), in which the progress the *Bodhisattva* has made so far becomes almost irreversible. He is destined to the supreme Buddhahood. Therefore, he cannot revert to the paths of the *Arahat*. Having perfected in wisdom and all other perfections, the Law of *Karma* has no influence on the life of the *Bodhisattva* at this stage. If he takes a rebirth to help sentient beings, it is done because of his own free will, and not due to the causality of the *Karma*. Free from the trap of *Karma*, the *Bodhisattva* at this stage is considered as a Great Being (*Mahaasattva*). He enjoys various psychic powers, such as being in various heavenly realms at the same time and projecting himself magically to different worlds to impart the *Buddha-Dharma*. At this stage there arises in the *Bodhisattva* perfection of skilled means (*Upaayakausalya*), with the help of which he can skillfully teach the *Dharma*. The skillful means consist in his capacity to function most effectively and efficiently for the sake of communicating the *Dharma*. He practices ten perfections: giving – by giving his root of virtue in his desire for Buddha-knowledge; morality – in extinguishing all defilements; patience – in his pity and love for all beings; heroism – in acts of extreme goodness; meditation – in aiming at omniscience; wisdom – in considering with approval the doctrine of the non-arising of all things; skillful expedients – for converting beings and for attaining unlimited knowledge; the vow – in his efforts to make the supremely highest vow; power – in being able to change his form and teach beings of other careers according to their dispositions; and knowledge – in acquiring the true knowledge of all things. The *Bodhisattva* also practices, at this stage, four elements of popularity (*Samgrahavastu*): liberality, pleasant speech, beneficent conduct and impartiality. The *Bodhisattva* is involved in the world in ever so many acts of kindness towards others, but any earthly things never defile him. He has the knowledge of a Buddha and exercises his full ability in saving all peoples. But he has not reached the state of *Nirvaana*.[233]

5.2.2.4.8. Stage of the Immovable

The eighth stage is the Immovable (*Acalaa*). Here the *Bodhisattva* knows that things of this world are non-existing, and he is beyond the pleasures of body, speech and mind. At this stage the *Bodhisattva* is like a man who has awakened form a dream. He knows the reality of this world is only as real as a dream. He sees the world as false conceptualization. There is no striving and wanting in the *Bodhisattva* at this stage. In many aspects he is like the Buddhas, as he has a number of powers the Buddha possesses. For instance, he can split his body into many pieces and appear in different forms. Similarly, the *Bodhisattva* can manifest himself in the form of the Buddha for the benefit of others. All the Buddhas appear to him and ask him to acquire Buddhahood and to obtain all the powers associated with it, so that he can help sentient beings.[234]

5.2.2.4.9. Stage of the Righteous One

The ninth stage is the stage of the Righteous One (*Saadhumatii*). Here the *Bodhisattva* attains the perfection of powers (*Balapaaramitaa*). For instance, he has the power to understand different questions from all different beings in the entire cosmos at one go. The powers point to the spiritual maturity of the *Bodhisttva* at this state. The purpose of the possession of these powers is to help people to attain enlightenment. The *Bodhisattva* at this stage attains four forms of analytical knowledge (*Pratisvamvit*): firstly, analysis of the meaning (*Artha*) of terms; secondly, the analysis of the *Dharma*, which consists in the knowledge of the causes of things; thirdly, analysis of grammar (*Nitrutti*); and fourthly, analysis of the power of ready exposition (*Patibhaana*). It is through these four analytical abilities that the *Bodhisattva* not only attains the essence of Buddhist doctrine, but also gains power to communicate it to others. He is a preacher *par excellence*.[235]

5.2.2.4.10. Stage of the Cloud of the Norm

The tenth stage is the stage of the Cloud of the Norm (*Dharmameghaa*). This stage is called the Cloud of the Norm, for three reasons: firstly, at this stage *Dharma* falls like rain and extinguishes the very glow of conflicting emotions in sentient beings; secondly, the meditative absorption at this stage is compared to the sky with clouds; thirdly, at the time of the consecration of the *Bodhisattva* as the Buddha, all the other Buddhas assembled there send clouds of *Dharma* to the *Bodhisattva*, which rest on his head. This stage is also called consecration (*Abhisheka*), as the *Bodhisattva* is consecrated as the Buddha at this stage. At this stage arises the perfection of knowledge (*Jnanaa-paaramitaa*). The *Bodhisattva* at this stage achieves complete concentration. He is seated on the lotus in the concentration known as the knowledge of omniscience. On other lotuses are seated the *Bodhisattvas* of all the ten quarters, gazing at the Buddha-to-be. An earthquake shakes the earth, and the rays of light that come forth appease the pains of all creatures. The rays of light that issue from the foreheads of the assembled Buddhas rest on the head of the Buddha-to-be. Thus, he is consecrated as the Buddha. With the help of his skill in remembering, the newly consecrated Buddha is able to keep in his mind all clouds of the *Dharma*, which the Buddhas have showered on him. The consecration ceremony takes place in the *Tushita* heaven. The newly consecrated Buddha is born once again in this world, ready to do all needed actions in saving the creatures as the Buddha. Thus, moving though the ten stages, the *Bodhisattva* becomes the Buddha.[236]

In this essay we have looked into the *Mahaayaana* tradition, and the new thinking that has emerged in comparison with the *Hiinayaana* tradition. Unlike the latter, the former represents a worldview that is more open, free and wide. Thus, the name "*Mahaayaana*", i.e., 'the Large Vehicle' is truly proper to it. It is a 'Vehicle' that carries to the Buddhahood every individual person, whether he is a layperson or a monk; it is open to adapt and integrate into it a number of elements from other cultures and religions; and it presents itself as a religion that stresses the role of self-effort and the merit of the Divinities, such as, the *Bodhisttvas* and the Buddhas, to experience the final enlightenment. Thus, *Mahaayaana* is a religion of both self-power and other-power, as it counts on the cooperation of the individual seeker and the grace of the Divinities. It proposes a rich and elaborate path of religious practice, besides the moral path and the path of meditaion – that takes the seeker to Buddhist wisdom – in order to lead the seeker to the final attainment of the Buddhahood. The *Mahaayaana* Buddhism is also messianic in its perception of the future and man's destiny. The later *Mahaayaana* sects, such as, the schools of Pure Land Buddhism, are very apocalyptic in their presentation of the future and man's destiny. They propose the future destiny of man in an ideal land, which is far superior and very different from present existence. Then they propose the spiritual means to live the life of today in contemplation of the Pure Land and its Buddha and the *Bodhisattvas*, thereby inviting them to be born in this ideal land in their next birth. In this manner, *Mahaayaana* Buddhism instills in the seeker a deep sense of hope for the future, as he struggles with the everyday life of the present existence. Another interesting feature of the *Mahaayaana* Buddhism is the interest, concern and compassion the *Bodhisattvas* manifest towards all sentient beings. Unlike the gods of Hinduism, the *Bodhisattvas* of the *Mahaayaana* Buddhism are ready to help and transfer the vast amount of the merits they have accumulated to every sentient being out of compassion for them. The *Bodhisattvas* are Divinities, who are ready to help even without the seeker asking them. *Mahaayaana* Buddhism gives the seeker of enlightenment a way in which he is not alone: but as he walks the path there is divine assistance, especially through the compassionate activities of the *Bodhisatvas* and the Buddhas. Thus, *Mahaayaana* Buddhism is a religion that appeals to the seeker's head and heart. Its Divinities are warm, loving, and compassionate. Its path fascinates both the intelligent and the emotional. It is a religion of diversity. Yet it leads divergent people through divergent means to the one goal of Buddha-realization. One of the significant schools, among differing schools of the *Mahaayaana* tradition, is the *Vajrayaana* Buddhism. In the next essay we shall attempt to elaborate the reality of the Divine in *Vajrayaana* Buddhism and the path it proposes to arrive at the Divine.

5.3. *VAJRAYAANA* BUDDHISM

The word "*Vajrayaana*", which derives from the terms "*Vajra*" and "*Yaana*", literally means 'thunderbolt' and 'vehicle' respectively. The *Vajra* is the weapon the Vedic god *Indra* uses to slay the evil ones. As a weapon, the *Vajra* is unbreakable, while it breaks everything else. In later Buddhism, *Vajra* refers to the supernatural substance that is as hard as the diamond, as clear as empty space and as uncontrollable as the thunderbolt. For this reason *Vajrayaana* is called 'the thunderbolt vehicle' or "the diamond vehicle". Now the term "*Vajra*" is identified with ultimate reality, the *Dharma* and the enlightenment. As a school of thought and religious practice, *Vajrayaana* idolizes the doctrine of emptiness (*Suunyataa*) and helps the seeker to take possession of his diamond body and to realize his true nature (*Vajra-dhaatu*), thereby transforming into a diamond being (*Vajrasattva*). To achieve the goal of becoming the *Vajrasattva*, the *Vajrayaana* makes use of combinations of Tantric rites. *Vajrayaana* claims that the use of these rites can speed up the process of attainment of the enlightenment, so much so that it can be attained even within one life span of the seeker. In non-Tantric Buddhism, the aspirant sits cross-legged to control the body, sits in silence to restrain from speech and aims at one-pointedness of mind in *Samaadhi*. Thus, a non-Tantric seeker attains true linkage with the Divine only in the third stage, i.e. that of *Samaadhi*, thereby slows down the process of enlightenment. But the Tantric process quickens the adept's journey towards enlightenment, because the Tantric rites enable him to share directly in the three levels of the mystery of the Buddha: in Buddha's body by way of the Tantric gesture (*Mudraa*); in Buddha's speech by way of incantations of spells (*Dhaaranii*); and in Buddha's mind by way of concentration (*Samaadhi*) on the deity or the circle

(*Mandala*).[237] In the following pages, we attempt to explore the *Vajrayaana* pantheon and the path it proposes to arrive at the stage of Buddhahood.

5.3.1. DIVINITIES OF THE VAJRAAYAANA PANTHEON

Buddhism, in its origins, knows no theistic gods. By the emergence of *Mahaayaana* Buddhism, there comes about belief in the reality of many divine beings, such as, the Buddhas, *Bodhisattvas*, *Pretyekabuddhas*, *Arahats* and other deities. In the *Vajrayaana* Buddhism, we find a full-fledged belief in one Supreme Being, from which emanate various levels of divinities. We also find a great number of minor deities, their female counterparts and other spiritual beings. In this section, we consider the various divinities that form the pantheon of *Vajrayaana* Buddhism.

5.3.1.1. PRIMORDIAL BUDDHA

The Primordial Buddha (*Aadi-Buddha*) stands at the top of the *Vajrayaana* pantheon. The *Aadi-Buddha* is the one eternal living principle of the whole universe. The primeval Buddha is the source and originator of all things. The *Aadhi-Buddha* is the Primordial Wisdom, the one eternally existing, spiritual Essence from which everything else in the universe emanates. Thus, the *Aadi-Buddha* enjoys a divine supremacy as the sole and self-existing spirit that pervades the universe. There are a few accounts of the creation of the universe by the power of the *Aadi-Buddha*. One creation account says that the *Aadi-Buddha*, the omnipotent and omniscient primeval principle of the universe, originates everything in the universe though his meditation. According to another account, the *Aadi-Buddha* produces everything in the universe through the union with the 'Transcendent Wisdom' (*Prajnaa Paaramitaa*). A third account of creation says that the *Aadi-Buddha*, with the help of forms and thoughts that are without blemish, causes the five elements to arise, in the process giving rise to the five Buddhas, *Bodhisattvas* and the human Buddhas. Thus, *Aadi-Buddha* is the Primordial Wisdom, whose executive power is manifested in the collective intelligence of the five Buddhas, the corresponding *Bodhisattvas* and the human Buddhas.[238]

5.3.1.2. FIVE BUDDHAS, BODHISATTVAS AND HUMAN BUDDHAS

The five Buddhas are believed to be emanations from the One Original *Aadi-Buddha*. Sometimes they are referred to as *Dhyaani-Buddhas*. The term "*Dhyaana*" stands for the four grades of mystic meditations, which have corresponding ethereal spaces, i.e., the heavenly worlds. The *Dhyaani-Buddhas* are those Buddhas who exist as spiritual Essences in the higher region of ethereal spaces. They are also known as the five *Tathaagatas* or the five *Jinas*. The five *Jinas* are: *Vairocana* – the Illuminator; *Akshobya* – the Imperturbable; *Ratna-sambhava* – the Jewel-born; *Amitaabha* – the Infinite Light; and *Amoghasiddha* – the Unfailing Success. They occupy the central, eastern, southern, western and northern cardinal points respectively. These Buddhas differ from the Buddhas known to Buddhism up to the eighth century A.D. The Buddhas of the pre-*Tantra* period began their careers as ordinary human beings or even as animals and worked out their salvation by purification through different births and rebirths, gradually moving up to the state of Buddhahood. But these five *Jinas* were always Buddhas and never were anyone else. They constitute the body of the universe and mystically correspond to the five constituents of the universe. Similarly, they correspond to the five senses, the sense objects, the five cardinal points, letters of the alphabet, parts of the body, the vital breaths, colors and sounds. Besides, each of the *Jinas* inspires the cyclic stage of evolution (*Kalpa*).[239]

Each of the *Jinas* manifests in a celestial *Bodhisattva*, who is sometimes referred to as *Dhyaani-Bodhisattva*. The *Bodhisattva* is brought into existence by the process of emanation from the *Jinas*. The *Bodhisattva* acts as the practical head and guardian of the Buddhist community during the interval between the death of each human Buddha and the advent of his successor. Thus, we have five celestial *Bodhisattvas*, viz., *Samanta-bhadra*, *Vajra-paani*, *Ratna-paani*, *Patma-paani* (*Avalokitesvara*) and *Visva-paani*. Corresponding to the five celestial *Bodhisattvas*, there are the human Buddhas. They are: *Kraku-cchanda*, *Kanaka-muni*, *Kaasyapa*, *Gautama* and *Maitreya*, the future Buddha. Thus, each *Jina* is reflected in a celestial *Bodhisttva* and in a human Buddha, and is united with a feminine force, *Sakti*. Similarly, a *Jina* is said to preside over 'a mystical family of gods', which includes many deities and accessory divinities, besides the celestial *Bodhisattva* and the human Buddha.[240] Thus, we find a well-organized system of Divinities in the *Vajrayaana* Buddhism, starting from *Aadi-Buddha*, the *Jinas*, the celestial *Bodhisattvas*, the human Buddhas, the associated female deities, the other deities and accessory divinities.

5.3.1.3. FEMALE DEITIES

The old Buddhism gives importance to masculinity. Only a few subservient feminine deities are accepted. The higher gods and the inhabitants of the Buddha-fields are often seen as sexless. Femininity is seen as a bar to the highest spiritual attainment. But with the emergence of the left-handed Tantric Buddhism, the worship of female deities, as *Saktis*, becomes a very popular religious practice. They are seen as united with the male deities in loving union, from which the energy of the gods is derived. The use of sexual intercourse as a ritual practice becomes a common phenomena in Tantric Buddhism.[241] In this section, we consider some of the popular female deities of *Vajrayaana* Buddhism.

5.3.1.3.1. Prajnaa-paaramita

Prajnaa-paaramita is an autonomous Buddhist female deity. In the *Mahaayaana* tradition *Prajnaa-paaramita* is a virtue, a collection of writing that contains the wisdom literature and a *Mantra*. In the *Vajrayaana* tradition, the term "*Prajnaa-paaramita*" stands for the female deity of Wisdom. It is the personification of 'the transcendental wisdom'. The worship of *Prajnaa-paaramita* originates among the small group of ascetic metaphysicians. As a goddess, she is referred to as 'the Mother of all the Buddhas'. Just as the child is born of the mother, the full enlightenment of a Buddha comes forth from the perfection of Wisdom. As the mother, she is not barren, but fertile and bears the fruits of many good deeds. In her representation her motherhood is stressed by presenting her with full breasts. Yet she remains a virgin, unaffected and untouched. In this manner, the *Vajrayaana* Buddhism sees the female deity of wisdom as one who shows the people how to go about in the world. Thus, *Vajrayaana* places this feminine principle on a par with the Buddha, and to a certain extent even superior to him.[242]

5.3.1.3.2. TAARAA

The cult of *Taaraa* emerges as a popular movement. She is believed to be a savioress, who helps the seeker to cross over to the other shore. She is considered the most lovable of all Buddhist deities. She represents the feminine aspect of compassion more adequately than any other deity. *Taaraa* dwells on the Potalaka Mountain. She is closely associated with *Avalokitesvara*. According to one legend, *Taaraa* is born out of the teardrop of *Avalokitesvara's* compassion. She is born to help him to perform his acts of compassion. According to another myth *Taaraa* is born from a blue lotus, which grew in the tears of *Avalokitesvara*. It is said of *Taaraa* that she, in her desire to perform works of compassion for all sentient beings, vows that she should change her sex in order to develop fully in the path of enlightenment. When she achieves full enlightenment, she wants to work for the benefit of all the sentient beings. In Tibet it is believed that *Taaraa* is a fully enlightened Buddha. It is said that she removes from a person eight great fears: the fear of lions, the fear of elephants, the fear of fires, the fear of snakes, the fear of bandits, the fear of captivity, the fear of shipwreck and the fear of demons. *Taaraa* is also called 'the mother of all the Buddhas'. Yet she is said to be perpetually the sixteen-year-old. She is young in age, yet old in her wisdom and acts of compassion.[243]

Ichnographically *Taaraa* is presented in many forms. The most common forms are the green *Taaraas* and the white *Taaraas*. The green form consists in *Taaraa* seated on a moon and resting on a lotus. As she is seated, her legs are drawn up and the foot of the right leg is on the lotus footstool. She is adorned with the ornaments and paraphernalia of a *Bodhisattva*. Her left hand, which is placed in front of her heart, holds the stem of a blue lotus, while the right arm and hand are extended, palm open, as if she hands down her blessings. In some paintings this hand also holds a blue lotus. The white *Taaraa*, which is associated with Tibetan Buddhism, represents *Taaraa* as seated in lotus position and dressed in white. Her left hand is placed at her heart, holding the stem of a white lotus. The right arm and the hand are extended, bestowing blessings. She is easily recognized, since she has seven eyes, three on her face and one in each palm and foot.[244]

5.3.1.3.3. Female Avalokitesvara

In the East Asian Buddhist practice, *Avalokitesvara* takes a female form. Some authors are of the opinion that the male *Avalokitesvara* is the 'doctrinal' *Bodhisattva*, while the female *Avalokitesvara* is the 'popular' *Bodhisattva*. Whether we accept or reject this opinion, *Avalokitesvara*, in the female form, has given rise to very interesting stories in Buddhist folk literature and beautiful art forms in the world of Buddhist religious art. *Avalokitesvara* is known in China as *Kuan-yin*. In the female expressions of *Kuan-yin*, *Avalokitesvara* is represented as 'the giver of children' – the Chinese Madonna and the child. Similarly, she is depicted as 'Lion's Roar' – as seated on the back of a playful Chinese lion. Again, the female *Avalokitesvara* is represented as 'the holder of lotus'. We also find paintings, in which *Avalokitesvara* is portrayed at the same time as male and female, with broad shoulders and soft face, reflecting compassion, gentleness, inner strength, willingness and ability to help. We also find pictures of *Kuan-yin* as 'the holder of the Willow Branch'. Likewise we find figures of *Kuan-yin* holding a slender-necked vase containing the drink of immortality. In the same way, *Avalokitesvara* is presented as the white robed *Kuan-yin*. In Japan, *Avalokitesvara* is known as *Kwannon*. In Japanese Buddhist religious art, we also find various representations of the female *Kwannon*. The female *Avalokitesvara* is a very popular deity in the East Asian Buddhist religious practice.[245]

5.3.1.4. FATHER-MOTHER DEITY

The introduction of female deities in the Buddhist pantheon has brought about in the Buddhist religious thinking an attempt to bring the masculine and feminine elements together to explain the spiritual phenomena. This trend finds full expression in the Left-handed *Tantra*, which depicts the pursuit of perfect wisdom as a love affair with the absolute. In other words, the seeker of wisdom should pursue wisdom with the intensity and exclusiveness with which a man thinks of a beautiful woman with whom he has made a date. In the Buddhist *Sakti*-cults, this attitude is brought into the open. The Ultimate Reality is perceived as a union of the masculine – the active principle, and the feminine – the passive principle. Masculinity is viewed as 'the skill-in-means', while femininity is conceived as the wisdom. The enlightenment can come about only when there comes about a union between these two principles, as the act of union leads one to the highest bliss. In Tibetan religious art, this attitude is expressed through the sexual union of the Buddhas and the *Bodhisattvas* with their female counterparts. Thus, there emerges the idea of the Father-Mother deity (*Yab-Yum*).[246]

5.3.1.5. OTHER SPIRITUAL BEINGS

Below the above-mentioned deities ranks the vast number of personified natural forces, spirits, devils and demons. They range from the manifestation of these spirits in human saints to a host of godlings, which are difficult to identify. Ichnographically some of these spiritual beings are represented as beautiful, the others are represented as repulsive, and still others are depicted as ferocious. It is believed that these spirits and demons have the power to cause or avert diseases and disasters, to control the destinies of men and to determine the fate of lower animals. Spells and incantations are recited and chanted to avoid their evil influences and to receive their favors. The worship of these spiritual beings is based on superstitious beliefs and practices. To those who criticize such superstitious beliefs in spiritual forces and superstitious practices to appease them, to avoid their trouble and receive their blessings, the learned *Laamas* of Tibet say that people are ignorant and they are not able to understand deeper teachings of Buddhism. By their nature, they are superstitious. Left to themselves they invent their own superstitions, which may not, in fact, help them. Therefore, it is better to devise superstitious beliefs and practices for them with specific objects in mind. This enables them to find a way out of the troubles of everyday life. Thus, the learned *Laamas* find the belief in these personified natural forces and spirits, and the cultic and ritual practices to appease them useful means to help people to move into deeper realms of spiritual existence. The belief in these spiritual beings, especially in Tibet, has emerged from the original *Boen* religion of Tibet, which is a form of *Shamanism* that makes use of various spells to counter the influences of these spiritual beings.[247]

5.3.1.6. AVATAARA LAAMAS

Laama (*bLama*) is a Tibetan name for a superior teacher. It is an equivalent of the Sanskrit '*Guru*'. Laamaism is a form of Buddhism, which, though based on the *Hiinayaana* and the *Mahaayaana* Buddhist traditions, due to the influence of *Shamanism*, *Siva*-worship, magic and the use of Tantric practices has become a genuine expression of *Vajrayaana* Buddhism. It holds for the hierarchy of teachers called the *Laamas*. The Laamisic hierarchy consists of two categories, a lower grade of *Laamas* and a higher grade of *Laamas*. The first category of the lower grade includes three levels of *Laamas*. The lowest in rank in the first category is the junior monk (*Gethsul*). He, in fact, is a novice, who is admitted to the first stage of monkhood. He shaves off his hair and wears monkish garments and observes one 112 rules. Usually a person is 15 years old when he is admitted to the first stage of monkhood. The second rank in the first category is the full-fledged monk (*Gelong*). He is the *Bhikshu*, who has received the complete consecration. He is often referred to as a *Laama*, even though he has no real right to this title. Though he is not a priest, he performs sacerdotal functions. He is expected to follow 253 rules of discipline. A person must be 20 years old before he is admitted to the second stage of the hierarchy of the *Laamas*. The third rank in the first category is the superior *Gelong*, known as *Khanpo*. He is called a *Laama*, by right. He is known for his higher knowledge and sanctity. He is often the head teacher (*Upaadhyaaya*), and usually is the chief-monk of the monastery.[248]

The second category, the higher grade of *Laamas*, is called the *Avataara Laamaas*. Unlike the first group, the *Laamas* of the second group are believed to be incarnations of certain Buddhas, *Bodhisattvas* or other great saints. Thus, though the *Avataara Laamas* are human beings, they are powerful spiritual beings, as the power of the great spiritual beings resides in them. There are three ranks of the *Avataara Laaamas*. The lowest in rank among the *Avataara Laamas* is called an ordinary incarnated *Laama* (*Khubilghan*). He represents the continuous re-embodiment of an ordinary canonized saint or a founder of a great monastery. He usually presides over a more important monastery. The second rank of *Avataara Laaamas* is called *Khutuktu*. He represents the incarnation of a Buddha, a higher *Bodhisattva* or a deified saint. He exercises jurisdiction over a larger and a more significant monastery than the one that the *Khubilghan* presides over. The highest of the *Avataara Laaamas* is the Supreme *Laama* or the Grand *Laama*. He is not a mere incarnation of an ordinary *Bodhisattva*, but rather that of a Supreme Buddha or of his *Bodhisattva*. Two *Laamas* belong to this rank of *Avataara Laamas*, viz., the *Dalai Laama*, who is believed to be the continuous incarnation of *Avalokiteshvara*, and the *Pancen Laama*, who is said to be the continuous incarnation of *Amitaabha-Buddha*. They exercise authority over large regions outside their monasteries.[249]

These two are the most significant divine persons in Tibetan Buddhism. The *Dalai Laama* is the Grand *Laama* at Lhaassa. His name '*Dalai Laama*' is a combination of the Mongolian term "*Dalai*", which means 'ocean' and the Tibetan term "*Laama*", which means 'a great teacher'. Thus, the name "*Dalai Laama*" means 'a superior teacher, whose learning and power are as great as the ocean'. He also has a Tibetan title '*Gyamthso Rinpoce*', which means 'the Ocean Jewel'. He exercises both temporal and spiritual power over a great number of believers. The other Grand *Laama*, the *Pancen Laama*, resides at the monastery at Tashi Lunpo, and is commonly known as the Tashi *Laama*. His Tibetan title '*Pancen Rinpoce*' means 'the Great Pandit Jewel'. He does not exercise any political power outside his own province, but he holds great spiritual authority over the believers.[250]

The manner in which successors are appointed to these two offices, when the holder of the office dies, is very interesting. It is said that the departing *Laama*, before he transfers himself to another body, reveals the conditions in which he is incarnated. It is also said that children of two or three years old, due to some spiritual influence, speak of themselves as the living Buddha and as the chief of a particular monastery. Normally the sacred books are consulted and the official soothsayer's opinion is sought to identify the person in which the dead *Lamaa* has incarnated. Guided by these directives, the monks after fasting and prayers look for the child in whom the dead *Laama* is incarnated. When such a child is identified, it is brought to the main monastery and enthroned as the Grand *Laama*. Due worship and veneration is given to him. Until the child grows up to take up the task of being the spiritual head, the elected regent, called *Nomun-khan*, governs the monastery and the believers. He is said to be the most powerful Tibetan official. The final authority to determine the incarnated living Buddha rests with the *Dalai Laama* and the *Pancen Laama*. When the *Dalai Laama* dies, it is the duty of the *Pancen Laama* to interpret the traditions, listen to the oracles about his incarnation and identify the child in whom the *Dalai Lamma* is reborn. When *Pancen Laama* dies, the *Dalai Laama* performs the task of choosing the next *Pancen Laama*.[251]

5.3.2. VAJRAYAANA PATH TO THE DIVINE

So far in this essay we have been looking into the various divinities that constitute the *Vajrayaana* pantheon. Besides the major divinities, both invisible and visible, there are a number of minor deities. While holding on to the multiplicity of divinities, the *Vajrayaana* also proposes a number of paths that enables the seeker to arrive at the Divinity in question. In the next section of the essay, we attempt to explore the *Vajrayaana* path to the Divine.

5.3.2.1. RECITATION OF MANTRAS

In *Vajrayaana* Buddhism the use of *Mantras* is seen as a powerful means to achieve emancipation. Etymologically, the Sanskrit term "*Mantra*" is connected with the Greek word "*Meimao*" and the Old High German term "*Minn-ia*". The former term means 'eager desire', 'yearning' and 'intensity of purpose', while the latter term expresses the idea of 'making love to'. Thus, pronouncing a *Mantra* that honors a deity amounts to wooing the deity and making him act on behalf of the one reciting the *Mantra*. Besides, the *Mantras* are considered to be very powerful, as they contain the effects of the original vows the Buddhas and the *Bodhisattvas* make. The *Mantras* are meritorious and bring success to all the endeavors of the humans, because the Buddhas and the *Bodhisattvas* have consecrated them.[252] The *Mahaa-Vairocana-Suutra* explains the power of the *Mantras* as follows:

> Thanks to the original vow of the Buddhas and *Bodhisattvas*, a miraculous force resides in the *Mantras*, so that by pronouncing them one acquires merit without limits. …[Similarly] success in our plans through *Mantras* is due to their consecration by the Buddha, which exerts upon them a deep and inconceivable influence.[253]

Because of the power inherent in the *Mantras*, the recitation of the *Mantras* is seen as a sure vehicle of salvation. As a result, the vehicle of the *Mantras* (*Mantrayaana*) becomes an important element of the *Vajrayaana* Buddhism. It is a belief of *Tantrism* that the recitation and meditation on the *Mantras* is a key to the removal of fetters and the attainment of the Buddhahood, but it is important that it be used according to the rules. If used according to the rules, there is nothing the *Mantras* cannot achieve. But the rules that are numerous and minute must be strictly followed. For instance, the *Mantra* addressed to the male deity must end with the words "*Huum*" or "*Phat*", and the *Mantra* recited to honor a female deity must end with the word "*Svaaha*". Thus we have the famous six-syllable *Mantra* addressed to *Avalokitesvara* which reads as "*Om Mani Padme Huum*" and the ten-syllable *Mantra* addressed to the female goddess *Taaraa* reads as "*Om Taare Tutaare Ture Svaaha*". The recitation of such *Mantras* helps the seeker's mind to get in touch with these deities and truly brings about identity with these deities.[254]

The Tantric Buddhist sacred text the *Mahaa-Vairocana-Suutra* distinguishes four levels in the recitation of the *Mantras*. The first level is the contemplative recitation. It consists of four elements: recitation of the *Mantra*, while contemplating in one's heart the shape of the letters; then one distinguishes the sound of different letters as one continues one's contemplation; next comes the grasp of the significance of phrases contained in the *Mantra*; and one practices breathing with the aim of contemplating the mutual interpenetration of the seeker and the Buddha. In the second and the third levels, while the seeker continues his contemplative recitation of the *Mantra*, he presents to the deity offerings of flower, perfumes and other similar objects. The fourth level is the recitation of realization, where one achieves the realization of the Buddhahood (*Siddhi*) through the power of the *Mantras*.[255]

The Diamond *Suutra* speaks of the fivefold contemplation of the *Mantras* leading the seeker to five Manifest enlightenments (*Abhisambodhi*), which bring in the seeker final enlightenment. This is the pathway, which Gautama Saakyamuni has walked as the *Bodhisattva*, and any seeker of enlightenment needs to follow. Firstly, the initiated contemplates the *Mantra*, "I perform mind penetration", which makes him realize the true nature of the mind (*Citta-dharmataa*) and its 16 stages of emptiness (*Suunyataa*). As the result of this contemplation the seeker realizes the shape of his mind as a moon disk in his own heart and attains the 'mirror of wisdom', which is the nature of Buddha *Akshobhya*. The Manifest Enlightenment in this case is the one resulting from discrimination. Secondly, the seeker contemplates the meaning of the *Mantra* "*Om*, I generate the Mind of Enlightenment". The consequence of this contemplation is the realization of his mind as void, undefiled and in the form of a full moon disk in his own heart. As the result of the second contemplation, one attains 'equality wisdom', which is the nature of Buddha *Ratnasambhava*. The Manifest Enlightenment one experiences as the result is the generation of the Mind of Supreme Enlightenment. Thirdly, the seeker contemplates the *Mantra*, "Stand up, O *Vajra!*" It leads to 'discriminative wisdom', which is the nature of the Buddha *Amitaabha*. Fourthly, he contemplates the *Mantra* "I consist of Diamond". This contemplation leads to the realization that all the elements of one's Body-*Vajra*, Speech-*Vajra* and Mind-*Vajra* are, in fact, of the same nature as the finest atoms of the

Vajras of all the *Tathaagatas*. It leads to the attainment of the 'duty-fulfillment wisdom', which is of the nature of *Amoghasiddha* Buddha. Finally, the seeker contemplates the *Mantra* "*Om*. Like all the Thus-gone, so am I". At this stage, because of the transformation of the *Vajra* and moon in his own heart, the one who meditates appears as *Mahaavairocana*. His nature is that of the *Sambhogakaaya*, consisting of 32 characteristics and 80 minor marks, thereby manifesting the Complete Buddha. He attains '*Dharmadhaatu* wisdom' which is of the nature of Vairocana. It is clear that the contemplative recitation of the *Mantras* brings about in the seeker genuine ascent towards the goal of Buddhahood.[256]

5.3.2.2. PERFORMANCE OF RITUAL WORSHIP

The *Vajrayaana* Buddhist practice involves the performance of a number of rituals. Some of these ritual practices have, besides religious values, social meaning. In this section, we consider a few ritual practices that are common in *Vajrayaana* Buddhism.

5.3.2.2.1. Daily Ritual Worship

In Tibetan and Mongolian Buddhist religious practice the Laamistic priests gather three times a day – at sunrise, at midday and at sunset – to perform the prescribed ritual. Before the commencement of the ritual, they gather in the temple or in the hall of worship, coming in a procession and seating themselves in their respective places in the order of importance. When it is time to start the ceremony, the choirmaster signals with a bell. Then the prayer formularies are recited or chanted, sections from the Law are read and litanies are sung with the accompaniment of noisy music and clapping of hands. The singing is done either all together or alternatively with responses. At other times, each monk repeats ejaculatory prayers in praise of the Buddha or the *Bodhisattva* individually, resulting in confusion of voices. When the Living Buddha is present for ritual worship, the ritual is performed in a much more solemn manner. A gilded seat is arranged for him in front of the chief idol, at the level of the altar. When all are assembled in the temple, a conch-shell trumpet is blown three times announcing the arrival of the Living Buddha. As he comes and takes his seat, all venerate him by threefold prostrations. Then the director of ceremonies rings a bell to indicate the start of the ritual. All pray the prescribed prayers using prayer formularies, which are followed by a brief silent pause. There is another bell to indicate the next stage of the ritual, which consists in singing two choruses accompanied by the use of bells, cymbals, drums, tambourines, conch shells, trumpets and pipes. Some other elements that are part of the Tibetan religious services are the consecration and distribution of holy water and grains by the chief *Laamas*. Perfumes are usually burnt and vessels containing incense are swung backwards and forwards during the ceremony. The main instruments that are used at the religious rites are a spiral shell, a long trumpet made of copper or brass about ten feet long, a large drum, flutes, cymbals and horns, which are usually made of human thigh-bones.[257]

5.3.2.2.2. Tea Drinking Ceremony

The ceremonial drinking of tea forms an important part of the Laamistic rituals. There are a number of ways in which this ceremony is performed. The priests and monks go in procession to the chapel and take their seats in the order of importance. They chant for about ten minutes. Tea is served. When the tea drinking is completed a short chant follows, after which all come out of the chapel in procession. There is another form of the tea drinking ceremony, in which, while the monks are seated in the chapel and praying, they take small cups out of the folds of their robes and drink tea with it, after which they place the cups back into the folds of their robes. After a while they repeat the action of taking the cup out and drinking the tea without interrupting the continuous repetition of prayers and chants. Another tea ceremony that is held after morning service in the temple, in which each monk drinks in silence, carefully placing his scarf before his cup, as if to prevent the unbecoming sight of drinking tea in a sacred place like the chapel.[258]

5.3.2.2.3. Ceremony for Transferring the Soul to Heavenly Mansions

This is a rite with the help of which the soul of a chief *Laamaa* (*Khanpo*) of a monastery is sent to the heavenly dwelling place. It usually takes place on the 49th day after his death. The *Dalai Laama* is the chief celebrant of the ceremony. He sits on his throne and chants a hymn in a low voice, and all the monks present repeat the same hymn. Then a venerable *Laama* from the gathering rises, addresses the Grand *Laama* as the incarnate Lord *Avalokitesvara* and proclaims the many acts of mercy the Grand *Laama* does, as the patron saint of Tibet, for the benefit of the people. After the proclamation of good deeds, he makes a number of offerings including the seven mythical treasures that belong to every universal monarch – a wheel, an elephant, a flying horse, a jewel that illumines the dark night for seven miles, a good queen, a good minister who has the power to discover hidden treasures and a good general – for the benefit of the soul of late *Khanpo*. Finally, he prostrates himself before the throne of the Grand *Laama* three times, after which there is a solemn pause. The Grand *Laama* leaves the assembly. With the help of this ceremony, the soul of the chief *Laamaa* is transferred to the heavenly mansions.[259]

5.3.2.2.4. Ceremonies Involving Fasting and Abstinence

A ceremony called *Nyungne* involves fasting and abstinence for four days. The first two days are preparatory in nature, and participants are given the following schedule to guide them. The participants of the ceremony rise early in the morning, have a bath and prostrate themselves before *Avalokitesvara*.

They also make their confessions and meditate on the evil effects of demerit. Reading extracts from the book of confessions follows. After tea, prayer recitals continue about two o'clock, when a vegetarian meal is served. Then comes a pause, after which prayers continue until late night, having tea at regular intervals. As they retire for the night, the chief *Laama* gives them specific duties and penances to be performed and directs them to sleep in 'the lion-posture', i.e., to lie on the right side, to stretch out the feet and to support the head with the right hand. On the third day, the devotees follow a strict fasting, which involves abstinence from all forms of food and drink. They are not even allowed to swallow saliva. They are to spit out the saliva in a vessel kept near them. They are expected to keep absolute silence throughout the day, praying and confessing their sins. The strict abstinence continues till sunrise of the fourth day.[260]

The practice of fasting (*Uposatha*) on the full moon, black moon and the intermediate quarter moon days has been a strict practice in the Tibetan Buddhism. On these days the monks recited the Law regarding the confession of sin (*Paatimokkha*), which accompanies strict fasting. On these days the monks eat nothing between the sunrise and the sunset except drinking tea. The laity is exhorted to join these fasting days and repeat prayers according to the three refuge formulas, the jewel-lotus formula, to make declaration to avoid the five great sins, to walk up to the image-altar and place offerings on it, to bow before the *Laama* and to get his blessings. The observance of days of fast is meant to bring to the seeker spiritually invigorating and enriching experiences.[261]

5.3.2.3. RITUAL GESTURES

Other than the use of *Mantras* and ritual ceremonies of worship, Tantric Buddhism makes use of ritual gestures (*Mudraas*), which involve various forms of magically efficacious positions of the hands and different parts of the body. Bowing is one form of ritual gesture. Even in social interactions, bowing plays an important role, as children bow to the parents, layperson bows to the monk and a junior monk bows to a senior monk. Bowing stands for one's humility before the other and one's respect for the other. In worship, bowing is an important ritual gesture. A devotee bows to a Buddha image, a *Bodhi* tree, a *Stuupa* and many other such sacred objects. Bowing before the sacred objects is usually done three times. *Namaskaara* is a form of bowing, which consists in a person standing or kneeling with palms joined. Usually *Namaskaara* is done by placing the joined palms on the forehead, on the lips and on the chest symbolizing the respect shown through the body, speech and mind respectively. The *Vajrayaana* Buddhist practice of the 'grand prostration', which involves lying full-length on the ground, is a common practice. Similarly, the practice of circumambulation, which consists in walking around temples, monasteries, *Stuupas* and sacred walls, is also very common. During such walks people carry enormous amounts of weight on them. Sometimes they perform circumambulation by measuring the ground with the extended body. The prostrations and circumambulations are done despite the severity of the weather. Whether it is raining, snowing, hot summer or cold winter, devotees carry on these gestures to manifest their devotion to the deities. These acts also manifest the spirit of repentance and penance of the people who perform them.[262]

Offering is another ritual gesture, which often accompanies the use of *Mantras*. Flower offering, incense offering and light offering are the most common forms of offerings. The flower offering can symbolize the flowering of the mind and its blooming into enlightenment. The incense offering points to the 'odor of sanctity' of the Buddha, his glorious character and virtues. The light offering symbolizes the Buddha, the enlightened. In Tibetan Buddhism, there are usually seven types of offerings, viz., water, grains, flowers, incense, lamps, perfume and food. Water is given to wash the face and the feet. Water and grains symbolize hospitality. The other five, viz., flowers, incense, lamps, perfumes and food represent the five senses. Thus, the seven offerings point to the devotees' dedication to spiritual development. They are often placed before the Buddha-image in seven bowls. When other *Mudraas*, like pelting with flower petals, waving lamps or incense sticks and *Mantras* accompany these seven offerings, they become powerful means to help people on their way to enlightenment.[263]

Religious dances and religious dramas can also be included in the ritual gestures. In northern Buddhism, religious dances are associated with the festival of 'the chase of the spirit-king', which is held on the 30th of the second month. This festival involves dancing, wearing of masks, mummery and buffoonery. Similar to the devil dancing in Sri Lanka, these dances are also based on a belief in demons and spirits and aim at warding them off, or at least preventing their evil effects. Similarly, religious dramas are performed with the intention of helping humans to escape the evil influences of the evil spirits. In Tibetan religious dramas, usually there are three characters: the tutelary deities, which are good *Genii*; the evil demons; and men. Different types of masks are used to distinguish these three characters in the plays. The dramas begin with the recital of hymns, prayers and loud music. The theme of these religious dramas involves the evil spirits tempting men to go astray. Guided by other men and helped by the tutelary deities, men do not give in to the insinuations of the evil spirits. Finally the tutelary deities punish the evil spirits. The religious dramas usually end with men praising the tutelary deities for helping them to have victory over evil spirits. At the concluding scene of the play, all the characters come to the stage and sing hymns in honor of the victorious tutelary *Genii*. Thus, the performances of religious dances and dramas are powerful ritual gestures, which bring in the people a sense of well-being and courage to overcome the evils that come in their lives.[264]

5.3.2.4. MEDITATION: MEANS OF UNION WITH DEITIES

The *Vajrayaana* Buddhist practice of *Tantra* has a system of meditation on deities. It takes place in four stages. Firstly, by way of contemplation one identifies one's 'self' with emptiness, in the process sinking one's individuality into emptiness. When the concept of emptiness becomes real to the seeker, the five aggregates (*Skandhas*) are destroyed without return. This awareness of oneself as emptiness leads to 'the mind of enlightenment' (*Bodhicitta*). Having arrived at the state of *Bodhicitta*, the seeker repeats and visualizes 'the germ-syllables' (*Bija*). Thirdly, the repetition and visualization of 'the germ-syllables' help the seeker to form an external representation of the deity, as shown in statues, paintings and other images. Finally, deeper level contemplation and visualization of the deity leads to identification with it. Thus, the seeker becomes the deity, as there takes place the subject-object identification in the deepest level of concentration (*Smaadhi*) or trance (*Dhyaana*).[265] A number of means are used to arrive at the identity of the seeker.

5.3.2.4.1. Meditation on the Magical Circles

The most significant help to Tantric meditation is 'the magical circles' (*Mandalas*). Usually the *Mandalas* are painted on cloth or paper, drawn on the ground with rice or pebbles, or engraved on a stone or metal. The Mandala is a diagram that shows the deities in their spiritual or cosmic connection. In the *Mandalas*, the deities are found in pictorial images, in their visible forms, in form of alphabets, in germ-syllables or in various symbolic forms. The *Mandalas* are in direct line with the ancient tradition of magic. They give a detailed, though condensed representation of the whole universe. They include the Buddhas, the *Bodhisattvas*, the gods, the spirits, mountains and seas, the zodiac and even the great heretical teachers. Hence, they can provide insight into the spiritual law, which the deities represent. Thus, the more one meditates on the *Mandalas*, the more one comes to the closer experience of the deity and all spiritual reality that deity embodies.[266]

5.3.2.4.2. Six Stages of Kariyaa Tantra

Other than meditation on the *Mandalas*, various *Vajrayaana* texts propose different meditational practices with the help of which one can establish union with the deities. The *Vajravidaarana-naama-dhaaranii*, which leads with *Kariyaa Tantra*, speaks of six meditational stages through which one can bring about union with the deity. Firstly, the seeker, by using Maadhyamika dialectics, denies the concepts of singleness and multiplicity, thereby recognizing the voidness of his own mind. These two accomplishments lead the seeker to the realization that the deity to be contemplated and the 'self-reality' are one and the same. As the result of the above procedures, the seeker attains 'the deity stage', i.e., 'the Reality-Deity'. Secondly, having realized the voidness of his mind and the inseparableness of 'the self-reality and the deity, the seeker imagines the sounds of the *Mantra* as the very deity to be contemplated, thus, the mind's only object of meditation becomes 'the Sound Deity'. Thirdly, the seeker imagines that his mind is a moon disk in the sky, carrying the letters that are identified with the deity to be contemplated, thus forming 'the Letter Deity'. Fourthly, the seeker contemplates that from these letters emerge rays of light that form the body of the deity, – purifying all sentient beings from their sins and delighting the Buddhas. Then he imagines that the rays are withdrawn on to the moon disk, and thus withdrawn into his heart, where the moon-mind and the letters are transformed into the perfect body of 'the Form Deity'. Fifthly, the seeker touches with *Mudraa* the crown of his head, the space between the eyebrows, the eyes, the shoulders, the neck, the heart and the navel, as he recites ritual formulas. As a result, these parts of the body one empowered, thereby achieving 'the *Mudraa* Deity'. Finally, as the Deity is so vivid in the mind of the seeker, he strengthens his ego by contemplating sentences, such as, "*Om*. I am entirely identical with the intrinsic nature of the *Dharmadhaatu* by *Yoga*". As a consequence, the seeker experiences a vivid vision of the deity, who becomes the sole meditative object of the seeker. It is referred to as 'the Sign Deity'. In this manner, deeper identification between the seeker and the deity is established.[267]

5.3.2.4.3. Four Steps of Caryaa Tantra

The *Vairocanaabhisambodhi-tantra*, which deals with *Caryaa Tantra*, speaks of the four steps with the help of which identity between the seeker and the deity is brought about. The first step is the subjective foundation. It consists in the seeker going through ascending imaginative stages, which end imagining himself to be identical with the *Vairocana* Buddha. The second step is the objective foundation. Here the seeker imagines that he is in front of Buddha *Vairocana* and identifies with him. The third step is the identification with the Mind of Enlightenment (*Bodhicitta*). Now the seeker imagines that his mind is in the shape of the moon disk within the heart of the Buddha *Vairocana* who is in front of him. The fourth step is the immersion in sound. Here one imagines that on the moon disk the syllables of the *Mantra* to be recited. Then he recites the *Mantra* 100,000 times. As the seeker masters this *Yoga*, 'the Sign Deity' stays in his mind with great brightness and vividness. This intense contemplation on the deity effects such genuine brightness in the inner mind of the seeker that the body-image of the deity appears as a mere illusion. His identification with the deity makes the external image of the deity meaningless, as he has experienced the deity directly, and so he needs no external signs, such as the image of the deity.[268]

5.3.2.4.4. Thirteen Visualizations of a Yogin

Tantric ritual texts also speak of 13 visualizations of a *Yogin*. Texts prescribe special place, posture and other requirements for the right practice of these visions. The place must be a temple hall, a monk's cell or a room sanctified for this purpose in a home. At the altar the icon of the deity, the Buddhist sacred books, and a *Stuupa* are placed. Special offerings are placed near the altar. The *Yogin* recites ritual formulas. The *Yogin* adopts the sitting

Mahaavairocana posture: he sits with legs interlocked; the hands are in *Samaadhi Mudraa*, i.e., the palms open with fingers on one hand on those of the other, the two thumbs touching the apex; the spinal column erect; the diaphragm relaxed; the head bent like a hook; the tongue touching the palate; and the eyes focused on a point two feet in front of the body. Before he begins the visualizations, he takes refuge in his *Guru* and the Three Jewels. He also takes a vow to become a Buddha out of compassion for all sentient beings.[269]

With these external and internal preparations, he begins the 13 visualizations. Firstly, the *Yogin* imagines his father and mother standing on his right and left respectively. He also sees various forms of sentient beings in different levels of existence. He imagines that every one of these beings could have been his father or mother during their innumerable births and rebirths. He decides to save them from their pain and sorrow. Secondly, he visualizes the deity he serves as seated on a high throne consisting of eight lions, transformed from eight *Bodhisattvas*. He sees the deity as transformed into many *Dharma*-transmitting *Gurus*. The *Gurus* confer the initiation of Fivefold Wisdom on him, by pouring sanctified water upon the crown of his head. As they do the initiation, he imagines the water passing out of his pores, taking with it all the sinful material from his body. Thirdly, he visualizes the deity as himself and becomes one with the deity. He sees the symbols of *Dharma*, *Sangha* and the protectors of *Dharma* shining brightly on his right, left and behind. Fourthly, he visualizes Saakyamuni, the founder Buddhism, seated on a lion-throne with his golden body. His right hand touches the ground, while the left hand makes the *Samaadhi Mudraa* and holds an alms-bowl. He sees a great light issuing forth from the heart of the Buddha and recognizes him as the primordial teacher. Another light emerges from Buddha's head, which makes visible the throne of *Vajradhaara*, the primordial Buddha, dark blue in color. The throne is enveloped by transparent light. The primordial Buddha is seated there, wearing a jeweled diadem in the company of the 84 great masters (*Mahaasiddhas*) of the past ages. Fifthly, another light that emerges from the heart of the Buddha manifests the future Buddha *Maitreya* seated on his right side, in the company of Asanga, Vasubandhu and others who belong to the Yogaacaara School. Sixthly, another light that comes from the heart of the Buddha reveals the *Boddhisattva Manjusrii* seated on his left, surrounded by the spiritual helpers, who belong to the School of Naagaarjuna. Seventhly, rays that appears from the heart of Saakyamuni light up the foreground, and here the *Yogin* sees his own immediate teachers, the ones who initiated him into the mysteries. Below them are the deities of the Buddha families, the *Bodhisattvas*, the *Pratyekabuddhas*, *Sraavakas*, deities of the mysteries (*Dakiniis*), the protectors of faith (*Dharmapaalas*) and the books of the scriptures, which they reveal – all emitting rays of light.[270]

Eighthly, the *Yogin* renews and strengthens in himself the Mind of Enlightenment (*Bodhicitta*), which he sees under 22 images. They are the following: earth, gold, moon, fire, treasure, jewel, ocean, diamond, mountain, cure-alls, great friend, wish-granting jewel, sun, *Gandharva*-voice, kind, gem storehouse, great road, vehicle, fountain, pleasant sound, great river and cloud.

540   Buddhist Tradition

Ninthly, the *Yogin* pronounces *Mantras* that express the four immeasurables (*Brahma-vihaaras*), viz., loving kindness, compassion, sympathetic joy and equanimity. While he recites the *Mantras*, he imagines that the form of a supreme teacher on a throne enters him through the top of his head and passes down to his heart. Tenthly, he imagines the *Vajra* standing upright in his heart on the moon disk, leading to the Mind of Enlightenment. He recites a *Mantra*, which reads as "*Om*! All the *Dharmas* are intrinsically pure; I am intrinsically pure", in the process realizing his oneness with the pure *Dharma*-nature (*Dharmadaatu*). Eleventhly, the *Yogin* begins the process of mystic death and resurrection. His body passes through the water, and he experiences the first sign, namely, a mirage. As fluid dries up and fire emerges, he has the second sign, viz., smoke. At this stage his ability to eat, drink and digest fails. When fire passes into wind, he has the third sign, i.e., the fireflies. As life winds are transferred from their normal bodily centers and as he acquires the understanding principle (*Vijnaana*), he has the fourth sign, a changeable lamp in the heart. When the understanding principle leaves the body and passes to the Clear Light, he abandons his body of works and obtains a diamond body. Then the body, thus purified in Clear Light, returns by a reverse process, recreating the elements. Twelfthly, the *Yogin* utters the four mystic syllables, viz., *Jah Huum Bam Hoh*, which takes him to the four levels of the Gnostic aspects (*Jnaanaruupa*) of the Lord. As the result, he realizes that the god enters him and he enters the god. Finally, he visualizes, in his heart, the germ-syllable, in the process emiting light that illumines the realm of desire (*Kaama-loka*) and the realm of form (*Ruupa-loka*). Then the rays of light are drawn back into the germ-syllable. The *Yogin*, then, invokes the appropriate deities to bestow initiation on his disciples. In this manner, identification with the deity is established and the *Yogin* becomes a master who can initiate and lead others to the experience of the Buddhahood. The 13 visualizations can be used to come in contact with any of the various divinities of the *Vajrayaana* pantheon.[271]

5.3.2.5. INITIATION RITES

The *Vajrayaana* Buddhism, with its Tantric ritual and meditational practices, emphasizes on initiation rites (*Diikshaa*). It distinguishes between the uninitiated and the initiated, just as it demarcates between the exoteric and esoteric doctrine. Any person can study the exoteric doctrines from the sacred books; they need no special initiation. But the esoteric doctrines are intended only for those who are initiated, i.e., the small circle of followers or disciples, who are directly under the direction of a *Guru*, who is known as *Vajraacaarya*. Thus, Tantric Buddhism claims that truly efficacious means of attainment of Buddhahood can never be learned from books, but rather they can be taught only by way of personal contact with the specialized instructor, the *Vajraacaarya*. The one who wants to be initiated must submit himself in complete obedience to the *Vajraacaarya*. He must recognize the *Vajraacaarya* as the one who stands in the place of the Buddha and who can transfer to him the true secrets and mysteries of the esoteric doctrine. According to *Tantrism*, genuine truth is what the *Vajraacaarya* teaches to the small circle of the initiated, and what is taught outside the circle in public is far from the truth. Thus, Tantric masters maintain an air of secrecy about what is taught to the initiated, and no one outside the circle of the initiated can have access to the rites and practices of the initiated.[272]

This is especially true of Left-handed *Tantrism*, in which the esoteric relationship – between the experiences of bliss in sexual union and the primordial bliss of the mind – is drawn. It believes that passions in their direct and unsublimated form can be used as vehicles of salvation. Therefore, the initial consecration and practice associated with the supreme *Yoga Tantras* may involve sexual union with a consort, representing the underlying symbolism of the union between the female, representing wisdom, and the male, symbolizing compassion. The monks, who have taken a vow to abstain from sexual activity, may perform such practices as visualizations, whereas for others such ritual practices imply the actual performance of sexual activity. The final aim of such rituals is not to feed on one's desires, but their final transformation and eradication. The Left-handed *Tantra* believes that immoral conduct is a necessary stage of transition for the attainment of a-moral conduct. Desire is used to make the initiated understand its peripheral and superficial nature, thereby helping him to overcome it. In order to avoid the abuse of such practices, to use such means at the right stage of the spiritual journey of the initiated and to achieve true liberation from desire and passions, there is the need for a true guide. For this reason *Tantrism* holds that without initiation one cannot begin a spiritual training.[273]

The Sanskrit word for initiation is *Abhisheka*, which literally means 'besprinkling'. Sprinkling the holy water at the time of initiation consecrates the initiated. The initiation ceremony is derived from the ancient Indian ritual of the inauguration of the Crown Prince. By the power of this rite of inauguration of the Crown Prince, he is transformed from the status of the Crown Prince into the status of a world ruler. In the same way, the Buddhist initiation ceremony fills the initiate with the true waters of knowledge, thereby enabling him to become a spiritual world ruler, i.e., a Buddha. The actual initiation rites differ from one sect to the other. But, some of the common elements are esoteric doctrine, secrecy of doctrine and practice, learning under the direction of a *Vajraacaarya* and different types of *Abhisheka* ceremonies.[274]

5.3.2.6. PRIESTHOOD

In many of the *Vajrayaana* Tantric Buddhist Sects, priesthood is considered as something very sacred, and elaborate rites are associated with the consecration of a priest, who is commonly called *Vajra*-Master (*Vajraacaarya*), though each Sect may have its own name to refer to a priest. The rite by which a person is raised to the office of priesthood is known as the consecration of a *Vajra*-Master (*Vajraacaarya-abhisheka*). This right is different from the rite of Tantric initiation (*Diikshaa*). In many Buddhist Sects, priesthood is hereditary, as only sons of the *Vajra*-Master may be consecrated as priests. Usually a *Vajra*-Master performs the Fire Sacrifice, acts as a priest and serves the people in performing various rites, including the Tantric initiation rites. Generally most of the *Vajraacaaryas* before they become priests go through the initiation rites. The consecration of *Vajraacaarya* takes place in the Tantric shrines of the monastery. The persons who oversee the rites are monastery officials, such as the senior *Vajraacaarya* (*Cakresvara*) and the ritual officer (*Betaaju*). After the consecration, the new priest's family priest assists him in performing the Fire Sacrifice, which takes place outside the monastery's courtyard. Among the other ceremonies, nine different types of consecrations (*Abhishekas*) are done over the candidate. The first is the Flask Consecration (*Kalasaabhisheka*), which consists in sprinkling water over the candidate from the main Flask. The second is the Crown Consecration (*Mukutaabhisheka*). It is a rite by which the neophyte is given the *Vajraacaarya's* ceremonial crown. The third is the *Vajra* Consecration (*Vajraabhisheka*). During this rite the *Vajraacaarya's Vajra* is placed in the right hand of the neophyte. The fourth is the Bell Consecration (*Ghantaabhisheka*). This rite consists in the candidate receiving the *Vajra*-Master's bell his left hand. The fifth is the Name Consecration (*Naamaabhisheka*). During this rite the candidate receives a new name, by which he is known thereafter. The sixth is the Consecration of the *Vajra*-Master (*Vajraacaarya-abhisheka*), which consists in the neophyte performing the *Aalinganaa Mudraa*, i.e., holding the bell and the *Vajra* with fingers splayed and wrists crossed, as if embracing his consort. The seventh is the Headband Consecration (*Pataakaabhisheka*). According to this rite, the chief celebrant places a headband around the neophyte's forehead and gives him a rosary. The eighth is the Lampblack Consecration (*Anjanaabhisheka*). During this rite a lampblack is placed on the candidate's eyes with the tip of the chief celebrant's *Vajra*. The ninth is the Mirror Consecration (*Darpanaabhisheka*). This rite consists in the neophyte receiving the yogurt and oil mix on his eyes with the help of which he is expected to perceive the ultimate emptiness of all things. By the use of these ninefold consecrations the *Vajraacaarya* is consecrated and raised to the order of priesthood.[275]

5.3.2.7. SACRED SYMBOLS

Some objects are considered sacred symbols. Some of the important Buddhist sacred symbols are the following: the Three Jewels (*Tri-ratna*), the Wheel (*Cakra*), the Lotus Flower, the *Svastika*, the Throne of the Buddha, the *Stuupa*, the Umbrella, the Conch-shell (*Sankha*), the flying horse and the *Norbu* gem. The first emblem is the *Tri-ratna*, viz., the Buddha, the *Dharma* and the *Sangha*. It is often used as an ornament. The second emblem is the Wheel. It symbolizes the Buddhist doctrine that the origin of the world is unknowable. It also points to the circle of cause and effect without beginning and end. The third symbol is the lotus flower. Its use as a Buddhist emblem comes from the fact that it resembles the wheel, the petals taking the place of spokes. It typifies the doctrine of perpetual cycles of existence. The fourth symbol is the

Svastika mark. Though its origin is controversial, it symbolizes good luck. It is similar to a wheel having four spokes. Its four spokes represent the four groups of worlds, i.e., the three regions of the heaven and the lower region of the universe. The fifth symbol is the throne of the Buddha. It is a favorite emblem that many Buddhist scriptures speak of. The throne of the Buddha is represented under the *Bodhi* tree. The sixth symbol is the *Stuupa*. As it holds the relics of the Buddha, *Bodhisattva* or a saint, it is often considered an object of adoration in itself. The seventh symbol is the umbrella. It is a sign of power and supremacy. When a king is present, he alone carries an umbrella. The eighth symbol is the conch shell. It is a very auspicious symbol. The ninth symbol is the flying horse. It can carry a man around the world in one day. The tenth symbol is the *Norbu* gem. It has the power to illuminate the earth for seven miles round, even on the darkest night. All these symbols are important in the life of a genuine Buddhist. They are also objects of true devotion.[276]

5.3.2.8. PRAYER AND FORMULARIES OF PRAYER

Prayer forms an important form of worship in the *Vajrayaana* Buddhist tradition. As the people who follow the Tantric tradition are religious minded and superstitious, they accord a significant place to prayer in their lives. Though their prayer is often mechanical repetition, inscribed on rocks and written on paper, their thoughts and hearts are very much involved when they pray. They pray at all times, according to their needs. They usually pray in the morning, at noon and in the evening. They pray in public and in private, at home and outside home, in moments of labor or idleness, whether they are lying down or standing up, on mournful and joyful occasions. There is no hesitation and inhibition to pray aloud or to pray together. In Lhaassa, there is a custom of praying in the public squares, known as *Monlam Chenpo*, which is a form of congregational prayer. In the evening, just as the day is setting, all Tibetans – men, women and children – stop their work, meet together in the principal town squares with the intention of praying together. As soon as the group is formed, everyone kneels down and begins chanting prayers. In this way, praying, in private and public, as an individual and a community, plays an important role in the spiritual life of the *Vajrayaana* Buddhists.[277]

While praying a number of prayer formularies are used. They are those things that are used as aids to prayer. Since the most common form of prayer among the *Vajrayaana* Buddhists is the repetition of sacred syllables, *Mantras* are used as an aid to prayer. The most common *Mantra* is the six-syllabled *Mantra* "*Om Mani Padme Huum*". It is a mystical sentence, which the *Bodhisattva Padma-paani* (*Avalokitesvara*), the patron saint of Tibet uses. It is believed that the six syllables represent the six realms of *Samsaara* existence, and the constant repetition of this mystical sentence helps a person to escape all the realms of *Samsaara* existence. As the result, the continuous repetition of this *Mantra* has become an important form of prayer. To make the repetition easier, prayer wheels and prayer cylinders are made in which this mystic sentence is written many times. The revolving of the wheel or the cylinder once amounts to repetition of the mystic syllable as many times as it is written in the wheel or the cylinder. The greater the number of revolutions made, the greater the prayer force or prayer merits that are accumulated. In this manner, the prayer wheels of various size and length become prayer merit producing machinery.[278]

Similarly, the mystic syllable is written or carved on the rocks, the stones, the monuments, the *Stuupas*, the trees and on every object that is visible to any person that passes by. We also find praying walls, which are long stone structures that are erected on the sides of the high roads and often-frequented thoroughfares. Some of these praying walls are a few feet long, six feet high and from six to twelve feet broad, while others are over 1000 yards long, built on the sides of pyramidal *Stuupas* or *Caityas*. On these praying walls the six-syllabled mystic sentence and other prayer formulas are written many times, along with the carved images of saints and are dedicated as votive offerings. Those who travel by the road acquire prayer-merit just by following the letters, without reading or repeating them. Other prayer formularies used to spread prayer all over the village and town are the praying staffs and the praying flags. On these the six-syllabled *Mantra* is written many times, and the images of the flying horse and *Norbu* gem are drawn. They spread the prayer merit all around the area where the flags are hoisted. It is believed that erecting praying staffs and hoisting praying flags are works of great merit. Thus, the most conspicuous feature that we find in Tibet is the presence of the praying staffs and prying flags on the hills, in the valleys, by the roadside, on the river bank, on walls, on the top of the houses, in the streets, squares and public places.[279]

Another prayer formulary often used to pray the six-syllabled mystic formula is the rosary. The rosary helps the accurate and complete repetition of the *Mantras*. In Northern Buddhist countries, including Tibet, the rosaries have 108 beads, representing the 108 volumes of *Kanjur*, the Tibetan scripture. The most common Buddhist rosaries are made of wood, pebbles, berries, bones, turquoise, coral, amber, silver, pearls or gems. The rosaries that are made of the bones of the holy *Laamas* are the costliest, as they radiate greater holiness. Sometimes a *Vajra* (*Dorje*) is attached to the rosary. By using the rosary the people repeat the ejaculatory prayers dedicated to *Bodhisattva Padma-paani* and other prayer formulas. Another prayer formulary used while reciting, especially while chanting the *Mantra*, is the sacred drum (*Damaru*). It is shaped like two hemispheres, joined on their convex sides and encircled by sacred shells. It is sounded by means of buttons attached to two strips of leather. The sound it produces depends on its size. A prayer formulary, which performs a function similar to that of the *Damaru*, is the prayer bell. It is used in the performance of the daily ceremonies. Usually it is rung to accompany the repetition and chanting of prayers. The bell is also rung to fill up the intervals of worship. The upper part of the handle of the bell is a half *Dorje*. In the handle, as well as on the body of the bell, are carved various mystical symbols. The purpose of ringing the bell during prayer is the call the attention of the deities to whom worship is offered. Prayer books and daily manuals of prayer are other prayer formularies that aid people in their prayer. All such prayer formularies aid the people to repeat the *Mantras* and gain prayer merits.[280]

5.3.2.9. SUPERSTITIOUS PRACTICES

The *Vajrayaana* Buddhism believes in the existence of malignant spirits that bring harm to the humans. These demons and evil spirits cause illnesses, accidents, death, natural calamities and similar dangers. There is a constant struggle between these evil forces and human beings. Hence, there is the need to ward off the evil influences of the demons and to bring positive good in the life of the human person. In order to protect the human beings from all such dangers, the Tantric masters propose a number of practices, viz., the use of protective weapons against evil spirits, the use of amulets and *Paritta*-cord, and the use of spells. In this section, we consider the manner in which *Tantrism* attempts to counter these evil forces as humans move towards their ultimate destiny.

5.3.2.9.1. Protective Weapons against Evil Spirits

The *Vajrayaana* Buddhist religious practice proposes a number of protective weapons that have the power to counter the evil influences of the demons and evil spirits. The possession and the use of these weapons can help one to prevent evil from having any effect on one's life. Some of these protective weapons are the following: the thunderbolt (*Vajra* or *Dorje*), the protective bell, the protective sacred drum, the nail (*Phrubu*) and the protective flag. The most powerful protective weapon against evil spirits is the *Dorje* or *Vajra*. In Tibet it is part of the equipment of a full monk. *Dorje* is shaped like an imaginary thunderbolt of the gods *Siva* and *Indra*. According to a myth, the original *Dorje* fell from *Indra's* heaven and is preserved in the Sera monastery at Lhaassa. According to another legend, the original instrument belongs to Gautama Buddha, and it traveled through the air from India to Tibet as the Buddha passed into his *Pari-Nirvaana*. The main purpose of the *Dorje* is the exorcising and driving away of evil spirits. It can also secure good fortune and ward off evil influences of all kinds. The *Laamas* using the *Vajra* are considered to be very powerful. Because of its power as a protective weapon against evil and that which brings good fortune, the original *Dorje*, preserved in Sera monastery, is considered an object of actual worship. People fall prostrate in adoration before the original *Dorje*. At the New Year festival, it is taken in procession for public veneration.[281]

The sacred bell, besides being a prayer formulary, is also a protective weapon. The handle of the bell is made of a half *Dorje*. The combination of the bell sound and the waving of the *Dorje* in the handle of the bell serve the purpose of keeping off evil spirits and their influence on human beings. Just like the sacred bell, the sacred drum also serves as a protective weapon, besides being a prayer formulary. The sound of the sacred drum is heard at great distances.

It is believed that the sound of the sacred drum is a highly efficacious means of frightening away the evil spirits, who are averse to all forms of loud noise. Thus, larger sacred drums are used to make louder sounds, thereby keeping the evil spirits from human habitations. Another important protective weapon is the nail (*Phurbu*). It is a triangular wedge-shaped instrument with a thin and sharp-pointed head, and having a half *Dorje* handle. It is usually made of cardboard or metal on which spells (*Dhaaraniis*) and other mystical words are written. These *Dhaaraniis* are directed against the demons of the South, the East and the Southeast. The *Laamas* use the *Phurbu* to cure illnesses that have come about as the result of the evil influences of the evil spirits. They go around the house turning the point of the *Phurbu* in all directions while uttering spells. The *Phurbu*, on which the spells composed by the *Dalai Laama* or the *Pancen Laama* are written, is believed to be very powerful and is sold for large sums of money. The *Phurbu* is a powerful protective weapon as on it is written spells against the demons, and it has a half *Dorje* handle. The combination of these two keeps all evil influences of demons from the humans. The last of the commonly used protective weapons is the protective flag. The flag, besides being a prayer formulary, is also a protective weapon. On the flag, that is used as protective weapon, is drawn the symbols of the flying horse, the *Norbu* gem and the *Phurbu*, besides the six-syllabled *Mantra* of *Pandma-paani*. The use of these symbols, especially that of the *Phurbu*, along with the *Mantra* in the flag makes it a protective weapon that efficaciously wards off and counteracts the diseases the demons would inflict on human beings. Similarly, flags on which the representations of four animals, viz., the tiger, lion, eagle and dragon, are also said to act against evil spirits. When these protective flags fly in different parts of a town or a village it is believed that the malicious and mischievous ghosts and demons that trouble the people of that town or village, are chased away. Thus, the protective flags perform the same tasks for the whole town or village, as talismans and charms do for an individual when he uses them. With the use of all these protective weapons, a person can live peacefully without being affected by the influence of the evil spirits.[282]

5.3.2.9.2. Use of Amulets and the Paritta-cord

The use of amulets (*Kavaca*) is a universal practice in Northern Buddhism, especially in Tibetan Buddhist religious practice. The amulets are ornamental boxes, which contain relics of saints, little images of saints, pictures of saints and prayer formularies. Sometimes the amulets are also filled with charms against evil spirits. They are made of wood, bones and filigree silver, and are marked with turquoise. The shape is square, circular or curved. Usually the amulets are attached to a string and worn round a person's neck. At other times, they are worn as breastplates or as phylacteries.[283]

The use of the *Paritta*-cord around a person's wrist is a common practice, the aim of which is to ward off the evil influences of the demons. The *Paritta*-cord is associated with protective chanting (*Paritta*). Even a layperson can chant the words of the Buddha to bring about protection through the words of the Buddha. But it is more efficacious when the members of the monastic *Sangha* chant the *Dharma* as the Buddha taught, as through such protective chanting the people who listen come under divine protection. To symbolize the protective power passing from the monk, he holds a cord, the other end of which is tied to the Buddha-image. The implication is that the Buddha image and the cord are filled with the *Paritta*-power, and the worship of the Buddha image brings protection on all those present. To indicate the presence of the *Paritta*-power symbolically, after the completion of the protective chanting ceremony, pieces of the *Paritta*-cord are tied to the laypeople's wrists. The *Paritta*-cord becomes not only a reminder of the protection against evil spirits, but also the actual storehouse of the *Paritta's* protective power. Thus, the person has continuous protection from the evil influences of the demons.[284]

5.3.2.9.3. Use of Spells

In *Vajrayaana* Buddhism, the spells (*Dhaaranii*) are used as magical formulae that bring protection from danger and furtherance of one's worldly interests. The use of spells for these purposes is based on two assumptions: firstly, the misfortunes and troubles of the humans are due to demonic powers, and secondly, the *Dhaaraniis* have the power to counter the spiritual powers that affect the humans. The *Dhaaraniis* are capable of dealing with the demon by forcing him out, by causing him to move away or by mustering the support of a more powerful and benevolent power against him. Thus, the spells are incantations that work wonders when one utters them rightly. There are various types of *Dhaaraniis*: there are the purificatory *Dhaaraniis*, that are said to remove the sins of the dead person and help him reach Sukhaavatii, the Pure Land of *Amitaabha* Buddha; the *Dhaaraniis* of the female goddess *Taaraa* are read against ghosts; the *Dhaaraniis* of *Bhaishjya-guru* are said against illness; the *Dhaaraniis* of *Vairocanna* are read as part of the daily worship of the Buddha-image; and the *Dhaaraniis* of *Aparamitaa* is read on one's birthday, for the purpose of attaining long life. Thus, the incantation of various spells, in the final analysis brings about the well-being of the people, freeing them from the evil influences of demons and evil spirits.[285]

When a seeker of the *Vajrayaana* path makes use of the above-mentioned paths in the context of his everyday living, he frees himself from all evil influences and attachments, and experiences the ultimate emptiness of reality. This helps to attain the *Vajra* nature with its *Vajra* body thereby transforming him into a *Vajrasattva*, which ultimately takes him to the final goal of the Buddhahood.

In this essay we have elaborated *Vajrayaana* Buddhism, focusing on the Divine and the path it proposes to arrive at the supreme goal of Buddhahood. The Divine of *Vajrayaana* Buddhism presents a picture that is a bit different from the other two traditions. Firstly, we see, for the first time in the Buddhist thought, the reality of the Primordial Buddha (*Aadi-*

Buddha), who is seen as the absolute and ultimate creator of the universe. The five Buddhas, their respective *Bodhisattvas* and the corresponding human Buddhas are seen as emanations of the Primordial Buddha. Thus, we find an emanationist worldview that is founded on one ultimate creator of the universe. This is something very new to the Buddhist tradition. Secondly, *Vajrayaana* Buddhism gives importance to the *Sakti* dimension, thereby providing a prominent place for female deities in its pantheon. They are often referred to as 'Mother of the Buddhas'. Thirdly, the concept of Father-Mother deity, representing two important truths of Buddhist beliefs, viz., compassion and wisdom respectively, and the sexual implication that is inherent in this concept, is something new in *Vajrayaana* Buddhism. Fourthly, in *Vajrayaana* Buddhism, especially in its Laamistic form, we have the *Avataara Laamas*, who are incarnations of divine *Bodhisattvas* and the Buddhas. Thus, the perception of the Divine in *Vajrayaana* Buddhism has some marked differences from other Buddhist traditions. We find a similar trend with regard to the *Vajrayaana* path to the Divine. The use of Tantric rites and Tantric gestures (*Mudraas*) are typically specific to *Vajrayaana* Buddhism. The attempt to identify with the Tantric deities by way of meditation on the *Mandalas* and prolonged meditative visualizations is another religious practice that we particularly find in *Vajrayaana* Buddhism. The widespread use of protective weapons, spells and amulets against evil spirits, ghosts and demons, thereby neutralizes their evil influences and brings rich blessings as the aspirant walks to his ultimate destiny. Thus, we find in the *Vajrayaana* Buddhist tradition a number of elements that are new. At the same time, it is not totally different from that of the original Buddhist tradition. It is definitely a further development of the original Buddhism, in the context of new cultural and religious backgrounds.

CONCLUSION

To the vast history of 2,500 years of Buddhism and its practice in its three major traditions of *Hiinayaana*, *Mahaayaana* and *Vajrayaana*, we need to add a consideration of the living Buddhism of the present in order to understand Buddhism and its present-day practice. The Buddhist tradition of today falls into three broad categories. The first is the *Theravaada* tradition, which the later *Mahaayaanist* tradition refers to as the *Hiinayaana*. The scriptures of this branch of Buddhism are preserved in the Paali language. In comparison with other Buddhist traditions, the *Theravaada* tradition is conservative, and therefore it is closer in doctrine and practice to the original Buddhism, which the Buddha preached. The *Theravaada* tradition is the religion of over 100,000,000 people in Sri Lanka and the South East Asian countries like Burma, Thailand, Cambodia and Laos. The second is the *Mahaayaana* tradition. It is a tradition that advocates a religious doctrine and practice that is more liberal. Its scriptures are preserved in the Chinese language. The *Mahaayaana* tradition is very diverse, as it has emerged as a result of the interaction of original Buddhism with a number of other native religious traditions. Besides being varied, the *Mahayaana* tradition has the largest number of adherents in comparison to other traditions. About 1,000,000,000 people adhere to this tradition in countries like China, Korea, Japan and Vietnam. The third is the *Vajrayaana* tradition. The general beliefs of this tradition are that of the *Mahaayaana* tradition, but its specific orientation is Tantric. As a result, it is also referred to as Tantric Buddhism. The canon of scriptures of this tradition is preserved in the Tibetan language. The *Vajrayaana* tradition has about 20,000,000 adherents, mostly in countries like Tibet, Mongolia, Nepal and the Himalayan India. All these living Buddhist traditions of today trace their origin back to the *Buddha Dharma*, taught by the Saakyamuni in the land of India, though it disappeared from this land centuries ago.[286]

Though all these Buddhist traditions are practiced in different parts of the world, in recent times there is an earnest desire among the adherents of the various traditions to come together as a united fold and to propagate the religion of the Buddha by way of missionary activities. Thus, instead of *Hiinayaana*, *Mahaayaana* and *Vajrayaana*, the slogan is *Ekayaana*, i.e., 'the One Vehicle'. In order to actualize this ideal, a common Buddhist forum named "the World Federation of Buddhists" has been founded with the aim of using Buddhist principles for effecting peace and freedom in the world. This forum organized a Council (*Sangiiti*) of 4,000 delegates, from 1954 to 1956 with the task of fixing the canonical texts (*Tripitaka*) in Paali, basing it on the oral recitation. As the texts are finalized, they are printed. Besides, a concise three-volume *Tripitaka* is published in Paali, Hindi and English, with the view of making Buddhism popular once again in India and in the English-speaking world. The World Federation of Buddhists is making an all-out effort to step up missionary activities in the western countries, like Switzerland, Holland, Belgium, Finland, France and United States. These activities include construction of Buddhist temples and monasteries, starting English branches of the societies like the *Mahaabodhi* Society, running Buddhist bookshops, bringing out periodicals containing Buddha *Dharma* and regular meetings of study groups to deepen the knowledge of Buddhism. All these activities are done with the view of finding a common basis for all the Buddhist traditions. Thus, there is a great revival of Buddhism in the contemporary period, not in a sectarian way, but to establish the *Ekayaana* Buddhism that would take all to true liberation.[287]

NOTES

1 Christmas Humphreys, *Buddhism*, (Middlesex: Penguin Books, 1962), p.11.

2 Cf. Rupert Gethin, *The Foundations of Buddhism*, (New York: Oxford University Press, 1998), pp. 1-2.

3 Cf. Damien Keown, *Buddhism: A Short Introduction*, (Oxford: Oxford University Press), pp. 3-15. Cf. also Edward Conze, *Buddhism: Its Essence and Development*, (New Delhi: Munshiram Manoharlal Publishers Pvt. Ltd., 1999), pp. 38-43.

4 Cf. P.V. Bapat, ed., *2500 Years of Buddhism*, (New Delhi: Publication Division, Ministry of Information and Broadcasting, Government of India, 1997), pp. 1-4.

5 Cf. Ibid., pp. 8-17.

6 The historians debate regarding the dates of Siddhartha Gautama's life. As controversies still persist, there is no agreement among the scholars. Probably he was born in 563 B.C; left home at the age of 29; attained enlightenment after six years of wandering at the age of 35 and passed away in 583 B. C., when he was 80 years old. Cf. Christmas Humphreys, p. 30.

7 Cf. E.H. Johnston, trans., *Asvaghosha's Buddhacarita or Acts of the Buddha*, (Delhi: Motilal Banarsidass Publishers Private Limited, 1995), I, 1-89. Cf. also Jack Maguire, *Essential Buddhism: A Complete Guide to Beliefs and Practices*, (New York: Pocket Books, 2001), pp. 3-4.

8 Cf. E.H. Johnston, II, 1-56. Cf. also Jack Maguire, p. 4.

9 Cf. E.H. Johnston, III – IX. Cf. also Jack Maguire, pp. 5-6.

10 Cf. Ibid., XII – XIV. Cf. also Christmas Humphreys, pp. 31-34. Cf. also Damien Keown, pp. 22-30.

11 Cf. Damien Keown, p. 59.

12 The term "*Sangiiti*" literally means 'recital' or 'chanting together'. In such *Sangiitis*, amidst the gathering of the monks, those who have committed the words of the Buddha to memory are invited to recite them. After the recitation, questions are raised regarding the sayings of Buddha, the occasion in which they are given, the person to whom they are given, the rule of life related to them and further rules resulting from these sayings and the offence resulting from the violation of the sayings in question. In this manner, the truth and authenticity of the sayings of Buddha are verified and determined. Cf. Edward J. Thomas, *The History of Buddhist Thought*, (New Delhi: Munshiram Manoharlal Publishers Pvt. Ltd., 1997), pp. 27-28.

13 According to some authorities, the fourth Council took place in Jalandhar. Cf. also P.V. Bapat, p. 42.

14 Cf. Edward J. Thomas, pp. 27-37. Cf. also P.V. Bapat, 31-49. Cf. also Helmer Ringgren, pp. 375-376.

15 Cf. Edward J. Thomas, pp. 37-41. Cf. also P.V. Bapat, pp. 86-96. Cf. also Damien Keown, pp. 59-60. Cf. also Edward Conze, *Buddhism: Its Essence and Development*, pp. 66-67, 69.

16 Cf. P.V. Bapat, pp. 96-102. Cf. also Helmer Ringgren, p. 376.

17 Rupert Gethin, p. 225. Cf. also Paul Williams, *Mahaayaana Buddhism: The Doctrinal Foundations*, (London: Routledge, 1996), pp. 20-26.

18 Cf. Christmas Humphreys, pp. 48-49. Cf. also Helmer Ringgren, p. 379. Cf. also Edward Cronze, *Buddhism: Its Essence and Development*, pp. 121-123.

19 Cf. Edward Conze, *Buddhism: Its Essence and Development*, pp. 67-69.

20 Cf. Christmas Humphreys, pp. 60-61.

21 Cf. Rupert Gethin, pp. 252-256. Cf. also Christmas Humphreys, pp. 62-66. Helmer Ringgren, pp. 382-386. Cf. also P.V. Bapat, pp. 75-82.

22 Cf. P.V. Bapat, pp. 82-85.
23 Cf. Rupert Gethin, pp. 257-266. Cf. also Christmas Humphreys, pp. 66-71. Cf. P.V. Bapat, pp. 110-120.
24 Cf. Helmer Ringgren, pp. 386-388. Cf. also P.V. Bapat, pp. 65-74. Cf. also Rupert Gethin, pp. 266-273.
25 Cf. Damien Keown, pp. 116-132. Cf. also Rupert Gethin, pp. 273-276.
26 Cf. Nisha Singh, *The Origin and Development of Buddhist Monastic Education in India*, (Delhi: Indo-Asian Publishing House, 1997), pp. 41-42. Cf. also Edward Cronze, *Buddhism: Its Essence and Development*, pp. 28-29.
27 Cf. Nisha Singh, pp. 42-43. Cf. also Edward Cronze, *Buddhism: Its Essence and Development*, pp. 28-29.
28 Cf. U Ko Lay, comp., *Guide to Tipitka*, (Delhi: Sri Satguru Publications, 1990), pp. 5-18. Cf. also Nisha Singh, pp. 49-50. Cf. also Edward J. Thomas, pp. 266-267. Cf. also Helmer Ringgren, p. 359.
29 Cf. U Ko Lay, pp. 19-24. Cf. also Edward J. Thomas, pp. 268-269.
30 Cf. U Ko Lay, pp. 25-44. Cf. also Edward J. Thomas, pp. 269-270.
31 Cf. U Ko Lay, pp. 45-82. Cf. also Edward J. Thomas, pp. 270-271.
32 Cf. U Ko Lay, pp. 83-109. Cf. also Edward J. Thomas, p. 271.
33 Cf. U Ko Lay, pp. 110-124. Cf. also Edward J. Thomas, p. 271.
34 Cf. U Ko Lay, pp. 125-142. Cf. also Edward J. Thomas, pp. 271-273.
35 Cf. Nisha Singh, pp. 51-52. Cf. also Edward J. Thomas, p. 276.
36 Cf. Edward J. Thomas, pp. 274-275. Cf. also U Ko Lay, pp. 143-153.
37 Cf. P.V. Bapat, p. 122.
38 Cf. Edward J. Thomas, pp. 283-284. Cf. also Christmas Humphreys, p. 53. Cf. also Helmer Ringgren, p. 361.
39 Cf. Moti Lal Pandit, *Suunyataa: The Essence of Mahaayaana Spirituality*, (New Delhi: Munshiram Manoharlal Publishers Pvt. Ltd., 1998), pp. 291-322. Cf. Christmas Humphreys, pp. 53-56. Cf. also Helmer Ringgren, p. 361. Cf. also Rupert Gethin, pp. 225-226.
40 Cf. Rupert Gethin, p. 267. Cf. also Helmer Ringgren, p. 361.
41 Cf. Rupert Gethin, p. 267.
42 Cf. Ibid. Cf. also Edward J. Thomas, pp. 285-287. Cf. Alex Wayman, "The Diamond Vehicle", *Buddhist Spirituality*, ed. Takeuchi Yoshinori, (New York: SCM Press Ltd., 1993), pp. 221-222. Cf. also Gethin Rupert, p. 269.
43 Cf. Edward J. Thomas, p. 287. Cf. also Edward Conze, *Buddhism: Its Essence and Development*, p. 32.
44 Cf. Rupert Gethin, p. 85.
45 Cf. Christmas Humphreys, pp. 132-134, 137-139.
46 Cf. Ibid., pp. 134-136.
47 Cf. Ibid., pp. 139-141.
48 Cf. Rupert Gethin, pp. 90-91.

49 Cf. Ibid., p. 91. Cf. also M. Monier-Williams: *Buddhism*, (New Delhi: Munshiram Manoharlal Publishers Pvt. Ltd., 1995), pp. 86-87.
50 Cf. M. Monier-Williams, pp. 87-91. Cf. also Rupert Gethin, pp. 107-110.
51 Cf. Christmas Humphreys, pp. 73-76.
52 Cf. Edward Conze, *Buddhism: Its Essence and Development*, pp. 38-42. Cf. also Rupert Gethin, pp. 126-132. Cf. also Ananda K. Coomaraswamy, *Buddha and the Gospel of Buddhism*, (New Delhi: Munshiram Manoharlal Publishers Pvt. Ltd., 1985), p. 101.
53 Cf. Edward Conze, *Buddhism: Its Essence and Development*, p. 40.
54 Cf. Damien Keown, pp. 31-32. Cf. also Rupert Gethin, pp. 112-113. Cf. also Edward Conze, *Buddhism: Its Essence and Development*, pp. 48-50.
55 Cf. Damien Keown, pp. 32-34. Cf. also Edward Conze, *Buddhism: Its Essence and Development*, pp. 49-50.
56 Cf. Damien Keown, p. 34.
57 Cf. M. Monier-Williams, p. 120. Cf. also Rupert Gethin, p. 118. The older Buddhist sources list only five world-realms and five classes of inhabitants, but the later sources speak of six world realms and six types of inhabitants. Cf. Edward Conze, *Buddhism: Its Essence and Development*, pp. 50. Cf. also Damien Keown, p. 34.
58 Cf. Damien Keown, pp. 34-35. Cf. also M. Monier-William, p. 121.
59 Cf. Damien Keown, p. 35. Cf. also M. Monier-Williams, pp. 120-121.
60 Cf. Damien Keown, p. 35. Cf. also Edward Conze, *Buddhism: Its Essence and Development*, p. 51.
61 Cf. Damien Keown, p. 36.
62 Cf. Edward Conze, *Buddhism: Its Essence and Development*, p. 51. Damien Keown, p.36.
63 Cf. Damien Keown, pp. 36-39. Cf. also Ananda K. Coomaraswamy, p. 102. Cf. also Rupert Gethin, pp. 116-117
64 Cf. M. Monier-Williams, p. 206.
65 Cf. Ibid., pp. 206-208.
66 Cf. Ibid., p. 208.
67 Cf. Ibid., pp. 210-211.
68 Cf. Ibid., pp. 211-212.
69 Cf. Ibid., p. 212.
70 Cf. Ibid., pp. 212-213.
71 Cf. Ibid., p. 213. Cf. also Damien Keown, p. 39. Cf. also Ananda K. Coomaraswamy, p. 102.
72 Isaline Blew Horner, *The Early Buddhist Theory of Man Perfected*, (New Delhi: Oriental Books Reprint Corporation, 1979), pp. 98-99. The *Mahaayaana* Schools do not recognize the *Arahat* as the final stage, as they consider *Boddhisattva* and Buddha stages superior to that of the *Arahat*. It is a later development. But the early Schools of *Hiinaayaana* tradition consider *Arahat* as the ultimate ideal of a Buddhist. They do not make any distinction between the *Arahat* and the Buddha. In fact, Buddha himself is identified with

the *Arahat*. It is only after three or four centuries that the distinction between the Buddha and the *Arahat* became a serious point of discussion among the Buddhists due to the influence of *Mahaayaana* Buddhism. We shall elaborate the *Mahaayaana* view in the next essay that deals with *Mahaayaana* concept of the Divine and the path to the Divine. Cf. Edward Conze, *Buddhism: Its Essence and Development*, p. 94.

73 Cf. Ibid., pp. 93-94. Cf. also Edward J. Thomas, pp. 120-121.

74 Cf. M. Monier-Williams, p. 133. Cf. also Edward Conze, *Buddhism: Its Essence and Development*, pp. 93-94.

75 Edward Conze, *Buddhism: Its Essence and Development*, p. 94.

76 Cf. Moti Lal Pandit, pp. 64-65.

77 Ibid., p. 68.

78 Cf. Ibid., p. 76. Cf. also Bhikkhuni T.N. Tin Lien, *Concepts of Dhamma in Dhammapada*, (Delhi: Eastern Book Linkers, 1996), pp. 91-111.

79 Christmas Humphreys, pp. 125-126.

80 Cf. Ibid., 126.

81 Cf. Ibid.

82 Cf. Ibid.

83 Cf. Antony Fernando, *Buddhism Made Plain: An Introduction for Christians*, (Indore: Satprakashan Sanchar Kendra, 1985), pp. 60-61.

84 Cf. Christmas Humphreys, p. 127.

85 Cf. Ibid. Cf. also Antony Fernando, pp. 57. Cf. also M. Monier-Williams, pp. 139-142. Cf. also Damien Keown, pp. 55-56.

86 Cf. Christmas Humphreys, p. 127. Cf. also M. Monier-Williams, p. 142. Cf. also Damien Keown, pp. 55-56.

87 Antony Fernando, p. 59.

88 Damien, Keown, pp. 48, 51, 54, 57.

89 Cf. Ibid., pp. 56-58. Cf. also Rupert Gethin, pp. 81-84.

90 Cf. Edward Conze, *Buddhism: Its Essence and Development*, p. 105.

91 Cf. Trevor Ling, *The Buddha: Buddhist Civilization in India and Ceylon*, (New York: Pelican Books, 1976), Christmas Humphreys, pp. 80-84. Cf. also Edward Conze, *Buddhism: Its Essence and Development*, pp. 51-52.

92 Cf. Trevor Ling, p. 135. Cf. also Damien keown, p. 54.

93 Cf. Rupert Gethin, pp. 133-139. Cf. also Edward Conze, *Buddhism: Its Essence and Development*, pp. 106-108. Cf. also Christmas Humphreys, pp. 85-89. Just as the *Hiinayaana* tradition denies the reality of the individual self behind the psychophysical complex of individual experiences, so also it denies the reality of an Absolute Self, who is the source of the cosmic activity. Thus, strictly speaking 'the no-soul theory, amounts to 'the no-God theory' as well. Cf. Christmas Humphreys, pp. 79-80.

94 Cf. Rupert Gethin, pp. 140, 145.

95 Cf. Ibid., pp, 141-143. Cf. also Trevor Ling, pp. 132-134.

96 Cf. Rupert Gethin, pp. 143-144.

97 Cf. Damien Keown, pp. 39-42.

98 Cf. Trevor Ling, pp. 136-137.

99 Cf. Antony Fernando, pp. 80-82. Cf. also Christmas Humphreys, p. 110. Cf. also Rupert Gethin, p. 81.
100 Cf. Antony Fernando, pp. 82-84. Cf. also Christmas Humphreys, p. 110. Cf. also Rupert Gethin, p. 81.
101 Cf. Christmas Humphreys, p. 240.
102 Ibid., p. 241.
103 Cf. pp. 111-115.
104 Cf. M. Monier-Williams, pp. 76-79. The novices are expected to learn the spiritual discipline of renunciation. Hence during their time of novitiate they are must even give up even those things which a person can normally receive from others and own for onelf. For this reason they are asked to follow the ten prohibitions.
105 Cf. Ibid., pp. 79-81.
106 Cf. Ibid., pp. 83-84.
107 Cf. Ibid., p. 84. Cf. also Edward J. Thomas, pp. 14-16.
108 Cf. Edward J. Thomas, pp. 16-26.
109 Cf. Antony Fernando, pp. 88-92.
110 Cf. Antony Fernando, pp. 93-95. Cf. also Christmas Humphreys, pp. 115-116. Cf. also Rupert Gethin, p. 81. Cf. also Bhikkhuni T.N. Tin Lien, pp. 99-101.
111 Cf. also Bhikkhuni T.N. Tin Lien, pp.101-111.
112 Cf. Bhikkhuni T.N. Tin Lien, pp. 95-99.
113 Cf. Rupert Gethin, p. 174. Cf. also Damien Keown, p. 58.
114 Cf. Rupert Gethin, pp. 174-176.
115 Cf. Damien Keown, pp. 91-92.
116 Cf. Ibid., pp. 92-94. Cf. also Rupert Gethin, pp. 176-179.
117 Cf. Damien Keown, pp. 97-98.
118 Cf. Damien Keown, pp. 93-95. Cf. also M. Monier-Williams, pp. 209-210.
119 Cf. Damien Keown, pp. 93, 95.
120 Cf. Ibid., p. 98, Cf. also Rupert Gethin, p. 187.
121 Cf. Damien Keown, pp. 98-99.
122 Cf. Ibid., pp. 99-100.
123 Cf. Rupert Gethin, pp. 198-199.
124 Cf. Damien Keown, p. 98.
125 Cf. Ananda K. Coomaraswamy, pp. 92-93.
126 Cf. Christmas Humphreys, pp. 119-120. Cf. also M. Monier-William, p. 132. Cf. also Ananda K. coomaraswamy, p. 92.
127 Cf. Christmas Humphreys, pp. 120-121. Cf. also M. Monier-Willaims, p. 132. Cf. also Ananda K. Coomaraswamy, pp. 92-93.
128 Cf. Christmas Hunphreys, pp. 120-121. Cf. also Ananda K. Coomaraswamy, p. 92.
129 Cf. Christmas Humphreys, pp. 121-122. Cf. also Ananda K. Coomaraswamy, pp. 93-94.
130 Cf. Motilal Pandit, p. 1. Cf. also Christmas Humphreys, p. 147.
131 Cf. M. Monier-Williams, pp. 205-206.

132 Cf. Ibid., pp. 215, 217-218.
133 Cf. Ibid., pp. 218-221. Cf. also Rupert Gethin, pp. 126-128.
134 Cf. Ibid.
135 Cf. Ibid.
136 Cf. Moti Lal Pundit, p. 105. Cf. also M. Monier-Williams, pp. 18181.
137 Cf. Moti Lal Pundit, pp. 80-83. Cf. also Edward Conze, *Buddhism: Its Essence and Development*, pp. 126-127.
138 Cf. M. Monier-Williams, p. 134. Cf. also David N. Gellner, *Monk, Householder and Tantric Priest: Newar Buddhism and its Hierarchy of Ritual*, (New Delhi: Fountain Books, 1996), p. 112.
139 Cf. Moti Lal Pundit, pp. 104-105. Cf. also Christmas Humphreys, p. 158. Cf. also Edward Conze, *Buddhism: Its Essence and Development*, p. 125.
140 Paul Williams, p. 49. Cf. also Moti Lal Pundit, p. 105.
141 Cf. Paul Williams, p. 49. Christmas Humphreys, p. 158.
142 Cf. Moti Lal Pundit, p. 106.
143 Cf. Ibid., 106-107.
144 Paul Williams, p. 50.
145 Edward Conze, *Buddhism: Its Essence and Development*, p. 128
146 Cf. Christmas Humphreys, pp. 160-161. Cf. also Paul Williams, pp. 51-54. Cf. also Moti Lal Pundit, pp. 80-83.
147 Cf. Paul Williams, pp. 228-230. Cf. also Moti Lal Pundit, p. 90. Cf. also M. Monier-Williams, p. 187.
148 Cf. Paul Williams, p. 228.
149 Ibid.
150 Cf. Paul Williams, pp. 231-132. Cf. also M. Monier-Williams, pp.195-199. Cf. also Moti Lal Pundit, pp. 90-91.
151 Paul Williams, p. 233.
152 Cf. Ibid., pp. 232-234.
153 Cf. Paul Williams, pp. 238-241. Cf. also Moti Lal Pundit, p. 91. Cf. also M. Monier-Williams, p. 201.
154 Cf. Paul Williams, pp. 241-243. Cf. also Moti Lal Pundit, p. 91.
155 Cf. M. Monier-Williams, pp. 201.
156 Cf. Ibid., p. 136.
157 Cf. M. Monier-Williams, pp. 134. Cf. also Moti Lal Pundit, pp. 42-43.
158 Ibid., pp. 134-135.
159 Cf. Paul J. Griffiths, *On Being Buddha: The Classical Doctrine of Buddhahood*, (Delhi: Sri Satguru Publication, 1995), PP.60-66.
160 Cf. Moti Lal Pundit, pp. 43-45.
161 Cf. Paul Williams, pp. 175-177. Cf. also M. Monier-Williams, p. 246. Cf. also Moti Lal pundit, p. 45. Cf. also Damien Keown, pp. 62-63.
162 Cf. Paul Williams, pp. 177-178. Cf. also M. Monier-Williams, p. 247. Cf. also Moti Lal Pundit, p. 45. Cf. also Damien Keown, pp. 62-63.
163 Cf. Paul Williams, pp. 178-179. Cf. also M. Monier-Williams, p.

247. Cf. also Moti Lal Pundit, pp. 45-46. Cf. also Damien Keown, pp. 62-63.
    164 Cf. Paul Griffiths, pp. 70-75.
    165 Cf. Ibid., pp. 67-68. Cf. also Moti Lal Pundit, p. 65.
    166 Cf. Paul J. Griffiths, pp. 68-70. Cf. also M. Monier- Williams, p. 128.
    167 Cf. Paul Williams, pp. 243-245.
    168 Cf. Ibid., pp. 245-246.
    169 Cf. Ibid., pp. 246-247.
    170 Cf. Paul Williams, pp. 247-249.
    171 Cf. Ibid., 247, 249. Cf. also Moti Lal Pundit, p. 90.
    172 Cf. Paul Williams, pp. 251 254. Christmas Humphreys, pp. 161-162.
    173 Cf. Paul Williams, pp. 254-256.
    174 Cf. Ibid., pp. 256-276. Cf. also Christmas Humphreys, 162-165.
    175 Cf. Moti Lal Pundit, pp. 132-133.
    176 Cf. Moti Lal Pundit, pp. 134-135, 136. Cf. also Damien kewon, p. 66. Cf. also Kajiyama Yuichi, "Prajnaapaaramitaa and the Rise of Mahaayaana", *Buddhist Spirituality*, ed. Takeuchi Yoshinori, pp. 147-148.
    177 Cf. Moti Lal Pundit, p. 135.
    178 Cf. Ibid., 137.
    179 Cf. Ibid., pp. 135-136.
    180 Cf. Ibid., p. 136.
    181 Cf. Ibid., p. 137.
    182 Cf. Ibid., pp. 137-139.
    183 Ibid., p. 138.
    184 Cf. Ibid., pp. 149-150.
    185 Cf. Ibid., pp. 150-151.
    186 Cf. Paul Williams, pp. 217-220. Cf. also Paul J. Griffiths, pp. 97-101.
    187 Cf. Paul Williams, pp. 224-227. Cf. also Edward Conze, *Buddhism: Its Essence and Development*, pp. 154-157.
    188 Cf. Paul Williams, pp. 255-256.
    189 Cf. Ibid., pp. 199-200.
    190 Cf. Ibid., pp. 200-201.
    191 Cf. Ibid., pp. 201-202.
    192 Cf. Edward Conze, *Buddhism: Its Essence and Development*, pp. 147-149.
    193 Ibid., p. 149.
    194 Cf. Edward Conze, *Buddhism: Its Essence and Development*, pp. 152-157.
    195 Cf. Ibid., pp. 157-159.
    196 Cf. Jean Holm, ed., *Worship*, (London: Pinter Publishers, 1994), pp. 20-21, 22-23.
    197 Cf. Ibid., pp. 24-25.
    198 Cf. Ibid., pp. 25-26.

199 Cf. Paul Williams, pp. 249-250. Cf. also Jean Holm, pp. 26-27.

200 Cf. M. Monier-Williams, pp. 465-474. There are many theories that attempt to explain the knobby hair on Buddha's head. Some say that curly hair is an auspicious sign, and so it is kept in Buddha-icons. Some others say that curl-like knobs indicate that Buddha is a Negro. Another opinion is that at the moment of renunciation when Buddha cut his hair with the sword, the stumps were formed and in the course of time they turned into permanent short curls. Still another opinion says that the curl on the head of the Buddha is kept there to resemble the topknot on the crown of the head in the Siva images. Some others maintain that it is a peculiar growth of the skull of the Buddha, which indicates his supernatural intelligence. It is said that this outgrowth of the skull is preserved as a sacred relic in Afghanistan. Cf. Ibid., pp. 474-475.

201 Cf. Ibid., pp. 475-476.
202 Cf. Ibid., pp. 477-483.
203 Cf. Ibid., pp. 483-492. Cf. also Jean Holms, pp. 17-20.
204 Cf. M. Monier Williams, pp. 494-495.
205 Cf. Ibid., 493-503.
206 Cf. Ibid., pp. 503-506.
207 Cf. Ibid., pp. 506-514. Cf. also Jean Holm, pp. 17-18.
208 Cf. M.Monier-Williams, pp. 514- 519. Cf. also Jean Holm, pp. 17-18
209 Cf. M. Monier-Williams, p. 495.
210 Cf. Ibid., pp. 353-357
211 Cf. Ibid., pp. 353-356.
212 Cf. Ibid., pp. 360-361.
213 Cf. Ibid., pp. 365-369.
214 Cf. Ibid., pp. 307-308.
215 Cf. Jean Holm, p. 29. Cf. also M. Monier-Williams, pp. 340-342.
216 Cf. Jean Holm, pp. 29, 31-32
217 Cf. Ibid., p. 30.
218 Cf. Ibid.
219 Cf. Ibid., pp. 31-32.
220 Cf. M. Monier-Williams, pp. 387-425.
221 Cf. Ibid., pp. 426-464.
222 Cf. Jean Holm, p. 28.
223 M. Monier-Williams, p. 387.
224 Cf. Moti Lal Pundit, pp. 118-125
225 Cf. Ibid.
226 Cf. Ibid., pp. 139-142.
227 Cf. Moti Lal Pundit, pp. 144-145. Cf. also Paul Williams, pp. 204-208. Cf. Edward J. Thomas, pp. 206-207.
228 Cf. Moti Lal Pundit, pp. 145-146. Cf. also Paul Williams, p. 209.
229 Cf. Moti Lal Pundit, pp. 146-148. Cf. also Paul Williams, pp. 209-210.
230 Cf. Moti Lal Pundit, pp. 148-149. Cf. also Paul Williams, p. 210.

231 Cf. Moti Lal Pundit, pp. 149-151. Cf. also Paul Williams, pp. 210-211. Cf. Edward J. Thomas, p. 208.
232 Cf. Moti Lal Pundit, pp. 151-153. Cf. also Paul Williams, p. 211. Cf. also Edward J. Thomas, p. 208.
233 Cf. Edward J. Thomas, pp. 208-209. Cf. also Moti Lal Pundit, p. 154. Paul Williams, p. 212.
234 Cf. Paul Williams, p. 212. Cf. Moti Lal Pundit, pp. 154-155. Cf. also Edward J. Thomas, p. 209.
235 Cf. Moti Lal Pundit, pp. 155-156. Cf. also Paul Williams, p. 212. Cf. also Edward J. Thomas, pp. 159,159.
236 Cf. Edward J. Thomas, pp. 209-210. Cf. also Moti Lal Pundit, p. 156. Cf. also Paul Williams, pp. 213-214.
237 Cf. Edward Conze, *Buddhism: Its Essence and Development*, p. 178. Cf. also Alex Wayman, p. 220.
238 Cf. Edward Conze, *Buddhism Its Essence and Development*, pp. 43, 190. Cf. also M. Monier-Williams, pp. 202, 204 -205. Cf. also David N. Gellner, pp. 129-130, 293. Cf. also Christmas Humphreys, p. 197. The doctrine of the *Aadi-Buddha* belongs to the secret part of the teachings of the various Tantric schools. Hence it is difficult for us to show clearly what each school holds regarding the doctrine of the *Aadi-Buddha*. Many schools consider one of the five Buddhas, usually *Vairocana*, as the chief of the Buddhas, while the other schools postulate a sixth Buddha, as the one who presides over the other five, and call him by names, such as *Mahaavairocana*, *Vajradhara* and *Aadi-Buddha*. Cf. Edward Conze, *Buddhism: Its Essence and Development*, p. 190.
239 Cf. Ibid., pp. 189-190. Cf. M. Monier-Williams, pp. 202, 204. Cf. also Ananda K. Coomaraswamy, p. 250.
240 Cf. Edward Conze, *Buddhism: Its Essence and Development*, p. 190. Cf. also M. Monier-Williams, pp. 202-204. Cf. also Ananda K. Coomaraswamy, p. 250.
241 Cf. Edward Cronze, *Buddhism: Its Essence and Development*, pp. 191-192.
242 Cf. Ibid., pp. 192-193.
243 Cf. Ibid., p. 192. Cf. also Paul Williams, pp. 236-237.
244 Cf. Paul Williams, pp. 237-238.
245 Cf. Ibid., p. 234-236.
246 Cf. Edward Conze, *Buddhism: Its Essence and Development*, pp. 193-194.
247 Cf. Christmas Humphreys, pp. 198-199, 200. Cf. also M. Monier-Williams, p. 262.
248 Cf. M. Monier-Williams, pp. 262-265.
249 Cf. M. Monier-Williams, pp. 265-266, 282-283, 285. Cf. also Christmas Humphreys, p. 199.
250 Cf. M. Monier-Williams, pp. 284-285. Cf. also Christmas Humphreys, pp. 199-200.

251 Cf. M. Monier-Williams, pp. 285-290. Cf. also Christmas Humphreys, p. 200.
252 Cf. Edward Conze, *Buddhism: Its Essence and Development*, p. 183.
253 Ibid.
254 Cf. Ibid., pp. 182-183. Cf. also Alex Wayman, p.226.
255 Cf. Edward Conze, Buddhism: *Its Essence and Development*, pp. 183-184.
256 Cf. Alex Wayman, pp. 232-233.
257 Cf. M. Monier-Williams, pp.327-329.
258 Cf. Ibid., pp. 329-330.
259 Cf. Ibid., pp. 333-334, 528.
260 Cf. Ibid., pp. 335-336.
261 Cf. Ibid., pp. 336-337.
262 Cf. Ibid., pp. 337-338. Cf. also Jean Holm, pp. 17-18.
263 Cf. Jean Holms, pp. 18-19.
264 Cf. M. Monier- Williams, pp. 347-350.
265 Cf. Edward Conze, *Buddhism: Its Essence and Development*, pp. 184-187.
266 Cf. Ibid., pp. 187-188.
267 Cf. Alex Wayman, p. 222.
268 Cf. Ibid., p. 231.
269 Cf. Ibid., p. 233.
270 Cf. Ibid., pp. 233-234.
271 Cf. Ibid., pp. 234-235.
272 Cf. Edward Conze, *Buddhism: Its Essence and Development*, p. 180.
273 Cf. Rupert Gethin, p. 269. Cf. also Edward Conze, *Buddhism: Its Essence and Development*, pp. 180, 191-197.
274 Cf. Edward Conze, *Buddhism: Its Essence and Development*, pp. 180-181. The Newar Buddhist initiation involves an elaborate set of ceremonies that are spread over ten days. The initiation rites include 14 different types of consecrations (*Abhisheka*). Cf. David A. Gellner, pp. 273-281.
275 Cf. David A. Gellner, pp. 266-268.
276 Cf. M. Monier-Williams, pp. 520-523.
277 Cf. M. Monier-Williams, pp. 371, 386.
278 Cf. Ibid., 371-378.
279 Cf. Ibid., pp. 379-382.
280 Cf. Ibid., pp. 323-324, 383-385, 526-527.
281 Cf. Ibid., pp. 322-323.
282 Cf. Ibid., pp. 323-324, 351-352, 381-382, 384-385,
283 Cf. Ibid., pp. 357-358.
284 Cf. Jean Holm, p. 21.
285 Cf. Edward Conze, *Buddhism: Its Essence and Development*, pp. 181-182. Cf. also David N. Gellner, p.128.
286 Cf. Rupert Gethin, pp. 1-2.

Chapter 6

Sikh Tradition

INTRODUCTION

Sikhism is the youngest of the world religions, having barely over 500 years of history. It is said to be the most recent, the most modern and the most scientific religion among the religions of the world. It is a religion that preaches a particular way of life, rather than a philosophy. Sikhism is often described as a body of devotees, who believe in One Immortal Being, in the ten *Gurus*, in the *Guru Granth Sahib* – their scripture and the Word (*Baanii*), and in the teaching of the ten *Gurus*, and who do not believe in any other religion. The Punjabi term "*Sikh*" derives from the Sanskrit term "*Sishya*", meaning 'a disciple' or 'a learner'. Thus, the Sikhs are disciples of the ten *Gurus* who learn from their teaching. So Sikhism is a religion of those who learn their way to God from the ten *Gurus*. Some of the basic features of Sikhism as a religion and a way of life are briefly:

Firstly, Sikhism stresses the importance of organization. The Sikh community is one the most organized communities in India. The sense of organization that is characteristic of the ten *Gurus* is the reason for the continuance of Sikhism as a religion for the first 200 years of its existence, despite persecution from politically and religiously hostile forces.

Secondly, Sikhism favors the life of the householder over the life of the ascetic. This is clear from the *Guru* Naanak's act of choosing a family man as his successor instead of an ascetic.

Thirdly, Sikhism teaches its adherents to be loyal to their *Gurus*.

Fourthly, Sikhism promotes a sense of service to the community among its believers.

Fifthly, Sikhism preaches a form of fatalism, as it believes in the absolute will of God (*Hukam*), which is due to the influence of the Hindu notion of the Law of *Karma* and the Islamic notion of *Qismet* or *Taqdir*.

Sixthly, Sikhism speaks of equality and the brotherhood of all, especially those within the Sikh community (*Panth*).[1]

In this introductory essay, we attempt to sketch a brief history of Sikhism, Sikh scriptures, the Sikh community and Sikh philosophy.

1. A BRIEF HISTORY OF SIKHISM

We can speak of the following phases in the historical development of Sikhism: the phase of the *Gurus*; the phase of Sikh imperialism; the colonial phase and the contemporary phase. Let us briefly consider each of these phases.

1.1. PHASE OF THE GURUS

The emergence of Sikhism is not an isolated event in the religious history of medieval India. It is only a part of the medieval reformation that originated from the *Bhakti* movement. A great number of saints like the *Adayaars*, the *Alvars*, Shankara, Ramaanuja, Nimbarka, Vallabha, Raamaananda, Kabir, the Nath *Yogis*, the Sufis and the *Bhagats* spearheaded the *Bhakti* movement in different parts of India.[2] Of these the most significant group that exercised a lasting impact on *Guru* Naanak is the *Bhagats*, whose compositions are integrated into the *Aadi-Granth*. Some of the main *Bhagats* are the following: Jaideev, Naamdeev, Triloochan, Parmaanand, Sadhnaa, Beenii, Raamaanand, Dhannaa, Piipaa, Sain, Kabiir, Ravi Daas, Mira Bai, Sheekh Fariid, Sheih Brahm, Bhiikhan and Suurdaas.[3] Strictly speaking, we cannot speak of *Guru* Naanak as the founder of Sikhism, as it has its antecedence in the teachings of the *Bhagats*. Yet we can also say that Sikh history begins with *Guru* Naanak, because though he has received the heritage from the others, he transforms it. Thus, Sikh history begins with *Guru* Naanak and continues through the line of nine successors for two centuries.[4] The ten *Gurus* are the following: *Guru* Naanak (1469-1539), *Guru* Angad (1539-1552), *Guru* Amar Daas (1552-1574), *Guru* Raam Daas (1574-1581), *Guru* Arjun (1581-1606), *Guru* Hargobind (1606-1645), *Guru* Hari Rai (1645-1661), *Guru* Har Krishnan (1661-1664), *Guru* Teeg Bahaadur (1664-1675) and *Guru* Gobind Singh (1675- 1708}.[5]

The political situation in Punjab at the time of *Guru* Naanak was not conducive to the well being of the people. For about 50 years the people of Punjab had neither an effective government nor a peaceful life. Due to the failure of the administration, lawlessness had become part of everyday life. The law and order situation had degenerated as the result of political chaos and administrative weakness. Due to political instability the social and cultural life of the society had come to a standstill. Corruption and immoral attitudes had prevailed in every sphere of social life. The caste system, too, had destroyed the social fabric. Superstition was widespread in the religious life of the people. Religious practice had become very formal and ritualistic. Evil practices, such as, thefts, adultery, robbery, utterance of falsehood and similar acts had become the order of the day. Thus, during the time of *Guru* Naanak there existed a totally degenerated social, moral and spiritual situation.[6]

In this context *Guru* Naanak began his ministry of preaching the Sikh faith, calling to people's attention his synthesis of Hinduism and Islam in proposing the Sikh religion. Though a married man, he had been constantly on the move from Sri Lanka in the South to Tibet in the North and from Assam in the East to Mecca in the West. His decision to appoint a householder, as his successor surpassing his own ascetic son was momentous and it shaped the future development of the Sikh faith, which since its inception has remained an organization of laypersons. To remove caste distinctions and to actualize the oneness of the Sikhs, *Guru* Naanak introduces worship together in mixed congregation (*Sangat*), after which they sat together to eat (*Pangat*) in the common free community kitchen. The second *Guru* Angad popularized the *Gurmukhi* script, which was a big step in separating Sikhism from Hinduism, the scriptures of which are in the *Devanagari* alphabet. Besides, it developed the Punjabi vernacular for religious writing. Since the time of *Guru* Angad, *Gurmukhi* script has been the sacred script of Sikhism. The third *Guru*, Amar Daas, organized the Sikh Church into 22 parishes placing each under one lay preacher. He also widened the scope of the free kitchen in *Gurdwaras* (*Langar*), which *Guru* Naanak had introduced, and made it the only place for meals, whether the person is from low or high background. He also introduces new marriage and death ceremonies, and Sikh festivals in place of Hindu festivals. The fourth *Guru*, Raam Daas, founded the Holy City of Raamdaaspur, later known as Amritsar, which is the religious capital of the world-Sikhism. The fifth *Guru*, Arjun, built the Golden Temple at Amritsar, which serves as the mother Church for Sikhs throughout the world. Besides, he also built the city of Tarn Taran in Amritsar district and the town of Kartarpur in Jullundur District. He also constructed the *Gurudwara* in the city of Tran Taran about 15 miles away form Amritsar, which is second in sanctity only to the Golden Temple among the Sikh holy places. Another important contribution of *Guru* Arjun is the compilation of the canonical scripture, the *Aadi-Granth*, in the year 1604. He died a martyr's death for his faith at the hand of the Muslim emperor Jahangir. The sixth *Guru*, Hargobind, a soldier-saint who, seeing war clouds after the brutal killing of his predecessor, builts up the Sikhs as a military power and fought some six battles, winning all of them. Besides being a spiritual leader, he was also acclaimed as the first military hero of the people of Punjab in 600 years. The seventh *Guru*, Har Rai, continued the military might of his predecessor. He fought a war against the forces of Aurangazeb. He also had to face the apostasy of his son, Raam Rai, who later founds a heretical sect with the help of Aurangazeb in Dehra Dun. He is also known for his missionary activities. The eighth Guru, Har Krishnan, became *Guru* when he was five years old. On a visit to Delhi to meet emperor Shah Jahaan, he contracted small pox and died there. His last words "Baba Bakale" indicated the place where his successor to *Guruship* is to be found. The ninth *Guru*, Teeg Bahaadur, is the youngest son of *Guru* Hargobind. Since his predecessor has proclaimed him as the *Guru*, he assumes office when he is 44. He founded the city of Anandapur in the foothills of Hymalayas. As a zealous preacher he made two missionary journeys to Bengal and Assam, where he founds more *Gurudwaras*. Emperor Aurangzeb arrested him and beheaded him publicly in Delhi.[7]

The tenth *Guru*, Gobind Singh, was proclaimed *Guru* when he is just nine years old according to the wish of his father. His father's death affected him very deeply. He received an all-round education both in learning and warfare. He strengthened the Sikh fortifications, especially in Anandpur, and encouraged the people to fight against aggression and injustice, especially from the Muslim emperors. When the imperial army attempted to close in on Anandpur, he decided to organize his disciples into the *Khaalsaa*, which literally means '*Guru's* own', a group of saint-soldiers. On the Hindu New

Year Day in 1699, he conducted an initiation rite for the first five persons who join the *Khaalsaa*. Of these five, one is a *Bhrahman*, one a *Kshatrya*, and the other three are members of the lower castes. The initiation rite consists in drinking sugared water (*Amrt*) from the same bowl, which they stir with a double-edged dagger (*Khanda*). These first five, known as 'the beloved ones' (*Panca Pyaaraas*), give up all their caste distinctions and form the nucleus of the *Kaalsaa*. The members of the *Kaalsaa*, after their baptism, take a new surname: men take the name "*Singh*", which means 'a lion', while women take the name "*Kaur*" which means princes. They resolve to wear the five K's: the uncut hair (*Kes*), the comb in the hair (*Kangaa*), the steal bangle on the right wrist (*Karaa*), the short drawers (*Kacc*) and the sword (*Kirpaan*). They refrain from having their hair cut. They also abstain from the use of tobacco, alcohol, having adulterous acts with Muslim women and meat obtained by illegal animal slaughter. They shun belief in astrology and join together, both men and woman, in congregational prayers. With these practices – in physical attire, spiritual worship and moral living – the members of the *Kaalsaa* cannot hide their identity. The member of the *Kaalsaa* is a soldier-saint. While he is deeply attached to the peaceful devotional religion of the *Aadi-Granth*, he is, like the lion, ready to fight, especially against the Moguls. The *Kaalsaa* brotherhood believes that when all other means have failed, it is righteous to draw the sword. One must keep oneself, on such occasions, from timidity, for one *Singh* is called to fight a legion. Anyone who joins the *Kaalsaa* must accept death as the supreme sacrifice for the *Guru's* mission of social freedom and national sovereignty. Under the command of *Guru* Gobind Singh, the members of the *Kaalsaa* fought 20 battles with the hill *Raajaas* and Mughal forces, from which they emerge successful in 16.[8]

In spite of these early victories, the *Kaalsaa* brotherhood failed to withstand the military might of the Muslim power. Gobind Sing fled to the Punjab. Despite his busy life in the formation of the *Kaalsaa* and waging wars, he found time for literary activities as well. He brought together 52 poets and had them write war stories after the model of the Indian *Puraanas* to instill in his followers the new spirit of resistance to all forms of injustice. Though many of them are lost different battles, some of them are preserved in his famous work 'the *Dasam Granth*', i.e., the *Granth* of the tenth *Guru*. Besides, he also gave the *Adi-Granth* its final form adding to the collection of *Guru* Arjun, a short *Sloka* of his own and many hymns of *Guru* Teg Bahadur. Finally, as he was on his way to the Southern kingdom of Hyderabad, he died due to stab injuries. Before his death, *Guru* Gobind Singh declared that with his departure the line of the personal *Gurus* had come to an end. Hence, the authority and function of the *Guru*, thenceforth, is vested with the *Aadi-Granth*, the *Guru Granth Sahib*. The practical decisions regarding religious and social sanctions, which the person of the *Guru* has been handling, were transferred to the *Kaalsaa*, i.e., the Sikh community, (*Sikh-Panth*). All such sanctions, thenceforth, depend on the corporate decisions of the *Kaalsaa*. Though, many scholars doubt that the last declarations of *Guru* Gobind Singh – the ending of the line of personal *Gurus*, the empowering of the *Aadi-Granth* as the 'manifest body of the *Guru*' in all matters and the empowering of the *Sikh-Panth* to govern all matters of sanctions – were made at this death-bed, these doctrines are never in doubt among the believers of Sikhism. Thus, the *Aadi-Granth* and the Sikh *Panth* replaced the personal *Gurus* even before the eighteenth century.[9]

1.2. PHASE OF SIKH IMPERIALISM

Very little is know about the state of affairs of the religious life of the Sikh-*Panth* during the period of over 100 years that intervene between the death of *Guru* Gobind Singh and the emergence of Ranjit Singh's Sikh empire, though we have some knowledge about the military and political activities of the Sikhs during this period. The seven years immediately after the death of *Guru* Gobind Singh were ones of turmoil and confusion in the Punjab, as the Mughals unleashed a reign of terror and persecution against the Sikhs. But Bandraa Singh Bahaadur, the ascetic whom *Guru* Gobind Singh converted at Nander, took up the cause of the Sikhs and won decisive victories over the Mughals. Besides their victories, he brought about a number of social reforms, such as, abolition of the zamindari system to free the poor landless people from the tyranny of the landlords. He also minted his own coin in the name of *Guru* Naanak. Later, the Mughals with their military power captured Bandraa Singh and tortured him to death along with many other Sikhs, in 1716.[10]

The valor of Bandraa Singh Bahaadur and his military leadership inspired the ordinary Sikhs resist the tyranny of the Mughals. The scattered members of the *Kaalsaa* fraternity also begin to organize themselves and the next 50 years were a matter of life and death for the Sikhs. The Mughals took every step to destroy the power of the Sikhs and to wipe out their community. In order to protect themselves, they began living in the forests in small groups, and trained themselves in guerilla warfare. These groups develop into 12 confederacies (*Misals*). While attacking the Mughals, they also attacked each other. Eventually Ranjit Singh, with his *Misal,* gained the upper hand over the other 11 *Misals* and becomes the *Mahaaraajaa* of Punjab. His kingdom included the greater portion of present Punjab, Jammu and Kashmir, the North-West Frontier and the areas the 12 *Misals* had been occupying, with Lahore as his capital. The Sikh states of Patiala, Nabha, Jind, Faridkot, Kulsia and Kapurthalla were founded during the period of emperor Ranjit Singh. Though militarily and politically the Sikhs were better off during this period, religiously they have deviated far from the truth. The teachings of the *Gurus* are totally forgotten and Hindu *Braahmanical* practices were adhered to in religious and social life. For instance, when emperor Ranjit Singh's funeral pyre is lit, the rite of *Sati* is performed for four of his queens and seven maidservants. Besides, the Hindu influence entered the *Grudwaras. Sati*, widow burning and the installation of idols in the *Gurdwaras* were common which the *Gurus* often condemned. Thus, religious life of the Sikhs was far from being what is should have been at this time.[11]

1.2. COLONIAL PHASE

After the death of emperor Ranjit Singh in 1839, confusion and struggle prevailed for power in the Sikh empire. These internal intrigues and quarrels made the kingdom weak. The British waited for an opportunity to take control of the Punjab. The Sikhs fought two battles with the British in defense of their country, but the British defeated the Sikhs and attached the kingdom to the British Empire. In the initial period after the annexation of the Punjab, the relationship between the Sikhs and the British government was good. In the Mutiny of 1857, the Sikhs gave their full support to the British. On the government's part, it backed Singhism by allowing the army recruits to wear the five K's, in the process helping them not to lapse into Hinduism. But later the relationship suffered. During the colonial phase, several religious reformist movements ensued, which also broadened the gulf between the Sikhs and the British government. The *Naamdhaari* Movement, *Nirankaari* Movement, the *Gurdwara* Reform Movement and the *Akaali* Movement were some of the important movements. The *Naamdhaari* propagated the gospel of *Naam*. In preaching the gospel of the Name of God as the way to reach God, it condemned the interference of the British government in matters of Sikh worship. The *Nirankaari* Movement wants to purify the Sikh community from all external influences and insist on worshiping the one God. The *Gurdwara* Reform Movement tried to put an end to Hindu influences in Sikh religious worship. It aimed to purify the *Gurdwars* of Hindu idols and to put a stop to such Hindu rites, as *Sati* and widow burning. Closely related to this movement is the *Akaali* Movement, which begans with the *Singh Sabha* Movement, in the later half of the 19th century, demanding the handing over of the administration of all the *Gurdwaras* to the elected body of the Sikh *Panth*, viz., the Shromani *Gurdwara* Parbandhak Committee, the headquarters of which is in Amritsar. All these movements widened the separation between the Government and the Sikhs, as the latter wanted to remove corrupt priests controlling the *Gurdwaras*, while the former supported the continuation of the state of affairs in the administration and worship in the *Gurdwaras*. The response of the British government to the Jallianwala massacre of 1919 – General Dyer's killing of 1,500 people – and the Nankana massacre of 1921 – Hindu Mahant Narain Daas' killing of 130 *Akaalis* as they took possession of the *Gurdwara* at *Guru* Naanak's birth-place – also soured the relationship between the British government and the Sikhs. All these events caused the Sikhs to take an active part in fighting the British during Indian independence struggle.[12]

1.4 CONTEMPORARY PHASE

Independence from the British brought with it the two states, India and Pakistan. In the partition of the country, the Sikhs suffered much, as their territory was split into two. Whatever the Sikhs created before partition was ruined during partition. After partition, the Sikhs resettled in the Indian state of Punjab. But the problems were not yet over. In 1968 the state further divided on linguistic grounds into three states: the states of Punjab, Haryana and Himachal Predesh. The language of Punjab is Punbjabi in the *Gurmukhi* script; the language of Haryana is Hindi in the *Devanagari* script; and the language of Himachal Predesh a mixture of these and *Pahari* in the *Devanagari* script. Similarly, there were problems of Chandigarh's status as the capital, distribution of river water among the three states carved out of the original state of Punjab and territorial disputes among the three states. Since independence there have been a number of efforts on the part of the Government of India and the people of Punjab to settle most of these issues. Above all these are the demands for a separate Kalistan state and the terrorism that emerged as the result of it. Though there are still a few foreign voices that speak of Kalistan, most of the Indian Sikhs are not in favor of a Kalistan. At long last, terrorism in the state of Punjab has subsided to a great extent. The people's life has become normal and peaceful.[13]

2. SIKH SCRIPTURES

Having surveyed the history of the Sikhs, we now focus our attention on their scriptures. The sacred literature of the Sikhs is the body of writings that contains basically the teachings of their *Gurus*. Their present form is a result of the compilation work of the *Gurus* or their disciples. Not all Sikh scriptures are of the same significance. The most important scriptural text is the *Aadi-Granth*. Besides, we have the *Dasam Granth*, which is said to be the work of the tenth *Guru* Gobind Singh. There is the hagiographical and biographical collection known as the *Jnana-Saakhiis*. There are the interpretative works of Bhaaii Gurdaas, viz., *Vaars* and *Kabits*. Finally, there are texts that deal with injunctions and laws guiding the life of the Sikhs. In this section, we attempt to study this body of Sikh sacred literatures.

2.1. AADI-GRANTH

The *Aadi-Granth* is the primary scripture of the Sikhs. It is considered the highest authority within the community, both on religious and moral questions. The term "*Aadi*" means 'the first' or 'the original'. The term "*Granth*" means 'a book'. Literally *Adi-Granth* means 'the first book' or 'the original book' and is the first scripture of the Sikhs. The term "*Aadi*" is also used to distinguish this book from the next important sacred text of the Sikhs, the *Dasam Granth*, which is the 'Book of the Tenth (*Guru*)'. The *Aadi-Granth* is also referred to as the *Granth Saahib* and the *Guru Granth Saahib*. The term "*Saahib*" is attached to the title as the designation of sanctity the Sikhs attach to this book. It is prefixed with the term "*Guru*" to indicate the particular status of this scripture, as after the death of *Guru* Gobind Singh, as per his declaration the *Aadi-Granth* take the place of the person of the *Guru* in guiding the people on their path to salvation. Therefore, for the Sikhs the *Aadi-Granth* is not a mere sacred text, but rather it is the textual manifestation of the person of the *Guru*. The standard title used for the published editions of this scripture is *Aadi Srii Guru Granth Saahib*; in popular usage it is often referred to as the *Gurbaanii*.[14]

The fifth *Guru* Arjun made the first compilation of the *Aadi-Granth* in 1603-1604, with the help of Bhaaii Gurdaas. According to tradition, the main reason for the compilation was to preserve the purity of the Sikh faith, especially in the context of the heretic Prithii Chand, who had been circulating spurious works bearing the name of *Guru* Naanak. As the Sikh community had been spreading especially in the North India, a number of copies of the compilation of *Guru* Arjun were made and there are minor differences between the original and the copies. About a 100 years later, the last *Guru* Gobind Singh made the final compilation of *Aadi-Granth*, adding a number of hymns from the ninth *Guru* Teeg Bahaadur and adding one hymn of his own. Thus, we have three editions (*Biirs*) of the *Aadi-Granth*: *Kartaarpur Vaalii Biir*, *Bhaai Banno Vaalii Biir* and the *Dam Damaa Vaalii Biir*. The first is the edition of *Guru* Arjun; the second is the edition based on copies of the original, which *Guru* Arjan compiled; and the last is the edition based on the compilation of the last *Guru,* Gobind Singh. The final and complete edition is the last one, and normally is used for the worship in the *Gurdwaras*. The Singh Sabha and the Shriomanii *Gurdwara* Parbandhak Committee have made every effort to finalize an authorized version of the *Aadi-Granth*.[15]

The *Aadi-Granth*, presently recognized as authentic, is a large volume consisting of nearly 6,000 hymns. Those who have contributed to the making of the *Aadi-Granth* fall in four categories: The Sikh *Gurus*, the Pre-Naanak *Bagats*, the poet-saints of the time of the *Gurus* and other contributors. Of the ten Sikh *Gurus*, the first five, ninth and the tenth have contributed: *Guru* Naanak has 974 hymns; *Guru* Angad has contributed 62 hymns; *Guru* Amar Daas's 907 hymns are included; *Guru* Raam Daas has 679 hymns; *Guru* Arjun has contributed 2,218 hymns; Teeg Bahaadur's contribution is 115 hymns; and *Guru* Gobind Singh contributed just one hymn. The second category consists of 16 Pre-Naanak saints, known as the *Baghats*. They are from different parts of North India. We place them here in chronological order: Jaideev from Bengal; Fariid comes from Punjab; Naam Deev, Triloochan and Paramaanand from Maharastra; Sadhnaa is a Sindhi; Beenii and Raamaananda from Utterpredesh; Dhannaa belongs to Rajasthan; Piipaa, Sain, Kabiir and Ravidaas from Utterpredesh; Miira Baai from Rajasthan; Bhikhan from Utterpredesh; and Suur Daas – the blind poet from Oudh. This part of the *Aadi-Granth* represents four centuries of Indian religious thought. The third category of contributors is the poet-saints (*Bhatts*). They are contemporaries of the *Gurus* and have served as bards in the courts of the *Gurus*. Their compositions consist mostly of praise of the *Gurus*, who were their masters. The bards are the following: Bhalhau, Bhikaa, Daas, Gangaa, Haribans, Jalan, Jaalap, Kal, Kalasu, Kalasaahaar, Kiiratu, Mathuraa, Nal, Rad and Sal. The *Bhagats* and the *Bhatts* have contributed together 937 hymns. The fourth category of contributors includes people like Mardaana, the Muslim companion and disciple of *Guru* Naanak and Sunder, who is the author of an elegy, the *Raam Kalii Sad* and the eulogistic ballard (*Vaar*) of Satta and Balwand.[16]

The *Aadi-Granth* is divided into three major sections: the opening section, the main body of the *Aadi-Granth* (*Raagas*) and the epilogue or the conclusion of the *Granth* (*Bhoog*). The opening section of the *Aadi-Granth*, the liturgical section, consists of the daily prayers of the Sikhs: firstly, the meditation (*Japjii*), a composition of *Guru* Naanak, which includes 38 stanzas and two couplets; secondly the supplication (*Rahiraas*), which is a collection of nine hymns composed by *Guru* Naanak (four hymns), *Guru* Raam Daas (three hymns) and *Guru* Arjun (two hymns); and thirdly, the praise (*Sohilaa*), which is a collection of five hymns composed by *Guru* Naanak (three hymns), *Guru* Raam Daas (one hymn) and *Guru* Arjun (one hymn). The *Japji* is said at sunrise; the *Rahiraas* are said at sunset and the *Sohilaa* is said before one goes to sleep at night. The main body of the *Aadi-Granth* consists of 31 separate sections called *Raagas*, which are set in musical mode, to help the devotee to sing in praise of the Almighty God. The thirty-one *Raagas* are the following: *Sirii Raaga, Raaga Maajh, Raaga Gaurii, Raaga Aasaa, Raaga Guujrii, Raaga Deevagandhaarii, Raaga Bihaagraa, Raaga Vadhansu, Raaga Soorathi, Raaga Dhanaasarii, Raaga Jaitsirii, Raaga Toodii, Raaga Bairaarii, Raaga Tilang, Raaga Suuhii, Raaga Bilaavalu, Raaga Gaud, Raaga Raamakalii, Raaga Natnaaraain, Raaga Maaliigauraa, Ragga Maaruu, Raaga Tukhaarii, Raaga Keedaaraa, Raaga Bhairau, Raaga Basantu, Raaga Saarang, Raaga Malaar, Raaga Kaanaraa, Ragga Kaliaan, Raaga Prabhaataa* and *Raaga Jaijaavantii*. Of these 31 *Raagas*, the first four are the most important and largest, while the other *Raggas* are minor. Each *Raaga* section begins with hymns of four stanzas (*Chupaas*) and includes hymns of eight stanzas (*Ashtapadis*), four stanzas of six verses each (*Chhants*) and other longer compositions containing a sequence of couplets and stanzas (*Vaars*). The smaller units within each section open with hymns of *Guru* Naanak, and include hymns of his successors, those of Sikh bards and the *Bhagats*. Thus, there is a good organization of the *Raagas*. The final section of the *Aadi-Granth* is the epilogue. It is composed of various hymns not set in musical mode. These compositions include couplets belonging to *Guru* Naanak, *Guru* Arjun, *Guru* Amar Dass, *Guru* Raam Daas and *Guru* Teeg Bahaadur. Besides, there are *Slookas* attributed to Kabiir, Sheekh Fariid and a collection of panegyrics (*Savaiiye*) composed by the bards. The epilogue ends with a garland of musical mode (*Raagamaala*), a hymn of 12 stanzas, the authorship of which is not known.[17]

2.2. DASAM GRANTH

The *Dasam Granth* is the second major collection of Sikh sacred literature attributed to *Guru* Gobind Singh. Its full name is *Dasven Paadsaah Kaa Granth*. It consists of 18 works: *Jap Saahib, Akaal Ustat, Bicitra Naatak, Candii Caritr* I, *Candii Caritr* II, *Candii Vaar, Gyaan Prabodh, Caubiis Avataar, Mehdii Miir Budh, Brahmaa Avataar, Rudra Avataar, Sabad

Hazaare, Srii Mukh baak Savaiiye, Khaalse dii Mehimaa, Sastra Naam Maalaa, Pakhyaan Caritr, Zafarnaama and *Hikaayats*. The languages the author uses in writing these books are Braj, Hindi, Persian and Panjabi. The compilation can be classified in four sections: mythological, philosophical, autobiographical and erotic. The largest collection is mythological and aims at telling the commonly known Hindu mythological tales that deal with battles of the Hindu goddess of destruction and incarnations of different gods of the Hindu Trinity, and their great deeds of war. The philosophical section consists of some hymns that are philosophical and devotional hymns, which have been used in ritual and prayer since the time of the *Guru*. The autobiographical section deals with recounting the mission of the *Guru* Gobind Singh himself. This section also includes a letter of the *Guru* to emperor Aurangazeb in reply to his letter to surrender. The erotic section deals with stories of the deceitful women in a corrupt and decadent society. Though the stories are not original, they include many erotic passages. Most parts of the *Dasam Granth* are composed in Anandpur, but the final compilation may have taken place in Dam Damaa. The present version is attributed to Mani Singh. Many question the authenticity of authorship of *Dasam Granth*. But it is very difficult to determine the question of authorship of this book. Some sections of *Dasam Granth* certainly belong to *Guru* Gobind Singh, while others can be ascribed to his poets.[18]

2.3. JANAM-SAAKHIIS

The other collection of Sikh sacred texts is the *Janam-Saakhiis*, which literally means 'birth stories'. They are basically concerned about giving detailed account of the life and works of *Guru* Naanak. Though there are many biographical elements in the *Janam-Saakhiis*, still their main purpose is hagiographical rather than biographical. Many of the *Janam-Saakhiis* present the *Guru* Naanak as a holy and miracle-working saint. Except for a few, in general the *Janam-Saakhiis* are written by semi-literate scribes to illiterate people. They are full of miraculous stories about the *Guru* and often they contradict each other on details regarding the saint's life. Besides, the statements Guru Naanak himself makes in the Aadi-Granth and the statements of Bhaaii Gurdaas in his Vaars contradict a number of materials found in the Janam-Saakhiis. The authors speak of four stages in the development of the *Janam-Saakhiis*: firstly, the *Janam-Saakhii* material is transmitted by way of oral tradition; the second stage records various events from the life of the saint, without much regard for chronology; the third stage is writing the *Janam-Saakhii* material in a consistent way, taking into account the chronology of the events from the *Guru's* life; and in the fourth stage of development of the *Janam-Saakhiis,* the writer adds his own exegesis regarding the event from the life of the *Guru*.[19]

It is not known who is the first one to write a *Janam-Saakhiis* or from where he has taken the material. But once the first was written, others followed. Each author added material that suited his way of looking at the

Guru, while deleting those materials that do not fit his perception. There are four traditions of *Janam-Saakhiis* that are commonly known, even though, according to some scholars, there are more than 6 different *Janam-Saakhiis*. The main four traditions are the following: the *Puraatan Janam-Saakhiis*, which are more ancient and follow a common source, have never been found; the *Miharbaan Janam-Saakhiis*, which is the most neglected tradition as they are associated with the *Miinaa* sect of the Sikhs that is antagonistic to the *Gurus*; the *Bhaaii Baalaa Janam-Saakhiis* are a not so reliable tradition, as they contain a number of errors; and *Bhaaii Manii Singh Janam-Saakhiis* is said to be the most recent and the most reliable among the *Janam-Saakhiis*. Since the nature of the *Janam-Saakhiis* is more hagiographical, and the authors of *Janam-Saakhiis* attempt only to present the saint as a person rather than presenting the actual facts about the person, they have only relative value. Hence a historian can neither totally disregard the material of the *Janam-Saakhiis*, nor accept them in their entirety, but needs to test every statement in the *Janam-Saakhiis* in the light of the available facts before determining its truth.[20]

2.4. VAARS AND KBITS OF BHAAII GURDAAS

Bhaaii Gurdaas, the one who has helped *Guru* Arjun to compile the *Aadi-Granth*, has also contributed to the Sikh sacred literature by way of writing 39 ballads in heroic meter (*Vaars*), which are written in Punjabi and 556 couplets (*Kabits*), which are composed in the Braj language. Strictly speaking, a *Vaar* is a heroic ballad or ode. But Gurdaas has turned it into a text that extensively covers Sikh history, belief and biography. These *Vaars* are the only authentic references we have regarding the history of the periods of the third, fourth, fifth and the sixth *Gurus*. His commentary on the Sikh practice indicates the way things were at that particular time. Hence his writing is the key to understanding the Sikh scriptures, especially the *Aadi-Granth*. Though his *Vaars* are read in the *Gurdwaras*, philologists and historians do not give them the attention they deserve. Similarly, the 556 *Kabits* are also ignored in the *Sikh-Panth*, perhaps because of the difficulty emerging from the Braj language in which they are written.[21]

2.5. TEXTS DEALING WITH LAW

Besides the above-mentioned texts, there are the texts that give injunctions regarding what should be done and what should not be done. Some of the texts are the following: *Rehatnaama* of Bhaaii Dayaa Singh, *Rehatnaama* of Bhaaii Nand Laal, *Rehatnaama* of Bhaaii Desaa Singh, *Rehatnaama* of Bhaaii Chapuaa Singh, *Rehatnaama* of Bhaaii Prehlaad Singh, *Prem Sumaarag Granth*, *Sudhaaram Maarag Granth*, *Sudhaaram*, *Tankhaah Naama*, *Mukat Nama* and *Wajibul Arz*. All these texts contain injunctions that regulate the life and activities of the individuals within the *Sikh-Panth*.[22]

3. THE SIKH COMMUNITY

The Sikh community originated when in 1520 *Guru* Naanak obtained a piece of agricultural land on the banks of the River Ravi and founded the town of Kartarpur, which literally means 'the City of God'. The families that were gathered around the *Guru* at Kartarpur form the original center of the later Sikh community. At this community at Kartarpur began the patterns of social and religious life that form the foundations of later development of the *Sikh-Panth*. The principle of guidance the *Guru* gives to this community to direct their social and religious life consist of three elements, viz., meditation on the divine name (*Naam*), purity (*Ishnan*) and charity (*Daan*). Meditation on the divine name and purity guide members of the community in developing a religious attitude towards God in his personal life, while charity opens them to the social obligation they must undertake for the sake of the other members in the community. In *Guru* Naanak's perception, a Sikhs attains their liberation only when they are open to God and to his community, in loving service. In this community the *Guru* is the center of the group; he gives direction to the life of the people. *Guru* Naanak's decision to appoint a successor after him shows clearly that he intended centrality for the *Guru* in the Sikh community. The *Guru's* lifestyle, his compositions, sermons and teachings generate a way of life and a daily routine for the people of Kartarpur. This way of life, as developed in Kartarpur, includes the following: meditation on the divine name (*Naam*), purity of life (*Ishnan*), charity towards other members in the community (*Daan*), hard work in the farms (*Ghal Khae*), service (*Seeva*), self-respect (*Pati*) and taking one's rightful share (*Haq Halal*). To maintain the religious life, of the people of Kartarpur *Guru* Naanak introduced the recital of three prayers: prayer recital at sunrise (*Japjii*), prayer recital at sunset (*Rahiraas*) and the prayer recital at the end of the day (*Sohilaa*). He also establishes the community kitchen (*Langar*), in order to stress the central features of Sikh piety, viz., sharing of food with the poor, social and gender equality within the community and provision of a forum for community service. In this manner, the first *Guru* laid the foundations of the Sikh community.[23]

The other nine *Gurus* continued what the first *Guru* had begun. Practically all of them established communities similar to that of Kartarpur, following the example of the *Guru* Naanak, while directing the already existing communities both in their social and religious life. *Guru* Angad built such a community in his native town of Khadur. *Guru* Amar Daas founded the township of Goindval, building the Sikh community there. *Guru* Raam Daas develop the city of Raamdaaspur, i.e., Amritsar. *Guru* Arjun establishes Sikh communities after building three townships: a new Kartarpur, Hargobinpur and Tran Taraan. *Guru* Hargobind built the city of Kirtapur, while the next *Guru* Hari Rai developed the community at Kirtapur. *Guru* Teeg Bhaadur founded Anandpur and built that Sikh community. The last *Guru* Gobind Singh founded Paunta, Dam Damaa and Bhatinda. Thus, every *Guru* has taken great trouble to build up townships and develop communities of Sikh people, guiding them spiritually, religiously and socially. In this manner, the early Sikh community developed.[24]

The original Sikh community, which had remained a community of peace-loving people as directed by the first five *Gurus*, turned out to be a militant group under the guidance of the sixth *Guru* Hargobind. This was due to the martyrdom of Arjun at the hand of the Mughal emperor. This movement, which Hargobind started, reached its culmination in the founding of the *Kaalsaa* by *Guru* Gobind Singh. Thus, the Sikh community, which was still a peace-loving one, took up arms when it came to the question of survival. The termination of the person of the *Guru*, the establishment of the *Guru Granth Saahib* in the place of the personal *Guru* and the founding of the *Kaalsaa* as the body that guides the everyday religious and social life of the community paved the foundation of the future development of the *Sikh-Panth*. The formal establishment of the Shiromanii *Gurdwara* Parbandhak Committee, an elected body, to guide the affairs of the religious life of the Sikh people, especially the administration of all the *Gurdwaras* was, in fact, an act done fully within the spirit of *Guru* Gobind Singh, the founder of the *Kaalsaa*. Due to the interference of politicians into this body, it failed to maintain the unity of the *Sikh-Panth*. But in terms of the formal observance and personal piety, the *Gurdwaras* still continue to provide the sense of oneness of the Sikh people all over the world and thus form the symbol and bond of Sikh-Panthic unity.[25]

4. BASIC TENETS OF SIKHISM

Many people consider Sikhism as an outgrowth of the medieval *Bhakti* Movement in India. Others consider Sikhism as a mere amalgamation of Hindu metaphysics and Islamic monotheism. Both Hindus and Muslims consider *Guru* Naanak, the founder of Sikhism, as a saint who belongs to their religious tradition. For this reason, after his death people belonging to both the religions claimed his body to conduct funeral rites in the tradition of both religions. There is no doubt that in Sikhism there are certain elements of Semitic, as well as of Oriental religion. Sikhism has integrated both in such a way that something new has emerged from this union. Hence, Sikhism cannot be reduced to either to Hinduism or to Islam. It is a religion of its own with its own beliefs, practices and philosophical worldview.[26] In this section, we consider Sikhism as a monotheistic religion, its conception of man, the ideal of life and its attainment.

4.1. SIKHISM: A MONOTHEISTIC RELIGION

Sikhism is a strictly monotheistic religion. It believes in One Supreme God, who is the cause of the universe. Though absolute in nature, He is involved in the world. Though by nature transcendent, He is also immanent. He is the Creator, Sustainer and Destroyer of the universe. He is without hate, enmity and jealousy. He is against no nation, race, caste, creed or class of people, as He is not the God of one nation or people. He is the God of humankind. Everything, both good and evil, emerges from his Will (*Hukam*), as He knows what is good for man, if He brings evil on man, there must be a reason. He is the God of grace, He is good, kind, merciful, loving and just. He reveals the moral law within the conscience of man. Different people know and call on this reality with the help of different names.[27]

Faith in the absolute God, who is the God of all, finds expression in different aspects of the Sikh way of life. Sikhism shuns all forms of caste distinction among its adherents, no one who is greater than the other because of his caste. It is interesting to note that in the *Aadi-Granth*, the sacred scripture of the Sikhs, there are sections that are compositions of persons who do not believe in the Sikh religion. The act of accepting truths from other persons, wherever he may come from, points to the open-mindedness that is inherent in Sikhism, which in fact derives from its belief in One God for all humankind. The tolerance we find in Sikhism comes also from its belief in One God. Thus, the Sikh religion, its belief and practices are founded on the absolute truth of the One God, who is the Father of all humankind.[28]

4.2. THE SIKH CONCEPTION OF MAN

According to Sikhism, man is composed of five elements, viz., the body, the breath (*Praanas*), the mind (*Manas*), the intellect and the soul. Of these five, only the soul is real. The soul is the self of man, which is part of the infinite and imperishable Divine Self of God. The other four components of the body are mere instruments of the soul, limited to the spatio-temporal world, while the soul is eternal and free. The sense world is passing in nature, and the true nature of man does not belong to the world of sense. The true nature of man belongs to the world of the spirit, as man is the supreme creation of God. He is different from all forms of living beings, because in him there resides the Divine element. As a result, he has the faculties of observation, comparison, evaluation, selection, judgment and memory. Besides, man has a curiosity to know, which makes him capable of knowing and unlocking the mysteries of the cosmos. He also has a sense of wonder and a passion for the truth, which moves him towards Absolute Truth, the Supreme Spirit. He achieves the final goal of being united with the Supreme Being through his education and his socio-religious life.[29]

4.3. SIKH IDEAL OF LIFE AND ITS ATTAINMENT

The ideal of life Sikhism proposes to man consists in making him recognize that the Divine dwells in him and to work towards the actual realization of the Supreme that is within him. Due to physical, psychic, social and spiritual bondage, humans are imprisoned within the bounds of his body and mind, which prevent them from knowing his true divine nature. Attaining freedom from these bonds makes them realize their immortal nature. To achieve this is the real liberation (*Moksha*). Sikhism believes in one's attaining *Moksha* while one is living in this life. A person, who attains liberation while still here on earth, is called a *Jiivanmukta*. A person attains *Jiivanmukti* when one possesses the Love of God, lives a virtuous life, gets rid of all cravings of the ego and lives under the Will of God (*Hukam*). When this happens, one experiences the state of God-consciousness, transcending all that is non-self, including one's ego; this is the state of Universal Consciousness (*Tuuriyaa Avasta*). As a person reaches this state, one is free from the transmigrations and conditions, which the Law of *Karma* imposes on man, as he places himself totally under the Holy Will of God. A person must continue maintaining this state of God-consciousness as he lives his life as a psychophysical and psychosocial being. To achieve this state a Sikh need not leave secular existence and embrace the asceticism of a *Sannyaasin*; one need only practice asceticism within the secular world. The attainment of *Mukti* in this world automatically guarantees *Moksha* in the next world.[30]

So far, by way of introduction, we have been looking into the history of Sikhism, its scriptures, its community and its basic tenets. Now, in the two following essays, we shall explore the reality of God in Sikhism and the various paths it proposes to lead man to the realization of God.

6.1. GOD IN SIKHISM

Sikhism is a monotheistic religion. In the *Aadi*-Granth, here are references to other deities from the Hindu pantheon. But, they are always considered as sub-deities totally under the control of the Almighty God. The following passage from the *Japjii* pictures the scene of the Kingdom of the One God, where lower deities sing the praises of the Supreme God, while sages and men sing his praises here on earth.

> Where is the gate, where the mansion
> From Whence Thou watchest all creation,
> Where sounds of musical melodies,
> Of instruments playing, minstrel singing,
> Are joined in divine harmony?
> In various measures celestial musicians sing of Thee.
> There the breezes blow, the waters run and the fires burn,
> There *Dharmaraaj*, the kind of death, sits in state;
> There the recording angels *Chitra* and *Gupta* write
> For *Dhanaraaj* to read and adjudicate;
> There are the gods *Iishvara* and *Brahmaa*,
> The goddess *Paarvatii* adorned in beauty,
> There *Indra* sits on his celestial throne
> And lesser gods, each in his place;
> One and all sing of Thee.
> There ascetics in deep meditation,
> Holy men in contemplation,
> The pure of heart, the continent,

Doughty warriors never yielding
Thy praises ever singing.
From age to age, pundits and the sage
Do Thee exalt in their studies;
There maidens fair heart bewitching,
Who inhabit the earth, the upper and the lower regions,
Thy praises chant in their singing. [31]

Hence, Sikhism, in spite of the fact that it recognizes subordinate deities, proclaims God as the One Absolute Being. He is Self-existent, as He does not need anything else for His existence. Though God is the Source of creation, He Himself is uncreated and eternal Being. Though eternal and transcendent in His Being, God does not remain within Himself, but communicates with man. God communicates Himself to man not because it is what man deserves, but rather He wants to reveal Himself to man. Thus, God's Self-expression, in fact, is His revelation of Himself to man. Man's right response to God's Self-revelation makes man move towards the Almighty God as partner and in relationship. This ascending movement towards God helps man enter into deeper union with Him. In order to explore the reality of God in Sikhism, in this section we shall clarify the nature of God, His characteristics and His Divine Self-expressions.

6.1.1. NATURE OF GOD

The best description of God's nature, as given in the *Aadi-Granth*, is the *Muul Mantra*. To a Sikh who is devoted to God, this simple formula conveys a wealth of meaning, as he understands the meaning of each word of the *Mantra*. It reads as follows:

There is one God,
Eternal Truth is His Name;
Maker of All things,
Fearing nothing and at enmity with nothing,
Timeless is His Image;
Not begotten, being of His own Being:
By the grace of the *Guru* [i.e., by the grace of His own Self-expression, He is], made known to men.[32]

This formula, though seemingly simple, contains the main elements of the nature of God as the Sikhs understand it. It expresses various aspects of the nature of God: the unity of God, the *Nirguna-Saguna* dimensions of God, God in His creative function, God in His sustaining function, God in His destroying function, God as the Sovereign, the eternity of God, the formlessness of God, the ineffability of God, God as the immanent, the divine initiative of God and God's Greatness. We, now, consider in detail each of the elements constituting the nature of God.

6.1.1.1. UNITY OF GOD

Describing the nature of God, the first dimension the *Muul Mantra* declares is God's oneness. God is one; there is no other but Him. The Punjabai term *"Oankar"* refers to the one indivisible Supreme Being, whose power, majesty and eternity cannot be matched with any other deity. When Sikhism holds for the absolute unity of God, it is not referring to a monistic perception of God, but rather a monotheistic view of God. The perception of God as one and as the absence of duality (*Dubidhaa*) brings to the fore the mystical dimension of God. In other words, it highlights the point that the ultimate essence of God is beyond all human categories and all human expressions fail to communicate the true nature of God. Only when a person surrenders all human powers to the Holy Will of God, is He known through the inner mystical experience. Even this depth level experience can communicate to us only a glimpse of the ultimate reality.[33] The following hymn expresses this truth clearly:

> It is not through thought that He is to be comprehended
> Though we strive to grasp Him a hundred thousand times;
> Nor by outer silence and long deep meditation
> Can the inner silence [mystical experience of God] be reached;
> Nor is man's hunger for God appeasable
> By piling up world-loads of wealth.
> All the innumerable devices of worldly wisdom
> Leave a man disappointed; not one avails.
> How then shall we know the Truth?
> How shall we rend the veils of untruth away?
> Abide thou by His Will, and make thine own,
> His will, O Naanak that is written in thy heart.[34]

The God of Sikhism, though unique and standing apart from everything else, is perceived as a personal God, who is the God of grace and to whom man can respond in love and devotion. There is no trace of strict pantheism in the way Sikhs understand their God, as they believe in both the immanence and transcendence of God. In fact, the transcendence of God is manifested through His immanence, i.e., in the infinite plurality of creation. Though Sikhism holds for the absolute oneness of God, there are hymns that speak of other deities of the Hindu mythology, such as, *Brahmaa*, *Vishnu* and *Siva* as being active in creation. But, the Hindu *Trimuurti* and other sub-deities are never seen as independent and above the one God, but are seen as dependent on God for their activity. In other words, God, the Absolute Being, performs the creative act through them. Thus, even when other deities are brought into the picture, they are seen as absolutely subservient to the one God, who is primal and above every other deity.[35] The following hymn from the *Japjii* illustrates the absolute oneness of God, even though He is referred to in relation to other deities.

Maayaa, the mythical goddess,
Sprang from the One, and her womb brought forth
Three acceptable disciples of the One:
Brahmaa, Vishnu and *Siva*.
Brahma, it is said bodies forth the world,
Vishnu it is who sustains it;
Siva the destroyer who absorbs,
He controls death and judgment.
God makes them to work as He wills,
He sees them ever, they see Him not:
That of all is the greatest wonder.
Hail, all hail unto Him,
Let your greetings be to the Primal Lord;
Pure and without beginning, changeless,
The same from age to age.[36]

Thus, belief in the absolute oneness and unity of God forms the foundation of the Sikh monotheism.

6.1.1.2. NIRGUNA-SAGUNA DIMENSIONS OF GOD

God, the One, is *Nirguna* and *Saguna*, the unconditioned and the conditioned, the unmanifest and the manifest. In His primal aspect, we cannot speak of God having any qualities, as He is absolute, unconditioned and devoid of all attributes. In this absolute dimension God is unknowable, as he is totally beyond the range of human comprehension. But, in His manifest aspect, He endows Himself with qualities that bring him within the range of man's comprehension. Thus, God, the *Nirguna*, makes Himself *Saguna*, by His own Will, in order that man may know Him and enter into a relationship of union with Him. But, the act of the Pure One, the *Nirguna*, moving from the absolute condition and becoming the Manifest One, the *Saguna*, does not amount to the *Saguna* as an *Avataara* of the *Nirguna*. *Avataara* involves God becoming. It means that God belongs to a human family, goes through endless cycle of birth and rebirth and that He is mortal. All these go against the very nature of God. Therefore, the concept of *Avataara* has no place in the Sikh conception of God. The transition of God from the primal condition to the manifest condition has to be understood in terms of God's divine immanence in the created world. It is in this aspect of divine immanence that God becomes manifest to man. This *Saguna* aspect of God is the object of a Sikh's meditation and worship. Since the *Nirguna* nature of God can never be brought to the grasp of human understanding, nothing can be said about it, nor can man strictly participate in it. Hence, in the ultimate condition of man, union with God, man does not participate in God's *Nirguna* condition, but he only participates in God's *Saguna* condition. Thus, the Sikh way to God (*Saadhanaa*) is concerned only with the *Saguna* expression of God.[37]

6.1.1.3. GOD IN HIS CREATIVE FUNCTION

According to Sikh cosmology, for innumerable *Aeons* there is indescribable darkness everywhere, without the heaven or the earth, the day or the night, the sun or the moon. At this time, none other than the infinite Will of God, i.e., the Divine Order (*Hukam*), exists. Then, when it pleases Him, He does create the whole universe without the support of any others. He is also said to have created the lower deities and remains unaffected by the allurements of the goddess *Maayaa*. All creation is said to have emerged effortlessly, as it is by the One Word of God that everything comes to be. Having made all creatures in the universe, God is said to have written all their names, kinds and colors. The world God created is beautiful, which manifests His beauty and bounty.[38] The following text from the *Japjii* illustrates God's creative act and the wisdom with which He has done it all.

All that they [the chosen saints of God] say is wisdom, but by what wisdom

> Can we number the works of the Lord? ...
> One ever-flowing pen inscribed the names
> Of all the creatures, in their kinds and colors;
> But which of us would seek to pen that record,
> Or if we could, how great the scroll would be.
> How can one describe Thy beauty and might of Thy Works?
> And Who has power to estimate Thy Bounty, O Lord?
> All creation emerging from Thy One Word,
> Flowing out like a multitude of rivers.
> How can an insignificant creature like myself
> Express the vastness and wonder of Thy creation?
> I am too petty to have anything to offer Thee;
> I cannot, even once, be sacrificed unto Thee.
> To abide by Thy Will, O Formless One, is man's best offering;
> Thou who art Eternal, abiding in Thy Peace.[39]

6.1.1.4. GOD'S SUSTAINING FUNCTION

God is not a mere creator of the universe, but also its sustainer. He does not only create, but also watches over everything in the world and cares for it. When God has created all things, He makes Himself immanent in all He has created. He pervades the waters, land and all that is between heaven and earth, and indwells in all. In doing so He fills all with the power of sustenance. Having filled everything with His power of sustenance, God orders them and watches over all. For instance, having created the sun and the moon, God directs them to rule the day and night respectively. Thus, for the Sikhs, the nature of God is that He is a participant in the life of the universe, which He has established. He is involved with His creation; He watches over the universe, directs and upholds it. God has the power to sustain the universe because He is Self-existent (*Saibhan*). He does not need anything else for His existence, as He is the cause of His own existence. God's Self-existence gives Him absolute power over everything and brings everything under His Holy Will. Thus, the Self-existence of God is the basis of His being the sustainer of the universe.[40] The following passage from the *Japjii* clearly points to God's role of sustaining and ordaining everything according to His Divine Will.

> The regions of the earth, the heavens and the Universe
> That Thou didst make and dost sustain,
> Sing to Thee and praise Thy Name.
> Only those Thou lovest and have Thy grace
> Can give Thee praise and Thy love be steeped.
> Others too there must be who Thee acclaim,
>   I have no memory of knowing them
> Nor of knowledge, O Naanak, make a claim.
> He alone is the Master true, Lord of the World, ever the same.
> He who made creation, is, shall be and shall ever remain;
> He who made things of diverse species, shapes and hews,
> Beholds that His handiwork His greatness proves.
> What He Wills He ordains,
> To Him no one can an order give,
> For He, O Naanak, is the King of Kings,
> As He Wills so we must live.[41]

6.1.1.5. GOD IN HIS DESTROYING FUNCTION

God is not only the creator and the sustainer of everything in the universe, but also its destroyer. The created world does not have a form that lasts forever. Just as it has a beginning, it also has an end, which comes from the destructive activity that flows from the power of God. God has not only the power to create and sustain the world but also has the power to destroy it. Just as God does not consult anyone in His activity of creation and sustaining, so also He does not have to consult anyone for His destruction of the world. After destruction God does not leave the world in the state of destruction, but He re-creates the world anew. Having destroyed it, He builds it up; casting down, He raises up; breaking down, He reconstructs. With His absolute power He performs the third function of destruction, just as He performs the former two.[42]

6.1.1.6. GOD AS THE SOVEREIGN

As the creator, sustainer and the destroyer God exercises absolute sovereignty over the whole of creation. Since God is the sovereign, whatever He wills comes to pass. As the sovereign, God possesses unqualified power and wields absolute authority over the totality of existence. Since God is the sovereign Lord, everything happens as He pleases. Hence, man's exaltation, renouncing the world and going begging, the floods flowing over the desert, lotus blooming in the sky, a man crossing the ocean of fear, his boat getting filled with water and sinking, all man's pains and gains happen because it is the pleasure of God. Therefore, the Sovereign Lord is omnipotent (*Anaath*) and omniscient. As omniscient, the Sovereign Lord sees all, comprehends all, and knows all – permeating all creation both from within and without.[43]

6.1.1.7. ETERNITY OF GOD

Unlike the creation that is limited, composed, contingent and changeable, God is eternal (*Abinaasii*). It means that He is without beginning (*Anaadi*), beyond time (*Akaal*), the one who is ever firm and constant in His existence. As eternal, God is wholly detached (*Niranjan*), completely opposed to *Maayaa*, which is His own creation, and possessing fullness of perfection. Eternity of God also implies that God is unborn and non-incarnated (*Ajuunii*). Incarnation (*Avataara*) of God implies attachment to the unstable, mutable and the corruptible. Besides, it implies being caught up in the cycle of birth, death, rebirth and the endless cycles of life within the *Samsaara* existence. For this reason, the eternal God can never be thought of as being incarnated or being born.[44]

6.1.1.8. FORMLESSNESS OF GOD

Since God is absolute and eternal by His very nature, we cannot speak of God concretely. It implies that we firmly reject not merely the idea of *Avataars*, but also the use of idols for worship of God and the use of anthropomorphic language to speak of God. He is basically without form (*Aruup*), and hence is the Formless one (*Nirankar*). Thus, God is the eternally unchanging Formless one. No form (*Ruupa*) can fully express the nature of God. Similarly, no material sign (*Rekhiaa*) is able to capture the eternal and formless Being of God. Believing in the formless nature of God, Sikhism rejects all forms of idol worship.[45]

6.1.1.9. INEFFABILITY OF GOD

The ineffable nature of God comes from the fact that He is the formless One, uncreated, unborn and not incarnate. Since nothing tangible can express God fully, His nature becomes ineffable. God's ineffability consists in that His nature and Being cannot be fully comprehended by human intelligence. God is beyond human grasp. To bring God, who is beyond the bounds of human intellect, to its narrow bounds is nearly an impossible task. Since God's nature is ineffable, man's proper response to the infinite God is that of awe (*Visamaad*), fear and wonder before Him whose nature baffles the human mind. As ineffable, God can be described as inscrutable (*Agam*), beyond the reach of the human intellect (*Agochar*), unfathomable (*Agah*), surpassing wonder (*Acharaj*), beyond the reach of the intellect, beyond seeing or perception (*Adrisht*), beyond time (*akaal*), unsearchable (*Alabh*), infinite (*Anant*), boundless (*Apaar*) and beyond utterance (*abol*).[46] The following passage describes the ineffability of God in clear terms:

> [He is] ... beyond human grasp or understanding, boundless, infinite, the all-powerful Supreme God! He who existed before time began, who has existed through out all ages, and who shall eternally exist, (He alone is true). Spurn all else as false. ... Beyond understanding, infinite, unreachable, beyond perception, free from death and *Karma*, without caste, never incarnate, self-existent, subject to neither love (of worldly things) nor doubt. Thou, the ultimate Truth, to Thee I sacrifice myself. Thou hast neither form, color, nor material sign, but Thou dost reveal Thyself in the true Word (*Sabad*).[47]

6.1.1.10. GOD AS THE IMMANENT EXISTENCE

The elements of God's nature, such as His eternity, formless and ineffable nature, makes God infinite and beyond human comprehension. In spite of the limitation of the human intellect to grasp the nature of God, we can have knowledge of God, though it is partial. This knowledge comes from our experience of God in His immanent presence in the world. Within each creature, the light of God is present, through which the reality of God is revealed, though in a limited way, to all. This all-pervading light of God is present in the waters and the land, and all that exists between heaven and earth is the presence of the ineffable, infinite, formless and eternal God in spatio-temporal existence. The omnipotent and omniscient God is also omnipresent. In a unique manner, His immanent presence is made available in the human heart. The following quotation clearly points to the truth that God's immanent presence in the created world and in a unique way, in the heart of man reveals to man the true nature of God, despite His transcendence and ineffability.[48]

> Wondrous, my Master, are Thy ways! Thou doest pervade the waters, the land and all that is between the heavens and the earth, indwelling in all. Wherever I look I see Thy light. ... The Lord pervades every heart. ...through the Word of the *Guru* He is revealed. By His Grace the *Guru*, the True *Guru*, revealed Him to me in this world where all dies, in the nether world, and in the heavens. The non-incarnated *Brahmaa* is and eternally will be. Behold the Lord within yourself. ... The one *Omkaar*, wholly apart, immortal, unborn, without caste, wholly free, ineffable, without form or visible sign, but searching I perceived Him in every heart. ... Wearing Ochre garments they [seekers of God] wander around, but without the True *Guru* none have

found Thee. Roaming in all countries and in all directions they have grown weary (but their efforts are in vain for) Thou are concealed within. ... Know Him who creates and destroys the world, know Him by His creation. Do not look far off for the True One, but recognize Him in the guise of the Word in every heart. He who established this creation, recognize Him as the true Word and do not imagine Him to be far distant. He who meditates on the Name finds peace. Without the Name the game (of life) is lost.[49]

Therefore, to find the infinite God, one need not go too far, as He is visible in every creature He has made, and in a special way in the human heart.

6.1.1.11. DIVINE INITIATIVE OF GOD

Another dimension of God's nature is that He takes the initiative in bringing about the union of love between the devotee and God. Ultimately it is God who is responsible for final union, which is the end of the process of emancipation. But man also must open himself to the invitation of God and take the steps required in order that this union is brought about. Basically, however, it is due to the Divine initiative that the whole salvational process gets started. It is the grace of God that instills in the seeker a desire for salvation, it guides the seeker through the journey, and finally it assists him to establish the deeper union with God. Thus, the grace of God is operative both in the created order and in the interior realms of the human heart. The Divine initiative with the help of Divine grace is operative in the inner realms of a person. Without this Divine assistance man is helpless. When God chooses to impart his grace to a person, the process of union with God gets started. But the human decision of saying 'yes' to the Divine grace and cooperating with the Divine initiative is very vital for man's ascent towards union with God.[50]

6.1.1.12. GREATNESS OF GOD

The greatness of God is another important element of God's nature. By His very nature God is a highly exalted personality. The recognition of the greatness of God is the first step one takes into his spiritual journey. One of the most important dimensions of the spiritual journey of the seeker is to realize the greatness of the goal towards which he is moving. The goal of his journey is God, the eternal, ineffable and formless Being. All through the various stages of the journey, it is God who leads and guides the seekers journey. The more the seeker understands the glory and worth of God, whom he is seeking in his life, and acknowledges it in gratitude, the greater is the depth of his spiritual existence. The admiration, love and the tenderness of heart the devotee feels towards God, facilitates and quickens the journey towards the ultimate Goal. One of the ways in which the devotee can acknowledge the greatness of God is to call on the Name of God constantly. Sikhism proposes the *Naamamaarga*, i.e., calling on the name of God as a sure means of the actualization of his union with God. In calling on the Name of God, the devotee acknowledges the greatness of God and gives Him the reverence and honor due to God.[51]

6.1.2. CHARACTERISTICS OF GOD

We have looked into the various elements that constitute the nature of God. Though God in His *Nirguna* aspect is incomprehensible, as the *Saguna* He is the treasure house of attributes (*Gunii-Nidhaan*). As God is infinite, His qualities are countless, inexpressible and unreachable. But finite beings can have access to these Godly qualities, when God bestows them. The devotee of God accepts various attributes of God, in His *Saguna* aspect, as the ideal to be followed in his journey towards God-realization. The more the seeker becomes God-like in acquiring these qualities, to that extent he realizes union with God. Some of the qualities the *Aadi-Granth* attributes to God are purity, justice, fearlessness, love, mercifulness, generosity, tolerance, sweetness, goodness and beauty. In this section, we consider these Godly qualities that God, in his *Saguna* aspect possesses.

6.1.2.1. PURITY

Purity is an important quality that is characteristic of God. He is infinitely pure and there is no trace of impurity in God. The world and the elements that constitute the world, viz., earth, air, fire and water are impure. The *Jiiva* and every other form of living being are impure. Their impurity comes from the fact they are associated with ego and *Maayaa*. God is free from ego and *Maayaa*. Hence, He is truly pure. Since God is pure, He resides in the pure body and soul. When a person is pure in body and soul, acts according to the instructions of the *Guru* and keeps oneself away from falsehood, then one becomes the dwelling place of God, who is pure. A body does not become pure just by external cleanliness, but can be called pure only if the true Name of the Lord dwells there. God, who is pure, flows into the heart of the devotee, who is pure. Thus God dwells in a heart that is pure, and a heart that is pure also dwells in God, who is the ultimate purity.[52]

6.1.2.2. JUSTICE

True justice emerges from a heart that is pure. The works of God are just. Before the eyes of God, all human beings are equal. He is impartial; there is no prejudice, bias or unequal treatment in God. As the creator, sustainer and destroyer of the universe, God exercises perfect justice. Every activity of God is based on the equality of justice; the justice of God is ever true. The justice God measures out is based on His Holy Will, i.e., in the Divine Order God establishes (*Hukam*). When a devotee remains submissive to the Holy Will of God, he also becomes just in his way of thinking and acting. Often people think that no justice is measured out in this world, as we find inequality and blame God as being unjust. But the reason for such inequality is not God, but the Law of *Karma*, which is part of the Divine Order and which measures out justly according to a person's past *Karma*. Every person reaps according to the fruit of his own actions. Thus, even in the execution of the Divine Order God is supremely just.[53]

6.1.2.3. FEARLESSNESS

Another characteristic of God is fearlessness. Since God is the absolute Being and there is nothing above Him, we cannot speak of God as fearful. Often fear is associated with a person having to deal with others who are more powerful and gifted physically or mentally. But with regard to God, as there is none more gifted than Him, we cannot think of Him as possessing fearfulness. When a human person is totally under the loving protection of God, he, like God, becomes fearless. But, in order to become fearless, a devotee must genuinely cultivate the fear of God. Every creature, whether great or small, must fear God. The fear of God which creatures are expected to cultivate is a sacred fear. No person can become fearless in his everyday living if he does not fear God. The fear of the Lord consists in taking refuge at His feet. When a devotee approaches God with this devout fear, all fearfulness and timidity to face life and the world vanishes as the fearlessness of God takes hold of him. Since the devotee has surrendered to the Will of God in complete trust – which, in fact, is the fear of God – he feels secure, and no power on earth can have any control over the devotee who fears God.[54]

6.1.2.4. LOVE

Love is another divine attribute of God. God is Divine Love. Unlike man, God does not keep any form of enmity, evil intent of malevolence. Instead, God is friendly, well intended and benevolent. He bestows all good things on people, provides for their needs and generously showers His blessings on the devotees. The God of Sikhism is like a friend, who stands by the devotee in his needs. Human friends, at times, can have selfish interests and can act out of self-centeredness. But God never acts out of selfishness, as He is ego-less. Just as God loves us, we need to love others. When we do this, we become worthy of His love, in the process a loving union between God and the devotee takes place.[55]

6.1.2.5. MERCIFULNESS

The mercifulness of God flows from the fact that He is Divine Love. When a person opens himself to the mercy of God, He truly becomes the *Bhakta* of God and devotedly practices meditation on the Holy Name of God. As this happens, the light of knowledge dawns on the *Bhakta* and his mind is filled with the mercy of God. The devotee, as the result, is able to treat others mercifully as God treats him. One of the most meritorious acts in the Sikh religious practice is to show mercifulness towards *Jiivas*. When a devotee is filled with the spirit of the mercy of God, he does not do any harm to the *Jiivas*, and such a devotee is received with great honor when he arrives at the house of God. A person who is imbued with the mercy of God is able to consider every other *Jiiva* like himself and be compassionate as God is compassionate to him.[56]

6.1.2.6. GENEROSITY

The generosity of God grows out of His mercifulness. It is natural that the feeling of compassion for someone moves a person to help him out in his trouble. Hence, the generosity of God is nothing else but a concretization in action of the compassion He feels for His devotees. Speaking of the generosity of God, Sikhism addresses God as the Giver, the Generous, the Provider and the Bestower. For a Sikh, God is the true Giver, as His stores are never empty. Besides, God is the Giver, who is eternally present to man, knowing all his needs: God is the true Giver, because He is always there to give and His stock never fails. God is Generous, as, unlike men, He never grows tired of giving to everyone what he needs. God is the Provider, for receiving from Him is something we can always count on. God is also the Bestower of divine riches. God guides the seeker all through his journey towards union with Him. When a devotee lives out these fourfold aspects of generosity, as does God, he gains merits that lead him to his final destiny of being united with God.[57]

6.1.2.7. TOLERANCE

Tolerance is another quality of God. It consists in bearing with the failures of others. Hence, it is related to forgiveness. A father does not punish a child who commits mistakes, but accepts the child in spite of the failures and leads it in the right path. Similarly, God bears with the past sins of a devotee and places him in the right path. In the face of tolerance, anger dies down and revenge recedes into the background. If a devotee truly practices the godly quality of tolerance, God truly dwells in him. A life of tolerance brings good conduct and contentment to the devotee.[58]

6.1.2.8. SWEETNESS, GOODNESS AND BEAUTY

Sweetness of speech is another attribute of God. The speech of God brings sweetness to the ears of the devotee. He never speaks a bitter word that hurts and destroys the person. The language in which God communicates is the language of limitless love. It relieves the troubles of the devotee and instills in him a sense of peace and tranquility. Hence, in order to be united with God, who speaks the sweet language of love, the devotee must also practice the sweet language of love as he communicates to others. Goodness is another attribute of God. It is out of God's goodness that the abundance of all these attributes of God flows. Sikh scriptures also attribute to God the quality of beauty. God is said to be beautiful. The reference here is the beauty of the spirit, rather than that of the body. Beauty consists in being absorbed in the love of the Lord, reciting His name and ever growing in the true wisdom of the spirit.[59]

6.1 3. SELF-EXPRESSIONS OF GOD

So far in this study we have explored the nature and characteristics of God. He is the Supreme and Eternal Being, who, in His *Saguna* aspect, manifests innumerable qualities. Besides being transcendent, God is also immanent in every level of existence, especially in the human heart. It is at this level of the heart that genuine communication between God and man takes place. Thus, it is at the interior level of the heart of man that God gives Himself to man in Divine Self-expression. Now the question arises as to the manner in which this self-communication of God to man takes place. According to Sikh theology, God reveals Himself to man in six ways: through the Divine Word (*Sabad*), through the Divine Name (*Naam*), through the Divine Preceptor (*Guru*), through the Divine Order (*Hukam*), through the Divine Truth (*Sach*) and through the Divine Grace (*Nadar*).[60] In this section, we shall explain the manner of God's revelation of Himself to the devotee in these six fold ways.

6.1 3.1. DIVINE WORD

The Divine Word (*Sabad*) is the vehicle of revelation of God to the seeker. The function of the Word is that it makes available the means to know God and the path that leads to God. In other words, the Word provides the means whereby an individual is able to free oneself from all his bonds, thereby attaining union with God. The Divine Word is the essential means for the attainment of salvation. The Divine Word, when contemplated, helps one to conform one's life to its dictates, thereby aiding in controlling one's self-centeredness. When one's self-centeredness is cast out, one grows nearer to God, until they attain the likeness of God, in the process reaching a state of union with God, which transcends the cycle of deaths and rebirths. Without the help of the Divine Word one is condemned to wander and gets sunk in worldly affections. But when the Word is there to guide him, he knows God, whom he is seeking and the place to find Him. Thus, the Word reveals to the seeker the true nature of God and helps him to experience union with Him in the depth of his heart.[61]

Though at times the term "*Sabad*" stands by itself, often it is used with the term "*Guru*". Normally the Word is 'the *Guru's* Word' (*Guru Kaa Sabad*) or '*Guru*-Word' (*Guru-Sabad*). For the Sikhs, the Divine Word in its true form always comes from the *Guru*. God communicates to the devotee through His Word, which always comes through the person of the *Guru*. The Word is always the expression of God's truth, which the *Guru* imparts to man (*Gurupades*). Though man experiences the Word in the depths of his heart as an inward experience, the revelation of the Word itself is not limited to the inner experience, as it primarily comes to the seeker from the *Guru*. Thus, the seeker's experience of the Word has both an external dimension of listening to the Word from the *Guru* and the inner dimension of experiencing it in the depths of his being. In fact the inner contemplation of the Word is based on the external hearing of the Word from the *Guru*. Since there is the external dimension of hearing the Word from the *Guru*, the adept is able to know with clarity God, whom he is seeking and the path that needs to be followed in attaining union with God. This implies besides that there are stages (*Khands*) in the path the seeker has to follow, as the continuous guidance of the *Guru* in understanding the Word is necessary to achieve the goal. Thus, God communicates His Divine Word, through the proclamation of the *Guru*, thereby making it concretely reach the seeker. When the seeker opens his heart to the proclaimed Word and contemplates it, he moves towards union with God in the level of his inner being.[62]

6.1 3.2. DIVINE NAME

The second means with the help of which God communicates Himself to the devotee is the Divine Name (*Naam*). For all practical purposes, The Divine Name is considered synonymous with the Divine Word. Hence whatever we have said about The Divine Word is applicable to the Divine Name, as well. In some texts the terms "*Sabad*" and "*Naam*" are used as synonyms; in other texts they are used in such a way that they can replace each other; yet in some other texts these two terms are substituted for each other, and some texts from *Aadi-Granth* make an implied and subtle distinction between the Divine Word and the Divine Name. The Divine Word is considered as the medium of communication, whereas the Divine Name is seen as the object of communication. But both remain expressions of God's Truth. These two terms have a difference in their meaning when they are understood in relations to Truth. When a *Guru* meditates upon the Truth, it is referred to as "*Sabad*", while, when a believer contemplates on the Truth, it is referred to as "*Naam*". In spite of these minor differences between these two terms, they both are means of revealing God's Being. Strictly speaking, the Divine Name is the proper object of contemplation. The contemplation of the Divine Name is an essential means of purification and salvation. The created world is the manifestation of the Truth of God, and when a seeker perceives this manifested Truth, he perceives the Divine Word or the Divine Name. Some authors distinguish between the 'Name of God' and the 'names of God'. The phrase 'Name of God' refers to the name that is primarily proper to God, while the phrase 'names of God' stands for the non-essential secondary names attributed to God. For instance, names, such as, *Hari*, *Raam*, *Paramesvar*, *Jagadiis*, *Prabhu*, *Gopaal*, *Allaah*, *Khudaa* and *Saahib* are non-essential secondary names. Some names, such as, *Nirankaar* and *Niranjan* are significant, but they do not constitute the 'Name of God', as they express only certain aspects of what is implied in True Name of God. The 'Name of God' is "*Sati Naam*" – His Name is Truth. [63]

6.1 3.3. DIVINE PRECEPTOR

Sikhism gives primary significance to the doctrine of *Guru*. If we attempt a general description of *Guru*, we can speak of him as 'the communicator of Divine Truth. Again we can describe him as 'a creative and perfect personality, who stands as a guide and an example'. Sikhism sees the person of the *Guru* as an absolute necessity to guide the devotee on his path to God. The ten personal *Gurus* are such personalities. But after *Guru* Gobind Singh, the personal *Gurus* cease to exist and the *Guru Granth Saahib* and the Sikh community have taken the place of the personal *Gurus*.[64] Here, we quote some of the statements about the *Guru* in the Sikh scriptures:

> The *Guru* is the ladder, the dinghy, the raft by means of which one reaches God;
> The *Guru* is the lake, the ocean, the boat, the sacred place of pilgrimage, the river.
> If it pleases thee I am cleansed by bathing in the lack of Truth.
> Without the *Guru* there can be no *Bhakti,* no love.
> Without the *Guru* there is no access to the company of *Saints*;
> Without the *Guru* one blindly engages in futile endeavor;
> But with the *Guru* one's *man* is purified, for its filth is purged by the Word.
> When the True *Guru* is merciful faith is perfected;
> When the True *Guru* is merciful, there is no grief;
> When the True *Guru* is merciful no sorrow is shown.
> When the True *Guru* is merciful the love of God is enjoyed;
> When the True *Guru* is merciful there is no fear of death;
> When the True *Guru* is merciful there is eternal peace;
> When the True *Guru* is merciful the nine treasures are obtained;
> When the True *Guru* is merciful one blends in union with the True One.[65]

Besides the personal *Gurus*, there are three senses in which the term "*Guru*" is spoken of in many scriptural texts. Firstly, it refers to God Himself, as the ultimate *Guru*. Secondly, the *Guru* is described as the voice of God. Thirdly, the *Guru* is the Truth of God. Thus, in the Sikh tradition the office of the *Guru* is given a very significant place, as the one through whom the Divine life of God descends in the life of the humans.[66]

6.1 3.4. DIVINE ORDER

The Arabic word *"Hukam"* literally means 'Will'. In Islamic usage, it refers to the 'Divine Will', i.e., 'the Order of Judgment of God'. Islamic theologians apply this term to 'the Order of Judgment of the Prophet Muhammad', besides applying it to 'the Order of Judgment of God. But in Sikh usage, especially that of *Guru* Naanak, *Hukam* stands for the divinely instituted principle of governing the existence and direction of the universe. It is not a capricious principle, but a constant and regular principle. Hence, it can be comprehended in its functioning in a predictable pattern. The regularity and the consistency of the functioning of the *Hukam* make it totally and completely dependable. The Sikh use of the term *"Hukam"* can be best translated as 'the Divine Order'.[67]

Guru Naanak gives a good description of *Hukam* in the *Japjii*, which explains the nature, meaning and scope of the Divine Order, as understood in Sikh religious thought. To quote:

> By (his) order [*Hukam*] are made the forms (of all things),
>   his order (however) cannot be told.
> By his order are made the living beings, by his order
>   greatness is obtained
> By his order are the high and the low, by his order pain
>   and pleasure are set down.
> By his order some are pardoned, some are by his order
>   caused to wander about (in transmigrations).
> Every one under (within) his order, exempt from his order
>   is no one.
> O Naanak! If one understands his order, he will not speak
>   in self-conceit.[68]

The description of the Divine Order indicates the following. Firstly, just as the fullness of God is beyond human comprehension, the total range of the *Hukam* (Divine Order) is beyond the complete grasp of man. Secondly, it can be understood to some extent, and man knows it as the principle that determines the human condition of greatness, the distinction between high and low, misery and happiness, transmigration or salvation. Thirdly, every created entity, including man, is within the power of the *Hukam*. There is no exception to the rule of the Divine Order. Finally, when a person fully understands the truth about the Divine Order, he experiences the destruction of the self and attains true salvation.[69]

The Divine Order manifests itself in the universe in ever so many ways. It is presented as the agent of creation. The *Hukam* also determines the regular cycle of human existence. A person is born in a particular culture, family and caste at the direction of the Divine Order. Every activity of man, like speaking, seeing, moving, living and dying, takes place within the *Hukam*. The sum total of all activity of God, whether it is creative, sustaining or destructive activity, takes place according to the Divine Order. Not only the physical laws directing the physical sphere of the universe, but also the moral law of *Karma* is also totally with the direction and control of the *Hukam*. Hence, the fact of each person's reaping in this world as determined in relation to what he has sown in the past, is decided according to the direction of the Divine Order. Thus, every aspect of every creature in the universe is within the control of the *Hukam*.[70] The following quote clearly points to the all-embracing nature of the Divine Order:

> Through His *Hukam* He creates and dissociates
> Through His *Hukam* everything is created and also dissolved.
> Through His *Hukam* He becomes high-up and lowly
> Through His *Hukam* He manifests Himself in several ways.
> ...
> *Jiiva* was conceived with His *Hukam*, O dear! It came to the womb.
> It was born with His *Hukam*, O dear! With its head downwards
> It came with His *Hukam* O dear! And goes with His *Hukam*.
> The evildoer is tied up with His *Hukam*, O dear! And punished
> The Word is recognized with His *Hukam*, O dear! And it goes in His presence
> It falls into accounts with His *Hukam*, O dear! And is seized by ego and duality.
> It experiences births and deaths with His *Hukam*, O dear! The evildoer weeps.
> If the *Hukam* of the Lord is recognized, O dear! The *Jiiva* realizes truth and receives respect. ...
> One comes in the world through *Hukam*
> One merges in the Lord through *Hukam*
> All the created world works under *Hukam*
> The heavens, the seas, the nether-world are under His *Hukam*
> His power works under His *Hukam*.
> The earth and the bull bearing it are under His *Hukam*.
> The wind, water and the sky are under His *Hukam*.
> The *Jiiva* resides in the house of *Shakti* under His *Hukam*.
> The sport of the world is under His *Hukam*.
> The wide expanse of the sky is under his *Hukam*.
> The seas, plains, all the three worlds are under His *Hukam*.
> All our breaths are under His *Hukam*.

And He sees everything under His *Hukam*.
He created the ten incarnations under His *Hukam* ...
He who accepts the *Hukam* goes in His presence and
    merges in the true Lord. ...
All is Thy Nature; Thou art the Creator, the Pure *OM*
He sees everything under His *Hukam* and acts consciously
...
The One Name is His *Hukam*.[71]

Thus, the Divine Order, the *Hukam*, is an all-embracing principle, the sum total of all the laws that are divinely instituted, with the help of which the universe is directed.

Since the *Hukam* envelops the totality of existence, including every sphere of the activity of man, one might say that the *Hukam* totally destroys man's freedom. But such a view is incorrect from the Sikh perspective. Man does have the necessary freedom to make decisions in his life. Though the totality of human existence falls within the domain of the *Hukam*, still there are areas in which he is truly free to do what he wishes. For instance, man is still free and capable of determining the future course of events, by his good actions. If he performs good actions, he can change his destiny for good. Besides, man is free to live his life either in discord or in harmony with the *Hukam*. Hence, though directed by the *Hukam*, still it is man's decision if he moves towards salvation or continues in a life of transmigrations. If he lives his life in harmony with the *Hukam*, he moves towards salvation; and if he decides to live in disharmony with the *Hukam*, he chooses to continue in a life of transmigrations. If a person chooses to submit himself to the Divine Order, he moves towards union with God, which in fact takes him to the true freedom. Thus, the *Hukam* is the revelation of the Will of God. When man recognizes the revelation of God though *Hukam* brings his life in conformity to it, he thereby ascends to the eternal union with God, who is his final happiness. In this manner, the *Hukam* becomes truly a self-expression of God to man.[72]

6.1 3.5. DIVINE TRUTH

Another medium through which God reveals Himself to the devotee is the Divine Truth (*Sach*). Truth is the essential element of the nature of God. Truth exists from all ages; it exists in the present, and it will exist in the future as well. Hence, Truth is ever-existent. The ever-existent Truth is as eternal as God Himself. God, as the eternal Truth, manifests Himself in His Word, in His Name, in the *Guru*, in His Order and through His Grace. The True Lord (*Sat Purakh*) is realized when the devotee remembers in his contemplation the True Name (*Sat Naam*) that the True *Guru* (*Sat Guru*) gives. The mind of the devotee is controlled and directed when the True Name is remembered in the True Company (*Sat Sangat*) of the True believers of God. Similarly, when the devotee opens himself to the Divine Order and Divine Grace, he experiences God, the Divine Truth. Since Truth is God, living a truthful life is the same as living a Godly life. Hence, for a Sikh, possession of Truth is a sign of God's blessing. Hence in every sphere of existence God manifests as the Truth. God, the truth, is revealed in a special way in the heart of man, for Truth is genuinely known only when God dwells deep in the devotee's heart. The presence of Truth in the life of a person removes all forms of evil from him and the True Light of God shines forth in him. Genuine possession of Truth leads to the possession of God and helps the seeker enter into deeper union with Him. Thus, a truthful person becomes Godlike as he lives his earthly existence and merges with the Truth, who is God, as he bids goodbye to his present existence.[73] The following quote highlights the significance of the Truth in the life of the devotee:

> Truth is known then, when the True one [God] resides in the heart.
> The dirt of falsehood is removed; the body is washed clean.
> Truth is known then when Truth [God] is loved.
> The mind is gladdened by hearing the Name of the Lord and thereby obtains salvation.
> Truth is known then, when he knows the way of life [God gives].
> He prepares the field of the body and puts the seed of (the Name of) the Creator.
> Truth is known then, when he receives true instruction [from God].
> He observes mercy towards creatures and gives alms (to the needy).
> Truth is known then, when he resides at the holy abode of the soul [where God dwells].
> He receives instruction from the True *Guru* and resides there.
> Truth is the remedy of all ills; it washes away sins.[74]

6.1 3.6. DIVINE GRACE

Divine Grace (*Nadar*) is another means with the help of which God reaches out to the devotee. Grace consists in God's special attention being focused on someone, even though every creature always remains in His sight. In moments of Grace, the devotee comes under the extraordinary thought of God; His eyes are particularly focused on the devotee. Many long to be the focus of God's attention, but, only a few meet Him, the True *Guru*, as man cannot force God to turn His face towards him. It is up to God to determine on whom He casts His gentle and loving look.[75] The following scriptural statement expresses the faith of the Sikhs on God's right to be gracious to some: "This cup of love [God's special attention] belongs to the Lord. And whomsoever the Lord wants, He gives this cup to him."[76]

This doctrine of Grace seemingly goes against the doctrine of *Karma* and the value of human effort and to points to partiality and injustice on the part of God, as He looks kindly on some while not on others. This perception is not true. In fact, the Grace of the Lord begins with the seeker's acceptance of the true Path in life. The fact that the seeker is able to open himself to the true path is due to the Grace of the Lord. God's intervention with His grace in the life of the seeker requires his endeavors to walk the right path. In fact it is not salvation that is given to the seeker through the grace of the Lord, as it must be attained through the individual's efforts. What is given to the seeker at the moment of Grace is the perception to appreciate the need for salvation, and the means the seeker must follow in order to attain it. In other words, the Grace of God does not do away with all the efforts the seeker is required to make to attain salvation, but rather it only places him, as it were, at the 'doorstep of salvation', so that knowing the way and assisted by the Lord, he can attain that deeper union with the Lord, in which consists his salvation. Thus, the Grace of God is not the result of any arbitrary activity of the Lord, but rather begins and matures as the seeker, guided by the Grace of the Lord, makes all efforts to walk the path of God-realization. From the beginning of the seeker's journey towards God up to his arrival at the final goal of God-realization, he carries on his spiritual living within the framework of Grace. The Grace of God does not make a person lazy in his spiritual journey, but rather only facilitates and sanctifies the efforts of the seeker.[77] The following quote highlights this point:

> Whosoever comes within His Grace, in him is born the
> faith and love, following the path of truth and contentment
> the pure mind is engrossed with the Word. ...
> Whosoever falls within His Grace meets the *Guru*. ...
> Through His Grace we serve the *Guru*. ...
> Though His Grace we serve (humanity).
> Through His Grace this mind can be controlled
> Though His Grace the mind becomes pure. ...
> Truth is always Pure, the Truthful are also pure
> Whosoever comes within His Grace, O Brother!
> Attains truthfulness. ...
> Through His Grace this attachment ceases.
> And one merges in the Lord.[78]

Thus, the Grace of the Lord, which is a special focusing of God's attention on the seeker, becomes real to the seeker only when he, himself, turns his face towards God, whose light is focused towards Him. Without this effort of turning the seeker's face towards God, the Grace of God is of no avail, as in his freedom man is free to say 'no' to God and walk in his own ways. If he takes the trouble to respond to the Divine Initiative that comes through Divine Grace by moving towards God, then the light of God that comes through the Grace of God lightens his path and envelops his life.

Everything he does, from then on, he does by the grace of God. God's doing and the seeker's doing go hand-in-hand, and what he achieves as the result of his cooperation with God's Grace is at the same time God's work and his work. When this happens, the seeker's ego vanishes, and he moves towards the final goal of God-realization with ease.[79]

In this section we have seen the reality of God in Sikhism, by clarifying His nature, outlining His characteristics and unfolding His ways of communication with creation, especially with humans. Though the Sikhs do recognize subordinate deities, often taken from the Hindu pantheon, they hold for the absolute supremacy of the One Eternal God. Though eternal, God is immanent in the universe, especially in His act of creation, sustaining and destruction. Besides, He communicates with humans in the depths of their hearts, through the Divine Word, Divine Name, Divine *Guru*, Divine Order, Divine Truth and Divine Grace. Through these six fold ways, God enters into relationship with man and calls man, in turn, to relate to Him. When man responds to God's six fold biddings, he moves towards union with Him. The next section will unfold the path, which takes the seeker to God.

6.2. THE SIKH PATH TO THE DIVINE

In Sikh religion, salvation depends on both Divine Grace and the efforts of the seeker. He must cleanse himself of all evil, that the salvation that is offered to him through the Grace of God can be owned and personalized. The Sikh path to God-realization (*Saadhanaa*), therefore, is nothing else but the individual seeker's necessary response to the offer of salvation that God communicates through the Divine Word, Divine Name, Divine *Guru*, Divine Order, Divine Truth and Divine Grace. The ultimate aim of this path is to bring about release from transmigrations, thereby attaining union with God. One prerequisite that the adept needs to have is the recognition of God in the whole of creation and particularly within the person. The path itself involves the performance of a number of religious practices, both personal and communal, which cleanse and discipline the aspirant, and progressively take him to the complete surrender of his will to the Divine Order (*Hukam*). Once this submission of man's will to the Divine Will takes place, the ascending of the seeker towards the final goal begins.[80] Here we shall explore the various religious practices of the Sikh path to God-realization and its stages.

6.2.1. RELIGIOUS PRACTICES OF THE SIKH PATH

There are numerous religious practices a devout Sikh is expected to follow. In this section, we classify them into three, viz., the interior path, the ritual path and the communal path. The interior path concentrates on the inner dimension of an adept's approach to God by way of contemplation and meditation. The ritual path deals with the ritual dimension of Sikh life. Finally, the communal path deals with those religious practices in which the larger Sikh community is involved. Though, at times, there is some overlapping in the classification, it brings a certain amount of clarity in our perception of Sikh religious practices. We shall consider each these paths.

6.2.1.1. INTERIOR PATH

The interior path attempts to highlight the foundational inner orientation of the Sikh religion. Though many external practices sustain the religious life of the Sikhs, yet Sikhism emphasizes that the ultimate experience, union with God, takes place in the interiority of oneself. Hence, it stresses the way of loving devotion to God (*Bhakti Maarga*), the way of contemplation on the Divine Name (*Naama Maarga*) and the inner purity of one's surrender of one's self to God. Thus, in this section, we briefly consider Sikhism as an interior religion, the way of loving devotion and the way of Name of God.

6.2.1.1.1. Interior Religion

Guru Naanak, the founder of Sikhism, lived at a time, when the richness and depth of a person's spiritual life was measured in terms of his birth, scriptures, ceremonies, caste and ascetical practices. The *Sant* tradition, to which *Guru* Naanak belonged, condemns such parameters to understand the spiritual worth of a person, as it amounts to making religion totally external. The *Sant* tradition in general and *Guru* Naanak in particular attempt to highlight the interior dimension of true religion.[81] The following quote clarifies this point:

> They who read (scriptures) continually and forget (their spiritual duty) suffer punishment (of spiritual death). For all their wisdom they continue to transmigrate. They who remember the Name and make fear (of God) their (spiritual) food – such servants, with the *Guru's* aid, dwell in union (with their Master). If the *man* is unclean how can it be purified by worshipping stones, visiting places of pilgrimage, living in jungles, wandering around as an ascetic? He who is united with the True One, he it is who acquires (eternal) honor. ...Hear me Pundit, you who put your trust in all your religious works. The work, which brings peace, is meditation upon spiritual reality. You stand up and recite the *Saastras* and *Vedas*, but your actions are those of the world. Inner filth and evil are not cleansed by hypocrisy. You are like a spider caught upside down (in the web you have spun)! ... One may have a cooking-square of gold with utensils of gold, (marked off) with lines of silver immensely protracted, water from the Ganges, a fire kindled with flint, and light food soaked in milk. But all these things are of no account, O *man*, unless one is imbued

with the true Name. One may have a hand-written copy of the eighteen *Puraanas* and be able to recite the four *Vedas* by heart, one may bathe on auspicious days, give to each according to the rules prescribed for each caste, fast and observe regulations day and night; one may be a *Qaazii*, a *Mullah*, or a *Sheikh*, a *Yogii*, a *Jangan*, or one wearing ochre robes; one may be a householder and living accordingly, but without the understanding (which comes from meditation upon the Name) all are bound and driven off to the abode of *Yam*).[82]

This statement from *Guru* Naanak clearly shows that he condemns a religion based on caste status, notions of purity and contaminations that arise out of caste differences, and the idea that caste standing is vital for one's approach to God. It is not birth, scriptures, ceremonies, ascetical practices and caste distinctions that determine who one is before God, but rather one's interior attitude towards God. The one who shelters God and His Name deep in his heart is the true servant of God. Hence, impurity does not come from birth or caste status, but rather from disorientation of the individual's mind. Sikhism expresses this interiority of religion concretely through the inter-communal refectory (*Langar*), where people of all castes eat together, and in the founding of the *Kaalsaa*, which again is a group that is formed of people of all castes.[83]

Similarly, Sikh religious practice condemns idolatry. Since idols are made of stone or other similar material, they are blind and dumb. Hence, they can neither see nor hear their worshippers. Therefore, the worship of idols can never carry one out of the ocean of existence. In the same way, bathing in places of pilgrimages (*Tiirath*) is also ineffective in leading one to union with God. The true *Tiirath* is not the waters of these places of pilgrimage, but the Divine Name. The inner contemplation of the Divine Word brings true knowledge, which, in turn, washes away the evils that stem from the body, mind and heart. Likewise, salvation is not found in ascetical practices, renouncing the world and pursuing the life of a solitary hermit or a wandering monk. That which is required for genuine interior life is not the renunciation of the world, but a life of disciplined worldliness. The way of Truth consists in living in the world, yet being unaffected by the attractions of the world. A true Sikh must be like a lotus that blooms in filthy and muddy water. Just as the beauty of the lotus is never affected by the dirty surrounding in which it grows, in the same way a Sikh who meditates on the Name of God is never affected by his life in the world. Hence, freedom from attachment, while living in the midst of temptation to attachment, is the ideal of a true believer. True religion is not to be found in mere external religious practices, but in the inward disciplines of love, faith, mercy and humility, which manifest themselves in virtuous and sympathetic actions, always upholding what is true.[84] The following passage clarifies the true nature of the interior religion a true seeker is called to live:

The true *Yogi* is he who recognizes the Way, who by the *Guru's* grace knows the One. The true *Qaazii* is he who turns away (from the world) and by the *Guru's* grace dies while remaining alive. The true *Braahman* is he who meditates on *Brahman*; he saves himself and all his kin.
Make mercy your mosque, faith your prayer-mat, and righteousness your *Qur'aan*. Make Humility your circumcision, uprightness your fasting, and so you will be a (true) Muslim. Make good works your *Ka'bah*, Truth your *Piir*, and compassion your creed and your prayer. Make the performance of what pleases (God) your rosary and, Naanak, He will uphold your honor.
(Make the Merciful Lord) your *Saalgraam*, your object of worship, O Pundit, and good deeds your garland of *Tulsii*. Construct a boat by repeating the name of God and pray that the Merciful One may show mercy towards you. Why waste your life in irrigating sterile land? Why plaster a mud wall when it will surely fall?[85]

6.2.1.1.2. The Way of Bhakti

Since Sikhism holds for an interior religion, its basic expression is one of loving devotion (*Bhakti*) to God. *Bhakti* is the devotee's response directed towards the formless God, whose presence he experiences in every aspect of the created world. The devotee, who worships the One True Formless God, with adoring love, thirsts for His supreme love, seeks it and finally finds true peace, as the love of God he seeks is experienced deep in his heart. The loving devotion the devotee feels towards his God instills in him a genuine fear of God, as he recognizes God's infinite immensity and absolute authority. The sentiment of the fear of God helps the devotee to make a complete surrender of himself to God's Divine Will (*Hukam*). This surrender is an unconditional submission to God in faith. It, in turn, makes the devotee sing the praises of the One Supreme God, whom he loves, fears and has accepted as his refuge. Unlike the Vaishnava *Bhakti* tradition, in the Sikh *Bhakti* tradition there is no place for the *Avataaras* of God, and worship in loving devotion, fear and surrender is offered directly to the One True Formless Supreme God. The Sikh expression of this loving devotion to God is found in the contemplation of the Divine Name,[86] to which we next turn our attention.

6.2.1.1.3. Contemplation on the Name of God

The contemplation of the Divine Name is done with the help of a meditative technique called *Naam Japan* or *Naam Simaran*. It is a method of remembering by way of repeating the Name of God, such as, *Vaahiguru* or *Satguru*. It cleanses the mind of the devotee instantly from *Haumai*, which is the cause of individuation and egocentricity in the human person. The term

"*Naam*", as we have already explained, stands for the Divine Name, which reveals God's Being, the sum total of all His attributes and the collection of everything that can be affirmed of God. The two verbs that are associated with the term "*Naam*", in this meditative technique, are "*Japanaa*" and "*Simaranaa*". The term "*Japanaa*" means 'to repeat'. It is used in connection with the repetition of a *Mantra*. It often refers to the mechanical repetition of a *Mantra* with the help of a rosary. But what *Guru* Naanak means by this term when it is used in association with the term "*Naam*", is a repetition that aims at understanding the deepest meaning of the term "*Naam*", interiorizing its meaning and exposing the devotees total being to its deepest meaning. The second verb "*Simaranaa*" means 'to remember' or 'to hold in remembrance'. Thus, *Naam Simaran* means remembering the Name of God, while repeating it. It is a meditation technique with the help of which the devotee can meditate on the nature and qualities of God. The remembrance involved in this meditation includes remembrance of the Lord in one's thought (*Mani*), word (*Bach*) and deed (*Karami Karakai*). In this meditative process, the seeker takes into his personality more and more godly qualities by contemplation on the Name of God, while all that is evil within the devotee is given away. As the meditation progresses, the devotee becomes more like God, thereby leading him to ultimate union with God.[87]

The remembrance of the Lord by way of *Naam Simaran* takes place in a few progressive stages, leading to final union with the Lord. The first stage is the repetition of the Holy Name of God with the tongue. It consists in the vocal recital of the Name, which involves repeating the Name aloud. The *Aadi-Granth* urges a devotee to repeat the *Naam* continuously and sing praises to the Name, especially in the gathering of the congregation (*Sat Sangat*). In such gatherings of true believers, *Naam Simaran*, in the level of vocal repetition, is done with the accompaniment of music. But this loud repetition, whether it is sung or recited, must accompany devout and loving meditation on the Name of the Lord. The best time for such meditative repetition is the early hours of the morning, which are known as the ambrosial time. Starting the day's work with the repetition of the Name of God helps the devotee to feel the presence of the Lord throughout the day, amidst the various activities he is expected to do. The loud vocal repetition of the Name of God moves into the second stage, when *Naam* is silently uttered. In this utterance the tongue and the throat are involved in uttering the *Naam*, but no sound is heard outside. Thus the recitation of the *Naam* moves through from the gross body to the subtler layers of the devotee's personality, filling these layers with the power of *Naam*. At this stage, the cleansing of the ego-sense (*Antahkaran*) takes place through the silent meditative repetition of the *Naam*.[88]

The third stage of *Naam Simaran* consists in repeating the Name of God through the activity of breath. Here the devotee repeats and remembers the *Naam* throughout the day as he inhales and exhales the breath in a natural way. One part of the Holy name is repeated while he inhales, and the other part is repeated as he exhales. In practicing the *Naam Simaran* in the third stage, the devotee remembers the Lord during the day and night. At this stage, the internal faculties, such as, the mind (*Citta*), the intellect (*Buddhi*) and the I-sense (*Ahankaara*), are imbued with the *Naam*. This results in the obliteration of negative and egoistic urges and tendencies that lead the devotee to evil actions, which, in turn, brings stillness, peace and tranquility. As the devotee continues to practice the *Naam Simaran* in the third stage, and as he remembers the Name of God lovingly and devotedly, he begins to experience feelings of wonder and bliss, which the Sikhs refer to as the state of *Visamaad*. It is a state of mystical experience, in which the devotee loses the awareness of duality and experiences a deep sense of oneness. Thus, he views God, the world and the self as merged into one reality. The mind of the devotee, without getting lost in the phenomenal world, remains fixed in the *Naam*, in the process moving from the phenomenal realm to the realm of noumena. As the result, he experiences feelings of tranquility (*Shaanti*), equipoise (*Sahaj*), wonder and bliss (*Visamaad*).[89] The following passage from the *Japjii* describes the devotee's experience of the state of *Visamaad*:

> Infinite is His Goodness, and infinite its praise;
> Infinite are His Works and infinite His Gifts;
> Where are the bounds of His seeing or His hearing?
> Unfathomable is the infinity of His mind;
> There are no bounds even to His creation.
> How many vex their hearts to know His limits
> But seeking to explore Infinity, can find no bounds;
> The more we say, the more there is left to say;
> High is our Lord and very High is His throne;
> His holy Name is higher than the highest.
> He that would know His height must be of the same
>   height;
> Only the Lord knoweth the greatness of the Lord;
> Saith Naanak, only by God's grace and bounty
> Are God's gifts bestowed on man.[90]

With the experience of the state of *Visamaad*, the adept gradually moves into the fourth stage of remembrance of the *Naam*. Here, the tongue, throat and the breath are not involved in the repetition of the Name of God. The mind of the devotee is imbued with the power of the *Naam*, and he goes through depth level mystical experiences. These experiences energize his intellect with the power of the Name of God, and as the result it becomes transparent with the nectar of universal love (*Prem Ras*), which is intuitively experienced as the result of the mystical experiences. When *Prem Ras* takes hold of the devotee, the ego-centered intellect is wiped out and perfect reason (*Bibek Buddhi*) takes its place. It leads to the demolition of doubts, removal of all illusions and the destruction of the effects of the *Maayaa*. The total personality of the devotee is filled with the power of the *Naam*, and he comes in face-to-face relationship with the True Self (*Aatam Darshan*). At this stage, the devotee fully experiences his union with the God, Whose Name he has been contemplating. Having experienced the True Self, the devotee takes up the following religious practices: to be baptized and become a member of the *Kaalsaa* (*Pio Pahun Khandedhaar*) and follow strictly the rules of the *Kaalsaa*; he meditates on the *Naam* (*Naam Japo*); he listens and sings verses from the *Aadi-Granth* (*Hari Kiirtan*), which help him to understand the instructions of the *Gurus* and induce a meditative spirit in him or her; to induce dignity of labor and self respect in man so that one earns an honest living (*Kirat Karo*); to bring about effectively the collective welfare and upliftment of the society, to subdue his egoistic desires, to bring temperance and avoid over-indulgence, he shares his honest earnings (*Vand Chhako*); he practices service to the helpless and the needy, both individually and collectively, in the secular and spiritual life (*Sevaa*); to ensure social justice, to make the dignity of mankind a reality, to protect the weaker and the helpless people from exploitation, oppression and tyranny, he fights even in the face of death, without yielding to tyranny timidly (*Gauu Garib Di Rakshaa*); and he joins all to work for the welfare of humankind as a whole, without differentiating people according to caste, creed race or religion (*Sarbat-daa-bhalaa*). Deep experiences and the practice of many social-service activities lead the adept to become the *Jiivanmukta*, spending his life in service to all.[91]

6.2.1.2. RITUAL PATH

Though Sikhism stresses the significance of the interior dimension of spiritual existence, it does not ignore the external dimension of spiritual living. Hence, within Sikh religious practice we find meaningful rituals and ceremonies. This section attempts to look into some Sikh rituals.

6.2.1.2.1. Daily Ritual of a Sikh

The daily ritual of the Sikhs is known as *Nitya Karmas*. It is elaborate and demands a lot of time and energy on the part of the devout Sikh. The life of a Sikh begins as early as four o'clock in the morning, as early hours are the best time for concentration and for prayer. As soon as the Sikh arises, he finishes his ablutions, takes a coldwater bath, cleanses his clothes and sits to begin his meditation and prayer. His prayer consists of portions of his Daily Rule (*Nitnem*), such as, the *Japjii*, which is the Sikh morning prayer. It also includes *Jap Sahib* and ten *Swayaas* of *Guru* Gobind Singh. He also may repeat the Name of God, on which he is expected to concentrate at all times. After completing the morning portion of the *Nitnem*, the devout Sikh is expected to go to a *Grudwara*, the true abode of the *Guru* for *Darshan* of the *Guru Granth Saahib* and for instructions. When he is in the *Gurudwara*, he takes part in the rite associated with the ritual opening of the *Aadi-Granth*. As he participates in the congregational prayer (*Sat Sangat*), he attentively listens to the instruction of the *Guru*, either as a recitation directly from the *Guru Granth Saahib* or in the form of *Kiirtan*, divine music, when the hymns of the *Gurus* are sung. A longer poem of *Guru* Naanak entitled, *Asa Ki Var*, is daily recited as a *Kiirtan*. A longer hymn of *Guru* Amar Daas, entitled *Anand Saahib* brings the *Sat Sangat* to a close. The *Sloka* at the end of the *Japjii* is also recited at this time. Thus, the individual and congregational prayer comes to an end.[92]

After the twofold prayers, the Sikh takes breakfast. Then he goes on with his worldly duties, with the help of which he earns bread for himself and his family. Lunch is taken at noon. After his work, he returns home and prays the evening prayers (*Rahiraas*). Depending on the availability of time, he goes to the *Gurdwara* for prayers. After dinner he prays the bedtime prayer (*Sohilaa*). In addition there are other practices a true Sikh has to follow. For instance, when a Sikh enters a *Gurudwara*, he has to take off his shoes, wash his feet and then proceed to the presence of the *Guru* and venerate the *Guru Grant Saahib* with a prostration, i.e., bowing to the ground with folded hands. Thus, the whole day of a devout Sikh, from early morning to late at night, is lived in the presence of the Absolute Being, during which he opens his life to the grace and blessing of God.[93]

6.2.1.2.2. Rituals at the Gurdwara

The Sikhs are encouraged to visit *Gurdwara* and worship there as often as possible, as the *Guru* is said to manifest himself both in the *Guru Granth Saahib* and the gathering of the community in worship (*Sat Sangat*). All the rites that take place in the *Gurdwara* call for the installation of the *Guru Granth Saahib* upon its throne (*Manjii*). The *Guru Granth Saahib* is opened to take orders for the day and for the daily reading of *Gurbaanii*. The basic worship at the *Gurdwara* consists in people meeting there for the congregational reading of the *Guru Granth Saahib*, for the rites of passage and for the everyday routine rites of the *Gurdwara*. The routine rites are more complex in historical shrines, where there are a number of officials to perform them. But in a small village *Gurdwara*, there may be only a reader (*Granthii*), who opens the *Guru Granth Saahib* in the morning, and people come for *Darsan*. Similarly, the people come to the *Gurdwara* to worship and offer special prayers during festivals.[94]

When the people gather in the *Gurdwara* for worship, they follow certain customary ways of action. They remove their shoes as they enter the *Gurdwara*. While the rite is in progress all cover their heads. Those men who wear turban have already covered their heads. For others, the use of a hat or placing a handkerchief over the head is sufficient. Women cover their heads with a scarf or a thin veil. As one enters the *Gurdwara*, one bows, kneels and then touches the floor with the forehead, as the sign of showing reverence for God. This gesture is called *Mathaa Teknaa*. In case a person is late for the service, he sees that he does not disturb the praying congregation as he enters the *Gurdwara*. Usually women and men sit in separate sides. There is a special reason for this practice. Women are given equal roles in Sikhism, and they are conduct services in the *Gurdwara* or even take part in the running of the *Gurdwara*. The assembly gathered in worship always sits on the floor during worship. People bring offerings in kind as they come to the *Gurdwara* for worship. These offerings are left at the side of the throne on which the *Guru Granth Saahib* is placed. The usual offerings brought to the *Gurdwara* are milk, rice, flour, sugar, lentils, sweets, flowers and fruits. People also offer money in the collection box that is kept for the purpose. Everyone offers something when they come to the *Gurdwara* for worship. After placing the offerings at the side of the *Manjii*, they move to their place without showing their backs to the *Guru Grantt Saahib*.[95]

Another prayer, which is regularly recited in the Gurdwara, is the *Ardaas*. It is the only recital read in the *Gurdwaras*, which is not taken from the *Guru Granth Saahib*. The term "*Ardaas*" literally means petition. Hence, it is a prayer of petition with which most of the ceremonies in the Sikh *Gurdwara* conclude. In first part of the *Ardaas*, words are quoted from the *Candii di Vaar* of the *Dasem Granth*, which recalls the Sikh *Gurus*, the *Guru Granth Saahib* and various events from Sikh history. In the second part, specific prayer requests are added. Usually at this part people pray for the sick, suffering and all in need. They also pray for the blessings of God to rest on humankind. People stand facing the *Guru Granth Saahib*, with folded hands, while the *Ardaas* is prayed.[96]

6.2.1.2.3. Rites Related to Aadi-Granth

Every Sikh believes in the sanctity of the *Guru Granth Saahib* because the spirit that was present in the ten *Gurus* for over two centuries is present in the *Aadi-Granth*. Thus, the Sacred Book is given a sacred personality of its own. Though the Sikhs reject worship of the *Aadi-Granth*, saying that worship belongs to God alone, some of the acts of reverence they offer to the Book amount to worship, as they are similar to the worship the Hindus offer to the idols. The sacred book is placed on a special throne in an elevated position. If the worshipers sit on the floor, a low but raised dais is used for the purpose. The books are always wrapped in expensive cloths (*Rumaalaas*). When the *Guru Granth Saahib* is opened for reading, it is protected by the use of flywhisks (*Chaur*), a symbol of royalty. Whenever the book is moved, the person holding it carries it on the head. When it is taken in procession, people are informed that proper respect must be given to the sacred book. Similarly, when one enters the *Gurdwara,* one falls in prostration before the Book. Elaborate rituals are associated with the opening of the Book in the morning and its closing in the evening. Similarly, offerings are made to the sacred Book and people accept *Prasaad* from the reader. Because of the sanctity the Sikhs accord to this Book, they read from it on every important occasion of their lives.[97]

The Sikhs give prominence to the *Guru Granth Saahib* in regular *Gurdwara* worship and to all other special ceremonies. Devout Sikhs read from the sacred book in the morning, in the evening and at bedtime. At the marriage ceremony of the Sikhs, the couple circumambulates the *Guru Granth Saahib*, instead of the sacred fire, as the Hindus do. As Sikhs begin their daily tasks in the morning, they take commands from the sacred scripture. It is the custom among the Sikhs to open the sacred book at random, reading the text that appears at the top of the left page and considering it as the will of God for them for that day. The Sikhs use similar procedures to choose a name for a newborn child and to give guidance on an issue that affects the life of the *Sikh-panth*. In the latter use, the procedure of opening the sacred book to find the will of God serves as the public oracle.[98]

Another ceremony that involves reading the *Guru Granth Saahib* is the *Akhand Paath*. It consists in unbroken reading from the sacred book. It is usually restricted to the wealthier members of the *Sikh-Panth*. It is usually kept on special occasions as a sign of thanksgiving, supplication for a special grace from God or as a means to avert a disaster that is predicted in the future. For instance, a wedding in the family may call for the rite of *Akhand Paath*. Similarly, opening of a new business, the return of a son from overseas, a serious illness of someone in the family and similar occasions can warrant the rite of *Akhand Paath*. The rite consists in continuous reading of the whole of the *Aadi-Granth* without any interruption. It is comparable to the Hindu *Yajna*. The readers gather and continue reading, relieving each other, seeing to it that no interruption takes place. The whole reading may take two days and two nights. The people are free to be present while the *Akhand Paath* is in progress. Usually the people who arrange the performance of the rite gather before the reading approaches the conclusion (*Bhog*) of the sacred Book. It is believed that this rite brings God's blessings, averts an evil and causes the general well-being of the family that organizes it. In the principal *Gurdwaras*, the rite of *Akhand Paath* is carried on continuously without any interruption, while in the smaller *Gurdwaras* it is done as a preparation for the festivals. It has become the recent custom among certain sections of the *Sikh-Panth* to perform the rite of *Akhand Paath* with the help of loudspeakers to obtain the well-being of the wider community.[99]

A few variations of these forms of reading the sacred book are in vogue. For instance, the *Saptaah Paath* is the continuous recital for seven days. Another variation of such recital is to read one favorite hymn after each hymn in the *Aadi-Granth* is recited. It is called *Sampat Paath*. The non-stop recital of this kind takes about 15 days. None of these forms of ceremonial recitation has any sanction from the *Gurus*. It is possible that these forms of recital came into practice only at the end of the 19th century.[100]

6.2.1.2.4. Officials of the Sacred Rites

Strictly speaking there is no priesthood in Sikh religion. It is basically the religion of householders. But over the 500 years of Sikh history, especially from the time of emperor Ranjit Singh, the running of the *Gurdwaras* becomes hereditary. There have been two orders of people, viz., the *Mahants*, who are descendants of *Gurus* and the *Purohits*, the descendents of *Brahmans*. Later, when the *Singh Sabha* begins its *Gurdwara* Reform Movement, there is a clash between those controlling the *Gurdwaras* and the members of the *Singh*

Sabha. A lot of blood is shed on this count, the *Mahants* and the *Prohits* move out of the scene of Sikh religious life, and readers (*Granthiis*) and singers (*Raagiis*) take their place in running the *Gurdwaras*. In recent times, *Granthiis* run the *Gurdwara*. They are usually married, middle-aged men. Their task is to attend to the *Guru Granth Saahib*, reading aloud and looking after the *Gurdwara*. The *Granthiis*, who are well intentioned, avoid all temptations, especially that of involvement in the *Gurdwara* politics. Strictly speaking, the *Granthiis* has no pastoral role, as he is basically the administrator of the *Gurdwara*. Usually men hold this office, as a woman may find it difficult to manage living alone in a *Gurdwara*. The *Granthi* has no special authority or position in the *Sikh-panth*, as all Sikhs are equal. There are also others who assist at the worship the *Gurdwara,* like those who sing and play music. Besides there are the pious men, to whom people come to listen for their teaching. Some of these are descendents of the *Gurus*, while others attract people due to their personal authority. Thus, Sikhism still remains a religion without an established priesthood.[101]

6.2.1.3. COMMUNAL PATH

Besides, the interior and ritual paths, there is also the communal path. The communal path includes those socio-religious practices and ceremonies, the performance of which involves the larger community, viz., the family, the village or the gathering of Sikhs from all over the world. This includes sacramental acts, festivals, the congregational assemblies and the congregational sharing of *Prasaad, Guru's* kitchen, and other religious practices in the community. We consider these in this section.

6.2.1.3.1. Sacramental Acts

The *Aadi-Granth* speaks of three distinct stages of human existence, viz., childhood, youth and old age. In between these stages, there are also other significant stages, such as, naming the child, the first entry into school, wearing the sacred thread, getting engaged, marriage, death and cremation. Hinduism proposes the sacramental acts (*Samskaaras*), with the help of which the community opens an individual's life to the influence of the Divine. *Guru* Naanak himself sees such acts as superfluous and extraneous. But over the period of time, perhaps due to Hindu and Muslim influence, these practices have become common in the Sikh community.[102] In this section, we briefly explore the Sikh birth ceremony, other childhood ceremonies, the initiation ceremony, betrothal and marriage ceremonies, and the death and cremation ceremony.

6.2.1.3.1.1. Birth Ceremony

The birth of a child is something mysterious, which ancient peoples attributed to the activity of some superhuman agency. The birth of a child, especially a male child, brings great happiness in the family. The birth of a son strengthens the status of the woman in the family and unites the husband and wife. The birth ceremony and the rites associated with it emerge from the natural helplessness of the child and the mother. Though, the rites originate from the physical conditions of childbirth, they gain socio-religious character over the period of time. Immediately after the birth of the child, the navel-cord is detached; the child is washed and breast-fed. The father of the child places honey in the mouth of the child. Prayers are offered to ward off the evil spirits. A light is kept burning in the room where the mother and the child are. Scriptural verses are recited. The poor are given money and other goods. The *Pandit* prepares the horoscope (*Janampatri*) of the child. After childbirth the mother is considered as impure (*Sutak*). After the stipulated days, the house is washed and purified, the mother and the child are bathed and the purification rite is performed. *Guru* Naanak and other *Gurus* condemn the practice of the writing of the horoscope and the concept of physical impurity, as the real impurities are internal and not merely external.[103]

6.2.1.3.1.2. Other Childhood Ceremonies

Some of the other childhood ceremonies are the name-giving ceremony (*Naamakarna*), ear-boring ceremony, food-giving ceremony (*Annaprasana*) and hair cutting ceremony. These are usually performed during the tenth or the twelfth month after the birth. A purification rite precedes the actual name-giving ceremony. In includes the bathing of the child and the mother, the walls of the room are smeared with cowdung, and the room in which the mother has given birth is washed. The *Purohit*, after consulting the horoscope, names the child. The Sikhs have the practice of finding the name of the child by a random opening the *Aadhi-Granth*. Another childhood ceremony is the ear-boring ceremony. It is usually done on the same day as the name-giving ceremony. Usually the ears of the boys are bored, while the ears and the nose of the girls are bored. The girls wear nose-rings (*Nath*) and earrings (*Bunde*). The food-giving ceremony is the third childhood ceremony. It consists in giving food for the first time to the child. The cutting of the hair of the child for the first time is another ceremony. These practices are more popular among the Hindus and the Muslims. We do find indirect references to these ceremonies in the hymns of *Guru* Naanak. He himself does not believe in the efficacy of these ceremonies and views them as hindering the ascent towards the Almighty God.[104]

Another important childhood ceremony is the school-going ceremony (*Vidhaarambha Samskaara*). It is performed when the child is five or seven years old. An auspicious day is fixed for sending the child to the preceptor. There are references in the hymns of *Guru* Naanak mentioning preceptors (*Chatras*), young students with wooden board (*Phatti*), pen (*Qalam*), ink (*Mas*) and students studying under the guidance of the *Pundits*, though he does not speak of it as a special sacramental act. Naanak himself goes though this rite as a child. As Naanak is against all forms of worldly education that lead to egoism and love of money, he does not give much importance to these rites. But as a sacramental act, it is a common practice in later Sikhism.[105]

6.2.1.3.1.3. Initiation Ceremony

In the ancient Hindu and Muslim tradition, initiation ceremonies (*Upanayana*) are performed. The Muslims circumcise boys at the age of seven, while the Hindus wear the sacred thread according to the age regulations of different castes. Usually an auspicious day is fixed for the ceremony. The boy is bathed before the actual ceremony and is seated on a wooden stool. His father sits opposite the boy. The sacred fire is lit and sacred *Mantras* are recited. The most important part of the ceremony is the consecration of the sacred thread and girding the boy with it. At the age of nine, *Guru* Naanak himself goes through this initiation ceremony. But he does not attach much significance and religious sanctity to this ceremony. Though he goes through this ceremony as a boy, he does not wear the sacred thread. According to him, formal wearing of the sacred thread is of no use to the one who wears it. Instead of merely wearing the sacred thread, one must practice the eternal values of mercy, contentment and self-control. For *Guru* Naanak, the praise of the Lord should be one's sacred thread. This true sacred thread never breaks, but takes one to the Lord's court.[106]

6.2.1.3.1.4. Betrothal and Marriage Ceremonies

Marriage (*Vivaaha*) is the most important of all ceremonies that constitute the Sikh family. The betrothal ceremony (*Mangni* or *Kurmai*) precedes the marriage ceremony. The betrothal ceremony consists in the formal recognition of the husband and wife to be. It is the occasion of great joy for the families of the bride and the bridegroom. After the betrothal, an auspicious day and time is fixed for the marriage ceremony, with the help of a *Pundit*. The rite of fixing the date and time is called *Saha Kadhna*. On this occasion, the members of the family shower blessings on the young bride and wish that her union with her husband may bring her unending joy. When the date and time are fixed, the actual preparation for marriage begins. For about a week before the marriage ceremony, every evening the neighboring women gather at the bride's house and sing songs meant for the occasion of marriage (*Ghorian* and *Suhag*). *Guru* Naanak calls these songs *Mangal*. The invitation for the ceremony is sent through special messengers to all relatives and friends. On the marriage day, all the invited guests arrive at the place of marriage. The bridegroom comes to the house of the bride in solemn procession, as a music party heads the procession. As the procession arrives at the bride's house, the bridegroom is welcomed by songs and greetings (*Vadhai*). They are served rich and sumptuous meals. The principal marriage rituals commence at a time that is already fixed. The main marriage ceremony consists of the bride and the groom circling the sacred fire seven times, while *Mantras* are recited. Among the Sikhs there is the practice of the bride and the bridegroom encircling the

Aadi-Granth seven times while texts from the *Aadi-Granth* are recited. The main rite also includes the presentation of the dowry in the form of various gifts to the bride from her father's family. The other rites are secondary in nature. When the marriage ceremony is completed, the bride accompanies her husband to her new home, bidding goodbye to her father, mother and the family members. On arrival at the bridegroom's house, the newlywed couple is received with great joy. Before the newlyweds enter the house, the threshold of the house is smeared with mustard and oil and water is sprinkled over the couple as the sign of welcoming. Thus, begins the married life of the newly weds in their new home. Sikh *Gurus* condemn the extravagance of the dowry practice. They also encourage the practice of widow re-marriage.[107]

6.2.1.3.1.5. Death and Cremation Ceremonies

In the hymns of *Guru* Naanak, we find a clear description of the death and cremation ceremonies. When a person is about to die, his body is laid on the floor, people gather around it and the *Pundits* recite *Mantras*. Food and gifts are distributed to the poor to help the dying person's soul to pass into the next life. After the person dies usually three forms of disposal of the body may be practiced. The most common form is cremation. The other two are throwing the body in running water and throwing it to be consumed by the animals. Before the dead person's body is placed on the funeral bier, it is washed in fresh water, perfumed and adorned with garlands and flowers. The body is covered with silk or cotton cloths depending on the age, sex and other circumstances of the dead person. The body, then, is placed on a bier made of bamboo and wood. It is carried on the shoulders of four persons to the cremation ground – which is usually in the bank of a river - with the accompaniment of music and dancing. The mourners, the relatives and friends of the dead person also join the procession. The conch is also blown during the procession. As the procession reaches the cremation ground, the cremation ceremony begins. The body is placed on a pyre of either ordinary wood or sandalwood. *Ghee* is poured into the eyes, nostrils, ears, mouth and other parts of the body. Accompanied by the recitation of the *Mantras*, the eldest son or a male relative of the dead person lights the fire on the dead body. All remain at the cremation ground until the fire consumes the dead body. They, then, leave the cremation ground and bathe themselves before they enter their houses. On the third day of cremation, the relatives of the dead gather to collect the ashes (*Asthi-chayana*), and they are immersed in the sacred rivers, like that of the Ganges. There are a number of superstitious practices, such as, placing earthen lamps to show the dead the way to heaven, considering the house of the dead as impure for ten days, the performance of the *Sharadha* ceremony of giving food and water to the dead to sustain his life until his soul enters another body, and the offering of rice-balls (*Pind-daan*) to the dead on the last day of the year. *Guru* Naanak condemns all such superstitious practices and says in clear terms that one is saved not by the efficacy of these superstitious practices, but by 'the remembrance of the name of God'.[108]

6.2.1.3.2. Festivals

The Sikh Books of Law (*Rahit*) do not prescribe the observance of any festival. Strictly speaking, no Sikh festival is universally observed. The Sikhs celebrate and commemorate significant events of their history in the local places where they have taken place. Usually the Sikhs do not celebrate universally the deaths and martyrdom of their *Gurus* and holy men. But there are local *Gurudwaras*, where the lives and events of these holy men are recalled and remembered. Nowadays, it is more common to celebrate the birth and death days of *Guru* Naanak and *Guru* Gobind Singh. The main feature of such commemorations is the *Akhand Paath*, that is the prolonged recitation of the *Aadi-Granth*.[109]

The most important festival of the Sikhs is the New Year festival, known as the *Baisaakhii*, which is celebrated on the 13th of April. It is a festival of thanksgiving. Strictly speaking it is not a religious festival, but rather it is a fair (*Melaa*). For the Sikhs the *Baisaakhii* festival is significant, as it is the commemoration of the founding of the *Khaalsaa* by *Guru* Gobind Singh. Usually a religious note to this festival is added by the recitation of the *Akhand Paath*. There is also a ceremony centered on the flagpole that is usually found outside the *Gurdwara*. It consists in lowering of the flagpole, removing the cloth with which it is wrapped, washing the flagpole with yogurt, re-wrapping the flagpole with new cloths and attaching the new *Nisaan Saahib*, the Sikh symbol, on the top of the flagpole. The whole Sikh community gathers at the *Gurdwara* on this occasion. Besides, on this day those who wish to take initiation as members of the *Khaalsaa* join the *Khaalsaa* community, and their relatives and friends join the rite of initiation. This initiation rite is meant only for the members of the *Khaalsaa*. The people who gather for the *Baisaakhii* festival sit in the *Gurdwara* to listen to the *Kiirtan* chanting, and everyone eats in the community kitchen (*Langar*). Another important festival the Sikhs celebrate is the *Diivaalii*, the festival of light, which is usually celebrated in October or November. Historically this festival commemorates the release of *Guru* Hargovind from prison. Thus, this festival points out to the Sikhs the victory of good over evil. The *Gurdwaras* are illuminated with lights and lamps. It is a festival of fun and joy. On this occasion the people enjoy the fireworks at night. They exchange gifts and give sweets to their friends. *Diivaalii* is a festival in which the whole Sikh community takes active part in the celebrations.[110]

6.2.1.3.3. Congregational Assemblies and Congregational Sharing of Karaah Prasaad

Besides the gathering of the community at festival times, there is also the gathering of the congregational assemblies called the *Diiwaan*. It is usually held on Sundays and holidays, as people are free to attend them only on such days. When it gathers, the *Diiwaan* lasts for several hours. At the gathering of the *Diiwaan*, the *Guru Granth Saahib* is opened solemnly.

The people gathered sing *Kiirtans*. Usually a lecture, which contains the explanation of the hymn that is sung, is delivered. The speaker may use different methods in explaining the hymn: he may explain the hymn line by line, or may use different stories, sayings, or anecdotes from the Sikh history to explain the hymn. In some *Diiwaan* gatherings the speaker also may talk of current affairs, local events and happenings, and even local political situations. At times the speakers at the *Diiwaan* refer to other religions and their sacred books, but they are referred to with much respect. Sometimes the people of other faiths are called to address the gathering (*Sangat*). In this manner, the *Diiwaan* encourages inter-faith dialogue and understanding. At the end of the *Diiwaan*, the gathered members of the congregation share in the *Karaah Prasaad*, which is a special food distributed in the *Gurdwaras*. It is made of semolina or wheat flour, *ghee* and sugar, and is prepared in clean conditions. While it is prepared, certain sections of the *Gurbaanii* are recited. Any person can prepare it, if he follows the accepted manner of making it. In the *Gurdwara*, the *Karaah Prasaad* is placed near the *Guru Granth Saahib*. At the end of the congregational assembly, it is touched with a sword, after which it is distributed to the members of the congregational assembly. It is received in cupped hands and is treated with respect. Usually people eat it immediately, though at times people take some home for other members of the family, who for some reason have not attended the *Diiwaan*.[111]

6.2.1.3.4. Guru's Kitchen

The *Guru's* kitchen (*Langar*) is an ancient Sikh traditional institution. It seems to have begun from the time of *Guru* Naanak. Those who come to worship and pray, sit together to eat and clean up after the meal. The origin of the practice of *Guru's* kitchen is not known. Probably it is borrowed from the practice of the Sufis. The *Guru's* kitchen stands for the equality of all, in spite of their caste and social status. When people sit in one line to eat together, caste bonds are broken and status distinctions cease to exist. No one knows the one who brings the food, the one who prepares the food and serves it. Thus, the *Guru's* kitchen breaks all social distinctions. The members of the *Kaalsaa* live this spirit totally and fully. The Sikh practice of *Langar* also has the aim of charity. According to the Sikhs, no one should ever go hungry, as the *Guru's* kitchen is open to all. The *Langar* also provides an opportunity to serve the community. The preparation of the food and its distribution is a service a Sikh can offer to the *Gurdwara* and to the congregation (*Sangat*). If this service is performed selflessly, it is one of the best forms of worship a Sikh can offer to God. In this manner, the *Guru's* kitchen is a great institution the Sikh community cherishes.[112]

6.2.1.3.5. Other Religious Practices in the Community

In the Sikh community, there is the expiatory practice of confession of a person's sins before the congregation (*Sangat*). When a Sikh commits a major or minor offence, he makes his confession before the congregation. The congregation takes the disciplinary action against him by imposing a penalty according to the nature of the offence. The act of confession is already an act of repentance, and the penalty given is usually light. The recitation of hymns, service at the congregation and the *Kaalsaa* brotherhood – such as, providing drinking water, grinding flour, helping at the *Guru's* kitchen, cleaning the utensils and doing ordinary chores at the *Gurdwara* – are some of the penalties normally imposed on the offenders of the *Sikh-Panth*. The performance of such acts of penance creates in the offender attitudes of humility, love, thoughtfulness of others and genuine love of God. While cultivating these qualities in the offender, these penances also make him open to the grace of God.[113]

Besides, there is the practice of issuing *Hukamnama* and *Gurmatta* in the Sikh community. An order from the *Guru* to a particular congregation or to an individual is known as the *Hukamnama*. The order of the *Guru* is often determined by the random selection and the recitation of a hymn from the *Guru Granth Saahib*. Such an order becomes the Will of God (*Hukam*) for the one to whom it is issued. He is bound it follow it. Similarly, a decision, which the holy congregation passes for the welfare of the Sikh community, is called *Gurmatta*. The *Gurmatta* are originally passed in the *Akaal Takhat*. They are considered as orders binding on Sikhs of all ranks. These twofold regulations of *Hukamnama* and *Gurmatta* direct the everyday life of the groups and individuals within the *Sikh-Panth*.[114]

The practice of holy pilgrimage is a common practice among devout Sikhs. The *Gurdwara* is a place of pilgrimage for a Sikh. The pilgrimage becomes special when he visits historic *Gurdwaras*. The main purpose of such pilgrimages is to join the congregations of these historic *Gurdwaras* and to meet the ideal Sikhs in order to learn from them their experiences in the spiritual realm. Usually a Sikh makes pilgrimages to four important *Gurdwaras*, which are Sikh Thrones (*Takhats*) or seats of authority. They are the following: Shri Takhat Amritsar; Shri Takhat Patna Saahib; Shri Takhat Keshgarh Saahib, Anandpur; and Shri Takhat Hazur Saahib, Nanded. The heads of these four centers of pilgrimage are considered authorities on Sikh religion. They are usually saints, soldiers and scholars. The pilgrimage, especially made to these four spiritual centers, helps a Sikh to build up his spiritual well-being.[115]

6.2.2. STAGES OF THE SIKH PATH

The genuine practice of interior ritual and communal paths brings in the seeker an ever-widening wonder about the reality of God (*Visamaad*), which, in turn, results in progressive subjugation of all evil inclinations and tendencies. The removal of evil inclinations and the ever-increasing awareness of God help the seeker to develop a sense of peace and joy. The seeker ascends to higher levels of understanding and experience of God. According to *Guru* Naanak, the aspirant ascends through five realms or stages of spiritual progress

(*Khands*) on his way to union with God. The five realms are the following: the realm of righteousness (*Dharam Khand*), the realm of knowledge (*Jnaan Khand*), the realm of effort, happiness and surrender (*Saram Khand*), 'the realm of Grace, Action and Fulfillment (*Karam Khand*) and the realm of Truth (*Sach Khand*).[116] We consider each of these in the following sections.

6.2.2.1. REALM OF RIGHTEOUSNESS

The stage of righteousness (*Dharam Khand*) refers to the life of creatures on this earth, whose lives are directed according to the law of cause and effect (*Karma*). In this world, we find beings of different kinds and habits. Each of them is judged according to one's acts. Hence, at this stage, the stress is on living a righteous life, by performing one's duty. Those persons, who do their duty, are called 'the elect', and they are honored in the court of God.[117] The *Japjii* describes the first stage of spiritual progress as follows:

> God made the night and the day,
> The days of the week and the months,
> And He made the seasons;
> He made winds to blow and water to run,
> He made fire; He made the lower regions;
> In the midst of all this He set the earth as a temple,
> On it He set a diversity of creatures,
> Various in kinds and color
> Endless the number of their names.
> All these lives are judged by their actions.
> God is True and in His Court is truth dispensed;
> There the elects are acceptable to Him,
> And by His Grace and His mercy
> Honored in His presence.
> In the Court the bad shall be sifted from the good
> When we reach His Court, O Naanak
> We shall know this to be true.[118]

Thus, the first stage of spiritual development points to the need to live a genuine moral and righteous life, in order that a person can move towards the final goal of union with God.

6.2.2.2. REALM OF KNOWLEDGE

The second stage is the stage of knowledge (*Jnaan Khand*). In this stage, the aspirant of salvation moves beyond the narrow vision the visible world. He experiences the vastness of the universe and its endless winds, waters and fires. He also has the vision of the realms of various gods, goddesses, demigods, demons and other spiritual beings. The experiences of the aspirant widen his understanding so that his knowledge becomes similar to that of 'the light of divine knowledge'. It results in the weakening of his self-centeredness, and he experiences deep feelings of joy in the levels of his speech, sight and action.[119] The *Japjii* describes this stage as follows:

> Now I shall describe ream of knowledge:
> How many are the winds, the fires, the waters,
> How many are the *Krishnas* and *Sivas*,
> How many are the *Brahmaas* fashioning the worlds,
> Of many kinds and shapes and colors;
> How many worlds, like our own there are,
> Where action produces the consequences.
> How many holy mountains to be climbed,
> With how many sages, like *Dhruva's* teacher, *Naarada*
> On the top of them.
> How many adepts, Buddhas and *Yogis* are there,
> How many goddesses and how many the images of the goddesses;
> How many gods and demons and how many sages;
> How many hidden jewels in how many oceans,
> How many the sources of life;
> How many the modes and diversities of speech,
> How many are the kings, the rulers and the guides of men;
> How many the devoted there are, who pursue this divine
>   knowledge,
> His worshippers are numberless ...[120]

Thus, in the second stage, the adept is filled with true knowledge so that the self-centeredness begins to vanish, and he moves towards God in an ascending manner. The knowledge that he is moving towards God makes him glad and fills in him a sense of complete joy.

6.2.2.3. REALM OF EFFORT, HAPPINESS AND SURRENDER

The third stage, viz., the *Saram Khand*, is interpreted in three different ways. The three interpretations show marked differences and emerge from the three different meanings of the word "*Saram*". Firstly, there are those thinkers, who understand the term "*Saram*" in its Sanskrit meaning, viz., 'labor' or 'toil. Taken in this sense, *Saram Khand* means 'the realm of effort'. There are other scholars who derive the term "*Saram*" from the Sanskrit "*Sarman*", which means 'happiness'. When we consider this sense, *Saram Khand* means 'the realm of bliss'. A third group of scholars derive the term "*Saram*" from the Persian "*Saram*", which means 'shame'. Taken in this sense, *Saram Khand* refers to 'the realm of humility' or 'the realm of surrender'. The real meaning of this stage is unclear. The description given in the *Japjii* does not clarify the exact nature of this stage.[121] To quote:

As in the realm of knowledge wisdom shines forth,
And Music is heard from the myriad joys proceed;
So in the realm of spiritual endeavor
The presiding deity is Beauty.
All things are shaped there incomparably,
The beauty of the place is beyond description;
And whosoever even attempts to describe it,
Will certainly afterwards feel deep remorse:
Understanding, discernment, the deepest wisdom is fashioned there.
There are created the gifts of the sages and seers.[122]

This quote indicates that *Saram Khand* is similar to the realm of knowledge, as genuine wisdom emerges from this stage. It is also portrayed as indescribable, and one may not succeed in describing it. All three meanings of the term "*Saram*" might help us to understand the reality of this stage. The realization of one's humble nature induces the seeker to make honest effort and surrender himself to God. Once this happens, one experiences within oneself a deep sense of joy and contentment. Though, strictly indescribable, this state stands for a deep spiritual experience which the adept goes through as he moves towards his final and ultimate union with God.[123]

6.2.2.4. REALM OF GRACE, ACTION AND FULFILLMENT

Karam Khand is the fourth stage. The term "*Karam*", when taken in the Persian meaning refers to 'Grace'. Hence *Karam Khand* stands for 'the realm of grace'. The second opinion states that the term "*Karam*" is derived from the Sanskrit term '*Karma*'. In this sense *Karam Khand* refers to 'the realm of action'. The fourth realm is the realm of grace. It can also be said to be the state achieved as the result of the good actions performed in the previous life. Hence, in the *Kharam Khand*, the seeker, both by the grace of God and by his own past actions, achieves a high state of spiritual existence. Therefore, *Karam Khand* can be translated as 'the realm of fulfillment'. But complete fulfillment of union with God is achieved only in the last stage.[124] The *Japjii* says the following regarding the *Karam Khand*:

In the realm of Grace, spiritual power is supreme,
Nothing else avails;
There dwell doughty warriors brave and strong,
In whom is the Lord's Spirit,
And who by His praise are blended in Him.
Their beauty is beyond telling,
In their hearts the Lord dwelleth,
They do not die and they are not deceived.
There dwell also the congregations of the blessed,
In bliss they dwell, with the true one in their hearts.[125]

6.2.2.5. REALM OF TRUTH

The realm of truth (*Sach Khand*) is the fifth and the final realm of God-realization. In this stage, the seeker moves into the dwelling place of the formless one. At this stage, the seeker realizes a unity with God, which can only be described in terms of infinity. It is a stage of ultimate climax of the seeker's search for truth, where the seeker is in perfect harmony with the Divine Order (*Hukam*). Thus, *Sach Khand* is the ultimate purpose of human existence and the final consummation of one's ascend to God. This realm is to be conceived in terms of the complete union of the individual with God, the Supreme Soul. This union with God completely ends all forms of transmigrations and the external and internal sufferings associated with it. The true nature of this state is beyond description, as it needs to be experienced rather than discussed. Yet we shall attempt to describe this realm, as far as human intelligence is capable. In the *Sach Khand*, the individual soul is finally absorbed in the Absolute God, leaving no trace or consciousness of duality. Thus, at the end of the spiritual journey, the blessed individual has no separate identity, as the Almighty God fills and pervades (*Samaanaa*) the individual soul. The individual soul merges and blends with the Supreme Being. It is the blending of the individual light in the Light of God (*Jotii joti Samaaunaa*). The *Aatma* of the individual is dissolved and becomes one with the *Parmaatmaa*. Besides, the individual union of the finite human being with the infinite, every reality and its truth is found in this realm of truth.[126] The following quote from the *Japjii* illustrates this point:

> In the realm of Truth,
> Dwelleth the Formless One
> Who, having created, watcheth His creation
> And where He looks upon them with Grace;
> And his creatures are happy.
> All continents, worlds, and universes
> Are contained in this supreme realm;
> Were one to strive to make an account of them all,
> There would be no end to the count.
> World there is on world there, form upon form there,
> And all have their functions as God's will ordaineth;
> The Lord seeth His creation and seeing it He rejoiceth.
> O Naanak, the telling is hard, as iron is hard to hand.[127]

When the seeker arrives at the realm of Truth, he transcends all transmigrations and lives in the condition of supreme wonder, contemplating the nature and beauty of God. At this condition, one experiences peace, perfect joy and complete tranquility. This experience is unutterable and beyond human description.

In this essay we have explored the Sikh path to the Divine and the various stages of this path. We have attempted to classify the Sikh path into three categories, viz., the interior path, the ritual path and the communal path. The interior path stresses the significance of the personal dimension in one's movement towards God. The ritual path focuses its attention on the external forms of worship, which are equally important aspects of man's movement towards God, as man is not only a spirit, but also is a bodily being. Tangible and ritual expressions of the interior life of the spirit are vital for a balanced journey towards God. The communal path points to the truth that a Sikh is not merely an isolated individual who journeys towards God all alone, but he is part of a larger community, which also strives to experience God. The community not only encourages the individual on his way to God, but also guides and directs his life with the help of prescribed laws and common forms of worship. In this manner, the Sikh religion presents to its adherents a well-balanced path, which takes care of the individual's journey towards God in its internal, external and communal dimensions.

CONCLUSION

The emergence of Sikhism, as a religion, responded to an historical need. At a time when bitter battles are waged between the Hindus and the Muslims, a belief and an outlook that takes one beyond the differing external forms, practices and schools is a necessity. *Guru* Naanak and his successors succeeded in presenting a system of beliefs that can take to God everyone, irrespective of caste, creed and sex. In so doing, the Sikh *Gurus* established a loose synthesis of Hindu *Bhakti* and Muslim Suufism. Thus, the religion of the Sikhs, as expressed in the *Aadi-Granth*, is a casteless and internal religion, which blends the tender devotion of a Hindu and the monotheistic belief of a Muslim. Though Sikhism originates as a peace-loving religion in the context of warring Hindus and Muslims with the aim of transcending both, due to historical expediency it turns out to be a religion that propagates militarism in practice. Only when their existence was threatened by the unjust acts of the Muslim emperors of Northern India did the *Gurus* take to militarism in self-defense. The belief behind such change in outlook is that 'when all other means fail, it is righteous to draw a sword'. Thus, in spite of their adherence of militarism as the last resort, Sikhism basically remains a religion that advocates pacifism.[128]

Sikhism, as a religion, is basically eclectic. The *Aadi-Granth*, the Sikh scripture, contains selections from not only the Sikh *Gurus*, but also from the *Bhagats*, the poets and the Suufi saints. After the time of the ten *Gurus*, there is the absence of true authority to guide the *Sikh-Panth* and to point out to them the great ideals of Sikhism. As a result, there came about a number of schisms within the Sikh religion. Besides, after the death of *Guru* Gobind Singh, Hindu practices became common in the *Gurdwaras*. Socially evil acts, such as Sati, began to exert influence among the Sikhs. For instance, at the death of the Sikh emperor Ranjit Singh his four widows and their seven maids are burnt with the king. The Sikh reform movements, such as, the *Niraankaari* Movement, the *Naamdhaari* Movement and the *Akaalii* Movement, have taken great trouble to weed out such evil practices and restore Sikhism to its original purity. Similarly, though Sikhism, in theory, is against all forms of caste and class distinctions, within the Sikh community, if we look at the present situation of the *Sikh-Panth*, we do find caste and class distinctions. Thus, to some extent Sikhism has fallen from its original ideal.[129]

In spite of these limitations, Sikhism is one of the recognized world religions. The immigration of the Sikhs to countries like United States, Canada and the European continent and their persistence in holding on to their heritage have brought about a better understanding of their religion. Besides, attempts are made to popularize the Sikh way of life and culture with the help of journals and other literature on Sikhism. Similarly, efforts are made to present the *Aadi-Granth*, the Sikh scripture, in modern versions and translations. These efforts have led to the joining of a small group of Euro-Americans to the Sikh-fold. These new converts have taken trouble to learn the Gurmukhi and Panjabi languages and are able to read the *Aadi-Granth* in the original. In this manner, Sikhism has become a religion that fulfills the religious aspiration of not only of Indian Sikhs, but also of others, converted to this religion.[130]

NOTES

1 Cf. Cf. C.H. Loehlin, *The Sikhs and Their Scriptures: An Introduction*, (Delhi: ISPCK – LPH, 1974), pp. 17-22,42. Cf. also K.S. Duggal, *The Sikh People: Yesterday &Today*, (New Delhi: UBS Publisher' Distributors Ltd, 1994), p. 23. Cf. also Surindar Singh Kohli, *Sikh Ethics*, (New Delhi: Munshiram Manoharlal Pvt. Ltd., 1974), p. 1. Cf. also Lajwanti Lahori, *The Concept of Man in Sikhism*, (New Delhi: Munshiram Manoharlal Publishers Pvt. Ltd., 1985), pp. 1-2.

2 Cf. Anil Chandra Banerjee, *The Sikh Gurus and the Sikh Religion*, (New Delhi: Munshiram Manoharlal Publishers Pvt. Ltd., 1983), pp. 1-41.

3 Cf. C.H. Loehlin, pp. 106-107.

4 Cf. W.H. McLeod, *Guruu Naanak* and the Sikh Religion, (New Delhi: Oxford University Press, 2001), p.1

5 Cf. Santokh Singh, *Philosophical Foundations of the Sikh Value System*, (New Delhi: Munshiram Manoharlal Publishers Pvt. Ltd., 1982), p. 7. Cf. also C.H. Loehlin, pp. 4-9.

6 Cf. Anil Chandra Banerjee, pp. 42-58.

7 Cf. C.H. Loehlin, pp. 3-8, 11. Cf. also Lajwanti Lahori, pp. 2-11. Cf. also Gurbhkhsh Singh, *A Panorama of Sikh Religion & Philosophy*, (Delhi: Bahubali Publications, 1985), pp.1-47.

8 Cf. Jesuit Scholars, pp. 266-267. Cf. also C. H. Loehlin, pp. 8-10. Cf. also Lajwanti Lahori, pp. 11-12.

9 Cf. C.H. Loehlin, pp. 10-11. Cf. also W.H. McLeod, *Guruu Naanak and the Sikh Religion*, p. 2.

10 Cf. C.H. Loehlin, pp. 27-28. Cf. also W.H. McLeod, *Guruu Naanak and the Sikh Religion*, p. 2. Cf. also Lajwanti Lahori, pp. 12-13.

11 Cf. Lajwanti Lahori, pp. 13. Cf. W.H. McLeod, *Guruu Naanak and the Sikh Religion*, pp. 2-3. Cf. also C.H. Loehlin, p. 28.

12 Cf. C.H. Loehlin, pp. 28-30. Cf. also Lajwanti Lahori, pp. 13-14. Cf. also Kushwant Singh, *A History of the Sikhs*, Vol. 2, (New Delhi: Oxford University Press, 1999), pp. 3-150.

13 Cf. Kushwant Singh, Vol. 2, pp. 239-420. Cf. also C.H. Loehlin, pp. 30-33. Cf. also Lajwanti Lahori, p. 14.

14 Cf. W.H. McLeod, *The Evolution of the Sikh Community*, (Delhi: Oxford University Press, 1998), pp. 59-60. Cf. also Gruinder Singh Mann, *The making of the Sikh Scripture*, (New Delhi: Oxford University Press, 2001), p. 4.

15 Cf. Kushwant Singh, Vol. 1, pp. 304-305. Cf. also W.H. MeLeod, *The Evolution of the Sikh Community*, pp. 60-63.

16 Cf. Ernest Trumpp, trans., *The Aadi Granth Or The Holy Scriptures of the Sikhs*, (New Delhi: Munshiram Manoharlal Publishers Pvt. Ltd., 1989), pp. cxix-cxx. Cf. also Kushwant Singh, Vol. 1, pp. 306-307. Cf. also Gurbaksh Singh, pp. 69-74.

17 Cf. Ernest Trumpp, pp. cxx-cxxi. Cf. also Gurinder Singh Mann, p. 5. Cf. also W.H. McLeod, *The Evolution of the Sikh Community*, pp. 70-73.

18 Cf. Kushwant Singh, Vol. I, pp. 313-318. Cf. also W.H. McLeod, *The Evolution of the Sikh Community*, pp. 79-81. Cf. also C.H. Loehlin, pp. 40-41.

19 Cf. Kushwant Singh, Vol. 1, p. 299. Cf. also W.H. McLeod, *The Evolution of the Sikh Community*, pp. 20-24.

20 Cf. W.H. McLeod, *Guruu Naanak and the Sikh Religion*, pp. 8-33. Cf. also W.H. McLeod, *The Evolution of the Sikh Community*, pp. 25-36. Cf. also Kushwant Singh, Vol. 1, pp. 299-301.

21 Cf. Kushwnt Singh, pp. 310-312. Cf. also W.H. McLeod, *The Evolution of the Sikh Community*, p. 81.

22 Cf. Santokh Singh, p. 10. Cf. also Surindar Singh Kohli, *Sikh Ethics*, pp. 68-74.

23 Cf. Gruinder Singh Mann, pp. 6-9.

24 Cf. Ibid., p. 9.

25 Cf. W.H. McLeod, *The Evolution of the Sikh Community*, pp. 1-19, 37-58.

26 Cf. Lajwanti Lahori, pp. 16-17.

27 Cf. Ibid., pp. 17-18.

28 Cf. Ibid., p. 17.

29 Cf. Ibid., p. 18.

30 Cf. Ibid., pp. 18-25.

31 Trilochan Singh, et al., trans., *Selections from the Sacred Writings of the Sikhs*, (London: George Allen & Unwin Ltd., 1973), p. 44.

32 Ibid., p. 28.

33 Cf. W.H. McLeod, *Guruu Naaanak and the Sikh Religion*, pp. 164-165. Cf. also Anil Chandra Banerjee, pp. 100-101.

34 Trilochan Singh, et al., p. 29.

35 Cf. W.H. McLeod, *Gruu Naanak and the Sikh Religion*, pp. 165-167. Cf. also Anil Chandra Banerjee, pp. 101-102.
36 Trilochan Singh, et al., pp. 46-47.
37 Cf. W.H. McLeod, *Guruu Naanak and the Sikh Religion*, pp. 167-168. Cf. also Anil Chandra Banerjee, pp. 102-103.
38 Cf. W.H. McLeod, *Guruu Naanak and the Sikh Religion*, p. 168. Cf. also Anil Chandra Banerjee, p. 104.
39 Trilochan Singh, et al., pp. 36-37.
40 Cf. W.H. McLeod, *Guruu Naanak and the Sikh Religion*, p. 169. Cf. also Anil Chandra Banerjee, p. 104.
41 Trilochan Singh et al., p. 45.
42 Cf. W.H. McLeod, *Gruu Naanak and the Sikh Religion*, pp. 169-170. Cf. also Anil Chandra Banerjee, p. 104.
43 Cf. W.H. McLeod, *Guruu Naanak and the Sikh Religion*, pp. 179. Cf. also Anil Chandra Banerjee, p. 105.
44 Cf. W.H. McLeod, *Guruu Naanak and the Sikh Religion*, pp. 170-172.
45 Cf. Ibid., p. 172.
46 Cf. Ibid., pp. 172-173.
47 Ibid., p. 173.
48 Cf. Ibid., pp. 173-175.
49 Ibid., pp. 174-175.
50 Cf. Ibid. pp. 175-176.
51 Cf. Ibid., pp. 176-177.
52 Cf. Surindar Singh Kohli, *Sikh Ethics*, p. 24.
53 Cf. Ibid., p. 25.
54 Cf. Ibid., pp. 25-26.
55 Cf. Ibid., p. 26.
56 Cf. Ibid., p. 27.
57 Cf. Ibid., p. 27.
58 Cf. Ibid., p. 28.
59 Cf. Ibid., pp. 28-29.
60 Cf. W.H. McLeod, *Guruu Naanak and the Sikh Religion*, pp. 189-191.
61 Cf. Ibid., pp. 191-193.
62 Cf. Ibid., pp. 193-194.
63 Cf. Ibid., pp. 195-196.
64 Cf. Ibid., pp. 196-197.
65 Ibid., pp. 197-198.
66 Cf. Ibid., pp. 198-199.
67 Cf. Ibid., p. 201. Cf. also Surindar Singh Kohli, *Outlines of Sikh Thought*, (New Delhi: Munshiram Manoharlal Publishers Pvt. Ltd., 1978), pp. 45-46.
68 Ernest Trumpp, p. 2.
69 Cf. W.H. McLeod, *Guruu Naanak and the Sikh Religion*, p. 200.
70 Cf. Ibid., pp. 201-202.

71 Surindar Singh Kohli, *Outlines of Sikh Thought*, pp. 47-48.
72 Cf. Cf. W.H. McLeod, *Guruu Naanak and the Sikh Religion*, p. 202.
73 Cf. Surindar Singh Kohli, *The Sikh Ethics*, pp. 22, 23-24.
74 Ibid., p. 23.
75 Cf. Surindar Singh Kohli, *Outlines of Sikh Thought*, p. 50.
76 Cf. Ibid., p. 49.
77 Cf. Ibid. Cf. also W.H. McLeod, *Guruu Naanak and the Sikh Religion*, pp. 204-207.
78 Surindar Singh Kohli, *Outlines of Sikh Thought*, pp. 49-50.
79 Cf. Ibid., p. 50.
80 Cf. W.H. McLeod, *Guruu Naanak and the Sikh Religion*, pp. 207-208.
81 Cf. Ibid., p. 208.
82 Ibid., pp. 208-209.
83 Cf. Ibid., pp. 209-210
84 Cf. Ibid., pp.210-212.
85 Ibid., pp. 212-213.
86 Cf. Ibid., pp. 213-214.
87 Cf. Ibid., pp. 214-217.
88 Cf. Lajwanti Lahori, pp. 107-108. Cf. also W.H. McLeod, *Guruu Naanak and the Sikh Religion*, pp. 217-219.
89 Cf. Lajwanti Lahori, pp.109-110. Cf. also W.H. McLeod, *Guruu Naanak and the Sikh Religion*, pp. 219-221.
90 Trilochan Singh, et al., pp. 41-42.
91 Cf. Lajwanti Lahori, pp. 110-112. Cf. also Santokh Singh, pp. 85-86.
92 Cf. Surindar Singh Kohli, *Outlines of Sikh Thought*, p. 104.
93 Cf. Surindar Singh Kohli, *Outlines of Sikh Thought*, pp. 104-105. Cf. also W. Owen Cole and Piara Singh Sambhi, *A Popular Dictionary of Sikhism*, (Calcutta: Rupa & Co., 1990), pp. 122-123.
94 Cf. Jean Holms, pp. 145, 153-154.
95 Cf. Ibid., p. 154.
96 Cf. Ibid., pp. 149-150.
97 Cf. Kushwant Singh, Vol. 1, pp. 307-308. Cf. also W.H. McLeod, *The Evolution of Sikh Community*, pp. 63-66. Cf. also Jean Holm, pp. 153-154.
98 Cf. W.H. McLeod, *The Evolution of the Sikh Community*, pp. 66-68.
99 Cf. Ibid., p. 68. Cf. also Kushwant Singh, Vol. 1, p. 308.
100 Cf. Kushwant Singh, Vol. 1, p. 308.
101 Cf. Jean Holm, pp. 155-156.
102 Cf. Harbans Kaur Sagoo, *Guru Nanak and the Indian Society*, (New Delhi: Deep & Deep Publications, 1992), p. 100.
103 Cf. Ibid., pp. 100-103.
104 Cf. Ibid., p. 103.
105 Cf. Ibid., pp. 104-105.
106 Cf. Ibid., pp. 105-106.
107 Cf. Ibid., pp. 106-112.

Paths to the Divine 621

108 Cf. Ibid., pp. 112-118.
109 Cf. Jean Holm, p. 152.
110 Cf. Ibid., pp. 152-153.
111 Cf. Ibid., pp. 156-157.
112 Cf. Ibid., p. 157.
113 Cf. Surindar Singh Kohli, *Outlines of Sikh Thought*, pp. 106-107.
114 Cf. Ibid., p. 107.
115 Cf. Ibid.
116 Cf. W.H. McLeod, *Guruu Naanak and the Sikh Religion*, p. 221.
117 Cf. Anil Chandra Banerjee, p. 106. Cf. also W.H. McLeod, *Guruu Naanak and the Sikh Religion*, p. 221.
118 Trilochan Singh et al., p. 48.
119 Cf. Anil Chandra Banerjee, p. 106. Cf. also W.H. McLeod, *Guruu Naanak and the Sikh Religion*, pp. 221-222.
120 Trilochan Singh, et al., p. 49.
121 Cf. W.H. McLeod, *Guruu Naanak and the Sikh Religion*, p. 222. Cf. also Anil Chandra Banerjee, pp. 106-107.
122 Trilochan Singh et al., pp. 49-50.
123 Cf. W.H. McLeod, *Guruu Naanak and the Sikh Religion*, pp. 222-223.
124 Cf. W.H. McLeod, *Guruu Naanak and the Sikh Religion*, p. 223. Cf. also Anil Chandra Banerjee, p. 107.
125 Trilochan Singh, et al., p. 50.
126 Cf. W.H. McLeod, *Guruu Naanak and the Sikh Religion*, pp. 223-226. Cf. also Anil Chandra Banerjee, p. 107.
127 Trilochan Singh, et al., p. 50.
128 Cf. Jesuit Scholars, p. 270. Cf. also John A. Hardon, Vol. 1, pp. 251-252.
129 Cf. Jesuit Scholars, p. 270. Cf. also W.H. McLeod, *The Evolution of the Sikh Community*, pp. 83-104. Cf. also John A. Hardon, Vol. 1, p. 250.
130 Cf. Mark Juergensmeyer and N. Gerald Barrier, eds.: *Sikh Studies: Comparative Perspectives on a Changing Tradition*, (Berkeley: Berkeley Religious Studies Series Graduate Theological Union, 1979), pp. 127-213. Cf. also Gurinder Singh Mann, pp. 134-136.

Bibliography

General Studies on Religion

Bowker, John: *Worship*, in *Themes in Religious Studies*, ed. Jean Holm and John Bowker. London: Pinter Publishers, 1994.

Brown, David A.: *A Guide to Religion*. London: SPCK, 1980.

Eastman, Roger, ed.: *The Ways of Religion: An Introductions to the Major Traditions*. New York: Oxford University Press, 1993.

Editorial Staff of Life: *The World's Great Religions*. New York: Golden Press, 1958.

Hardon, John A.: *Religions of the World*, 2 Vols. New York: Image Books, 1969.

Herod, F.G.: *World Religions*. Illinois: Argus Communications, 1975.

Holmn, Jean: *Worship*. London: Pinter Publishers Ltd., 1994.

Jurji, Edward J., ed.: *The Great Religions of the Modern World*. Princeton New Jersey: Princeton University Press, 1967.

Lala, Chhaganlal: *Bhakti in the Religions of the World*. Delhi: B.R. Publishing Corporation, 1986.

Macnicol, Nicol: *The Living Religions of Indian People*. New Delhi: Oriental Books Reprint Corporation, 1979.

Pandit, M.P.: *Traditions in Mysticism*. Bangalore: Sterling Publishers Private Ltd., 1987.

Perry, A.E.: *How People Worship*. Surrey: Denholm House Press, 1974.

Ringgren, Helmer and Ake V. Stroem, *Religions of Mankind: Today & Yesterday*. Philadelphia: Fortress Press, 1967.

Singh, Herbert Jai: *My Neighbors: Men of Different Faiths*. Bangalore: Christian Institute For the Study of Religion and Society, 1966.

Srivastava, Rama Shanker: *Comparative Religion*. New Delhi: Munshiram Manoharlal Publishers Pvt. Ltd., 1974.

Smart, Ninian: *The Religious Experience of Mankind*. New York: Found Paperbacks, 1977.

Woolson, Gayle: *Divine Symphony*. New Delhi: Baha'i Publishing Trust, 1976.

Primitive Religious Tradition

Best, Esdon: *The Maori*. Wellington: Publication of the Board of Maori Ethnological Research on behalf of the Polynesian Society, 1924.

Codrington, R.H.: *The Melanesians: Their Anthropology and Folklore*. London: O.U.P., 1891.

Handy, E.S.C.: *Polynesian Religion*. Honolulu: Bayard Dominique Publications, 1927.

Idowu, E. Bolaji: "Errors in Terminology" *The Ways of Religion: An Introduction to Major Traditions*, ed. Roger Eastman, 2nd edition. New York: Oxford University press, 1993.

Idowu, E. Bolaji: *African Traditional Religion*. London: SCM Press Ltd., 1973.

Mbiti, John S.: "Divinities, Spirits, and the Living-Dead", *The Ways of Religion: An Introduction to Major Traditions*, ed. Roger Eastman, 2nd edition. New York: Oxford University press, 1993.

Mbiti, John S.: *African Religions and Philosophy*. New York: Doubleday, 1970.

Murray, ed.: *Cultural Atlas of Africa*. New York: Facts on File, 1981.

Parrinder, E. Geoffrey: "God in African Belief", *The Ways of Religion: An Introduction to Major Traditions*, ed. Roger Eastman, 2nd edition. New York: Oxford University press, 1993.

Parrinder, E. Geoffrey: *Religion in Africa*. London: Penguin Books Ltd., 1969.

Smith, Edwin, ed.: *African Ideas of God*. London: Edinburgh House Press, 1950.

Zuesse, Evan M.: *Ritual Cosmos: The Sanctification in African Religion*. Athens, Ohio: Ohio University Press, 1979.

Greek-Hellenistic-Roman Tradition

Apuleius: *The Golden Ass*, trans. S. Gaselee. London: Leob Library, W. Heinemann, 1922.

Armstrong, A.H. (ed.): *Classical Mediterranean Spirituality: Egyptian, Greek, Roman*. New York: SCM Press Ltd., 1986.

Armstrong, A.H.: "The Ancient and Continuing Pieties of the Greek World". *Classical Mediterranean Spirituality: Egyptian, Greek, Roman*, ed. A.H. Armstrong, pp. 66-101.

Bailey, C.: *Phases in the Religion of Ancient Rome. Sather Classical Lectures 10.* Oxford: Clarendon Press, 1932.

Bowra, C.M. and the Editors of Time-Life Books: *Classical Greece*. United States: Time-Life International (Nederland) N.V., 1971.

Budge, Wallis: *Osiris*. Vol. II. London: Medici Society, 1911.

Dodds, E.R.: *The Greeks and the Irrational*. Berkeley and Los Angeles: University of California Press, 1951.

Festugiere, A.J.: *Personal Religion among the Greeks. Sather Classical Lectures 26.* Berkeley and Los Angeles: University of California Press, 1960.

Fowler, W. Warde: *The Roman Festivals of the Period of the Republic. Handbook of Archeology and Antiquities*. London: Macmillan, 1899.

Fowler, W. Warde: *The Religious Experience of the Roman People from the Earliest Times to the Age of Augustus. Gifford Lectures for 1909-1910.* London: Macmillan, 1911.

Fowler, W. Warde: *Roman Ideas of Deity in the Last Century before the Christian Era.* London: Macmillan, 1914.

Guthrie, W.D.C.: *Greeks and Their Gods.* London: Methuen, 1950.

Guthrie, W.D.C.: *Orpheus and Greek Religion.* 2nd rev. ed. London: Methuen, 1950.

Gow, A.S.F. (ed. & trans.): *Theocritus*, Vol. I. London: C.U.P., 1950

Halliday, W.R.: *Lectures on the History of Roman Religion: From Numa to Augustus.* London: Hodder & Stoughton, 1922.

Harrison, Jane: *A Prolegomena to the Study of Greek Religion.* London: O.U.P., 1922.

Liebeschutz, J.H.W.: *Continuity and Change in Roman Religion.* Oxford: Clarendon Press, 1979.

MacMullen, Ramsay: *Paganism in the Roman Empire.* New Haven: Yale University Press, 1981.

Moris, William Sir, trans.: *The Iliad of Homer.* London: O.U.P., 1934.

Nilsson, Martin P.: *Greek Popular Religion.* Oxford: Clarendon Press, 1948.

Nilsson, Martin P.: *The Dionysiac Mysteries of the Hellenistic and Roman Age.* Acta Instituti Atheniensis Regni Sueciae 8.5. Lund: Gleerup, 1957.

Ogilvie, R.M.: *The Romans and Their Gods in the Age of Augustus. Ancient Culture and Society.* London: Chatto & Windus, 1969.

Otto, W.F.: *Homeric Gods: The Spiritual Significance of Greek Religion.* London: Thames & Hudson, 1954.

Paley, F.A., trans.: *The Odes of Pindar.* Cambridge: Deighton Bell & Co., 1868.

Perowne, Stewart: *Roman Mythology.* London: Hamlyn, 1988.

Pinsent, John: "Roman Spirituality". *Classical Mediterranean Spirituality: Egyptian, Greek, Roman*, ed. A.H. Armstrong, pp. 154-194.

Rose, H.J.: *A Handbook of Greek Mythology.* 3rd rev. ed. London: Methuen, 1945.

Rose, H.J.: *Ancient Roman Religion. Hutchinson's University Library 27.* London: Hillary House, 1948.

Scullard, H.H.: *Festivals and Ceremonies of the Roman Republic. Aspects of Greek and Roman Life.* London: Thames & Hudson, 1981.

Smyth, W.H. (ed. & trans.): *Aischylus*, Vol. II. London: Loeb Library, W. Heinemann, 1950.

Storr, F., ed. & trans.: *Sophocles*, Vol. II. London: Loeb Library, William Heinemann, 1919.

White, Hugh Evelyn, ed. & trans.: *Hesiod, the Homeric Hymns, and Homerica.* London: Leob Library, W. Heinemann, 1914.

Hindu Tradition

Bahadur, Om Lata: *The Book of Hindu Festivals and Ceremonies*. New Delhi: UBSPD, 1997.

Basham, A.L.: *The Origins and Development of Classical Hinduism*. Delhi: Oxford University Press, 1990.

Bloomfield, Maurice: *Hymns of the Athava-Veda*. Sacred Books of the East, ed. F. Max Mueller. Vol. 42. Delhi: Motilal Banarsidass, 1979.

Bhattacharyya, Narendra Nath: *Indian Puberty Rites*. New Delhi: Munshiram Manoharlal Publishers Pvt. Ltd., 1980.

Buehler, G., trans.: *The Laws of Manu*. The Sacred Book of the East, ed. F. Max Mueller. Vol. 25. Delhi: Motilal Banarsidass, 1979.

Carman, John Braisted: *The Theology of Raamaanuja*. Indian Reprint. Bombay: Ananthacharya Indological Research Institute, 1981.

Chari, S.M. Srinivasa: *Vaishnavism: Its Philosophy, Theology and Religious Discipline*. Delhi: Motilal Banarsidass Publishers Private Limited, 2000.

Chaudhuri, Nirad C.: *Hinduism: A Religion to Live By*. 5th Impression. Oxford: Oxford University Press, 1999.

Danielou, Alain: *Hindu Polytheism*. London: Routledge & Kegan Paul, Ltd., 1964

Dasgupta, S.N.: *Hindu Mysticism*: Delhi: Motilal Banarsidass, 1987.

Deusen, Paul: *The Philosophy of the Upanishads*. New York: Dover Publications Inc., 1966.

Deutsch, Eliot: *Advaita Vedaanta – A Philosophical Reconstruction*, 2nd ed. Honolulu: The University Press of Hawaii, 1962.

Eggeling, Julies, trans.: *The Satapatha-Braahmana*. Sacred Books of the East, ed. F.Max Mueller. Vols. 12, 26, 41, 43, 44. Delhi: Motilal Banarsidass, 1978, 1978, 1972, 1978,1972.

Gambhirananda, Swami, trans.: *Brahma-Suutra Bhaashya*, 3rd ed. Calcutta: Advaita Ashrama, 1977.

Griffith, Ralph T.H., trans.: *The Hymns of the Rig Veda*. Delhi: Motilal Banarsidass Publishers Private Limited, 1986.

Harshananda, Swami: *Hindu Gods and Goddesses*. Madras: Sri Ramakrishna Math, 1982.

Hume R.E., ed.: *The Thirteen Principal Upanishads*. New York: Princeton University Press, 1973.

Jaiswal, Suvira: *The Origin and Development of Vaishnavism*. New Delhi: Munshiram Manoharlal Publishers Pvt. Ltd., 1981.

Jesuit Scholars: *Religious Hinduism: A Presentation and Appraisal*. Allahabad: St. Paul Publications, 1964.

Jee, Swami Lakshman: *Kashmir Shaivism: The Secret Supreme*. Delhi: Sri Satguru Publications, 1991.

Kaul, H. Kumar: *Aspects of Yoga*. Delhi: B.R. Publishing Corporation, 1994.

Keith, A.B.: *Religion and Philosophy of the Veda*. London: Oxford University, 1925.

Kinsley, David: *Hindu Goddesses: Visions of the Divine Feminine in the Hindu Religious Tradition*. Delhi: Motilal Banarsidass, 1986.

Kumar, Frederick L.: *Philosophy of Saivism: An Existential Analysis of Its Underlying Experiences*. New Delhi: Oxford & IBH Publishing Co. Pvt. Ltd., 1988.

Macnicol, Nicol: *Indian Theism: From the Vedic to the Muhammadan Period*. Delhi: Muhshiram Manoharlal, 1968.

Mathothu, Kurian: *The Development of the Concept of Trimuurthi in Hinduism*. Palai: St. Paul's Press Training School, 1974.

Mishra, Kamalakar: *Kashmir Saivism: The Central Philosophy of Tantrism*. Delhi: Sri Satguru Publications, 1999.

Murthy, H.V. Sreenivasa: *Vaishnavism of Samkaradeva and Raamaanuja*. Delhi: Motilal Banarsidass, 1973.

Nikhilananda, Swami: *Hinduism: Its Meaning for the Liberation of the Spirit*. Madras: Sri Ramakrishna Math, 1982.

Nihilananda, Swami, trans.: *Vedaantasaara of Sadaananda Yorindra*, Calcutta: Advaita Ashrama, 1968.

Pandey, Rajbali: *Hindu Samskaaras: Socio-Religious Study of the Hindu Sacraments*. Delhi: Motilal Banarsidas, 1987.

Pandey, R.K.: *The Concept of Avatars*. Delhi: B.R. Publishing Corporation, 1979.

Parthasarathy, A.: *The Symbolism of Hindu Gods and Rituals*. Bombay: Vedanta Life Institute, 1989.

Parthasarathy, A.: *Vedaanta Treatise*, 3rd ed. Bombay: Vedaanta Life Institute, 1989.

Pavgee, N.B.: "Soma Juice Is Not Liquor", *Proceedings and Transactions of the Third Oriental Conference*. Madras: University of Madras, 1924.

Radhakrishnan S.: *The Bhagavadgiitaa*. 15th Impression. New Delhi: HarperColins Publishers India Pvt. Ltd., 2000.

Radhakrishnan S.: *The Hindu View of Life*. New York: Macmillan, 1927.

Radhakrishnan, S.: *The Principal Upanishads*, 3rd impression. London: George Allen & Unwin Ltd., 1969.

Ramamurthi A.: *Advaitic Mysticism of Shankara*. West Bengal: The Center of Advanced Study in Philosophy, Vishva Bharati, Shanti Niketan, 1974.

Sen, K.M.: *Hinduism*. Middlesex: Penguin Books, 1975.

Shankara: *Aatmabhoodha [Knowledge of the Self]*, trans. A. Parthasarathy, 3rd ed. Bombay: Vedaanta Life Institute, 1960

Shankara: *Aprokshaanubhuuti (Self-realization) of Sri Shankaraachaariya*, trans. Swami Vimuktananda. Calcutta: Advaita Ashrama, 1977.

Shankara: *Crest-Jewel of Discrimination (Viveka-Chudaamani)*, trans. Swami Prabhavananda and Christopher Isherwood, 3rd ed. California: Vedanta Press, 1978.

Shankara: *Self-knowledge (Aatmabhooda)*, trans. Swami Niilananda. New York: Ramakrishana Vivekananta Centre, 1980.

Shankara: "Statasloki", *The Works of Shankara*, Vol. XV. Srirangam: Srivanivilas, 1910.

Shankara: *Upanishad Bhaasyas (Aitareeya, Iisha, Kaatha, Keena, Mundaka, Prasana and Taittiiriya Upanishads)*, trans. Swamin Gambhirananda, 2 Vols. Calcutta: Advaita Ashrama, 1957.

Sharma, B.N.K.: *Philosophy of Srii Madhvaacaarya*. Delhi: Motilal Barsidass, 1986

Sharma, D.S.: *What is Hinduism?* Madras: G.S. Press, 1939.

Sharma, D.S.: *Essence of Hinduism*. Bombay: Bharatiya Vidya Bhavan, 1971.

Sharma, Krishna: *Bhakti and the Bhakti Movement: A New Perspective*. New Delhi: Munshiram Manoharlal Publishers Pvt. Ltd., 1987.

Sharma, L.N.: *Kashmir Savism*. Delhi: Bharatiya Vidya Prakashan, 1996.

Siddhantashastree, Rabindra Kumar: *Saivism through the Ages*. New Delhi: Munshiram Manoharlal Publishers Pvt. Ltd., 1975.

Siddhantashastree, Rabindra Kumar: *Vaishnavism through the Ages*. New Delhi: Munshiram Manhorlal Pvt. Ltd., 1985.

Sinari, Ramkant A.: *The Structure of Indian Thought*. Illinois: Charles E. Thomas Publisher, 1970.

Sinha, Jadunath: *Schools of Saivism*. Calcutta: Jadunath Sinha Foundation, 1975.

Sircar, Mahendranath: The *System of Vedic Thought and Culture*. Delhi: Anmol Publications, 1987.

Sivananda, Sri Swami: *Lord Shiva and His Worship*. Tehri-Garhwal: The Divine Life Society, 1984.

Sivananda, Sri Swami: *Science of Yoga*, Vol. 5, Tehri-Garhwal: The Divine Life Society, 1981.

Sivaraman, K.: *Saivism in Philosophical Perspective*. Delhi: Motilal Banarsidass, 1973.

Tagare, Ganesh Vasudeo, trans.: *The Bhaagavata Puraana, Ancient Indian Tradition & Mythology*, ed. J.L. Shastri, Vols. 7-11, Parts 1-5. Delhi: Motilal Banarsidass, 1986, 1986, 1987,1988, 1989.

Thibaut, George, tans.: *Brahma-Sutras*. Mayavata: Advaita Ashrama, 1948

Zaehner, R.C.: *Hinduism*. London: Oxford University Press, 1966.

Jaina Tradition

Babb, Lawrence A.: *Ascetics and Kings in a Jain Ritual Culture, Lala Sundarlal Jain Research Series*, ed. Satya Ranjan Banerjee, Vol. XI. Delhi: Motilal Banarsidass Publishers, 1998.

Bhattacharyya, Narendra Nath: *Jain Philosophy: Historical Outline*. New Delhi: Munshiram Manoharal Publishers Pvt. Ltd., 1976

Chaatterjee, Asim Kumar: *A Comprehensive History of Jainism*. Calcutta: Firma KLM Private Limited, 1978.

Glasenapp, Helmuth Von: *Jainism: An Indian Religion of Salvation*, trans. Shridhar B. Shrotri, *Lala Sundarlal Jain Research Series*, ed. Satya Ranjan Banerjee, Vol. XIV. Delhi: Motilal Banarsidass Publishers Private Limited, 1999.

Jain, Shri Satish Kumar, ed.: *Perspectives in Jaina Philosophy and Culture*. New Delhi: Ahimsa International, 1985.

Jaini, Padmanabh S., ed.: *Collected Papers on Jaina Studies*. Delhi: Motilal Banarsidass Publishers Private Limited, 2000.

Jaini, Padmanabh S.: *The Jaina Path of Purification*. Delhi: Motilal Banarsidass Publishers Private Limited, 1998.

Nahar, P.C. and K.C. Ghosh, eds.: *An Encyclopaedia of Jainism, Sri Garib Dass Oriental Series*, No. 40. Delhi: Sri Satguru Publications, 1996.

Saastrii, Saahitya Vaacspati Srii Devendra Muni: *Jaina Religion and Philosophy: An Introduction*, trans. Kewal Krishan Mittal. Udaipur: Srii Taarak Guru Jain Granthaalya, 1985.

Schubring, Walther: *The Doctrine of the Jainas: Described after the Old Sources*, trans. Woflgang Beurlen, *Lala Sundarlal Jain Research Series*, ed. Satya Ranjan Banerjee, Vol. XV. Delhi: Motilal Bararsidass Publishers Private Lmited.

Shah, Nagin J., ed.: *Jaina Theory of Multiple Facets of Reality and Truth, BLII Series*, No. 13. Delhi: Motilal Banarsidass Publisher Private Limited & Bhogilal Leherchand Institute of Indology, 2000.

Sharma, Arvind: *A Jaina Perspective on the Philosophy of Religion, Lala Sundarlal Research Series*, ed. Satya Ranjan Banerjee, Vol. XVI. Delhi: Motilal Banarsidass Publishers Private Limited, 2001.

Stevenson, Sinclair: *The Heart of Jainism*. New Delhi: Munshiram Manoharlal Publishers Pvt. Ltd., 1984.

Buddhist Tradition

Bapat, P.V., ed.: *2500 Years of Buddhism*. New Delhi: Publication Division, Ministry of Information and Broadcasting, Government of India, 1997.

Bu-ston: *The History of Buddhism in India and Tibet*, trans. E. Obermiller. Delhi: Sri Satguru Publications, 1999.

Coomaraswamy, Ananda K.: *Buddha and the Gospel of Buddhism*. Delhi: Munshiram Manoharlal Publishers Pvt. Ltd., 1985.

Cowell, E.B., et al., trans.: *Buddhist Mahaayaana Texts, The Sacred Books of the East*, ed. F. Max Mueller, Vol. XLIX. Delhi: Motilal Banarsidass, 1978.

Cronze, Edward: *Buddhism: Its Essence and Development*. Delhi: Munshiram Manoharlal Publishers, Pvt. Ltd., 1999.

Cronze, Edward, trans.: *Buddhist Scriptures*. Middlesex: Penguin Books, 1976.

Davids, T.W. Rhys, trans.: *Buddhist-Sutras, The Sacred Books of the East*, ed. F. Max Mueller. Vol. XI. Motilal Banarsidass, 1973.

Dutt, Sukumar: *The Buddha and Five After-centuries*. Calcutta: Sahitya Samsad, 1978.

Fernando, Antony: *Buddhism Made Plain: An Introduction for Christians*. Indore: Satprakshan Sanchar Kendra, 1981.

Gellner, David N.: *Monk, Householder, and Tantric Priest: Newar Buddhism and its Hierarchy of Ritual*. New Delhi: Foundation Books, 1996.

Gethin, Rupert: *The Foundations of Buddhism*. New York: Oxford University press, 1998.

Gour, Sri Hari Singh: *The Spirit of Buddhism*, 2 Vols. New Delhi: Cosmo Publications, 1986.

Griffiths, Paul J.: *On Being Buddha: The Classical Doctrine of Buddhahood*. Delhi: Sri Satguru Publications, 1995.

Guenther, Herbert V.: *Buddhist Philosophy: In Theory and Practice*. Baltimore: Pelican Books, 1972.

Hazra, Kanai Lal: *The Rise and Decline of Buddhism in India*. Delhi: Munshiram Manoharlal Publishers Pvt. Ltd., 1995.

Horner, Isaline Blew: *The Early Buddhist Theory of Man Perfected*. New Delhi: Oriental Books Reprint Corporation, 1979.

Humphreys, Christmas: *Buddhism*. Middlesex: Penguin Books, 1962.

Johnston, E.H., trans.: *Asvaghosha's Buddhacarita or Acts of the Buddha*. Delhi: Motilal Banarsidass Publishers Private Limited, 1995.

Kalupahana, David J.: *A History of Buddhist Philosophy: Continuities and Discontinuities*. Delhi: Motilal Banarsidass Publishers Private Limited, 1994.

Kawamura, L.S. and G.M. Nagao, eds.: *Maadhyamika and Yogaacaara: A Study of Mahyaanaaya Philosophies*. Delhi: Sri Satguru Publications, 1992.

Keith, A. Berriedale: *Buddhist Philosophy in India and Ceylon*. Oxford: The Clarendon Press, 1923.

Keown, Damien: *Buddhism: A Very Short Introduction*. Oxford: Oxford University Press, 1996.

Kirthisinghe, Buddhadasa P., ed.: *Buddhist Concepts: Old and New*. Delhi: Sri Satguru Publications, 1983.

Kiyota, Minoru and Elvin W. Jones, eds.: *Mahaayaana Buddhist Meditation: Theory and Practice*. Delhi: Motilal Banarsidass Publishers Pvt. Ltd., 1991.

Kopp, Sheldon: *If You Meet the Buddha on the Road, Kill Him!.* London: Sheldon Press, 1980.

Lay, U Ko, comp.: *Guide to Tipitaka*. Delhi: Sri Satguru Publications, 1990.

Lien, Bhikkhunii T.N. Tin: *Concepts of Dhamma in Dhammapada*. Delhi: Eastern Book Linkers, 1996.

Ling, Trevor: *The Buddha: Buddhist Civilization in India and Ceylon*. New York: Pelican Books, 1976.

Maguire, Jack: *Essential Buddhism: A Complete Guide to Beliefs and Practices*. New York: Pocket Books, 2001.

Merton, Thomas: *Thomas Merton on Zen*. London: Sheldon Press, 1976.

Monier-Williams, M.: *Buddhism: In Its Connection with Braahmanism and Hinduism, and Its Contrast with Christianity*. Delhi: Munshiram Manoharlal Publishers Pvt. Ltd., 1995.

Mueller, F. Max, trans.: *The Dhammapada, The Sacred Books of the East*, ed. F. Max Mueller. Vol. X. Delhi: Motilal Banarsidass, 1973.

Mullin, Glenn H., ed.: *The Path to Enlightenment*. New York: Snow Lion Publications, 1995.

Nyanatiloka: *Buddhist Dictionary: Manual of Buddhist Terms and Doctrines*, ed. Nyanapomika. Colombo: Frewin & Co., Ltd., 1972.

Oldenberg, Hermann: *Buddha: His Life, His Doctrine, His Order*, trans. William Hoey. Delhi: Motilal Banarsidass Publishers Private Limited, 1997.

Pandit, Moti Lal: *Suunyataa: The Essence of Mahaayaana Spirituality*. New Delhi: Munshiram Manoharlal Publishers Pvt. Ltd., 1998.

Poussin, L. De La Vallee: *The Way to Nirvaana*. Delhi: Sri Satguru Publications, 1982.

Saher, P.J.: *Zen-Yoga: A Creative Psychotherapy to Self-Integration*. Delhi: Motilal Banarsidass Publishers Private Limited, 1999.

Santina, Peter Della: *Madhyamaka Schools in India*. Delhi: Motilal Banarsidass Private Limited, 1995.

Sayama, Mike K.: *Samadhi: Self-Development in Zen, Swordsmanship, and Psychology*. Delhi: Satguru Publications, 1991.

Singh, Nisha: *The Origin and Development of Buddhist Monastic Education in India*. Delhi: Indo-Asian Publishing House, 1997.

Stcherbatsky, Th.: *The Conception of Buddhist Nirvaana*. Delhi: Motilal Banarsidass Publishers Private Limited, 1999.

Suzuki, Daisetz Teitaro: *Living by Zen*, ed. Christmas Humphreys. London: Rider, 1990.

Takakusu, Junjiroo: *The Essentials of Buddhist Philosophy*, eds. Wing-

tsit Chan and Charles A. Moore. Delhi: Motilal Bararsidass Publishers Private Limited, 1998.
Thomas, Edward J.: *The History of Buddhist Thought*. Delhi: Munshram Manoharlal Publishers Pvt. Ltd., 1997.
Watts, Alan: *This Is It and Other Essays on Zen and Spiritual Experience*. New York: Vintage Books, 1973.
Williams, Paul: *Mahaayaana Buddhism: The Doctrinal Foundations*. London: Routledge, 1996.
Wright, Dale S.: *Philosophical Meditations on Zen Buddhism*. New York: Cambridge University Press, 1998.
Zen Buddhism. New York: The Peter Pauper Press, 1959.

Sikh Tradition

Banerjee, Anil Chandra: *The Sikh Gurus and the Sikh Religion*. New Delhi: Munshiram Manoharlal Publishers Pvt. Ltd., 1983.
Cole, W. Owen and Piara Singh Sambhi, eds.: *A Popular Dictionary of Sikhism*. Calcutta: Rupa & Co., 1990.
Deora, Man Singh: *Guru Gobind Singh: A Literary Survey*. New Delhi: Anmol Publications, 1989.
Duggal, K.S.: *The Sikh Gurus: Their Lives and Teachings*. New Delhi: Vikas Publishing House Pvt. Ltd., 1980.
Duggal, K.S.: *The Sikh People: Yesterday and Today*. New Delhi: UBS Publishers' Distributors Ltd., 1994.
Grewal, J.S. and Indu Banga, eds.: *The Khalsa over 300 Years*. New Delhi: Tulika, 1999.
Jain, Nirmal Kumar: *Sikh Religion and Philosophy*. New Delhi: Sterling Publishers Pvt. Ltd., 1979.
Jain, S.C.: *A Panorama of Sikh Religion and Philosophy*. Delhi: Bahubali Publications, 1985.
Juergensmeyer, Mark and N. Gerald Barrier, eds.: *Sikh Studies: Comparative Perspectives on a Changing Tradition*. Berkeley: Berkeley Religious Studies Series Graduate Theological Union, 1979.
Kapoor, Sukhbir Singh: *Philosophy: Facts and Fundamentals of Sikh Religion*. New Delhi: Hemkunt Press, 1994.
Kohli, Surindar Singh: *Sikh Ethics*. New Delhi: Munshiram Manoharlal Publishers Pvt. Ltd., 1975.
Kohli, Surindar Singh: *Outlines of Sikh Thought*. New Delhi: Munshiram Manoharlal Publishers Pvt. Ltd., 1978.
Lahori, Lajwanti: *The Concept of Man in Sikhism*. New Delhi: Munshiram Manoharlal Publishers Pvt. Ltd., 1985.
Loehlin, C.H.: *The Sikhs and Their Scriptures: An Introduction*. Delhi: ISPCK-LPH, 1974.

Mann, Gurinder Singh: *The Making of Sikh Scripture*. New Delhi: Oxford University Press, 2001.

Macauliffe, Max Arthur: *The Sikh Religion: Its Gurus, Sacred Writings and Authors*. 6 Vols. Delhi: Low Price Publications, 1996.

McLeod, W.H.: *The Evolution of the Sikh Community*. Delhi: Oxford University Press, 1998.

McLeod, W.H.: *Gruu Naanak and the Sikh Religion*. New Delhi: Oxford University Press, 2001.

Ray, Niharranjan: *The Sikh Gurus and the Sikh Society: A Study in Social Analysis*. New Delhi: Munshiram Manoharlal Publishers Pvt. Ltd., 1975.

Sagoo, Harbans Kaur: *Guru Naanak and the Indian Society*. New Delhi: Deep and Deep Publications, 1992.

Singh, Kushwant, *The History of the Sikhs*. 2 Vols. New Delhi: Oxford University Press, 1999.

Singh, Santokh: *Philosophical Foundations of the Sikh Value System*. New Delhi: Munshiram Manoharlal Publishers Pvt. Ltd., 1982.

Singh, Sewaram: *The Divine Master: Life and Teachings of Guru Nanak Dev*. New Delhi: Gian Publishing House, 1989.

Singh, Trilochan et al., trans.: *Selections from the Sacred Writings of the Sikhs*. London: George Allen & Unwin Ltd., 1973.

Trumpp, Ernest, trans.: *The Aadi Grant or The Holy Scriptures of the Sikhs*. New Delhi: Munshiram Manoharlal Publishers Pvt. Ltd., 1989.

Others

Augustine, Saint: *The City of God*, trans. Gerald G. Walsh, et al. New York: Image Books, 1958.

Duff, J. Wight: *A Literary History of Rome*. London: Leob Library, 1960.

Fry, Plantagenet Somerset: *The Hamlyn Children's History of the World*. London: Hamlyn, 1974.

Hooper, V.D. and H. Ash (eds. & trans.): *De Re Rustica*. London: Leob Library, W. Heinemann), 1934.

Kent, R.G., ed. & trans.: *De Lingua Latina*. Vol. II. London: Leob Library, W.Heinemann), 1938.

Postgate, J.P., trans.: *Catullus, Tibulus, Perviligium Veneris*. London: Leob Library, W. Heinemann, 1919.

Index

A

Aacaarya 167, 178, 350-351, 377, 382-384, 387-388, 397
Aagamas 133-134, 226, 260, 325
Aalaara 515
Aatman 194-197, 203, 208-209, 226, 228, 252, 306
Achaeans 55, 73
Alexander the Great 55, 106
Alwars 246
Amulet 46, 48
Animism 7, 20, 46
Apuleius 100, 109, 113, 120-121, 128-129, 624
Arahat 382, 411, 414-415, 422-423, 436, 443-451, 471-478, 485, 521-522, 553
Armstrong 56, 123-126, 624-625
Ascetic 373
Ash 127-128, 633
Ashanti people 18, 21
Asuras 227-230, 333, 347, 438-441, 453, 475, 499
Attis Mysteries 112
Augustine 83, 90, 127, 633

B

Babb 345, 403-407, 629
Bacchus-Dionysius cult 99
Bahadur 313, 316, 564, 626
Bailey 624
Banerjee 402-403, 617-619, 621, 629, 632
Banga 632
Bapat 550, 551, 629
Barrier 621, 632
Basham 626
Benevolence 15, 230, 245, 258, 270, 291, 456, 457
Best 52, 623
Bhattacharyya 402, 403, 626, 629
Bhrahman 564
Blavatsky 418
Blessings 31, 37-40, 45, 50, 69, 70, 75, 80, 91, 94, 96, 103-105, 116, 133, 147, 151-152, 157, 161, 165-166, 169-174, 181, 185, 189, 227, 251, 263, 275-276, 280, 376, 389, 400, 448, 489, 491, 493, 503-506, 516-517, 527-529, 535, 548, 585, 603, 604, 607
Bliss 79, 107, 145, 192, 197, 200-201, 208, 214, 246-247, 265, 268, 270, 277-278, 287, 349, 350, 375, 377, 436, 453, 476, 486, 528, 541, 600, 613-614
Bodisattva 477
Bowker 623
Bowra 123, 124, 624
Brahman 143, 180, 187-209, 225-226, 228-229, 305, 598

Breathing 158, 182, 190, 204, 222, 284-285, 288, 424, 464, 466, 468, 502, 532
Brown 51, 52, 53, 54, 623
Buddha 234, 239-41, 310, 318, 411-459, 462-478, 480-495, 498-558, 630-631
Buddha-Dharma 430-431, 435, 439, 450, 452, 457, 459, 463, 465, 476, 480, 483, 485, 494, 499, 510, 519, 520-521
Buddhahood 414, 427, 473, 476, 478-480, 484, 486, 489-497, 503-507, 510, 515, 517, 521-526, 532, 533, 540, 547, 555, 630
Buddhist Tradition iii, 3, 411
Budge 128, 624
Buehler 296, 626

C

Carman 306, 626
Caste 118, 135-137, 143, 162-166, 176, 227, 240, 247-250, 259, 261, 295, 319, 331, 340, 351, 356, 364, 383, 390-391, 422, 499, 562, 564, 573-574, 582, 590, 596-597, 601, 610, 616-617
Chan 632
Chari 308-313, 626
Charity 215-216, 257, 346, 360, 392, 394-493, 572, 610
Chastity 93, 104, 168, 179, 362, 373, 385, 481
Childhood sacramental act 176-177
Chthonian Gods 66, 68
Clinging 423, 479, 493, 518
Codrington 623
Cole 620, 632
Compassion 210, 215, 229, 245, 248, 257-258, 325, 412-413, 416, 430-433, 447-449, 457, 459, 461, 466, 472, 476-489, 494-496, 499-505, 518-519, 521, 524, 527-528, 539-541, 548, 586, 598
Consciousness 42, 180, 187-191, 194-197, 200-203, 208-209, 211-214, 220, 224-225, 246, 260-271, 278, 281, 283, 286-287, 293, 325, 377, 413, 423, 425, 434, 443, 447, 449, 453-455, 464-467, 469, 472, 486-487, 575, 615
Constantine the Great 106, 116
Contemplation 131, 192, 211, 213, 216, 269, 281, 284-285, 292-293, 325, 332, 351, 416, 452, 488, 523, 532, 536-538, 575, 588, 592, 595-599
Conze 550-551, 558, 630
Coomaraswamy 552, 554, 558, 630
Cowell 630
Creation 12, 14, 18, 66, 108, 152-153, 167, 186, 189-190, 198-201, 229-230, 233-234, 241, 264-268, 271-277, 309, 353, 434, 453, 480, 525, 574-581, 583, 590, 595, 600, 615
Creation of the universe 234, 273, 525
Creative act 17, 153, 267, 577, 579
Cremation 91, 183, 392, 475, 489, 511-512, 605, 608
Cult 56, 67, 70-71, 75-79, 82-93, 99-101, 106-108, 110-123, 128, 145, 159, 164, 166, 170, 185, 249, 255, 262, 294-295, 314, 323, 353-354, 376, 379-382, 384-385, 393, 400, 412, 415, 474, 481, 484, 489-492, 527
Cult of Cybele 99

D

Dahomey people 30
Danielou 314, 626
Darsanas 133, 134
Dasgupta 626
Davis 418
Death 2, 10-13, 16-33, 37, 40-41, 46, 58-69, 74, 77, 81, 87, 89, 91, 93, 100, 108-116, 119, 123, 137, 145, 150, 156-157, 161, 167-168, 170-174, 182-186, 210, 236, 238-239, 255, 269, 319, 321, 325, 328, 333-335, 338, 340, 343-344, 351, 359-360, 365, 368-371, 374, 386, 388, 392, 396, 399, 414, 419-420, 422, 427-430, 433, 436, 439, 444, 447, 449-456, 466, 479, 487, 490, 500-501, 508, 510-517, 526, 534, 540, 545, 563-567, 573, 575, 578, 581-582, 589, 596, 601, 605, 608-609, 616
Deliverance 273, 329, 350, 434
Deora 632
Despair 16, 139, 245, 449, 451, 453, 455
Destruction of the universe 230, 273-274
Detachment 205, 211, 215-219, 245-247, 257-258, 289, 290, 364, 368, 371, 396, 447-450, 457, 467, 489, 492, 495
Deusen 305, 626
Deutsch 305, 626
Devotion 62, 72-73, 132, 142, 148, 198-199, 202, 210-216, 221, 226, 236, 242-249, 253-258, 261, 276, 279-282, 291, 294-295, 312, 367, 443, 485-486, 503-506, 509, 513, 536, 543, 577, 596, 598, 616
Dharma 133-134, 138, 197, 227, 233, 238, 240, 257-258, 303, 317, 349, 356, 360, 365-367, 370, 413-414, 417, 419, 421-425, 430-432, 435, 439, 444, 446-450, 452, 457, 459, 463, 466, 473-474, 476, 480, 483-494, 499-500, 504, 507-508, 510, 515, 518-524, 539-540, 542, 547, 549
Dhyaana 220, 223-224, 282-285, 370, 466, 520-521, 525, 537
Dignity 198, 342, 351, 485, 507, 601
Divinations 400
Divine *passim*
Divine cosmos 107
Diviners 26, 48
Divinities iii, 3-4, 9-10, 20-27, 30-35, 38-46, 50, 52, 55, 57, 69-70, 74, 79, 82-87, 90-96, 104-105, 115, 120, 140, 162, 170, 330, 332, 335, 344, 352, 429, 436, 474, 524-525, 526, 531, 540, 624
Dodds 624
Dorians 55
Dualism 107, 191, 246, 294
Duff 127, 633
Duggal 617, 632
Duties 43, 93-94, 133, 136-137, 157, 162, 164, 211, 215, 218, 221, 230, 245, 253, 269, 282, 327-328, 346, 356, 358, 364, 387, 390, 421, 431, 459, 461, 535, 602
Dutt 630

E

Eastman 50-52, 623-624
Educational sacramental act 178, 180
Eggeling 301, 626
Eightfold Path 434, 447, 451-452, 457-458, 461-465, 470, 472, 495
Eleusinian Mystical Cult 77
Emanations of Siva 273
Energy 9, 39, 40, 46, 137, 149, 154, 177, 203-205, 217-218, 229, 252, 260-261, 266, 270, 274, 289-290, 349, 429, 433, 440, 447, 464, 471, 506, 520, 526, 601
Enlightenment 270, 282, 318, 329, 347, 378, 394, 413, 422, 425, 427, 430-434, 437, 442, 444, 446-449, 452, 464-465, 473, 477, 479, 481-505, 510, 513, 515-519, 522-524, 527-528, 532, 536-540, 550, 631
Equanimity 447-448, 464-467, 487, 496, 506, 519, 540
Evil 1, 7-8, 10, 16, 20-23, 26-28, 32, 34, 37-38, 40, 43-50, 58, 63, 66-68, 77, 89, 91, 97-98, 101, 107-108, 110, 114-115, 137-138, 152, 154, 158, 161-162, 170-172, 175, 184-85, 190, 197-198, 203, 210-211, 215, 218, 222, 226, 233, 235-241, 252, 256, 270, 272, 281, 283, 289, 293-295, 314, 325, 328, 333, 336, 340, 343-344, 354-358, 367, 372, 384, 388, 397-400, 413, 422, 434, 437-438, 447, 456, 463, 474-475, 481-482, 484, 487, 495, 498-499, 503-504, 512, 524, 529, 535, 536, 545-548, 562, 574, 585, 593-596, 599, 600, 604, 606, 609, 611, 616-617
Evolution 200, 286, 333, 437, 526, 618, 620-621, 633
Ewe people 13, 31-32
Expiation 44-46, 69, 75, 81, 95-97, 104-105, 121, 162, 171-172, 185, 230, 294, 394, 462

F

Fernando 553-554, 630
Fertility cult 75, 255
Festugiere 624
Fetish 3, 7, 46-49
Forgiveness 15, 163, 171-172, 183, 222, 252, 257, 364, 371, 386, 396, 519, 586
Fortitude 229, 245, 257, 488
Fowler 624, 625
Freedom 10, 19, 50, 107, 121-122, 138-139, 164, 192, 199, 217, 219, 224-225, 232, 241, 257, 264-270, 349, 351, 356, 364, 368, 383, 423, 444-445, 468-469, 488, 492, 506, 520, 549, 564, 574, 592, 594, 597
Free spirits 10, 24, 26-27, 30, 41
Fry 633
Funeral rite 182-183, 392

G

Gambhirananda 307, 626, 628
Ga people 14, 23-28, 35, 36, 38-39, 45, 47, 53
Gellner 555, 558-559, 630
Generosity 198, 229, 328, 432, 466, 475, 493-495, 505, 518, 584, 586

Gentleness 257, 528
Gethin 549-555, 559, 630
Gnosticism 107
Gour 630
Gow 124, 625
Grace 19, 31, 83, 103, 113, 116, 119, 139, 145, 180, 183, 201, 210-216, 226-227, 244-245, 249, 251, 260-261, 273, 279-284, 291, 352-353, 400, 402, 472, 480, 510, 513, 523, 574, 576-577, 580, 582-583, 587, 592-595, 598, 600, 602, 604, 611-615
Grammar 429
Greco-Roman-Hellenistic Tradition iii, 3
Greed 136, 215, 220, 222, 340, 348, 356, 364, 369-377, 445, 449, 456, 464, 483, 496, 503
Grewal 632
Grief 58, 100, 183, 363, 374, 449, 451, 453, 455, 464, 589
Griffith 296, 626
Griffiths 555-556, 630
Guenther 630
Guru 136, 204, 206-207, 215, 245, 247, 253, 281-282, 287, 291, 331, 352, 354, 359-360, 367, 369, 372-373, 384, 386-395, 402, 489, 490-491, 506, 529, 539-540, 547, 561-573, 576, 582, 584, 587-611, 616, 620, 629, 632-633
Gurudwaras 563, 609
Guthrie 125, 625

H

Halliday 625
Handy 624
Happiness 32, 59, 120, 147-149, 182, 227, 231, 239-240, 340, 343-344, 352, 365, 389, 401, 436, 453, 481, 489, 496, 499, 501-502, 590, 592, 606, 612-13
Hardon 19, 47, 51-54, 131, 296, 301-302, 621, 623
Harrison 625
Hatred 60, 211, 233, 346, 348, 362, 378, 445, 449, 456, 464, 470-471, 497, 518
Hazra 630
Hermit 136-137, 230, 476, 597
Herod 623
Hiinayaana iii, 3, 416-417, 420, 429, 435-436, 444, 446, 449-451, 470-473, 476, 481, 502-503, 523, 529, 548-549, 553
Hinduism iii, 1, 3, 131-143, 149, 151, 155, 165, 170-173, 185-187, 190, 202, 225-226, 235, 240, 259, 262, 294-297, 302, 304, 308, 311, 314, 322, 326, 398, 412, 417, 435, 474, 477, 510, 524, 562-563, 566, 573, 605, 626-628, 631
Holmn 623
Honor 8, 32, 34, 42, 66, 71, 74-77, 81, 90, 94, 96-99, 102, 104, 109-110, 137, 139, 279, 293, 342, 360, 377, 380, 382, 385, 389, 394, 397-398, 445, 459, 474, 485, 504-505, 508-510, 532, 536, 584, 586, 596, 598
Hooper 127, 633
Hope 23, 34, 68, 77-78, 91, 106, 112, 120, 217-218, 236, 295, 358, 391, 503, 524
Horner 552, 630

Householder 458, 555, 630
Hukam 561, 574-575, 579, 584, 587, 590-592, 595, 598, 611, 615
Hume 305, 626
Humility 44, 139, 152, 206, 209-210, 215, 244, 246, 252, 257-258, 364, 369, 376-377, 396, 535, 597-598, 611, 613
Humphreys 411, 418, 549-559, 630, 631

I

Idowu 50, 624
Ignorance 16, 195, 198, 200, 203, 206-209, 233, 261, 273, 283, 287, 292, 331, 348, 355, 365, 367, 415, 433, 444-445, 449, 452, 455, 457, 470, 472, 483, 492
Imperfect 11, 212, 262, 468
Impermanence 203, 365, 423, 433, 447, 452-453, 468, 470, 500, 511, 521
Incarnation 115, 166, 211, 226, 233-241, 310, 353, 490, 530-531
Initiation rites 36, 43, 119, 136, 253, 386-387, 392, 408, 540-542, 559
Insight meditation 465, 468-470, 497-498, 521
Installation 89, 168, 253, 254, 384-385, 506, 565, 602
Instruction 56, 113, 232-233, 238, 247, 253, 282, 391, 421, 461, 593, 601
Integrity 209, 237, 245
Intellectual preparation 203, 205-206
Intelligence 175, 191, 193, 195, 201-202, 261, 335, 442, 525, 557, 581, 615
Invincible sun 110, 117
Ionians 55
Isherwood 306, 628
Isis Mysteries 112

J

Jaina community 295, 317-329, 332, 344-345, 350-351, 355, 359, 376, 378, 380, 384, 387, 394-396, 401-408, 629, 632
Jaini 402, 405, 408-409, 629
Jaiswal 309, 310, 312, 313, 626
Jesuit Scholars 296-297, 301-308, 313-315, 403, 406, 617, 621, 626
Jones 631
Joy 58, 75-76, 80, 107, 120, 147, 154, 181, 196, 211, 213, 221-222, 241, 245-246, 255, 258, 267, 270, 276, 278, 280, 290, 338, 351, 363, 366, 374, 377, 396, 412, 447-449, 464, 466-467, 481, 487, 489, 496, 499, 506, 519, 540, 607-609, 611, 613-615
Juergensmeyer 621, 632
Jurji 312, 314, 623
Justice 15, 63, 79-80, 86, 90, 109, 114, 138, 153, 219, 239, 584-585, 601

K

Kalupahana 630
Kapoor 632
Karma 135, 138-139, 170, 183, 190, 197-198, 216-218, 222, 225, 255, 261, 266-267, 272, 282, 317, 320, 328-338, 343-354, 361-372, 375-378, 393-394,

398-402, 427, 433, 436-440, 443-448, 451-456, 460, 473, 476, 490, 500, 502, 521, 561, 575, 582, 585, 591, 593, 612, 614
Karmayogi 216-219
Kaul 308, 627
Kawamura 630
Keith 297-298, 300, 306, 627, 630
Kent 127, 633
Keown 549-556, 630
Kinsley 158, 160, 297, 299, 301, 310, 627
Kirthisinghe 630
Kiyota 631
Kohli 617-621, 632
Kopp 631
Kumar 308-315, 403-407, 627-629, 632

L

Lahori 617-620, 632
Lakshmi 230-233, 243, 309, 397
Lala 402, 403, 623, 629
Laypeople 327, 351, 363, 370-371, 380, 387-388, 396, 401, 403, 415, 461, 514, 547, 551, 631
Liberation 107-110, 118, 123, 137-138, 191, 199, 201, 205, 220, 227, 232, 244-245, 273, 280, 284, 287, 290, 332-335, 344-346, 350, 352, 355, 361-362, 365, 367, 370-371, 376-379, 382-383, 393-397, 400-401, 412, 416, 433, 436, 443, 450-451, 487, 541, 549, 572-75
Liebeschutz 625
Lien 553, 554, 631
Ling 553, 631
Livelihood 91, 164, 326, 434, 451, 457, 462-463, 493, 495
Living-dead 24, 26-30, 41, 47
Loehlin 617, 618, 632
Logic 165, 188, 193, 329, 427, 429
Lordship 22, 190, 229, 231, 252
Love 59, 60-65, 78, 150, 172, 181-182, 198, 210-218, 222, 233, 243-248, 261, 265, 276, 279-282, 286-291, 311-312, 338, 346, 348, 362, 367-378, 391, 396, 401, 447-448, 471, 479-480, 493, 496, 500-505, 522, 528, 531, 577, 580-589, 593-594, 597-600, 607, 611

M

Maadhavadeva 246
Macauliffe 633
MacMullen 625
Macnicol 623, 627
Madhva 187, 191, 199-202, 226, 294, 323
Magic 3, 7-8, 26, 28, 31, 41, 43, 46-49, 87, 93, 134, 177, 317, 399, 429, 529, 537
Maguire 550, 631

642 *Index*

Mahaayaana iii, 3, 415-418, 420, 426-428, 431, 435, 473-474, 476-478, 480-493, 497-498, 500-508, 517-519, 523-526, 529, 548-553, 556, 630-632
Maitreya 422, 428, 480-481, 489, 508, 526, 539
Mana 7, 369
Mann 618, 621, 633
Maori people 15, 17, 22-23, 28, 31-33, 41-42
Marriage 22, 43, 62, 67, 75, 93, 103, 119, 135, 148, 167, 173-175, 181-184, 295, 357, 387, 391, 398, 494, 510-511, 514, 563, 603-608
Mathothu 297-300, 304, 309-315, 627
Mawu 13, 15, 18, 31-32
Mbiti 29, 52-53, 624
McLeod 617-621, 633
Meaning 5, 22, 38, 44, 97, 101, 122, 134, 174, 177, 187, 191, 206-210, 214, 222, 225, 228-233, 248, 252, 263, 277, 285, 288, 304-305, 308, 314, 345, 377, 397, 421, 426, 433-434, 450, 452, 477, 488, 491, 521-522, 532-533, 261, 576, 588, 590, 599, 613-614, 627
Medicine 21, 26, 28, 47, 64, 97, 359, 391, 421, 429, 461, 484, 490, 502
Meditation 134, 190, 192, 199, 202, 206-209, 220, 223-225, 230, 234, 240, 245-246, 260-262, 277-282, 285, 292, 294, 327, 351, 359, 365-371, 375, 378-379, 385, 393-396, 411, 413, 416, 423-424, 427-428, 431, 434, 443, 451-452, 457, 461, 463-472, 476-477, 481, 483, 487-507, 514-517, 520-525, 531, 536-537, 548, 569, 572, 575-578, 585, 595-601, 631
Merit 148, 170, 173-174, 183, 246, 328, 351, 354-355, 373, 385, 427, 439, 445, 460, 480, 483, 489, 493, 502-503, 518, 523, 531, 544
Merton 631
Mindfulness 447, 451, 463-466, 494-497
Mishra 313-316, 627
Missionary zeal 326, 417
Moksha 138, 205, 244-245, 276, 287, 290, 317, 321-322, 325, 328-330, 343, 346, 350, 356, 373-377, 382, 392, 394, 574-575
Monier-Williams 552-559, 631
Monks 319-328, 345, 349, 351, 359-363, 366-371, 380, 386-388, 391-396, 401, 413-417, 421, 424-425, 430-434, 460-462, 473-475, 494, 506-509, 511-516, 530, 534-535, 541, 550
Moore 632
Moral code 3, 31, 42-44, 49, 111
Moral path 353-356, 370-375, 378, 400, 457-460, 492-493, 497, 517, 523
Moral preparation 203-205
Moris 125, 625
Mueller 296, 299, 626, 630-631
Muni 402, 406, 629
Murray 624
Murthy 309, 312, 313, 627
Mystery cults 67, 69, 75-78, 82, 84-85, 91, 99-107, 110-112, 115-123, 128
Mysticism iv, 4, 68, 134, 246, 307, 623, 626, 627
Mythology 19, 66, 68, 83, 112, 126, 140, 145-148, 165-167, 289, 311, 318, 474, 484, 577, 625, 628

N

Nagao 630
Nahar 629
New Wisdom Worldview 415
Nhialic 14, 21, 32-34
Nikhilananda 627
Nilsson 125, 625
Nirvaana 281-282, 319, 345, 347, 349, 351-352, 376, 380, 394-397, 401, 416, 423, 434, 436-439, 443-444, 449-453, 457-458, 462-465, 468-473, 476-485, 489, 496, 502, 504-507, 516, 521-522, 545, 631
Non-dual 187, 191-193, 202, 246, 264-265, 268, 294, 478, 486
Non-violence 209, 245, 257, 318-319, 325, 328
Noumena 203, 600
Nuns 321, 326-328, 330, 345, 349, 359, 380, 387, 393, 395-396, 401, 408, 421, 424, 430-432
Nyanapomika 631
Nyanatiloka 631

O

Oaths 15, 59, 86, 90, 114
Ogilvie 625
Olcott 418
Oldenberg 418, 631
Olympian Gods 61
Omnipotence 14, 270
Omniscience 22, 198, 270, 278, 317, 319, 345-346, 347, 350-353, 363, 375-378, 380, 383, 478, 488, 494, 498, 519, 522-523
Oracles 22, 64, 69, 70, 79, 82, 102, 105, 107, 185, 531
Orgiastic Dionysian Cult 76-77
Otto 625

P

Paali 419, 420, 426, 466, 477, 506, 548, 549
Pandey 303-304, 310-311, 627
Pandit 350, 530, 551-554, 606, 623, 631
Parrinder 51-53, 624
Parthasarathy 305-309, 314-315, 627
Passion 65, 211, 340, 368, 374-377, 444-445, 481, 488-489, 505, 574
Paterfamilias 164
Path of devotion 202, 211-212, 215, 245, 294
Path of Knowledge 202, 294
Patience 209, 281, 350, 488, 493, 518-519, 522
Pavgee 297, 627
Peace 23, 32, 38, 44, 58, 83, 87-90, 93, 104-107, 150, 204-206, 211-213, 219, 221, 224, 238, 241, 245, 247, 280, 293, 356, 364, 396, 434, 436, 438, 448-450, 466, 468-469, 496, 506, 549, 573, 583, 586, 589, 596, 598, 600, 611, 615-616

644   Index

Penances 230, 254, 291, 367, 393, 461-462, 535, 611
Perfection 11, 139, 197-200, 212-213, 218-219, 265, 269, 329-330, 346, 351, 360, 371, 374, 377, 379, 427-428, 444, 453, 476, 478, 487, 493-494, 518-523, 527, 581
Perfect knowledge 240, 377, 472, 484
Permanence 200, 232, 431
Perowne 126-128, 625
Perry 623
Personality 2, 25-27, 64, 68, 82, 89, 105-106, 173, 205, 209, 214, 216, 220, 228, 233, 241, 243, 262-264, 268-272, 290, 311, 343, 412, 450, 456, 464-465, 468, 478, 485, 487, 498, 583, 589, 599-600, 603
Pinsent 126-129, 625
Plinius Major 83
Postgate 128, 633
Posture 203-204, 220-221, 262, 269, 273, 277, 284, 369, 370, 379, 381, 396, 462, 465, 466, 490, 507, 535, 538-539
Poussin 631
Power 7-8, 14-22, 25, 27, 34, 37-40, 46-48, 50, 57-61, 65, 68, 83, 87, 89, 92, 108-116, 123, 134-135, 138-141, 147-155, 165-168, 173, 183-187, 198, 204, 211-212, 218-219, 228-232, 237-241, 244-261, 265-269, 273-275, 278-281, 289, 293, 297, 309, 327, 330, 338, 343, 348-349, 351-353, 356, 370, 372-375, 397-399, 412, 436, 439, 441, 446, 448, 453, 458, 478, 481-487, 490-491, 504-505, 508, 511, 514-517, 522-525, 529-532, 534, 541, 543, 545, 547, 563-566, 577-580, 585, 590-591, 599-600, 614
Prabhavananda 306, 628
Prayer 3, 19, 30-39, 44, 49, 57, 72, 81, 94-95, 134, 137, 145, 147, 157, 159, 161-163, 171-172, 175, 177, 187, 215, 221, 244-245, 248-249, 251, 260, 350, 359, 376, 386, 388, 396, 434, 461, 481, 504, 511, 533, 535, 543-546, 570, 572, 598, 601-603
Pre-natal sacramental act 174
Preservation of the universe 227, 273
Pride 80, 209, 236, 257-356, 364, 369, 372-374, 444-445, 470, 472, 479, 480
Priests 3, 26, 28, 31, 35, 38-41, 45, 48-49, 56, 70, 79, 82, 84, 86, 90-94, 97, 99, 102-103, 118, 120, 132, 164-168, 253, 259, 283, 293, 399, 533-534, 542, 566
Primitive Religious Tradition iii, 5, 623
Prosperity 8, 19, 31, 59, 95, 105, 141, 148, 166, 173, 175, 181-184, 232, 253, 276, 280, 293, 389, 398, 506
Psychic 1, 219, 258, 447, 463-464, 480, 521, 574
Puraanas 133-134, 226, 241, 247, 249, 250, 254, 260, 269, 271, 273, 275, 296, 310-312, 326, 391, 564, 597
Pure being 189, 197

Q

Qualified Non-dualism 191, 246

R

Radhakrishnan 131, 196, 211, 216, 218, 296, 304, 305, 306, 307, 309, 627
Ramaanuja 323, 562

Ramamurthi 207, 307, 627
Ray 633
Rebirth 40, 68, 100, 113, 117, 120-121, 138, 200, 245, 328, 365, 406, 433, 436, 438, 444, 449, 451-456, 475, 489-491, 496-501, 506, 521, 578, 581
Reflection 1, 169, 193, 201-203, 206-208, 214, 217, 221, 265, 277-287, 317, 334, 341, 356, 365, 378, 468, 470-471, 497-498, 511, 520
Religious festivals 3, 31, 38, 49, 98
Removal of ignorance 206-208, 292
Righteousness 153, 233, 236, 350, 352, 375, 470, 472, 598, 612
Right View 451
Ringgren 51-54, 123-129, 298-300, 302, 550-551, 623
Rite 39-40, 44-46, 67, 73, 76-77, 81-84, 91-92, 96-101, 107-108, 112-119, 121, 167-169, 173-183, 243, 245, 249-252, 279, 282-383, 386, 388-394, 460-461, 511-514, 534, 541-542, 564-565, 601-602, 604-609
Roman culture 55, 105, 106
Roman Pantheon 84, 90, 122
Rose 625

S

Saadhu 350-351, 373, 377, 382-387, 397
Sacramental act 174-182, 390-393, 606-607
Sacred places 42, 69, 71-72, 82, 94, 105, 259, 515-517
Sacrifice 1, 3, 7-8, 31-34, 40, 42, 45, 49, 64, 72-75, 84, 95-97, 114, 143-145, 151, 161, 164-170, 185, 216, 227, 236, 237, 238, 247, 248, 252, 271, 276, 367, 418, 464, 479, 518, 542, 564, 582
Sagoo 620, 633
Saher 631
Saiva Siddhaanta 134, 261
Saivism iii, 3, 133, 139, 226, 249, 258-263, 275, 282, 287, 293-295, 313-315, 627-628
Salvation 106-108, 110-111, 213-215, 219, 226, 243-246, 249, 255, 259, 273, 317, 320-321, 325, 327-328, 330, 334, 338, 344-346, 352-353, 360-361, 368, 370-371, 373-376, 394, 397, 401, 404, 406, 416, 433-434, 476, 478, 480, 484, 492, 502-503, 526, 531, 541, 567, 583, 587-588, 590, 592-597, 612
Samaadhi 209, 219-220, 224-225, 292, 427-429, 434, 451, 464-465, 493, 524, 539
Sambhi 620, 632
Samsaara 135, 138-139, 199, 280, 328, 345, 351-353, 365, 412, 436-437, 445, 449, 451, 463, 472, 476, 478, 485, 500, 543, 581
Samskaara 173-183, 252, 303, 390-392, 454, 606
Sangha 322, 351, 411, 414, 421, 430-432, 459, 460-462, 466, 473, 508, 539, 542, 547
Sannyaasa 136, 137
Sanskrit 135, 146, 153, 155, 165, 173, 194, 203, 210, 221, 229, 233, 244, 261, 272, 274, 297, 392, 403, 419, 420, 466, 477, 481, 505, 529, 531, 541, 561, 613-614
Santina 631
Sayama 631
Schopenhauer 418

Schubring 629
Scullard 625
Seers 48, 140, 614
Self-consciousness 214, 265
Self-control 115, 205, 210, 219, 221, 257, 258, 362, 367, 413, 607
Self-mastery 258, 377
Self-realization 192, 202, 205, 209, 264, 283, 284, 287, 305, 377, 433, 628
Self-restraint 378, 396
Self-salvation 433
Selfishness 211-212, 215, 233, 290-291, 295, 432-433, 457, 469, 479, 495, 585
Sen 296, 627
Shah 407, 563, 629
Shamanism 35-37, 416, 529
Shamkaradeva 246
Shankara 187, 191, 193-197, 199, 202-208, 305-307, 323, 562, 627-628
Sharma 134, 296-297, 306, 313-314, 628-629
Shrotri 402, 629
Siddha 211, 333, 350-353, 362, 365, 374-377, 382, 396-397
Siddhantashastree 309-315, 628
Siddhartha 412-413, 550
Siddhas 352, 375, 379, 381, 396
Sikh tradition 589
Sinari 304, 628
Singh 403, 551, 562-573, 589, 601, 604, 609, 616-623, 630-633
Sinha 313, 628
Sircar 304, 305, 306, 307, 308, 628
Siva 133, 189-190, 239, 259-295, 298, 314-316, 474, 482-484, 529, 545, 557, 577-578
Sivalinga 259, 274-279, 285, 293, 315
Sivananda 308, 315, 316, 628
Smart 51-53, 124, 125-129, 296-297, 300, 304, 308, 623
Smith 624
Smrti 131-134, 296
Smyth 124, 625
Sorcerers 49, 399
Sorrow 57, 65, 107, 133, 172, 211, 216, 218, 258, 274, 351, 448-449, 451-455, 464, 539, 589
Splendor 113, 229, 232
Spontaneity 266, 290
Sramana 318, 361, 411-412
Srivastava 51, 53, 623
Sruti 131-132, 134, 296
St. Augustine 83, 90
Stcherbatsky 418, 631
Stevenson 402-409, 629
Storr 126, 625
Stroem 51, 623
Stupidity 445, 449, 482
Success 33, 40, 59, 83, 115, 236-237, 258, 293, 418, 525, 531
Suffering 16, 57, 65, 239, 240, 258, 317, 333, 360, 371, 413, 423, 433-435,

439-440, 451-458, 464, 470, 472, 479, 480-485, 490, 496-499, 501-502, 506, 521, 603
Superimposition 192, 264
Supernatural 7, 47-49, 69, 91, 140, 174, 176, 249, 297, 352, 411, 424, 427, 435, 459, 461, 474, 485, 488, 519, 524, 557
Supreme Being 3, 10-24, 30-35, 39, 42-43, 46, 50, 109, 134-137, 143, 154, 186, 197-199, 210, 227-229, 230, 233-234, 239, 244, 259, 298, 311, 402, 436, 485, 525, 574, 577, 615
Suutra-Pitaka 42-421, 425
Suzuki 418, 631
Swami Lakshman 286, 315-316, 626
Syncretism 11, 121

T

Taboos 35, 40-42, 46, 48, 56, 81, 91-93, 104, 135, 167, 174, 221, 263
Tagare 311, 628
Takakusu 631
Talisman 48
Tantra 275, 287, 418, 428-429, 526, 528, 536-538, 541
Temple worship 162, 169, 170, 185, 243, 253, 258, 294, 382-385
Terentius Varro 83
Thibaut 191, 305, 628
Thiruvannamalai 291
Thomas 304, 550-554, 557-558, 628, 631-632
Tiirthankara 317-319, 325, 330-331, 342-354, 359-360, 373-390, 393-398, 401, 404, 407
Totemism 7-8
Trans-empirical 200
Transcendental 187-191, 200-203, 234, 266-268, 278, 294, 349, 486, 488, 527
True Pure Land School 419
Trumpp 618-619, 633
Truthfulness 15, 136, 215, 245, 362, 372, 594
Tsang 259
Tullius Cicero 83

U

Uddaka 413, 515
Universe 10-14, 17-23, 59- 62, 109-110, 114, 131, 134, 140-146, 149-160, 186-191, 195-199, 202, 209, 214, 227- 236, 258-261, 263-278, 281, 286, 289, 293, 295, 300, 309, 317, 328-335, 339, 365, 370, 403, 422, 433-437, 440, 447-448, 451, 453, 474, 482, 484, 499, 509, 521, 525-526, 537, 543, 548, 573, 579, 580, 584, 590-592, 595, 612
Upanishads 132, 143, 186-190, 19-198, 202, 207, 226- 229, 304-309, 412, 626-628

V

Vaishnavism iii, 3, 133, 139, 226-229, 233, 235, 243, 246-249, 254, 257-259, 294-295, 308-312, 626-628
Vaisnavism 230, 246, 249
Vajryaana 420
Vasudeva 238-239
Vedaantic Hinduism iii, 3, 139, 186-187, 190, 202, 225-226, 294-295
Vedic Hinduism iii, 3, 139-143, 149, 151, 170-171, 185, 225, 294
Veneration 42, 85-86, 253, 331, 347, 350, 379, 427, 436, 443-446, 472, 476, 508-513, 531, 545
Vishnu 133, 142, 146, 149, 154-158, 189, 198, 226-259, 271-272, 275-276, 289, 294-295, 309-310, 331, 445, 474, 577-578

W

Watts 632
White 124-126, 625
Williams 550, 552-559, 631-632
Will of God 575-579, 584-585, 592, 611
Woolson 623
Worship 1, 3, 7, 9, 13, 17-19, 30-38, 46-50, 56-58, 68-72, 75, 79, 82-91, 94, 99, 101, 106, 109-112, 116-117, 122-123, 132-134, 141-145, 152, 162-171, 177, 185, 198, 210-212, 214, 226-227, 234, 237, 239-243, 248-261, 268, 274-294, 310, 314-315, 322, 330-332, 336, 344, 347, 350-354, 360, 375-376, 379-393, 397-402, 405-408, 411-419, 427, 432, 445-446, 474, 481-485, 498, 503-513, 516, 526, 527, 529, 531-535, 543-547, 562, 564-568, 578, 581, 597-598, 602-605, 610, 616
Wright 632

Y

Yoga 134, 203-204, 219, 230, 251-252, 260-261, 269-270, 272, 279, 281-282, 284, 286, 308-309, 350, 374, 378-379, 407, 429, 465, 538, 541, 627-628, 631

Z

Zaehner 297, 300, 628
Zen 419, 427, 631-632
Zuesse 624

THE COUNCIL FOR RESEARCH IN VALUES AND PHILOSOPHY

PURPOSE

Today there is urgent need to attend to the nature and dignity of the person, to the quality of human life, to the purpose and goal of the physical transformation of our environment, and to the relation of all this to the development of social and political life. This, in turn, requires philosophic clarification of the base upon which freedom is exercised, that is, of the values which provide stability and guidance to one's decisions.

Such studies must be able to reach deeply into one's culture and that of other parts of the world as mutually reinforcing and enriching in order to uncover the roots of the dignity of persons and of their societies. They must be able to identify the conceptual forms in terms of which modern industrial and technological developments are structured and how these impact upon human self-understanding. Above all, they must be able to bring these elements together in the creative understanding essential for setting our goals and determining our modes of interaction. In the present complex global circumstances this is a condition for growing together with trust and justice, honest dedication and mutual concern.

The Council for Studies in Values and Philosophy (RVP) unites scholars who share these concerns and are interested in the application thereto of existing capabilities in the field of philosophy and other disciplines. Its work is to identify areas in which study is needed, the intellectual resources which can be brought to bear thereupon, and the means for publication and interchange of the work from the various regions of the world. In bringing these together its goal is scientific discovery and publication which contributes to the present promotion of humankind.

In sum, our times present both the need and the opportunity for deeper and ever more progressive understanding of the person and of the foundations of social life. The development of such understanding is the goal of the RVP.

PROJECTS

A set of related research efforts is currently in process:

1. *Cultural Heritage and Contemporary Change: Philosophical Foundations for Social Life.* Focused, mutually coordinated research teams in university centers prepare volumes as part of an integrated philosophic search for self-understanding differentiated by culture and civilization. These evolve more adequate understandings of the person in society and look to the cultural heritage of each for the resources to respond to the challenges of its own specific contemporary transformation.

2. *Seminars on Culture and Contemporary Issues.* This series of 10 week crosscultural and interdisciplinary seminars is coordinated by the RVP in Washington.

3. *Joint-Colloquia* with Institutes of Philosophy of the National Academies of Science, university philosophy departments, and societies. Underway since 1976 in Eastern Europe and, since 1987, in China, these concern the person in contemporary society.

4. *Foundations of Moral Education and Character Development.* A study in values and education which unites philosophers, psychologists, social scientists and scholars in education in the elaboration of ways of enriching the moral content of education and character development. This work has been underway since 1980.

The personnel for these projects consists of established scholars willing to contribute their time and research as part of their professional commitment to life in contemporary society. For resources to implement this work the Council, as 501 C3 a non-profit organization incorporated in the District of Colombia, looks to various private foundations, public programs and enterprises.

PUBLICATIONS ON CULTURAL HERITAGE AND CONTEMPORARY CHANGE

Series I. Culture and Values
Series II. Africa
Series IIA. Islam
Series III. Asia
Series IV. W. Europe and North America
Series IVA. Central and Eastern Europe
Series V. Latin America
Series VI. Foundations of Moral Education
Series VII. Seminars on Culture and Values

CULTURAL HERITAGE AND CONTEMPORARY CHANGE

Series I. Culture and Values

I.1 *Research on Culture and Values: Intersection of Universities, Churches and Nations*. George F. McLean, ed. ISBN 0819173533 (paper); 081917352-5 (cloth).

I.2 *The Knowledge of Values: A Methodological Introduction to the Study of Values;* A. Lopez Quintas, ed. ISBN 081917419x (paper); 0819174181 (cloth).

I.3 *Reading Philosophy for the XXIst Century*. George F. McLean, ed. ISBN 0819174157 (paper); 0819174149 (cloth).

I.4 *Relations Between Cultures*. John A. Kromkowski, ed. ISBN 1565180089 (paper); 1565180097 (cloth).

I.5 *Urbanization and Values*. John A. Kromkowski, ed. ISBN 1565180100 (paper); 1565180119 (cloth).

I.6 *The Place of the Person in Social Life*. Paul Peachey and John A. Kromkowski, eds. ISBN 1565180127 (paper); 156518013-5 (cloth).

I.7 *Abrahamic Faiths, Ethnicity and Ethnic Conflicts*. Paul Peachey, George F. McLean and John A. Kromkowski, eds. ISBN 1565181042 (paper).

I.8 *Ancient Western Philosophy: The Hellenic Emergence*. George F. McLean and Patrick J. Aspell, eds. ISBN 156518100X (paper).

I.9 *Medieval Western Philosophy: The European Emergence*. Patrick J. Aspell, ed. ISBN 1565180941 (paper).

I.10 *The Ethical Implications of Unity and the Divine in Nicholas of Cusa*. David L. De Leonardis. ISBN 1565181123 (paper).

I.11 *Ethics at the Crossroads: 1.Normative Ethics and Objective Reason*. George F. McLean, ed. ISBN 1565180224 (paper).

I.12 *Ethics at the Crossroads: 2.Personalist Ethics and Human Subjectivity*. George F. McLean, ed. ISBN 1565180240 (paper).

I.13 *The Emancipative Theory of Jürgen Habermas and Metaphysics*. Robert Badillo. ISBN 1565180429 (paper); 1565180437 (cloth).

I.14 *The Deficient Cause of Moral Evil According to Thomas Aquinas*. Edward Cook. ISBN 1565180704 (paper).

I.15 *Human Love: Its Meaning and Scope, a Phenomenology of Gift and Encounter*. Alfonso Lopez Quintas. ISBN 1565180747 (paper).

I.16 *Civil Society and Social Reconstruction*. George F. McLean, ed. ISBN 1565180860 (paper).

I.17 *Ways to God, Personal and Social at the Turn of Millennia: The Iqbal Lecture, Lahore*. George F. McLean. ISBN 1565181239 (paper).

I.18 *The Role of the Sublime in Kant's Moral Metaphysics*. John R. Goodreau. ISBN 1565181247 (paper).

1.19 *Philosophical Challenges and Opportunities of Globalization.* Oliva Blanchette, Tomonobu Imamichi and George F. McLean, eds. ISBN 1565181298 (paper).

1.20 *Faith, Reason and Philosophy: Lectures at The al-Azhar, Qom, Tehran, Lahore and Beijing; Appendix: The Encyclical Letter: Fides et Ratio.* George F. McLean. ISBN 156518130 (paper).

1.21 *Religion and the Relation between Civilizations: Lectures on Cooperation between Islamic and Christian Cultures in a Global Horizon.* George F. McLean. ISBN 1565181522 (paper).

1.22 *Freedom, Cultural Traditions and Progress: Philosophy in Civil Society and Nation Building, Tashkent Lectures, 1999.* George F. McLean. ISBN 1565181514 (paper).

1.23 *Ecology of Knowledge.* Jerzy A. Wojciechowski. ISBN 1565181581 (paper).

1.24 *God and the Challenge of Evil: A Critical Examination of Some Serious Objections to the Good and Omnipotent God.* John L. Yardan. ISBN 1565181603 (paper).

1.25 *Reason, Rationality and Reasonableness, Vietnamese Philosophical Studies, I.* Tran Van Doan. ISBN 1565181662 (paper).

1.26 *The Culture of Citizenship: Inventing Postmodern Civic Culture.* Thomas Bridges. ISBN 1565181689 (paper).

1.27 *The Historicity of Understanding and the Problem of Relativism in Gadamer's Philosophical Hermeneutics.* Osman Bilen. ISBN 1565181670 (paper).

1.28 *Speaking of God.* Carlo Huber. ISBN 1565181697 (paper).

1.29 *Persons, Peoples and Cultures in a Global Age: Metaphysical Bases for Peace between Civilizations.* George F. McLean. ISBN 1565181875 (paper).

1.30 *Hermeneutics, Tradition and Contemporary Change: Lectures In Chennai/Madras, India.* George F. McLean. ISBN 1565181883 (paper).

1.31 *Husserl and Stein.* Richard Feist and William Sweet, eds. ISBN 1565181948 (paper).

1.32 *Paul Hanly Furfey's Quest for a Good Society.* Bronislaw Misztal, Francesco Villa, and Eric Sean Williams, eds. ISBN 1565182278 (paper).

1.33 *Three Theories of Society.* Paul Hanly Furfey. ISBN 978-1565182288 (paper).

1.34 *Building Peace In Civil Society: An Autobiographical Report from a Believers' Church.* Paul Peachey. ISBN 978-1565182325 (paper).

1.35 *Karol Wojtyla's Philosophical Legacy.* George F. McLean, Agnes B. Curry and *Nancy Mardas,* eds. ISBN 9781565182479 (paper).

Series II. Africa

II.1 *Person and Community: Ghanaian Philosophical Studies: I.* Kwasi Wiredu and Kwame Gyeke, eds. ISBN 1565180046 (paper); 1565180054 (cloth).

II.2 *The Foundations of Social Life: Ugandan Philosophical Studies: I.* A.T. Dalfovo, ed. ISBN 1565180062 (paper); 156518007-0 (cloth).

II.3 *Identity and Change in Nigeria: Nigerian Philosophical Studies, I.* Theophilus Okere, ed. ISBN 1565180682 (paper).

II.4 *Social Reconstruction in Africa: Ugandan Philosophical studies, II.* E. Wamala, A.R. Byaruhanga, A.T. Dalfovo, J.K.Kigongo, S.A.Mwanahewa and G.Tusabe, eds. ISBN 1565181182 (paper).

II.5 *Ghana: Changing Values/Chaning Technologies: Ghanaian Philosophical Studies, II.* Helen Lauer, ed. ISBN 1565181441 (paper).

II.6 *Sameness and Difference: Problems and Potentials in South African Civil Society: South African Philosophical Studies, I.* James R.Cochrane and Bastienne Klein, eds. ISBN 1565181557 (paper).

II.7 *Protest and Engagement: Philosophy after Apartheid at an Historically Black South African University: South African Philosophical Studies, II.* Patrick

Giddy, ed. ISBN 1565181638 (paper).

II.8 *Ethics, Human Rights and Development in Africa: Ugandan Philosophical Studies, III.* A.T. Dalfovo, J.K. Kigongo, J. Kisekka, G. Tusabe, E. Wamala, R. Munyonyo, A.B. Rukooko, A.B.T. Byaruhanga-akiiki, M. Mawa, eds. ISBN 1565181727 (paper).

II.9 *Beyond Cultures: Perceiving a Common Humanity: Ghanian Philosophical Studies, III.* Kwame Gyekye ISBN 156518193X (paper).

II.10 *Social and Religious Concerns of East African: A Wajibu Anthology: Kenyan Philosophical Studies, I.* Gerald J. Wanjohi and G. Wakuraya Wanjohi, eds. ISBN 1565182219 (paper).

II.11 *The Idea of an African University: The Nigerian Experience: Nigerian Philosophical Studies, II.* Joseph Kenny, ed. ISBN 978-1565182301 (paper).

II.12 *The Struggles after the Struggles: Zimbabwean Philosophical Study, I.* David Kaulemu, ed. ISBN 9781565182318 (paper).

Series IIA. Islam

IIA.1 *Islam and the Political Order.* Muhammad Saïd al-Ashmawy. ISBN ISBN 156518047X (paper); 156518046-1 (cloth).

IIA.2 *Al-Ghazali Deliverance from Error and Mystical Union with the Almighty: Al-munqidh Min Al-dalil.* Critical edition of English translation with introduction by Muhammad Abulaylah and Nurshif Abdul-Rahim Rifat; Introduction and notes by George F. McLean. ISBN 1565181530 (Arabic-English edition, paper), ISBN 1565180828 (Arabic edition, paper), ISBN 156518081X (English edition, paper)

IIA.3 *Philosophy in Pakistan.* Naeem Ahmad, ed. ISBN 1565181085 (paper).

IIA.4 *The Authenticity of the Text in Hermeneutics.* Seyed Musa Dibadj. ISBN 1565181174 (paper).

IIA.5 *Interpretation and the Problem of the Intention of the Author: H.-G.Gadamer vs E.D.Hirsch.* Burhanettin Tatar. ISBN 156518121 (paper).

IIA.6 *Ways to God, Personal and Social at the Turn of Millennia: The Iqbal Lecture, Lahore.* George F. McLean. ISBN 1565181239 (paper).

IIA.7 *Faith, Reason and Philosophy: Lectures at The al-Azhar, Qom, Tehran, Lahore and Beijing; Appendix: The Encyclical Letter: Fides et Ratio.* George F. McLean. ISBN 1565181301 (paper).

IIA.8 *Islamic and Christian Cultures: Conflict or Dialogue: Bulgarian Philosophical Studies, III.* Plament Makariev, ed. ISBN 156518162X (paper).

IIA.9 *Values of Islamic Culture and the Experience of History, Russian Philosophical Studies, I.* Nur Kirabaev, Yuriy Pochta, eds. ISBN 1565181336 (paper).

IIA.10 *Christian-Islamic Preambles of Faith.* Joseph Kenny. ISBN 1565181387 (paper).

IIA.11 *The Historicity of Understanding and the Problem of Relativism in Gadamer's Philosophical Hermeneutics.* Osman Bilen. ISBN 1565181670 (paper).

IIA.12 *Religion and the Relation between Civilizations: Lectures on Cooperation between Islamic and Christian Cultures in a Global Horizon.* George F. McLean. ISBN 1565181522 (paper).

IIA.13 *Modern Western Christian Theological Understandings of Muslims since the Second Vatican Council.* Mahmut Aydin. ISBN 1565181719 (paper).

IIA.14 *Philosophy of the Muslim World; Authors and Principal Themes.* Joseph Kenny. ISBN 1565181794 (paper).

IIA.15 *Islam and Its Quest for Peace: Jihad, Justice and Education.* Mustafa Köylü. ISBN 1565181808 (paper).

IIA.16 *Islamic Thought on the Existence of God: Contributions and Contrasts with Contemporary Western Philosophy of Religion.* Cafer S. Yaran. ISBN 1565181921 (paper).

IIA.17 *Hermeneutics, Faith, and Relations between Cultures: Lectures in Qom, Iran.* George F. McLean. ISBN 1565181913 (paper).

IIA.18 *Change and Essence: Dialectical Relations between Change and Continuity in the Turkish Intellectual Tradition.* Sinasi Gunduz and Cafer S. Yaran, eds. ISBN 1565182227 (paper).

Series III.Asia

III.1 *Man and Nature: Chinese Philosophical Studies, I.* Tang Yi-jie, Li Zhen, eds. ISBN 0819174130 (paper); 0819174122 (cloth).

III.2 *Chinese Foundations for Moral Education and Character Development: Chinese Philosophical Studies, II.* Tran van Doan, ed. ISBN 1565180321 (paper); 156518033X (cloth).

III.3 *Confucianism, Buddhism, Taoism, Christianity and Chinese Culture: Chinese Philosophical Studies, III.* Tang Yijie. ISBN 1565180348 (paper); 156518035-6 (cloth).

III.4 *Morality, Metaphysics and Chinese Culture (Metaphysics, Culture and Morality, I).* Vincent Shen and Tran van Doan, eds. ISBN 1565180275 (paper); 156518026-7 (cloth).

III.5 *Tradition, Harmony and Transcendence.* George F. McLean. ISBN 1565180313 (paper); 156518030-5 (cloth).

III.6 *Psychology, Phenomenology and Chinese Philosophy: Chinese Philosophical Studies, VI.* Vincent Shen, Richard Knowles and Tran Van Doan, eds. ISBN 1565180453 (paper); 1565180445 (cloth).

III.7 *Values in Philippine Culture and Education: Philippine Philosophical Studies, I.* Manuel B. Dy, Jr., ed. ISBN 1565180412 (paper); 156518040-2 (cloth).

III.7A *The Human Person and Society: Chinese Philosophical Studies, VIIA.* Zhu Dasheng, Jin Xiping and George F. McLean, eds. ISBN 1565180887.

III.8 *The Filipino Mind: Philippine Philosophical Studies II.* Leonardo N. Mercado. ISBN 156518064X (paper); 156518063-1 (cloth).

III.9 *Philosophy of Science and Education: Chinese Philosophical Studies IX.* Vincent Shen and Tran Van Doan, eds. ISBN 1565180763 (paper); 156518075-5 (cloth).

III.10 *Chinese Cultural Traditions and Modernization: Chinese Philosophical Studies, X.* Wang Miaoyang, Yu Xuanmeng and George F. McLean, eds. ISBN 1565180682 (paper).

III.11 *The Humanization of Technology and Chinese Culture: Chinese Philosophical Studies XI.* Tomonobu Imamichi, Wang Miaoyang and Liu Fangtong, eds. ISBN 1565181166 (paper).

III.12 *Beyond Modernization: Chinese Roots of Global Awareness: Chinese Philosophical Studies, XII.* Wang Miaoyang, Yu Xuanmeng and George F. McLean, eds. ISBN 1565180909 (paper).

III.13 *Philosophy and Modernization in China: Chinese Philosophical Studies XIII.* Liu Fangtong, Huang Songjie and George F. McLean, eds. ISBN 1565180666 (paper).

III.14 *Economic Ethics and Chinese Culture: Chinese Philosophical Studies, XIV.* Yu Xuanmeng, Lu Xiaohe, Liu Fangtong, Zhang Rulun and Georges Enderle, eds. ISBN 1565180925 (paper).

III.15 *Civil Society in a Chinese Context: Chinese Philosophical Studies XV.* Wang Miaoyang, Yu Xuanmeng and Manuel B. Dy, eds. ISBN 1565180844 (paper).

III.16 *The Bases of Values in a Time of Change: Chinese and Western: Chinese Philosophical Studies, XVI.* Kirti Bunchua, Liu Fangtong, Yu Xuanmeng, Yu Wujin, eds. ISBN 156518114X (paper).

III.17 *Dialogue between Christian Philosophy and Chinese Culture: Philosophical Perspectives for the Third Millennium: Chinese Philosophical Studies, XVII.* Paschal Ting, Marian Kao and Bernard Li, eds. ISBN 1565181735 (paper).

III.18 *The Poverty of Ideological Education: Chinese Philosophical Studies, XVIII.* Tran Van Doan. ISBN 1565181646 (paper).

III.19 *God and the Discovery of Man: Classical and Contemporary Approaches: Lectures in Wuhan, China.* George F. McLean. ISBN 1565181891 (paper).
III.20 *Cultural Impact on International Relations: Chinese Philosophical Studies, XX.* Yu Xintian, ed. ISBN 156518176X (paper).
III.21 *Cultural Factors in International Relations: Chinese Philosophical Studies, XXI.* Yu Xintian, ed. ISBN 1565182049 (paper).
III.22 *Wisdom in China and the West: Chinese Philosophical Studies, XXII.* Vincent Shen and Willard Oxtoby †. ISBN 1565182057 (paper)
III.23 *China's Contemporary Philosophical Journey: Western Philosophy and Marxism ChineseP hilosophical Studies: Chinese Philosophical Studies, XXIII.* Liu Fangtong. ISBN 1565182065 (paper).
III.24 *Shanghai : Its Urbanization and Culture: Chinese Philosophical Studies, XXIV.* Yu Xuanmeng and He Xirong, eds. ISBN 1565182073 (paper).
III.25 *Dialogue of Philosophies, Religions and Civilizations in the Era of Globalization: Chinese Philosophical Studies, XXV.* Zhao Dunhua, ed. ISBN 9781565182431 (paper).
III.26 *Rethinking Marx: Chinese Philosophical Studies, XXVI.* Zou Shipeng and Yang Xuegong, eds. ISBN 9781565182448 (paper).
III.27 *Confucian Ethics in Retrospect and Prospect: Chinese Philosophical Studies XXVII.* Vincent Shen and Kwong-loi Shun, eds. ISBN 9781565182455 (paper).
IIIB.1 *Authentic Human Destiny: The Paths of Shankara and Heidegger: Indian Philosophical Studies, I.* Vensus A. George. ISBN 1565181190 (paper).
IIIB.2 *The Experience of Being as Goal of Human Existence: The Heideggerian Approach: Indian Philosophical Studies, II.* Vensus A. George. ISBN 156518145X (paper).
IIIB.3 *Religious Dialogue as Hermeneutics: Bede Griffiths's Advaitic Approach: Indian Philosophical Studies, III.* Kuruvilla Pandikattu. ISBN 1565181395 (paper).
IIIB.4 *Self-Realization [Brahmaanubhava]: The Advaitic Perspective of Shankara: Indian Philosophical Studies, IV.* Vensus A. George. ISBN 1565181549 (paper).
IIIB.5 *Gandhi: The Meaning of Mahatma for the Millennium: Indian Philosophical Studies, V.* Kuruvilla Pandikattu, ed. ISBN 1565181565 (paper).
IIIB.6 *Civil Society in Indian Cultures: Indian Philosophical Studies, VI.* Asha Mukherjee, Sabujkali Sen (Mitra) and K. Bagchi, eds. ISBN 1565181573 (paper).
IIIB.7 *Hermeneutics, Tradition and Contemporary Change: Lectures In Chennai/Madras, India.* George F. McLean. ISBN 1565181883 (paper).
IIIB.8 *Plenitude and Participation: The Life of God in Man: Lectures in Chennai/Madras, India.* George F. McLean. ISBN 1565181999 (paper).
IIIB.9 *Sufism and Bhakti, a Comparative Study.* Md. Sirajul Islam. ISBN 1565181980 (paper).
IIIB.10 *Reasons for Hope: Its Nature, Role and Future.* Kuruvilla Pandikattu, ed. ISBN 156518 2162 (paper).
IIB.11 *Lifeworlds and Ethics: Studies in Several Keys.* Margaret Chatterjee. ISBN 9781565182332 (paper).
IIIC.1 *Spiritual Values and Social Progress: Uzbekistan Philosophical Studies, I.* Said Shermukhamedov and Victoriya Levinskaya, eds. ISBN 1565181433 (paper).
IIIC.2 *Kazakhstan: Cultural Inheritance and Social Transformation: Kazakh Philosophical Studies, I.* Abdumalik Nysanbayev. ISBN 1565182022 (paper).
IIIC.3 *Social Memory and Contemporaneity: Kyrgyz Philosophical Studies, I.* Gulnara A. Bakieva. ISBN 9781565182349 (paper).
IIID.1 *Reason, Rationality and Reasonableness: Vietnamese Philosophical Studies, I.* Tran Van Doan. ISBN 1565181662 (paper).
IIID.2 *Hermeneutics for a Global Age: Lectures in Shanghai and Hanoi.* George F. McLean. ISBN 1565181905 (paper).
IIID.3 *Cultural Traditions and Contemporary Challenges in Southeast Asia.*

Warayuth Sriwarakuel, Manuel B.Dy, J.Haryatmoko, Nguyen Trong Chuan, and Chhay Yiheang, eds. ISBN 1565182138 (paper).
IIID.4 *Filipino Cultural Traits: Claro R.Ceniza Lectures*. Rolando M. Gripaldo, ed. ISBN 1565182251 (paper).
IIID.5 *The History of Buddhism in Vietnam*. Chief editor: Nguyen Tai Thu; Authors: Dinh Minh Chi, Ly Kim Hoa, Ha thuc Minh, Ha Van Tan, Nguyen Tai Thu. ISBN 1565180984 (paper).

Series IV. Western Europe and North America

IV.1 *Italy in Transition: The Long Road from the First to the Second Republic: The Edmund D. Pellegrino Lectures*. Paolo Janni, ed. ISBN 1565181204 (paper).
IV.2 *Italy and The European Monetary Union: The Edmund D. Pellegrino Lectures*. Paolo Janni, ed. ISBN 156518128X (paper).
IV.3 *Italy at the Millennium: Economy, Politics, Literature and Journalism: The Edmund D. Pellegrino Lectures*. Paolo Janni, ed. ISBN 1565181581 (paper).
IV.4 *Speaking of God*. Carlo Huber. ISBN 1565181697 (paper).
IV.5 *The Essence of Italian Culture and the Challenge of a Global Age*. Paulo Janni and George F. McLean, eds. ISBB 1565181778 (paper).
IV.6 *Italic Identity in Pluralistic Contexts: Toward the Development of Intercultural Competencies*. Piero Bassetti and Paolo Janni, eds. ISBN 1565181441 (paper).

Series IVA. Central and Eastern Europe

IVA.1 *The Philosophy of Person: Solidarity and Cultural Creativity: Polish Philosophical Studies, I*. A. Tischner, J.M. Zycinski, eds. ISBN 1565180496 (paper); 156518048-8 (cloth).
IVA.2 *Public and Private Social Inventions in Modern Societies: Polish Philosophical Studies, II*. L. Dyczewski, P. Peachey, J.A. Kromkowski, eds. ISBN.paper 1565180518 (paper); 156518050X (cloth).
IVA.3 *Traditions and Present Problems of Czech Political Culture: Czechoslovak Philosophical Studies, I*. M. Bednár and M. Vejraka, eds. ISBN 1565180577 (paper); 156518056-9 (cloth).
IVA.4 *Czech Philosophy in the XXth Century: Czech Philosophical Studies, II*. Lubomír Nový and Jirí Gabriel, eds. ISBN 1565180291 (paper); 156518028-3 (cloth).
IVA.5 *Language, Values and the Slovak Nation: Slovak Philosophical Studies, I*. Tibor Pichler and Jana Gašparíková, eds. ISBN 1565180372 (paper); 156518036-4 (cloth).
IVA.6 *Morality and Public Life in a Time of Change: Bulgarian Philosophical Studies, I*. V. Prodanov and M. Stoyanova, eds. ISBN 1565180550 (paper); 1565180542 (cloth).
IVA.7 *Knowledge and Morality: Georgian Philosophical Studies, I*. N.V. Chavchavadze, G. Nodia and P. Peachey, eds. ISBN 1565180534 (paper); 1565180526 (cloth).
IVA.8 *Cultural Heritage and Social Change: Lithuanian Philosophical Studies, I*. Bronius Kuzmickas and Aleksandr Dobrynin, eds. ISBN 1565180399 (paper); 1565180380 (cloth).
IVA.9 *National, Cultural and Ethnic Identities: Harmony beyond Conflict: Czech Philosophical Studies, IV*. Jaroslav Hroch, David Hollan, George F. McLean, eds. ISBN 1565181131 (paper).
IVA.10 *Models of Identities in Postcommunist Societies: Yugoslav Philosophical Studies, I*. Zagorka Golubovic and George F. McLean, eds. ISBN 1565181211 (paper).
IVA.11 *Interests and Values: The Spirit of Venture in a Time of Change: Slovak Philosophical Studies, II*. Tibor Pichler and Jana Gasparikova, eds. ISBN

1565181255 (paper).
IVA.12 *Creating Democratic Societies: Values and Norms: Bulgarian Philosophical Studies, II.* Plamen Makariev, Andrew M.Blasko and Asen Davidov, eds. ISBN 156518131X (paper).
IVA.13 *Values of Islamic Culture and the Experience of History: Russian Philosophical Studies, I.* Nur Kirabaev and Yuriy Pochta, eds. ISBN 1565181336 (paper).
IVA.14 *Values and Education in Romania Today: Romanian Philosophical Studies,* Marin Calin and Magdalena Dumitrana, eds. ISBN 1565181344 (paper).
IVA.15 *Between Words and Reality, Studies on the Politics of Recognition and the Changes of Regime in Contemporary Romania.* Victor Neumann. ISBN 1565181611 (paper).
IVA.16 *Culture and Freedom: Romanian Philosophical Studies, III.* Marin Aiftinca, ed. ISBN 1565181360 (paper).
IVA.17 *Lithuanian Philosophy: Persons and Ideas Lithuanian Philosophical Studies, II.* Jurate Baranova, ed. ISBN 1565181379 (paper).
IVA.18 *Human Dignity: Values and Justice: Czech Philosophical Studies, III.* Miloslav Bednar, ed. ISBN 1565181409 (paper).
IVA.19 *Values in the Polish Cultural Tradition: Polish Philosophical Studies, III.* Leon Dyczewski, ed. ISBN 1565181425 (paper).
IVA.20 *Liberalization and Transformation of Morality in Post-communist Countries: Polish Philosophical Studies, IV.* Tadeusz Buksinski. ISBN 1565181786 (paper).
IVA.21 *Islamic and Christian Cultures: Conflict or Dialogue: Bulgarian Philosophical Studies, III.* Plament Makariev, ed. ISBN 156518162X (paper).
IVA.22 *Moral, Legal and Political Values in Romanian Culture: Romanian Philosophical Studies, IV.* Mihaela Czobor-Lupp and J. Stefan Lupp, eds. ISBN 1565181700 (paper).
IVA.23 *Social Philosophy: Paradigm of Contemporary Thinking: Lithuanian Philosophical Studies, III.* Jurate Morkuniene. ISBN 1565182030 (paper).
IVA.24 *Romania: Cultural Identity and Education for Civil Society.* Magdalena Dumitrana, ed. ISBN 156518209X (paper).
IVA.25 *Polish Axiology: the 20th Century and Beyond: Polish Philosophical Studies, V.* Stanislaw Jedynak, ed. ISBN 1565181417 (paper).
IVA.26 *Contemporary Philosophical Discourse in Lithuania: Lithuanian Philosophical Studies, IV.* Jurate Baranova, ed. ISBN 156518-2154 (paper).
IVA.27 *Eastern Europe and the Challenges of Globalization: Polish Philosophical Studies, VI.* Tadeusz Buksinski and Dariusz Dobrzanski, ed. ISBN 1565182189 (paper).
IVA.28 *Church, State, and Society in Eastern Europe: Hungarian Philosophical Studies, I.* Miklós Tomka. ISBN 156518226X.
IVA.29 *Politics, Ethics, and the Challenges to Democracy in 'New Independent States'.* Tinatin Bochorishvili, William Sweet, Daniel Ahern, eds. ISBN 9781565182240.
IVA.30 *Comparative Ethics in a Global Age.* Marietta T. Stepanyants, eds. ISBN 978-1565182356.
IVA.31 *Identity and Values of Lithuanians: Lithuanian Philosophical Studies, V.* Aida Savicka, eds. ISBN 9781565182367.
IVA.32 *The Challenge of Our Hope: Christian Faith in Dialogue: Polish Philosophical Studies, VII.* Waclaw Hryniewicz. ISBN 9781565182370.
IVA.33 *Diversity and Dialogue: Culture and Values in the Age of Globalization: Essays in Honour of Professor George F. McLean.* Andrew Blasko and Plamen Makariev, eds. ISBN 9781565182387.

Series V. Latin America

V.1 *The Social Context and Values: Perspectives of the Americas.* O. Pegoraro,

ed. ISBN 081917355X (paper); 0819173541 (cloth).
V.2 *Culture, Human Rights and Peace in Central America.* Raul Molina and Timothy Ready, eds. ISBN 0819173576 (paper); 0-8191-7356-8 (cloth).
V.3 *El Cristianismo Aymara: Inculturacion o Culturizacion?* Luis Jolicoeur. ISBN 1565181042.
V.4 *Love as the Foundation of Moral Education and Character Development.* Luis Ugalde, Nicolas Barros and George F. McLean, eds. ISBN 1565180801.
V.5 *Human Rights, Solidarity and Subsidiarity: Essays towards a Social Ontology.* Carlos E.A. Maldonado ISBN 1565181107.

Series VI. Foundations of Moral Education

VI.1 *Philosophical Foundations for Moral Education and Character Development: Act and Agent.* G. McLean and F. Ellrod, eds. ISBN 156518001-1 (cloth) (paper); ISBN 1565180003.
VI.2 *Psychological Foundations for Moral Education and Character Development: An Integrated Theory of Moral Development.* R. Knowles, ed. ISBN 156518002X (paper); 156518003-8 (cloth).
VI.3 *Character Development in Schools and Beyond.* Kevin Ryan and Thomas Lickona, eds. ISBN 1565180593 (paper); 156518058-5 (cloth).
VI.4 *The Social Context and Values: Perspectives of the Americas.* O. Pegoraro, ed. ISBN 081917355X (paper); 0819173541 (cloth).
VI.5 *Chinese Foundations for Moral Education and Character Development.* Tran van Doan, ed. ISBN 1565180321 (paper); 156518033 (cloth).
VI.6 *Love as the Foundation of Moral Education and Character Development.* Luis Ugalde, Nicolas Barros and George F. McLean, eds. ISBN 1565180801.

Series VII. Seminars on Culture and Values

VII.1 *The Social Context and Values: Perspectives of the Americas.* O. Pegoraro, ed. ISBN 081917355X (paper); 0819173541 (cloth).
VII.2 *Culture, Human Rights and Peace in Central America.* Raul Molina and Timothy Ready, eds. ISBN 0819173576 (paper); 0819173568 (cloth).
VII.3 *Relations Between Cultures.* John A. Kromkowski, ed. ISBN 1565180089 (paper); 1565180097 (cloth).
VII.4 *Moral Imagination and Character Development: Volume I, The Imagination.* George F. McLean and John A. Kromkowski, eds. ISBN 1565181743 (paper).
VII.5 *Moral Imagination and Character Development: Volume II, Moral Imagination in Personal Formation and Character Development.* George F. McLean and Richard Knowles, eds. ISBN 1565181816 (paper).
VII.6 *Moral Imagination and Character Development: Volume III, Imagination in Religion and Social Life.* George F. McLean and John K. White, eds. ISBN 1565181824 (paper).
VII.7 *Hermeneutics and Inculturation.* George F. McLean, Antonio Gallo, Robert Magliola, eds. ISBN 1565181840 (paper).
VII.8 *Culture, Evangelization, and Dialogue.* Antonio Gallo and Robert Magliola, eds. ISBN 1565181832 (paper).
VII.9 *The Place of the Person in Social Life.* Paul Peachey and John A. Kromkowski, eds. ISBN 1565180127 (paper); 156518013-5 (cloth).
VII.10 *Urbanization and Values.* John A. Kromkowski, ed. ISBN 1565180100 (paper); 1565180119 (cloth).
VII.11 *Freedom and Choice in a Democracy, Volume I: Meanings of Freedom.* Robert Magliola and John Farrelly, eds. ISBN 1565181867 (paper).
VII.12 *Freedom and Choice in a Democracy, Volume II: The Difficult Passage to Freedom.* Robert Magliola and Richard Khuri, eds. ISBN 1565181859 (paper).
VII 13 *Cultural Identity, Pluralism and Globalization* (2 volumes). John P.

Hogan, ed. ISBN 1565182170 (paper).

VII.14 *Democracy: In the Throes of Liberalism and Totalitarianism.* George F. McLean, Robert Magliola, William Fox, eds. ISBN 1565181956 (paper).

VII.15 *Democracy and Values in Global Times: With Nigeria as a Case Study.* George F. McLean, Robert Magliola, Joseph Abah, eds. ISBN 1565181956 (paper).

VII.16 *Civil Society and Social Reconstruction.* George F. McLean, ed. ISBN 1565180860 (paper).

VII.17 *Civil Society: Who Belongs?* William A.Barbieri, Robert Magliola, Rosemary Winslow, eds. ISBN 1565181972 (paper).

VII.18 *The Humanization of Social Life: Theory and Challenges.* Christopher Wheatley, Robert P. Badillo, Rose B. Calabretta, Robert Magliola, eds. ISBN 1565182006 (paper).

VII.19 *The Humanization of Social Life: Cultural Resources and Historical Responses.* Ronald S. Calinger, Robert P. Badillo, Rose B. Calabretta, Robert Magliola, eds. ISBN 1565182006 (paper).

VII.20 *Religious Inspiration for Public Life: Religion in Public Life, Volume I.* George F. McLean, John A. Kromkowski and Robert Magliola, eds. ISBN 1565182103 (paper).

VII.21 *Religion and Political Structures from Fundamentalism to Public Service: Religion in Public Life, Volume II.* John T. Ford, Robert A. Destro and Charles R. Dechert, eds. ISBN 1565182111 (paper).

VII.22 *Civil Society as Democratic Practice.* Antonio F. Perez, Semou Pathé Gueye, Yang Fenggang, eds. ISBN 1565182146 (paper).

VII.23 *Ecumenism and Nostra Aetate in the 21st Century.* George F. McLean and John P. Hogan, eds. ISBN 1565182197 (paper).

VII.24 *Multiple Paths to God: Nostra Aetate: 40 years Later.* John P. Hogan and George F. McLean, eds. ISBN 1565182200 (paper).

VII.25 *Globalization and Identity.* Andrew Blasko, Taras Dobko, Pham Van Duc and George Pattery, eds. ISBN 1565182200 (paper).

The International Society for Metaphysics

ISM.1 *Person and Nature.* George F. McLean and Hugo Meynell, eds. ISBN 0819170267 (paper); 0819170259 (cloth).

ISM.2 *Person and Society.* George F. McLean and Hugo Meynell, eds. ISBN 0819169250 (paper); 0819169242 (cloth).

ISM.3 *Person and God.* George F. McLean and Hugo Meynell, eds. ISBN 0819169382 (paper); 0819169374 (cloth).

ISM.4 *The Nature of Metaphysical Knowledge.* George F. McLean and Hugo Meynell, eds. ISBN 0819169277 (paper); 0819169269 (cloth).

ISM.5 *Philosophhical Challenges and Opportunities of Globalization.* Oliva Blanchette, Tomonobu Imamichi and George F. McLean, eds. ISBN 1565181298 (paper).

The series is published and distributed by: The Council for Research in Values and Philosophy, Cardinal Station, P.O.Box 261, Washington, D.C.20064, Tel./Fax.202/319-6089; e-mail: cua-rvp@cua.edu (paper); website: http://www.crvp.org. All titles are available in paper except as noted. Prices: $17.50 (paper).